Newsmakers®

ISSN 0899-0417

Newsmakers®

The People Behind Today's Headlines

Laura Avery

Project Editor

2003

Cumulation

Includes Indexes from
1985 through 2003

GALE®

THOMSON ™

GALE

Detroit • New York • San Diego • San Francisco • Cleveland • New Haven, Conn. • Waterville, Maine • London • Munich

Newsmakers 2003, Cumulation

Project Editor
Laura Avery

Editorial
Angela Pilchak

Research
Barbara McNeil

Editorial Support Services
Venus Little

Permissions
Margaret Chamberlain, Lori Hines, Shalice Shah-Caldwell

Imaging and Multimedia
Dean Dauphinais, Lezlie Light, Dave G. Oblender, Luke A. Rademacher

Product Design
Cynthia Baldwin

Composition and Electronic Capture
Carolyn A. Roney

Manufacturing
Mike Logusz, Stacy L. Melson

ISBN 0-7876-6391-3
ISSN 0899-0417

Printed in the United States of America
10 9 8 7 6 5 4 3 2 1

Contents

Obituaries

Introduction

Newsmakers provides informative profiles of the world's most interesting people in a crisp, concise, contemporary format. Make *Newsmakers* the first place you look for biographical information on the people making today's headlines.

Important Features

- **Attractive, modern page design** pleases the eye while making it easy to locate the information you need.

- **Coverage of all the newsmakers** you want to know about people in business, education, technology, law, politics, religion, entertainment, labor, sports, medicine, and other fields.

- **Clearly labeled data sections** allow quick access to vital personal statistics, career information, major awards, and mailing addresses.

- **Informative sidelights essays** include the kind of in-depth analysis you're looking for.

- **Sources for additional information** provide lists of books, magazines, newspapers, and internet sites where you can find out even more about *Newsmakers* listees.

- **Enlightening photographs** are specially selected to further enhance your knowledge of the subject.

- **Separate obituaries section** provides you with concise profiles of recently deceased newsmakers.

- **Publication schedule and price** fit your budget. *Newsmakers* is published in three paperback issues per year, each containing approximately 50 entries, and a hardcover cumulation, containing approximately 200 entries (those from the preceding three paperback issues plus an additional 50 entries), *all at a price you can afford!*

- And much, much more!

Indexes Provide Easy Access

Familiar and indispensable: The *Newsmakers* indexes! You can easily locate entries in a variety of ways through our four versatile, comprehensive indexes. The Nationality, Occupation, and Subject Indexes list names from the current year's *Newsmakers* issues. These are cumulated in the annual hardbound volume to include all names from the entire *Contemporary Newsmakers* and *Newsmakers* series. The Newsmakers Index is cumulated in all issues as well as the hardbound annuals to provide concise coverage of the entire series.

- **Nationality Index**—Names of newsmakers are arranged alphabetically under their respective nationalities.

- **Occupation Index**—Names are listed alphabetically under broad occupational categories.

- **Subject Index**—Includes key subjects, topical issues, company names, products, organizations, etc., that are discussed in *Newsmakers*. Under each subject heading are listed names of newsmakers associated with that topic. So the unique Subject Index provides access to the information in *Newsmakers* even when readers are unable to connect a name with a particular topic. This index also invites browsing, allowing *Newsmakers* users to discover topics they may wish to explore further.

- **Cumulative Newsmakers Index**—Listee names, along with birth and death dates, when available, are arranged alphabetically followed by the year and issue number in which their entries appear.

Available in Electronic Formats

Diskette/Magnetic Tape. *Newsmakers* is available for licensing on magnetic tape or diskette in a fielded format. The database is available for internal data processing and nonpublishing purposes only. For more information, call 1-800-877-GALE.

Online. *Newsmakers* is available online as part of the Gale Biographies (GALBIO) database accessible through LEXIS-NEXIS, P.O. Box 933, Dayton, OH 45401-0933; phone: (937) 865-6800; toll-free: 1-800-227-9597.

Suggestions Are Appreciated

The editors welcome your comments and suggestions. In fact, many popular *Newsmakers* features were implemented as a result of readers' suggestions. We will continue to shape the series to best meet the needs of the greatest number of users. Send comments or suggestions to:

The Editor
Newsmakers
The Gale Group
27500 Drake Rd.
Farmington Hills, MI 48331-3535

Or, call toll-free at 1-800-877-GALE

S. Daniel Abraham

Executive

Born in 1924 in Long Beach, NY; married and divorced; married Ewa Sebzda; children: five.

Addresses: *Home*—West Palm Beach, FL. *Office*—c/o Thompson Medical Company, Inc., 222 Lakeview Ave., Floor 17, West Palm Beach, FL 33401–6150.

Career

Bought Thompson Medical Company in the late 1940s; served as board chair, president, and chief executive officer of the West Palm Beach, FL–based diet–aid marketer until 2000; company launched Slim–Mint gum, 1956, Figure–Aid appetite suppressant, 1960, Dexatrim diet pill, 1976, and Slim–Fast meal replacement drink, 1977. Has also contributed to pro–peace initiatives between Israel and its neighbors, and is co–founder of the Center for Middle East Peace and Economic Cooperation.

Sidelights

Slim–Fast founder S. Daniel Abraham is one of the most reclusive billionaires on the *Forbes* 400 list of the wealthiest Americans. In 2002, Abraham's estimated net worth of $1.8 billion placed him between Edgar Bronfman, head of the Seagram liquor fortune, and McDonald's heiress Joan Kroc in the rankings. Abraham's genius in cornering the diet–product market in postwar America created his fortune: he began in the 1950s with a small pharmaceutical firm that sold an appetite suppressant, and before creating the phenomenally successful Slim–Fast meal–replacement product, his company was the maker and marketer of the top–selling diet pill in the United States in the 1970s.

Born in 1924, Abraham grew up in an Orthodox Jewish family in Long Beach, New York. His father was both a pharmacist and dentist, but Abraham eschewed a college education for himself. After a stint in the U.S. Army during World War II, Abraham went to work for an uncle who owned a small drug company. Yearning to start his own business, he found a small firm for sale that made an itch–relief balm called San–Cura with annual sales of only $5,000. Abraham bought the company, Thompson Medical, with his savings and the funds of his brother–in–law. He was determined to make his venture a success, and peddled its sole product to pharmacies himself; he offered pharmacists free samples to give away to customers if they agreed to display a poster for San–Cura in their store window.

Abraham's Thompson Medical Company began marketing its first diet product in 1956, Slim–Mint gum, which contained an appetite–dulling ingredient called benzocaine. Four years later, the company began making Figure–Aid, an appetite–suppressant candy, and enjoyed steady sales into the 1970s with it. In 1976, the company launched the Dexatrim diet pill, which contained the appetite–suppressing ingredient phenylpropanolamine (PPA). The powerful Dexatrim soon cornered the entire diet–aid market, bolstered by a major advertising campaign that trumpeted the fact that users could take just one a day for it to be effective.

Abraham introduced Slim–Fast, the company's first meal–replacement product, in 1977. But a spate of deaths from liquid–protein diet drinks, which contained far fewer calories than Slim–Fast, made national headlines that year, and Abraham curtailed production and took the remaining products off shelves. Slim–Fast was reintroduced in 1984, and sales skyrocketed over the next few years. In 1988 the company launched a $100–million ad campaign with celebrity endorsements; the product's most popular spokesperson was Tommy Lasorda, manager of the Los Angeles Dodgers baseball team, which helped boost the number of male Slim–Fast users immensely. Between 1989 and 1990, sales of the canned shake or powder mix doubled, and it was spun off from Thompson Medical entirely.

With sales of $500 million for his company by 1991, the famously reclusive Abraham allowed himself to be interviewed by *New York Times* writer Peter Kerr in conjunction with Slim–Fast's soon–to–be launched line of food products. The 60–item Slim-Fast Foods line, sold in grocery stores via a manufacturing and distribution deal with food giant ConAgra, would compete directly with similar low-calorie frozen and prepared edibles from Weight Watchers International, Lean Cuisine, and Healthy Choice. Kerr noted that it was a risky move, because Thompson had no real experience in the food business, but Abraham remained nonplussed. "This company has been dedicated to always giving the consumer something better, a little extra for his money," he told Kerr. "Neither Healthy Choice nor Weight Watchers offer the same healthy nutrients."

When Slim–Fast Foods was launched in earnest in early 1992, Abraham spent lavishly on a ten–page coupon newspaper insert that reached 61 million United States households; at the time, it was the biggest single newspaper promotional event in history. Its early–January launch was timed to coincide with the traditional post–holiday weight gain and corresponding New Year's resolution to get in shape among consumers, but Abraham knew that the market was undergoing a more subtle shift. "Slim–Fast's new products come at a time when researchers say consumers are turning away from the relentless desire to be almost instantly skinny that typified much of the 1980s," wrote Kerr in the *New York Times*. "In this decade, analysts say, consumers are more likely to search harder for foods that appear healthful than for products that promise a quick shortcut to shedding pounds."

Despite the massive success, Abraham maintains his aversion to publicity. In 1991, *Forbes* writers Phyllis Berman and Amy Feldman attempted to pro-file him, but noted that it had been extremely difficult to find any business or social acquaintance of his that was willing to talk to a reporter. Berman and Feldman did learn some details, however. "Abraham practices what he preaches," the *Forbes* article noted. "He's a fitness fanatic. His daily routine begins with serious exercise in the private workout room built into his marble– and glass–decorated Manhattan apartment, followed by a swim in the pool atop the building. At night, he occasionally winds down with a boxing match with a friend."

Privately, Abraham is a major philanthropist and has contributed heavily to Middle East peace initiatives. For many years he worked with a Utah Democrat, Wayne Owens, and together they co-founded the Center for Middle East Peace and Economic Cooperation. Abraham takes a rather liberal—and somewhat controversial—stance on the Israeli–Palestinian question, believing that true security as a state for Israel is possible only through peace with its neighbors, not war. He has also funded a program called Birthright Israel, which sponsors trips for young American Jews to the religious homeland. Abraham is also known as a large Democratic Party donor, and was a quiet supporter of the Clinton White House. The business school of Bar Ilan University in Ramat Gan, Israel, was created from Abraham's largesse, and for several years in the late 1990s he unsuccessfully fought the zoning board in Florida's posh Palm Beach enclave in the hopes of establishing a new Orthodox synagogue on an expensive parcel of beachfront property there. Abraham also has a vacation home in Netanya, Israel. He sold the Thomson Medical Company in 1998 for $200 million, and Unilever bought Slim–Fast in 2000 for $2.3 billion; the sale landed him on *Forbes* magazine's "Rich List" of the 400 wealthiest Americans.

Sources

Chain Drug Review, January 13, 1992, p. 2.
Forbes, December 9, 1991, p. 10, p. 136; September 30, 2002, pp. 228–230.
New York Times, August 31, 1991, p. 33.
Palm Beach Post, May 25, 2000, p. 1D.

—*Carol Brennan*

Linda Allard

Fashion designer

Born May 27, 1940, in Akron, OH; daughter of Carroll (a civil engineer) and Zella (a homemaker) Allard; married Herb Gallen, March 18, 2000. *Education:* Kent State University, Kent, OH, B.F.A., 1962.

Addresses: *Office*—575 Seventh Ave., New York, NY 10018.

Career

Design assistant, Ellen Tracy, New York, 1962–64; director of design, Ellen Tracy, 1964—; Linda Allard label introduced, 1984; design critic, Fashion Institute of Technology, New York; visiting professor, International Academy of Merchandising and Design, Chicago.

Member: Board of directors, Kent State University; member of The Fashion Group International, Inc., Council of Fashion Designers of America.

Awards: Dallas Fashion Award, 1986; Dallas Fashion Award, 1987.

Sidelights

Linda Allard is the visionary behind the Ellen Tracy fashion label. There never was an Ellen Tracy—the name is a fictional moniker for the brand—but Allard has help make the very real com-

pany one of the leading women's apparel manufacturers in the United States. Her clothes are casual and understated, designed for modern, professional women.

Allard was born May 27, 1940, in Akron, Ohio, the eldest of six children, and grew up in Doylestown, Ohio. Her father, Carroll, was a civil engineer, and her mother, Zella, was a homemaker and 4–H advisor who taught her daughters the arts of gardening, canning and preserving, baking, and sewing. "She was a perfectionist, which has been a really good thing for my career," Allard said in an interview with Lynne Thompson of *Inside Business.* "If I sewed a seam and it wasn't exactly to her liking, I had to rip it out until it was perfect in her eyes." At the age of ten, Allard designed clothes for her paper dolls, and became a swift designer and seamstress for herself, her sisters, and her friends as a teen. "I really wanted to do something with my life that had to do with clothes," Allard told Thompson, "but I wasn't sophisticated enough to know that there were so many fashion schools ... all over the country."

As an art major in her senior year at Kent State University in Kent, Ohio, Allard had to compile a portfolio of her work. She used her friends as models, offering to design an outfit for each of them if they would buy the materials. One of her art teachers secured a photo shoot location for her at a traveling circus that was passing through town. The event turned out to be more complicated than Allard had bargained for—the art teacher had negotiated a deal that his students would repaint the circus wagons in exchange for their use as props in Allard's photo shoot. The story became campus legend at Kent State.

In the 1960s, it was traditional for young women with fine arts degrees to pursue careers as art teachers, and to work on their own art during summer breaks. Allard had a different plan. She earned her Bachelor of Fine Arts degree from Kent State University in 1962. Soon after, with a gift of $200 from her parents in her pocket, she boarded a bus bound for New York City. Once there, she moved into a women's hotel and began searching for a job. Three weeks into her search, she walked out of a downpour into the offices of Ellen Tracy, which was just a junior blouse manufacturer at the time. Company founder and chairman Herb Gallen hired Allard, despite the fact that she was dripping wet. "Her head was wet—she was soaked," Gallen told *Inside Business*. "But she acted like she knew what she was talking about."

Gallen had founded Ellen Tracy in 1949. He invented the name himself; he thought it sounded feminine. After two years as a design assistant, Allard was promoted to design director when Ellen Tracy's designer left the company. She and Gallen worked together to expand Ellen Tracy into a full junior–sportswear manufacturer. In 1979, the company introduced its first designer sportswear line. Linda Allard's name went on Ellen Tracy fashions in 1984, on a line called Linda Allard for Ellen Tracy. A reasonably priced line of weekend and casual office wear, called Company Ellen Tracy, was unveiled in 1990.

Allard and her 15–person design staff churn out three collections a year for both the Ellen Tracy and Company Ellen Tracy lines. She travels to five or six cities each spring and fall to meet face–to–face with the women who wear her clothes. Allard is not only the designer and visionary behind Ellen Tracy; she also is, in a sense, her own model. "I only wear Ellen Tracy," she told *Inside Business*. "When I'm designing, I'm thinking partly for myself, partly for women like me." While other labels present outrageous garments each season, Allard keeps her designs beautifully styled but wearable. "I'm not here

to make art for art's sake or to make some sort of statement by doing something that's never been done before," Allard told Irene Daria of *Women's Wear Daily* (*WWD*) in 1986. "The people who do that sort of thing make a big splash and then, after they've splashed, they sink." She later told *WWD*'s Janet Ozzard, "We study our customer, we have the same viewpoint. I design for a woman who has a career or a profession and wants to feel fabulous in her clothes, but it isn't the be–all and end–all of her world."

"People can relate to Linda's garments—they're attractive, they look good on you, they function well for you," Elizabeth Rhodes, director of Kent State's fashion school, told *Inside Business*. "Customers can become loyal to it," Lynne Ronon of Saks Fifth Avenue told *WWD*'s Ozzard. "Linda Allard is very much in touch with who her customer is." Apparently, many women agree: Ellen Tracy generated gross revenue of $250 million in 2000, and is one of the largest privately held companies in New York's Seventh Avenue fashion district. Ellen Tracy jackets sell for about $395, trousers $200, skirts $175, and shirts $150 to $250. Eveningwear prices are slightly higher. The label is available in the United States at Macy's, Saks Fifth Avenue, and Neiman Marcus department stores.

Allard wed for the first time when she was nearly 60. She has cited dedication to her career for keeping her single. She married Gallen, a widower almost 25 years her senior, on March 18, 2000. Though she has no children of her own, Allard has 13 nieces and nephews, and Gallen has two daughters, seven grandchildren, and nine great–grandchildren. The two split their time between his home in New Jersey and her country estate in Connecticut. There, she loves cooking and entertaining. Her extensive gardens have been featured in several home and garden publications. She wrote a cookbook, *Absolutely Delicious*, which also features her watercolor paintings.

Sources

Atlanta Journal–Constitution, April 14, 2002, p. M6.
Boston Globe, September 5, 1994, p. 38.
Inside Business, September 2001, p. 41.
New York Times, March 19, 2000, p. 9.
Women's Wear Daily (New York), June 2, 1986, p. S29; December 14, 1994, p. 8.

—*Brenna Sanchez*

Avi Arad

President and Chief Executive Officer of Marvel Studios

Born in 1948 in Israel; son of immigrants from Eastern Europe. *Education:* Hofstra University, Hempstead, NY.

Addresses: *Office*—Marvel Studios, 10880 Wilshire Blvd., Los Angeles, CA 90024. *Website*—http://www.marvel.com.

Career

Began his career as a designer of toys, working for companies such as Mattel, Hasbro, and Tyco; joined Ike Perlmutter at Toy Biz, late 1980s; named president and chief executive officer of Marvel Studios, 1998.

Sidelights

Like the superheroes that people the pages of Marvel's popular comic books, Avi Arad, president and chief executive officer of Marvel Studios, has proved himself capable of some pretty incredible feats. In early May of 2002, Arad pulled off what has to be his most impressive accomplishment to date: *Spiderman*, the film based on one of Marvel's most popular comic book heroes, opened to a weekend box office take of more than $100 million, the only film ever to do so. By the end of its second week, the film, starring Tobey Maguire as Marvel's web–slinging hero, had racked up a mind–boggling $240 million at the box office. The film's domestic gross had topped $400 million by the end of the summer of 2002.

Spiderman, on which Arad shared executive producer responsibilities with Stan Lee, co–creator of the character, is just one of the first in a series of Marvel characters scheduled to make their way to the big screen over the next year or so. Arad is personally overseeing the leap of those characters from the comics to film. With more than 4,700 proprietary characters in Marvel's library, the film projects alone should keep Arad busy for a very long time.

No less amazing has been Arad's role in reviving the fortunes of Marvel Enterprises. The company, then known as Marvel Entertainment, filed for bankruptcy in 1998 after a battle of the titans between Ron Perelman and Carl Icahn for its control brought Marvel to the brink of collapse. In 1998, Arad and Ike Perlmutter, partners in Toy Biz, rode to the rescue, winning the approval of a federal judge to take over Marvel. They promptly renamed the combined company, including the toy business, Marvel Enterprises, and installed Arad as president and CEO of Marvel Studios. In that post, Arad is responsible for bringing Marvel's comic book characters to life in toys, film, and television. His first big success came in 2000 with the release of *X–Men*, which had grossed nearly $160 million by the end of the summer of 2002. Although *X–Men* was handily eclipsed by *Spiderman* in 2002, it nevertheless ranked right up there on *Variety*'s list of top all–

time domestic grossers, holding position number 69 as of end–September 2002. Sequels to both *X–Men* and *Spiderman* are already in the works, with the latter scheduled to hit theaters on May 7, 2004.

Hardly your typical corporate executive in appearance, Arad is a walking advertisement for the Marvel franchise. When interviewed in mid–2001 by Patrick Goldstein of the *Los Angeles Times,* Arad wore a black t–shirt emblazoned with the image of one of Marvel's trademark superheroes and a Harley–Davidson belt buckle, all accessorized with a flashy Spiderman ring and lapel button. Arad's offices in West Los Angeles were decorated with a number of X–Men action figures, a Spiderman blow–up doll, and assorted other Marvel memorabilia.

Arad was born in Israel in 1948, the son of parents who had only recently immigrated to the country from Eastern Europe. He was educated in Israel and at the age of 17 joined the Israeli Army, serving from 1965 until 1968. During the Six–Day War in 1967, Arad was seriously injured and spent about 15 months in the hospital, although he declines to discuss the circumstances in any greater detail. He left Israel for New York City in 1970 and put himself through college at nearby Hofstra University in Hempstead on Long Island. After college, he went to work as a toy designer, working for such industry notables as Mattel, Hasbro, and Tyco. In the late 1980s Arad joined forces with fellow Israeli immigrant Ike Perlmutter at Toy Biz.

In 1993 Arad and Perlmutter struck an agreement with Ron Perelman, the then–chairman of Marvel Entertainment, that gave Toy Biz a perpetual license to manufacture toys based on Marvel characters without paying royalties in exchange for 46 percent of the toy company. However, it was not long before the two entrepreneurs discovered that they had a very different vision of Marvel's future than Perelman. In 1995, as Marvel's sales of comic books and baseball cards slumped, Arad and Perlmutter implored Perelman to take advantage of the riches of Marvel's franchise by spinning off TV and film projects built around Marvel's comic book characters. To their dismay Perelman showed little interest. Marvel suffered its first unprofitable year ever in 1995, and 1996 was even worse. Faltering under the burden of its enormous bank debt and troubled by lagging sales, Marvel filed for protection from its creditors under Chapter 11 of the U.S. Bankruptcy Code on December 27, 1996. Marvel bondholders, led by Carl Icahn, blamed Perelman for the company's financial crisis and managed to oust him as chairman. Icahn took over as chairman,

and Arad and Perlmutter sought to work with him to get Marvel back on its feet, but Icahn proved unreceptive to their overtures.

Just short of a year after he took over at Marvel, Icahn was ousted by a federal judge, who then installed a trustee to administer the company. Finally, in June of 1998 Toy Biz won approval from a federal judge to take over Marvel. The transaction was completed in October of 1998, putting Marvel in the hands of Arad and Perlmutter. The two entrepreneurs emerged the unlikely victors in a battle dubbed *Comic Wars* by writer/CBS news correspondent Dan Raviv in his book–length study of the struggle for control of Marvel. Arad and Perlmutter merged their prize, Marvel Entertainment, and Toy Biz into a new company they called Marvel Enterprises. Arad was made president and CEO of Marvel Studios, the arm of the new company responsible for film and television projects. His first big box office success, *X–Men,* came out less than two years after his takeover of Marvel with Perlmutter.

With Marvel's vast library of proprietary characters, the possibilities for film and TV projects are virtually endless. In his interview with the *Los Angeles Times*'s Goldstein, Arad observed that when kids graduate today from the prestigious film school at the University of Southern California, "their first phone call is to us, saying, 'I want to make a movie out of your comic books.'" Already in the pipeline, in addition to the *X–Men* and *Spiderman* sequels, are *The Fantastic Four* and *Daredevil* from Twentieth–Century Fox; *The Incredible Hulk* and *Namor the Submariner* from Universal; and *Werewolf by Night* and *Ghost Rider* from Miramax's Dimension Films. Artisan Films also signed an agreement with Arad signaling its commitment to produce films, television shows, and videos based on 15 popular Marvel characters, including Captain America and Black Panther.

Very protective of Marvel's comic book heroes, Arad turned thumbs down on an early script for *Spiderman* because it had the hero slashing one of his opponents's throats. "That would be the end of everything," Arad told the *Los Angeles Times.* "Spiderman kills nobody!" It's a sure bet that Arad will be keeping a close eye on the treatment that all Marvel's characters receive at the hands of Hollywood's filmmakers. In view of the rapidly growing interest in all things Marvel, that should keep him busy.

Sources

Books

Raviv, Dan, *Comic Wars,* Broadway Books, 2002.

Periodicals

Entertainment Weekly, May 10, 2002.
Los Angeles Times, July 10, 2001.
United Press International, May 13, 2002.
Variety, July 13, 1999; May 19, 2002.

Online

"A Comic Wars Timeline," Random House, http://www.randomhouse.com/features/comicwars/timeline.html (September 28, 2002).

"Avi Arad: Biography," Cinema.com, http://www.cinema.com/search/person_detail.phtml?ID=2983 (September 28, 2002).
"*Cloak and Dagger* Comic Coming to Big Screen," Jam! Showbiz, http://www.canoe.ca/JamMovies ArtistsA/arad_avi.html (September 28, 2002).
"Highlights from *Comic Wars*," Random House, http://www.randomhouse.com/features/comicwars/highlights.html (September 28, 2002).
"Marvel Enterprises Inc.," Hoovers Online, http://www.hoovers.com/co/capsule/5/0,2163,42835,00.html (September 28, 2002).

—*Don Amerman*

Scott Bakula

Actor, director, and producer

Born Scott Stewart Bakula, October 9, 1954, in St. Louis, MO; son of Stewart (a corporate lawyer) and Sally Bakula; married Krista Neumann, 1981 (divorced, 1995); children: Chelsy, Cody (with Neumann), Wil, Owen (with Chelsea Field, a dancer and actress). *Education*—Attended Jefferson Junior College, Hillsboro, MO, and University of Kansas.

Addresses: *Office*—15300 Ventura Blvd., Ste. 315, Sherman Oaks, CA 91403.

Career

Actor in television, including: *V* (uncredited), 1983; *My Sister Sam*, 1986; *I–Man*, ABC, 1986; *Gung Ho*, ABC, 1986–87; *Designing Women*, CBS, 1986–88; *The Last Fling* (movie), ABC, 1987; *Matlock*, 1987; *Infiltrator* (movie), 1987; *Eisenhower and Lutz*, CBS, 1988; *Quantum Leap*, NBC, 1989–93; *In the Shadow of a Killer* (movie), NBC, 1992; *Mercy Mission: The Rescue of Flight 771* (movie), NBC, 1987; *Murphy Brown*, CBS, 1993–96; *Dream On*, HBO, 1994; *Carol Burnett: Men, Movies and Carol*, HBO, 1994; *Nowhere to Hide* (movie), ABC, 1994; *The Invaders* (miniseries), Fox, 1995; *The Bachelor's Baby* (movie), CBS, 1996; *Adventures from the Book of Virtues* (voice), PBS, 1996; *Mr. & Mrs. Smith*, CBS, 1996; *Tom Clancy's Netforce* (miniseries), ABC, 1999; *Mean Streak* (movie), Showtime, 1999; *In the Name of the People* (movie), CBS, 2000; *Papa's Angels* (movie), 2000; *A Girl Thing* (miniseries), 2001; *What Girls Learn* (movie), 2001; *Role of a Lifetime*, 2001; *Enterprise*, Paramount, 2001—. Television producer, including: *Mr. & Mrs. Smith*, 1996; *The Bachelor's Baby* (movie), 1996; *Papa's Angels* (movie), 2000; *What Girls Learn* (movie), 2001. Television director, including: *Quantum Leap*, 1990–93.

Film appearances include: *Sibling Rivalry*, 1990; *Necessary Roughness*, 1991; *L.A. Story*, 1991; *For Goodness Sake*, 1993; *A Passion to Kill* (also known as *Rules of Obsession*), 1994; *Color of Night*, 1994; *My Family* (also known as *East L.A.*, *My Family*, *Mi Familia*, and *Café con leche*), 1994; *Lord of Illusions* (also known as *Clive Barker's Lord of Illusions*), 1995; *Cats Don't Dance* (voice), 1997; *Major League: Back to the Minors* (also known as *Major League: The Minors, Major League 3: Back to the Minors,* and *Major League 3: The Minors*), 1998; *Luminarias*, 1999; *American Beauty*, 1999; *The Trial of Old Drum*, 2000; *Above Suspicion*, 2000; *Life as a House*, 2001.

Stage appearances include: *Shenandoah*, New York, NY, 1976; *Keystone*, GeVa Theatre, Rochester, NY, 1981; *Marilyn: An American Fable*, Minskoff Theatre, New York, NY, 1983; *Broadway Babylon—The Musical that Never Was!*, Paper Moon Cabaret, New York, NY, 1984; *Three Guys Naked from the Waist Down*, Minetta Lane Theatre, New York, NY, 1985; *Romance, Romance*, Helen Hayes Theatre, New York, NY, 1988; *The Importance of Being Wilde*, 1995; *Anyone Can Whistle*, Carnegie Hall, 1995; *Nite Club Confidential*, Tiffany Theatre, Los Angeles, CA, 1995. Also appeared in *Accentuate the Positive*, Bottom Line, New York, NY; *Godspell*, Equity Library Theatre, New York, NY; *The Baker's Wife*, Cincinnati Playhouse, Cincinnati, OH; *Fiddler on the Roof, I Love My Wife,*

Joseph and the Amazing Technicolor Dreamcoat, Magic To Do, The Pirates of Penzance. Recording appearances include: *Quantum Leap* (soundtrack), Crescendo Records, 1994; "Somewhere in the Night" (single), Crescendo Records, 1994; *Stars of the Musical Stage*, Madacy Records, 1996; *Cats Don't Dance* (soundtrack), Polygram, 1997.

Awards: DramaLogue Award for best actor for *Nite Club Confidential*, 1986; Viewers for Quality Television Award for best actor in a quality series for *Quantum Leap*, 1991; Golden Globe Award for best performance by an actor in a television series (drama), Hollywood Foreign Press Association, for *Quantum Leap*, 1992.

Sidelights

Since appearing as a singer in a Canada Dry national advertising campaign in the early 1980s, Golden Globe winner Scott Bakula has become one of the most widely recognized faces on contemporary television. He received numerous Emmy Award nominations for his role in the science–fiction dramatic series *Quantum Leap*. He also starred in the short–lived programs *Gung Ho, Eisenhower and Lutz, The Invaders,* and *Mr. and Mrs. Smith.* Plus, he was a series regular and romantic interest for Candice Bergen on the situation comedy *Murphy Brown* for the 1993 through 1996 seasons. In 2001, he debuted as Captain Jonathon Archer on the United Paramount Network *Star Trek* franchise drama, *Enterprise.*

Born in St. Louis, Missouri, Bakula displayed an interest in theater and music at an early age. When he was four years old, a white streak appeared in his hair that has remained there ever since. He began putting together musical groups when he was a fourth grader, and won the starring role in a local church production of *Amahl and the Night Visitors.* After graduating from Kirkwood High School in St. Louis, he briefly attended Jefferson Junior College in Hillsboro, Missouri. For one year, he studied business and pre–law at the University of Kansas, but changed his major to theater. He moved to New York in 1976, playing in several Off–Broadway productions before landing the role of Joe DiMaggio in the Broadway production of *Marilyn: An American Fable* in 1983. He appeared in television commercials for Canada Dry ginger ale and Folgers coffee. From 1986 to 1988, he guest–starred on the television shows *Designing Women, Matlock,* and *My Sister Sam,* as well as landing his first regular series work in the short–lived series *Gung Ho* and *Eisenhower and Lutz.* Following the cancellation of the latter series—which coincided with a Screenwriters Guild

strike—Bakula accepted the role of Alfred/Sam in the Barry Harmon–written Broadway musical *Romance/Romance.* Given the role after it was turned down by Armand Assante, Bakula's performance in *Romance/Romance* earned him a 1988 Tony Award nomination, but he lost to Michael Crawford, who had starred in Andrew Lloyd Webber's blockbuster musical *The Phantom of the Opera.* Offered another leading role in a television series in 1989, Bakula left *Romance/Romance* and was replaced by Barry Williams.

Bakula moved back to Hollywood to star opposite veteran actor Dean Stockwell in the NBC science–fiction television series *Quantum Leap,* which was broadcast on network television from 1989 to 1993. It subsequently became a popular program in syndication. His performance on this show resulted in several Golden Globe and Emmy Award nominations. He was awarded a Golden Globe for best performance by an actor in a television series for *Quantum Leap* in 1992. The program was cancelled for the 1993 through 1994 season, but Bakula rebounded with a recurring role on *Murphy Brown* as television reporter Peter Hunt. He also appeared in a 1994 televised Carol Burnett special, *Carol Burnett: Men, Movies and Carol.* That same year, Bakula was a guest star on the HBO comedy series *Dream On.* In 1995, he acted in *The Importance of Being Wilde,* a benefit play that also starred Malcolm McDowell. Later that year, he starred in a Carnegie Hall performance of the Stephen Sondheim musical *Anyone Can Whistle.* In 1996, he teamed again with Burnett at the Hollywood Bowl to honor Hollywood musicals. Also in 1996, Bakula introduced Bakula Productions Incorporated, which produced the television series *Mr. and Mrs. Smith,* in which he starred. The show was unsuccessful, however, and lasted only one season. The same year, Bakula and Chelsea Fields, his girlfriend and the mother of two of his four children, starred in the television film *The Bachelor's Babies.*

Throughout the remainder of the 1990s, Bakula appeared in a series of mostly forgettable films. He portrayed a therapist friend of Bruce Willis in *The Color of Night,* released in 1994, and it is the murder of Bakula's character that sets the film's plot in motion. In 1995, he portrayed a hard–boiled detective in Clive Barker's *Lord of Illusions.* While assessing Bakula's performance as unconvincing in a videotape review, *Entertainment Weekly* critic Glenn Kenny wrote: "This story of a David Copperfield type who fakes his own death to escape a cult leader is horror maestro Barker's most accomplished filmmaking effort. It features a cohesive plot and a nifty hook: the wobbly line between illusion as entertainment and the actual black arts." *Entertainment*

Weekly film critic Owen Gleiberman was less generous: "A magician (Kevin J. O'Conner) fakes his own onstage death with a series of swords that 'accidentally' plunge into his torso. The rest of the movie is turgid cop–thriller nonsense, with Scott Bakula, looking as bored as I was, chasing down the source of O'Conner's black magic, a desert cult leader who's become a blue–cheese mummy."

Bakula was able to exercise his singing talents as the voice of Danny the cat in the animated musical, *Cats Don't Dance.* In this 1997 film, Danny is a feline from Kokomo, Indiana, who is obsessed with breaking into show business. He takes a bus to Hollywood in an effort to fulfill his dream, but learns that a child film star is ensuring that the film studios discriminate against the use of cats in film. The film enabled Bakula to duet with singer Natalie Cole on songs written by Randy Newman. In 1998, Bakula appeared with Corbin Bernsen in the film comedy *Major League: Back to the Minors,* the third film in the *Major League* trilogy. In this film, Bakula portrayed a former pitcher who takes over the management of a minor league farm team to the Minnesota Twins. A *People* critic wrote: "The always easygoing and welcome Bakula portrays a washed–up pitcher who proves a whiz at managing a ragtag minor league team owned by ML series star Bernson, who has little to do. The jokes here are broad enough to be read from the bleacher seats." Daniel M. Kimmel, writing in *Variety,* dissented: "It's an amusing film in its own right and should enjoy a ham ancillary life on cable and homevid."

In 1999, Bakula starred in the ABC network miniseries *Tom Clancy's NetForce* with actors Kris Kristofferson, Brian Dennehy, Joanna Going, and Judge Reinhold. In the production, Bakula portrayed Alex Michaels, the commander of NetForce, a division of the FBI dedicated to policing rampant technology in the year 2005. According to Laura Fries, writing in *Variety,* "The movie poses an interesting question about the rapid growth of technology and its place in the New World Order. After all, the Web's true potential has yet to be tested, and this flick preys on our fears and hopes for the future." Fries appreciated Bakula's performance, which she described as "[bringing] a charismatic everyman feel to his role, although traditionally this kind of part calls for more of a he–man character. His Alex Michaels is more comfortable with bear hugs than SWAT team raids. He even orders his security guard to 'lighten up.'" Bakula also had a brief role in the 1999 Academy Award Best Picture winner, *American Beauty,* which starred Kevin Spacey. He appeared with Kevin Kline in the 2001 film *Life as a House.*

In 2001, Paramount announced that Bakula would star in the fifth *Star Trek* series, *Enterprise.* The show reunited him with producers Kerry McCluggage and Garry Hart, both of whom he work with on *Quantum Leap.* A prequel to the original series that starred William Shatner for three years in the 1960s, *Enterprise* was also preceded by the *Star Trek* series *Star Trek: The Next Generation, Deep Space Nine,* and *Voyager.* The show is more adventure–based than its predecessors, focusing on the development of the technology and galactic politics that became more sophisticated and commonplace in the previous series. In the series, Bakula plays Captain Jonathon Archer, a far more physical Starship captain than any *Star Trek* commander. A Paramount press release described Archer as an "intensely curious captain with a bold personality. Although he has a strong sense of duty, he is a bit of a renegade and is not afraid to question orders or even disobey them if he feels in his gut that he is right." *Entertainment Weekly* television critic Ken Tucker wrote: "The tone of the series is set neither by sci–fi pie–in–the–sky fantasy nor by slavish adherence to Star Trek mythology, but by Bakula's fine, easygoing yet tough demeanor as Capt. Jonathon Archer." Tucker continued: "Archer is a space cowboy who, more in the spirit of John Wayne or Gary Cooper than Shatner or [*Next Generation*'s] Patrick Stewart, rankles at being reined in: In the year 2151, he's burned that the United States long ago decided to defer to the apparently superior knowledge and self–control of Vulcan 'ambassadors.'"

Bakula's likeable familiarity brought a new audience to the Star Trek franchise—an audience with whom he had ingratiated himself through his numerous television, theater, and film appearances. Traditional Star Trek audiences benefited from Bakula's extensive background in drama, romantic comedy, and music—a performing trifecta that viewers and critics alike believed reinvigorated the franchise. Because of Bakula's acting range, episodes of *Enterprise* focused more on the action and adventure concept of original series creator Gene Roddenberry, instead of the mostly serious dramatic episodes of the previous series. With his successful new series, Bakula should continue be a familiar face in television.

Sources

Books

Contemporary Theatre, Film and Television, volume 27, Gale Group, 2000.

Periodicals

Entertainment Weekly, February 3, 1995, p. 60; September 15, 1995, p. 87; January 19, 1996, p. 60; March 15, 1996, p. 51; September 27, 1996, p. 61; September 28, 2001, p. 58.
Parade, February 5, 1995, p. 23.

People, April 7, 1997; May 4, 1998, p. 31.
PR Newswire, May 11, 2001, p. 7380.
Variety, March 24, 1997, p. 34; April 20, 1998, p. 43;
    February 1, 1999, p. 29.

Online

Scott Bakula: Biographical Info, Apus Apus.com,
    http://www.apusapus.demon.co.uk/ailsa/
    bakula/biograph.htm (September 30, 2002).

"Scott Bakula," E! Online, http://www.eonline.
    com/Facts/People/Bio/0,128,17731,00.html
    (October 9, 2002).

"Scott Bakula," Internet Movie Database, http://us.
    imdb.com/Bio?Bakula,+Scott (September 30,
    2002).

—*Bruce Walker*

Clive Barker

Author

Born October 5, 1952, in Liverpool, England; son of Len (a shipping clerk) and Joan (a homemaker) Barker. *Education:* University of Liverpool, B.A., 1974.

Addresses: *Home*—Los Angeles, CA. *Correspondence*—P.O. Box 691885, Los Angeles, CA 90069.

Career

Playwright for the Dog Company, Liverpool and London, 1974–82. Author of short story collections and novels, and writer of screenplays. Producer of films, including: *Hellbound: Hellraiser II,* 1989; *Hellraiser III: Hell on Earth,* 1992; *Candyman,* 1992; *Candyman II: Farewell to the Flesh,* 1995; *Hellraiser: Bloodline,* 1995; *Lord of Illusions,* 1995; *Gods and Monsters,* 1998; *Saint Sinner* (television movie), 2002; *Tortured Souls: Animae Damnatae,* 2002. Director of films, including: *Salome,* 1973; *The Forbidden,* 1978; *Hellraiser,* 1987; *Nightbreed,* 1990; *Lord of Illusions,* 1995; *Tortured Souls: Animae Damnatae,* 2002. Artwork has appeared in shows, including: Bess Cutler Gallery, New York, NY, 1993; South Coast Plaza branch of the Laguna Art Museum, Costa Mesa, CA, 1995.

Awards: British Fantasy Award for best collection, for *Books of Blood,* 1985; World Fantasy Award for best collection, for *Books of Blood,* 1985; Borders Original Voices Award for young adult fiction, for *Abarat,* 2003.

Sidelights

The British author Clive Barker has become one of the most successful horror writers in the history of the field. With books such as *The Books of Blood* and *Weaveworld,* Barker established himself as a bestselling author in the 1980s and 1990s. Master of the genre Stephen King (author of *Carrie, The Shining,* and many other horror novels) has said of Barker, quoted by Douglas E. Winter in the book *Clive Barker: The Dark Fantastic,* "I think Clive Barker is so good that I am almost literally tongue–tied." Like King, Barker has expanded his efforts to include writing for film, most notably the horror film series *Hellraiser.* He has also begun to write books for children, making his first foray into this field with *Abarat,* published to critical and popular acclaim in 2002.

Barker was born in Liverpool, England, in 1952, the son of a shipping clerk and a homemaker. Barker's working class parents, Len and Joan Barker, also ran a boarding house to help make ends met, and it was through the family's paying guests, who were often actors, that the young Barker was introduced to the world of theater—a world which was to have a profound influence on the course Barker's life would take.

Barker's mother was an avid storyteller, and instead of simply reading bedtimes stories to Barker and his younger brother, Roy, she would make them up, often using characters from well–known books. Thus was Barker introduced to the joys of storytelling. That Barker's own stories were later drenched in bloodshed and other horrors normally kept unspoken might just be traced to an incident that occurred when Barker was still very young. When Barker was four years old, he and his family went to see an air show at a nearby airport. The show featured a parachutist who made several successful jumps that day, until, on his final jump, his equipment failed. Horrified, the family looked on as the man fell to his death. As Barker later told Winter, "[I]f my early work is marked by a certain hunger to see what should not be seen … the beginning of that appetite may be here, at the edge of the cornfield with the men watching the sky, and me, struggling in my mother's arms because I was forbidden the sight."

Growing up, Barker became an avid reader of horror fiction, especially that of Edgar Allan Poe. He also developed an interest in theater, and in constructing sculptures out of wire and other objects he found around the house. All three interests—horror fiction, theater, and making art—were to become lifelong preoccupations. Moving from primary to secondary school, Barker began to develop his writing talents in English classes, greatly impressing his teachers with his talent with words. Also at this time, he began to write and perform in plays. One of these, a piece called *The Holly and the Ivy,* raised the hackles of conservative faculty members because it featured a marriage between two men. Undaunted, Barker began to publish an underground newspaper at the school featuring, among other things, illustrations and provocative fiction.

After graduating from secondary school, Barker moved on to the University of Liverpool, focusing first on philosophy, and then majoring in English literature. Barker found college to be stultifying; he found his escape by forming a theater company with some friends. Called the Hydra Theatre Company, the group presented, among other works, plays written by Barker. Barker graduated from the university in 1974, and he continued making theater with Hydra. Money was tight, and the group found it increasing difficult to stay afloat. In 1976, Barker and his friends decided to relocate to London, where there were bigger audiences. In London, the theater company established itself as a professional company called the Dog Company. The company, after an initial struggle, achieved critical and popular success, but by 1982, the company's members agreed to go their separate ways. Barker continued

his playwrighting efforts after his theater company disbanded, but it was his fiction, which he began writing seriously in the final months of the Dog Company's existence, that would bring him his first taste of fame and fortune.

In 1984, Barker published his first work of fiction, a short story collection titled *Clive Barker's Books of Blood.* The stories that make up the collection began as an interesting diversion from Barker's playwrighting activities. As Barker later explained to Winter in *Clive Barker: The Dark Fantastic,* "I was writing them at odd moments and just enjoyed doing them for the benefit of friends or my own pleasure." Originally conceived by Barker as a single book, the collection was published by Sphere in three volumes, without fanfare, advertising, or promotion of any kind. The books at first struggled, and then, as word of mouth spread, they became more and more popular, eventually reaching bestseller status. The books were reprinted in the United States, where they proved equally popular. In the U.S. edition, no less a figure than bestselling horror author Stephen King graced the covers with the words "I have seen the future of the horror genre … and his name is Clive Barker."

Buoyed by the success of his first venture into writing and publishing fiction, Barker went to work on a novel, under contract with Sphere. The book was called *The Damnation Game,* and it was published in 1985. Also in 1985, Barker won both the British Fantasy Award and the World Fantasy Award for the *Books of Blood* for the best collection of 1984. Just in time to capitalize on the prestige brought by the awards Barker published three more *Books of Blood,* bringing the total to six. Barker wrote at a furious pace during this time, publishing two more novels in rapid succession, *Weaveworld,* published in 1987, and *Cabal,* which came out in 1988. His career as fiction author was assured, but he was to add one more title to the list which already included playwright, short story writer, and novelist: screenwriter.

Barker had enjoyed watching horror movies since he was a child, and in the early 1980s he had begun a collaboration with filmmaker George Pavlou, who wanted to adapt some of Barker's work in the *Books of Blood* into a feature film. The result was *Underworld,* which was released in 1985. Shot on an extremely low budget in England, with limited distribution, and plagued by conflicts, personal and otherwise, the feature nevertheless let Barker enter the world of screenwriting, and he found that he liked it.

After *Underworld,* Barker began work on *Rawhead Rex,* based on another of the *Books of Blood* stories, and, like *Underworld,* shot on a limited budget, this time in Ireland. *Rex* was released in 1986. Barker, although gracious about the result, was ultimately disappointed. He realized that he only way to properly present his work on screen was to direct it himself. He got his chance with the film that was to introduce him to a wide audience of moviegoers for the first time. This was *Hellraiser,* released in 1987, and based on a short novel written by Barker called *The Hellbound Heart,* which was published in 1986 in a small press anthology along with works by other authors (the novel was later published separately in 1991). Barker found financing from New World Pictures in the form of a $4.2 million budget.

With no prior experience directing for the big screen Barker quickly found himself with his hands full. As he told Winter in *Clive Barker: The Dark Fantastic,* "A book speaks for itself. But a movie is perpetually in progress. Everything you do in a given day—your screw-ups, your occasional moments of triumph—are visible the next day. And when your producer asks you what happened or why you did such and such, you've got to have answers." Still, making the film proved a very satisfying experience for Barker, and the film quickly gained popularity both among critics and at the box office. In fact, the film was so successful that it spawned two sequels: *Hellbound: Hellraiser II,* released in 1988, and *Hellraiser III: Hell on Earth,* which hit theaters in 1992. Although Barker supplied the ideas in both films, he wrote neither screenplay.

The Hellraiser movies established Barker as a master of the macabre not just among readers, but among moviegoers as well, and his fortunes rose accordingly. His next film project was *Nightbreed.* Released in 1990, this film was the first big-budget Hollywood film that Barker wrote. In spite of the fact that the process of making films required him to give up the supreme creative control that he enjoyed when writing books, Barker continued to enjoy the process of making films, and, armed with his new prominence in Hollywood, he moved in 1991 from London to Beverly Hills, California, to be closer to the action. Also that year he published his next novel, *Imajica.*

Barker wrote both fiction and for the screen through the 1990s. In 1992 came the book *The Thief of Always.* The novel *Everville* saw publication in 1994, and the film *Lord of Illusions,* based on a *Books of Blood* story, hit movie theaters in 1995. The novel *Sacrament* followed in 1996.

Also in 1996, Barker met the man who would become his partner in life, a fashion photographer named David Armstrong. Armstrong later described his chance meeting with Barker as love at first sight, and although the State of California where they lived had yet to recognize same-sex marriages, the two participated in a wedding ceremony at the end of 1997. As Armstrong explained to Winter in *Clive Barker: The Dark Fantastic,* "We did it before God, and that's all that matters. We recognize it, and our friends, and whoever we meet on the street. We're married."

In 1999, Barker's father died after a more-than-three-year battle with leukemia. Partly as a way to come to terms with his grief, Barker conceived of an ambitious quartet of books based on a series of paintings and drawings he had started working on at the time his father had become ill. These illustrated books, about a mystical chain of islands called the Abarat, would be called the *Abarat Quartet,* and their primary audience, far from the horror fans who devoured his previous books, would be children.

Called simply *Abarat,* the first book features a 14-year-old girl as the heroine, based partly on Barker's stepdaughter (Armstrong's daughter), Nicole. The book was published at the end of 2002. Barker also secured a deal with Disney to turn the quartet into a series of films, bringing the theatrical, literary, and artistic influences of Barker's childhood full circle. On March 3, 2003, the book won the Borders Original Voices award for young adult fiction.

Selected writings

Novels

Clive Barker's Books of Blood Volume One, Sphere (London), 1984.
Clive Barker's Books of Blood Volume Two, Sphere (London), 1984.
Clive Barker's Books of Blood Volume Three, Sphere (London), 1984.
Clive Barker's Books of Blood Volume Four, Sphere (London), 1985.
Clive Barker's Books of Blood Volume Five, Sphere (London), 1985.
Clive Barker's Books of Blood Volume Six, Sphere (London), 1985.
The Damnation Game, Weidenfeld & Nicolson (London), 1985.
Weaveworld, Collins (London), 1987.
Cabal, Poseidon (New York), 1988.
The Great and Secret Show, Collins (London), 1989.
The Hellbound Heart, Fontana (London), 1991.

Imajica, HarperCollins (London and New York), 1991.

The Thief of Always: A Fable, HarperCollins (London and New York), 1992.

Everville, HarperCollins (London and New York), 1994.

Incarnations: Three Plays, HarperCollins (London and New York), 1995.

Forms of Heaven: Three Plays, HarperCollins (London and New York), 1996.

Sacrament, HarperCollins (London and New York), 1996.

Galilee, HarperCollins (London and New York), 1998.

The Essential Clive Barker, HarperCollins (London), 1999.

Coldheart Canyon, HarperCollins (London and New York), 2001.

Abarat, HarperCollins (New York), 2002.

Screenplays

Underworld (with James Caplin), 1985.
Rawhead Rex, 1986.
Hellraiser, 1987.
Nightbreed, 1990.
Lord of Illusions, 1995.
The Thief of Always (with Bernard Rose), 1998.

Sources

Books

St. James Guide to Horror, Ghost & Gothic Writers, St. James Press, 1998.

Winter, Douglas E., *Clive Barker: The Dark Fantastic*, HarperCollins, 2002.

Periodicals

Entertainment Weekly, October 4, 2002, p. 21.

New York Times, October 13, 2002, magazine section, p. 62.

San Francisco Chronicle, October 19, 2002, p. D1.

Online

Contemporary Authors Online, Gale, 2002.

—*Michael Belfiore*

David Beckham

Professional soccer player

Born David Robert Joseph Beckham, May 2, 1975, in Leytonstone, London, England; son of Ted (a kitchen equipment fitter) and Sandra (a hairdresser) Beckham; married Victoria Adams (a pop singer), July 4, 1999; children: Brooklyn (son), Romeo (son).

Addresses: *Office*—c/o Manchester United Football, Sir Matt Busby Way, Old Trafford, Manchester M16 0RA, England.

Career

Signed with Manchester United (soccer team) development league, 1989; joined team, 1991; made home debut as right midfielder, April, 1995; became midfielder; named to English national team for 1998 World Cup; became captain of English national team, 2000; signed on to Spain's Real Madrid team, 2003.

Awards: Sky Sports/Panasonic Young Player of Year, 1996; best midfielder, Union Des Associations Europennes de Football, 1999; Most Valuable Player, Union Des Associations Europennes de Football, 1999; Britain's Sportsman of the Year, 2001; British Broadcasting Corporation's Sports Personality of the Year, 2001.

Sidelights

David Beckham is inarguably one of the most celebrated—and celebrity–conscious—athletes of his era. He has spent his entire career in profes-

sional soccer with the Manchester United team, bolstering that organization's already legendary status in English football. "Becks," as Britain's newspapers have dubbed him, is one of his country's most popular pin–up boys, and his face appears in advertisements for products ranging from hair gel to sausages. Married to pop star Victoria "Posh" Adams, Beckham's every move—including joint shopping excursions with his wife—is avidly chronicled in the British tabloids. Notwithstanding his telegenic looks, Beckham's prowess on the soccer pitch remains unparalleled. "There is nothing more beautiful in the English game than the sight of one of Mr. Beckham's free kicks arching over the defenders's wall and curling into a corner of the net, or one of his signature cross shots cannoning off his foot and speeding like a guided missile toward one of his leaping teammates," opined *New York Times* writer Warren Hoge. Closer to home, he has been termed "English football's willowy, floppy–haired poster boy, the living symbol of the new affluence which has enabled the game to shake itself free of its roots," asserted *Independent* writer Richard Williams.

Beckham was born on May 2, 1975, in Leytonstone, England. He grew up in a solidly middle–class area of Essex called Chingford, where his father, Ted, was a kitchen renovator and his mother worked as a hairdresser. Winning a soccer skills tournament at the age of eleven, Beckham won a place at a soccer academy for youth run by the Tottenham Spurs team. As a teen, however, he was rejected for a spot in the English junior league. One of the country's most celebrated teams, however, took an interest in him, and Beckham entered the legendary Manchester United club organization as a 14–year–old recruit in its development league in 1989; two years later, he began playing on its youth team. In 1992, Beckham led his team to a national championship with their win in the Football Association (FA) Youth Cup finals.

Manchester United, rivals to cross–town Manchester City, overcame an infamous tragedy in 1957 when a plane crash killed several team members en route from a game in West Germany. Eleven years later, they became the first English team in history to win the prized European Cup. Over the years, Manchester's fortunes rose, and it became a leader in the FA, known for its mix of veteran players and young upstarts. "Manchester United is to Britain what the New York Yankees are to the United States," explained Hoge in the *New York Times*, "a collection of highly paid athletes who win with a dynastic consistency, which makes them adored in Manchester and loathed elsewhere."

Beckham made his first appearance in the signature Manchester red jersey in a game against Brighton on September 23, 1994. He made his home debut at Old Trafford, Manchester's legendary pitch, in April of 1995. He was put in during the second half in a match against Aston Villa, and scored a goal. Loaned out to the Preston North End team for a time, Beckham originally played right wing before being switched by coach Glen Hoddle to a central midfield position. During his first game in the 1996–97 season, Beckham made a stunning shot that brought him overnight fame and a place in the annals of soccer: he scored a goal from inside his own half of the field in a game against Wimbledon, a shot of nearly 60 yards.

Beckham was given a spot on the English national squad within a few days—another impressive honor for such a novice player—and continued to play well for Manchester, scoring an impressive eleven goals during his first season. His ability to "bend" a shot—to send it flying in an arc that eludes opposing players—soon became legendary, and some medical experts even theorized that an unusual combination of joints in his knees and ankles helps him achieve such aerodynamic precision. Beckham, explained *New Statesman*'s Hunter Davies, "is bandy–legged–but only from the knees down....

Above the knee, his legs and thighs go straight up and are what we call normal. But below the knees, each leg is curved inwards like a boomerang. Very weird. This abnormality explains how he can bend the ball when taking corners and free kicks."

As the 1998 World Cup in France loomed, Beckham was increasingly tagged as the player to watch, the one who would take England to a long–awaited finals finish. Hoddle, who also coached the national squad, attempted to check some of this anticipation by keeping Beckham out of the first match. He was sent in to a game against Romania after another player was injured, and then against Colombia scored his first goal for England, a fantastic free–kick shot.

Thus emotions ran high when England began its next game in the second round, a match against bitter foe Argentina on the St. Etienne pitch on June 30. The two nations had gone to war in 1982, and four years later Argentine footballer Diego Maradona, considered one of the sport's greatest players, scored a winning goal with his hand in a move that was overlooked by referees. Maradona later claimed that it was "the hand of God" that put that ball into the net, and all subsequent World Cup matches between the two countries were marked by intense play and even more ardent crowd reactions. At the start of the second half in the 1998 game, England was down 1–0 when the captain of the Argentine team, Diego Simeone, smashed into Beckham's back. Beckham fell over, and flicked his heel at Simeone, who then collapsed in the melodramatic theatrics which are often a hallmark of international soccer play. The referee showed up and gave Simeone a yellow card for the first foul, but then flashed a red card at Beckham, ejecting him from the game.

England lost the match, and Beckham was vilified as a loose cannon, a player whose recklessness had yielded another blow to English national pride. Even Hoddle made negative remarks in the next day's papers, and one infamous newspaper photo showed an effigy of Beckham—clad in his Manchester jersey and a sarong that had once made headlines of a different sort for him—on fire outside a pub. "I will always regret my actions," the *Independent* quoted him as saying not long after the debacle. "I have apologised to the England players and management and I want every England supporter to know how deeply sorry I am.... I was absolutely staggered when [the referee] produced the red and sent me off. I felt sick and numb. I couldn't believe what was happening to me." The apology failed to stem the tide of negative press. In the respected *Times* of London, writer Rob Hughes wryly noted that a dozen "years on from Diego Maradona's infamy in Mexico City, comes David Beckham, a gifted but flawed player, to show that the English are well capable of defeating themselves."

Fans and reporters even besieged the Beckham family home in Chingford, and when the new season started, he was given police protection. Crowds booed him every time he had the ball, and sang vicious chants. Though Beckham publicly apologized, he also flew to New York City to be with his girlfriend immediately after the St. Etienne game. He had been dating former Spice Girl Victoria Adams for several months, and the pair had just found out that they were expecting a baby. Beckham later told Kate Thornton in *Sunday Times* that Adams's support was crucial during those tough months. "I couldn't have got through it without her; she was my saviour," he told the paper, and claimed that what "hurt the most about the World Cup was how my family were treated—I thought that was really out of order.... At first I couldn't see any light at the end of the tunnel because by the time I got back from France it was totally out of control, there was nothing I could do or say to make it stop."

Beckham's lot improved considerably during 1999. His son, Brooklyn, was born on March 4, 1999, and he led Manchester United to an impressive season finish: the team won the Premier League championship, the FA Carling Premiership, and the European Champions's Cup in what is known as a Treble victory. He and Adams were married on July 4, 1999, at Luttrellstown Castle in Ireland in a ceremony reported to have cost almost $800,000. Over the next year, he returned to his vaulted status in the British tabloids—though there were sometimes rumors that he might defect to play for an Italian team—and earned impressive contractual endorsements that upped his income considerably. Beckham, wrote Andrew Longmore in the *Independent Sunday*, "has epitomised the ultimate fusion of football and popular culture, the family trees of Manchester United and the Spice Girls, of ancient traditions and disposable fashion joined together in one big money-making enterprise to be known hereafter as Mr and Mrs D Beckham Ltd."

In October of 2001, Beckham made a free kick in the last moments of a World Cup qualifying match against Greece that won the game and gave England a cherished place in the finals. Now the captain of the English national team, Beckham inspired a frenzy of new headlines in April of 2002, just weeks before the May 31 start of the 2002 World Cup in Japan and South Korea, when he injured his second metatarsal, one of the bones between the

ankle and toes, during a game against Spanish team Deportivo La Coruña. Literally adding insult to injury, Beckham's pain was caused by a two-footed tackle from an Argentine player for La Coruña. One newspaper printed a photograph and asked readers to lay their hands on it in with healing wishes, and even British Prime Minister Tony Blair's spokesperson told the press, according to *Sports Illustrated,* that "nothing is more important to England's preparations than the state of David Beckham's foot." Okayed to play by doctors just in time, Beckham atoned for his 1998 red card when he scored with a penalty kick in the 44th minute of the first half. Argentina never scored, and England won the game 1–0. At the finish, Beckham ran to the Argentine side of stadium and waved his jersey, giving out a jubilant yell.

The British press concurred. Headlines and commentary deployed laudatory, heroic terms to describe his performance. "Leadership. Calm. Maturity. Responsibility. All the words that could never have been applied to Beckham four years ago have been raining down on him for months," wrote Simon Barnes in the *Times* of London. "You can tell a great sportsman not merely by his skill, but by the way he deals with an occasion.... Yesterday was the most massive occasion of his life. And he rose." Barnes also stated that "the emotion he displayed in scoring showed clearly that this was an exorcism of four years of grief and misery, of shame and humiliation. For his mistake four years ago was not the error of a footballer, it was the error of a man. Not technique, but character."

Prior to his World Cup feat, Beckham was signed to another three years by Manchester for 14 million British pounds, which tripled his salary. The contract—which took a year of negotiation to finalize—would keep him wearing the Manchester red until the end of June in 2005. For all of the press items that chronicle his haircuts, his clothes, his cars—Ferrari, Porsche, and Jaguar are his preferred rides—and the lavish lifestyle of "Posh" and "Becks," Beckham remains a down-to-earth celebrity athlete. He is not known for his carousing ways, is often photographed nuzzling his son, and his father still attends every one of his games. He calls his wife "the only woman I've ever loved," as he told Thornton in the *Sunday Times.* Beckham's prowess on the soccer pitch has even been honored with an independent film, *Bend It Like Beckham,* a 2002 release from *Bhaji on the Beach* director Gurinder Chadha. The story centers on a teenage girl who dreams of a professional soccer career, much to the dismay of her Indian Sikh parents. Beckham took on a new project in 2002, designing a line of clothing for boys aged six to 14. Beckham told the BBC that the apparel, which will be sold in Britain's Marks & Spencer stores, is "the kind of clothes which I would have wanted to wear when I was younger." On September 1, 2002, Beckham and his wife welcomed the birth of their second son, Romeo, in London, England.

In June of 2003, the Spanish soccer club FC Barcelona agreed to a conditional deal with Manchester United to sign Beckham for $50 million. However, later that month, Manchester United confirmed that they had agreed to sell Beckham to Real Madrid, FC Barcelona's rival (Beckham had two years remaining on his Manchester United contract). On July 1, 2003, Beckham signed a four-year contract with Real Madrid, worth $40 million.

Sources

Periodicals

Birmingham Post (England), June 3, 1999, p. 35.

Daily Mail (London, England), October 6, 2001, p. 93.

Europe, July–August 2002, p. 20.

Financial Times, June 16, 2000, p. 17.

Grocer, May 4, 2002, p. 70.

Guardian (London, England), August 24, 1996, p. 20; February 22, 2000, p. 2; June 20, 2002, p. 6.

Independent (London, England), May 15, 1999, p. 5; May 26, 1999, p. 30; June 4, 1999, p. 32; June 8, 2002, p. 1.

Independent Sunday (London, England), August 18, 1996, p. 32; September 29, 1996, p. 22; June 28, 1998, p. 27; July 5, 1998, p. 23; June 16, 2002, p. 4.

Marketing, March 14, 2002, p. 3.

Mirror (London, England), January 15, 2000, p. 18.

News of the World (London, England), May 12, 2002, p. 66.

New Statesman, April 22, 2002, p. 59.

Newsweek, October 16, 2000, p. 64.

New York Times, December 18, 2001, p. A4; June 8, 2002, p. D3; July 21, 2002, p. 1.

People, May 4, 1998, p. 71; July 19, 1999, p. 58.

Revolution, June 12, 2002, p. 38.

Sports Illustrated, September 7, 1998, p. 28D; April 22, 2002, p. 30.

Sun (London, England), October 26, 1998, p. 7.

Sunday Mirror (London, England), August 25, 1996, p. 60; March 16, 1997, p. 19.

Sunday Times (London, England), March 28, 1999, p. 4.

Time International, April 22, 2002, p. 52.

Times (London, England), February 11, 1997, p. 44; July 1, 1998, p. 45; July 6, 1998, p. 31; August 22, 1998, p. 29; May 26, 1999, p. 52; May 27, 1999, p. 30; June 8, 2002, p. 31.

Western Mail (Cardiff, Wales), April 12, 2002, p. 15.

Online

"Beckham Signs Real Deal," CNN.com, http://www.cnn.com/2003/WORLD/europe/07/01/bechham.medical/index.html (July 14, 2003).

"Beckham To Join Real Madrid," CNN.com, http://www.cnn.com/2003/WORLD/europe/06/17/beckham.madrid.deal/index.html (July 21, 2003).

"Barcelona Wants Beckham's Answer," CNN.com, http://www.cnn.com/2003/WORLD/europe/06/17/uk.beckham.barcelona.index.html (July 21, 2003).

"Dress Becks–style at M&S," BBC.com, http://news.bbc.co.uk/cbbcnews/hi/uk/newsid_1834000/1834303.stm (September 13, 2002).

"Victoria Beckham leaves hospital," BBC.com, http://www.news.bbc.co.uk/2/hi/entertainment/2233700.stm (September 4, 2002).

—Carol Brennan

Jennifer and Laura Berman

Courtesy of Discovery Health Channel

Sex researchers

Jennifer born c. 1964, Laura born c. 1968, in New York, NY; daughters of Irwin (a colorectal surgeon) and Linda (a broker's assistant) Berman; Jennifer married Greg Moore (a professional sailor), 1998; children: Max; Laura married a Spanish businessman, 1995 (divorced, 1998); children: Ethan. *Education:* Jennifer graduated from Hollins College in Roanoke, VA, B.A., 1986; University of Maryland School of Medicine in Baltimore, MD, M.S., 1988; Boston University School of Medicine, M.D., 1992. Laura graduated from the University of Vermont in Burlington, VT, B.A., 1990; New York University, M.A., 1992, M.S.W., 1994, Ph.D., 1997.

Addresses: *Office*—924 Westwood Boulevard, Ste. 515, Los Angeles, CA 90024. *Website*—NewShe, http://www.newshe.com/.

Career

Jennifer trained in the University of Maryland Department of Surgery, 1992–94; served her residency in urology at the University of Maryland Medical Center, Division of Urology, 1994–98; American Foundation of Urologic Disease Research Scholar at Boston University Medical Center, 1998–2000; served at the UCLA Medical Center with a Female Urology/Pelvic Floor Reconstructive Surgery Fellowship, 2000–01; co–founded Women's Sexual Health Clinic at the Boston Medical Center, 1998–2001; co–founded Female Sexual Medicine Center at UCLA's Medical Center, 2001—. Laura completed her fellowship training in sex therapy at the New York University Medical Center, 1996; co–founded Women's Sexual Health Clinic at the Boston Medical Center, 1998–2001; co–founded Female Sexual Medicine Center at UCLA's Medical Center, 2001—.

Awards: Jennifer has earned the American Foundation of Urologic Disease Research Scholar, 1998–2000; the Pfizer Scholar in Urology Award, 1998; the Pfizer Scholar in Urology Award, 1999; first prize essay winner, Society for the Study of Impotence, for "Clinical Evaluation of Female Sexual Function: Effects of Age and Estrogen Status on Physiologic and Subjective Sexual Responses," 1999; first prize essay winner, Female Sexual Function Forum, for "Effect of Sildenafil of Subjective and Physiologic Parameters of the Female Sexual Response," 1999; third prize, Society of Uroradiology Meeting, for "Doppler Evaluation of the Effects of Sildenafil Citrate on Perineal Blood Flow in Women," 1999.

Sidelights

Doctors Jennifer and Laura Berman have been called many names, including the Viagra Twins, Doctors of Desire, Sex Sisters, and Baby Ruths (referring to the grandmotherly sex expert Dr. Ruth Westheimer). The nicknames originate from their pioneering work on the physiology and psychology of female sexual desire and its corresponding dysfunctions. They have co–directed two of America's first health clinics focused exclusively on female sexuality. Their ability to talk straight about concerns that make many people blush has made them media darlings who have made appearances on various television talk shows including *The Oprah Winfrey Show*. Working in tandem they are able to combine their specialties. Laura is a licensed sex therapist and Jennifer is a medical doctor specializing in urology. Their work has demystified and explained dysfunctions related to female sexuality. They have generated groundbreaking scientific information, which some have called revolutionary.

Jennifer was born around 1964, and Laura was born around 1968, in New York, New York, to Irwin and Linda Berman. The Berman sisters grew up in the luxury of Upper East Side Manhattan, where their father was a colorectal surgeon and their mother was a broker's assistant on Wall Street. The girls attended prestigious private schools and took lessons in ballet and drama. Eventually, Irwin grew tired of the pace of life in the big city. He explained to Rebecca Johnson in an interview in *Vogue*, "I was bouncing off my patients instead of relating to them." To escape the city, Irwin moved the family to St. Simons, a small island off the coast of Georgia. Laura and Jennifer faced the challenge of adjusting to a new world that included bias against their Jewish heritage. Laura told Johnson, "My first day of school one of my classmates asked where my horns and tail were." Eventually they settled into the community and began to thrive, most likely because of their parents's ability to face questions directly.

One area in particular was always addressed honestly and succinctly—sex. Jennifer told Barbara Davies of the *Mirror*, "Our father was strict with us, but very comfortable talking about sex." Their mother was also straightforward with her daughters's questions. Laura described her mother to Nick Charles and Karen Grigsby Bates in a *People* interview, "My mother would always answer every question without blinking." In addition, Jennifer and Laura were exposed to their father's work, opening their eyes in different ways to medicine. Irwin would take the girls with him on his rounds at the hospital. It was during this time that Jennifer realized she wanted to become a surgeon. Their mother first thought medicine would be in Jennifer's future when she spent a day caring for her horse that had had an accident. At the same time Laura realized that she did not want to be a medical doctor. Her curiosity and interests would lead her down a different professional path.

Jennifer attended undergraduate school at Hollins College in Roanoke, Virginia. She studied Spanish and psychology and thought about becoming a writer. The only problem was that she hated writing.

After graduating from Hollins in 1986, Jennifer took a pre–med course that ignited once again her earlier interest in medicine. She ended up earning a master of science in human anatomy and physiology at the University of Maryland in 1988. From there she went to medical school at Boston University's School of Medicine. After graduation in 1992, she decided to do her residency in urology.

Medical school itself is a challenge and can be even more of a challenge for an attractive woman. Jennifer's father often advised her to act like a man when faced with challenges while in medical school. She also wore glasses that she didn't need to appear more serious based on the advice of one of her mentors. By choosing to focus on urology, Jennifer further challenged herself by entering a field in which the majority of practitioners are men. After her residency, she became one of about 150 board–certified female urologists in the United States.

During her residency in urology, Jennifer realized that there was a lack of scientific information about women's physiology. One particular example astounded her: the nerves that function for men's sexual organs are known in detail and mapped out so that surgeons can avoid them. The same was not true for these nerves in women. Jennifer decided to focus on female sexual dysfunction. This decision was often met with derision. She told *Vogue*'s Johnson about the reaction of her peers to her area of study, "Their attitude was 'Who cares?' Or not even that—more an uncomfortable kind of laughing. Jokes and then dismissal."

Without realizing it, Laura was taking a path that would eventually cross with her sister's. Laura earned an undergraduate degree from the University of Vermont studying the anthropological aspects of sexuality. She continued her studies at New York University (NYU). At NYU, she earned a master's degree in 1992 focusing on human sexuality, marriage, and family life. She proceeded to get a master of social work in 1994, followed by a doctorate in human sexuality, marriage, and family life in 1997. She studied in programs sponsored by the New York State Department of Health as well as the New York University Medical Center.

One of the most important steps in Laura's becoming a therapist was learning how to normalize sex practices. In therapy, she must address and discuss many kinds of sex practices while making patients feel comfortable. To reach that level of comfort, Laura had to become desensitized to the multitudes of sexual expression. She explained to *Vogue*'s

Johnson, "Anything I was remotely uptight about was pounded out of me.... Now my only criterion for unacceptable behavior is anything nonconsensual."

While the two were completing their studies, their father often joked that they would end up in practice together. Eventually, they did discover that their studies were complementary. Laura explained the realization to Mariko Thompson of the *Daily News*, "We very quickly realized we were working in vacuums in our respective fields. We picked each others's brains. She [Jennifer] became more cognizant of the role that emotions and relationships play. I gained a better appreciation for the role physiology plays. We filled in the blanks for each other." In 1998, the opportunity arose for Jennifer and Laura to begin practicing together.

Laura had married in 1995. After finishing graduate school, she moved to Spain to be with her husband. By 1998, the marriage had fallen apart, and Laura was left trying to figure out what to do with her life. She was newly divorced and caring for her toddler son, Ethan. Meanwhile, as Laura was adjusting to being a divorced mother, Jennifer was getting married. She had met Greg Moore, a professional sailor, while on vacation and the two married in 1998. In 1999, their son Max was born. Soon afterward, Moore gave up professional sailing and went to school to study public health.

In the midst of these changes in their personal lives, a major change was initiated in their professional lives. In 1998, Jennifer received an American Foundation of Urologic Disease research scholarship. Along with her mentor from medical school, Irwin Goldstein, M.D., Jennifer opened the Women's Sexual Health Clinic, the first of its kind in the United States, at the Boston Medical Center. Jennifer invited Laura to be on her staff.

One of their first projects at the Women's Sexual Health Clinic was a study on whether or not the drug Viagra, which had benefited the sexual lives of countless men, could also help women. Their studies showed that some women did benefit from the use of Viagra. They also realized and are vehement in pointing out that no pill can cure all forms of sexual dysfunction. Their research has shown that the intimate connection between mind and body cannot be discounted.

The Bermans's unique system for studying female dysfunction involves several levels of inquiry. When a woman first comes to their clinic, Laura interviews her. This interview helps establish any possible emotional or psychological basis for the dysfunction. After the interview, she is given a complete physical, usually by Jennifer. The third stage of the process involves testing the woman's sexual responsiveness using equipment that measures blood flow and response to stimulation in the genitals. Their method has helped women realize that something they once thought was all in their head—a thought readily encouraged by prevalent attitudes regarding female sexuality—actually has physiological origins. They have also helped many couples come to terms with the emotional problems that inhibit sexual function, helping them to regain the intimacy that is necessary to maintain a committed relationship.

The sisters worked for three years at the Women's Sexual Health Clinic. During that time, their studies started getting the attention of the media. They were making appearances on television talk shows like *Good Morning America, 48 Hours,* and *Larry King Live.* Their honest answers to women's questions about sexuality made them so popular that they appeared on *The Oprah Winfrey Show* twice. According to *Vogue*'s Johnson, Shelley Ross, the executive producer of *Good Morning America,* has called the sisters revolutionary because they can make the show's hosts, Charles Gibson and Diane Sawyer, feel comfortable discussing sex. Although their work is based in sound scientific practice, the two have been criticized for being too media friendly. Jennifer explained to the *Mirror*'s Davies, "I think initially, that the rest of the medical community didn't really take us seriously. But there's science behind what we talk about. People are taking notice."

In 2001, the University of California–Los Angeles (UCLA) Department of Urology took notice and invited the sisters to open a clinic in Los Angeles. Jennifer had just completed a fellowship at the UCLA Medical Center studying female urology and pelvic floor reconstruction. The Bermans took the offer and packed up their families and moved their operations to the West Coast. In addition to establishing the Female Sexual Medicine Center at UCLA's Medical Center, Jennifer and Laura published their first book. *For Women Only: A Revolutionary Guide to Overcoming Sexual Dysfunction and Reclaiming Your Sex Life* has been described as one of the most thorough and understandable guides to female sexuality. By combining the knowledge they have accumulated from case studies and writing in a style that communicates without confusing, the sisters created a usable and reader–friendly book that extends their contact with the public.

The sisters continued to reach an even wider audience with the establishment of the Network for Excellence in Women's Sexual Health. The network is primarily represented by the web site http://www. newshe.com. Through the site, women can access articles by the Bermans and other sexual health professionals, find links to other sites that provide relevant information, and also find out the schedule for the Bermans's television show. Their show debuted on April 15, 2002, on the Discovery Health Channel. *Berman and Berman: For Women Only* is taped in front of a live audience. The daily talk and magazine show provides an intimate space for women to discuss and learn about sexual health issues.

Jennifer and Laura have a good relationship that is evident in their comfort with each other. Growing up they had a typical sibling relationship in which the older Jennifer often teased the younger Laura. Living so close to each other, Laura now has the guilty pleasure of watching her son, Ethan, who is slightly older than Jennifer's son, Max, take on the role of tormentor. They have worked together professionally since 1998, and continue to make gains in their studies of female sexual dysfunction. Combining a commitment to sound science with a highly public image, the Bermans feel that they are achieving the goal that they've set for themselves. Jennifer explained this goal to Davies, "The message we are trying to get out is that something can be done and women don't have to suffer in silence any more." Laura's anthropology professor, Helen Fisher, put their success in a broader context when she spoke to *Vogue*'s Johnson, "The rise of women's sexuality will be one of the big stories of this century, and their approach of looking at problems in the broader context of your emotional and personal life is the next wave of medicine."

Selected writings

For Women Only: A Revolutionary Guide to Overcoming Sexual Dysfunction and Reclaiming Your Sex Life, Henry Holt (New York City), 2001.

Sources

Periodicals

Daily News (Los Angeles), June 10, 2002, p. U4.
Mirror (London), May 30, 2001, p. 24.
People, March 26, 2001, p. 95.
Vogue, December 2000, p. 342.

Online

"Jennifer Berman," FSM Center at UCLA, http://www.urology.medsch.ucla.edu/fsmc–jberman.html (November 14, 2002).
"Laura Berman," FSM Center at UCLA, http://www.urology.medsch.ucla.edu/fsmc–lberman.html (November 14, 2002).

—*Eve M. B. Hermann*

Carole Black

Chief Executive Officer of Lifetime

Born in 1945; married and divorced; children: Eric. *Education*—Ohio State University, B.A. in English literature.

Addresses: *Office*—Lifetime Entertainment Services, 309 West 49th St., New York, NY 10019.

Career

Marketing executive for Proctor & Gamble; worked at the advertising firm DDB Needham, 1983–86; joined the Walt Disney Company as a marketing executive and became vice president in charge of marketing and television, 1986–93; joined NBC4 in Beverly Hills, California, as general manager, becoming the first woman to head a Los Angeles area commercial television station, 1994; left NBC4 to become the first female chief executive officer of the Lifetime cable television network, 1999.

Sidelights

In 2001, under the leadership of chief executive officer Carole Black, the Lifetime cable television network became the most–watched cable television network for prime–time programming in the United States, edging out TBS Superstation and USA Network for the number–one spot. In leading her company up from the number–five spot, Black proved that serious television programming for and about women could be as successful as any other type of programming.

Before Black became CEO in 1999, Lifetime, which had always been led by men, was known for overly sentimental programming featuring women in peril. Under Black, the network matured after 17 years in operation, becoming serious competition for the likes of ESPN and other high–profile cable networks (cable networks as a whole still attracted far fewer viewers than their broadcast counterparts). As Jack Myers, a television advertising analyst, put it in *BusinessWeek,* the Lifetime network had become less about "women in jeopardy, and much more women achieving against the odds."

Some steps Black took to improve Lifetime's offerings included increasing the network's budget for original programming by a factor of three in a period of less than three years. She also doubled the network's budget for marketing, and made women's health issues—such as breast cancer and domestic violence—a priority for network programming.

Black grew up in the Ohio Valley. Her parents divorced when she was just six months old, and Black and her sister were sent to be raised by her maternal grandparents. Their grandparents were immigrants from Armenia and co–managed both a candy store and a real estate office. Black described her childhood to Robin Finn in the *New York Times* as "pretty idyllic." She told *People* that her hard–working grandmother "made me feel I could do everything in life." A leader even in high school, Black was the first girl to be elected president of a student body in Cincinnati, Ohio.

After high school, Black attended Ohio State University; she graduated with an undergraduate degree in English literature. After graduation, Black returned to her hometown of Cincinnati, and married a dentist. She and her husband produced a son named Eric. Also in Cincinnati, Black began her professional life, taking a job at Procter & Gamble as a marketing executive, helping to sell brands like Head & Shoulders and Crest. "It was branding boot camp there," she told the *New York Time*'s Finn, "understanding what the user wants, and delivering on it. And connecting your product with the emotions of the user."

In the early 1980s, Black divorced her husband. She told Finn years later that her marriage was "the first thing I'd ever failed at." Also during this period, Black left Proctor & Gamble, joining the Chicago–based advertising firm DDB Needham in 1983. She remained at that company until 1986. While there, one of her main responsibilities was to help the Sears department store chain appeal more to women.

Black moved from the Midwest for the first time in 1986, establishing a home in Los Angeles, California, to work for the entertainment giant Walt Disney. She rose through the corporate ranks to become vice president of marketing and television. By the time she left Disney in 1993, Black had greatly increased home video sales at the company, partly by focusing marketing efforts on working mothers.

In 1994, Black became the first woman to head a Los Angeles–area commercial television station. With no previous television experience, Black was hired to run the NBC affiliate NBC4. As at DDB Needham, one of her main tasks was to increase the number of women consuming her employer's products; in this case, television programming. NBC president and CEO Bob Wright recalled in *USA Today* that Black's experience in advertising is what made her an ideal choice for leading NBC4 to greater profitability. "That sophistication in reaching people with messages," said Wright, "was a big idea to bring into Los Angeles."

Black's work at NBC4 was an unqualified success; during her time there, her station became the number–one television news station in the area, and

pulled in more revenue than at any other time in its then 50–year existence. Black's success at the television station made her the prime candidate to run Lifetime when the then–current CEO's contract with the cable network ran out. At the time, Lifetime was ranked number five among cable networks, and not considered likely to advance in ranking because women's programming was not seen as lucrative enough.

But Lifetime's corporate parents, Disney and the Hearst Corporation, thought the network had more potential than had been realized thus far, and they thought Black specifically could give the network the boost it needed. Anne M. Sweeney was the Disney executive who ultimately hired Black to head Lifetime. Sweeney outlined her reasoning in *BusinessWeek:* "Nothing was broken, but Carole saw the chance to have a much deeper and stronger relationship with viewers."

Black, initially reluctant to leave a good job in a city she had come to love, finally made her decision after a male colleague tried to talk her out of moving to New York City and the Lifetime network. As she told Finn in the *New York Times,* "He told me, 'You can't go there; if you go there, you'll be number five, you'll never be number one, and you're not the kind of person who can take it if your team isn't number one.'" He didn't know it, but Black's colleague had presented Black with an irresistible challenge.

Black became the first female president of Lifetime in March of 1999. She shook things up right from the beginning, immediately replacing four of the company's top executives. She also added an in–house production arm to allow the network to produce its own daytime shows, because, as she told Keith Alexander in *USA Today,* "[C]ontent is king. I mean, should I say, queen." As at her previous job, her hard work paid off, increasing advertising revenue by 12 percent in a single year, and raising her network to a new respectability among women who had never given it more than a passing glance.

After Lifetime became the number–one prime–time cable network, Black set her sights even higher. "I think we can be bigger," she told Finn. And she told *USA Today*'s Alexander, "Lifetime will emerge as one of the strongest brands for women in this country, not just in TV.... The extensions to this brand are endless."

Black also sees her position at Lifetime as a way to influence issues that are important to women in every aspect of society, not just in entertainment.

"Women are 52 percent of the population," she told Finn. "It's time we had a woman in the White House and not Mrs. Somebody."

Accordingly, Lifetime has become a lobbyist in Washington, working to convince federal officials that issues important to women deserve greater attention. At Black's initiative, the network has produced documentaries on issues such as domestic violence and breast cancer, and has dealt with these topics in its dramatic programming as well. Lifetime has also sponsored hearings on domestic violence in Washington, D.C., supported legislation that would require hospitals to keep mastectomy patients under their care for at least 48 hours, and legislation that would require nurses to be trained in how to collect rape evidence. "The bigger we become," Black told the *Washington Post*, "the more women we can reach. And the bigger difference we can make."

Sources

BusinessWeek, December 24, 2001, pp. 56–57.
New York Times, February 6, 2001, p. B2.
People, May 14, 2001, p. 132.
USA Today, July 29, 1999, p. 1B.
Washington Post, July 21, 2002, p. Y6.

—Michael Belfiore

David Blaine

Entertainer

Born April 4, 1973, in Brooklyn, NY; son of Patrice White.

Addresses: *Office*—c/o Jan Podell, International Creative Management, 40 West 57th St., New York, NY 10019–4001.

Career

Began performing magic tricks for private parties in his late teens; starred in first television special, *David Blaine: Street Magic*, ABC–TV, 1997; second special, *David Blaine: Magic Man*, ABC–TV, 1999; third special, *David Blaine: Frozen in Time*, ABC–TV, 2000; fourth special, *David Blaine's Vertigo*, ABC–TV, 2002.

Sidelights

Almost as amazing as illusionist David Blaine's widely publicized death–defying feats has been his meteoric rise from virtual obscurity to the ranks of top magicians whose names are instantly recognizable worldwide. The Brooklyn–born Blaine first exploded on the scene in the late 1990s, electrifying television audiences with eye–catching demonstrations of his seemingly superhuman powers. To win the hearts and minds of his far–flung audience, Blaine has done everything from being encased in ice for more than two and a half days to balancing himself atop a 90–foot tower for 35 hours before plummeting from his perch into a collection of cardboard boxes on the ground below.

For Blaine the challenge lately has become trying to find stunts even more daring than those he's performed in the past. In early 2003 the illusionist was preparing for still another Houdini–like escapade. Blaine was planning to jump into London's River Thames wearing boots made of lead and handcuffed and bound with rope. As of late February, he had not yet decided whether to make his May of 2003 leap into the Thames from the top of the Tower Bridge—a distance of nearly 190 feet—or from a helicopter hovering even higher above the river's surface. Whichever way he eventually chooses to enter the river, he estimates he will need to hold his breath for seven minutes to work his way out of his bonds and swim to the surface of the river. At last report, he'd only managed to go three and a half minutes without taking a breath.

Blaine was born in Brooklyn, New York, on April 4, 1973, and was raised by his mother, Patrice White, after his father—a Vietnam veteran of Italian and Puerto Rican descent—abandoned the family when Blaine was three years old. The family sometimes survived on welfare alone, although his mother worked as a waitress when she could. Fascinated by magic from an early age, he learned his first card trick—the pencil through the playing card illusion—when he was only four years old. As a boy, he carried a deck of cards with him everywhere he went, willing to perform feats of legerdemain for friends or strangers at the drop of a hat.

When Blaine was ten, his mother remarried, and the family moved to New Jersey. Around this time, Blaine became interested in acting and began commuting to a performing arts school in Manhattan. Through the school, he managed to pick up some jobs in television commercials and bit parts in soap operas. But he continued to practice his magic and during his teens began booking himself engagements at private parties. When he was 17, he struck out on his own, moving to the Hell's Kitchen neighborhood of West Side Manhattan where he began to develop a reputation as a promising street performer.

In his late teens, Blaine suffered a devastating personal blow. His mother was diagnosed with ovarian cancer. After a long struggle with the disease, she died in 1994 when Blaine was 21. To take his mind off his loss, he threw himself even more feverishly into his magic. Booking himself into celebrity functions, Blaine developed a following among the city's stars of film, music, and sports. Among those for whom he performed were Leonardo DiCaprio, Robert De Niro, David Geffen, Al Pacino, and Mike Tyson.

Increasingly confident in his abilities as an illusionist, Blaine decided to try to win a broader audience. He mailed off a videotape of one of his performances to executives at ABC–TV. To the surprise of everyone but Blaine, his bold gambit worked. Called in for an interview by ABC, the supremely confident Blaine talked himself into a long–term television deal. His first outing for the network—*David Blaine: Street Magic*—was broadcast in 1997 and earned high ratings. It was followed two years later by *David Blaine: Magic Man*, which also turned out to be a big hit with the viewing audience. To drum up interest for his 1999 TV special, Blaine spent more than a week submerged under thousands of gallons of water, emerging 24 pounds lighter.

Blaine got even more daring on his next television outing. For the November of 2000 special, *David Blaine: Frozen in Time*, the magician spent 61 hours entombed in a six–ton block of ice in the middle of New York's Times Square. For two and a half days, Blaine, who'd been fitted with a catheter, stood upright in his icy prison as thousands of curious bypassers looked on. More a feat of endurance than magic, the stunt predictably generated a blizzard of publicity for Blaine and was criticized by many for being overhyped. It certainly gave Blaine plenty to talk about as he made the rounds of the television talk shows.

For his fourth TV special in May of 2002, Blaine decided to face down one of his personal demons. Troubled all his life by a fear of heights, he proposed to stand for more than 30 hours atop a tiny platform 90 feet above New York City's Bryant Park. To cap off this marathon balancing act, the magician plunged from his perch into a foundation of cardboard boxes at the base of the tower on which he'd stood. The latter feat was done live before the television audience. Blaine disappeared into the maze of boxes below and for a few seconds it was unclear whether he'd hurt himself or not. Then with a flourish he picked his way out of the boxes, making it clear to all that he was fine. At the end of 2002, Blaine's book, *Mysterious Stranger,* was published. The book was "a hybrid of history, memoir and, of course, marketing," according to Dan Jewel in *People.*

Blaine, who uses his middle name as his last name, has managed somehow to keep his real last name a secret. Although he loves performing in public, he prefers to keep his private life as mysterious as possible. As for labels, he doesn't like them, particularly the label of magician. "I don't like to categorize," he told Barbara Davies of the *Mirror* of London. "I like to think of myself as somebody who likes to perform. I like to inspire; I like to cause wonder, intrigue. That's my goal."

Selected writings

Mysterious Stranger, Villard, 2002.

Sources

Books

Complete Marquis Who's Who, Marquis Who's Who, 2001.

Periodicals

Entertainment Weekly, November 22, 2002, p. 36.
Mirror, November 28, 2002, p. 16.
Newsday, November 5, 2002, p. B6.

People, May 26, 1997, p. 124; December 29, 1997, p. 14; December 23, 2002, p. 43.
Time, May 19, 1997, p. 97.

Online

Biography Resource Center Online, Gale Group, 2001.
"David Blaine," AskMen.com, http://www.askmen.com/men/entertainment_60/79_david_blaine.html (February 18, 2003).
"David Blaine Bio," Trickshop.com, http://www.trickshop.com/blaine.html (February 18, 2003).
"Street Magician: David Blaine," Magic Directory, http://www.magicdirectory.com/blaine/biography.shtml (February 18, 2003).

—Don Amerman

Lee C. Bollinger

AP/Wide World Photos

President of Columbia University

Born Lee Carroll Bollinger, April 30, 1946, in Santa Rosa, CA; son of Lee and Pat Bollinger; married Jean Magnano (an artist), 1968; children: Lee (son), Carey (daughter). *Education:* University of Oregon, B.S., 1968; Columbia University Law School, J.D., 1971.

Addresses: *Office*—2960 Broadway, New York, NY 10027–6902, Mail Code 4309.

Career

Law clerk for Judge Wilfred Feinberg, U.S. Court of Appeals for the Second Circuit, 1971–72; law clerk for Chief Justice Warren Burger, U.S. Supreme Court, 1972–73; assistant professor, University of Michigan, Ann Arbor, 1973–76; associate professor, University of Michigan, 1976–1979; professor of law, University of Michigan, 1979–94; dean of law school, University of Michigan, 1987–94; provost and professor of government, Dartmouth College, 1994–96; president, University of Michigan, Ann Arbor, 1996–2002; president, Columbia University, 2002—.

Awards: National Humanitarian Award, National Conference on Community and Justice, for strong defense of affirmative action in higher education; Herbert W. Nickens, M.D., Award for Diversity, Association of American Medical Colleges, 2001; Columbia Law School Association's Medal for Excellence, 2002.

Sidelights

Senator Carl Levin called him a "dynamic and visionary leader" in a tribute delivered on the floor of the Senate. The *Christian Science Monitor* dubbed him a "Renaissance man." *Newsweek* said that he was "part of a new, visionary breed of college presidents." Having risen to the level of an Ivy League school president, one might think that Lee C. Bollinger would be tempted to retreat to his ivory tower and rest on his laurels. However, Bollinger is a man fundamentally incapable of such passivity. While university presidents must satisfy a wide range of constituencies—from alumni and potential donors to students and faculty—Bollinger demonstrated at the University of Michigan that he could at once expand the sciences, enhance the arts, stand up for his principles, and help grow its endowment to be the fourth largest among public universities.

A highly recognized First Amendment scholar who has championed the cause of affirmative action, Bollinger is on the front lines of a battle over whether it is constitutional to consider race in the admissions process—a battle that has made it to the United States Supreme Court. His interest in freedom–of–speech issues and his advocacy for diversity in higher education both stem from his belief that we cannot truly understand the world without exposure to a full spectrum of perspectives, and that for higher education to be successful, it must create an environment in which these perspectives can be shared. Indeed, he sees the university not as an ivory tower where academics and researchers can hide away with their books and test tubes, but as an evolving, responsive institution that is engaged with and contributes to the world at large.

Bollinger was born in 1946 in Santa Rosa, California, and was raised there and in Baker, Oregon, where his father owned a newspaper. He attended the University of Oregon, where he met his future wife, Jean Magnano. In an article on the University of Oregon College of Arts and Sciences website, Bollinger said that it was in college that he had his intellectual awakening: "My senior year was one of the best years of my life," he recalled. "I lived alone and read—it was a wonderful opportunity to digest an incredible array of novels, philosophy, and social theory, and to be around great intellectuals." He graduated in 1968, and soon after, he and Magnano were married.

Bollinger and his wife then moved to New York, where they both enrolled at Columbia University in the fall—Magnano at the Teachers College, and Bollinger at the Law School, where he was an articles editor at the *Columbia Law Review*. He graduated in 1971, and went to work as a law clerk for Judge Wilfred Feinberg on the United States Court of Appeals for the second circuit. In 1972, he became a law clerk for Chief Justice Warren Burger on the United States Supreme Court. Bollinger then joined the faculty of the University of Michigan in 1973 as an assistant professor, becoming an associate professor in 1976, and a professor of law in 1979.

Bollinger was named Dean of the University of Michigan Law School in 1987, where he continued to teach. He made headlines in 1989, along with Francis X. Beytagh, Dean of the Ohio State University College of Law, after a United States district court ruled that the FBI had systematically discriminated against Latino agents. Both deans barred the FBI from recruiting on campus (though Beytagh did allow the distribution of literature) because their non–discrimination policies prohibit the use of school facilities to contact students. Bollinger imposed a ban of one year after several student groups complained. "It was deeply offensive to own our students to assist that organization in hiring," Bollinger told the *Los Angeles Times*.

After seven years as dean of the University of Michigan law school, Bollinger became provost of Dartmouth College, and a government professor in July of 1994. James O. Freedman, president of Dartmouth at the time, said that Bollinger had "unerring judgment," according to the Columbia College Today website. In November of 1996, Bollinger moved on to become the president of the University of Michigan, where he was known for his warmth and accessibility. He hosted an open house to celebrate the Wolverines's appearance in the 1998 Rose Bowl, and often held "fireside chats" with students. Bollinger's accomplishments at Michigan include the construction of the Walgreen Drama Center, which houses a 450–seat theater; bringing the Royal Shakespeare Company of Great Britain to campus; and development of the Life Sciences Initiative, which included a $100 million facility and 20 to 30 world–renowned research teams.

While at the University of Michigan, Bollinger again made headlines when in 1997 he was named as a defendant in two separate lawsuits filed by three white students who were denied admission. The suits claimed that the university's affirmative action policies unfairly discriminated against the students because of their race. Bollinger worked hard to garner national support from higher education leaders and organizations, and from dozens of major corporations, which filed briefs on behalf of the university. Bollinger told the *Los Angeles Times*'s Kenneth R. Weiss that the lawsuits held implications for the world beyond the university: "I decided to use this case to educate society about this issue. This is not just a Michigan issue—it's a higher–education issue, it's a business issue, and a military issue." He got the backing of multinational corporations because "[i]n their judgment, good business requires workers who can function well in a racially and ethnically diverse environment," he said. Bollinger further explained that, in his understanding, "military academies take race into account as a factor in admissions … [b]ecause of the belief that we need an integrated officer corps, given the racial composition of the military." So far, the University of Michigan has spent more than $4 million in defending the cases.

In October of 2001, Columbia University chose Bollinger to be its nineteenth president; he officially took up the post on June 1, 2002. Part of what attracted Columbia to Bollinger was his willingness to speak out for the causes in which he believes. Barbara Kantrowitz wrote in *Newsweek* that "Bollinger's outspoken advocacy of affirmative action has made him a role model for those who would like to see more college presidents speak out on social issues in the tradition of such august educators as James Bryant Conant, who ran Harvard University from 1933 to 1953 and then went on to help reform American high schools." But maintaining diversity is only one of Bollinger's concerns. While he understands the vital importance of investing in the sciences for a research university, he is also passionate about the arts and the humanities. "What is happening to classics, to literary criticism, to poetry? Are we making the right choices in the allocation of resources?" Bollinger asked in an interview with Mark Clayton of the *Christian Science Monitor.*

Bollinger strongly believes that a university must strive to integrate the various academic disciplines whenever possible. "Bollinger worries that the 'lack of integration of knowledge' is a pitfall for society," wrote Clayton. This desire for learning across disciplines led to a lot of controversy on July 23, 2002, when Bollinger announced that he was calling off the search for a new dean for the Columbia School of Journalism, and was forming a task force to re-think the school's mission. School administrators were swamped with e-mails and phone calls following the announcement, some voicing support, others angry.

"My interest is not in fixing a particular problem, but in addressing and exploring what a modern journalism school should look like," Bollinger told Brent Cunningham of the *Columbia Journalism Review.* "My sense is that it is possible to enhance what is already a very fine program by looking at opportunities to relate the school to other parts of the university," he added. This might include allowing journalism students to concentrate on one specific area—medicine, for example—and then to take courses from that particular curriculum; or it might mean allowing for exposure to an array of subjects, such as political or economic theory, the arts, or scientific practices. Bollinger told Cunningham that ethics is the one thing that should be incorporated into all courses, not just in the School of Journalism.

At Columbia University, Bollinger continues to teach an undergraduate course on one of his favorite topics—freedom of speech and the press (he has written several books and numerous journal articles on the topic); and he continues to run four to five miles a day. He's drawing his interests in the arts and education together in a book examining the role of museums, universities, and other public cultural institutions. Plus, the United States Supreme Court was slated to hear the two affirmative action cases in which Bollinger is a defendant. While Columbia, being a private university, is not directly affected by the outcome (though all federal funding could be threatened if the plaintiffs win), Bollinger will once again be in the spotlight, standing up for what he believes in—and he'll have a lot of people standing behind him.

On June 23, 2003, the Supreme Court ruled that race can be used in university admission decisions. But the court also "seemed to put limits on how much of a factor race can play in giving minority students an advantage in the admissions process," according to National Public Radio (NPR). The justices "decided on two separate but parallel cases—they voted 5-4 to uphold the University of Michigan's law school affirmative action policy, which favors minorities. But in a 6-3 vote, the justices struck down the affirmative action policy for undergraduate admissions, which awards 20 points for blacks, Hispanics, and Native Americans on an admissions rating scale. The cases tested whether the university is allowed to discriminate because it values diversity in its student body, or whether discrimination is only justified to reverse past racial injustice," NPR reported.

Selected writings

Contract Law in Modern Society: Cases and Materials, West Publishing Co., 1980.

Tolerance and the First Amendment, Marshall–Wythe School of Law, College of William and Mary, 1986.

The Tolerant Society: Freedom of Speech and Extremist Speech in America, Oxford University Press, 1986.

Images of a Free Press, University of Chicago Press, 1991.

Eternally Vigilant: Free Speech in the Modern Era, University of Chicago Press, 2002.

Sources

Periodicals

Christian Science Monitor, November 20, 2001, p. 15.
Los Angeles Times, February 22, 1989, section 1, p. 14; February 4, 2001, Opinion, section M, p. 3.
Newsweek, March 11, 2002, pp. 54–56.
New York Times, July 25, 2002, p. 6.

Online

"Biography," *President's Office of Columbia University,* http://www.columbia.edu/cu/president/biography.html (December 3, 2002).
"Carl Levin Senate Floor Statement—In Recognition of Lee Bollinger's Service as President of the University of Michigan," *U.S. Senate,* http://www.levin.senate.gov/floor/120701fs1.htm (December 3, 2002).

"Split Ruling On Affirmative Action," National Public Radio, http://www.npr.org/news/specials/michigan (July 21, 2003).

"In His Own Words: Lee Bollinger," *Columbia Journalism Review,* http://www.cjr.org/year/02/6/bollinger.asp (December 3, 2002).

"The Life of the Mind," *Columbia College Today,* http://www.college.columbia.edu/cct/sep02/sep02_cover_mind.html (December 4, 2002).

"UO Alum Lee Bollinger Takes Top Job at Columbia," *CAS Alumni & Development,* http://www.cas.uoregon.edu/alumnidev/cascade/200205bollinger.html (December 3, 2002).

—*Michael Geffen*

Robert C. Bonner

AP/Wide World Photos

United States government official

Born c. 1942, in Wichita, KS; married Kimiko, c. 1970; children: Justine. *Education:* Earned degrees from the University of Maryland, Georgetown University School of Law, and Harvard University.

Addresses: *Office*—Office of the Commissioner, U.S. Bureau of Customs and Border Protection, Department of Homeland Security, Washington, D.C. 20528.

Career

Served in U.S. Navy, with the Judge Advocate General's Corps; assistant U.S. Attorney, Los Angeles, CA, until 1975; attorney in private practice; appointed United States Attorney for the Central District of California by President Ronald Reagan, 1984; appointed United States District Judge, Central District of California, by President George H.W. Bush, 1989, and Administrator of the Drug Enforcement Administration, Washington, D.C., 1990; partner in the law firm Gibson, Dunn & Crutcher, Los Angeles, c. 1993–2001; U.S. Department of Treasury, Washington, D.C., Commissioner of Customs, 2001— (renamed U.S. Bureau of Customs and Border Protection and placed under the Department of Homeland Security, February, 2003).

Sidelights

California attorney Robert C. Bonner has earned high marks for his management of the U.S. Customs Service since September of 2001. Bonner became commissioner of what was once an arm of the Department of Treasury just days after the terrorist attacks on the World Trade Center and the Pentagon, when national–security concerns emerged overnight as a top White House priority. Bonner's tough executive skills helped re–shape the Customs Service for the new era, and defuse inter–agency wrangling as well; it also continued to ensure that United States trade was not obstructed as a result of these new measures. "The U.S. Customs Service has twin goals: increasing security and facilitating trade," an article by *Transportation & Distribution* journalist Lisa H. Harrington quoted him as saying. "I reject the notion that these goals are mutually exclusive."

Born in the early 1940s, Bonner earned a political science degree from the University of Maryland before going on to law school at Georgetown University. He served in the U.S. Navy for three years on active duty in the Judge Advocate General's Corps, the office that handles all legal matters for the Navy. From there he spent four years as an assistant U.S. Attorney in Los Angeles, California. In 1975, he entered private practice and rose to prominence in the Los Angeles area for his legal expertise and growing involvement in Republican circles.

In 1984, President Ronald Reagan appointed Bonner U.S. Attorney for the Central District of California, the top prosecutorial job in Los Angeles and several surrounding counties. He won praise for his zeal in handling a notorious case involving a slain U.S. Drug Enforcement Administration agent, Enrique (Kiki) Camarena. He also gained a reputation for being a tough, no–nonsense boss. "As far as being one of the guys, that's just not my image," *Washington Post* writer Michael Isikoff quoted him as saying. "I am required to put some demands on the assistants that require a little more distance than being just another attorney in the office."

Bonner's reputation attracted the notice of Reagan's successor, George H.W. Bush, who in 1989 appointed him Judge on the U.S. District Court for the Central District of California. Bonner spent a year on the bench before another presidential appointment, this time as chief of the Drug Enforcement Administration. During his three–year tenure at this government agency, which is charged with eradicating illegal drug trafficking, Bonner became known for the success of his office in obstructing money-laundering trails, thereby robbing the drug cartels of their source of cash. Bonner left the DEA when a new Democratic administration entered the White House, and went back to Los Angeles and into private law practice as a partner at Gibson, Dunn & Crutcher.

Bonner was nominated to become the next U.S. Customs Service commissioner in June of 2001 by the George W. Bush White House, and passed a Senate confirmation hearing in July. His formal appointment, however, was hamstrung by internecine arguments in Congress over textile–trade policy, and was still pending on September 11 of that year. National–security concerns ended much of the partisan bickering, and Bonner was formally confirmed on September 19. He became head of a Customs Service with some 22,000 employees, including 2,000 agents, whose duty it is to inspect goods entering the United States via 301 official points of entry. After the September 11 attacks, a Level One Security Alert was immediately declared at all borders, and Customs agents began thoroughly inspecting all cars and trucks at the border crossings. Bonner asked Canadian authorities for extra help in the cargo inspections, and the 12–hour waits to enter the United States quickly diminished.

Another of Bonner's pressing concerns was the security of U.S. ports, where some 50,000 cargo containers were unloaded from ships daily. Such yards–long units, which hold imported goods ranging from electronics to textiles, are called intermodal containers, and Bonner warned that should terrorists even use just one cargo container for an attack, "the shipping of containers would stop cold for a period of time. This is not a lesson we want to learn," *WWD* writer Joanna Ramey quoted Bonner as saying. "The stakes are high and the system is vulnerable." Within a few months he had won widespread support for his "Container Security Initiative." Announced in January of 2002, the new Customs Service program asked foreign port agents at ten major world cities, from Hong Kong to Rotterdam, to inspect outgoing containers before they arrived at United States ports. The plan fit in with Bonner's goal of a "smart" border perimeter—the extension of security measures beyond the physical borders of the United States. "Trade experts express amazement at the speed with which Bonner has persuaded foreign trade ministries to join in—and with minimal help from other U.S. agencies," remarked *Washington Post* writer John Mintz.

In early 2003, several government agencies were reshuffled, and Bonner's Customs Service came under the umbrella of the Department of Homeland Security, and was renamed the Bureau of Customs and Border Protection (CBP). By this time, Bonner and the Customs service had put in place other new measures to guard against future terrorist attacks. One of them was the 24–hour rule, which forced ocean carriers to transmit advance cargo manifests to U.S. Customs agents prior to ships being loaded at foreign ports with U.S.–bound goods. Bonner's expertise in cracking international drug cartels has also led to the creation of Operation Green Quest, a hunt for the furtive financial transactions that provide clues into underground terrorist networks.

Outside the office, Bonner reportedly likes to play chess and tennis for recreation. Observers assert that the new leadership role is the perfect challenge for him. A year and half after the September 11 attacks, he presided over a ribbon–cutting ceremony at a new Customs House in lower Manhattan that replaced the one at 6 World Trade Center, destroyed when the North Tower fell. According to a CBP press release, Bonner told the assembled guests that the day was "an important event for the trade community, it's an important event for CBP, and it's an important event for me as Commissioner. I am thrilled that we are back here in lower Manhattan, and I am committed to continuing to our efforts to reestablish a presence here."

Sources

Periodicals

American Banker, June 21, 2001, p. 10.
Atlanta Journal–Constitution, January 18, 2002, p. A10.

Business Travel News, March 25, 2002, p. 6.

Insight on the News, February 11, 2002, p. 6.

JoC Week, May 13, 2002, p. 28; May 27, 2002, p. 28.

Los Angeles Times, January 28, 2002, p. A8.

San Francisco Chronicle, February 19, 1996, p. A15.

Time, June 29, 1992, p. 27.

Transportation & Distribution, January 2003, p. 4.

Washington Post, May 14, 1990, p. A9; November 11, 2002, p. A23.

WWD, November 28, 2001, p. 15; January 18, 2002, p. 2.

Online

"Remarks of CBP Commissioner Robert C. Bonner," Customs & Border Protection, http://www.customs.ustreas.gov/xp/cgov/newsroom/commissioner/speeches_statements/mar31003.xml (April 9, 2003).

"Robert C. Bonner Formally Nominated To Serve As Commissioner Of The U.S. Customs Service," United States Department of the Treasury, http://www.ustreas.gov/press/releases/po448.htm (April 8, 2003).

—Carol Brennan

Lara Flynn Boyle

Actress

Born March 24, 1970, in Davenport, IA; daughter of Sally Boyle (her manager); married John Patrick Dee III, August 11, 1996 (divorced, 1998). *Education:* Attended Chicago Academy for the Arts, Chicago, IL.

Addresses: *Office*—ABC, Inc., 500 S. Buena Vista St., Burbank, CA 91521–4551.

Career

Actress in television, including: *Amerika* (miniseries), 1987; *Sable*, 1987; *Terror on Highway 91* (movie), 1989; *The Preppie Murder* (movie), 1989; *Twin Peaks*, 1990–92; *The Hidden Room*, 1991; *Jacob* (movie), 1994; *Past Tense* (movie), 1994; *Legend* (uncredited), 1995; *Cafe Society*, 1996; *The Practice*, 1997–2003; *Ally McBeal*, 1998, 2002; *Since You've Been Gone* (movie), 1999; *Saturday Night Live*, 2001. Film appearances include *Poltergeist III*, 1988; *How I Got Into College*, 1989; *Dead Poets Society*, 1989; *The Rookie*, 1990; *May Wine*, 1990; *The Dark Backward*, 1991; *Eye of the Storm*, 1991; *Mobsters* (also known as *The Evil Empire*), 1991; *Wayne's World*, 1992; *Where the Day Takes You*, 1992; *The Temp*, 1993; *Red Rock West*, 1992; *Equinox*, 1992; *Baby's Day Out*, 1994; *The Road to Wellville*, 1994; *Threesome*, 1994; *Past Tense*, 1994; *Farmer & Chase*, 1995; *Cafe Society*, 1995; *The Big Squeeze* (also known as *Body of a Woman*), 1996; *Afterglow*, 1997; *Red Meat*, 1997; *Happiness*, 1998; *Susan's Plan* (aka *Dying To Get Rich*), 1998; *Chain of Fools*, 2000; *Speaking of Sex*, 2001; *Men in Black II*, 2002.

Awards: Ensemble Performance Award, National Board of Review, for *Happiness*, 1998.

Steve Granitz/WireImage.com

Sidelights

Perhaps best known for her role as Helen Gamble on the hit ABC–TV series *The Practice*, Lara Flynn Boyle got her start at the age of 20 when she landed a recurring role on the David Lynch television series *Twin Peaks*. On *Twin Peaks*, she played Donna Hayward, who was the best friend of series main character Laura Palmer. That show debuted in 1990, and Boyle has worked steadily since then, expanding her roles to include film as well as television roles. Other roles in the 1990s included parts in the 1993 film *Red Rock West,* which also starred Nicholas Cage and Dennis Hopper, 1994's *Threesome,* in which she played the college roommate of two male students, *Afterglow* in 1997, the ironically named *Happiness* in 1998, and *Men in Black II* in 2002.

Boyle was born in 1970 in Davenport, Iowa. Her mother, Sally Boyle, loved the film *Doctor Zhivago,* and she named her daughter after one of the film's characters, Lara, who was played by Julie Christie. When Boyle was six years old, her father left the family, and Boyle and her mother moved to Chicago, Illinois, and were left to scrape by as best they could, living in a succession of small, low–rent apartments. Boyle never saw her father again after he left the family.

Those early years in Chicago were difficult for Boyle and her mother. Boyle's mother was at times forced to work two jobs to support her and her daughter, including stints as a clerk in an insurance company, and as a retail sales clerk. At one point she worked as the caretaker of the housing project where she and Boyle lived. In the evenings, Boyle's mother would put out rat traps and poison, and in the mornings, before school, Boyle would have to dispose of the dead rats. These hard times bonded Boyle and her mother, and their close relationship remained strong into Boyle's adulthood.

Boyle was shy and introverted as a girl, initially had few friends, and was a poor student. The fact that she had no brothers or sisters compounded her feelings of loneliness. To help her overcome these difficulties, her mother enrolled her in acting improvisation classes at Chicago's Piven Theater when she was ten years old. Boyle's transformation into a performer was almost immediate; she had found her element.

Her first acting class was to become one of Boyle's fondest memories. "I remember the car ride home," she later told Maree Curtis in Australia's *Courier Mail.* "I remember how excited I was. I was making friends and I felt I had something to offer these people." Years later, Boyle's mother told Michael Kilian in the *Chicago Tribune* that acting was her daughter's salvation. "She would have been a high school dropout. She hated school, and was only interested in acting." Also at a young age, Boyle was found to have dyslexia, a learning disorder in which letters and words appear to be reversed. Because of this, Boyle had trouble reading, and so she learned to memorize grocery lists, directions, and other materials that others would normally read. The memorization skills she developed served her well in her later acting career. To this day, she reads scripts twice to make sure she understands them, but she memorizes them very quickly.

In 1984, at the age of 14, Boyle won a scholarship to study at the Chicago Academy for the Arts, where she continued her acting training. She was only 15 years old when she landed her first television role, a part in the miniseries *Amerika.* Boyle wanted to move to Los Angeles, California, immediately to begin her acting career in earnest, but her mother convinced her to stay in school. "I told her that if she would give me two more years and graduate," Boyle's mother explained to the *Chicago Tribune's* Kilian. "I would help her."

Boyle stayed in school, and continued to rack up film and television credits. She made her film debut in a small role in the horror film *Poltergeist III* in 1988. She graduated from the Chicago Academy for the Arts in 1989, and true to her word, Boyle's mother moved with Boyle to Los Angeles so that Boyle could devote all her time to her acting career. Hollywood was everything Boyle wanted it to be. "When I first arrived it was dreamy," she later told Martyn Palmer in the London *Times.* "I was this inner–city kid who'd dreamed of this place with palm trees since I was eleven."

The move to Los Angeles quickly paid off. Boyle immediately obtained an agent, and was soon attending three or four auditions every day. Within two weeks of her arrival in Los Angeles, she landed a recurring role in the TV series *Twin Peaks.* The show, which debuted in 1990, became a hit, and Boyle has never found herself wanting for work since.

Boyle has fond memories of her time working on *Twin Peaks* with director David Lynch. She told Palmer in the *Times,* "I was very naïve when I worked with David and I thought that's what it would always be like, so I wasn't able to be wholly grateful for what was happening to me at the time." *Twin Peaks* ended its run in 1992, and Boyle moved on to roles in films such as the 1992 film *Wayne's World,* in which she played opposite Mike Myers as the ex–girlfriend of the main character.

Other notable film roles for Boyle in the 1990s included a part in *Equinox,* in which she played the girlfriend of a character played by Matthew Modine, and *Red Rock West,* which featured her as the target of a hit man played by Dennis Hopper. Notable TV performances at this time included a role in a Biblical miniseries on the TNT network called *Jacob,* which aired in 1994, and which paired her again with Modine. In 1995, she appeared in *Cafe Society* as a 1950s homemaker pushed into being a prostitute by her husband.

Although Boyle worked steadily through the 1990s, most of the films and TV shows she appeared in during this time had a low profile, and so, consequently, did she. She initially found her lack of fame disappointing, but she sought to put her experiences in perspective. She acknowledged that actors are some of the few hardworking professionals who even expect to achieve broad recognition outside of their professions, and that she should just be happy to be working. She also sought to cultivate this grateful attitude on the sets of the films and television shows she worked on. As she explained to Palmer in the *Times,* "Actresses are a dime a dozen in Hollywood, and if you are difficult to work with there is somebody waiting to take your place.... I try to remember why I started doing this, what I loved about it."

From the very beginning of her career, Boyle has always preferred film and television to acting in theater. Although many actors feel just the reverse, she finds working on camera more challenging, and therefore more satisfying than acting in front of a live audience. Nothing, Boyle has said, reveals an actor's inner life the way a camera does. Therefore, she told the *Chicago Tribune*'s Kilian, "There's less you can get away with, in terms of honesty, in film."

Boyle and her mother continued to live together for some time after they moved to Los Angeles. Her mother remained an active partner in her career, acting as her manager and script–reader, as well as advising her on career issues. Although the two no longer live together, Boyle and her mother remain very close, and the elder Boyle continues to act as her daughter's manager.

Boyle has admitted that she is consumed by her work, preferring to spend her off–time looking for new projects and reading new scripts. "I can't express enough how much life I get from work," she told Kilian in the *Chicago Tribune*. "I'm one of those people. I tend to become very much of a homebody and go into my shell when I'm not working."

In 1997, Boyle landed a recurring role as an attorney on the hit TV series about a law firm called *The Practice*. On the show, she played a hard–nosed District Attorney named Helen Gamble, who acted as a foil and love interest for attorney Bobby Donnell, played by Dylan McDermott. *The Practice* became a hit, and for the first time, Boyle began to experience the broad recognition that she had always felt she deserved.

Also in 1997, Boyle appeared in a film called *Afterglow*. Directed by Alan Rudolph, this film starred the woman whose character in *Doctor Zhivago* Boyle had been named after: Julie Christie. Boyle later called the experience of working with Christie a high point of her career. Along with Christie, actresses Boyle has cited as influences in her work include Joan Crawford, Marlene Dietrich, Bette Davis, and Katharine Hepburn—people who lived lives of glamour, soaking in the adoration of their fans. "That's my whole thing," she told the *Courier Mail*'s Curtis. "I want to copy and rip them all off, but you can't even come close." She also told Curtis that one of the attributes she admires most in those actresses is their supreme confidence. "They were like the men—they didn't have to prove anything."

Like the movie stars of old, Boyle enjoys looking the part, even when she is not on set. Going out in public is an event to her. As she explained to the *Times*'s Palmer, "I'm from the old school where I don't like it when people go to the theatre and look like they are going to work out or hang around on a street corner asking for dimes." She said of dressing up, "I think it's part of my job. If I go to a movie premiere or an awards show, it's like being a bride over and over again. I enjoy it."

In 2002, Boyle appeared in her first big–budget Hollywood film, *Men in Black II*, which starred Will Smith and Tommy Lee Jones as immigration agents chasing illegal space aliens. In the film, Boyle plays a ravenous space alien named Serleena. She opens the film in a scene in which she uses her good looks to attract a would–be rapist in a deserted park at night, and then devours him. Used to acting mostly in independent films and on television, Boyle found the experience of appearing in a big budget Hollywood film exhilarating. As she told Tom Charity in *Time Out*, "to see yourself the size of a first–story building, your face the size of a Dodge, that is awesome."

All in all, Boyle, who makes her home in Beverly Hills, California, is grateful for the path her life and career have taken. "My life," she told Palmer in the *Times*, "has surpassed my dreams and what I hoped would happen by marathons. I've got a great gig."

In May of 2003, Boyle, along with six of her fellow cast members, was dropped from *The Practice*. The ABC network, striving to cut costs in the face of sliding ratings throughout its programming lineup, required producer David E. Kelley to cut his budget for the show in half—from $6.5 million to $3.5 million. Kelley told reporters that the decision to cut so many cast members was extremely painful, but necessary if the show was to stay on the air.

Sources

Periodicals

Chicago Tribune, October 5, 1997, p. 7.
Courier Mail (Queensland, Australia), July 13, 2002, p. L4.
Entertainment Weekly, June 28/July 5, 2002, p. 37.
Time Out, July 31, 2002, pp. 22–23.
Times (London, England), July 27, 2002, magazine section, p. 36.
USA Today, May 21, 2003, p. D3.

Online

"Biography for Lara Flynn Boyle," Internet Movie Database, http://us.imdb.com/Bio?Boyle,%20 Lara%20Flynn (April 11, 2003).

"Lara Flynn Boyle," ABC.com, http://abc.abcnews. go.com/primetime/thepractice/bios/lara_flynn_ boyle.html (April 11, 2003).

"Lara Flynn Boyle," All Movie Guide, http://www. allmovie.com/cg/avg.dll?p=avg&sql=B7850~C (April 11, 2003).

"Lara Flynn Boyle Biography," Hollywood.com, http://www.hollywood.com/celebs/bio/celeb/ 1674052 (April 11, 2003).

"The Facts: Lara Flynn Boyle," E! Online, http:// eonline.com/Facts/People/Bio/0,128,1996,00. html (April 11, 2003).

—Michael Belfiore

Todd Bradley

President and Chief Executive Officer of Palm, Inc. Solutions Group

Born November 29, 1958, in Baltimore, MD; married; children: a son. *Education:* Towson State University, B.S (business administration).

Addresses: *Office*—Palm, Inc., 400 N McCarthy Blvd., Milpitas, CA 95035.

Career

Manager in charge of production and quality control at the Miller Brewing Company, early 1980s; executive in charge of logistics at Federal Express Corporation (FedEx), 1984–1993; executive (eventually serving as president) at NCH Promotional Services, 1993–97; president and chief executive officer of Transport International Pool, a GE Capital Services company, 1997–98; executive vice president of global operations, Gateway, Inc., 1998–2001; executive vice president and chief operating officer, Palm, Inc. Solutions Group, 2001–02; president and chief executive officer, Palm, Inc. Solutions Group, 2002—.

Sidelights

Todd Bradley was named Chief Executive Officer (CEO) of handheld computer maker Palm, Inc.'s Solutions Group in June of 2002. He officially took on the job in September of 2002. He had previously been the company's Chief Operating Officer (COO), and the new posting was made to help Palm, Inc. split into two separate companies, one (headed by Bradley) making Palm–branded hardware, and the other developing software. This dramatic restructuring of Palm was seen as a way to rescue the company from declining sales, and Bradley was placed firmly at the forefront of this effort.

Bradley was born and raised in Baltimore, Maryland, where his father worked as a teacher. After completing high school, Bradley went on to Towson State University, outside of Baltimore. Immediately after earning a bachelor's degree in business administration, Bradley took a job at the Miller Brewing Company, where he became a manager in charge of production and quality control.

Moving on from Miller Brewing in 1984, Bradley landed next at Federal Express (FedEx). At FedEx, Bradley worked to help the company expand its next–day delivery services throughout Europe, managing 2,500 employees and $200 million in revenues. After his stint at Federal Express, which lasted nine years, Bradley worked at NCH Promotional Services, a Dun & Bradstreet Corporation subsidiary, where he was directly responsible for 6,500 employees based in 45 different countries.

Moving on to the GE Capital Corporation, Bradley took over management of a transportation equipment rental and leasing business worth $1.5 billion, leading 3,000 employees based both in North America and in Europe. This business was a wholly GE Capital–owned company called Transport International Pool, and Bradley served as its president and CEO.

Bradley's next job was at computer maker Gateway, Inc., where for a time he was placed in charge of the company's international operations, and based in Dublin, Ireland. His official title at the time was executive vice president of global operations. Gateway, then the second–largest computer manufacturer in the world, created the position specifically for Bradley. Bradley stepped into this position in the summer of 1998, and he was tasked with making Gateway as popular worldwide as it was in the United States. In a move that foreshadowed his later efforts at Palm, Bradley sought to accomplish this in part by introducing Gateway–branded Internet and information services that customers would access on his company's products.

While at Gateway, Bradley was also responsible for boosting sales from Gateway's online presence, Gateway.com, from three percent to fully ten percent of the company's total revenues. He also helped Gateway expand its retail presence in the United States, and he was in charge of a business strategy that had Gateway selling computers in partnership with major chain store retail outlets. His last position at Gateway was as senior vice president of the company's consumer division.

In January of 2001, Bradley came to Palm, Inc. from Gateway. Palm manufactured popular handheld personal computers called Personal Digital Assistants, or PDAs, and had made the Palm brand almost synonymous with this type of product. Initially appointed to the position of Palm, Inc. Solutions Group's President and Chief Operating Officer (COO), he was named the Solutions Group's CEO the following year. This put Bradley, then 43 years old, firmly in charge of Palm's hardware division. The shift was said by Palm's chief executive, Eric A. Benhamou, to be in preparation for the company's splitting its hardware and software divisions into two separate companies. This split occurred later in 2002.

Palm, although blessed with fully two–thirds of the world market share for handheld computers, nevertheless faced increasingly stiff competition from such computer manufacturing giants as Hewlett Packard on the hardware side, and Microsoft on the software side of things. The split at Palm into separate hardware and software companies was seen as a way to strengthen each of the company's enterprises.

Bradley, just as he had at Gateway, quickly moved to the forefront of a movement at Palm to integrate his company's devices with Internet access and services. "The new [Palm] devices," he boasted to *New Media Age*, "are totally built around wireless connectivity, access to the Internet and Web–enabled applications." This new focus would be built into devices marketed under the brand name of Tungsten.

In addition, Bradley hoped to extend Palm's reach to a market of ordinary consumers, including students, homemakers, and others who had previously not responded to Palm's business–centric marketing and manufacturing efforts. A large part of this new push would involve lowering the prices of some of Palm's products, and designing them to be more friendly to non–business consumers.

The first of these consumer devices was priced under $100, marketed under the brand name of Zire, and sold in shrink–wrap packaging at supermarket checkout counters. At the end of 2002, speaking to Chana R. Schoenberger in *Forbes*, Bradley called his then–17–year–old son a representative of Zire's target market. "He wants something that looks cool, can play games, has an address book, and some basic calendar functions."

These actions represented bold moves for the once high–flying Palm, Inc. But bold moves were exactly what was required of Palm if it wanted to stay afloat in an increasingly competitive market. After suffering major sales slumps in the preceding years, some observers doubted whether the company would even survive.

But Bradley had no doubt of the outcome of his business strategies. In fact, he was already looking ahead to one of the biggest markets of all: mainland China. Although he refused to comment about his specific plans, he said in a statement made public by Anh–Thu Phan in the *South China Morning Post*, "We're currently reviewing various strategies and business models for entering the China market. With a population of one billion people, the China market offers tremendous growth potential...."

In addition to his duties at Palm, Inc., Bradley serves on the advisory boards of both the Consumer Electronics Association of America and the Sonic Wall Corporation.

Sources

Periodicals

Forbes, October 14, 2002, pp. 98–99.
Irish Times, March 26, 1999, p. 54.
New Media Age, November 21, 2002, p. 26.

New York Times, May 3, 2002, p. C4.
PC Magazine, May 2, 2002.
South China Morning Post, July 18, 2002, p. 10.

Online

"Palm Board of Directors: Todd Bradley," Palm, Inc., http://www.palm.com/about/corporate/ directors.html#todd (February 26, 2003).

"Palm Management Team: Todd Bradley," Palm, Inc., http://www.palm.com/about/corporate/ executive.html#todd (February 24, 2003).

Additional information was provided by Palm, Inc.'s Corporate Communications department on March 5, 2003.

—Michael Belfiore

Erin Brockovich-Ellis

Sebastian Artz/Getty Images

Environmental crusader

Born Erin L.E. Pattee, June, 1960, in Lawrence, KS; daughter of Frank (an industrial engineer) and Betty Jo (a journalist; maiden name, O'Neal) Pattee; married Shawn Brown (a restaurant manager), 1982 (divorced, 1987); married Steven Brockovich (a stockbroker), 1989 (divorced, 1990); married Eric Ellis (an actor), 1999; children: Matthew (from first marriage), Katie (from first marriage), Elizabeth (from second marriage). *Education:* Attended Kansas State University; Miss Wade's Fashion Merchandising College, Dallas, TX, associate's degree.

Addresses: *Office*—Masry & Vititoe, 5707 Corsa Ave., Westlake Village, CA 91362.

Career

Management trainee, K–Mart, Orange, CA, 1981; electrical design engineer trainee, Fluor Engineers and Constructors, until 1982; secretary, E.F. Hutton, Reno, NV, 1987; file clerk, Masry & Vititoe, early 1990s; asked approval to research unusual pattern of illness in Hinckley, California, that formed the basis for a lawsuit against Pacific Gas & Electric Company; named director of research at Masry & Vititoe; hosted television specials; host of *Final Justice*, Lifetime Television Network, 2003—.

Awards: Consumer Advocate of the Year and Presidential Award of Merit, Consumer Attorneys of California; Profile in Courage Award, Santa Clara County Trial Lawyers Association; Scales of Justice Award, Court TV; Justice Armand Arabian Law and Media Award, San Fernando Valley Bar Association; Special Citizen Award, Children's Health Environmental Coalition; Champion of Justice Award, Civil Justice Foundation of ATLA; President's Award, Oregon Trial Lawyers Association; Mothers & Shakers Award, *Redbook* Magazine; Consumer Advocate of the Year, Themis Capital Corporation; Debbie Cole Award, Silicon Valley Toxics Coalition; Lifesaver Award, Lymphoma Research Foundation of America; Champions of Children Award, Cystic Fibrosis Foundation.

Sidelights

Thanks to the hit movie starring Julia Roberts, the story of Erin Brockovich–Ellis's role in winning the largest legal settlement in American history is fairly well known. As a lowly legal file clerk for a Southern California law firm, the brash, mini–skirted Brockovich uncovered a disturbing pattern of serious illness among residents of Hinckley, California. She prevailed upon her bosses to let her investigate the matter further, leading to the conclusion that much of the sickness in Hinckley was attributable to toxic chromium 6 that had leaked into the town's groundwater from the unlined holding ponds of Pacific Gas & Electric Company (PG&E). Brockovich–Ellis then signed up more than 600

Hinckley residents in a massive lawsuit against the giant California utility, leading in 1996 to the largest direct–action settlement in United States history: $333 million.

That PG&E lawsuit brought Brockovich–Ellis wide recognition within the legal community, and the film story of the file clerk's investigation and subsequent legal victory spread her fame to a far broader audience. What is perhaps less widely known is that Brockovich–Ellis continues to do her thing as an environmental crusader, winning a number of notable victories along the way. No longer a file clerk, Brockovich–Ellis now works as director of research at Masry & Vititoe. Most of her investigatory efforts have been focused on cases of groundwater contamination, including another chromium 6 case against PG&E in Kettleman, California; a trichloroethylene (TCE) contamination case against Lockheed Martin in Redlands, California; and dibromochloropropane (DBCP) and ethylene dibromide (EDB) cases involving Dole and Del Monte Foods in Hawaii.

Brockovich–Ellis was born Erin L.E. Pattee in June of 1960 in Lawrence, Kansas, home of the University of Kansas. The youngest of four children of Frank and Betty Jo Pattee, she grew up in Lawrence with her brothers, Frank Jr. and Tom, and sister, Jodie. In a 2001 interview with Dan Levin, editor of *Conservation Matters,* Brockovich–Ellis discussed some of her childhood aspirations and the path her life has followed since girlhood. "I wanted to be a doctor when I was a kid, but I was a dyslexic. Everyone called me stupid and told me I would never achieve anything great. When I realized how difficult it was going to be just getting through high school, I thought, well, maybe I won't be a doctor, but I could see myself as a model, or as an actress. I'd always had high hopes for myself, but I never thought I'd do a toxic litigation, and have a movie made about it named after me, starring someone like Julia Roberts. If I had said anything like that, people would have called me crazy."

Brockovich–Ellis somehow managed to overcome the obstacles and in 1978 graduated from Lawrence High School. Although both her parents were graduates of the University of Kansas in Lawrence, Brockovich–Ellis opted instead to enroll at Kansas State University (KSU) in Manhattan, Kansas. "Like a lot of kids she wanted to get out of her hometown," her mother, Betty Jo, told the *Kansas State Collegian.* "Some of her friends were going there, too." However, her stay at KSU was very brief. "It was one semester," her father told Eric Adler of the *Kansas City Star.* "She majored in partying. It was

pretty obvious, based on her grades and what was going on, college wasn't for her." Always interested in fashion, Brockovich–Ellis in 1979 headed to Dallas, Texas, where she enrolled in Miss Wade's Fashion Merchandising College.

After earning her associate's degree from Miss Wade's, Brockovich–Ellis followed her brother, Frank, to the West Coast where in 1981 she landed a job as a management trainee with a K–Mart store in Orange, California. She stayed with K–Mart only a few months before taking a job with Fluor Engineers and Constructors to work and train as an electrical design engineer. During her stay at Fluor, Brockovich–Ellis began making the rounds of Southern California beauty pageants. She won the title of Miss Pacific Coast. After meeting restaurant manager Shawn Brown, she dropped out of the beauty pageant circuit. She and Brown were married in 1982. The newlyweds returned to Kansas, where Brockovich–Ellis gave birth to their son, Michael, and daughter, Katie. In the mid–1980s the couple headed westward again, this time settling in Reno, Nevada. They were divorced in 1987.

A single mom with two young children to support, Brockovich–Ellis took a job as a secretary at the Reno office of stock brokerage E.F. Hutton. It was at this job that she met stockbroker Steven Brockovich, whom she married in 1989. Although their marriage was short–lived, ending in divorce the following year, it did produce Brockovich–Ellis's third child, a daughter named Elizabeth. Not long after the divorce, Brockovich–Ellis was seriously injured in a traffic accident in Reno. Temporarily unable to work, Brockovich–Ellis moved her three children to Southern California. Her first encounter with Masry & Vititoe came in 1991 when she retained the law firm's services to sue the driver of the other car involved in the Reno auto accident. Although Masry & Vititoe managed to hammer out a settlement of $17,000 for Brockovich–Ellis, the money didn't go very far in covering not only her medical expenses but the cost of raising three children alone in South California.

Desperate, Brockovich–Ellis appealed to Jim Vititoe, the partner who had represented her in the auto injury case, to give her some sort of job that would provide additional income on which to live. Although Vititoe was somewhat concerned that the buxom, mini–skirted Brockovich–Ellis wasn't exactly an ideal fit for the law office, he reluctantly agreed to give her a job as a clerk. In her interview with Levin in *Conservation Matters,* Brockovich–Ellis recalled what happened next: "So the next day he told me to come in, and I did. Ed [Masry, Vititoe's law partner] looked out of his office ... and he went, 'What the hell is she doing here?' Jim took him into the office and told him that he'd hired me, and Ed said, 'With the exception of being able to sit up by herself, Jimmy, what can she do?' And Jimmy, who's very busy, said, 'I'm going to have her answer my calls,' and that's what I started out doing."

Not long after starting work at Masry & Vititoe, Brockovich–Ellis was approached by Masry, who asked if she knew how to open a real estate file. Although she was clueless about how to proceed, she wanted to favorably impress Masry, so she assured him she could handle the job. As it turned out, the files Masry gave Brockovich–Ellis involved residential properties in Hinkley, California, and were littered with medical reports documenting an alarmingly high illness rate among the citizens of the high desert town of 1,000. Alarmed by the high incidence of serious illness she discovered in the files, Brockovich–Ellis prevailed upon her bosses to let her take a trip to Hinkley. It was on this trip that the file clerk began to suspect that the culprit in Hinkley might be chromium 6, a toxic chemical that Brockovich–Ellis suspected had leached into the town's water supply from holding ponds at PG&E's massive compressor station nearby.

To further build her case against PG&E, Brockovich–Ellis spent hours at the University of California, Los Angeles, library researching chromium 6. As she told Levin in *Conservation Matters,* "I found thousands of reports, and what was interesting to me was that in all the studies of animals there were nosebleeds, strange rashes, and respiratory problems. I made an association between the animals and the people of Hinkley, because they—unbeknownst to one another—were presenting the same symptoms. It made no sense to me why a group of 20, then 30, then 40, then 80 people all complained of the same symptoms."

Even in Hinkley, Brockovich–Ellis's appearance was a bit offputting to the local citizenry. Hinkley resident Valerie Bruce told *People,* "When I saw Erin get out of her car, I thought, 'Oh my God.' But she's more than a great body. She's smart and honest and forthcoming." Whatever personal qualities or physical assets she used are unclear, but one thing is certain: Brockovich–Ellis—with help from Masry—managed to sign up more than 600 of Hinkley's townspeople as plaintiffs in a massive lawsuit against PG&E. In 1996 the giant California utility agreed to pay Hinkley's plaintiffs $333 million in damages in the largest toxic tort settlement in United States history.

For her part in the successful lawsuit, Brockovich–Ellis, who was then earning a monthly salary of $800 as a file clerk, earned a bonus of about $2

million. Her title at Masry & Vititoe was immediately elevated from file clerk to director of environmental research. She's since been further promoted to director of research at the law firm. With her newfound wealth, Brockovich–Ellis was able to move out of a bug–infested apartment in Agoura Hills to a grand mansion in the San Fernando Valley suburbs of Los Angeles.

As often happens, Brockovich–Ellis's sudden reversal of fortune was not without its drawbacks. Her older children, Matt and Katie, both developed substance abuse problems and spent time in rehabilitation. Interviewed by *The Guardian* about the changes in her life since winning the Hinkley lawsuit, Brockovich–Ellis said, "Sometimes I think this house is a curse. My children weren't used to this kind of home. It was like going from rags to riches overnight, and I think it catapulted them into a faster lifestyle than they were used to, a peer group they weren't used to, material possessions, experimenting with drugs. I was so guilt–ridden, having been gone and working, that I found myself going overboard and giving and giving and giving." On the upside, however, Brockovich–Ellis met and married her third husband, Eric Ellis, a native of Burbank who doubles as both a country and western disc jockey and an actor. She and Ellis were married in Hawaii in 1999.

Perhaps most importantly for Brockovich–Ellis, she continues to do what she has come to love the best—fighting for the rights of the weak and those with no voice of their own against the excesses of big business. Although the bulk of her investigations continue to focus on the contamination of water supplies from toxic substances released by large industrial operations, she has recently developed an interest in the problem of toxic mold. The mold issue has particular resonance for Brockovich–Ellis whose San Fernando Valley home was found contaminated by three serious forms of mold—specifically *Aspergillus, Stachybotrys,* and *Penicillium.* She began hosting her own Lifetime television show called *Final Justice* in 2003. The show deals with women who have taken life experiences, challenged the legal system, and made it better for others who follow. On April 28, 2003, Brockovich–Ellis and Masry filed claims with Beverly Hills High School and the city of Beverly Hills on behalf of 25 alumni who allegedly contracted cancer from gases lurking beneath the campus. According to CNN.com, the claims are a precursor to lawsuits Brockovich–Ellis and Masry plan to file against the city and the school, along with five oil companies.

Through all the ups and downs that life has brought her, Brockovich–Ellis retains a strong belief in the power of people to do almost anything if they band together in pursuit of a noble cause. She's seen that power unleashed in Hinkley and dozens of other towns and cities around the country. After more than a decade working with the attorneys of Masry & Vititoe, you might think that Brockovich–Ellis would be aspiring to a career in the law herself, but as she told *Time,* "I don't want to—it's boring. I have great respect for lawyers, but a good deal of their job is writing motions and being in court all day. I like to be around people. I'm afraid that as a lawyer, I'd lose my ability to do that."

Selected writings

Take It From Me: Life's a Struggle But You Can Win, McGraw–Hill/Contemporary, 2001.

Sources

Periodicals

Conservation Matters, Summer 2001.
Forbes, May 28, 2001, p. 64.
Guardian, December 10, 2001.
Kansas City Collegian, March 27, 2000.
Maclean's, February 19, 2001, p. 51.
People, April 3, 2000.
Time, May 20, 2002, p. 8.

Online

Biography Resource Center Online, Gale Group, 2000.
"Brockovich takes on Beverly Hills High," CNN. com, http://www.cnn.com/2003/TECH/science/04/29/california.brockovich.reut/index.html (April 30, 2003).
"Erin Brockovich–Ellis," Masry & Vititoe, http://www.masryvititoe.com/erin.htm (February 19, 2003).
"Erin Brockovich–Ellis," NPR, http://www.npr.org/programs/npc/2001/010816.ebrockovich.html (February 22, 2003).
"Erin Brockovich Is a Real Person Dealing with Real Problems," *Southern Life,* http://www.stp.gasou.edu/George–Anne/arc5/spr00/0405life.html (February 22, 2003).
"Erin Brockovich," *TV Tome,* http://www.tvtome.com/tvtome/servlet/PersonDetail/personid–173090 (February 21, 2003).
"The Power of One," Commonwealth Club of California, http://www.commonwealthclub.org/archive/01/01–02brockovich–speech.html (February 22, 2003).

—Don Amerman

Mel Brooks

Filmmaker and comedian

Born Melvin Kaminsky, June 28, 1926, in Brooklyn, NY, son of Max (a process server) and Kate (Brookman) Kaminsky; married Florence Baum (a dancer), 1952 (divorced, 1959); married Anne Bancroft (an actress), August 5, 1964; children: Stefanie, Nicky, Edward (with Baum), Maximilian (with Bancroft).

Addresses: *Office*—Culver Studios, 9336 West Washington Blvd., Culver City, CA 90232.

Career

Worked as a stand–up comedian, handyman, musician, and social director in Catskill Mountains resort area after World War II. Sketch writer for Sid Caesar, collaborating on television shows, including: *Broadway Revue*, NBC, 1949–50; *Your Show of Shows*, NBC, 1950–54; *Caesar's Hour*, NBC, 1954–57; *Sid Caesar Invites You*, ABC, 1957–58. Writer for television specials starring such performers as Andy Williams, Jerry Lewis, Victor Borge, and Anne Bancroft, 1958–70. Creator of television series, including: *Get Smart*, with Buck Henry, NBC, 1965; *When Things Were Rotten*, with John Boni, Norman Steinberg, and Norman Stiles, ABC, 1975. Actor and or director in films made from his own and co–authored screenplays, including: *The Producers*, 1968; *The Twelve Chairs*, 1970; *Blazing Saddles*, 1974; *Young Frankenstein*, 1974; *Silent Movie*, 1976; *High Anxiety*, 1977; *History of the World—Part I*, 1981; *Spaceballs*, 1987; *Life Stinks*, 1991; *Robin Hood: Men in Tights*, 1993; *Dracula: Dead and Loving It*, 1995. Actor in films written by others, including: *Putney Swope*,

1969; *The Muppet Movie*, 1979; *To Be or Not to Be*, 1983; *The Silence of the Hams*, 1994; *Screw Loose*, 1999. Formed movie production company Brooksfilms, 1980. Producer of films, including: *The Elephant Man*, 1980; *My Favorite Year*, 1982; *Frances*, 1982; *To Be or Not to Be*, 1983.

Awards: Academy Award for best short subject, Academy of Motion Picture Arts and Sciences, for *The Critic*, 1963; Emmy Award for outstanding writing achievement in variety, Academy of Television Arts and Sciences, for *The Sid Caesar, Imogene Coca, Carl Reiner, Howard Morris Special*, 1967; Academy Award for best screenplay, Academy of Motion Picture Arts and Sciences, for *The Producers*, 1968; Writers Guild Award for best original screenplay, for *The Producers*, 1968; Writers Guild Award for best original screenplay, for *Blazing Saddles*, 1975; Nebula Award for dramatic writing, for *Young Frankenstein*, 1976; Writers Guild Award, for *Young Frankenstein*, 1976; Emmy Award for outstanding guest actor, Academy of Television Arts and Sciences, for *Mad About You*, 1997; Emmy Award for outstanding guest actor, Academy of Television Arts and Sciences, for *Mad About You*, 1998; Emmy Award for outstanding guest actor, Academy of Television Arts and Sciences, for *Mad About You*, 1999; Grammy Award for best spoken comedy album, Recording Academy, for *The 2000–Year–Old Man in the Year 2000*, 1999; Drama Desk Award for outstanding new musical, for *The Producers*, 2001; Antoinette Perry Award (Tony) for best musical, League of American Theaters and Producers and the American Theatre Wing, for *The Producers*, 2001; Antoinette Perry Award (Tony) for best book of a musical, League of American Theaters and Producers and the American Theatre Wing, for *The Producers*, 2001.

Sidelights

A comic genius of unparalleled talent, Mel Brooks is a jack of all trades in the entertainment business. Over the years he's done just about everything there is to do in show business. Brooks got his start more than 50 years ago as a stand–up comedian but in the years following he's been an actor, comedy writer, producer, and director. His influence has been felt in film, theater, television, and stand–up comedy. Brooks has even written the musical score for a handful of films, including his own *Blazing Saddles* and *High Anxiety.*

Of all his multivaried show business projects, Brooks is undoubtedly best known for his work in motion pictures. His first venture into feature films came in the late 1960s with *The Producers*, a low–budget satire of the Broadway theater world. The film, a box office disappointment when it was first released in 1968, has since become a cult favorite and in 2001 was transformed into a smash Broadway musical that garnered a record 12 Tony Award nominations. In 1974 Brooks hit pay dirt on the silver screen with *Blazing Saddles,* a box office hit that he co–wrote and directed. He also co–starred in the film and wrote its musical score.

Brooks was born Melvin Kaminsky in Brooklyn, New York, on June 28, 1926. His stage name is an adaptation of his mother's maiden name, Brookman. Son of Max and Kate, both of Russian Jewish origin, he was a small and often sickly child. His father, a process server, died when Brooks was only two years old. The death left him with a sense of loss that persisted into adulthood. In a profile of Brooks written for *New Yorker*, critic Kenneth Tynan observed that later in life Brooks recognized "that his relationship with Sid Caesar [during his years with *Your Show of Shows* in the early 1950s] was that of a child clamoring for the attention of a father. When Brooks went into analysis in 1951, his purpose ... was 'to learn how to be a father instead of a son.'" Growing up in Depression–era Brighton Beach, a neighborhood in southern Brooklyn, Brooks, the youngest of four sons, was spoiled by his mother and three older brothers.

While still a boy, Brooks became a big fan of the movies. One of his favorite films as a child was the 1931 horror film *Frankenstein*, directed by James Whale. After seeing the film, Brooks found he could send his closest childhood friend into hysterics with his rendition of "Putting on the Ritz," as it might be performed by Boris Karloff as The Monster. Years later, he incorporated the routine into his own film, *Young Frankenstein.* Humor became a haven for Brooks as a boy, a safe harbor that allowed him—at least for a while—to forget his small stature and sickly nature.

In his teens, Brooks found summer work in the Borscht Belt resort hotels of New York's Catskills Mountains, working at a variety of tasks, including washing dishes, cleaning the pool and tennis courts, and reminding guests when their time in the hotel's rental rowboats was up. His bosses, recognizing his love—and obvious talent—for comedy, occasionally rewarded him by allowing him to perform for the hotel's guests. In one poolside routine developed by Brooks, he would walk out onto the diving board, clad in a black overcoat and derby hat and carrying two suitcases. According to Tynan's profile in the *New Yorker,* the budding comic would pause at the end of the diving board, exclaim "Business is terrible. I can't go on!" and suddenly plunge, fully clothed, into the pool.

Back in Brooklyn during the school year, Brooks attended Eastern District High School. One of his closest friends growing up was next–door neighbor Buddy Rich, who later taught Brooks how to play the drums. When World War II broke out, Brooks joined the U.S. Army and was eventually assigned duty as a combat engineer. He helped to clear German land mines after the Battle of the Bulge. But even in the military he found it impossible to leave his passion for entertainment behind, spending his spare time organizing shows for the American troops.

After the war, Brooks returned to his old stomping grounds in the Catskills, working in a variety of menial positions until he eventually landed the coveted job of social director. His comic instincts, however, were not to be denied. Whenever possible, he used his position to wheedle his way onto stage where he told jokes, did impersonations, and played the drums. It was during one such performance that he was spotted by Sid Caesar, himself a young comedian and saxophone player. Only a few years later, Brooks worked with Caesar on *Your Show of Shows* and *Caesar's Hour,* two of the most popular variety shows of television's Golden Age in the

1950s. Brooks joined Caesar's writing team, a genuine comedy "dream team," whose members include Larry Gelbart, creator of *Mash;* Carl Reiner; brothers Danny and future playwright Neil Simon; and Woody Allen. At the outset of his employment with Caesar, Brooks earned a very modest $50 weekly; but before long, still in his twenties, he was bringing home $2,500 a week. This radical change in his financial circumstances, coupled with the breakup of his first marriage to dancer Florence Baum and a couple of failed musicals (*Shinbone Alley* and *All–American*) on Broadway, propelled Brooks into years of psychoanalysis.

During his years with Caesar, Brooks developed a particularly close relationship with Reiner, who played second banana to Caesar on air and also pitched in to write comedy sketches with Brooks and other members of Caesar's comedy brain trust. After they had both left the Caesar show, the two decided to bring to life two characters they had created for themselves while writing for Caesar as an in–office shtick. Those unforgettable characters were the 2,000–Year–Old Man and the intrepid reporter in search of enlightenment. Reiner, playing the reporter, was straight man for Brooks's inimitable characterization of the 2,000–Year–Old Man, a miracle of modern science who has survived for more than two millennia and speaks with a thick Jewish–American accent.

First performed publicly in the early 1960s, the 2,000–Year–Old Man routine has survived for more than four decades. After a 2000 revival of the sketch, marked by the release of a new comedy CD and a book, Brooks and Reiner were interviewed by Scott Simon of National Public Radio's *Weekend Saturday.* Brooks, asked what makes a good straight man, told Simon: "What makes a good straight man is somebody who honestly pursues the question, who wants proof of ... the insanities that you're spouting. Carl never lets up. Carl is the best straight man that ever lived." For his part, Reiner said he was successful as a straight man "because I found a guy [Brooks] who makes me laugh. I can't wait to ask him questions. He calls me 'the pest' because he knows that when I ask him a question, I'm looking for ... humor. And sometimes he doesn't feel humorous."

In 1963 Brooks decided to try his hand at directing a film. For his first venture, he selected an animated short subject entitled *The Critic,* for which he also supplied the voice of the film's central character. For his debut in filmmaking, Brooks won an Academy Award for best short subject. The following year, he married actress Anne Bancroft. Brooks next teamed up with comedy actor/writer Buck Henry to create the teleplay for a sitcom called *Get Smart,* which enjoyed great popularity on TV from 1965 until 1970. While still working on *Get Smart,* Brooks dusted off an unpublished novel, *Springtime for Hitler,* he'd written a decade earlier, and adapted it to the screenplay for *The Producers.* In the motion picture, Gene Wilder and Zero Mostel played shady Broadway producers who scheme to sell shares in a sure–to–fail musical entitled *Springtime for Hitler.* Although the film was both a critical and commercial failure when it was first released, it has since become a cult favorite. Next up for Brooks the moviemaker was *Twelve Chairs,* a 1970 film based on the 1928 novel of the same name by Russian authors Ilya Ilf and Yevgeni Petrov. Brooks not only wrote the screenplay and directed the film but acted in it as well. Although critics applauded his acting job, most panned the film as a whole.

Far more successful was Brooks's next film, *Blazing Saddles,* a spoof of traditional western movies that featured just about every stereotypical western character ever seen on the big screen, including a cowpuncher who actually knocks out his horse. Movie critics were mixed in their views on *Saddles.* Vincent Canby of the *New York Times,* as quoted in *Entertainment Weekly,* observed that the film "was funny in the way ... a rude burp in church can be," while the *Wall Street Journal,* as quoted in *Entertainment Weekly,* called it "an undisciplined mess." However, mixed reviews or not, *Saddles* became one of the highest grossing motion pictures of 1974. The movie's title song, composed by Brooks, was nominated for a best song Oscar.

From spoofing westerns, Brooks next turned to movies in the horror genre. His first target was the tale of Dr. Frankenstein, parodied to a fare thee well in the director's 1974 film *Young Frankenstein.* In his review of the film for *Newsweek,* Paul D. Zimmerman hailed it as "an uproarious homage to the horror classic." For his next film spoof, *Silent Movie,* Brooks relied on sight gags and the simplest of plots to make up for its almost total absence of dialogue (the only word is spoken by French mime Marcel Marceau). Just to prove that no one was safe from the Brooks parody machine, he next took on no less a target than master filmmaker Alfred Hitchcock. *High Anxiety,* released in 1977, spoofed several of Hitchcock's best known films, including *North by Northwest, Vertigo, Psycho, The Birds,* and *The Man Who Knew Too Much.*

After the release of *High Anxiety,* Brooks turned his attention for a few years to the production of films by other creative artists. In 1980 he formed a movie production company called Brooksfilms Inc., which turned out such non–Brooksian films as 1980's *The Elephant Man,* and 1982's *My Favorite Year* and *Frances.* He also spent some time before the camera in other people's films, including roles as a mad German scientist in *The Muppet Movie* and opposite wife Anne Bancroft in director Alan Johnston's 1983 remake of the classic farce *To Be or Not to Be.* In 1981 Brooks returned to the director's chair with his production of *History of the World—Part I,* featuring a series of vaudeville skits depicting various periods in history. Next up for Brooks as director was 1987's *Spaceballs,* his parody of the science fiction genre, followed in 1991 by *Life Stinks,* in which he also starred. Other Brooks films during the 1990s included 1993's *Robin Hood: Men in Tights* and 1995's *Dracula: Dead and Loving It.* In the late 1990s, Brooks appeared as actor Paul Reiser's Uncle Phil on the sitcom *Mad About You.* For his role, Brooks received three Outstanding Guest Actor Emmy awards.

One year into the new millennium, Brooks enjoyed one of his greatest triumphs yet with the smashingly successful transformation of *The Producers* into a musical comedy for the Broadway stage. The production, starring Nathan Lane and Matthew Broderick, opened on Broadway in April of 2001. Interviewed on National Public Radio's *All Things Considered* by Robert Siegel, Brooks said: "I haven't been this happy … since the original shooting of the original *Producers,* the movie, at Lincoln Center when the fountain went off and Gene Wilder said, 'I want everything I've ever seen in the movies,' because that was the happiest moment of my life."

Sources

Books

Authors and Artists for Young Adults, volumes 7–26, Gale Research, 1992–96.

Periodicals

Entertainment Weekly, February 11, 2000, p. 84.

Online

Contemporary Authors Online, Gale Group, 2001.
"Mel Brooks: Biography," Hollywood.com, http://www.hollywood.com/celebs/bio/celeb/348201 (August 21, 2002).
"Mel Brooks—Director, Actor, Writer, and Producer," BBC, http://www.bbc.co.uk/dna/h2g2/alabaster/A650594 (August 21, 2002).
"Mel Brooks," E! Online, http://www.eonline.com/Facts/People/Bio/0,128,2222,00.html (October 11, 2002).
"Mel's Biography," Mel Brooks Humor Site, http://www.tmbhs.com/tmbhs/biography.asp (August 21, 2002).

Transcripts

All Things Considered, National Public Radio, May 14, 2001.
Good Morning America, ABC, October 7, 1997.
Weekend Saturday, National Public Radio, October 18, 1997.

—*Don Amerman*

Mark Burnett

Television producer

Born in 1960 in England; married Dianne; children: two.

Addresses: *Office*—c/o Survivor Entertainment Group, 9899 Santa Monica Blvd., PMB 346, Santa Monica, CA 90404.

Career

Joined British Army Paratroop Regiment, c. 1978; served in Northern Ireland and Falkland Islands, early 1980s; moved to California, mid–1980s; worked as a childcare provider and chauffeur, sold insurance and used clothing, worked in advertising and marketing, late 1980s; created *Eco–Challenge,* 1995; bought *Survivor* concept from Charlie Parsons, 1996; *Survivor* debuted on CBS network, 2000; published *Dare to Succeed: How to Survive and Thrive in the Game of Life,* 2002; created *Combat Missions* and *Destination Space* reality television programs, 2002.

Awards: Emmy Award for outstanding non–fiction program (special class), Academy of Television Arts and Sciences, for *Survivor,* 2001.

Sidelights

The producer behind the popular–culture phenomenon *Survivor,* a reality television series on CBS, Mark Burnett has gained success through his creation of such programs as *Eco–Challenge* and *Combat Missions* that mix elements of danger, humor, fun, competition, and the occasional ingestion of ro-

dents, slugs, and insects. Burnett told *Esquire* that the success of *Surviver* is attributable to the recognition factor of the show's contestants: "We've all met people like this. We've all experienced workplace politics. It's duplicity and hardball. It's serious emotions. We can identify."

Born in 1960 in England, Burnett grew up in East London. He told *New York Times Magazine:* "I was an only child and never criticized my whole life. Unconditional love. You can't ask for more." He claimed to *Los Angeles* magazine that he was brought up in a family that struggled financially. When he was 18, he joined the British Army Paratroop Regiment, serving active duty in the Falkland Islands and Northern Ireland. "Real stuff. Horrific. But on the other hand, in a sick way, exciting," he recalled to *New York Times Magazine.* Upon completing active duty, Burnett relocated to Los Angeles, California. He contemplated a career as a mercenary weapons and tactics adviser in Central America, but reconsidered after prompting from his mother, who thought the enterprise too dangerous. For a while, he paid the bills by chauffeuring and working in childcare. He also coached soccer and basketball and taught swimming. In the late 1980s, Burnett received his work permit and completed a management–training program. He worked subsequent jobs as an insurance salesmen and selling used clothing. He later worked in advertising and marketing, and eventually found success marketing his ideas for tax preparation programs and low-interest credit cards. The latter venture, called Public Action, was so successful, it is estimated that Burnett made $1 million when he sold the company in 1992. While he found financial success, he told *Interview,* he had yet to attain satisfaction: "If I'd been born 200 years ago, I would have been an explorer."

Burnett explored the world of adventure racing in the early 1990s, and was inspired to create *Eco-Challenge.* He incorporated Eco-Challenge Lifestyles in 1992, and teamed with New York investment banker Brian Terkelsen, who told *Los Angeles* magazine, "I didn't jump in blind.... I could see that people who were doing marathons in the 1960s, triathlons in the 1970s and the Ironman in the 1980s were looking for the next step." The event "would be a great marketing–television kind of thing—people on the edge of death, racing for a prize," Burnett told *New York Times Magazine.*

Adventure racing began in the mid–1980s in New Zealand. Sponsored by the French cigarette company Gauloises, the races were called raids. A relatively unheard-of activity in the mid–1990s, adventure racing inspired Burnett and his business partner, Terkelsen, to participate in two ten-day outings in Madagascar and Oman. Burnett formed Team American Pride and spent nine months training for his first raid. Team American Pride didn't fare well on their first outing. According to team member Michael Carson, interviewed by *Los Angeles* magazine, "We finally ran out of food and water, but we found a Bedouin who, through hand signals, led us to some stagnant water with dead animals in it. That kept us alive." The group was lost in the desert for four days, and was eventually disqualified after two team members quit during the competition. But Burnett and two others persevered, continuing on to the next phase of the race—kayaking in the Persian Gulf. According to Burnett, as quoted in *Los Angeles* magazine, "An adventure race is a brutal thing." He continued, "But that's what it's designed to be. It's designed to take you to your absolute lowest low, so that you learn something about yourself." His participation in these events presented tremendous challenges. According to *Los Angeles* magazine, "Burnett had hallucinated, been non compos mentis from sleep deprivation, suffered dehydration and diarrhea from drinking pond scum, and huddled with shivering teammates—all bloodied, bandaged, bitten, and blistered." In 1993, Raid Gauloises was held in Madagascar. Contestants parachuted into the jungle and were forced to deal with such extreme heat that the film emulsifier

melted in the ESPN cameras that Burnett had arranged to accompany Team American Pride. This time, Team American Pride finished the course intact, winding up in ninth place.

Burnett and Terkelson took the Raid Gauloises concept back to the United States. Determined to introduce adventure racing to the United States, the two men created a more organized version. Participation in the raids, however, was costly—sometimes the entry fees alone were $25,000. He brought the concept to a more financially manageable level by securing television backing money and office space from MTV and sponsorship money to bring the entry fee down to $10,000 for his first race. Burnett and Terkelson formed the Eco–Challenge race in 1995. The point of the race was to endure harsh climates and terrains while competing for $50,000 in prize money. "I had two goals in mind when I founded *Eco–Challenge,*" he told Mountainzone.com. "One was obviously very commercial. It's a for-profit business and I hoped to make excellent returns on my investment. Number two, I'd hoped to have a really good time making that money."

The first *Eco–Challenge* involved racers competing by bicycle, hiking, horseback, raft, canoe, and mountaineering 370 miles of remote Utah terrain. The Southern Utah Wilderness Alliance, however, protested to stop the race, and Terkelson and Burnett were forced to pay $400,000 in legal fees in order to proceed on schedule. The race featured 50 five-member teams, with each team required to include at least one woman. Of the initial 50 teams, only 21 finished the race. The first race cost $2.5 million to produce, and Burnett subsequently organized mini *Eco Challenge* races for ESPN's *Extreme Games* in Maine, and a second large-scale event in British Columbia. Burnett successfully produced *Eco–Challenge* races for the next six years, making certain to offset any negative publicity with several environmental–service projects. During the British Columbia *Eco–Challenge,* for example, he helped organize the preservation of a salmon–spawning tributary. Likewise, he organized a reforestation project on an eroded riverbank during the Australian *Eco–Challenge.*

Burnett had a chance meeting with British producer Charlie Parsons in 1996 that would spark another adventure. Parsons had created the popular British television series *The Big Breakfast* and had an idea for another series involving stranding 16 castaways on a deserted island. Burnett bought the idea, and spent four years trying to sell the concept to American television networks. Finally, in 2000, CBS was looking for a way to increase moribund summer ratings with a new and exciting original program. Burnett's new program, *Survivor,* fit the bill. An instant hit, *Survivor* attracted swarms of viewers who were intrigued by the challenges presented to the two tribes of castaways. The tribe members could earn immunity by performing such challenges as eating slugs, starting fires, spearing fish, or running obstacle courses. Members participated in tribal councils wherein one of the tribe would be voted off the show until, eventually, there was only one survivor. CBS had a enormously successful hit on its hands. Radio and television talk shows reflected America's obsession with the program. Members who were voted off the show appeared as guests on other television programs to discuss their experiences.

The success of *Survivor* created pressure on Burnett to deliver even more compelling programming. "It used to be that I felt that I was being paid for having adventures," he told *Electronic Media.* "Now it's much more serious … having the responsibility of delivering results for CBS on my shoulders is a huge thing." The following three installments of *Survivor,* which were set in such exotic locales as the Australian Outback, Kenya, and Thailand, failed to match the ratings success of the original program, but continued to garner impressive ratings for CBS nonetheless. Burnett boasted to *Electronic Media* that the success of *Survivor* is due to "good storytelling with a decent pace and a compelling idea executed well." The drama of watching real people competing with each other for the physical and psychological advantage wasn't the only reason viewers tuned in, according to Josef Adalian in *Variety:* "Burnett knew American viewers expect top–notch production values in primetime programs, so he eschewed the cheap–is–better conventions of most reality shows and gave *Survivor* a virtually cinematic look that made the show look as good as (if not better than) the typical network drama." Burnett's method of paying himself directly from the network's advertising revenues was also innovative, and netted him an estimated $15 million for the first installment of *Survivor.* Typically, a producer will sell the rights of a program to a network for an agreed–upon fee.

In 2002, Burnett published his book *Dare to Succeed: How to Survive and Thrive in the Game of Life.* He also created two new shows, *Combat Missions* and *Desti-*

nation Mir. The former show featured former elite members of United States combat units—Navy Seals, Army Green Berets, and Recon Marines—pitted against each other and their own physical limitations. The latter show was to feature 15 contestants vying for the opportunity to spend ten days on the Russian space station Mir with two cosmonauts. The contestants were to compete at a Russian space station. However, when it was decided that Mir was in too poor condition to continue to be used, the space station was brought down to Earth; as a result, Burnett's show fell through. His reputation as the king of reality television prompted him to reflect on success and failure: "Realize you're going to fail all the time, and accept it," he told *Entrepreneur.* "That doesn't mean I'm not frightened of it…. [But] if you don't take risks, you're not going to make it big. You have to embrace uncertainty." Burnett continues to plan bigger and better adventure programming, with an eye on keeping audiences enthralled.

Sources

Periodicals

Broadcasting and Cable, August 14, 2000, p. 6.
Electronic Media, February 19, 2001.
Entertainment Weekly, May 18, 2001, p. 13.
Entrepreneur, March 2002, p. 32.
Esquire, July 2001.
Forbes, March 19, 2001, p. 152.
Interview, February 2001, p. 32.
Los Angeles, January 1996, p. 56.
New York Times Magazine, January 28, 2001.
Publishers Weekly, August 27, 2001, p. 71.
Variety; September 25, 2000, p. 1; November 27, 2000, p. 62; January 15, 2001, p. 42; February 15, 2001, p. 46.

Online

Biography Resource Center Online, Gale Group, 2002.
"Eco–Challenge '98: Mark Burnett—Interview," Mountainzone.com, http://classic.mountainzone.com/features/ecochallenge98/burnett.html (October 9, 2002).

—*Bruce Walker*

Jeb Bush

AP/Wide World Photos

Governor of Florida

Born John Ellis Bush, February 11, 1953, in Midland, TX; son of George H.W. (a former United States president) and Barbara Bush; married Columba Garnica Gallo, 1973; children: George, Noelle, John Ellis "Jeb" Jr. *Education*—University of Texas at Austin, B.A. in Latin American Affairs, 1973.

Addresses: *Office*—The Capitol, Tallahassee, FL 32399.

Career

Became head of Dade County (Florida) Republican Party, 1981; was appointed Florida's secretary of commerce, 1987, served until 1988; ran for the office of governor of Florida but was defeated, 1994; elected governor of Florida, 1998; reelected governor, 2002.

Sidelights

When Jeb Bush, a son of former United States President George H.W. Bush, was elected Governor of Florida in 1998, the event marked the first time since the 1960s that two brothers simultaneously held positions as governors of states; his older brother, George W. Bush, had just been elected governor of Texas. Bush was also part of history when his state became the focus of a crisis in the 2000 U.S. presidential elections. Presidential hopeful George W. and his opponent, outgoing vice president Al Gore, were separated at the polls by a tiny,

difficult–to–determine fraction of a percent in the state of Florida, throwing the outcome of the presidential race into question for weeks to come.

Born in Midland, Texas, one of five children of George and Barbara Bush, who later became president and First Lady of the United States, John Ellis Bush was raised in Midland and in Houston, Texas. From an early age, he has been known by the nickname of "Jeb" (his initials). During summers off from high school at Phillips Academy in Andover, Massachusetts, Bush worked odd jobs, including stints at a fast–food restaurant and as a door–to-door salesman. He was also a high school exchange student in Mexico at the age of 17, and there he met the woman who was to become his wife, Columba Garnica Gallo. He said later that he took many of those odd jobs in summers in order to earn money so that he could spend time in Mexico with his then–girlfriend. He also became a fluent speaker of Spanish. Bush attended college at the University of Texas at Austin. He graduated in only two and a half years instead of the usual four, earning Phi Beta Kappa honors along with a bachelor's degree in Latin American Affairs. Bush and Columba were married in 1973, shortly before his graduation.

David Bates, a childhood friend of Bush's, described his early years this way to Mary Leonard of the *Bos-*

ton Globe: "Jeb was always very disciplined, very focused, and in a hurry. He matured quicker than the rest of us, graduated faster, got married sooner, and was ready to go out in the world and get down to business."

"Business" for the young Bush right out of college turned out to be a job as a banker, and he held this position until he and his family moved to Miami, Florida, from Texas in 1981. The year before, Bush's father, George Bush, had been elected vice president of the United States, and Bush wanted to establish himself apart from his father's rising star.

In 1981, Bush helped to found a commercial real estate development firm called Codina Group. The company was based in Miami, and it later became one of South Florida's largest real estate developers. At the beginning of the venture, Bush revisited his door–to–door salesman days by pounding the pavement to sell land. He earned $41,000 a year this way before commissions and some of his own investments began to boost his income.

Real estate in Miami during the 1980s was at times a dicey business; at least two of Bush's clients were later revealed to be international criminals. But Bush managed to stay clear of any deals that might involve him in legal entanglements, and he also avoided conducting business with the U.S. government to order to avoid any appearance of profiting from his relationship with his powerful father. His hard work paid off; his real estate ventures eventually made him a millionaire. During this time, he pursued a parallel career in politics, in 1984 becoming head of the Dade County Republican Party. One of his tasks in this position was to register newly minted U.S. citizens to vote as soon as they were sworn in.

Bush also worked on his father's campaigns for vice president and president from 1980 to 1992. From 1987 to 1988, he also served as secretary of commerce for the state of Florida. He was appointed to this position by then–Governor Bob Martinez, and his major assignment there was to promote Florida's business interests around the world.

Bush first ran for Florida governor in 1994, selling his stake in Codina Group to devote full time to do so. It was a stretch for Bush, who was said to be uncomfortable making speeches and promoting himself. "He was never a guy who bragged about himself," his mother told Ellen Debenport of the *St. Petersburg Times* of her involvement in his campaign. "Jeb might be the last one I thought I'd be doing this for."

Bush's opponent was sitting Democratic governor Lawton Chiles, and he campaigned on a platform that included cracking down harder on crime in Florida. "The solution," he then told Bill Moss of the *St. Petersburg Times,* "must begin with getting today's predators off the streets. More cops. More prosecutors. More prisons. And a tough new juvenile justice system run by law enforcement professionals, not social workers." He also cited the fact that he was not a native of Florida as a selling point, telling the *St. Petersburg Times*'s Moss, "I haven't been up here my entire adult life inside a process that is broken." Also in this campaign, Bush advocated cutting welfare spending, and was quoted by Richard Berke in the *New York Times* as saying in one speech that women who were dependent on welfare "should be able to get their life together and find a husband."

In this campaign Bush also spoke against gay rights measures and abortion, and came out in favor of prayer in public schools and capital punishment. As he told Steve Berg in the *Star Tribune,* "It's an unbelievable denial of justice that it now takes over 12 years for someone who has committed an atrocious act before he is executed." He also took pains to acknowledge his relationship with his famous father, while at the same time seeking to establish his own reputation. "I want people to know that I'm not trying to disengage myself from this obvious relationship I have with the former President of the United States," he told the *New York Times*'s Berke. "I won't dissociate myself. I long ago overcame any insecurities about being the son of a famous man. A lot of sons of famous people jump out windows."

Bush was defeated in 1994, but the race was very close. He went on to start a non–profit organization called Foundation for Florida's Future, which worked to influence public policy on issues ranging from battered women to education. In his capacity as the head of the foundation, Bush also helped to start the first charter school in the state, Liberty City Charter School. Also during this time, he found time to write a book called *Profiles in Character,* which features profiles of 14 notable Floridians.

Bush ran for governor of Florida again in 1998, and he looked to his older brother, George W. Bush (then–governor of Texas), for advice on how to improve his campaign. As Bates told the *Boston Globe,* "George W. was very, very supportive in this election." This time, Bush won, edging out his opponent, Lieutenant Governor Kenneth "Buddy" McKay, with 55 percent of the vote to become Florida's 43rd governor. Bush was 45 years old when he took the oath of office.

One of Bush's stated goals as governor has been to improve public education in Florida. With this in mind, he approved an increase of $2.4 for funding of public schools. Delivered over a three–year period, the money represents the largest increase in public school funding (23 percent) in the state's history. He has also pushed for the introduction of school vouchers, which would allow parents to receive money from the state to send their children to private schools, and he has worked to cut state taxes.

Bush found himself in the center of a political hurricane during the 2000 elections for president of the United States. George W. was tied with his opponent, the then–current vice president Al Gore, for the office. Only three hundredths of one percent of Florida votes separated the opponents, and on the evening of election day, first Gore, than George W., then Gore, and then George W. again were announced as the nation's next president—all based on votes counted in Florida. "I hope I'll never have to go through another evening like I did," Jeb Bush said to David Firestone in the *New York Times,* "and I'm sure the Gore family would say the same thing. It was one of the most amazing and emotionally intense evenings of my life."

Bush blamed himself for the fact that the presidential race was so close in his own state. "I decided," he told the *New York Times*'s Firestone, "after apologizing to my brother, that I didn't do what I had hoped I would be able to do, which was to help him carry the state. So I started making phone calls around to talk radio in Sacramento and Seattle and Medford, Oregon, and other places where the polls were still open, to urge people to vote for my brother in those places. Then, somehow the results were overturned, so there was a period of a couple of hours of incredible anxious anxiety, then the results were changed again, and I thought prematurely on the last one. It was a very emotional time."

Some speculated that a backlash from African American voters might have helped to create the election crisis. Bush had earlier pushed to end affirmative action at state universities in Florida, angering African Americans in the state. Two African American legislators had even conducted a sit–in at the governor's offices. In the end, votes that had been cast in Florida were painstakingly recounted, and after Supreme Court intervention, George W. Bush became the 43rd president of the United States. Jeb Bush dismissed any notion that he had pulled strings to get his older brother into the White House, telling the *Los Angeles Times,* "Vote fraud in our state is a felony. We will prosecute it to the fullest extent of the law."

Bush did have a brush with felony in early 2002, when his daughter Noelle, then 24 years old, was arrested after trying to pass a fake prescription for Xanax at a pharmacy in Tallahassee. Her crime carried a potential prison sentence of up to five years. Bush issued a statement after his daughter was arrested, reported by CNN.com, "This is a very serious problem. Unfortunately, substance abuse is an issue confronting many families across our nation."

Noelle was spared a jail term after she agreed to enter a drug treatment program in Orlando later that year. However, she was later caught with mood–altering prescription drugs at the treatment facility, and sentenced to three days in jail. After returning to the drug facility, Noelle was found with a substance that tested positive for cocaine. No charges were filed, and she remained at the facility. Said Bush in the *St. Petersburg Times,* "We know there are thousands of families across Florida who share in this unfortunate experience with their own children and feel as Columba and I do today. We love Noelle, but she is an adult and I respect the role of the courts in carrying out our state's drug treatment policies."

Bush's first term in office was to expire in 2003, with elections held in November of 2002. Bush defeated Democratic challenger Bill McBride on November 5, 2002, to be reelected governor of Florida.

Sources

Periodicals

Boston Globe, November 18, 1998, p. A1.

Campaigns & Elections, June 2002, p. 18.

Los Angeles Times, November 10, 2000, p. 29.

New York Times, September 2, 1994, p. A1; November 9, 2000, p. B7.

Star Tribune (Minneapolis and St. Paul), October 17, 1994, p. 1A.

St. Petersburg Times, October 5, 1993, p. 4B; August 23, 1994, p. 1A; January 6, 1999, p. 1A; July 18, 2002, p. 1A.

Online

"Bush defeats McBride in Florida governor's race, CNN projects," CNN.com, http://www.cnn.com/2002/ALLPOLITICS/11/05/elec02.fl.g.hotrace/index.html (November 8, 2002).

"Governor Jeb Bush of Florida," National Governors Association, http:www.nga.org/governors/1,1169,C_GOVERNOR_INFO_124,00.html (August 13, 2002).

"Jeb Bush, Portrait and Biography," Florida Division of Historical Resources, http://dhr.dos.state.fl.us/governors/jebbush.html (August 13, 2002).

"Jeb Bush's Daughter Charged with Prescription Fraud," CNN.com, http://www.cnn.com/2002/US/01/29/jeb.bush.daughter.drugs/ (August 13, 2002).

"Meet Governor Jeb Bush—Biography," Government of Florida, http://www.myflorida.com/myflorida/government/meetgovernor/jebbush.html (August 13, 2002).

"Police investigate Jeb Bush's daughter," CNN.com, http://www.cnn.com/2002/US/09/10/noelle.bush/index.html (September 16, 2002).

—Michael Belfiore

Andrew H. Card, Jr.

Chief of staff to United States President George W. Bush

Born May 10, 1947, in Brockton, MA; married Kathleene Bryan, August 27, 1967; children: three. *Education:* University of South Carolina, B.S. in engineering, 1971; attended U.S. Merchant Marine Academy and the John F. Kennedy School of Government at Harvard University. *Military service:* U.S. Navy, 1965–67.

Addresses: *Office*—The White House, 1600 Pennsylvania Ave. NW, Washington, D.C. 20500.

Career

Member of the Massachusetts House of Representatives, 1975–83; Massachusetts chairman and part–time driver for George Bush's unsuccessful run for the Republican Party's presidential nomination, 1980; candidate for Massachusetts Governor, 1982; special assistant to the President for Intergovernmental Affairs during the Reagan administration, 1983–87; New Hampshire campaign manager for George H. W. Bush, 1987–88; assistant to the President and Deputy Chief of Staff during the Bush administration, 1988–92; U.S. Secretary of Transportation, 1992–93; led disaster relief effort for Hurricane Andrew, 1992; president and chief executive officer of the American Automobile Manufacturers Association (AAMA), 1993–98; vice president of government relations, General Motors Corp., 1999–2000; chairman of the "Bush for President" operation, 2000; chief of staff to President George W. Bush, 2000—.

Awards: Legislator of the Year, Republican Legislators Association, 1982; Distinguished Legislator Award, Massachusetts Municipal Association, 1982; numerous honorary degrees and other awards.

Sidelights

When Andrew H. Card, Jr. was named chief of staff of President George W. Bush's administration in 2000, many saw it as a reward for years of loyalty to the Bush family's political dynasty. The appointment was another in a long line of positions he has filled for the Bushes, as he also served in the first President Bush's administration, and for President Ronald Reagan before him. The "true soldier of the Republican Party," as he was called in *Traffic Management* magazine, earned his reputation as an effective, solution–minded politician as he resolved many a partisan debate during his years in the Democrat–led Massachusetts State House. The former lobbyist for the auto industry was treated with suspicion by environmentalists, but Card's colleagues and friends laud him for his integrity, pragmatism, and moderate politics. He outlined the secrets of his success in *Campaigns and Elections:* "Listen. Have the courage to make decisions. Pay attention to your conscience and sleep well at night."

Card was born on May 10, 1947, in Brockton, Massachusetts, and raised in the strongly Democratic town of Holbrook, Massachusetts. He served two years in the U.S. Navy before earning his Bachelor of Science degree in engineering from the University of South Carolina in 1971. He later studied at the U.S. Merchant Marine Academy and the John F. Kennedy School of Government at Harvard University. He married the former Kathleene Bryan on August 27, 1967. The two have three children and four grandchildren.

Card first entered politics and public service as a member of the Massachusetts House of Representatives from 1975–1983. He was a member of the Republican minority in the Democrat–dominated Statehouse and earned a reputation for his ability to overcome party differences in the largely Democratic state. In fact, he counts Democrat and former colleague Philip W. Johnston, who entered the Massachusetts House with him in 1975, as a longtime friend. The two led a campaign against contract corruption between the government and construction companies. They also headed a bipartisan movement to open up the state's House with more elected rather than appointed positions. Card and Johnston had left office by the time any changes were instituted, but they bore a strong resemblance to the program the two had championed. "Massachusetts was one of the most corrupt states in the country. There was a lot of public attention and internal opposition to what we were doing, but Andy was unflappable the whole time," Johnston told Claire Moore of ABCNews.com. "He's of the more moderate, progressive, New England–style of Republican. He's not a rigid ideologue. Andy is very practical. He understands how to compromise and make a deal." Card was named Legislator of the Year by the National Republican Legislators Association and received the Distinguished Legislator Award from the Massachusetts Municipal Association in 1982.

Card served in Republican President Ronald Reagan's administration as special assistant to the president for Intergovernmental Affairs from 1983–87. In the low–profile but well–respected position, he acted as a liaison between the White House and state and other elected officials. When George H. W. Bush ran for president in the 1988 election, Card led the campaign to victory in New Hampshire as Bush's campaign manager in the state. For his trouble, Card was promoted in 1988 and served in President Bush's administration as an assistant to the president and Deputy Chief of Staff under John Sununu until 1992. "Even then Card's quiet style contrasted sharply with the more brash Sununu," according to ABCNews.com's Moore. Card managed the daily operations of the White House staff and was involved with the process of economic, foreign, and domestic policy development.

Bush named Card the eleventh U.S. Secretary of Transportation in 1992, an appointment many saw as a reward for his years of loyalty and hard work. During his brief leadership of the Department of Transportation, Card pushed strongly for deregulation of the shipping industry. The position only lasted until 1993, when Democrat Bill Clinton was inaugurated president. Also in 1992, Bush assigned Card to head the federal disaster relief effort after Hurricane Andrew devastated South Florida. He skillfully facilitated the often–slow bureaucratic response to major natural disasters. He counted the experience as his "claim to fame," according to *Campaigns and Elections.* When it was time for President Bush's administration to vacate the White House and make way for Clinton's, Card was named outgoing administrations chief to head the transition.

With a Democrat in the White House, Card entered the private sector in 1993 as the President and Chief Executive Officer of the American Automobile Manufacturers Association (AAMA), which is the trade association of the Big Three American car companies. He remained with the group until it disbanded in December of 1998, when Daimler Benz AG took over Chrysler. Card then merged into a position as vice president of government relations at General Motors (GM), where he lobbied for the company before Congress and in the White House. He also headed GM's international, national, state, and local government affairs activities.

Card first served President George W. Bush during his 2000 presidential election. Bush looked to Card to bring focus to his campaign during the 2000 Republican National Convention in Philadelphia, Pennsylvania. When he dropped behind Democratic nominee Al Gore in the opinion polls during the campaign, Bush called on Card to help him prepare for debates. Card took a leave of absence from GM when he was appointed to be chief of staff of the presidential administration of then–governor Bush on November 26, 2000, as anticipation of Bush's win grew during that year's drawn–out election debacle.

Environmentalists opposed Card's appointment, arguing the former senior lobbyist for the automotive industry would have a hard time leaving those alliances behind. They questioned whom Card might favor in decisions regarding toughening emissions standards on new and more environmentally sound vehicles. But Bush was not alone in his support of Card as chief of staff. "He's perfect for the job," Ron Kaufman, a Republican activist and Card's brother–in–law, told ABCNews.com's Moore, "because he's a unifier, not a divider, and because he and Bush are so similar stylistically."

Sources

Periodicals

Campaigns & Elections, June 2000, p. 19.
Traffic Management, October 1992, p. 45.

Online

"Chief of Staff Andrew H. Card," White House, http://www.whitehouse.gov/government/card–bio.html (December 23, 2002).

"Former lobbyist and longtime Bush family friend," ABCNews.com, http://abcnews.go.com/sections/politics/DailyNews/profile_card.html (December 23, 2002).

—Brenna Sanchez

Pierre Cardin

Fashion designer

Born Pietro Cardin, July 2, 1922, in San Biaggio di Callalta, Italy; son of wine merchants. *Education:* Studied architecture in Saint–Etienne, France.

Addresses: *Home*—Paris and Cote d'Azur, France. *Office*—59 Rue de Faubourg Saint–Honoré, 75008 Paris, France.

Career

Began as a tailor's apprentice, Saint–Etienne, France, late 1930s; worked as an accountant in Paris for the French Red Cross, early 1940s; designer for Paquin fashion house and for Elsa Schiaparelli, both Paris, c. 1945–46; designed the costumes for Jean Cocteau's film *La Belle et la Bete,* 1946; head of workrooms, Christian Dior fashion house, Paris, 1946–50; founded own house, Pierre Cardin, Paris, 1950; showed first haute couture collection, Paris, 1957; joined Chambre Syndicale de la Couture (Couture Employers' Federation; ousted, 1959; reinstated, 1963); made first women's ready–to–wear collections, 1959; introduced men's line, 1960; began licensing name to an array of products, late 1960s; founder–director, Theatres des Ambassadeurs–Cardin (now Espace Cardin complex), Paris, from 1970; chairman, Maxim's Restaurant, Paris, from 1981; UNESCO ambassador, 1991—.

Awards: Gold Thimble Award, Paris, 1977, 1979, 1982; Chevalier de la Légion d'Honneur, France, 1983; Fashion Oscar, Paris, 1985; Prize of the Foundation for Garment and Apparel Advancement, Tokyo, Japan, 1988; Grand Officer, Order of Merit, Italy, 1988; honorary ambassador to UNESCO, 1991; Officier de la Légion d'Honneur, 1991; Décoration de l'Ordre du Trésor Sacré au Japon, 1991; Académicien des Beaux Arts, 1992.

Sidelights

French designer Pierre Cardin sent forth innovative, space–age themed fashions in the 1960s that defined the progressive zeitgeist of the era. Yet Cardin was also far ahead of his time in recognizing the value of his name as a brand, and he was first in France's rarified world of haute couture to lend his signature to a line of lesser–priced clothing. His daring act—which made him a pariah for a time among his more elitist Parisian colleagues in 1959—was said to have launched the designer craze. "Cardin saw the future before anyone else," noted *New York Times Magazine* writers Lisa Eisner and Roman Alonso. In the years since, Cardin has sometimes been criticized for becoming so ubiquitous, and many have forgotten his pioneering futurist wear. "Still, those that would criticize his licensing strategy should remember this," pointed out Thomas Cunningham in a *Daily News Record* article. "Pierre Cardin is still one of the most recognized brand names in the world.... Fashion's leaders, from Ralph Lauren to Bernard Arnault, are influenced by Cardin's expansive vision."

Cardin was born in July of 1922, near Venice, Italy, to French parents who had a wine–merchant business. A few years later, they returned to France and settled in Saint–Etienne, an industrial city near Lyon. Fascinated by clothes at an early age, Cardin reportedly sewed items for a neighbor's doll collection as a child, and at the age of 14 began working as an apprentice to a tailor. After a brief stint studying architecture in Saint–Etienne, he took a job as an accountant with the French Red Cross in Paris during World War II. As the city moved from Nazi occupation to peacetime with the close of the war, Cardin returned to his first passion. In 1945, he found work as a designer for the Paquin fashion house, where he was invited to design the costumes for a film by Jean Cocteau, *La Belle et la Bete* ("Beauty and the Beast"). Soon he was hired at the atelier of Elsa Schiaparelli, and left that to take a post as workroom director at Christian Dior.

Cardin worked at Dior on the coat and suit line when the couture house made international headlines with its revolutionary "New Look:" after years of wartime austerity and related fabric shortages, in 1947 Dior introduced an ultra–feminine silhouette characterized by a nipped–in waist and voluminous skirts made from yards of fabric. Bolstered by his experiences at Dior, Cardin moved on and founded his own company in Paris in 1950. Initially concentrating on custom ball gowns and costume design, within a few years he had attracted a devoted clientele, and formally opened the House of Cardin in eighteenth–century quarters on the rue de Faubourg Saint–Honoré in 1954. "When I was a young couturier, women didn't work; they dressed in haute couture, their clothes had not yet evolved like the male wardrobe and pants had not yet taken such an important place," he recalled about this era in an interview with *International Herald Tribune* fashion writer Suzy Menkes. To obtain the property, however, Cardin had to agree to a real–estate deal that allowed the menswear store on the ground level to remain open, and so he divided the space into two boutiques: Eve, for women, and Adam, the men's shop, for which he began designing rather avant–garde shirts and ties.

Cardin formally presented his first haute–couture collection on a Paris runway in 1957, and it was well–received. Eschewing the extravagant mood of the era, Cardin created clothing with clean, minimalist lines. His next innovation was an even more daring one: in 1959, he contracted with a company that manufactured women's dresses; the line would use his name and sell at Paris's Printemps department store. No other French couture designer had ventured into mass–market retailing at the time, and for his transgression Cardin was vilified and even ousted from the prestigious Chambre Syndicale de la Couture, the governing body of French fashion designers. His cheeky attitude bore some blame for the rancor with which he was treated at the time, for Cardin told the press that "he wanted to bring fashion to the secretaries," reported *Financial Times* writer Vanessa Friedman.

Cardin's move proved so financially lucrative that he was soon able to launch a line of menswear, and began distributing both to stores outside of Paris. As with the designs he had done a few years earlier for his Adam store, Cardin made some daring items for men, including suits without lapels or even collars, often in far brighter fabrics than were standard for men at the time. Even the Beatles wore matching Pierre Cardin suits. "Through the rest of the decade he would continue to push the envelope of men's fashion," wrote Cunningham in the *Daily News Record*, "evolving a narrow–shouldered, quintessentially French silhouette that captivated Europeans."

Cardin was also interested in expanding his business outside the Paris–London–New York style axis. In 1957, he was the first European designer ever to venture into Japan—after dismissing warnings that the Japanese were not fashion–conscious—and five years later he caused a stir when he invited a young Japanese model, Hiroko, to appear in one of his runway shows. Cardin's designs arrived in American stores like Bonwit Teller in 1966. That same year, his "Cosmos" women's line broke new ground during this era, tapping into the interest in space exploration along with another French designer, Andre Courreges, and the promise that conquering outer space seemed to hold for humankind. Cardin's look included inventive, unisex–style clothing like tunics, fitted sweaters, leggings, and even matching helmets. "Cardin was also extraordinarily inventive with cut, taking the circle as a persistent motif and using the twirl of a compass to create swing backs, cocoon coats, petal sleeves and collars as satellite circles of fabric," wrote Menkes in the *International Herald Tribune*. He was also one of first designers to use synthetic materials—including his own, which he trademarked as "Cardine"—and spurred a fad for colored tights.

Cardin's brand–licensing deals grew in number in the late 1960s, when he began to design "lifestyle" items to enhance an environment in which his clothes were displayed. He began making kitchenware in 1968, and over the next decade introduced a dizzying array of products, from fragrances to luggage to hair dryers. "Indeed, today, it's easy to forget how revolutionary Pierre Cardin was," noted

Independent journalist Natasha Edwards some years later. "The brand's image seems to have become fossilized in memories of 1970s ads of young, blow-waved men in waisted suits, while the instantly recognizable, rounded, lower-case Pierre Cardin logo, that adorns watches, cologne, pens, socks and saucepans across the world, means that Cardin seems as much a part of supermarket shelves as salubrious Faubourg-St.-Honoré shop windows." Products with the Pierre Cardin logo included wigs, golf clubs, mattresses, and even cigarettes. Cardin defended himself against critics, noting that "it's not easy to sell chocolates with a name," he told *WWD* writer Andrew Collier. "Try it." In 1970, Cardin made a move to expand his vision outside of fashion, purchasing and renovating a nightclub in Paris called Les Ambassadeurs and renaming it Espace Cardin. It served as a restaurant, film theater, concert hall, and art gallery. Several years later, he purchased the Maxim's de Paris restaurant, and the esteemed name itself, for $20 million. A fixture in the city since 1893, it had recently fallen on hard times, and Cardin made it a chain with eateries in several other major cities. At the same time, Cardin continued to expand globally. In 1978 he and his associates made a trip to China to present a fashion show for the wives of top Communist Party officials. Eight years later he signed an historic licensing deal with the Soviet government for the manufacture and distribution of apparel under his name; it made him the first Western fashion designer with products available outside the diplomatic store circuit, which accepted only foreign dollars and thus were off-limits to the majority of Soviet citizens.

Cardin has been honored with museum retrospectives on a number of occasions. He was made a UNESCO peace ambassador in 1991, and in 1993 became the first French designer to be inducted into the Academie des Beaux Arts. After the 1993 death of his longtime fashion director Andre Oliver in 1993, Cardin bowed out of couture formally with his last collection in 1996. At the close of the twentieth century, there were more than 800 products bearing Cardin's name being sold in some 140 countries. These included a well-received furniture line, boasting the clean modernist lines of his 1960s couture designs, and eleven fragrances. He still owned the Maxim's boites as well as a few others in Paris, three magazines, and a trio of theaters. It was also believed that he owned several valuable parcels of real estate in the pricey Eighth Arrondissement of Paris. Nearing the age of 80, he began courting buyers for his empire. Some press reports noted that his privately held warren of companies and licensees made $1 million a day, and he was estimated to be the 44th richest man in France. "There is no one like me at the head of their own [international] house anymore," he told the *Financial Times*'s Friedman in 2000. "Now the great houses are run by bankers, not createurs. No other name has been around for 50 years; I am the last one. But I am not worried; the name will continue. It is that powerful."

Cardin's empire remained unsold until the end of 2002, when reports surfaced that his business was faltering and carried a large debt load. The designer, who owned some 32 homes and even part of a town on the French Riviera, dismissed this. "That's completely false," he told *WWD* writer Robert Murphy. "I have more money than I know what to do with. That's a rumor started by someone—someone malicious—who owes me tons of cash."

Forty years after his first dresses began appearing at the Printemps department store, Cardin was amused by a world in which designer underwear had become de rigueur. "Cardin is commonly thought to be the richest man in fashion," wrote Lauren Goldstein in a 2002 article for *Time International*. "He's also probably the most satisfied and the most mocked." He remained philosophical about his critics. "I don't have any regrets," he declared to *WWD* writer Godfrey Deeny. "I've always done what I wanted. When I thought I should do something, I just went ahead and did it. How many other people can you say that about?" In the 2002 *New York Times Magazine* profile, Cardin was asked by Eisner and Alonso what he hoped his legacy might be. "There were people before me, and there will be people after me," he mused. "I epitomized a moment in fashion. Historically, I think I was important to fashion. A legacy is not my goal. I did what I did driven by passion, enthusiasm and talent."

Sources

Books

Contemporary Designers, third edition, St. James Press, 1997.
Encyclopedia of World Biography Supplement, volume 18, Gale, 1998.

Periodicals

Daily News Record, March 26, 1990, p. 14; December 31, 2001, p. 86.
Financial Times, November 25, 2000, p. 3.
Forbes, May 2, 1988, p. 90; October 14, 2002, p. 46.
Guardian (London, England), January 9, 1999; January 12, 2002, p. 56.

Independent (London, England), September 24, 2000, p. 41.

Interior Design, January 2002, p. 164.

International Herald Tribune, April 18, 2000, p. 11.

Nation's Restaurant News, August 17, 1992, p. 3.

New York Times Magazine, August 18, 2002, p. 201.

Time, September 21, 1998, p. 11.

Time International, March 15, 2002, p. 20.

WWD, November 8, 1983, p. 1; March 7, 1985, p. 1; December 20, 1985, p. 6; November 24, 1986, p. 1; November 12, 1990, p. 8; December 2, 1992, p. 20; January 14, 1994, p. 10; March 17, 1999, p. 4; February 8, 2002, p. 11; February 27, 2002, p. 11; December 2, 2002, p. 2.

—*Carol Brennan*

Richard Carmona

United States Surgeon General

Born Richard Henry Carmona, November 22, 1949, in New York, NY; married Diana Sanchez; children: four (three adopted). *Education:* University of California at San Francisco, B.S., 1976; University of California at San Francisco Medical School, M.D., 1979; University of Arizona, M.A. in public health, 1998.

Addresses: *Office*—Office of the Surgeon General, 5600 Fishers Lane, Room 18–66, Rockville, MD 20857.

Career

Served in the U.S. Army, 1967–70; served in the Vietnam War as a medic and weapons specialist with the Green Berets; served in Army Special Forces; helped start Tucson Medical Center's new trauma unit, 1985; joined Tucson's Special Operations Section (SWAT) team, 1986; became chief executive officer and medical director of Kino Community Hospital, Tucson, Arizona, 1995; promoted to oversee Pima County's healthcare system, 1997; served as Clinical Professor of Surgery, Public Health, and Family and Community Medicine; sworn in as United States Surgeon General, 2002.

Awards: Two Purple Hearts, Vietnam War; Bronze Star, Vietnam War; Physician of the Year, Pima County, 1993; National S.W.A.T. Officer of the Year; National "Top Cop" Award, National Association of Police Organizations, 2000; Alumnus of the Year, University of Arizona, 2000.

AP/Wide World Photos

Sidelights

When United States President George W. Bush named Richard Carmona as his selection for Surgeon General in 2002, newspapers and television were flooded with stories about the Hispanic–American doctor's colorful life and career. A former Green Beret, a two–time Purple Heart recipient, and a SWAT team member, Carmona garnered a reputation as a man of extraordinary valor and extensive and broad–ranging experience. His rise from a high school dropout from the Harlem barrio to a successful Arizona surgeon and hospital administrator seemed to epitomize the American Dream, and the heroic tales of his SWAT team experiences seemed straight out of a Wild West action movie. Yet Carmona also had a reputation for an aggressive administrative style and a tendency to generate conflicts with his colleagues. Early in his tenure as Surgeon General, he allayed critics's fears, emerging as a compassionate and concerned public health spokesperson whose goals include closing the gap in health care disparities in a racially diverse nation.

Born in 1949 in New York City's Spanish Harlem section, Carmona was a street kid from a poor Puerto Rican family. His father was the youngest of 27 children. Growing up in the barrio, Carmona received infrequent health care and dental care only to treat toothaches; both of his parents struggled with alcoholism. Many of his friends became involved in a life of crime; like most of them, Carmona dropped out of high school. Yet, at age 17, he made a decision that saved him from the fate of many a street youth: He enlisted in the United States Army.

Soon after, he served in the Vietnam War, as a medic and a weapons specialist with the Green Berets. "I was fortunate I went away to Vietnam," Carmona said in a 1999 interview, quoted by Joe Salkowski in the *Arizona Daily Star*. "When I came back, I was a changed man." During his service in Vietnam, Carmona earned a Bronze Star and two Purple Hearts for combat wounds. Later, he received his high school equivalency diploma (G.E.D.) and went on to serve in the Army Special Forces.

In the mid–1970s, Carmona became the first in his family to attend college. His parents disapproved of his desire to study, and encouraged him instead to take an electrician's job and start raising a family. Nevertheless, he went to school, studying biology and chemistry at the University of California at San Francisco; he obtained a bachelor's degree in 1976. Three years later, he earned a medical degree from the same university, graduating at the top of his class. Carmona completed his residency and a fellowship at San Francisco's university hospitals, becoming a vascular and general surgeon with subspecialties in trauma, critical care, and burns.

Carmona relocated to Tucson, Arizona, where he helped start Tucson Medical Center's new trauma unit in 1985. The facility would become Southern Arizona's first level–one trauma center—that is, a center designated to treat the region's most severe trauma injuries. Carmona went on to become director of the unit. In 1986 he began his long–standing service as a doctor for the Pima County Sheriff's Department; later, he would become a leader of the department's SWAT team.

Moonlighting as a SWAT team member, Carmona earned many accolades and awards. The fearless doctor made headlines in 1992, when he dangled out of a helicopter to rescue a helicopter crash survivor who was stranded on a cliff. The incident earned Carmona a reputation as a real–life Indiana Jones, and the story became inspiration for a 1997 made–for–television movie.

At Tucson Medical Center, however, Carmona held a less positive reputation—that of a street fighter. While he was acknowledged for having a remark-able rapport with patients, he clashed with some of his coworkers and hospital administrators. Within his first year on the job, he sued the hospital over the terms of his contract; the two parties reached a settlement out of court. In 1991 Carmona demanded the resignation of a nurse who questioned his medical judgment, and in other incidents, Carmona accused colleagues of age and racial discrimination.

Among his coworkers, Carmona developed a reputation as a difficult colleague who fought to prove he was right, and who sued or threatened to sue anyone whom he believed had wronged him. In one administrative conflict, the hospital questioned the status of Carmona's board certification for general surgery. While most doctors pass the boards within a year or two after completing their residencies, Carmona passed the boards eight years later.

Preparing to merge its trauma center with that of the nearby University Medical Center, Tucson Medical Center chose to eliminate Carmona's position. He was dismissed in July of 1993—much to the dismay of his patients, who rallied in Carmona's defense and sang his praises. Some patients even compared him to a saint. Meanwhile, Carmona sued the hospital for a breach of contract. A settlement was reached out of court, awarding Carmona some $3.9 million and a printed public apology. Per his usual pattern, Carmona received praise and criticism in equally strong doses. The same year of his dismissal, Pima County, Arizona, presented Carmona with its Physician of the Year award.

By 1995 Carmona had secured another administrative position—that of chief executive officer and medical director of Kino Community Hospital in Tucson. Here he immediately clashed with the hospital's chief of surgery, Dr. Eric Ramsey; the two maintained differences of opinion on everything from the hospital's residency program to its staffing. After a 37–year relationship with the hospital, Ramsay resigned in 1996, distraught over what he considered to be Carmona's aggressive and uncooperative behavior.

Nevertheless, Carmona was promoted in 1997, when Pima County appointed him to oversee its healthcare system. He would stay in the position for only two years, however, and negotiated with county health commissioners for his resignation in July of 1999. The commissioners questioned Carmona's ability to resuscitate the county's financially troubled system, citing the public hospital's monthly deficit of more than $1 million. Carmona's supporters rose to his defense, noting that the financial problems long predated Carmona's appointment.

While he served Pima County, Carmona did not escape from clashes with colleagues and health commissioners. Two months before his resignation, he had a conflict with one commissioner over an incident regarding a drug–abusing Kino doctor who had written false prescriptions to obtain drugs. After the commissioner, Sylvia Campoy, reported allegations about the doctor to the county attorney, Carmona grew angry and accused her of violating the doctor's confidentiality. Yet it was the commissioner and her colleagues who began to lose confidence in Carmona. Apparently, shortly before he announced his resignation, the county health commissioners had planned to vote Carmona out.

Meanwhile, Carmona received a master's degree in public health from the University of Arizona in 1998. At the university, he served as Clinical Professor of Surgery, Public Health, and Family and Community Medicine. Throughout all of his ventures since 1987, Carmona continued to moonlight as a SWAT team member and surgeon. He was such a busy man that he seemed to have "three sets of legs and six arms," Pima County Sheriff Clarence Dupnick told Robert Pear of the *New York Times.*

One of his most dramatic SWAT team moments came when Carmona was off duty. The scene was a busy Tucson intersection, where a minor traffic accident had gotten out of hand, with an enraged male driver attacking a female driver. When Carmona stepped forward to help the woman, the gathering crowd warned that the man was armed. A shootout ensued, during which Carmona fired seven shots. Three of these hit and critically wounded the man.

The incident, which occurred in 1999, has earned Carmona both praise and criticism. It was discovered later that the shooter was a mentally ill man who had stabbed his father to death that day; thus, Carmona's actions were seen not only as justified but as heroic. Yet others involved in the incident questioned Carmona's actions, stating that the doctor should have recognized and responded to the shooter's mentally ill behavior. Moreover, others have complained that Carmona's actions violated the Hippocratic Oath, which prohibits a doctor from intentionally taking a life. Nevertheless, Carmona garnered more praise than criticism, and in 2000 was named one of the nation's "Top Cops" by the National Association of Police Organizations. Two

years later, the University of Arizona at Tucson presented Carmona with its Alumnus of the Year award. When United States Surgeon General David Satcher stepped down in February of 2002, Carmona emerged as a strong contender for the illustrious position. At the time, he was continuing his professorship at the University of Arizona and holding several other positions, including attending surgeon at the U.A. Campus Student Health center, medical director at the Arizona Department of Public Safety Air Rescue Unit, and SWAT team training officer.

Carmona's background in bioterrorism prevention made him a virtual shoo–in for the surgeon general position. During his work in Arizona, he had helped coordinate the state's efforts in bioterrorism preparedness and response. Long before the September 11, 2001, terrorist attacks on the United States, Carmona had warned that American cities were unprepared for bioterrorist strikes and other menaces. "When we take into account the threats of the future, we are not prepared," Carmona said at a September 1996 conference, quoted by the *Arizona Daily Star*'s Salkowski.

In March of 2002, United States President George W. Bush announced Carmona as his selection for Surgeon General. Four months later, the U.S. Senate confirmed Carmona's appointment, despite some brief controversy over the conflicts that have marred the Arizona doctor's professional career. According to CNN.com, U.S. Senator Edward Kennedy, who presided over Carmona's confirmation hearings, said, "Dr. Carmona impressed us with his commitment to preventive health, and made particularly clear his intention to aggressively oppose tobacco use by children and youth and to combat the HIV/ AIDS epidemic."

Carmona was sworn in as Surgeon General on August 5, 2002, becoming the 17th American doctor to serve in the post. Among his responsibilities is the administration of the 5,600–member Public Health Service Commission Corps—the on–call emergency medical team that was deployed during the September 11 attacks and during anthrax attacks that occurred a few months later.

Carmona's most important role during his four–year term will be as the nation's leading public–health spokesperson. Although he has only a small staff, the Surgeon General has recourse to this "bully pulpit," which he can use to influence public health policy. In one of his first public speeches, to a group of Hispanic healthcare professionals on August 16, 2002, Carmona called upon the medical community to "close the gap in [racial] disparities," according to Todd Ackerman of the *Houston Chronicle.* "We must create a seamless, easily accessible, cost–effective and culturally and linguistically sensitive health care system that serves all citizens," he said.

Carmona is married to his high school sweetheart, Diana Sanchez, with whom he has two sons and two daughters.

Sources

Periodicals

Arizona Daily Star, March 27, 2002.
Houston Chronicle, August 17, 2002, p. A33.
Los Angeles Times, July 8, 2002, p. A1; July 24, 2002, p. 12.
New York Times, March 27, 2002, p. A16.
Plain Dealer, September 25, 2002, p. B1.

Online

"New Surgeon General Richard Carmona," About. com, http://phoenix.about.com/library/weekly/aasurgeongenerala.htm (October 10, 2002).

Office of the Surgeon General, http://www.surgeongeneral.gov/sg/default.htm (October 9, 2002).

"Surgeon General Nominee Wins Approval," CNN. com, http://www.cnn.com/2002/ALLPOLITICS/07/23/surgeon.general.reut/index.html (July 25, 2002).

"Who Is Dr. Richard Carmona?" CNN.com, http://fyi.cnn.com/2002/HEALTH/07/17/carmona.profile (October 9, 2002).

—*Wendy Kagan*

Kim Cattrall

Jim Spellman/WireImage.com

Actress

Born August 21, 1956, in Liverpool, England; daughter of Dennis (a construction engineer), and Shane (a homemaker) Cattrall; married Larry Davis, 1975 (divorced); married Andre J. Lyson, 1982 (divorced, 1989); married Mark Levinson, 1998 (separated, 2003). *Education:* Attended American Academy of Dramatic Arts, New York, NY.

Addresses: *Agent*—Jeffrey Witjas, William Morris Agency, 151 El Camino Dr., Beverly Hills, CA 90212.

Career

Actress in films, including: *Rosebud*, 1975; *Deadly Harvest*, 1977; *Tribute*, 1980; *Ticket to Heaven*, 1981; *Porky's*, 1981; *Police Academy*, 1984; *Turk 182!*, 1985; *City Limits*, 1985; *Hold–Up*, 1985; *Big Trouble in Little China*, 1986; *Mannequin*, 1987; *Masquerade*, 1988; *Palais Royale*, 1988; *Midnight Crossing*, 1988; *Return of the Musketeers*, 1989; *La Famiglia Buonanotte*, 1989; *Honeymoon Academy*, 1990; *The Bonfire of the Vanities*, 1990; *Star Trek VI: The Undiscovered Country*, 1991; *Split Second*, 1992; *Breaking Point*, 1993; *Above Suspicion*, 1995; *Live Nude Girls*, 1995; *Unforgettable*, 1996; *Where Truth Lies*, 1996; *Exception to the Rule*, 1997; *Modern Vampires*, 1998; *Baby Geniuses*, 1999; *15 Minutes*, 2001; *The Devil and Daniel Webster*, 2001; *Crossroads*, 2002. Television appearances include: *Quincy*, 1976; *Logan's Run*, 1977; *Switch*, 1977; *Good Against Evil* (movie), 1977; *Family*, 1978; *The Hardy Boys/Nancy Drew Mysteries*, 1978; *Starsky and Hutch*, 1978; *Columbo: How to Dial a Murder* (movie), 1978; *The Bastard* (movie), 1978; *The Incredible Hulk*, 1979; *How The West Was Won*, 1979; *Vega$*, 1979; *Charlie's Angels*, 1979; *Trapper John, M.D.*, 1979; *The Rebels* (mini-series), 1979; *Night Rider*, 1979; *Crossbar* (movie), 1979; *The Gossip Columnist* (movie), 1979; *Hagen*, 1980; *Scruples* (miniseries), 1980; *Tales of the Gold Monkey*, 1983; *Sins of the Past* (movie), 1984; *Miracle in the Wilderness* (movie), 1992; *Double Vision* (movie), 1992; *Wild Palms* (miniseries), 1993; *Angel Falls*, 1993; *Dream On*, 1994; *Running Delilah* (movie), 1994; *Two Golden Balls* (movie), 1994; *OP Center* (movie), 1995; *The Heidi Chronicles* (movie), 1995; *Every Woman's Dream* (movie), 1996; *The Outer Limits*, 1997; *Rugrats* (voice), 1997; *Duckman*, 1997; *Invasion* (miniseries), 1997; *Creature*, 1998; *Sex and the City*, 1998–2004; *36 Hours to Die* (movie), 1999.

Awards: Golden Globe Award for best performance by an actress in a supporting role in a series, miniseries, or motion picture made for television, Hollywood Foreign Press Association, for *Sex and the City*, 2003.

Sidelights

By the time most actresses hit their mid–forties, they are typecast into playing wife and mother roles. Not so for Kim Cattrall, who plays the steamy seductress Samantha Jones on HBO's Emmy–winning comedy *Sex and the City*. Cattrall has proven that television's femme fatale roles need no longer be reserved for younger actors.

Cattrall was born in Liverpool, England, on August 21, 1956, though her family moved to Vancouver Island, Canada, before her first birthday. Cattrall's father, Dennis, worked in construction, and her mother, Shane, worked on and off as a secretary to make ends meet. With three children to support, the Cattrall family was often short on cash but long on love. "It was basically the old story of the immigrant coming over with $20 and a bicycle," Cattrall told *People*.

From an early age, Cattrall knew she wanted to act. When she was eleven, Cattrall went to London for a family visit and decided to stay with her great–aunt so she could study at the London Academy of Music and Dramatic Art. It was Cattrall's father who encouraged the young girl to achieve her dreams—even forbidding her to prepare for a career to fall back on. "I remember in school, I wanted to take a typing class and my father wouldn't let me.... He said, 'I don't want you to cover your bases. I want you to reach for your dreams,'" Cattrall recalled in an E! Online interview.

By the age of 16, Cattrall had graduated from high school in Vancouver. She moved to New York City on a scholarship to attend the American Academy of Dramatic Arts. New York overwhelmed Cattrall. "I really felt like Andy Griffith from Mayberry," she told *People*. "I was such a country bumpkin." During her final year at the academy, Cattrall made her movie debut in the 1975 political drama, *Rosebud*. After completing this work, Cattrall decided she preferred the stage and found work in a repertory theater in Toronto, Canada.

Cattrall returned to film in the 1980s, starring in several screwball comedies including 1981's *Porky's*, where Cattrall played a sex–crazed gym teacher. She also played a skimpy–shirted recruit in 1984's *Police Academy*, and a plastic doll come to life in 1987's *Mannequin*. In 1991, Cattrall landed one of her all–time favorite roles, playing Spock's pointy-eared Vulcan love interest Valeris in *Star Trek VI: The Undiscovered Country*. Cattrall had so much fun working on the movie that during her last day on the set, she flubbed her lines and ended up in tears because she did not want the experience to end.

Though Cattrall has starred in nearly 50 films, the role most people will forever remember her for is that of Samantha Jones on HBO's *Sex and the City*, which made its debut in 1998 and boosted the cable network's profile considerably. Cattrall's character, Samantha, is the one people discuss during their coffee breaks. Over the years, Cattrall's character has earned a reputation as the queen of television kinkiness, having tried everything from threesomes to bondage on air. Though some critics have characterized her character as too slutty, Cattrall sees her as a role model. "She has a positive attitude about everything," Cattrall told *InStyle*. "Opportunities present themselves and she says, 'Why not experience them? We're here to live life, not to sit on the shelf and judge.'"

Cattrall played the role so well that she snatched up a seven–figure salary and received both Emmy and Golden Globe nominations for supporting actress in a comedy series. The show itself won the 2001 Emmy Award for Outstanding Comedy, making it the first–ever cable series to win an Emmy in that category. The much–loved show will come to an end with a final season airing in early 2004.

The demands of her career have taken their toll on three of Cattrall's marriages. "I think the hardest thing I gave up over the years was a personal life," Cattrall told E! Online. "There were a lot of hotel rooms with no family around. It was a tough life. Very, very hard—but I got to the other end."

Cattrall met her third husband, audio equipment executive Mark Levinson, at a Manhattan nightspot in January of 1998. They were married eight months later. What Levinson discovered is that Cattrall is so much more than her television persona. "Kim's a sexy, beautiful woman," Levinson told *People*. "But there's much more to her. She loves to read, she loves the ocean, and she loves her Dalmation, Dot." The husband–wife duo collaborated on a book, *Satisfaction: The Art of the Female Orgasm*, which was released in 2001. Despite the closeness the couple seemed to share in their book, by 2003 their marriage was faltering, and they officially separated in February of that year.

While Cattrall has enjoyed her time in the spotlight, she does not intend to have plastic surgery to maintain her youthful appearance. According to *People*, Cattrall told Britain's *Red* magazine: "I don't think the answer is plastic surgery. I see women my age, like Melanie Griffith, who have had surgery, but I don't want to look at myself and see Joker from Batman staring back." She later retracted that, telling the Europe Intelligence Wire that plastic surgery is "every woman's decision.... I'm not there yet, but who can say?"

Cattrall won a Golden Globe award for her role as Samantha on *Sex and the City* in 2003. Upon winning the award, Cattrall gave a heartfelt acceptance speech, as reported by the *Hollywood Reporter.* "I never expected to have a career in my 40s. The amount of job opportunities I had was cut in half, the agency I had wasn't even interested in me anymore, and even I believed the myth that women are not supposed to be sexy in their 40s. That is why I am so proud and pleased to be able to play characters like this one that breaks stereotypes."

Sources

Periodicals

Europe Intelligence Wire, October 28, 2002.
Hollywood Reporter, January 28, 2003.
InStyle, August 1, 2000.

People, January 20, 1992; June 1, 2001; December 31, 2001; January 28, 2002; March 17, 2003.
PR Newswire, October 29, 2002.

Online

"Fact Sheet: Kim Cattrall," E! Online, http://www.eonline.com/Facts/People/Bio/0,128,2898,00.html (February 4, 2002).
Golden Globe Awards 2003, http://www.hfpa.org (March 7, 2003).
"Q&A: Kim Cattrall," E! Online, http://www.eonline.com/Celebs/Qa/Cattrall/interview2.html (February 4, 2002).

—Lisa Frick

Tom Cavanagh

Actor

Born Thomas Cavanagh, October 26, 1968, in Ottawa, Ontario, Canada. *Education*—Queens University, Kingston, Ontario, bachelor's degrees in English and biology, 1987, bachelor's degree in education, 1988.

Addresses: *Office*—c/o Viewer Relations, NBC, 30 Rockefeller Plaza, New York, NY 10112.

Career

Actor on television, films, and stage. Television appearances include: *Beyond Reality*, 1991; *Sherlock Holmes Returns* (movie), 1993; *Other Women's Children* (movie), 1993; *Madison*, 1993; *A Vow to Kill* (movie), 1995; *Jake and the Kid*, 1995; *The Outer Limits*, 1995; *Bloodhounds II* (movie), 1996; *Viper*, 1996; *The Sentinel*, 1996; *Northern Lights* (movie), 1997; *Mentors*, 1998; *Eyes of a Cowboy*, 1998; *Sports Night*, 1998; *Providence*, 1999; *Anya's Bell* (movie), 1999; *Oh Grow Up*, 1999; *Ed*, 2000—, *Bang, Bang, You're Dead* (movie), 2002; *Scrubs*, 2002. Film appearances include: *Dangerous Intentions*, 1995; *Magic in the Water*, 1995; *Mask of Death*, 1996; *Profile for Murder*, 1997; *Honeymoon*, 1997; *Something More*, 1999. Stage appearances include: *Grease*, c. 1988; *Shenandoah*, 1989.

Awards: Favorite actor in a new series, TV Guide Awards, for *Ed*, 2001.

Sidelights

A relatively unknown actor, Tom Cavanagh became an international celebrity after he was cast in the starring role in the popular NBC television series *Ed*, which first aired in 2000. Winner of a People's Choice Award for Favorite New Comedy Series, the show features Cavanagh as a likeable young lawyer who moves from New York City back to his hometown of Stuckeyville, Ohio, after losing his job and breaking up with his wife.

Born in Ottawa, Canada, Tom Cavanagh was the second born of five children, and was raised by his schoolteacher parents in Canada and Ghana, West Africa. He was six years old when his family moved to Ghana from Canada. There, his father ran a school to train schoolteachers, while his mother taught in area schools. "We had one movie a month on some screen in some village somewhere," Cavanagh told *Entertainment Tonight* of this time of his life. "We didn't have a television, so for all of those formative years, I didn't have a channeling that says, 'This is how you do this thing'—which I think can be occasionally dangerous. You feel that you have to copy that."

The family returned to Canada in time for Cavanagh to start high school in a small town in southern Quebec. He studied French intensively immediately upon his return, and then attended a French-speaking high school. In many ways, the town in which his family lived at this time resembled the fictional setting of *Ed*. "Literally," Cavanagh told *Entertainment Tonight*, "it was the same type of town—3,000 people, where everybody knew everybody, you got a crush on a girl for a long time, people didn't lock their doors, they nodded hello to each other on the streets, and it was beautiful."

Leaving high school, Cavanagh attended Queens University in Kingston, Ontario. He played on the basketball team there, and graduated in 1988 with triple degrees in English, biology, and education. He began his professional acting career when he was cast as the lead in a Canadian production of *Grease*. He went on to New York's famed Broadway to play in a musical called *Shenandoah*. Roles on television followed, including an ongoing role on the NBC series *Providence*, and a starring role in the made–for–TV movie *Anya's Bell*. He also acted in feature films, landing roles in such movies as *Magic in the Water* and *Mask of Death*.

But it wasn't until 2000 when *Ed* was shown for the first time that Cavanagh achieved celebrity status. The project appealed to Cavanagh immediately. "In Hollywood," he told Australia's *Herald Sun*, "you run into a lot of writing you can never make work. Then you get lucky and read stuff you hope you can live up to. When I read the scripts, I thought, 'Wow, if only I could get a crack at this.'"

Ed was originally planned for CBS, but that network decided not to air it, and it was moved to NBC two years after the pilot was shot. As Cavanagh told *Entertainment Tonight*, "We got together and we were doing the show for a network (CBS) and we really thought it would go, but they didn't think we were a good fit. So then you have this basically two–year process before you shoot the next pilot for NBC, and nobody knew if it was going to go. I think that experience brought us closer together, and we all just became genuine friends."

The show centers around a bowling alley in a fictional town in Ohio called Stuckeyville. Cavanagh plays a lawyer who, after being fired from his corporate job, and losing his wife to the mailman, has returned to his hometown from New York City and bought the town's bowling alley. There, he runs the bowling alley and practices law in the back room. "They have functioning lanes," Cavanagh said of the set to *Entertainment Tonight*, "and we have a full–time bowling technician. So at lunch hour you can rev up and go."

Cavanagh also told *Entertainment Tonight* that he enjoys playing a lawyer since his brother is a practicing attorney. In an early incarnation of the script,

Cavanagh's character was first a stockbroker before being changed to a lawyer. "It was a smart move," Cavanagh told *Entertainment Tonight*, since as a practicing lawyer, his character has the opportunity to meet and interact with people throughout Stuckeyville, adding interest to the show.

During a break between shooting seasons of *Ed* in 2002, Cavanagh took the time to act in a drama for the Showtime network. Called *Bang, Bang, You're Dead*, it was based on a one–act play of the same name by William Mastrosimone that had become tremendously popular on high school stages. The play and the Showtime movie are about shootings by students in high school. The play was first performed in 1999 by students who had actually witnessed a high school shooting.

Cavanagh found the movie an interesting change of pace from his work on *Ed*. "There's always the value of entertainment, like our show (*Ed*) in this business," Cavanagh told the *Rocky Mountain News*. "But an actor doesn't often get the chance to do something that may be important or has a modicum of social importance. That's why I was drawn to *Bang, Bang, You're Dead*.... I simply wanted to get involved in a project that might, in some way, explain to viewers the hows and whys of school violence."

Cavanagh has taken his newfound fame in stride, telling Australia's *Sunday Mail*, "I think the older you are, you realize that celebrity is fleeting and fame is just a notion and there are very few concrete or character building things to pull from.... Because somebody's job happens to land them in the public eye does not make them any more or less special than anyone else."

Since *Ed* is shot in New Jersey, Cavanagh makes his home in nearby New York City, where he lives by himself. "I am doing what I love to do," he told *Entertainment Tonight* when asked if would ever consider giving up his acting career and moving to a small town like Stuckeyville. "I can see the appeal of that. But as actors, we have to be in a major [city]. You hear about the actors who reach a certain level and they go out and buy farmland. For me, anyway, that is appealing."

Sources

Periodicals

Herald Sun (Australia), May 2, 2001, p. H4.
Maclean's, October 30, 2000, p. 59.
Rocky Mountain News (Denver), July 15, 2002, p. 2D.

Sunday Mail (Australia), May 13, 2001, p. 8.

Time, December 25, 2000, p. 130.

Time, International Edition/Time Canada, August 6, 2001, p. 48.

Online

"Biography for Thomas Cavanagh," Internet Movie Database, http://us.imdb.com/Bio?Cavanagh, +Thomas (August 27, 2002).

"Bowling Alley Lawyer," *Entertainment Tonight,* http://www.etonline.com/television/a7273.htm (August 27, 2002).

"Cast Biographies: Tom Cavanagh," NBC, http://www.nbc.com/Ed/bios/Tom_Cavanagh.html (August 5, 2002).

"Notable Alumni," Queen's University, http://www.queensu.ca/artsci/alumni/notablealumni.html (August 27, 2002).

"People Profiles: Tom Cavanagh," *People.com,* http://people.aol.com/people/profiles/basicfacts/0,9855,128287,00.html (August 27, 2002).

—Michael Belfiore

Hussein Chalayan

Fashion designer

Born in 1970 in Nicosia, Cyprus. *Education:* Graduated from St. Martin's School of Art in London, 1993.

Addresses: *Office*—71 Endall St., London, England WC2H 9AJ. *Website*—http://www.husseinchalayan. com.

Career

Sold his graduation designs to Browns, a London fashion emporium, 1993; worked under tailor Timothy Everest; launched his own label, 1994; designed for TSE Cashmere, 1998–2001; liquidated and relaunched his own label, 2001.

Awards: Designer of the Year, British Fashion Awards, 1999; Designer of the Year, British Fashion Awards, 2000.

Sidelights

Hussein Chalayan is renowned for his unorthodox design sense—"the word 'genius' is not infrequently used," according to the *Guardian*. His deconstructionist designs for his own label, along with the more accessible TSE Cashmere line and the British clothing chain Top Shop earned him the Designer of the Year honors at the British Fashion Awards in both 1999 and 2000. He is known as the philosopher of fashion, as he is much more reserved than his wild peers, London designers Alexander McQueen and John Galliano, who are known for stirring up controversy. Rather, Chalayan takes his inspiration from outside the fashion world. His elegant, minimalist designs are far from conventional, however. He has used prints from meteorological charts and photographically printed washable paper as fabric. In his fall 2000 show, one model wore a circular wood table as a dress.

Chalayan (pronounced sha–LY–on) was born in 1970 in Nicosia, the capital of the Mediterranean island of Cyprus, where his family owns a restaurant. For centuries, the island's Greek and Turkish inhabitants had coexisted peacefully. In 1974, fearing the Greeks were starting a campaign of ethnic cleansing, the Turkish Army arrived on the island. By 1975, the United Nations divided the island into northern and southern regions and the Greeks and Turkish Cypriots went their separate ways. The island remains bisected by a wall and series of barbed wire fences. It is inevitable that his homeland's history and the territorial split he experienced as a child would have an effect on Chalayan's creativity. "As a kid I used to feel that at the very tip of the island you could imagine Cyprus in its entirety," Chalayan told Neville Wakefield of the *New York Times*, "There was something very liberating about being here, like being able to see something you already know from a vantage point outside of yourself."

Chalayan attended Highgate boarding school in England, an environment so strict he has likened it to being in the army. He studied fashion at St. Martin's School of Art in London, where one teacher told him he should pursue sculpture because he was no good at fashion. His curious approach to fashion started early—he buried his graduation line in a friend's backyard to see how they would decompose. Chalayan proved the teacher wrong when, after graduating in 1993, he sold that graduation collection to Browns, a London fashion emporium. After a stint working under tailor Timothy Everest, Chalayan launched his own label in 1994. He began to build his reputation "on clothing that is both wearable and intellectually engaging," according to the CelebrityTrendZ fashion website.

Chalayan signed on to design for TSE Cashmere in 1998, but practically dismissed the work he did for the American company: "It's not the collection I'd do for myself," he told Ginia Bellafante in the *New York Times*. He did not renew his contract when it expired in March of 2001, and the fall 2001 TSE collection was his last. "TSE has benefited enormously from the colossal talents of Hussein Chalayan since fall 1998," TSE's executive vice president said in a statement, according to the *New York Times*. Though critics praised the six collections he designed for TSE, they received a mixed response in stores.

Unlike many designers, Chalayan finds his inspiration outside the fashion world. He introduced his spring 2001 line for TSE Cashmere with these words: "I don't refer to anything really, anything historical, anything about clothes from the '60s, anything at all. It's based on the idea of a circle, a square, and a triangle," according to the *New York Times*'s Bellafante. He also has used shapes and materials inspired by airplane wings, coffee tables, voodoo, and mail. Many fashion critics have observed the architectural influences in his work. In his fall/winter 1998–99 fashion show, models wore wooden cones on their heads and red plastic squares over their mouths—adornments that were thought–provoking, if nothing else. Chalayan readily admits his seasonal fashion showpieces aren't created for purchase or wear, like his more accessible clothes. "These pieces might not sell," he told Michelle Orecklin in *Time*, "but they express the concept behind each collection."

In addition to his geometric inspirations, Chalayan is often moved by influences in world culture. In his spring/summer 1998 collection, he addressed the role of women in Islamic society—a row of his models wore Islamic chadors of varying lengths—from naked but masked at one end of the row to covered from head to toe in a full–length chador at the other. Chalayan's fall 2000 show is perhaps his crowning achievement. Set in a sparsely furnished living room, "clothes, surroundings, and people became one," according to the *New York Times*'s Wakefield. Piece by piece, models removed items from the room, stowing them in specially designed

pockets in their clothes. Chair covers were taken off and worn as tailored dresses and "in what has become Chalayan's most iconic image," Wakefield continued, "a model stepped into a circular wood table and walked off wearing it as a skirt."

In 2001, when he parted ways with TSE, Chalayan also announced he was liquidating his own company. Burdened by upwards of $450,000 in debt, Chalayan did not have the capital to meet production demands—his sales were steadily increasing, but he could not afford to fill the orders. Far from an indication of failure, fashion industry analysts took the move as a sign that he was trying to attract investors. "Basically, they're not interested in you if you have debt," he told the *New York Times*. As a result, Chalayan's fall/winter 2001 London runway show was cancelled, and he released a significantly smaller collection for the season. He signed on to design for the Autograph collection by London's Marks & Spencer early in 2001.

By March of 2001, Chalayan was back in business with a newly restructured company and a new line. His fall 2001 collection included 50 pieces in fabrics such as denim, leather, sheepskin, wool, and shirting. For his spring 2002 ready–to–wear collection, Cathy Horyn of the *New York Times* wrote that Chalayan "must have clung to that ideal of making deconstruction seem alive and organic—and in common fabrics like cotton and washed silk that anybody can understand...." Despite his previous claims to the contrary, Chalayan was obviously influenced by historical fashion for this line. His fashions were inventive and unconventional, as always, but clearly echoed fashion references as far back as the Greeks and Victorians, as well as 1920s and 1960s styles.

The *New York Times*'s Bellafante, who had praised Chalayan's work in the past, was highly critical in her October of 2002 review of his spring 2003 collection. His show was titled "Manifest Destiny" and featured what "looked like gym wear put through a document shredder," Bellafante wrote. The show was accompanied by a droning live band, a far cry from the elegant Philip Glass music he had used in the past. The idea he presented was one "with which most inhabitants of six continents are familiar," Bellafante continued, "and that Mr. Chalayan didn't contribute something fresh to the subject seemed imperious on his part, as if he was suggesting that he could now do whatever he wanted because his gifts have been well recognized."

Chalayan's "well recognized" gifts went a long way in making him a hot spot on the fashion industry's radar early in his career, and carried him through financial troubles that could have ruined a lesser talent. Although reviews of Chalayan's Spring 2003 show generally were critical, that he was even able to launch a collection is a testament to his significant standing in the highly competitive fashion industry.

Sources

Periodicals

New York Times, September 20, 2000, p. B11; January 9, 2001, p. 8; July 8, 2001; October 9, 2001, p. A20; October 7, 2002, p. 9.
Time, July 17, 2000, p. 62.

Online

"Chalayan Returns," *Daily Telegraph,* http://www.telegraph.co.uk/fashion/main.jhtml?xml=%2Ffashion%2F2001%2F03%2F21%2Fefhush21.xml (December 23, 2002).
"Deconstructing Chalayan," *Daily Telegraph,* http://www.telegraph.co.uk/fashion/main.jhtml?xml=%2Ffashion%2F2001%2F12%2F05%2Fefhuss.xml (December 23, 2002).
"Designer: Hussein Chalayan," CelebrityTrendZ, http://www.celebritytrendz.com/fashion/designers/husseinchalayan1.html (December 23, 2002).
"Table talk: Hussein Chalayan named fashion designer of the year," *Guardian,* http://www.guardian.co.uk/fashion/article/0,2763,191600,00.html (December 23, 2002).
"Time to collect an autograph," *Daily Telegraph,* http://www.telegraph.co.uk/fashion/main.jhtml?xml=%2Ffashion%2F2001%2F01%2F17%2Fefhussein17.xml (December 23, 2002).

—*Brenna Sanchez*

Mohammed ibn Chambas

AP/Wide World Photos

Diplomat

Born December 7, 1950, in Bimbilla, Ghana; son of Alhaji Alhassan (a district commissioner) Chambas; married Khadija; children: a daughter, Shakira. *Education:* University of Ghana, Legon, B.A., 1973; Cornell University, Ph.D., 1980; Case Western Reserve University, J.D., 1984.

Addresses: *Office*—ECOWAS Secretariat, 60, Yakubu Gowon Crescent, Asokoro District P.M.B., 401 Abuja, Nigeria.

Career

Worked in the law firm of Forbes, Forbes, and Teamor, Cleveland, OH, mid–1980s; teacher, Oberlin College, Ohio; took first government position as Deputy Foreign Secretary of Ghana, 1987; played central role in the peace talks that led to the end of civil war in Liberia, 1991–96; elected to the First Parliament of the Fourth Republic of Ghana, 1992; served as First Deputy Speaker of the Parliament, 1993–94; elected Deputy Foreign Minister; lost bid for re–election to Parliament, 1996; appointed Deputy Minister of Education, 1997–2000; re–elected to Parliament, 2000; took post of Executive Secretary of ECOWAS, 2002; played key role as mediator in Ivory Coast civil conflicts, 2002—.

Sidelights

The Ghanaian diplomat Mohammed ibn Chambas has earned a reputation as a skillful mediator and peacemaker with wide–ranging influence throughout West Africa. A former member of Parliament and Deputy Foreign Minister in Ghana, Chambas played a key role in helping to resolve the civil war in Liberia in the 1990s. Serving as the Executive Secretary of the Economic Community of West African States (ECOWAS) since February of 2002, he has been charged with seeking a peaceful solution to civil conflicts that have wracked war–torn Ivory Coast since September of 2002. A U.S.–educated lawyer and political scientist, Chambas has been described by *Africa News* as a "dapper diplomat ... whose genteel demeanour masks his resilience and inner strength."

Born on December 7, 1950, Chambas grew up in Bimbilla, in North Ghana. He is the son of Alhaji Alhassan Chambas, a district commissioner in the government of Dr. Kwame Nkrumah. As a child he attended a missionary school where teachers renamed students with Christian names; he was known as David. Chambas, a Muslim, later reclaimed his birth name, though friends often referred to him by the nickname Chambo. The name Chambas refers to an ethnic group with an ancestry spread throughout northern Ghana, Togo, and Nigeria. "Ibn Chambas" literally means "son of the Chamba people."

At the University of Ghana in Legon, Chambas studied political science and was active in student politics. An excellent student, he showed the promise of a budding statesman when he served as secretary of the school's Student Representative Council. Chambas then went to the United States to do graduate work. He earned a Ph.D. in political science from Cornell University in 1980. He then studied law at Case Western Reserve University, earning a J.D. in 1984. Admitted to practice law in Ghana as well as in the state of Ohio, Chambas worked in the Cleveland law firm of Forbes, Forbes, and Teamor in the mid–1980s. Chambas also held a teaching position at Oberlin College in Ohio.

Returning to Africa, Chambas took his first government position in 1987, when he became Deputy Foreign Secretary of Ghana. In this role he served as a member of the Head of State's summit delegations to several countries, including the United States, China, the United Kingdom, France, Malaysia, and Nigeria. Chambas also led a number of Ghana's delegations and conferences, including the United Nations General Assembly, the ministerial meetings of the Organization of African Unity (OAU), and ECOWAS conferences.

In December of 1992 Chambas, running on the National Democratic Congress (NDC) party ticket, was elected to the First Parliament of the Fourth Republic of Ghana, representing his hometown of Bimbilla. He served as First Deputy Speaker of the Parliament from January of 1993 to March of 1994. During this time he was elected Deputy Foreign Minister. He also served as chairman of the Appointments and Privileges Committee, which was responsible for holding public hearings on the ministerial and court nominees chosen by the President of Ghana.

Between 1991 and 1996, Chambas proved himself to be skillful in conflict resolutions and negotiations. As Ghana's Deputy Foreign Minister, he took a central role in the peace talks that led to the end of civil war in Liberia. Credited with facilitating the signing of peace agreements in Monrovia, Chambas gained a reputation as a very capable mediator. In 1996 Chambas was an important member of Ghana's campaign team for the election of Kofi Annan to his first term as Secretary–General of the United Nations Organization. As a member of the Commonwealth Ministerial Action Group, Chambas helped bring about a transition to constitutional governance in Nigeria, Sierra Leone, and Gambia.

However, despite these achievements Chambas lost his bid for re–election to Parliament in 1996. He remained popular among Ghanaians, who acknowl-

edged his accomplishments in a 1997 radio poll, when he was chosen by the people as Minister of the Year. The same year, the administration of Ghanaian president Jerry Rawlings inexplicably removed Chambas from the foreign ministry. Instead he was appointed Deputy Minister of Education, a position that made him responsible for Ghana's five universities, ten polytechnics, and other higher–education institutions.

The move was a drastic one. Instead of facilitating international negotiations, Chambas was now presiding at college graduations. Moreover, the Rawlings administration repeatedly overlooked Chambas in favor of dignitaries with less experience. The Minister of Education position was given to Mr. Ekwow Spio–Garbrah, who ranked lower than Chambas in education and office.

Yet while many government dignitaries would have protested this drop in status, Chambas took it in stride. Indeed, he was able to use his conflict–resolution skills during a period of volatile student protests and university–administration disputes. Chambas served as Deputy Minister of Education until December of 2000.

That year, he regained his Parliament seat in the general election on December 7. Running on the NDC party ticket, Chambas was elected to the Third Parliament of the Fourth Republic of Ghana. As a member of Parliament, he resumed his work on foreign affairs, serving as the ranking member of the Parliamentary Select Committee on Foreign Affairs, as well as the minority NDC "shadow minister" for foreign affairs. Yet Ghanaian President John Kufor had other plans for Chambas, naming him for the top job at the Economic Community of West African States (ECOWAS). As a candidate for the prestigious position of Executive Secretary, Chambas was in competition with several other West African diplomats.

As with many political nominations, controversy surrounded Kufor's choice of Chambas for the job. Inside Ghana, some critics accused the president of choosing Chambas in order to free up a seat on the Parliament for the majority party. Outside Ghana, some West African nations accused Kufor of putting only Ghanaians in control of ECOWAS. The organization already had a Ghanaian serving as president of the ECOWAS Bank for Finance and Development. About Chambas's character, however, there was no controversy. He was regarded as a man of fairness, tact, conviction, and great diplomatic skill.

Ultimately, Kufor's influence proved weighty, and Chambas was elected Executive Secretary of ECOWAS at the 25th session of the Authority of Heads of State and Government in Dakar. He would replace the Guinean incumbent, who had announced his retirement. Chambas took office at the ECOWAS Secretariat in Abuja, Nigeria, on February 1, 2002.

Shortly after taking office, Chambas expressed his vision of ECOWAS under his leadership. He told *Africa News*, "[West Africans] want to be able to move about freely [between countries], engage in legitimate business, seek opportunities in neighboring countries. They believe that ECOWAS was established precisely for that purpose so they expect ECOWAS to facilitate the free movement of persons, goods and services." Chambas pointed to the importance of ECOWAS in promoting free trade in West Africa, as well as in promoting peace and security in the sub–region and in Africa as a whole.

In summer of 2002, Chambas announced that ECOWAS planned to establish two military bases for the storage of equipment. Plans were also afoot to establish standby troops as forces for peacekeeping and humanitarian initiatives. The goal, Chambas told *Africa News*, was to promote "long term conditions for development and security, building the capacity of African institutions for early warning, as well as enhancing the capacity of African institutions to prevent, manage, and resolve conflicts."

With financial assistance from the European Union and the United States, ECOWAS was further able to develop its peacekeeping capabilities. A \$5.3 million satellite communication network, a gift of the U.S. European Command, would help ECOWAS observe and monitor the sub–region for conflict–prevention, peacekeeping, and security. The communications equipment would also help monitor any terrorist activity, which would be a potential concern of the United States and the European Union.

By September of 2002, Chambas found that all of his prior military planning had become indispensable to control a volatile situation that had erupted in Ivory Coast. On September 19 of that year, about 700 Ivory Coast soldiers began to mutiny in three cities after certain troops discovered they were slated for demobilization. By the end of the month, at least 300 people had been killed in the bloody mutiny, which pitted rebel forces against loyalist troops. ECOWAS was prepared to stage a military intervention to restore peace to the region.

On October 1, at the close of an ECOWAS emergency summit held in Accra, Ghana, Chambas delivered a communiqué that urged forces on both sides to cease fire and settle their dispute through

diplomatic means. Chambas also encouraged the rebel leaders to contact him, and said that he would travel to occupied areas to meet with them. The rebel soldiers, who now called themselves the Patriotic Movement of Ivory Coast, claimed to have occupied about 40 percent of the country.

Thus began several weeks of intense mediation spearheaded by Chambas and ECOWAS. Although the conflict seemed far from over, Chambas's ability to keep the two sides talking was regarded as a sign of progress. Meanwhile, the rebel soldiers gained ground, banding together with other disenfranchised groups in Ivory Coast. These insurgents carried a message of freedom from what they called the dictatorship of the current regime under President Laurent Gbagdo. At the root of the conflict was tension between the largely Muslim rebels and a government based in southern, predominantly Christian Ivory Coast. The conflict had spawned widespread ethnic violence, and the United States and European countries had issued warnings urging their citizens to leave the region.

In October, two plans for a cease–fire had failed because Gbagdo's administration had insisted that the rebels disarm first. Along with Senegalese President Abdoulaye Wade, Chambas helped put together a new agreement that was acceptable to both the rebels and the government. As negotiations pressed on, Chambas urged both sides to make concessions. "Tolerance is absolutely essential," Chambas said at a summit in Abidjan, Ivory Coast, according to Clar Ni Chonghaile of the Associated Press. "People who have been to war must appreciate the need ... to reconcile, to forgive, and move forward."

But by late November it appeared that the peace talks had reached a stalemate, with the rebels rejecting the peace plan because it appeared to favor the government. The peace plan also failed to meet the rebels's demands that President Gbagdo resign and that a new election be held within six months. Sympathizers throughout Western Africa began to criticize Chambas and his fellow mediators for their inability to reach a diplomatic compromise.

The situation had worsened by early December of 2002, with both sides accusing the other of mass killings. After a mass grave was uncovered in the Ivory Coast village of Monoko–Zohi, the government claimed it contained the bodies of rebel soldiers, but surviving villagers said the victims were innocent civilians. Chambas's job as mediator became even more difficult, with the rebels refusing to negotiate with a government that resorted to genocide.

By March of 2003, with no end to the conflict in sight, Chambas and ECOWAS had helped create a proposed coalition government to take over war–torn Ivory Coast. A cease–fire had been reached, and French troops had arrived in the former French colony to uphold the truce. Meanwhile, West African army chiefs called for an influx of peacekeeping personnel from all ECOWAS member countries. "We have to do what is needed to bring peace," Chambas told Reuters, according to the *New York Times,* in a phone call from the peace talks in Accra, Ghana.

Whether or not peace in Ivory Coast can be achieved and maintained remains to be seen. All eyes remain fixed on Chambas, the one man who may be capable of calming the troubled West African nation.

Sources

Periodicals

Accra Mail, October 1, 2002; October 3, 2002.
Africa News, June 29, 2001; July 12, 2001; March 12, 2002; July 24, 2002; July 29, 2002; October 11, 2002.

Agence France Presse, September 26, 2002.
Associated Press, October 17, 2002; October 23, 2002; December 8, 2002.
Ghanaian Chronicle, March 11, 2002; November 28, 2002.
Xinhua General News Service, October 5, 2002.

Online

"Profile of Hon. Dr. Mohamed ibn Chambas," ECOWAS Official Website, http://www.sec.ecowas.int/sitecedeao/english/kouyate–cv.htm (March 5, 2003).
"Profile: Mohammed ibn Chambas," BBC News, http://news.bbc.co.uk/2/hi/africa/2299229.stm (October 4, 2002).
"West Africa Wants Ivory Coast Peace Force Trebled," *New York Times,* http://www.nytimes.com/reuters/international/international–ivorycoast.html (March 6, 2003).

—Wendy Kagan

Michael Chiklis

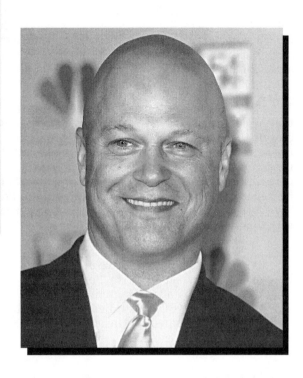

Actor

Born August 30, 1963, in Lowell, MA; son of Charles Chiklis; married Michelle Moran, 1992; children: Autumn, Odessa. *Education:* Boston University School of Fine Arts, B.F.A., 1989.

Addresses: *Home*—Sherman Oaks, CA. *Office*—FX Networks, LLC, 10000 Santa Monica Blvd., Los Angeles, CA 90067.

Career

Actor in films, including: *Wired,* 1989; *The Rain Killer,* 1990; *Nixon,* 1995; *Soldier,* 1998; *Body and Soul,* 1998; *The Taxman,* 1999; *Do Not Disturb,* 1999; *Last Request,* 1999; *Carlo's Wake,* 1999; *Spirited Away,* 2002. Television appearances include: *Miami Vice,* 1989; *B.L. Stryker,* 1989; *Wiseguy,* 1989; *L.A. Law,* 1990; *Murphy Brown,* 1990; *Seinfeld,* 1991; *The Commish,* 1991–95; *Touched by an Angel,* 1998; *The Three Stooges* (movie), 2000; *Daddio,* 2000; *Family Guy,* 2001; *The Shield,* 2002—.

Awards: Emmy Award for best actor in a drama series, Academy of Television Arts and Sciences, for *The Shield,* 2002; Golden Globe Award for best actor in a drama series, Hollywood Foreign Press Association, for *The Shield,* 2003.

Sidelights

Michael Chiklis built a solid career as a character actor in films and on television through the 1980s and 1990s, creating roles that earned him the respect of his peers but nevertheless kept him from achieving a star status. That changed in 2002 when he was cast in the role of hard–nosed detective Vic Mackey on *The Shield,* a television series on the FX network. The show received critical and popular acclaim when it debuted, and Chiklis, then 39 years old, won an Emmy Award for best lead actor in a drama series for his work on it.

Chiklis was born in Lowell, Massachusetts, in 1963, and grew up in Andover. He wanted to be an actor from the time he was five years old. His brother, Peter, in later years recalled that Chiklis wanted to be a rich and famous actor. Chiklis landed his first professional acting role when he was 13 years old, in a summer stock production at the Town and Country Playhouse in Salem, New Hampshire. This role was the beginning of a long association with the man who was to become Chiklis's theatrical mentor, Mark Kaufman. Kaufman took Chiklis with him to a new theater called the Merrimack Repertory Theater, which went on to become one of the most successful theaters in Massachusetts. Chiklis went on to appear in many theatrical productions at theaters around the East Coast.

In high school, Chiklis was an athlete as well as an actor. He was captain of the Andover High School football team and lettered in two other sports. He also played the lead in every high school theater production throughout his high school career. For about ten years, from the late 1970s through the late 1980s, Chiklis was the lead singer in a band. The band's members had met each other in elementary school, and they stayed friends through junior and senior high.

The band members all stayed in touch, even after they went their separate ways professionally (only one of the band members became a professional musician). One of the former band members attributed Chiklis's later success as an actor to perseverance. "I've seen him down a few times, but he never gave up," he told Joyce Crane in the *Boston Globe*. "He kept plugging away, and that's the way you make it in this business."

Chiklis's parents were supportive of their son's ambitions, and they sent him to Boston University School of Fine Arts after his graduation from high school in 1985. At BU he studied acting, and the day after he graduated, he headed to New York City to start his acting career.

Not long after his arrival in New York, Chiklis landed his first big break, in the form of a starring role in a film called *Wired,* about the life of the late comedian John Belushi. At first overjoyed to find himself in a major film playing one of his idols, Chiklis soon found that this project was extremely unpopular in Hollywood because it portrayed in a negative light many of Belushi's associates—not a few of whom were powerful Hollywood figures.

Belushi's former associates tried to prevent the film's release, embroiling Chiklis in a controversy he later admitted almost ended his film career before it began. Still, Chiklis soon afterward managed to land supporting and guest roles on major television shows like *Seinfeld, L.A. Law, Murphy Brown,* and *Miami Vice.*

In 1991, Chiklis was cast as the lead in a new ABC television series called *The Commish.* Chiklis played a good-natured police commissioner named Tony Scali. Although Chiklis was then in his late 20s, the character he played was in his late 30s. Chiklis gained weight in order to make himself look older, assuming a softer, older persona. So successful was his transformation to a character utterly unlike himself, that Chiklis was afterward sharply limited in the kind of roles for which he would be considered. While he had pulled off a remarkable transformation, this transformation was known only to people who knew Chiklis beforehand; the rest of world

had yet to realize what the actor was truly capable of. After *The Commish* ended its run, "People were passing on me even reading for parts. They thought I was 50 and fat. I was only 33," he later told Laurence in the *San Diego Union–Tribune.*

Still, his work on *The Commish* was a powerfully positive experience for Chiklis. It was also during this time that he met and married his wife, Michelle; they had their first child, a daughter named Autumn, in 1993. Their second daughter, Odessa, was born in 1999.

After his stint on *The Commish,* which lasted from 1991 to 1995, Chiklis starred for six months in a one-man show on Broadway called *Defending the Caveman.* This show, which featured other actors in the role both before and after Chiklis made his appearance, made Broadway history by becoming the longest-running show on the Great White Way. More feature film roles followed for Chiklis, including *The Taxman, Soldier, Body and Soul,* and *Do Not Disturb.*

Chiklis's next major TV role was that of Curly in the ABC television movie *The Three Stooges.* Chiklis, still smarting from his unpleasant experience following his work on *Wired,* was at first reluctant to take on another role portraying a real-life comedian. But his agent prevailed upon him to focus on the material rather than whatever controversy might or might not follow it, and after reading the script, Chiklis was hooked.

It didn't hurt that the producer of *The Three Stooges* was the famous actor Mel Gibson, a longtime Three Stooges fan who was committed to an extremely thorough and accurate portrayal of the classic comedy team. Also, as Chiklis told Tim Feran in the *Columbus Dispatch* at the time, "It's so far after the fact, as opposed to *Wired.* This was a much more comfortable endeavor to me. The fact that I was going to play homage to one of my all-time favorites...."

The movie aired in 2000. It was a big year for Chiklis—that year he also starred in the NBC-TV series *Daddio,* in which he played a stay-at-home dad. This show proved unsuccessful, however, running only one full season. After *Daddio* tanked, Chiklis hit a low point, and he stopped to reevaluate the direction his career was taking. His wife, who Chiklis has called the major driving force in his life, played a crucial role at this juncture. She got him to realize that casting directors would only see what he looked like when he approached them, not what he could become. She encouraged him to turn down roles that would only further his previous image, even if that meant earning less money for the family.

With this powerful encouragement, Chiklis hit the gym, dropped 45 pounds of fat, gained a lot of muscle, and shaved his head, dramatically changing his appearance. He also began work on a script about a rough–and–tumble Miami cop, the kind of hard–boiled, tough–as–nails role no casting director would ever cast him in in his previous incarnation.

As it happened, another script—for a new show called *The Shield*—about just such a cop was in development at the Fox–owned FX network. Chiklis managed to obtain a copy, and he knew that this could be the break he had been looking for. Beefed up, looking years younger than he did in *The Commish*, Chiklis auditioned for the show, and was cast in its lead role. The show premiered in early 2002 to critical and popular acclaim.

The Shield features, in addition to Chiklis as a hardened cop, graphic violence, nudity, and foul language—characteristics that have caused several advertisers, including Burger King, Gillette, and the United States Army to stop advertising on the show. Chiklis himself has admitted that he does not want his kids to watch the show, which he termed strictly for adults.

The premier episode of *The Shield* introduced Chiklis as Mackey, the head of an elite squad of Los Angeles police officers who get the job done by any means necessary, including excessive violence. They also steal money and drugs, and kill anyone who gets in their way. Mackey himself kills another police officer after it appears that the officer would report Mackey and company's illegal activities.

It was a welcome change for Chiklis, who until then was typecast because of his role on *The Commish* as a "roly–poly, daddy type," he told Robert P. Laurence in the *San Diego Union–Tribune*. While he didn't mind playing such roles, he felt it expressed only one narrow portion of his true range as an actor. "Those were the only parts I was considered for," he complained to Laurence. "It was a major frustration for me, because I knew I was capable of far more than that."

Chiklis has said that his role on *The Shield* is no more like him that his role on *The Commish*. And that's just the way he likes it. Like his role on *The Commish*, it is a stretch that allows him to express his range as a performer. He also relished this role

which required him to play a character who was simultaneously the villain and the hero. Then, too, Chiklis saw *The Shield* as part of a welcome shift in focus in television toward morally ambiguous main characters—characters Chiklis saw as more realistic, complex, and thought–provoking than their progenitors.

The Shield proved hugely successfully, drawing the biggest audience in its premier episode than any other series debut in basic cable history. It also earned Chiklis an Emmy Award for best actor in a drama series. In winning his Emmy Award, Chiklis beat out the likes of Martin Sheen, who had been nominated three times running for *West Wing*, Kiefer Sutherland for his work in *24*, and Michael C. Hall for *Six Feet Under*.

The win shocked Chiklis, as well as many observers, who did not think the show, broadcast on a relatively little–watched basic cable network, would stand a chance against the larger networks that were home to the competing shows. Nevertheless, Chiklis saw his win as a long–overdue public recognition of what he had known from the beginning was one of his major strengths as a performer—his ability to transform himself. He was also delighted by the reactions of two of his competitors for the award, Sheen and Sutherland, both of whom he had long admired, to his Emmy win—both of them offered heartfelt congratulations.

Although he has relocated to Sherman Oaks, California, and is an Emmy award–winning television star, Chiklis still maintains close ties to his hometown and his family and friends there. "I guess I'm a New England boy, still," he told the *Boston Globe*'s Joyce Crane. He also has not lost sight of what he considers his most important priorities—his focus on his home life. He has said that his single most important goal is to provide the best possible lives he can for his children.

Sources

Periodicals

Boston Globe, April 30, 2002, p. E1; October 20, 2002, p. 4.
Buffalo News, January 7, 2003, p. C7.
Chicago Sun–Times, May 7, 2002, p. 37.
Columbus Dispatch, April 23, 2000, p. 4G; January 21, 2003, p. 7E.
Los Angeles Times, September 25, 2002, Calendar, p. 1.
San Diego Union Tribune, January 5, 2003, p. F9.

USA Today, January 7, 2003, p. 3D.
Washington Post, January 14, 2003, p. C1.

Online

"Fact Sheet: Michael Chiklis," E! Online, http://www.eonline.com/Facts/People/Bio/0,128,3122,00.html (March 4, 2002).

"Michael Chiklis," Internet Movie Database, http://us.imdb.com/Name?Chiklis,+Michael (March 4, 2003).
Michael Chiklis Official Web Site, http://www.michaelchiklis.com (March 4, 2003).

—Michael Belfiore

Hayden Christensen

Michael Caulfield/WireImage.com

Actor

Born April 19, 1981, in Vancouver, British Columbia, Canada; son of David (a public relations consultant) and Alie (a public relations consultant) Christensen. *Education:* Attended Actors Studio, New York.

Addresses: *Office*—Lucasfilm Ltd., P.O. Box 2009, San Rafael, CA 94912.

Career

Actor in films, including: *Street Law,* 1995; *In the Mouth of Madness,* 1995; *Strike!,* 1998; *The Virgin Suicides,* 1999; *Life as a House,* 2001; *Star Wars: Episode II—Attack of the Clones,* 2002; *Shattered Glass,* 2003; *Nailed Right In,* 2003. Television appearances include: *Family Passions,* 1993; *Love and Betrayal: The Mia Farrow Story* (movie), 1995; *Harrison Bergeron* (movie), 1995; *No Greater Love* (movie), 1996; *Forever Knight,* 1996; *Goosebumps,* 1997; *Real Kids, Real Adventures,* 1999; *Freefall* (movie), 1999; *Are You Afraid of the Dark?,* 1999; *The Famous Jett Jackson,* 1999; *Higher Ground,* 2000; *Trapped in a Purple Haze* (movie), 2000. Stage appearances include: *This Is Our Youth,* 2002.

Awards: Breakthrough Performance of the Year Award, U.S. National Board of Review, for *Life as a House,* 2001.

Sidelights

The Canadian actor Hayden Christensen became an international star in his early 20s when he appeared in the role of Anakin Skywalker in the blockbuster film *Star Wars: Episode II—Attack of the Clones,* released in 2002. He had already received critical acclaim for his work in the 2001 film *Life as a House,* in which he starred opposite Kevin Kline, and had been an actor in films and on television throughout his teens.

Christensen was born in Vancouver in 1981, the son of a pair of self–employed public relations experts. He was one of four children born to the couple, and the second youngest. When he was six years old, his family moved to a suburb of Toronto called Thornhill. Christensen took to sports at an early age, starting to play hockey when he was seven years old. Sports ran in the Christensen family; his older sister, Hejsa, became a junior world champion on the trampoline when she was 13 years old.

Christensen got his start as a professional actor on television when he was still a boy. It all started when he accompanied Hejsa to a meeting with a talent agent who had signed her after she was cast in a television commercial. The agent, perhaps seeing something of Christensen's innate talent, offered to represent him as well as his sister.

In high school in Toronto, Christensen enrolled in a performing arts program and appeared in many school theater productions. He also continued to play hockey, and began to play tennis. His grandmother, Rose Schwartz, lived in Long Island, New York, and he typically spent his summers with her, taking tennis lessons during the week, and visiting Manhattan on weekends to take acting lessons at the famous Actors Studio.

Although classmates were later to say that Christensen did not stand out particularly among a student body that contained many talented actors, Christensen pursued his dream during and after high school, landing roles in such films as *Street Law, In the Mouth of Madness, Strike!,* and *The Virgin Suicides,* before rising to prominence in the Fox television series *Higher Ground* in 2000, when he was 18 years old. In the show, he played a troubled teenager who, after being seduced by his stepmother, tries to find comfort in drugs.

One of Christensen's major roles coming out of high school was a starring role in the film *Life as a House,* released in 2001. In this film, Christensen plays Sam, a brooding teen with a father, played by Kevin Kline, who has terminal cancer. Christensen first appears in the film wearing mascara, with a pierced chin, engaged in autoerotic asphyxiation—quite a contrast to the wholesome entertainment offered by the *Star Wars* films.

The pierced chin proved difficult to work with for Christensen. It was held on magnetically, and it had a tendency to fly off at inopportune moments during filming. He threw himself into the role with gusto, at one point slamming his fist into a wall to make a point during a scene. Afterward, he told Joan Krzys in the *Herald Sun,* "I turned around [to face the camera] and I was crying. My hand was bleeding real blood. It was great!" Unfortunately, the director decided not to use that particular take.

Although Christensen completed his work in *Attack of the Clones* before *Life as a House* was shot, *Life as a House* was the first to hit the theaters. When *Life as a House* director Irwin Winkler cast Christensen, he did not know about Christensen's role in *Attack of the Clones.* But both Winkler and *Attack of the Clones*

director George Lucas cited the same reason for casting Christensen in their two very different projects. As Winkler explained it to Krzys in the *Herald Sun,* "There is a sense of toughness about him behind this very sweet guy." Kline, Christensen's costar in *Life as a House,* was deeply impressed by Christensen's work in that film, telling Brian D. Johnson in *Maclean's,* "He's astonishing. He's the genuine article, and there's nothing flash in the pan about him."

To audition for *Attack of the Clones,* Christensen was flown to Lucas's sprawling studio complex outside of San Francisco, California, to screen test with the director and future costar Natalie Portman. Christensen, who was a longtime *Star Wars* fan, and who had admired Portman's good looks and talent in the previous *Star Wars* film was doubly nervous at not only meeting both of them, but having to prove himself to them as well. He was so nervous, in fact, that he threw up on the plane ride.

To keep himself calm, he reasoned with himself that he really had very little chance of landing this role of a lifetime, and that he should just enjoy the opportunity to meet Lucas and Portman. He need not have been so modest. Casting director Robin Gurland later described Christensen as a godsend, saying that it was obvious that he was ideal for the role as soon as he walked in the door. As Gurland told Cindy Pearlman in the *Sunday Telegraph,* "[H]e had two of the characteristics we were seeking for the character: vulnerability and edginess."

Christensen, then 21 years old, beat out more than 400 other hopefuls for the role of Anakin Skywalker. He remained modest in his speculation about why he had been chosen over so many other actors: his best guess was that it was because he looked most like the eight–year–old boy who had played Anakin as a child in the previous *Star Wars* film.

After being cast in the pivotal role in *Attack of the Clones,* Christensen was asked by the producers to keep his new job a secret. It was perhaps one of the most difficult aspects of his new job. Christensen spent the next several weeks before shooting started with a kind of permanent smile affixed to his face—but could tell no one why.

Once he began to get used to the idea that he would have such a major role in the next installment of the *Star Was* saga, Christensen began to think about what life after the film's release might be like. He realized that he would not be anonymous anymore, and would be recognized by millions of people around the world. He began to take pleasure in simple things that he had always taken for granted. As he told Derek Tse in the *Toronto Sun*, of his feelings at this time, "I relish riding the bus because that's something I feel like maybe I won't be able to do when *Star Wars* comes out."

Star Wars: Episode II—Attack of the Clones was released in 2002. In it, Christensen plays Anakin Skywalker as the hero of the piece, although at later points during the *Star Wars* saga, Anakin becomes Darth Vader, the hooded, deep-breathing villain everyone loves to hate. Playing such a well-known character, established in *Star Wars* movies going back to 1977, presented a unique challenge to Christensen. On the one hand, he wanted to bring the character to life as believably as possible, which required adding his own spin on the character. On the other hand, as he explained to Krzys in the *Herald Sun*, "I wasn't walking into a part which I could openly explore." He had to live up to the expectations of legions of *Star Wars* fans, himself included.

To complete his transformation into Anakin Skywalker, fair-skinned Christensen had to acquire a deep tan (Anakin is from a desert planet), and wear hair extensions to recover from a haircut inflicted on him by his older brother, Tove. Making the film required Christensen to spend three months on location in Sydney, Australia. A full third of that time, Christensen was required to learn the light sabre choreography that is a mainstay of the *Star Wars* saga. It was time well-spent; he had some bad habits to unlearn. As a boy he had spent hours pretending to be characters in the previous *Star Wars* films, fighting with light sabres. In his pretend battles, he would supply his own sound effects by making whooshing noises with his mouth. When he first took up his light sabre on the set of *Attack of the Clones*, Christensen unconsciously began mouthing the same whooshing noises. Lucas had to tell him to cut it out, joking that he appreciated Christensen's effort, but that the film had a big enough budget to supply sound effects in postproduction.

Two additional months were spent shooting the film, mostly on soundstages in Australia. Only about ten percent of the time was spent on actual sets—the remaining 90 percent of the film was shot in front of blue screens, upon which virtual sets were digitally inserted in postproduction. Working with as-yet imaginary scenery was a challenge to Christensen, who at times found the process somewhat disconcerting. He rose to the occasion, though, ultimately finding it not unlike acting in theater because, as he told Krzys in the *Herald Sun*, "[Y]ou have to use your imagination for that, too."

Rumors started during the course of shooting that Christensen and costar Natalie Portman might have actually shared a real-life romance as well as their screen romance. Nothing could have been further from the truth. Christensen later compared his kiss scenes with Portman to changing the oil on his car. He said that the scenes were precisely choreographed and allowed no room for spontaneity on the part of the performers. One of the aspects of his performance in *Attack of the Clones* of which Christensen is particularly proud is the fact that he performed all of his own stunts in the film, including a lot of Hong Kong action film-style wire work.

In spite of his fears to the contrary, Christensen found that his life remained largely unchanged following the release of *Attack of the Clones*. He still lived with his mother and father in the house he had grown up in. His mother still cooked his breakfast and folded his laundry. He even had to do chores around the house. Best of all, he found that he could still ride public transportation unmolested.

Emboldened by this, Christensen moved to Los Angeles with his brother Tove, and together they put together a small production company called Forest Park Pictures. One of the production company's first projects was a co-production with actor/producer Tom Cruise's production company, C/W Productions, on a film called *Shattered Glass*. This film is the true story of Stephen Glass, a journalist whose career was ruined after he was caught inventing a lot of the material for his articles. Christensen plays Glass in the film, which went into production in 2002.

The film, with a small production budget, and made outside of the Hollywood system, might seem a strange choice for an actor now used to acting in one of the biggest-budget Hollywood films of all time. But, as Christensen explained to Brendan Kelly in the *Montreal Gazette*, "Budget doesn't really factor into what you choose to spend your time on. You just judge it by the quality of the script. It has to be a character that interests you." Also in 2002, Christensen began gearing up for *Star Wars: Episode III*, slated to begin production in Australia in June of 2003.

Sources

Periodicals

Herald Sun (Melbourne, Australia), May 11, 2002, p.W4.

Maclean's, October 29, 2001, p. 57.

Montreal Gazette, August 9, 2002, p. A1.

People, May 13, 2002, p. 104.

Sunday Telegraph (Sydney, Australia), April 21, 2002, p. 93.

Toronto Sun, May 12, 2002, p. S14.

Online

"Hayden Christensen," E! Online, http://www.eonline.com/Features/Features/Sizzlin2002/Guys/christensen.html (January 10, 2002).

"Hayden Christensen," IMDB.com, http://us.imdb.com/Name?Christensen,+Hayden (March 18, 2003).

—Michael Belfiore

Kelly Clarkson

Singer

Born in 1982, in Texas; daughter of Jeanne Taylor (a school teacher); stepdaughter of Jimmy Taylor (a contractor).

Addresses: *Office*—c/o RCA Records, 6363 Sunset Blvd., #429, Los Angeles, CA 90028.

Career

Worked as a waitress in a Texas comedy club and as a pharmacy clerk, 2000–01; relocated to Los Angeles, CA, and worked with songwriter Gerry Goffin, 2002; won the grand prize in the *American Idol: The Search for a Superstar* televised talent search, September, 2002, and with it a contract from RCA Records; released first single, "Before Your Love"/"A Moment Like This," 2002; filmed scenes for first film, 2003; appeared at the MGM Grand Hotel in Las Vegas; first full–length album released, 2003.

Sidelights

Texas native Kelly Clarkson became a household name in September of 2002 when she took first prize in *American Idol: The Search for a Superstar*, a weekly talent/elimination contest that aired for several weeks on the Fox television network. Clarkson's impressive ability to belt out rhythm–and–blues standards won over judges as well as millions of viewers, who phoned each week to cast their votes. Critics noted that despite the manufactured nature of the contest, Clarkson's sincerity gave her the added boost over the equally talented unknowns she competed against. "I just try to be as real as I can be," the 20–year–old said in interview with Andrew Marton of the *Houston Chronicle*, "the kind of person who doesn't really care if she is caught without makeup, not some ultra–professional musician who is only 'on' when in front of the camera."

Born in 1982, Clarkson grew up in Burleson, a town outside of Fort Worth. Her mother, Jeanne, was an elementary–school teacher, and her stepfather worked as a contractor. A performer for her family and friends from an early age, Clarkson was a standout in her high school choir and regularly won the lead parts in school musicals. Her Burleson High music teacher told the *Houston Chronicle*'s Marton that even as a teen, "Kelly could do any and all musical styles," Philip Glenn said. "She could sing the classical literature but didn't sound like a rhythm–and–blues singer trying to sing classical." Already writing her own songs, Clarkson was determined to forego college and concentrate on a career in music. After graduating from Burleson High in 2000, she worked as a waitress in a comedy club and as a clerk at a pharmacy. In January of 2002 she moved to Los Angeles, California, with a friend. There, Clarkson's talent caught the attention of legendary singer–songwriter Gerry Goffin, but Goffin became ill, and there was a fire at Clarkson's apartment. Her roommate moved out and a dejected Clarkson decided to return to Texas as well. She found work passing out samples of the Red Bull energy drink, and had to be convinced by a friend to try out for *American Idol*. Known as a late sleeper, Clarkson was worried enough about missing her chance that she stayed up all night before driving to Dallas for the open audition. The lack of sleep did not hamper her chances, however, and she made the first cut. After several more auditions, Clarkson and the other top 30 finalists were flown to Los Angeles and given a rented mansion of their own on the posh Mulholland Drive neighborhood of the stars. Once the show began airing in late June of 2002, contestants who did not make the cut had just a few hours to pack and leave.

American Idol proved the surprise television hit of the summer of 2002. Based on a successful British show, it featured contestants dueling onstage by singing standards from the pop canon, and then enduring sometimes–harsh critiques from a trio of judges. Their decisions eliminated Clarkson's competitors one by one. Singer Paula Abdul and music producer Randy Jackson were two of the panel, but audiences tuned in to listen to Simon Cowell's sometimes–barbed comments. The British record–company executive was known for his ability to reduce finalists to tears, but Clarkson won him over with renditions of "(You Make Me Feel Like) A Natural Woman" from Aretha Franklin and "Walk on By," once a Dionne Warwick hit. Viewers also registered their approval, via special call–in phone numbers, for Clarkson's powerful voice; it was a set of pipes which seemed to belie her diminutive frame, and she was early on predicted to be the winner on fan Internet sites for the show. Marton of the *Houston Chronicle* believed that it was her genuineness that showed through and helped her advance to the finals—Clarkson, he noted, seemed to perform "her songs with the nakedly smoldering gaze of someone utterly invested in her material's primal emotion."

As the show neared its grand finale, just Clarkson and Justin Guarini of Doylestown, Pennsylvania, remained. Before the final show, which aired on September 4, Clarkson had to drink olive oil before taking the stage to sooth her strained vocal cords. Some 15 million viewers called in to register their votes that night, and her victory netted her a recording contract from RCA. Her first single, "Before Your Love"/"A Moment Like This," was released on September 17, 2002. Within the first week, it sold 236,000 copies—an impressive figure given what had been described as the moribund state of the record industry of late. "The music business, which is anxiously seeking out new ways to sell records as a way of boosting its flagging revenues, is watching

closely," *Financial Times* journalist Peter Thal Larsen wrote of the *American Idol* phenomenon. "In theory, Ms Clarkson should be a godsend for the record business. The programme's judges have done the expensive and time–consuming work of weeding out potential talent from thousands of applicants. And millions of people have already endorsed the winner." *San Francisco Chronicle* writer Neva Chonin also commented on the hype surrounding *American Idol* in her review of the single, and wondered if Clarkson could "deliver the goods." Chonin found Clarkson's talents up to the job. "So far, the answer is a qualified yes—her voice has a sleek elasticity that does its best with banal material such as 'Before Your Love' and 'A Moment Like This,' a pair of faux–Whitney, wannabe–Celine power ballads so inoffensively generic they could carpet an elevator."

Clarkson embarked upon a whirlwind publicity tour along with her studio recording sessions and a video shoot, at times logging in 20–hour days. At the same time, she filmed scenes for *From Justin to Kelly,* a musical set at a beach which co–starred Guarini; the film was scheduled for release in June of 2003. In Las Vegas, Nevada, she performed with other the *American Idol* finalists at the MGM Grand Hotel, and despite the demands of her newfound celebrity, she remained upbeat. "I've always been busy, and this is just a different kind of busy," she confessed to *Los Angeles Times* writer Greg Braxton. "I don't feel that much pressure," she told the paper. "They prepared all of us for a lot of this stuff in the beginning. This is fun." Clarkson's first full–length record, *Thankful,* was released on April 15, 2003. Her plans for the future were to "work on writing scripts, because I really like the whole behind–the–scenes aspect of entertainment, and I hope to do some Broadway acting," she told Marton in the *Houston Chronicle*.

Selected discography

Thankful, RCA, 2003.

Sources

Entertainment Weekly, December 20, 2002, p. 24; April 25, 2003, p. 67.
Financial Times, September 14, 2002, p. 15.
Houston Chronicle, September 9, 2002, p. 3.
Los Angeles Times, September 23, 2002, p. F14.
New York Post, December 13, 2002, p. 149.
New York Times, September 6, 2002, p. C1.
People, September 9, 2002, p. 52.
San Francisco Chronicle, September 17, 2002, p. D1.

—*Carol Brennan*

Kenneth Cole

Fashion designer

Born c. 1954, in New York; son of Charles (a shoe–factory owner) and Gladys (a homemaker) Cole; married Maria Cuomo, 1987; children: Emily, Amanda, Catie. *Education*—Attended Emory University.

Addresses: *Home*—Westchester County, NY. *Office*—Kenneth Cole Productions, Inc., 603 W 50th St., New York, NY 10019.

Career

Became factory manager of El Greco Leather Products Company, Brooklyn, NY, 1976; marketed popular "Candie's" mules, late 1970s; founded Kenneth Cole Productions, Inc., of New York City, 1982; launched Kenneth Cole "Reaction" and "Unlisted" shoe lines; created accessory lines for both men and women; men's clothing line introduced, 1997; "Kenneth Cole New York" women's line launched, 2000.

Awards: Man of the Year, *Footwear News*, for business success and social activism, 1997; Humanitarian of the Year Award, Devine Design, 1996; Dom Perignon Award for Humanitarian Leadership, Council of Fashion Designers of America, 1997; Media Spotlight Award, Amnesty International, 1998; Milton Margolis Humanitarian Award, National Father's Day Committee, 2002.

Sidelights

American designer Kenneth Cole heads an eponymous fashion empire with several phenomenally successful lines. Cole started out in the early 1980s as a small–time shoe designer, and in just under two decades his company had grown so exponentially that it was able to launch clothing collections for men and women. Retail analysts predict that the corporate logo may reach the level of a Calvin Klein– or Ralph Lauren–type of megabrand—especially if Cole takes his company into the home–furnishings market. By 2001, Kenneth Cole manufactured or had licensing agreements for shoes, outerwear, men's suits, women's separates, accessories, fragrance, and children's wear. Sales from the upscale department stores that sold his gear and the freestanding Kenneth Cole retail emporiums were $364 million in 2001.

Yet Cole, a New York native, is also somewhat of a rarity: a fashion–industry player with a well–run, solidly performing company whose stock is highly touted among Wall Street analysts. Moreover, Cole is also an ardently political CEO. Since the company's earliest days, its ads were known for their cheeky irreverence, either poking fun at the established political order or urging consumers to be more socially conscious. The company credo, borrowed from one ad's tag line, asserts: "To be aware is more important than what you wear." As Cole explained to *Daily News Record* writer Annmarie Dodd, "I am absolutely intrigued about what is going on in the world and how it drives our life choices. And I do believe that what clothes you wear are really not that important, but we can make it tie into what is."

Growing up in Great Neck, Long Island, in the 1950s and '60s, Cole had no plans to make fashion design or the apparel industry his career. After attending Emory University, he was slated to enter law school at New York University in the fall of 1976. Cole's father, who built a vending machine company and then retired, acquired a Brooklyn shoe factory in the early 1960s called El Greco Leather Products. When a manager there quit that Bicentennial summer, Cole agreed to postpone his studies for a short period to fill in.

El Greco made sandals and mundane women's footwear. Out of the blue one day, Cole sketched a shoe that jokingly wed two major shoe trends of the decade—the espadrille and the earth shoe. He called it the "Earthpadrille" and El Greco began making it, with minor success. In 1977, the Coles discovered a wooden high–heeled slide shoe at a trade show in Italy, and bought it and its "Candie's" logo. El Greco began producing them for the United States, and Cole became responsible for the marketing strategy. The style was a perfect match for the glitzy, disco–fashion era, and sales of Candie's stunned the footwear industry: women actually bought the heels, whose upper came in an array of different colors and materials, in multiple pairs.

El Greco grew into a $100–million–plus conglomerate, with five footwear divisions and several license agreements for other products, but Cole decided to strike out on his own in 1982. Hinting that the rapid growth may have caused internal dissension among the family members—brothers Neil and Evan and sister Abby were also executives—Cole would only tell *Footwear News* writer Rosalind Resnick, "It's hard being the boss's son." With a nest egg of $200,000, he decided to launch his own women's shoe line. He designed several pairs, contracted with a manufacturer in Italy to produce some samples, and came up with a creative—and inexpensive—way to hawk them at the important New York trade show for the footwear industry that December: he borrowed a large tractor–trailer from a friend and applied for a film permit with the New York City Police Department, calling his company

"Kenneth Cole Productions." The bogus permit allowed him to park the trailer in the street near a New York hotel used by the other manufacturers to sell their lines. The buyers coming to and fro were intrigued by the apparent documentary film being produced right there, for Cole had a fake director and crew, replete with lights and cameras. Onlookers were invited to come inside and have a look at the making of a film titled "The Birth of a Shoe Company," but instead they found his shoe line. By the time the trade show was over, Cole had inked deals with Bergdorf Goodman, Bloomingdale's and Macy's.

Cole's business had an impressive first year: $1 million in profit on sales of $5 million. With shoe styles that were knock–offs of pricey designer looks from Europe, Cole entered the market at a crucial juncture: women's shoes ran to two styles, either the pump or the penny loafer, and younger, more fashion–conscious buyers were willing to try out daring new looks. By early 1984, the first Kenneth Cole store had opened on Columbus Avenue in Manhattan, and the company was producing men's shoes for sale there as well. Over time, borrowing from London's punk–rock scene, Cole's shoes helped set the standard for the 1980s look of a clunkier, heavy–soled shoe for both sexes.

Cole, already a savvy marketer after his Candie's ad–campaign experience, handled this end of his new business himself. But it was also a new era in America, seemingly light years away from the care-free disco days, with a conservative Republican White House and the menace of a mysterious new epidemic called AIDS. Some of the first Kenneth Cole print ads blended the political and the personal with an irreverent humor that would become a hallmark of the company's campaigns. In 1985, Cole took a great leap and began promoting AIDS awareness in some ads, and began to devote his personal time and assets to the cause as well. "I corporately decided to get involved in helping to fight AIDS through fund–raising because it's the first disease we've had in my generation that plagues everyone," Cole said in an interview with *Daily News Record* journalist Elena Hart. "The only vehicle to combat AIDS is awareness."

In 1987, Cole's company launched his lesser–priced shoe line, Unlisted, ventured into handbags and other accessories, and by 1990 was selling men's socks and neckwear. In June of 1994 Kenneth Cole became a publicly traded firm, which helped finance the opening of more company stores. Reaction, a moderately priced line of accessories and footwear for women wedged between the more upscale Kenneth Cole brand and the Unlisted one, appeared in 1995. The year 1996 was one of spectacular growth—in sales, the number of stores up and running, and new licensees. Sales climbed to the $200–million mark in 1997, and by the following year the Kenneth Cole logo was appearing on men's suits, jeans and sportswear, men and women's outerwear, ties, watches, handbags, sunglasses and optical eyewear, and even a line of silver jewelry. The expansion seemed a natural one, as Cole told Samantha Critchell in a report published in the *Fresno Bee*. "A business takes on a life of its own," he reflected. "You make a commitment that you're going to suit a customer's lifestyle, then you become a lifestyle brand, and then you decide that you're going to serve a variety of their wardrobe needs."

Around this time Cole began adding to his existing 47 retail outlets with some impressive flagship stores in high–profile urban areas, including San Francisco's Grant Avenue, Michigan Avenue in Chicago, and Grand Central Terminal in Manhattan. Watching the growth—and the impressive handling of licensee quality and management—retail analysts pegged the brand as the next name to watch in affordable designer gear, and viewed him as the next Calvin Klein or Ralph Lauren. Cole was sanguine about his design strategy, realizing that following his own instincts was key. "Every day I walk into my closet and see what is there and what isn't," he told Critchell in the *Fresno Bee* article. "Then I ask 'What do I wish was there?'"

Cole's impressive track record continued with a women's clothing line, launched in the fall of 2000 as Kenneth Cole New York. Though his company had grown swiftly in recent years, Cole continued to create all of its socially conscious ad copy himself. The coolly understated ads promoted a variety of causes, from increased funding for AIDS research to gun control to reproductive rights. In the fall of 2000, as the United States presidential race heated up, Cole presented his new line for Spring 2001 at the Council of Fashion Designers of America's (CFDA) "7th on Sixth" industry event. Promotional giveaways for his show included pencils with the caveat, "Everyone needs to vote for a change" and blank New York State voter registration cards.

On other occasions, Cole has requested that the buyers and journalists invited to view his new line bring a pair of shoes to donate to a charity run by his wife, Maria, that provides assistance for homeless and low–income families. Despite his phenomenal success, Cole remains as wary of the fashion industry as he had back when he rented his trailer and parked it on the street in order to sell his first line.

"It's a waste, an extravagance and offensive in many, many ways," he told Dodd for the *Daily News Record* about the seasonal runway collections in New York, which lure celebrities and involve a heady round of parties. "I'm floored at the thousands of dollars spent for a half–hour show. It's very unsettling and it is stressful and it is the reality of this business."

Just once has a Kenneth Cole ad attracted a negative response: in the fall of 2001, just weeks after the September 11 attacks on the World Trade Center and the Pentagon, the company was criticized for a print ad that showed a model sitting on a curb near the intersection of Bush Avenue and Cheney Lane, references to U.S. President George W. Bush and Vice President Dick Cheney; another sign in the frame is the symbol for a dead–end street. In the national climate of unease and renewed patriotism after the first–ever attacks on American soil, the company was forced to pull the ads and issue a statement. "We had several complaints," Meredith Wollins, vice president of corporate communications at Kenneth Cole, told Knight–Ridder/Tribune News Service reporter Candace Murphy. "Kenneth Cole really supports the administration."

Expansion of the Kenneth Cole brand continued through 2002, with new stores added in Venezuela, London, and Seoul, South Korea. A fragrance line was launched in the fall of 2002. Its namesake remained dedicated to a variety of philanthropic causes: since 1986 he has served on the board of the American Foundation for AIDS Research (AmFAR), and his wife's HELP USA Homeless Project thrives. An endowment given to his alma mater, Emory University, established the Kenneth Cole Fellowship in Community Building and Social Change there. Cole has been honored with several awards, including the Dom Perignon Award for Humanitarian Leadership from the CFDA in 1997 and the Milton Margolis Humanitarian Award in 2002 from the National Father's Day Committee. "I find the humanitarian concept staggering," he told *Footwear News* writer Maryann Lorusso. "... I'm lucky to have been able to create a business that can serve more than just my professional needs, and to energize the people I work with by getting them involved in trying to achieve a higher level."

Cole enjoys social and family ties to the upper stratospheres of American Democratic politics. Wife Maria, whom Cole wed in 1987, is the daughter of former New York governor Mario Cuomo; her brother Andrew is a rising political figure in his own right and the former Secretary of Housing and Urban Development in the Clinton administration.

Cole's brother–in–law, moreover, is married to the daughter of slain presidential candidate Robert F. Kennedy. Cole fishes with Kennedy's son, Robert Jr., off the coast of the Cole summer home in Martha's Vineyard, Massachusetts. There, Cole, his wife, and their three daughters decamp for the entire summer; they also have a home in Westchester County, just outside of New York City. The company's name remains, as it read on the application for that 1982 film permit, Kenneth Cole Productions. He recognizes the oddity of becoming so entirely ubiquitous. "When I come home for dinner I call out, 'Maria, the brand is home!'" he joked with *InStyle* writer Leslie Marshall. "Then I change hats from the brand to the person."

Sources

Periodicals

Brandweek, September 11, 2000, p. 94.
Crain's New York Business, January 5, 1998, p. 1.
Daily News Record, September 3, 1990, p. 38; March 9, 1992, p. 10; February 10, 1999, p. 6; March 4, 2002, p. 5; June 17, 2002, p. 48.
Footwear News, February 13, 1984, p. 8; February 5, 1996, p. 16; December 23, 1996, p. 10; December 25, 2000, p. 6.
Footwear News Magazine, February 1984, p. 14.
Forbes, November 20, 1995, p. 190.
Fresno Bee, August 10, 1999, p. E3.
InStyle, July 2002, p. 224.
Knight–Ridder/Tribune News Service, October 10, 2001.
Los Angeles Times, January 15, 1998, p. 4.
New York Times, April 9, 2002, p. C4.
Palm Beach Post, February 27, 2002, p. 6D.
WWD, July 24, 1995, p. S12; December 29, 1998, p. 9; March 16, 2001, p. 2; April 11, 2002, p. 3; July 31, 2002, p. 19.

Online

"The Birth of a Shoe Company," Kenneth Cole Online, http://www.kennethcole.com/scripts/aboutus/ourstory.asp (September 5, 2002).

—*Carol Brennan*

Patricia Cornwell

Author

B orn Patricia Daniels, June 9, 1956, in Miami, FL; daughter of Sam (an attorney) and Marilyn (a secretary; maiden name, Zenner) Daniels; married Charles Cornwell (a college professor), June 14, 1980 (divorced, 1989). *Education*—Davidson College, North Carolina, B.A. in English, 1979.

Addresses: *Home*—Richmond, VA, and London, England. *Agent*—International Creative Management, 40 W. 57th St., New York, NY 10019.

Career

B egan career as police reporter for the *Charlotte Observer*, Charlotte, NC, 1979; technical writer and computer analyst, Office of the Chief Medical Examiner, Richmond, VA, 1985–91; author, 1983—; board chair, Virginia Institute of Forensic Science and Medicine.

Awards: Investigative reporting award, North Carolina Press Association, 1980; Gold Medallion Book Award for biography, Evangelical Christian Publishers Association, for *A Time for Remembering: The Story of Ruth Bell Graham,* 1985; John Creasey Award for best first crime novel, British Crime Writers Association, for *Postmortem,* 1990; Edgar Award for best first crime novel, Mystery Writers of America, for *Postmortem,* 1990; Anthony Award for best first crime novel, Boucheron, for *Postmortem,* 1990; Macavity Award for best first crime novel, Mystery Readers International, for *Postmortem,* 1990; French Prix du Roman d'Aventure for *Postmortem,* 1991; Gold Dagger award, for *Cruel and Unusual.*

AP/Wide World Photos

Sidelights

P atricia Cornwell's forensic–detective novels featuring her inscrutable heroine, Dr. Kay Scarpetta, have won her a devoted readership and interest from Hollywood studios. Cornwell's books regularly debut on the *New York Times*'s bestseller list and have a reputation for putting readers through the occasional stomach–turning passage in their graphic descriptions of dismemberment, murder, autopsies, and forensic pathology. The author—reputedly one of the highest–paid writers in North America, earning more than $8 million for each Scarpetta book—"can write engagingly for pages on techniques for reading blood splatter," remarked *Entertainment Weekly* writer Gillian Flynn.

Cornwell was born in 1956 in Miami, Florida, and moved to Montreat, a small North Carolina town, when she was seven with her newly divorced mother. There they became neighbors of American evangelist Billy Graham and his wife, Ruth, who would provide Cornwell with an important source of emotional support in her life. When Cornwell's mother became clinically depressed, the Grahams stepped in and Cornwell and her two brothers were put in foster care for a period of four months. Cornwell later said that their caregiver was verbally and emotionally abusive. "If I ever said, 'When's my mommy coming home?', she'd say, 'Don't you ever say that,'" Cornwell recalled in an interview with *Independent* journalist Dina Rabinovitch. She noted that even as an adult, "I still have not completely emotionally dealt with it. It will take me a long time to deal with, because I was so powerless."

In high school, Cornwell earned top grades, but pushed herself in other areas as well, battling anorexia and bulimia. She was briefly hospitalized for depression in the same facility where her mother had once stayed. Ruth Graham encouraged her to pursue her education, and Cornwell went on to graduate from Davidson College in North Carolina with an English degree in 1979. With a year, Cornwell graduated, married her former professor Charles Cornwell, and began working at the *Charlotte Observer,* where she was quickly promoted to crime reporter. Her prostitution series for the paper won the investigative reporting award from the North Carolina Press Association in 1980, but her promising journalism career was cut short when Cornwell's husband felt drawn to the ministry and moved to Richmond, Virginia, to attend its Union Theological Seminary.

Cornwell wrote her first book, a biography of Ruth Graham, in 1983. Graham had always encouraged her to write more, so Cornwell decided to try a crime novel based on her reporting experience. Feeling that more research was necessary, she asked officials at the Virginia morgue if she could spend some time at the facility. There Cornwell met pathologist Dr. Marcella Fierro, one of just 50 women practicing in the field in the United States, and was impressed by Fierro's non–nonsense approach to the autopsy business. Cornwell would later base her Scarpetta character on Fierro.

Cornwell was fascinated by the morgue, and began taking classes at the Forensic Science Academy of the Commonwealth of Virginia, which trains police officers in the state. Cornwell also worked as a volunteer police officer in Richmond, riding along with a pair of cops on the evening shift. She attended her first autopsy in 1985, and admitted that when she saw her first corpse, "I went weak in the knees," she told *American Medical News* writer Peter Macpherson. She began spending so much time there that the chief medical examiner offered her a job as a technical writer, which involved taking notes while autopsies were underway. She also worked as a computer analyst.

Cornwell wrote her first crime–story manuscript in 1985, which featured a male detective and medical examiner Kay Scarpetta as a secondary character.

Both this and a second try were rejected by publishers. "I began to think I'd ruined my life," Cornwell told Macpherson in the *American Medical News* interview. "I remember thinking, 'I used to get paid for my writing. Now I work in a morgue and I'm surrounded by dead people all day long.'" It was a tough time for Cornwell, with her marriage disintegrating as well, for her interest in morgues and autopsies began to supersede her status as a minister's wife. Unable to even find a literary agent with her third manuscript, Cornwell finally had a heart–to–heart talk with an editor who had rejected her submissions, who told her to "write about what I knew, instead of esoteric poisonings set in river mansions somewhere," as Cornwell recalled in an interview with Joanne Tangora in *Publishers Weekly.* "And she advised me to make Scarpetta the main character."

Dutifully Cornwell began what would become her first published novel, *Postmortem,* in 1988, following the editor's advice and basing it on a more localized crime scenario: in the previous year, a serial rapist had murdered professional women in their homes in quiet residential neighborhoods in Richmond. Cornwell had followed the slayings and then arrest and subsequent conviction with interest, stunned by the affinity she felt for the victims. "It was almost as crazy as lightning striking you. It can't happen to me, but these people were very much like me," she told Macpherson.

Cornwell's publishing luck changed when she met Edna Buchanan, the *Miami Herald* crime reporter and novelist, who introduced her to a literary agent. Still, *Postmortem* was rejected by several editors, but Scribners showed interest and the work appeared in print in 1990. In it, forensic pathologist Scarpetta anchors the plot. Cornwell presents her as an ambitious, determined woman in her mid–40s who is the first of her gender to hold the office of chief medical examiner in Virginia. Despite her status, she battles sexism on the job, and becomes absorbed in solving the case of a serial killer preying on Richmond women. Cornwell's debut won praise for the vividly reconstructed world of forensic pathology it presented, and even her colleagues at the Virginia morgue commended it as technically accurate. In addition to its good reviews, *Postmortem* sold well, but it was the slew of mystery–fiction awards Cornwell received for it that launched her writing career in earnest. It won the Edgar, John Creasey, Anthony, Macavity, and the French Prix du Roman d'Aventure awards.

Cornwell lured readers into Scarpetta's world through several subsequent books. In *All That Remains,* published in 1992, she must solve a case in which just fragments of two bodies are found, along with a jack–of–hearts playing card. In *Body of Evidence,* author Beryl Madison faces death threats which prove true, and Scarpetta is perplexed as to why this intelligent, street–savvy woman allowed serial killer Temple Gault into her home. In 1993's *Cruel and Unusual,* Scarpetta is baffled by the crime–scene fingerprints found that match those of an executed killer, prompting *Entertainment Weekly* writer Mark Harris to note that, with this fourth book, "Cornwell has become an increasingly skilled plotter."

Cornwell's crime–solving skills, based on her sharp eye for a piece of seemingly insignificant forensic evidence, are aided by a cast of secondary characters, including police detective Pete Marino, who comes to possess a grudging respect for the shrewd Scarpetta, FBI agent Mark James—a former paramour of Scarpetta's—and her computer–whiz niece Lucy Farinelli. In the sixth novel in the series, 1995's *From Potter's Field,* Scarpetta journeys to New York City to solve the slaying of a homeless woman in Central Park. Temple Gault is still tailing her, and the plot wraps up with a chase scene through the New York City subway system. It earned more mixed reviews than her earlier novels, but its author consistently won praise for her attention to gruesome detail. "Cornwell is superb in evoking the cold, bare, tawdry facts of murder and their aftermath on the mortuary tray," remarked *New Statesman & Society* critic Mary Scott.

In 1996, Cornwell jumped ship and signed a lucrative contract with publisher Penguin Putnam, reportedly in the realm of $24 million for three books. *Cause of Death,* which appeared in 1996, was her first for the house. But around this time Cornwell's name was linked to a bit of scandal in real life, when an FBI agent held his wife's minister hostage in suburban Washington; in divorce papers, the man accused his wife, a former FBI agent, with being romantically involved with Cornwell. In her books, Scarpetta's niece Lucy is presented as a gay character in sympathetic tones, but the author has shied away from discussing her own views on the matter. "My personal life is not anybody else's business," she told *Newsweek* reporters Mark Miller and Katrine Ames that same year.

Cornwell has said that her books often attract a bad element. "I've been stalked, blackmailed," she said in the *Newsweek* interview. "I have a huge list of inmates who can't wait to meet me." She also attracted a contentious lawsuit brought by a Virginia couple. Their daughter had been slain some years before, and many details of the murder were simi-

lar to those in *All That Remains.* Cornwell, who had quit working at the Virginia morgue by the time that novel was published, was defended by Dr. Fierro, who said that any similarities had been culled from published newspaper accounts, not sealed forensic evidence. *Independent Sunday* writer Lucretia Stewart discussed the author's intriguing background and its relation to her fiction. "In Cornwell's writing, it is possible to discern both the impulse that led her to write about Ruth Bell Graham and to marry a minister, and the impulse that drove her to work in a mortuary. She is a particularly moral writer: right and wrong, good and evil, black and white—there are no shades of grey in her books. Scarpetta is [a] lone crusader against evil, an avenging angel holding a flaming scalpel in her hand."

Cornwell's impressive sales figures continued with *Unnatural Exposure* in 1997, *Point of Origin,* published in 1998, and a new, lighter series of crime fiction featuring Andy Brazil, a young police detective with a journalism background. *Hornet's Nest, Southern Cross,* and *Isle of Dogs* belong to this latter series. Cornwell explained the move in the interview with the *Independent's* Rabinovitch, noting that for her the Brazil stories were a respite. "Scarpetta takes a tremendous amount of energy," Cornwell confessed. "It's very painful, writing about Scarpetta, because of her world, and I have to go back into that world to write about it. People think I get some kind of great personal satisfaction from going into the morgue, but it isn't true." She has also somewhat improbably (given the fact that one of Cornwell's Scarpetta novels was once awarded "the Lose Your Lunch Award" by *New York Times* crime–fiction writer Marilyn Stasio for a vividly chronicled autopsy) penned a novelette centered on a holiday–season get–together, *Scarpetta's Winter Table* and another, *Food to Die For: Secrets from Kay Scarpetta's Kitchen.*

Cornwell has forced Scarpetta to evolve as the fictional character ages. Beginning with *Black Notice,* a decade into the series, Scarpetta seeks therapy and displays a more vulnerable side. In this particular story, she tracks the murderous Jean–Baptiste Chandonne, nicknamed the Werewolf for his rare condition of hyper–hirsuteness. Chandonne is suspected in the death of Scarpetta's foe, police officer Diane Bray, but in 2000's *The Last Precinct,* Scarpetta is attacked in her home by the Werewolf and then finds herself the prime suspect in a grand jury investigation into the Bray death. *Entertainment Weekly's* Flynn liked the new twist, as Scarpetta "slips into her past and pokes at her own wounds. She is, finally, losing her cool—and it's a truly enjoyable jolt."

Cornwell signed a new contract with Penguin Putnam in 2002, and Columbia Pictures was planning a film treatment of the *Cruel and Unusual* and *Unnatural Exposure* stories. The writer's homes in Richmond and London—where she worked on a nonfiction book about the Victorian–era killer Jack the Ripper—contain identical offices, down to the last forensic pathology textbook. Despite the trappings, Cornwell remains surprised at her success. "I've always wanted to write, just because I love it," she told Dorman T. Shindler in *Writer.* "My dream was just to get published. I never thought in terms of making money. And I never thought I'd be on a bestseller list or that anybody would know who I am."

Selected writings

A Time for Remembering: The Story of Ruth Bell Graham (biography), Harper (New York City), 1983.
Postmortem, Scribner (New York City), 1990.
Body of Evidence, Scribner, 1991.
All That Remains, Scribner, 1992.
Cruel and Unusual, Scribner, 1993.
The Body Farm, Scribner, 1994.
From Potter's Field, Scribner, 1995.
Cause of Death, Putnam (New York City), 1996.
Hornet's Nest, Putnam, 1997.
Unnatural Exposure, Putnam, 1997.
Three Complete Novels: Postmortem, Body of Evidence, All That Remains, Smithmark Publishers (New York City), 1997.
Point of Origin, G.P. Putnam's Sons (New York City), 1998.
Southern Cross, G.P. Putnam's Sons, 1998.
Scarpetta's Winter Table, Wyrick & Co. (Charleston, SC), 1998.
Life's Little Fable, illustrated by Barbara Leonard Gibson, Putnam, 1999.
Black Notice, Putnam, 1999.
The Last Precinct, G. P. Putnam's Sons, 2000.
Isle of Dogs, Little, Brown, 2001.
(With Marlene Brown) *Food to Die For: Secrets from Kay Scarpetta's Kitchen,* G. P. Putnam's Sons, 2001.

Sources

Books

Contemporary Popular Writers, St. James Press, 1997.

Periodicals

American Medical News, April 27, 1990, p. 31.
Booklist, May 15, 1996, p. 1547; May 15, 1997, p. 1540; October 15, 2001, p. 370.
Bookseller, December 14, 2001, p. 23.
Daily Variety, January 10, 2002, p. 6.
Economist, December 13, 1997, p. S14; June 19, 1999, p. 4.
Entertainment Weekly, June 26, 1992, p. 73; October 16, 1992, p. 70; June 25, 1993, p. 98; August 25, 1995, p. 106; July 12, 1996, p. 50; August 9, 1996, p. 52; January 10, 1997, p. 50; December 1, 2000, p. 89; January 25, 2002, p. 97.
Esquire, January 1997, p. 14.
Independent (London, England), November 17, 2001, p. 10.
Independent Sunday (London, England), June 30, 1996, p. 19.
Library Journal, April 15, 1999, p. 142; September 1, 1999, p. 252; November 15, 1999, p. 116.
Maclean's, August 25, 1997, p. 73.
New Statesman, October 13, 1995, p. 32; October 30, 1998; October 30, 2000, p. 58.
Newsweek, July 22, 1996, p. 70.
New York Times, August 2, 1998; August 8, 1999; November 5, 2000.
People, May 13, 1991, p. 35; August 24, 1992, p. 71; July 22, 1996, p. 44; February 3, 1997, p. 33; September 8, 1997, p. 108; July 13, 1998, p. 47.
Publishers Weekly, December 7, 1990, p. 76; February 15, 1991, p. 71; March 22, 1993, p. 72; July 18, 1994, p. 237; September 12, 1994, p. 16; August 4, 1995, p. 51; January 27, 1997, p. 19; April 28, 1997, p. 53; August 18, 1997, p. 12; August 25, 1997, p. 64; January 4, 1999, p. 76; July 31, 2000, p. 18; September 25, 2000, p. 90; October 30, 2000, p. 24; January 8, 2001, p. 35; October 22, 2001, p. 16.
Time, October 3, 1994, p. 84.
Variety, April 9, 2001, p. 12.
Writer, December 2000, p. 7; March 2001, p. 30.

—*Carol Brennan*

Simon Cowell

Music executive and television producer

Born October 7, 1959, in England; son of Eric P. (a music executive) and Julie (a dancer) Cowell.

Addresses: *Home*—London, England, and Beverly Hills, CA. *Office*—S Records, Bedford House, 69–79 Fulham High St., London, England SW6 3JW.

Career

With EMI Music Publishing, 1977–82; founder and co–owner, Fanfare Records, 1982–89; A&R consultant, BMG records, 1989—; founder and co–owner, S Records, 2001—; judge, *Pop Idol*, 2001–02, *American Idol*, 2002—; producer, *Cupid*, 2003—.

Awards: Record Executive of the Year, 1998, 1999; A&R Man of the Year, 1999.

Sidelights

Music executive Simon Cowell has been work-ing in the entertainment business since 1977, and is the founder of S Records, a joint venture with BMG. He has also converted animated television shows, such as *Teletubbies* and *The Power Rangers*, into musical successes. However, he has achieved his most widespread notoriety as a judge of the tele-vision talent show *American Idol*. Cowell's acidic, blunt remarks about the performers's abilities are often true, but also often controversial.

Cowell grew up outside London, England, one of two sons of a dancer mother, Julie, and a music ex-ecutive father, Eric. His family also included four half–siblings. Cowell was often bored in school, and as a result, he behaved badly, leading teachers to tell him he would never amount to anything. He moved from school to school, dropped out at age 17, and in 1977 began working in the mailroom of EMI, his father's music company. He then moved into the A&R (Artist and Repertory) field of this business.

When he was 22, Cowell and his partner, Iain Bur-ton, started a music publishing company, Fanfare, but the venture failed. A few years later, while working at a small record label, he met Pete Water-man, a successful music producer for BMG. Water-man told Cowell that his business tactics were "ab-solutely useless," according to *People*. Cowell was initially hurt by this cruelly accurate comment, but he accepted a position in A&R at BMG and followed Waterman around for the next three years, learning how the business really worked and building a list of pop stars. This venture took off, and between 1997 and 2002, Cowell's pop acts sold more than 25 million albums in the United Kingdom and had 17 Number One singles. In 2001, Cowell created S Records, a joint venture with BMG. He also con-verted television shows, such as *The Power Rangers* and *Teletubbies*, into musical successes.

In 2001, Cowell and a partner decided to create a television show that would showcase amateur singers hoping for a break into the business. The show began as *Pop Idol* in the United Kingdom, and then crossed the Atlantic as *American Idol. American Idol—The Search for a Superstar* debuted in 2002. In the show, singers looking for fame and fortune compete and, one by one, are weeded out by judges. The first season's judges included singer Paula Abdul, music executive Randy Jackson, and Cowell.

The show's ratings increased steadily over the course of its first season, with as many as 15 million viewers watching the season finale on September 3 and 4, 2002. Over the course of the season, Cowell became known for his biting assessments of the singers. According to *Daily Variety*'s Phil Gallo, "Abdul tends to give out warm fuzzies; Jackson is hit–or–miss in giving a direct assessment but generally forgiving of minor slips; Cowell tells it like it is. And while what he says may be hurtful to the performer ... his directness is immensely refreshing." Cowell's comments to performers included remarks that their singing was "rubbish," "pathetic," or that it sounded "like a train going off the rails," according to *People*. He told one contestant, "You will never, ever, ever have a career in singing." According to James Poniewozik in *Time,* he told another, "Who's your [singing] teacher? Get a lawyer and sue her."

Cowell's harsh assessments often rankled the more moderate Abdul, and led some contestants to speculate that Cowell was being particularly harsh because the controversy he created raised the show's ratings. *Time*'s Poniewozik noted that many viewers were entertained and even gratified by Cowell's devastating honesty: "You may wince at Cowell's barbs, but you also welcome them when Abdul or Jackson offers a wimpy 'Good job' to a singer who has scraped the fingernails of her ambition down the chalkboard of her limited ability."

In *Daily Variety*, Timothy M. Gray wrote, "The show has finally found its real star: judge Simon Cowell." As Gray noted, Cowell received more media attention than any of the singers on the show, "and in the process has become America's favorite new villain." Gray quoted Cowell, who explained his brutal honesty by saying, "I tell them the truth. I think I am being nice, because I'm saving them a lot of anguish in the future." Gray speculated that Cowell's image as a villain might be intensified by his posh English accent, and Cowell agreed: "Who the hell is this Englishman coming in and telling us what we're good at doing or not doing? If we [in the United Kingdom] had a loudmouth American telling us what we should or shouldn't be doing, we'd probably feel the same way." Some contestants were so angered by his remarks that after being rejected, they lurked outside the studio with baseball bats, forcing the show to hire more security guards.

For the show's second season, Cowell received $2 million (up from $250,000); with the larger salary, he purchased a mansion in Beverly Hills, California. In 2002, Cowell was named one of *People*'s sexiest men alive.

On May 19, 2003, Cowell began working with CBS on a new relationship reality show, called *Cupid,* scheduled for broadcast starting July 9, 2003. In the show, Cowell and a young woman named Lisa Shannon, an advertising executive from Detroit, Michigan, traveled the United States looking for "Mr. Right" for Shannon. Two of Shannon's best friends joined the entourage to judge young men, who "auditioned" for the part of Mr. Right. Each man had just 30 seconds to impress Shannon and her friends with his sense of humor or other characteristics. In the fourth episode, Shannon began going on dates with those who passed this initial screening; after eleven episodes, viewers would choose which of these suitors would propose marriage to Shannon. If she accepted, she and the man would split the $1 million "dowry." Cowell did not appear on the show, but was heavily involved in behind–the–scenes decisions.

In July of 2003, Cowell signed a three–year deal with Fox to remain on *American Idol,* as well as develop new projects for the network. According to CNN.com, he would earn about $150,000 per episode for the third edition of the show, which was scheduled for January of 2004. On July 15, 2003, Cowell's agent announced that he had signed a $2 million deal with Random House for a book about *American Idol.* The book, to be titled *I Don't Mean to be Rude, But ...,* was scheduled to be published on December 2, 2003 by Broadway Books, an imprint of the Doubleday Broadway Publishing Group under the Random House division of Bertelsmann AG. Co–authored by his older brother, Tony, the book will provide an insider's view of the show and chronicle his career.

Despite his reputation for having a sharp tongue, Cowell still has legions of fans. According to *People,* Cowell's friend Terri Seymour said, "Women are just desperate to get near him." The article noted that Cowell has a softer side: when he is not working, he volunteers at an animal shelter near his home in London, has lunch with his mother every Sunday, and takes bubble baths when he wants to relax. Another article in *People* told a story that revealed Cowell's sensitive side: One day Cowell was driving in London and saw a man kicking a dog. He promptly "screeched to a halt, leapt out of the car, and kicked the man," *People* quoted Cowell's friend Jackie St. Clair, who said this showed that, "Underneath it all, he's a big softy. He's a really sensitive, kind man."

Sensitive or not, Cowell warned *People* that he was not interested in settling down; in relationships, he enjoyed the chase, but quickly became bored once he had the object of his affection. In addition, in other areas of his life, he was driven by the need to make more money. His main aim in life, he told Sathnam Sanghera in the *Financial Times*, was to find a singer who would sell millions of records for his label: "If I wasn't selling records on the back of this, it would all be a waste of time."

Sources

Books

Debrett's People of Today, Debrett's Peerage Ltd, 2002.

Periodicals

Daily Variety, August 20, 2002, p. 5; September 4, 2002, p. 19.
Entertainment Weekly, August 9, 2002, pp. 20–25.
Financial Times, September 24, 2002, p. 10.
Mediaweek, May 12, 2003, p. 5.
New York Post, May 9, 2003, p. 133.
People, July 8, 2002, p. 107; December 2, 2002, p. 117; May 26, 2003, p. 56.
PR Week, December 7, 2001, p. 28.
Time, July 1, 2002, p. 61.

Online

Biography Resource Center Online, Gale Group, 2002.
"Cowell signs for 3 more years of Idol," CNN.com, http://www.cnn.com/2003/SHOWBIZ/TV/07/08/television.cowell.reut/index.html (July 8, 2003).
"*Idol* judge lands $2 million book deal," CNN.com, http://www.cnn.com/2003/SHOWBIZ/books/07/16/books.simon.reut/index.html (July 18, 2003).

—*Kelly Winters*

Michael Cunningham

AP/Wide World Photos

Author

Born November 6, 1952, in Cincinnati, OH; son of Don (an advertising executive) and Dorothy (a real estate agent) Cunningham. *Education:* Stanford University, B.A. (English literature), 1975; University of Iowa, M.F.A. (writing program), 1980.

Addresses: *Agency*—Steven Barclay Agency, 12 Western Ave., Petaluma, CA 94952. *Publisher*—Picador USA, 175 5th Ave., New York, NY 10010.

Career

Author. Published works include the novel *Golden States*, 1980; *White Angel* published in *Best American Short Stories*, 1989; novel, *A Home at the End of the World*, 1990; novel, *Flesh and Blood*, 1995; novel, *The Hours*, 1999; walking tour book, *Land's End: A Walk Through Provincetown*, 2002. Contributor of fiction and nonfiction to periodicals, including *New Yorker, Atlantic, Los Angeles Times, Mother Jones,* and *Paris Review.*

Awards: Michener fellowship, University of Iowa, 1982; National Endowment for the Arts fellowship, 1988; Guggenheim fellowship, 1993; PEN/Faulkner Award for *The Hours,* 1999; Pulitzer Award for fiction for *The Hours,* 1999.

Sidelights

Michael Cunningham has built his career on writing novels and short stories that explore the motivations of everyday people. For many years his style was appreciated by critics, but a large audience was elusive. Then Cunningham decided to work on the story he had yearned to write since he was in the tenth grade. "I wanted to write about the power of reading a great book," he told Allison Adato and Liza Hamm in *People.* The result was *The Hours,* a moving tale of three women in three different decades, linked together by one brief moment. *The Hours* won the PEN/Faulkner and the Pulitzer awards, hit the New York Times best–seller list and was adapted into a movie that received nine Oscar nominations in 2003, including Best Picture.

Cunningham was born in 1952 in Cincinnati, Ohio. When his father, Don, found a job opportunity in Europe the family packed up and left the United States. They moved around for a couple of years until his stint was complete and then decided California was where they should settle for the remainder of the children's schooling. At the age of ten the young Cunningham, by his own account, lived the "nuclear family" life: with mother at home, father at work and he and his sister attending the same high school. Cunningham was a smart but somewhat quiet kid who was intrigued by the artist's life. By the time he reached the tenth grade Cunningham considered himself something of a painter and hoped to pursue that career path in college.

But, according to Cunningham, he fashioned himself many things, and most of it was just skin deep. He met his match in the parking lot of his high school, in 1967, in a moment that would end up changing his life forever. He was trying to impress a girl he liked with his knowledge of folk music, but apparently he did not know much at all. "[The girl asked], 'Have you ever thought of being less stupid?' I *had* been thinking about being less stupid," he told Adato and Hamm in *People*. The young woman recommended he read a book; he decided to start with *Mrs. Dalloway*, a novel by Virginia Woolf. After finding a copy in the library, he devoured it. He was so moved by the story that he would always remember that feeling of reading a brilliant novel and, as a result, being a changed person.

So he spent his years in Stanford writing instead of painting. He impressed his professors with a strong style that was quickly developing into a mature voice. His pieces, even at an early stage, showed his fascination with a human being's hidden motivations and emotions. But he was beginning to understand how hard the work was and wondered if the writing life was for him. Then, in a moment of decisiveness, he found himself enjoying the creative process enough to send his work to the University of Iowa's prestigious M.F.A. writing program. He hoped to get in but did not consider it very likely. Much to his surprise, he received his acceptance letter in early 1978.

Cunningham told Michael Coffey of *Publishers Weekly*, "I went to Iowa in 1978 with real trepidations about whether I wanted to be a writer.... I found myself among 60 plus people, some of them extremely talented, who were just about willing to commit murder over a paragraph.... [S]omething about it made me snap to." His experience there was a testament to the program's strength and his own perseverance. He quickly found a mentor in novelist Hilma Wolitzer and had shorts published in *Paris Review* and a number of other publications. This was all before he had even received his M.F.A. degree. But his run of good luck would quickly come to an end as he left academia and entered the professional world.

It was as if the well had run dry. For ten years, Cunningham took jobs ranging from waiting on tables to farming. By the time he reached the age of 30 he began to worry his whole life would be the story of a man with a lot of promise who never quite reached his potential. But amidst the doubts, he managed to write a book called *Golden States*, which was published by Crown in 1980. It told the story of a 12–year–old boy in southern California, who grapples with a family that always seems to be on the verge of falling apart. The book was generally well–received by critics but the sales were not impressive. By the time his first novel was published he had already started on his next work, but ten years passed before it would see print.

A Home at the End of the World, published in 1990, is a story of two young men, Jonathan and Bobby, who become boyhood friends and eventually move to New York. They hook up with Clare, who ends up having Bobby's child, but soon disappears from their lives as the three of them try their hand at the country lifestyle. Again, reviewers loved the book; *Nation*'s David Kaufman declared, "Cunningham is in a league with Sybille Bedford for his exquisite way with words and for his uncanny felicity in conveying both his characters and their story through their own internalized impressions. This is quite simply one of those rare novels imbued with graceful insights on every page." The book sold better than *Golden States* and even helped to garner Cunningham the esteemed Guggenheim Fellowship in 1993. By most accounts this book was considered his breakthrough piece. At the very least, the literary world knew he was alive and he was building a very loyal fan base. He was also developing a reputation amongst his readers for being obsessed with family. He found this ironic, since all of the families he wrote about were very untraditional. But his next book would only build on the reputation.

Flesh and Blood, published in 1995, was a tale about friction between generations. The Stassos family is an All–American family in appearance only. In reality the husband's selfishness slowly tears the family apart, leaving the children to find lives separate from each other. Interestingly, Cunningham experimented with telling the tale over a number of decades, in a fashion that is similar to the style of his following work. Again, the reviews came in with a glow to them. "Michael Cunningham is one of the most gifted writers around," wrote Paul Burston of *Guardian Unlimited*. "[Flesh and Blood] is an ambitious book, epic in scale...."

It was while working on *A Home at the End of the World* that Cunningham began writing the novel which would make his career one of the most celebrated of his generation. This time he was going to tell the story he had wanted to tell for decades. His deep connection to the novel *Mrs. Dalloway* and Virginia Woolf's tragic life had sparked an idea in him way back when he first read it in the tenth grade. He decided it was time to get the story down on paper. He set out to craft a tale that most men would never dare to try—a story about three women doing their best to keep their lives together. Each one of the women walks a fine line between being what other people expect from them and who they really are. By tackling this theme, Cunningham set out to get into the minds of three women: the result was *The Hours*. Robert Plunket of the *Advocate* wrote about the finished novel, "[Cunningham] is that rarest of writers, combining intellectual and emotional depth with an astonishing command of technique. *The Hours* is one of the best books I've read in years, profoundly sad, perhaps, but always exhilarating." Then, in an ironic comment, Plunket went on to write," And best of all, it's a real book. It could never, ever be a movie." But Hollywood producer Scott Rudin, of *Sister Act* and *The Addams Family* fame, thought differently. *The Hours*'s interplay between three women in three different decades appealed to him. So he hired David Hare, a playwright known for his play, *Plenty*, to adapt the novel into a script.

Cunningham was as surprised as his fans that Hollywood was interested. "[I thought it would] sell a few thousand copies," he told Adato and Hamm in *People*, "then march with whatever dignity it could muster to the remainders table." The opposite happened. The novel won Cunningham the PEN/Faulkner, an award which is judged by a group of fiction writers who identify five outstanding works of fiction each year. From those five they choose a winner. Then, also in 1999, his book won what is arguably the most coveted literary prize, the Pulitzer. He took the sudden rush of success in stride. "I haven't changed my view that prizes are mostly stupid and embarrassing, but I do like the fact that this odd little book was deemed in some way to be about the American experience," Cunningham told Nicholas Wroe of *Guardian Unlimited*.

Once the power players in Hollywood got their hands on the thoughtful, quiet script the stars started lining up: Nicole Kidman, Julianne Moore, and Meryl Streep read the script and loved it. "It was masterfully constructed," Streep told Adato and Hamm in *People*, "Three interior stories about the wars waged inside people's heads and hearts." The movie debuted in the winter of 2002 in select theaters, but once buzz began to build it added screens and quickly became a Top 10 film and a frontrunner for Best Picture at the Academy Awards. Ironically, in the midst of his surge in popularity, Cunningham wrote a simple book called *Land's End: A Walk Through Provincetown*. The walking tour book takes the reader through Provincetown, Massachusetts, a place on the tip of Cape Cod, that is known by writers and artists as having an almost mythic quality.

While the film adaptation of *The Hours* did not win Best Picture, it did pick up Best Actress with Nicole Kidman receiving the statue for her performance as Virginia Woolf, the same writer Cunningham admired and based the book on. The writer himself could not be happier with how the film turned out. "I loved it," he told Tony Peregrin of the *Gay & Lesbian Review*. "I can't describe or compare the look of the film to any other film I've ever seen. It's like any true work of art in that it looks like itself, it has its own particular quality that is wholly unique." The writer struggled to keep things in perspective, though, and insisted his new book would be very different from *The Hours*. He told Stephanie Schorow of the *Boston Herald*. "The only thing you must not do is try to write the same book again. You want to be loved all your life, but that's a kiss of death."

Cunningham lives in Provincetown, Massachusetts, and Manhattan with his partner of 15 years, psychotherapist Ken Corbett.

Selected writings

Golden States, Crown (New York City), 1984.
A Home at the End of the World, Farrar, Straus (New York City), 1990.
Flesh and Blood, Farrar, Straus, 1995.
The Hours, Farrar, Straus, 1998.
Land's End: A Walk Through Provincetown, Crown, 2002.

Sources

Periodicals

Advocate, December 8, 1998, p. 87; May 1999, p. 83.
Boston Herald, December 6, 2002, p. 43.
Gay & Lesbian Review, March/April 2003, pp. 30–31.
Nation, July 1, 1991, pp. 21–24.
People, February 10, 2003, pp. 105–106.
Publishers Weekly, November 2, 1998, pp. 53–55.

Online

"About the Author," Literati.net, http://www.literati.net/Cunningham (March 27, 2003).
"Driving Mrs. Dalloway," Guardian Unlimited, http://books.guardian.co.uk/departments/generalfiction/story/0,6000,103050,00.html (March 27, 2003).
"Paul Burston's favorite gay fiction," Guardian Unlimited, http://books.guardian.co.uk/top10s/top10/0,6109,523071,00.html (March 27, 2003).

—Ben Zackheim

Larry David

Writer, producer, and director

Born in 1948 in Brooklyn, New York; married Laurie Lennard, 1993; children: two.

Addresses: *Office*—LD Productions, 3000 Olympic Blvd., Santa Monica, CA 90404.

Career

Performed stand–up on comedy circuit, 1974–79; staff writer for *Fridays* TV series, 1979–82; staff writer, *Saturday Night Live*, 1982–83; creator and writer of *Norman's Corner*, 1989; co–creator and co–executive producer, *Seinfeld*, 1990–96; director and screenwriter, *Sour Grapes*, 1998; creator and actor, *Curb Your Enthusiasm*, 2000—. Film appearances include: *Second Thoughts*, 1983; *Can She Bake a Cherry Pie?* 1983; *Radio Days*, 1987; *New York Stories*, 1989; *Sour Grapes*, 1998.

Sidelights

Previously best known for his behind–the–scenes work as co–creator and executive producer of the immensely popular *Seinfeld* comedy series, Larry David kicked off the new millennium by going public in a big way. With the October of 2000 premiere of *Curb Your Enthusiasm* on HBO, David came out from behind the camera to play himself, a character that on TV somehow manages to embody all the worst personality defects of the entire *Seinfeld* ensemble. At first glance, David, bespectacled, bald, and deceptively mild in appearance, hardly seems the type of character you'd expect to find in the

midst of such utter chaos that he encounters in every episode of the hit comedy. However, you won't have to watch *Curb* for long to begin to understand how David's cynicism and overall misanthropy make him a lightning rod for trouble. Each show is largely improvised by David and his fellow cast members, including Cheryl Hines, who plays his wife, and Jeff Garlin, who plays his manager. The cast regulars are joined each week by one or more guest stars, who in the show's first three seasons included Richard Lewis, Ted Danson, Martin Short, and *Seinfeld* veterans Jason Alexander and Julia Louis–Dreyfuss. For each episode, David sketches out a rough outline that the actors then bring to life through improvisation.

At HBO's website for *Curb Your Enthusiasm*, Peter Mehlman, a writer for *Seinfeld* and a longtime associate of David, offers this assessment of the show's creator and star: "Larry is very in tune with his own deepest, darkest, most embarrassing thoughts—and he's utterly unabashed about sharing them." In fact, many of David's real–life experiences have found their way to the small screen in episodes of both *Seinfeld and Curb Your Enthusiasm*. For the memorable *Seinfeld* episode in which bumbling George Costanza (played by Alexander) quit his job in a fit of anger and then returned to work as though nothing had happened, David drew upon a similar incident from his year as a writer for *Saturday Night Live* (*SNL*). As he related to *Onion* interviewer Stephen Thompson, David, incensed that a sketch he had written had been dropped by *SNL* executive producer Dick Ebersol, stormed into Ebersol's office minutes before showtime to vent his anger. As Ebersol sat in his director's chair with headphones on, waiting for the show to begin, David exploded, "That's it, I quit! ... I've had it! I'm gone! I'm out of here! Goodbye!" After David got home, it dawned on him that his outburst was likely to cost him a lot of money in lost salary, so on Monday morning he returned to work as though nothing had happened; the gambit worked.

Born and raised in Brooklyn, New York, David, according to his biography at Hollywood.com, said that he enjoyed "a wonderful childhood, which is tough, because it's hard to adjust to a miserable adulthood." In his mid–20s, he hit the comedy circuit, doing stand–up mostly in the comedy clubs of New York City. It was during his stand–up years that David first met fellow comic and future collaborator Jerry Seinfeld. Although he developed a reputation as a "comic's comic," which David told Hollywood.com is just a polite way of saying he stank as a comedian, he has few fond memories of his years as a comic. Asked in 1994 by an interviewer for *Laugh Factory* if he missed stand–up at all, David, in a flood of typical Davidian sarcasm, replied: "Well, as you know, I'm really only happy when I'm on stage. I just feed off the energy of the audience. That's what I'm all about—people and laughter." David went on to say, "Yeah, I'd much rather be on stage talking to a couple of [idiots] for 20 bucks than sitting at my desk thinking up jokes for ... well, let's say, a few dollars more."

In late 1979 David signed on as both a writer and a performer for the upcoming ABC comedy variety show *Fridays*, modeled after *SNL*. The show premiered in April of 1980 and ran until October of 1982. However, David left *Fridays* and joined *SNL* as a writer for the 1982–83 season. It was not one of the more pleasant experiences of his career. As he told Thompson of the *Onion*, he spent the year at *SNL* in agonizing isolation, with nobody talking to him. "I had an office that faced the elevator, and hordes of people would go out to lunch, and my door would be open, and I would be sitting there looking at them, and I'm waiting for the wave of, 'Come on, Lar, we're going to lunch! Come on with us! You want to have lunch with us?' No. It was the only place I ever worked where I really, truly did not make a friend. I couldn't believe it."

The year at *SNL* proved almost as barren professionally as it was socially for David. Only one of the sketches he'd written made it onto the show, he told Thompson. "It was the last sketch of the night, the one that's on at, like, five to one in the morning. I had a lot of them cut after dress rehearsal. I hated the executive producer, Dick Ebersol."

After leaving *SNL*, David spent the next few years working on a varied assortment of projects. He played small film roles in 1983's *Second Thoughts* and *Can She Bake a Cherry Pie?*, and Woody Allen's 1987 film *Radio Days* and 1989 film *New York Stories*. David also created and wrote a TV sitcom pilot (*Norman's Corner*) for comedian Gilbert Gottfried. The 1989 pilot crashed and burned, never making it onto the prime–time schedule. Gottfried, interviewed by Neil Gladstone at *Philadelphia Citypaper.net* in 1996, was asked if he considered it odd that David had such a big hit with *Seinfeld* but had failed to get *Norman's Corner* off the ground. He replied: "I guess he was saving his good writing for later on. Why couldn't he have written *Norman's Corner* for Jerry Seinfeld and a sitcom called *Gottfried* for me?"

Not long after the failure of *Norman's Corner*, David's old pal Seinfeld came in search of his help. Seinfeld was working with NBC executives to develop a comedy project, and he thought David might be able to offer some helpful suggestions. Together, huddled over a table at a New York City coffee shop, Seinfeld and David developed the concept for what was to become one of television's most influential situation comedies ever. Curiously, the sitcom was not an immediate success. When it first aired in 1990, *Seinfeld* had some trouble developing an audience, attributable perhaps in part to the show's unique format. It did not take long, however, for the show to catch on. Asked to discuss the factors that had helped to give the show life, David told *Laugh Factory*: "To be honest with you, I think the only thing that really worked in my favor is that right from the beginning I really didn't give a [expletive] whether or not the show was a success. That's not to say I didn't want to do good work, but I wasn't about to let myself be judged by network standards. When you're not concerned with succeeding, you can work with complete freedom."

Although the show bore Seinfeld's name, much of its content was inspired by incidents in David's life, as well as his unique outlook on life. Of David's contribution to the plot lines of the show, Seinfeld told Joe Rhodes of *Entertainment Weekly*, "Our senses of humor dovetail in such a way that the words sound right coming out of my mouth, but most of the time they're [David's] words. I'd say 90 percent of the show comes from Larry." Whatever its formula for success may have been, *Seinfeld* eventually became one of television's biggest comedy hits ever, earning David, Seinfeld, and its regular cast members millions during the show's nine–year run. Worn down by the grind of turning out scripts for the weekly sitcom, David left the *Seinfeld* team in 1996, although he returned to help write the script for the show's finale in 1998.

David left *Seinfeld* not just to get some rest but also to try his hand at writing for the big screen. His first such project, 1998's *Sour Grapes,* which also marked David's debut as a film director, failed to duplicate the magic of *Seinfeld.* In fact, the film, which starred Craig Bierko and Steven Weber, was largely savaged by the critics, as were David's contributions as writer and director. Bridget Byrne, in her review of the film for *Boxoffice* magazine, wrote: "Mean–spirited and witless, *Sour Grapes* lacks all the subtle quirkiness anticipated by the writing and directing credit. If Larry David is truly responsible for making something out of nothing as co–creator of *Seinfeld,* there is not a glimmer of that talent visible in this movie." Almost equally unkind was Paul Tatara of CNN, who observed: "David, whose work for *Seinfeld* was undeniably brilliant, evidently never bothered to consider that you can't get away with that sort of streamlined–but–meandering illogic for an entire movie, and *Sour Grapes* pays for it, big time."

Undeterred by his failure at the box office, David began casting about for a new project. When fellow comedian and longtime friend Jeff Garlin suggested that David revisit his years as a stand–up comic, David came up with an idea for an HBO special that blended some of his old stand–up routines with a mockumentary view of action behind the scenes. The special, which was dubbed *Larry David: Curb Your Enthusiasm,* so impressed HBO executives that they commissioned David to develop a sitcom centered around some of the comedian's pet peeves as encountered during his day–to–day life as a successful television producer. The sitcom, which borrowed the title *Curb Your Enthusiasm* from David's 1999 HBO special, debuted on Sunday, October 15, 2000, to almost universal critical praise. And, thanks to HBO's strong Sunday night schedule, the show also enjoyed a substantial audience, at least measured by the standards of a premium cable channel.

Typical of the critics's praise for *Curb Your Enthusiasm* was this review from the *New York Daily News,* reprinted on HBO's website: "Curb my enthusiasm? No way. [*Curb*] has given HBO its best sitcom since *The Larry Sanders Show* and given all of television the best sitcom since *Seinfeld.* Not too shabby for a show that isn't even scripted. [It's] so real and so absurdly comic precisely because the rhythms are so natural."

For his part, David is having the time of his life. Married since 1993 to Laurie Lennard, David and his wife make their home in Los Angeles, California, where they live with their two children. As to his work on *Curb,* where almost every episode finds him the butt of the joke, David couldn't be happier. As he told Scott Simon on National Public Radio's *Weekend Edition,* "I don't mind playing the fool. It's fun. Most of the scenes I can't even get through; I have so many people cursing me all the time, and calling me all these obscene names, and I find it hilarious, because it never happens to me in life where people are actually calling me the vilest names. And when I hear it, I just burst out laughing. It's a strange thing. So I'm having a good time."

Sources

Books

Complete Marquis Who's Who, Marquis Who's Who, 2001.
Contemporary Theatre, Film, and Television, volume 23, Gale Group, 1999.

Periodicals

Boxoffice, April 1998.
Entertainment Weekly, March 6, 1992, p. 48; September 14, 2001, p. 74; June 28/July 5, 2002, p. 64; September 20, 2002, pp. 64–69.
Laugh Factory, April 1994.
New Republic, January 13, 2003, p. 23.
New Statesman, March 3, 2003, p. 47.
Onion, April 23, 1998.
Time, November 8, 1993, p. 78.
Toronto Star, February 12, 2003.
Washington Post, September 11, 2001, p. C1.

Online

"About the Show," *HBO: Curb Your Enthusiasm,* http://www.hbo.com/larrydavid/about/ (April 23, 2003).
"Gilbert Gottfried," *Philadelphia Citypaper.net,* http://www.citypaper.net/articles/022996/article001.shtml (April 23, 2003).
"Larry David: Biography," Hollywood.com, http://www.hollywood.com/celebs/bio/celeb/1678551 (April 22, 2003).

"Larry David Is Himself," HBO.com, http://www.hbo.com/larrydavid/cast_and_crew/index.html (April 23, 2003).

"Review: 'Sour Grapes' Unpalatable," CNN.com, http://www.cnn.com/SHOWBIZ/9804/24/review.sour.grapes/ (April 23, 2003).

Transcripts

Weekend Edition, National Public Radio, October 27, 2001.

—*Don Amerman*

Fred DeLuca

Chief Executive Officer and President of Subway Restaurants

Born Frederick DeLuca in 1947 in Brooklyn, NY; married; children: one son.

Addresses: *Home*—Orlando, FL. *Office*—Subway Restaurants, 325 Bic Dr., Milford, CT 06460.

Career

Co–founder, chief executive officer, and president of Subway Restaurants. Opened Pete's Super Submarine Sandwiches, in Bridgeport, CT, 1965; expanded through franchising agreements after 1974; opened first Subway in Canada, 1986, and in Australia, 1987; expanded into Europe and the Middle East, 1990s; launched Micro Investment Lending Enterprise (MILE), a nonprofit organization for small businesses, 1996.

Sidelights

Fred DeLuca's Subway Restaurants fast–food empire surpassed McDonald's as the largest fast–food company in the United States in 2001. The Brooklyn, New York, native founded his company with a $1,000 loan as a teenager, and has since expanded it into more than 16,000 outlets in 75 countries. The $3–billion annual business grew exponentially in the 1990s, as Subway began a marketing campaign that trumpeted its menu as a fresh, low–fat, lunchtime alternative. The company seems to have finally hit its stride after some lean early years, noted *BusinessWeek Online* writer Diane Brady. "With weight–conscious consumers losing their appetites for french fries and grilled burgers—even going so far as to sue chains that allegedly made them fat—it can only bode well for outfits like Subway."

DeLuca spent the first ten years of his life in Brooklyn, where his family lived in a public–housing project and he collected pop bottles in the neighborhood to earn pocket money. His father was a factory worker and relocated the family to Schenectady, New York, in the late 1950s, where DeLuca again displayed an early entrepreneurial streak with a newspaper route that grew to some 400 homes. As a teen, he moved once again with his family to Bridgeport, Connecticut. With dreams of becoming a doctor, he planned to enter the pre–med program at the University of Bridgeport, but needed money for tuition. He took a job in a hardware store, but found it impossible to save on the $1.25 hourly wage he earned. Hoping for advice, he asked a neighbor and friend of his parents, Dr. Peter Buck, for suggestions. Buck believed that a submarine sandwich shop might be profitable, and offered to bankroll one if DeLuca would run it. The two became partners in the business, and Pete's Super Submarine Sandwiches opened in Bridgeport in August of 1965.

DeLuca realized in his first day on the job that he had never made a submarine sandwich before in his life. Learning by trial and error, he persevered, but the business was a money–loser. Buck suggested opening a second outlet, on the principle that it would at least make them appear to be thriving financially, but that outlet lost money as well; a third followed, with predictably dire results. "The following winter instead of having one really low volume, money–losing store, we had three low volume, money–losing stores," *Fairfield County Business Journal*'s Dan Strempel quoted DeLuca as saying. Finally, at the end of their first year in business De-Luca and Buck had made a $7,000 profit, and changed the name of the business to "Subway."

DeLuca did finish college, but settled on an undergraduate degree in psychology rather than a medical license, realizing that he enjoyed working for himself and running a business. DeLuca and Buck set a goal to have 32 stores by the end of Subway's first decade. "The reason why we picked that number, we both knew of a sandwich shop in upstate New York called Mike's Submarines and they had 32 stores, so that was our goal," he told *Fairfield County Business Journal*'s Strempel. Only halfway to making his goal by 1974, he realized that there was only one of him and that quick–minded managers were necessary. So he offered to loan a friend, Brian Dixon, the $14,000 himself to "franchise" a Subway, and even offered to let him out of the agreement if it didn't work out; Dixon liked his steady paycheck and declined—but then went to work one day and found the company door padlocked by the sheriff. Out of work, Dixon agreed to become Subway's first franchisee, and his store was so successful that DeLuca decided to make this his business plan for the future.

Franchising involves an initial up–front payment, or franchise fee, to an established company with a product or service to offer. The franchisee is granted the right to operate that business, using a marketing plan or system already devised, and pays the parent company a percentage of annual sales. In return, advertising costs are covered by the parent company. DeLuca's idea to expand Subway through franchising worked immediately. The fee was not exorbitant, and running the business was a relatively easy operation, since the stores had a limited menu, no fryer, and not very much space for seating. A husband–and–wife team could usually handle the business themselves, even at peak busy hours. The initial costs—around $85,000 in 2000— were much lower than those of other fast–food franchises; a McDonald's restaurant, for example, required a minimum half–million–dollar investment.

By 1978, Subway had opened its 100th store, and reached the 1,000–mark in 1987. *Entrepreneur* magazine began to list it as the number–one franchise opportunity in the United States, and by 1995 there were some 5,000 stores, including outlets in Canada, Mexico, and Australia. DeLuca maintained tight control of the business, and even signed every single check issued until 1990, when his accountant explained that a CEO's time was far more valuable. He did make some executive decisions that were unwise along the way, however, such as a series of television commercials in the late 1990s that starred two fictitious cab drivers and purported Subway fans. "When the commercials were shown, sales would go down," DeLuca told Brady in *Business-Week Online*.

DeLuca's company hit another low point around this same time with a spate of bad publicity over its franchising practices; a 1998 *Fortune* article appeared with the title, "Why Subway is 'the biggest problem in franchising,'" and listed a number of grievances from franchisees. Some of them involved a loss of sales when Subway, in violation of a "protected area" clause of the franchise agreement, allowed a new franchisee to open a store nearby. The Federal Trade Commission investigated Subway, but dropped the case due to lack of evidence. DeLuca, interviewed by Nichole Torres for *Entrepreneur.com*, said that his company's numbers spoke for themselves. "Somewhere between 60 and 70 percent of the new stores we build every year are built by existing franchisees who are expanding," he told the reporter. "I feel really good about that."

DeLuca and Subway received a much–needed jolt of good exposure when a college student from Indiana, Jared Fogle, wrote to tell them he had lost 245 pounds by eating two of Subway's lower–fat offerings daily for several months. Subway hired Fogle to star in a new national advertising campaign, and the Midwesterner became a household name after the ads began appearing in 2000. Subway's sales skyrocketed, and soon afterward the company posted a growth of 19 percent in the past year, far ahead of the fast–food industry average of just four percent. The timing was fortuitous, DeLuca told *Sunday Herald* writer Darran Gardner. "There is big concern about obesity in children and adults," he said. "And I personally have never before seen this much interest in what people are eating. Studies have shown that about a third of Americans are now making food choices based on what's good for them. That's good for us because Subway sandwiches can be customized according to dietary requirements."

In 2001, Subway reached the 14,000–outlet mark, making it—by sheer number at least—the largest fast–food franchise in the United States. DeLuca was busy with an overseas expansion plan as well, and Subway franchises had sprung up in Britain, Germany, India, Israel, Saudi Arabia, Austria, Brazil, and Russia. It had been a risky move to venture outside of North America, because the submarine sandwich was a food item relatively unknown outside of the United States. DeLuca was savvy enough to realize the universal appeal, however. "I think a good way to gauge the potential of any market is the presence of chain branded fast food outlets," he said in the interview with Gardner of the *Sunday Herald*. "If you see chains there and they are doing well that means that there will also be demand for additional choices. In many ways McDonald's is doing the groundwork for us in countries such as India or China as they are teaching people to go and eat there."

Despite the tremendous success, DeLuca is still an active boss and is uninterested in giving up any of that control, no matter how lucrative the prospect. He has dismissed the idea of taking his company public with an initial public offering (IPO) of its stock, telling Brady in *Business Week Online* that in the late 1980s, "We talked about it for half an hour," but then reconsidered. "Do we want a bunch of additional people—shareholders—to distract us from our mission? We did the calculations and decided we didn't have to go public." Even business rivals praise DeLuca's vision. Anthony Conza, cofounder of Blimpie's, a subway chain launched the same year as DeLuca's, voiced awe at Subway's impressive growth. "DeLuca created the segment," Conza told *Nation's Restaurant News* writers Suzanne Kapner and Peter O. Keegan. "It hardly existed before Subway's expansion. It was a real wake–up call to us."

As Subway's boss, DeLuca likes to make anonymous visits to stores. One franchisee, Charlie Serabian, recalled in the *Nation's Restaurant News* article by Kapner and Keegan that one day in Florida, DeLuca "was being given a ride to the airport when he saw … a little freestanding unit on a major road with cars whizzing by. You couldn't miss it. Fred thought it was so fantastic that he ripped the for–rent sign down and threw it in the bushes so no one else would lease the space." In time, this Fort Lauderdale Subway outlet became one of the highest–grossing in the United States. At other times, DeLuca has taken a more hands–off approach. The Subway company structure was a relatively decentralized one, he noted. "I learned early on that, with a corporate store, I could ask the manager to get the window cleaned and it would be done," he told *Financial Times* journalist Christopher Swann. "With a franchise unit, if you tell them to wash the windows it does not mean they will do it. There is a greater element of persuasion and cooperation involved."

DeLuca put his ideas to paper with John P. Hayes in the book *Start Small. Finish Big: Fifteen Key Lessons to Start—and Run—Your Own Successful Business*, published by Warner Books in 2001. He recounts his own empire–building story, as well as those of other successful franchise operations like Kinko's and Little Caesar's. DeLuca was already a firm believer in small–business opportunities, having started Micro Investment Lending Enterprise (MILE) in 1996, a nonprofit organization that makes loans to small start–ups.

Subway's CEO lives in Orlando, Florida, and described himself as "married to the job" when interviewed by Torres for *Entrepreneur.com*. He considered other prospects, "and then I think to myself, well geez, what would I do? If I didn't do this, I would probably do something else that would just get me in trouble, you know…. I know a lot of people at some point in their business careers decide they'll just cash in and do something else, but for some reason, I've never had that feeling." DeLuca admits that he has made some missteps along the way, but has learned a lot by listening to his franchisees' suggestions. "At least half of the time I find I would have done things differently," he said in the interview with Swann in the *Financial Times*. "But this does not mean that I would have been doing things any better."

Selected writings

(With John P. Hayes) *Start Small. Finish Big: Fifteen Key Lessons to Start—and Run—Your Own Successful Business*, Warner Books, 2001.

Sources

Books

Business Leader Profiles for Students, Volume 1, Gale, 1999.

Periodicals

Booklist, July 2000, p. 1983.
Entrepreneur, January 1996, p. 192; October 2000, p. 136.
Express on Sunday (London, England), June 16, 2002, p. 7.
Fairfield County Business Journal, May 27, 2002, p. 3.
Financial Times, June 26, 2001, p. 4.
Forbes, September 3, 2001, p. 85.

Fortune, March 16, 1998, p. 126.

Grocer, March 31, 2001, p. 5; June 29, 2002, p. 6.

Inc., November 1990, p. 24; November 1995, p. 102.

Library Journal, July 2000, p. 111.

Nation's Restaurant News, August 27, 1990, p. 7; January 1995, p. 49.

New York Times, March 3, 2003.

Orange County Business Journal, March 18, 1991, p. 6.

Publishers Weekly, July 3, 2000, p. 2.

Sunday Herald (Glasgow, Scotland), June 23, 2002, p. 5.

Online

"The Man Behind Subway's Success," *Entrepreneur. com,* http://www.entrepreneur.com/franzone/article/0,5847,306152,00.html (March 1, 2003).

"Why Subway Is on a Roll," *BusinessWeek Online,* http://www.businessweek.com/bwdaily/dnflash/aug2002/nf20020819_6308.htm (January 11, 2003).

—Carol Brennan

Catherine Deneuve

Actress

Born Catherine Dorléac, October 22, 1943, in Paris, France; daughter of Maurice (an actor) and Renée (an actress; maiden name: Deneuve) Dorléac; married David Bailey (a photographer), 1965 (divorced, 1972); children: Christian Vadim (son, with director Roger Vadim), Chiara Mastroianni (daughter, with actor Marcello Mastroianni).

Addresses: *Office*—76 Rue Bonaparte, 75006 Paris, France.

Career

Actress in films, including: *Les Collegiennes*, 1957; *Les Portes claquent*, 1960; *Ladies Man*, 1960; *Tales of Paris*, 1962; *Vice and Virtue*, 1962; *Satan Leads the Dance*, 1962; *Portuguese Vacation*, 1963; *The Umbrellas of Cherbourg*, 1964; *The Beautiful Swindlers*, 1964; *La Costanza della ragione*, 1964; *Male Hunt*, 1964; *Repulsion*, 1965; *Wild Roots of Love*, 1965; *Song of the World*, 1965; *Male Companion*, 1965; *Who Wants to Sleep?*, 1965; *A Matter of Resistance*, 1966; *Belle de Jour*, 1967; *The Young Girls of Rochefort*, 1968; *Benjamin*, 1968; *Mayerling*, 1968; *Manon 70*, 1968; *Mississippi Mermaid*, 1969; *The Creatures*, 1969; *Heartbeat*, 1969; *The April Fools*, 1969; *Tristana*, 1970; *Donkey Skin*, 1970; *It Only Happens to Others*, 1971; *Liza*, 1972; *A Slightly Pregnant Man*, 1973; *Don't Touch the White Woman!*, 1974; *The Lady with Red Boots*, 1974; *Zig-Zag*, 1974; *Drama of the Rich*, 1974; *The Savage*, 1975; *Hustle*, 1975; *Dirty Money*, 1975; *Act of Aggression*, 1975; *If I Had to Do It All Over Again*, 1976; *The Forbidden Room*, 1977; *March or Die*, 1977; *Beach House*, 1977; *Other People's Money*, 1978; *Look See....*, 1978; *These Kids Are Grown-Ups*, 1979; *Us Two*, 1979; *Courage—Let's Run*, 1979; *The Last Metro*, 1980; *I Love You All*, 1980; *Hotel des Ameriques*, 1981; *Choice of Arms*, 1981; *Contract In Blood*, 1982; *The Hunger*, 1983; *The African*, 1983; *Le Bon plaisir*, 1984; *Fort Saganne*, 1984; *Love Songs*, 1984; *Let's Hope It's a Girl*, 1985; *Scene of the Crime*, 1986; *Agent Trouble*, 1987; *A Strange Place to Meet*, 1988; *Listening in the Dark*, 1988; *La Reine blanche*, 1991; *Against Oblivion*, 1991; *Indochine*, 1992; *My Favorite Season*, 1993; *François Truffaut: Stolen Portraits*, 1993; *The Young Girls Turn 25*, 1993; *The Chess Game*, 1994; *The Convent*, 1995; *A Hundred and One Nights*, 1995; *Thieves*, 1996; *Genealogies of a Crime*, 1997; *Sans titre*, 1997; *Place Vendome*, 1998; *The Wind of the Night*, 1999; *Beautiful Mother*, 1999; *Le Temps Retrouvé*, 1999; *East-West*, 1999; *Dancer in the Dark*, 2000; *I'm Going Home*, 2001; *Clouds: Letters to My Son* (narrator), 2001; *The Musketeer*, 2001; *Tom Thumb*, 2001; *8 Femmes*, 2002; *Nearest to Heaven*, 2002. Television appearances include: commercials for Chanel, c. mid-1970s; *Court toujours: L'inconnu* (movie), 1996; *Pierre ou les ambigütés* (movie), 1999; *Les Liaisons dangereuses* (miniseries), 2002. Producer of *A Strange Place To Meet*, 1988.

Awards: Best actress, Berlin International Film Festival, for *Repulsion*, 1965; Cesar for best actress, French Film Academy, for *The Last Metro*, 1980; Cesar for best actress, French Film Academy, for *Indochine*, 1992; Honorary Golden Bear award for lifetime achievement, Berlin International Film Festival, 1998; best actress, Venice International Film Festival, for *Place Vendome,* 1998; lifetime achievement award, Cairo International Film Festival, 1999; Actor's Mission Award for contributions toward developing world cinema, International Art Film Festival Trencianske Teplice, 2000; career award, Vasto Film Festival, 2002; Silver Bear award for Best Individual Artistic Contribution, Berlin International Film Festival, presented to cast of *8 Femmes,* 2002.

Sidelights

For more than 40 years, Catherine Deneuve has graced the film screen. Her varied films include the musical *The Umbrellas of Cherbourg,* the thriller *Repulsion,* and the Academy Award–nominated *Indochine.* Her beauty has inspired directors, actors, and fashion designers. Her image was even used as the model for the image of the French Republic, Marianne, which adorned posters, coins, and stamps throughout France. She has worked steadily throughout the decades since she first appeared in film. She continues to create memorable and fascinating female characters while adhering to a high standard for herself and her films.

Born Catherine Dorléac on October 22, 1943, in Paris, France, Deneuve was one of four daughters of actors Maurice and Renée Dorléac. Her father's career spanned from the 1940s to the '70s. He often appeared in films under the name Maurice Teynac. Deneuve adopted her mother's maiden name when she began acting at the age of 13. Her older sister, Françoise Dorléac, had already begun a successful career in acting and was influential in getting Deneuve some of her early roles. Even though she began acting at a young age, Deneuve was never sure if acting was truly her calling. It wasn't until after her success in the film *The Umbrellas of Cherbourg* that she truly dedicated herself to acting.

Deneuve's first film role was in 1957 in *Les Collegiennes.* In 1960, she appeared in *Les Portes Claquent,* which also featured her sister. She appeared in several other films without garnering much attention until 1964 when she appeared in *The Umbrellas of Cherbourg.* In the film she played the daughter of an umbrella store owner. She falls in love with a car mechanic right before he is sent off to the war in Algeria. Despite professing her love and promising to marry, Deneuve's character ends up marrying a kind, rich young man who she does not love because she is pregnant with the mechanic's child. The two meet again years later having settled into their respective lives, hers as an upper–class wife and mother, his as a middle–class

gas station owner. The film was made as a musical with the actors singing all of their lines. The sung dialogue in combination with the vivid colors of the film made it an enchanting and heartbreaking love story. For her performance, Deneuve gained an international audience and impressed upon the film–going public her freshness and innocence.

In Deneuve's next film, she strayed from the innocence portrayed in *The Umbrellas of Cherbourg* to successfully embody the neurotic and sexually repressed Carol Ledoux in *Repulsion.* The film was directed by the controversial Roman Polanski, who fled the United States in 1978 to avoid serving jail time for rape charges. *Repulsion* helped establish the cold yet sexual persona that has been identified with Deneuve for the majority of her career. That persona was solidified in the film *Belle de Jour* in which Deneuve portrayed a bored housewife, Severine, who relieves her boredom by working in a brothel during the day. *Belle de Jour* was directed by Spanish director Luis Bunuel, who was famous for his earlier surrealist film, *Un Chien Andelou.*

Deneuve worked steadily throughout the 1970s. She earned her first Cesar nomination, the French Academy Award, in 1976 for her performance in *The Savage.* From 1982 to 1999, she was nominated for the Cesar nine times for Best Actress. The films she was nominated for include *Hotels des Ameriques, Agent Trouble, A Strange Place to Meet, My Favorite Season, The Thieves,* and *Place Vendome.* Besides acting she modeled frequently, appearing as the face of Chanel No. 5 perfume in the United States from 1969–77. With her as the representative of the perfume, Chanel No. 5 sold more bottles in eight years than it had sold in the previous 20. In the 1980s, Deneuve launched her own perfume through Avon. In 1985, the French Ministry of Culture acknowledged Deneuve's inspirational beauty by selecting her to be the model for Marianne, symbol of the French republic. As Marianne, Deneuve's face appeared on stamps and coins throughout France, replacing the previous model, the sexy French star, Brigitte Bardot.

Deneuve's beauty wasn't only used as an enticement to buy perfume or inspire loyalty among the French. Designer Yves Saint Laurent met Deneuve on the set of *Belle de Jour* and immediately made her his lifelong muse. For more than 20 years, since they first worked together, Laurent has designed clothes for Deneuve. He told David Hutchings of *InStyle,* "She's a radiant beauty who chooses her clothes admirably so they correspond with her personality." In 2002, Saint Laurent announced his retirement from the fashion industry. The last item of clothing ever stitched at his headquarters in Paris, France, was a gold–embroidered black wool jacket that was given to Deneuve.

Early in her career, Deneuve's personal life was filled with drama and tragedy. When she was 17, she met director Roger Vadim when he was directing her in the film *Vice and Virtue*. Vadim was known for discovering and marrying Brigitte Bardot. His other relationships included such '70s beauties as Jane Fonda and Angie Dickinson. Deneuve moved out of her childhood home to live with Vadim. In 1963, their son Christian was born.

In 1965, she married British photographer, David Bailey. The two met through Polanski while they were filming *Repulsion*. Polanski convinced Bailey to shoot a series of photographs of Deneuve for the men's magazine *Playboy* to promote the film. Bailey, who is famous for his portraits of rock stars, actors, and models, particularly during the late '60s, invited his friend Mick Jagger to be the best man at their wedding. Deneuve shocked many by wearing a black dress instead of the traditional white gown.

By 1971, Deneuve had become involved with Italian actor Marcello Mastroianni, who was also married. Bailey and Deneuve divorced in 1972. In May of that year Deneuve had her second child, a daughter named Chiara, fathered by Mastroianni. Speaking of her children, Deneuve noted to Bob Thompson of the *Toronto Sun*, "I thought I would stop worrying about my children, but I worry about them more now that they are grown up. I always thought there would be an age when I wouldn't worry anymore, but there isn't."

The great tragedy of Deneuve's life was the death of her sister, Françoise Dorléac, at age 25. Despite having chosen the same career, Deneuve claims that they were not competitive. Dorléac's outgoing personality contrasted and complemented Deneuve's more reserved personality. Deneuve told Stephen Schaefer of the *Boston Herald*, "We were never rivals because we were so different, she was much more the extrovert, the redhead." In 1967, the two starred in the follow–up film to *The Umbrellas of Cherbourg*, *The Young Girls of Rochefort*. The film had a lighter theme and featured the sisters in the starring roles as musically inclined twins. Before the release of the film in 1968, Dorléac was killed in a car accident. Speaking to the *Boston Herald*'s Schaefer, Deneuve explained her family's reaction to Dorléac's death, "It was a very painful, silent thing in my family for a very long time." Thirty years after her sister's death, Deneuve hosted a French television special

about her. She credits the show with helping her to come to terms with her sister's death. In particular, she related to Schaefer the effect watching *The Young Girls of Rochefort* had upon her: "It's a mixture of everything, but that fact that it's a film and we're there laughing and happy, when you see it, it's like a perfume—something comes back."

While she created some memorable and award–winning roles during the '70s and '80s, Deneuve's work in the 1990s has consistently earned recognition and accolades. In 1992, Deneuve's performance in the historical drama *Indochine* earned her an Academy Award nomination for Best Actress. In the film, she played Eliane Devries, a French rubber tree plantation owner who must come to terms with her adopted Vietnamese daughter's love affair as well as the increasing uselessness of colonialism in a nation working toward independence. Although she did not win the award, the film did receive an Academy Award for Best Foreign Film.

Other notable films of hers from the '90s include *My Favorite Season, The Convent*, and *Thieves*. In 1998, Deneuve earned a Best Actress nomination for her role in *Place Vendome*. She played the alcoholic wife of a diamond merchant. When he commits suicide she is forced to overcome her addiction and deal with her past. Kevin Thomas wrote of her performance in the *Los Angeles Times*: "This is a rich, dense film, its bits and pieces gradually coming together with clarity and allowing the timelessly beautiful Deneuve the range and depth, subtleties and nuances, she demands of her roles and fulfills so glowingly."

Deneuve has worked consistently in French cinema but has rarely ventured to Hollywood to make films. She starred opposite Burt Reynolds in 1975's *Hustle*. In 1981 she starred in the vampire film *The Hunger* with David Bowie and Susan Sarandon. While not an award–winning movie, the film has become a cult favorite. Her other American films have been few and far between. One reason for this is that Deneuve is very selective of the films in which she appears. She explained to Paul Fischer of *Film Monthly*, "I'm not going to do a film in America that I would refuse to do in France." She also has issues with how films and celebrity are made in America. She believes that too many films that come out of Hollywood rely on technology rather than creating interesting characters or using good acting technique. She told Jane Barrett of the *Manilla Times* that with all the special effects, "[I]t seems the soul has been taken out of things."

She also values her privacy and believes that Hollywood enforces a lifestyle she's not interested in. In France she feels she can live her life normally because actors are not treated like stars and don't need all the accoutrements, including bodyguards. France also has stricter rules about the use of a celebrity's image, which makes it easier for Deneuve to control her exposure to the public. When she does interviews she does not allow photographs. She refuses most television invitations unless the show is scripted beforehand. She explained her opinion about television to Laurence Chollet of the *Record*, "In France, I see the television as something that eats you.... It demands things, and it is never enough if you start to respond to the demand. There is no limit. And I find that inhuman."

When Deneuve chooses a role it is because she wants to work with a particular director or actor, or because the script intrigues her. One thing she is sure to avoid is any film that would use her for her persona rather than engaging her acting skills. She explained to *Film Monthly*'s Fischer, "I want to at least give the impression that I'm doing something I haven't done before. I want to feel endangered and scared by a film." She is also interested in portraying characters that are in step with her age. While there are limited opportunities for mature actresses in Hollywood, Deneuve has been able to continue working in the French cinema in challenging roles that reflect her maturity as an actress and with regard to her age. She told Nicole Winfield of the Associated Press, "I don't want to grow older than I am, but I don't want to try to be very resistant to reality either. I want to be in harmony with my image and what I feel about my age."

With an average of two films per year, Deneuve has worked with some of the world's best directors. The impressive list includes Jacques Demy, who directed *The Umbrellas of Cherbourg*, and the famed New Wave director Francois Truffaut, whom she worked with in the award–winning *The Last Metro*.

Deneuve has more directors on her list, including several American directors such as Quentin Tarantino, Martin Scorsese, and Jonathan Demme. Her goal with regard to her career is to continue to create meaningful characters that entertain. In addition to that, she tries to combine her work so that it fits in easily with her life. She views her work as an important part of living. She explained to Laurence Challet of the *Record*, "There are a lot of people I would like to work with, too. And that's the thing that keeps me alive."

Sources

Periodicals

Associated Press, December 20, 1996.
Boston Herald, September 30, 1998, p. 45.
InStyle, October 2000, pp. 304–12.
Los Angeles Times, December 22, 2000.
Record (Bergen County, New Jersey), March 30, 1998, p. Y1.
Star–Ledger (Newark, New Jersey), April 14, 1996, p. 1.
Toronto Sun, July 13, 1995.

Online

"Catherine Deneuve bemoans focus on special effects," *The Manilla Times*, http://www.manilatimes.net/national/2002/sept/05/enter/20020905ent2.html (October 17, 2002).
"Catherine Deneuve," IMDB.com, http://us.imdb.com/Name?Deneuve,+Catherine (December 20, 2002).
"Catherine the Great," *Film Monthly*, http://www.filmmonthly.com/Profiles/Articles/CDeneuve/CDeueuve.html (October 17, 2002).

—Eve M. B. Hermann

John M. Devine

Chief Financial Officer for General Motors

Born John Martin Devine, May 13, 1944, in Pittsburgh, PA; son of John Patrick (a salesperson) and Camilla (Durkin) Devine; married Patricia McGee; children: Sean, Bridget. *Education:* Duquesne University, B.S., 1967; University of Michigan, M.B.A., 1972.

Addresses: *Office*—General Motors Corp., 300 Renaissance Ctr., Detroit, MI 48265–3000.

Career

Began career at Ford Motor Company, Dearborn, MI, as analyst in finance department, 1967; held various positions until 1980; controller for product development for Ford of Europe, 1981–83; staff director of finance, Ford of Asia, 1983–85; vice president for Pacific operations, Ford Asia, 1985–86; executive director for Pacific business development Ford Asia, 1986–87; controller for truck operations, Ford U.S., 1987; First Nationwide Bank (a division of Ford Motor Company), San Francisco, CA, vice chairman and chief executive officer, 1988–91, president, 1991–94; chief financial officer and controller for Ford Motor Co., 1994–99, and group vice-president and chief financial officer, 1995–99; Fluid Ventures LLC, San Francisco, chief executive officer, 1999–2000; General Motors Corporation, Detroit, MI, chief financial officer, 2000—.

Sidelights

Automotive–industry analysts were stunned when General Motors, the world's largest carmaker, announced that retired Ford Motor Company executive John M. Devine would become the company's newest chief financial officer. Devine's first day on the job, in January of 2001, came at a time of change for General Motors (GM), as it struggled to maintain a slipping share of the domestic auto market and seemed perpetually stymied in its bid to arouse consumer excitement in its models. Within a year, Devine and other top GM executives were heralded by business journalists for effecting a turnaround at the Detroit company that was deemed nothing short of miraculous. Though to his wife Devine had seemed happy in his early retirement, he later said the GM offer was one he found hard to resist. "You don't get too many opportunities to be part of significant changes at one of the world's largest companies," he told *Business Week* writer David Welch.

Born in 1944, Devine grew in Pittsburgh, Pennsylvania, where his father worked as a sales representative for the Sunshine Biscuit Company. He graduated from Duquesne University with an economics degree in 1967 and was hired by Ford as financial analyst that same year. He spent the next five years at its Dearborn headquarters, while taking classes to earn a graduate business degree from the University of Michigan in his spare time. At one point, Devine tired of the corporate grind, attempted to resign so that he and his wife could take a cross-country trip in a motor home. Instead, his Ford bosses granted him a year–long sabbatical.

Returning to Ford's "Glass House" headquarters, Devine quickly advanced through the ranks of the company's finance department. In 1981, he was transferred to London to serve as controller for product development at Ford's European division, and spent the next few years in various other posts around the world, including staff director of finance for Ford Asia, and executive director for the company's Pacific business development. In 1987, he and his family returned to Dearborn when Ford made him controller for its truck operations in the United States. Devine already had a reputation within the company for his shrewd financial judgment calls, and within a year he was tapped to take over First Nationwide Bank, a Ford banking subsidiary in San Francisco. He restructured the money–losing institution and then oversaw its sale, at a profit, in 1994.

Later that year Devine was again recalled to Dearborn and named Ford's chief financial officer and controller. The company was desperately trying to reorganize itself and capture a greater share of the global auto market, and Devine's advancement was viewed as portent of a new era for the oldest of the three United States automakers. "Positively nomadic by Detroit standards, Devine's eclectic global background exemplifies the flexibility and range of training that large, global companies now increasingly require of CFOs," explained *Institutional Investor* writer Ida Picker.

Devine's name was often mentioned as a possible successor to Ford CEO Alex Trotman, and in 1995 he was made a group vice–president as well. But Trotman was replaced by Jacques Nasser, and Devine announced his own retirement, at the age of just 55, in October of 1999. He and his wife had planned to spend more time at their Southern California vacation home, but instead Devine took a job as CEO of an e–business firm in San Francisco.

An executive search firm ventured Devine's name to GM executives in late 2000 when the company was searching for a replacement for ousted CFO Michael Losh. GM CEO G. Richard "Rick" Wagoner, known as somewhat of a maverick among Detroit's automotive–executive cadre, announced that the former Ford veteran would be joining GM effective January 1, 2001. "Because of his intimate knowledge of the industry, he will be able to contribute immediately," *Financial Times* writer Nikki Tait quoted Wagoner as saying at the time.

Devine's first duty was to increase value of the GM stock price for shareholders, but it was a job that also gave him, as a finance executive, an unusually high level of input into product development as well. Much–needed revenue increases at the company, which had consistently lost market share for the past 38 years, were dependent on the company's ability to produce new and exciting cars and trucks. "I feel very passionate about getting the products right," Devine told Welch in the *Business Week* interview after three months on the job.

Some unexpected changes at GM over the next year helped Devine and a new executive team turn the automaker around. In August of 2001 the company hired retired Chrysler executive Robert Lutz to serve as vice chair and head of product development. Known for his outspoken manner and daredevil hobbies, Lutz was widely credited with rescuing Chrysler in 1990s. Later in 2001, GM announced interest–free financing deals for certain makes, and by the end of the year was the sole domestic carmaker to post a profit. Early in 2002, Devine announced that GM was raising its earnings estimate for the first quarter, after continued strong sales and a corresponding improvement in its manufacturing costs per vehicle. Moreover, his cordial relationship with Wall Street—unlike that of his predecessor Losh—was credited with helping bring a healthy 50 percent rise in GM's price per share over the past six months.

Devine was GM's highest paid executive in 2001, with a total salary and bonus package of $4.3 million. The father of two, Devine professes a penchant for vintage GM models like the Corvette, but also stows two Porsche sports cars in his home garage. Industry analysts believe he may be next in line for the job of chief operating officer at GM. He remains sanguine about his rise to the highest echelons of American business, remembering when he was ready to resign from Ford at the age of 30. "I never was very good at career planning," he admitted in the interview with Picker for *Institutional Investor*. "I was too busy dealing with what was on my plate."

Sources

Automotive News, May 24, 1999, p. 4; December 18, 2000, p. 6; March 26, 2001, p. 16; April 22, 2002, p. 2.
BusinessWeek, April 2, 2001, p. 82.
Detroit News, October 16, 2002, p. 1.
Financial Times, December 14, 2000, p. 34.
Fortune, April 1, 2002, p. 68.
Institutional Investor, March 1995, p. 55.
New York Times, February 26, 2002, p. C1.
San Francisco Business Times, February 8, 1991, p. 12.

—*Carol Brennan*

Bruce Downey

Chairman and Chief Executive Officer of Barr Laboratories

Born November 12, 1947, in Athens, OH; married Deborah, 1984; children: one son, one daughter. *Education*—Miami University, B.A. in economics, 1969; law degree, Ohio State University College of Law, 1973.

Addresses: *Office*—Barr Laboratories, 2 Quaker Rd., Pomona, NY 10970–0519.

Career

Prosecutor, U.S. Department of Justice, 1970s; moved to the legal staff of the U.S. Department of Energy; partner, Bishop, Cook, Purcell and Reynolds, Washington D.C., 1981–90; firm merged into Winston & Strawn, 1990–93; outside attorney, Barr Laboratories, 1991; president and chief operating officer, Barr Laboratories, 1993; chairman and chief executive officer, Barr Laboratories, 1994—.

Sidelights

With nearly two decades of legal experience, it really shouldn't have come as any surprise that Bruce Downey would incorporate litigation as a fundamental element of his strategy for leading generic drugmaker Barr Laboratories Inc. to financial success. And that strategy has proved phenomenally successful for Barr, which in fiscal 2002, ending June 30, 2002, more than doubled its sales to nearly $1.2 billion, up from $509.7 million in fiscal 2001 and $482.3 million in fiscal 2000. Under Downey's leadership, Barr's net income climbed in fiscal 2002 to $212.2 million, a sharp increase from profits of $62.5 million in fiscal 2001 and $42.3 million in fiscal 2000.

In one of his most notable victories, Downey led Barr's lengthy legal battle with the giant Eli Lilly & Co. pharmaceutical company, owner of the patent on the popular antidepressant Prozac. That fight ended in victory for Barr in the summer of 2001, when the small but aggressive generic pharmaceuticals manufacturer won the exclusive right to market fluoxetine, a generic version of Prozac, for the next six months. Barr's exclusive marketing period for fluoxetine, which gave the company's sales a much–needed shot in the arm, began on August 2, 2001. Although Barr's exclusivity on fluoxetine ended in early 2002, the sales spurt it provided helped the company to double its sales for fiscal 2002.

Although the bulk of Barr's business comes from the sale of generic drugs, Downey has utilized merger as a strategy to steer the company into the development of proprietary products. Only a couple of months before Barr won its victory in the Prozac case, Downey engineered a $450 million stock deal to acquire Duramed Pharmaceuticals, which specializes in women's health products. A year later Barr acquired key assets of Enhance Pharmaceuticals Inc., which has developed a novel vaginal drug delivery system that Downey believes "presents an opportunity to expand Barr's female healthcare franchise," according to a company news release. The acquisition of Duramed not only gave Barr some new products for its proprietary line but beefed up the company's sales force, which Downey hopes to utilize in the marketing of the company's other proprietary products.

Born in Athens, Ohio, on November 12, 1947, Downey grew up on a 200–acre farm in the rural countryside of southeastern Ohio. Even as a teenager, there were signs of the entrepreneurial spirit that would eventually bring Downey to the helm of one of the country's leading generic drugmakers. Looking back on his early money–making enterprises, Downey told *BusinessWeek*, "I was a hustler." As a boy, he maintained a trap line of about 80 traps along the nearby Hocking River. Downey would skin the muskrats he caught in the traps in the family garage and then sell the harvested pelts for approximately $3 each. He showed a real spark of entrepreneurialism in the early 1960s when the river overflowed in Athens, flooding many of the city's streets. Downey borrowed his father's boat and earned a couple of hundred dollars ferrying stranded college students from home to campus and back.

After his graduation from high school, Downey studied economics at Miami University in Athens, Ohio, earning his bachelor's degree in 1969. He next studied law at the College of Law of Ohio State University in Columbus, from which he received his law degree in 1973. Fresh out of college, Downey spent the next few years working as a prosecutor for the Justice Department. He specialized in civil rights litigation. He later joined the legal staff at the U.S. Department of Energy. However, by the early 1980s Downey had decided to leave government service and get into private practice. He joined the prestigious Washington, D.C., law firm of Bishop, Cook, Purcell and Reynolds, which in 1990 merged into Winston & Strawn.

It was while working as a partner at Winston & Strawn that Downey first became involved with Barr Labs. The small generic drugmaker, founded in 1970 and based in Pomona, New York, brought in Downey as an outside attorney in its fight with the Food and Drug Administration (FDA). Barr, according to the FDA, had serious problems in its manufacturing procedures, particularly in the realm of quality control. The government agency wanted to shut Barr down. Downey came up with a unique strategy, suing the FDA on the grounds that its move against Barr were without legal justification. Although in the end, Barr was forced to adopt many of the manufacturing reforms sought by the FDA, it did manage to remain in operation, thanks in large part to its lawyer. Of his initial battle with FDA on behalf of Barr, Downey told Bethany McLean of *Fortune*, "We fought 'em to a standstill."

Impressed by Downey's performance as an outside consultant, Barr Labs in January of 1993 named him president and chief operating officer. Thirteen months later he moved up to chairman and chief executive officer upon the retirement of Edwin A. Cohen, Barr's founder. Under Downey, the company has pursued a three–point strategy: the development and marketing of proprietary products, the development and marketing of generic pharmaceuticals that have one or more barriers to entry, and the development of a generic versions of select brand pharmaceuticals, the patents for which Barr believes are invalid, unenforceable, or not infringed by Barr's product. It is in this third area of corporate strategy that Downey's mark is seen most clearly.

Downey has led attacks on the patents of a number of pharmaceutical products, often going head to head with some of the industry's biggest players. He admits he gets a certain amount of satisfaction from these legal showdowns, telling Amy Barrett of *BusinessWeek:* "You have to either be prepared to do battle with the people who want to do you in, or whine about it. We aren't in the whining category."

The success of Downey's leadership at Barr is impressive. Barr's revenues have skyrocketed—more than sextupling since Downey came on board—to almost $1.2 billion in fiscal 2002. The company's surge in profits is equally eye–opening, climbing from less than $10 million to $212 million in fiscal 2002. The key difference between Barr and its competitors in the generic drug business is Barr's raw aggressiveness in pursuing the patents of the giants of the pharmaceutical industry. These giants maintain legions of lobbyists in the nation's capital; Barr, however, is the only generic drug producer to have a legislative office in Washington. As CIBC security analyst Elliott Wilbur told *Fortune*'s McLean, "There's a perception that Bruce Downey stays up late at night searching the patent lists." Although Downey himself makes no claim to expertise in patent law, Barr does employ a staff of outside patent attorneys to do just that. In this connection, according to McLean, Downey told an investment conference: "We see no end to the patent–challenge opportunities as long as branded firms continue to get patents. I look at it as them generating business opportunities for Barr."

In his years at the helm of Barr Labs, Downey has led the company in battle against the patent claims of such pharmaceutical giants as Bayer and AstraZeneca. Barr's litigation against Bayer ended in a settlement that calls for the German drugmaker to sell Cipro—an antibiotic that is used in the treatment of anthrax and many other bacterial infections and generates United States annual sales of about $1 billion—to Barr, which would resell the drug, or pay Barr $30 million a year. Although Bayer has chosen thus far to pay Barr the $30 million annually, another part of the settlement will force it to begin selling Cipro to Barr six months before the expiration of its patent in December of 2003. Barr's suit against AstraZeneca also resulted in a settlement, which requires the larger company to sell Barr the cancer drug tamoxifen, which Barr then markets at a discount of 15 percent. Barr hasn't won all its patent challenges, although its losses have been few. One such loss came in litigation against GlaxoSmithKline and involved the AIDS drug Retrovir.

Although Downey's patent challenges have generated a lot of negative criticism and even prompted the Federal Trade Commission to announce in April of 2001 an investigation into the company's practices, none of it seems to ruffle Downey's feathers. "You can settle murder one," Downey told *Fortune*'s McLean. "Why should you have to fight a patent battle to the death?"

As competition in the generic drug market intensifies, Downey realizes that it's becoming increasingly difficult to generate strong revenue growth in this arena alone. For that reason Barr Labs has been focusing increasing attention on the development of proprietary products since 1997. The company took a major step forward in that direction in January of 2000 when it founded Barr Research. The company's research arm, headquartered in Philadelphia and led by Carole Ben–Maimon, M.D., has been charged with the continuing development of Barr's proprietary product strategies and the expansion of its proprietary product activities through the successful development of New Drug Application (NDA) products. Thus far the company's proprietary product activities have focused on the areas of cancer agents, female healthcare products (including oral contraceptives and hormone replacement therapy), and anti–infective/anti–viral products.

Under Downey's direction, Barr Labs now markets three proprietary products: Cenestin, Trexall, and ViaSpan. Cenestin, acquired as part of Barr's 2001 acquisition of Duramed, is the market's only slow–release, plant–derived synthetic conjugated estrogens product with no animal precursors. Trexall is the company's trade name for its 5mg, 7.5mg, 10mg, and 15mg tablets used in the treatment of some cancers, severe psoriasis, and adult rheumatoid arthritis. ViaSpan is a solution used for hypothermic flushing and storage of organs, including kidney, liver, and pancreas at the time of their removal from the donor in preparation for storage, transportation, and eventual transplantation into a recipient. Barr began producing ViaSpan in August of 2000 under a license granted by DuPont Pharmaceuticals, which is now part of Bristol–Myers Squibb. Other proprietary products that are being developed by Barr include an adenovirus vaccine, additions to its Cenestin product line, an extended regimen oral contraceptive called SEASONALE, vaginal ring products, and DP3 oral contraceptive.

Barr's exclusive right to market fluoxetine, a generic version of Prozac, for six months during fiscal 2002 played a major role in the company's spectacular financial showing during that period. In fact, fiscal 2002 sales of fluoxetine totaled almost $368 million, accounting for more than a quarter of the company's total revenue for the year. Addressing analysts and investors in a conference call after the earnings announcement, Downey said, "We did have a terrific quarter and a terrific year," according to Lewis Krauskopf, staff writer for the *Record*. Since the exclusive fluoxetine marketing arrangement ended in February of 2002, Downey predicted that Barr Labs anticipated a decline in overall product sales during fiscal 2003.

Downey and his wife, Deborah, who married in 1984, have two children, a son and a daughter. One of Downey's biggest passions is to go on an annual quail hunt. And he's not forgotten his roots growing up as a boy on an Ohio farm. In fact, he told *BusinessWeek*'s Amy Barrett that he hopes someday to buy the farmhouse in which he grew up from its current owners.

Sources

Periodicals

BusinessWeek, October 1, 2001, p. 76.
Fortune, August 13, 2001, p. 118.
Money, October 2002, p. 41.
PRNewswire, June 6, 2002.
Record (Bergen County, NJ), August 15, 2002.
USA Today, June 6, 2002, p. 2A.

Transcripts

CNBC/Dow Jones Business Video, August 14, 2002.

—*Don Amerman*

Henry Duarte

Fashion designer

Born c. 1963, in Torrance, CA; son of Henry (a longshoreman) and Irene (a homemaker) Duarte; married Daina Jackson, c. 1987; children: Julian. *Education:* Attended Los Angeles Fashion Institute of Design and Merchandising and Otis College of Art and Design.

Addresses: *Office*—Henry Duarte, 7977 Melrose Ave., Los Angeles, CA 90046.

Career

Started Sqwear fashion line with William Berenck, 1986; first exhibition at California Mart, 1987; makes first pair of leather pants for rock musician Lenny Kravitz, 1991; partners with Mink Vox and opens a store on Sunset Plaza, 1998; walks away from Mink Vox partnership, loses rights to name, designs singer Nikka Costa's Polaroid i–Zone outfit for MTV Video Music Awards, 2001; opens his own boutique on Melrose Avenue, 2002; exhibitor at Threads ... That Rock the World Trade Show and Conference, 2003.

Awards: Woolmark Cutting Edge Award, 1992; Fashion Windows Award for Best Lowriders, 2001.

Sidelights

With 17 years in the fashion industry, Henry Duarte has had a significant influence on the look and style of many of rock and roll's hitmakers. Duarte's clothes are de rigueur for relative new-comers like Sheryl Crow and Lenny Kravitz as well as rock legends like Neil Young, Bob Dylan, and Aerosmith's Steven Tyler. He outfits the stars personally for their tours, awards ceremonies, and everyday living in deerskin lace–up pants and leather coats with price tags often reaching the $3,000 mark. The *Australian*'s Sharon Krum described his style: "His design aesthetic is Jim Morrison meets California surfer dude meets Carnaby Street, all done in the softest leather."

Born around 1963 in Torrance, California, Duarte is the only son of Henry and Irene Duarte. Duarte's father worked as a longshoreman until his retirement, and his mother was a homemaker. He grew up surfing, listening to rock and roll, and indulging in his love for fashion. When he wasn't surfing, he was listening to albums imagining his idols onstage. He described such a scene to Mary Melton of the *Los Angeles Times:* "I'd be listening to Robert Plant [of Led Zeppelin], imagining this guy in these really tight jeans, a shirt halfway out but unbuttoned.... Back then, you didn't look like the audience.... You looked like a rock star." He would draw inspiration for his later designs not only from the early 1970s look made popular by the Doors's singer Jim Morrison but also the appliqued and well–worn jeans he found in resale shops.

When he graduated from high school, Duarte took classes at a local junior college but eventually dropped out. He focused most of his energy on surfing at Hermosa Beach until coming to the conclusion that he wanted to go into fashion design. At age 23, he began taking classes at the Otis College of Art and Design as well as Los Angeles's Fashion Institute of Design and Merchandising.

Right away he started designing surf trunks. In 1986, he and a fellow surfer, William Berenck, formed Sqwear. Their designs ranged from sportswear to what Duarte called "rock and roll suits" in a *People* article. Duarte's timing could not have been more perfect. His designs had a special flare and style that appealed to the eye, making them popular with pop stars in the new arena of music video production. Duarte did not even know that his clothes were being used this way until he saw them by accident in a video. He told *People,* "That's how I discovered that celebrities were wearing my clothes."

From then on, Duarte's fashions were in demand. Music stars like Janet Jackson and Bobby Brown were asking him to fulfill their fashion desires. Sqwear was even responsible for decking out the all–boy group New Kids on the Block. He explained to David Wharton of the *Los Angeles Times,* "Once you met one rock guy, he told another rock guy who told a stylist who told a producer…. The next day, a new client walked in the door." In 1991, Duarte went on tour with Kravitz, executing one–of–a–kind designs while on the road. He made his first pair of leather pants during this time, pants that have become a trademark of Duarte's fashion sense.

As Sqwear, Duarte and Berenck worked together until 1990. Berenck left to form his own company, designing his own line of high fashion suits called William B. They had owned a shop on Beverly Boulevard; with the split, Duarte needed a new venue to show his wares. He partnered with his wife, Daina Jackson, and began focusing on his trendsetting designs. For several years afterward, Duarte worked out of a three–story house he rented with Jackson. The basement held sewing machines, the first and second floors were showrooms, and the third floor was their living area. The house was also home to frequent parties hosted by Duarte, who not only designed for the rock and roll lifestyle, but also lived it.

In 1998, Duarte formed a partnership with a company called Mink Vox and opened a store in Sunset Plaza—the cafe and boutique district of Sunset Boulevard. From his tony new boutique, Duarte continued to work on custom orders. His designs were now in demand from movie stars like Meg Ryan and Gwyneth Paltrow and fashion models like Naomi Campbell. The store became a combination retail store, fitting room, and art gallery. As a retail store, the shop offered racks of items to those willing to pay anywhere from $185 for denim jeans to $550 for leather pants and $1,200 for coats. As a custom fitting room, well–heeled stars like Tyler could lay down more than $3,000 for handmade, custom–designed, deerskin pants. When Tyler won the VH1/Vogue Fashion Award for rock style in 2002, he accepted the award by giving thanks to Duarte. As an art gallery, Duarte collaborated with Los Angeles art curator Seth Kaufman who helped set up site–specific installations created by local artists every couple of months.

Eventually Duarte found that working as an employee of Mink Vox created tension for the free–spirited and self–directed fashion designer. He explained to Rose Apodaca Jones of *WWD,* "I just decided this isn't really my future. I need to open my own store, own my own future." He walked out on his partnership with Mink Vox in February of 2001. Unfortunately, Duarte's plan for independence hit a roadblock.

When he left Mink Vox he neglected to secure the rights to his name, which had been trademarked by the other partners involved who comprised Mink Vox. The store Duarte left behind continued to operate, but with a different designer putting out clothes similar to his designs and carrying a nametag that sported the Henry Duarte name in addition to Mink Vox. Four months after his walkout, Mink Vox filed a civil complaint against Duarte and Jackson stating trademark infringement. According to Mink Vox, Duarte cannot use any part of the trademarked name to market clothing or any other fashion products.

Undeterred, Duarte set out to open his own shop on Melrose Avenue. Partnering once again with his wife as well as a former sales agent, Duarte started working behind blacked–out windows and locked doors at his Melrose Avenue store. After several postponements, the sleek new store opened in early November of 2002. While he often states that he is not interested in marketing his brand and becoming a major fashion house, his sales for 2002 were expected to reach the $2 million mark.

Duarte approaches his designs like an artist, creating a collision of fashion and art that thrives on his excessive attention to the details of his designs. Ever since he made that first pair of leather pants for Kravitz, Duarte has been perfecting the design and translating it into other fabrics, particularly denim. He told the *Australian*'s Krum, "Chanel has her jacket and I have my pant. The Henry Duarte pant. Designers work a lifetime to create a signature piece. And this is mine." His signature piece involves hip–hugger jeans that contain 84 pieces of denim which are tinted to achieve Duarte's particular faded look. The buckles, rivets, and grommets for his jeans are all hammered by hand. He explained to Krum, "I don't make more than 150 pairs a year.... To get the pants to look the way I want, there is no other way to do this."

Despite being labor intensive, Duarte has managed to manufacture enough of his designs that his line is represented all over the world. His clothes, shoes, and jewelry are sold in New York City at Barneys New York and Jeffrey, in Chicago at Ultimo, in Paris at Colette, and in Boston at Louis Boston. It's been hard for Duarte to let go of the control of every creation. His first attempt to sell clothes wholesale, back in 1991, only lasted two years before his output could no longer match the orders he was receiving. Even as his designs begin to make it into the retail side of the market, Duarte insisted to *WWD*'s Jones, "I'm not interested in putting out basic jeans."

In 2001, one of Duarte's designs doubled as a work of art and commercialism. He partnered with Polaroid to create an outfit for singer Nikka Costa, who was nominated for a best new artist award at the MTV Video Music Awards that year. The suede and knit halter–dress he designed was decorated with i–Zone photos. In a statement to PR Newswire, Duarte described the design as his "first creative collaboration of [his] career. Our efforts have resulted in a fusion of fashion, fun and photography—and the synergy between us is just plain cool."

Duarte invests a lot of energy and passion in making his clothes, but there is a part of him that has not outgrown his surfer roots. He and Jackson still manage to hit the waves often. Once he became old enough, their son, Julian, began joining them; he received his first surfboard when he was eight years old. As Duarte explained to *People*, "My main goal is to go back to that surfing life." In fact, Duarte was still deeply involved in surfing when he met Jackson at an after–hours bar. The two were married around 1987, and have worked together ever since developing his career and designs. His home doubles as his studio with its doors wide open to a rock and roll who's who visiting at all hours of the day and night to talk music and fashion.

If there is one thing from which Duarte derives the most inspiration, it is music. He explained to Melton in the *Los Angeles Times*, "My whole fashion is driven from music." Whether he is hanging out with rock stars or listening to some obscure band from the 1960s, Duarte is always trying to find ways to translate the music he loves into his designs. He told Elizabeth Kaye of *Los Angeles Magazine* how hearing songs he really likes inspires him: "That's so great. How can I do the same kind of thing in clothing?" What he's doing in his studio doesn't seem much different than what he used to do in his bedroom when he was a teenager, imagining the look of the band as he listened to their music.

Duarte has been described as an artist by ardent fans such as actress Rosanna Arquette. Kaye characterized him as "an arts and crafts type gone Hollywood." Others cite his surfing days as a way to define him. When it comes down to it, Duarte seems to have found his own perfect description of his style and who he is. He told Wharton in the *Los Angeles Times*, "You know, the French designers say they are really French. Ralph Lauren has the WASP thing and Tommy Hilfiger has the Connecticut look. Well, I'm fourth–generation Californian. I'm really Californian."

Sources

Artweek, March 1999, p. 5.
Australian (Sydney, Australia), December 14, 2001, p. 19.
Harper's Bazaar, October 2000, p. 172.
Los Angeles Magazine, April 2002, p. 42.
Los Angeles Times, February 16, 1990, p. E10; February 15, 1998, p. 12; June 3, 2001, p. 26.
People, August 26, 2002, pp. 93–94.
WWD, April 23, 2001, p. 12; November 27, 2002, p. 11.

—Eve M. B. Hermann

Eduardo Duhalde

AP/Wide World Photos

President of Argentina

Born October 5, 1941, in Lomas de Zamora, Argentina; son of Hijo de Tomas Duhalde and Maria Esther Maldonado; married Hilda Beatriz Gonzalez; children: Juliana, Analía, María Eva, Agustina, Tomas. *Education:* University of Buenos Aires, J.D., 1970.

Addresses: *Office*—Office of Vice President, Buenos Aires, Argentina. *Website*—Eduardo Duhalde Official Presidential Website: http://www.presidencia.gov.ar.

Career

Professor of economics at the University of Lomas de Zamora prior to entering politics; elected to Lomas de Zamora city council, 1971; became mayor of Lomas de Zamora, 1983; elected to Argentina's National Congress, 1987; became vice–president of Argentina, 1989; left vice–presidency, 1991; governor of Buenos Aires, 1991–99; represented Buenos Aires in national Senate, 2001; assumed presidency, 2002.

Sidelights

On January 2, 2002, Eduardo Duhalde became the fifth president to lead Argentina in just two weeks. The sudden ascendancy for this longtime member of the Partido Justicialista–Peronista (PJ), or Peron Party, occurred as a result of political and economic turmoil that reached a crisis point when Latin America's third largest economy neared collapse. Duhalde had a daunting task ahead of him,

and won praise for avoiding partisan overtones in his first speech. "We Peronists are part of the problem," *New York Times* correspondent Larry Rohter quoted him as saying, "just like all the others who have governed this country, civilian and military."

Duhalde was born on October 5, 1941, and raised in Lomas de Zamora, one of the sprawling suburbs of Argentina's capital, Buenos Aires, where Juan Peron's socialist–spirited party first gained widespread support in that decade. Duhalde came from a working–class family, of whose ilk benefited from Peron's popular programs; indeed, changes made by Peron's government enabled Duhalde to study law at the university for free. In 1971, at the age of 30, he was elected to the Lomas de Zamora city council, his first political office. He eventually became mayor of the city. In 1987, Duhalde ran for and won a seat in the lower house of Argentina's Congress. Two years later, he was invited to become the running mate of Carlos Saul Menem, whose PJ ticket won that presidential election.

Duhalde spent two years as Menem's vice president, but their ideology began to differ, and they eventually became political enemies. Menem reversed many of the Peronist–type social programs that had benefited Argentina's poor and working class for many years. In 1991 he made a significant decision to tie the exchange rate of Argentina's peso to that of the United States dollar. The United States and International Monetary Fund (IMF) had long urged such a change as a way to combat Argentina's legendary hyperinflation. Menem's government also instituted a program of free–market reforms, but over the next decade Argentina struggled to stay solvent, and regularly received emergency–aid loans from the IMF.

Meanwhile, Duhalde ran for and won the governorship of Buenos Aires Province in 1991. He served in this position for the next eight years, and implemented many popular social–service programs during that time. Duhalde won praise for forging cooperation among the province's feuding political parties and for taking a strong stand against police corruption and brutality. His critics, however, claimed that the governor was bankrupting the province with his generous social–service expenditures. In 1999, Duhalde stepped down as governor to run for the presidency of Argentina, but lost to Fernando de la Rua.

Over the next two years, Argentina's public debt swelled to $141 billion—much of it in foreign loans. Attempts to adhere to a repayment schedule forced the government to economize under an austerity program urged by the IMF, and unemployment rose to 18 percent. Some worried that the dollar–peso peg was the culprit for the economic woes, and that the de la Rua government would soon suspend the monetary policy. This would likely cause the peso's value to plummet immediately. As fears over savings grew, many Argentines began exchanging pesos for dollars, and reserves in Argentina's Central Bank dropped precipitously throughout 2001.

In late 2001, Duhalde won a seat in Argentina's upper house, the Senate, by a large margin of votes. In early December, the IMF refused to disburse a loan of $1.3 billion, which plunged the national treasury into crisis. On December 3, the government announced a limit on bank withdrawals to $1,000 a month. The decree angered the country's middle class, and on December 13 a 24–hour strike took place. From there followed riots and protests, and a December 17 government announcement of more spending cuts incited a new wave of rioting that included the looting of shops and supermarkets. By December 20, 27 people had died, and de la Rua declared a state of siege. He resigned later that night.

Congress then elected Adolfo Rodriguez Saa, who was sworn in on December 23. A government announcement that a third currency, the argentino,

would be introduced brought still more protests, and Rodriguez Saa resigned on December 30. After his departure, power passed under the constitution to Senate leader Ramos Puerta, but he resigned minutes later on grounds of ill health. The constitution then dictated that Congressional leader Eduardo Camano should take office. However, Camano only held the post until a replacement could be found; he said he did not have the support of colleagues in his own Peronist party to take on the country's economic crisis. Duhalde was Congress's next choice, and was elected by a vote of 262–21, with 18 abstentions. Both houses of Congress contained a majority of PJ legislators, but adherents of the Radical and Frepaso parties also voted for Duhalde.

Duhalde was sworn in on January 2, 2002, and told the nation, according to a report in *NotiSur—South American Political and Economic Affairs,* "We have been left today without a peso. My commitment, starting today, is to do away with an exhausted economic model that has brought desperation to a vast majority ... and to lay the foundations of a new model that can help our market recover and ensure a better distribution of wealth." One of his first acts was to declare a moratorium on repayment on foreign loans, and he also secured from Congress approval of an emergency economic plan.

In February of 2002, Duhalde introduced a three–month program aimed at reversing the economic downward trend and shoring up the country's banks. One dramatic measure the Duhalde government had taken immediately upon assuming office was to eliminate the one–to–one conversion of the peso with the United States dollar, noting that artificially keeping the peso strong had launched the four–year–old recession. Duhalde converted more than US$40 billion in bank deposits, recorded in dollars, into devalued pesos; the citizenry responded with street protests, vandalism, and attacks on government officials. Since the government allowed the peso's value to float against the dollar, the peso's value plummeted by 70 percent and consumer prices were increasing by 10 percent per quarter.

Duhalde was in the unenviable position of trying to pilot the Argentine economy to recovery. In February of 2002, he presented a budget and announced elections for 2003, urging citizens to be patient as he and his advisors implemented economic recovery measures. The budget contained some several billion dollars in cuts, a large percentage of which were to be accomplished by suspending scheduled debt payments.

Duhalde faced an uphill battle to win support for his tough recovery measures from the Argentine citizens, many of whom saw their life savings disappear when the currency's peg to the United States dollar was eliminated. The historically placid Argentine middle class took to the streets in noisy protest as they saw their financial security destabilizing in the economic crisis of early 2002.

Duhalde's term was originally supposed to last until December of 2003, but he announced in July of 2002 that he would cut his term short and hold elections earlier than planned. The election that Duhalde originally scheduled for late April of 2003, with the elected president to be sworn in on May 25—the country's national day—was postponed indefinitely in the first quarter of 2003. Those close to Duhalde say the primary election was cancelled because of the possibility of violence erupting during the election. Skeptics think that he may have cancelled the primary because of the very real chance that Menem, running again for the presidency, would win the primary and most likely, the election. Menem opposed the cancellation of the primary, and the matter worked its way through the court system in early 2003 and would most likely end up in the Argentine Supreme Court.

Duhalde is the father of Juliana, Analía, María Eva, Agustina, and Tomas, and is an avid chess player. His wife, Hilda "Chiche" Duhalde, is considered his closest political advisor, and they live in Lomas de Zamora. Duhalde has emphasized the importance of a national consensus during this time of economic crisis. In a rather unpresidential move, but one with clear Peronist roots, he began appearing on a radio show three times a week, fielding calls from listeners. One Argentine political consultant, Felipe Noguera, told Rohter in the *New York Times* that the new president "is not necessarily the man to lay the foundation for long–term prosperity, but he can pacify Argentina and give it a sense of stability, which does seem to make him a man for this moment."

Prior to entering political life, Duhalde was professor of economics at the University of Lomas de Zamora. In 1996, an unauthorized biography, *El Otro* (The Other) by investigative reporter Hernán López Echague, alleged that Duhalde had ties to drug trafficking, had engaged in vote–rigging, and had accumulated unexplainable personal wealth since 1984. Duhalde called the author a criminal, and broke down in tears during a televised interview about the publication. When he assumed the office of the presidency in 2002, Duhalde was considered one of the most powerful men in Argentine politics.

Sources

Periodicals

Economist, January 5, 2002; November 16, 2002; February 1, 2003.

Financial Times, January 14, 2002.

Los Angeles Times, January 2, 2002.

New York Times, January 3, 2002; January 4, 2002; January 6, 2002; January 27, 2002; February 1, 2002.

NotiSur—South American Political and Economic Affairs, January 11, 2002.

Washington Post, January 2, 2002; January 6, 2002; January 14, 2002; January 26, 2002.

Online

"New Man Takes Helm in Argentina," BBC.com, http://news.bbc.co.uk/2/hi/americas/1737562/stm (May 2, 2003).

—*Carol Brennan*

Carroll Dunham

Artist

Born in 1949 in New Haven, CT. *Education:* Trinity College, B.A. (studio art), 1979.

Addresses: *Office*—c/o Columbia University School of the Arts, 305 Dodge Hall, 2960 Broadway, New York, NY 10027.

Career

Interned as assistant to painter Dorothea Rockburne, early 1970s; moved to New York City to paint at the age of 23; enjoyed first commercial and critical success, early 1980s; work exhibited widely in Europe and North America, c. 1985—; teaches in the Visual Arts graduate program at Columbia University's School of the Arts.

Sidelights

One of the most influential American artists of the late 20th and early 21st centuries, Carroll Dunham has a style distinctly his own. The artist, whose work mirrors the sometimes–chaotic cultural changes of the times, is perhaps best known for the cartoon–like beings that inhabit his paintings, many of which are also marked by Dunham's flashy use of color. Dunham clearly dances to a different drummer, adhering to none of the art world's stylistic norms while still drawing upon elements from some of the best of the past. His work blends the influences of Mayan art, pop culture, and Minimalism with the traditions of Modernism, Surrealism, and Abstract Expressionism.

In a 1995 appraisal of Dunham's work, art critic Ronald Jones observed, as quoted at Hoopycake. com, "The coin of Dunham's art is the outward expression of inward self–experience, but rather than locating that exchange within painting's official culture, his encounter arises from a deep comprehension of the self centered by our media culture, high and low. His pictures insist that meaningful experiences of the self are available within the real as it has been assembled by popular culture and, as a result, redefine what it means to issue authentic and unnamable emotion through paint. It must be said that with this accomplishment, Dunham, and a very few others, restored painting's integrity at a particularly fragile moment in its history."

On October 31, 2002, New York's New Museum of Contemporary Art opened a three–month, 40–painting retrospective of Dunham's work, a clear indication that the artist had finally attained star status. In the view of many art critics, this recognition was long overdue. In announcing the retrospective, New Museum curator Dan Cameron told Peter Plagens in *Newsweek* that no other American artist of the late–20th century had "treated the transformed cultural interaction of nature and humanity with anything approaching the intensity and depth of Carroll Dunham."

Born in New Haven, Connecticut, in 1949, Dunham was raised in nearby Old Lyme, Connecticut; he was known by family and friends as "Chip." He began to draw as a boy and after high school enrolled at Trinity College in Hartford to study studio art. Before completing his degree, however, Dunham moved to New York City to pursue his art career.

(He eventually earned his bachelor's degree from Trinity College in 1979.) Once in the city he found himself drawn to the work of such contemporary artists as Mel Bochner, Barry Le Va, and Dorothea Rockburne, the influence of all of whom can be seen in Dunham's earliest work. He interned as an assistant for Rockburne and began in his spare time to develop his own distinctive style.

In his paintings of the early 1980s, Dunham opted to use panels with wood–veneered surfaces rather than canvas. The artist allowed the natural pattern of the wood to guide and influence him. One such painting from this period—"Fourth Pine"—reveals the wood's surface through the paint, an acknowledgement by Dunham of the integral role played by the natural world in his work. Most of Dunham's paintings from this period are made up largely of tubular shapes, sweeping lines, and floating ovals. Writing in *NY Arts,* art critic Matthew Bourbon said of Dunham's work of the 1980s: "They are chock full of painterly and drawing touches, as if Dunham wants to display a form of aesthetic babbling. These essentially formalist paintings are like doodles from an attention–deficit teenager distracted during trigonometry class. Freudian slips occur frequently. Pointless as the paintings may appear, the contrast between crudity and sophistication attaches an unexpected gravity to these works, enabling them to feel nostalgic while remaining available to our current polymath tendencies."

In the late 1980s and early 1990s Dunham's painting style underwent a significant change. The artist returned to canvas, rendering large–scale paintings filled with shapes and signs resembling lips, teeth, and tumors. He also did some of his work during this period on multi–part ragboard panels. Adding a three–dimensional depth to his work, Dunham began affixing Styrofoam balls to the surface of his paintings. "Mound A," painted in the early 1990s and part of Dunham's Mound series, depicts an unearthly world of the painter's imagination. The shapes that inhabited the artist's earlier works began to take on more pronounced form, seeming to emerge from the background of his paintings as if demanding to be seen. In commentary written for Dunham's New Museum retrospective, Johanna Burton observed: "By the time Dunham painted *Red Studies Itself* (1994), however, the shape has assumed definite (and aggressive) form. Sprouting upside down, like a creeping fungus, the creature is interpretable as a large square head, its complexion an angry magenta. The no–longer ambiguous slit has acquired teeth, which are clenched and bared. The canvas is dotted with a coagulated viscous substance (actually paint–drenched Styrofoam balls), which continues to expel itself from deep inside the beast's head—an exploding pustule or cyst buried in the core of the organism in which it grows."

The mid–1990s witnessed yet another change in Dunham's painting style. Creeping into his paintings were tiny caricatures of men and women engaged in sexual and violent behavior. Even normally inanimate objects in Dunham's paintings began to take on human characteristics, behaving as if driven by some mysterious primordial urges. Dunham's cartoon–like characters, according to Hilarie Sheets of the *New York Times* (as quoted by *Newsweek*'s Plagens), emanate from "the sludge of the subconscious, feeling their way blind through the painterly terrain by means of phallic protuberances and bared teeth."

The art world has been somewhat slower to embrace Dunham's work than that of other painters of his generation. The New Museum retrospective of 2002–2003 appears to signal the artist's attainment of star status, but with or without it, it's clear that Dunham has been extremely influential among younger artists, notably Matthew Ritchie and Fred Tomaselli. For his part, Dunham seems content to continue painting as his own, personal muse dictates. As he told Ritchie in a 2002 interview published in an exhibition catalog, "I want to make art that feels true, that can function as a window into realms that aren't part of the day to day. I know that my art exists in this kind of tension between irrational, almost goofy things and extremely tight, formal, organized things. That tension is where I live."

Sources

Periodicals

Independent, November 14, 1994, p. 4; March 22, 2003, p. 12.
Newsweek, December 9, 2002, p. 86.
New York, December 2, 2002.
NY Arts, December 2002.
St. Louis Post–Dispatch, April 20, 1997, p. 3C.

Online

"Carroll Dunham (b. 1949) American," ArtNet, http://www.artnet.com/ag/artistdetails.asp?aid=5542 (May 5, 2003).
"Carroll Dunham," *Frieze.com,* http://www.frieze.com/review_single.asp?r=1794 (May 5, 2003).

"Carroll Dunham," Hoopycake.com, http://www.hoopycake.com/metro/cd/cdmain.htm (May 5, 2003).

"Carroll Dunham," New Museum of Contemporary Art, http://www.newmuseum.org/now_cur_c_dunham.php (May 5, 2003).

"Carroll Dunham's First Major Museum Survey," *AbsoluteArts.com,* http://www.absolutearts.com/artsnews/2002/11/01/30438.html (May 5, 2003).

"New Museum of Contemporary Art Presents the Paintings of Carroll Dunham," New Museum of Contemporary Art, http://www.newmuseum.org/Press_Office/Press_Releases/CarrollDunham.htm (May 5, 2003).

"The Paintings of Carroll Dunham," ArtFacts.net, http://www.artfacts.net/index.php/pageType/exhibitionInfo/exhibition/10153/lang/1/name/The–Paintings–of–Carroll–Dunham (May 5, 2003).

—Don Amerman

Missy Elliott

AP/Wide World Photos

Rap musician, songwriter, and music producer

Born Melissa Arnette Elliott in 1971, in Portsmouth, VA; daughter of Ronnie and Pat Elliott.

Addresses: *Fan club*—Missy Elliott Fan Club, c/o Gejel Enterprise, P.O. Box 923, Temple Hills, MD 20757. *Record company*—Elektra Entertainment Group, 75 Rockefeller Plaza, New York City, NY 10019. *Website*—Missy Elliott Official Website: http://www.missy–elliott.com.

Career

Auditioned with group Sista for Devante Swing of Jodeci, 1991; with partner Timbaland, began writing and producing, 1992; Sista cut first and only album, *Brand New*, 1995; wrote seven tracks for Aaliyah's *One In A Million*, 1996; received major songwriting, recording, and production deal, including a label of her own from Elektra Entertainment, 1996; worked with Jodeci, Raven–Symone, 702, Whitney Houston, Janet Jackson, Mariah Carey, Paula Cole, Scary Spice, and Nicole; released debut solo album, *Supa Dupa Fly*, 1997; released *Da Real World*, 1999; released *Missy E ... So Addictive*, 2001; released *Under Construction*, 2002.

Awards: Grammy award for best rap solo performance, Recording Academy, for "Get Ur Freak On," 2001; BET award for best female hip–hop artist, Black Entertainment Television, 2002; Grammy award for best female rap solo performance, Recording Academy, for "Scream a.k.a. Itchin,'" 2003; BET award for best female hip–hop artist, Black Entertainment Television, 2003; Soul Train Award, The Michael Jackson Award for Best R&B/Soul or Rap Music Video for "Work It," 2003.

Sidelights

Missy "Misdemeanor" Elliott is a phenomenon. She did not merely take the traditionally male–dominated recording industry by storm as a rapper, songwriter, arranger, producer, and head of her own label, she did so in one of the most macho, testosterone–laden of all genres, hip–hop—and remarkably, she achieved all of this in only a few years time. Besides Elliott's work writing for and producing the cream of hip–hop and R&B, she has released four CDs to critical and popular acclaim. She was the first hip–hop artist to perform on the Lilith Fair tour. Elliott has been featured in a major ad campaign for the Gap, but she has not hesitated to have fun at the expense of her image in her videos. "Puff Mommy," as Elliott is known to her fans, has "established herself as a singer–rapper–writer with a welcome penchant for humor and positivity," wrote Michael Musto in *Interview*. Elliott has become known for her versatility and originality. "Missy is one of those talented artists who always finds a way to reinvent herself," Sean R. Taylor, music director for WQHT in New York, told *Billboard*. "Her music is always pounding, moving, vibrant."

Elliott was born in Portsmouth, Virginia. Her earliest musical experiences were with a church choir. Elliott knew at an early age that she was going to be a star, and she told her mother so repeatedly. She began playing the part of the star singer early, too. Elliott would sing in her room with a broomstick microphone to an audience of her dolls. "In my mind I pictured them screaming for me. I would go into a whole other zone," she told *Essence*. Elliott wrote her own songs about butterflies, birds, whatever happened to be around. She sang them to passing cars from overturned trash cans, or to her family from atop picnic tables in the park.

Elliott not only vividly imagined herself on stage, she could see her heroes coming to take her to music stardom. "I remember in school writing Janet Jackson and Michael Jackson and asking them to come get me out of class," she told *Interview*. "I would imagine them running down the hall and asking my teacher, 'Ms. Daniels, can we get Missy out of class? We're here to see Missy.' My imagination was always wild like that. So when I got a call from Janet, just to hear her say she loved my music, it was like a blessing. It was a dream come true to get a call from Mariah [Carey] and now I'm just waiting for Michael Jackson to call."

Despite the fact that many of her dreams came true and she accumulated impressive power in the recording industry, Elliott remains a little star–struck by the artists who used to be just voices on records. Whitney Houston once called her, and, she told *Interview*, "when I got off the phone I screamed so loud." Elliott's feet remain firmly planted on the ground, however, and she often signs autographs patiently for the fans who recognize her on the streets of Manhattan, New York. More significantly, Elliott has courageously made public her father's physical abuse of her mother and her own sexual abuse at the hands of a cousin. For her, speaking out publicly was a way of taking control of a past that had previously controlled her, as well as drawing attention to a serious social problem that frequently gets swept under the rug.

Elliott got her first musical break in 1991 when the R&B group Jodeci came to Portsmouth. She took her group, Sista, made up of some of her friends from junior high, to the hotel where Devante Swing, one of the members of Jodeci was staying. He was so impressed by their performance—a set of original tunes written by Elliott—that he signed them to his production company. "We thought we were too hot," Elliott told Imusic.com. "We tried to look just like Jodeci during that audition. We had our pants tucked in our boots. We had begged our mothers to get us these outfits. We even had our canes. We thought we were four hot Devantes."

Sista cut their first album in 1995, and broke up when it became clear that Elektra Records could not afford to release it. Elliott then formed a production team at the company with Timbaland (aka Tim Mosley), a childhood friend, and began writing songs for artists such as Jodeci, Raven–Symone, and 702; Timbaland produced the records. It was a combination that worked. "When we come together, we are able to be a lot more creative because there are no bars," Elliott told the *New York Times Upfront*. "We're just, 'Let's do it,' instead of worrying about what people might say."

Despite Sista's apparent failure, Elliott had gotten noticed. "People started to call for songs, or ask me to rap or something," she told Imusic.com. One call came from the late singer Aaliyah, who was looking for a new producer. Elliott and Timbaland entered the picture and the result was four big singles from Aaliyah's CD *One In A Million*: "4 Page Letter," "Hot Like Fire," "If Your Girl Only Knew" and the title track. Sylvia Rhone, the chairman and CEO of the Elektra Entertainment Group, took notice. She offered Elliott, then a mere 22 years old, a deal that included writing and producing opportunities, her own recording label (The Gold Mind, Inc.), and eventually a contract as an artist. "You could recognize instantly that Missy possessed star potential," Rhone told *Essence*.

Elliott has since worked with a number of other superstar singers, including Houston, Carey, Janet Jackson, Paula Cole, and Scary Spice. In addition to writing, arranging and producing, Elliott began making guest appearances, notably on Gina Thompson's "The Things You Do," in which she displayed her infectious laughter and did a one-of-a–kind slide. "That one caused people to start coming up to me on the street and say 'Ain't you the 'Hee Ha' girl?,'" she told Imusic.com. "They don't even know my name and they'll say, 'Hee Ha girl, do that slide across the floor.'"

Michael Musto asked Elliott in *Interview* if she ever worried that her work as a label executive, songwriter, and producer would distract her from making her own music. "No," she replied, "because I really enjoy writing and producing for other artists. Some people save their best songs for their own albums. I'd rather give another artist one of my songs. At the end of the day, it still represents me."

Despite the fact that the world seemed to be waiting with baited breath, it took Elliott some time before she finally released the first CD of her own. "I was not going to make a record just to make one, if you know what I mean," she told Imusic.com. "I wasn't going to do a record if I couldn't mix it up." The result was 1997's *Supa Dupa Fly,* a record critically praised as forging an innovative new direction for hip–hop. In "The Rain (Supa Dupa Fly)," for example, she deliberately distanced herself from the violent themes that run through so much other hip–hop. "I don't knock nobody's hustle," she told Imusic.com, "but everybody don't want to hear that. You get that on the news and it depresses you enough." *Supa Dupa Fly* ended up going platinum and receiving a Grammy nomination.

Her second album, *Da Real World,* had more of a street feel. It produced a controversial single, "She's a B****," a song which addressed her power—and attitude—as a woman. "Music is a male–dominated field," Elliott explained to *Interview.* "Women are not always taken as seriously as we should be, so sometimes we have to put our foot down. To other people, that may come across as being a b****, but it's just knowing what we want and being confident." *Da Real World* also went platinum, and garnered a Grammy nomination.

Elliott stepped back out of the spotlight in 2000, concentrating on her record label, Gold Mind, Inc. With releases from artists T.C., Mocha, and Nicole slated for release that year, Elliott found herself busy overseeing these new projects. "These are my babies," Elliott said in *Billboard.* "I'm very proud of the work they're doing; they're kicking it hard."

For the 2001 film *Moulin Rouge,* Elliott produced and was briefly featured in a cover of Patti LaBelle's "Lady Marmalade." Performed by Christina Aguilera, Lil' Kim, Mya, and Pink, the song was an instant hit. The video for the song went into heavy rotation, and won both the Best Video from a Film and Video of the Year awards at the MTV Video Music Awards.

Also in 2001, Elliott released her third album, *Missy E … So Addictive. Interview*'s Dimitri Ehrlich said that the album served up "frenetic, freaky soundscapes that seem to have no precedent anywhere." The album's first single, "Get Ur Freak On," featured, according to Gareth Thomas of *Music & Media,* "a hypnotic, looped riff that sticks in your head." Pop singer Nelly Furtado appeared on the remixed version, much to Elliott's delight. "People are going to bug out when they hear it," Elliott enthused in *Billboard.*

Produced by Timbaland, the album also included several collaborations. "One Minute Man," the album's second single featured rappers Jay–Z and Ludacris on two separate versions. On "This Is for My People," rising rap star Eve added, according to *Billboard*'s Marci Kenon, "an out of character flow on the hot techno number." R&B singer Ginuwine appeared on "Take Away" and gospel singers Kim Burrell, Yolanda Adams, and Mary Mary joined Elliott on the inspirational "I'm Moving On." Elliott was accompanied by Redman and Method Man on "Dog in Heat." "They can always add party to a track," Elliott told *Billboard.* "There's something about both their voices that gives energy to a track."

Elliott returned in 2002 with a new album, *Under Construction,* and a new look, courtesy of a 70–pound weight loss. The album quickly went platinum on the strength of the first single, "Work It," which features the chorus "Is it worth it? Let me work it. I put my thang down, flip it, and reverse it," rapped both forward and in reverse, a "marvelous example of hip–hop cryptography," deemed *Salon*'s Stephen Weiss. It's also something that only Elliott, light years ahead of the rest of hip–hop, would dream up. Ludacris, Jay–Z, Beyoncé Knowles, and the remaining members of TLC all contributed to the album, most notably Ludacris's contribution to the second single "Gossip Folks" (a tune built around Frankie Smith's 1980s hit "Double Dutch Bus") and Jay–Z's verse on "Back in the Day." Elliott's inspiration for *Under Construction* was old school rap and artists like Run–D.M.C., Salt–N–Pepa, and Big Daddy Kane. "When hip–hop was beginning for me, people weren't making the kind of money that they make now," she told *Entertainment Weekly*'s Rob Brunner. "It was for the love of doing it and having fun with it…. [That] is what's missing in music right now."

While already spending mornings in meetings at her label and afternoons and evenings in the studio, Elliott intended to continue expanding her activities. She has done ads for the Gap and Sprite, made television appearances, and hopes to break into producing movies. "It ain't easy but I've got goals in life. And I'm going to step forth and do all of them," she told *Essence.* But with her music, Elliott remained committed to creating something fresh and new. "Once you make an impact on the world you kinda gotta come back and make sure your new music don't really sound like the last time," Elliott told *Interview.* "I'm never scared to try whatever," she added, "and I feel that's what people like me are for, for doing something different."

Selected discography

With Sista

Brand New, Elektra, 1995.

Solo

Supa Dupa Fly, Elektra, 1997.
Da Real World, Elektra, 1999.
Miss E ... So Addictive, Elektra, 2001.
Under Construction, Elektra, 2002.

Sources

Books

Contemporary Black Biography, volume 31, Gale Group, 2001.
Contemporary Musicians, volume 30, Gale Group, 2001.

Periodicals

Asia Africa Intelligence Wire, February 5, 2003.
Billboard, March 11, 2000; April 14, 2001.
Dallas Morning News, September 7, 2001.

Entertainment Weekly, November 22, 2002.
Essence, March 2000.
Interview, June 1999; May 2001.
Knight Ridder/Tribune News Service, November 14, 2002, p. K6463.
Music & Media, April 28, 2001.
New York Times Upfront, May 14, 2001.
People, January 20, 2003, p. 77.

Online

"Missy Elliott," All Music Guide, http://allmusicguide.com (May 27, 2003).
Missy Elliott Official Website, http://www.missy-elliott.com (May 27, 2003).
"Missy Elliott on the Network," Imusic, http://imusic.com/showcase/urban/missy.html (May 27, 2003).
"Missy Elliott: *Under Construction,*" *Salon,* http://archive.salon.com/audio/music/2003/01/09/missy_elliott/ (May 27, 2003).

—Evelyn Hauser

James Ellroy

Author

Born Lee Earle Ellroy, March 4, 1948, in Los Angeles, CA; son of Armand (an accountant) and Geneva (a nurse; maiden name, Hilliker) Ellroy; married Mary Doherty, 1988 (divorced, 1991); married Helen Knode (a journalist and author).

Addresses: *Agent*—Nat Sobel, Sobel Weber Associates, 146 E. 19th St., New York, NY 10003. *Home*—Kansas City, MO.

Career

Served briefly in the U.S. Army, 1965; worked as a golf caddy at the Bel–Air and Hillcrest Country Clubs, Los Angeles, CA, 1977–81, and at the Wycagyl Country Club in Long Island, NY, 1981–84; first novel, *Brown's Requiem,* published in paperback by Avon Books, 1981; several of his subsequent novels have been made into films, including *Blood on the Moon,* adapted as the 1988 movie *Cop,* and *L.A. Confidential* in 1997.

Awards: Prix Mystere Award, 1990, for *The Big Nowhere.*

Sidelights

James Ellroy's noirish crime fiction does not flinch from scenes of graphic violence or human depravity, and Ellroy has been candid about his life and its own horrors. Ellroy's mother was strangled in a 1958 case that remains unsolved, and the author spent the next 20 years on an odyssey that included homelessness and alcohol–induced memory loss. His was truly a case where writing saved his life, and when he began putting pen to paper, he wrote about what he knew best: the dark underbelly of Los Angeles, California. His novels feature corrupt cops, byzantine plots, and explicit episodes of murder and mayhem, all delivered in his trademark staccato prose style. *Esquire* reviewer David Thomas described his works as "a fascinating cross between literature and slangy pulp."

Born in 1948 in Los Angeles, Ellroy was the product of a union between an accountant and a registered nurse, "a great–looking cheap couple," Ellroy wrote in *My Dark Places: An L.A. Crime Memoir,* "along the lines of Robert Mitchum and Jane Russell in *Macao."* The union was tempestuous and shortlived, and after they divorced Ellroy lived primarily with his mother in El Monte, a far–from–idyllic town in the San Gabriel Valley. "El Monte was a smoggy void," he wrote in *My Dark Places.* "People parked on their lawns and hosed down their cars in their underwear. The sky was carcinogenic tan." Poisoned by his father's contempt of his mother, Ellroy came to see her as a drinker and woman of dubious morals. When he was ten years old, his father returned him after a weekend visit to find the house overrun by police officers and homicide detectives: his mother had been assaulted and strangled, and her body was found by some boys in a field near the local high school. She had been seen leaving a bar the night before with a couple, and as Ellroy theorized in an interview with *People's* Steve Dougherty, her murder was likely "a sex deal that went bad. She was sharp–tongued, articulate, and bad–tempered. She mouthed off to the last guy in the world she should have."

Ellroy did not even attend the funeral, and was thankful that he could finally escape the hated El Monte area. He went to live with his father in Los Angeles, and the household was a permissive one. Not surprisingly, Ellroy emerged as a troubled teenager. He cultivated an anti–social personality, drawing swastikas on his notebooks that offended fellow Jewish students at Fairfax High School; a habitual truant, he was eventually expelled. His father died of cancer a few months later, and his last words to his son were, according to the Dougherty interview in *People*, "'Try to pick up every waitress who serves you.'" With nowhere to turn, Ellroy decided to enlist in the U.S. Army, but changed his mind during boot camp and managed to get himself discharged by faking a stutter and running around the camp naked. He returned to the Los Angeles area and began his 12–year hiatus from the mainstream world.

Ellroy slept in parks, drank heavily, and injected speed. To support his habits, he broke into homes; to eat, he shoplifted from stores. Sometimes he slept in a Goodwill dumpster box near Fifth Street and Western Avenue. Once, he did have a more permanent place to stay, but was often so incapacitated that he worried he would forget his own name. "I wrote it on the wall behind my bed as a reminder," he recalled in *My Dark Places*. "I wrote 'I will not go insane' beside it."

Ellroy's sojourn was not without its brief respites: he spent hours at the public library, drinking surreptitiously while reading through the canon of twentieth–century American fiction. He also amassed, through shoplifting, a collection of some 200 crime and pulp–fiction novels. Finally, a 1977 bout with double pneumonia scared him and he began attending Alcoholics Anonymous meetings. A friend from the program helped him land a job as a golf caddy at the Bel–Air and Hillcrest Country Clubs in the Los Angeles area, where he toted clubs for celebrities like George C. Scott, Telly Savalas, and Dinah Shore.

In 1979, Ellroy began writing his first novel, inspired in part by *The Onion Field*, Joseph Wambaugh's 1973 nonfiction account of the murder of a Los Angeles police officer by two small–time hoods ten years before. He wrote for ten months, in longhand, while standing at his dresser in a room at the Westwood Hotel. After coming up with the $850 to have it typed, he sent the manuscript to four agents he found in the *Writer's Market*, and one of them sold it to Avon Books for $3,500. Published in 1981, *Brown's Requiem* recounted the sordid experience of a Los Angeles private investigator who runs afoul

of a group of killer extortionists. Both this and Ellroy's next work, *Clandestine*, were "the work of a gifted but unpracticed author: disturbed cops corrupted by the crime world they are supposed to combat; redeeming women who are (or were) hookers; sprawling, ill–managed plots loaded with depravity and violence," assessed *Contemporary Novelists*.

Ellroy did not earn very much for the first two books, but *Clandestine* was nominated in 1982 for a Edgar Award by the Mystery Writers of America, a career boost. He decided to leave Southern California behind, and settled in Eastchester, New York, near a golf club that hired him as a caddy. On his first–ever visit to New York City, he chanced upon the Mysterious Bookshop, a renowned crime–and–mystery novel seller, and introduced himself to its owner, Otto Penzler. Penzler helped Ellroy land a new agent, Nat Sobel, who represented a stable of solid writers like Andrew Greeley, and also offered to publish Ellroy's next book, *Blood on the Moon*, through his Mysterious Press imprint. When that book appeared in 1984, Ellroy was finally able to quit his caddying job.

Ellroy wrote three more books during the 1980s before attracting serious literary notice with 1987's *The Black Dahlia*. This was the name given to an unsolved 1947 murder case of Elizabeth Short that Ellroy felt had eerie similarities to that of his mother. After coming across an account of it once, he told *People*'s Dougherty that the details of the case "brought my mother's death home in very brutal terms," he says. "I began to have awful nightmares of Elizabeth Short being killed. I was afraid to sleep." Short was a known prostitute who liked to wear black and frequented seedy bars. Her severed torso found in a vacant lot at 39th and Norton. As Ellroy told Dougherty in *People*, Short was like many other women who came to Hollywood looking for film stardom and fell on hard times instead. "Rather than dump this girl who wouldn't be missed in the ocean or bury her," Ellroy noted, "the killer drives around with two halves of a naked body in the trunk and deposits it six inches off the sidewalk in the middle of Los Angeles."

The Black Dahlia was immediately hailed upon publication as a tour–de–force, though some critics did decry it as sensationalistic. It was the first in what would become Ellroy's "L.A. Quartet" series, followed by the *The Big Nowhere* in 1988. The intricate plot of this book involves a serial killer in the gay community; the hunt becomes intertwined with 1950s anti–communist fervor and the rooting out of political "subversives" within the Hollywood film industry. *L.A. Confidential*, the next in Ellroy's series, was similarly complex, involving a trio of police officers in Los Angeles in 1953 and a series of unsolved slayings. *White Jazz* was the last in the quartet of novels before the author, now critically acclaimed, turned away from Los Angeles and tackled a much larger criminal underworld. *American Tabloid*, published in 1995, attempts to present a portrait of late–1950s America by focusing on a network of fictional events leading up to the greatest "unsolved" crime of decade—the assassination of American president John F. Kennedy in Dallas, Texas, in 1963. Its plot centers around two Federal Bureau of Investigation agents and a Central Intelligence Agency operative, and the exhaustive action moves from Miami, Florida, to Chicago, Illinois, to Los Angeles, California, and New Orleans, Louisiana. "This ground," noted an essay in *Contemporary Novelists*, "is traversed with extreme modern facility by the novel's three maculate heroes: Kemper Boyd, a stone–souled free agent of conspiracy and a genius at multiple role–playing; Ward Littell, a guilt–infected repository of self–destructiveness and Jesuit–schooled moral absolutism, deteriorating sympathetically into a helpless American amorality; and Pete Bondurant, the hired hitman and dope–runner carried over from his minor role in *White Jazz* to discharge the duties of an old–fashioned fictional heavy who turns out to be a romantic."

American Tabloid landed on the bestseller lists and helped secure Ellroy's place in American letters. In 1996, he revisited the trauma of his mother's still–unsolved murder in *My Dark Places*. Recruiting a retired detective from the Los Angeles County Sheriff's Department, Ellroy examined the police reports and tried to track down those who had known his mother before her death. In the end, the case remains a mystery, but he learns much about a woman he barely knew, and about himself as well. "I ran from my mother for a long time," he told *People* writers Kim Hubbard and Stanley Young. "I finally saw that she tried to give me a decent life, and she fought the more self–destructive side of her nature to do it. I love her fiercely now." *My Dark Places* earned a positive review from *New York Times* book critic Michiko Kakutani, who described it as "half confessional memoir, half hard–boiled crime chronicle." Kakutani found similarities in it with Ellroy's fiction: "There's the same scabrous, staccato prose, the same eye for grisly details, the same intimate knowledge of the seamy side of life."

Ellroy's reputation advanced further in 1997 with the release of the film version of *L.A. Confidential*. Director Curtis Hanson and Brian Helgeland co-wrote the script, based on Ellroy's novel, and the resulting film made Hanson's career. The work starred Russell Crowe as a violence–prone LAPD cop, Bud White; Kevin Spacey played the corrupt detective, Jack Vincennes, and the role of rookie cop/resident good guy of the trio, Ed Exley, was taken by newcomer Guy Pearce. Danny DeVito also appeared as the publisher of a crime scandal–sheet, and Kim Basinger as a prostitute. The film version, like the novel, was a scathing fictionalization of the endemic racism and corruption in the LAPD in the 1950s. "Like most of Ellroy's novels, *L.A. Confidential* is a dark–side–of–the–moon reverie, a neo–Chandler pulp fantasia that wears its rotting organs on the outside," noted *Entertainment Weekly* reviewer Owen Gleiberman. The critic went on to note that Hanson's tour–de–force was "the first film that has truly gotten Ellroy on screen and, in many ways, it's a sleeker and more pleasurable experience than his hard–boiled–bebop prose. With its plot that zigs and zags like knife slashes, its cynicism stoked to the melting point, the movie brings the thrill of corruption crackingly to life."

Ellroy's next work, *The Cold Six Thousand*, was a sequel of sorts to *American Tabloid*, picking up the threads of the plot in the moments just following the Kennedy assassination. The 2001 novel weighs in at a hefty 700 pages, and takes readers on a journey that involves shady casino operators in Las Vegas, Nevada; the Vietnamese opium trade, Cuban exiles, the Mormon church, a white supremacist group, and the assassinations of Robert F. Kennedy and civil–rights leader Martin Luther King, Jr. "As uniformly depraved and vicious as the world he depicts may be, as grim as his take on human nature, Ellroy never seems truly cynical because he's so endlessly jazzed by it all," *New York Times* critic Laura Miller wrote. "His enthusiasm for picking up rocks and detailing everything squirming beneath them is bizarrely puppyish and perversely endearing."

Ellroy lives in Kansas City, Missouri, with his second wife, the writer Helen Knode. Assessing the dozen or so years of his life as a young man on the streets of Los Angeles, he said he was happy to have found his calling, and was grateful, he said in a *Publishers Weekly* interview with Fleming Meeks, "for not being holed up, drinking myself to death in some L.A. rathole. Grateful for the ability to write books and see them published...."

Selected writings

Brown's Requiem, Avon (New York, NY), 1981.
Clandestine, Avon (New York, NY), 1982.

Blood on the Moon, Mysterious Press (New York, NY), 1984.

Because the Night, Mysterious Press (New York, NY), 1984.

Killer on the Road, Avon (New York, NY), 1986.

Suicide Hill, Mysterious Press (New York, NY), 1986.

Silent Terror, introduction by Jonathan Kellerman, Avon (New York, NY), 1986.

The Black Dahlia, Mysterious Press (New York, NY), 1987.

The Big Nowhere, Mysterious Press (New York, NY), 1988.

L.A. Confidential, Mysterious Press (New York, NY), 1990.

White Jazz, Knopf (New York, NY), 1992.

Hollywood Nocturnes (short stories), O. Penzler Books (New York, NY), 1994.

American Tabloid, Knopf (New York, NY), 1995.

My Dark Places: An L.A. Crime Memoir, Knopf (New York, NY), 1996.

Crime Wave: Reportage and Fiction from the Underside of L.A., Random House (New York, NY), 1999.

The Cold Six Thousand, Knopf (New York, NY), 2001.

Sources

Books

Contemporary Novelists, seventh edition, St. James Press, 2001.

My Dark Places: An L.A. Crime Memoir, Knopf (New York, NY), 1996.

Periodicals

Entertainment Weekly, September 19, 1997, p. 54.

Esquire, October 1997, p. 50.

Los Angeles Times, July 2, 2002, p. E2.

New Statesman, November 8, 1996, p. 46.

New York Times, November 5, 1996, p. C16; May 20, 2001, p. 9.

People, December 14, 1987, p. 122; November 25, 1996, p. 93.

Publishers Weekly, June 15, 1990, p. 53; February 22, 1999, p. 69.

Time, April 10, 1995, p. 74.

USA Today Magazine, January 1999, p. 81.

—Carol Brennan

Thomas J. Engibous

Chief Executive Officer of Texas Instruments

Born in 1953, in St. Louis, MO; married; children: two sons. *Education:* Attended Purdue University, BSEE, 1975, MSEE (engineering), 1976.

Addresses: *Office*—Texas Instruments Incorporated, 12500 TI Blvd., Dallas, TX 75243–4136.

Career

Integrated circuit design engineer, Texas Instruments, 1976; promoted to section manager for the design and development of high voltage display circuits, 1979; promoted to a senior member of the technical staff, 1980; elected semiconductor group vice president, 1986; promoted to applications specific products manager, 1991; became president of same department and executive vice president of the company, 1993; named president and chief executive officer, 1996; chairman of the board, 1998—.

Member: Board of Directors of J.C. Penney Company, Inc.; The Business Roundtable, the Business Council; Institute of Electrical and Electronics Engineers; Purdue University Engineering Visiting Committee; chairman of the board for Catalyst, a group formed to advance women in the workplace; trustee, Southern Methodist University; director, Dallas Citizens Council; director, Southwest Medical Foundation; director, U.S.–Japan Business Council; director, National Center for Educational Accountability; trustee, foundation for the Malcolm Baldrige National Quality Award, Inc.; serves on the Engineering Visiting Committee at Purdue University.

Awards: Named a Purdue Distinguished Engineering Alumnus, 1990; honorary degree of Doctor of Engineering at Purdue, 1997; "Champions of Diversity" award, *Working Mother,* for practicing diversity in the workplace, 2001.

Sidelights

During the downtrend in the tech sector that began in 2001, there were not many bright spots for Wall Street or corporate America to look to. While companies like Intel were scaling back on semiconductor production, Texas Instruments was shedding its reputation as an old–school company by ramping up production and, by all analysts's accounts, was headed toward healthy growth for the foreseeable future. The company's remarkable turn-around and stability began when Thomas J. Engibous took over as chief executive officer of the company under tragic circumstances.

Engibous was born in 1953 in St. Louis, Missouri. He was a teacher's dream come true as he displayed an intelligence that put him at the top of his class and a demeanor that made him popular with his fellow students. He was also a good athlete and took to playing hockey once he was old enough to wear skates. But it was his fascination with computers that his parents knew would take him somewhere. He did not just like to use them—he was interested in how they worked. When it came time to choose a college he went with Purdue University's School of Electrical and Computer Engineering due to its reputation for having a solid and influential engineering program. His intent was to be the talent behind the computer chip but his peers soon found that he had a charm to him as well. His straight–talk and humble demeanor endeared him to his fellow students and his professors. Whether he knew it or not he had a knack for business that rivaled his natural talent as an engineer.

Engibous completed his bachelors degree in electrical engineering (BSEE) at Purdue in 1975 and his masters (MSEE) in 1976. In September of the same year, he was hired to his first job out of college at Texas Instruments (TI), a leading company in the development of computer chips. In the 1980s TI was one of the few big companies to set their sights on the fledgling personal computer industry. Though they focused on designing semiconductors for many different types of hardware, they would build their reputation in the private sector as the company that drove the size of chips to their smallest size ever. But TI suffered from corporate sprawl. On one hand they designed notebooks and printers and on the other hand they secured multi–billion dollar defense contracts with the United States government. This lack of focus was about to become a big drag on their bottom line.

Engibous joined the team as an integrated circuit design engineer specializing in high voltage circuits. The same charm he had shown in college quickly developed in the business world and his seniors were taking notice. It was clear to them that Engibous not only understood the technology he designed but he understood how it could fit into the world around him. He rose through the ranks of the company quickly. First he was promoted to section manager for the design and development of high voltage display circuits in 1979. It was in this division that he was able to put his "analog" sensibilities to use. While the rest of the world was becoming fascinated with what digital could do for them, Engibous found his niche in what we see and hear. The analog output of TI's digital processors was what he thought the future held. And his company appreciated that perspective, as radical as it was. In 1980, he was promoted yet again to become a senior member of the technical staff. By 1986 he was elected semiconductor group vice president.

From his new position Engibous began to enjoy credit for injecting a focus on the company's future. He was a big fan of an up–and–coming technology that would eventually catapult him to the top: the Digital Signal Processor (DSP). The DSP is a computer chip dedicated to making digital signals sound and look good to the human senses. Unlike a computer's Central Processing Unit, the DSP doesn't need to be everything to everyone. It has one job

and, if Engibous had anything to say about it, TI would be the leading manufacturer for computer makers, home theater devices, emerging telephony technologies, and media makers around the world. With this focus, in 1991 Engibous was promoted again to oversee the design and manufacturing of all digital and graphic signal processors, standard cell logic, LAN processors, microprocessors, and floating point processors. Only a year and a half later, in 1993, he became president of the same division and an executive vice president for the entire company.

But the company was dealt a major blow when its CEO died suddenly. Jerry R. Junkins was in Germany when he suffered a massive heart attack on his way to a meeting. Junkins was a very well–respected CEO who was in the midst of making bold moves with the company, selling off divisions that no longer met the company's needs and acquiring new ones that he hoped would take TI into the future. William Weber immediately took control of the company as an interim CEO until the Board could decide on a new chief executive. Most people expected Weber would secure the job permanently but the entire business world was shocked when TI installed Engibous as the new CEO. TI was beginning to show its age by this point and many wondered if it had the resources to survive with powerful competitors such as Intel and IBM. But Engibous, who was just as surprised as everyone else by his appointment, had a plan.

Engibous decided to shed a lot of the semiconductor design that assumed the world would be "PC–centric" and opted to go with what we see and hear. His focus on the DSP might have seemed like a big risk at the time but he was determined to position the company at the forefront of the fledgling industry. His gamble was that consumers would need streamlined ways to see and hear the digital information that technology promises them. His gamble paid off. As cell phones became more a part of modern life, TI was there to provide the chips to make them work. Currently, a TI chip is in 80 percent of all cellphones distributed in the United States. TI aggressively entered the home theater industry as well, partnering with huge companies like Yamaha to create the chips that lets consumers see and hear digital content. By 1999 the DSP market had ballooned to a $6 billion industry and, of that, TI owned 48 percent of the pie. Under Engibous's leadership the company shed 13 divisions that did not meet his vision for TI's future and acquired ten that did. But a lot of people wondered if the company was focusing too much on one technology. When asked about that in *Institutional Investor*, Engibous responded, "[I]n reality, a

DSP goes into a diverse, wide variety of applications: disc drives, digital cellular phones, digital TVs, digital still cameras, digital modems, motor controls. There are literally thousands of applications for DSPs. So we spend a lot of time trying to figure out which areas we should be covering...." His guess was that consumers come across a DSP in one form or another around 200 times before noon everyday and Engibous estimated that will grow to 2,000 times within five years.

Engibous attributed the company's success to a number of factors: a strong succession plan put in place by the previous CEO, a strong development team, and diversity in the workforce. Engibous has been an advocate for women and diversity at TI for many years. In the '80s, he headed his group's diversity steering team and developed the TI diversity standards in use today.

The result is a company that has bucked the trend. Instead of suffering the worst of the economic downturn that began in the year 2001, TI consistently posted growth quarters, with only the occasional bad news. The company, under Engibous's optimistic vision, is not sitting on its accomplishments. They spend approximately 15 percent of their profits on research and development, up from six percent before Engibous took the reins. A primary focus for the company moving forward is Internet telephony, which is the use of voice over the World Wide Web infrastructure. Engibous summed up his company's future in an interview with *BusinessWeek*. His conclusion is that the electronics industry has seen four eras: the mainframe computer in the 1970s, the minicomputer in the 1980s, the home PC in the 1990s, and communications in the 21st century. "Instead of one computer per person, it's several computers—a phone, an organizer, or an MP3 player. It's an era of real-time signal processing. Players that are in that space—analog chips, DSPs, and other types of signal processing—are the champions of this era."

Sources

BusinessWeek, Spring 2001, p. 36; June 24, 2002, p. 26B.
Fortune, October 11, 1999, p. 44.
Institutional Investor, March 1999, p. 33.

—Ben Zackheim

Theo Epstein

AP/Wide World Photos

General manager of the Boston Red Sox

Born December 29, 1973, in New York, NY; son of Leslie (an author and college professor) and Ilene (an owner of a women's clothing store) Epstein. *Education:* Yale University, B.A., 1995; University of San Diego Law School, 1999.

Addresses: *Office*—c/o Boston Red Sox, 4 Yawkey Way, Boston, MA 02215–3496.

Career

Worked as an intern in the public relations department of the Baltimore Orioles during summer breaks from college, 1992–95; moved to San Diego to work in media relations department of San Diego Padres, 1995; became baseball operations assistant for the Padres; named director of baseball operations, 2000; named assistant general manager of Boston Red Sox, 2002; named general manager, 2002.

Sidelights

Just over a month before his 29th birthday, Theo Epstein in November of 2002 was named general manager of baseball's Boston Red Sox, becoming the youngest general manager in baseball history. To those who knew Epstein growing up in the Boston suburb of Brookline, his selection for the job came as no big surprise. For them, it seemed almost preordained that Epstein, who'd been working in baseball since his college days, would eventually become a member of the Red Sox family. As Epstein told Bella English of the *Boston Globe,* "I was probably a Red Sox fan before I even knew it." Although his family moved to the Boston area from New York when Epstein was only four years old, his father, who despised the hometown Yankees, had been a Sox fan long before the move. It was a bias that Epstein and his twin brother, Paul, absorbed early on. To further cement the Epstein family ties to Boston's beloved baseball team, the family's home in Brookline was located only a mile from Fenway Park.

Every step of Epstein's climb through the ranks of baseball management had been shepherded by Larry Luchino, who became president and chief executive officer of the Red Sox organization shortly after the team was purchased in early 2002 by an investment group headed by Florida financier John W. Henry and Tom Werner. This made it almost inevitable that some skeptics would speculate that Epstein would be little more than Lucchino's puppet. For his part, Epstein wasted no time in moving to shoot down such suggestions. "They're dead wrong," the new general manager told Daniel

G. Habib of *Sports Illustrated*. "We have healthy debates. On baseball issues we disagree more often than we agree. I don't think he exercises any more control over me than most presidents do over their G.M.'s."

Born December 29, 1973, in New York City, Epstein spent the first four years of his life on Manhattan's Upper West Side, where he lived with his parents, Leslie and Ilene, twin brother, Paul, and older sister, Anya. The family moved from New York to Brookline, Massachusetts, after Epstein's father, an author, accepted a job with the English department at Boston University (BU). For more than two decades, he has served as director of BU's creative writing program.

As boys, even before their move to Brookline, Epstein and his brother, Paul, were both active in sports, playing soccer and baseball. While Epstein was drawn more to baseball, his twin preferred soccer. Epstein told the *Globe*'s English that his baseball skills peaked at the age of three when his dad would take him to nearby Central Park in New York and pitch balls to him. "I'd hit them over the fence. People would gather to watch the little kid. But that came about 20 years too early to maximize my earning potential." In Brookline, he pitched for his high school baseball team but describes himself to the *Globe*'s English as only "a second–tier player." Despite their different preferences in sports, Epstein and his brother shared a passion for watching sports events on television. Somewhat alarmed by their growing obsession with sports, their father laid down a new household rule: for every minute of television watched, a minute had to be spent reading a book.

After high school, Epstein and his brother went their separate ways: Theo off to Yale and Paul to Connecticut's Wesleyan University. During the spring break of his freshman year, Epstein traveled to Baltimore to interview for an internship with the public relations department of the Baltimore Orioles. It was the beginning of his career in baseball's front offices. Shortly after Orioles CEO Larry Lucchino moved to San Diego to take up similar duties with the Padres, Epstein graduated from Yale and followed Lucchino westward. He worked for a couple of years in the Padres media relations department, following which he became the team's baseball operations assistant. In 2000, he was named director of baseball operations for the Padres. During his years in San Diego, Epstein studied law at the University of San Diego Law School.

When the investors group led by Henry and Werner purchased the Red Sox in early 2002, Lucchino came to Boston to take over as Red Sox president and CEO. Not far behind was Epstein, who in February of 2002 assumed the post of assistant general manager under interim general manager Mike Port. Throughout the 2002 season, the team's new owners scouted the field for a new general manager to replace Dan Duquette, who was fired shortly after the team changed hands. Leading candidates for the job, besides Epstein, included Port, Oakland general manager Billy Beane, J.P. Ricciardi of Toronto, Mets assistant G.M. Jim Duquette, Orioles adviser Mike Flanagan, former White Sox G.M. Ron Schueler, Cincinnati's director of player personnel Leland Maddox, and Phillies assistant G.M. Mike Arbuckle. In the end, the new owners decided that the best choice was right under their nose. "Irrespective of his age, we are confident Theo is among the best and the brightest in baseball," Red Sox chairman Werner told CNNSI.com. "We believe that the team he'll assemble will achieve results for which we so yearn."

Diving into his new job, Epstein moved quickly to put his personal imprint on the Sox. He and his staff have written software programs to help them evaluate players. Only two days after he was named general manager, Epstein claimed Tampa Bay Devil Rays pitcher Ryan Rupe off waivers. To those critics who pointed to Rupe's dismal earned–run average (ERA) of 5.60 for Tampa in 2002, Epstein replied, "An ERA is not perfect, and there's a little bit of luck involved," according to *USA Today*. To try to more accurately pinpoint Rupe's pitching ability, Epstein and his Red Sox assistants ran a software program that showed his statistics in a somewhat different light. The program computed Rupe's strikeouts, walks, and homers per inning but stripped away the runs that had been charged to the pitcher after he left the mound. Suddenly, Rupe's ERA dropped to 3.60, a sharp improvement.

As for his ultimate goal for the Red Sox, Epstein makes it clear that a World Series win would suit him just fine. As to the so–called curse that has kept the Sox from that elusive goal for more eight decades, Epstein told the *Boston Globe*'s English, "I don't really believe in curses. Look, I can't sit here and deny that the Red Sox have broken their fans's hearts for the better part of a century. But I think with the right approach, tremendous resources, great ownership, and hard work, we can put ourselves in a position to win the World Series. It's just a matter of time."

Sources

Periodicals

AP Online, November 30, 2002.
Boston Globe, December 5, 2002, p. B10.
Sports Illustrated, December 23, 2002, pp. 60–63.
USA Today, December 11, 2002, p. 3C.

Online

"Youthful enthusiasm," CNNSI.com, http://sportsillustrated.cnn.com/baseball/news/2002/11/24/redsox_epstein_ap/ (November 26, 2002).

—*Don Amerman*

Rupert Everett

Actor

Born May 29, 1959, in Norfolk, England; son of Anthony (an army officer) and Sarah (a homemaker) Everett. *Education:* Attended School of Speech and Drama, London.

Addresses: *Agent*—ICM, 8942 Wilshire Blvd., Beverly Hills, CA 90211.

Career

Actor in films, including: *Another Country*, 1984; *Dance With a Stranger*, 1985; *The Right Hand Man*, 1986; *Duet for One*, 1986; *Hearts of Fire*, 1987; *The Comfort of Strangers*, 1991; *Inside Monkey Zetterland*, 1992; *Ready to Wear*, 1994; *The Madness of King George*, 1994; *Cemetary Man*, 1996; *Dunston Checks In*, 1996; *O Casamento Do Meu Melhor Amigo*, 1997; *My Best Friend's Wedding*, 1997; *Shakespeare in Love*, 1998; *An Ideal Husband*, 1999; *Inspector Gadget*, 1999; *A Midsummer Night's Dream*, 1999; *B. Monkey*, 1999; *The Next Best Thing*, 2000; *Unconditional Love*, 2002; *The Importance of Being Earnest*, 2002. Television appearances include: *The Far Pavilions*, 1984; *Arthur the King*, 1985; *The Victoria's Secret Fashion Show* (host), 2001; *One Night with Robbie Williams* (host), 2001; *Les Liaisons Dangereuses*, 2002. Stage appearances include: *Don Juan*, 1980; *A Waste of Time*, 1981; *Another Country*, 1982; *Heartbreak House*, 1985; *The Vortex*, 1988; *Picture of Dorian Gray*, 1993; *The Milk Train Doesn't Stop Here Anymore*, 1994; *Private Lives*, 1994; *Picture of Dorian Gray* (second time in play), 2001; *The Importance of Being Earnest*; *Some Fine Day*.

Awards: Critics's Circle Award for most promising new actor, for *Another Country*, 1984; American Comedy Award for funniest supporting actor in a motion picture, for *My Best Friend's Wedding*, 1998; Favorite Supporting Actor Award—Comedy, Blockbuster Entertainment Awards, 1998; Florida Film Critics's Circle Award for best supporting actor, for *My Best Friend's Wedding*, 1998; Golden Space Needle Award for best actor, for *An Ideal Husband*, Seattle International Film Festival, 1999.

Sidelights

Rupert Everett became the next big thing when he appeared as Julia Roberts's co–conspirator in the hit film *My Best Friend's Wedding* in 1997. He was witty, charming, engaging, and irreverent, and audiences loved him. In reality, though, the film was a curtain call for the second act of Everett's career, one that had begun more than 15 years earlier on stages in London, England, and Glasgow, Scotland. His first chance at being the next big thing came originally in 1984 when he starred in the film *Another Country*, which fictionalized the school days of famous British turncoat Guy Burgess. He starred in a few other well–received films before losing credibility in England with fans, critics, and the movie industry due to temperamental outbursts and outrageous demands. With a newly gained sense of humility and a tempered wisdom, Everett has returned to being a highly admired, desired, and employed actor.

Born on May 29, 1959, in Norfolk, England, he is the son of Anthony and Sarah Everett. Everett grew up in a wealthy household. As a child he was forced to go fox hunting every weekend. Although surrounded by wealth, Everett's life was very strict and reserved. He is descended from a long line of military men; his uncles and grandfathers have served in both world wars. His father was in the army and moved the family around often while Everett was a child. When he was seven years old, Everett was sent to school at Ampleforth College, a prestigious school for boys that is run by Benedictine monks. Everett related to Ryan Gilbey of the *Sunday Times* what it was like to leave home at that age: "That was the biggest event of my whole life.... That rejection ... it calcifies your heart somewhere.... It was just the most unpleasant thing."

The experience may have been unpleasant for Everett but he seemed to make the most of it at the time. At Ampleforth, Everett was trained in classical piano. He enjoyed having the skill but harbored secret desires to be a rock star. Eventually his desire switched from rock star to actor. By the time he was 15, Everett was driven to become an actor. He dropped out of Ampleforth and went to London to attend the Central School of Speech and Drama.

Everett had expected drama school to be wild and exciting and challenging. Instead he felt he had ventured into a tame, middle-class world. Dissatisfied with his courses and classmates, he began acting out. After two years, he was expelled from the school.

Determined to make a go of his acting career, Everett headed to Scotland. Forced for the first time to support himself, Everett found himself working odd jobs. One day a man propositioned him for sex. Everett says the huge sum of money that was offered to him was something he couldn't turn down. Thus began his brief career as a male escort. In the meantime, Everett was also apprenticing with the Glasgow Citizens Theater. He started out with small roles in plays like *Don Juan* and *A Waste of Time*. By 1985, he was playing more substantial characters, including a well-received performance as Nicky, a drug-addicted young man, in the play *The Vortex*.

By this time, Everett had been noticed for his performance in the role of Guy Bennett (a fictional character based on Guy Burgess) in the stage production of *Another Country* and had recreated the role equally well in the film of the same name. The film was released in 1984 and earned Everett a Critics's Circle Award for Most Promising New Actor. While continuing to perform on the stage, Everett added to his filmography the tense and tragic film *Dance with a Stranger* starring opposite Miranda Richardson. Based on a true story, Everett played an upper class race car driver, David Blakely, who meets up with the decidedly lower class Ruth Ellis. Their affair ends with Ellis murdering Blakely. She was the last woman in England to be hanged.

As Everett's career rose, his ego also grew. He described his attitude at the time to Gilbey in the *Sunday Times* interview, "I was excessively egocentric." In return for being chastised by an audience member for being lazy during his performance, Everett sent the disgruntled audience member cuttings of his pubic hair. He was also demanding and often argumentative during productions. That attitude changed when Everett went to Hollywood in 1985 at the invitation of Orson Welles. Welles had believed Everett was perfect for a role in his film *Cradle Will Rock*. But the weeks that the two spent together were strained. Everett says that Welles seemed disappointed with him and the project eventually fell through. He stayed in Hollywood for a while attempting to find work. He discovered that mid-'80s Hollywood was more interested in Brat Pack stars like Emilio Estevez and Rob Lowe and couldn't find a place for Everett's more refined and continental style.

Everett returned to Europe and bought a villa on the southern coast of France. His house ended up being a money pit that put him into financial difficulties. He continued to find work in several French and Italian films. He had a string of regrettable films, including *Hearts of Fire* in which he co-starred with singer Bob Dylan. For a short time he moved to Moscow to work on a film with Russian director Sergei Bondarchuk, best known for his award-winning adaptation of *War and Peace*. Everett described that time in Moscow as very exciting. He felt like he was in the middle of something very important, watching as governmental policies shifted and their effects rippled through the country.

Like a modern day Renaissance man, Everett has dabbled in music and literature. In the early '80s, he indulged his earlier desire to be a rock star by releasing two albums, *Into the Vortex* and *Generation of Loneliness*. His singing talents were also evident in *Hearts of Fire*, having contributed to the soundtrack. Everett hasn't let his singing career go completely, despite the negative reviews he received for his early albums. In 2000, he sang backup to Madonna's remake of the pop classic *American Pie* (a remake that he takes credit for convincing Madonna to make). The next year when he hosted the television special *One Night with Robbie Williams*, he sang with the British pop star.

His literary pursuits have been more successful than his musical ones. In 1991, he wrote a semi–autobiographical book called *Hello Darling, Are You Working?* The book became a bestseller despite receiving less–than–stellar critical reviews. In 1994, he published another semi–autobiographical book, *The Hairdressers of St. Tropez.* This, too, made it onto the bestseller lists.

Having effectively disappeared off the radar in the early '90s by appearing only in European films which were never exported to England and which have never been recognized by American cinema, Everett made a significant reappearance in the mid–'90s. His turn as the scheming son of a fashion industry leader in director Robert Altman's *Ready to Wear* in 1994 increased his visibility. He also gained ground through his performance as the Prince of Wales in the critically acclaimed film *The Madness of King George.* It would be another supporting role that would rocket Everett into his second chance at stardom.

In the Julia Roberts vehicle *My Best Friend's Wedding,* Everett originally had a small role as her editor and friend helping her to regain the love of her life. Initial screenings of the film convinced the director to recut the film when audiences couldn't seem to get enough of Everett's onscreen wit and deviance. Several edits later, he got 17 more minutes of film time and effectively stole each scene he was in from Roberts. The chemistry between Everett and Roberts was palpable. His cool confidence in contrast to her edgy nervousness created an on-screen pairing that charmed millions of moviegoers. Off screen Everett seemed to have charmed his co-star. Roberts told Reggie Nadelson of *Vogue,* "I think the planet is a better place with Rupert on it."

With his newfound success and notoriety, Everett embarked on what seemed like a whirlwind schedule of filmmaking. He explained to Margot Dougherty of *Los Angeles Magazine,* "I got opportunities to do all sorts of things." Apparently, he turned few of these opportunities down. He had a bit part in the 1998 film *Shakespeare in Love*; appeared opposite Cate Blanchett and Minnie Driver in the comedy *An Ideal Husband*; and had roles in three other films released in 1999: *Inspector Gadget, A Midsummer Night's Dream,* and *B. Monkey.* In 2000, he teamed up with his friend Madonna to make the film *The Next Big Thing.*

Everett's classically English looks inspire admiration from men and women alike. In 1995, his looks garnered him a contract as the face of the cologne Opium for Men. When he was younger, he spent some time in Milan modeling. In 1987, long before he became one of Hollywood's leading men, he openly admitted his homosexuality. In 1997, he revealed his past history as a male escort. His reasoning for these admissions, which haven't seemed to have harmed his career (although he admits they have alarmed and hurt his family), was that he expected to be in the acting business for a long time. With that expected longevity, he decided he didn't want to have any skeletons in his closet. He has only discussed the issue of prostitution once, and chooses not to discuss it any further. As for his sexuality, he believes that if he should have any label it should be that of "actor." He explained to Gilbey, "I hate this new climate where private lives are up for debate, and celebrities have to wave whatever banner is applicable."

In contrast to his earlier hedonistic tendencies, Everett's life is much quieter these days. He lives alone and enjoys it, as he told Gilbey, "I'm very happy being alone." He shares his homes in New York, Miami, Los Angeles, and England with his constant companion, a black Labrador named Moise, nicknamed "Mo." He had once stated that he loved living in New York because he felt invigorated by the city's level of activity, but that he would never live in Los Angeles because it was boring. However, in 1999 he bought a home in Los Angeles because Mo was suffering from arthritis and his beloved pet would be better able to regain her health there.

One of the advantages of the success he's enjoyed in the past few years is being able to find more time to write. Everett is working on a new novel tentatively titled *Guilt without Sex.* He has also been developing several different scripts for films that he hopes to get into production. One of them is another vehicle for him and his former co–star Julia Roberts. He also seems to relish the ability to pick and choose his films, confident in the knowledge that he won't be out of work anytime soon.

Sources

Periodicals

Los Angeles Magazine, April 2000.
Sunday Times (London), August 11, 2002, p. 4.
Vogue, February 1998, p. 228; December 1999, p. 125.

Online

"Biography for Rupert Everett," Internet Movie Database, http://us.imdb.com/Bio?Everett,+Rupert (September 29, 2002).

—*Eve M. B. Hermann*

Ian Falconer

Author

B orn c. 1960, in Ridgefield, CT. *Education*—Attended New York University, Parsons School of Design, and Otis Art Institute.

Addresses: *Office*—c/o Atheneum Books For Young Readers, 1230 Avenue of the Americas, New York, NY 10020–1513.

Career

I llustrator for the *New Yorker.* Stage and costume designer for productions at the Los Angeles Opera, Chicago Lyric Opera, London's Covent Garden, and the New York City Ballet, among others; painter and designer of floats for Disneyland. Author of children's book series, 1997—.

Awards: Parents' Choice Gold Award for *Olivia*, 2000; Caldecott Honor Book, American Library Association, for *Olivia*, 2001; Book Sense Book of the Year Award for Children's Illustrated Winner, American Booksellers Association, for *Olivia*, 2001; Book Sense Book of the Year Award for Children's Illustrated Winner, American Booksellers Association, for *Olivia Saves the Circus*, 2002.

Sidelights

I an Falconer's first–ever book, which he both wrote and illustrated, was a stunning commercial success and took one of the highest honors in children's book publishing. *Olivia*, Falconer's artfully rendered tale of an endearing little piglet–girl with a love of clothes and penchant for the occasional self–aggrandizing remark, was named a 2001 Caldecott Honor Book by the American Library Association. Sales for it and a follow–up, *Olivia Saves the Circus*, hit the million–copy mark in 2002, and the books were translated into 17 languages. Falconer, a professional illustrator and theater set designer, shies from the limelight. His editor at Simon & Schuster, Anne Schwartz, told *Publishers Weekly* writer Gayle Feldman that in her experience, some of "the best children's authors and illustrators ... are those who are so in touch with the child in themselves that they're almost children. They're the most brilliant, and Ian is one of them."

Falconer is a native of Connecticut and was in his early forties when *Olivia Saves the Circus* appeared in print. He attended New York University, the Parsons School of Design, and Otis Art Institute, and enjoyed some early career success when he teamed with painter David Hockney. The two have designed sets and costumes for opera productions of *Tristan and Isolde* and *Turandot* for the Los Angeles Opera and London's Covent Garden house, among others. Falconer has also designed floats for Disneyland and served as a contributing illustrator to the esteemed *New Yorker* magazine.

In 1997, Falconer decided to write a book for his four–year–old niece, Olivia Crane. "She was my first niece," Falconer recalled in an interview with *People*. "I was all excited about her." He created an adorable piglet of the same name. "I just did drawings first—I drew a whole story—and then I wrote it afterwards," Falconer told *Publishers Weekly* interviewer Jennifer M. Brown. His sister and the mother of that real–life Olivia, Victoria Falconer, loved it, recalling that when she first read it, "I was crying," she said in the *People* article, "it was so touching and funny."

Falconer showed his Olivia book to an agent at the William Morris Agency, who suggested finding an established children's writer to provide the text—an idea he nixed. In the fall of 1998, Falconer received a call from Schwartz, editor of her own imprint at Atheneum Books for Young Readers. She had a book project that needed an illustrator, and knew Falconer's work from the *New Yorker*. Falconer met with Schwartz, confessing that he was not interested in illustrating a book written by somebody else, and then showed her the Olivia sketches. "It was the best work I've ever seen come from a portfolio," Schwartz told Feldman in *Publishers Weekly*. "It was contemporary but timeless."

Olivia was published by Atheneum, an imprint of Simon & Schuster, in the fall of 2000. A first printing of 30,000 copies was rapidly depleted by advance buzz surrounding the title, and within a month it had gone through five more printings and landed on the *New York Times* children's bestseller list. Critics raved over *Olivia*. Falconer's creation, an imaginative, irrepressible piglet who adores elaborate outfits, was depicted in elegant charcoal illustrations in a black, gray, red, and pink color scheme. *Olivia* chronicles a typical day for the title character, which of course involves several costume changes. The text asserts that Olivia "is good at lots of things." At the beach, she builds an Empire State Building sandcastle; visiting a museum, she scoffs at a work by American abstract expressionist painter Jackson Pollock, and then re–creates it on her wall at home. Falconer writes that Olivia is also "very good at wearing people out," and concludes with an exhausted Olivia and the line, "She even wears herself out."

"The genius of the volume is its economy: the brief text brilliantly plays off the artwork, rendered only in shades of red and black with an occasional background setting," noted a *Publishers Weekly* review, which termed it an "extraordinary debut." *Book*'s Kathleen Odean predicted that "Olivia has star quality," while *New York Times* critic Sam Swope liked the simple yet familiar scenes illustrated by Falconer that depicted parents, siblings, and even a dog and cat. Swope described Olivia's world as "*Leave It to Beaver* peopled by porkers.... Adding to this pleasant undercurrent of nostalgia is the fact that Olivia doesn't have a computer. Her family doesn't pile into an S.U.V. We never see a television set. Her room isn't overwhelmed with toys. She doesn't even own a teddy bear. (She does ride a scooter, but it's not a newfangled one.) Without the distractions of modern childhood, Olivia is left to her own devices, and they never fail her."

Falconer's heroine earned comparisons to Miss Piggy from Muppets fame, and also to the elegant, self–confident Eloise from the Kay Thompson series, illustrated by Hilary Knight, about a little girl who lives in New York's Plaza Hotel. Atheneum quickly signed Falconer for another *Olivia* book, and when he ventured the idea of a circus theme, Schwartz and others tried to dissuade him, since such books have a reputation for failure in the children's book industry. He was adamant, however, and in 2001 *Olivia Saves the Circus* appeared. Here, the porcine star delivers a "what I did on my summer vacation" tale before her classroom, and Falconer's illustrations depict her adventures in flashback. As she relates, when she attended the circus with her mother one day its stars were sick, so Olivia, with typical aplomb, stepped in. She tamed a lion, rode an elephant, and executed some impressive acrobatic feats on the trapeze and trampoline. "Falconer has successfully sustained and built upon his delightfully original portrayal of the feisty Olivia, her vivid imagination, and her strong sense of self," opined *School Library Journal* reviewer Dorian Chong. *Olivia Saves the Circus* won Falconer the Book Sense Award for Best Children's Illustrated Book, the same award Falconer won for *Olivia* only one year earlier.

Falconer has also produced two board books for younger children, *Olivia Counts* and *Olivia's Opposites*. When the first Olivia tome was published, he presented a first edition to the namesake niece, but she "took it in stride," he told Brown in the *Publishers Weekly* interview, "as though it were perfectly natural for someone to write a book about her."

Selected writings

Olivia, Atheneum (New York, NY), 2000.
Olivia Saves the Circus, Atheneum, 2001.
Olivia Counts, Simon & Schuster/Anne Schwartz, 2002.
Olivia's Opposites, Simon & Schuster/Anne Schwartz, 2002.

Sources

Periodicals

Book, May 2001, p. 80; November–December 2001, p. 75.
Booklist, August 2000, p. 2134; August 2001, p. 2116; February 15, 2002, p. 1022; July 2002, p. 1857.

Entertainment Weekly, December 8, 2000, p. 85.

Family Life, February 1, 2001, p. 93.

Financial Times, October 27, 2001, p. 5;

Horn Book, November–December 2001, p. 735.

Instructor, April 2002, p. 14.

New York Times, November 18, 2001, p. 46; January 20, 2002, p. 14.

People, February 4, 2002, p. 123.

Publishers Weekly, July 17, 2000, p. 193; November 20, 2000, p. 19; December 18, 2000, p. 26; August 27, 2001, p. 83; September 10, 2001, p. 54; December 17, 2001, p. 32; May 6, 2002, p. 60.

School Library Journal, September 2000, p. 196; October 2001, p. 114; June 2002, p. 94.

Online

"Book Sense Book of the Year Award," BookWeb. org, http://www.bookweb.org/news/awards/3433.html (October 28, 2002).

—Carol Brennan

Jimmy Fallon

George De Sota/Getty Images

Actor and comedian

Born James Thomas Fallon, September 19, 1974, in Brooklyn, NY; son of Jim and Gloria Fallon. *Education*—Attended St. Rose College, Albany, NY.

Addresses: *Management*—Green Room Productions, 2609 Kennedy Court, Franklin, TN 37064. *Office*—*Saturday Night Live*, 30 Rockefeller Plaza, New York, NY 10112.

Career

Actor on television, including: *Saturday Night Live*, 1998—; *Band of Brothers*, HBO, 2001; *MTV Movie Awards* (as host), 2001; *MTV Video Music Awards* (as host), 2002. Film appearances include: *Almost Famous*, 2000. Co–author, *I Hate This Place: The Pessimist's Guide to Life*, 1999. Released album, *The Bathroom Wall*, 2002.

Sidelights

Comedian Jimmy Fallon used to blow out the candles on his birthday cake and wish that one day he'd appear on the weekly live TV comedy show *Saturday Night Live* (*SNL*). After he made it, at age 23, he quickly became one of the troupe's leading players, known for his dead–on impressions, hilarious characters, charm, and easy good looks. Fallon has fans galore—die–hard *SNL* fans praise him on the streets of New York City, and the Internet abounds with adoring female fans who call him "sweet," "goofball," "adorable," and "cutie–pie."

Fallon was born James Thomas Fallon to Jim and Gloria Fallon, who named their two children Jim and Gloria. Born in Brooklyn, New York, and raised in Saugerties, in upstate New York, Fallon dreamed of appearing on *Saturday Night Live* as a kid. He and his sister watched the show religiously—their parents taped *SNL* weekly and edited out any questionable material. The siblings did impersonations of the show's "Two Wild and Crazy Guys" and "King Tut." As a student at Saugerties High, he and his friends came up with a *SNL* spoof called *Saugerties Night Live*. "Ever since I can remember, it's just what I wanted to do," Fallon told *US Weekly*.

Fallon began his career in comedy at age 17, when he won a "Best Impressionist" contest in a local club for his impression of the Paul Reubens character, Pee Wee Herman. In college at St. Rose College in Albany, New York, Fallon regularly passed on Saturday night party plans to watch his favorite show. He left school 15 credits shy of earning his bachelor's degree in computer science to pursue a career in comedy. He went to Los Angeles, where he studied with the famed Groundlings troupe. He has performed his stand–up, characters, and impressions in comedy clubs across the country, including the Improv in Los Angeles, and Caroline's Comedy Club in New York. Following the advice of fellow comedian and *SNL* alum Adam Sandler, Fallon continues to tour and do stand–up in his time off.

Fallon's childhood wish came true when he joined the cast of *SNL* as a featured player during the 1998–99 season. One year after failing his first audition with the show's executive producer, Lorne Michaels, Fallon got the job. He can do uncanny impressions of such stars as Robert De Niro, John Lennon, and Howard Stern, and comedians Adam Sandler, Jerry Seinfeld, and Chris Rock. His obsession with rock music has given Fallon an edge parodying such musicians as Rolling Stone Mick Jagger, singer–songwriter Alanis Morrisette, rapper Eminem, and rock groups Blink 182, Creed, and Counting Crows.

Fallon's characters include the dreadlocked college talk–show host Jarrett, the heavily accented Bostonian teen Sully, the know–it–all computer geek Nick Burns, and the cooler–than–thou clerk of the high–fashion boutique Jeffrey's. "The people who pop first on this show are the ones who you believe you can see right into their hearts," *SNL* producer Michaels told *New York*. "It was true of Gilda [Radner], it was true of John Belushi, and it's true of Jimmy. You just feel you know them."

Michaels isn't the only person to lump Fallon in with famed *SNL* greats—critics and fans liken him to the cast members of the show's best years. Although he says he gets "tired of being compared to other comedians," according to *Mean*, he still exudes a fan's excitement for *SNL* and its history. In the interview in *New York*, he called a wall of headshots "the coolest thing" in the entire *SNL* studio. The wall features *SNL* alumni, including Belushi, Chevy Chase, Eddie Murphy, Chris Farley, and Julia Louis–Dreyfus, all next to a picture of Fallon himself. "It's lunacy, right? Every time I see this, I totally flip out," he said in *New York*.

In 1999, Fallon and his sister released the book *I Hate This Place: The Pessimist's Guide to Life*. The book consists of humorous, if bleak, e–mails the two wrote cross–country to each other while he was living in Los Angeles, she in Boston. Fallon has always been close to his sister and his parents. He remembers playing sick in high school to stay home with his mom.

During *SNL*'s 2000–01 season, Fallon became co–anchor of the show's "Weekend Update" segment opposite the show's head writer, Tina Fey. He expanded his talents to more serious acting, picking up small roles in director Cameron Crowe's Oscar–winning film *Almost Famous* and in Tom Hanks's HBO World War II miniseries *Band of Brothers*. "I always wanted to die in a war movie," but didn't get the chance, he told *Teen People*. "I had to be the tough guy. I'm honking the horn of a jeep going, 'I got the ammo!'" He also co–hosted the 2001 *MTV Movie Awards* with actress Kirsten Dunst. His other television appearances include *Late Night with Conan O'Brien*, *Late Show with David Letterman*, the *Rosie O'Donnell Show*, and the *Oprah Winfrey Show*.

In 2002, Fallon released what he insisted is not an attempt to "cross over"—a record that is one–half rock songs, and one–half stand–up comedy, called *The Bathroom Wall*, to mostly favorable reviews. Fallon returned to MTV in 2002 to host the *Video Music Awards*, where he spoofed nominees Eminem, Nelly, Avril Lavigne, and the White Stripes in true Fallon fashion. "I have the greatest, most fun job ever," Fallon said in an interview with *Spin*. "Sometimes I still can't believe it."

Sources

Periodicals

Boston Globe, October 6, 1999, p. E3.
Green Bay Press–Gazette (Green Bay, WI), April 18, 2002, p. 12.
Mean (Los Angeles), June 2001.
New York, October 18, 1999, p. 40.
Paper (New York), November 2001.
People, May 13, 2002, p. 173.
Rolling Stone, July 5, 2001, p. 153.
Spin, March 2002.
Teen People, October 1, 2001, p. 118.
US Weekly, November 6, 2000, p. 20.

Online

"Eminem wins four MTV video music awards," USATODAY.com, http://www.usatoday.com/life/music/awards/mtvmusicawards/2002–08–30–mtv–awards_x.htm (October 3, 2002).
"Jimmy Fallon," NBC.com, http://www.nbc.com/Saturday_Night_Live/bios/Jimmy_Fallon.html (June 21, 2002).

—Brenna Sanchez

Frederic Fekkai

Hairstylist and beauty consultant

Born c. 1959 in Aix–en–Provence, France; children: Alexander (with Elizabeth Schiell). *Education:* Studied hairstyling under Jacques Dessange.

Addresses: *Home*—New York, NY. *Office*—c/o Beaute de Provence, 15 East 57th St., New York, NY 10022.

Career

Began as a hairstylist for Bruno Dessange Salon in New York, NY; opened Beaute de Provence salon, 1996, in New York City and Beverly Hills, CA; began Frederic Fekkai Beaute line of hair products, cosmetics, and accessories. Author, *A Year of Beauty,* 2001.

Sidelights

Beauty, according to Frederic Fekkai, is about a woman's confidence and attitude. His custom–designed coiffeurs merely help complete the picture. Recognized in the United States and internationally as a hairstylist, makeup artist, and accessories expert, Fekkai is the proprietor of the Beaute de Provence salons in New York City and Beverly Hills, California. Known by the fashion elite for his creations, Fekkai is equally familiar to the general public as a "stylist to the stars" whose clientele includes Claudia Schiffer, Martha Stewart, and Salma Hayek.

Born in Aix–en–Provence, France, Fekkai realizes his nationality is virtually associated with high style. But "being French doesn't automatically make me an authority on sexiness," he asserted in *People.* Fekkai studied hairstyling with mentor Jacques Dessange, and helped launch the Bruno Dessange Salon in New York. "I'll never forget my first day in New York," he recalled in a *Salon News* interview. He had exited a cab outside his new apartment, then "I rang the bell, but of course no one answered, and there I was on the sidewalk, bewildered. I expected America to be like the movies, certainly nothing like the cramped and funky Manhattan."

But Fekkai got the lay of the land quickly enough, to the point where he made New York City his permanent home. Fekkai was affiliated with the retailer Bergdorf Goodman, running a New York salon from their premises. But in 1996 the hairstylist entered into a joint venture with Chanel, Inc., and marked the occasion with a new business, opening Beaute de Provence in the Chanel building. The five–floor Manhattan salon's theme comes from Fekkai's birthplace; the décor features an eighteenth–century stone Provencal fountain in the reception area. The idea of channeling France "seemed natural," Fekkai noted to Jenny Fine in a *WWD* interview. "When you say Provence, people think of the Pierre Deux country look, but Provence to me has a very modern feeling. There is beautiful architecture, fabrics and colors, and that is what I wanted to recreate."

Hued in ocher and terra–cotta, the salon was designed to create what Fekkai called "a serene, intimate atmosphere, where you can still feel the buzz and meet your friends or see someone famous." Later in 1996, Beaute de Provence headed westward, opening on exclusive Rodeo Drive in Beverly Hills, California. "There will be one difference between the two salons," commented Fine in a *WWD* report. "The Beverly Hills version will—of course—offer valet parking."

Catering to those who would not find outrageous a four–month wait for a $250–plus hair appointment, Beaute de Provence salon soon took off, due in no small part to its owner's personal magnetism. "When I cut hair I perform a little dance," he admitted in *Salon News*. "I walk in circles around my client to observe her and her hair from every angle. I may ask her to stand up, sit down, I move with her." One notable customer, television newswoman Paula Zahn, told *People*, "Ninety–nine percent of the women who come to his salon fall in love" with Fekkai. But while he enjoyed a playboy image while in his twenties, the stylist changed his ways with the arrival of his son, Alexander, with art dealer Elizabeth Schiell.

The salons are run according to Fekkai's personal credo: Less is more. Nor does he cater just to the supermodel type. Indeed, "style is not about age or height or weight," he wrote in his book *A Year of Style*. "It's about a sense of ease, a sense of dignity, and a sense of individuality shining through." Fekkai's arrangement with Chanel included the introduction of a line of beauty products branded by the stylist's name. As Frederic Fekkai Beaute senior vice president Michelle Taylor stated in *WWD*, "Fekkai is to Chanel what Prescriptives is to Estee Lauder," meaning a signature cosmetics line tied to a major player in the beauty business.

The new Frederic Fekkai Beaute line incorporated two categories of cosmetics—Basics and Accents. Included in the Basics are liquid makeup, crème powder, loose powder, and concealer. With the foundation in place, a customer can then move to the Accents: lip color, eyeshadow, brow definers, blushes, and a collection of nail enamels. But even with all the variety, Fekkai stressed that moderation is key in creating personal style. "Do wear red," he advised in a *Salon News* "do's and don'ts" section. "Do simplify your makeup routine.... Don't be too serious.... Don't hide your character. Don't try to look picture perfect...."

Over the next few years the Fekkai line expanded to include fragrances, handbags, and sunglasses.

However, not every venture was successful; by 2002 the organization had retired the over–competitive cosmetics and handbag market to refocus on hair and body products. Fekkai for Men, a line of shampoo, gel, and pomade, was launched in April of 2002. To the stylist, this marked a natural transition: "I'm a very good barber," he remarked to Dana Wood in a *W Men's Portfolio* article. "There are techniques to understand, like scissors–over–comb, but once you get that, it's a *fait accompli*."

During its retail debut, Frederic Fekkai Beaute products were available only at the signature salons and through a toll–free number. The gradual rollout was intentional, Taylor asserted, giving the startup time to establish its client base and experiment with ways to grow the business. What's more, the limited access gave the fledgling line an air of exclusivity, a Fekkai spokeswoman told *WWD*'s Peter Braunstein. "Plus, a lot of people still feel uncomfortable about transacting online and using their credit cards," the spokeswoman continued. According to his website, by 2002 Fekkai products were also located in such venues as Neiman Marcus, Saks Fifth Avenue, Bloomingdale's and Lord & Taylor stores. But Fekkai did go the cyber–route when he launched Fredericfekkai.com in late 2001. While selling Fekkai products was part of the launch, the site "is avoiding full–blown transactional e–commerce," according to Braunstein. "[I]t is more than a simple online vanity site," because it highlights the toll–free number customers can call to order products.

Though he has made his name in the service of high fashion, Fekkai often finds the simplest answers the most effective. He confessed in *People* that he even gives himself the conditioner–and–gel treatment to overcome a "bad hair day."

Sources

Books

Fekkai, Frederic, *Frederic Fekkai: A Year of Style*, Clarkson Potter, 2000.

Periodicals

People, May 8, 1995, p. 162; November 6, 2000, p. 53.
Salon News, January 2001, p. 64.
Town & Country, November 2000, p. 228.
WWD, July 11, 1995, p. 2; February 8, 1996, p. 2; August 9, 1996, p. 5; December 2, 1996, p. 8; July 11, 1997, p. 12; August 4, 1997, p. 20; April 17, 1998, p. 6; April 20, 1998, p. 8; June 19, 1998, p. 7; No-

vember 26, 2001, p. 3; February 13, 2002, p. 19; February 15, 2002, p. 13.

Online

Frederic Fekkai website, http://www.fredericfekkai. com (November 23, 2002).

"Haircut 101," *W Men's Portfolio,* http://www. geocities.com/FashionAvenue/1122/fashion_ men/haircut.html (November 23, 2002).

—*Susan Salter*

Albert Finney

Actor and director

Born Albert Finney, Jr., May 9, 1936, in Salford, Lancashire, England; son of Albert Finney, Sr. (a bookmaker) and Alice (Hobson) Finney; married Jane Wenham (an actress), 1957 (divorced, 1961); married Anouk Aimee (an actress), 1970 (divorced, 1978); children: Simon (from first marriage). *Education:* Graduated from Royal Academy of Dramatic Arts, 1955.

Addresses: *Agent*—International Creative Management, 76 Oxford St., London W1D 1BS, United Kingdom.

Career

Actor on stage, including: *Julius Caesar*, Birmingham, England, 1956; *Caesar and Cleopatra*, London, England, 1956; *The Beaux Stratagem*, Birmingham, 1956–58; *The Alchemist*, Birmingham, 1956–58; *The Lizard on the Rock*, Birmingham, 1956–58; *Henry V*, Birmingham, 1956–58; *Macbeth*, Birmingham, 1958; *The Party*, London, 1958; *King Lear*, Stratford–upon–Avon, England, 1959; *Othello*, Stratford–upon–Avon, 1959; *A Midsummer Night's Dream*, Stratford–upon–Avon, 1959; *Coriolanus*, Stratford–upon–Avon, 1959; *The Lily–White Boys*, London, 1960; *Luther*, Paris, France, and London, 1961; *Twelfth Night*, London, 1962; *Luther*, New York, New York (Broadway), 1963; *Henry IV*, Glasgow, Scotland, 1963; *Much Ado About Nothing*, London, 1965; *Armstrong's Last Goodnight*, Chichester, England, 1966; *Miss Julie*, Chichester, 1966; *Black Comedy*, Chichester, 1966; *A Day in the Death of Joe Egg*, Broadway, 1968; *Alpha Beta*, London, 1972; *Krapp's Last Tape*, London, 1973; *Cromwell*, London, 1973; *Chez Nous*, London, 1974; *Ham-*

let, London, 1975; *Tambulaine the Great*, London, 1976; *Hamlet*, Lyttelton Theatre, England, 1976; *Tribute to a Lady*, London, 1976; *The Country Wife*, London, 1977; *The Cherry Orchard*, London, 1978; *Macbeth*, London, 1978; *Uncle Vanya*, Manchester, England, 1978; *Present Laughter*, Manchester, 1978; *Has Washington Legs?*, London, 1978; *Armstrong's Last Goodnight*, London, 1983; *Sergeant Musgrave's Dance*, London, 1984; *The Biko Inquest*, London, 1984; *Orphans*, London, 1986; *J.J. Farr*, London, 1987; *Another Time*, London; *Reflected Glory*, London, 1992. Joined Birmingham Repertory Theatre, 1955; joined Britain's National Theatre Company, 1965; partnered with Michael Medwin to form Memorial Enterprises Ltd., 1965; associate artistic director, Royal Court Theatre, 1972–75. Director for the stage, including: *The Birthday Party*, Glasgow, 1973; *The School for Scandal*, Glasgow, 1973; *Armstrong's Last Goodnight*, London, 1975; *The Freedom of the City*, London, 1973; *Loot*, London, 1975; *Armstrong's Last Goodnight*, London; *The Biko Inquest*, London, 1984; *Sergeant Musgrave's Dance*, London, 1984. Producer for the stage, including: *A Day in the Death of Joe Egg*, London, 1967.

Film appearances include: *The Entertainer*, 1960; *Saturday Night and Sunday Morning*, 1960; *The Victors*, 1963; *Tom Jones*, 1963; *Night Must Fall*, 1964; *Two for the Road*, 1967; *Charlie Bubbles*, 1967; *The Picasso Sum-*

mer, 1969; *Scrooge,* 1970; *Gumshoe,* 1972; *Bleak Moments,* 1972; *Alpha Beta,* 1973; *Murder on the Orient Express,* 1974; *The Adventures of Sherlock Holmes' Smarter Brother,* 1975; *The Duellists,* 1978; *Loophole,* 1980; *Looker,* 1981; *Wolfen,* 1981; *Shoot the Moon,* 1982; *Annie,* 1982; *The Dresser,* 1983; *Under the Volcano,* 1984; *Orphans,* 1987; *Miller's Crossing,* 1990; *Rich in Love,* 1992; *The Playboys,* 1992; *The Browning Version,* 1992; *A Man of No Importance,* 1994; *The Run of the Country,* 1995; *Washington Square,* 1997; *Breakfast of Champions,* 1999; *Simpatico,* 1999; *Erin Brockovich,* 2000; *Traffic,* 2000; *Joan of Arc: the Virgin Warrior,* 2000; *Delivering Milo,* 2000; *Hemingway, the Hunter of Death,* 2001. Director of films, including: *Charlie Bubbles,* 1967. Producer of films, including: *Gumshoe,* 1963; *Night Must Fall,* 1964; *Charlie Bubbles,* 1967; *If ...,* 1969; *Bleak Moments,* 1972; *O Lucky Man!* 1973.

Television appearances include: *Forget–Me–Not Lane* (movie), 1975; *Pope John Paul II* (movie), 1984; *The Biko Inquest* (movie), 1984; *The Image* (movie), 1990; *The Endless Game* (movie), 1990; *The Green Man* (movie), 1990; *Karaoke* (miniseries), 1996; *Cold Lazarus* (miniseries), 1996; *Nostromo* (miniseries), 1996; *My Uncle Silas,* 2000; *The Gathering Storm* (movie), 2002.

Awards: BAFTA Award for most promising newcomer, British Academy of Film and Television Arts, for *Saturday Night and Sunday Morning,* 1960; best actor, National Board of Review, for *Saturday Night and Sunday Morning,* 1961; best actor, Mar del Plata Film Festival, for *Saturday Night and Sunday Morning,* 1961; best actor, New York Film Critics Circle, for *Tom Jones,* 1963; best actor, Venice Film Festival, for *Tom Jones,* 1963; Golden Globe Award for most promising newcomer, Hollywood Foreign Press Association, 1964; Golden Globe Award for best actor, Hollywood Foreign Press Association, for *Scrooge,* 1971; best actor, Berlin International Film Festival, for *The Dresser,* 1984; acting award, U.K. Film Critics's Circle, for *Under the Volcano,* 1984; best actor, Los Angeles Film Critics, for *Under the Volcano,* 1984; Dilys Powell Award, London Critics Circle, 1999; Emmy Award for best actor in a miniseries or made–for–television film, Academy of Television Arts and Sciences, for *The Gathering Storm,* 2002.

Sidelights

Part of the vanguard of northern actors who took the British stage by storm in the latter half of the 1950s, Albert Finney remains today one of the most dynamic British actors of stage, screen, and television. Although he first won attention on the stage, he rose to international prominence in film during the British New Wave's surge in social realism of the early 1960s. His searing portrayal of working class anti–hero Arthur Seaton in *Saturday Night and Sunday Morning,* director Karl Reisz's classic "angry young man" drama, won Finney wide acclaim in his homeland and around the world. His early reputation as a film actor of tremendous range was further bolstered in 1963 by his award–winning portrayal of the title character in director Tony Richardson's immensely popular film production of *Tom Jones.*

Early in his stage career, Finney appeared with Sir Laurence Olivier in a 1958 production of Shakespeare's *Coriolanus.* Years later, in an interview with Louis B. Hobson of the *Calgary Sun,* Finney recalled, "I went on for him [Olivier] once at the last moment.... Olivier pulled a ligament. I had a small role in the play and had understudied him, so with just a few hours rehearsal, I went on. I was not prepared for how difficult a task that was because Olivier always made it look so easy. That was his genius." At the time, Olivier was 41 and Finney was 22. When Olivier died in 1989, the British press dubbed Finney the great Olivier's successor as Britain's leading stage actor.

Born in Salford, Lancashire, England, on May 9, 1936, Finney, the son of bookmaker Albert Finney and his wife, Alice, grew up in the industrial heart of northern England, not far from the city of Manchester. As a boy he was exposed to the economic hardship and social injustice common to the gritty factory town in which he was raised. After graduating from Salford Grammar School, Finney attended the Royal Academy of Dramatic Arts in London, graduating in 1955.

Fresh out of drama school, Finney joined the Birmingham Repertory Company and in 1956 made his stage debut in the role of Decius Brutus in a production of William Shakespeare's *Julius Caesar.* After seeing Finney's portrayal of Henry V, a reviewer from the *Times* of London observed, as quoted in the *International Dictionary of Theatre,* that the young actor displayed considerable stature and emotional maturity, "sturdy rather than royal, in the Burton tradition rather than the Olivier." Word of the dynamic young actor's talent spread, and noted actor Charles Laughton traveled to Birmingham to see Finney play the title role in *Macbeth.* In 1958 Finney won critical acclaim opposite Laughton in a West End production of *The Party,* after which Finney joined the Shakespeare Memorial Theatre at Stratford–on–Avon for its centennial season.

In 1957, Finney married actress Jane Wenham, who appeared on London's West End in a number of musicals, including 1956's *Grab Me a Gondola,* 1963's

Virtue in Danger, and 1971's *Tyger.* The couple had a son, Simon, who works as a film technician. Finney and Wenham were divorced in 1961.

Among other roles at Stratford–on–Avon, Finney played Cassio opposite Paul Robeson's Othello in a production directed by Tony Richardson and reunited with Laughton in a production of *A Midsummer Night's Dream.* It was at Stratford that the young actor understudied Olivier in *Coriolanus.* In a 2000 interview with Cindy Pearlman of the *Chicago Sun-Times,* Finney recalled: "[Olivier] was at the peak of his powers, and each night I watched him make this role his own. He pushed the possibilities. He told me, 'Albert, that's what real imagination can do.'"

Finney's brief encounter with Olivier in Stratford eventually led to a small role as the actor's son in *The Entertainer,* Finney's film debut in 1960. Later that same year, Finney electrified film audiences everywhere with his searing portrait of Arthur Seaton, the cocky, belligerent anti–hero of *Saturday Night and Sunday Morning,* directed by Reisz. When the film was reissued by the British Film Institute in the fall of 2002, BBC reviewer Jamie Sullivan wrote, "Set in Nottingham at the end of the '50s, *Saturday Night* offered newcomer Finney the chance to really show what he could do on–screen. The result is a smoldering, poison pen letter of a film in which Finney's working class hero—a rarity in the stuffy days of postwar British cinema—battles the system with a near–religious fervor.... Finney exhibits a talent and screen presence here that helped make him a star."

Finney's vibrant portrayal of Seaton won him the title role in the 1963 film adaptation of Henry Fielding's *Tom Jones,* directed by Richardson, who had produced *Saturday Night.* Audiences everywhere were captivated by Finney's portrayal of Fielding's rakish hero, which earned him his first Academy Award nomination as Best Actor. That same year, the actor made his Broadway debut in the title role of John Osborne's *Luther,* also directed by Richardson. In 1964 Finney reunited with director Reisz for a remake of *Night Must Fall,* which Finney also produced.

Finney and fellow actor Michael Medwin teamed up in 1965 to found Memorial Enterprises Ltd., a film and theater production company. On one of Memorial's first film productions, *Charlie Bubbles,* Finney made his directorial debut. He also starred in the film. Memorial's other ventures included the 1968 motion picture adaptation of *If ...,* directed by

Lindsay Anderson, and 1973's *O Lucky Man!,* as well as the successful play, *A Day in the Life of Joe Egg,* written by Peter Nichols. Finney proved himself a very credible leading man when he teamed up with Audrey Hepburn for the romantic film comedy–drama *Two for the Road* in 1967. For his performance in the title role in the 1970 musical *Scrooge,* Finney won the 1971 Golden Globe Award for Best Performance by an Actor in a Motion Picture—Comedy or Musical. In 1970 Finney married French actress Anouk Aimee. They divorced in 1978.

Finney continued to confound audiences and critics with his incredible range. He followed his dead–on portrayal of a 20th–century art enthusiast in 1969's *Picasso Summer* with his award–winning turn as Ebenezer Scrooge in the musical version of Charles Dickens' beloved *A Christmas Carol* in 1970. Other diverse roles from this period included that of a bickering husband in 1973's *Alpha Beta,* Belgian sleuth Hercule Poirot in 1974's *Murder on the Orient Express,* a Frenchman of the Napoleonic Era in 1978's *The Duellists,* a werewolf hunter in 1981's *Wolfen,* and a plastic surgeon/murder suspect in *Looker* that same year. His portrayal of Hercule Poirot won for Finney his second Academy Award nomination as Best Actor.

Between 1974 and 1981, Finney appeared in only one film—*The Duellists*—devoting himself instead to the stage. As a member of the the National Theatre beginning in 1975, Finney played the title roles in *Hamlet, Macbeth, Tamburlaine the Great,* and *Uncle Vanya.*

Returning to film, Finney earned his third Academy Award Best Actor nomination for his portrayal in *Shoot the Moon* (1982) of an award–winning novelist who has left his wife of 15 years to live with his lover. In his review of the film for the *Boston Globe,* Michael Blowen wrote: "Finney, playing an older version of his character in *Saturday Night and Sunday Morning,* conveys both the guilt and joy of a man in crisis. In scenes of tenderness with his children and rage with his wife, he communicates the extremes of a man experiencing what is jingoistically called a mid–life crisis." Although Finney's performance was almost universally acclaimed, *Shoot the Moon* was a financial failure. In 1983, Finney appeared in Peter Yates' *The Dresser,* which won the actor his fourth Academy Award nomination as Best Actor. Finney played Sir, an aging Shakespearean actor whose tragic life in many ways parallels that of one of the characters—King Lear—he plays on stage.

The following year Finney collected still another Academy Award Best Actor nomination—and a Golden Globe nomination as well—for his portrayal of a hopelessly alcoholic British diplomat in director John Huston's *Under the Volcano.* In its review of the film, *Magill's Survey of Cinema* observed that "Albert Finney's performance ... is superb. His modulations from utterly incoherent inebriation to tequila–sodden lucidity and wit, the intensity of his pain in recalling the past he is cursed never to be able to forget, and the incomparable physical presence of a man struggling to stay upright (both physically and psychologically) while pulled down by drink and conscience—all of these qualities of the Consul's character are brilliantly captured in Finney's singularly successful portrayal."

In 1987 Finney demonstrated his flair for dialects with his portrayal of a deceptive, alcoholic Chicago gangster in *Orphans,* a role he originated on stage. *Orphans* was followed by a series of made–for–TV films, including *The Green Man, Karaoke, Cold Lazarus,* and Joseph Conrad's *Nostromo.* Finney returned to the big screen in 1990 with the Coen brothers' *Miller's Crossing,* in which he played an Irish gang leader. He followed this with a trio of portrayals of Irish characters in 1992's *The Playboys,* 1994's *A Man of No Importance,* and 1995's *The Run of the Country.* Sandwiched in between his Irish roles was Finney's portrayal of hapless Southerner Warren Odom in 1993's *Rich in Love.* In his review of *Rich in Love,* James Berardinelli wrote: "Albert Finney, who seems at home in almost any role, conquers this one with aplomb. He masters Warren with as much ease as he does the Southern accent. As written, Finney's character might not be the most interesting of men, but the actor infuses him with life and keeps him from becoming the maudlin cliché that is the unfortunate destiny of many abandoned motion picture spouses."

For the remainder of the 1990s, Finney divided himself between stage and film ventures. In 1996 he reunited with Tom Courtenay, his co–star in *The Dresser,* for the London stage production of *Art.* He and Courtenay teamed up again at the end of the decade for *A Rather English Marriage,* which was aired in the United States on the Public Broadcasting Service's *Masterpiece Theatre* series. On the big screen, Finney also portrayed eccentric author Kilgore Trout in 1999's *Breakfast of Champions* and a former racing commissioner in Sam Shepard's *Simpatico* that same year.

With his memorable performance in the 2000 box office hit *Erin Brockovich,* Finney won the widest audience he'd enjoyed in years. His portrayal of Brockovich's lawyer boss, opposite Julia Roberts in the title role, won Finney another Academy Award nomination, this time as Best Supporting Actor.

Steven Soderbergh, who directed *Erin Brockovich,* also persuaded Finney to take a cameo role in the director's *Traffic,* another big commercial hit also released in 2000.

Finney's portrayal of Winston Churchill in HBO's 2002 made–for–television production of *The Gathering Storm* won for the actor some of the most lavish praise of his career. The television drama, in which Finney played opposite Vanessa Redgrave in the role of Churchill's wife, Clementine, is an acid–etched portrait of the Churchills' marriage in the years leading up to World War II. Typical of the critical praise for Finney's work was this observation from Tom Shales of the *Washington Post:* "Albert Finney's portrayal of Churchill must be the best ever done anywhere by anyone, with the exception of Churchill's portrayal of himself on the world stage. Finney's performance transcends all the usual limitations of imitating real–life figures. It transcends even the notion of performance. The acting is invisible. From his first appearance, preceded by the end of a cigar and the tip of a cane, Albert Finney steps aside and lets Churchill take over." The performance won Finney an Emmy Award as Best Actor in a Miniseries or Made–for–Television Film.

Sources

Books

Complete Marquis Who's Who, Marquis Who's Who, 2001.
Contemporary Theatre, Film, and Television, volume 35, Gale Group, 2001.
International Dictionary of Films and Filmmakers, Volume 3: Actors and Actresses, St. James Press, 1996.
International Dictionary of Theatre, Volume 3: Actors, Directors, and Designers, St. James Press, 1996.

Periodicals

Birmingham Post, September 24, 2002, p. 9.
Boston Globe, April 3, 1983.
Calgary Sun, March 15, 2000.
Chicago Sun Times, March 13, 2000.
Independent on Sunday, January 26, 1997, p. 18.
Magill's Survey of Cinema, June 15, 1995.
Minneapolis Star Tribune, February 26, 1995, p. 6F.
Washington Post, April 27, 2002, p. C1.

Online

"Albert Finney," Yahoo! Movies, http://movies.yahoo.com/shop?d=hc&id=1800018748&cf=biog&intl=us (February 17, 2003).

"Albert Finney—Awards," Thespian.net, http://www.thespiannet.com/actors/F/finney_albert/awards.shtml (February 17, 2003).

"Albert Finney Biography," Britmovie, http://www.britmovie.co.uk/actors/f/005.html (February 17, 2003).

"Albert Finney: Biography," Hollywood.com, http://www.hollywood.com/celebs/bio/celeb/1677461 (February 17, 2003).

Rich in Love, ReelViews, http://www.movie–reviews.colossus.net/movies/r/rich_in.html (February 18, 2003).

Saturday Night and Sunday Morning, BBC.com, http://www.bbc.co.uk/kent/films/reviews/saturday_night.shtml (March 1, 2003).

"*Shoot the Moon* Deserves Notice; Portrait of Domestic Reality Should Be Seen More Than Once," Acme Web Pages, http://www.acmewebpages.com/articles/8304glob.htm (March 1, 2003).

—Don Amerman

Ari Fleischer

AP/Wide World Photos

Former White House press secretary

Born Lawrence Ari Fleischer in 1960, in Pound Ridge, NY. *Education*—Middlebury College, B.A. 1982 (political science). *Politics*—Republican.

Addresses: *Office*—c/o The White House, 1600 Pennsylvania Ave. NW, Washington, D.C. 20500.

Career

Press secretary for Jon Fossel, 1982; worked phone banks for Republican National Committee; press secretary for Congressman Norman Lent; press secretary for Senator Pete Domenici, 1989–92; depute communications director for President George H.W. Bush, 1992; ran lobbying firm, 1992–1994; spokesman, House Ways and Means Committee, 1994–99; communications director, Elizabeth Dole for President campaign, 1999; White House press secretary, 2000–03.

Sidelights

Ari Fleischer became the official spokesperson for President–elect George W. Bush in December of 2000. As White House press secretary, Fleischer was in charge of handling media queries and disseminating information about the administration, its policies, and its goals to reporters. His notoriously tough job became even more difficult in the wake of the attacks on the World Trade Center and the Pentagon on September 11, 2001, and the subsequent U.S. military assault on Afghanistan, but Fleischer won high marks for his performance.

Joe Lockhart, Fleischer's predecessor who worked for the Clinton White House, described the role of White House press secretary to *People* as "an impossible job. If you can avoid making yourself the story and reflect the President's beliefs, you've done a good job. And so far he's done that."

Fleischer, who turned 40 the year that Bush was inaugurated, grew up in Pound Ridge, a suburban enclave near New York City. His father was an executive recruiter, while his mother worked as a computer programmer at IBM. He attended Fox Lane High School, where twice he was elected president of his class. Both Fleischer parents were committed Democrats, and admitted later that their youngest son's Republican sympathies, which emerged during his years at Middlebury College, surprised them. After graduating with a degree in political science in 1982, Fleischer found work as press secretary to Jon Fossel, a Republican from New York who was running for a Congressional seat. Fossel lost, but Fleischer was still determined to work in politics, and so he moved to Washington and lived with his older brother. He first worked the phone banks for the Republican National Committee, and was eventually hired as press secretary to New York congressman Norman Lent. From there he took a job with New Mexico senator Pete Domenici in 1989.

Fleischer became a trusted up–and–comer in Republican Party circles. He served as deputy communications director for incumbent President George H.W. Bush in his failed 1992 re–election campaign. During the Clinton years, Fleischer ran his own lobbying firm for aircraft makers and cattle ranchers, and returned to the back halls of Congress when he took a job with a Republican from Texas, Bill Archer, who chaired the House Ways and Means Committee. He quit that job when he was hired by American Red Cross president Elizabeth Dole as communications director in her campaign to become the Republican Party nominee for the White House in 2000.

Fleischer quit the Dole team in September of 1999, and Dole herself dropped out of the race when the presidential campaign of another Republican, Texas governor George W. Bush, began to gain momentum. When the communications director for the Bush team, Karen Hughes, learned that Fleischer had quit the Dole campaign, she offered him a job. He initially declined, but Archer urged him to take the job, and so he interviewed with Hughes. "I remember him telling me what he really wanted to do was find a nice Jewish woman and get married and have children," Hughes told Washington Post writer Howard Kurtz.

After the election dispute between Bush and Democratic hopeful Al Gore was resolved in the Texas governor's favor, Bush began making his staff appointments, and Fleischer was named the next White House press secretary. Fleischer endured some initial trials during his first few months on the job. Members of the White House Correspondents's Association complained that he called press conferences on too short a notice, and in June of 2001, a Washington Post article allowed Fleischer to voice his ire about acts of vandalism he claimed were committed by outgoing Clinton staffers. At times, he was derided as a member of a tightly controlled Bush White House staff, and termed an official spokesperson who appears to be tied to "a very short leash," as four–decade White House correspondent Helen Thomas told New York Times writer Alessandra Stanley. In response, Fleischer stated, "My job is to faithfully represent the president at all times. The French use the expression 'porte parole,' which means 'carries the words,' and that is what I do."

Barely a year into his high–profile job, Fleischer rose to new challenges when suspected militant Islamic extremists launched devastating attacks on the World Trade Center and the Pentagon. On September 11, 2001, Fleischer was at the side of the commander–in–chief for the entire day aboard Air Force One, Bush's plane, which ferried him and his staff to two different military bases and then back to the nation's capital in the evening.

Fleischer weathered a small crisis when he commented, not long after the September 11 attacks, that Americans needed to "watch what they say." The quote was mentioned in newspaper articles exploring issues of censorship in the new, highly charged atmosphere of national uncertainty, and critics attacked his statement as an unprecedented restriction on free speech in modern times. "Fleischer says he was also directing his remarks at GOP Rep. John Cooksey, who made the dopey remark that 'diaper heads' should be pulled over on the highway," reported Newsweek's Jonathan Adler, who noted that the White House official then rescinded his remark and stated that he hoped that in such times of crisis, everyone would become "much more thoughtful" in their remarks. Fleischer, as Adler wrote, "went out of his way to note that 'the press has an unlimited right to do what it sees fit—in war and peace.'" Fleischer weathered another storm with the crisis that emerged following reports that the White House had prior knowledge of the terrorist attacks. Time named him their "Person of the Week" for his cool–headed handling of the potentially damaging accusations.

In his highly visible job, Fleischer earned high marks for being unflappable and stoic in his demeanor before a determined group of media representatives. He became engaged to Rebecca Davis, a staff member of the Budget Director's office, in April of 2002; they married later that year. An ardent New York Yankees fan, he was known to play catch sometimes with the president, who called him "Ari Bob," because "in Texas, you have two first names," People quoted Bush as saying, "and as far as I'm concerned he's a Texan."

On May 19, 2003, Fleischer announced he would step down to pursue a career in the private sector. In an interview with CNN, he said he would seek paid speaking engagements, do some writing, and do whatever he could to assist the president's re-election campaign. He left the post on July 14, 2003, and was replaced by Deputy press secretary Scott McClellan. Fleischer has plans to open Ari Fleischer Communications, a Washington consulting firm that will advise corporate executives on handling the news media.

Sources

Periodicals

Christian Science Monitor, July 3, 2001.
Editor and Publisher, January 1, 2001.
Newsweek, October 8, 2001.
New York Times, April 22, 2001; October 30, 2001.
People, November 19, 2001.
Time, May 17, 2002.
Washington Post, December 29, 2000; April 3, 2001; June 4, 2001.

Online

"Fleischer resigning White House post," CNN.com, http://www.cnn.com/2003/ALLPOLITICS/05/19/fleischer.resigns.index.html (May 19, 2003).

"McClellan to be new White House spokesman," CNN.com, http://www.cnn.com/2003/ALLPOLITICS/06/21/mclellan/index.html (July 21, 2003).

—Carol Brennan

Mike Fleiss

Vince Bucci/Getty Images

Film and television producer, director, and writer

Born Michael Fleiss, April 14, 1964, in Fullerton, CA; married to Alex; children: Aaron, Devin. *Education:* University of California, Berkeley, B.A. (journalism), 1987.

Addresses: *Office*—c/o Next Entertainment, 14622 Ventura Blvd., Ste. 1019, Sherman Oaks, CA 91403.

Career

Worked as a sportswriter for Associated Press, *Sacramento Union,* and *Santa Rosa Press Democrat,* late 1980s; became briefly involved in book publishing; wrote stunts for Fox TV's *Totally Hidden Video;* signed on with Nash Entertainment, where he worked on *Before They Were Stars;* formed Next Entertainment, which produced *Who Wants to Marry a Multi–Millionaire?,* 1999; went on to produce series of successful reality shows, including *The Bachelor, The Bachelorette,* and *High School Reunion.*

Sidelights

Like the mythical phoenix, Mike Fleiss has managed to rise from the ashes of the disaster surrounding his role as creator and producer of the scandal–tainted *Who Wants to Marry a Multi–Millionaire?* to become one of the hottest properties in television today. Fleiss, a journalism major at Berkeley and former sportswriter, has quickly climbed the ladder to television success with his dead–on grasp of the public's almost voyeuristic appetite for real life (or a reasonable facsimile thereof) on the small screen. Quickly recovering from the debacle that followed *Multi–Millionaire* in February of 2000, Fleiss won the hearts of American television viewers with such blockbuster hits as *The Bachelor, The Bachelorette, High School Reunion,* and *Are You Hot?.* Confident that viewers's appetites for reality are far from sated, Fleiss continues to consider new ways in which to bring real life into their homes.

A little over a decade ago, Fleiss, temporarily out of work, found himself spending an inordinate amount of his time in front of the television. After hundreds of hours spent watching the unremarkable fare being served up on network TV, Fleiss made a momentous decision. He felt confident that he could write material at least as good, if not far better than what he was seeing on the small screen. On just such a whim were the seeds planted for his eventually successful television career. At first, he found it difficult to break into the business, and when he eventually did, the first jobs he managed to snare paid less than he'd made as a journalist. However, he stuck with it, and today Fleiss is one of the most sought–after players in network television.

Fleiss was born on April 14, 1964, in Fullerton, California, a suburb of Los Angeles in neighboring Orange County. An enthusiastic athlete as a boy, he spent much of his free time on the ball fields of his hometown. His love of sports and interest in journalism led him to dream of a career as a sportswriter. After finishing high school, he enrolled in the University of California, Berkeley, to major in journalism. He worked for the school paper, *The Daily Californian,* as a student, serving as its editor for a time. After graduating in 1987, he went to work as a sportswriter for the *Sacramento Union,* which has since ceased publication. For Fleiss, his first job out of college seemed to be everything he'd ever wanted. As he told Chuck Barney of the *Contra Costa Times,* "I thought it was the dream job. I got tears in my eyes the first time I walked into Arco Arena."

Laid off by the *Union* in 1989, Fleiss moved back to the Bay Area where he landed a job with the *Santa Rosa Press Democrat.* That job lasted less than a year, ending when Fleiss blew up at his supervisor after being passed over for a promotion. "I guess I can be a bit of a loose cannon," he told Barney. "I just got in my little Jetta, drove home, and never went back to sportswriting." As it turned out, journalism's loss was television's gain, but it took a little time to make the transition. Temporarily at loose ends, Fleiss spent the next several months mulling his future at the Benicia apartment he shared with his pregnant wife, Alex.

It was while watching TV that Fleiss got his inspiration about a future career possibility. After watching hours of inane programming on television, he decided, as he told the *Contra Costa Times*'s Barney, "I can write this stuff." Setting out to prove it, Fleiss began turning out scripts for a variety of TV shows then on the air but had no luck in selling any of them. He eventually managed to win a job dreaming up stunts for the Fox TV series *Totally Hidden Video* but was discouraged to find that it paid even less than he'd been earning as a sportswriter. However, the job did provide Fleiss with an opportunity to learn the business and before long he was coming up with his own proposals for TV programming. He soon hooked up with Bruce Nash of Nash Entertainment, one of the pioneers of reality TV, and began working on such shows as *Before They Were Stars* and *Breaking the Magician's Code: Magic Secrets Finally Revealed.*

After having a falling out with Nash, Fleiss in 1999 formed Next Entertainment, which a year later produced the now–infamous *Who Wants to Marry a Multi–Millionaire.* At first blush, the special, aired on Fox TV in February of 2000, was a smashing success, attracting an audience of more than 23 million viewers. But less than a week after the broadcast,

Fleiss found himself awash in controversy when it was revealed that the show's "multi–millionaire," was not really as rich as billed and, moreover, had once been accused of assaulting a girlfriend. In an interview with Craig Tomashoff of *Emmy* magazine, Fleiss recalled *Multi–Millionaire* and its aftermath: "The show aired on a Monday, ratings came out on Tuesday, the scandal broke on Sunday, so I had five days of glory. It took me a few years to get back to the point where some of my publicity wasn't negative. People loved that show, though.... It started at a 13 share, and by the end of the two hours it was a 28 share. How did it double in the course of one airing? It's because people were calling friends, saying, 'Oh, my God! You have to look at this thing!' Three years later, people still talk about it. I mean, nobody is talking about *Wings* now."

In the days immediately following the *Multi–Millionaire* scandal, Fleiss was publicly shunned by most TV executives, but it soon became clear that the show had struck a responsive chord. "I was so radioactive that no one would publicly embrace me, but I still got calls from network presidents saying they thought the show was the best they'd ever seen," he told Allison Hope Weiner in *Entertainment Weekly.* "Within a month, I'd sold two shows to Fox."

Just over two years after the "Multi–Millionaire" debacle, Fleiss hit pay dirt with *The Bachelor,* a new entry in the reality TV sweepstakes in which one man chooses a possible spouse from among 25 candidates. Debuting on ABC on March 25, 2002, the show quickly won a loyal audience. Executives at ABC, desperate for a spark to reignite the network's falling ratings, recognized they had a hit on their hands and told Fleiss and Next Entertainment to prepare a second installment of the popular show. The second round of *The Bachelor,* which wrapped up in the late fall of 2002, proved an even bigger hit than the first installment had been, with a finale that drew more than 26 million viewers. Expressing the network's gratitude for Fleiss's contribution, Susan Lyne, president of ABC Entertainment, told the *Contra Costa Times*'s Barney: "Mike Fleiss has been a gift. He just seems to understand today's young audience and what they're looking for."

For his part, Fleiss is not surprised at all by the overwhelming popularity of reality programming and, more specifically, the success of *The Bachelor.* As he told Weiner of *Entertainment Weekly,* "Shows like *The Bachelor* make network television relevant. What I hate to see are knockoffs. I'd really like to see some of those crappy reality shows fail." Asked if he included NBC's *Fear Factor* among the latter category, he said, "That show is the most purely degrading thing on TV. They're eating a horse's a** for only $50,000." But Fleiss admitted that, given the opportunity, he would produce the show, "but I'd give a bigger prize."

So popular was *The Bachelor* that ABC cleared it for four installments, the third of which concluded in May of 2003. To answer some of the criticism from feminists upset at the spectacle of 25 women fighting and making fools of themselves over a man, Fleiss was also asked to produce a show that used the same formula but with the genders reversed. The resulting series, *The Bachelorette*, debuted in January of 2003. Fleiss gives ABC executives credit for getting the ball rolling on the gender–swapped version of his hit series. Interviewed by Marc Peyser of *Newsweek*, Fleiss said, "I was sort of dragging my feet on this one. My theory is if it's working, leave it alone. But the network wanted to silence some of our feminist critics, and rightfully so." The fourth installment of *The Bachelor* will feature one of the rejected men from *The Bachelorette.*

With all the positive buzz surrounding Fleiss's successful *Bachelor* franchise, it was almost inevitable that he would seek to find new ways of satisfying the American demand for more reality TV. The wunderkind producer's first non–*Bachelor* show out of the blocks was *High School Reunion*, which began its six–episode run on the WB network in early January of 2003. The show brought together 17 former classmates from the 1992 graduating class of Oak Park and River Forest High School in suburban Chicago, Illinois. Fleiss invited the carefully selected twenty–somethings to a jury–rigged reunion at a beachfront hotel in Maui, hoping that during their two weeks together, enough sparks—both romantic and other—would fly to make for riveting viewing. He got what he was angling for, as he told Barney. "I had hoped the drama would intensify quickly, and it really did. In one day of filming, we'd get as much drama as two to three weeks of a show like *The Bachelor.*"

The following month, Fleiss's Next Entertainment trotted out *Are You Hot? The Search for America's Sexiest People*, which pitted scantily clad young men and women against one another in competition for the titles of "hottest" man and woman. Predictably, the show was widely panned by critics and further savaged by women's groups. Despite the criticism, the show did well in the ratings. Fleiss made no pretensions to high ideals with this entry, telling *USA Today*'s Bill Keveney, "We say upfront that this is the most superficial show in TV history."

Not content to rest on his television laurels, Fleiss has branched out into film. As of the spring of 2003, the producer had two feature projects in the can, one of them an attempt to transfer the popular reality format from TV to the big screen. That project, entitled *The Quest*, documents the antics of seven friends from the University of Colorado during a hedonistic spring break in Mexico's Cabo San Lucas. Originally scheduled to premiere in early May, *The Quest* was briefly put on hold after the disastrous debut of a similarly themed film, *The Real Cancun*. In a totally different vein, Fleiss's company has also finished production of a remake of the horror classic, *The Texas Chainsaw Massacre*, scheduled to be released in the fall of 2003.

In the meantime, Fleiss toils diligently at the Sherman Oaks headquarters of Next Entertainment, looking for still–new avenues of reality to explore on the small screen. Asked by *Time* to describe his criteria for deciding to take a concept public, Fleiss said, "I like to make a show where people say, 'You can't put that on TV.' Then I put it on TV."

Sources

Periodicals

Contra Costa Times, January 4, 2003; February 18, 2003.
Daily Californian, January 22, 2003.
Entertainment Weekly, February 14, 2003, p. 29; May 2, 2003, p. 44.
Emmy, April 2003.
Newsday, January 6, 2003, p. B2.
Newsweek, January 13, 2003, pp. 62–64.
St. Louis Post–Dispatch, April 20, 1997, p. 3C.
Time, February 17, 2003, p. 64.
USA Today, February 13, 2003, p. 3D.
Variety, October 9, 2002.

Online

"*The Bachelor*," *Extratv.com*, http://extratv. warnerbros.com/dailynews/extra/03_02/03_ 11d.html (May 7, 2003).
"Man Power," *EW.com*, http://www.ew.com/ew/ report/0,6115,230206~3|42805|10~,00.html (May 6, 2003).
"Mike Fleiss," Internet Movie Database, http://us. imdb.com/Name?Fleiss,+Mike (May 6, 2003).
"The WB to Keep It Real in January," TheWB.com, http://www.thewb.com/PressRelease/Index/ 0,8341,82785,00.html (May 7, 2003).

—Don Amerman

Sutton Foster

Actress

Born March 18, 1975, in Statesboro, GA; daughter of a retired General Motors sales representative. *Education:* Attended Carnegie–Mellon University, 1993–94; student at Hunter College, c. 2001.

Addresses: *Home*—New York, NY. *Office*—c/o Marquis Theater Stage Door, 211 W. 45th St., New York, NY 10036.

Career

Began performing in children's theater in Georgia and Michigan; appeared in the national touring company of *The Will Rogers Follies,* c. 1992; appeared in national touring company of *Grease* as Sandy, c. 1995, and in same role in the Broadway production; ensemble member of *The Scarlet Pimpernel;* cast as Jennifer in *What the World Needs Now;* appeared in national tour of *Les Miserables* as Eponine, c. 2000; originated role of "Millie Dillmount" in the Broadway production of *Thoroughly Modern Millie,* 2002.

Awards: Drama Desk Award for leading actress in a musical, for *Thoroughly Modern Millie,* 2002; Antoinette (Tony) Perry Award for best actress in a musical, League of American Theatres and Producers/ American Theatre Wing, for *Thoroughly Modern Millie,* 2002; Antoinette and Astaire Award for best female dancer in a Broadway musical, Theater Development Fund, for *Thoroughly Modern Millie,* 2002.

Sidelights

Sutton Foster won the prestigious Antoinette (Tony) Perry Award in 2002 for best actress in a musical for her title role in *Thoroughly Modern Millie,* that year's surprise Broadway hit. Just 27 years old and a relative newcomer to the world of professional musical theater, Foster earned critical accolades for her portrayal of a small–town ingénue and her adventures in a madcap 1920s New York City.

Foster was born in Georgia and began taking dance classes at the age of four. She performed in youth theater in two Peach State cities, Athens and Augusta, and starred as the lead in the musical *Annie* at the age of ten. After relocating with her family to suburban Detroit, Michigan, in the late 1980s, she joined a local theater group there, and as a high schooler tried out for and won a spot in the touring company of *The Will Rogers Follies.* After a year at Pittsburgh's Carnegie Mellon University, Foster moved back home with her parents, who were then living in Memphis, Tennessee, at the time, and waited tables at a local Macaroni Grill.

Foster's older brother, Hunter, was by then living and working as an actor in New York City, and she joined him there to try her luck in auditions. She won the part of Sandy, the lead female role, in the national tour of *Grease,* and appeared in a revival of *The Scarlet Pimpernel.* She also appeared in the hit Andrew Lloyd Webber musical, *Les Miserables,* as Eponine, in its third national tour.

In between jobs, Foster joined a workshop for a planned stage version of *Thoroughly Modern Millie,* a musical whose origins were a kitschy 1967 Hollywood film starring Julie Andrews as the lead. For the live musical adaptation, the songbook had been entirely rewritten, and director Michael Mayer took the finished version to the La Jolla Playhouse in suburban San Diego in late 2000 for its pre–New York tryout. The starring role was originally slated for Kristin Chenoweth, who was compelled to drop out when she won her own television series. Foster, originally with a small cast part and serving as the understudy for the new lead, was invited to try the Millie role just weeks before it opened when Mayer was dissatisfied with Chenoweth's replacement.

Foster had just three days to learn the lead role of a young Kansas ingénue who arrives in New York City in 1922 by bus. Determined to be "modern," she bobs her hair and announces her intention to marry for money rather than love. She takes up residence at an ostensibly respectable women's hotel, and sets her sights on her new boss, the owner of an insurance agency. Millie's designs on him are continually thwarted by a penniless young man she keeps bumping into around Manhattan, and she also becomes involved in uncovering the kidnapping/white–slavery ring that lurks behind her hotel's front desk.

Thoroughly Modern Millie's La Jolla performances earned positive reviews and garnered interest from Broadway producers. *Variety*'s Steven Oxman saw it there, and noted that there had been some last–minute changes made to tailor the part more specifically to Foster's talents. "The superbly slick result displays no signs of trauma," Oxman noted. "Only a week into its official run, the show is remarkably tight and moves along so briskly that it accomplishes what few musicals can brag about these days: It leaves the audience wanting more." The *Variety* critic called Foster "ideal" as Millie, "and she demonstrates some serious triple–threat potential, acting, singing and dancing the role with a confident ease. She brings to Millie a kind of brassy American boldness" that Oxman asserted had been lacking in Julie Andrews's characterization.

A Broadway production of *Thoroughly Modern Millie* was planned, but producers nervous about their collective $9.5 million investment were unsure about letting an unknown like Foster take the lead. The names of pop stars/actresses Britney Spears, Jennifer Love Hewitt, and even Jewel were mentioned, but director Mayer was adamant that Foster open the show in New York. "I didn't want a star in the part," Mayer told *New York Post* just before the show's April of 2002 Broadway premiere. "The audience should receive her as Millie, the new girl in town."

Foster was understandably nervous about opening night at the Marquis Theater. She recalled it as initially "one of the best nights of my life," she told *New York Times* writer by Don Shewey, remembering how she walked home with her actor boyfriend afterward. She was crushed to read the first negative newspaper reviews. The *New York Times*'s Ben Brantley had labeled *Thoroughly Modern Millie* a "hard sell…. Watching this aggressively eager show is like being stampeded by circus ponies. It's all whinnying and clomping and brightly decorated bouncing heads, and it never lets up for a second." Brantley asserted Foster "has the pearly toothed, clean–scrubbed glow of the young Marie Osmond and works like a Trojan throughout."

Foster recalled in the interview with Shewey that upon reading such critiques, "the pressure of the show came rushing into me," she said, "and I thought: 'Oh, no! I'm playing the lead and I've let everyone down!'" But subsequent reviews were more upbeat in their assessment of the Broadway newcomer. *Back Stage*'s Julius Novick called Foster "a lanky, likeable belter with plenty of easy energy, quite up to the job of carrying a 10–million–dollar musical," and Stefan Kanfer in the *New Leader* described her as "a leggy singer/dancer/actress of extraordinary energy and high style."

Foster's name was among those nominated for several Tony awards for *Thoroughly Modern Millie.* She and her brother also made Broadway history, as the first brother–and–sister team nominated in the same Tony slot—best lead in a musical—in their respective gender categories; Hunter Foster was nominated for his role in *Urinetown: The Musical. Thoroughly Modern Millie* won several Tonys in June of 2002, including best actress honors for Foster and best new musical; the resulting publicity boosted ticket sales immensely. The actress, whose dressing room at the Marquis was larger than her New York City apartment, was optimistic about her future. When interviewed with her brother for *Entertainment Weekly,* she admitted to admiring former childhood *Annie* star and *Sex and the City* actress Sarah Jessica Parker, along with Parker's husband Matthew Broderick, as role models. "She's famous but not out of control," said Foster, "and they're unbelievably talented and keep doing things that stretch them."

Selected discography

Thoroughly Modern Millie (cast recording), RCA, 2002.

Sources

Back Stage, May 3, 2002, p. 48.
Daily Variety, May 17, 2002, p. 4.
Entertainment Weekly, June 28, 2002, p. 100.

New Leader, May–June 2002, p. 53.
New York Post, April 16, 2002, p. 37.
New York Times, April 19, 2002; May 19, 2002, p. 12; May 20, 2002, p. E6; June 4, 2002, p. E3.
People, June 3, 2002, p. 120.
Record (Bergen County, N.J.), April 14, 2002, p. E4; April 19, 2002, p. 20; June 3, 2002, p. F7.
Variety, November 6, 2000, p. 28.

—*Carol Brennan*

Charles Frazier

Author

Born Charles Robinson Frazier, November 4, 1950, in Asheville, NC; son of Charles O. (a high school principal) and Betty (a school librarian and administrator) Frazier; married Katherine (a professor of accounting), 1976; children: Annie. *Education:* University of North Carolina, B.A., 1973; graduate studies at Appalachian State University; University of South Carolina, Ph.D., 1986.

Addresses: *Agent*—Amanda Urban, International Creative Management, Inc., 40 West 57th St., New York, NY 10019. *Home*—North Carolina.

Career

Author. University of Colorado, professor of English until 1986; North Carolina State University, professor of English until 1989.

Awards: National Book Award for fiction, National Book Foundation, for *Cold Mountain,* 1997.

Sidelights

Charles Frazier stunned the American literary scene with his debut novel, *Cold Mountain,* the story of a Civil War veteran and his long journey home. Published in 1997 to extravagant critical accolades, it dominated the *New York Times* bestseller list for weeks and sold three million copies; it made Frazier, a former part–time literature professor and househusband who spent eight years writing it, an overnight literary sensation. The success of *Cold*

AP/Wide World Photos

Mountain was trumpeted as proof that literary fiction had not been forever banished from bestseller lists. "Just when many people in publishing were decrying the dominance of chain stores and megaselling pop fiction," remarked Malcolm Jones Jr. in *Newsweek,* "Frazier's book proved that literary fiction by an unknown writer could succeed wildly." Five years after its publication, the story was filmed by director Anthony Minghella (*The English Patient*) with stars Jude Law and Nicole Kidman. Frazier, meanwhile, was working on his next book, for which he had signed a contract reportedly in the neighborhood of $8 million.

Born in 1950, Frazier grew up in the mountainous part of western North Carolina in which *Cold Mountain* is set, near the Nantahala Mountain range. A native of Asheville, the largest city in the area, he lived in the towns of Andrews and Franklin; in the latter, his father served as principal of his high school. After graduation in 1969, he went on to the University of North Carolina at Chapel Hill, finishing his degree in 1973. While doing graduate work at Appalachian State University he met his future wife, Katherine, and went on to earn a Ph.D. in English from the University of South Carolina. He taught literature courses at the University of Colorado and co–authored an Andes Mountain guide for the Sierra Club, but returned to North Carolina in 1986 around the time that he and his wife's daughter, Annie, was born.

Frazier taught at North Carolina State University part–time and raised show ponies on the family's property outside of Raleigh. He had the occasional short story published, but it was a bit of family history that his father told him one day that sparked his interest in writing a much larger fiction project. While researching the family's ancestry, the elder Frazier came across a reference to a great–great–grandfather who had served in the Confederate Army, was injured, and then deserted a military hospital to make his way back to Cold Mountain in western North Carolina. Fascinated by the meager story—little else was known about the rest of the man's life—Frazier began researching local and state archives for old journals and letters from the Civil War era. From there he began his story of the fictional Inman. In 1989, his wife urged him to quit his teaching job in order to write full–time.

Over the next few years, Frazier also pored over journals written by Frederick Law Olmsted, the landscape architect of New York City's Central Park who had traveled the Great Smoky Mountains; he also drew upon the writings of naturalist William Bartram, whom the Cherokee called Flower–Gatherer, to re–create the landscape of a rural, genuinely rustic American South just after the war. In *Cold Mountain*, the fictional Inman has fled a Confederate military hospital in Raleigh, disgusted by the war and its carnage. Though it was a neck wound that he was not expected to survive and did anyway, Inman feels permanently scarred inside by his experience. "He had seen the metal face of the age and had been so stunned by it that when he thought into the future, all he could envision was a world from which everything he counted important had been banished or had willingly fled," Frazier wrote, according to the *St. Louis Post–Dispatch*.

Inman is determined to return home to Cold Mountain and the love of his life, Ada. His journey takes him across the Blue Ridge Mountains during the last weeks of the war, and he must elude the deadly "Home Guard," a posse that seeks out deserters and carries out summary executions. Ada, meanwhile, is enduring struggles of her own. A former Charleston debutante, too independent–minded for her era, she is bereft after the death of her father, and impoverished as well. She has inherited his Cold Mountain estate, but it is not a true working farm; only with the help of a young teen from the area, Ruby, does Ada learn the land and the chores necessary to make the property solvent. In her dwindling spare moments at night, Ada reads aloud to Ruby from *The Odyssey*, the classic work of literature from ancient Greece about a returning war veteran and the dangers he faces.

Frazier mined many sources to come up with the period detail and archaic vocabulary that helped make *Cold Mountain* such a compelling read. When his daughter came home from school, she would read his drafts from that day aloud. "It really helped to hear it in somebody else's voice and to see if she was getting the rhythm of the sentences," Frazier told *People*'s Michelle Green. The 12–year–old also served as another important catalyst in what became her father's stunning literary celebrity: Frazier and his wife knew North Carolina novelist Kaye Gibbons from a school carpool group. Frazier's wife suggested that Gibbons read some of his manuscript. "I was so stunned," Gibbons told Green in *People*, "that my left arm went numb. Outside of Eudora Welty and William Faulkner, I had never seen anything like it." Gibbons put Frazier in touch with a literary agent, who then sent the still–unfinished manuscript to a small house, Atlantic Monthly Press. The publisher bought it in late 1995 for a six–figure sum—a record at Atlantic at the time for a first novel.

But the Press and its parent company, Grove/ Atlantic, liked the manuscript so much that as Frazier worked with an editor over the next year to shape it into final form, they sent out pre-publication galleys to publishing–industry insiders, and positive word–of–mouth soon circulated about *Cold Mountain*. As Frazier's publisher, Morgan Entrekin, told *Newsweek*'s Jeff Giles, "*Cold Mountain* came out of the gate selling," Entrekin said. "I think that's because it's a beautiful book and because there's still a network of people in this industry with big mouths."

Published in June of 1997, *Cold Mountain* had reached the number–nine spot on the *New York Times* bestseller list within a month, and the paperback and film rights soon fetched high price tags at auction. The critical response was largely positive. *Publishers Weekly* hailed it as "rich in evocative physical detail and timeless human insight," while a lengthier critique from *America*'s John B. Breslin asserted that "Frazier gives us an exquisite diptych: in Inman's story, an unstinting epic of war and its ravages, on and off the battlefield; and in Ada's, an account of life's stubborn refusal to surrender to either man or nature's relentless onslaught." A *National Review* assessment from James Gardner described it as "an ambitious example of the historical novel. But unlike most specimens of the genre—and very much to its credit—the book treats the past as if it were, in a way, present." *National Review*'s Gardner noted that though it was the author's literary debut, "in certain details, Frazier reveals a genuine novelistic talent and tact which simply cannot be faked."

The commendatory words from reviewers seemed to vindicate Frazier and the extraordinary amount of time it took him to write *Cold Mountain*. "One thing people like—and it's something I worked real hard on," he told Jones in the *Newsweek* interview, "is the physical texture of another time and place. What interests me about historical fiction is, how do you, the reader, connect those characters and that situation to your own life? But at the same time, I want the diction of the book to make people understand this is a different world." *Cold Mountain*, as a novel of the Civil War period, also won praise for giving the ideological underpinnings of the conflict rather short shrift in comparison to others of its genre. As Frazier told the *St. Louis Post–Dispatch*, "what I tried to capture in Inman was the weariness I read in" his ancestor's letters; his own ancestor-veteran, he told the paper, had been one of a quartet of brothers who "went off to war and all four of them just had a horrible experience. And these were men who did not own any slaves and had very little connection to the Southern economy or that of the North."

Critics heralded *Cold Mountain* as the return of the commercially successful piece of literary fiction. It spent 18 weeks at No. 1 on the *New York Times* list, and almost ten months there overall. Grove/Atlantic sent Frazier out on a lengthy book tour, where hundreds lined up to have him sign their editions—an entirely new world for the shy, taciturn author. His novel was sometimes grouped alongside two other recent works, *Snow Falling on Cedars* from David Guterson, winner of the 1995 PEN/Faulkner Award for fiction, and Cormac McCarthy's *All the Pretty Horses*, the National Book Award honoree from 1992. "All three novels are seen as proof that a strong literary work by an unknown writer can still find a huge audience and proof that Americans will read beyond the usual potboilers, thrillers, romances, and other formulaic concoctions," noted the *St. Louis Post–Dispatch* writer. Frazier's literary status was secured when *Cold Mountain* took the National Book Award for fiction from the National Book Foundation later in 1997. It beat out a heavily favored contender, Don DeLillo's *Underworld*. Writing in the *National Review*, Gardner hinted that there had been some backlash behind closed doors in the publishing world because of Frazier's win, assessing *Cold Mountain* as "self–consciously literary without being opaque." The novel, Gardner continued, "presents us with characters of the requisite complexity, neither as complicated and self–absorbed as those in Mr. DeLillo's indubitably highbrow books, nor as subordinated to the dictates of compelling action as in your basic [John] Grisham or [Tom] Clancy novel."

Frazier concluded his publicity rounds and began planning his next work. In April of 2002, nearly five years since the appearance of *Cold Mountain* in book stores, he signed a deal for a second book at a sum rumored to be $8.25 million. The deal was inked on the basis of one–page outline Frazier had submitted to Random House, and the story idea came from research he had come across while writing *Cold Mountain*: around 1900, a North Carolina state psychiatric hospital housed a 100–year–old man who sometimes refused to speak any language but Cherokee. He was not a Native American, but rather had grown up among the Cherokee in North Carolina, and represented them in Washington for a time. "His life spans the time from when the southern Appalachians were still a white space on the map to the time when there were early automobiles and sound recordings and light bulbs and telephones ringing," Frazier told Jones in *Newsweek* about why the man's life fascinated him so. Though slated for completion in 2005, the as–yet–untitled work even attracted the interest of Hollywood, and the film rights were sold for $3 million; director Peter Weir (*The Truman Show*) was interested in helming it.

Later in 2002, shooting in the Carolinas and Romania began on Minghella's film version of *Cold Mountain*. Frazier, meanwhile, was ensconced on his eleven–acre ranch writing his second book and raising show ponies, which his daughter rides in competitions. The appeal of *Cold Mountain* and historical fiction in general was not a surprise to him. As he told *Newsweek*'s Jones, people seem to want to reconnect with the past. "We have this desire to look back and think that we were closer to it than we are now," Frazier mused. "How did we get where we are? A way to answer that question is to see where we've been."

Selected writings

(With Donald Seacrest) *Adventuring in the Andes: The Sierra Club Guide to Peru, Bolivia, the Amazon Basin, and the Galapagos*, Sierra Club Press (San Francisco, CA), 1985.
Cold Mountain (novel), Atlantic Monthly Press (New York, NY), 1997.

Sources

Books

Contemporary Southern Writers, St. James Press, 1999.

Periodicals

America, January 31, 1998, p. 33.

Entertainment Weekly, September 26, 1997, p. 46.

Esquire, November 1998, p. 70.

National Review, December 31, 1997, p. 54.

Newsweek, July 28, 1997, p. 64; April 6, 1998, p. 62; April 15, 2002, p. 54.

New York Times, April 7, 2002, p. 24.

People, February 23, 1998, p. 107.

Publishers Weekly, May 5, 1997, p. 196; November 24, 1997, p. 14.

Roanoke Times, January 17, 1999, p. 1.

Southern Review, Winter 2000, p. 188.

St. Louis Post–Dispatch, November 13, 1997, p. G1.

—*Carol Brennan*

Patricia A. Friend

Tim Boyle/Getty Images

Labor union executive

Born August 28, 1946; married and divorced. *Education:* Attended Northeastern State College, Tahlequah, OK, mid–1960s.

Addresses: *Home*—Washington, D.C. *Office*—Association of Flight Attendants, AFL–CIO, 1275 K St. NW, 5th Fl., Washington, DC 20005.

Career

Began career as a flight attendant with United Airlines, 1966; head of United Council 8/ORD Chicago local of the Association of Flight Attendants, 1980–82; chaired grievance committee after 1982; named to ESOP (Employee Stock Ownership Plan) Committee, 1993; elected president of the union, 1995; re–elected twice; also serves as a vice president in the American Federal of Labor Unions–Congress of Industrial Organizations (AFL–CIO).

Sidelights

Patricia A. Friend has headed the Association of Flight Attendants as its international president since 1995. Friend represents some 50,000 American flight attendants at 26 airlines in the largest union of flight attendants in the world. Once an ardent champion to improve working conditions for flight crews, who were increasingly beleaguered as airlines struggled to cut costs, since 2001 Friend has concentrated on calling attention to new work–safety rules in the wake of the deadly commercial-passenger jet hijackings that destroyed the World Trade Center and part of the Pentagon on Septem-

ber 11 of that year. "The old view of a hijacker is a dissident who wants to go to Cuba or take a tour of the Middle East," Lou Gonzales, a reporter for the Colorado Springs *Gazette*, quoted Friend as saying. "We've been trained to negotiate with them. They are not interested in negotiating anymore."

Born in 1946, Friend grew up in Oklahoma and studied at Northeastern State College in Tahlequah. She left school after applying to become a flight attendant, who were then called "stewardesses," with United Airlines in 1966. She was surprised to land the job, she told *Newsmakers* in a telephone interview, for there was a certain glamour attached to it, and applicants were many. Most airlines had specific height and weight requirements for female flight attendants—who were usually required to be single as well—and Friend was obliged, in a practice that was standard at the time in the industry, to sign a document stating that she would give up the job when she reached the age of 32.

Friend was drawn into union activism during the 1970s, as new federal civil–rights legislation made such age strictures increasingly unsupportable in the courts. As contentious contract negotiations were underway in 1977 and a strike loomed at United, she called her local union office to volunteer, and remained active after the walkout was averted. In 1980, she was elected head of her local United Airlines chapter of the Association of Flight Attendants in Chicago, and served for two years. Over the next decade she became increasingly active in union duties and work committees. At the onset of the 1990s, Friend took a sabbatical from her union work, but continued to fly United on its international route based out of London. Transferring to Washington, D.C., she resumed duties part–time at the union while continuing to fly. In 1995, she was elected to her first term as international president of the union, which is also part of the American Federal of Labor Unions–Congress of Industrial Organizations (AFL–CIO). She was re–elected to her third term in 2001.

Much of Friend's job takes place in Washington, meeting with members of Congress and officials in the Department of Transportation and the Federal Aviation Authority. Her terms as AFA president had already achieved some notable gains: the union was able to secure federal whistleblower–protection laws that shielded employees from reprisals when they called attention to safety or other types of violations; the union also secured increased penalties for passengers charged with interfering with the flight crews after several well–publicized incidents of "air rage."

The September 11, 2001, hijackings of United Airlines planes by a network of men with links to Afghanistan's Al–Qaeda terrorist organization brought renewed calls from Friend and her union to protect crews and passengers alike. Shortly after the tragedy, U.S. Secretary of Transportation Norman Mineta appointed her to a special Department of Transportation Rapid Response Team for Aircraft Security, which met to make recommendations, both immediate and long–term, for improvements that could make passenger planes safer and immune to such attacks in the future. Friend argued foremost for better defense training for flight crews. "Every day flight attendants go to work as unprepared for an attack as we were on September 10, 2001," *Time* quoted her as saying. Federal funds were allocated to the airlines for defense training, but months later Friend again spoke out, claiming that the airlines had been lax in offering the classes to their employees, and charged that some of the ones that were offered were woefully inadequate 45–minute lectures.

Later in 2001, Friend called attention to increased security measures at airports in the wake of the terrorist attacks. Speaking for several union members who had filed complaints claiming that airport security guards had inappropriately fondled female flight attendants, Friend lodged a formal complaint to Secretary Mineta. A few weeks later, Friend testified before a Congressional committee on aviation security, pointing out that after "September 11th, the American people have made it abundantly clear that they expect the government to correct fundamental problems in the air security system before they will resume normal travel patterns. Our nation's flight attendants have not had the similar luxury of picking and choosing when they would fly—they went right back to work after September 11th. They comforted anxious passengers, while they coped with not only their own concerns and fears about personal safety, but their grief for fellow flight attendants who lost their lives." Friend concluded her testimony by voicing her union's approval of the recently passed Aviation and Transportation Security Act of 2001, which established a program to train professional passenger screeners at airports, among other measures. She noted that there were still other areas for improvement, such as better industry–wide limits for carry–on bags, hands–on defense training for flight crews, and permission to carry non–lethal weapons in the cabin. "If we leave one loophole in the system, terrorists will find it," Friend asserted. "I urge you to help us move swiftly on these additional security needs in order to build a truly secure and safe aviation environment."

Friend's job as union president has become even more important, after economic repercussions from September 11 landed several major airlines in financial trouble—United among them. In December of 2002, the company went bankrupt, the largest bankruptcy in aviation history. Retiree health benefits are one of the main bargaining points as the airline's unions, the AFA among them, struggle to avoid widespread layoffs and cutbacks. Though she has not flown since 1996, Friend remains on the international flight crew seniority list with United. Her career has witnessed many changes since she began in the mid–1960s, at a time when nearly all benefit packages for flight attendants, save for the free travel, were almost nonexistent. "Women weren't expected to stay on the job for long," back then, Friend told *Newsmakers*.

Sources

Periodicals

Atlanta Journal–Constitution, February 29, 2000, p. C1.
Gazette (Colorado Springs, CO), September 19, 2001.
New York Times, December 5, 2001.
Los Angeles Times, October 19, 2001, p. C4.

Star Tribune (Minneapolis, MN), August 8, 2002, p. 3D.
Time, August 19, 2002, p. 17.

Online

"Federal Regulations Needed To Ensure Aviation Security," Committee On Government Reform, http://reform.house.gov/reg/hearings/112701AirSecurity/Friend.htm (January 11, 2003).

Additional information was obtained through a telephone interview with Patricia Friend on February 25, 2003.

—Carol Brennan

Bill Frist

AP/Wide World Photos

Senate Majority Leader

Born William Harrison Frist, February 22, 1952, in Nashville, TN; son of Thomas Sr. (a physician) and Dorothy Harrison (a homemaker; maiden name, Cate) Frist; married Karyn (a homemaker), March 14, 1981; children: Harrison, Jonathan, Bryan. *Education:* Princeton University, A.B., 1974; Harvard University Medical School, M.D. (honors), 1978.

Addresses: *Home*—Nashville, TN. *Office*—The Hon. Bill Frist, United States Senate. 416 Russell Senate Office Building, Washington, D.C. 20510.

Career

Began medical residency in surgery at Massachusetts General Hospital in Boston, 1978; became chief resident and fellow in cardiothoracic surgery at the hospital, 1984; senior fellow and chief resident in cardiovascular surgery at Cardiac Transplant Service, Stanford University, Stanford, CA, 1985–86; assistant professor of cardiac and thoracic surgery, surgical director of Multi–Organ Transplant Center, Vanderbilt University, Nashville, TN, 1986–94; chair of the Center's executive committee, 1989–94; elected to the U.S. Senate from Tennessee, 1994 and 2000; named head of the National Republican Senatorial Committee; elected Senate majority leader, December, 2002.

Awards: President's Award for best scientific paper, Southern Thoracic Surgical Association, 1986.

Sidelights

Tennessee's Republican Senator Bill Frist was the surprise choice to become United States Senate majority leader in December of 2002, after colleague Trent Lott was forced out of the job when racially insensitive remarks the Mississippi legislator made incited a national furor. Often termed the epitome of compassionate conservatism, Frist was a nationally renowned thoracic surgeon and heart–and–lung transplant expert before winning his first–ever bid for electoral office in 1994. *Christian Science Monitor* writer Gail Russell Chaddock called his appointment "one of the most unlikely rises to power in Senate history," but pundits noted it was Frist's background as a physician—and an eleventh–hour, life–saving one at that—that seemed to make him a natural choice to heal the rifts within the GOP.

Frist hails from a prominent Tennessee family. An ancestor was one of the first 52 settlers of Chattanooga, and by the time Frist was born in 1952, his father's career was rapidly advancing as a heart specialist in Nashville. The senior Frist would serve as personal physician to no less than seven successive Tennessee governors. Frist's two older brothers became doctors as well, and one eventually founded the Hospital Corporation of America with their father. It would later become the largest chain of investor–owned hospitals in United States. Politically, the Frist family was conservative, but mother Dorothy Cate Frist had a reputation as somewhat of a dissident and liked to challenge her husband and neighbors on such topics as the United States military presence in Vietnam.

Frist enjoyed a successful, accomplished high-school career at Montgomery Bell Academy, an all-boys prep school. He served as yearbook editor and class president, and though he suffered a motor-cycle accident that shattered his knee, he recovered well enough to play the starting quarterback position on the school's football team during his senior year. He was the first in his family to leave the South to attend college, choosing Princeton University. He graduated in 1974 with a degree in health–care policy from its Woodrow Wilson School of Public and International Affairs, and went on to earn his M.D. from Harvard Medical School in 1978.

Frist planned to specialize in cardiac surgery. He completed a five–year surgical residency at Massachusetts General Hospital in 1983, but during this time became interested in organ–transplant medicine. He headed to Stanford University Medical Center, which was a leader in transplant surgery at the time, and in 1986 returned to Nashville and established the Transplant Center at Vanderbilt University's Medical Center. It was one of the first multi–specialty organ transplant centers in the United States, and Frist served as its director for a number of years. He performed more than 200 heart and lung transplant procedures, and chronicled those experiences in a 1989 book, *Transplant*, published by Atlantic Monthly Press.

Frist had, to date, displayed little interest in politics. He voted for the first time in his life in 1988, at the age of 36. But in 1992, Tennessee governor Ned McWherter made him head of a commission to reform the state's Medicaid program, and not long after that Frist decided—with what many termed an impractical streak of ambition—to make a bid for one of Tennessee's two Senate seats. Running as a Republican, he went up against an 18–year Democratic incumbent, Jim Sasser, and spent heavily. He hired a tough, media–savvy Republican campaign strategist, and Frist's televisions ads and campaign speeches excoriated Sasser's voting record in Washington. Tennesseans seemed to like this relative newcomer to politics, with a well–known local name and a stellar career as a heart surgeon, and Frist wound up beating Sasser by 14 percentage points.

Frist's election–day triumph in November of 1994 landed him on the cover of *Time* with another long-shot winner of the Senate races, Republican Steve Stockman of Texas. Frist also became the first practicing physician elected to the United States Senate since 1928. During his first six–year term, he made a name for himself as a staunch supporter of Republican politics, and by the last year of that term had been named the Senate's deputy whip. As a physician, Frist made health–care issues his focus, and argued for more private–sector initiatives that would aid the underinsured and uninsured, such as tax credits for those who must buy private health insurance. He supported the Medicare Prescription Drug and Modernization Act of 2000 and the Patient Privacy Act, and championed President George W. Bush's Medicare reform plan. As a conservative Republican, he opposes women's reproductive rights, but also managed to craft a compromise for the controversial stem–cell research proposal.

In 2000, when Frist ran for re–election, he also headed the National Republican Senatorial Committee and served as the Senate's official liaison to the George W. Bush for President Committee. In the Tennessee voting, Frist trounced Democratic challenger Jeff Clark by the largest margin in Tennessee election history. The Senate's Republicans gained a majority finally after the 2002 elections, and Frist continued his rise in the GOP. That year, noted *New York Times* writer Richard W. Stevenson, "Frist impressed the White House, including Karl Rove, the president's chief political adviser, and Mr. Bush himself with his astute judgment, diligent preparation, and sheer hard work. In doing so he went from being a talented up–and–comer to the administration's favorite senator, Republican strategists and allies of the White House said."

After the November balloting, Senate GOP members elected Trent Lott of Mississippi to the important post of Senate majority leader. A few weeks later, however, footage surfaced of a speech Lott gave on December 5 at a 100th–birthday dinner for South Carolina Senator Strom Thurmond. In the 1948 presidential race, Thurmond had run on a platform that championed racial segregation. Speaking about his home state in the tribute, Lott asserted, "When Strom Thurmond ran for president, we voted for him. We're proud of it," he told the audience, according to a *New York Times* report by Robin Toner. "And if the rest of the country had followed our lead, we wouldn't have had all these problems over all these years, either." The remarks caused an outcry, and though Lott claimed he had been speaking off the cuff, a similar quote surfaced from a 1980 speech he had made. The remarks became front-page headlines across the United States and were debated internationally as well; pundits called them evidence that the Republican Party was deeply insensitive to minorities. Lott's colleague, Senator Don Nickles of Oklahoma, called for his resignation as Senate majority leader, and others asserted that he should give up his Senate seat altogether.

Frist quickly emerged as the frontrunner to replace Lott as the Senate's GOP leader, and reportedly enjoyed the crucial behind–the–scenes backing of President Bush. Finally, Lott agreed to step down from the job, but not resign, and an emergency conference call among all Republican senators and senators–elect on December 24 elected Frist to the job unanimously. It was the first time in Senate history that such a vote had taken place over telephone lines, and was also the only instance of a Senate majority leader being ousted, though such maneuvers are common in the House of Representatives. In his first speech after the vote, Frist said, "a few moments ago something unprecedented in the history of the country happened with my election to the United States Senate under circumstances that nobody had anticipated," a *New York Times* report quoted him as saying. The new Senate majority leader promised to work "to ensure that the United States Senate as an institution does stand united, that indeed the Republican Party in the broadest sense stands united."

Frist became the least–experienced senator ever to hold the Senate majority leader job from either party. It was an appointment described by the *New York Times*'s Toner as "the most challenging and byzantine of political jobs, one that has humbled far more experienced politicians: managing an agonizingly small majority in a profoundly polarized Senate." Frist's main duty was to move legislation through the Senate, by securing the necessary number of votes to get Republican–sponsored bills passed, or stymie the legislative goals of Democrats with voting blocks. His new post also required a grasp of the complex rules and procedures of the Senate. Yet Frist's rise was viewed as a symbolic gesture from an embattled Republican Party; his status as a cardiac surgeon, and the general respect that physicians enjoyed as healers, was also mentioned repeatedly in the press as the Lott controversy faded. *New Yorker* writer Hendrik Hertzberg described it as a "a nice, clean trade–in, which not only substituted an attractive–seeming fellow for an unctuous incompetent but also changed the question of the day from 'How come these guys are always pining for Jim Crow and white supremacy?' to 'Isn't it reassuring that they got rid of that terrible man?'"

After the vote that elected Frist Senate majority leader, Congress shut down for the Christmas holidays and convened again on January 8, 2003. Cus-

tomarily, the Senate leader holds a news conference that day and announces his political priorities for the coming year, but Frist had no time to prepare such a statement. After his first day on the job, during which he began to master the complex procedural rules of the job, he spoke with *New York Times* journalist David Firestone and compared it to "my first heart transplant. It's a good day, and I'm excited, but I can't forget the enormous responsibility I have now assumed."

Frist asserts he is a firm believer in term limits, and has said he will only serve until 2006. Even prior to assuming the Senate majority leader post, his name had been mentioned as a possible Republican contender for the presidential nomination in 2008. He still keeps his doctor's bag in his Senate desk, and has worked as a medical missionary in Africa with an organization called Samaritan's Purse, run by Franklin Graham, son of the evangelist Billy Graham. Known for own good–samaritan deeds closer to home, Frist rushed to aid Thurmond when he collapsed on the Senate floor in 2001, and also put his medical training to use when a gunman took aim at several people on Capitol Hill in 1998. Not long after he became Senate majority leader, Frist happened upon a highway accident in Florida on New Year's Day; he pulled over to help before emergency medical personnel arrived, clearing the windpipe of one victim and resuscitating two others. During the nationwide anthrax scare in October of 2001, Frist's medical expertise landed him on a bipartisan emergency committee to help deal with the crisis. From his experiences, Frist authored another book, *When Every Moment Counts: What You Need to Know About Bioterrorism from the Senate's Only Doctor.*

Known for his tireless work ethic, Frist reportedly still eschews sleep one night per week, as he has done since his medical–residency days. He also flies his own plane and has completed both marathons and triathlons. Stock in his family's company—placed in a blind trust when he was first elected, to avoid conflict–of–interest worries—gives him an estimated fortune of $20 million, making him one of the Senate's wealthier members. Married with three sons, Frist's home base remains in Nashville, where he lives in the house his parents once owned.

Selected writings

Transplant, Atlantic Monthly Press, 1989.
(Editor with J. Harold Helderman) *Grand Rounds in Transplantation,* Chapman & Hall (New York), 1995.
(With J. Lee Annis, Jr.) *Tennessee Senators, 1911–2001: Portraits of Leadership in a Century of Change,* Madison Books (Lanham, MD), 1999.

When Every Moment Counts: What You Need to Know About Bioterrorism from the Senate's Only Doctor, Rowman & Littlefield (Lanham, MD), 2002.

Sources

ADWEEK Southwest, January 6, 2003, p. 3.
Christian Science Monitor, December 23, 2002, p. 1.
Good Housekeeping, April 2002, p. 50.
Independent (London, England), January 31, 2003, p. 14.

Medical Economics, January 9, 1995, p. 93.
New Republic, January 27, 2003, p. 16.
New Yorker, January 27, 2003, p. 27.
New York Times, December 15, 2002, p. 1, p. 5; December 21, 2002, p. A1; December 22, 2002, p. 1; December 23, 2002, p. A23; December 24, 2002, p. A1, p. A18; January 8, 2003, p. A16.
Time, November 21, 1994, p. 54; January 13, 2003, pp. 32–34.

—*Carol Brennan*

Victor Ganzi

Chief Executive Officer and President of Hearst Corporation

Born Victor F. Ganzi in 1947, in Queens, NY; married Patricia; children: twin daughters. *Education:* Fordham University, 1968; Harvard University Law School, J.D., 1971; New York University, L.L.M. in taxation, 1981.

Addresses: *Office*—Hearst Corporation, 959 8th Ave., New York, NY 10019.

Career

Tax attorney at the law firm of Roger & Wells, 1970–90; general council and vice president, Hearst Corporation, 1990–92; chief financial and legal officer, and senior vice president, Hearst Corp., 1992–95; director, Hearst Business Media, 1995–99; executive vice president, Hearst Corp., 1997–98; chief operating officer, Hearst Corp., 1998–2002; chief executive officer and president, Hearst Corporation, 2002—.

Sidelights

Victor Ganzi became the chief executive officer (CEO) and president of the Hearst Corporation, one of America's oldest media conglomerates, in 2002. He had risen through the corporate ranks at Hearst over the previous 12 years, most recently serving as the company's number two in command under outgoing CEO Frank Bennack, Jr. Hailed by Bennack as the best possible choice for the job, Ganzi took over leadership in the venerable company at a time when declining advertising revenue and stiff competition from bigger conglomerates promised to make his job challenging.

Ganzi was born in the New York City borough of Queens in 1947. His father worked as a typesetter during the 1930s at the *New York Mirror,* a newspaper owned by the Hearst Corporation, setting the stage for Ganzi's later career path. After receiving his undergraduate degree at New York City's Fordham University, Ganzi went on to the Harvard Law School, where he specialized in tax law.

In 1970, Ganzi joined the law firm of Rogers & Wells, which subsequently became Clifford Chance Rogers & Wells, one of the biggest international law firms in the world. Rising through the firm's ranks, Ganzi became managing partner at the firm. His duties in this regard included managing the firm's day–to–day operations as well as its staff of attorneys and their support teams.

Ganzi's association with the Hearst Corporation began as early as 1970. Ganzi was then a tax associate with Rogers & Wells, and Hearst had just hired the firm to represent it on tax matters. Ganzi was assigned to the new account, and over the next 20 years, he became intimately familiar with Hearst's financial operations. Ganzi first went to work directly for Hearst in 1990, when he took on a job as general council to the corporation, also becoming a vice president at the company. He moved up in 1992 to the position of chief financial and legal officer, and was elected to the position of senior vice president.

In 1995, Ganzi was chosen to head the Hearst Books/Business Publishing Group, a position he held until the Group was reorganized in the summer of 1999 as Hearst Business Media. In 1997, Ganzi was elected executive vice president of the company. In 1998, following a one–year trial period, he became chief operating officer (COO) of the company, second in command only to CEO Frank Bennack, Jr. As 2002 began, Bennack announced that Ganzi would succeed him as CEO. In his announcement, Bennack warmly described Ganzi as "my partner" and said he was "the best possible successor," according to Paul D. Colford of the *Daily News*.

Bennack's retirement as Hearst CEO at the end of May of 2002 was marked by a gala event with more than 500 invited guests. It was held in a white tent at New York's Lincoln Center. Bennack had served as CEO for 24 years, and he was going out in style. Music was played by the New York Philharmonic as well as by the country music band Brooks & Dunn, Bennack's favorite musical group. Significantly, in sharp contrast to most such high profile corporate events, the party was successfully kept out of the press by Bennack and company. But that was typical of this enormously influential, but intensely private media company.

With $5.2 billion in revenues at the time of Bennack's retirement, the Hearst Corporation is a privately held company. Founded by William Randolph Hearst at the end of the 1880s, the Hearst Corporation owns, in addition to a dozen newspapers around the United States, 16 magazines—including *Good Housekeeping, Cosmopolitan, Esquire,* and *Harper's Bazaar*—numerous television stations, and substantial holdings in cable TV channels such as the History Channel, ESPN, A&E, and Lifetime.

William Randolph Hearst left very specific instructions in his will that his company was to remain in his family. The company is overseen by a board of trustees made up of 13 people, five of whom are direct Hearst descendants. A board of directors also helps to manage the company. Seven of the 20 members of the board of directors are Hearst family members.

Ganzi, 55 at the time of his appointment as Hearst CEO, had big shoes to fill. Bennack was largely credited with having transformed the Hearst Corporation over the course of two decades from what some had termed a staid, unassuming publishing company past its heyday, into a vast media empire. Under Bennack, Hearst's revenues increased sixfold through the 1980s and 1990s.

Then too, Ganzi was challenged by a softening economy that had severely weakened advertising revenue across all media outlets. With fully 60% of Hearst's revenue derived from advertising sales, Ganzi had his work cut out for him if he wanted to see the company's revenues continue to swell, especially when faced with formidable competition in the form of such media giants as AOL Time Warner and the publishing conglomerate Bertelsmann.

Although Ganzi told Colford in the *Daily News* that "radical change within Hearst is an oxymoron," he did announce initial plans following his ascension to purchase more television stations and more magazines. He was also considering leading Hearst back into the business of providing cable television services, something the company had not been involved in since it had sold a San Francisco Bay area cable company at the end of the 1980s.

Ganzi was modest in his assessment of what he could accomplish as CEO of Hearst, and effusive in his praise of his predecessor, telling Colford, "My hope is that I can be as successful as Frank was...."

In addition to his duties at Hearst, Ganzi serves on the boards of ESPN, the PGA Tour, and Palm Management Corporation. This last organization runs the Palm restaurant chain, which has branches all over the United States. Ganzi's family has owned a 50% stake in the restaurant for more than 75 years. Ganzi also contributes his time to several civic charities in the New York City area.

Sources

Periodicals

BusinessWeek, July 8, 2002, pp. 78–81.
Daily News (New York), January 2, 2002, p. 48.
Media Week, April, 6, 1998; December 10, 2001.

Online

"Corporate Biographies: Victor F. Ganzi—President and CEO," Hearst Corporation, http://www.hearstcorp.com/biographies/corp_bio_ganzi.html (March 2, 2003).

—*Michael Belfiore*

Jennifer Garner

Actress

Born Jennifer Anne Garner, April 17, 1972, in Houston, TX; daughter of Bill (a chemical engineer) and Pat (a teacher) Garner; married Scott Foley (an actor), October 19, 2000 (divorced). *Education:* Earned performing arts degree from Denison University, 1994.

Addresses: *Agent*—Endeavor, 9701 Wilshire Blvd., 10th floor, Beverly Hills, CA 90212. *Home*—Los Angeles, CA.

Career

Actress on television, including: *Spin City,* 1996; *Swift Justice,* 1996; *Fantasy Island,* 1998; *Felicity,* 1998; *The Pretender,* 1998; *Significant Others,* 1998; *The Time of Your Life,* 1999; *Alias,* 2001—. Television movie appearances include: *Harvest of Fire,* 1996; *Rose Hill,* 1997. Miniseries appearances include: *Danielle Steel's "Zoya,"* 1995; *Larry McMurtry's Dead Man's Walk,* 1996; *Aftershock: Earthquake in New York,* 1999. Film appearances include: *Deconstructing Harry,* 1997; *Mr. Magoo,* 1997; *Washington Square,* 1997; *1999,* 1998; *Dude, Where's My Car?,* 2000; *Pearl Harbor,* 2001; *Catch Me If You Can,* 2002.

Awards: Golden Globe award for best actress in a TV drama, Hollywood Foreign Press Association, for *Alias,* 2002.

Sidelights

Jennifer Garner stars in *Alias,* a sci–fi/spy thriller on the ABC network that emerged as one of the 2001–2002 television season's surprise hits. Her casting as Sydney Bristow called for Garner to don outrageous latex gear and perform daring action sequences, but also, in quieter on–camera moments, to win sympathy for her character's tragedy–plagued personal life. *Alias* was both a ratings success and a hit with critics, and Garner emerged as one of Hollywood's newest celebrities by the time of the show's cliffhanger first–season finale in May of 2002. "Garner's agile, soulful performance is one of the many pleasures of this stylish action show," declared *New York Times* writer Joyce Millman, and *Entertainment Weekly* writer Ken Tucker concurred. "Garner is exceptionally adroit as Sydney," Tucker noted, adding that the novice lead proved to be "a full–blown action star with acting chops...."

Garner was born in 1972 in Houston, Texas, but grew up in Charleston, West Virginia, in a family of three daughters. Her father was a chemical engineer, and her mother a teacher, and Garner was a dedicated ballet student for much of her adolescence. Upon enrolling in Denison University in Ohio, she planned to study chemistry, but the stage still lured. She eventually switched to drama and earned her performing–arts degree in 1994. She lived in New York City for a time before an increasing number of television roles began coming her way and she headed to the West Coast. Her credits include a television miniseries, *Danielle Steel's*

"Zoya," episodes of *Spin City, The Pretender,* and *Fantasy Island,* and two made–for–TV movies, *Harvest of Fire* and *Rose Hill.* In 1998, she made her feature–film debut as Annabell in *1999.*

Garner was also cast in two television series, both created by writer/producer teams involved in the hit *Party of Five* drama, but both *Significant Others* in 1998 and the following season's *Time of Your Life* (which starred Jennifer Love Hewitt) failed to catch on with viewers and were cancelled. Her break came when she won a small part on the hit WB network series *Felicity* during its 1998–99 debut season. Cast in the role of Hanna, the former girlfriend of one of the lead characters, Garner impressed the show's creator and writer, J. J. Abrams, as well as the actor playing her fictional ex, Scott Foley. Expanding on the joke that someone had ventured during a script meeting—What if Felicity was actually an international spy?—Abrams began planning a new action series, and invited Garner to audition for the lead.

Meanwhile Garner had wed Foley in the fall of 2000, and appeared in the films *Pearl Harbor* and *Dude, Where's My Car?* She was somewhat taken aback by the prospect of carrying her own television series, and began a serious fitness regimen once *Alias* was greenlighted by ABC executives. In the nearly 70–minute commercial–free pilot episode, Sydney Bristow's intriguing life was sketched out for viewers: at age 26, she is a part–time graduate student and works for what she believes is a covert branch of the Central Intelligence Agency (CIA). To the outside world and even her devoted boyfriend, Sydney appears to be a rising junior bank executive, but her Los Angeles financial institution is actually a front for the shadowy SD–6 organization.

Sydney's mother allegedly died when she was young, and she is estranged from her father, whom she believes to be an airplane–part exporter. When her boyfriend, Danny, proposes marriage, she confesses her dual life, and soon afterward he is slain in a robbery. Sydney learns that SD–6 is actually an anti–CIA organization and her father is also a member; she begins to wonder if Danny's death—and perhaps that of her mother's long ago—were indeed accidental. Irate, she offers her services to the CIA and becomes a double agent. The first season follows Garner's character as she balances work, school, and a personal life now marred by tragedy. Her father, played by Victor Garber, remains a central figure in the plot lines, and other pivotal characters include her journalist friend Will (Bradley Cooper), roommate Francie (Merrin Dungey), and her shady boss at SD–6, Arvin Sloane (Ron Rifkin). A romance seems to be developing between Sydney and her CIA handler, Michael Vaughn (Michael Vartan).

The show's premise, while somewhat fantastic, hinged upon Garner's abilities to pull it off convincingly, and a majority of the critics found her up to the challenge. "The quick–change demands of student Sydney and spy Sydney could easily have seemed ludicrous," noted *Entertainment Weekly*'s Tucker, "but she's completely in tune with Abrams's storytelling style, which slithers between the naturalistic ... and the hyper (the secret–agent hugger-mugger is as deftly edited and as exciting as a James Bond feature)." *Los Angeles Times* television critic Howard Rosenberg asserted that the show "delivers spectacular fun with great style edged in melancholy," and like many of his colleagues, singled out Garner for especial praise. Rosenberg described her as the classic action heroine, "lithe and leggy in sweats or an evening gown, a seething, smash–face fantasy heroine whose self–doubt and other human frailties lower her to mortal status and make her all the more interesting to watch." *Variety*'s Phil Gallo compared her to other popular television power–babes, finding that her role offers "none of that 'Dark Angel'–bionic humans stuff—she's all flesh and blood."

Alias also earned comparisons to cult–favorite *X–Files* for its intricate story lines and convoluted plot twists, but critics also noted that Garner's ability to defuse nuclear devices and elude danger while wearing a rubber dress and stilettos gave the show a unique edge. Gallo remarked that the lead "gets stuck in fight scenes that are so stagy one can count out the steps," and faulted an on–screen wardrobe—"in a world populated by men in suits, she's almost always showing cleavage or midriff," the *Variety* critic noted—but did concede that Garner "plays the more human side with aplomb."

Other reviews were also effusive. The *New York Times*'s Millman called it "a brisk and involving entertainment that balances action and heart. And Ms. Garner's Sydney is an appealing heroine who exudes authenticity even when she's being duplicitous. Her full–lipped mouth, her most expressive feature, is a mercurial canvas depicting determination, worry, delight, sorrow, calculation." Amy Amatangelo, critic for the *Boston Herald,* called the show "one of those rare action dramas where all the elements—plot, characters, production design, costumes, soundtrack, and performances—come together to form one perfect hour of television." Aside from the escapist thrill, however, Amatangelo also felt the show possessed a certain amount of depth, especially in Garner's portrayal of a heroine haunted by tragedy; her character's "heartbreak and her struggle for revenge and understanding are very real," Amatangelo asserted.

Garner's regimen of weight training, running, and tae kwon do for her *Alias* role was crucial, but she noted that her years of ballet class also proved advantageous. As she told Bruce Fretts in *Entertainment Weekly,* if a script sequence called for Sydney to kick another character near their ear, "chances are I'm going to hit right next to their head and not take off their nose," Garner joked. The show's creator, Abrams, ventured in another interview with the same magazine that his lead actress was using her own form of Method training. "The more risky physical stuff that she does, the more I think she feels like she's closer to who Sydney really is," Abrams told *Entertainment Weekly*'s Dan Snierson. "Gung ho is an understatement. If anything, she's sometimes too enthusiastic.... There was a big explosion thing we wouldn't let her do. I'm sure she's still depressed about that."

Garner and *Alias* won several first–season honors, including eleven Emmy nominations, and she took the Golden Globe award for Best Actress in a TV drama from the Hollywood Foreign Press Association. *Time*'s Belinda Luscombe noted that the Golden Globe in this category was rarely bestowed on action stars, but theorized it was "Garner's ability to plausibly embody Bristow's many identities—cheerful graduate student, plucky double agent, vulnerable loner and (this part is key) killer clotheshorse" that helped her beat competitors like Sela Ward, Edie Falco, and Lorraine Bracco. When her name was announced as the winner, Garner was visibly stunned, and made a self–deprecating joke when she took to the podium. "I know I was good in *Dude, Where's My Car?,* but seriously...." she was quoted as saying by Darrell Giles, writer for the Australian *Courier–Mail* in Brisbane.

During its first season, *Alias* scored high in the Nielsen ratings, pulling in nearly ten million viewers weekly. "Part frenetic espionage adventure, part precious twentysomething drama, *Alias* has emerged as the thrill ride of the 2001–02 TV season," declared Snierson in *Entertainment Weekly,* and described it as "a spy–fi roller coaster of killer gadgets, double roundkicks, triple crosses, poignant confessionals, cliff–hangers, sliced–off fingers, conspiracies, outrageous outfits, exotic locales, flirtations, [and] mythologies." Tellingly, ABC executives had scheduled it to compete with the *X–Files* on Sunday nights, an intelligent thriller not unlike *Alias,* but one whose audience had been dwindling in recent seasons. Even *X–Files* creator Chris Carter mentioned *Alias* when it was announced that his show was being cancelled. "I felt we were counter–programmed [by *Alias*]," the *New York Post* quoted Carter as saying.

After finishing the cliffhanger final episode for *Alias*'s first season—which found Sydney once again in danger, her CIA contact Vaughn vanished into a gelatinous red orb, and international peril looming—Garner spent her break working on a film project, *Daredevil,* an adaptation of the Marvel Comics series. She also appeared with Leonardo DiCaprio in another project, *Catch Me If You Can,* the true story of a con artist who eluded authorities for years. When *Alias*'s second season opened on September 29, 2002, viewers were eager to learn more about Sydney's rather complicated relationship with her mother, who proved to be very much alive and very much a threat. Swedish actress Lena Olin signed on to play the part of this deadly agent. Millman, writing in the *New York Times,* found an inspiring modern feminist message in the show. "*Alias* is really about a woman unraveling the mystery of herself by trying on and discarding personalities, learning how much of her strength and courage is for show and how much is the real thing," Millman theorized. "Sydney is refracted, but paradoxically, she's one of the most together women in prime time."

Garner's television persona has been infiltrating her personal life, as she confessed in an interview with *Esquire*'s Brendon Vaughan for the magazine's "Women We Love" issue. Her martial–arts training was the reason, she believed. "I'm starting to have all these violent dreams," she admitted. When one of her pets triggered a security alarm at their home one night, she and Foley "were creeping down the hall to make sure no one was in the house. He had a baseball bat, and I was behind him, and I was thinking, What can I do first? Elbow? Knee to the crotch? Backspin hook kick?"

In February of 2003, Twentieth Century Fox and Regency Enterprises confirmed that they were developing a feature film based on the character Elektra, who Garner played in the movie *Daredevil.* While things were going well career-wise, her personal life was having problems. On May 12, 2003, Garner filed for divorce from Foley, citing irreconcilable differences.

Sources

Books

Contemporary Theatre, Film, and Television, volume 28, Gale, 2000.

Periodicals

Boston Herald, September 30, 2001, p. 56.
Courier–Mail (Brisbane, Australia), February 7, 2002, p. 4.

Daily Variety, January 14, 2002, p. 5; February 20, 2002, p. 7; April 10, 2002, p. A4.

Entertainment Weekly, April 18, 1997, p. 53; March 20, 1998, p. 64; October 12, 2001, p. 70; November 23, 2001, p. 30; December 21, 2001, p. 51; March 8, 2002, p. 24; April 12, 2002, p. 60; September 13, 2002, p. 30.

Esquire, June 2001, p. 29; February 2002, p. 100.

Los Angeles Times, September 29, 2001, p. F16.

New York Post, January 22, 2002, p. 71.

New York Times, November 18, 2001, p. 34.

People, March 16, 1998, p. 15; March 18, 2002, p. 121; May 13, 2002, p. 119.

Teen, February 2002, p. 30.

Time, February 4, 2002, p. 62; June 10, 2002, p. 75.

Variety, October 25, 1999, p. 30; October 1, 2001, p. 46.

Online

"Garner Files For Divorce," E! Online, http://www.eonline.com/News/Items/0,1,11781,00.html (May 14, 2003).

"Garner Gets Daredevil Spinoff," E! Online, http://www.eonline.com/News/Items/0,1,11347,00.html?eol.tkr (February 28, 2003).

—Carol Brennan

Laurent Gbagbo

AP/Wide World Photos

President of Ivory Coast

Born May 31, 1945, in Gagnoa, Ivory Coast; son of Zepe Paul Koudou and Gado Marguerite Koudou Paul; married Jaqueline Chanoos, July 20, 1967 (divorced, June, 1982); married Simone Ehivet, January 19, 1989; children: Koudou Michel, Gado Lea (from first marriage), Gado Marie–Patrice, Popo Marie–Laurence, three stepchildren (from second marriage). *Education:* University of Abidjan, B.A. (history), 1969; University of Paris, Sorbonne, M.A. (history), 1970; University of Paris VII, Doctorate 3rd cycle (Contemporary History), 1979. *Politics:* Ivorian Popular Front (FPI). *Ethnicity:* Bété. *Religion:* Roman Catholic.

Addresses: *Office:* Présidence de la République, 01 BP 1354, Abidjan 01, Côte d'Ivoire.

Career

Taught history and geography at the Classical College (Lycée Classique) of Abidjan, 1970; arrested and held for two years for "subversive" teaching, March 31, 1971; released from prison, January, 1973; held post in education department, 1973; researcher at the Institute of History, Art, and African Archaeology (IHAAA) at the University of Abidjan, 1974–80; director of IHAAA, 1980–82; fled to France, 1982; established unauthorized opposition political party, Ivorian Popular Front, or Front Populaire Ivoirien (FPI), in exile, 1982; returned to Ivory Coast, September, 1988; elected Secretary General at the founding congress of the FPI, November, 1988; challenged President Félix Houphouët–Boigny in presidential election, October, 1990; won seat in National Assembly in parliamentary elections, No-

vember, 1990; incarcerated in Abidjan prison for leading protest demonstrations, February 21–July 31, 1992; along with other opposition parties, boycotted presidential election, October, 1995; president of Ivory Coast, October 26, 2000—.

Sidelights

Laurent Gbagbo is a man of contradictions. Though he was instrumental in bringing about multi–party democracy in Ivory Coast, he became president, in part, because the only other major opposition party candidate, Alassane Ouattara, had been barred from participating due to having only "partial" Ivorian parentage. Moreover, he refused to hold new, more inclusive elections, and prevented Ouattara from running in the December parliamentary elections based on the same legal precedent. While Gbagbo had fought for 30 years for socialist issues such as workers's rights and better healthcare, he has been unable or unwilling to control his government forces, who human rights groups say are responsible for numerous human rights abuses, including extra–judicial killings, torture, and rape. It is doubtful that he directed any of these actions himself, but many analysts say that he used the same methods of incitement and ethnic division that his predecessor had. His country in the midst of civil war, they say he must choose the rule of law over military impunity if he is to prevent Ivory Coast from descending into the chaos that has plagued so many West African countries before.

Gbagbo was born on May 31, 1945, in Gagnoa, a major city in the west central part of Ivory Coast (La République de Côte d'Ivoire). His parents were of the Bété tribe, rivals of the Baoulé, the tribe that controlled Ivorian politics from independence in 1960 until 1999. He was reportedly an intelligent and single-minded student. He attended high school at the Traditional College of Abidjan, and received his diploma in 1965.

Gbagbo then studied at the University of Lyon, France, for a time, returning to Ivory Coast to earn a Bachelor of Arts degree in history from the University of Abidjan in 1969, the year that he was first arrested for his political activism; he spent two weeks in jail. He then went back to France and attended the University of Paris at the Sorbonne, where, in 1970, he obtained a Master of Arts degree in history. That same year he returned yet again to Ivory Coast, and took a position teaching geography and history at the Classical College of Abidjan, where he stayed until he was arrested in 1971 for his unauthorized teachings and for publishing politically subversive pamphlets. He was held at the Seguela military camp without trial, and not released until January of 1973.

In 1974, Gbagbo was hired as a researcher by the Institute of History, Art, and African Archaeology (IHAAA) at the University of Abidjan. Taking time out to study at the Paris VII University (part of the Sorbonne), he successfully defended his doctoral thesis, and obtained his Ph.D in 1979. He continued lecturing at the IHAAA until he became its director in 1980. His reputation as a dissident grew, and President Félix Houphouët-Boigny, who had ruled the country now for more than 20 years with little tolerance for political competition, saw him as a growing threat.

Not one to be intimidated, Gbagbo continued to speak out. In 1982 he secretly distributed a "speech" that called for multi-party democracy. It was at this time that he began to form what would become the Ivorian Popular Front (FPI), and helped lead a large-scale teachers strike, raising the ire of Houphouët-Boigny, who accused Gbagbo of being behind the alleged "teachers's plot" to overthrow the government. His group became a target of government harassment, so Gbagbo went into "voluntary" exile in France. He would not return to Ivory Coast for another six years.

In France, Gbagbo worked to fight against what he called the dictatorship of the Democratic Party of Ivory Coast (PDCI), which controlled all levels of government. To this end, he published *La Côte d'Ivoire: Pour une Alternative Démocratique* in 1983, and, in 1987, he published a collective work, *Les Propositions pour Gouverner*, which presented the FPI's program for governance. Gbagbo was officially granted political asylum in 1985, but when Jacques Chirac became Prime Minister in 1986, Gbagbo was pressured by police to leave France, presumably in some part due to his involvement with the Unified Socialist Party (PSU), and the journal *Libération Afrique*.

Gbagbo returned to Ivory Coast on September 13, 1988. On September 18 and 19 of that year, the inaugural congress of the FPI was held, and Gbagbo was elected secretary general. At the time, the FPI was still an unauthorized political party, so he was harassed again by PDCI officials. Nevertheless, the FPI held another congress in the fall of 1989. Houphouët-Boigny was under outside pressure from the World Bank, the International Monetary fund (IMF), and foreign supporters who all wanted the political system opened up for a possible successor; and he was under internal pressure from frequent public protests, so Houphouët-Boigny finally relented, and, in April of 1990, announced that there would be multi-party elections for the first time in the history of Ivory Coast. The FPI's candidate was, of course, Gbagbo. No other party dared to offer anyone up to challenge the president, who was known as "the old man."

With only six months to openly campaign, an opponent with 30 years of political machinery to back him up, and incidents of violence that the FPI claimed made the process unfair, Gbagbo was easily defeated, 81.7 percent to 18.3 percent. He disputed the election results, but the Supreme Court rejected his appeal. Gbagbo and eight other FPI candidates did, however, manage to win seats in the National Assembly in the parliamentary elections that followed in November. But the PDCI still had overwhelming control, winning 163 seats. Dissatisfaction with what was essentially still a single-party government continued, and Houphouët-Boigny continued his policy of political oppression.

In 1991, students and academics held protests over planned salary reductions, and were subjected to brutal treatment by security forces, leading in January of 1992 to a commission of inquiry, which concluded that General Robert Guei had been responsible for the violence. Houphouët-Boigny responded by backing his army chief of staff. Gbagbo led some

20,000 outraged protesters onto the streets. Violence broke out, and Gbagbo was arrested three days later under a new law that allowed organizers of public demonstrations to be held accountable for disturbances. Though he was sentenced to two years in prison, Gbagbo was released four months later after Houphouët–Boigny declared an amnesty for all who had been involved in the riots.

Houphouët–Boigny was diagnosed with prostate cancer in June of 1993. Since he had never chosen a vice president, succession would, under recent amendments to the constitution, go to the president of the National Assembly were he to die or become incapacitated. Gbagbo met with Houphouët–Boigny to ask that the constitutional provision be changed, but the President refused. He died on December 7, 1993, leaving Finance Minister Henri Konan Bédié to take his place. Prime Minister Alassane Ouattara, a Muslim from the North, didn't have time to call a government of national unity in order to hold new elections, so he gave up his challenge, resigning two days later. In May he abandoned his supporters within the PDCI to become deputy–managing director of the IMF in Washington, D.C. His departure prompted the formation of a new, moderate centrist party, the Rally of Republicans (RDR).

In 1994, Bédié passed legislation that required that both parents of a candidate had been born in Ivory Coast, and that the candidate had lived in the country for the past five years. It was no coincidence that Ouattara failed to qualify on both counts (his father was from Burkina Faso), and so this was seen as a move both to disqualify Bédié's main rival, and to further widen the growing rift between the Muslim North and the Christian South. This and other electoral irregularities brought the two main opposition parties—the RDR and the FPI—together to boycott the October of 1995 presidential election. Bédié, of course, won in a landslide.

Bédié tried to further enhance his power by amending the constitution yet again, but Gbagbo responded by leading another boycott by the FPI and other opposition deputies in June of 1998. He led a demonstration in Abidjan in September, and by December he had persuaded Bédié to establish an independent national electoral commission. But, as Alan Rake wrote in *African Leaders: Guiding the New Millennium*, "Bédié was not popular and did not have the healing touch of Houphouët–[Boigny]. The country was seething with discontent. Teachers and students renewed their strikes. The army was restless over pay and conditions. The once flourishing Ivorian economy was collapsing into stagnation and debt." And so, on December 24, 1999, a group of soldiers mutinied, taking to the streets of Abidjan. Three days later they brought in General Guei to lead them, and Bédié was overthrown in a bloodless coup.

Guei agreed to hold elections on October 22, 2000. But he was no more for democratic reform than his predecessors had been. Ouattara was again excluded from the election, and Guei stood for election himself, in spite of having claimed that he wanted to return the country to civilian rule. Thus his only opponent was Gbagbo. When elections returns began to point to Gbagbo as the winner, Guei dissolved the Electoral Commission, and an official from the Interior Ministry declared Guei the victor, citing "massive fraud." On October 24, tens of thousands of protesters, mainly from the FPI and the RDR, took to the streets of Abidjan. The Presidential Guard and other forces loyal to Guei opened fire on the crowd with little warning, killing about 60 people. Violent acts and other human rights abuses by security forces continued throughout the city. The next day, the paramilitary police, or gendarmes, joined the protesters, and persuaded some in the military to abandon their general. Guei fled the country, and Gbagbo declared himself president.

On October 26, supporters of Ouattara's RDR, who were mainly Muslims from the North, took to the streets to call for new elections, setting up barricades of burning tires. According to a Human Rights Watch Report, "[w]hile the military stayed in their barracks, the paramilitary gendarme and police launched operations to aggressively impede RDR militants from demonstrating. In many cases, paramilitary gendarmes and police actively sided with FPI mobs," who were mainly Christians from the South. In the end, more than 200 people were killed, and hundreds more wounded. Gbagbo refused to hold new elections, claiming that, as people had voted for the referendum that amended the constitution, he was merely following the law. But since many northerners who supported Ouattara had boycotted the polls, and much of the international community viewed the election as far from free and fair precisely because of the electoral laws, Gbagbo was standing on shaky ground from the moment he took office.

In January of 2001, opposition forces in the army attempted a coup, but were put down. Gbagbo publicly blamed foreigners for it, which, wrote Ross Herbert in *Business Day* (Johannesburg), "sparked a frenzy of violence." In October of 2001, Gbagbo set up a National Reconcilliation Forum, and held several meetings with Bédié and Ouattara, but, wrote Herbert, "he made no fundamental concessions and continued to spout ethnically divisive rhetoric." When a full–scale rebellion erupted on September 19, 2002, Gbagbo again blamed foreigners; Muslim northerners and foreigners were then attacked by security forces in Abidjan townships.

The fighting continued in the North, and the rebels, who called themselves the Patriotic Movement of Ivory Coast, began to gain ground, stopping only briefly for a ceasefire brokered by six other West African countries on October 3, 2002. On October 17 another ceasefire was signed and French troops came in to monitor the truce. As peace talks continued, ethnic and religious violence went on unabated since the failed coup attempt. Most observers blamed so–called death squads backed by government forces for the killings, but Gbagbo claimed that the rebels themselves were responsible, and were trying to implicate the government and destabilize the country even further.

In late November of that year, two new rebel groups, the Patriotic Movement for the Greater West and the Movement for Justice and Peace, appeared in the western part of Ivory Coast. Western diplomats believe many in these groups were supporters of General Guei, who was killed at the start of the rebellion. As Gbagbo's troops moved in to try to secure that part of the country, the peace talks with the rebels in the North became threatened. Because nearly half the population is composed of Muslims and immigrants, many observers believe that Gbagbo must end his polarizing rhetoric, and reign in his security forces if there is to be any hope of stopping Ivory Coast from following in the footsteps of its war–ravished neighbors, Sierra Leon and Liberia. Gbagbo has overcome obstacle after obstacle to get to the top, but he may find it harder to stay there.

Selected writings

Réflexions sur la Conférence de Brazzaville, Éditions CLE (Yaoundé), 1978.

Soundjata: le Lion du Manding, éditions CEDA (Abidjan), 1979.

(With Robert Bourgi) *Débat sur la Conférence de Brazzaville et la Décolonisation de l'Afrique Noire*, Institut d'Histoire, d'Art et d'Archéologie Africains (Abidjan), 1981.

La Côte d'Ivoire: économie et Société à la Veille de l'Indipendence, 1940–1960, L'Harmattan (Paris), 1982.

(With A.L. Téty Gauze) *Histoire des Magwe: Contribution à la Connaissance des peuples de la Côte d'Ivoire Occidentale*, Université Nationale de Côte d'Ivoire, Centre Réprographique de l'Enseignement Supérieur (Abidjan), 1982.

Côte d'Ivoire: pour une Alternative Démocratique, L'Hartmann (Paris), 1983.

Côte d'Ivoire: Histoire d'un Retour, L'Hartmann (Paris), 1989.

Adresse à la Jeunesse de Côte d'Ivoire: Treichville, 12 Août 1990, Front Populaire Ivoirien (Abidjan), 1990.

Côte d'Ivoire: Agir pour les Libertés, L'Hartmann (Paris), 1991.

(With Honoré De Sumo) *Le Temps de l'Espoir: Entretiens avec Honoré De Sumo*, éditions Continentales (Johannesburg), 1995.

Sources

Books

Complete Marquis Who's Who, Marquis Who's Who, 2001.

Rake, Alan, *African Leaders: Guiding the New Millennium*, The Scarecrow Press, 2001.

Uwechue, Ralph, editor, *Makers of Modern Africa: Profiles in History*, Africa Books Limited, 1996.

Periodicals

Economist (London, England), October 7, 1995, p. 48.
Economist (United States), October 28, 2000, p. 42; November 11, 2000, p. 60.
New African, December, 2000, p. 43.

Online

"Adresses Utiles du Gouvernement," *Abidjan.net*, http://www.abidjan.net/gouvernement/adresse.htm (December 2, 2002).

"An African Calamity in the Making," *allAfrica.com*, http://www.allafrica.com/stories/printable200211140278.html (November 30, 2002).

"Biographie du Président," *Le Site Officiel de la Présidence de la République de Côte d'Ivoire*, http://www.presidence.gov.ci/biographie.html (December 1, 2002).

"Côte d'Ivoire or Ivory Coast," *Africana.com*, http://www.africana.com/Articles/tt_255.html (November 24, 2002).

"Election Violence in Abidjan: October 24–26, 2000," *Human Rights Watch*, http://www.hrw.org/backgrounder/africa/IvoryCoastbrf.htm (November 24, 2002).

"Ivory Coast's Death Squads Leave Terrifying Trail," *New York Times*, http://www.nytimes.com/reuters/international/international–ivorycoast-killings.html (November 29, 2002).

"Renewed Fighting in Ivory Coast Threatens to Halt Peace Talks," *New York Times*, http://www.nytimes.com/2002/11/30/international/africa/301VOR.html (December 2, 2002).

—*Michael Geffen*

Elizabeth George

Author

Born Susan Elizabeth George, February 26, 1949, in Warren, OH; daughter of Robert (a salesman) and Anne (a nurse; maiden name, Rivelle) George; married Ira Toibin (a business manager), May 28, 1971 (divorced, 1995). *Education:* Foothill Community College, A.A., 1969; University of California at Riverside, B.A., 1970; California State University, Fullerton, M.A., 1979.

Addresses: *Agent*—Deborah Schneider, John Farquharson Ltd., 157 West 57th St., New York, NY 10107. *Home*—611 13th St., Huntington Beach, CA 92648.

Career

Teacher of English, Mater Dei High School, Santa Ana, CA, 1974–75; teacher, El Toro High School, El Toro, CA, 1975–87; writer, 1988—; instructor in creative writing, Irvine Valley College, 1989; instructor in creative writing, University of California, Irvine, 1990; conductor of writing seminars; visiting professor, University of British Columbia; visiting professor, Exeter College; teacher, annual Maui Writer's Retreat.

Awards: Named teacher of the year, Orange County, CA, 1981; Anthony award for best first novel, for *A Great Deliverance,* 1989; Agatha award for best first novel, for *A Great Deliverance,* 1989; Le Grand Prix de Litterature Policiere, 1990; MIMI award (Germany), for *Well–Schooled in Murder.*

Elizabeth George is not British. That may come as a surprise to readers of her mystery novels, which star a team of Scotland Yard sleuths. But the American–born author joins such names as Sue Grafton, Janet Evanovich, and Kathy Reichs as the successors to Dorothy Sayers and Agatha Christie, the trailblazing women who broke into the crime fiction market. George has distinguished herself from her peers, however, as a writer of length (her novel *A Traitor to Memory* runs more than 700 pages) and depth. She is, in the words of *Los Angeles Times Book Review* writer Margo Kaufman, "arguably the finest writer working in the mystery genre today."

George was born in Warren, Ohio, in 1949, the daughter of a salesman and a nurse. The family relocated to the San Francisco, California, area when George was a baby; as a child she took command of an old 1939 manual typewriter and began tapping out her first stories. "I first became interested in England in the 1960s when the Beatles made their initial invasion into pop culture in the United States," she wrote on her website. "On the heels of the Beatles came not only a score of other British pop music groups, but also fashion in the person of Mary Quant." As a high–schooler George took a trip to London for a Shakespeare seminar and found herself hooked. "We were given the freedom to explore the city, and I fell in love with it," she noted. But

George trained not as a writer but as a teacher, receiving her undergraduate degree from the University of California at Riverside and earning her master's in counseling and psychology from California State University.

A stint teaching high school followed, but George lost that job after trying to organize the other teachers into a labor union. By the time the courts ordered the fired teachers back to work, George had already secured employment at a different school. She found more success at El Toro High School in El Toro, California. George stayed there for 13 years, specializing in remedial students. She was named Orange County Teacher of the Year in 1981.

But within the careerwoman was a novelist waiting to emerge. In 1983 George's then–husband, Ira Toibin, facilitated her ambition when he brought home a new novelty—one of the first IBM personal computers available on the market. "Once the computer came into my home," George related to Galina Espinoza of *People*, "it was a simple jump from thinking about writing a novel to actually doing it." An early attempt at publishing brought rejection—and an important lesson—for the would–be novelist. "I was very lucky when [my first book] was rejected, because the editor explained to me why," she told a *Meet the Writers* site on barnes&noble.com. "I had written a very Agatha Christie–esque book and she said that wasn't the way it was done. The modern crime novel doesn't have the detective call everyone into the library. It must deal with more topical crimes and the motive must be more psychological because the things you kill for are different now."

So George retooled her style and in 1988 her first detective novel, *A Great Deliverance*, was published by Bantam to acclaim and awards. The tale introduces George's series heroes, two Britons dissimilar in gender, class, and approach. In one corner is suave, Bentley–driving Inspector Thomas Lynley, eighth earl of Asherton; in the other his blunt-talking, working–class partner, Detective Sergeant Barbara Havers. The clashing personalities, George noted to *USA Today* reporter Anita Manning, is deliberate: "I wanted to have a partner for Lynley who was his antithesis, because he was a character who might be somewhat unbelievable—a detective inspector with a title in the family for 250 years, a belted earl, handsome, rich." As for Havers, she is "his polar opposite," as the author noted on her website. "Since Barbara hated [Lynley] so much in that first novel and since she herself was fairly unlikable, it seemed to me reasonable to conclude that however she felt about someone, the reader was likely to feel the opposite."

Along with Lynley's pathologist pal Simon St. James, the sleuths investigate the beheading of a wealthy family's patriarch in *A Great Deliverance*. "At a time when other American women writers were just beginning to publish mysteries featuring hardboiled women detectives," Lisa See noted in *Publishers Weekly*, "George elected to create a contained English mystery." The author told See what appealed to her about the genre: "The English tradition offers the great tapestry novel, where you have the emotional aspects of a detective's personal life, the circumstances of the crime and, most important, the atmosphere of the English countryside that functions as another character."

A Great Deliverance won the Agatha Award for best debut crime novel, but George was not content to sit on her laurels. She published her follow–up mystery, *Payment in Blood*, in 1989. In this tale Lynley and Havers travel to a Glasgow estate to investigate the gruesome stabbing death of a playwright. Evidence points to two aristocrats, one a woman with whom Lynley has fallen in love. With the detective distracted by romance, it is up to Havers to take over the investigation, which leads to an aging stage director. Some "wonderfully drawn tensions and bonds between the characters" distinguish *Payment in Blood*, remarked *Washington Post* critic Carolyn Banks.

As George's reputation grew, so did the number of books in the Lynley–Havers series. Five novels— *Well–Schooled in Murder*, *A Suitable Vengeance*, *For the Sake of Elena*, *Missing Joseph*, and *Playing for the Ashes*—appeared with clocklike regularity over the next five years. For each novel George follows a writing pattern that draws on her schooling in psychology. "She starts with the killer, the motive and the method, then creates lengthy psychological profiles of each character," according to *Publishers Weekly*'s See. As George remarked in that article, "It's not about who's going to get the inheritance, but what their emotional pathology is." Nor is George obsessed with keeping "whodunit" a secret until the final page. "I don't mind if [readers] know who the killer is," she told See. "I'm happy to surprise them with the psychology behind the crime."

George reached a personal milestone in her life when she and Ira Toibin, her husband of 24 years, divorced. He had played a key role in George's career, beginning with his purchase of the computer that helped her write. In 1993 George told Marjorie Rosen of *People* that Toibin offered plot suggestions, including the time George was struck with writer's block concerning a murder in *Payment in Blood*. "I came downstairs, upset, and said, 'I don't know what to do,'" she remarked to Rosen. "He casually suggested, 'Kill somebody else.' And all of a sudden it started to go right again." With the breakup of her marriage in 1995, "I've built a family among my friends," the author told See. "Divorce has allowed me to enrich my friendships by becoming vulnerable and allowing my friends to give me support." She noted that her ex–husband has remained in the picture, acting as her business manager: "He does a bang–up job."

The year following her divorce the author released her eighth mystery, *In the Presence of the Enemy*. The impetus for this book's plot was the shocking real–life kidnap and murder of 12–year–old Polly Klaas, which took place in George's home state of California. In the author's version, the young kidnap victim, Charlotte Bowen, is the product of what *Entertainment Weekly*'s Mark Harris called "a loveless fling" between an Eve Bowen, a ruthlessly ambitious up–and–coming Parliament member, and Dennis Luxford, a tabloid journalist whom she actually detests. "When both parents receive notes demanding they go public in order to save Charlotte's life," Harris wrote in *Entertainment Weekly*, "a furious standoff pits two of England's most Machiavellian institutions—Parliament and Fleet Street—against each other." Because the child's mother does not want Scotland Yard involved, it is up to independent agent Simon St. James to lead the investigation. But when the child turns up dead, Lynley and Havers enter the scene. Beyond being a murder mystery, the book "raises questions of parental love and responsibility on several levels," said a *Publishers Weekly* contributor. To *People* critic Susan Toepfer, "George serves up a splendid, unsettling novel that readers will race to finish, yet not soon forget."

Hard–boiled Havers, whose character heretofore had served as a foil to Lynley, takes center stage in George's 1997 release, *Deception on His Mind*. On leave from Scotland Yard "to recuperate from injuries suffered in *In the Presence of the Enemy*," according to a *Publishers Weekly* reviewer, Havers finds herself drawn to her neighbors, a family of Pakistani immigrants. She is concerned about the recent murder of a Pakistani and fears for the safety of Hadiyyah, the young daughter of microbiologist Taymulla Azhar. So when the family leaves London to visit the seacoast city of Essex, Havers follows. The trail takes Havers to Balford, where she is asked to investigate the murder of a man who was engaged to the daughter of Azhar's wealthy uncle. "Although the killing has racial overtones," noted the *Publishers Weekly* writer, "other motives arise—love, jealousy, sexuality, religion, greed." *Entertainment Weekly*'s Harris saw the novel as a "compassionate look at two cultures glowering at one another across an abyss."

Following *In Pursuit of the Proper Sinner*, a 1999 Lynley–Havers whodunit, George produced the opus–sized *A Traitor to Memory*. Several reviewers commented on the length (736 pages) of this mystery, in which violinist Gideon Davies, under hypnotic therapy to help regain his lost ability to play, begins to dredge up memories of murder. Lynley and Havers are summoned in to find out if the past memories hold any connection to a contemporary hit–and–run murder. "Too long and predictable," decided Jane la Plante of *Library Journal*, though *Booklist*'s Connie Fletcher was more welcoming of the novel, calling *A Traitor to Memory* "first–rate suspense with a stunner of an ending." *Entertainment Weekly*'s Harris noticed that "working–class Havers is increasingly crowding out the aristocrat Lynley—and although she's richly drawn, her ongoing personal and professional miseries … are beginning to reek of masochism."

Apart from her mystery series, George branched out into short stories with *The Evidence Exposed* in 1999 and *I, Richard* in 2002. In the latter title, George shows in five tales "how the most ordinary people can turn murderous," according to Jeff Johnson of the *Post and Courier*. The title story concerns a schoolteacher's unhealthy fascination with Richard III, whose treatment of the two young princes in the tower made him one of history's great villains. In "Remember I'll Always Love You" a young widow makes a disturbing discovery about her late husband, a biotech expert who led a frightening double life. "Jealousy, greed, obsession, rats, Richard III, and bioterror," summed up Connie Fletcher of *Booklist*. "What more could a crime collection have?"

George's work made it to the small screen in a two–part BBC adaptation of her first novel, *A Great Deliverance*, which aired on the Public Broadcasting System (PBS) in July of 2002. At the same time George was working on her twelfth Lynley–Havers book, *A Place of Hiding*. The author shared her workday schedule with *People*'s Espinoza: wake at six a.m., an hour of aerobics, then down to work in book–lined study. "If I waited for the moment of inspiration to strike," she remarked, "it probably wouldn't." She also shared the news of her new relationship, with firefighter Tom McCabe.

For all her success, George is still the object of curiosity as an American writer of British mysteries. Indeed, "how many Americans can get away with using words like 'suzerainty' and 'pellucid'—in addition to the seven that can't be said on the radio—or feature lead investigators who drop classical allusions like 'Medea in Derbyshire' into the middle of their conversations?," noted *Star–Ledger* writer Tom Curran. To the author, the fuss is unwarranted. "Why on earth do people find it so weird that I write about England?," she declared on her website. "It worked well enough for Henry James."

Selected writings

A Great Deliverance, Bantam (New York City), 1988.
Payment in Blood, Bantam (New York City), 1989.
Well–Schooled in Murder, Bantam (New York City), 1990.
A Suitable Vengeance, Bantam (New York City), 1991.
For the Sake of Elena, Bantam (New York City), 1992.
Missing Joseph, Bantam (New York City), 1993.
Playing for the Ashes, Bantam (New York City), 1994.
In the Presence of the Enemy, Bantam (New York City), 1996.
Deception on His Mind, Bantam (New York City), 1997.
The Evidence Exposed (short stories) Hodder & Stoughton (London, England), 1999.
In Pursuit of the Proper Sinner, Bantam (New York City), 1999.
A Traitor to Memory, Bantam (New York City), 2001.
I, Richard (short stories), ASAP Publishing (Mission Viejo, CA), 2002.
(Editor) *Crime from the Mind of a Woman* (anthology), Hodder & Stoughton (London, England), 2002.
A Place of Hiding, Bantam Doubleday Dell (New York City), 2003.

Sources

Periodicals

Booklist, July 1999, p. 1893; May 1, 2001, p. 1632; September 1, 2002, p. 5.
Daily Telegraph (Surry Hills, Australia), August 15, 2002, p. T04.
Denver Post, July 13, 1997, p. E6.
Entertainment Weekly, September 18, 1992, p. 73; March 15, 1996, p. 56; July 18, 1997, p. 78; December 12, 1997, p. 77; August 10, 2001, p. 66.
Guardian (London, England), February 1, 2003, p. 11.
Library Journal, June 1, 2001, p. 214.
Los Angeles Times, May 26, 1996.
Los Angeles Times Book Review, August 13, 1989, p. 8; June 9, 1991; July 12, 1992, p. 8; July 10, 1994, p. 8; May 12, 1996, p. 11; October 31, 1999, p. 11.
New Yorker, August 23, 1993, p. 165.
People, October 1, 1990, p. 32; August 31, 1992, p. 26; August 23, 1993, p. 59; August 22, 1994, p. 24; March 18, 1996, p. 34; July 21, 1997, p. 29; August 26, 2002, pp. 107–108.
Post and Courier (Charleston, SC), January 5, 2003, p. E3.
Publishers Weekly, April 12, 1991, p. 46; May 11, 1992, p. 56; May 23, 1994, p. 80; January 8, 1996, p. 60; March 11, 1996, p. 38; June 2, 1997, p. 56; October 7, 2002, p. 56.
Star–Ledger (Newark, NJ), March 24, 1996, p. 6; October 10, 1999, p. 5.
Sunday Herald (Glasgow, Scotland), May 5, 2002, p. 15.
USA Today, March 26, 1996, p. 8D.
Washington Post, August 29, 1989; February 29, 1996, p. C2.

Online

Elizabeth George Website, http://www.elizabethgeorgeonline.com/ (February 23, 2003).
"Meet the Writers," Barnes&Noble.com, http://www.barnesandnoble.com/writers/writerdetails.asp?userid=6U6WK3STPy&cid=99 (February 23, 2003).

—Susan Salter

Troy Glaus

AP/Wide World Photos

Professional baseball player

B orn Troy Edward Glaus, August 3, 1976, in Newport Beach, CA; son of Tom and Karen Glaus. *Education:* Attended UCLA, 1994–97.

Addresses: *Office*—c/o Anaheim Angels, 2000 Gene Autry Way, Anaheim, CA 92806.

Career

P rofessional baseball player; made professional debut with the Anaheim Angels, 1998.

Awards: Most Valuable Player, Major League Baseball, 2000.

Sidelights

P ublicity shy and almost painfully modest, Troy Glaus, third baseman for the Anaheim Angels, batted .385 in baseball's 2002 World Series to carry his team to the world championship over the San Francisco Giants. In the process, Glaus (pronounced Gloss) won for himself Most Valuable Player (MVP) honors for the series, capturing four times as many votes as Barry Bonds of the Giants. But he made it clear that to him the important trophy was not for MVP but for the world championship itself. "It's a great honor, obviously," he told Ken Davidoff of *Newsday*. "But we play for the big trophy with the pennants on it, not for these. No one guy on this

team has gotten us to this point or carried us through this point. It's been a team effort all the way through, 25 guys."

In the five seasons since Glaus made his debut in major league baseball on July 31, 1998, he's compiled a very respectable batting average of .253, but more importantly he's shown himself capable of coming through in the clutch, delivering an extraordinary performance just when it is needed most. Of his performance in the 2002 American League (A.L.) playoff game against the New York Yankees, Angels hitting coach Mickey Hatcher told Associated Press sports writer Beth Harris, "He's capable of carrying a team for a short period of time, especially when he gets hot. He's the guy in that lineup that everybody's afraid of."

Making Glaus's spectacular performance in 2002's post–season all the more impressive was the fact that he'd been fighting a slump during the regular season. Although the Angels as a team had been shining throughout 2002, Glaus hit only 30 home runs, down sharply from 47 and 41 in 2000 and 2001, respectively. But from the very first game of the post–season, the big third baseman (he stands 6 feet, 5 inches tall and weighs in at nearly 250 pounds), Glaus proved he can deliver the goods when it really counts. In Game 1 of the A.L. division series against the Yankees, he homered twice; in Game 2, he blasted the game–winning homer off Orlando Hernandez. All in all, it was a remarkable October for Glaus, who homered seven times in the post–season.

Glaus was born on August 3, 1976, in Newport Beach, California, and is the son of Tom and Karen Glaus. He was raised by his mother, who divorced Tom Glaus when Troy was only two years old. Glaus has had almost no contact with his father since his teens. To support Troy and herself, his mother operated an air freight courier service. Their home in Los Angeles usually had two or three trucks parked in its driveway at all times. As Glaus told Tom Verducci of Sports Illustrated, "As a little kid it was the coolest thing to have 20–foot trucks in your driveway to play in all the time. But it was never anything I wanted to do when I grew up. For as long as I can remember, the only thing I wanted to be was a baseball player. That was it."

In the late 1980s his mother quit the trucking business and moved with eleven–year–old Glaus to Carlsbad, California, where she opened a small accounting business. Glaus attended Carlsbad High School and played shortstop for the school's baseball team, lettering in the sport all four years of high school. Shortly after he graduated from high school in 1994, Glaus was drafted in the second round (37th pick overall) of the free agent draft by the San Diego Padres, but he decided to pass. Of his failure to reach an agreement with the Padres, Glaus told Sports Illustrated's Verducci, "That's when they were going through their fire sale, and they just never got close." Glaus was the highest draft choice in the June of 1994 draft to ultimately decide against signing professionally.

Instead of going into baseball straight out of high school, Glaus decided to attend college, accepting a baseball scholarship to the University of California, Los Angeles (UCLA). During his three seasons playing for the UCLA Bruins, he posted a college career batting average of .344. He racked up a total of 180 runs batted in (RBIs), including 39 doubles, two triples, and 62 home runs, and 24 stolen bases. In his junior year—the last year he played for UCLA— Glaus batted an awesome .409 and scored 100 runs, including 15 doubles, one triple, and 34 home runs. In his final year with the Bruins, he set a Pac–10 Conference record for home runs in a single season (34), surpassing the previous record of 32 set in 1984 by Mark McGwire of the University of Southern California. He also became the third player in collegiate baseball history to hit 30 home runs and steal 10 bases in a single season.

Between his sophomore and junior years at UCLA, Glaus started at third base for the U.S. Olympic baseball team at the 1996 Summer Games in Atlanta, Georgia. The U.S. team eventually took bronze in the competition. During his summer with Team U.S.A., Glaus batted .342 with a total of 15 home runs and 34 RBIs. During the Atlanta games, he hit four home runs at Atlanta–Fulton County Stadium.

After finishing his junior year at UCLA, Glaus decided to declare himself eligible for the 1997 baseball draft. He was picked up quickly—third pick overall—by the Anaheim Angels, who made it clear from the start that they needed his services not as a shortstop but at third base. Anaheim already had a solid shortstop—Gary DiSarcina—but needed to strengthen its defense at third base. To groom him for his major league debut, Glaus was sent off to the minors, where he served a relatively brief apprenticeship of only 109 games. His professional debut came on July 31, 1998.

In his first two seasons with the Angels, Glaus didn't really live up to the team's expectations for him. Although he'd compiled a college career batting average of .344, Glaus managed to bat only .218 in his debut season. Things didn't get much better in 1999, when he batted .240. Some observers attributed Glaus's lackluster batting performance to the fact that he and Rod Carew, the team's hitting coach in 1999, never really got along that well. On top of that, Glaus seemed to be having difficulty focusing on the task at hand when he stepped to the plate. As he admitted to Sports Illustrated's Verducci, he found himself thinking about his hands, his feet, his stride, his weight shift, and his hips. "Everything except the ball and the pitcher."

Things started to turn around for Glaus during spring training in 2000. New hitting coach Mickey Hatcher helped him to regain his focus. Hatcher suggested that Glaus go back to the batting style that had proved so successful for him in college. Between them, they agreed that Glaus should drop his hands in his batting stance and bring his feet closer together. Hatcher urged Glaus to forget everything else but the ball and connecting with it. For about an hour the two worked on perfecting Glaus's batting style. Hatcher tossed balls to Glaus, who blasted them into a net. "Nobody else around," Glaus told Verducci in Sports Illustrated. "Just Mickey, me, and a kid with a golf cart picking up balls in the outfield."

Hatcher's tutorial did Glaus a world of good. By early June of 2000 the third baseman was awash in impressive stats: second in walks (43), on–base percentage (.450), and doubles (19); third in extra–base hits (35) and in runs (44); fifth in total bases (133); sixth in slugging (.668); seventh in batting average (.332); and ninth in home runs (16). By the end of his second full season, Glaus had pushed his home run total to a dazzling total of 47 and posted 102 RBIs. His batting average for the season as a whole was .284, up sharply from .240 the previous year.

Another contribution to Glaus's improved performance in 2000 may well have been athroscopic surgery done on both his knees after the 1999 season. Doctors recommended the surgery to clean out both knees because of the ballplayer's rapid growth spurt as a boy. In the spring of 1990, Glaus had finished eighth grade at 5 feet, 6 inches, but entered Carlsbad High School three months later at 6 feet, 2 inches. Once he'd recovered from the minor knee surgeries, Glaus began fitness training with a former boxer, focusing on flexibility, sprinting, and weight-lifting that wouldn't add bulk. Of his new fitness routine, Glaus told Verducci in *Sports Illustrated,* "At my size I have to be careful not to get too big. Think about it: A boxer has to get the most strength out of his body while staying within a certain weight class. I worked harder than I ever have in my life. It was really the first time I set up that kind of program. I have no doubt I'm seeing the results now."

Although his batting average slipped in 2001 to .250, Glaus still managed to turn in a creditable performance, compiling a total of 41 home runs for the season and batting in 108 runs. The third baseman experienced something of a slump during the regular season of 2002. He posted only 30 home runs but still managed to bat in 111 runs. For the 2002 regular season, Glaus again posted a batting average of .250.

It was in the 2002 post–season that Glaus truly came into his own. When the Angels faced off against the New York Yankees in the first round of the A.L. playoffs, Glaus blasted two homers in the first game and another in the second game to help power the Angels to the division title in only four games. Next up against the Minnesota Twins for the A.L. championship, Glaus hit a go–ahead homer in Game 3 to lead his team to a 2–1 victory over the Twins. In Game 4, he hit the go–ahead single. The Angels won the A.L. championship series against the Twins by four games to one.

The crowning glory of Glaus's brilliant 2002 post–season romp came with his performance in the World Series against the San Francisco Giants. In the first four games against the Giants, Glaus had become a real thorn in the side of the San Francisco team, scoring seven hits off Giants pitchers, including three home runs and five RBIs. To shut down the Glaus machine, Giants pitchers got tough in Game 5. In his first at–bat, Glaus got knocked down by a fastball pitched by righthander Jason Schmidt. In Game 6, Giants righthander Russ Ortiz sent another fastball buzzing past Glaus's chin, prompting the third baseman to drop to the ground to avoid it. For most of Games 5 and 6, the Giants strategy worked, but by the seventh inning of Game 6, Glaus had had enough. With the Angels trailing the Giants 5–0, Glaus drew on his pent–up anger to smash a single to left field. Glaus's hit sparked a three–run rally. The very next inning, Glaus drove in the tying and winning runs with a double off closer Robb Nen. In Game 7, the Angels wrapped it up, beating the Giants 4–1.

Perhaps teammate Scott Spezio summed it up best. In an interview with Stephen Cannella of *Sports Illustrated,* Spezio, the Angels first baseman, said, "A lot of people say we don't have superstars, but Troy's one. He may not get a lot of publicity, but hopefully he will now."

Sources

Periodicals

AP Online, October 3, 2002; October 28, 2002.
Baseball Digest, October 2000.
Newsday, October 28, 2002, p. A64.
Sports Illustrated, June 12, 2000, p. 46; November 4, 2002, p. 38.

Online

"Troy Glaus," *Baseball–Reference.com,* http://www.baseball–reference.com/g/glaustr01.shtml (February 27, 2003).
"Troy Glaus: Bio," *Baseball Babes,* http://baseballbabes.tripod.com/troyglaus/id1.html (February 27, 2003).
"Troy Glaus, #25," *BigLeaguers.com,* http://bigleaguers.yahoo.com/mlbpa/players/6/6063 (February 25, 2003).
"Troy Glaus, #25, 3B," *Anaheim Angels,* http://anaheim.angels.mlb.com/NASApp/mlb/ana/team/ana_player_bio.jsp?club_context=ana&playerid=136267 (February 25, 2003).

—*Don Amerman*

Thelma Golden

Museum curator

Born in 1965. *Education:* Smith College, B.A. (art history), 1987.

Addresses: *Office*— Studio Museum in Harlem, 144 West 125th St., New York, NY 10027. *Website*—www. studiomuseuminharlem.org

Career

Assistant, Whitney Museum of Art; curator of eight shows at Jamaica Art Center; director and exhibition coordinator, Whitney Museum of Art, 1991–93; associate curator, 1993–96; curator and director of branch museums, 1996–99; special projects curator for Peter and Ellen Norton, 1999–2000; deputy director, Studio Museum in Harlem, 2000—.

Member: Graduate Committee, Center for Curatorial Studies at Bard College.

Awards: New York Award for Art (for work at the Studio Museum in Harlem), 2001.

Sidelights

As a young child, Thelma Golden's interest in art was awakened by the prints of famous works on the playing cards for the board game "Masterpiece." Although she wasn't interested in playing the game, the images on the cards fascinated her. After visiting some of New York's many art museums, Golden realized that someone had to select and display the artwork there, and decided at an early age that she wanted to be that someone. Golden was also inspired to pursue a curatorial career when she read about Lowery Stokes Sims, the African–American woman who was curator at the Metropolitan Museum of Art in New York City.

By the time she was a senior in high school, Golden was working as a curatorial apprentice at the Metropolitan Museum of Art. She later graduated from Smith College in Northampton, Massachusetts, with a degree in art history and African–American studies. Interestingly, noted Greg Tate in the *Village Voice,* "Golden found that Smith's Afro–Am people didn't bother with visual art while their art history people didn't discuss African Americans." Golden decided to link these two interests in her work.

While in college, Golden worked as a curatorial intern at the Studio Museum. The museum felt stuffy to her, "like my parents' museum," she told the *Village Voice*'s Tate. Like many museums, it emphasized the past, and treated the paintings as artifacts, separate from the lives of their creators. She knew that she wanted to work in a place where the ideas and opinions of the artists were integrated with their works, and where the works were displayed in an approachable, aesthetically pleasing manner.

Golden then worked as an assistant at the Whitney Museum of Art, which exactly fit these criteria. After this, she moved on to the Jamaica Arts Center, where she curated eight shows. She became director and exhibition coordinator at the Whitney Museum of Art in 1991. This began a long association with the Whitney; Golden was promoted to associate curator in 1993, and to curator and director of branch museums from 1996 to 1999. As branch director at the Whitney, Golden's mission was to present the work of artists who were not receiving the recognition they deserved—largely women and people of color.

In 1994, Golden presented a show titled "Black Male: Representations of Masculinity in Contemporary American Art." The exhibit traveled throughout the United States, and featured images of African–American males in films, photography, paintings, sculpture, television, and video. Although the show included work by well–respected artists, it also featured images from "blaxploitation" films, such as *Shaft*, as well as other pop culture venues. In its sheer breadth, however, the exhibit was intended to bring viewers beyond negative stereotypes of African–American men. Golden's ambition for the show was that it open up the art world, which, she told Veronica Chambers in *Essence*, is "the last bastion of exclusivity." In addition, she said, she hoped that the exhibit would encourage African–American artists and art lovers to participate more in the art world: "[T]he museum belongs to them, too."

However, the show aroused a great deal of controversy, both in the art world and among African Americans. According to an article by Tate in *Vibe*, some African Americans were dismayed by the presentations of negative images of black men, and some conservative white critics expressed disdain for black political art. Golden was annoyed by these comments, and believed that those who made them simply misunderstood the purpose of the exhibit and the artwork in it. She told Tate, "The contemporary black artists I'm interested in have found a way to combine aesthetic and formal issues with the political in a way that one is not sacrificed for the other."

Golden followed "Black Male" with many other exhibitions, including 1998's "Heart, Mind, Body, Soul: New Work from the Collection" and "Bob Thompson: A Retrospective," and 1999's "Hindsight: Recent Work from the Permanent Collection." As Golden told Tate, she did not want to be considered a "curator of Afro–American art," but she was interested only in African American artists. David

Ross, director of the Whitney museum, understood that she wanted the freedom and power to focus on these artists without being labeled, and he gave her free rein to follow her instincts.

In 1999, Golden left the Whitney to work as special projects curator for Peter and Ellen Norton, who were collectors of contemporary art in Los Angeles, California. In 2000, Golden joined the woman who had inspired her to become a curator, Lowery Stokes Sims, at the Studio Museum in Harlem. Sims became director of the museum and Golden was deputy director. Although Sims had a more traditional background and Golden had become known for her adventurous and sometimes controversial choices, they worked well together, and within two years had doubled membership at the museum.

In a diary she kept for *Slate*, Golden wrote that she took the Studio Museum position "at a moment when I was seriously considering if perhaps there might be a life beyond art for me. I didn't get far. I ended up in Harlem."

In 2001, Golden presented "Freestyle," featuring the work of 28 African–American postmodernists. She told Tate in the *Village Voice*, "'Freestyle' is me trying to begin the process of finding the next group of artists I'd be working with for the next ten years." Golden had been working with some of the same artists since the beginning of their careers in the early 1990s, and this exhibit allowed her to reach out and become familiar with a whole new generation of artists.

The show was widely acclaimed; according to Suzanne Muchnic in the *Los Angeles Times*, *New Yorker* art critic Peter Schjeldahl called Golden "a superb judge of quality." In the *New York Times*, Holland Cotter wrote that the exhibit provided an important look at "the notion of what 'black art' means in a country, a neighborhood, even an art world where racial balances are shifting."

In 2002, Golden presented "Black Romantic," which emphasized figure paintings by 30 African–American artists. Some of these artists had a background in fine arts, while others were self–taught artists. In contrast to Golden's earlier shows, many of the paintings featured here were already widely available as posters or postcards, and were widely known in the African–American community.

Although Golden commented in the show's catalog that this exhibit was not intended to be "a corrective or compensation" for the controversy aroused by "Black Male," Michael Kimmelman wrote in the *New York Times* that the show "seems as if it were Ms. Golden's response to the attacks on 'Black Male.'" However, he also noted that the show brought up important questions about why art by white artists is often treated differently than that by African–American artists. For example, some of the artists in "Black Romantic" are considered kitschy because they imitate the style of some old masters, whereas white artists who do this are viewed as doing homage to those masters. Kimmelman commented, "'Black Romantic' forces all this into the open, where it should be."

In addition to her museum work, Golden has also worked as a guest lecturer, essayist, and guest curator at a variety of institutions, including the Guggenheim Museum, the Museum of Modern Art, the ICA/Philadelphia, Harvard University, the ICA/London, and the Miami Art Museum. She has served as a selector for the Pew Charitable Trust, the MacArthur Foundation, the Federal Advisory Committee on International Exhibitions, the Alpert Foundation, and the National Endowment for the Arts.

Golden also teaches, writes, and lectures about curatorial work, contemporary art, and cultural issues. She is an adjunct professor at the Columbia University School of the Arts, and has taught at Yale University and Cornell University. She is a member of the Graduate Committee at the Center for Curatorial Studies at Bard College.

Golden wrote in *Slate* that a "secret truth" of her work as a curator is "relationship and (perhaps more importantly) an ongoing conversation [with the artist] that creates an intellectual bond, that usually results in a project."

Selected writings

(With Guillermo Gomez–Pena and David Deitcher) *The Decade Show,* New Museum of Contemporary Art, 1990.

(With Elisabeth Sussman, John G. Hanhardt, Lisa Phillips, Homi K. Bhabha, Coco Fusco, B. Ruby Rich, Avital Ronell) *1993 Biennnial Exhibition: Whitney Museum of American Art,* Harry N. Abrams, 1993.

(Contributor) *Ancestral Dialogues: The Photographs of Albert Chong,* edited by Michael Read, Friends of Photography, 1994.

(With Elizabeth Alexander) *Black Male: Representations of Masculinity in Contemporary American Art,* Harry N. Abrams, 1994.

(With Gail Gelburd) *Romare Bearden in Black and White,* Harry N. Abrams, 1996.

(With Judith Wilson) *Bob Thompson,* University of California Press, 1998.

(With Byron Kin, Richard Meyer, and Judith Tannenbaum) *Glenn Ligon: Unbecoming,* University of Pennsylvania Institute of Contemporary Art, 1998.

(With Thomas Piche, Jr.) *Carrie Mae Weems: Recent Work, 1992–1998,* George Braziller, 1999.

(With Thomas McEvilley and Charles Merewether) *Converge,* Miami Art Museum, 2000.

(With Robert Storr, Lynn M. Herbert, Katy Siegel, and Susan Sollins) *Art 21: Art in the 21st Century,* Harry N. Abrams, 2001.

(With Maurice Berger and Franklin Simons) *Gary Simmons,* Chicago Museum of Contemporary Art, 2002.

(With Annette Dixon and Robert Reid–Pharr) *Kara Walker: Pictures from Another Time,* Distributed Art Publishers, 2002.

Sources

Periodicals

Essence, November 1994, p. 64; July 2002, p. 74.
Los Angeles Times, September 29, 2001, p. F1.
New York Times, July 29, 2001; April 26, 2002, p. E29.
Vibe, October 1994, p. 34.
Village Voice, May 16–22, 2001.

Online

"Art: Thelma Golden and Lowery Sims," 2001 New York Awards, http://www.newyorkmetro.com/ (February 18, 2003).

"Thelma Golden," Institute of International Visual Arts, http://www.iniva.org/general/info_bio12 (February 18, 2003).

"Thelma Golden," *Slate,* http://www.slate.msn.com/id/2062296/entry/2062304/ (February 18, 2003).

—Kelly Winters

Lauren Graham

Actress

Born March 16, 1967, in Honolulu, HI; daughter of Lawrence Graham (a lobbyist) and Donna Grant (a retail buyer); stepdaughter of Karen (a corporate meeting planner). *Education:* Barnard College, Columbia University, New York, B.A., English; Southern Methodist University, Dallas, TX, M.F.A., acting, 1992.

Addresses: *Agent*—Writers and Artists Agency, 924 Westwood Blvd., Suite 900, Los Angeles, CA 90024. *Office*—c/o Gilmore Girls, Warner Brothers, 4000 Warner Blvd., Burbank, CA 91522.

Career

Actress in films, including: *Confessions of a Sexist Pig*, 1998; *Nightwatch*, 1998; *One True Thing*, 1998; *Dill Scallion*, 1999; *Sweet November*, 2001. Television appearances include: *Good Company*, ABC, 1995–96; *Townies*, ABC, 1996–97; *Conrad Bloom*, NBC, 1998–99; *MYOB*, 2000; *Gilmore Girls*, 2000—. Television guest appearances include: *Caroline in the City*, NBC, 1995; *3rd Rock from the Sun*, NBC, 1996; *Law and Order*, NBC, 1996; *Seinfeld*, NBC, 1996; *NewsRadio*, NBC, 1997.

Sidelights

Lauren Graham is an actress who has appeared in several well–regarded film and television roles. She has played both comedic and dramatic roles. Graham is currently the star of *Gilmore Girls*, a popular situation comedy produced by Warner Brothers.

Graham was born in Honolulu, Hawaii, but grew up in northern Virginia, where she was an avid equestrian and competed in horse shows. In 1971, when she was five years old, her mother divorced her father and left to pursue a singing career. The split was amicable, according to Graham, who wrote in *InStyle*, "They parted as friends, determined to find the best way to raise me, even if it didn't turn out to be the most conventional."

Graham was raised by her father, Lawrence, who was a lawyer and chief aide to a congressional representative. Growing up in a dad–only household had certain perks, Graham told *People*. She and her father ate out frequently, and she did not have to keep her room neat. She wrote in *InStyle*, "We had a white leather couch in the living room and didn't own two pieces of silverware that matched. What's more, there wasn't a chair that you couldn't put your feet up on or share with the dog." Her friends liked her father, and some of them almost envied Graham's relaxed, unconventional family life. One result of her upbringing was that Graham became more independent than most teenagers. She enjoyed spending time alone, reading or playing games, and was studious and self–reliant.

In 1981, when Graham was 15, her father married again, and Graham developed a good relationship with his new wife, Karen. It was "so important to have a woman come into my life," Graham told *People*. She wrote in *InStyle*, "Suddenly there was someone who could properly hem my jeans with a sewing machine instead of a stapler, who took hair issues seriously, and who didn't think lipstick was funny at all."

Graham earned a bachelor's degree in English from Barnard University, and then earned an M.F.A. degree in acting from Southern Methodist University in 1992. She then spent a couple of years working in Chicago, Illinois, at the Ann Sathers restaurant. "I just was slaving away, putting icing on rolls," she told Allan Johnson in a Knight Ridder/Tribune News Service article. At night, she worked waiting tables at the Improv comedy club. Graham told Johnson that she originally moved to Chicago to be with a boyfriend, but that she also seriously considered living there permanently. She thought she would become a member of a local theater company and settle down there.

Instead, Graham moved to New York City, where she worked at the Barneys New York department store by day and that city's Improv venue by night. "I just never stopped working to make enough money to take [an acting] class," she told Johnson. However, she did eventually find work in commercials and in the NBC daytime drama *Another World*.

In 1995, Graham moved to Los Angeles, California, seeking acting roles and sleeping on an aunt's couch until she found one. Unlike many other would–be actors who struggle to find work, within six months Graham was chosen for a recurring role in the first season of *Caroline in the City*, for which she played a main character's relentlessly optimistic girlfriend. She followed this with other recurring roles: an efficiency expert on *NewsRadio*, and a Los Angeles studio executive on *Law and Order*. In *MYOB*, Graham starred as a high school administrator who must deal with her disruptive niece, and she was a regular on the comedy series *Conrad Bloom, Good Company,* and *Townies*. She was also a guest star on the sitcoms *Seinfeld* and *3rd Rock from the Sun*.

Although *Townies, Good Company, MYOB,* and *Conrad Bloom* were canceled almost as soon as they started, Graham did not view them as failures. She told Larry Bonko in the *Virginian Pilot*, "I realized from those shows how ambitious I'd become. I couldn't wait to progress from the quirky, wacky character to the pretty girlfriend to the place I really wanted to be as an actress."

Graham appeared in the 1998 feature film *Nightwatch*, which starred Patricia Arquette and Ewan McGregor. In the Meryl Streep drama *One True Thing* released that same year, she played a main character's confidante and best friend. She also appeared as Keanu Reeves's girlfriend in the 2001 film *Sweet November*.

In 2002, Graham got her big break with a starring role in the WB network's *Gilmore Girls*. The show's creator, Amy Sherman–Palladino, told Bonko, "The role required someone who can act, who can make you cry, who can break your heart, who is funny and gorgeous and tough and sexy and vulnerable. We looked and looked and couldn't find that actress." Just as Sherman–Palladino was ready to settle for anyone she could get, in walked Graham. "She gave us everything we wanted...."

In *Gilmore Girls*, Graham plays Lorelei Gilmore, a single parent who is raising her 16–year–old daugher. Young–looking, she could pass for her daughter's sister, and the two are close. Gilmore dreams of opening her own inn, with the help of her best friend, and sending her daughter to an Ivy League college. In *Redbook*, Katherine Dykstra described the character as "the caring yet cool mother every teenage girl dreams of. The kind of mother who will discuss the nuances of high school dating while ironing a shirt and cooking dinner." In *Variety*, Laura Fries wrote that *Gilmore Girls*, unlike Graham's previous short–lived television series, "is a better fit with [Graham's] innate comic ability and appealing nature."

Gilmore told Dykstra that her role as a mother who is deeply connected to her daughter is ironic, since she didn't have that bond in her own childhood. However, she said, "One thing I do identify with is the sense of community on *Gilmore Girls*. I was raised by a community of people who knew my father, similar to the situation on the show."

Graham's work in *Gilmore Girls* led to nominations for a Golden Globe and a Screen Actors Guild award, as well as appearances on the *The Tonight Show with Jay Leno* and *Late Show with David Letterman*. The show has received critical acclaim and has legions of devoted viewers.

Sources

Books

Contemporary Theatre, Film, and Television, Volume 25, Gale Group, 2000.

Periodicals

Daily News (Los Angeles, California), October 9, 2001, p. L6.

InStyle, June 1, 2002, p. 219.

Knight Ridder/Tribune News Service, August 20, 2001, p. K6344.

Los Angeles Times, October 1, 2000, p. 16.

New York Post, February 25, 2001, p. 44.

People, May 7, 2000, p. 77.

Redbook, March, 2002, p. 54.

Variety, October 2, 2000, p. 32.

Virginian Pilot, February 12, 2002, p. E1.

Online

"The Facts: Lauren Graham," E! Online, http://www.eonline.com/Facts/People/Bio/0,128,46120,00.html (May 15, 2003).

Gilmore Girls, http://www.gilmoregirls.org/lauren.html (May 15, 2003).

—Kelly Winters

Jennifer Granholm

Governor of Michigan

Born February 5, 1959, in Vancouver, British Columbia, Canada; daughter of Civtor Ivar (a banking consultant) and Shirley Alfreda (a homemaker) Granholm; married Daniel Mulhern, May 23, 1986; children: Kathryn, Cecelia, Jack. *Education:* University of California–Berkeley, B.S., 1984; Harvard Law School, J.D, 1987.

Addresses: *Office*—P.O. Box 30013, Lansing, MI 48909. *Website*—Jennifer Granholm Official Website: http://www.michigan.gov/gov.

Career

Judicial law clerk in U.S. Circuit Court of Appeals in Detroit, 1987; admitted to Michigan bar, 1987; executive assistant, Wayne County, Michigan; 1988–90; U.S. prosecutor, Department of Justice, 1990–94; corporation counsel, Wayne County, Michigan, 1994–96; general counsel, Detroit and Wayne County Stadium Authority, 1996–98; Michigan Attorney General, 1998–2001; Michigan Governor, 2002—.

Awards: Special Achievement Award, U.S. Department of Justice; Newsmaker of the Year, *Crain's Detroit Business,* 2002.

Sidelights

In 1998 Jennifer Granholm became the first woman ever to be elected as attorney general of the State of Michigan. Four years later, she placed her hat in the political ring again, hoping to be elected as the first female governor of that state. The ambition became reality in November of 2002, when Michigan voters picked her over her Republican opponent, Michigan Lieutenant Governor Dick Posthumus. *Newsweek,* calling Granholm a "compelling mix of tough–minded prosecutor and down–to–earth mom," recognized her importance to the Democratic party at a time when it was searching for new leaders.

Born on February 5, 1959, the daughter of Civtor, a banking consultant, and Shirley, a homemaker, Granholm is Canadian by birth. She immigrated with her family to the United States from her hometown of Vancouver, British Columbia, as a three–year–old child in 1962. She grew up in the San Francisco Bay area in California along with her brother, a member of the Mennonite clergy.

After graduating from San Carlos High School in 1977, Granholm moved to Los Angeles, California, with the intention of becoming an actress. With her photogenic features and blonde hair, she seemed a natural. However, even Hollywood couldn't distract her from a natural affinity for politics. While working for the 1978 presidential campaign of independent candidate John Anderson, she applied for United States citizenship, not wishing to miss out on the chance of voting in future elections.

Eventually Granholm enrolled as an undergraduate at the University of California in Berkeley. By funding her own education with jobs and student loans, she became the first member of her family to graduate from college. Her request for citizenship was approved while she was at Berkeley, and she took the oath at age 21. Also during that time, she spent a year in Europe, largely in France. Her time abroad also included two side trips to the former Soviet Union, in support of that country's displaced Jewish population called refuseniks.

She graduated from the University of California with a bachelor's degree in political science in 1984, then enrolled in Harvard Law School in Cambridge, Massachusetts. Once again unable to distance herself from politics, Granholm served as editor-in-chief of the *Harvard Civil Rights/Civil Liberties Law Review*. She focused her efforts on boycotts of companies doing business with South Africa during apartheid.

After earning a J.D. degree from Harvard in 1987, she moved to Michigan where she began her career as a judicial law clerk for Judge Damon Keith of the U.S. Circuit Court of Appeals in Detroit. She was admitted to the Michigan Bar, the U.S. District Court (eastern district) of Michigan, and the U.S. Court of Appeals 6th Circuit that year. She spent the next two years as an executive assistant for Wayne County, contributing her time in 1988 as a field coordinator for the Michael Dukakis presidential campaign.

Granholm joined the Department of Justice as a United States prosecutor in Detroit in 1990, achieving a 98 percent conviction rate. She then served as corporation counsel for Wayne County in 1994, overseeing a staff of 75 and a budget of $9.5 million. With practical experience in municipal, real estate, and criminal law, she became the general counsel for the Detroit and Wayne County Stadium Authority in 1996. She first joined a ticket in 1998, with Democratic gubernatorial candidate Geoffrey Fieger. At the time, she was practically a political unknown. Ironically Fieger lost the election, but Granholm—running for attorney general of Michigan—won the election, thus becoming a lone Democrat in a largely Republican administration.

Upon being elected she retained her residence in Northville in southeastern Michigan, opting to alternate her commute between the attorney general's offices in Lansing and Detroit. Availing herself of a job perk in the form of a state limousine, she put her commute time to practical use, working by car phone and laptop while riding to work.

By the time Granholm entered the Michigan governor's race in 2001, she had established a bond of trust with her constituency. Even more, she was committed to bridging the chasms of partisan politics in the interest of progress. She announced her candidacy for governor early in March of 2001. In her candidacy, she was anti–big tobacco and pro–environment, and she spoke out as an advocate for seniors and touted better health care. Additionally she took aim at the oppressive policies of large corporations and at computer crimes, especially identity theft and child pornography.

Tireless in her campaigning, she has been known to traverse the entire state of Michigan in a single day, seemingly making stops on the fly. Those who know her describe Granholm as decisive and quick, and relentless yet humane. "I have rarely seen people running for office who are as good at working through a crowd and making a real contact with people," said former Michigan Representative Maxine Berman in the *Battle Creek Enquirer*. "I've never seen anything like her," said prosecutor Michael Duggan, quoted by the *Detroit Free Press*.

Granholm was quickly confronted with problems once she was inaugurated as governor in January of 2003. In her second week in office, she discovered a surprise $277 million deficit in the current year's budget. That amount was small compared to the budget deficit she then had to deal with for the 2003–04 year: $1.9 billion dollars had to be slashed from the state budget. She presented her plan for a balanced budget on March 6, 2003, which included a $1.1 billion reduction of state spending, the largest in Michigan's history. Areas that faced deep cuts included arts funding, public universities, scholarships for outstanding students, and local governments. She didn't cut money from K–12 education, Medicaid, public safety, and senior citizen care. In her presentation, Granholm said she was often forced to choose between "the important and the vital," but urged citizens to really think about the decisions she made. Speaking to the *Detroit Free Press*, she rhetorically asked, "The question: Is it college, or is it K–12? Is it college, or is it letting people out of jail? Is it college, or is it providing health care for senior citizens who have no other way to go?" She urged people to set partisanship aside and work together to find ways to overcome the huge deficit the state faced.

Granholm was extremely popular with the media, the citizens, and other governors at her first National Governors' Association conference in Washington, D.C., in February of 2003. *Meet the Press*, CNN, and *The NewsHour with Jim Lehrer* all approached Granholm about interviews. She turned them down, opting instead to focus on the issues at hand at the conference. This approach served her well, as she made an outstanding impression among the other governors. "She's a star, she's incredible," Washington governor Gary Locke told Knight Ridder/Tribune Business News Service. "She speaks up, she has incredibly good questions. She asked a question today of the president. People are very impressed with her."

Community service is an important facet of Granholm's life. Her membership in Leadership Detroit dates back to 1990. In 1995 she served as the vice president of the board of directors of the YWCA in Inkster, Michigan. She went as a delegate to the 1996 Democratic National Convention in Chicago, Illinois, and she chaired the selection committee for U.S. Senator in Detroit in 1997. In addition to her membership in the Detroit Bar Association and the Women's Law Association, she is a member of the Society of Irish Lawyers. Granholm holds a Phi Beta Kappa key and is a respected contributor to professional journals. A Roman Catholic, she is active in her church and serves as a lector at her parish.

She is married to Daniel Mulhern, an author and co-founder of Mulhern Hastings Group, a leadership and organizational development firm. The couple met at the Boston airport when they were fellow law students at Harvard returning from a spring break. Within weeks they were engaged. They were married on May 23, 1986. As both are inspired by Irish culture, they honeymooned in Ireland. Their children, Kathryn, Cecelia, and Jack, were born in the 1990s. In a unique display of gender equality, Granholm and Mulhern each uses the other's surname as a middle name.

Sources

Periodicals

Battle Creek Enquirer, July 31, 2002.
Crain's Detroit Business, January 20, 2003.
Detroit Free Press, February 20, 2003.
Economist, September 21, 2002, p. 54.
Grand Rapids Press, October 18, 1998.
Knight Ridder/Tribune Business News Service, February 25, 2003; March 5, 2003.
Michigan Daily, November 5, 1998.
Newsweek, December 30, 2002.

Online

"Fiscal Year '04 Budget Presentation," Office of the Governor, http://www.michigan.gov/gov/0,1607,7–168—62782—,00.html (March 7, 2003).
"Jennifer Granholm: Campaigning On Character," *Detroit Free Press*, http://www.freep.com/news/politics/gran17_20020717.htm (October 16, 2002).
"Jennifer Granholm, Democrat Candidate For Attorney General," *State News*, http://www.statenews.com/editionsfall98/102898/election/granholm.html (October 16, 2002).

—*Gloria Cooksey*

Robert Greenberg

Chief Executive Officer of Skechers USA, Inc.

Born c. 1940; son of Harry and Belle Greenberg; married and divorced; children: five sons, one daughter. *Education:* Attended hairdressing school.

Addresses: *Office*—228 Manhattan Beach Blvd., Manhattan Beach, CA 90266.

Career

Worked in his father's produce store; owned a chain of beauty salons called Talk of the Town, 1962–69; owned Wig Bazaar, 1965–68; opened a shop called Wigs 'n' Things, and sold wigs and men's toupees via mail order, 1968; began importing clocks from Korea, 1973; bought the publicly traded Medata Computer Systems and renamed it Europa Hair, 1971–74; started a jeans importing company called Wild Oats, 1974; funded Removatron, 1977; ran Roller Skates of America, 1979–83; founder and chief executive officer, L.A. Gear, 1983–92; chief executive officer, Skechers USA, Inc., 1992—.

Sidelights

Entrepreneur Robert Greenberg has had his share of ups and downs in the shoe business, and has made an astounding comeback. After starting a series of businesses—from wig and clock importers to a roller–skate rental shop—he found his place in shoes. The first footwear company he founded, L.A. Gear, became the third–largest shoe manufacturer in the United States in the late 1980s. By 1991, trends shifted radically, resulting in a massive sales plunge

that effectively forced Greenberg out of the business. Six months after he wrote off L.A. Gear, Greenberg and his son Michael co–founded Skechers USA, Inc., to import the trendy Dr. Martens brand of clunky British shoes and work boots. Soon, Skechers was manufacturing its own popular line of shoes targeted at men, women, children, and teens. By 2002, Greenberg was once again chief executive officer (CEO) of the nation's third–largest footwear seller, with sales nearing $1 billion.

Greenberg grew up in Boston, Massachusetts, the son of Harry and Belle Greenberg. The young Greenberg worked at the produce and grocery store his father opened in the 1930s and named Belle's Market after his wife. He later attended hairdressing school and opened a beauty salon called Talk of the Town in Brookline, Massachusetts, in 1962, which grew into a chain of salons. As wigs became popular, Greenberg got into the lucrative wig–importing business with a company called Wig Bazaar in 1965. He bought wigs for $50 and sold them for $300 and got his first taste of how profitable a wholesale business can be. He sold Wig Bazaar in 1968 and opened a shop called Wigs 'n' Things, and started selling wigs and men's toupees via mail order. He sold Talk of the Town in 1969 and began importing $16 clocks from Korea and selling them for $129. He bought the publicly traded Medata Computer Systems in 1971 and renamed it Europa Hair. He traded it as a penny stock until selling the company in 1974, when he started importing jeans in a company called Wild Oats. He put up the money to start Removatron, an electronic–tweezers company, in 1977.

After his divorce, Greenberg moved with his children to Los Angeles, California, in 1979 to escape the bitter East Coast winters. Once in sunny California, he acquired the license for Hang Ten shoe skates and opened a roller skate–rental store called Roller Skates of America. His involvement in footwear landed him at a shoe–industry trade show where he "saw a lot of people who weren't working too hard and looked wealthy. And I decided to go into it," he told Nancy Rotenier in *Forbes*. He earned $3 million in 1982 after buying the license to sell shoelaces with *E.T.: The Extra Terrestrial* movie characters printed on them. Greenberg went into the shoe business in 1983, when he launched L.A. Gear, a women's clothing store and shoe importer in Los Angeles. L.A. Gear became the third–largest shoe manufacturer in the United States after Greenberg closed the store to focus on making his own shoes in 1984. L.A. Gear's quick rise was fueled by the aerobics craze of the 1980s and the company became known for its stylish aerobic shoes. Greenberg bought out his partner and took the company public in 1986, and L.A. Gear was Wall Street's best–performing firm in 1989, with sales of $900 million.

As the trends of the 1980s rapidly evolved, L.A. Gear styles did not keep up. Greenberg tried unsuccessfully to move the company into the "performance" athletic shoe and apparel market dominated by Nike and Reebok. Sales plunged 25 percent in 1991, costing the company $45 million. Greenberg also defaulted on a bank agreement in 1990, which sent the company's stock further downward. An investment company paid $100 million for 34 percent of the company in 1992 and forced Greenberg out soon after. Greenberg was one of L.A. Gear's former executives who were sued by the company's stockholders, who claimed they had been given misleading profit information intended to inflate share prices, a violation of securities laws. The defendants agreed to pay a $29.3 million settlement in December of 1992, which they claimed was not an admission of guilt. L.A. Gear filed for Chapter Eleven bankruptcy protection in 1998 and still operates as a minor footwear company, though Greenberg is not at all involved in the business.

Six months after he was ousted from L.A. Gear, Greenberg founded Skechers, which is based in Manhattan Beach, California. The name describes a nervous, fidgety person in the parlance of 1990s youth, and was suggested by Greenberg's son Josh. Greenberg didn't move on the idea until his daughter's girlfriend seconded it. "I didn't think it would work," he told Leslie Earnest of the *Los Angeles Times*. The company started as an exclusive importer of the popular Dr. (Doc) Martens shoes and boots, and soon was knocking off the British shoe company's clunky styles and manufacturing its own line of Skechers shoes. Skechers shoes were only available in such department stores as Macy's, Nordstrom, and Bloomingdale's until the company opened 85 stores of its own across the country. Skechers USA, Inc. is a family affair: Greenberg is CEO of Skechers and his son Michael is president of the company. Greenberg's four other sons, his daughter, and a niece and nephew also work for the company. "I have the best employees," he told *Forbes* in 1993. The siblings all live in Los Angeles and vacation and socialize together. Pushed by a massive celebrity advertising campaign that has featured actors Matt Dillon and Robert Downey Jr., L.A. Laker Rick Fox, and pop star Britney Spears, Skechers sold nearly $1 billion worth of trendy shoes by 2002. The company advertises in more than 100 United States magazines each month. While most shoe companies offer 100 to 200 styles, Skechers produces 1,500 designs, including sneakers, boots, slippers, conservative loafers, wild platform styles, and even sneakers with pop–out wheels on the bottom for skating. That range of styles, targeted to women, men, children, and teens, fueled a 42 percent sales growth in 2001 when overall footwear sales had been sluggish.

In the last half of 2001, Skechers earnings dropped about 50 percent, resulting in layoffs at the company and costly inventory backups. But by mid–2002, the stock price had risen encouragingly. While things were looking good on the horizon for the company, some trouble arose at the end of 2002. On December 23, 2002, Spears sued Skechers for $1.5 million, contending the footwear firm exploited her in international print ads, but failed to market Britney–branded skating accessories. A lawyer for Skechers threatened a counter suit, saying Spears "rejected design after design … leaving Skechers out in the cold with nothing to sell," according to *Entertainment Weekly*.

Despite his legal troubles, Greenberg has set his sights on the European market because he is not content with being number three in the United States. Greenberg looks to Europe to promote Skechers growth in the future. "The potential is enormous," he told the *Los Angeles Times*'s Earnest. Fawn Evenson, vice president of the American Apparel & Footwear Association, told Earnest, "To take this company and make it a premier brand, I think people just look at it in awe."

Sources

Periodicals

Entertainment Weekly, January 10, 2003, p. 16.

Forbes, September 27, 1993, p. 154; August 6, 2001,
  p. 62.
Los Angeles Business Journal, August 10, 1998, p. 3.
Los Angeles Times, June 16, 2002, p. C1.

Online

Skechers USA, Inc., http://www.skechers.com
  (October 30, 2002).

—Brenna Sanchez

Brian Greene

Physicist

Born February 9, 1963, in New York, NY; son of Alan Greene (a voice coach and composer). *Education:* Harvard University, Cambridge, MA, B.S., 1984; Oxford University, England, Ph.D., 1987.

Addresses: *Office*—Columbia University, Department of Physics, 538 W. 120th St., New York, NY 10027.

Career

Associate professor of physics, Cornell University, 1990–95; named full professor, 1995; director, Theoretical Advanced Study Institute, 1996; co-director, Institute for Strings, Cosmology, and Astroparticle Physics (ISCAP); professor of physics and mathematics, Columbia University, 1996—.

Awards: Phi Beta Kappa Book Award for science, 1999; Aventis Prize for Science Books, 2000; Public Understanding of Science Award, 2001; New York Mayor's Award for Excellence in Science and Technology, 2002; Andrew Gemant, American Institute of Physics, 2003.

Sidelights

Brian Greene is one of world's experts in the field of superstring theory, which could potentially explain the origin of everything down to the smallest particle and including the universe itself. His best-selling book, *The Elegant Universe,* sold more than half a million copies and made it to the 17th spot on the New York Times best–sellers list. His ability to explain some of physics most–complex theories has led to a popular explosion of interest in science. His charisma, good looks, and ability to explain the complexities of physics to the layperson have made him a media darling.

Born February 9, 1963, in New York City, Greene's father was a former vaudeville performer turned voice coach and composer. Greene was precocious and excelled in math. At the age of six he multiplied 30–digit numbers by taping together sheets of paper. By the time he was in sixth grade, he had learned all the math that the public school he attended had to offer. With a note from one of his teachers in hand, Greene canvassed the campus of Columbia University searching for a tutor. A graduate student in math, Neil Bellinson, agreed to help Greene, and assisted him until Greene graduated from high school.

In 1980, Greene began his studies at Harvard University where he majored in physics. His interests were not one–sided, though. At Harvard, Greene ran cross country and acted in musicals. He graduated in 1984 and on a Rhodes Scholarship attended Oxford University where he earned his doctorate in only three years. A chance event led Greene to string theory: he attended a lecture that introduced him to the theory. He explained his reaction to Diana Steele in *21stC,* "I really got hooked on the ideas and basically jumped in at that moment."

After graduating from Oxford University, Greene returned to the United States. He went back to Harvard for a short while and then began teaching at Cornell University in 1990. He was named a full professor in 1995. The following year he accepted a position at Columbia University teaching math and physics. He is the co–director of the Institute for Strings, Cosmology, and Astroparticle Physics. In 1996, he acted as director for the Theoretical Advanced Study Institute at the University of Colorado in Boulder. He also teaches at Cornell and Duke University through videoconferencing.

Greene's research involves mathematical formulas that attempt to deal with one of string theory's main propositions, which is that there are more than three dimensions. Greene wrote on his website, "Much of my research has focused on the physical implications and mathematical properties of these extra dimensions." In 1992, Greene, along with Duke University scientists Paul Aspinwall and David Morrison, was able to prove theoretically that the fabric of space tears and subsequently repairs itself.

In the late 1990s, Greene decided to write a book about string theory with a general audience in mind. He was reluctant at first, as he told Steele, "I just wanted to throw it away and forget about the whole thing." Fortunately, he didn't and in 1999, *The Elegant Universe: Superstrings, Hidden Dimensions, and the Quest for the Ultimate Theory* was published. It went on to record–breaking sales, including making it to the top of sales on the online sales site Amazon.com. The book was also a finalist in the running for a Pulitzer Prize in nonfiction writing. Its accessibility and popularity led to a media blitz.

He made appearances on the talk show *Late Night with Conan O'Brien*, and was a guest on National Public Radio's (NPR) *Science Friday* as well as *Newshour with Jim Lehrer*, CNN, and *Charlie Rose*. Greene helped a friend, a writer for the sitcom *Third Rock from the Sun*, with scientifically accurate dialogue. He advised Alan Alda in his role as physicist Richard Feynman in a play performed at Lincoln Center. He was also a scientific advisor for the 2000 film *Frequency* and appeared briefly in the film as himself.

Before his popularity made it impossible to keep up, Greene answered all the e–mail that he received. The classes he teaches at Columbia fill up consistently. Students and non–students show up hoping to sit in on his lectures. Even though he is teaching an obscure and esoteric subject, he tries to make his lectures understandable and enjoyable. He

explained to Shira J. Boss of *Columbia College Today*, "I can't imagine feeling worse than coming home realizing you've bored people for the last hour...."

He has hopes of inspiring even more people to take an interest in science in general and physics in particular. Plans are in the works for him to teach a class that illuminates physics for creative writers. He was also on a panel discussing the portrayal of science and scientists in films. One of the purposes of the panel was to encourage film students at Columbia University to consider making more films with science as the focus and portraying scientists more realistically and less stereotypically.

Greene's popularity is a combination of his excellent ability to communicate, his deep knowledge of the subject, plus his good looks. His background in acting and improvisational theater adds another element of entertainment to his speaking style. In May of 1999, he took lecturing to the level of performance art by collaborating with the Emerson String Quartet. He lectured while the quartet performed at an event at the Guggenheim Museum. The evening was such a hit that another was scheduled for later in the year.

Although Greene has easily adapted to the spotlight, he doesn't want the attention he's received to interfere with his research. He is excited that he may have made science less intimidating for many people, but there's much work to be done in string theory. He and other string theorists need to prove that the theory is physically possible. Greene has to face the possibility that string theory is an improbability. He told Boss, "You can find yourself momentarily gripped with fear that you're spending a working lifetime on something and in the end still couldn't know if it's right or wrong."

Selected writings

The Elegant Universe: Superstrings, Hidden Dimensions, and the Quest for the Ultimate Theory, W.W. Norton & Company (New York City), 1999.

Sources

Periodicals

Forbes, February 4, 2002, pp. 68–69.
Scientific American, April 2000, pp. 36–40.

Online

"Advanced physics, accelerated for mass consumption," 21st C, http://www.columbia.edu/cu/21stC/issue–4.2/steele.html (April 17, 2003).

"Brian Greene," Department of Physics, Columbia University, http://phys.columbia.edu/faculty/greene.htm (April 17, 2003).

"World On A String," *Columbia College Today,* http://www.college.columbia.edu/cct/sep99/12a.html (April 17, 2003).

—*Eve M. B. Hermann*

Jon Gruden

AP/Wide World Photos

Head coach of the Tampa Bay Buccaneers

Born August 17, 1963, in Sandusky, OH; son of Jim (a football coach) and Kathy (a teacher) Gruden; married Cindy; children: three sons. *Education:* Attended Muskingum College, OH; University of Dayton, Dayton, OH, 1985.

Addresses: *Office*—c/o Tampa Bay Buccaneers, One Buccaneer Place, Tampa, FL 33607.

Career

Graduate assistant, Tennessee Volunteers, 1986–87; passing game coordinator, Southeast Missouri State; wide receivers coach, University of the Pacific, 1989; assistant coach, San Francisco 49ers, 1990; assistant offensive coach, Green Bay Packers, 1992–93; wide receivers coach, Green Bay Packers, 1993–94; offensive coach, Philadelphia Eagles, 1995–97; head coach, Oakland Raiders, 1998–2001; head coach, Tampa Bay Buccaneers, 2002—.

Awards: AFC West Division Title, 2000; NFC South Division Title, 2002; NFC Conference Championship, 2002; Super Bowl, 2003.

Sidelights

In 2003, at the age of 39, professional football coach Jon Gruden led the Tampa Bay Buccaneers to their first Super Bowl victory, thus becoming the youngest coach ever to win the title.

Gruden grew up in Orlando, Florida, one of three sons of Jim, a football coach, and Kathy, an elementary school teacher, who was an ardent supporter of her husband and children's interest in sports. Once, when Gruden and his brothers were playing in a Little League game and their mother's car broke down, she went anyway—by riding one of her sons's bikes seven miles to the game. She arrived in time to cheer for the last seven innings. Gruden told Mike Bianchi in a Knight Ridder/Tribune News Service article, "She was relentless in her devotion to us. She was our everything."

As a teenager, Gruden dreamed of becoming the star quarterback at Notre Dame University, and he focused all his time and energy on football. He became a reasonably good quarterback at South Bend Clay High School, and was known for his temper, once beating up a fan who criticized the Notre Dame coaching staff.

Unfortunately, Gruden lacked the athletic talent to make his football dreams come true at a college level, and he was also doing poorly in school. In contrast, his older brother, James, was an excellent student, and they frequently fought with each other. "He was a 4.0 student, and I was about a 2.0," Gruden told S.L. Price in *Sports Illustrated.* "People thought something was wrong with me. Teachers would ask, and my brother thought something was wrong with me, too." In addition to having an academically gifted older brother, Gruden also suffered because his younger brother, Jay, was a naturally talented athlete. Gruden often felt insecure and displaced by his siblings and their obvious talents.

Gruden's father became assistant football coach at Notre Dame in 1978, and although Gruden could have gotten free tuition to the university, his parents thought it would be better for him to go to a different school where there was not as much competition to play on the football team. Gruden still wanted to play football, and he wasn't good enough to play at Notre Dame, so his parents suggested a smaller school, Muskingum College in Ohio. Gruden spent a year at Muskingum before transferring to Dayton. At Dayton, he worked hard, practicing passes, lifting weights to bulk up and increase his strength, and running, believing that through sheer will and hard work he could mold himself into a star player.

At the time, Gruden's brother, Jay, was spending his free time watching television and eating snacks. Gruden, irritated, and at the same time confident in his intense training regimen, harassed Jay about his laziness until Jay finally challenged Gruden to a two–mile race. They were evenly matched until the last two–tenths of a mile, when Jay put in a finishing kick that left Gruden in the dust. "Talk about getting humiliated," Gruden told Price in *Sports Illustrated*. "Hey, loser. That's when I knew."

What Gruden had realized was that all the drive and hard work in the world would not make him into a great player, because he lacked the innate athletic talent. He told Price, "The most disappointing thing in my whole life is not being able to be anything [on the football field] but a ham–and–egger." Jay moved on to become a star player at Louisville, and Gruden became his biggest fan, listening to Jay's games every Saturday on the radio, no matter where he was or what else he was doing.

Gruden graduated from Dayton in 1985, then moved to Tennessee, where he worked as a graduate assistant for the Tennessee Volunteers football team. He specialized in studying the team's films of games, organizing them and customizing them for each coach. Walt Harris, offensive coordinator for the Volunteers, was impressed by Gruden's meticulous work, and in 1986, when Harris accepted a job as coach at the University of the Pacific, he offered Gruden a job as a wide receivers coach.

After working with Harris for a season, Gruden moved on to work for the San Francisco 49ers and then, in 1992, accepted a position as assistant offen-

sive coach for the Green Bay Packers under head coach Mike Holmgren. After one season, he had impressed Holmgren enough to become the Packers's wide receivers coach. He stayed with the Packers until 1994.

During the early stages of his career, Gruden became aware that he was different from other people because he had a much higher energy level, needed little sleep, and became agitated very easily. He thought this might be a problem, but when he asked a doctor about it, the doctor told him that he should consider his high energy level as a gift, accept it as part of his personality, and devote his extra time to something he loved. Gruden followed this advice, and has customarily woken up at 3:17 every morning (317 is his lucky number) and worked until 10 or 11 at night, concentrating on his team and how to improve it. His speed is legendary among his family and friends. His wife, Cindy, told *Sports Illustrated*'s Price, "He's awake while he sleeps.... Everything is just *bam–bam–bam* high intensity." She also noted, "One time we brought a movie home, and I went up to put the kids to bed. When I came down, he was previewing the movie in fast–forward. I was like 'Can't we just watch it at regular speed?'" Buccaneers safety John Lynch told Price, "His energy is unreal."

Gruden is also notable for his hatred of fidgeting or the sounds other people make while chewing. His brother, Jay, told *Sports Illustrated*'s Price, "We got along great, but the thing that worried me was, if you're in the same room with him for a long period of time, he's going to find something you're doing that bothers him." Gruden hates the sound of other people eating so much that when his wife and sons sit down to eat, he moves his own plate to another room, where he can't hear them. His wife told Price, "If he's in a movie theater and someone's chewing too loudly or talking, we get up and move. One time we moved five times. I was so embarrassed. It's just the chewing thing. Is that weird?"

Gruden became the offensive coach for the Philadelphia Eagles in 1995, when he was 31 years old. This was considered a very young age for a coach, but Gruden's youth proved not to be a handicap. In 1996, the Eagles finished in the top five of the National Football League (NFL), with 363 points. In the same year, they were fourth in the league in passing yards. In 1997, they came in sixth in the league in passing yards.

Gruden told Paul Domowitch of the Knight Ridder/Tribune News Service, "Coaching in Philadelphia, where nothing is bigger than Eagles football, was really exciting. Working underneath that big stadium every day, that was cool, man." Gruden stood a good chance of moving up to head coach if he stayed with the Eagles, but after three years with the team, he moved on to become head coach of the Oakland Raiders. He spent four years with the Raiders, taking the team to the NFC title game in 2000 and to the division playoffs in 2001. During this time, his ability drew the attention of his old dream-school, Notre Dame, which offered him a job, as did Ohio State. Gruden turned both schools down. His father told Price, "I don't know many guys who had a chance to coach Ohio State and Notre Dame ... and turned them down."

In 2001, Gruden was named one of *People*'s 50 Most Beautiful People. However, his players joked about the dark side of Gruden's good looks, calling him "Chucky" after the malevolent, homicidal doll in a horror movie of the same name. Gruden has cheerfully embraced the nickname, and often signs Chucky dolls for admiring fans.

According to the *Holland Sentinel*, during Gruden's time with the Raiders, there were persistent rumors that Gruden was having trouble getting along with Al Davis, owner of the Raiders; when he had one year left on his contract, he told Davis that he wanted an extension and a raise, or he would leave the team. John Madden, former Raiders coach and a television football analyst, told the *Holland Sentinel*, "Bottom line was, Al Davis wasn't going to pay Jon Gruden four or five million dollars." In addition, it was believed that Gruden was annoyed because he did not have enough decision-making ability regarding team personnel. Davis made those decisions, and this annoyed Gruden because it led many people to think Davis was the real coach of the team, and Gruden was just a figurehead. Past Raiders coaches had also struggled with this issue; unlike some other team owners, Davis was always present at practice and in the locker room.

Gruden denied these rumors of personal problems with Davis. He told the *Holland Sentinel* that members of the media did not have all the information about the issue, although they could think whatever they wanted to about it. He said he had never had trouble getting along with people or in taking charge of his job. However, he added, "At the same time, when it comes to calling plays, when it comes to organizing players, that's the job of a coach."

In 2002, the Tampa Bay Buccaneers released head coach Tony Dungy, who had worked with the Buccaneers for five years. They offered the Raiders two first-round draft picks, two second-round draft picks, and $8 million in exchange for Gruden. Buccaneers executive vice president Joel Glazer told

Price, "He's special. When you're dealing with special, sometimes you do special things." However, when some observers of football called him an "offensive genius," Gruden modestly told Price, "[Other coaches] deserve to be called geniuses. I'm just a grunt.... I wouldn't be getting up this early if I was a genius, man."

The Raiders accepted the offer, and so did Gruden. Shortly afterward, the NFL changed the draft rules, prohibiting deals in which teams traded a coach for draft picks. At first, Gruden had a rocky start: by October of 2002, the Buccaneers lost for the fourth straight time against Philadelphia, leading *Sports Illustrated* writer Jeffri Chadiha to comment, "The Bucs's offense looks as feeble as ever." Despite this slow start, Gruden soon turned the team around, leading them to the NFC South Division title, the NFC Conference Championship, and, on January 26, 2003, a Super Bowl XXXVII win against his old team, the Raiders. After the win, Gruden began writing an autobiography, *Do You Love Football? Winning With Heart, Passion and Not Much Sleep*, to be published in the fall of 2003.

The Buccaneers won the Super Bowl 48–21, the first NFL championship for the team and the third-highest-scoring Super Bowl in history. CNNSI.com wrote, "The Tampa Bay defense won by a mile, returning three of a record five interceptions for touchdowns and shutting down any hope the Raiders had of a late comeback." Buccaneers defensive tackle Warren Sapp added, "There was nothing [the Raiders] could do to us. Nothing." Buccaneers owner Malcolm Glazer said, "We were waiting for the right man and the right man came—Jon Gruden."

In the *Sporting News*, former Raiders tight end Roland Williams told Dan Pompei that Gruden was "the best coach in the NFL," and added, "He knows how to get us going, and his love for the game comes through. I'd play for him forever." Bill Callahan, offensive coordinator for the Raiders, told Pompei, "He's probably the most creative offensive mind in the league." A scout for an opposing team told *Sports Illustrated*'s Josh Elliott, "Jon Gruden is the best coach in the NFL, and he'll add to that reputation. He's the perfect mix of old- and new-school values. He schemes well and exploits his opponents's weaknesses better than anyone."

As a result of his Super Bowl success, and because of his youth, good looks, and hard-driving style, Gruden became a sought-after spokesperson for a wide variety of companies, who asked him to sell everything from cars to financial services. Steve Nudelberg, chief executive officer of a sports marketing firm, told Gary Haber in the *Tampa Tribune,* "I can't imagine him not being attractive to any company." Gruden resisted these offers, however; he had already refused offers to do local commercials in Tampa, Florida, and had only appeared in two commercials, one for a hotel chain and one for a satellite television service.

Gruden described his style to Domowitch: "I'm intense on game day. I enjoy competing. I want to win. When you're down there calling plays and something goes bad, you wonder what happened. I love the game. I get fired up. I don't know what's wrong with that." Gruden remains modest about his abilities; when asked "Would you make a good general or CEO?" by *Men's Health*'s Bruce Schoenfeld, Gruden replied, "Probably not. All I know is football."

Sources

Periodicals

Knight Ridder/Tribune News Service, January 13, 2001; October 19, 2002; May 4, 2003, p. K4237; May 10, 2003, p. K0319.

Men's Health, September 2002, p. 80.

Sporting News, September 9, 2002.

Sports Illustrated, September 2, 2002, p. 112; September 9, 2002, p. 42; October 28, 2002, p. 63.

Tampa Tribune, January 30, 2003, p. 1.

Time for Kids, February 7, 2003, p. 8.

Online

Biography Resource Center Online, Gale Group, 2003.

"Buc Kickin'," CNNSI.com, http://sportsillustrated. cnn.com/football/2003/playoffs/news/2003/ 01/26/sb_gamer_ap/ (January 27, 2003).

"Strange Reunion for Jon Gruden," *Holland Sentinel,* http://www.thehollandsentinel.net/stories/ 012203/spo_012203052.shtml (May 20, 2003).

Tampa Bay Buccaneers, http://www.buccaneers. com/ (May 21, 2003).

—Kelly Winters

Daniel Handler

Children's book author

Born in 1970 in San Francisco, CA; son of Louis (a certified public accountant) and Sandra (a college dean) Handler; married Lisa Brown (a graphic artist), 1998. *Education:* Wesleyan University, B.A.

Addresses: *Agent*—c/o HarperCollins Children's Books, 1350 Avenue of the Americas, New York, NY 10019. *Email*—lsnicket@harpercollins.com.

Career

Novelist and screenwriter. Adult novels published under name Daniel Handler include: *The Basic Eight*, 1999; *Watch Your Mouth*, 2000. Author of youth novels "A Series of Unfortunate Events," published under pen name Lemony Snicket. Worked as a comedy writer, *House of Blues Radio Hour*. Has written for periodicals including *Voice Literary Supplement*, *Salon*, and the *New York Times*.

Awards: Academy of American Poets Prize, 1990; Olin Fellowship, 1992.

Sidelights

Who is Lemony Snicket? According to many reports, he is an unpleasant fellow who writes accounts of put–upon orphans in constant danger of being eliminated in nasty ways. Snicket is not much given to interviews, but his spokesman, novelist Daniel Handler, is more forthcoming. In fact, it's whispered that Handler is the brains behind the Lemony Snicket publishing phenomenon. Indeed, it is Handler who is reaping the acclaim for Snicket's "A Series of Unfortunate Events," which has challenged *Harry Potter* and *Captain Underpants* on the children's bestseller lists.

In Handler's words, Snicket was "born before you were, and is likely to die before you as well." As for Handler, he was born in San Francisco, California, in 1970, the son of an accountant and a college dean. At age seven the boy began writing his first stories, strongly influenced by the morbid stylings of Roald Dahl and Edward Gorey. Her son could "see the humor in everything," Handler's mother, Sandra, told Richard Jerome of *People*. After graduating from San Francisco's prestigious and demanding Lowell High School (where he tied for Best Personality of his class), Handler enrolled in Connecticut's Wesleyan University. At that time the young man specialized in verse, winning the 1990 Poets Prize from the Academy of American Poets. But soon fiction would emerge as Handler's forte. It was destined to happen: "My poems were getting longer and longer, and more proselike," he said in an interview posted on CNN.com.

Around the same time he met his wife–to–be, graphic artist Lisa Brown, in an "aptly Snick-etesque" way, according to *People*'s Jerome. "At the time Handler suffered periodic blackouts (the cause was never determined), and one day in Chaucer class he collapsed on Brown." After living in New York City for several years, the couple moved to San Francisco where Handler took a job writing comedy pieces for the syndicated *House of Blues Radio Hour.* By 1998 he had finished the manuscript of his first novel, *The Basic Eight.* Though written for adults, *The Basic Eight* is set in an upscale high school where a clique of eight overprivileged teens includes narrator Flannery Culp. Among Flan's seven confidantes are "Queen Bee" Kate, attractive Natasha, secret crush Gabriel, and "V," who uses only her initial to protect the identity of her wealthy family. Flan's story begins in prison and unfolds backward in time to reveal how she and her group turn from pranks to real menace when they begin experimenting with absinthe. Natasha comes to Flan's rescue by poisoning a biology teacher. Another student, Adam, is the object of Flan's unrequited love; he meets his fate via a croquet mallet to the head. As news of the murders becomes public, the Basic Eight become tabloid celebrities.

The publication of *The Basic Eight* in 1999 brought respectful if not rave reviews—the author is "a charming writer with a lovely mastery of voice," said a contributor to the *New Yorker,* "but the book is weakened by his attempt to turn a clever idea into a social satire." Handler's novel was also the object of some unintended publicity when its students–as–killers storyline coincided with the fatal shootings of students and staff at Littleton, Colorado's Columbine High School by two teenage boys.

For his second adult novel, *Watch Your Mouth,* Handler returned to youthful characters and incendiary themes. This time the action revolves around college junior Joseph, who finds love and lust with classmate Cynthia ("Cyn") Glass. Visiting her house over summer break, Joseph begins to notice something amiss with the respectable–appearing Glass family: father Ben is a little too attentive to his comely daughter, while mother Mimi makes barely hidden overtures to her teenage son, Stephen. Joseph begins to wonder if he's only imagining what sexual escapades may be taking place in the Glass household. Billed as an "incest comedy," *Watch Your Mouth* gained some critical notice. *Salon's* Edward Neuert felt the author "is more than ready to pick up the torch [of Kurt Vonnegut] and write the kind of deftly funny absurdist story that both horrifies with its subject matter and hooks you with its humor."

Having established himself as a writer of black comedy, Handler struck out into the children's market in 1999 via the emergence of Lemony Snicket. That Jiminy Cricket–like *nom de plume* was born when Handler was contacting right–wing reactionary groups to research *The Basic Eight.* He wanted literature and information, "but I was paranoid," Handler told Daniel Fierman of *Entertainment Weekly.* "What would happen in two years, if I'm a major novelist, and I'm exposed as a member of the John Birch Society? So I was on the phone with some organization and they said, 'What's your name?' And I said, *Lemony Snicket.* I have no idea where it came from." Soon Lemony Snicket was adopted as a pet name among Handler and his friends, who used it for everything from dinner reservations to business cards.

At the urging of an editor friend, Handler refashioned a drafted novel into a gothic tale for young readers. The result, volume one of "A Series of Unfortunate Events," was released as *The Bad Beginning* by HarperCollins in 1999. The book opens with a cautionary note from Snicket: "If you are interested in stories with happy endings, you would be better off reading some other book." (Nor would there be any happy beginnings or middles, he adds.) Then Snicket introduces the Baudelaire children—brainy Violet, bookworm Klaus, and baby Sunny. Orphaned under mysterious circumstances, the children find themselves bumped from one comically inept guardian to the next—until they meet their distant cousin, Count Olaf.

Olaf's mission is to get his hands on the orphans's inheritance and will stop at nothing, including putting Sunny in a cage, to achieve his goal. This kind of edginess distinguished Handler's writing and made some of his associates nervous. "We had mothers in our publicity department telling us: You put a baby in a cage in this book," HarperCollins editor Susan Rich remarked to *Entertainment Weekly's* Fierman. "You. Put. A BABY. In a CAGE!" Nor was controversy avoided when Olaf revealed his evil intentions to marry 14–year–old Violet. In one scene he strokes her hair; she imagines spending the night with her nemesis. "There's a wisp of sexuality over the paragraph," the author acknowledged to Joel Rickett of *Independent Sunday.* "It should be disturbing. I wanted the notion of marrying him to make people shudder."

But what mainly sets Handler's books apart is the aura of mounting doom and the constant, unhappy, unlucky happenstance that befalls the poor Baudelaires. In the author's view, it's important to expose youngsters to such darker aspects of life. He thinks this sense of honesty is missing in some children's literature: "It annoys me that there are these books about going to hospital for young children that say it is really not so bad," he told Rickett. "If you're a child going to the hospital you're going to have a miserable time; you're probably going to be in pain, you're going to be lonely, it's going to be scary, there are people in masks poking at you. A book that says it is going to be fun is a desperate lie."

Handler, however, offsets the scares with Lemony Snicket's dry wit. As narrator of the series, Snicket adopts a tone—according to Handler—that is "mock moralizing;" he is "ten times more depressed and horrified and scared than any of his readers," the author was quoted by Patrick Reardon in a Knight Ridder/Tribune New Service article. Snicket's air of melodrama, added Handler, "mocks the condescending and certain voice that children hear from most adults." The author kept a wary eye out for adult reaction to his Baudelaire books, telling Sam Whiting of the *San Francisco Chronicle,* "I thought kids would like [the books] but I thought they'd never get in the hands of kids. I thought teachers would be revolted and librarians would be offended and all the guardians of children's culture would be horrified. I didn't think these books would sell any. I thought these books would be miserable failures."

Handler's fears proved unfounded when the "Unfortunate Events" series became widely read and well received. "The author uses formal, Latinate language and intrusive commentary to hilarious effect," noted a *Publishers Weekly* reviewer, while Susan Dove Lempke of *Booklist* assessed *The Bad Beginning* and *The Reptile Room* as two books that will make children "laugh at the over–the–top satire, hiss at the creepy, nefarious villains, and root for the intelligent, courageous, unfortunate Baudelaire orphans."

In *The Reptile Room,* the second Snicket novel, the orphans find slimy adventure with their herpetologist uncle. *The Wide Window,* "Book the Third" of the Baudelaire series, has the children living with elderly Aunt Josephine, a frightful grammarian. When Count Olaf catches up with the orphans, he tricks Josephine into thinking he's a sea captain, then tosses the woman into leech–infested waters. The fourth installment, *The Miserable Mill,* features a rescue of Klaus, who is under the hypnotic clutches of Olaf.

Handler showed his penchant for vocabulary–building titles with *The Austere Academy* and *The Ersatz Elevator.* In the former title, the Baudelaires find themselves enrolled in Prufrock Preparatory School, best remembered for its snapping crabs and dripping fungus. *The Ersatz Elevator* introduces two new guardians, well–meaning Jerome and his social–climbing wife, Esme, who, according to *Booklist's* Carolyn Phelan, is obsessed with "'what's in' (aqueous martinis, pinstripe suits, and orphans) and 'what's out' (alcoholic martinis, light, and elevators)."

The author makes light of the saying, "It takes a village to raise a child" when, in *The Vile Village,* an entire community adopts the Beaudelaires. It soon becomes evident, however, that the townspeople see the orphans as little more than a source of free labor. In "Book the Eighth," *The Hostile Hospital,* the children escape various dangers—including having Violet's head cut off—but end up on the final page stuffed into the trunk of Count Olaf's car, "hurtling toward whatever destiny awaits in volume nine," as Phelan put it in a *Booklist* review. That destiny was revealed in "Book the Ninth," *The Carnivorous Carnival,* released in 2002. When the Baudelaires are framed for a murder they didn't commit, the orphans take refuge in Madame Lulu's House of Freaks, with Violet and Klaus impersonating the two–headed Beverly/Elliot, and Sunny portraying Chabo the Wolf Baby.

Snicket interrupted the flow of his 13–volume series to pen his own story. *Lemony Snicket: The Unauthorized Biography* was released in 2002. Handler got the job of publicizing the book, telling a *Publishers Weekly* interviewer that when the Snicket manuscript fell into his hands, "the first thing I did … was lock all the doors and windows of the hotel at which I was staying. It was a big hotel so this took some time." Certain that Snicket would not want the details of his past brought to light, Handler added that what he feared were "not 'repercussions' but 'percussions,' as there seem to be several suspicious drummers who have appeared in my life since publication was announced."

As dark tales of danger and woe, "A Series of Unfortunate Events" has been compared to J. K. Rowling's blockbuster *Harry Potter* books. But Handler sees less similarity: "If I were South American, they would probably say, 'How are you like or unlike Gabriel Garcia Marquez?'" the author said to *Los Angeles Times* reporter Susan Carpenter. "I really don't like that it's turned into a contest," he added. "There's no question that thousands and thousands of people have picked up my books because somebody said to them, 'If you like Harry Potter, you'll like this,' so it's great to be writing children's books at a time when that's going on."

"Unfortunate Events" also followed Harry Potter to the big screen when a film adaptation was announced in 2002. Handler wrote the script, and Jim Carrey was signed to play Count Olaf. But by February of 2003, *Entertainment Weekly's* Josh Young was reporting rancor on the set when the picture's budget was slashed by the production company, Paramount. Producer Scott Rudin and director Barry Sonnenfeld left the project, leaving the fate of the film, in the words of Young, "as precarious as that of the woefully orphaned Baudelaire siblings." In April of 2003, it was announced in *Entertainment Weekly* that the film was due to start shooting in October of that year and be directed by Brad Silberling.

The young fans of Lemony Snicket often contact the author with questions; until the volume of correspondence got oppressive, Handler used to read and answer every letter in the character of Snicket. Following the terrorist attacks on America of September 11, 2001, there was a different tenor to the feedback. "Children asked if Count Olaf was a terrorist," Reardon explained in the Knight Ridder/Tribune New Service article. "They wanted to know if the Baudelaire orphans had been near the World Trade Center on the day of the attacks." At the same time, demand for the books increased in the days following the national trauma. "Our best guess," librarian Cynthia Oakes told the Knight Ridder/Tribune New Service's Reardon, "was that [a scary book] was a safe place to put their fear." In the subsequent weeks and months, the children's questions returned to more everyday issues of "complaining about their grumpy teacher or the curfew they have," as Handler noted in the article.

A popular speaker at schools, where he tells tales of Lemony Snicket, Handler says he's taking his fame in stride. "I have eavesdropped on large groups of people debating the minutiae of my plots," Handler wrote in the *Daily Telegraph.* "I have received more letters and e-mails than I can count, saying that I am the best author who has ever lived. I have attended cocktail parties and encountered the response: 'I can't believe I'm actually meeting you!' when introduced to a stranger. Five cats have been named after me, and those are just the ones I know about."

Selected writings

The Basic Eight, St. Martin's Press (New York City), 1999.

The Bad Beginning (volume one of "A Series of Unfortunate Events"), HarperCollins (New York City), 1999.

The Reptile Room (volume two of "A Series of Unfortunate Events"), HarperCollins (New York City), 1999.

Watch Your Mouth, St. Martin's Press (New York City), 2000.

The Wide Window (volume three of "A Series of Unfortunate Events"), HarperCollins (New York City), 2000.

The Miserable Mill (volume four of "A Series of Unfortunate Events"), HarperCollins (New York City), 2000.

The Austere Academy (volume five of "A Series of Unfortunate Events"), HarperCollins (New York City), 2000.

The Ersatz Elevator (volume six of "A Series of Unfortunate Events"), HarperCollins (New York City), 2001.

The Vile Village (volume seven of "A Series of Unfortunate Events") HarperCollins (New York City), 2001.

The Hostile Hospital (volume eight of "A Series of Unfortunate Events"), HarperCollins (New York City), 2001.

The Carnivorous Carnival, (volume nine of "A Series of Unfortunate Events"), HarperCollins (New York City), 2002.

Lemony Snicket: The Unauthorized Biography, HarperCollins (New York City), 2002.

Sources

Periodicals

Booklist, March 15, 1999, p. 1289; December 1, 1999, p. 707; June 1, 2000, p. 1857; August 2001, p. 2122.

Daily Telegraph (London, England), August 14, 2002, p. 14.

Entertainment Weekly, June 29, 2001, p. 90; May 24, 2002, pp. 56–59; February 7, 2003, p. 8; April 25, 2003, pp. 32–36.

Herald Sun (Melbourne, Australia), May 18, 2002, p. W28.

Independent (London, England), September 21, 2002, p. 26.

Independent Sunday, June 10, 2001, p. 43.

Knight Ridder/Tribune News Service, December 11, 2001, p. K3644.

Los Angeles Times, September 9, 2001, p. E1.

Newsweek, June 24, 2002, p. 95.

New Yorker, June 21, 1999.

New York Times Magazine, April 29, 2001.

People, May 27, 2002, pp. 155–156.

Publishers Weekly, March 1, 1999, p. 59; September 6, 1999, p. 104; May 29, 2000, p. 42; June 19, 2000, p. 60; May 6, 2002, p. 59.

San Francisco Chronicle, August 5, 2001, p. 8.

Online

A Series of Unfortunate Events Website, http://www.lemonysnicket.com (February 18, 2003).

"Author Suggests You Read Something Else," CNN.com, http://www.cnn.com/2002/SHOWBIZ/books/08/08/lemony.snicket/index.html (August 8, 2002).

Contemporary Authors Online, Gale, 2002.

"What To Read," *Salon,* http://www.salonmag.com/ (July 24, 2000).

"Wry 'Series of Unfortunate Events' Books Earn Fans, Praise," CNN.com, http://www.cnn.com/2000/fyi/news/ (May 12, 2000).

—Susan Salter

Jill Hennessy

Actress

Born Jillian Hennessy, November 25, 1969, in Edmunton, Alberta, Canada; daughter of John (a meat salesman) and Maxine Hennessey; married Paolo Mastropietro (an actor, businessman, and restaurant owner), 2000.

Addresses: *Email*—CrossingJordan@nbc.com. *Television network*—NBC–TV Viewer Relations, 30 Rockefeller Plaza, New York, NY 10112.

Career

Actress in films, including: *Dead Ringers,* 1988; *Robocop 3,* 1993; *The Paper,* 1994; *I Shot Andy Warhol,* 1996; *A Smile Like Yours,* 1997; *Chutney Popcorn,* 1999; *Molly,* 1999; *The Acting Class,* 2000; *Autumn in New York,* 2000; *Love in the Time of Money,* 2002. Television appearances include: *Law & Order,* NBC, 1993–96; *Nuremburg* (miniseries), TNT, 2000; *Jackie, Ethel, and Joan: The Women of Camelot* (miniseries), NBC, 2001; *Crossing Jordan,* NBC, 2001—. Stage appearances include: *Buddy: The Buddy Holly Story* (Broadway debut), 1990. Studied with improvisational comedy troupe Second City.

Awards: Golden Satellite Award, International Press Academy, for TNT miniseries *Nuremburg,* 2000.

Sidelights

The Canadian–born actress Jill Hennessy is best known for her television roles and her portrayals of strong, brainy women. From 1993 to 1996 she played the part of Claire Kincaid, the staid assistant district attorney on NBC's popular courtroom drama *Law & Order.* In 2001, after acting in a series of film roles, Hennessy returned to network television as the lead on NBC's acclaimed forensics drama *Crossing Jordan.* As the tough, working–class coroner Jordan Cavanaugh, Hennessy garnered critical praise for her portrayal of a complex, not–always–likable character. The actress also starred as Jacqueline Kennedy in 2001's NBC miniseries *Jackie, Ethel, and Joan: The Women of Camelot,* and has appeared in a diverse range of film roles, including Laura in 1996's *I Shot Andy Warhol* and Lynn in 2000's *Autumn in New York.*

Jillian Hennessy was born in Edmunton, Canada, on November 25, 1969, three minutes after her identical twin sister, Jacqueline. Known as "Jacq and Jill," the twins were 12 years old when their parents separated. Hennessy's mother, Maxine, moved far away, leaving the girls and their younger brother to be raised by their father, John, a meat salesman. Their paternal grandmother relocated to Canada from Arizona to help care for Hennessy and her siblings.

"I was affected by the loss of my mother in lots of ways," Hennessy told Eirik Knutzen of Copley News Service. "First of all, I'm fascinated by mothers, good mothers, mothers who stay with their kids. And femininity in general. I'm entranced by how women put on their makeup and do their hair. I remember my mother sitting in front of the mirror, but I still had to learn those things by myself."

Since Hennessy's father's job involved constant travel, the family moved often. Hennessy had lived in nine communities across Canada by the time she had graduated from high school in Kitchener, Ontario. Both Hennessy and her sister studied music, and later sang together in local clubs and pubs. The guitar–playing Hennessy has told reporters that she hopes to put together a duo band with her twin, and perhaps release an album.

In addition to music, the twins shared a passion for acting. Hennessy acted in her first school plays at age 12. Although she took up modeling in Toronto at age 15, Hennessy does not fondly remember her childhood looks. "I was so unattractive, sort of the outcast drama geek," she told Jenelle Riley of Back Stage West. "I didn't date, my clothes were never cool, and I never thought there would be a day when people would be asking me what beauty products I use."

Early in her career, Hennessy studied with the improvisational comedy troupe Second City, and also worked with a Toronto–based comedy troupe. She had her share of discouragements as a wannabe–actress teen. "When I was about 19 or 20, I worked incredibly hard with an acting coach for a part that I wanted very badly," she told Cosmopolitan, as quoted at iVillage.com. "I went in for the audition, and I felt really good about how I did. But as soon as I finished, [the casting director] took one look at me and said, 'I know a girl like you thinks she can get by on her looks. But it's going to take a hell of a lot more than that to be a good actor, and God knows you need a lot of training!'"

It wasn't long, though, before Hennessy got a break, appearing with her sister in David Cronenberg's 1988 thriller Dead Ringers, starring Jeremy Irons. "[P]laying a twin, I needed my sister to audition, too," Hennessy told Eirik Knutzen of Copley News Service. "Jacqueline had final exams on the day of the audition, of course, but she somehow managed to postpone the tests for a few days." Jacqueline later pursued a career as a writer, becoming an award–winning reporter for the Canadian women's magazine Chatelaine.

In 1990 Hennessy made her Broadway debut as singer Buddy Holly's Puerto Rican wife in Buddy: The Buddy Holly Story. A series of small television roles followed for Hennessy, until her big break came in 1993, when she was cast as Claire Kincaid on the NBC drama series Law & Order. The same year she played Robocop's chemist, Dr. Marie Lazarus, in the action–movie sequel Robocop 3.

It was Law & Order that would bring Hennessy into the spotlight. The Emmy Award–winning program had already aired for three seasons and the cast had undergone a few changeovers. Hennessy fit right in as a confident, straight–laced New York lawyer. Despite the fact that Law & Order was a plot–driven rather than a character–driven program, Hennessy's character attracted a loyal following of viewers. Rumor has it that Hennessy's twin, Jacqueline, occasionally stepped in to play Claire Kincaid when her sister was unavailable.

Looking to broaden her career—and to avoid the actor's pitfall of becoming typecast—Hennessy decided to leave Law & Order after her third season. Rather than replace the actress, the program's creators decided to write Hennessy's character out of the story. In an emotional episode, Claire died in a car accident, leaving the show's fans surprised and saddened. Hennessy hadn't realized that audience members had bonded so strongly with her character. "When I was on the show I was just focusing on the show and you don't have an audience there," she told Riley of Back Stage West. "It's only been since I left that people come up to me and say they cried the day I died."

Although she was sad to leave the show, Hennessy was enthusiastic about venturing into new territory as an actress. While she was on Law & Order, she had appeared in 1996's I Shot Andy Warhol, and the experience of working on an independent film had inspired her. In the world of independent filmmaking, Hennessy found that directors were more willing to let her portray a range of diverse characters and were less liable to typecast her. She also found the subject matter of independent films to be more daring and less conventional.

During the late 1990s Hennessy sought out more roles in independent films. In 1999's Chutney Popcorn she portrayed the lesbian lover of an Indian woman. Comfortable in the roll–up–your–sleeves environment of a low–budget film set, Hennessy not only acted but also moved equipment, brought her own wardrobe, and styled her own hair. The same year, she played a doctor who breaks through to an autistic patient played by Elisabeth Shue in Molly, which received tepid reviews.

Hennessy has also tried her hand at making her own films. In 2000 she starred in the comedic short The Acting Class, in which she served as the writer, co–director (with Elizabeth Holder), producer, cinematographer, makeup artist, and even the catering coordinator. The film—which included performances by her sister; her husband, Paolo Mastropietro; and former *Law & Order* costars Chris Noth and Benjamin Bratt—told the story of a dysfunctional acting teacher. That same year, Hennessy appeared in the TNT miniseries *Nuremburg,* playing Elsie Douglas, a lawyer who prosecutes Nazi war criminals. For this role she received a Golden Satellite Award from the International Press Academy.

Hollywood film credits for Hennessy include a small role in 1994's *The Paper,* a satirical comedy–drama by director Ron Howard, in which she portrayed Robert Duvall's daughter. Just after her *Law & Order* stint, she turned away from drama and toward comedy in 1997's *A Smile Like Yours,* playing an architect who tries to seduce a married man played by Greg Kinnear. Other Hollywood roles include 1999's *Dead Broke;* 2001's action flick *Exit Wounds,* with Steven Seagal; and 2000's *Autumn in New York,* with Richard Gere.

In December of 2000 Hennessy was offered the lead role in the pilot episode of NBC's *Crossing Jordan.* It was the script, and particularly the role of Dr. Jordan Cavanaugh, that inspired Hennessy to take a hiatus from film work and return to network television. As the hot–tempered, headstrong Jordan, Hennessy would play a Boston medical examiner with a penchant for crime–solving. "You never see [women] portrayed that way," Hennessy told Riley of*Back Stage West.* "Actresses are always demanded or required to be likable. Men aren't."

Hennessy was also intrigued by similarities between Jordan's childhood and her own. Like her television alter ego, Hennessy was raised by a single father, to whom she remains very close. Yet while her own father was a salesman, Jordan's father was a tough ex–cop. And while her own mother had abandoned her family, Jordan's mother had been murdered—explaining the character's obsession with sleuthing. Understanding the huge void created by the absence of Jordan's mother, Hennessy was able to quickly grasp the emotional aspects of her character. To learn about being a medical examiner, the actress spent time doing research in the Los Angeles County Coroner's Office, where she observed real–life autopsies.

In its first season, critics were slow to praise the *Crossing Jordan,* suggesting it too closely resembled another show about sleuthing coroners, CBS–TV's *CSI.* But at the start of the second year, *TV Guide* lauded the season premiere. It seemed that the program had gained a following. The popularity of its star had been a key to the show's success.

Hennessy married Mastropietro, her boyfriend of six years, in October of 2000. A former lawyer, Mastropietro is a businessman and restaurant owner as well as an actor. One of his businesses is Hennessy's Tavern, a bar and grill in Northvale, New Jersey—next door to the sound stage where NBC's *Ed* is filmed. Serving "comfort food," the restaurant is a favorite hangout for *Ed*'s cast and crew. Mastropietro also manages his wife's personal appearance schedule as well as most of her publicity. The couple had a second wedding ceremony, with Mayor Rudolph Guiliani officiating, in New York's City Hall, in January of 2001.

In 2001 Hennessy portrayed Jacqueline Kennedy Onassis in CBS's two–part, four–hour miniseries *Jackie, Ethel, and Joan: Women of Camelot.* Bearing a strong resemblance to the dark–haired beauty, Hennessy was aptly cast as the American icon. Although the miniseries spawned mixed reviews, Hennessy received raves for her performance. Among praise from critics was a nod to Hennessy's convincing approximation of Jackie O's soft, breathy voice. To complete her transformation, Hennessy was costumed in outfits by popular 1960s designer Oleg Cassini, and donned a series of wigs resembling Jackie O's hairstyles.

Hennessy shared the screen with Steve Buscemi and Rosario Dawson in 2002's *Love in the Time of Money,* which premiered at the Sundance Film Festival. An independent feature from first–time director Peter Mattei, the film found Hennessy in the role of Ellen Walker, a lonely, scared housewife whose husband falls for another man. The film was a modern adaptation of Arthur Schnitzler's play *La Ronde,* bringing disparate characters together in intersecting stories about love and sex.

Although her surname is Irish, Hennessy shares her Celtic heritage along with Ukrainian, Italian, French, and Swedish ancestries. She is fluent in French, Spanish, and Italian. The actress also has a song named after her, "The Ballad of Jill Hennessy," by Minnesota band Mollycuddle. In 2002 *Cosmopolitan* voted Hennessy one of the year's most "Fun Fearless Females."

Sources

Periodicals

Advertiser, May 29, 2002, p. 49.
Back Stage West, October 16, 2002.
Copley News Service, September 2, 2002.
Ottawa Citizen, March 2, 2001, p. E6.

Online

"Biography for Jill Hennessy," Internet Movie Database, http://us.imdb.com/Bio?Hennessy,+Jill (November 11, 2002).

"Fun Fearless Females 2002: Jill Hennessy: TV Titan," iVillage.com, http://magazines.ivillage.com/cosmopolitan/connect/fearless/spc/0,12859,284424_294212,00.html (November 11, 2002).

"Jill Hennessy," Hollywood.com, http://www.hollywood.com/celebs/bio/celeb/1677013 (November 4, 2002).

"Jill Hennessy," NBC.com, http://www.nbc.com/Crossing_Jordan/bios/Jill_Hennessy.html (November 4, 2002).

—Wendy Kagan

Betsy Holden

Co-Chief Executive Officer of Kraft

Born Elizabeth DeHaas in 1955 in Lubbock, TX; married Arthur Holden (chairman and CEO of SNP Consortium), 1982; children: Andy, Julie. *Education:* Duke University, Durham, NC, B.A. (education), 1977; Northwestern University Graduate School of Education and Social Policy, Evanston, IL, M.A. (education), 1978; Northwestern University Kellogg Graduate School of Management, M.A. (management and finance), 1982.

Addresses: *Office*—Kraft Foods North America, Inc., 3 Lakes Dr., Northfield, IL 60093–2753.

Career

Taught fourth grade in public schools of Glencoe, Illinois, 1978–80; consulted for Playskool; joined General Foods Corporation, which later was merged into Kraft Inc., as an assistant product manager in the Desserts Division, 1982; moved into Kraft's Venture Division as a brand manager, new products, 1984; became brand manager of Miracle Whip, 1985; promoted to group brand manager for Confections and Snacks, 1987; named vice president of new product development and strategy, 1990; named vice president of marketing, Dinners and Enhancers, 1992; became president of Tombstone Pizza Division, 1993; named executive vice president and general manager of Kraft Cheese Division; promoted to president of Cheese Division, 1997; promoted to executive vice president of Kraft Foods Inc., responsible for overseeing the operations of Kraft's Consumer Insights & Communications,

Courtesy of Kraft Foods

E–Commerce, Operations, Procurement, and Research & Development divisions, 1998; named president and chief executive officer of Kraft Foods North America, 2000; promoted to co–CEO of Kraft Foods Inc., 2001.

Member: Board member of Tupperware Corporation, the Grocery Manufacturers of America, and Kellogg Graduate School of Management.

Sidelights

One of the most powerful executives in the country, Betsy Holden, as president and co–chief executive officer (CEO) of Kraft Foods Inc., is responsible for the North American operations of America's largest food company. Sales of Kraft Foods North America Inc., a Kraft subsidiary that Holden leads as president and CEO, rocketed to $25.1 billion in 2001, up an impressive 36 percent from the previous year. She shares CEO chores for its parent company with Roger Deromedi, who's responsible for Kraft's sales outside North America. Holden is based at Kraft's corporate headquarters in suburban Chicago, while Deromedi, who also holds the title of president and CEO of Kraft Foods International Inc., works out of the company's international headquarters in Rye Brook, New York.

From her offices at Kraft headquarters in Northfield, Illinois, Holden helps to map marketing strategy for such powerhouse brand names as Oreo, Ritz, Velveeta, Kool–Aid, Miracle Whip, LifeSavers, and Philadelphia Cream Cheese. Kraft Foods Inc., the parent of both Kraft Food North America Inc. and Kraft Foods International Inc., in 2001 posted revenue of almost $33.9 billion, up about 27.7 percent from $26.5 billion in 2000. Worldwide, Kraft is second only to Swiss–based Nestle in terms of food sales. At first glance, Holden's appearance, which conjures up images of an elementary school teacher or soccer mom, belies the awesome responsibility she wields. But don't let her appearance deceive you. Holden is a mighty savvy and skillful executive, her skills well honed by more than two decades in the food business. Of Holden's grasp of the business, Merrill Lynch food and agribusiness analyst Leonard Teitlebaum told the *Chicago Sun–Times*: "Here we have an executive who can explain the numbers, the business, and the company's position, and produce good results."

Holden was born in Lubbock, Texas, in 1955. Her father, an obstetrician–gynecologist stationed at Reese Air Force Base, delivered his daughter. "He said it was the only time he ever spanked me," Holden told Sandra Guy, a business reporter for the *Chicago Sun–Times*. As soon as her father had fulfilled his military obligation, the DeHaas family moved to the Pittsburgh area. During Holden's childhood, the family lived in three small towns outside Pittsburgh, spending the most time in the blue–collar town of Washington, Pennsylvania. She attended public schools in Washington and went to a high school where only about a third of the students went on to college. After finishing high school, Holden, who'd set her sights on becoming a teacher, headed to Duke University in Durham, North Carolina, where she earned a bachelor's degree in education in 1977.

During her senior year at Duke, Holden was approached by a recruiter from Northwestern University who told her about the school's master's teaching program, which allowed students to teach during the day and pursue their master's degree in classes at night. The idea appealed to her, so shortly after graduation she moved to Evanston, Illinois, to join the program. During the master's program, she taught during the day in the public school system of Park Ridge, Illinois. After earning her master's degree from Northwestern's Graduate School of Education and Social Policy, she took a job teaching fourth graders in Glencoe, Illinois. While teaching in Glencoe, Holden took on a freelance project that was to bring a dramatic change in the direction of her career.

"I worked for Playskool and helped to develop kids's toys and games when I was teaching," Holden told Terry Stephan, a writer for *Northwestern*, the university's alumni magazine. "I was on the R&D [research and development] side, but I saw what the business people were doing and thought it looked pretty fun." Not long thereafter, she returned to Northwestern and enrolled at its Kellogg Graduate School of Management to pursue a master's degree in management, finance, and marketing. While there, she met and began dating fellow student Arthur Holden. The couple married in 1982, the same year she received her master's degree from Kellogg. In 1982 the Holdens moved to New York where she took a job in the Desserts Division of General Foods Corporation in nearby White Plains.

When her husband moved back to the Chicago area to take a job with Baxter Travenol, Holden followed and went to work as a brand manager for the Venture Division of Kraft Foods Inc. She rose quickly through the management ranks at Kraft, serving briefly as group brand manager, vice president of new product development and strategy, president of Kraft's Tombstone Pizza Division, executive vice president and general manager of the Cheese Division and, in December of 1998, executive vice president of Kraft Foods Inc.

About 18 months later, Holden was named president and CEO of Kraft Foods North America, the Kraft subsidiary responsible for roughly 75 percent of the total annual revenue of Kraft Foods Inc. The following year she and Roger Deromedi, president and CEO of Kraft Foods International, were named co–CEOs of Kraft Foods Inc. Analysts and other food industry observers initially looked askance at Kraft's decision to split CEO responsibilities in this fashion, but Holden and Deromedi have made believers of most of them. Holden said the power–sharing arrangement works largely because she and Deromedi spent more than a dozen years working together before they reached the executive suite.

Kraft's results for the first half of 2002 clearly signaled that the unique power–sharing arrangement between Holden and Deromedi was continuing to work its magic. Revenue for Kraft Foods Inc. rose to nearly $1.6 billion in the first half, almost double the $831 million posted in the first half of 2001. In announcing Kraft's second quarter results, according to a company news release, Holden observed: "Kraft delivered strong earnings growth in the quarter, keeping us in line with our earnings projections for the full year. The Nabisco integration, our productivity programs and new product initiatives are all tracking well, and we are benefiting from lower interest expense. We continue to expect pro forma diluted earnings per share for the year in the range of \$2.00 to \$2.05, representing a 14 percent to 16 percent increase versus 2001."

Holden lives in Winnetka, Illinois, with her husband, chairman and CEO of SNP Consortium, a bioscience company, and their children, Andy and Julie. In addition to her responsibilities with Kraft, Holden serves on the boards of Tupperware Corporation, the Grocery Manufacturers of America, and Kellogg Graduate School of Management.

Sources

Periodicals

Advertising Age, February 2, 1998.
BusinessWeek, June 27, 2000.
Chicago Sun–Times, May 21, 2000; September 30, 2002.
Forbes, April 15, 2002, p. 129.
Inquiry, Spring 2002.
Northwestern, Winter 2000.

Online

"Kraft Foods Inc.," Hoover's Online, http://www.hoovers.com/co/capsule/2/0,2163,103392,00.html (October 12, 2002).

"Kraft Foods Inc. Reports 2002 Second–Quarter Results," Kraft Foods, http://www.corporate–ir.net/ireye/ir_site.zhtml?ticker=kft&script=410&layout=–6&item_id=316322 (December 20, 2002).

"Newsroom: Management Bios: Betsy D. Holden," Kraft Foods, http://www.kraft.com/newsroom/biosholden.html (October 11, 2002).

—Don Amerman

Steven Holl

Architect

Born Steven Myron Holl, December 9, 1947, in Bremerton, WA; son of Myron Leroy (a sheet–metal shop owner and furnace installer) and Helen May Holl; married Solange Fabiao (an artist), 1999. *Education:* University of Washington, Seattle, WA, B.A., 1971; Architecture Association, London, England, post–graduate work, 1976.

Addresses: *Home*—435 Hudson St., New York, NY 10014. *Office*—450 West 31 St., 11th Floor, New York, NY 10001; email: mail@stevenholl.com. *Website*—http://www.stevenholl.com/.

Career

First drafting job, Bellevue, WA, 1967; interned in San Francisco, CA; taught at Architecture Association, 1975–76; established Steven Holl Architects, 1976; part–time drafting job, New York, 1977; taught at Parsons School of Design, University of Washington, Pratt Institute; co–founded *Pamphlet Architecture*; started teaching at Columbia University, 1981; first commission, pool house and sculpture studio, 1980–81; designer of award–winning buildings and interiors including Stretto House, 1990–92, D. E. Shaw & Co. office interiors, 1992, residential complex in Makuhari, Japan, 1992–96, Helsinki Museum of Contemporary Art (Kiasma), 1993–98, Chapel of St. Ignatius, 1995–97, Bellevue Art Museum, 2000; Artist in Residence, MIT, Cambridge, MA, 2001.

Awards: National Endowment for the Arts (NEA) Award, 1982; American Institute of Architects (AIA), New York Chapter Award, for Andrew Cohen apartment, 1985; AIA, New York Chapter Award, for Pace Collection Showroom, 1986; AIA, New York Chapter Awards, for Urban Proposal, Milan, Italy, and Giada Clothing Shop, New York, NY, 1988; NEA, Graham Foundation, and NYSCA grants, 1988; National AIA Honors Award, for Berkowitz–Odgis House, Martha's Vineyard, MA, 1989; Progressive Architecture Awards, for College of Architecture and Landscape Architecture, University of Minnesota and American Memorial Library, West Germany, 1990; Arnold W. Brunner Prize in Architecture, American Academy and Institute of Arts and Letters, 1990; Progressive Architecture Award, for Void Space/Hinged Space housing, Fukuoka, Japan, 1991; National AIA Honors Award, for Hybrid Building, Seaside, FL, 1991; Excellence in Design Award, New York City Art Commission, for Strand Theater renovation, 1991; AIA, New York Chapter Honors Award, for Void Space/Hinged Space, 1992; National AIA Interiors Award, for D. E. Shaw & Co. offices, 1992; National AIA Honor Award for Excellence in Design, for the Stretto House, Dallas, TX, 1993; Graham Foundation Grant, 1992; AIA New York Chapter Architecture Project Award, for Makuhari Housing, Japan, 1993; AIA New York Chapter Design Awards, for the Chapel of St. Ignatius, Seattle, WA, and the Cranbrook Institute of Science addition and renovation, Bloomfield Hills, MI, 1995; National AIA Design Award, 1995; National AIA Design Award, 1996; Progressive Architecture Award, for the Knut Hamsun Museum in Norway and the Museum of the City in Cassino, Italy, 1996; AIA New York Chapter Medal of Honor Award, 1997; National AIA Religious Architecture Award, for Chapel of St. Ignatius, Seattle, WA, 1997; Japanese Building Contractors Society Award, Makuhari

Housing, Japan, 1997; National AIA Design Award, for the Chapel of St. Ignatius, 1998; Alvar Aalto Medal, 1998; Chrysler Design Award, 1998; National AIA Design Award, for Helsinki Museum of Contemporary Art (Kiasma), 1999; AIA New York Chapter Project Award, for Nelson–Atkins Museum of Art, Kansas City, MO, 1999; AIA New York Chapter Design Award, for Cranbrook Institute of Science, Bloomfield Hills, MI, 1999; Progressive Architecture Award, for Nelson–Atkins Museum of Art, Kansas City, MO, 2000.

Sidelights

Steven Holl's work is characterized by an attention to the smallest details, knowledge of the requirements of the human body in space, and a dedication to bringing architecture down to the human scale. He bases much of his design practice on the philosophical discipline known as phenomenology, which attempts to study an individual's ways of experiencing objects or situations outside his/herself. Holl has written influential books on architecture and co–founded a magazine. He has earned numerous prestigious awards for his designs for buildings and interiors, which can be found throughout Europe, Asia, and the United States. His approach creates unique buildings that do not readily reflect a specific style that can be identified as Holl's. He explained to Joseph Masheck of *Bomb*, "That's what I strive for in my work, a conceptual stratagem in response to the special conditions of every project."

Holl (pronounced Hall) was born on December 7, 1947, in Bremerton, Washington, to Myron and Helen Holl. Holl's father was largely self–employed, operating a sheet–metal shop and selling and installing furnaces. Holl accompanied his father on his jobs and gained early insight into the inner workings of homes from his experience installing furnaces. Holl's father is also a natural artist, an accomplished draftsman, and a perfectionist, qualities that Holl also embodies. Growing up, Holl spent much time at home building tree houses and forts. In 1962, a trip to the World's Fair in Seattle where he saw the Space Needle impressed him with the possibilities of architecture.

Holl's interests span philosophy, science, and mathematics. He starts his mornings by painting in watercolors or penciling out ideas and designs. Because he travels often, Holl carries a sketchpad and portable watercolor kit with him for sketching in hotel rooms or while on airplanes. His admiration for the composer Bela Bartok inspired the design for the award–winning Stretto House in Dallas, Texas. His vision extends beyond just buildings to entire cities. He described his ideal city to Abe Fra-

jndlich of *Esquire* as having "... shifting strips of sunlight and birds flying daredevil between oblique gaps in buildings." Holl believes that most buildings today are too big. Fellow architect James Cheng, a former classmate, described Holl to Richard Seven of the *Seattle Times*, "Steven is an architect's architect.... He's an intellectual.... His buildings have warmth, but above all they have integrity."

Holl attended college at the University of Washington in Seattle. His studies there were frustrating; he almost dropped out mid–course because he felt that the classes and the professors were not inspiring. It was his professor of architectural history, Herman Pundt, who encouraged him to study architecture more thoroughly and to spend a year in Rome. It was that year in Rome that sparked Holl to continue his studies. He told the *Seattle Times*'s Seven, "Rome was the first time that I was truly inspired by architecture." Holl visited the Pantheon daily and observed how light and weather would change the characteristics of the buildings. He returned to the University of Washington and completed his studies in 1971.

Holl left the northwest region soon after graduating because of a distaste for the direction that its architecture and planning were going. He spent some time interning in San Francisco, California, before returning to Europe. This time he ended up in London, England, where he studied and taught at the Architecture Association for a year.

Holl returned to the United States in 1976 and established himself in New York City. He started his own business, Steven Holl Architects, and worked part–time drafting. Any other time he had he spent conceptualizing and designing for make–believe clients. Another project he worked on was an alternative magazine, *Pamphlet Architecture*, which he founded to focus on fledgling architects who he thought deserved attention. He taught at the Parson's School of Design, and through that position earned his first commission, designing a pool house for one of his student's fathers.

Holl eventually began to establish a reputation. A selection of his designs were purchased by the Museum of Modern Art in 1989 and exhibited. By that time Holl had designed approximately a dozen buildings and interiors. Despite his standing as an up–and–coming architect, Holl was not shy about making demands upon the museum with regard to the exhibition of his designs; it's a testament to his insistence on integrity and his attention to detail. Only black–and–white photographs of his work were allowed; some walls had to be covered in plaster; and details of certain apartments were installed into the walls of the exhibit. In 1991, the Walker Art Center in Minneapolis, Minnesota, hosted Holl's *Edge of a City* exhibition.

Holl also has a collection of dinner plates and candlesticks he designed for Swid Powell, a company that commissions tableware items from designers and architects. However, he didn't seem too proud of the tableware collection, telling Kurt Anderson of *Time,* "It's too much about selling and not enough about ideas and hopes and dreams." For his interiors, he has been known to design down to the smallest detail, including such items as chairs, lighting fixtures, rugs, windows, and door handles.

In 1992, Holl completed one of his most exciting home designs, the Texas Stretto House. The house was designed to replicate in architecture Bartok's *Music for Strings, Percussion, and Celeste.* The concept was described on the website for Steven Holl Architects as follows, "Where music has a materiality in instrumentation and sound, this architecture attempts an analogue in light and space." The house was built using concrete block and metal as contrasting elements. The concrete sections function as dams that stop the eyes while also representing the percussion element of Bartok's composition. The metal sections function as a fluid element, representing both water and the strings of the inspirational music. The Stretto House won the 1992 National American Institute of Architects (AIA) Design Award.

In 1993, Holl was one of only four international architects invited to compete against those from the Nordic and Baltic countries in designing the new Museum of Contemporary Art in Helsinki, Finland. In a stiff competition involving 516 entries, Holl's design was eventually chosen. He called his concept for the new museum "Chiasma." The meaning of the term, as he told Nancy Marmer of *Art in America,* relates to "the intertwining of the building's mass with the geometry of the city and landscape."

When the project began, renamed "Kiasma" to fit with Finnish spelling practices, it faced opposition on many fronts. Many opposed the fact that Holl was American; others disliked the design. Some were opposed to the site on which the museum was being built, and others questioned the purpose of the museum in the first place. Despite the opposition, which at times became very vocal, the project moved forward and was completed in 1998. Kiasma was described on the Steven Holl Architects website as follows, "With Kiasma, there is a hope to confirm that architecture, art, and culture are, rather than separate disciplines, integral parts of the city and

the landscape. The geometry has an interior mystery and an exterior horizon which, like two hands clasping each other, form the architectonic equivalent of a public invitation." At its inauguration on May 29, 1998, the museum was well received by a large crowd. It received the 1999 National AIA Design Award.

Holl returned to his home state of Washington to design two very different types of buildings, the Chapel of St. Ignatius in Seattle and the Bellevue Art Museum in Bellevue. The chapel is situated on the campus of Seattle University, which was founded by Jesuit priests. Holl described his concept for the chapel as "seven bottles of light in a stone box." Colored glass, painted walls that reflect light from windows, as well as colored glass lenses, illuminate the interior of the chapel with varying shades of colors often in unexpected combinations. Holl not only designed the building but many of the furnishings, including the pulpit, lighting fixtures, and a carpet representing the life of St. Ignatius. Begun in 1995, the chapel was completed in 1997. The chapel's design won an award from the New York chapter of the AIA, and a scale model of the chapel is part of the Museum of Modern Art's permanent collection.

His other contribution to his former home is the Bellevue Art Museum. The *Seattle Times*'s Seven described the building as "brick–red, wide–mouthed, and built right to the street, an edgy urban building in a city still searching for a center." While still working on the Chapel of St. Ignatius, Holl was convinced by fellow architect Alan Sclater of Seattle to submit a design for the proposed museum. Despite hectic scheduling problems that forced Holl to interview for the job from 3,000 miles away, the project was awarded to Holl and Sclater. For Holl, getting this project was a victory of sorts. He told Seven, "One of the special things about this particular project ... is working in a town I had criticized so heavily because of how badly it was being developed." The concept for the building was based on the idea of "tripleness," which coincided with the museum's goal of intersecting art, science, and technology as well as creation, exploration, and education in the arts. The museum was opened on New Year's Eve in 2000.

Holl has been known to collaborate with artists on several projects. One of the more interesting collaborations has been his work with multimedia artist Vito Acconci. Acconci and Holl approach their works from what seems like entirely opposite sides of the spectrum. Acconci is a poet, photographer, print–maker, video artist, filmmaker, and installation artist. He began his career by examining himself in the minutest details. His primary concern was with his body in the world. While Holl is concerned about the body and its relation to the world, his view encompasses the relationship of many bodies interacting with the buildings and forms around them. The two first collaborated in 1988 on a plan for an urban arts community in Washington, D.C. In 1992, the two were commissioned to renovate a SoHo gallery called Storefront for Art and Architecture. The finished project created an atmosphere for the gallery that allowed it to appear to flow out onto the sidewalk by controlling panels that could be opened or shut.

Another artist that Holl has collaborated with is his wife, Solange Fabiao. She is a Brazilian–born artist who originally worked as a set designer, but expanded into painting and photography. She has worked with Holl's firm on several submissions to design competitions. The two originally met at a concert by the avant–garde composer, John Cage. Years later, in 1999, they married in the Paula Cooper gallery where the concert had been held.

Holl's work, which has been described as futuristic while still referencing the best of 20th century architecture, continues to surprise and excite the architectural community. He is a tireless intellectual, who doggedly adheres to the concepts he devises for his projects. Holl seems dedicated to the future of architecture through his constant teaching. In addition to a position at Columbia University, Holl is often a guest lecturer at architectural schools throughout the United States and Europe. More than anything, it would seem that Holl is dedicated to the people who use his buildings. As far as he's concerned, as he told Linda Mack of the *Star Tribune*, "architecture should be about people's experience of the space." His refreshing, exciting, and challenging designs will continue to make people want to experience the spaces he creates.

Selected works

Pool house and sculpture studio, Scarsdale, New York, 1981.
Berkowitz–Odgis House, Martha's Vineyard, Massachusetts, 1988.
Stretto House, Dallas, Texas, 1992.
D. E. Shaw & Co. office building, New York, New York, 1992.
Cranbrook Institute of Science extension, Bloomfield Hills, Michigan, 1995.
Museum of the City, Cassino, Italy, 1996.
Chapel of St. Ignatius, Seattle, Washington, 1997.
Y House, Catskill Mountains, New York, 1997.

Museum of Contemporary Art (Kiasma), Helsinki, Finland, 1998.
Bellevue Art Museum, Bellevue, Washington, 2000.

Selected writings

The Alphabetical City, Pamphlet Architecture (New York), 1980.
Anchoring: Selected Projects, 1975–1988, Princeton Architectural Press (New York, NY), 1989; reprinted, 1991.
Intertwining: Selected Projects 1989–1995, Princeton Architectural Press, 1998.
Parallax, Princeton Architectural Press, 2000.

Selected exhibitions

Steven Holl, Museum of Modern Art, New York, 1989.
Edge of a City, Walker Art Center, Minneapolis, Minnesota, 1991.
The Un–Private House, Museum of Modern Art, New York, 1999.
Steven Holl, Max Protetch Gallery, New York, 2000.
Idea and Phenomenon, MuseumsQuartier Wien, Austria, 2002.
Living in Motion—Design and Architecture for Flexible Dwelling, Vitra Design Museum, Germany, 2002.

Sources

Periodicals

Art in America, October 1998.
ARTNews, November 1999, p. 50.
Artweek, August 1997.
Esquire, May 1991, p. 31.
Seattle Times, December 3, 2000, p. 18.
Star Tribune, April 1, 2001, p. 2F.
Time, March 20, 1989, p. 75.

Online

"About Chapel," The Chapel of St. Ignatius, http://www.seattleu.edu/chapel/about/ (September 24, 2002).
"Museum of Contemporary Art, Helsinki, Finland," Steven Holl Architects, http://www.stevenholl.com/pages/helsinki.html (September 24, 2002).
"Texas Stretto House," Steven Holl Architects, http://www.stevenholl.com/pages/texasstretto.html (September 24, 2002).

—*Eve M. B. Hermann*

Walter Isaacson

Journalist

Born Walter Seff Isaacson, May 20, 1952, in New Orleans, LA; son of Irwin, Jr., and Betsy (Seff) Isaacson; married Cathy Wright, September 15, 1984; children: Elizabeth. *Education:* Harvard University, B.A., 1974; Pembroke College, Oxford, M.A., 1976.

Addresses: *Agent*—Amanda Urban, International Creative Management, 40 West 57th St., New York, NY 10019. *Office*—CNN: Cable News Network and CNN Headline News, Box 105366, 1 CNN Center, Atlanta, GA 30348.

Career

Reporter, *Sunday Times*, London, England, 1976–77; reporter, *Times–Picayune/States–Item,* New Orleans, LA, 1977–78; *Time*, New York City, staff writer, 1978–79, Washington, D.C., correspondent, 1979–81, associate editor, 1981–84, senior editor, then assistant managing editor, 1984–93; new–media division editor, Time Inc., New York City, 1993–95; managing editor, *Time* magazine, 1996–2000; editorial director, Time Inc., 2000–01; CEO and chair, CNN News Group, 2001–03; member of the Aspen Institute, 2003&msdash;.

Awards: Mary Hemingway Award, Overseas Press Club of America, for article "The Colombian Connection," 1979; Overseas Press Club of America Award for foreign news interpretation, for article "Arming the World," 1982; Harry Truman Book Prize, Truman Library Institute, for *The Wise Men*, 1987.

Sidelights

Veteran print journalist Walter Isaacson became chair and chief executive officer of the CNN News Group in the summer of 2001. A former editor at *Time*, Isaacson was credited with reviving the venerable American newsweekly by infusing it with a more contemporary focus. His hire at the pioneering Cable News Network was viewed as a portent of a new era for the 24–hour cable news service. "I travel around the world, travel around the country, and [CNN] is the most important, most trusted source for information anywhere—and it needs a little bit of juicing up," he was quoted as saying by *New York Observer* journalist Jason Gay the day following announcement of his promotion. "It needs to get really comfortable with the mandate of great journalism. There was a perception that it was losing its way."

Isaacson was born in 1952 in New Orleans and is a 1974 graduate of Harvard University. He was a Rhodes Scholar at Oxford University, from which he earned a graduate degree in 1976. After a stint with London's *Sunday Times* and at a hometown Louisiana newspaper, Isaacson was hired by *Time* in 1978. He covered stories on its national desk, including the 1980 presidential race, and became assistant managing editor in 1984. By this time Isaacson had already written his first book, *Pro and Con*, which addressed both sides of several newsworthy topics, including reproductive rights, legalized gambling, and term limits for politicians. He also co–authored the 1986 book *The Wise Men: Six Friends and the World They Made* with *Newsweek* editor Evan Thomas. The work profiled six men who played important roles in shaping American postwar diplomatic policy.

Not long after the publication of his third book, a biography of American foreign–policy advisor Henry Kissinger, Isaacson was tapped to head the new–media division of Time Inc., the parent company of *Time* and several other magazines. Isaacson's job was to oversee the new Internet presence and news–delivery capabilities for all company publications. He saw great potential, as he told Michael Krantz in *Adweek Eastern Edition* at the time. "I truly believe the digital revolution is going to change the nature of journalism more than anything since the invention of television," Isaacson declared.

Isaacson returned to print in 1996 when he advanced to the job of managing editor at *Time*. Industry analysts credit him with giving the magazine a fresh spin by bringing in younger staff writers and emphasizing lengthy feature stories on the Internet boom, consumer health issues, and public education debates. In 2000, Isaacson advanced to one of the top posts at the Time, Inc. print empire when he was named editorial director. He was on board during the company's historic merger with the Internet service provider America Online (AOL), which created the AOL/Time Warner entertainment empire.

AOL/Time Warner was the parent company of the Atlanta, Georgia–based CNN News channel, and on July 9, 2001, Isaacson was made chair and chief executive officer of the cable mainstay. Given his lack of television experience, Isaacson's hire was somewhat of a surprise, but it was heralded as the onset of a new era for CNN. A former colleague from the Time, Inc. media empire told *Cablevision* magazine that CNN's new chief was "very bright, well–respected, energetic, and well–connected. As a journalist and editor he's the real deal, with an extraordinary intellect and tremendous versatility. He'll look at stories quite carefully, and people at CNN can expect quick feedback. They better be on their toes."

At that point, the first–ever all–news television network had slipped in ratings after losing viewers to MSNBC, a joint venture between Microsoft and NBC, and the Fox News channel. While MSNBC attracted a younger viewership with its lifestyle focus, Fox lured a more conservative element with celebrity anchors and often incendiary political–panelist shows. Isaacson vowed that CNN would not take the Fox approach to win market share. "I don't think we have to do wacky, tabloidy things to get ratings," Isaacson told *Newsweek*'s Peg Tyre. "Just bring a passion back to journalism."

Ratings at CNN jumped dramatically in the aftermath of the terrorist attacks on the United States on September 11, 2001—a common occurrence in the history of the network, long heralded for its coverage of breaking stories—but Isaacson was already working to ensure that viewers remained tuned in during the weeks following. He hired high–profile television journalists Paula Zahn and Connie Chung, and onetime ABC correspondent Aaron Brown was given his own prime time news hour. CNN stalwart Larry King, host of a popular nightly CNN interview show, was signed to a new $30 million contract. As Isaacson told *Broadcasting & Cable*, it was with this personality– and programming–based strategy that he hoped to eclipse Fox. "I would love to build programs that get us good ratings when there's a lull in the news, just as we get good ratings when there's a spike in the news. You can create networks based on ideological talk. You can base it on people parachuting into various places around the world, or you can base it on a long–term commitment to covering the world. We've done the latter."

Isaacson commutes between CNN's Atlanta headquarters and suburban New York City, where his wife and daughter still live. That is likely to change when CNN's new high–tech studios at the AOL/Time Warner skyscraper, under construction near Lincoln Center in New York City, go on–air in 2004. When asked by *Broadcasting & Cable* whether he missed the print world at all, Isaacson responded with a characteristically pragmatic assessment. "I've been impressed by how much fun it is to pull together the various elements of a package in television," he told the magazine. "Whereas, in print, it's much easier, just usually words and still photographs, TV gives you a broader range of tools by which to communicate."

On January 13, 2002, Isaacson announced that he was leaving CNN in the spring to become the head of a Washington–based political thinktank called the Aspen Institute.

Selected writings

Pro and Con, Putnam (New York, NY), 1983.

(With Evan Thomas) *The Wise Men: Six Friends and the World They Made: Acheson, Bohlen, Harriman, Kennan, Lovett, McCloy,* Simon & Schuster (New York, NY), 1986.

Kissinger: A Biography, Simon & Schuster, 1992.

Sources

Periodicals

Adweek Eastern Edition, February 27, 1995, p. MQ4.
Atlantic, March 1984, p. 132.
Broadcasting & Cable, February 18, 2002, p. 16.
Cablevision, July 23, 2001, p. 14.
Crain's New York Business, April 29, 1996, p. 1.
Electronic Media, September 10, 2001, p. 13; January 21, 2002, p. 44.
National Review, December 14, 1992, p. 49; January 29, 1996, p. 60.
New Republic, Feb 9, 1987, p. 40.
New York Observer, July 16, 2001, p. 1.
Newsweek, July 23, 2001, p. 48.
Publishers Weekly, September 7, 1992, p. 72.
Time, November 27, 2000, p. 8; July 23, 2001, p. 48.

Online

"First Look," E! Online, http://www.eonline.com/News/Items/0,1,11104,00.html (February 4, 2003).

—Carol Brennan

Alan Jackson

Country singer

Born Alan Eugene Jackson, October 17, 1958, in Newnan, GA; son of Eugene (an autoworker) and Ruth (a homemaker) Jackson; married Denise, December 15, 1979; children: Mattie, Alexandra, Dani.

Addresses: *Home*—Nashville, TN. *Record company*—Arista, 6 West 57th St., New York, NY 10019.

Career

Hired by Glen Campbell Enterprises as a songwriter; signed to Arista Records, 1989; released first album *Here in the Real World,* 1990; the title song becomes a number–one hit; became member of the Grand Ole Opry, 1991; success continued with more than 30 number–one hits such as "Midnight in Montgomery," "Chattahoochee," "Little Bitty," "I'll Go on Loving You," and "Where Were You;" opened the Alan Jackson Showcar Café in Pigeon Forge, TN, 1998.

Awards: Academy of Country Music (ACM) top new male vocalist, 1990; TNN/Music City News song of the year for "Here in the Real World," 1990; TNN/Music City News star of tomorrow, 1991; TNN/Music City News album of the year, 1991; ACM country music album of the year, 1991; ACM country music single of the year, 1991; Country Music Association (CMA) music video of the year, 1992; ASCAP song of the year, 1992; TNN/Music City News male artist, 1992; TNN/Music City News single, 1992; TNN/Music City News album of the year, 1992; CMA single of the year, 1993; ASCAP songwriter of the year, 1993; ASCAP songwriter of the year, 1994; American Music Awards (AMA) favorite album, 1994; AMA single of the year, 1994; CMA album of the year, 1994; CMA song of the year, 1994; CMA entertainer of the year, 1995; ACM male vocalist of the year, 1995; ACM male vocalist of the year, 1996; TNN/Music City News entertainer of the year, 1996; TNN/Music City News entertainer of the year, 1997; ASCAP songwriter of the year, 1998; CMA vocal event of the year, 2000.

Sidelights

Traditions are sometimes forgotten in favor of the new and improved. In the early 1980s, the weeds of a fad—the synthesized pop music of the urban cowboy—had trampled country music's roots. However, in 1989 a new group of country singer/songwriters—which included a tall, white–hatted Georgia boy, Alan Jackson, tore out those weeds and planted a new tradition. Jackson hit number one on the country music charts more than 30 times and won more than 45 awards. However, Jackson remained humble, telling WAMZ FM that he is "just a guy who sings [and who] hopes I'm keeping a little bit of traditional country music alive for the next generation so they'll know what it is."

Jackson was born on October 17, 1958 in Newnan, Georgia. His father, Eugene, an autoworker, and mother, Ruth, a homemaker, married in 1952 and moved into Eugene's dad's 12' x 12' tool shed. As their family expanded—it included Alan and his sisters Diane, Connie, and twins Cathy and Carol—so did the tool shed. While still in high school, Jackson met his future wife, Denise, at a Dairy Queen. He married his sweetheart in 1979. Soon after, they moved to Nashville so Jackson could pursue his music career. While Denise worked as a flight attendant, Jackson worked odd jobs including a stint as a used car salesman and mailman for cable TV's The Nashville Network (TNN). During his lunch breaks Jackson would study what type of country music hit the charts, what fans liked, and what they were buying.

In the early 1980s, country music fans seemed to like and buy the bland, "pop-ified" country music of the urban cowboy while everyone else seemed to be riding bucking broncos in bars, wearing cowboy boots, hats, and tight blue jeans. Country music, according to *Country Weekly* reporter Gerry Wood, "got very plasticized strings everywhere. Traditional roots were just getting ground under like plowed ground." As the 1980s urban cowboy fad cooled off, as stated by Ken Kragen on TNN's *The Life and Times of the All-Star Class of '89*, "country music started to retrench and almost as a reaction against this popularizing of country music, traditionalists came along." One of these new traditionalists was Jackson. However, it would be Denise, not Jackson himself, who found his big break. On one of Denise's flights, she ran into country superstar Glen Campbell. She told him about Jackson's desire to be a country singer/songwriter and asked Campbell for advice. Campbell gave Denise the name of his company's manager, Marty Gamblin, and told Jackson to call. Soon after, Gamblin hired Jackson to write songs for Glen Campbell Enterprises. Thus, a chance meeting on an airplane had started Jackson's career.

By the late 1980s, country music fans had had enough of the synthesized pop that was passing for country music. A new class of country music superstars—musicians who sounded a lot like country music legends Hank Williams, Faron Young, Merle Haggard, and George Jones—emerged, led by Randy Travis. In 1989, seeing this return to tradition, record labels signed their own "new traditionalists" including Jackson, Clint Black, Travis Tritt, Vince Gill, and Garth Brooks. In 1990, the year of the birth of his first daughter, Mattie, Jackson's first album, *Here in the Real World*, was released on Arista Records. *Here in the Real World* produced four number-one singles: "Wanted," "Chasin' That Neon Rainbow," "I'd Love You All Over Again," and the

title track. Jackson also won two major awards that year: TNN/Music City News Song of the Year for "Here in the Real World," and the Academy of Country Music (ACM) award for Top New Male Vocalist.

In 1991, Jackson released his second album, *Don't Rock the Jukebox*. Five songs, four of which Jackson wrote or co-wrote, topped the country music charts: "Someday," "Dallas," "Love's Got a Hold on You," "Midnight in Montgomery," and the title track. In two of these number-one hits, Jackson paid respect to his musical inspirations: Hank Williams and George Jones. "Midnight in Montgomery" honors the legendary country singer/songwriter Williams. In "Don't Rock the Jukebox," Jackson wrote what *Country Music Culture's* Curtis W. Ellison called, "a homage to George Jones—another Hank Williams admirer—and to honky tonk music, a statement against rock and roll in favor of country music." Jackson won four awards that year including TNN/Music City News Star of Tomorrow and Album of the Year, and ACM's Country Music Single and Album of the Year.

In 1992, Jackson's success continued with two new albums: *Honky Tonk Christmas* and *A Lot 'Bout Livin' (and a Little 'Bout Love)*, the latter producing five number-one hit singles including "Chattahoochee." Jackson not only won five awards that year including CMA Music Video of the Year, ASCAP Song of the Year, and TNN/Music City News Male Artist, Single, and Album of the Year, but also welcomed another baby daughter, Alexandra.

In 1994, Jackson's fifth album, *Who I Am* was released. This album, according to *Entertainment Weekly* music reviewer Alanna Nash, seemed to "show him to be more emotionally vulnerable." With hits like "Let's Get Back to Me and You" and "Job Description," Nash wrote that "seldom has a star made his life away from home sound so lonely." Thus, for the first time, Jackson seemed to be feeling the pressures of success. Jackson told *People* that "[My career] is like a movie or something [and my home] is more like the real world for me, in the woods with my family." He further commented that he was "realizing that all those things that you wanted so bad aren't gonna make you happy or keep you happy." In the same vein, Jackson told *People* that he realized that "my life is really like a fairy tale [and] you gotta be happy with yourself and with your spouse and with your life. All the rest is just icing on the cake." Jackson won ten awards in 1994 including ASCAP Song and Songwriter of the Year as well as ACM Top Male Vocalist and American Music Awards Favorite Album and Single of the Year.

Throughout the mid–to–late 1990s, Jackson's star continued to burn brightly. In 1995, Jackson released his *Greatest Hits* album and won eight major awards including CMA Entertainer of the Year. In 1996 Jackson released his seventh album, *Everything I Love*, his first album of all new material in three years. This album included the number–one single "Little Bitty," written by songwriting great Tom T. Hall, which told people to enjoy life "because it goes on only for a little bitty while." Speaking on his approach to music, Jackson told WAMZ FM that "I just try to have fun with it and pick songs and write songs that I like. I don't really worry about what's going to happen to it commercially." Country music fans loved what Jackson liked and awarded him TNN/Music City News Entertainer of the Year in 1996 and 1997. Dani, Jackson's third daughter, was also born in 1997. However, though Jackson's music career and home life seemed to be on a solid ground, Jackson's marriage was crumbling.

In February of 1998, *USA Today* announced that Jackson and his wife had separated. Jackson told *USA Today*'s Brian Mansfield that "what was happening was, I couldn't be happy. I kept trying to let everything else make me happy. Maybe that's why I'm successful. I worked so hard to get all this stuff to make me happy." Jackson continued, "Then that didn't do it. It actually got worse. This career added other problems to it. I isolated myself more." After months of therapy, Jackson and Denise reconciled and renewed their wedding vows on December 15, their nineteenth wedding anniversary. Denise told *Life* that "I see that separation as a gift. It forced us to put our attention back on our relationship." Jackson told *Life* that "I realize what makes you happy: It's having someone to love and someone who loves you."

In September of 1998, Jackson released his eighth album, *High Mileage. Life* called this album "an ode to marriage" while Artist Direct stated that "the album is Jackson's take on life's latest chapter, both the home runs and the curve balls as it came rushing to him." *High Mileage*'s first single, "I'll Go On Loving You," written by Kieran Kane, "is sure to set tongues wagging," Mansfield said, because, "[it] is a markedly different sound for Jackson [who] recites much of the song's intimate lyrics in which the singer watches his lover step out of her dress, yet speaks of a love that will last after the passing 'pleasures of the flesh.'" After ten years in country music, which *Chicago Sun–Times* reporter Dave Hoekstra described as, "like a new snakeskin boot. You have to grow into it," Jackson had not only grown a successful music career that helped revive traditional country music, but had grown into a happy man, as well. As he told *People*, "You can have ev-

erything, but if you ain't got nobody to enjoy it with, it ain't no fun."

Jackson paid tribute to those artists who influenced and impacted his career on his next album, *Under the Influence,* released in 1999. He covered songs by artists as varied as Charley Pride, Merle Haggard, and Jimmy Buffett on the album, which *Newsweek* called a "refreshing" standout and *People* added that "those honored should feel rightly proud." Jackson paid a different sort of tribute to another idol, George Jones, that same year. At the 1999 Country Music Awards, Jones was only slotted one minute to perform his hit song, "Choices." When he declined to play because of the time constraint, Jackson used his (considerably longer) amount of time to break into an impromptu version of Jones's hit song. *Entertainment Weekly* writer Chris Willman called his performance "the moment that forever made Jackson a hero in many fans's minds." Jones himself was pleased: "That shows he takes up for his peers," he told Willman.

Jackson released an album of original material, *When Somebody Loves You*, in 2000. Three hit singles, including "www.memory," came from that album. However, Jackson's biggest hit was yet to come. "Where Were You (When the World Stopped Turning)," a song penned in reaction to the September 11, 2001, terrorist attacks on the United States, was Jackson's biggest hit to date. He described the process he went through to write the song to *Entertainment Weekly*'s Willman. "After the 11th, I was pretty disturbed, like most people. For a few weeks, I thought about writing something, but ... couldn't think of anything that didn't feel like you'd be taking advantage of [the tragedy] commercially." He continued, "I wrote what I felt; I didn't premeditate anything. I'm just a singer of simple songs...." That simple song touched the heart of a nation, and became the unofficial anthem of the post–9/11 United States. Willman described it as "a ballad that crystallized [that] moment in history like no other song, with its mixture of shell shock and hope."

"Where Were You" was released in two forms on Jackson's 2002 album, *Drive:* a studio version and a live version, which was recorded at the Country Music Awards in November of 2001. A second hit single from the album, "Drive (for Daddy Gene)" is Jackson's tribute to his late father, Eugene, who passed away in 2000. More than a decade after it began, Jackson's career just keeps soaring higher. He earned an unprecedented ten Country Music Award nominations in 2002, making him the second most nominated singer in CMA history. (George Strait, one of Jackson's early idols, is the most nominated.) Jackson realizes that as a traditionalist, he is an anomaly in the current country music scene. He shared his thoughts with *Newsweek*'s Lorraine Ali, "If I were a new artist today, it'd be real difficult to get on the radio. It's hard when you're a traditionalist, or whatever they call me…. I may be naïve, but I believe that good songs are what's allowed me to hang in this long."

Selected discography

Here in the Real World, Arista, 1990.
Don't Rock the Jukebox, Arista, 1991.
Honky Tonk Christmas, Arista, 1992.
A Lot 'Bout Livin' (and a Little 'Bout Love), Arista, 1992.
Who I Am, Arista, 1994.
Greatest Hits, Arista, 1995.
Everything I Love, Arista, 1996.
High Mileage, Arista, 1998.
Under the Influence, Arista, 1999.
When Somebody Loves You, Arista, 2000.
Drive, Arista, 2002.

Sources

Books

Ellison, Curtis, *Country Music Culture: From Hard Times to Heaven*, University Press of Mississippi, 1995.

Periodicals

Chicago Sun–Times, September 21, 1998.
Entertainment Weekly, July 7, 1998; March 15, 2002.
Good Housekeeping, June 1995.
Life, February 1999.
Newsweek, November 8, 1999; February 18, 2002.
People, Special Issue, 1994; November 22, 1999.
Tennessean, August 30, 2002.
USA Today, February 20, 1998; September 1, 1998.

Online

"Alan Jackson," Artist Direct, http://imusic. artistdirect.com/showcase/country/ajackson. html (October 2, 2002).

Alan Jackson Official Website, http://www. alanjackson.com (September 16, 2002).

"Alan Jackson," WAMZ 97 FM, http://www.wamz. com/gossip/gossip3.html (September 13, 2002).

Additional information provided by *The Life and Times of the All–Star Class of '89*, a TNN special program broadcast January 25, 1999, and from liner notes from Alan Jackson's albums.

—*Ann M. Schwalboski*

Allison Janney

Actress

Born Allison Brooke Janney, November 19, 1959, in Dayton, OH; daughter of Jervis (a real estate executive and amateur jazz musician) and Macy (a homemaker and former actress) Janney. *Education:* Kenyon College, Gambier, OH, B.A., 1982; attended Royal Academy of Dramatic Arts, London, England.

Addresses: *Business*—The West Wing, c/o Allison Janney, 4000 Warner Blvd., Trailer 8, Burbank, CA 91522.

Career

Actress in films, including: *Who Shot Patakango?*, 1989; *Dead Funny*, 1994; *The Cowboy Way*, 1994; *Heading Home*, 1995; *Walking and Talking*, 1996; *Big Night*, 1996; *Faithful*, 1996; *The Associate*, 1996; *Flux*, 1996; *Private Parts*, 1997; *The Ice Storm*, 1997; *Tears of Julian Po*, 1997; *Anita Liberty*, 1997; *Primary Colors*, 1998; *The Object of My Affection*, 1998; *Six Days Seven Nights*, 1998; *Celebrity*, 1998; *The Impostors*, 1998; *10 Things I Hate About You*, 1999; *Drop Dead Gorgeous*, 1999; *American Beauty*, 1999; *The Debtors*, 1999; *Nurse Betty*, 2000; *Leaving Drew*, 2000; *The Hours*, 2002; *Finding Nemo* (voice), 2003; *How to Deal*, 2003. Television appearances include: *Law and Order*, 1990; *Morton and Hayes*, 1991; *Frasier*, 1993; *Blind Spot* (movie), 1993; *The Guiding Light*, 1993–95; *New York Undercover*, 1994; *The Wright Verdicts*, 1995; *Aliens in the Family*, 1996; *Cosby*, 1996; *First Do No Harm* (movie), 1997; *Path to Paradise: The Untold Story of the World Trade Center Bombing* (movie), 1997; *David and Lisa* (movie), 1998; *LateLine*, 1998; *The West Wing*, 1999—; *A Girl Thing* (mini–series), 2001; *Intimate Portrait: Allison Janney*, 2001. Stage appearances in-

clude: *Breaking Up*, 1990; *Inspecting Carol*, 1992; *Alone at the Beach*, 1993; *Five Women Wearing the Same Dress*, 1993; *Fat Men in Skirts*, 1994; *New England*, 1995; *Blue Window*, 1996; *Present Laughter*, 1996; *A View From the Bridge*, 1998; *Taming of the Shrew*, 1999.

Awards: Outer Critics Circle Award for outstanding featured actress in a play (three–way tie with Deborah Findlay and Celia Weston), for *Present Laughter*, 1997; Theatre World Award for *Present Laughter*, 1997; Drama League Award for outstanding artist, 1997; Outer Critics Circle Award for outstanding featured actress in a play, for *A View From the Bridge*, 1998; Drama Desk Award for outstanding featured actress in a play, for *A View From the Bridge*, 1998; best ensemble, Online Film Critics Society, for *American Beauty* (shared), 1999; outstanding performance by a cast, Screen Actors Guild, for *American Beauty* (shared), 1999; Emmy Award for best supporting actress in a drama, Academy of Television Arts and Sciences, for *West Wing*, 2000; Emmy Award for best supporting actress in a drama, Academy of Television Arts and Sciences, for *West Wing*, 2001; outstanding performance by a female actor in a drama series, Screen Actors Guild, for *West Wing*, 2002; outstanding performance by an ensemble in a drama series, Screen Actors Guild, for *West Wing* (shared), 2002; Emmy Award for best actress in a drama, Academy of Television Arts and Sciences, for *West Wing*, 2002.

Sidelights

It took determination and years of hard work, but Allison Janney has proven herself a gifted actress in a wide range of roles in theater, film, and television. From critical success on Broadway to her Emmy Award–winning turn as C. J. Cregg on NBC's *The West Wing*, Janney has proven that a six–foot–tall actress can play roles other than a man, an alien, or a lesbian.

Born on November 19, 1959, in Dayton, Ohio, Janney is the only daughter of Jervis and Macy Janney. Her father owns a real estate firm in Dayton, and was once an amateur musician. Her brothers followed in her father's musical footsteps and went on to become professional musicians. Her mother studied acting in New York before giving it up to become a homemaker.

As a child Janney had hopes of becoming an Olympic figure skater. She trained and practiced with that goal in mind. However, circumstances prevented her from attaining that goal. After years of training with one coach, she was devastated when the coach suddenly and inexplicably left town. She also suffered a near–fatal accident when she was 17. Someone stepped on the hem of her strapless gown when she was at a dance. As she was running from the room holding her dress up, she ran into a plate–glass door, shattering it. The resulting wounds caused her to lose more than 50 percent of her blood and put her in the hospital for eight weeks. Janney uses the memory of that event to help her in her acting when she needs to portray vulnerability.

After high school, Janney attended Kenyon College in Gambier, Ohio. She had first thought she would study psychology, but classes involving animal dissection turned her off of the idea. Instead, she chose drama. As luck would have it, actor Paul Newman, an alum of Kenyon College, was directing a play at the school her freshman year. During the open audition Janney impressed Newman. The auditions were set up to allow each student two minutes to talk on any topic. She chose to tell him that she could get to the school from home 45 minutes faster than the usual amount of time it took, hoping to appeal to his love of race–car driving.

While working on the play, Janney was encouraged by Newman's wife, actress Joanne Woodward, who felt confident that Janney could make it as an ac-

tress in New York. With Woodward's advice to embolden her, Janney moved to New York immediately after graduating from college in 1982 at 21 years old. Newman and Woodward would continue to encourage Janney throughout the years, attending many of her opening nights, including her Broadway debut years later.

Janney's first years in New York were rough. Agents didn't know how to sell her, feeling that her height was a hindrance. Casting directors often put her in roles as men or 40–year–old women for the same reason. She was also embarrassed to admit that she was an actress and instead often told people that she was a freelance photographer. She explained why it was hard for her to find roles during her twenties to Blake Green of *Newsday*: "My height and my presence read older on stage and people didn't know what to do with me." In between acting and auditioning she held various odd jobs including scooping ice cream and working the night shift as a receptionist for a recording studio.

Janney endured insults and slights, ever hopeful that her day would arrive. She told *Newsday*'s Green, "I always knew time was on my side." She watched as some of her fellow actors found stardom at an early age, while she toiled away in the background. Even though she worked hard to overcome the drawbacks inherent in her height, she admitted to Phil Kloer of the *Atlanta Journal–Constitution*, "Growing up, it was a total drawback. There was nothing good about it at all." Despite her height, her parents enrolled her in ballet classes. The dance and figure skating lessons helped her to gain control over her body, a control that she often uses to great comedic and dramatic effect.

She studied and acted at the Neighborhood Playhouse in New York, where she was once again mentored by Woodward who was directing there when Janney arrived. Janney also studied at the Royal Academy of Dramatic Arts in London, England. It wasn't until the early 1990s that her acting career began to pick up. She was getting roles in small Off–Off–Broadway plays. She appeared in a couple episodes of the television crime drama *Law and Order*. In 1993, she landed the role of Ginger on the soap opera *Guiding Light*. She appeared on *Guiding Light* for two years before her theater and film career began to take hold.

In 1996, at the age of 36, Janney made her Broadway debut in *Present Laughter*, a revival of Noel Coward's 1939 comedy. Janney's performance as Liz, the sophisticated former wife of a movie star, won her praises across the board. She almost walked out on the role though. She explained to Degen Pener of *InStyle* her insecurity about being cast in the lead role, "I was a nervous wreck. I called the director to say, 'You can fire me now, because I know it's coming.'" Luckily, the director ignored her plea.

Jean Nathan of the *New York Times* quoted fellow *New York Times* writer Ben Brantley, who applauded Janney's performance, "The most fully accomplished performance on the stage comes from Allison Janney.... Everyone should have a Liz in his life, as Ms. Janney plays her." For her performance, Janney won an Outer Critics Circle Award for Outstanding Featured Actress in a Play, an award granted to her and two other actresses that year, Deborah Findlay and Celia Weston.

That same year Janney appeared in the critically acclaimed film *Big Night* as the quiet florist who is the love interest of Tony Shaloub's character, a chef with extremely high standards. Over the next three years, Janney would appear in many more acclaimed films with her roles growing progressively bigger. She had small roles in films such as *The Ice Storm* and Woody Allen's *Celebrity*. Her brief role as the bumbling yet attractive public school teacher in *Primary Colors* showed her talent for physical comedy. In the Jennifer Aniston vehicle *The Object of My Affection*, she played Aniston's sister who is married to a name–dropping book agent played by Alan Alda.

Even though she was turning in remarkable performances in film, it would be her stage credits that would begin to gain notoriety for her. In 1998, Janney was nominated for a Tony Award for Best Actress in a Play for her role in *A View From the Bridge*. The revival of Arthur Miller's 1955 play had her starring opposite Anthony LaPaglia. She excelled as a middle–aged wife who must come to terms with her husband's desire for his niece who lives with them. The revival was critically acclaimed, and LaPaglia won a Tony for his performance.

Janney continued to appear in supporting roles in well–received films. She was deftly handling comedic roles in films like *10 Things I Hate About You* and *Drop Dead Gorgeous*. At the same time she was turning in emotionally powerful performances like that of a quiet, broken–down housewife of a strict military husband in *American Beauty*. Her role in *Nurse Betty* as a conniving manager for Greg Kinnear's character brought her further into the public's eye.

In 1999, her agent sent her the script for a drama being developed by NBC called *The West Wing*. She was impressed with the writing, "I thought Aaron Sorkin just wrote a beautiful pilot and I thought, 'I can see doing this,'" she told Susan King of the *Los Angeles Times*. Auditioning for the role was more trying than she had expected, especially since it was her first time. She explained to Sylvia Ruben of the *San Francisco Chronicle*, "It's just a huge deal. I've heard about it, testing for the network, but here I am in my late thirties doing it for the first time. I had to read three times. It's just terrifying. Thirty people you don't know, and you just have to wow them, basically."

Not only did Janney's audition register with those 30 people, she went on to impress audiences and eventually the Academy of Television Arts and Sciences. Nancy Reichardt of the *Austin American–Statesman* described *West Wing* as a "behind–the-scenes glimpse into the inner workings of the Oval Office as seen through the eyes of its eclectic group of frenzied staffers." Janney portrays C. J. Cregg, the former Hollywood public relations guru now working as press secretary. Her costar Bradley Whitford noted to *InStyle*'s Pener, "Few people can combine glamour and goofiness as perfectly as she does."

For her role as Cregg, opposite fellow Daytonians Martin Sheen and Rob Lowe, Janney apprenticed with Dee Dee Myers who was a press secretary during one of former president Bill Clinton's administrations. Janney felt working with Myers was beneficial in helping her understand being a woman within a male–dominated inner circle. Her work on the show was rewarded when she won Emmy Awards in 2000 and 2001 as Best Supporting Actress in a Drama. In 2002, she won an Emmy for Best Actress in a Drama. The show itself has been popular with the Emmys as well, winning nine awards in 2000 and eight in 2001. In 2002, the award total went down to four.

Despite her success in television, Janney did not forsake her film or theater career. In the summer of 1999, she appeared in performances of *The Taming of the Shrew* in Central Park in New York City. Her role as Kate was highly acclaimed. In 2002, she also appeared in a supporting role in the critically successful film *The Hours* as Meryl Streep's lover.

After years of renting apartments and hoping for the next big break, Janney began to feel a sense of accomplishment and stability with her recurring role on *The West Wing*. At first she was unsure of the show's lasting power, so she rented a house in Los Angeles and left her boyfriend of several years in New York. She explained her insecurity to Mary

Melton of *Los Angeles Magazine*, "I'm still wondering if we're going to go to next season.... Most things I do that are supposed to have a life after the pilot, or after the first run on Broadway—the money falls through or something happens. So I try not to get my hopes up." Eventually, Janney realized she could trust that the show would be renewed. In June of 2001 she bought her first house. "It was the most terrifying thing I've ever done," she told *InStyle*'s Pener.

Janney's experience and skill as an actress are evident in all the roles she plays. As her career continues to move forward, hopefully more opportunities will arise for this tenacious actress. She may have had many difficulties in getting to where she is but she has proven that sticking to her goals pays off. She told *Newsday*'s Green, "Now I feel that the better part of my career is in front of me."

Sources

Atlanta Journal–Constitution, October 4, 2000, p. D7; July 18, 2001, p. C3.

Austin American–Statesman, January 9, 2000, p. 37.

Dayton Daily News, May 14, 2001, p. 1C; October 29, 2001, p. 1C; September 24, 2002, p. C1.

InStyle, May 2002, pp. 402–07.

Los Angeles Magazine, January 2001, p. 15.

Los Angeles Times, July 22, 1999, p. F10.

Newsday (New York), April 23, 1998, p. B03.

New York Times, December 22, 1996, section 2, p. 5.

San Francisco Chronicle, September 12, 1999, p. 40.

Star–Ledger (Newark, NJ), May 5, 1998, p. 69.

—*Eve M. B. Hermann*

Mary E. Junck

Chairman, President, and Chief Executive Officer of Lee Enterprises

Born c. 1948, in Iowa; married Ralph Gibson (a business owner); children: one daughter, one stepson. *Education:* Valparaiso University, B.A., 1969; University of North Carolina at Chapel Hill, Master's (journalism), 1971.

Addresses: *Home*—Pleasant Valley, IA. *Office*—Lee Enterprises Inc, 215 N. Main St., Ste. 400, Davenport, IA 52801–1924.

Career

Began career at the *Charlotte Observer*, Charlotte, NC, as a marketing researcher, 1972, became retail advertising manager; advertising marketing manager, *Miami Herald*, Miami, FL, 1977, later became assistant advertising director; *St. Paul Pioneer Press*, St. Paul, MN, president, general manager and senior vice president after 1985, became publisher, 1990; joined the Times–Mirror newspaper chain, 1992; served as publisher and chief executive officer of its *Baltimore Sun* newspaper, 1993–97; became president of the Times–Mirror's eastern newspapers, 1997; Lee Enterprises, Davenport, IA, chief operating officer, 1999, became chief executive officer, 2001, and board chair, 2002.

Member: Board of directors, Newspaper Association of America; board of directors, Mercantile Bankshares Corporation of Baltimore; board member, Putnum Museum.

Sidelights

Journalism executive Mary E. Junck serves as president and chief executive officer of the Lee Enterprises newspaper chain in Davenport, Iowa. A $525 million business with roots stretching back to the nineteenth century, Lee publishes several dozen daily newspapers in scores of cities across the American Midwest and beyond, and serves more than a million readers. Junck concedes that her realm of journalism is far removed from such stalwarts as the *New York Times* or the *Washington Post*, but points out that her company's newspapers serve as an important community voice in a changing world, especially by focusing on local issues. "What we do is important to [our] democracy," she told *BusinessWeek* writer Joseph Weber.

Junck is a product of the same heartland–based American community that her papers typically serve. Her family had a farm outside of Ogden, Iowa, where she grew up as the only daughter. She studied English at Valparaiso University in Indiana, where a stint as yearbook editor gave her a taste for journalism. In an interview with *Editor & Publisher*'s Mark Fitzgerald, she later realized her error. "I thought that qualified me as a journalist," Junck joked about her yearbook duties. "Of course, it doesn't qualify you to be anything." But she did realize that she enjoyed the business and managerial side of publishing, and after graduating from Valparaiso in 1969, she went on to earn a graduate degree in journalism from the University of North Carolina at Chapel Hill. In 1972, she began her career as a marketing researcher at the *Charlotte Observer* in North Carolina. After a stint as head of the *Observer*'s retail advertising, its parent company, the Knight–Ridder newspaper chain, offered her a job at the *Miami Herald* as an advertising–marketing manager there in 1977. She spent several years in Florida and in 1982 was given a Knight–Ridder executive slot as assistant to the senior vice president of operations. Three years later, she was sent to another of Knight–Ridder's flagship papers, the *St. Paul Pioneer Press,* as president, general manager and senior vice president. In 1990 she was made that paper's publisher.

Junck left Knight–Ridder in 1992 for the Times–Mirror newspaper company, where from 1993 to 1997 she served as publisher and chief executive officer of its *Baltimore Sun* daily. Five years later, Times–Mirror executives promoted her to president of its Eastern U.S. newspaper division, a realm that included *Newsday* and Connecticut's *Hartford Courant.* When she was offered a job as chief operating officer of the Iowa–based Lee Enterprises in 1999, Junck made a surprising move and accepted it; having been dissatisfied with her career in recent years, she felt ready for a new challenge. Problems within the Times–Mirror group were exacerbated when the Tribune Company, another newspaper and media giant, acquired it in 2000.

At Lee, Junck was promoted to chief executive officer in 2001 and board chair the following year. Not only was Junck the first woman to run Lee, but she was also the first person in charge who was not related to its founding Lee and Adler families. As one of the highest–ranking female executives within the American newspaper business, Junck was apolitical about her achievements to date. "I'm actually not sure whether being a woman has helped or hindered my career," she told Fitzgerald in the *Editor & Publisher* interview. "A bigger factor, I think, is that I've been fortunate throughout my career to work with many talented people and I've had great bosses."

Under Junck, Lee Enterprises—founded in 1890—returned to its original mission by selling off a number of television–station properties in order to redirect its energies into print publishing. With the capital from that sale, it moved to acquire Howard

Publications and its 16 newspapers in the spring of 2002. The merger made Lee the twelfth–largest newspaper chain in United States, and was deemed a wise move by industry analysts. Revenues increased, as did overall circulation figures; in all, Junck oversaw 44 daily newspapers across 18 states, plus 175 weekly papers. The largest in the chain, acquired through Howard, was the *North County Times* of Escondido, California. Lee also published the *Billings Gazette* in Montana, Iowa's *Sioux City Journal,* and the *Bismarck Tribune* of North Dakota. In such markets, as Americans migrate from the larger, older urban areas to new exurbs centered around smaller cities, newspaper circulation has bucked a downward 20–year downward national trend and actually increased. "It helps, of course, that Junck's papers are potent little cash machines," noted Weber in the *BusinessWeek* article. "Such papers as Iowa's *Muscatine Journal*—which Mark Twain once wrote for—and the *Chippewa* (Wis.) *Herald* own their markets in ways big–city papers can only envy. Where the *Chicago Tribune* might reach 20 percent of households in its markets, Lee papers go to more than 60 percent of their households." Acclaimed American writers Willa Cather and Thornton Wilder also worked for Lee papers during their early career years.

Junck is married to Ralph Gibson, who owns a plumbing, heating, and air–conditioning supply company in the Davenport area. She has a stepson and a daughter, and serves as a local Girl Scout troop leader. At Lee, she has earned high marks for her managerial skills at the office, too. "Mary has the best way of saying 'No,'" Michael E. Phelps, an executive with the Davenport *Quad–City Times* told *Editor & Publisher*'s Fitzgerald. "She'll say, 'You know, that's a great idea, and there are a lot of great ideas, and we're not going to do that one.' Mary is wonderfully Midwestern, but she can say 'No'—there's no question about it."

Sources

Periodicals

Business Record (Des Moines), December 25, 2000, p. 17.
BusinessWeek, July 1, 2002, p. 94.
Editor & Publisher, September 25, 2000, p. 7; January 28, 2002, p. 6; February 10, 2003, p. 10.

Online

Lee Enterprises, http://www.lee.net/insidelee/ (March 27, 2003).

—*Carol Brennan*

Joseph Kabila

AP/Wide World Photos

President of Democratic Republic of Congo

Born on June 4, 1971, in Ankoro, North Katanga, Congo; son of Laurent Kabila (president of Congo) and Sifa Maanya; children: Josephine (with girlfriend, Olive). *Education:* Received basic military training in Rwanda, 1995; attended university in Uganda, 1996. *Religion:* Christian.

Addresses: *Office*—Presidence de la Republique, Kinshasa, Democratic Republic of Congo, Africa. *Representation in the United States*—Ambassador Faida Mitifu, 1800 New Hampshire Avenue NW, Washington D.C. 20009.

Career

Major–general in Democratic Republic of Congo army and army chief of staff, 1997–2001; president of Democratic Republic of Congo, 2001—.

Sidelights

After three decades of corrupt government and three years of civil and foreign war, the Democratic Republic of Congo (DRC) was in dire need of peace. DRC's president, Laurent Kabila, spoke of peace, but was unable—or unwilling—to forge it. After Kabila was murdered in January of 2001, his son, Joseph, was named president. Reluctant to be president, the younger Kabila had no political experience and little military experience. The Congolese knew little about him and feared he would be as difficult and corrupt as his father. But Kabila used the first months of his presidency to restructure

DRC government and to visit with heads of Europe and the United States, promoting his willingness to work for peace in DRC.

Even while Kabila took the oath of office on January 27, 2001, crucial details of his life gave rise to a flurry of speculation; questions concerning his ancestry in particular plagued the onset of his administration. An official statement issued by the Congolese supreme court on the occasion of Kabila's inauguration listed his date of birth as June 4, 1971, quelling a variety of rumors that fixed his birth as early as 1968 and as late as 1972. Kabila was known to be the eldest of ten children who were fathered by the former president, Laurent D. Kabila. Of the ten siblings, Kabila, along with a twin sister, Jane, and a younger brother named Saide, were the children of Mrs. Sifa Maanya. Maanya's nationality, believed by many to be Tutsi, was reported as Bango–Bango soon after her son was named to succeed his father as the DRC president. Likewise, in the official statement of the supreme court, the younger Kabila was identified as being of pure Congolese descent, having been born in South Kivu in the eastern portion of the DRC, contrary to popular reports that he was born in Rwanda.

Kabila's early and intermediate education transpired in Tanzania, where he attended Anglo–style schools and grew up fluent in both English and Swahili. He later underwent military training in Rwanda in 1995. In 1996, while preparing to attend college in Uganda, Kabila heeded a summons from his father to join in a campaign to oust the regime of Mobutu Sese Seko, who controlled the DRC at that time. After the elder Kabila met with success in his political aspiration and assumed the presidency, he reinstated the country's original name of Democratic Republic of Congo, from the interim name of Zaire, which the nation was called under Seko. The elder Kabila subsequently sent his son to China for six months during 1998, to undergo further military training. President Kabila then appointed his own son as chief-of-staff of the Congolese Armed Forces (FAC) upon the younger's return to the DRC in August of 1998.

The DRC is the third-largest African nation—about the size of Western Europe—and is, for natural resources, one of the richest lands in the world. The country abounds with diamonds, copper, uranium, oil, timber, and coffee. Decades of corrupt government weakened the country's infrastructure. Taking advantage of this, six of DRC's neighboring countries—Rwanda, Uganda, Burundi, Namibia, Zimbabwe, and Angola—and several rebel groups put military troops on DRC soil, fighting for a piece of the wealth, and in the process ravaging the country. In the confusion, many Congolese became impoverished. Food and gas prices skyrocketed. The inflation rate was the highest in the world, at 500 percent. The food markets in the nation's capital, Kinshasa, were half empty. Orphans and the destitute roamed the streets, and some families ate whatever they could find—cooked cow skin, bats, caterpillars.

On January 16, 2001, Laurent Kabila was murdered in his palace by a guard. Though conspiracy theories abounded—many believe the Angolans were responsible—the official position was that the assassination was personal. Soon after the murder, the DRC's top military and political advisors sat down to choose his replacement. "Joseph was the best man, as he is accepted by all sides," DRC Justice Minister Mwenze Kongolo told the *Christian Science Monitor*. The general belief was that Joseph would be more interested in resolving the war than his hard-line father was.

In the days before he became president, Kabila moved from the modest military villa, where he lived with his girlfriend, Olive, and their young daughter, Josephine, to live in the official palaces. He spent the days after his father's murder in private meetings with foreign diplomats and represen-

tatives of various Congolese religious, social, and commercial groups. On January 27, 2001—eleven days after his father's death—Kabila became president of DRC and the youngest head of state in the world.

The Congolese did not know what to expect from their new president. They did not know if he was strong enough to hold the country together or whether he would pursue war or peace. Many were unhappy with the way he had come to power. Many Congolese objected to the fact that he was chosen secretly and automatically. Congolese government sources and Western diplomats said that Kabila did not want to become president, only that he did so at the insistence of his father's Cabinet ministers. Others disapproved of the choice because they were unhappy with his father. Many believed the son was easily influenced and a puppet to his father's advisors.

The people of DRC were not confident that Kabila was capable of being president, and there was immense pressure on him to move quickly. He had no political experience and little military experience. Though fluent in English and Swahili, Kabila is not fluent in French, the official language of DRC, or Lingala, the tribal language spoken by most Congolese. Kabila does not smoke, drink, like to dine out, or dress lavishly. He is by all accounts a shy, down-to-earth man who has few good friends. He reads the Bible and enjoys sports and computer games.

The new president spent his first three months in office "cleaning house." He removed extremists and ineffective old-timers. He restructured the government and promised to "democratize the political process and liberalize the economy," according to the *Christian Science Monitor*. "We are trying to change a whole system of misery, give the Congolese people breathing space, and start with programs of recovery," he was quoted as saying in the same article. Many worried that his promises needed to be fulfilled quickly for the Congolese to be satisfied. "I always back my words with action," Kabila responded in the *Christian Science Monitor*. "When I promise something I have to do it. That is what dignity is all about."

Kabila's first goal was peace. He traveled to the United States, France, Belgium, the Nordic countries, and Britain, to talk with heads of state, and push his message of peace. He reopened talks with the International Monetary Fund and World Bank. He appeared willing to cooperate with the United

Nations (UN) in following the Lusaka accord, which outlined a withdrawal of foreign armies from the DRC and an end to the DRC's war, and which his father had reluctantly signed in 1999 but made no attempt to implement.

Three months into his presidency, the *Economist* reported that, despite the positive steps Kabila appeared to have taken, he lacked "legitimacy and power" and "the authority and the political skill" to keep DRC together. By May of 2001, however, the *Economist* reported that Kabila had "been more flexible, thus winning the authority and status his father lacked.... [Compared to his father, he was] cleverer and more statesmanlike."

Kabila felt progress was being made. He allowed UN monitors and guards to enter the country to help facilitate peace and the withdrawal of military troops. "As far as I'm concerned," he told the *Christian Science Monitor*, "the peace process is on track." David Meyer, chief of staff for the UN observer force in the DRC agreed. "It is going pretty well," he said in the *Christian Science Monitor*, "Broadly speaking we are on track and we are pleased."

Kabila won allies in the West by agreeing to economic reform. He believed that, within a year's time, the DRC would have a different look, a different feel—that the fuel problems would be solved, roads would be built. "There are plans, there are visions, there are expectations," he told the *Christian Science Monitor*. Indeed, Kabila made significant strides in the following months that took him even closer to his goal of regional peace.

The United Nations Mission in the Democratic Republic of Congo (better known by its French acronym, MONUC) was extended through June of 2003. The MONUC is, by its mandate, supposed to "protect civilians under imminent threat of physical violence." Kabila was pleased with the extension and the additional UN troops dispatched to the DRC at his request to aid in the peace progress. He argued that if additional troops were not deployed, the whole mission would be a waste, since the region couldn't be helped by the small numbers that were originally there—he called it a "waste of time [and] a waste of money," according to the *Africa News Service*.

Kabila signed a peace agreement with Rwanda in July of 2002, ending a four-year war between the two countries. The agreement, signed in the South African capital of Pretoria, called for the withdrawal of Rwandan troops from the DRC. In turn, Kabila's government agreed to disarm and repatriate DRC–based Rwandan Hutu rebel militias hiding out in the country within a three-month time frame. The Hutus are thought to be responsible for the genocide that took place in 1994. Kabila and Rwandan leader Paul Kagame agreed to meet regularly following the agreement to review the progress being made. In a press conference, Kabila spoke of his commitment to making and keeping a lasting peace in the Great Lakes region of Africa, as the *Africa News Service* reported: "I sense that this time there is a genuine commitment by the political leaders to ensure that we succeed in reaching our aim of peace. The people of the Great Lakes region will be granted their peace reward. I shall play my part to ensure that peace succeeds."

At the first post–agreement meeting between Kabila and Kagame in early October of 2002, both sides were able to show efforts made toward fulfilling the peace agreements. In late October, Congolese allies Angola, Namibia, and Zimbabwe announced they would pull the remainder of their armed forces out of the DRC by October 31, 2002. While announcing their intent to withdraw from the region, they also called for a strengthening of the United Nations MONUC mandate and for a verification that all Rwandan troops had left the DRC.

Another important advancement toward peace in the Great Lakes region came in November of 2002, when Kabila and Ugandan president Yoweri Museveni signed a peace agreement that included the withdrawal of Ugandan troops from the DRC. The agreement was signed at a summit called by Tanzanian president Benjamin Mkapa aimed at achieving peace between the DRC and Uganda.

Kabila made plans for a transitional government that was scheduled to be in place by January of 2003. Under the terms of the transitional government reached after meeting with Rwandan president Kagame and South African president Thabo Mbeki, Kabila would remain president of the DRC and four vice presidents would be put into office. One vice president would be from the present government, one would represent the rebel group Congolese Rally for Democracy, another would represent the rebel group Congolese Liberation Movement, and the fourth would represent the unarmed opposition parties within the country.

Sources

Africa News Service, June 17, 2002; July 30, 2002; November 2, 2002.

Asia Africa Intelligence Wire, October 18, 2002; October 26, 2002; November 2, 2002; November 26, 2002.

Christian Science Monitor, January 23, 2001, p. 1; January 25, 2001, p. 6; May 7, 2001, p. 1.

Economist, March 17, 2001, p. 1; May 5, 2001, p. 5.

Knight–Ridder/Tribune News Service, January 25, 2001, p. K47.

New York Times Upfront, March 5, 2001, p. 14.

—*Brenna Sanchez*

Dean Kamen

Inventor

Born c. 1951; son of Jack (a magazine illustrator) and Evelyn (an accountant) Kamen. *Education:* Attended Worcester Polytechnic Institute.

Addresses: *Office*—DEKA Research and Development Corporation, Technology Center, 340 Commercial St., Manchester, NH 03101.

Career

Founded AutoSyringe, 1976; demonstrated first portable infusion pump, 1978; sold infusion pump product rights, became multi–millionaire, 1982; founded DEKA Research and Development, 1982; invented portable dialysis machine, 1993; invented the iBot, a wheelchair able to climb stairs, 1995; introduced the Segway, self–balancing, electric–powered transportation machine, 2001.

Awards: The Kilby Award; the Heinz Award in Technology, the Economy, and Employment; the Hoover Medal, 1993; the National Medal of Technology, 2000; Lemelson–MIT prize, 2002.

Sidelights

Inventor Dean Kamen holds more than 150 United States and foreign patents for devices ranging from medical devices to innovative personal transportation. He was still a college undergraduate when he devised the first wearable infusion pump, which found applications in chemotherapy, neona-tology, and endocrinology. He founded AutoSyringe, Inc., in 1976 to manufacture and market the infusion pumps. Using the same principals he used to invent the infusion pump, he developed the first insulin pump for diabetics. He later sold AutoSyringe to Baxter International Corporation. He founded DEKA Research and Development in 1982 to facilitate his inventions as well as to provide research and development for corporate clients. Some of the inventions Kamen developed with DEKA include the HomeChoice kidney dialysis machine and the INDEPENDENCE IBOT Mobility System. He later developed a cardiac "stent" that improves blood flow. He also designed the iBot, a wheelchair that can climb stairs. Kamen received international attention in 2001, when he introduced the Segway, a self–balancing, electric–powered transportation machine.

A college dropout from Worcester Polytechnic Institute, Kamen professed to *Boston Herald* reporter Stephanie Schorow that he doesn't like "anything about school." He was raised with his older brother, Barton, by Jack, an illustrator for *MAD* magazine, and Evelyn Kamen. Kamen's father is employed by his son to draw sketches of his son's inventions, and his mother is employed as an accountant at DEKA. Barton became a noted oncologist. Kamen told CNN.com that he built his first invention when he was five years old: "... I figured out a way to make my bed without having to run from one side of the bed to another." He invented the fusion pump after conversations with his brother. The *Boston Herald*'s Schorow described Kamen: "[H]e showed up at Babson College to accept an honorary degree dressed in jeans and work boots, with a pen in his breast pocket, a phone at his hip, and a joke about stuffy Harvard on his lips." Schorow continued: "Quick–witted and self–mocking, Kamen seems to shrewdly play his celebrity for all it's worth. Behind his easy demeanor, his eyes dance with impatience."

In the 1990s, Kamen founded For Inspiration and Recognition of Science and Technology (FIRST), a program intended to motivate young people to pursue careers in science and technology. Three of FIRST's national robotics competitions set attendance records for non–Disney events at Walt Disney World's Epcot Center. Kamen explained to the *Boston Herald*'s Schorow that he might have appreciated school more if there were a program similar to FIRST when he attended. "But I have to say [FIRST] would have come a lot closer to any of the other garbage I had to sit through." He also explained to Schorow why he believed FIRST is relevant to students: "It's not important if a kid even touches a robot. What is important is that sponsoring companies shower kids with resources and 'dazzle' them. At the end of six weeks, kids have a perspective of what's possible in this world."

In 2001, articles began to appear in the press concerning a new Kamen invention, which was alternately code–named "IT" and "Ginger." The name Ginger was intended as a joke to indicate the invention's technical relationship to Kamen's iBot, which had been described as Fred Astaire because of the nimbleness the iBot displayed. (Fred Astaire's most famous dancing partner was Ginger Rogers.) In 2001, he unveiled the Segway, an invention that he claimed in a *Time* article quoted in *The Independent*, would make automobiles "not only undesirable, but unnecessary." *Independent* reporter Charles Arthur described the Segway as looking "like nothing more than ... an overlarge scooter with the back end lopped off. But what it actually does is more subtle. By all accounts, it is a marvellous piece of technology." Arthur continued: "It is two–wheeled, concealing in its base a complex array of gyroscopes, computer chips, and tilt sensors that monitor the center of gravity of the person standing on its platform 100 times a second and which prevent you from tipping over, while moving in the direction that you're leaning." Kamen described the experience to Arthur as "skiing without the snow." The

Segway's initial top speed was clocked at 17 miles per hour, or 27 kilometers per hour.

Most of the reaction to the Segway was enthusiastic. Steve Jobs of Apple Computer saw a prototype and, according to Arthur, proclaimed: "[I]f enough people see the machine you won't have to convince them to architect cities around it. It'll just happen." Amazon founder Jeff Bezos, who also saw the prototype, was quoted by Arthur as declaring: "You'll have no problem selling it. The question is, are people going to be allowed to use it?" The mystery surrounding these early reports spurred speculation that Kamen had developed a hydrogen–powered car that would replace the internal–combustion engine or an anti–gravity device. After introducing the Segway to the public on the ABC television program *Good Morning America*, Kamen remarked to *Time*, as quoted by Arthur: "Most people in the developing world can't afford cars, and if they could, it would be a complete disaster. If you were building one of the new cities of China, would you do it the way we have? Wouldn't it make more sense to build a mass–transit system around the city and leave the central couple of square miles for pedestrians only?" Critics, however, pointed out that the first Segway introduced does not allow for the carrying of cargo other than the rider. Kamen countered the latter argument by displaying a $10,000 Segway that is able to carry luggage. The smaller Segway will be sold for $3,000. Kamen announced that the United States Post Office, the United States National Parks Service, General Electric, and Amazon had already ordered Segways for corporate fleet purposes.

Kamen's resourcefulness has made him an extremely wealthy man. He designed a 32,000–square–foot home in Manchester, New Hampshire, and purchased an island off the coast of Connecticut, which he has called a sovereign state. He also designed and built a personal helicopter which he has used to commute to the DEKA offices.

Sources

Periodicals

Atlanta Journal–Constitution, December 4, 2001, p. E2.
Boston Herald, May 22, 2001, p. 48.
Christian Science Monitor, December 7, 2001, p. 11.
Grand Rapids Press (Grand Rapids, Michigan), April 23, 2002, p. A2.
Independent (London, England), December 4, 2001, p. 1.

Online

DEKA Research and Development Corporation, http://www.informagen.com/Resource_Informagen/Full/1/8561.php (October 1, 2002).

"Ginger inventor garners coveted prize," CNN.com, http://www.cnn.com/2002/TECH/industry/04/23/inventor.prize.ap/index.html (April 23, 2002).

—Bruce Walker

Mwai Kibaki

AP/Wide World Photos

President of Kenya

Born in November 15, 1931, in Othaya, Kenya; married Lucy Muthoni; children: Judy, Jimi (son), David, Tonny. *Education:* Makerere University College, B.Sc., 1955; attended the London School of Economics.

Addresses: *Home*—Nairobi, Kenya. *Office*—Harambee House, Office of the President, P.O. Box 30510, Nairobi, Kenya.

Career

Lecturer at Makerere University; became national executive officer of Kenya African National Union, a new political party, 1960; Central Legislative Assembly of East African Common Services Organization, representative from Kenya, 1962; elected to Kenya's House of Representatives, 1963; parliamentary secretary to treasury, 1963; assistant minister of economics, planning, and development, 1964–66; minister for commerce and industry, 1966–69; minister of finance, 1969–70, 1978–82; minister of finance and economic planning, 1970–78; minister of home affairs, 1978–79, 1982–88; vice president of Kenya under President Daniel arap Moi, 1978–88; minister of health, 1988–91; National Democratic Party of Kenya, leader after 1991; elected president of Kenya, 2002.

Kenyans elected 71–year–old Mwai Kibaki by a landslide vote as the country's third president in its history in December of 2002. His rise signaled a new era for the country, which had been ruled—and some say ruined—by Kibaki's former mentor,

Daniel arap Moi, since 1978. Kibaki broke from Moi in 1991 after a ban was lifted on opposition parties. Kibaki's 2002 electoral win on the ticket of the party he founded, the National Democratic Party of Kenya, was also the first time that Kenya's longtime ruling party relinquished power since independence from Britain in 1963. A journalist for Britain's *Independent* newspaper, Declan Walsh, described him as "one of the great gentlemen of Kenyan politics."

Kibaki was born in 1931 in Othaya, not far from Mount Kenya. His family belonged to the Kikuyu ethnic group, and his early years were spent living in a mud hut and herding the family cattle. Sent to Nyeri Boys' School for a formal education in 1939, he slept on a bed made from a wooden board and hay; despite the hardships, his academic performance earned him a scholarship to Uganda's Makerere University College. Makerere was the top school in East Africa, and at the time was educating many of the young adults who, like Kibaki, would go on to play crucial roles in their respective countries' bids for political independence. While at Makerere, Kibaki served as chair of the Kenya Students Association and won a scholarship to study at a British university of his choice. He enrolled at the prestigious London School of Economics, but while there learned that his brother had been killed in Kenya's Mau Mau uprising, an armed revolt against

British rule. He returned to Africa and took a teaching post at Makerere University, but once things in Kenya had calmed down, Kibaki went to visit his family on the Easter holiday. At the African Corner Bar in Nairobi, he met with friends who were involved in forming a new political party as Kenya readied for independence, and on that day he helped draft what would be his country's first constitution.

Kibaki played several important roles in these early years of Kenyan independence. He served as national executive officer of the Kenya African National Union (KANU), the country's new political vanguard party from 1960 to 1962, and was elected to Kenya's first legislative assembly. In 1964 President Jomo Kenyatta appointed him assistant minister of economics, planning, and development, and two years later Kibaki took a full cabinet post as minister for commerce and industry. In 1969 he was made Kenya's minister of finance, keeping the job after Kenyatta's 1978 death and Moi's ascendancy; at that time, Kibaki was also made the country's vice president. He was ousted from that post in a political fracas in 1988, but Moi gave him the Ministry of Health portfolio.

Moi's regime became an increasingly authoritarian one during his first decade in power. He fostered a cult of personality, outlawed political opposition parties, and allowed corruption to flourish. Moi finally bowed to international pressure in 1991 and agreed to allow multi–party elections the following year; Kibaki broke with Moi's KANU at this time and became leader of the newly formed National Democratic Party of Kenya. Twice he ran against Moi for the presidency, in 1992 and 1997, but was trounced in elections marked by violence and suspected vote fraud. After nearly 25 years in power, many believed the moment was ripe for a change. "Moi's Kenya has become a land of stark contrasts," wrote *New York Times* correspondent Marc Lacey. "Dire poverty and fabulous, mostly stolen, wealth; natural beauty and collapsing infrastructure.... Known for its luxury safaris in remote unspoiled regions, it is also a place where the bulk of the population gets by on less than a dollar a day."

Elections were again scheduled to take place at the end of 2002, and this time Moi was constitutionally prohibited from running for re–election. He chose Kenyatta's son, Uhuru, as the KANU candidate, but it was a move that angered many within the party. Some debarked to form their own groups, and these, in turn, united under a newly formed "National Rainbow Coalition" with Kibaki as its front–runner. As before, he ran a clean campaign, absent of hired thugs and political venom, and won sympathy when he was injured in a car accident just weeks before the election and had to campaign from a wheelchair. His platform promises included free primary education for all children; he also pledged to improve the country's dismal economic performance, launch an independent inquiry into the endemic corruption, and begin a constitutional review process that would remove some of the power from the presidential office.

Kibaki trounced Kenyatta in the polls on December 29. News of the victory prompted Kenyans to take to the street in celebration. "It is a very humbling occasion," the *New York Times* report by Lacey quoted Kibaki as saying in his victory speech. "It means, in effect, Kenyans have given me a challenge." He was sworn in two days later, with Nairobians turning out in droves to catch a glimpse of the new president. "When Mr. Kibaki arrived," reported Lacey in the next day's paper, "they exploded into a frenzy that some said equaled the celebrations held at the time of independence in 1963."

Once in place, Kibaki's new administration soon announced an investigation of one notorious debacle from the Moi regime in which a fake gold–and–diamond export ring had netted millions for those with connections to certain government ministries. Repercussions from it were said to have ruined the Kenyan economy in the early 1990s. Such new anti–corruption measures inspired many Kenyans to suddenly refuse to pay the bribes that were once an everyday part of life in the country.

Kibaki is married and the father of four. He lives in the Muthaiga district of Nairobi, Kenya, and is an avid golfer. As he told Lacey in the *New York Times*, he did not plan to follow Moi's example and allow his image to be used on Kenya's shilling notes. "What is important is that we should have a stable currency, not whose picture is there," Kibaki told the newspaper. "A president should prove himself by things he's going to do that change the life of ordinary Kenyans, not by naming every street and every corner."

Sources

Independent (London, England), January 4, 2003, p. 14.
Los Angeles Times, February 27, 2003, p. A5.
Malawi Standard January 2, 2003.
New York Times, December 30, 2002, p. A1, p. A6; December 31, 2002, p. A8.
Time, January 13, 2003, p. 38.

—*Carol Brennan*

Jason Kidd

Professional basketball player

Born Jason Fredrick Kidd, March 23, 1973, in San Francisco, CA; son of Steve (a supervisor with Trans World Airlines) and Anne (a bank bookkeeper) Kidd; married Joumana Samaha, 1997; children: Jason (from previous relationship), T.J., Jazelle and Miah (twin daughters). *Education:* Attended University of California, Berkeley.

Addresses: *Office*—New Jersey Nets, 390 Murray Hill Parkway, East Rutherford, NJ 07073.

Career

Drafted by Dallas Mavericks, 1994; traded by Mavericks to Phoenix Suns, 1996; traded to New Jersey Nets, 2001; led the New Jersey Nets to the NBA finals for the first time in the team's history, 2002.

Awards: Naismith Award for nation's top high school basketball player, 1991–92; *Parade* high school basketball player of the year, 1992; *USA Today* high school basketball player of the year, 1992; Pac–10 player of the year, 1993–94; National Basketball Association rookie of the year award (shared with Grant Hill), 1994–95.

Sidelights

Although his brilliance on the basketball court has at times been overshadowed by news of his problems off the court, there can be no doubt that Jason Kidd is one of the most outstanding pro-

fessional basketball players in history. Kidd, a point guard, was traded by the Phoenix Suns to the down–on–their–luck New Jersey Nets in July of 2001 after being charged with punching his wife in the face during an argument over feeding their two–year–old son, Trey Jason, known by his parents as T.J. With this shadow still hanging over his head, Kidd arrived in the Jersey Meadowlands, vowing to take the hapless Nets to the National Basketball Association (NBA) finals. Despite his boasts, neither his new Nets teammates nor the team's fans expected much. After all, in its 18 seasons, the team had only once advanced beyond the first round of the NBA playoffs, and that was in 1984.

However, Kidd made good on his promise, leading the Nets to the NBA finals against the Los Angeles Lakers in 2002. Although the Lakers made short work of the Nets in the finals, winning four games in a row to take their third consecutive NBA championship, it was hardly a runaway. The Nets acquitted themselves well for a team that had never before played in the finals, losing by six or less points in three of the four games. Even in defeat, Kidd managed to see a silver lining. He told Curtis Bunn of the *Atlanta Journal and Constitution*, "We had a great season. No one picked us to get this far. But we can't be satisfied. We have to use this to be the first step to becoming a great team." On the eve of the 2002–03 season, he said he hoped the Nets could win a total of 60 games, eight more than in the previous season. "I think we can do it if we're healthy," Kidd told Barbara Barker, a staff writer for *Newsday*. "Last year everybody had something to prove. Now, we have to take the same approach. We have to prove we are a team that is not going to fall on our face. Everybody is waiting for us to fall. We didn't fall last year until we got to the finals, and that is not a bad place to fall."

Kidd was born in San Francisco, California, on March 23, 1973, to Steve and Anne Kidd, who later divorced. His father, an African American who died in 1999, was a longtime employee of Trans World Airlines, working his way up from baggage handler to ticket counter supervisor. His mother, Anne, who is Caucasian, works as a bookkeeper at a Bay Area bank. Kidd, along with his younger sisters, Denise and Kimberly, grew up in the solidly middle–class neighborhood of Oakland, across the bay from San Francisco. He spent much of his time playing basketball with neighborhood friends, most of them older than he. Early on, he learned that he could best fit in with the older boys if he helped them to score. By the time he reached junior high school, he'd developed into something of a local phenomenon on the basketball court. Things only got better in high school. Attending St. Joseph's of Notre Dame in nearby Alameda, Kidd proved himself to be a scoring sensation. During his high school ball playing years, he averaged 25 points, ten assists, seven rebounds, and seven steals per game, leading St. Joseph's to two consecutive California Division I state titles. Kidd was twice named California Player of the Year. In his senior year of high school, he was named High School Player of the Year by both *Parade* magazine and *USA Today* and also won the Naismith Award as the nation's top high school player in the 1991–92 season.

After graduating from high school, Kidd enrolled at the University of California in Berkeley. During his freshman season on the basketball court for the Golden Bears, he averaged 13 points, 7.7 assists, and 4.9 rebounds per game, earning himself a berth on the All–Pac–10 Team, making him only the fifth freshman in league history to make the team. During his sophomore year, Kidd averaged 16.7 points, 6.9 rebounds, and 9.1 assists per game and was named Pac–10 Player of the Year, the first sophomore ever to earn this honor. He was also a finalist for both the Naismith and John Wooden awards.

After his stunning performance as a college sophomore, Kidd decided that he was ready for pro ball and declared himself eligible for the 1994 draft. He was clearly the most heralded point guard prospect since 1979–80. The Dallas Mavericks, which held the second pick in the draft, had their eye on Kidd and snatched him up immediately. A lackluster team for most of its history, the Mavericks, with the potent combo of Kidd at point guard, Jimmy Jackson at shooting guard, and Jamal Mashburn at forward, quickly began to turn things around during Kidd's first season (1994–95). Kidd averaged 11.7 points, 7.7 assists, and 5.4 rebounds per game, winning him NBA Rookie of the Year honors, which he shared with Detroit's Grant Hill. He led the league with four triple–doubles. (A triple–double is awarded when a player earns double figures in points, assists, and rebounds in a single game.) Despite the team's dramatic turnaround, an injury sidelined Jackson for the second half of the season, putting an end to the Mavericks's hope for a playoff berth.

Kidd was even more impressive in his second season (1995–96) with the Mavericks, averaging 16.6 points, 9.7 assists, and 6.8 rebounds per game. He also posted nine triple–doubles to rank second in the NBA for the season. With a total of 783 assists and 553 rebounds for the season, Kidd became only the sixth player in NBA history to register at least 700 assists and 500 rebounds in a single season. The last NBA player to have done so was Magic Johnson in the 1990–91 season. While playing at Dallas, Kidd earned something of a reputation as a disruptive influence. After an argument with his teammate Jackson, Kidd refused to speak to him for six weeks. He also cut off communication the team's coach for two months after the two had a disagreement.

Kidd played the first 22 games of the 1996–97 season for the Mavericks before being traded to the Phoenix Suns in late December of 1996, along with Tony Dumas and Loren Meyer for Michael Finley, A.C. Green, and Sam Cassell. During his games for Dallas, Kidd averaged 9.9 points, 9.1 assists, and 2.05 steals per game. In the first half of his very first game for Phoenix, he suffered a sterno–clavicular joint sprain and a hairline fracture of his right collarbone. Nevertheless, he managed to post six points, nine assists, seven rebounds, and three steals before injury forced him from the game. The injury kept him on the sidelines for the next 21 games, during which the Suns compiled a disappointing record of nine wins and 12 losses. Kidd returned to the game on Valentine's Day and powered a winning streak that carried the Suns into the playoffs for the season. In his 32 games for Phoenix, the Suns posted a record of 23 wins and nine losses, and Kidd averaged 11.6 points, nine assists, and 2.4 steals per game. Unhappily, the Suns lost to Seattle in the playoffs, but Kidd performed impressively, averaging 12 points, 9.8 assists, six rebounds, and 2.2 steals in 41.2 minutes per game in the five games of the playoffs. During the 1997–98 season, Kidd once again led the Suns into the plays with a record of 56 wins and 26 losses. He averaged 9.1 assists per game, the second best performance in the league. In the Suns's four playoff games against the San Antonio Spurs, Kidd averaged 14.3 points, 7.5 assists, 5.7 rebounds, and four steals per game.

In the 1998–99 season, Kidd became the first Phoenix Sun ever to lead the NBA in assists, averaging 10.8 per game and he also topped the NBA with seven triple–doubles. He also led the Suns in rebounds, averaging 6.8 per game. He was named NBA Player of the Month in April of 1999. In his three playoff games against the Blazers, Kidd averaged 15 points, ten assists, 2.3 rebounds, and 1.7 steals per game. In the 1999–2000 season, Kidd once against topped the NBA in assists, averaging 10.1 per game. He suffered an ankle injury late in the season but returned to help the Suns beat the Spurs in the first round of the playoffs. In the Western Conference semifinals against the Los Angeles Lakers, Kidd averaged ten points, 8.6 assists, and 7.6 rebounds. The Lakers, however, bested the Suns to take the series.

In 2000–01, for the third straight season, Kidd led the NBA in assists, averaging 9.8 per game, becoming only the fourth player in history to lead the NBA in assists for three consecutive seasons. He also led the league with a total of seven triple–doubles. For the fifth consecutive season, Kidd appeared in the playoffs, averaging 14.3 points, six rebounds, and 13.3 assists in four playoff games. Kidd's brilliant play on the court, however, was overshadowed by his arrest in January of 2001 for striking his wife Joumana in the face in front of their two–year–old son, T.J. Although the Kidds quickly reconciled after the incident, the after–effects were to have a profound effect on Kidd's career. The domestic abuse charges were a major factor in the decision of Suns management to trade Kidd to the New Jersey Nets in July of 2001. After the incident, reported to Phoenix police by his wife, Kidd spent the night in jail and followed that up with six months of counseling. Both Kidd and his wife contend that as unfortunate as the incident was, it has had a positive effect on their marriage in the long run. Joumana told Juliet Macur of the *Dallas Morning News*, "People will always say, 'I can't believe she stayed with him.' To tell you the truth, I don't care what people say because we've never been this happy. If we could bottle all of this up and keep going like this forever, we'd do it."

Despite the circumstances of his trade to the lackluster New Jersey Nets, Kidd was determined to make the very best of it. He pulled it off on a spectacular scale, leading the team to the NBA finals for the first time in its history. In the regular season, his first at the Meadowlands, Kidd averaged 14.7 points, 9.9 assists, 2.13 steals, and 7.3 rebounds per game. He started in all 82 games of the Nets's season and led the NBA with eight triple–doubles, moving up to fifth on the NBA's all–time triple-double list with 46 posted during his career through the end of the season. Kidd became only the eighth individual Nets player to take the court in an All–Star game, posting five points and four assists. Although the Nets eventually fell to the Lakers in the NBA finals, the Nets's specatacular showing was largely powered by Kidd. The team compiled an impressive regular season record of 52 wins and 30 losses.

Kidd's hopes for another strong season in 2002–03 were based on some major changes made in the Nets's player lineup. The Nets traded Keith Van Horn and Todd MacCulloch to Philadelphia in exchange for Dikembe Mutombo, a four–time defensive player of the year. The team hopes that the loss of Van Horn from the Nets's offense will more than be made up by the addition of Rodney Rogers, who was signed as a free agent from Boston, and significant improvement in the game of rookie Richard Jefferson, who'd enjoyed an impressive debut season in 2001–2002. Of the addition of Mutombo to the starting lineup, Kidd told Barbara Barker of *Newsday*: "When you have the flyswatter back there, it helps us defensively in the sense we can be more aggressive on the perimeter."

Kidd and his wife live in Saddle River, New Jersey, with their son, T.J., and twin daughters, Miah and Jazelle. Kidd also has an older son, Jason, from an earlier relationship, who lives with his mother. Kidd knows he came close to losing his family after the assault on his wife in early 2001, and he feels blessed that the family remains intact and stronger than it was before the blow–up. He's also happy to be playing the best basketball of his life. "Everything is in place right now, and I feel so lucky," he told the *Dallas Morning News*. "A lot of things have happened since I came into the league, but I never would have expected this."

Sources

Books

Sports Stars, Series 1–4, U*X*L, 1994–98.

Periodicals

Atlanta Journal and Constitution, June 13, 2002, p. C6.
Dallas Morning News, June 5, 2002, p. 1B.

Newsday, May 31, 2002, p. A90; September 29, 2002, p. C16.

Record (Bergen County, NJ), May 3, 2002, p. S1.

Sports Illustrated, January 28, 2002, p. 58.

Time, June 10, 2002, p. 56.

Online

"Jason Kidd," NBA, http://www.nba.com/playerfile/jason_kidd/bio.html (October 10, 2002).

—Don Amerman

Craig Kilborn

Michael Caulfield/WireImage.com

Talk-show host

Born in 1964 in Hastings, MN; son of Hiram (an insurance executive) and Shirley Kilborn; children: Jonathon. *Education:* Graduate of Montana State University.

Addresses: *Agent*—c/o Creative Artists Agency, 9830 Wilshire Blvd., Beverly Hills, CA 90212–4545. *Home*—Los Angeles, CA.

Career

Began broadcasting career as a play–by–play announcer in Savannah, GA, and Anaheim, CA; sportscaster, KCBA–TV, Salinas, CA; anchor, *Sports-Center,* ESPN, 1993–96; host, *The Daily Show,* Comedy Central, 1996–99; host, *The Late Late Show,* CBS–TV, 1999—; guest editor, *Gear* magazine, September, 2001.

Sidelights

Craig Kilborn, it may be argued, was destined to become a talk–show host. As a child in Hastings, Minnesota, Kilborn would entertain at his parents's parties with his ventriloquist act. As he reached adulthood, Kilborn majored in film and television at Montana State University, also indulging in basketball, in which he excelled as a guard. In fact, he was approached to play professional basketball in Europe, but Kilborn turned down the opportunity to try his hand at being an actor and comedian. His instincts proved correct; just a few years later Kilborn would be launched on the career path that would lead to his own late–night network talk show.

Kilborn cut his broadcasting teeth doing play–by–play for the Savannah Spirits. But the lure of big–time success brought him to Hollywood in 1988, where he took improvisational acting courses and taught traffic school to stay afloat. Kilborn repeated his sports broadcasting stint by doing basketball commentary in Anaheim for Long Beach State University. By 1990 he had a more regular gig, as a television sportscaster on station KCBA in Salinas, California. At 26, the young comic began to be noticed by a viewing public that responded to Kilborn's off–the–cuff sports commentary and on–air comedy routines, such as the time he convinced two men in a bar to recreate a Pay–Per–View boxing title match for those who couldn't pay. In 1993, the all–sports cable station ESPN spied Kilborn in action and offered him his first big break: anchorman of their freewheeling show *SportsCenter.* He stayed at that post for three seasons, during which *Sport* reviewer Jeff Weinstock called Kilborn's performance "the greatest boon to the hack sports fan since the hatching of the slow pitch softball."

In 1996 Kilborn agreed to be represented by the high–powered Creative Artists Agency; that led to a job offer from cable's Comedy Central. He agreed to host their new *Daily Show,* in a slot recently vacated by comic Bill Maher's *Politically Incorrect,* which had moved to a broadcast network. *The Daily Show* provided a prime backdrop for the emerging Kilborn persona, that of a self–confident, sometimes cocky former jock. As Alyssa Katz described it in a *Nation* review, Kilborn "careers through a dada delivery of the day's news (interrupting himself for updates later in the show) and a chat with a B–list celebrity. The interviews are capped, in loving homage to the TV genre infotainment helped destroy, by a short quiz consisting of five questions, such as 'How high is the sky?'" Other features, such as the televangelist–clipfest "GodStuff," hinted at an edge behind the humor. The show's reporters were known to sign off with such niceties as, "Thanks, Craig, you manly white heterosexual." To Katz, "it all makes for a fine parody of infotainment's nonstop chatter, that insistently upbeat language that attempts to speak to as many people as possible while offending none, with the inevitable result of making viewers feel anything from bored to embarrassed to despairing." Kilborn received a Cable ACE award nomination for *The Daily Show.*

During Kilborn's tenure at the *Daily Show,* some news articles reported rancor on the set and a dissatisfied host. Kilborn himself told *Entertainment Weekly*'s Joe Flint that while the cable comedy "was obviously a great platform," still "from day one I wanted to leave." He got the opportunity in 1999 with his biggest booking to date: taking the reins of *The Late Late Show,* a CBS mainstay that had previously been hosted by Tom Snyder. "The irreverent Kilborn may seem an odd choice for the determinedly square Eye network," remarked Flint, "but really what's the net got to lose? For four seasons now, its late–night ratings have trailed behind NBC's." As for his new competition—Jay Leno, David Letterman, and especially timeslot rival Conan O'Brien, of NBC's established hit *Late Night,* Kilborn joked that he would deliver success "as long as expectations are low."

The Late Late Show began to thrive, helped along by Kilborn's fresh new approach. Revisiting the show after two seasons, an *Entertainment Weekly* reviewer felt that its host had "actually gotten better" with his network experience. "Of all the late–night hosts, [Kilborn's] the one who projects a false persona: that of a self–absorbed, horny cad (or at least, I HOPE it's false). This ironic distance leads him to make jokes about his own vanity." On at least one occasion, Kilborn's comedy went too far: During the presidential election campaign of 2000, *The Late Late Show* ran a picture of George W. Bush with the caption, "Snipers Wanted." The Federal Communications Commission was not amused; Kilborn apologized for the faux pas.

Then came September 11, 2001. After planes hijacked by terrorists wreaked havoc in New York City, Washington, D.C., and rural Pennsylvania, American broadcast television was pre–empted for days of around–the–clock news reports. When the networks began a tentative return to their regular schedule, the producers and stars of nightly entertainment faced a crisis of conscience. Suddenly, nothing was funny; the kind of cutting detachment that characterized late–night stand–up now seemed inappropriate. Manhattan–based David Letterman returned to the air with a "cold opening" (no music or monologue) and a conversation with newsman Dan Rather. In Los Angeles, Kilborn likewise opened his show from behind his desk. His welcoming remarks were serious. Speaking for Generation X, Kilborn said, "We weren't around for World War II [or] the Kennedy assassination," as he was quoted in an *Entertainment Weekly* article. "We have a dilemma on our show. When do we go back to comedy?" Kilborn brought on news analyst Lawrence O'Donnell, who pointed out entertainment during wartime was an American tradition that stretched as far back as Bob Hope's overseas tours during World War II.

As the nation slowly eased back into the realm of entertainment, Kilborn remained with *The Late, Late Show.* In January of 2002 *Star Tribune* reporter Neal Justin found the host and his writing staff preparing for an interview with Marlee Matlin by brainstorming a raft of jokes that took a less–than–tasteful approach to the actor's deafness. But, as Justin pointed out, none of the offensive material made it to the air; "[i]n fact, *Late, Late Show* is considerably more conservative than its primary competition, *Late Night with Conan O'Brien,* which boasts such characters as Triumph the Insult Comic Dog and the Masturbating Bear." To Kilborn, such edgy antics are not his style. "I don't do oral–sex jokes," he told Justin. "I don't like stuff that's too detailed, too graphic."

Among the crop of late–night talk–show hosts—Letterman, Leno, O'Brien—Kilborn distinguished himself with a different image—less the lively "frat boy" enamored of silly humor, and more what Justin called "the cool cat in the corner, sipping a martini." Indeed, Kilborn's role model was the mature Johnny Carson: "I thought he was smooth," the comic remarked in Justin's article. He brought his sensibilities to a stint as guest editor of the men's magazine, *Gear.* Foreswearing the monthly's regular "Sex" column, Kilborn told Lisa Granatstein of *Mediaweek* that he alerted the staff: "Listen, in my issue I want to read about hand–holding and neck–kissing. That's it."

Sources

Entertainment Weekly, April 4, 1997, p. 72; January 16, 1998, p. 53; March 26, 1999, p. 68; August 14, 2001; September 18, 2001; October 9, 2002.

Esquire, January, 1998, p. 40.

InStyle, November 1, 2002, p. 254.

Mediaweek, June 4, 2001, p. 44; May 6, 2002, p. 31.

Nation, December 23, 1996, p. 34.

People, March 10, 1997, p. 71; November 15, 1999, p. 139.

Rolling Stone, May 15, 1997, p. 122.

Sport, July, 1996, p. 14.

Star Tribune (Minneapolis–St. Paul, MN), January 2, 2002.

—*Susan Salter*

Judith Krantz

AP/Wide World Photos

Author

Born Judith Bluma Tarcher, January 9, 1928, in New York, NY; daughter of Jack D. (an advertising executive) and Mary (an attorney; maiden name, Braeger) Tarcher; married Stephen Krantz (an independent film producer and author), February, 1954; children: Nicholas, Anthony. *Education:* Wellesley College, B.A., 1948.

Addresses: *Agent*—Morton Janklow, 598 Madison Ave., New York, NY 10022. *Home*—Orange County, CA. *Office*—c/o Stephen Krantz Productions, 9601 Wilshire Blvd., Ste. 343, Beverly Hills, CA 90210.

Career

Worked as a fashion publicist in Paris, France, late 1940s; fashion editor, *Good Housekeeping* magazine, New York City, 1949–56; contributing writer, *McCall's,* 1956–59; contributing writer, *Ladies' Home Journal,* 1959–71; contributing West Coast editor, *Cosmopolitan,* 1971–79; published first novel, *Scruples,* 1978.

Sidelights

Though her career as a best–selling author began relatively late in life, Judith Krantz ranks as one of the best–selling writers of commercial fiction in late twentieth century. Beginning with her racy novel *Scruples* in 1978, this onetime magazine writer has penned nine other tales of love and redemption set against a backdrop of jet–set travel and lavish spending. Her heroines have struck a particular chord with women: they are universally beautiful, stylish, intelligent, ambitious, and ultimately irresistible to men. By 2000, Krantz's books had sold 80 million copies and been translated into 52 languages.

Krantz was born in 1928 into a family of Russian–Jewish heritage. At the time, her parents, Jack and Mary Tarcher, were living in New York City's bohemian enclave of Greenwich Village. Krantz's literary penchant for compelling female characters seems to have been rooted in her own family history: her paternal grandmother had abandoned three children and run away with a married man; Krantz and her younger siblings were warned never to speak of the matter to their father. Krantz's Brooklyn–born mother grew up in such poverty that as a teenager that she was forced to leave school to work in a candy factory; a fortuitous marriage to Jack Tarcher, then a rising advertising executive, enabled her to continue her education. At the time of Krantz's birth, her mother had just finished graduate degree work in economics at Columbia University, and went on to earn a law degree from New York University.

Krantz and her siblings grew up in a fabled New York City of the 1930s, ensconced in a grand apartment building on Central Park West. Their parents were friendly with many leading personalities drawn from the city's artistic community, and were active in numerous Jewish philanthropic causes as well. Krantz was enrolled in the private Birch Wathen School for girls in Manhattan from the first grade, and became a model student. Bookish but socially inept, she claimed to have never entertained "romantic fantasies" as a girl, she told *Redbook* writer Joan Smith. "I had clothes fantasies. I thought that if I had absolutely perfect clothes, everyone would like me," Krantz recalled. "Being unpopular as a child and not knowing why is one of the most traumatic experiences you can have. You spend the rest of your life making up for it."

Skipping her junior year of high school, Krantz entered Wellesley College in Massachusetts at the age of 16. She claims to have been the only Jewish girl from New York City to enter that class. Her social life improved considerably as she entered her teens when she discovered a talent for flirting. She dated several young, accomplished, Ivy League men, but retained her chastity until her 21st year, which she spent in Paris working for a public–relations firm tied to the couture industry. There, Krantz became involved with her American boss and was even living with him in a former brothel when her father visited; she announced that she had no intention of marrying her beau. "As far as I was concerned, marriage had always loomed as the gateway to slavery and I truly pitied the hordes of my classmates who'd rushed into it right after graduation," Krantz wrote in her autobiography, *Sex and Shopping: Confessions of a Nice Jewish Girl*. Her father ordered her to return home, and she dutifully obeyed.

A former classmate of hers at Birch Wathen, future television journalist Barbara Walters, introduced Krantz to her future husband, television executive Steve Krantz. The two were married in early 1954, despite Krantz's misgivings and her gulping of an enormous glass of bourbon just before the ceremony. As her husband's career accelerated, Krantz worked for a time as an accessories editor for *Good Housekeeping* magazine before giving birth to the first of their two sons. Over the next two decades, the Krantzes divided their time between New York City and a Westport, Long Island, summer home; they also traveled to Europe often and Krantz enjoyed a satisfying career as a freelance contributing writer to *McCall's* and *Ladies' Home Journal*. A longstanding acquaintance with film producer David Brown introduced Krantz to his wife Helen Gurley Brown, the legendary editor of *Cosmopolitan* magazine, and Krantz began writing for the publication in the early 1970s, when it became a must–read for sexually liberated women. She served as *Cosmo*'s West Coast editor after her family moved to Beverly Hills in 1977, and gained a small measure of fame for her article "The Myth of the Multiple Orgasm."

Krantz's husband had always encouraged her to write fiction, but a paper in a creative writing class at Wellesley—marked a "B" because of her poor spelling—had been her first and last attempt. She realized, however, that she had a talent for writing sex scenes when she was asked to do a feature for *Cosmopolitan* about women's fantasies and had to come up with some racy ones herself. Her shopping excursions on Beverly Hill's burgeoning new exclusive retail strip, Rodeo Drive, gave her the idea for a novel about a hip boutique. She went home one day and wrote some pages, and when she showed them to her husband, he told her to go and write more. "This was better than flying, it was better than anything I'd ever done at a typewriter before; it was like uncorking a bottle of champagne, it was as if I'd been meant to do this all my life, I realized, as I finished the first chapter of *Scruples*," she recalled in her autobiography.

"Scruples" was the name of a fictional boutique owned by the fabulous Wilhelmina "Billy" Ikehorn, the fictional heroine. Krantz had sent her manuscript to a friend, the powerful New York literary agent Morton L. Janklow, who then offered it to a highly regarded Simon & Schuster editor, Michael Korda. However, Korda declined the *Scruples* manuscript on the grounds that there were too many characters and plots, but it would be the only rejection letter that Krantz would ever receive. Crown published it instead in March of 1978. Within weeks, copies of *Scruples* were selling out across the country, and by summertime it had reached No. 1 on the *New York Times* bestseller list. In the end, Krantz's literary debut sold 220,000 copies in hardcover and more than three million in paperback.

Scruples was quickly adapted into a television miniseries starring Lindsay Wagner, and Krantz went straight to work on her second novel, *Princess Daisy*. She earned a $400,000 advance for it and the paperback rights were acquired by Bantam Books for $3.2 million, setting an industry record that broke that of Mario Puzo and *The Godfather* a few years earlier. The windfall prompted Krantz's mother to cut her out of her will, remarking that her daughter no longer needed the money. Like the rest of Krantz's books, *Princess Daisy* featured an improbably beautiful heroine who overcomes personal or financial hardship, some spectacularly failed romances, and various other crises to triumph both personally and professionally—often on an internationally impressive scale. Again, Krantz's work sold well and landed on the bestseller lists, though critics savaged it, as they had done with her debut work.

Krantz's third novel, *Mistral's Daughter*, was published in 1982 and centered on a fictional French painter and renowned cad, Julien Mistral, and the women in his life. Krantz told *Town & Country* interviewer Bill Higgins that despite the litany of designer names and jet–set enclaves that make up her plots, it is her protagonists's ambitions that drive her. "I start with a job," she told Higgins. "The first thing I look for is my heroine's profession. She has to work in an interesting field in which a woman can really make a mark. As soon as I find the right job for her, I know my heroine will come out of the ether." This formula worked well for Krantz's 1986 novel *I'll Take Manhattan,* in which plucky Maxi Amberville takes over her father's publishing empire and launches a terrifically successful women's magazine despite her brother's attempts at sabotage. Maxi is a characteristically vivacious beauty in the Krantzian style: she "was, somehow, more real than other people, more *there*," Krantz writes, "... formed like a great courtesan of the Belle Époque, with a tiny waist, excellent deep breasts, and sumptuous hips.... she would have been riveting in a room full of beautiful women, for she made mere beauty seem not only irrelevant but uninteresting."

Krantz's fifth novel, *Till We Meet Again,* featured Eve Coudert, a singer in France in the years before World War I who weds a champagne mogul. Her two spirited daughters, Freddy and Delphine, carry on her legacy. The 1990s began for Krantz with the publication of *Dazzle,* in which photographer Jazz Kilkullen emerges triumphant in love despite some initial bad calls and then battles to save her family's vast California coastal ranch. *Scruples Two* continues the Billy Ikehorn saga, while 1994's *Lovers* follows the trail of her stepdaughter Gigi. *Spring Collection,* from 1996, is set amidst the Paris fashion world and the supermodels who work for the lovely Justine Loring and her agency. Krantz's tenth novel, *The Jewels of Tessa Kent,* revolves around actress Tessa and the illegitimate child she bore as a teenager.

"Tessa" was a somewhat of a departure for Krantz, who preferred to tag her heroines with men's names. "When I was growing up, my parents knew George Gershwin's sister," she told *Los Angeles Magazine* writer Jessica Yellin. "Her name was Frankie, which struck me as being extremely glamorous." Critical response to Krantz's work over the years has been mixed; reviewers tend to view her works as a sex–and–shopping–fueled cotton candy for undiscriminating readers. *Buffalo News* writer Emily Simon remarked that Krantz has "always written great heroines—self–sufficient, strong–willed heroines who remain incredibly shallow in the face of insurmountable odds."

In 2000, Krantz published her *Sex and Shopping* autobiography, titling it in mock homage to her critics's slurs. In it, she confessed that her seemingly charmed life had not been without its challenging times. Engaging for a number of years in Freudian analysis—despite two unsatisfactory therapists—had, in the end, helped her deal with the legacy of an aloof father and bitter mother. It also brought insight that Krantz deployed in her novels. "I learned to forgive or ignore or deal with people who couldn't help being troubled and troublesome," she wrote about her years of psychoanalysis in *Sex and Shopping.* "I doubt seriously that I could have ever written fiction without analysis, since it's essential for me to know exactly why my characters act and react. They can do nothing without an inner psychological truth that satisfies me."

The irrepressible spirit of Krantz's heroines seems not far from her own sense of self: she once conquered her fear of flying by learning to fly a plane. She and her husband lived in Paris from 1983 to 1986—during the making of the miniseries of *Mistral's Daughter*—and reside in the upscale Balboa Peninsula enclave of Orange County in California. Married for 45 years when her autobiography was published, she writes of her own storybook romance. "Maybe the reason I couldn't make up my mind to marry Steve is that it was already made up and I just couldn't bring myself to admit it," Krantz reflects. "This must be the reason why so many characters in my books often, and convincingly, fall in love at first sight."

Selected writings

Scruples, Crown (New York City), 1978.
Princess Daisy, Crown, 1980.
Mistral's Daughter, Crown, 1982.
I'll Take Manhattan, Crown, 1986.
Till We Meet Again, Crown, 1988.
Dazzle, Crown, 1990.
Scruples Two, Crown, 1992.
Lovers, Crown, 1994.
Spring Collection, Crown, 1996.
The Jewels of Tessa Kent, Crown, 1998.
Sex and Shopping: Confessions of a Nice Jewish Girl, St. Martin's (New York City), 2000.

Sources

Books

Krantz, Judith, *Sex and Shopping: Confessions of a Nice Jewish Girl,* St. Martin's, 2000.

Periodicals

Booklist, March 1, 2000, p. 1146.
Buffalo News (Buffalo, NY), May 7, 2000, p. F7.
Daily News (Los Angeles, CA), April 18, 1996, p. L10.
Daily Record (Glasgow, Scotland), March 22, 2000, p. 28.
Entertainment Weekly, April 29, 1994, p. 74; April 19, 1996, p. 70.
Los Angeles Magazine, April 1996, p. 26.

New Republic, September 15, 1986, p. 38.
New York Times, March 19, 1978.
People, January 28, 1991, p. 22; April 4, 1994, p. 27.
Publishers Weekly, March 11, 1996, p. 42; August 17, 1998, p. 44; April 10, 2000, p. 80.
Redbook, May 2000, p. 76.
Town & Country, November 1998, p. 184.
Washington Post, April 1, 1996, p. D2.

—Carol Brennan

Ashton Kutcher

AP/Wide World Photos

Actor

Born Christopher Ashton Kutcher, February 7, 1978, in Cedar Rapids, IA; son of Larry and Diane Kutcher (both factory workers); stepson of Mark Portwood (a construction worker). *Education:* Attended University of Iowa, Iowa City.

Addresses: *Agent*—Endeavor, 9701 Wilshire Blvd., 10th Floor, Beverly Hills, CA 90212.

Career

Actor in films, including: *Distance,* 1997; *Coming Soon,* 1999; *Switch,* 1999; *Down to You,* 2000; *Reindeer Games,* 2000; *Dude, Where's My Car?* 2000; *Texas Rangers,* 2001; *The Guest,* 2001; *Just Married,* 2003; *The Boss's Daughter,* 2003; *The Butterfly Effect,* 2003. Producer of films, including: *The Boss's Daughter,* 2003; *The Butterfly Effect,* 2003. Television appearances include: *That '70s Show,* 1998—; *2000 MTV Movie Awards,* 2000; *Rocky Horror 25: Anniversary Special,* 2000; *My VH1 Music Awards,* 2000; *2001 MTV Movie Awards,* 2001; *Making the Band,* 2001; *Just Shoot Me,* 2001; *Punk'd,* 2003—.

Sidelights

Iowa–born Ashton Kutcher, star of Fox TV's popular sitcom, *That '70s Show,* clearly has a lot more on the ball than carefree and clueless Michael Kelso, the character he portrays on the long–running comedy series. Asked by Juan Morales of *InStyle* what he might be doing if he were not in show business, the young actor said he probably would be finishing up his master's degree at Purdue or Massachu-

setts Institute of Technology and going into genetic engineering, a field in which it's impossible to imagine Kelso at all. Whatever Kutcher might be doing, however, one thing is clear. It would be something that made him happy. As he told Morales, "I only do things that make me happy."

Although he's best known for his portrayal of the bumbling Kelso on TV, Kutcher is quickly making his presence known on the big screen. With about a dozen films under his belt by the spring of 2003, Kutcher looks forward to a long career in motion pictures. In fact, he told *Teen,* he is hoping to pattern his career after that of another actor who got his start in teen–oriented films such as *Taps, The Outsiders,* and *Risky Business:* "I want to be like Tom Cruise ... and go on and do amazing movies for a long time." To show fans and filmmakers alike that he's able to do more than play hapless stoner teens in comedy films, Kutcher took a far different role in the psychological thriller, *The Butterfly Effect.* In the film, Kutcher plays a young man tortured by repressed childhood memories who discovers a way to travel back in time to inhabit the body of his boyhood. "It's the first time I've done dark drama on film," he told Donna Freydkin of *USA Today,* "and it was great."

Kutcher made his debut as an impresario for the small screen in March of 2003, when MTV began airing *Punk'd,* of which the young star is co–creator, executive producer, and host. The show, which focuses on sometimes–complex practical jokes, played on such celebrity notables as singers Britney Spears, Justin Timberlake, Pink, Kelly Osbourne, and actor Frankie Muniz, got such a warm reception from the viewing public that MTV announced in June of 2003 it would air 20 more episodes of the show, beginning that fall.

Born Christopher Ashton Kutcher in Cedar Rapids, Iowa, on February 7, 1978, he beat his fraternal twin brother, Michael, into the world by five minutes. The son of Larry and Diane Kutcher, both of whom worked in factories, he spent the first 15 years of his life in Iowa's second largest city. In addition to his twin brother, Kutcher has an older sister, Tausha. When he was 13, Kutcher's parents divorced; he and his brother and sister stayed with their mother. Adding to the trauma of Kutcher's 13th year was the emergency heart transplant surgery of brother Michael, who went into cardiac arrest after suffering from myocarditis, a viral heart inflammation. Looking back on the family crisis, Michael told *People* that "Ashton never left my side. He showed me the love one brother has for another." For his part, Ashton told *People,* "If I could give him my heart so that he could live, I would have."

Two years after the divorce, Kutcher's mother remarried. With their mother and new stepfather, construction worker Mark Portwood, the Kutcher siblings moved to the small farm community of Homestead, about 30 miles southwest of Cedar Rapids. No longer could Kutcher stroll through the familiar surroundings of his neighborhood to Washington High School in Cedar Rapids; he now traveled 25 miles roundtrip each day by school bus to Clear Creek Amana High in Tiffin. However, he soon adjusted to the change and continued to pursue the two great passions of his school years— acting and wrestling. The student thespian had made his stage debut as a thief in a seventh–grade production of *The Crying Princess and the Golden Goose* and continued to appear in school plays and musicals whenever the opportunity arose. However, it was not until his senior year that Kutcher snared the meaty role for which he'd so long hungered. Selected to play Daddy Warbucks in the school's production of *Annie,* Kutcher dove into the role, going so far as to have his head shaven. However, before the musical was ever staged, Kutcher was caught trying to break into the school after hours (just a prank, he insisted) and was banned from all extra-curricular activities, *Annie* included. This was a bitter disappointment, but it did little to dampen Kutcher's interest in acting.

After graduating from high school in 1996, Kutcher decided to study biochemical engineering at the University of Iowa, hoping that someday he might be able to find a cure for the cardiomyopathy that had almost cost his brother his life. Once on campus in Iowa City, he pledged Delta Chi fraternity but found his free time limited as he struggled to earn the money he needed to help pay for college. To help ends meet, he took on a wide variety of part–time jobs, including sweeping up cereal dust at the local General Mills factory, washing dishes, roofing, and gutting and skinning deer. When all else failed, Kutcher donated blood to get a few extra dollars. Of his job at General Mills, Kutcher told *People:* "It was $12 an hour. Can't beat that! Except that I'd come home looking like a battered tenderloin."

Kutcher's big break came out of nowhere during his first year in college. As he told an interviewer for *TeenPeople.com,* "One night I was at a bar and a lady came up and asked if I wanted to be a model. I didn't even know that was real job. I thought Fabio was the only male model. Then I realized, 'Oh, the Marlboro Man isn't really a cowboy.' " So I thought I'd give it a shot." Kutcher entered the Fresh Faces of Iowa modeling contest and, much to his surprise, won. As the winner he was given an all–expenses–paid trip to New York City to compete in the 1997 International Model and Talent Agency competition. It was during this contest that Kutcher caught the attention of the Next agency, which quickly put him to work modeling for such top designers as Calvin Klein, Tommy Hilfiger, and Versace. It was during a shoot for the Abercrombie & Fitch catalog in the fall of 1997 that he met and was smitten by January Jones, an actress and model.

In the spring of 1998, Kutcher flew to Los Angeles to audition for a couple of upcoming TV shows. He tried out on the same day for roles in *Wind on Water,* the tale of two professional surfers who put their careers on hold to help their mother save the family's Hawaiian cattle ranch, and *That '70s Show,* a look at the lives of several teenage friends in mid–1970s Wisconsin. To complicate matters, Kutcher landed both of the roles for which he'd read, forcing him to make a very tough decision. In the end, he decided to go with the comedy, a fortuitous decision indeed, since *Wind on Water* was cancelled shortly after its debut.

A big part of the appeal of *That '70s Show* to Kutcher was the way in which the plight of its leading characters echoed some of the frustrations of his teenage years in Iowa's farm country. "You're sincerely believing you are living in the most boring town on the face of the earth," he told Gary Levin of *USA Today*. "You have to find your own fun. I kind of grew up doing that, so I'm able to relate to the character in the show." Terry Turner, one of the series' creators, told *People* that Kutcher impressed the show's producers with "his enthusiasm and innocence."

Although *That '70s Show* was panned by a handful of critics, most seemed impressed by the sitcom's largely successful effort to replicate the polyestered mindlessness of the disco decade. In naming the show to its 10 Best Shows of 1998, Ken Tucker in *Entertainment Weekly* observed, "People who dismiss it as conventional don't recognize *That '70s Show* as a heightened (and frequently high) version of the conventional '70s sitcom." Even more lavish in his praise for the show was *USA Today* critic Robert Bianco, who wrote, "Charm is not a word you normally associate with the Day–Glo, drug–drenched '70s. Yet charm is the strong suit of *That '70s Show*, a sweet comedy … that pokes gentle fun at the oddities of the bicentennial decade. Set in a Wisconsin suburb in 1976, this sitcom trip to the baby–boomer past should attract both those who are nostalgic for the '70s and those who are simply bemused by the era's excesses."

Away from the set of the popular Fox sitcom, Kutcher sought to translate his growing TV success into similar good fortune on the big screen. He picked up minor roles in 2000's *Down to You* and *Reindeer Games* but later that same year landed a starring role in *Dude, Where's My Car*. That film, which proved immensely popular with young moviegoers, paired Kutcher with Sean William Scott, who'd first hit it big in *American Pie*. The film capitalized on the same sort of dimwitted brilliance of his TV character. He followed up on his success in *Dude* with a somewhat more serious role opposite James Van Der Beek in 2001's *Texas Rangers*. In his critique of the film for Daily–Reviews.com, Chuck Dowling wrote that he "was hoping Ashton Kutcher wouldn't be playing another giddy dork. His role starts out deathly serious, and I was pleasantly surprised. But soon after he's bouncing around like a gibbon on crack."

Despite the disappointing showing of *Texas Rangers*, Kutcher bounced back in early 2003 with *Just Married*, in which he starred opposite Brittany Murphy. Although the notices for the film were lukewarm at best, *Just Married* proved a big hit with young moviegoers who kept it in the box office Top Ten for nearly a month. Kutcher also made his debut as a film producer in 2003, serving in that capacity on *The Boss's Daughter* and as executive producer of *The Butterfly Effect*. In July of 2003, Kutcher inked a deal to stay with *That '70s Show* through 2004–05; it was estimated that he would earn $5–7 million for that season.

Despite his immense popularity, Kutcher has somehow managed to remain grounded and true to his country roots. He cooks his own meals, watches wrestling on TV, plays basketball, and hangs out with his friends. His closest pals include Wilmer Valderrama, Danny Masterson, and other members of the cast of *That '70s Show*. On the romantic front, Kutcher in the spring of 2001 ended his longtime relationship with Jones. Not long thereafter he began dating actress Ashley Scott. When he and Scott broke up in the spring of 2002, Kutcher began a relationship with *Just Married* costar Brittany Murphy, which ended in April of 2003. Not long after the split with Murphy, he created a tabloid sensation when he started making the rounds in Hollywood with actress Demi Moore, 15 years his senior. Although he enjoys his time off, Kutcher feels most comfortable when he is working. As he told *USA Today*'s Freydkin, "I'm very awkward when I have time off—I don't know what to do with myself. It's weird not to work."

Sources

Books

Contemporary Theatre, Film, and Television, volume 39, Gale Group, 2002.

Periodicals

AP Online, June 23, 2003.
Entertainment Weekly, December 25, 1998, p. 124.
InStyle, February 2003, p. 121.
People, November 2, 1998, p. 75.
Teen, September 2000, p. 64.
USA Today, August 21, 1998, p. 6E; December 11, 1998, p. 12E; March 16, 2003, p. 1D.

Online

"Artist Biography: Ashton Kutcher," Blockbuster. com, http://www.blockbuster.com/bb/person/details/0,7621,BIO–P242492,00.html (March 27, 2003).
"Ashton Kutcher," Internet Movie Database, http://www.imdb.com/Name?Kutcher,%20Ashton (March 25, 2003).

"Spotlight Stats: Ashton Kutcher," *TeenPeople.com,* http://www.teenpeople.com/teenpeople/stars/spotlight/stats/0,8044,91181,00.html (March 21, 2003).

"Stuck in the '70s," E! Online, http://www.eonline.com/News/firstlook.html?tnews (July 7, 2003).

"Texas Rangers" Daily–Reviews.com, http://www.daily–reviews.com/t/texasrangers.htm (March 27, 2003).

—Don Amerman

A. G. Lafley

Chairman, President, and Chief Executive Officer of Procter & Gamble

Born Alan George Lafley, June 13, 1947, in Keene, NH; married Margaret; children: Patrick, Alex. *Education:* Hamilton College, B.A. (history), 1969; Harvard Business School, M.B.A., 1977.

Addresses: Procter & Gamble, Cincinnati, OH.

Career

U.S. Navy, 1970–75; Procter & Gamble (P&G), brand assistant for Joy, 1977; assistant brand manager for Tide, 1978; brand manager for Dawn and Ivory Snow, 1980; brand manager for special assignment and Ivory Snow, 1981; brand manager for Cheer, 1982; associate advertising manager, PS&D Division, 1983; advertising manager, PS&D Division, 1986; general manager for laundry products, PS&D Division, 1988; vice president—laundry and cleaning products, P&G USA, 1991; group vice president, P&G Company, 1992–95; president—laundry and cleaning products, P&G USA, 1992; president—laundry and cleaning products, P&G Far East, 1994; executive vice president, P&G Company, 1995; president—North America, P&G North America, 1998; president, Global Beauty Care and North America, 1999; president and chief executive, 2000; chairman, president, and chief executive, 2002—.

Member: General Motors Corporation Board of Directors; Business Council; Business Roundtable Board of Trustees; Hamilton College trustee; Lauder Institute Board of Governors; Cincinnati Institute of Fine Arts Board of Trustees; Cincinnati Playhouse in the Park.

Sidelights

After becoming head of Procter & Gamble (P&G) in 2000, A. G. Lafley, chairman, president, and chief executive, has put the ailing consumer–products giant back on its corporate feet. Refocusing the company on its big, successful, and well–known brands such as Tide and Crest resulted in net profits that rose to $910 million in 2002, after a loss of $320 million in the comparable 2001 period. Crest also regained its number–one spot in oral care brands in the United States. According to Lafley, this is the result of getting the company back to its basic selling techniques.

Silver–haired, soft–spoken Lafley had been a P&G veteran when he took over the top job. Typically self–effacing, he explained his swift success to Daniel Eisenberg in *Time*, "We had gotten into a mind–set where innovation had to flow into new categories and new brands exclusively, and all I did was open people's minds to [the possibility] that it could also flow through our established brands."

Lafley was born in Keene, New Hampshire, on June 13, 1947. He received a B.A. from Hamilton College in 1969 and an M.B.A. from Harvard Business

School in 1977. From 1970 to 1975, he served in the U.S. Navy. It was in the service that he gained his first experience in merchandising as a supply officer during the war in Vietnam. He also spent three years in Asia for P&G in the mid–1990s, where he built a booming business for the company in China and breathed new life into the cosmetics market in Japan.

Lafley has spent all his working life at P&G, joining the company in June of 1977 as a brand assistant. Lafley rose from the assistant brand manager for Tide in 1978 to brand manager for Dawn and Ivory Snow in 1980 and then Cheer in 1982. His next promotion was to associate advertising manager of the PS&D Division in 1983 and then advertising manager in 1986. Two years later he became general manager of laundry products, then vice president of laundry and cleaning products in 1991, and group vice president in 1992. After spending some time in Asia in the Far East division, he returned in 1998 to become executive vice president of the company and president—North America. He moved on to president of Global Beauty Care and North America in 1999, president and chief executive of the company in 2000, and also chairman in 2002.

P&G was formed in 1837 by a maker of candles, William Procter, and a producer of soap, James Gamble. Since that time, it climbed to the top of the corporate world, offering the everyday consumer a vast array of daily needs from beauty products to household products to food. Its name became a household term, with such a range of products that it became almost impossible for the American consumer *not* to buy a P&G brand.

In the 1990s, however, P&G became an ailing giant. Its stock dropped drastically. Many of its products were losing their top spots in the sales market. In early 1998, Durk Jager, a tough–talking native of the Netherlands, was brought in as chief executive to turn the company around and send it charging into the twenty–first century. Jager's idea was to boost the company's research and development end by pouring money into and hoping for the next "million–dollar product" with the launch of several new product brands. The last time P&G had scored big with a new product was with the introduction of Pampers disposable diapers in 1961. But the company was slow to respond to Jager's methods. Attempts to buy Warner–Lambert and American Home Products in the pharmaceutical industry failed. An aggressive restructuring program within the company left many of the 110,000 workers upset with their new jobs. Some new products, such as Febreeze, a fabric deodorizer, did become successful and Jager acquired Iams, a pet food business, and Recovery engineering, a water filter producer.

Yet overall, results were disappointing and morale, along with profits, was falling. By early 2002, P&G was in a slump. By mid–year, its stock had dropped by half in the previous six months, losing $70 billion in market value. Jager ended the shortest tenure for a P&G chief executive officer by abruptly resigning in June. Lafley, then a 23–year–veteran with the company, was named his successor. P&G stock dropped another $4 with the announcement and continued to slide over the next three weeks; no one had high hopes for the company's resurrection, especially in the midst of a worldwide economic depression.

Two years later, Procter & Gamble was reported in fine financial shape, its best record in ages. Besides its growth in net profits, net earnings per share rose almost 52% over the previous year. Revenues rose; the stock dividends climbed.

Lafley's approach was not innovative or earth shaking. He simply went back to basics. As he saw it, P&G did not need a big makeover, it just needed to sell more of its trusted brands. Instead of looking for the new blockbuster product, Lafley concentrated on the core brands of the company. As he said in an article for *Alochona* magazine in 2002, his basic strategy worked for him in the navy: "I learned there that even when you've got a complex business, there's a core, and the core is what generates most of the cash, most of the profits. The trick was to find the few things that were really going to sell, and sell as many of them as you could." It was so simple that it apparently worked. Everyone at P&G could see that it was easier to try and sell more boxes of well–known Pampers than to try and invent a new disposable diaper. However, if a tried–and–true product just is not selling, Lafly is not afraid to let it go; such was the case with Jif peanut butter.

Lafley is not sticking completely with faith in core brands only. He paid $5 billion for Clairol's hair care business. It is estimated that health care and beauty products could account for about 40 percent of P&G's annual sales by 2010. Other acquisitions were Cover Girl cosmetics, Olay skin products, and Herbal Essences shampoo. Iams pet food is now a mass–market brand. The demand for skin care products and over–the–counter remedies continues to grow at about four to six percent a year. Teenagers especially are big markets for Clairol hair coloring products. Sales for Cover Girl and Max Factor cosmetics are doing very well, although the success of such items tends to depend more on fashion than do the sale of standard household items. Analysts warn that P&G is relatively new in this field. Alliance Bernstein analyst Jim Gingrich told Eisenberg in *Time*, "P&G still has things to learn about how to market products where benefits are more intangible."

The example of the Crest Spinbrush indicates how Lafley has guided P&G to a new track. Steering away from the usual "P&G has to invent it" philosophy, the giant bought a small firm in the Cleveland area for $1.5 million. Its four inventors had come up with a battery–powered toothbrush that could be sold at a profit for about $6; most electric toothbrushes cost about $50 or more. The inventors deliberately set out to sell the product to P&G. Since they could not afford an advertising compaign, they put the toothbrush in stores with the "try me" approach, allowing people to turn the brush on. This caught the interest of Walgreens and then Wal–Mart in early 2000. With that great success, the inventors got an interview with P&G, and the company bought the product and the firm. Three of the inventors went on the P&G payroll for a year and a half to ensure the smooth operation. With P&G distribution and advertising behind it, the Crest Spinbrush turned into a $200 million megahit. It may not have hit its full potential yet, but the initial signs are excellent. In so doing, Crest has taken back its number–one title in the oral–care market, which it had lost to Colgate in 1998. After the Spinbrush, Colgate launched a new electric toothbrush for $19.95. A few months later, the price was cut to $12.

In a similar, less–expansive move, Lafley reacted to the introduction of a moist toilet paper by the Kimberly–Clark Corporation. He bought a company that made a similar product, an unheard–of move in the "old" P&G. But Lafley makes no secret that this new concept for the old company is one he encourages. He told *Time*'s Eisenberg, "I'd love to see a third to half of 'discovery' come from outside. I really want the doors open."

Under Lafley's direction, P&G is finding new ways to reach its markets. To sell its Actonel osteoporosis prescription medication, it set up screenings for bone density in such places as Wal–Mart. Pantene, a long–selling shampoo, is now classified not as the usual oily, normal, or dry, but by style, such as curly or straighter or thicker. Marketers hand out samples of Olay cleansing cloths at subways and train stations, or anywhere a consumer might be uncomfortably warm.

Lafley's approach to market research has been cited as a major factor in his success. In his type of consumer research, the researcher spends time in the consumer's world as he or she will use the product. This involves interviews on–site with consumers and hours of observation about how products are used. Instead of inviting groups to the company to focus on a product, Lafley believes in his researchers going to the people themselves, in their homes, to see what they are doing with the items that P&G sells. This takes a lot of time, but Lafley believes it is worth it.

Lafley, who admits to being a long–suffering Boston Red Sox fan, keeps himself in shape with swimming, biking, and workouts several times a week. He is married with two sons. Around the company headquarters, he is known as being approachable. He actually wants to hear bad results and is not afraid to give everyone a fair hearing. He urges his employees to get involved, to go see what retailers are doing with P&G products. His easy–going personality hides the crisp determination he has once he has made up his mind about a business decision. Thanks in large part to his own demeanor, the corporate image of P&G is changing from an insulated culture to one that is more open to learning from outsiders.

Some business analysts, however, predict that there will be big bumps for P&G along the road. Some items, such as the Swiffer electrostatic mop, are far from blockbusters, and the jury is still out on the pharmaceutical division. Cautious analysts think the company is better off sticking to what it knows how to do. For the immediate future, however, Lafley seems satisfied to follow his instincts as he leads Procter & Gamble back to the top of consumer minds and pocketbooks.

Sources

Periodicals

BusinessWeek, August 12, 2002, p. 58; July 7, 2003, pp. 52–63.
Journal of Business Strategy, September 2000.
Time, September 16, 2002, pp. 46–48.

Online

"Back to Basics," Alochona, http://magazine. alochona.org/magazine/2002/October/ business/business1.asp (March 15, 2003).
"New Dawn for P&G?," ABC News.com, http:// abcnews.go.com/sections/business/TheStreet/ PG_000609.html (March 15, 2003).

—Rose Blue and Corinne J. Naden

Liz Lange

Fashion designer

Born Elizabeth Steinberg, c. 1967, in New York; married Jeffrey Lange (a financial services entrepreneur), 1996; children: Gus, Alice. *Education:* Earned degree from Brown University, 1988.

Addresses: *Home*—New York, NY. *Office*—Liz Lange Maternity, 958 Madison Ave., New York, NY 10021-2636.

Career

Worked as an assistant editor at *Vogue*, New York City, before 1993; co–founded sportswear line in New York City, 1993; founded Liz Lange Maternity, 1997; opened first eponymous store, c. 1998; moved to larger location on Madison Avenue, 2000; opened first California Liz Lange boutique, 2000; showed line during New York's fashion week, 2001; launched maternity lines for Nike and Target, 2002.

Sidelights

New York City clothing designer Liz Lange is the force behind an extremely successful line of maternity wear that bears her name. Lange's designs have won legions of fans for their understated elegance, and have been hailed as the first of their kind designed for a woman who normally buys Prada or Gucci. In 2001, Lange's clothing line became the first maternity wear ever shown on a runway in the history of Seventh Avenue.

Born Elizabeth Steinberg in the mid–1960s, Lange grew up in New York City. Her father owned an insurance company, while her mother worked as a real–estate broker. She studied comparative literature at Rhode Island's Brown University, graduating in 1988, and after moving back to Manhattan she landed a highly coveted job at *Vogue* as an assistant editor. In 1993, Lange and two partners launched their own sportswear design business. Three years later Lange married, and then many in her circle of friends began to announce their impending parenthood. As stylish New York women, they carped about the dismal selection of maternity wear they found in stores. The few retailers that catered to this niche market offered tent–like shifts, Peter Pan collars, dated prints, and gauche colors. To help, Lange began altering some of her company's existing pieces for her pregnant friends, and the items were an immediate hit. They suggested she launch her own line, after "telling me that they couldn't find anything normal to wear," Lange recalled in an interview with *Inc.* Curious, Lange went on a spurious maternity–shopping field trip herself. "I was pretty horrified by what I saw," she told *Inc.*

Lange's parents loaned her $50,000 in seed money to launch her own maternity line. In October of 1997 she opened "Liz Lange Maternity" as a small, by–appointment–only business in a Manhattan office building. Her first line was made up of ten basic pieces, all with simple lines and in a palette of black, light blue, and camel. She assumed this would be a sedate little business, as she recalled in an interview with *People.* "I thought: Isn't this perfect? I'll make this little line of made–to–order clothing, and the rest of the time I'll be free being this married woman thinking about having a baby," Lange told the magazine. But word of Lange's stylish gear soon caught on, and a *New York Times* mention and then a blurb in *Vogue* caused her business to boom. Suddenly she was fielding calls from across the United States and even overseas. "I had no catalog," she told *Crain's New York Business* writer Ylonda Gault. "All I could do was describe the pieces. And I told everyone I had a no–return policy—which I don't, but I was so overwhelmed I wanted to discourage them." With items ranging from an $85 t–shirt to dress priced at $425, Lange's business earned $400,000 in its first six months of operation, in part from a website she quickly established to take orders. She soon was able to open an actual store on Lexington Avenue.

Lange entered the business at the juncture of a new era: many department stores had stopped stocking maternity lines, the few chain and specialty stores held much of the $450 million maternity–apparel market hostage with their aforementioned moribund styles, and pregnancy suddenly seemed kind of hip. Industry veterans initially scoffed at Lange, warning that it was an especially tough sector for newcomers. There is a six–month window during which expectant women buy clothes, but purchase patterns show that they usually shop ahead—thus stores need to carry several sizes and seasonal lines, and a large inventory is a deadly risk for most retail businesses. Lange planned to grow her business slowly, however. "The industry is underestimating this audience," she told Gault in the *Crain's New York Business* article. "Most women, especially professionals, want to look as sophisticated as they did before they were pregnant." This desire to look chic also seemed to coincide with a plethora of new high–visibility celebrity moms, such as pop star Madonna and model Cindy Crawford. Crawford became a client of Lange's, as did actresses Catherine Zeta–Jones and Téa Leoni. The birth of a son to *Sex and the City* star Sarah Jessica Parker in late 2002 landed both mom and newborn on the cover of *People* soon afterward. *New York Times* journalist Ruth La Ferla observed, in an article about impending motherhood as the new status symbol, that the Parker picture heralded a new mood. "There's a message implicit in such coverage: Step aside, all you single *Sex and the City* types, and make way for the glamazon mom," La Ferla wrote.

Lange became her own best focus group during her first year in business with her son, Gus, born in October of 1998. A daughter named Alice soon followed, as did a retail expansion: a Liz Lange flag-ship emporium opened on Madison Avenue in March of 2000, followed by a Beverly Hills, California, store later that year. In September of 2001, Lange's designs became the first maternity line ever shown in the history of Seventh Avenue, New York's fashion center, during its biannual Fashion Week. American designers from Calvin Klein to Michael Kors presented the coming season's lines to buyers and journalists in runway shows held at Bryant Park, and Lange showed her Spring 2002 line just before the tents were shut down because of the September 11 terrorist attacks on the United States.

Lange has witnessed a change just in the few years since she began her business, with expectant mothers becoming even more chicly attired and proud of their physiques. When she began, her line had a couple of "cover–up"–style items, but as she told the *New York Times*'s La Ferla, demand soon yielded to a more body–hugging look. "Now I couldn't sell anything oversize," Lange said. "Ninety–five percent of my things are closely fitted, and that is by customer demand." To meet the increase in interest for her designs, Lange signed with athletic–gear maker Nike to launch a line of exercise togs, called "Liz Lange for Nike," in 2002. Mass–market retailer Target began carrying an exclusive line of Liz Lange–brand maternity gear in its stores as well.

Lange lives on the Upper East Side with her husband and children, and walks three miles daily around the Central Park Reservoir for exercise.

Sources

Child, March 2002.
Crain's New York Business, June 22, 1998, p. 3; August 13, 2001, p. 19.
DSN Retail Fax, September 23, 2002, p. 1.
Fit Pregnancy, February–March 2002, p. 24.
Inc., November 1999, p. 17.
InStyle, June 1, 2000, p. 118.
Interior Design, April 2001, p. 217.
Los Angeles Business Journal, October 2, 2000, p. 9.
MMR, October 7, 2002, p. 1.
New York Times, November 10, 2002, p. 13.
People, June 21, 1999, p. 81.
Town & Country, May 1999, p. 102.
W, December 1999, p. 208.
WWD, July 5, 2002 p. 3.

—Carol Brennan

Robert S. Langer

Courtesy of Robert S. Langer

Chemical and biomedical engineer and educator

Born Robert Samuel Langer, Jr., August 29, 1948, in Albany, NY; son of Robert Samuel, Sr. (a liquor store owner) and Mary (a homemaker; maiden name, Swartz) Langer; married Laura Feigenbaum, July 31, 1988; children: Michael David, Susan Katherine, Samuel Alexander. *Education:* Cornell University, B.S. (chemical engineering), 1970; Massachusetts Institute of Technology (MIT), Sc.D. (chemical engineering), 1974.

Addresses: *Office*—MIT Department of Chemical Engineering, 77 Massachusetts Ave., Room 342, Cambridge, MA 02139–4307.

Career

Research associate, Children's Hospital, Boston, MA, 1974; assistant professor of chemical and biomedical engineering, MIT, 1978–81; associate professor of chemical and biomedical engineering, MIT, 1981–85; professor of chemical and biomedical engineering, MIT, 1985–89; Kenneth J. Germeshausen professor of chemical and biomedical engineering, MIT, 1989—.

Awards: Outstanding Patent in Massachusetts, Intellectual Property Owners Inc., 1989; John W. Hyatt Service to Mankind Award, Society of Plastic Engineers, 1995, International Award, 1996; Ebert Prize, American Pharmaceutical Association, 1995, 1996, 1999; Research Award, American Diabetes Association, 1996; International Award, Gairdner Foundation, 1996; Wiley Medal, U.S. Food and Drug Ad-

ministration, 1997; Killian Award, MIT, 1997; International Award, Nagai Foundation, 1998; Lemelson–MIT Prize, 1998; Charles Stark Draper Prize, National Academy of Engineering, 2002.

Sidelights

One of America's leading pioneers in the burgeoning field of biomedical engineering, Robert S. Langer is widely recognized as the father of controlled drug delivery and tissue engineering. The Kenneth J. Germeshausen professor of chemical and biomedical engineering at the prestigious Massachusetts Institute of Technology (MIT), Langer came to the field of biomedicine as an outsider, having been trained as a chemical engineer. However, the timing of his entry into biomedicine could not possibly have been more fortuitous. He became involved in the field at a time of impressive advances in both medicine and materials engineering. Drawing on the work of medical researchers and his own research into polymers, Langer has developed vastly improved systems of drug delivery and designed biodegradable polymers on which human tissue can be grown.

Langer and students at his MIT research laboratory hold nearly 400 patents and have published hundreds of scientific papers, most of them focusing on biomedical subjects. So widespread has been the impact of the work done in Langer's lab that one of his early doctoral students told TechTV that there is not a doctor or hospital patient in the United States who has not been touched in some fashion by the scientific processes developed there. In 1998, Langer was awarded the Lemelson–MIT Prize, recognizing the scientist as "one of history's most prolific inventors in medicine," according to MIT's website.

The son of a liquor store owner and a homemaker, Langer was born on August 28, 1948, in Albany, New York. His interest in science in general—and chemistry in particular—was first triggered by a Gilbert chemistry set he received as a gift when he was eleven years old. After high school, Langer enrolled in Cornell University, where he earned his bachelor's degree in chemical engineering in 1970. He next pursued graduate studies at MIT, where in 1974 he earned his doctoral degree in chemical engineering. Like many of his fellow graduates, Langer was deluged with offers from the major oil companies, which found themselves at the time in the midst of an oil crisis. Although he received four job offers from Exxon alone, Langer decided that he might be able to make a greater impact elsewhere.

The opportunity to do great things came when Langer in 1974 accepted a postdoctorate position working with renowned cancer researcher Judah Folkman at Children's Hospital in Boston, the primary pediatric teaching hospital of Harvard Medical School. Folkman had devised a pharmaceutical strategy for inhibiting malignant tumors' ability to create their own blood vessels, a process necessary to fuel tumor growth. However, Folkman needed a reliable system to deliver this inhibitor to tumors, sometimes deep within the body. Folkman assigned Langer to devise a way to gradually release a stream of large molecules into the tissue of lab animals. Polymer experts told Langer it could not be done, but he proved them wrong. Instead of drafting an existing polymer for use in the project, Langer went first to the lab to determine the precise physiological requirements for such a delivery system and them custom–designed a polymer to meet those specifications.

Langer's discovery in Folkman's lab revolutionized the world of drug delivery systems and was but the first such invention by Langer in this arena. In 1986 he collaborated with neurosurgeon Henry Brem in the development of a tiny, dime–sized chemotherapy wafer for the treatment of brain cancer. These wafers, positioned at the site from which a tumor has been surgically removed, slowly release cancer–killing medication to destroy any cancer cells that may have been missed by the surgeon. Because the drugs released by the wafers are largely confined to the tumor site, their impact on other organs is minimized. Similar drug delivery systems have been used to fight ovarian, prostate, and spinal cancers.

Langer has also been a pioneer in the development of remotely controlled drug delivery systems that allow the rate at which a drug is released to be varied using signals delivered by electric impulse, ultrasound, and magnetic field. At Langer's MIT research lab, he and his students in 1999 designed a prototype "pharmacy–on–a–chip" that they hope one day will be able to monitor a patient's blood chemistry and release a precisely measured dosage of medication when it is required. Such an implantable silicon chip could potentially replace injections and pills in the future.

In recent years, Langer has devoted much of his energy to the field of tissue engineering. Working with a framework of biodegradable polymer designed in the shape of a human heart, kidney, or liver, for example, Langer collects human cells from a stem or donor—or ideally from the host—and places them on the plastic framework. The framework is then placed in a carefully controlled environment where over time the cells regenerate and create a new organ. This laboratory–generated organ, along with its polymer scaffold, would then be implanted into a human where blood vessels would regenerate as the plastic framework gradually degraded until nothing of it remained. Already Langer's procedure has been approved by the U.S. Food and Drug Administration for human skin, and clinical trials for other human tissue, including cartilage, are under way. Of the procedure's potential, Langer told Monte Burke of Forbes, "It's plausible to think that in this century, many structures in the human body will be able to be replaced with living tissue that's virtually identical to the normal healthy tissue."

Langer's contributions to biotechnology have not gone unnoticed. Forbes magazine in 1999 named him one of the world's 25 most important individuals in the field, and three years later the magazine picked Langer as one of the 15 innovators most likely to reinvent our future. In 2001, Time and CNN spotlighted the scientist as one of America's top 18 people in science and medicine and one of the 100 most important people in the country. Married since 1988 to Laura Feigenbaum, Langer lives in the Boston suburbs with his wife and three children, Michael, Susan, and Samuel. The family also has a summer home on nearby Cape Cod, where Langer each summer hosts a beach barbecue for the staff of his MIT laboratory. An amateur magician, Langer manages to do the seemingly impossible both on the job and in his spare time. Folkman, with whom Langer remains close, told *Time,* "He's a true genius. He sees answers to problems in such unique ways you can't trace the steps he took."

Selected writings

(With Donald Wise, editor) *Medical Applications of Controlled Release,* volume 1, CRC Press, 1985.

(With Mark Chasin) *Biodegradable Polymers as Drug Delivery Systems,* Marcel Dekker, 1990.

(With William J.M. Hrushesky and Felix Theeuwes) *Temporal Control of Drug Delivery,* New York Academy of Sciences, 1991.

(With Rudolf Steiner and Paul B. Weisz) *Angiogenesis: Key Principles—Science—Technology—Medicine,* Springer Verlag, 1992.

(With Shalaby W. Shalaby, Yoshito Ikada, et al) *Polymers of Biological and Biomedical Significance,* American Chemical Society, 1993.

(With Jeffrey L. Cleland) *Formulation and Delivery of Proteins and Peptides,* American Chemical Society, 1994.

(With Robert P. Lanza and Joseph P. Vacanti) *Principles of Tissue Engineering,* 2nd ed., Academic Press, 2000.

Sources

Books

Complete Marquis Who's Who, Marquis Who's Who, 2003.

Periodicals

Forbes, December 23, 2002, pp. 296–98.
New York Times, January 7, 2002.
Time, August 20, 2001, p. 24, pp. 50–51.

Online

"Dr. Robert Langer," Lemelson–MIT Program, http://web.mit.edu/invent/a–winners/a–langer.html (April 25, 2003).

"MIT's Robert Langer Proves Nice Guys Deliver The Goods," Red Herring, http://www.redherring.com/insider/2002/0115/876.html (April 23, 2003).

"Professor Robert Langer," Langer Lab, http://web.mit.edu/cheme/langerlab/langer.html (April 23, 2003).

"Robert Langer: Engineering Miracles," TechTV, http://www.techtv.com/bigthinkers/features/story/0,23008,3341154,00.html (April 23, 2003).

"Show #102: Dr. Robert Langer," *Scientific American.com,* http://www.sciam.com/mastertech/langer.html (April 23, 2003).

—*Don Amerman*

Nigella Lawson

Journalist, chef, and television personality

Born Nigella Lucy Lawson, January 6, 1960, in England; daughter of Nigel (a politician and Lord Lawson of Blaby) and Vanessa Mary (Salmon) Lawson; married John Diamond (a journalist), September, 1992 (died, March, 2001); children: Cosima Thomasina, Bruno Paul Nigel. *Education:* Lady Margaret Hall College, Oxford University, B.A. (honors), early 1980s.

Addresses: *Home*—London, England. *Office*—c/o Jacquie Drewe, London Management, 2–4 Noel Street, London W1, England.

Career

Editor, Quartet Books, 1982–84; assistant in Arts & Review section, *Sunday Times* (London), 1984–86; deputy literary editor, *Sunday Times,* 1986–88; arts writer, *Sunday Times,* 1988–89; restaurant columnist, *Spectator* (London), 1985–96; columnist, *Evening Standard* (London), 1989–94; columnist, *Times* (London), 1995–98; food writer, *Vogue* (London), 1996—; columnist, *Observer* (London), 1998—; host of television cooking and lifestyle show, *Nigella Bites,* Channel 4, 2000— columnist, *New York Times.*

Awards: Author of the Year, British Book Awards, for *How to Be a Domestic Goddess,* 2000.

Sidelights

British food writer and cookbook author Nigella Lawson found her niche as host of a television show that instantly gained a cult viewership when it was launched in Britain in 2000. Late the next year, *Nigella Bites* began airing on North American cable channels and garnered fans across the Atlantic as well. With her plummy accent, voluptuous figure, and long tresses, Lawson indeed comes across as a "domestic goddess," a term that supplied the title of one of her cookbooks; she was even feted in *People* magazine's "50 Most Beautiful People" issue in 2002. Known for pinching food while cooking and emitting exultant sounds, Lawson also manages to make the recipes seem easy to replicate, and convince her viewers that having a dinner party is a stress–free pleasure. "Lawson certainly does play to the camera," remarked *New York Times* writer Amanda Hesser, "but beneath that satin veneer is a true cook with a valuable message and a groundbreaking show."

Lawson was born in 1960 into a Jewish family in London, England. Her father, Nigel, was a journalist for some years, and her mother, Vanessa, was an heiress to a chain of tea cafés in England. She grew up with two sisters and a brother, and the family lived in posh Kensington and Chelsea abodes, but Lawson had an admittedly difficult childhood. She attended no fewer than five schools, and once refused to take a compulsory math exam. "I was never expelled, although my parents may have been asked to take me out," she recalled in an interview with

Times journalist Catherine O'Brien. "I don't know. I was just difficult, disruptive, good at schoolwork, but rude, I suspect, and too highly strung." In 1970, Lawson's father formally entered politics by running for a seat in the House of Commons, and emerged as a rising Conservative (Tory) party leader. By 1983, he was serving as Britain's Chancellor of the Exchequer, or treasury secretary, under Prime Minister Margaret Thatcher.

Lawson studied medieval and modern languages at Oxford University, and found her first job as a book editor in 1982. Two years later, she was hired at the venerable *Sunday Times* newspaper in London, and became deputy literary editor in 1986. By then she was also writing restaurant reviews for the *Spectator,* and after stints as an arts writer and opinion columnist, Lawson signed on as *British Vogue*'s food writer and started to make guest appearances on celebrity–chef programs. Her husband, onetime *Times* colleague John Diamond, whom she married in Venice in 1992, encouraged her to write her first book, *How to Eat: The Pleasures and Principles of Good Food,* a compendium of recipes and entertaining tips. Sections were organized by topic, such as "Cooking in Advance" and "Weekend Lunch." Acclaimed author Salman Rushdie reviewed it for the *Observer* and admitted he had tested some of the recipes at the Lawson table already. He liked Lawson's mix of literary references and such intriguing personal recollections such as "'I first had salsa verde when I was a chambermaid in Florence....'" After describing it as "comfortingly down–to–earth," Rushdie concluded with the observation that Lawson's "prose is as nourishing as her recipes."

Lawson's second career as a celebrity chef was spurred, in part, by tragedy: in 1997 her husband was diagnosed with throat cancer. He chronicled his illness in his *Times* column, which evolved into a book and then stage play. By late 2000, her husband had his tongue removed and was subsisting on a liquid diet. "I think there must be a connection with the fact that I have become more absorbed in cooking since his illness," Lawson said at the time in the interview with O'Brien for the *Times.* "I can't feed him, so it has to be channelled elsewhere." Diamond died in March of 2001, leaving Lawson a widow at 41 and single parent to Cosima, aged seven, and three–year–old Bruno.

Lawson's show, *Nigella Bites,* was already a hit on Britain's Channel 4, and debuted to American and Canadian audiences late in 2001. Filmed at what was once her West London home with Diamond, the show featured practical and decidedly non-

perfectionist advice, and Lawson was immediately hailed as the antithesis of Martha Stewart. Pundits noted that it would be hard to imagine Lawson's American counterpart moaning rapturously after snatching a bite of torta rustica on–camera. "At its best, *Nigella Bites* makes you want to cook," wrote Hesser in the *New York Times.* "During the few minutes she was cracking eggs and whisking cheese and lemon juice for a pasta sauce, she anticipated and then seamlessly answered many natural questions—why she chose linguine over another pasta and what to do if there's not enough sauce."

Lawson scoffs at the term "gastro–porn," coined to describe her style. "[A]ll food images, if they are successful, have the power to arouse appetite," she told London's *Independent* newspaper. "They should be luscious and sexy. I have no embarrassment about the culinary come–on. But that's the limit of my erotic intent. I am always surprised when people read double entendres into my innocuous babble."

Lawson's other tomes include *How to be a Domestic Goddess,* a compendium of baking recipes and tips, *Nigella Bites: From Family Meals to Elegant Dinners— Easy, Delectable Recipes for Any Occasion,* and *Forever Summer,* the companion to a television show that aired in Britain in 2002. She writes a bi–monthly *New York Times* food column. Lawson lives with advertising–executive/art collector Charles Saatchi in London, and notes that she is far from a paragon of female virtue. "I do shout at the children sometimes," she admitted in the interview with O'Brien for the *Times.* "One of the reasons I spend so much time in the kitchen is so that I don't have to go outside and stand by the swings."

Selected writings

How to Eat: The Pleasures and Principles of Good Food, edited by Arthur Boehm, John Wiley & Sons (New York), 2000.
How to Be a Domestic Goddess: Baking and the Art of Comfort Cooking, photography by Petrina Tinslay, Chatto & Windus, 2000; Hyperion, 2001.
Nigella Bites: From Family Meals to Elegant Dinners— Easy, Delectable Recipes for Any Occasion, Hyperion, 2001.
Forever Summer, photographs by Petrina Tinslay, Hyperion (New York), 2003.

Sources

Guardian (London, England), September 2, 2002, p. 8.
Independent (London, England), December 18, 2001, p. 1; April 20, 2002, p. 50; September 12, 2002, p. 7.

Independent Sunday (London, England), July 12, 1998, p. 60.

New Statesman, October 16, 1998, p. 46; March 20, 2000, p. 49; January 29, 2001, p. 48; June 25, 2001, p. 50.

New York Times, January 9, 2002, p. F1.

Observer (London, England), September 27, 1998, p. 14.

People, May 13, 2002, p. 131.

Times (London, England), September 3, 1997, p. 16; October 13, 2000, p. 3.

—*Carol Brennan*

Blanche Lincoln

United States senator

Born Blanche Lambert, September 30, 1960, in Helena, AR; daughter of Jordan Bennett, Jr. (a judge and farmer) and Martha Kelly Lambert; married Steve Lincoln (an obstetrician and gynecologist), 1993; children: Bennett, Reece (twin sons). *Education:* Earned degree from Randolph–Macon Women's College, 1982.

Addresses: *Home*—North Arlington, VA. *Office*—355 Dirksen Senate Office Bldg., Washington, DC 20510; 912 West Fourth St., Little Rock, AR 72201.

Career

Worked as receptionist for Representative Bill Alexander (D–AR), late 1980s, and as lobbyist, early 1990s; ran for Arkansas's First Congressional District seat in U.S. House of Representatives, 1992; re–elected, 1994; resigned from Congress, 1996; won Arkansas seat in U.S. Senate, 1998.

Sidelights

Blanche Lambert Lincoln, a Democratic from Arkansas, is the youngest woman in American history to be elected a U. S. senator. Lincoln took her seat in the formidable upper chamber of Congress in 1999, joining just eight other female lawmakers among 100 senators. Her achievement was heralded by legions of working mothers in Arkansas and beyond, because just three years earlier Lincoln had retired from politics when she learned that she was expecting twins. "The most important thing to me

was to have a family," Lincoln told *People*'s Bill Hewitt in a 2002 profile. "I always knew there would be filler. I just didn't know that my filler would be the Senate."

Lincoln was born in 1960 in Helena, Arkansas, the youngest of four children. Her father was a local judge as well as a farmer, and the family's roots in the area stretched back six farming generations behind him. Interested in art, Lincoln studied at Randolph–Macon Women's College in Lynchburg, Virginia, and spent a semester abroad in London. After graduating in 1982, she obtained a coveted internship at Sotheby's, the prestigious auction house in New York City. Deciding Manhattan was too expensive, she relocated to Washington and found work as a receptionist in the office of one of the state's Democratic lawmakers, Representative Bill Alexander. She also worked at a Laura Ashley store to make ends meet, but over time established herself inside the Beltway as a professional lobbyist.

Feeling the need for a new challenge in her life, Lincoln decided to run for Alexander's seat in the First Congressional District. Her family and friends contributed money to finance her campaign, and her former boss initially scoffed at her long–shot bid, joking, "Why not run for the Senate?," the *New*

York Times quoted Alexander as telling her. It was a rather moribund campaign until revelations surfaced that Alexander had run up more than $200,000 in overdrafts at the House bank. Lincoln used the scandal to her political advantage, telling voters, "I'll promise you one thing—I can sure enough balance my checkbook!," according to *People.* She bested Alexander in the Democratic primary, then went on to beat Republican Terry Hayes in the general election in November of 1992.

Lincoln took her House seat in early 1993, sworn in with a record number of other newly elected women legislators that year. She won another term in 1994, though it was a close election in which her Republican opponent derided her as liberal, and compiled an impressively independent voting record during her two terms. A moderate Democrat, Lincoln sometimes voted against party lines, and was a key early member of the Blue Dog coalition, a group of conservative Democrats in the House. She ended her promising political career in 1996 when she announced that she would not seek another term that year. Married since 1993 to Steve Lincoln, an obstetrician and gynecologist, the lawmaker had recently learned that she and her husband were expecting twins.

Sons Bennett and Reece were born in 1996, and Lincoln enjoyed her time as a stay–at–home mother. In July of 1997, however, longtime Arkansas senator Dale Bumpers announced his retirement from Congress, and Lincoln decided to make a run for his seat. Her supporters were elated about her sudden return to politics, and she seemed to strike a particularly resonant chord with younger female voters in the state, women not unused to the demands of balancing a career and family. Lincoln campaigned on a moderate platform that stressed family issues and a balanced budget. One campaign ad showed her at home, with her family and husband, and the voice–over, "Daughter, wife, mother, Congresswoman. Living our rock–solid Arkansas values."

Lincoln bested her Republican opponent, religious conservative and state senator Fay Boozman, in November of 1998. At 37, she became the youngest woman ever elected to the U.S. Senate. Lincoln did admit to being slightly awed when she took her seat the following January, realizing that she was largely in the company of male colleagues with law degrees and years of political experience behind them. Confessing that her first days on the job "initially made me feel nervous," as she told the *Christian Science Monitor,* Lincoln quickly realized that she could bring a new focus to American politics.

"My perspective ... comes from a purely parental background," she told the newspaper. "I think of the discipline and the things I want my children to learn."

As a Senate Democrat, Lincoln again proved one of its moderates. In 2001, she sided with Senate Republicans in favor of President George W. Bush's tax–cut package. She belongs to the Senate's New Democrat Coalition, and is also a founding member of the bipartisan Senate Centrist Coalition. In other matters, she has displayed a more traditional Democratic stance: she journeyed to Cuba in 2000 as part of a delegation of Arkansas farmers to meet with trade and agriculture officials there, and returned home to speak out against the decades–old U.S. embargo against its Caribbean neighbor. Her Senate committee work has included stints on the Agriculture, Nutrition and Forestry panel, the Special Committee on Aging, the Select Committee on Ethics, the Social Security Task Force and the Rural Health Caucus; in January of 2001 she was appointed to the Senate Finance Committee, and became the only third woman in history to serve on that important, purse–controlling body. "She's turned out to be a very solid senator," Charles Cook of the *Cook Political Report* told Hewitt in *People.* "In a business dominated by middle–aged white guys, she brings a new perspective."

Lincoln moved her family to the suburban Washington area after her Senate win, where her husband established a Fairfax, Virginia, practice. They live in North Arlington, Virginia. In 2000, she contributed to the book *Nine and Counting* with the eight other women in the U.S. Senate. Lincoln, in an article penned for *Cosmopolitan* that same year, said that she and her co–authors try to get together on a monthly basis. Though it is a bipartisan group consisting of politicians from dissimilar backgrounds and with different agendas, a spirit of camaraderie nevertheless persists. "We work together on some issues and in opposition on others, but no matter where we stand, we always strive to treat one another as equals," Lincoln noted. She also stressed that "one of the few things we can all agree on is the need for more women senators!"

Selected writings

(With others) *Nine and Counting: The Women of the Senate,* William Morrow (New York City), 2000.

Sources

Periodicals

Arkansas Business, June 5, 2000, p. 6.
Christian Science Monitor, January 20, 1999, p. 1.
Cosmopolitan, July 2000, p. 70.

New York Times, June 13, 1998.

People, March 11, 2002, p. 129.

Rural Telecommunications, May 2001, p. 14.

Washington Times, October 16, 1996, p. 11.

Online

United States Senator Blanche Lincoln, http://lincoln.senate.gov/ (August 12, 2002).

—Carol Brennan

George Lopez

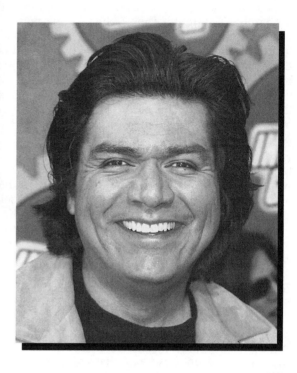

Comedian and actor

Born in 1963, in Mission Hills, CA; married Anna Serrano (a casting director and movie producer), c. 1994; children: Mayan (daughter).

Addresses: *Office*—ABC, Inc. 500 S. Buena Vista St., Burbank, CA 91521–4551. *Management*—Ron DeBlasio, SDM, Inc., 740 N. La Brea Ave., 1st Floor, Los Angeles, CA 90038. *Website*—George Lopez Official Website: http://www.georgelopez.com.

Career

Actor in films, including: *Fist of Fear, Touch of Death* (also known as *The Dragon and the Cobra*), 1980; *Ski Patrol*, 1990; *Fatal Instinct*, 1993; *Bread and Roses*, 2000; *Real Women Have Curves*, 2002; *Outta Time*, 2002; *Ali G Indahouse*, 2002; *The Original Latin Kings of Comedy*, 2002; *Tortilla Heaven*, 2003. Television appearances include: *Latino Laugh Festival*, 1997; *2nd Annual Latino Laugh Festival*, 1998; *Fidel*, 2002; *George Lopez*, 2002—; *30th Annual American Music Awards*, 2003.

Awards: National Hispanic Media Coalition Impact Award; Manny Mota Foundation Community Spirit Award; Vision Award, the Imagen Foundation, 2003.

Sidelights

George Lopez has made waves as the star of the most successful English–language prime time television series about Latin Americans since *Chico and the Man* left the air in the 1970s. His show, *George*

Lopez, is a sitcom featuring a fictionalized version of himself and his family. It debuted in 2002 and it has since become one of the most–watched shows on ABC.

A writer and producer as well as the star of his show, Lopez began his performing career as a standup comic in the Los Angeles, California, area in the 1980s. He also pursued a parallel career as an actor in film and television, and, in 2000, he became the first Latino to host his own radio show on an English–language radio station in Los Angeles. His show, on MEGA 92.3 F.M., was a morning drive–to–work show, and featured a radio–friendly version of some of his standup acts.

George Lopez was launched in part through the efforts of actress and show co–producer Sandra Bullock, who discovered Lopez at one of his standup comedy gigs. She had been looking for material for a new Latino television show, and she found that Lopez's stand–up acts exactly fit the bill. A Mexican American, Lopez draws heavily on his early life experiences for material for the TV show. However, these experiences do not immediately lend themselves to comedy; he had an extremely difficult childhood.

Born in 1963, Lopez grew up in Mission Hills, California. When he was two years old, his father left the family. Lopez and his mother moved in with his mother's parents. Then, when Lopez was ten years old, his mother moved out with her new husband to start a new life without him. From then on Lopez was raised by his maternal grandmother and her second husband. Lopez, who had been told that his father was dead, learned the truth about his father around the time his mother left him to be raised by his grandparents. By then, he and his family had no contact with Lopez's father.

Lopez admits that his upbringing left him with a warped sense of what is normal in a family. He has never been able to find a baby picture of himself, and as a child he never had a birthday party. "It's a form of abuse to not feel important," he later told Mireya Navarro in the New York Times. "It's considered being neglected."

To this day, Lopez rarely sees his mother, whom he has not completely forgiven for leaving him. Even his grandmother he sees only occasionally. His grandmother's husband has since died. He has largely left his early years behind; even though his show is based on these experiences, he maintains little or no contact with the people he knew when he was younger, including the man on which his character's best friend is based.

Lopez had his first experience as a standup comic at an open mic night at a club in Los Angeles in 1979 on the day he graduated from high school. He was inspired to take the plunge after watching the late Latino comedian Freddie Prinze in the TV show Chico and the Man, which had a popular run in the 1970s. Prinze remains a hero to Lopez to this day. Lopez has described the first time he saw Prinze on television as a life–changing experience, and, in fact, Prinze's former manager, Ron DeBlasio, now works for Lopez.

Being a standup comic did not come naturally to Lopez; his first experience terrified him, and he stayed away performing for four full years, working odd jobs to stay afloat. But he could not get standup comedy out of his system, and no other choice for making a living stuck, including a brief flirtation with a career in information technology. Finally, in the mid–1980s, he decided to become a full time comic. First picking up regular standup comedy gigs on stage, he also began to perform in small roles in films. In 2000 he found steady work as the host of a morning drive–time radio show.

It was during his years as a struggling standup comic that he first met the woman who would play his wife on TV, Constance Marie. Marie, like Lopez, was frustrated by the meager selection of roles available to Latinos in Hollywood, and the two hit it off. Together they conceived of a comic television series about a Latino couple. They worked well together, hashing out ideas for the possible show, which she later described as a Latin Honeymooners.

That particular idea did not find its way onto the small screen, but Marie was a natural choice to play Lopez's wife on the George Lopez show. Marie was delighted to be involved in this new project, not in small part because it represented an extremely refreshing change from the negative ways in which Latinos are often portrayed on TV and in movies. She was also delighted at the depth of the show's scripts, which are thought–provoking as well as funny.

Lopez's first major film role was as the character Eddie in the 1990 film Ski Patrol. It was at the premier of Ski Patrol that Lopez met his future wife, Ann Serrano, who is Cuban American. At the time Serrano worked as a casting director; she now works as an independent film producer. Lopez struggled through the 1990s, piecing together a living as best he could as a standup comic and in occasional film and television roles.

After putting many years as a standup comic, Lopez developed a loyal following of fans. One of these fans was Bullock, who approached Lopez after a show one night around 2000. She thought his material would make a great television series, and she told him so. Going against the advice of her own talent agents, Bullock helped Lopez get his own show. Lopez later expressed his gratitude for Bullock's help to Mark Sachs in the Los Angeles Times, saying, "I owe everything to her, because she didn't have to do this.... She did this out of a love for the culture and because of a lack of visibility for Latinos on TV."

Bullock, for her part, backs Lopez wholeheartedly. As she told the New York Times's Navarro, among the many things she appreciates about Lopez's work is his honesty: "George speaks the truth," she said. "It opens people's minds into other directions." Bullock remained a presence throughout the process of landing the show on the ABC network, and throughout the taping of the early episodes as an executive producer. Bullock also took on a recurring role on the show as an uncoordinated factory worker named Accident Amy.

Bullock has continued to guide the George Lopez show, helping to build its reputation as a sitcom with substance. In particular, after the first few episodes, she planned to work in more of the dark, edgy humor that has been a hallmark of Lopez's work as a standup comic. She admitted that this attempt would not be without risk. Her plan was to build the darker material into the show gradually to give audiences time to get used to it. If this approach didn't work, said Bullock to the *Los Angeles Times*'s Sachs, at least the show would "go out with a bang."

In the show, Lopez plays a manager at a factory that manufactures airplane parts. His character's mother also works at the plant. In real life, Lopez's grandmother was an inspector at such a plant at the same time that Lopez himself worked there. Lopez's character on the show, like the real–life Lopez, is married. On the show, his wife's name is Angie (played by Constance Marie). Also as in real life, Lopez's character and his wife have a daughter. The similarities end there; on the show, Lopez and his wife have a son named Max and a diabetic dog named Mr. Needles.

The *George Lopez* show debuted in an 8:30, Wednesday night time slot in 2002. The first episode features a storyline that closely paralleled Lopez's actual experience. In the episode, Lopez's character is told by a long–lost relative that his father, contrary to what Lopez had been told growing up, is still alive. Lopez's character becomes determined to track him down.

Critical responses and ratings were immediately positive, and the show soon climbed to the number–three spot in its time period. ABC executives were very pleased with the show's success. As chairman of ABC Entertainment Lloyd Braun told Navarro in the *New York Times*, "It exceeds even our most optimistic hopes in terms of performance." Braun said also that the show exactly filled the bill as the kind of comedy ABC had been looking for—appealing to family audiences with a fresh perspective.

In addition, no less a figure than Cheech Marin of the famed comedy team Cheech and Chong has credited Lopez with opening doors for English–language television shows featuring Latinos. Since the *George Lopez* show debuted, Marin himself has gotten the greenlight to do a sitcom called *The Ortegas*.

Lopez's grandmother, Benne Gutierrez, now proclaims herself one of Lopez's biggest fans. "I'm very proud of him, very proud," she told Navarro in the *New York Times*. When asked why she never celebrated Lopez's birthday when he was growing up, she replied, "Probably because I never had a birthday. I didn't know what birthdays were."

Lopez attributes the success of the show to its universal appeal; although it is about a Latino family living in the Los Angeles area, people from as far away as Russia have told him that they relate to the show and find it funny. That to Lopez means he is doing something right.

Meanwhile, he now performs standup to packed—and very appreciative—houses. Although he had been playing to sold–out audiences before his television show took off, his audiences were not quite as generous as they were after his show became popular. "At 41 years old," he told Peter Hartlaub in the *San Francisco Chronicle* in 2002, "it's really like having my first childhood again."

Sources

Periodicals

Los Angeles Times, January 12, 2003, p. E36.
New York Times, November 27, 2002, p. E1.
People, October 21, 2002, pp. 129–30.
San Francisco Chronicle, June 20, 2002, p. D7.

Online

"Biography for George Lopez," Internet Movie Database, http://us.imdb.com/Bio?Lopez,%20 George%20(I) (April 11, 2002).
"George Lopez Biography," George Lopez Online, http://www.georgelopez.com/bio/bioinfo.html (April 11, 2002).

—*Michael Belfiore*

Mike Lowell

Professional baseball player

Born Michael Averett Lowell, February 24, 1974, in San Juan, Puerto Rico; son of Carl (a dentist) and Beatriz Lowell; married Bertha Lopez (a dancer), November 7, 1998; children: Alexis. *Education:* Florida International University, Miami, FL, B.S., 1997.

Addresses: *Email*—fanfeedback@marlins.mlb.com. *Office*—Florida Marlins, Attn: Mike Lowell, 2267 Dan Marino Blvd., Miami, FL 33056.

Career

Second baseman, Florida International University Golden Panthers; third baseman, Greensboro Bats Class A team, 1996–98; third baseman, New York Yankees, 1998; third baseman, Florida Marlins, 1999—.

Awards: *Collegiate Baseball Magazine* Freshman All–American, 1993; All Trans American Conference player, 1993 95; American Baseball Coaches Association All–Region player, 1995; Division 1, College Sports Information Directors of America All–American, 1995; Trans America Athletic Conference Athlete of the Year, 1995; South Atlantic League All–Star player, 1996; National League Player of the Week, August 28–September 3, 2000; National League All–Star player, 2002.

Sidelights

Mike Lowell just might be able to say that baseball saved his life. Traded to the Florida Marlins in early 1999 after four years on the New York Yankees's farm team, Lowell's pre–season physical turned into a diagnosis of testicular cancer. Early detection, surgery, and treatment took him out of the line–up for a short time, but Lowell's determination helped him return to the field and soon thereafter hit his first major league home run. Lowell told *FIU Magazine,* "If I wasn't playing professional baseball, I probably wouldn't have had a physical. It might have taken years before my cancer was discovered, and it might have been too late at that point." Not one to take any opportunity for granted, Lowell has continued to improve his game as the Florida Marlins's third baseman and one of the team's top batters.

Lowell was born on February 24, 1974, in San Juan, Puerto Rico, to Carl and Beatriz Lowell. His last name comes from his paternal grandfather. A German–American, Lowell's grandfather could speak Spanish well enough that the meat packing company he worked for transferred him to Cuba. Eventually he moved the family to Puerto Rico from Cuba when Lowell's father was a child. Carl Lowell pitched for the Puerto Rican national team and even has a place in Puerto Rico's Hall of Fame. When Lowell was still a child his father moved the family to Coral Gables, Florida, and opened a dental practice. In addition to the practice, Carl Lowell coached his kids's Little League teams. Lowell told

Charlie Atkinson of the *News & Record*, "I can safely say my dad had the biggest influence on my life." One aspect that Lowell appreciated most was that despite his father's love of baseball, he was not pressured to play. Lowell explained to Atkinson, "He said, 'If you don't like it, don't do it.'"

Lowell liked baseball, and he was willing to devote himself to the sport. At the end of his sophomore year at Christopher Columbus High School, a private Catholic school in Miami, Lowell discovered that his baseball coach had no intention of playing him during his junior and senior years. Without regular game play, there was little chance that Lowell would be picked for a college team. With the help of his father, Lowell was able to convince his mother to let him transfer to Coral Gables High School, a large public high school. Lowell told *FIU Magazine*, "I developed there, I think in part because Coach Bisceglia really helped develop my confidence. He showed a lot of faith in me."

Along with confidence, Lowell developed the body needed to play college baseball. Despite his height, he was considered too lean for baseball. College teams did not court him until his senior year, by which time he had added 20 pounds to his six–foot frame. Florida International University took notice of Lowell and offered him an athletic scholarship. At FIU Lowell was able to juggle his dedication to baseball with the demands of academia, eventually being named an academic All–American.

In 1995, during his junior year at FIU, Lowell was drafted in the 20th round by the New York Yankees. Understanding that baseball was one option among many, Lowell signed with the Yankees but returned to school to finish his degree. He explained to *FIU Magazine*, "The guarantee to play in the big leagues is so small that I knew I had to get my degree." With a level–headedness he credits to his parents, he earned a degree in finance and graduated in 1997.

As a late–round draft for the Yankees, Lowell was placed on their farm team, the Greensboro Bats, to learn the Yankee code of conduct. He was moved around to different positions until settling into his spot as third baseman. While with the Greensboro team Lowell earned the respect of his coaches, teammates, and the press. He was considered the unofficial team leader, especially for the Hispanic members of the team who often needed help from Lowell adjusting to life in the United States as well as translating. Terms used to describe Lowell included quiet, professional, and solid. "Greensboro Bats

third baseman Mike Lowell is a refreshing change—a genuinely nice guy with big–league potential," according to *News & Record*'s Atkinson.

Lowell spent four years playing Class A baseball and credits the managers he had during that time with giving him the confidence to believe he could make it to the major leagues. A short discussion with the Yankees's owner, George Steinbrenner, only reinforced Lowell's work ethic. Steinbrenner explained to Lowell that everything any player needed to succeed was provided for, it was up to the player to make it happen. His batting coach, Gary Denbo, helped him become a better batter. His manager for the Bats, Jimmy Johnson, helped shore up his confidence in his abilities. Lowell told Joe Capozzi of the *Palm Beach Post*, "Jimmy Johnson saw me hit and he said, 'You know what? Your instincts are good enough that you're going to play in the big leagues.'" Lowell was eventually called up to play with the Yankees for eight games in the 1998 season. His tenure with the team was short–lived because the Yankees traded him in early 1999 for three minor–league pitchers from the Florida Marlins.

On February 19, 1999, Lowell was undergoing a routine physical after his trade to the Marlins when the doctor discovered a suspicious lump. The doctor sent Lowell for more tests, which revealed that Lowell had testicular cancer. Lowell told Ken Davidoff of New Jersey's *Record*, "The news was definitely a shock.... I didn't feel anything. There were no signs that said that something was going to happen." Two days later he went into surgery to remove one of his testicles. Following surgery, he underwent three weeks of radiation treatment. Five days a week for three weeks, Lowell endured the nausea and weakness associated with intensive radiation therapy. Another blow for Lowell, who has had to battle being underweight throughout his baseball career, was losing more than ten pounds during treatment.

While being forced to deal with the pressure of overcoming cancer, Lowell was also attempting to perform at the major league level. He explained to Adam Minichino of the *Athens Daily News*, "At first I was mad that the doctor found it because it kind of put a dent in my plans." He felt distracted by the appointments and tests he had to undergo. He told the *Florida Times Union*, "It was a pain because you don't want to be thinking about those things. I was trying to compete at a level I hadn't been at before, and I didn't really have all the bullets in the chamber." After treatment, Lowell ended up in Calgary playing Class AAA ball for a short while before being called back up to the Marlins on April 13, 1999. Physical strain and weakness caused by the radiation treatment put Lowell into physical therapy soon afterward for treatment of tendinitis.

On May 29 of that year, he returned to play for the Marlins. Less than a month later he played an impressive game in which he hit his first major league home run. Lowell told the *Seattle Times*, "Hitting a home run is always special, and that was a pretty big moment in the game." Lowell made an even more impressive play on August 9, 1999. That day he was one of five players who hit a grand slam, the only time in the history of baseball that five grand slams had ever been hit in the same day. For Lowell this was the first grand slam of his baseball career, and his home run helped even the score against the San Francisco Giants in the eighth inning. The Marlins ended up beating the Giants, 5–4. Because of his part in that record–breaking day, Lowell's bat is now displayed in the National Baseball Hall of Fame and Museum in Cooperstown, New York.

In 2000, Lowell returned for another season of major league baseball, but this time without the added distraction of dealing with cancer. Continued screening showed that he was cancer–free. In his first full season, Lowell hit 22 home runs, 91 RBIs, and had a team high of 38 doubles. He was named National League Player of the Week for August 23 to September 3 when he batted .471, with eight RBIs, and three home runs.

Lowell tries to enter each new season fit and ready to do his best for his team. He explained to Dave George of the *Palm Beach Post*, "I pride myself coming into spring training in good shape so that I don't have to use the whole spring on that." Because of his level of fitness at the beginning of the season, Lowell was able to play impressively from the start of both the 2001 and 2002 seasons, earning the somewhat tongue–in–cheek title of "Mr. April." In 2001, he earned 24 RBI's in that month before ending the season with 100. In April of 2002, he hit three doubles in one game that helped him achieve the leading place for doubles in the National League at that time.

Besides his considerable dedication to baseball, Lowell is also dedicated to his cultural heritage and his family. One of the great advantages for Lowell in being traded to the Marlins was being able to return to his hometown where he can live close to his family. In fact, his entire family often turns out for home games. Even though he is not easily identified by either looks or name as Latino, Lowell is proud of his family's background. He explained to George, "Maybe some people don't think of me and Luis Castillo as the same Latin guys, but we have the same culture, we eat the same foods, we celebrate Christmas the same way. I consider myself Latino." As part of that consideration, Lowell speaks only Spanish at home with his wife, Bertha, and daughter, Alexis.

Bertha Lopez and Lowell first met and began dating in high school. They dated through Lowell's college days while Bertha worked as a dancer for the Miami Heat. The two were married in November of 1998, right before Lowell's fortuitous trade to the Marlins brought him back to live full time in his hometown. Lopez's parents, who are Cuban exiles, had always liked Lowell. Lopez told George, "[M]y parents loved Mike way back when we started dating. He was a good kid, very well–mannered, very religious, and we liked a lot of the same things." In October of 2000, Lopez gave birth to their daughter.

Lowell's brush with cancer led him to create his own foundation and lend support to Miami's League Against Cancer. In 2001, he pledged $25 for every RBI he hit to the league. With 100 hits that year, he ended up donating $2,500. In 2002, he hosted the first ever Mike Lowell Foundation Charity Golf Classic, from which all proceeds were donated to the League Against Cancer as well as select local sports programs. Lowell also adopted a local fifth grade class through the Florida Marlins Community Foundation and the Adopt–a–Classroom program.

Lowell feels like he's living his childhood dreams playing baseball. One moment that made him feel like a kid again came in April of 2001. He was asked to catch the ceremonial opening pitch being thrown by the 1980 World Series Most Valuable Player, Mike Schmidt, who also played third base. From the time he was six, and the Philadelphia Phillies won the World Series, Lowell had idolized Schmidt along with the Philadelphia Phillies. Another dream–like moment came in August of 2002, when Lowell was selected to play on the National League All–Star team.

As a cancer survivor, Lowell was forced to recognize the place that baseball needed to take in his life. He was able to refocus on his family, friends, and his health while still maintaining his dedication to baseball. From his childhood, Lowell has exhibited determination to achieve beyond anyone else's expectations. His continued success and the contributions he's made to building the Florida Marlins into a championship team show that his strength and will to succeed are paying off.

Sources

Periodicals

Florida Times Union, April 22, 2000, p. C5.

News & Record (North Carolina), June 18, 1996, p. C1.

Palm Beach Post, April 8, 2001, p. 6C; July 15, 2001, p. 7C; April 28, 2002, p. 5B; July 9, 2002, p. 1C.

Record (Bergan County, New Jersey), June 12, 1999, p. S7.

Seattle Times, June 4, 1999, p. D4.

Online

"Florida Marlins Community," http://florida. marlins.mlb.com/NASApp/mlb/fla/ community/fla_community_players_lowell.jsp (October 21, 2002).

"Hitting his stride," *FIU Magazine,* http://news.fiu. edu/fiumag/spring_01/alumnus–profile.htm (October 21, 2002).

"Lowell fighting cancer battle one day at a time," *Athens Daily News,* http://www.onlineathens. com/stories/070999/spo_0709990021.shtml (October 21, 2002).

—*Eve M. B. Hermann*

Bernie Mac

Courtesy of Bernie Mac

Actor and comedian

Born Bernard Jeffrey McCullough in 1957 in Chicago, IL; married Rhonda, 1974, children: Je'Neice (daughter).

Addresses: *Office*—The Bernie Mac Show, P.O. Box 900, Beverly Hills, CA 90213–0900.

Career

Actor in films, including: *Mo' Money,* 1992; *Who's the Man,* 1993; *Above the Rim,* 1994; *The Walking Dead,* 1995; *Don't Be a Menace to South Central While Drinking Your Juice in the Hood,* 1996; *Get on the Bus,* 1996; *Booty Call,* 1997; *BAPS,* 1997; *How to Be a Player,* 1997; *The Player's Club,* 1998; *Life,* 1999; *The Original Kings of Comedy,* 2000; *What's the Worst that Could Happen?,* 2001; *Ocean's Eleven,* 2001. Television appearances include: *Midnight Mac,* HBO, 1995; *Moesha,* WB; *The Bernie Mac Show,* Fox, 2001—.

Sidelights

Bernie Mac became one of television's most critically applauded comedic stars following the debut of the situation comedy bearing his name, *The Bernie Mac Show.* A more sanitized version of the standup comedy routine that first brought him national attention in the Spike Lee film *The Original Kings of Comedy,* the television series presents an irreverent view of the travails of family life in the early years of the 21st century. Despite his irreverence and penchant for garnering laughs with off–color remarks and mannerisms, Mac has expressed a desire to deliver a message of self–respect to his audience.

Born in 1957 on Chicago's South Side, Mac was one of 15 children. He recalled that he was four years old when he witnessed his mother being driven to tears from laughter while watching comedian Bill Cosby on television. This sparked in him the desire to hone his natural comedic ability and he became the family clown. He told the *New York Daily News:* "I did two hours at my grandfather's funeral.... They asked me to say a few words, and I just started doing [mimicking] him. Imitating his walk and his laugh, and repeating his favorite line: 'I'l kil'yu.'" He was voted class clown by his high school graduation class, but turned it down. "I thought it was an insult at the time," he told *Entertainment Weekly.*

Upon leaving high school, Mac worked a succession of menial jobs, honing his craft by performing standup routines for tips on the platforms of Chicago's subway and elevated train tracks. A series of family tragedies about which he refuses to elaborate upon caused Mac to commit himself fully to comedy. During this period, he was encouraged by comedian Redd Foxx to take more chances with his comedic delivery. Mac told *Time* journalist James Poniewozik, "He said, 'Young man, you're funny.... But your problem is, you don't want to be funny. You want to be liked.'" Chicago's vibrant comedy club scene opened its doors to his burgeoning talent, and he eventually landed an appearance on

HBO's *Def Comedy Jam.* The host of the program was Damon Wayans, a member of the comedic Wayans family responsible at the time for the Fox television sketch comedy series *In Living Color.* Impressed by Mac's performance, Wayans cast Mac in a role in his 1992 film *Mo' Money,* based upon hustling African–American characters made popular on a series of sketches from *In Living Color.* The role opened the door for him to play a series of funny sidekicks in several films. In 1994, however, he expanded his acting range to include serious drama when he portrayed a homeless ex–basketball star named Flip in *Above the Rim.* He explained his decision to portray Flip to the *New York Daily News:* "Where you start is where you end up…. So before I got typecast, I wanted to establish that I could go deep." Before long, he was a regular fixture on television as well, making appearances on *The Arsenio Hall Show,* hosting an episode of NBC's *Later,* performing as a recurring character on the teen series *Moesha,* and writing and starring in his own HBO show, *Midnight Mac,* which was nominated for a Cable Ace Award.

With the ascendancy of Mac's Hollywood film and television careers, he also accelerated his live standup performance career. He leveraged his popularity on film by headlining in comedy clubs and theaters throughout the country. He estimated that he was touring 40 weeks out of the year in the mid–1990s, an era when a large contingent of talented black comedians came into their own. In a 1994 article, *Jet* noted that black comics "are among the hottest on the comedy circuit." *In Living Color, Showtime at the Apollo,* and *Russell Simmons's Def Comedy Jam* were tremendous avenues of exposure to black comics of the era. The focus on the talent of black comedians, however, resulted in an unforeseen backlash. The perception that black comics only concerned themselves with black audiences and African–American themes caused many white audiences to stay away. The segregation was unwarranted, Mac believed, because as he told the *Florida Times Union,* "People are missing out. The world isn't all black or all white." He underscored this statement in an interview with *Jet,* "I don't consider myself a Black Comic, I don't consider myself a White Comic. I consider myself a comedian…. I can make them all laugh."

Mac's increasing reputation for delivering hilarious, side–splitting performances landed him on the bill with three other comics in the 1997 tour, *The Original Kings of Comedy,* which secured his popularity. Mac received equal billing with such future television stars as Steve Harvey, Cedric the Entertainer, and D. L. Hughley. The show, which was created and produced by promoter Walter Latham, was a veritable Woodstock of comedic talent that presented two–and–a–half hours of adult humor. "It reminds you of when you were a kid and someone jumped on you to tickle you," Harvey told *Jet.* "After a while you just want him to stop. You can't take no more. That's what coming to see this show is like."

The Original Kings of Comedy was a smash success, moving from small theaters to 11,000–seat stadiums. Every venue in which the show was presented quickly sold out. Playing to packed houses each night resulted in the show becoming the highest–grossing comedy tour in history, eventually earning more than $40 million. Noting the tour's success, Mac commented to *Jet,* "We're doctors. We're medicine. We're something a lot of people wish they could be…. People come and can forget about their hardships. The world is hurting. Most of the people who come may be crying and arguing, but they come to get away and to laugh for a couple of hours."

The tour got an unexpected reprise in popularity when director Spike Lee brought 12 digital cameras on the tour to capture the comics' performances for a wide–release movie. Lee's film of *The Original Kings of Comedy* became a tremendously popular film in its theatrical release and later video release to audiences of all colors. The impact on Mac's career was incendiary, and his career took off like a Roman candle. In 2001, Mac appeared in director Steven Soderbergh's remake of *Ocean's Eleven,* appearing in an ensemble cast that included Brad Pitt, George Clooney, Julia Roberts, Matt Damon, and Andy Garcia. That same year he published the book *I Ain't Scared of You,* which he co–wrote with Darrell Dawsey, to coincide with the winter 2001 debut of his television series *The Bernie Mac Show.*

Of the book, *Library Journal* critic Norman Oder wrote, "[Mac] tells stories about his upbringing, his drive to succeed, religion, and the importance of self–reliance. He also riffs on sports and on his comedy career. Some of his topics are predictable, drawing on well–worn stereotypes of black and white (and gay) folk, but you can forgive a guy who says, 'I grew up hard, so all the money and fame I've achieved is gravy.'" A *Publishers Weekly* critic commented: "[Mac's] most compelling material stems from his inner–city childhood. He writes of sharing not only bathwater with his siblings but cereal milk, poured from bowl to bowl. He laments the erosion of communal structures, the disappearance of the strong maternal figure ('Your grandmama, now what—34?')." The critic continued, "Co–written by journalist Dawsey (*Living to Tell About It: Black Men in America Speak Their Piece)*, this book skillfully captures the rhythm and color of street vernacular." While finding much to praise, the critic also asserted that "the structure is loose and jumpy, fattened up with verbal chest puffing and relentless swearing. There are some perhaps overly confessional moments (e.g. physical fights with his wife), but Mac shows on more than one occasion that he can reach deep into the pockets of human distress and bring forth a smile."

The premise of *The Bernie Mac Show* concerns a successful comedian who becomes caregiver to his nephew and nieces while his sister struggles with a drug addiction. Eschewing the sensitive caring approach of many television situation comedy parents, Mac portrays an in–your–face proponent of tough love. Series creator Larry Wilmore told *Time*'s Poniewozik, "Bernie Mac does not feel it is important to be your kids's friend." Poniewozik also applauds the program for avoiding the clichés of black situation comedies by portraying the title character's financial success as commonplace rather than an African–American version of *The Beverly Hillbillies*—reminiscent of *The Jeffersons* and *The Fresh Prince of Bel Air*—in which the viewer is expected to find humor in the supposed irony of a lower class surrounded by a wealth and a culture they inherently cannot comprehend. Furthermore, Poniewozik asserted, the program avoids the treatment of the show's characters as specifically black: "Mac rarely mentions race—a sharp contrast to the netlet shows, which load their scripts with in–jokes." Wilmore told Poniewozik, "Bernie Mac doesn't need to remind us that he's black. We know that already." In a previous *Time* article written before the show's debut, Poniewozik observed, "Larry Wilmore (*The PJs*), has retained Mac's stand–up voice, but fleshed it out with strong supporting characters, especially the kids, who convey their rough history without falling into ghetto stereotypes." Poniewozik noted that the show's pilot deftly handled the sensitive topic of children removed from their birth parents by portraying one child as frequently wetting

himself. Rather than using this portrayal to garner easy laughs, however, Poniewozik noted, "It underscores the real emotional stakes for the uprooted kids. It also brings out a fatherly side in Bernie that Mac—who has more range than many a comic who has taken on sitcom parenthood—makes believable without getting sappy."

An instant success, *The Bernie Mac Show* has been lauded for consistently evoking laughter without succumbing to stereotypes. The softening of Mac's stage demeanor by eliminating four–letter words and violently aggressive behavior while retaining Mac's message of self–respect marked a new era in television comedy. *The Bernie Mac Show* proved itself a hit with viewers and critics by winning high ratings as well as a Peabody Award for broadcasting excellence and a 2002 Emmy Award for outstanding writing for a comedy series.

Sources

Books

Contemporary Black Biography, volume 29, Gale Group, 2001.

Periodicals

Daytona Beach News Journal, August 18, 2000.
Entertainment Weekly, August 11, 2001, p. 42.
Florida Times–Union, June 4, 1999.
Interview, August 2000, p. 57.
Jet, September 5, 1994, p. 34; September 20, 1999, p. 58.
Library Journal, May 15, 2002.
New York Daily News, March 28, 1994.
Time, November 5, 2001, p. 103; February 25, 2002, p. 64.

—Bruce Walker

Clint Mathis

Professional soccer player

Born November 25, 1976, in Conyers, GA; son of Phil (a Pentecostal minister) and Pat (a bank manager) Mathis. *Education:* Attended University of South Carolina, 1994–97.

Addresses: *Office*—New York/New Jersey MetroStars, One Harmon Plaza, 3rd Floor, Secaucus, NJ 07094.

Career

Led his high school soccer team to Georgia State Cup during his junior and senior years and was named 1993 Gatorade Player of the Year in Georgia; played stand–out soccer for the University of South Carolina, where he became the third all–time leading scorer, 1994–97; began his professional career for the Los Angeles Galaxy, 1998; picked up by the New York/New Jersey MetroStars, 2000; selected as starting forward by the U.S. National Team for World Cup play, 2002.

Sidelights

One of the most promising American soccer players of the new millennium, Clint Mathis helped advance the U.S. Men's National Team to new heights in 2002 World Cup play. However, plagued by recurring knee problems and publicly chided by U.S. coach Bruce Arena for not working hard enough, Mathis failed to fulfill the high hopes that had been held for him in advance of the international competition. His goal in the United States's World Cup face–off with South Korea tied the game, 1–1, and moved the U.S. team along in competition. But injury and differences with Arena kept Mathis off the field a good deal of the time, leaving unanswered the question of whether he's got the stuff to become the first U.S.–born soccer scoring sensation ever.

One thing is certain, however. At his best, Mathis is an inspired soccer player. Although his performance in World Cup play was somewhat disappointing, he still ended the year as the leading scorer for the U.S. Men's National Team. And with Mathis's help, the U.S. soccer team won new international respect after advancing to the World Cup quarterfinals. In the wake of the Americans's performance at Seoul, the U.S. team in August of 2002 was voted into the top ten of the Fédération Internationale de Football Association (FIFA) world rankings for the first time ever.

For his part, Mathis waxed philosophical about the U.S. team's experience in Seoul, telling *Atlanta Journal and Constitution* reporter Wendy Parker: "We got to the quarterfinals with a team effort. I was able to get a goal in a World Cup, which is a dream come true, and was able to assist in another one."

The son of Philip and Pat, Mathis was born in Conyers, Georgia, on November 25, 1976. His father, a Pentecostal minister, and mother, a bank manager, were divorced in 1988. Mathis was playing soccer with older brothers Phil and Andy by the age of 3 1/2. Hoping to mold their younger brother into as versatile a player as possible, they told him he could join them in soccer play only if he used his left foot exclusively. Looking back on his siblings's early training efforts, Mathis told *Sports Illustrated*, "They didn't want me to grow up playing just right-footed." His brothers also took pains to steer Mathis away from football, fearing the game was too dangerous for him. Although the early results of his brothers's training rule was awkward and sometimes comical, in the end it all paid off for Mathis, who is today one of the New York/New Jersey MetroStars's leading scorers, able to deliver the goods with either foot. Mathis eventually graduated from play with his brothers to participation in local youth leagues and plenty of kicking practice at home. However, Clint did some of that kicking inside the house, breaking the glass front of the family curio cabinet so many times that the repairman eventually stopped charging to replace it.

Mathis proved to be a standout player at Heritage High School in Conyers. During his junior and senior years, he led the Heritage soccer team to the Georgia State Cup, and in 1993 he was named Gatorade Player of the Year in Georgia. After high school, Mathis opted to play for the Gamecocks of the University of South Carolina. At the USC campus in Columbia, he studied exercise science, and on the soccer field he played brilliantly throughout his collegiate career, ending up as the college's third leading scorer in history. During all four years playing for the Gamecocks, the team, under the guidance of head coach Mark Berson, advanced to the NCAA Tournament. One of Mathis's fellow players on the Gamecocks soccer team was Josh Wolff, who now plays for Major League Soccer's Chicago Fire and also was a member of the U.S. Men's National Team in 2002 World Cup competition.

Mathis left the University of South Carolina one semester short of completing work on his degree in exercise science. He was drafted by Major League Soccer's (MLS) Los Angeles Galaxy in 1998. Although he showed flashes of brilliance while in Los Angeles, he was relegated to part–time starter and in his two years with the team, never scored more than seven goals. His big break came in the spring of 2000, when the Galaxy picked up Mexican star Luis Hernandez and was forced to spin off Mathis, Roy Myers, and Joey Franchino in a league–mandated dispersal draft. Mathis was quickly snatched up by the New York/New Jersey MetroStars, who were then in last place and badly in need of an infusion of new blood.

Mathis wasted no time in showing the New York fans what he was made of. In his first season with the MetroStars in 2000, he started in 20 of the 21 games in which he played and posted 13 goals and 13 assists. His impressive debut helped Mathis to finish second in the league's Most Valuable Player (MVP) voting. It also caught the attention of U.S. National Team coach Bruce Arena, who started Mathis in the American team's final two games of 2000. Mathis scored his first international goal in play against Barbados and also contributed two assists.

New York area fans of the MetroStars were quickly captivated by Mathis's country–boy ways. In his first season with the team, he wore an "I Love NY" t–shirt beneath his uniform jersey. Each time he scored, Mathis snatched off his jersey, much to the delight of hometown fans. For his part, Mathis found himself equally enraptured with New York, particularly the city's night life. "Everything has happened at the right time for me," he told Grant Wahl of *Sports Illustrated* in 2001.

Back with the MetroStars for the 2001 season, Mathis started in all ten games he played. Given the limited number of games he played, Mathis posted an impressive seven goals and five assists. He also turned in an impressive performance for the U.S. National Team in 2001, scoring two goals and three assists in the six matches he played. Perhaps his most valuable contribution came during a game against Honduras in San Pedro Sula. In the final minutes of the game, Mathis struck a dead ball to score the winning goal in the United States's 2–1 qualifying victory against the Hondurans.

One of Mathis's biggest fans is his mother, Pat. When he and former Gamecocks teammate Wolff were brought in as early substitutes in a World Cup–qualifier against Mexico in February of 2001, Pat called Wolff's mom and made an uncannily accurate prediction. According to a report in *Sports Illustrated*, Pat Mathis told Sandy Wolff: "You'd better watch now, 'cause they're fixin' to score!" Moments later, Mathis's made a pinpoint pass to Wolff, setting him up to score the team's first goal in a 2–0 victory.

Mathis's action with both the MetroStars and the U.S. National Team was limited in 2001 by June surgery to repair the torn anterior cruciate ligament in his right knee. Sidelined for months after his knee surgery, Mathis came roaring back in early 2002. He rejoined the U.S. National Team as a starter in a March 2, 2002, game against Honduras, scoring twice in the United States's 4–0 win. Only a week later, Mathis set up the game's only goal in a 1–0 United States win over Ecuador. Next up, Mathis scored both United States goals in the Americans's 4–2 loss to Germany, following which he scored the only goal in a 1–0 win over Mexico. Impressed by Mathis's blockbuster return to play after knee surgery, Arena announced on April 17, 2002, his intention to start Mathis as forward on the World Cup team. Before turning his full attention to preparations for the World Cup, Mathis also saw some early 2002 action with the MetroStars, scoring a goal in the team's March 23 game against New England and another in the April 27 game against San Jose.

Even before World Cup play began in Seoul, reports of friction between Mathis and Arena began to circulate. The reports focused on Arena's unhappiness with Mathis's apparent lack of commitment to get into better playing shape. By the end of May, Arena went public, telling the Associated Press (AP): "In the next couple of years, if Clint wants to move forward, he has to bend a bit, conform to the way professional players on big clubs act. He's got a really good future if he can develop some better habits." Mathis, for his part, didn't have much to say, but he did tell the AP, "Nobody complains when you win."

Citing continuing knee problems, Arena kept Mathis out of the United States's World Cup opener against Portugal. Although the coach's decision at first blush seemed something of a gamble, the United States team still managed to triumph, pulling off a 3–2 upset over the Portuguese. Frustrated and spending most of the time in his hotel room, Mathis next appeared in public sporting a freshly shorn Mohawk haircut.

After missing the opening United States game against Portugal, Mathis's brightest moment in World Cup play came in the Americans's game against co–host South Korea. Sporting his new hairdo, Mathis early in the game took a pass from John O'Brien, trapping the ball with his right foot and shooting it with his left. He scored the U.S. team's only goal in its 1–1 tie with South Korea. After the goal "I put up two peace signs, and the kiss was to the U.S. fans," he told Associated Press. "There was a small section of them, but they were supporting us 100 percent." The tie with South Korea, coupled with its earlier win over Portugal, helped the Americans to advance to the second round of World Cup play.

In his first MLS game after the World Cup, Mathis sprained and tore the meniscus in his right knee in play against Columbus on July 6, 2002. This new knee injury sidelined Mathis until the MetroStars's game with D.C. United on August 25, 2002. In that game, Mathis connected on a pass from Rodrigo Faria to score the game's winning goal.

In the flood of positive publicity during the run–up to the World Cup in Seoul, Mathis was widely rumored to be a prime candidate to be signed to one of the major European soccer clubs. In late April of 2002, with the permission of the MetroStars, Mathis flew to Germany to spend a day talking with officials of Bayern Munich, the leading team in Germany's Bundesliga soccer league. Not content to put all of his eggs in one basket, Mathis dispatched his agent, Craig Sharon, to Italy for talks with officials from the Series A club Perugia. Mathis let it be known that his personal preference would be a berth on the United Kingdom's Premier League. In an interview, Mathis told AP sports writer Ronald Blum, "I don't want to limit my opportunities. You don't know what will happen after an event like this. I'd like to explore my opportunities."

Despite his somewhat spotty performance at the World Cup, Mathis remained a property that Bayern Munich dearly wanted to acquire. In the end it was the MLS, the organization overseeing first–tier U.S. professional competition in the sport, that threw a monkey wrench into the works, putting any such deal on hold for at least 18 months. The league refused to negotiate with the German club, forcing Mathis to serve out the remaining 18 months of his contract with the MetroStars. Sharon, the player's agent, told Agence France Presse, "It's disappointing that the MLS won't even start a dialogue. In most cases a club takes into consideration the desires of the player. But unless something changes, Clint will be left with no option but to play out the last 18 months of his contract and make himself available on a free transfer."

Sources

Periodicals

Agence France Press, July 3, 2002.
Associated Press, June 10, 2002; August 25, 2002.
Atlanta Journal and Constitution, June 7, 2002, p. C7; June 23, 2002, p. D12; August 10, 2002, p. E6.
Dallas Morning News, June 30, 2002, p. 17B.
Sports Illustrated, May 14, 2001, p. R4; May 27, 2002, p. 61; September 2, 2002, p. R6.
USA Today, May 19, 2002, p. 9C.

Online

"Biographies: Clint Mathis," U.S. Soccer Federation, http://www.ussoccer.com/bio/bio.sps?iBiographyID=1707 (August 1, 2002).

"Former Gamecock Clint Mathis Graces the Cover of *Sports Illustrated*," USCsports.com, http://uscsports.ocsn.com/sports/m–soccer/spec–rel/052202aaa.html (September 23, 2002).

"#13, Clint Mathis, Forward," MetroStars, http://www.metrostars.com/yourteam/clint_mathis.htm (September 23, 2002).

"2000 MetroStars Stats," MetroStars, http://www.metrostars.com/stats2000.htm (September 23, 2002).

—Don Amerman

William McDonough

Architect and designer

Born February 21, 1951, in Tokyo, Japan. *Education:* Dartmouth College, B.A., 1973; Yale University School of Architecture, M.A., 1976.

Addresses: *Office*—William McDonough and Partners, 410 East Water St., Charlottesville, VA 22902. *Websites*—http://www.mcdonough.com, http://www.mbdc.com.

Career

Apprenticed at a major New York architectural firm; founded and headed his own firm, William McDonough Architects, in New York, 1981; firm known as McDonough, Rainey Architects, 1982–86; firm relocated to Charlottesville, VA, and renamed William McDonough + Partners, 1994; founded McDonough Braungart Design Chemistry in Charlottesville with Michael Braungart, 1994; dean, University of Virginia's School of Architecture, 1994–99; professor, University of Virginia's School of Architecture, 1994—.

Awards: Presidential Award for Sustainable Development, 1996.

Sidelights

At first glance, William McDonough seems a rather unlikely revolutionary. But if one listens closely to his ideas, it soon becomes clear that what he'd like to see amounts to nothing less than a second industrial revolution, a revolution that will bring greater harmony to what is now the frequently unhappy relationship between industry and the environment.

An architect of international repute for more than two decades, McDonough in recent years has devoted an increasing amount of his time to pushing for a commitment from industry to operate in a fashion that does no damage to the natural world. In 2002, he and chemist Michael Braungart, cofounders of McDonough Braungart Design Chemistry, spelled out their vision of a plan for "remaking the way we make things" in *Cradle to Cradle,* published by North Point Press. In their landmark book, the two argue that the current concepts of "reduce, reuse, recycle" are responsible for unconscionable amounts of waste and pollution.

In *Cradle to Cradle,* McDonough and Braungart point to the shining example of lesser creatures in their appeal for a new way of doing things. They write: "Consider this: all the ants on the planet, taken together, have a biomass greater than that of humans. Ants have been incredibly industrious for millions of years. Yet their productiveness nourishes plants, animals, and soil. Human industry has been in full swing for little over a century, yet it has brought about a decline in almost every ecosystem on the planet. Nature doesn't have a design problem. People do."

McDonough has been widely recognized for his work on behalf of the environment. In 1996, he received the Presidential Award for Sustainable Development, the United States's highest environmental honor. In 1999 *Time* cited him as a "Hero for the Planet," observing that "his utopianism is grounded in a unified philosophy that—in demonstrable and practical ways—is changing the design of the world."

McDonough was born in Tokyo, Japan, on February 21, 1951. His father was an executive with Seagrams International, so the family moved frequently, and McDonough's childhood was spent in Japan, Hong Kong, Canada, and the United States. His experiences abroad helped to shape his vision for the future. In an interview with editor Tom Gibson of *Progressive Engineer*, he shared this vivid recollection of his years in Hong Kong: "I grew up in Hong Kong before the pipeline from China. We had people dying at our doorstep of cholera. We had water every fourth day for four hours. So, I got to see what happens when six million people inhabit 40 square miles with no water."

His earliest years were spent in Japan where McDonough recalls being struck by the scarcity of land and resources but also the wonders of the traditional Japanese home with paper walls, futons, and steaming baths, as well as farmhouses with interiors kept warm in winter and cool in summer by thick walls of clay and straw.

For his undergraduate studies, McDonough went to Dartmouth College where he studied art. During his four years at Dartmouth, he accompanied an urban design professor to Jordan to develop housing for increasing numbers of Bedouins who were settling in the Jordan River valley. Once again he was struck by the local scarcity of natural resources, especially water, soil, energy, and food. Against this relatively bleak backdrop, however, the Bedouins had found a way to make the very most of what they had. The nomads' tents of woven goat hair, which drew hot air up and out and became ultra tight and waterproof when it rained, seemed proof positive to McDonough that good design could be simple, elegant, and ideally suited to the unique characteristics of the local environment. Even more conveniently, the goats that were the source of the fabric accompanied the nomadic Bedouins as they traveled. "This ingenious design, locally relevant, culturally rich, and using simple materials, contrasted sharply with the typical modern designs I had seen in my own country, designs that rarely made such good use of local material and energy flows," McDonough wrote in *Cradle to Cradle*.

After earning his bachelor's degree at Dartmouth, McDonough enrolled at Yale University's School of Architecture to study both architecture and photography. The former eventually emerged as his real passion, for it afforded him a much larger platform for his talents and also involved working with people, which he enjoyed. As part of a school project, McDonough designed and built a solar-heated house in Ireland, a particularly ambitious undertaking considering the limited amount of sunshine in Ireland. For the Irish project, a number of United States–based experts suggested that McDonough might want to build a huge rock storage bin to retain heat. McDonough acted on the suggestion, hauling more than 30 tons of rock to get it done, only to discover that the thick masonry walls of the typical Irish home made the effort totally redundant.

With his architectural degree in hand, McDonough in 1976 made the short hop from New Haven, Connecticut, to New York City, where he apprenticed at a firm that had earned a reputation for its sensitive and socially responsible approach to urban housing. Five years later, in 1981, the young architect started his own firm, William McDonough Architects. In 1984 the firm was commissioned to design the New York offices of the Environmental Defense Fund. The terms of the contract stipulated that the building was to contain no materials that might release volatile toxic substances. McDonough focused on the matter of indoor air quality, a subject that at that time had received little attention at all. He was particularly concerned about volatile organic compounds, carcinogenic materials, or anything else in the paints, wall coverings, carpets, flooring, and fixtures that could adversely affect air quality. He got little help in his research from manufacturers of these materials, most of whom said the information was proprietary and offered little more than the vague safety warnings mandated by law.

Thus frustrated, McDonough had little choice but to do "the best we could at the time," he recalled in *Cradle to Cradle*. "We used water–based paints. We tacked down carpet instead of gluing it. We provided 30 cubic feet per minute of fresh air per person instead of five. We had granite checked for radon. We used wood that was sustainably harvested. We tried to be less bad." When EDA project was completed in 1985, it helped to launch the green building movement.

In 1991 McDonough met the German–born Braungart, a chemist by trade and founder of the Environmental Protection Encouragement Agency (EPEA), a Hamburg–based agency launched to provide environmental chemistry research. The two struck up a conversation about toxicity and design, discovering that each felt strongly a need for more sensible product design. That same year, they coauthored *The Hannover Principles,* which outlined design guidelines for the 2000 World's Fair. In 1994 they founded McDonough Braungart Design Chemistry (MBDC), although both continued to work in their respective fields. MBDC helps its clients, which have included Nike, Ford Motor Company, BASF, Volvo, Herman Miller, and the city of Chicago, to implement the company's unique sustaining design protocol. More specifically, the company provides guidance to companies that seek to redesign their products, materials, and manufacturing processes to reduce or eliminate their negative impact on the environment, economy, and the communities in which they operate. MBDC is headquartered in Charlottesville, Virginia.

McDonough and Braungart developed a set of philosophies and theories that they call the Next Industrial Revolution, which goes well beyond the generally accepted principles of reducing, recycling, regulating, and sustainability. "Our culture has adopted a design stratagem that says if brute force or massive amounts of energy don't work, you're not using enough of it," McDonough explained to *Progressive Engineer.* "What is required is a completely different way of looking at taking, making, using, and consuming in the world."

The central concept behind McDonough's idea for a radical reform of product design and use is this: Waste equals food. He explains that there is no such thing as waste in nature, which means the first step in reform must be the elimination of waste. McDonough suggests that the world supports two fundamental metabolisms: one is the organic, natural world of which man is a part, while the other might be called technical metabolism, representing the operation of human industry apart from natural systems. McDonough told *Progressive Engineer:* "We need to design products into each of these metabolisms such that they nourish one metabolism without contaminating the other."

In 1994 McDonough relocated his architectural design firm from New York City to Charlottesville, Virginia, where it was renamed William McDonough + Partners. It is one of the few architectural firms to employ a fairly large research staff, which works doggedly to analyze materials and processes, develop advanced engineering solutions, and draw up estimates of operational cost savings. The company's portfolio includes such diverse projects as the Gap's headquarters in San Bruno, California; the Warsaw Trade Center Tower in Poland; the headquarters of Nike Europe; and the offices of the

Heinz Family Foundation. A particularly gratifying project for William McDonough + Partners was the design of the Adam Joseph Lewis Center for Environmental Studies at Ohio's Oberlin College. The center is unique in that it creates more energy than it consumes. Another project involved the design and development of the Coffee Creek Center community in Indiana, which was designed to fight suburban sprawl through the establishment of a compact yet pleasant residential community.

The relocation of his architectural design firm to Charlottesville was necessitated by McDonough's appointment in 1994 as dean of the University of Virginia's School of Architecture. He remained in this post until 1999. McDonough continues to teach both architecture and business administration at the University of Virginia. In addition to his academic responsibilities in Charlottesville, he serves as White Professor–at–Large at Cornell University in Ithaca, New York.

On the product design side of his busy agenda, McDonough and Braungart have worked on the behalf of several MBDC clients in the textile industry to develop environmentally friendly fabrics for use in both carpets and furniture. These new fabrics can be recycled or composted and are free of any potentially harmful chemicals. MBDC worked with Switzerland's Rohner Textil, a mill that supplies fabric for Designtex, to design a new fabric called Climatex Lifecycle, which can be used in commercial upholstery and wall coverings and is fully recyclable. To create the new fabric, MBDC suggested the removal of polyester from a blend that also contained wool and ramie, because its presence had made recycling of the fabric problematic. To follow MBDC's suggestion, Rohner had to rework the fabric so that its attractive durability and texture could be retained.

McDonough's work has only just begun. If his utopian vision of a world in which industry and nature live in perfect harmony is to be achieved, a vast amount of work must be done. And you can be sure that McDonough will continue to be in the forefront of those who will make it happen.

Sources

Books

McDonough, William, and Michael Braungart, *Cradle to Cradle,* North Point Press, 2002.

Periodicals

Forbes, April 15, 2002, p. 110.
Progressive Engineer, September/October 2000.
Time, February 15, 1999.

Online

"William McDonough, FAIA," William McDonough, http://www.mcdonough.com (September 23, 2002).

—Don Amerman

Andre Miller

Professional basketball player

Born Andre Lloyd Miller, March 19, 1976, in Los Angeles, CA; son of Andrea Robinson. *Education:* University of Utah, B.A. 1998 (sociology).

Addresses: *Office*—Los Angeles Clippers STAPLES Center, 1111 S. Figueroa St., Ste. 1100, Los Angeles, CA 90015, website: http://www.nba.com/clippers.

Career

Played guard position in basketball, University of Utah, 1994–98; graduated Utah with all–time record in steals and second in career assists, 1998; drafted in first round by Cleveland Cavaliers, 1999; played on All–Rookie first team, 1999–2000; led Cavaliers in scoring with 15.9 points per game average, 2000–01; traded to Los Angeles Clippers, 2001.

Awards: Gold medal, Goodwill Games, 1998; gold medal, Goodwill Games, 2002; World Championship team, 2002.

Sidelights

Basketball player Andre Miller is a point guard for the Los Angeles Clippers. He played with the Cleveland Cavaliers from 1999 to 2001. Miller grew up in a tough neighborhood of South Central Los Angeles and played basketball as a way of staying off the streets and dealing with the emotional pain of his younger brother Duane's illness. Duane, who suffered from viral encephalitis for six years, died at the age of eleven in 1988.

Miller's mother, Andrea Robinson, told Mark Whicker in the Knight–Ridder/Tribune News Service that Miller's interest in basketball started "when his kindergarten teacher's husband took him to the Inglewood YMCA. At that time in a child's life there are so many activities." She said that of all the activities Miller tried, basketball was his favorite. However, Robinson wanted him to be more than a basketball player; she wanted him to be educated.

A star player at Verbum Dei High School in Los Angeles, Miller went on to Utah University in 1994. His mother chose the school, forbidding him to go to the Southern California junior college he had chosen. According to Dave Kindred in the *Sporting News*, she said, "Go. And don't come back." Miller, who was not interested in studying, thought he would simply go to college and play ball, but received a rude awakening in his freshman year when his grades were too poor for him to make the team. He did not qualify for a basketball scholarship, and had to sit out for a year and work to improve his grades.

Miller felt out of place in Salt Lake City, where the university was located, and worried about being able to study hard enough to qualify. He was homesick for Los Angeles and felt shy with the other players. Instead of quitting, Miller stayed with the program, began playing in his sophomore year, and in the following years he did well enough to be allowed to play for a fourth year. He also graduated with a degree in sociology. While playing at Utah, he led the team to a 114–20 record and to competition in the 1998 NCAA Championship game, which the team lost to Kentucky.

Despite the loss, Miller was noted as the top player in the game by Mike DeCourcy in the *Sporting News*. DeCourcy praised Miller's "abilities to change speeds on the break and leave the defenders guessing about his intentions, to think as he moves, to make a tough lay–up." He also noted, "This tournament belonged to Miller. He shared it with everyone who appreciates the game."

In 1998 and 2002, Miller helped the United States basketball team win gold medals at the Goodwill Games. The Cleveland Cavaliers drafted Miller in 1999. During his rookie season with the team, Miller became known for his fearless persistence, even when players on opposing teams elbowed him, hit him in the face, or knocked him down during play. Miller told *Sports Illustrated* reporter David Fleming that by the end of that season, "People know I'm just gonna keep on coming no matter what, and that's all the respect I need."

In the 2000–01 season, Miller did not have a reliable backup for the final 33 games, and he began looking tired. Cavaliers coach John Lucas told Chris Tomasson in the Knight–Ridder/Tribune News Service, "Andre looks dead out there. But that's the hand he's been dealt. He has to adjust to it." Miller tried to adjust, and denied that he was wearing down because of the lack of a backup player, but eventually, when it became obvious that his game was suffering, he told Tomasson, "I'm not going to say that I'm not tired. I get tired at times. It depends on how the game is going."

At the end of the 2000–01 season Miller's agent, Lon Babby, asked the Cavaliers to trade him; he wanted a higher salary for Miller, but knew that the Cavaliers could not afford it. In the end, the Cavaliers agreed to a trade with the Clippers: they traded Miller for Clippers forward Darius Miles. An NBA scout quoted in *Sports Illustrated* felt that the trade was a good move. "At 24 and with his selflessness, Miller is the right guy to run [the Clippers]. He sets an example of how to play the right way."

In 2001, Miller became the second player since 1980–81 to lead the NBA in assists (averaging 10.9 per game) for a losing team.

In March of 2002, Miller became one of 12 players chosen for the United States team in the World Championships, held in Indianapolis, Indiana, in August of 2002. Players in the World Championships generally are on the inside track to compete in the Olympic Games, and Miller is expected to compete in the 2004 Olympics, to be held in Athens, Greece.

In 2002, the Clippers's general manager, Elgin Baylor, told Ian Thomsen in *Sports Illustrated*, "On paper we're as talented as any team. Andre was the one piece we were missing." Miller told Thomsen, "I'm just going to try to bring a hard–work mentality. If I lead by example rather than by running my mouth, I'll get respect."

Sources

Periodicals

Knight Ridder/Tribune News Service, March 4, 2002; March 11, 2002; April 5, 2002; July 31, 2002.
Sporting News, April 6, 1998.
Sports Illustrated, April 17, 2000; August 12, 2002; October 28, 2002.
Washington Post, March 28, 1998.

Online

"Andre Miller," ESPN.com, http://sports.espn.go.com/ (October 30, 2002).
"Andre Miller: John Lucas Has Made a Big Difference," *Hoopshype.com*, http://www.hoopshype.com/interviews/andre_lester.htm (October 30, 2002).
"Andre Miller Player Info," NBA.com, http://www.nba.com/playerfile/andre_miller (March 3, 2003).

—*Kelly Winters*

Malia Mills

Swimsuit designer

Born Malia Margaret Mills in 1966, in Honolulu, HI. *Education:* Attended La Chambre Syndicale de la Couture Parisienne; Cornell University, B.A., 1990.

Addresses: *Office*—255 W. 36th St., 8th Floor, New York, NY 10018.

Career

Took first sewing class, 1978; studied apparel design at Cornell University in Ithaca, NY, and in Paris, France, 1986–90; worked as assistant designer at Jessica McClintock, Inc., 1990–92; launched Malia Mills Swim Wear, 1992; first Malia Mills bikini appeared in *Sports Illustrated* swimsuit issue, 1993; opened flagship boutique, downtown New York City, 1998; opened second store, Los Angeles, CA, 1999; netted $1 million in profits, 1999; opened third store, Miami, FL, 2000.

Awards: Award for Excellence in New Design, from Vidal Sassoon/Intercoiffure, 1993.

Sidelights

Designer Malia Mills sewed her first bikini when she was in college, and by the time she was in her mid–twenties her swimwear had appeared in *Sports Illustrated*'s popular swimsuit issue. As the principal of a successful swimwear company, Mills specializes in two–piece, mix–and–match bathing suits in lingerie–inspired designs. Her company's mission—to create swimwear that makes women feel good about their bodies—has earned Mills the devotion of a growing number of customers worldwide.

Though her designs have graced the bodies of magazine–cover supermodels, Mills has made waves in the fashion world for modeling her swimsuits on "real women" with imperfect bodies. Her suits range in price from about $120 to $160, and her business has been gradually expanding to include lingerie and other fashions and accessories. After making only $10,000 in sales in its first year, in 1999 Malia Mills Swim Wear reported a profit of $1 million.

Born in Honolulu, Hawaii, Mills was never far from the beach throughout her childhood. She and her three sisters could often be spotted on Waikiki Beach wearing matching floral baby–doll bathing suits. It wasn't often that the girls would wear bikinis, though, because their mother disapproved of the skimpy bathing attire. "[She] thought they were vulgar," Mills told Faye Penn of *P.O.V.*, reprinted at MaliaMills.com. Yet when she was ten years old, Mills received her first bikini—in lemon–yellow nylon/spandex with yellow plastic rings—as a Christmas present.

At age 12, Mills took a summertime class at the Singer Sewing Center upon her mother's recommendation. "When I was a kid I was really, really shy and my mom was always trying to think of ways for me to sort of get out there," Mills told CNNfn's *Business Unusual*. "So she enrolled me in this Singer sewing class.... I decided to make these red corduroy overalls.... [M]y mom had those tapes that said Malia Mills, so she could sew them on my clothes. So I cut one off and sewed it on the back pocket and I was like, hey, that's pretty excellent and I just loved it."

Two years later Mills and her family moved from Honolulu to Hanover, New Hampshire. After attending high school in Hanover, Mills studied apparel design at Cornell University in Ithaca, New York. Spending her junior year in Paris, France, she attended La Chambre Syndicale de la Couture Parisienne to study fashion. It was here that she met role model Maryvonne Herzog, a custom swimsuit designer.

Upon graduating from Cornell in 1990, Mills drove across country, taking an assistant–designer position at Jessica McClintock, Inc., in San Francisco, California. More than a year after she started her job, she received a phone call from a college friend, Julie Stern. As a newly hired assistant in the fashion department at *Sports Illustrated,* Stern encouraged Mills to design swimsuits and submit them for the magazine's famed annual swimsuit issue. "I had seen Malia stay up 72 hours straight to prepare for fashion shows at school," Stern recalled to Faye Penn of *P.O.V.* "She used to sleep curled up on one of those huge pattern tables next to her sewing machine at school. I knew she had the drive and was excited to give her the opportunity."

Within six weeks, Mills had designed six swimsuits, which she sent by overnight mail to *Sports Illustrated.* Although the suits never made it into the 1992 issue, Mills was encouraged by the positive response of the issue's editors. Quitting her job in 1991, she moved to New York City with a vision to create her own swimsuit company. Mills took up residence in a 500–square–foot loft in downtown Manhattan's TriBeCa neighborhood, where she waited tables by night and designed and sewed bathing suits by day. She launched her company, Malia Mills Swim Wear, in 1992. In her small loft, she mixed fabric dyes in an oversize pasta pot. From the beginning, Mills established her signature style: feminine, lingerie-inspired bikinis sold as separates that customers could mix and match.

It wasn't long before Mills's *Sports Illustrated* connection paid off. The 1993 swimsuit issue featured one of her designs—a charcoal–grey string bikini bottom paired with a matching long–sleeve, tie-front top—worn by supermodel Kathy Ireland. Practically overnight, Mills's business took off. Phone orders came in faster than Mills could set up a toll–free number to handle them, and two stores bought the suits as well.

One year after the *Sports Illustrated* debut, Mills took on an investor and quit her restaurant job. Also in 1994, she incorporated her business and took on Stern as a partner in the company. That summer, she and Stern worked round–the–clock to prepare for the swimwear line's national launch at the Hotel Macklowe. In August, a Malia Mills suit graced the cover of *Vanity Fair* magazine.

By autumn of 1994, Mills had perfected the "zig-zag" stitch that would become one of her bathing suits' trademarks. The following month, Mills received a phone call from Bloomingdales, the popular New York City department store, which wanted to feature a Malia Mills bathing suit in their Christmas windows on Lexington Avenue.

In 1995, Mills moved into a 1,000–square–foot studio closer to Manhattan's garment district, on 28th Street. By then Mills business had grown considerably, but was still netting only about $200,000 in sales. Although Mills's family had invested in the enterprise, as had an ex–boyfriend, Mills and Stern both went deep into debt. "[W]e take the money that we generate and for the most part, buy more fabric or buy more goods to make bathing suits and as a result we end up living personally off of credit cards," Mills told *Business Unusual.* "It's not necessarily the savviest way to build a business, but it's definitely gotten us very far."

It wasn't until 1999 that the company turned a significant profit of $1 million. With sales increasing, and with stores nationwide carrying Malia Mills bathing suits, the business grew stronger. Meanwhile, Mills published swimsuit catalogs that shocked the fashion world because they featured imperfect "real women" instead of flawless supermodels. "We wanted to show that our suits fit all sorts of shapes, sizes, and styles," Mills told Esther Gross Kremer of New York's *Daily News.* Although some fashion pundits criticized Mills for using inexperienced models, the catalogs generated a favorable response from customers.

"You can do amazing things in your life if you stop worrying about what your body looks like," Mills told Gwen Kilvert of *Sports Illustrated Women* in

2002, summing up the philosophy that drives her swimwear company. Looking to the future, Mills told CNNfn's *Entrepreneurs Only* that she plans to launch a line of lingerie "since that's the inspiration for our swimwear."

Sources

Periodicals

Daily News (New York), May 28, 2000, p. 13.
New York Times, May 4, 1997, section 13, p. 4.
Sports Illustrated Women, July/August 2002, p. 44.
Women's Wear Daily Swimwear Supplement, July 1998, p. 14; August 2000, p. 50.

Online

"Bikinis for the Supermodels," *P.O.V.*, http://www.maliamills.com/pr/features/pov.html (August 12, 2002).
Malia Mills Official Web Site, http://www.maliamills.com (August 12, 2002).

Transcripts

Business Unusual, #97112001FN–L12, CNNfn, November 20, 1997; #00042001FN–112, April 20, 2000.
Entrepreneurs Only, #00031602FN–118, CNNfn, March 16, 2000.

—Wendy Kagan

Kylie Minogue

AP/Wide World Photos

Singer and actress

Born May 28, 1968, in Melbourne, Australia; daughter of Ron (an accountant) and Carol (a ballet dancer) Minogue.

Addresses: *Record company*—EMI/Parlophone, 43 Brook Green, 5th Floor, W6 7EF London, United Kingdom. *Website*—Kylie Minogue Official Website: http://www.kylie.com.

Career

Recorded "Locomotion" for Australian release on the Mushroom label; signed with PWL International label, c. 1987; released "I Should Be So Lucky," 1988; signed with DeConstruction label, 1993; released *Kylie Minogue*, 1994; signed with EMI/Parlophone, 1999; released *Light Years*, 2000; released *Fever*, 2002. Television appearances include: *Skyways*, 1979; *The Henderson Kids*, 1985; *The Zoo Family*, 1985; *Fame and Misfortune*, 1986; *Neighbours*, 1986–88. Film appearances include: *The Delinquents*, 1989; *Street Fighter*, 1994; *Hayride to Hell*, 1995; *Bio-Dome*, 1996; *Misfit*, 1996; *Cut*, 2000; *Sample People*, 2000; *Moulin Rouge*, 2001. Executive producer of films, including: *The Island*, 2000; *Subterrain*, 2001.

Awards: Australian Record Industry Association Awards: Highest Selling Single, Best Pop Release, Single of the Year, all for "Can't Get You Out of My Head," and Highest Selling Album for *Fever*, 2002; BRIT Awards, Best International Female and Best International Album for *Fever*, 2002; MTV Video Music Award for best choreography, for "Can't Get You Out of My Head," 2002.

Sidelights

With the release of her single "Spinning Around" in the summer of 2000, Australian singer and actress Kylie Minogue scored her twenty–seventh Top 20 hit in Great Britain, a feat she matched in numerous other countries in Europe, the Far East, and of course, Australia. Minogue also set a record with the estimated 220,000 concert tickets she sold in her home country for the tour in support of her album *Light Years*, making her Australia's best–selling female live performer. While Minogue had been successful since her debut on the pop charts in 1988, her latest accomplishments ensured her status as an international icon of popular music alongside the likes of Madonna, with whom she was often compared for her ever–changing image makeovers, diverse musical directions, and devoted fan base.

Born into a theatrical family in Melbourne, Australia, on May 28, 1968, Minogue gained her first professional experience on the Australian television drama series *Skyways* when she was ten years old. Shortly thereafter, she landed a continuing role on the children's show *The Henderson Kids*. As a teenage actress, however, Minogue found a breakthrough role as Charlene in *Neighbors*, an Australian soap opera that was also broadcast in Great Britain and Canada. Building on her popularity in the show, Minogue appeared at a charity concert in 1987, singing the 1960s Little Eva hit "Loco-Motion," which proved to be a highlight of the evening. Soon, the actress with only a minor aspiration to be a singer found herself in the recording studio to prepare the single for commercial release. When it went to the top of the charts in Australia in July of 1987, Minogue's singing career was suddenly underway.

Although her success as a singer was unexpected, the petite actress benefitted from her record company's connection to the legendary producers Mike Stock, Matt Aitken, and Pete Waterman (S–A–W), a London–based team that had worked with popular groups on the 1980s such as Bananarama and Dead or Alive. Sent to London to record a debut album to build on the initial success of "Loco-Motion," Minogue put herself fully in the care of S–A–W. The collaboration resulted in a collection of romantic, up–tempo tunes aimed squarely at the pop market. As she recounted in a 1995 interview with Britain's *New Musical Express*, "When I made my first album, what you heard was pretty much all there was to me as a person anyway. I never spoke my mind, didn't do what I really wanted, because I didn't really know what I wanted."

While the lyrical content of her 1988 debut album, *Kylie*, was lightweight, its success was astounding. By the end of 1988, Minogue had four top–five singles in Britain: "I Should Be So Lucky," a number–one debut hit that became her trademark song; "Got to Be Certain," another uptempo, romance–themed track; the rereleased "Loco-Motion," which also went into the top three in the United States; and "Je Ne Sais Pas Porquoi," a mid-tempo ballad. Minogue capped the year with the release of "Especially for You," a duet with *Neighbors* co–star Jason Donovan. The song hit Number One in Britain in January of 1989. Eventually, *Kylie* sold about two million copies in Britain, where Minogue earned the distinction of being the youngest female artist to score a number–one album up to that time. In the meantime, Minogue's younger sister, Dannii, who had also appeared on *Neighbors*, started to score on the pop charts as well; in 1991, Dannii Minogue had four hit singles, followed by some additional chart successes in the latter part of the decade.

Minogue's second album, *Enjoy Yourself*, marked the end of the singer's profile in the United States, where it failed to make an impact. In Britain, however, it was another stunning success, with the singles "Hand on Your Heart," "Wouldn't Change a Thing," "Never Too Late," and "Tears on My Pillow" hitting the top five. Yet Minogue increasingly felt constrained by the S–A–W production team. While their success was indisputable—in 1989, fully one–quarter of Britain's Top 40 singles of the year were S–A–W productions—Minogue felt compelled to break out of her squeaky–clean image. She began by taking charge of her video shoots, offering her fans a more provocative image than had been produced under the guidance of S–A–W. Minogue also returned to her work as an actress, although her roles—such as the romantic interest in the Pauly Shore film *Biosphere*—were quickly overshadowed by her musical career.

Minogue began appearing in more avant–garde British monthlies like *I–D* and *The Face*, rather than the teen pop magazines that had boosted her career in its initial years. In 1993, she surprised many by signing with a respected dance label, DeConstruction, owned by media giant BMG. *Kylie Minogue*, the first record she made for her new label, was released in 1994. *Billboard*'s Larry Flick described it as an "odd, yet mildly appealing, blend of ballads and sugar-disco." In 1994, the singer appeared opposite Jean-Claude Van Damme in the film *Street Fighter*, but it was her friendships with other musical personalities that broadened her horizons. She befriended fellow Australian Nick Cave—an unlikely match, for the longtime alternative rocker was famous for his somber, darkly lyrical songs. When they met, Cave confessed he had been a fan of Minogue's for years, and had even written several songs for her. She joined him in a duet for his *Murder Ballads* album, and he encouraged her to dig deeper into herself during songwriting bouts.

At one point in the mid–1990s, Minogue and her then–boyfriend, photographer Stephane Sednaoui, drove across the United States, and she took a notebook with her to write down song inspirations. Testifying to the unusual cult following that the singer enjoyed, a number of well–known figures from British music stepped in to help produce her next record, including members of the Manic Street Preachers and Brothers In Rhythm. The result was a series of songs for a 1997 DeConstruction release initially titled *Impossible Princess*. But, following the Paris, France, car crash that killed the Princess of Wales, the album's title was changed at the last minute to simply *Kylie Minogue*. Two singles were released in the United Kingdom before the album was sent to stores, and "Some Kind of Bliss" and "Did It Again" did well on the British charts. Writing in *Billboard*, Flick called the record "stunning," and singled out "Limbo" and "Say Hey" as "intense groove poems ... which sew intelligent, often self–examining words into timely music that darts back and forth between moody electro–funk and richly layered modern pop." One track, "Breathe," hit No. 14 in the United Kingdom, but some of the British music press mocked Minogue's alternative-music pretensions.

Although critics received her albums of the late-1990s with slightly more enthusiasm than her S–A–W productions, it seemed that Minogue's omnipresence on the pop charts had ended. Although her singles continued to make the Top 20 with regularity, her last album of the decade, *Kylie Minogue,* sold only 60,000 copies, a far cry from the double-platinum sales of her debut. Minogue also suffered a personal loss with the suicide of Michael Hutchence, singer for INXS, in November of 1997; they dated from 1989–91, and although they had not dated for several years, Minogue had often referred to Hutchence's role in her personal and artistic development. When asked about the late singer in a *Q* interview in April of 2001, Minogue said simply, "He was wonderful and inspirational."

Although she had engaged some darker themes on her post–S–A–W albums, Minogue returned to her roots with the 2000 release *Light Years.* As the singer told Malaysia's *New Straits–Management Times,* "The album is basically hot disco. It's an uplifting, vibrant album. When I first met with the different writers and producers, we discussed and vocalised the musical style. I gave them my keywords, which were 'pool side,' 'disco,' and 'cocktails.'" Minogue was richly rewarded for her decision to return to her pop roots: the album's first single, "Spinning Around," became another number–one hit in Britain, where it was followed by "Kids," a smash duet with British pop singer Robbie Williams.

As successful as *Light Years* was, it was Minogue's next album that reestablished her as a pop star in America. Bolstered by the aptly titled single "Can't Get You Out of My Head," her first hit single in the United States since "Loco–Motion," *Fever* went platinum in a matter of months and rose to Number Three on the *Billboard* charts. All Music Guide's Chris True praised *Fever* as "a very stylish Euro-flavored dance–pop record that will appeal to all ages. Not one weak track, not one misplaced syrupy ballad to ruin the groove." For her part, Kylie said with a laugh to *People*'s Kevin Airs, "It's nice not to be the one–hit wonder 'Loco–Motion' girl for the rest of my life."

Selected discography

Kylie, Geffen, 1988.
Enjoy Yourself, Geffen, 1989.
Rhythm of Love, Mushroom, 1990.
Let's Get To It, Mushroom, 1991.
Kylie Minogue, Deconstruction, 1994.
Impossible Princess (aka *Kylie Minogue*), Deconstruction, 1997.
Intimate & Live, Mushroom, 1999.
Light Years, Parlophone, 2000.
Hits, BMG, 2000.
Fever, Capitol, 2002.

Sources

Books

Contemporary Musicians, volume 32, Gale Group, 2003.

Periodicals

Australian, January 26, 2001; April 16, 2001; April 21, 2001.
Billboard, April 4, 1998; June 17, 2000.
Daily Variety, April 24, 2001; October 17, 2002.
Interview, May 2002, p. 88.
New Musical Express, October 7, 1995.
New Straits–Management Times (Malaysia), September 29, 2000.
People, August 12, 2002, p. 85–86.
Q, October 2000; April 2001.
Time, April 8, 2002, p. 68.

Online

"Fever," All Music Guide, http://www.allmusic.com/ (May 27, 2003).
"Kylie Minogue," All Music Guide, http://www.allmusic.com/ (May 22, 2003).
"Kylie Minogue," Internet Movie Database.com, http://us.imdb.com/Name?Minogue,+Kylie (June 30, 2003).

—*Carol Brennan*

Charles Moose

Former Chief of Police, Montgomery County, Maryland

Born Charles Alexander Moose, c. 1953, in New York, NY; married Linder (divorced); married Sandra Moose (an attorney), c. 1985; children: David (from first marriage). *Education:* University of North Carolina, B.A., 1975; Portland State University, M.P.A., 1984; Portland State University, Ph.D., 1993.

Addresses: *Office*—Montgomery County Police Headquarters, 2350 Research Blvd., Rockville, MD 20850.

Career

City of Portland, Oregon, patrol officer, 1975–81; sergeant, 1981–84; lieutenant, 1984–91; captain, 1991–92; deputy chief, 1992–93, chief of police, 1993–99; Oregon Air National Guard, major, 1987–98; Portland State University, adjunct faculty in criminal justice, 1994–99; Montgomery County Chief of Police, 1999–2003; District of Columbia, Air National Guard, major, 1999—; Montgomery College, adjunct faculty, 2000—.

Awards: Community Leadership Award, Federal Bureau of Investigation, 1995; Man of the Year Award, Boys and Girls Club, 1996–97; United States Community Relations Service Special Recognition Award, 1998; William French Smith Award for Outstanding Contribution to Cooperative Law Enforcement, 1998; Employer Support Freedom Award, Secretary of Defense William S. Cohen, 1998; Distinguished Community Service Award, Association for Retarded Citizens, 1998.

Sidelights

He had worked for years within the police community, making contributions that were honored within law enforcement. On October 2, 2002, a shooting spree began that would leave ten people dead and three wounded, and catapult Montgomery County, Maryland, Police Chief Charles Moose into the national spotlight. A 27–year veteran of police work, Moose led a task force comprised of police officers, federal agents, forensics specialists, firearms experts and other specialists to discover the identity of the snipers who terrorized the outlying suburbs of Washington, D.C., for three weeks.

Initially uncomfortable in the spotlight, Moose exhibited a willingness to learn and soon became adept at dealing with the media as well as initiating a dialogue with the snipers via news conferences. He endured international scrutiny that led some to question his effectiveness and call for his replacement as head of the investigation. Overall, he proved himself capable, and his team successfully apprehended the snipers, John Allen Muhammed and John Lee Malvo, on October 24, 2002.

Charles Alexander Moose was born in New York City while his father was finishing up his degree at Columbia University around 1953. Afterward, the

Moose family settled in Lexington, North Carolina, where Moose grew up in a segregated middle class neighborhood. His father taught biology at a local high school and his mother was a registered nurse.

Moose attended the University of North Carolina at Chapel Hill, where he earned a degree in history. During his senior year, a political science professor, Reuben Greenberg, encouraged Moose to apply for a job in Oregon with the City of Portland Police Department, which was seeking more minority officers. Even though he had never been to the city, Moose applied and was accepted for a position as a patrol officer.

Early in his career, Moose caught the media's attention. Working undercover, he was part of a team that infiltrated and busted a crime ring involved in stolen property. The story of their successful sting operation was picked up by the news show *60 Minutes*. Moose's concept of police work was tainted by the attention. He related to Kevin Chappell of *Ebony*, "I hadn't been on the job but two years and I was already being interviewed on *60 Minutes*. I thought it was going to be like that all of the time."

As it turned out, the job didn't involve constant media adoration. Moose spent 18 years working his way up within the ranks of the Portland Police Department. During those years he also acted as a major in the Oregon Air National Guard. In addition, he attended Portland State University where he earned a Master of Public Administration degree in 1984 and a doctorate in criminology and urban studies in 1993. After earning his doctorate, Moose taught at Portland State University as an adjunct faculty member.

Moose was known as an innovator, and was instrumental in establishing several special teams and units that increased positive community relations. He developed a team to deal with mentally ill criminals. He created standards and procedures on how to use less–than–lethal force when apprehending violent criminals. He also formed a team to help victims of violent crime and their families.

In 1993, Moose became the first African–American police chief in Portland's history. He began his six–year tenure by moving to one of Portland's worst neighborhoods. This bold move was symbolic of his intention to make all of Portland safe. Crime did decrease during his stint as police chief; it dropped by 18 percent. His success attracted the attention of the federal government. During the Clinton admin-

istration, he was invited to lead the newly formed Community Oriented Policing Services. He turned the offer down.

In 1999, a search committee trying to find a new police chief for Montgomery County, Maryland, tapped Moose as an appropriate candidate for the job. Initially uninterested because he was looking for a bigger city, Moose was persuaded to take the job by County Executive Doug Duncan. In his new position, Moose helped the department improve its relations with the community as well as increase staff morale.

All of Moose's abilities were tested during the month of October in 2002, when two snipers launched a shooting spree in Montgomery County. In 24 hours, five people were fatally shot and for the next three weeks the random shootings continued. Because the shootings had started in Moose's district he became the liaison between the press and the investigative team that he headed. For Moose, who had dealt with serial killings as police chief in Portland, the difference was the scope of the fear inspired by the sniper attacks. He explained to Chappell, "In terms of the actual investigation, the thing that was so different was so many people were scared.... They were killing so quickly. Most serial killers will kill one, then 18 months later, kill another.... but they don't start with five, then every 36 hours do another."

The sniper shootings garnered constant media attention, leaving Moose no choice but to use news conferences to help calm the panicked citizens of Montgomery County as well as the entire nation. Working on no more than five hours of sleep each night, the fatigue and frustration he felt was visible with each succeeding press conference. Moose had never had an easy relationship with the media. He explained to Chappell, "I feel like I got my fair share of media in Portland during my six years as chief."

Moose's frustration came to a head when the media leaked information to the public that he thought needed to be withheld. He vented his anger in a televised news conference in which he harshly criticized news outlets for interfering with police work. He sarcastically offered to let them solve the case and put his police force to work on other problems. Following his outburst at the press conference Moose began working more closely with FBI specialists who helped him script his conferences, often making statements directed specifically to the snipers.

Moose had to field even more media attention with the successful conclusion of the sniper investigation. On top of the requests for interviews that he received, he also needed to catch up with police work that was shelved during the ordeal. In the face of the trying circumstances of October of 2002, Moose showed his strengths and weaknesses. He wept for the victims and expressed anger at the snipers' willingness to target anyone. Despite constant criticism, Moose kept control of the investigation and often managed to soothe those terrified by the random shootings. With the capture of the snipers, he returned to his regular duties but Moose was changed by the events. He told Chappell, "You try to always remember to tell the people you love that you love them every day."

A county ethics commission ruled that Moose not finish writing his book, *Three Weeks in October: The Manhunt for the Serial Sniper*, which is scheduled for release in October of 2003. However, the book was posted on Amazon.com for preorder sales. Moose appealed the commission's decision, but state and federal courts have yet to rule. According to CNN.com, on March 20, the commission said Moose's request to write a book and consult on a movie project violated the county's code of ethics, which forbids employees from exploiting the prestige of public office for personal gain. In Moose's federal lawsuit, he maintains that any attempt to prevent him from writing the book violates his First Amendment rights. Montgomery County Council members Phil Andrews and Mike Knapp questioned whether Moose should remain chief of police because of the decision to list the book. Both councilmen said they thought it will be up to County Executive Douglas Duncan to decide what action should be taken. However, Duncan often stated that he supports Moose's desire to write the book and appeal the commission's decision. In June of 2003 Moose resigned as police chief in the wake of the conflict with county leaders. According to Salon.com, his attorney, Ron Karp, read a statement that said Moose felt it was time "to move on and explore other paths

in life." In July of 2003, Moose reached a settlement with the commission that allowed him to write the book and pursue a movie project.

Selected writings

(With Charles Fleming) *Three Weeks in October: The Manhunt for the Serial Sniper,* EP Dutton, 2003.

Sources

Periodicals

Ebony, April 2003, pp. 86–89.
Knight Ridder/Tribune News Service, October 25, 2002.
M2 Best Books, February 11, 2003.
New York Post, October 23, 2002, p. 5.
People, November 4, 2002, p. 75.
Time, December 30, 2002, p. 114.

Online

"Charles Moose given a send–off to mark his departure," CNN.com, http://www.cnn.com/2003/US/South/07/10/moose.farewell.ap/index.html (July 11, 2003).
"Despite Ruling, Chief Moose's Book For Sale," CNN.com, http://www.cnn.com/2003/SHOWBIZ/books/06/14/moose.book.ap/index.html (June 17, 2003).
"Police Chief Who Led Sniper Probe Resigns," Salon.com, http://www.salon.com/news/wire/2003/06/18/police/index.html (June 18, 2003).

—Eve M. B. Hermann

Viggo Mortensen

Actor and poet

Born October 20, 1958, in New York, NY; married Exene Cervenka (a musician), 1987 (divorced, 1997); children: Henry Blake. *Education:* Earned degree from St. Lawrence University, 1980.

Addresses: *Agent*—Creative Artists Agency, 9830 Wilshire Blvd., Beverly Hills, CA 90212–1825. *Home*—Los Angeles, CA.

Career

Actor in films, including: *Witness*, 1985; *Salvation! Have You Said Your Prayers Today*, 1987; *Fresh Horses*, 1988; *Prison*, 1988; *Leatherface: The Texas Chainsaw Massacre III*, 1990; *Young Guns II*, 1990; *The Reflecting Skin*, 1990; *Tripwire*, 1990; *The Indian Runner*, 1991; *Boiling Point*, 1993; *Carlito's Way*, 1993; *Ruby Cairo*, 1993; *Deception*, 1993; *The Gospel According to Harry*, 1993; *Two Small Bodies*, 1993; *The Young Americans*, 1993; *Desert Lunch*, 1994; *Floundering*, 1994; *The Crew*, 1994; *Crimson Tide*, 1995; *American Yakuza*, 1995; *Black Velvet Pantsuit*, 1995; *The Prophecy*, 1995; *The Passion of Darkly Noon*, 1995; *Gimlet*, 1995; *Daylight*, 1996; *Albino Alligator*, 1996; *The Portrait of a Lady*, 1996; *G.I. Jane*, 1997; *La Pistola de mi Hermano*, 1997; *A Perfect Murder*, 1998; *Psycho*, 1998; *A Walk on the Moon*, 1999; *28 Days*, 2000; *Original Sin*, 2000; *The Lord of the Rings: The Fellowship of the Ring*, 2001; *The Lord of the Rings: The Two Towers*, 2002; *The Alamo*, 2003; *Hidalgo*, 2003; *The Lord of the Rings: The Return of the King*, 2003. Television appearances include: *George Washington* (miniseries), CBS, 1984; *ABC Afterschool Special*, "High School Narc" episode, ABC, 1985; *Miami Vice*, 1987; *Once in a Blue Moon* (movie), 1990; *Vanishing Point*, Fox, 1997. Stage appearances include: *Romeo and Juliet*, Indiana Repertory Theatre, Indianapolis, IN, 1985–86; *Bent*, Coast Playhouse, Los Angeles, CA.

Sidelights

News that Viggo Mortensen would take the romantic warrior–hero role in the planned *Lord of the Rings* trilogy caused some media pundits to wonder whether the Danish–American actor was poised for major Hollywood stardom. Yet Mortensen had been working steadily for nearly 20 years by time the first *Lord of the Rings* story, *The Fellowship of the Ring*, was released in 2001. One of his more noteworthy performances prior to that was in the 1997 Demi Moore drama *G.I. Jane*, where he played a sadistic training officer. Mortensen remains sanguine about stardom and the publicity machine that has shadowed his career. "I've been told I had arrived many times in the past 20 years," he pointed out to *Los Angeles Times* writer Irene Lacher. "And presumably departed as well."

Mortensen was born in 1958 to a Danish father and an American mother. He lived in both Argentina and Denmark until the age of eleven, when his parents divorced and he and two older brothers settled with their mother in upstate New York. It was 1969, and Mortensen experienced culture shock. "When I came to the United States, the news was full of things like Woodstock and the moon landing and the Manson killings and *Easy Rider* and *Mad* magazine," he recalled in an interview with Amy Longsdorf of the Bergen County *Record*. "I got a crash course in pop culture that summer." After high school, Mortensen studied Spanish and government at St. Lawrence University in New York, and traveled extensively. He eventually settled in New York City and tended bar while attempting to establish himself as an actor. He made his first television appearance as Lieutenant LeBoeuf in a CBS miniseries about George Washington in 1984, and the following year appeared in an *ABC Afterschool Special* titled "High School Narc." He attracted notice for his role in the stage drama *Bent* at the Coast Playhouse in Los Angeles, California. Small parts in *The Purple Rose of Cairo* and *Swing Shift* followed, but Mortensen's scenes in these were cut and never made it to the screen. His first notable film appearance was as an Amish farmer in the 1985 Peter Weir–directed movie *Witness.*

In 1987 Mortensen wed punk pioneer Exene Cervenka, chanteuse of the late–1970s Los Angeles band X, and soon had a son; as a result, he began taking some of the more mainstream film offers that came his way, such as *Leatherface: The Texas Chainsaw Massacre III* and *Young Guns II.* "I had stayed away from commercial films because the characters didn't appeal to me," he told the *Record*'s Longsdorf, "but I needed to support my family." In 1991, Sean Penn cast him in *The Indian Runner* as a troubled Vietnam veteran who returns to his small Nebraska hometown and begins to make trouble for his police–officer brother. It was Penn's directorial debut, from a script he also wrote, and *New Republic* critic Stanley Kauffmann asserted that "the picture is held together—as Penn surely knew—by Viggo Mortensen's performance.... For this film, he embodies perfectly the truth of 'badness' as egomania: the person who sees the hypocrisy of society and the humiliations of docility and, instead of using these perceptions as an inverse power source for getting through the day, takes them as a license to hurt and steal and kill.... It's a part that Penn might have played himself, but, wisely, he directed Mortensen instead."

One of Mortensen's next intense performances, though it was a small one, came alongside Penn and Al Pacino in the 1993 Brian DePalma drama *Carlito's Way.* He went on to appear in four movies that year alone, before impressing critics again with a supporting role in the 1995 nuclear–submarine thriller *Crimson Tide* opposite Denzel Washington

and Gene Hackman. Mortensen worked steadily for the next few years, mostly in action or crime–drama fare, such as *American Yakuza, Daylight* (a 1996 Sylvester Stallone film), and the little–seen *Albino Alligator.* In 1996, he appeared in a surprise romantic turn in Jane Campion's lavish adaptation of the Henry James novel, *The Portrait of a Lady,* as one of the love interests of fictional Isabel Archer, played by Nicole Kidman.

Mortensen attracted a good deal of notice for his portrayal of a sadistic superior officer alongside Demi Moore in 1997's *G.I. Jane.* The film followed the travails of Moore's Lieutenant Jordan O'Neil, who becomes the first female accepted into the elite but rigorous Navy SEAL training program; Mortensen's Master Chief John Urgayle, opposed to the idea of a co–ed SEAL future, attempts to wear her down. He subjects her to the same abuse that other SEAL recruits endure, but also adds a dose of psychological cruelty. In one mock prisoner–of–war scene, Mortensen's character slugs O'Neil, but she clocks him in return. It was, declared *Newsweek*'s Jack Kroll, "the screen's all–time best intergender fight." Kroll noted that as foil for Moore's determined O'Neil, "Mortensen is splendid in this role; his excessive ferocity forces her to the extreme effort that is necessary if she is to succeed." *National Review* critic John Simon also liked Mortensen's intensity of character, which he found marked by "a sublime blend of patriotic fervor and flat–out sadism."

Mortensen's off–screen persona is a far different one than usually shown in his roles. He is a published poet, and has dabbled in the visual arts as well. When called to play an artist in a planned 1998 remake of an Alfred Hitchcock thriller, he asked if he could provide the canvases himself. *A Perfect Murder,* which found him in an on–screen romantic triangle alongside Gwyneth Paltrow and Michael Douglas, earned mostly dismal reviews, however. Mortensen played a dashing, unshaven artist, David Shaw, who is involved in an adulterous liaison with Paltrow's character, wife of Douglas's formidable and wealthy Wall Street trader. Incensed when he learns of the affair, the husband then learns that Shaw regularly cons wealthy heiresses out of their fortunes, and enters into a pact with Shaw to eliminate her. "Mortensen undergoes an interesting transformation in his key scene with Douglas," remarked *Chicago Sun–Times* reviewer Roger Ebert. "We believe him when he's a nice guy, and we believe him even more when he's not; he doesn't do a big style shift, he simply turns off his people–pleasing face."

After appearing in another Hitchcock remake, director Gus Van Sant's *Psycho* in 1998, Mortensen won critical acclaim for his role as an itinerant hippie who romances a 1960s Jewish wife and mother, played by Diane Lane, in *A Walk on the Moon*. The film's reviews usually mentioned a waterfall scene in which Lane's Brooklyn housewife trysts with the longhaired, free–spirited character played by Mortensen. He took on a straighter role helping Sandra Bullock's character come to terms with her alcoholism in *28 Days*, but around this time was tendered a surprise offer: director Peter Jackson asked him to take on a key role in the epic *Lord of the Rings* trilogy. Filming was about to start on the adaptation of the classic J. R. R. Tolkien novels in New Zealand, and Jackson was not happy with the original actor cast. Mortensen had just days to decide whether he wanted to take the part of Aragorn and spend 18 months in New Zealand; all told, the project required a three–year commitment for the actors involved.

Mortensen had never read the Tolkien books, but his adolescent son was familiar with them, and thrilled that his father was being offered the role of Lord Aragorn "Strider" Elessar, a mortal who was once heir to the throne of Gondor. As Mortensen told Marshall Fine, a writer with the *Journal News* of Westchester, New York, "I had one major consideration: It would have been a lengthy period of absence from my son," he says. "But when I expressed my misgivings, he said, 'You should do it.'" Mortensen felt that the exiled mortal was an appealingly ambiguous role to play, as he told *Independent* writer Ryan Gilbey. "I had read enough on the plane to see that the character had misgivings about the burden of the undertaking. He feels the weight of other people's expectations; it's one thing for someone to tell you that you're capable but it's quite another for you to know it yourself. I felt that in Aragorn, and I felt it too as an actor: 'You've hired me 'cos you think I can do it but privately I'm not sure.'"

The first film in the trilogy, *The Fellowship of the Ring*, was one of the most anticipated movies of 2001, and won rave reviews when released that December. Starring Elijah Wood as Frodo Baggins and Ian McClellen as the good wizard Gandalf, the tale is set in Middle Earth and starts off in the land of the Hobbits. Frodo inherits a powerful ring, which gives its wearer immense power, and teams with a band of renegades, Aragorn included, to return it to the only place where it can be destroyed—in a furnace called the Fire of Doom, located in the dreaded land of the Mordors. The evil wizard who forged it, Saruman, is desperate to have it returned to him, and pursues the band of elves and Hobbits, for which Aragorn serves as de facto leader. Along the way, Aragorn dallies with an elfin princess, Arwen, played by Liv Tyler. "Mortensen brings the magne-

tism of an anti–hero to Aragorn, the wandering outcast king," opined the *San Francisco Chronicle*'s Mick LaSalle. "Like Sean Bean, who is equally impressive as Boromir, Mortensen gives the sense of a great man in reduced times."

The first Lord of the Rings film was the second–highest–grossing release of 2001, earning $860 million worldwide. Its sequel, the *The Two Towers*, was released in late 2002 and took a darker turn, with more violence, doom, and an epic battle scene. Mortensen's Aragorn had a larger role in this story, urging King Theoden of Rohan to take a decisive stand against the beastly army assembled by Saruman's ally, the evil Sauron, and emerged as a swashbuckling horseman. The romance with Arwen is thwarted, but another to come is hinted at with King Theoden's niece, Eowyn, played by Miranda Otto. Peter Travers, writing in *Rolling Stone*, found the actor "growing steadily impressive in the role." Mortensen was reportedly so intense about his part that he was never without his sword on the set, rode his horse during his off–hours, and even slept out of doors at times.

The third film in the trilogy, *The Return of the King*, was set for a 2003 release. Mortensen undertook a minimal press tour in late 2002 to promote *The Two Towers*, but did appear wearing a t–shirt with a hand–painted anti–war message. Mortensen was blunt about the film being harnessed as a propaganda measure in relation to U.S. foreign policy against Iraq. Some reviewers had noted that Tolkien wrote the books in late–1930s England, when that country failed to recognize the threat that Germany's Nazi regime posed. Mortensen did not want any similarities drawn between the battle over good and evil forces in the film during a time of strong talk about a potential U.S.–led military action against Iraq to oust its leader, Saddam Hussein. "In our time, for better or worse, there are these simplistic comparisons made between the Middle East and our movie," Mortensen told Fine in the *Journal News* interview. "I do have a problem with comparisons to our movie," he said. "It's us against the bad guys and woe to them who question whether we're doing the right thing."

Divorced from Cervenka in 1997, Mortensen still paints and exhibits his work in galleries in Los Angeles and New York. He continues to write poetry, and founded Perceval Press to publish both his and the works of his girlfriend, Lola Schnabel, daughter of painter and director Julian Schnabel. One of his next projects, *Hidalgo*, also calls for some daring equestrianship: the film stars Mortensen as famed Pony Express rider Frank T. Hopkins, a distance racer who competed in the Arabian desert in the 1890s. Though he was named one of *People* magazine's 50 most beautiful people of 2002, Mortensen remains wary about the Hollywood star system. His forays into music, poetry, and painting serve to ground him, as he told *Entertainment Weekly*'s Gillian Flynn. The paintings, in particular, remain "something where I can look at the end product and—whether I like it or you like it—I can say that's something I did. That came out of me. That's not true of movies."

Selected writings

Ten Last Night (poetry), Illuminati Publishers, 1993.
Recent Forgeries (poetry), Smart Art Press, 1998.
Coincidence of Memory (poetry), Perceval Press, 2002.

Sources

Books

Contemporary Theatre, Film and Television, volume 31, Gale, 2000.

Periodicals

Boston Herald, June 3, 1998, p. 39.
Chicago Sun–Times, June 5, 1998.

Daily Record (Glasgow, Scotland), December 12, 2002, p. 8.
Daily Variety, December 6, 2002, p. 9.
Entertainment Weekly, November 3, 1995, p. 79; August 22, 1997, p. 105; June 19, 1998, p. 46; December 21, 2001, p. 36.
Guardian (London, England), December 13, 2002, p. 14.
Independent (London, England), December 14, 2001, p. 9.
Journal News (Westchester, NY), December 17, 2002, p. 1E.
Los Angeles Magazine, December 1998, p. 56.
Los Angeles Times, June 5, 1998, p. 6; February 5, 2002, p. E2; December 21, 2002, p. E1.
National Review, September 29, 1997, p. 60; July 20, 1998, p. 51.
New Republic, October 21, 1991, p. 26.
Newsweek, August 25, 1997, p. 73.
New York Times, December 27, 2002, p. E13.
Observer (London, England), December 16, 2001, p. 7; December 15, 2002, p. 7;
People, May 13, 2002, p. 184.
Record (Bergen County, NJ), March 25, 1999, p. Y1.
Rolling Stone, January 2, 2003.
San Francisco Chronicle, December 19, 2001, p. D1; December 18, 2002, p. D1.
Seattle Times, January 17, 1997, p. F1; August 22, 1997, p. G1.
Time, September 1, 1997, p. 77; April 12, 1999, p. 90.

—Carol Brennan

Walter Mosley

AP/Wide World Photos

Author

Born on January 12, 1952, in Los Angeles, CA; son of LeRoy (a school custodian) and Ella (a school personnel clerk) Mosley; married Joy Kellman (a dancer and choreographer), 1987. *Education:* Attended Goddard College, 1971; Johnson State College, B.A., 1977; attended writing program at City College of New York, 1985–89.

Addresses: *Home*—New York City. *Publisher*—W. W. Norton & Co., Inc., 500 Fifth Ave., New York, NY 10110. *Website*—Walter Mosley Official Website: http://www.waltermosley.com.

Career

Worked as a computer consultant for Mobil Oil, and as a computer programmer, potter, and caterer; full–time writer, 1986—.

Member: TransAfrica; National Book Foundation; Poetry Society of America; Manhattan Theater Club.

Awards: John Creasey Memorial Award and Shamus Award, both for outstanding mystery writing; winner of the Black Caucus of the American Library Association's Literary Award for *RL's Dream*, 1996; winner of the Annisfield–Wolf Book Award for *Always Outnumbered, Always Outgunned*, 1998; winner of the TransAfrica International Literary Prize.

Sidelights

Walter Mosley has broken new ground as a mystery writer by incorporating issues of race into novels that stand on their own as gripping detective fiction. His novels are all written from an African–American perspective. He has also branched out into the areas of science fiction and social commentary.

Critics have praised Mosley's writing for its realistic portrayal of street life in African–American neighborhoods of post–World War II Los Angeles, California. Much of Mosley's success has been due to the powerful recurring character of Ezekiel ("Easy") Rawlins, one of the most innovative private investigators to appear in fiction. Unlike many detectives who populate the pages of hard–boiled prose, Rawlins is a multidimensional character who stumbled into his sleuthing career as a means to pay mounting debts. Mosley has used Rawlins to expose the problems of getting by in a world where only a thin line lies between crime and business as usual.

Mosley was born in southeastern Los Angeles in 1952 and grew up in Watts and the Pico–Fairfax district. His father was an African American from the deep South, and his mother a white woman of Jewish descent whose family emigrated from Eastern Europe. This unique African American/Jewish heritage made prejudice a major topic in the household. An only child, Mosley grew up hearing about the woes of life for African Americans in the South, as well as the horrors of anti–Semitism across the Atlantic. However, he was also regaled by colorful accounts of partying and carrying on among his African–American relatives, along with tales of czars in old Russia.

After earning a bachelor's degree at Johnson State College in 1977, Mosley drifted for a number of years in various jobs. He and Joy Kellman, a dancer and choreographer, moved to New York City in 1982 and were married in 1987. The parents of Kellman, who is white and Jewish, reportedly did not speak to their daughter for five years after meeting Mosley.

Mosley settled down into a career as a computer programmer in the 1980s, but his work left him unfulfilled. Meanwhile, he read voraciously, including mysteries by Raymond Chandler, Dashiell Hammett, and Ross MacDonald, and existential novels such as *The Stranger* by Albert Camus. This blend of suspense and philosophy served him well in the mysteries he would later write.

According to a profile in *People*, Mosley's decision to become a writer was strongly influenced by his reading of *The Color Purple* by Alice Walker. That book rekindled the youthful urge to write that he had long since lost. He began writing feverishly whenever he could find time. Intent on devoting himself totally to his craft, Mosley quit his computer programming job in the mid–eighties and enrolled at the City College of New York.

In 1989 Mosley showed *Devil in a Blue Dress*, which he had first written as a screenplay, to his writing teacher. The teacher showed the book to his agent, who sold it to the W. W. Norton publishing company. When the novel came out in 1990, the *New York Times* said that it "marks the debut of a talented author." Rawlins's reappearance a year later in *A Red Death* caused *Publishers Weekly* to theorize that "Mosley ... may well be in the process of creating a genre classic." The author's reputation soared when Bill Clinton said during his 1992 U.S. presidential campaign that Mosley was his favorite mystery writer.

Many characters in the Easy Rawlins novels are based on the experiences of Mosley's father, with similarities between LeRoy Mosley and Easy Raw-

lins especially apparent. After being treated like a hero abroad during World War II, LeRoy Mosley was dismayed to find that he was still a second class citizen back in the United States. This disillusionment was also felt by veteran Easy Rawlins in *Devil in a Blue Dress.* However, the war made it clear to Rawlins that the white man was not much different from himself. Early in the novel, the character ruminates: "I had spent five years with white men, and women, from Africa to Italy, through Paris, and into the Fatherland itself. I ate with them and slept with them, and I killed enough blue–eyed young men to know that they were just as afraid to die as I was."

In a commentary in the *Los Angeles Times*, Mosley asserted that "black soldiers learned from World War II; they learned how to dream about freedom." LeRoy Mosley's dream of freedom took him to California, where endless jobs and opportunities were rumored to be waiting for everyone, including African Americans. In the *Los Angeles Times*, Mosley described the Los Angeles of Easy Rawlins as "a place where a black man can dream but he has to keep his wits about him. Easy lives among the immigrants from the western South. He dreams of owning property and standing on an equal footing with his white peers. Deep in his mind, he is indoctrinated with the terror of Southern racism. In his everyday life he faces the subtle, and not so subtle, inequalities of the American color line."

Similar to the canon of Chester Himes, an African–American author who wrote Harlem–based crime novels in the 1940s and 1950s, Mosley's works have consistently addressed social and racial issues. Drawing on his father's life and his own as a close observer of the Watts riots during the 1960s, Mosley shows in his books how racism infects the lives of inner–city African Americans. Double standards abound in *Devil in a Blue Dress*, in which a white man hires Rawlins to find a woman known to hang out in African–American jazz clubs. Easy was chosen because he was African American and regarded as a bridge into a world where the white man dare not go. In *White Butterfly*, the police show a keen interest in the case of a murdered white cocktail waitress—after basically ignoring the murders of a series of black waitresses that occurred earlier.

Mosley has also tapped his African American/ Jewish perspective to deal with Jewish suffering as perceived by African Americans. In *Devil in a Blue Dress*, two Jewish liquor store owners in the ghetto cause Easy Rawlins to remember when his unit broke open the gates of a Nazi extermination camp. This recollection leads to an understanding of similarities in the oppression suffered by African Americans in America and Jews abroad. The novel was nominated for an Edgar Award for best first novel by the Mystery Writers of America in 1990.

Mosley's novels have made it clear that morality cannot be judged the same for African Americans as it is for whites. The author wrote in the *Los Angeles Times* that "Easy tries to walk a moral line in a world where he is not treated equally by the law.... He's a man who, finding himself with dark skin, has decided that he's going to live his life and do what's right, in that order." Mosley has used Easy's moral flexibility to force his hero back into the private eye business, such as in *A Red Death* when Rawlins buys some buildings with stolen money. When the IRS threatens to look into his finances, Easy reluctantly agrees to spy on a suspected Jewish communist for an FBI man in exchange for protection from the taxman.

In 1994, Mosley published another installment in the Easy Rawlins series entitled *Black Betty*. The novel opens with Rawlins facing both the collapse of his real estate business, and the fact that his wife and daughter have walked out on him. In the midst of this turmoil, he is asked by a private eye to find Elizabeth Eady, a seductive former housekeeper who is known as Black Betty. Reviews of *Black Betty* were quite favorable. Barry Gifford, writing in the *New York Times Book Review,* remarked that "nobody will ever accuse Walter Mosley of lacking heart.... [H]is words prowl around the page before they pounce, knocking you not so much upside the head as around the body, where you feel them the longest."

Mosley's 1995 novel, *RL's Dream,* marked a departure from the Easy Rawlins mystery series. This novel tells the story of Atwater "Soupspoon" Wise, an aged and dying blues guitar player who is facing eviction from his New York apartment. He is soon befriended by an alcoholic white Southerner named Kiki Waters, who takes Wise into her home and cares for him. Wise longs to relive his glory days, and recalls to Waters about his struggles with racism and the time he played with a legendary Delta blues singer named Robert "RL" Johnson. As their friendship develops, the two share their individual stories, relive the pain of the past, and learn to heal their emotional wounds. Digby Diehl of *Playboy* noted that Mosley's mystery novels "don't prepare you for the emotional force of *RL's Dream.* Mosley mixes the nightmares of Soup's past with the immediate anguish of poverty, chemotherapy, and aging. The result is harsh, uplifting, and unforgettable."

Always Outnumbered, Always Outgunned, which was published in late 1997, presented another departure from Mosley's Easy Rawlins series. The book con-

sists of 14 stories which revolve around the character of Socrates Fortlow. Fortlow is an ex–convict who has been released from prison after serving 27 years for killing two acquaintances. He lives in an abandoned building in the Watts neighborhood of Los Angeles, and supports himself by delivering groceries for a supermarket. Throughout all 14 stories, Fortlow grapples with philosophical questions of morality in a world that is riddled with racism, crime, and poverty. Sven Birkerts, reviewing the novel for the *New York Times Book Review,* remarked that the book delves into "the implications of moral action in a society that has lost all purchase on the spirit of the law." Birkerts also noted that the book's 14 stories "incorporate the Platonic dialogues as a kind of ghost melody; signature strains of the classic are vamped up in the rough demotic of present–day Watts."

Mosley broke new ground in 1998 with the release of his first science fiction novel, *Blue Light.* Set in San Francisco during the 1960s, the plot focuses on a group of people who are struck by an extraterrestrial blue light. Some who are touched by the light die or go insane, while others are given supernatural abilities. Those with supernatural abilities are stalked by the Gray Man, an evil entity who seeks their destruction. Critical reviews of *Blue Light* were mixed. In the *New York Times Book Review,* Mel Watkins remarked that "for those readers accustomed to the gut–real encounters, sharp dialogue and quirky perceptions that enliven the first–person narrations of Mosley's Easy Rawlins mysteries ... the surreal nature of *Blue Light* may be a disappointment."

Mosley published the novel *Walkin' the Dog* in late 1999. This novel signaled the return of Socrates Fortlow, the philosophical ex–convict that Mosley first introduced in *Always Outnumbered, Always Outgunned.* In *Walkin' the Dog,* Fortlow is faced with challenges such as being evicted from his home, avoiding confrontations with police, and caring for his two–legged dog, Killer. Although Fortlow is trying to live an honest life, he remains burdened by the sins of his past. Despite his difficult circumstances, he tries to face each day with determination and hope. *Walkin' the Dog* received generally favorable reviews. Writing for the *New York Times Book Review,* Adam Goodheart noted that "in prose as plain and gritty as asphalt, Mosley ... adeptly builds a feeling of urgency and suspense around even seemingly ordinary episodes of his protagonist's life."

In early 2000, Mosley published a social commentary entitled *Workin' the Chain Gang: Shaking Off the Dead Hand of History.* In this book, he challenges the

American people to find imaginative and creative solutions to the political, social, racial, and economic problems within society. Among other things, he urges his readers to turn away from rampant consumerism and consumption, and cautions against overexposure to mass media. Mosley encourages readers to learn from the lessons and struggles of the African–American experience, and envision a brighter future. In *Booklist*, Mary Carroll noted that "free market fanatics will hate this book," but believed that readers who are "receptive to a progressive critique of the religion of the market will value Mosley's creative contribution."

Mosley published *Bad Boy Brawly Brown*, another Easy Rawlins novel, in 2002. Critics once again praised his use of the novel to examine the racial politics of America. "It takes only a few pages for Mosley to capture the anger and violence of the '60s, and he does it from the point of view of an African–American man who wants no part of radicalism and even less to do with the white power structure...." reviewer Malcolm Jones wrote in *Newsweek*. "The remarkable thing about this scene, though, is that it takes place not in some ambitious social novel about radical violence but in a detective story."

In the early 2000s, Mosley's publisher reissued in paperback six of the novels that preceded *Bad Boy Brawley Brown*. Each reprint contained an original short story featuring Easy Rawlins. In 2003, those stories and a seventh never before published were gathered together in a volume called *Six Easy Pieces*. That same year, Mosley released *Fear Itself: A Fearless Jones Novel*, the follow–up to 2001's *Fearless Jones*.

Walter Mosley has demonstrated a willingness to expand his horizons beyond the Easy Rawlins mystery series into the realms of science fiction and social commentary. He has actively used his popularity and influence to address the economic and social concerns of the day. As Emory Holmes II said in *Los Angeles Magazine*, Mosley has become "a rich and increasingly strident voice in publishing."

Selected writings

Devil in a Blue Dress, Norton, 1990.
A Red Death, Norton, 1991.
White Butterfly, Norton, 1992.
Black Betty, Norton, 1994.
RL's Dream, Norton, 1995.
A Little Yellow Dog, Norton, 1996.
Gone Fishin', Black Classic Press, 1997.
Always Outnumbered, Always Outgunned, Norton, 1997.
Blue Light, Little, Brown, 1998.
Walkin' the Dog, Little, Brown, 1999.
Workin' on the Chain Gang: Shaking Off the Dead Hand of History, Ballantine, 2000.
Fearless Jones: A Novel, Little, Brown, 2001.
Futureland, Warner, 2001.
What Next: An African American Initiative Toward World Peace, Black Classic Press, 2002.
Bad Boy Brawley Brown, Little, Brown, 2002.
Six Easy Pieces, Atria Books, 2003.
Fear Itself: A Mystery, Little, Brown, 2003.

Sources

American Visions, April/May 1992, pp. 32–34.
Booklist, May 1, 1996, p. 1469; January 1, 2000, p. 840.
California, August 1990, p. 115.
Cosmopolitan, July 1991, p. 28; July 1992, p. 30.
Detroit Free Press, November 17, 1991, p. 6.
Essence, January 1991, p. 32; October 1992, p. 50.
Kirkus Reviews, April 15, 1994; April 15, 1996.
Library Journal, June 1, 1991, p. 200; March 15, 1992, p. 68; February 1, 2000, p. 105.
Los Angeles Magazine, November 1998, p. 32.
Los Angeles Times, May 5, 1992, pp. B7, E1, E5; May 14, 1992, p. 6.
Los Angeles Times Book Review, July 14, 1991. pp. 1–2, p. 9.
New Statesman & Society, April 19, 1991, p. 37.
Newsweek, July 7, 1990, p. 65; June 24, 2002, p. 86.
New York Times, September 4, 1990, p. C13, p. C16.
New York Times Book Review, August 5, 1990, p. 29; June 5, 1994; January 26, 1997; November 15, 1998; November 7, 1999.
People, September 7, 1992, pp. 105–106; July 8, 2002, p. 35.
Playboy, October 1995, p. 34.
Publishers Weekly, May 17, 1991, p. 57; April 25, 1994; May 28, 2001, p. 54.
Vanity Fair, February 1993, pp. 46, 48, 50.

—Ed Decker

Anne M. Mulcahy

Courtesy of Xerox Corporation

President and Chief Executive Officer of Xerox

Born Anne Dolan, October 21, 1952, in Rockville Centre, NY; married Joseph Mulcahy (a retired sales manager); children: Michael, Kevin. *Education:* Marymount College, B.A., 1974.

Addresses: *Home*—Fairfield, CT. *Office*—Xerox Corporation, 800 Long Ridge Rd., Stamford, CT, 06902–1227.

Career

Began career as sales representative with the Xerox Corporation, Stamford, CT, 1976; held various management positions during the 1980s; vice president of human resources, 1992–95; vice president and staff officer for worldwide customer operations, 1996–97; senior vice president and chief staff officer, 1998; president for general markets operations, 1999; president and chief operating officer, 2000; chief executive officer, 2001—.

Sidelights

Longtime Xerox Corporation executive Anne M. Mulcahy became the company's first female president and chief executive officer (CEO) in 2001. Mulcahy's ascendancy to the top post at the Connecticut–based photocopier and computer–peripherals giant coincided with dire predictions among business analysts that Xerox teetered on the verge of bankruptcy. She became one of just a handful of female corporate executives at the helm of Fortune 500 companies in the United States, but when interviewed for the *Sunday Times* by Dominic Rushe, Mulcahy preferred to downplay her achievement. "I try not to do a lot of things that focus on my role as a woman executive," she told the paper. "I'm much more focused on my role as chief executive of Xerox. That's what's meaningful."

Born in 1952, Mulcahy grew up in Long Island, New York, the sole daughter among five children. She graduated from Marymount, a women's college in Tarrytown, New York, in 1974 and was hired at Xerox two years later. At the time, the company enjoyed dominance of the photocopier market worldwide, and would soon enter the nascent personal–computer industry. Mulcahy started as a sales representative at the company, and quickly advanced through its marketing and management ranks. She became vice president of human resources in 1992, and four years later was made vice president and staff officer for worldwide customer operations. In 1998, she was named corporate senior vice president, and as such oversaw the launch of Xerox's small–office and home business products division.

At the time, Xerox seemed to have lost its way in an industry it once dominated. Known for a deeply entrenched corporate culture that inspired the nickname "Burox," the company had missed out on several important information–technology turns in the past decade, and was attempting to remake itself into a "solution"–selling firm under CEO Rick Thoman, who had been lured away from International Business Machines, Inc. (IBM). But in 2000 Thoman was ousted by a Xerox board of directors unhappy with his leadership, and Mulcahy was named president and chief operating officer. Xerox's CEO duties were assigned to Paul Allaire, but within a year Allaire had resigned as well and Mulcahy was named CEO in his stead.

Mulcahy was faced with seemingly insurmountable problems when she took over in the summer of 2001. The American economy was moribund, Xerox's revenues were down, its stock was trading at less than $10 a share, and there were also some troubling internal problems as well. A reorganization of the sales and administrative billing divisions under Thoman had gone badly, and the company was carrying a debt load of $18.6 billion. "She could have inherited worse circumstances but it is hard to imagine them," remarked Rushe in the *Sunday Times.* Acting swiftly, Mulcahy named a cost–cutting team to trim down Xerox's crushing debt. Some 20,000 jobs were eliminated, bringing payroll numbers down to 73,000, and the company sold off or closed several divisions, including the consumer photocopier and inkjet printer arms. Within months it had sold off nearly $2.5 billion worth of assets, and reduced the debt to $12 billion.

Despite the hardships engendered by the budget cuts, Mulcahy enjoyed a surprising level of support and loyalty among the "Xeroid" ranks, as its dedicated employees are known. Some of this was inspired by her veteran status at the company, and Mulcahy was gracious enough to attribute her success to the internal support she'd enjoyed. As she recalled in an interview with *Financial Times* writer Simon London, she once discussed tough fiscal turnarounds with a fellow CEO who headed a similarly struggling company. That CEO, as she noted, had told her that only drastic change could revive their companies, and urged her "to break the culture to make the kind of progress you need to make—otherwise you'll totally fail." Mulcahy, however, was reluctant to agree with such sentiment. "I come from a different perspective," she told London. "I am the culture of the company. I've been with Xerox for 25 years. It is a culture that needs to be challenged and changed, but your ability to change depends on your ability to have the culture follow you."

In the spring of 2002, less than a year on the job, Mulcahy faced an entirely new set of problems when the U.S. Securities and Exchange Commission (SEC) accused the company of fraudulent accounting practices. The revelation came in the recent wake of some other major corporate balance–sheet scandals, most notably in the Enron Corporation bankruptcy, but Mulcahy and the Xerox board moved swiftly to maintain stockholder confidence. A settlement was reached with the SEC in which Xerox agreed to pay a $10 million fine in exchange for not admitting or denying the allegations, and it was also compelled to issue a 97–page restatement of pre–tax income and revenue for years 1997 through 2001. Mulcahy defended the restatement, when the financial numbers proved to have been even higher than the SEC had first claimed, and pointed out that it was simply an accounting strategy gone awry. "This was not something that was hidden from our auditors," she explained in an interview with *Daily Telegraph* journalist Andrew Cave. "Quite frankly, it was openly recorded. This was an accounting methodology debate that, quite frankly, we lost." She cautioned against overreaction and comparisons with Enron or Tyco, another failed giant. "I would like to think Xerox can be a role model that helps companies provide the transparency and governance that shareholders expect," she asserted in the same article.

Mulcahy's turnaround of Xerox seemed on firm footing, despite the mid–2002 worries. At the end of the third quarter for 2002, its stock had outperformed analysts's expectations. Should the company's success continue, Mulcahy would receive her full salary package: a $1 million base pay, plus more than $2 million more in performance–related bonuses and stock gifts. She one of a rare "One Percent Club," the number of female executives heading Fortune 500 companies. Her days begin with a gym workout near her Connecticut home, where she lives with her husband, Joseph, and two teenage sons. Her brother serves as head of Xerox Global Services. When asked by Cave if she might like to see her sons join the company where she met her husband, Mulcahy revealed herself a not untypical American parent in her reply. "I would love to see my kids work at Xerox," she told the *Daily Telegraph* journalist, and jokingly added, "I would love to see my kids work at all."

Sources

BusinessWeek, August 6, 2001, p. 47.
Computer Reseller News, June 26, 2000, p. 127.
Daily Telegraph (London, England), July 13, 2002, p. 31.
Electronic Publishing, July 2001, p. 14.
Financial Times, August 30, 2001, p. 28; March 15, 2002, p. 12; October 24, 2002, p. 21.
Sunday Times (London, England), October 20, 2002, p. 7.

—*Carol Brennan*

Francois Nars

Makeup artist and photographer

Born in 1959 in Tarbes, France; son of Jean–Jacques (an owner of a pork products factory) and Claudette (a housewife) Nars. *Education:* Attended Carita Makeup School, Paris, France.

Addresses: *Office*—Nars Cosmetics Inc., 580 Broadway, Ste. 901, New York, NY 10012. *Website*—http://www.narscosmetics.com.

Career

Moved to Paris at the age of 18 and began his career as an assistant to renowned makeup artist Olivier Echaudemaison; after a year he struck out on his own, working for various designers and fashion magazines, including Yves Saint Laurent, *Elle, Marie Claire,* and *Vogue;* came to New York, where found work with the city's leading fashion editors and photographers, 1984; launched a line of lipsticks, 1994; expanded to a full line of makeup, 1995; became interested in photography, mid–1990s; photographed first makeup campaign, 1996; published *X–Ray,* 1999.

Sidelights

It seems only fitting that the official biography of Francois Nars from NARS Cosmetics bears this observation about the nature of style from Diana Vreeland, the late fashion doyenne who for years was the editor of *Vogue:* "The energy of imagination, deliberation, and invention, which fall into a natural rhythm totally one's own, maintained by innate discipline and a keen sense of pleasure—these

are the ingredients of style. And all who have it share one thing: originality." Nars epitomizes the very essence of style, and he's nothing if not an original.

A makeup artist and photographer of international repute, Nars also serves as the creative director of the cosmetics company he founded in the mid–1990s. His approach to makeup has been described as revolutionary, for he believes fervently that makeup must never become a mask and should only serve to enhance the natural features of those who wear it, that the woman must shine through. The basic tenets of Nars's philosophy of makeup are being real and less is more. "I take a girl and make her look more beautiful as an individual," he told interviewer Susan Sargisson of *Drug & Cosmetic Industry.* And if at first you don't succeed, Nars told the *Mirror* of London: "Don't be afraid to start all over again if you mess up. Just wipe everything off. The great thing about makeup is that it's temporary."

Nars's artistry has adorned the faces of some of the world's most celebrated women, including Madonna, Sharon Stone, Michelle Pfeiffer, Isabella Rossellini, Catherine Deneuve, Anjelica Houston, and Lauren Hutton, as well as supermodels Naomi Campbell, Cindy Crawford, Claudia Schiffer, and others. The makeup artist's relationship with Madonna began in the early 1990s with a comment Nars made to photographer Steven Meisel about hating the singer/actress's eyebrows, according to *People.* Before long he found himself face to face with Madonna who told him: "Nice to meet you. I heard you hate my eyebrows. So we've got to do something about it." Thus began a lengthy collaboration during which Nars handled Madonna's makeup for a number of music videos as well as for *Sex,* her coffee table venture into published erotica. Nars told *People* that he gave the singer a new look that was "more beautiful and womanly. Not as crazy."

Nars was born in 1959 in the city of Tarbes, capital of the Hautes–Pyrenees region of southwestern France. His father, Jean–Jacques, operated a pork products factory in Tarbes, while his mother, Claudette, took care of things on the home front. Nars showed an early fascination with fashion magazines, poring through the pages of his mother's *Vogue* starting when he was only ten years old and sketching the faces of the models and celebrities he saw in the magazine. His mother told *People* that as a teenager Francois "would do my makeup. I'd be very chic, and he was delighted."

Nars was fascinated by the elegance and sophistication he found within the pages of the fashion magazines and quickly developed an appreciation for the contributions of designers, models, hair stylists, and makeup artists who collectively created and showcased the stylish fashions of the day. He was particularly taken with the work of visionaries like Yves St. Laurent, who embodied the culture, sophistication, and elegance that attracted Nars to the world of fashion.

At the age of 18, Nars left Tarbes for Paris, where he studied at the Carita Makeup School and worked briefly for leading makeup artist Olivier Echaudemaison. After about a year he struck out on his own, working first with fashion photographer Paolo Roversi and eventually handling the makeup for leading designers like St. Laurent and fashion magazines, including *Elle, Marie Claire,* and *Vogue.* Polly Mellen, who in the early 1980s edited the American edition of *Vogue,* was impressed by his work and encouraged Nars to come to New York.

Arriving in New York in 1984, Nars almost immediately began handling makeup assignments from the leading American fashion magazines, international designers, and photographers. His clients included *Vogue, Harper's Bazaar, Elle,* Bill Blass, Ralph Lauren, Marc Jacobs, Karl Lagerfeld, Anna Sui, Versace, Valentino, Alberta Ferretti, and Dolce & Gabbana, as well as such top photographers as Richard Avedon, Irving Penn, Patrick Demarchelier, Helmut Newton, and Steven Meisel. Of his successful move to New York, Nars told *People,* "I worked hard, but I got lucky. People really liked me right away."

Unhappy with the quality of most cosmetics then on the market, Nars in 1994 decided to do something about it. With financial help from his parents, he launched a line of ten lipsticks that at first were marketed exclusively by Barney's in New York. A year later it was expanded into a full line of cosmetics. NARS Cosmetics Inc., of which Nars himself is creative director, was sold in mid–2000 to Japan's Shiseido Company Ltd. The NARS product line, which is targeted at hip women of all ages, is available in some of the country's most exclusive department stores, including Saks Fifth Avenue and Neiman Marcus, as well as specialty cosmetics stores, such as Sephora.

When NARS Cosmetics decided to launch its first advertising campaign in 1996, it found itself short of the funds it needed to hire a top–notch photographer to shoot art for the campaign. Long fascinated with the art of photography, particularly after years of working closely with some of the world's best, Nars decided to shoot the art himself. The 1996 NARS campaign marked his debut as a professional photographer. He continues to shoot all of the company's advertising campaigns and has also been retained to shoot photo spreads and covers for a number of the world's top fashion magazines, including *Harper's Bazaar, Vanity Fair,* and the French and German editions of *Vogue.*

Nars's first book of photographs hit bookstores in 1999. *X–Ray,* loaded with striking photos of men and women who personified to the photographer the very essence of chic and style, proved wildly successful. In its review, the *New York Times* said the book "features portraits of members of the fashion elite in cosmetic overdrive, from socialite to porn star, from hairstylist to hat designer to Hollywood royalty." A review in *Paper* magazine observed that Nars's "clean, bright style magnifies his subjects's sensuality, while his makeup artistry—from a dab of lip gloss to full–fledged fantasy—showcases his vision, even if, he says with a laugh, it doubles the amount of work for each portrait." A second book, *Makeup Your Mind,* released in 2001, is more of a makeup instruction manual, featuring 63 before–and–after images of some of the world's most recognizable faces.

Nars, who is single, lives with his French bulldog Marcel in a one–bedroom apartment in New York City's SoHo neighborhood. Of his cosmetics company's continuing success, he told *People,* "Knowing that even when I go to sleep at night there are women in Europe or in Asia buying my cosmetics, that's quite a thrill."

Selected writings

X–Ray, New York: powerHouse Books, 1999.
Makeup Your Mind, powerHouse Books, 2001.

Sources

Periodicals

Drug & Cosmetic Industry, June 1, 1995, pp. 46–47.
Mirror, August 13, 2002, p. 30.
People, December 7, 1998, p. 91.

Online

"Jetsetera," Hint Fashion Magazine, http://www.hintmag.com/jetsetera/francoisnars.htm (September 30, 2002).

"Nars Review," Face Online, http://www.faceonline.com/reviews/nars.html (September 30, 2002).

"Shiseido to Acquire U.S. Makeup Brand 'Nars,'" Shiseido Co. Ltd., http://www.shiseido.co.jp/e/e9705grp/html/grp00089.htm (September 30, 2002).

"*X–Ray,*" French Culture, http://www.frenchculture.org/books/release/art/nars.html (September 30, 2002).

"*X–Ray,*" HallEntertainment, http://www.hallentertainment.com/pop_culture/274.shtml (September 30, 2002).

Additional information provided by NARS Cosmetics Inc., 2002.

—*Don Amerman*

David Neeleman

Chief Executive Officer of JetBlue Airways

Born in 1959, in Sao Paulo, Brazil; son of Gary (a former LA Times Syndicate International executive vice–president) and Rose (a personal assistant) Neeleman; married Vicki Vranes, 1980; children: nine sons and daughters. *Education:* Attended University of Utah, Salt Lake City. *Religion:* Mormon.

Addresses: *Home*—235 Oenoke Rdg., New Canaan, CT 06840. *Office*—JetBlue Airways Corporate Office, 80–02 Kew Gardens Rd., Kew Gardens, NY 11415. *Website*—http://www.jetblue.com/.

Career

Entrepreneur and corporate executive; opened his own travel agency, 1981; travel agency went bankrupt, 1983; executive vice–president, Morris Air, 1984–88; president and member of the board of directors, Morris Air Corporation, 1988–94; member executive planning committee, Southwest Airlines, 1994; CEO/member of the board of directors, Open Skies, 1995–98; member of board of directors, West-Jet, 1996–99; CEO/member of board of directors, JetBlue, 1998—.

Member: Honorary Chairman, Smart Kids with Learning Disabilities.

Awards: Top Ten Entrepreneurs of 2000, *Business-Week*; Travel Industry Innovator, *Time*; one of the Most Influential Business Travel Executives, *Business Travel News*.

Sidelights

David Neeleman has spent his entire career creating solid and profitable travel–oriented companies. Before his overwhelming success forming the low–fare carrier JetBlue, he helped launch two other low–fare airlines, both of which were competitive. Neeleman is credited with pioneering electronic ticketing. He is an innovative thinker who credits his creativity and energy to a self–diagnosed learning disability. A devout Mormon, Neeleman bases his business strategy and employee relations upon teachings in the Bible.

Neeleman was born in 1959, in Sao Paulo, Brazil, where his father, Gary, was stationed working for an international newswire service. His mother worked as Gary's personal assistant once he was promoted to executive vice–president for the Los Angeles Times Syndicate International. Neeleman was the second of seven children, and grew up in Salt Lake City, Utah.

As a child, Neeleman had trouble concentrating in just about all situations. At school his easily distracted nature led to an inability to read or write well. To this day Neeleman has trouble with writing. To get through school, he took the easiest classes he could, but the experience left him feeling like he was not smart. His father described Neeleman's impatience as a child to Chris Woodyard of *USA Today*, "David hated fishing. He didn't have the patience. He would start fishing, and two minutes later, [he'd be] throwing rocks in the pond."

Neeleman did have a knack for communicating with people, and learned valuable lessons in customer service from his grandfather. Back before convenience stores were a regular part of the American urban landscape, Neeleman's grandfather owned a small store that he called Miniature Mart. If customers came in asking for something that the Miniature Mart didn't carry, they would be given coffee and doughnuts while one of the clerks ran to the supermarket to purchase the item. Neeleman learned from that experience to try and provide for customers no matter what the effort.

After high school, Neeleman went on a two–year missionary trip to Brazil. All men in the Mormon church are expected to serve on a mission. In Brazil, Neeleman—who had experienced Brazil as a young child from the perspective of the well–to–do—immersed himself in the other side of life in that country. For his mission he preached to and converted inhabitants of rural poor villages. He told *BusinessWeek*, "It was really the first time I felt like I had some talent."

In 1980, after returning to the United States, Neeleman married his college sweetheart Vicki Vranes. The two have remained married for more than 20 years. They have nine children ranging from toddlers to college students. Part of living with Neeleman is dealing with his idiosyncratic ways. Vicki told *USA Today*'s Woodyard, "He's always intrigued me because he's a little off the beaten path, and I can't always read him." His oldest daughter told Jason Lynch Mark of *People*, "When I call him, I've got 20 seconds before he says, 'I gotta go!' There are so many things going through his mind."

Neeleman gave college a try, studying accounting at the University of Utah. After returning from his missionary service he soon gave up on college. In 1981, he dropped out to start his own travel agency. Unfortunately, within two years his agency went bankrupt, but business executive June Morris recognized Neeleman's talent and invited him to join her travel agency, Morris Air.

With Neeleman on board, Morris Air underwent significant changes. First he moved Morris Air from being just a travel agency into being a charter business. Based in Salt Lake City, Morris Air flew to high traffic destinations like Los Angeles, California, and Cancun, Mexico. By 1992, Neeleman had turned the company into a small airline with regular flights. He instituted time– and money–saving practices such as electronic ticketing, and allowing reservation agents to work from home. He was a charismatic salesman, who never seemed to turn off. He could be found trying to sell honeymoon packages at weddings he attended.

In 1993, Southwest Airlines bought Morris Air for $129 million. Neeleman was hired as a member of the executive planning board for Southwest, which seemed like a great opportunity to Neeleman at the time. He explained to Melanie Wells of *Forbes*, "Herb [Kelleher, CEO of Southwest] said, 'We need someone like you at Southwest.' I just assumed that when I got to Dallas it would be a love fest." With that assumption, Neeleman readily agreed to sign a five–year agreement that he would not form another airline company in the United States. Unfortunately, it only took a short time for the love fest to turn into torture for the independent and high–strung Neeleman.

As part of the executive planning committee, Neeleman was forced to sit through meetings that seemed to him to be a waste of time. He had once been the president of a company; now he was relegated to a managerial position that left him powerless to make the kind of innovative changes for which he was known. His outbursts of impatience as well as frustration with bureaucracy eventually led to his dismissal. His tenure with Southwest had lasted only five months.

After his dismissal from Southwest, Neeleman went on an entrepreneurial binge. He invested in several companies that failed, including a pretzel company. But his skill in the travel industry was still evident. He started a company called Open Skies in 1995. Open Skies created a system that allowed for ticketless airline reservations and also managed revenues. He built the company up over three years and sold it in 1998 to Hewlett Packard.

Because of his noncompete agreement, Neeleman could not work directly for any airline company in the United States. Instead, he looked to Canada. He became co–founder and a member of the board of directors for a low–fare carrier called WestJet. He served with WestJet from 1995 until 1999. The company continues to do well.

With five years to plan, Neeleman was set on the idea of creating another low–fare carrier in the United States. In 1997, Neeleman and associate Tom

Kelly began planning that airline. They studied all the other low–fare carriers, the successful as well as unsuccessful companies, trying to figure out the structure. Once the noncompete agreement expired, Neeleman set out to raise investment money and to hire the best people from all areas of the travel industry.

Neeleman pulled out all the stops to make his pitch to investors and potential employees. He already had several million dollars of his own to invest, and with his positive track record was able to convince venture capitalists that his carrier would be a good investment. He also hired the best and brightest from other airlines, including employees of England's Virgin Airways, even the human resources director who had dismissed him from Southwest Airlines. He went on to convince Senator Charles Schumer of New York to give him the needed slots for his airline at Kennedy International Airport.

With every aspect in place, Neeleman launched Jet-Blue Airways. On February 11, 2000, JetBlue made its inaugural flight from New York to Ft. Lauderdale, Florida. From the beginning, Neeleman's goal was to recreate the success of Southwest Airlines, but to update the operations. The advantages that JetBlue enjoyed as a start–up included having no legacy systems to upgrade or integrate. Neeleman continued his commitment to a ticketless operation, a unified reservation and accounting system, and allowing employees in customer service and reservations to work from home. After one year of service, JetBlue earned $14 million.

JetBlue distinguishes itself from other low–fare airlines in a number of ways, most of which is the direct result of Neeleman's business philosophy. His number–one goal is the comfort and convenience of his passengers. He eliminated first–class from his planes. "It's just kind of maddening. You've got these people perched up front and then stuff the others in back. I thought, why not do away with the class system, spread the cabin out a bit and give a little more legroom than other airlines?" he told Kris Grant of the *San Diego Union–Tribune*.

Other amenities that set JetBlue apart are the leather seats, individual television sets for each passenger, two or three bathrooms, and occasionally being served snacks by the CEO of the company himself. For Neeleman, JetBlue is a 24–hour–a–day investment. Once a week he hops a flight to meet with the crew, talk with the pilots, and get first–hand feedback from his passengers. He often works at the terminals as well, handling luggage or assisting with check–ins. His BlackBerry wireless device notifies him whenever a JetBlue flight is delayed for more than a minute—his wife claims he wears it to bed.

In an era during which most start–up low–fare carriers fail, JetBlue has had a promising start. Despite the financial problems that plagued the airline industry after the September 11, 2001, terrorist attacks, JetBlue continued to post profits far beyond the average. For just the first half of 2002, the company netted $27.6 million. All of the success has given Neeleman an optimistic outlook for the future. "I can't believe how quickly we got out of the gate and how profitable we became. Now I don't think there's a limit on how big JetBlue can get," he boasted to Wells in *Forbes*.

Neeleman's Mormon religion plays a large role in his dealings with his crew and his passengers. When he introduces himself and the company to new employees he preaches the value of saving money. Once he helped a widowed employee buy a house by loaning her money to make the down payment. His view of corporate structure is based on the structure of the Mormon church. He explained to Caroline Daniels of the *Financial Times*, "In our church of Jesus Christ, we have a very egalitarian view of things and it is an all lay ministry. There is no pastor. I try and treat all crew members the same."

Family is also very important to Neeleman. In 1999, he moved his wife and children from Utah to Connecticut. To ease the transition for his kids, he took them to see a different Broadway show every week. For his oldest daughter, Ashley, he convinced the family of her best friend to allow the friend to move with them for a short while. Ashley also returned to Utah to participate in her former class's graduation ceremony. In spite of the benefits that his financial success brings, Neeleman is quick to address the reality of money. "Wealth doesn't mean much except the ability to do a lot of good things and help a lot of good causes. I have nine kids. I have to make sure I have a normal upbringing for those nine kids. Life is rewarding but not easy," he told *Newsday*.

Several years ago, Neeleman self–diagnosed himself as having attention deficit disorder. He went through a list of 20 questions and found that he answered 19 of them with acute symptoms. Still, he refuses to take medication and has learned to live with his disability, seeing it as an asset, as the reason he's been able to accomplish all that he has in life. Even though he acknowledges the positive aspects of his disability, he has moments of regret, as he related to Mark in *People,*, "[I]t would be nice to sit and have a really long conversation with somebody."

Neeleman is a man of dedication. He is dedicated to his church, his family, his company, and his passengers. His skill and drive to succeed have led him from one venture to the next, always walking away with a lesson and often with a lot of money. He told Jeff Sweat of *Information Week,* "I love to work. I love my job. To me, there's no golf game on the planet that can compare with that."

Sources

Business Week, May 3, 1999, p. 182.
Financial Times, August 26, 2002, p. 8.
Forbes, October 14, 2002, pp. 131–38.
Information Week, January 1, 2001, p. 42.
Newsday, April 16, 2002, p. A46.
People, August 26, 2002, p. 89.
San Diego Union–Tribune, August 4, 2002, p. D2.
USA Today, October 8, 2002, p. 1B.

—Eve M. B. Hermann

Jeremy Northam

Gregg DeGuire/WireImage.com

Actor

Born Jeremy Philip Northam, December 1, 1961, in Cambridge, England; son of John (a literature and theater professor) and Rachel (an economics professor and pottery artist) Northam. *Education:* Studied English at University of London; studied theater at Bristol Old Vic Theater School.

Addresses: *Agent*—International Creative Management, 8942 Wilshire Blvd., Beverly Hills, CA 90211–1934.

Career

Actor in films, including: *Emily Bronte's Wuthering Heights* (also known as *Wuthering Heights*), 1992; *Soft Top, Hard Shoulder,* 1992; *A Village Affair,* 1994; *Voices* (also known as *Voices from a Locked Room*), 1995; *The Net,* 1995; *Carrington,* 1995; *Emma,* 1996; *Amistad,* 1997; *Mimic,* 1997; *The Misadventures of Margaret* (also known as *Les folies de Margaret*), 1998; *Happy, Texas,* 1998; *An Ideal Husband,* 1999; *Gloria,* 1999; *The Winslow Boy,* 1999; *The Golden Bowl* (also known as *La coupe d'or*), 2000; *Enigma,* 2001; *Gosford Park,* 2001; *Possession,* 2002; *Cypher,* 2002; *The Singing Detective,* 2003. Television appearances include: *Journey's End* (United Kingdom), 1988; *A Fatal Inversion,* 1991; *The Tribe,* 1998; "Dead Man's Mirror," *Poirot,* 1988; "Suspicion," *American Playhouse* (special), 1988; *Piece of Cake* (pilot), 1990; *Martin and Lewis,* 2002. Stage appearances include: *Hamlet,* National Theatre Company, Olivier Theatre, London, 1989; *The Voysey Inheritance,* National Theatre Company, Cottesloe Theatre, London, 1989; *The Gift of the Gorgon,* Royal Shakespeare Company, The Pit, London, 1992; *La bete,* Really Useful Theatre Company, 1993; *Love's Labour's Lost,* Royal Shakespeare Company, Barbican Theatre, London, 1994; *The Country Wife,* Royal Shakespeare Company, The Pit, 1994. Also appeared in a production of *School for Scandal.*

Awards: Laurence Olivier Award for most promising newcomer of the year in theatre, Society of West End Theatre, for *The Voysey Inheritance,* 1989; ALFS Award for British actor of the year, London Critics Circle, for *Happy, Texas,* 1999; British Film Award for best actor, *Evening Standard,* for *An Ideal Husband,* 1999; Edinburgh International Film Festival Award for best British performance, for *The Winslow Boy,* 1999.

Sidelights

Award–winning British film and stage actor Jeremy Northam is best known for his work in period pieces. He has played an upper–crust Britain in such films as *Emma, The Winslow Boy,* and *Gosford Park.* The first major break in his career came in 1989, when he was called onstage to replace Daniel Day–Lewis mid–performance in *Hamlet.* In contemporary Hollywood films, such as *The Net* and *Gloria,* he is often cast as the villain. He was a hit as an escaped American convict in the independent film *Happy, Texas*. In a seeming stretch, he portrayed American singing legend Dean Martin in the 2002 TV movie *Martin and Lewis*.

Born December 1, 1961, in Cambridge, England, Northam is the youngest of four children of John and Rachel Northam. John Northam was a professor of literature and theater at Cambridge University who is best known for his translations of the works of playwright Henrik Ibsen. His mother, a pottery artist, also was a professor of economics at Cambridge. The family moved to Bristol, England, when Northam was eleven years old. Northam followed in his parents's academic footsteps in college, majoring in English at London University. He started acting in 1986 when he was working one summer moving scenery for a local theater company. "I had so much fun and I envied the actors so much that I thought I'd give it a try," he told Canoe online.

Northam then began studying theater at Bristol's Old Vic Theater School. He began to make his way onstage in regional theater productions, and landed on the London stage as an understudy for Daniel Day–Lewis, who played the Prince of Denmark in the National Theater Company's production of *Hamlet*. Northam was playing the role of Osric when, in 1989, Day–Lewis suffered a nervous breakdown onstage and walked off stage half an hour into the show. A nervous Northam was called to the stage, where he barely made it through his lines to the end of the performance. He had not rehearsed the role in five months and had become unfamiliar with the dense text. "There was no indication I was going to have to go on," he recalled to Terry Gross on National Public Radio's *Fresh Air* in 2002. "It was fairly ridiculous. It was a bit of a one–sided fight between me and the text, and the text came out on top. And you could hear the flipping of seats," which meant people were leaving the theater. "It was one of the most terrifying experiences of my life. But it became—on subsequent nights—exhilarating and exciting."

Once he had more thoroughly learned his lines, Northam fully inhabited his roll in *Hamlet* and became a critical and popular hit on the London stage. He won the Laurence Olivier Award for most promising newcomer of the year in theatre for his portrayal of Edward Voysey in the National Theatre Company's revival of the 1905 play *The Voysey Inheritance*. He also appeared in the London productions of *The Gift of the Gorgon*, by the Royal Shakespeare Company in 1992, *La bete*, by the Really Useful Theatre Company in 1993, and *Love's Labour's Lost* and *The Country Wife*, both in 1994 by the Royal

Shakespeare Company. He also appeared on British television, including as Captain Stanhope in *Journey's End* in 1988 and Rufus Fletcher in *A Fatal Inversion* in 1991.

Northam played Hindley Earnshaw in *Emily Bronte's Wuthering Heights* in 1992, which was to become the first in a long line of period films he would appear in, including *Carrington* (1995), *Emma* (1996), *Amistad* (1997), *The Winslow Boy* (1999), *An Ideal Husband* (1999), *Gosford Park* (2001), and *Enigma* (2001). "It's rare that people see me as a contemporary guy—as an actor or as a person," he lamented in an interview with Merle Ginsberg of *WWD*. People see him "as if I'm some dinosaur from some bygone age." But he also admitted in the same interview that period pieces often offer dramatic challenges that contemporary films do not. "I am drawn, I have to admit, to the abstract and the complicated. I like density of character—not just a reduction of motives to one simple thing."

The British actor made his Hollywood debut playing in the 1995 computer–age thriller, *The Net*, opposite Sandra Bullock. The producers just happened to be looking for an unknown English actor to play the villainous Jack Devlin. "There I was in the proverbial right place at the right time," he said online at Canoe. In 1997's *Mimic* Northam battled giant, man–eating insects alongside Mira Sorvino. The film was a critical disappointment, though Northam was excited about taking a role in a horror film. "I grew up watching the old ... fright films in Britain," he told Canoe. "*Dracula, Prince of Darkness* was my favorite, so I have a lot of respect for the horror genre."

Northam perfected a working–class American accent for the independent comedy *Happy, Texas*, which was the hit of the 1998 Sundance Film Festival. In it, he played opposite Steve Zahn as one of two escaped convicts who are mistaken as gay beauty pageant judges. Northam redonned his accent and formal waistcoats as Welsh matinee idol Ivor Novello in Robert Altman's 2001 murder–mystery, *Gosford Park*. The all–star ensemble cast of upper–crust characters and servants spends a 1932 weekend hunting on an English estate. Despite the large cast, Northam's portrayal of Novello, in which he did his own singing, won kudos. Some critics found the plot forsaken for the great number of characters, but Northam "seems as quietly amused as Novello himself to be part of this tedious party," Stanley Kauffman wrote in the *New Republic*.

Northam portrayed Dean Martin opposite Sean Hayes in the 2002 TV movie *Martin and Lewis*. Northam was a "surprising choice" to play American lounge legend Martin, Terry Gross said on *Fresh Air.* First of all, she noted, he was British. Second, he is known for his formal, period roles—"characters that are the opposite of Martin's cool," she said. To overcome the inherent differences between himself and Martin, Northam carefully studied and attempted to emulate Martin's physical presence and the idiosyncratic way he used his voice, both when singing and speaking, though Martin's singing voice was used in the film. Despite some critical comments about flaws in his American accent as Martin, American TV critics generally approved of the Brit's portrayal of the crooner. Though considered by many to be the "heir apparent" to British acting, according to MovieThing.com, Northam seems equally poised to reign on both sides of the Atlantic.

Sources

Periodicals

New Republic, December 31, 2001, p. 24.
WWD, September 27, 1999, p. 4.

Online

"British actor Jeremy Northam," *Fresh Air,* http://freshair.npr.org/day_fa.jhtml?displayValue=day&todayDate=11/21/2002 (November 23, 2002).

"Fright of fancy," Canoe, http://www.canoe.ca/JamMoviesArtistsN/northam_jeremy.html (October 30, 2002).

"Jeremy Northam," Internet Movie Database, http://us.imdb.com/Name?Northam,+Jeremy (October 10, 2002).

"Jeremy Northam," MovieThing.com, http://moviething.com/cgi-bac/ecom9990057318529.cgi?itemid=9800057404743&action=viewad&page=1&placeonpage=1&totaldisplayed=25&categoryid=9990057318529 (October 30, 2002).

—*Brenna Sanchez*

Jorma Ollila

President, Chief Executive Officer, and Board Chair of Nokia

Born Jorma Jaakko Ollila, August 15, 1950, in Seinäjoki, Finland; married to Liisa Annikki (Metsola); children: Jaakko, Anna, Matti. *Education:* University of Helsinki, Master of Political Science degree, 1976; London School of Economics, M.S. (economics), 1978; Helsinki University of Technology, M.S. (engineering), 1981.

Addresses: *Office*—Nokia Corp., P.O. Box 226, Espoo, Finland 00045.

Career

Began career at Citibank N.A., London, England, as an account manager, 1978–80, Citibank Oy, Helsinki, Finland, account officer, 1980–82, board of management member, 1983–85; Nokia Group, Espoo, Finland, vice president for international operations, 1985–86, senior vice president for finance, 1986–89, deputy member of the board of directors, 1989–90, president of mobile phones division, 1990–92, president and chief executive officer, 1992—, board chair, 1999—.

Member: Vice chair, Otava Books and Magazines Group, Ltd.; board of directors, Ford Motor Company; board of directors, UPM–Kymmene Corporation; European Round Table of Industrialists.

AP/Wide World Photos

Sidelights

Jorma Ollila heads Nokia, the Finnish mobile–phone giant, and is widely credited with helping the brand attain global domination in its market. Of the estimated 930 million cell–phone users around the world, some 300 million of them use Nokia's advanced–design, easy–to–use devices. The company has posted spectacular profits under Ollila's watch, and is heading toward taking its loyal customers with it into the next age of wireless communications—when mobile–communication devices will serve as Web browsers, MP3 players, and even digital cameras. "In ten years' time, I would like Nokia to be dubbed as the company that brought mobility and the Internet together," Ollila told the *Economist* in 2000. "It's not going to be easy, but this organization loves discontinuity; we can jump on it and adapt. Finns live in a cold climate: we have to be adaptable to survive."

Born in 1950, Ollila hails from the city of Seinäjoki in the western part of Finland. He studied political science at the University of Helsinki and served as president of the Finnish National Union of Students during his time there. After he graduated in 1976, he moved to England and earned a graduate degree from the London School of Economics. Beginning his career in 1978 as an account manager at Citibank's London offices, Ollila returned to Finland's capital city and center of commerce two years later to take a position with Citibank there. Within a few years he had risen so quickly within the organization that he held a seat on the management board of Citibank's Finland group. During this period he also returned to school and earned an engineering degree from the Helsinki University of Technology.

Ollila left Citibank to join Nokia in 1985 as a vice president for international operations. At the time, Nokia was a venerable Finnish conglomerate, founded as a lumber mill in 1865 and named after the local river there. Over the decades, it had branched out from wood and paper products to make television sets, rubber boots, tires, and an array of other goods. The company first ventured into the proto–telecommunications market when it began making specialty radio telephones used in remoter areas of Scandinavia. In the mid–1980s, the company entered into a partnership with Ericsson, a Swedish company. Ericsson created the first cellular communications network in Scandinavia, and Nokia began producing the first car–based phones for it.

After a stint as a senior vice president for finance at Nokia, Ollila was made president of the company's mobile–phone division in 1990. He was interested in taking the company further into the burgeoning telecom market, yet Nokia was still an unwieldy corporate goliath, and some inside the company were resistant. However, political events helped shape the company's destiny: in 1991, Finland's eastern neighbor, the Soviet Union, collapsed. The Communist country had been one of Nokia's most important trade partners, and the company was left with a large inventory of products, including a warehouse of toilet paper, on its hands. As the company's fortunes began to flag, some executives argued that Nokia should exit the mobile–phone business altogether, a sector in which competition was growing increasingly keen.

Ollila, however, believed Nokia should instead make its mobile–phones unit a priority. He was given the go–ahead to make some changes in research and development as well as production, and Nokia's phones began selling in record numbers across Scandinavia. Profits followed, and in 1992 Ollila's foresight was rewarded by Nokia's board when he was named president and chief executive officer of the entire company. At that point, he began to turn Nokia into a global powerhouse. The

company sold off its other manufacturing divisions, and invested the money into cutting–edge research and phone design. As the decade progressed, Nokia's products were often the first affordable, lightweight, and stylish phones on the market. It also achieved several technological firsts in the market, including the first products designed exclusively for Asian consumers, and the first with a real–time chat function. Ollila also let the company's marketing division spend lavishly on international advertising to help promote the brand name over rivals Motorola and Ericsson.

As Nokia emerged as an industry leader, Ollila was once again rewarded for his leadership, and the title of board chair was added to those of president and chief executive officer in 1999. By 2000, the price of a Nokia share, traded on the New York Stock Exchange, had risen 2,000 percent in five years. It was largest company in Europe in market–capitalization numbers, and Ollila managed some 53,000 employees. Yet by this time the telecom industry had hit a downturn, and a cell–phone saturation level in the developed world was rapidly approaching. To remedy this, Ollila arranged a series of strategy meetings with Nokia managers throughout 2001. "We tried to respond to the realities of the marketplace, not to get mired in management philosophy and orthodoxy," he told *Business-Week* writer Andy Reinhardt. By the end of the year, Ollila and his team had announced an historic restructuring: it would be broken up into nine separate divisions; one would make technologically advanced phones, and the last in the chain would concentrate on flooding developing markets like Brazil and India with lower–priced products.

Ollila was certain that Nokia could remain an industry leader, especially by giving consumers new wireless communication devices that offered Internet access, MP3 capabilities, and what is called multimedia messaging (MMS), which allows users to send and view video images. In 2002, it introduced some 30 new products into the market, and though sales had slowed, Nokia's profits remained strong at $3.57 billion for the year. Ollila's contract has been extended through 2006, and he is a popular CEO at the company's modernist glass–and–wood headquarters in Espoo, on the Gulf of Finland. He eats in the company cafeteria, makes time for his family, which includes a wife and three children, and plays tennis three mornings a week. "This isn't a business where you do one big, strategic thing right and you're set for the next five years," he told *Fortune's* Janet Guyon. "It's a big orchestration task."

Sources

Periodicals

BusinessWeek, July 1, 2002, pp. 56–58; January 13, 2003, p. 70.
Economist, October 14, 2000, p. 83.
Fortune, March 4, 2002, p. 115.
Industry Week, November 20, 2000, p. 38.
InformationWeek, January 24, 2003.
International Management, July/August 1992, p. 52.

Time, May 29, 2000, p. 64.
Wireless Week, November 5, 2001, p. 3.

Online

"Biography: Jorma Ollila," Nokia, http://www.nokia.com/cda2/0,1083,2544,00.html (April 10, 2003).

—*Carol Brennan*

Suze Orman

James D. Wilson/Getty Images

Media personality

Born Susan Orman, c. 1951, in Chicago, IL; daughter of Morris (a landlord and deli operator) and Ann (a legal secretary) Orman. *Education:* Earned degree in social work, University of Illinois at Urbana–Champaign, early 1970s.

Addresses: *Agent*—c/o Riverhead Books, Putnam Berkley Group, 200 Madison Ave., New York, NY 10016.

Career

Account executive, Merrill Lynch, San Francisco, CA, 1980–83; vice president of investments, Prudential Bache Securities, San Francisco, 1983–87; president and chief executive officer, Suze Orman Financial Group, Emeryville, CA, 1987—. Host of PBS special *The Financial Freedom Hour.* Appears regularly on QVC–TV as host of *Financial Freedom,* and as a guest on the *Oprah Winfrey Show,* the *Today Show, NBC Nightly News,* and *Good Morning America.* Speaker and lecturer throughout the United States.

Sidelights

Best–selling author and ubiquitous television presence Suze Orman is America's most successful financial–advice guru. Orman first gained fame in 1997 with her second book, *The Nine Steps to Financial Freedom,* which attained the No. 1 spot on the *New York Times* bestseller list, as did its successor, *The Courage to Be Rich.* Orman's advice is less about the specifics of financial planning and investment strategies than it is a mission to help con-

sumers eradicate what she views as a pervasive fear of finance. Asserting that money is what people fear most—an apprehension which, she believes, leads to overspending and undersaving—Orman urges a healthier outlook based on some common–sense strategies combined with New Age tenets. "In my own way, I think money is one of the most spiritual things," Orman explained in an interview with *Kiplinger's Personal Finance* writer Robert Frick. "Money will not set you free. It's your control over your thoughts and fears about money that will set you free."

Orman was born in the early 1950s into a Jewish family that lived in a blue–collar neighborhood in south–side Chicago. As she has revealed in her books and in interviews, her family's struggle to make ends meet was a constant one. Her father and grandfather owned a boarding house, but a woman had a paralyzing accident there, sued them, and they lost the building. Orman's mother went to work as a legal secretary, while her father opened a delicatessen. This business was destroyed by fire when Orman was 13. She recalled a vivid memory of her father running into the burning store to save the cash register, because the till "was all the money we had," she told *People* journalist Erik Meers.

"When he dropped the register, everything came with it—his shirt, the skin on his arms. That's when I learned money was more important than life."

Growing up, Orman had a conflicted relationship with money, feeling that her family was poorer than the households of her friends. After high school, she enrolled in the University of Illinois at Urbana–Champaign to study social work, where comedian John Belushi and his future wife were roommates of hers. Feeling disconnected from her Jewish roots, she spent time in Israel, and moved to California in 1973. She found a waitressing job at the Buttercup Bakery in Berkeley, earning $100 a week, and managed to save enough to buy a small house within three years. "I never felt I would ever be anything more than a waitress," Orman recalled in the interview with Frick in *Kiplinger's Personal Finance*. "I was getting by. I loved serving people."

In northern California, Orman became interested in New Age ideas, and dreamed of opening her own place that would serve as both restaurant and a spa. She borrowed $50,000 from friends and customers at the Buttercup, and gave it to a broker at Merrill Lynch to invest—who then lost it trading. Desperate to pay back her investors, Orman applied for a job at Merrill Lynch, and though she arrived at her interview wearing red–and–white striped pants tucked into cowboy boots, she got the job. Some believed that her only other recourse would have been to sue Merrill Lynch for her loss, but Orman proved a surprisingly quick learner and compelling salesperson in her new career. Annuities quickly became her forte, and Merrill Lynch began sending her out to give retirement planning seminars to employees of Pacific Gas and Electric, a major utility company in the region.

Early on, Orman was fascinated by the relationship between money and self–esteem, and became a devotee of a perennially popular self–help book from 1953, *The Power of Positive Thinking*, by Norman Vincent Peale. She spent three years at Merrill Lynch in the early 1980s and achieved impressive financial success, took time off to travel to India and Nepal in 1983, and returned to the Bay Area and a job with Prudential Bache Securities. In 1987, she left her vice president's job there to launch her own firm, just around the time that Pacific Gas and Electric began offering employees an early–retirement package. She suddenly had an onslaught of clients, but Prudential Bache had retained her license for a month after her last day of work. So the new clients were signed on by her assistant, who had a license, but then the two had a falling–out over compensation and the woman took Orman's files. After three years and two legal battles, Orman obtained a small judgment in her favor, but the incident would come back to haunt her when she attained fame as a financial–planning guru.

Orman's business tanked in the late 1980s, and desperate to appear at least outwardly successful, she ran up large credit–card debts. In the early 1990s, Pacific Gas and Electric offered additional early–retirement inducements, and Orman's company once again found itself flush with clients. In 1994, Pacific Gas and Electric asked her to do a satellite pitch to 7,000 worldwide employees on retirement planning, and her seminar became the basis for her first book. She co–wrote *You've Earned It, Don't Lose It: Mistakes You Can't Afford to Make When You Retire* with Linda Mead, in which she offered tips on how to select a financial adviser; the book also outlined the basics of wills, trusts, and long–term–care insurance. Orman boosted its sales by appearing on the QVC shopping channel, and on her first early–morning spot in October of 1995, she sold 2,500 copies. A Super Bowl Sunday 1996 appearance on QVC resulted in even more remarkable numbers: in just 12 minutes, *You've Earned It, Don't Lose It* sold 10,000 copies.

Orman contracted for a regular spot on QVC, and its debut coincided with the publication of her next book, *The Nine Steps to Financial Freedom: Practical & Spiritual Steps So You Can Stop Worrying*, in 1997. In it, she recounts her childhood and the sense of inadequacy over money she experienced, and moves on to chronicle her success story as an investment specialist. She asserted that that people often spend money on themselves unnecessarily—a pricey coffee every morning, or a sale item worn only once—but she points out that if she asks someone to rip dollar bill in half, they will almost always balk. Her book urged readers to remove the distance between oneself and money, to cultivate a more personal relationship with it. The *San Francisco Chronicle's* Patricia Holt liked the case stories that Orman presented from her years as a financial planner: "Orman has a knack for making us feel the depth of the client's confusion and even terror about money, making each step toward financial independence all the more vivid and memorable." Noting that the book combined such self–help exhortations with more practical advice about living trusts, 401(k) plans, and the like, Holt conceded "such information has been provided endlessly in other books; it's the power of Orman's personality that makes it all seem so personal and valuable."

The Nine Steps to Financial Freedom sold 25,000 copies on her show's debut broadcast on QVC, which led to an offer from a PBS producer in Minneapolis/

St. Paul to put her on the air during pledge week. PBS often relied on personal–growth gurus like Deepak Chopra to boost their fund–raising efforts, but Orman enjoyed instantaneous success with her 21–city tour that raised $2.3 million. Her pitch involved discussing her book, and urging readers to donate to PBS for a copy or other Orman–related perk in return. Sales continued to climb outside of the PBS readership as well, and in early 1998 Orman was invited on to Oprah Winfrey's highly rated daytime show for the first time. By April, *Nine Steps* had landed on the *New York Times* self–help list, and would become the best–selling nonfiction title of 1998.

Sales for Orman's next book, *The Courage to Be Rich: Creating a Life of Material and Spiritual Abundance,* again surpassed expectations. In the 1999 title, she once more dissects the emotional relationship people have with money, usually tied to feelings of fear, anger, or shame, and urges readers to respect money, restrict unnecessary spending, and realize the difference between self–worth and net worth. The impetus behind the book, as Orman revealed in an interview with *Sales & Marketing Management* writer Erika Rasmusson, was tied to the rising divorce rate she witnessed among her friends and acquaintances. "A lot of them got divorced over money," she noted. "And a lot of them were treating their money the exact same way they treated their relationship: In essence, they weren't quite honest. So I started to realize that the way we related to people was the exact same way we related to money."

Orman's personal–empowerment creed made some of her financial–advisor competitors wary, claiming that her message was long on maxims and short on substance. In a *New Republic* critique of *The Nine Steps to Financial Freedom,* Christopher Caldwell asserted that "the structural resemblance between Alcoholics Anonymous's 12 steps and her nine is uncanny, and, outside of the recovery movement, Orman may be America's most forthright champion of slogans—and of their thought–eradicating potential." *Los Angeles Times* writer Josh Getlin pointed out that "Orman and others like her are simply the latest variation of an old theme in American intellectual life: The marriage of spirituality and good old–fashioned moolah," a strange–bedfellows mix that dates back to Puritan times and Benjamin Franklin.

In a *New York Times* article that compared Orman to other modern–day electronic–media icons like Martha Stewart and Oprah Winfrey, Edward Wyatt contended that Orman's pitch relies upon her "challenge ... to examine whether they are just not brave enough to be rich. It is an extremely effective sales technique, questioning the backbone of her audience." Wyatt continued with the observation that "the Orman oeuvre is no more ambitious than the scores of other volumes of financial advice that clog the shelves at local bookstores. What makes Ms. Orman special is her ability to equate the pursuit of money with some form of courage." Caldwell, writing in the *New Republic,* pegged her appeal as one that reflected our times. "Orman is implicitly questioning the viability of a debt–based, luxury–item–driven, millennial economy in which higher living standards have more to do with higher material expectations than greater means to afford them. We've seen this before. This is populism," Caldwell asserted, and clarified that he was using the term in its original, non–political definition. Populism, he defined, is in this case "a critique of a credit–based economy made by hardworking but generally overindebted people who've discovered too late that compound interest is a more benevolent friend and a more spiteful adversary than it at first appears."

Orman's critics, though biting, were far outnumbered by her fans. As she told Getlin in the *Los Angeles Times,* "I wrote the books for people who nobody pays attention to. They're people who have $50 a month and that's all they can afford to invest. This is not about sales," Orman asserted. "It's about souls." She continued to be a presence on the bestseller lists with her fourth book, *The Road to Wealth: A Comprehensive Guide to Your Money,* published in 2001. That same year, she began writing a monthly money–advice column for *O: The Oprah Magazine.* A few months after the terrorist attacks on the United States, Orman wrote in the magazine that a recession was already looming before the events of September 11, 2001, but asserted that the American economy would strengthen in the end. The trauma might even work toward reordering priorities, she noted, and predicted that credit–card debt would drop. "We have felt so much pain in the aftermath of the attacks on the World Trade Center and the Pentagon, and now the idea of trying to make ourselves feel better by spending money we don't have has lost its appeal," she wrote.

Orman began 2002 with another new book, *Financial Freedom: Creating True Wealth Now,* and the debut of a two–hour radio talk show, *The Suze Orman Show,* that aired in several American cities. In 1998, Orman was still living in a 1,000–square–foot home she bought in 1976 when working as a waitress, though she did acquire a Manhattan apartment in the late 1990s.

Selected writings

(With Linda Mead) *You've Earned It, Don't Lose It: Mistakes You Can't Afford to Make When You Retire,* Newmarket Press (New York City), 1994; revised and updated edition, 1999.

The Nine Steps to Financial Freedom: Practical & Spiritual Steps So You Can Stop Worrying, Crown (New York City), 1997.

The Courage to Be Rich: Creating a Life of Material and Spiritual Abundance, Riverhead Books (New York City), 1999.

The Road to Wealth: A Comprehensive Guide to Your Money, Riverhead Books, 2001.

Financial Freedom: Creating True Wealth Now, Riverhead Books, 2002

Sources

Best's Review, April 2002, p. 97.

Business Record (Des Moines), September 3, 2001, p. 17.

Forbes, December 28, 1998, p. 118.

Kiplinger's Personal Finance, November 1998, p. 96.

Library Journal, May 1, 1997, p. 118; March 1, 1999, p. 124; June 1, 1999, p. 207.

Los Angeles Times, June 22, 1999, p. A1.

Mediaweek, January 7, 2002, p. 20.

Money, May 1, 1999, p. 58.

National Underwriter Life & Health–Financial Services Edition, March 18, 2002, p. 14.

New Republic, October 18, 1999, p. 24.

New York Times, January 6, 2002, p. 16.

O: The Oprah Magazine, December 2001, p. 58.

People, May 17, 1999, p. 153.

Publishers Weekly, August 6, 2001, p. 19; December 24, 2001, p. 59; July 1, 2002, p. 33.

Sales & Marketing Management, August 1999, p. 120.

San Francisco Chronicle, July 27, 1997, p. 1; January 6, 1999, p. B1.

—*Carol Brennan*

The Osbournes

Entertainers

Members include Jack (born in 1985; son of Ozzy and Sharon); Kelly (born October 27, 1984; daughter of Ozzy and Sharon); Ozzy (born John Michael Osbourne, December 3, 1948, in Birmingham, England; son of Jack and Lillian Osbourne; married Thelma Mayfair, 1971 (divorced,

1981); married Sharon, 1982; children: Jessica, Louis (from first marriage), Aimee, Kelly, Jack); Sharon (maiden name, Arden; born in England; daughter of Don Arden; married Ozzy, 1982; children: Aimee, Kelly, Jack) Osbourne.

Addresses: *Television network*—MTV Networks, 2600 Colorado Ave., Santa Monica, CA 90404. *Website*—Official Osbournes Website: http://www.mtv.com/onair/osbournes/.

Career

Ozzy Osbourne rose to prominence as a member of the heavy metal rock band Black Sabbath, 1970s; Ozzy and his family starred in first season of the MTV reality series, *The Osbournes*, 2002; starred in second season of *The Osbournes*, 2002–03; began filming third season of *The Osbournes*, 2003.

Awards: Grammy Award for best metal performance (for Ozzy), Recording Academy, for "I Don't Want to Change the World," 1993; Grammy Award for best metal performance (for Black Sabbath), Recording Academy, for "Iron Man," 1999; star on Hollywood's Walk of Fame (for Ozzy), 2002; inducted into the Rock and Roll Hall of Fame (Ozzy), 2002.

Sidelights

On March 5, 2002, the MTV cable television network debuted a reality show featuring the family of heavy–metal rock legend Ozzy Osbourne. Called *The Osbournes*, the show featured the family at home in their Beverly Hills, California, mansion, arguing, swearing, making up, and just hanging out. The show quickly became the most successful program in the history of the network, attracting an average of six million viewers a week in the United States alone.

In their second season, which premiered November 26, 2002, the Osbournes found themselves enormously popular, and, astonishingly for a family in which alcohol and drug use has formed a major theme, looked up to as role models. Initially seen as a novelty show about an eccentric rocker and his zany family, the show has propelled the family into genuine celebrity status: Ozzy and his wife, Sharon, were invited to dine with the president of the United States and Ozzy performed at Buckingham Palace. The second season reportedly netted the Osbourne family a fee of $39 million for 20 half–hour episodes, up from less than $600,000 for the first season of 10 half–hour episodes.

The show also launched the music career of one of Ozzy and Sharon's daughters, Kelly, who first gained popularity as a musician by covering pop-star Madonna's "Papa Don't Preach" at the MTV Movie Awards in 2002. Released as a single, Kelly's version of the song quickly became a Top 40 hit. Kelly released her first album, *Shut Up*, on the Sony imprint Epic in 2002.

While admitting that she would not have a music career without the MTV show, Kelly has mixed feelings about being filmed for *The Osbournes*. She acknowledged that she tolerated being filmed at home, but that she hated being followed by cameras when she went out in public because she found it embarrassing.

Show biz is nothing new to Kelly, however. Three weeks after she was born, she was on the road for an Ozzy concert tour. She has described being babysat by the members of the heavy metal band Mötley Crüe while her father performed. "I've seen stuff people have never seen or would ever want to see," she told Cameron Adams in the *Advertiser*.

The Osbournes's son, Jack, who likes to wear combat fatigues and carry a knife, capitalized on his newfound fame by acting in the TV series *Dawson's Creek*. He also picked up a part–time job as a talent scout for the Epic record label. He remained in the public eye off–camera when he entered a drug rehabilitation program in Pasadena, California, on April 23, 2003. Jack returned home from rehab on June 18, 2003, and gave a tell–all interview to MTV News to discuss his drug abuse and recovery. According to E! Online, Jack's reality check came while partying with his friends: "I took myself out of the picture for a second, and I looked around at every single person in the room, at who they were, how old they were, and what they had going on in their lives. A lot of them were near 30, unemployed, living off their parents. There were heroin addicts; there were the world's biggest couch potatoes. And it was like, I don't want to be like that. I don't want my life to be controlled by a drug. I want to be in control of my life."

Only the Osbournes's oldest daughter, Aimee, has sought a normal life, declining to appear on the show. While the show was filmed, Aimee lived in the guest house. She is also pursuing a career in music. In July of 2003, it was announced that Aimee would make her acting debut in MTV's musical adaptation of *Wuthering Heights*, airing in September of 2003. The Osbournes as a family have also taken advantage of their time in the public spotlight by releasing merchandise, including pens, mugs, air fresheners, T–shirts, and even a line of underwear.

The second season of the *The Osbournes* also features Kelly's friend, Robert Marcato. After Marcato's mother died of cancer, Sharon took the 18–year–old under her wing, inviting him to move in with her family. She also told him that she would finance his education at the best acting school they could get him into.

Sharon Osbourne works as Ozzy's manager, and she is credited with reinventing her husband's career in the 1990s, making them multi–millionaires in the process. It was also Sharon's idea to have her family star in a reality–TV series about their lives. Like her husband, Sharon has indulged in her share of alcohol abuse, although she has drawn the line at illegal drugs. They fought constantly through the 1980s, often violently. Sharon cleaned up her act before Ozzy because as she later explained to Sue Crawford in the book *Ozzy Unauthorized*, "I realized that if we both carried on, we'd wind up a washed–up pair of old drunks, living in a hovel."

In episode two of the second season, Sharon, then 48 years old, was diagnosed with colon cancer. The diagnosis was real, and Ozzy's distress genuine. The show featured Ozzy on tour when he found out about his wife's illness, as well as his brief slide back into the self–destructive behavior that marked his early days as a rocker. Cameras followed Sharon into chemotherapy sessions, and her treatment quickly became an integral part of the real–life drama that is *The Osbournes*.

Ozzy first gained notoriety as a member of the heavy metal band Black Sabbath. The band found instant popularity among teens, and was quickly vilified by parents who claimed that the band's music was harmful to young minds. Ozzy was born John Michael Osbourne, one of six children of working–class parents Jack and Lillian Osbourne. He picked up the nickname Ozzy in high school, from which he frequently played hooky. He hated school, and he once attacked a teacher with an iron bar. He dropped out of school at the age of 15, going to work in a slaughterhouse. He later said that he enjoyed the work of killing animals.

Before Black Sabbath hit it big, Ozzy served a prison sentence for burglary and possession of marijuana. It was in prison that he acquired his first tattoo, the letters "O–Z–Z–Y" spelled out on his left knuckles. He applied the tattoo himself. Ozzy was released from prison after serving six weeks of a three–month sentence.

Black Sabbath came together in Birmingham, England, in 1969. Originally calling themselves Earth, the members of the band soon changed their name to honor their favorite horror film. First playing in local clubs, the band quickly gained a large following. Black Sabbath's self–titled debut album was an instant success, selling more than a million copies, and leading to the group's first American tour in 1970. It was the first time that a heavy–metal band had toured the United States.

Black Sabbath released its second album in 1970, *Paranoid,* followed by *Masters of Reality* in 1971, *Sabbath Bloody Sabbath* in 1974, and *Sabotage* in 1975. Meanwhile, Ozzy married his first wife, Thelma Mayfair, in 1971. Ozzy's involvement with Black Sabbath and his marriage ended at about the same time; Ozzy quit the band (some sources say he was thrown out) as the 1970s drew to a close, and his marriage was officially dissolved in 1981. The couple had two children, a daughter, Jessica, and a son, Louis.

Leaving Black Sabbath in 1978, Ozzy launched a solo career, with the help of his future second wife, Sharon. One of the songs Ozzy produced in the 1980s, "Suicide Solution," was said to advocate suicide among teenagers. In fact, Ozzy was the subject of a wrongful death lawsuit in which the parents of a young Ozzy fan who killed himself tried to hold Ozzy responsible for their son's death. Ozzy claimed the song "was written in relation to the effects of alcohol abuse," according to All Music Guide. In a concert video for the song "Bark at the Moon," he made waves by biting the head off a live bat, which, he later explained, he thought was fake. Ozzy's solo albums—including his solo debut, *Blizzard of Ozz* in 1980 and 1983's *Bark at the Moon*—sold more than 70 million copies.

Much of Ozzy's success as a solo artist was propelled by Sharon's talent as his manager. Sharon is the daughter of Don Arden, the head of Ozzy's former record label and the manager of Black Sabbath. Sharon convinced Ozzy to leave her father's record label and sign with CBS/Columbia Music. The move was a good business decision, but it caused an irreparable rift between Arden and the Osbournes. Sharon was forced by Arden to buy out Ozzy's recording contract for $3 million. It took Sharon almost 20 years to forgive her father for that, and the two only began speaking to each other again in 2001.

Meanwhile, Sharon built a reputation for being one of the best managers in the music business, winning widespread respect among other managers and executives. Ozzy learned to trust her completely. As he was quoted by Crawford in *Ozzy Unauthorized,*

"My wife is the ruler of the roost, she tells me what to do most of the time. It's a true old saying that behind every great man is a great woman, and I've got the greatest woman in the world working for me. It's fabulous." Ozzy does draw the line sometimes, though. Once, while helping to plan one of Ozzy's concerts, Sharon suggested that they fill up the stage with bubbles generated by a bubble-making machine. According to James Morrison in the *Independent*, Ozzy's response was one of exasperation: "Bubbles?!? Sharon, I'm the Prince of f***ing Darkness."

Ozzy and Sharon's relationship began as strictly business; Sharon saw potential in Ozzy for a music career beyond what he had had with Black Sabbath, and she was determined to help him realize it. After the two of them built a new career for Ozzy, their relationship deepened into something more. Ozzy started their new relationship in typical fashion, as he later explained to Crawford, "I got her drunk and leapt on her. I was never very subtle with relationships."

Ozzy and Sharon were married in 1981, soon after Ozzy's divorce from his first wife was finalized. Ozzy and Sharon's marriage was not without its rocky periods. Ozzy continued to drink heavily and use illicit drugs, including cocaine and heroin. His drug and alcohol problem came to a head in 1989, when drunk on three bottles of vodka, he attempted to strangle Sharon. He went to jail, and although Sharon did not press charges, she took him back only after he agreed to clean up his act.

Shortly after Ozzy kicked his drug and alcohol habits, he developed a slight limp. Doctors initially diagnosed him with multiple sclerosis. This diagnosis was eventually proven false; doctors finally came to the conclusion that years of hard drinking and drug use had caused a permanent imbalance in his brain chemistry. He now walks and moves slowly, is hard of hearing, has shaky hands, and has difficulty speaking at times.

Ozzy and Sharon's first child, Aimee, was born in 1983. She was followed by Kelly in 1984, and Jack in 1985. By all accounts, Ozzy is a devoted family man, lavishing attention on Sharon and their three children. As he was quoted as saying by Geoffrey Wansell in Australia's *Sunday Mail*, "If it wasn't for Sharon, I'd be dead by now, without a doubt. Career-wise, I would definitely be dead—and I would almost certainly have been physically dead as well." Ozzy further credited his wife with helping him to "grow up," and he expressed gratitude for her work as his manager, admitting that he has no aptitude for the business end of his career.

Ozzy's transition from wild rock 'n' roller accused of corrupting young minds to respectable family man is complete. On April 12, 2002, he received a star on Hollywood Boulevard's Walk of Fame. In May of that same year, he was inducted into the Rock and Roll Hall of Fame. Crawford explained Ozzy's newfound mainstream acceptance this way to Wansell in the *Sunday Mail*: "Ozzy's done awful things but he's not an awful person, which is why we feel affection for him. He's redeemed himself by being repentant."

Ozzy, who was once banned from the state of Texas for urinating on the Alamo monument, and who was often spoken of in the same breath as the devil for corrupting a generation of youngsters, has arrived in the mainstream as the star of his family's reality television series. He has been invited to dinners at the White House—at which he shouted to President George W. Bush that he should wear his hair long—and to perform his heavy-metal classics at Buckingham Palace.

Sharon underwent surgery for her colon cancer in Los Angeles, California, in July of 2002. The family was uncharacteristically tight-lipped about Sharon's prognosis, revealing only that her cancer was treatable. Ozzy left his OzzFest tour to be with her as she started chemotherapy, but returned to the tour after she insisted that he do so.

On May 9, 2003, Sharon announced that Ozzy was leaving the Sony Music label after 23 years; Kelly also left the label. Sharon said in a statement that her husband and daughter were looking for "fresh ideas," but she offered no specific explanation for their move. According to CNN.com, the Osbournes's publicist, Lisa Vega, said that Sharon and Sony had agreed that Kelly would leave the label after former CEO Tommy Mottola, who signed Kelly in 2002, left the company. "Sony has been a part of the family for years … and Tommy Mottola was the person they had dealt with all those years, and when he left, they decided it was time for a change as well," Vega explained. A later report by Bill Zwecker at the *Chicago Sun-Times* said it was because Kelly had actually been dropped from the label because of disappointing sales, and Ozzy and Sharon were furious with the label, so they terminated his association with Sony.

Continuing with their busy schedule, the Osbourne family did not fade away from the public's sight. The second half of the second season (sometimes referred to as the third season) of *The Osbournes* premiered on June 10, 2003. Kelly began a tour in the summer of 2003 with British pop star Robbie Williams, while Ozzy began a Canadian tour in June of that year and headlined the annual Ozzfest rock tour that summer. According to MTV.com, Sharon signed a deal with Telepictures Productions, a division of Warner Bros. Television, to host a syndicated talk show scheduled to premiere in fall of 2003; she was reported to receive between $3 million and $5 million for her efforts. On July 8, 2003, MTV announced that it had signed up the family for 20 more episodes of *The Osbournes*, scheduled to begin airing early in 2004.

Selected discography

Ozzy (with Black Sabbath)

Black Sabbath, Warner, 1970.
Paranoid, Warner, 1971.
Master of Reality, Warner, 1971.
Black Sabbath, Vol. 4, Warner, 1972.
Sabbath, Bloody Sabbath, Warner, 1973.
Sabotage, Warner, 1975.
We Sold Our Soul for Rock and Roll, Warner, 1976.
Technical Ecstasy, Warner, 1976.

Ozzy (solo)

Blizzard of Ozz, Jet, 1980.
Diary of a Madman, Jet, 1981.
Speak of the Devil, Jet, 1982.
Bark at the Moon, Epic, 1983.
The Ultimate Sin, Epic, 1986.
Tribute (live), Epic, 1987.
No Rest for the Wicked, Epic, 1989.
Just Say Ozzy (live), Epic, 1990.
No More Tears, Epic, 1991.
Ozzmosis, Epic, 1995.
OzzFest, Vol. 1: Live, Red Ant, 1997.
Down to Earth, Sony, 2001.
Live at Budokan, Epic, 2002.

Kelly (solo)

Shut Up, Sony, 2002.

Sources

Books

Crawford, Sue, *Ozzy Unauthorized*, HarperCollins, 2002.

Periodicals

Advertiser (Australia), October 5, 2002, p. W3.
Chicago Sun–Times, May 12, 2003, p. 38.
Courier Mail (Queensland, Australia), January 30, 2003, p. 24.
Independent (London, England), April 21, 2002, p. 9.
Los Angeles Times, May 13, 2003, business section, p. 3.
Newsday, June 5, 2003, p. A12.
Newsweek, November 25, 2002, pp. 80–81.
St. Louis Post–Dispatch, August 18, 2002, p. F3.
Sunday Mail (Australia), July 28, 2002, p. 58.
Time, November 25, 2002, p. 84.
Times (London, England), May 25, 2002.

Online

"Jack Osbourne Comes Clean," E! Online, http://www.eonline.com/News/Items/0,1,12092,00.html (July 7, 2003).
"Jack Osbourne Comes Clean," E! Online, http://www.eonline.com/News/Items/0,1,12092,00.html (July 7, 2003).
"Kelly Osbourne," All Music Guide, http://www.allmusic.com (April 11, 2003).
"Osbournes Up For More *Osbournes*," E! Online, http://www.eonline.com/News/Items/0,1,12118,00.html?tnews (July 9, 2003).
"Ozzy Osbourne," All Music Guide, http://www.allmusic.com (April 11, 2003).
"Ozzy Seeking Fresh Ideas," CNN.com, http://www.cnn.com/2003/SHOWBIZ/Music/05/10/ozzy.reut/index.html (May 12, 2003).
"Sharon Osbourne To Host TV Talk Show," MTV.com, http://www.mtv.com/news/articles/1458589/20021108/story.jhtml (May 28, 2003).

—*Michael Belfiore*

Rod Paige

United States Secretary of Education

Born Roderick Raynor Paige, June 17, 1933, in Monticello, MS; divorced. *Education:* Jackson State University, B.S., 1955; Indiana University, M.S., 1964, D.P.Ed, 1969.

Addresses: *Office*—U.S. Department of Education, 400 Maryland Ave., SW, Washington, D.C. 20202.

Career

Became head football coach at Utica Junior College in Mississippi, 1957; became head football coach of Jackson State University in Mississippi, 1962; began in several posts at Texas Southern University, among them head football coach, athletic director, and assistant professor, 1971; appointed dean of the School of Education at Texas Southern University, 1984; elected to the Houston Independent School District Board of Education, 1989; became president of the Houston Board of Education, 1992; became Houston Independent School District superintendent of schools, 1994; appointed U.S. Secretary of Education by president George W. Bush, 2000; confirmed by the U.S. Senate as the nation's seventh Secretary of Education, 2001.

Awards: Richard R. Green Award for outstanding urban educator of 1999, Council of the Great City Schools, 2000; Harold W. McGraw, Jr. Prize in Education, 2000; Superintendent of the Year Award, National Association of Black School Educators, 2000.

Sidelights

Rod Paige was nominated by President–elect George W. Bush to the post of Secretary of Education in 2000, and was confirmed by the Senate in 2001. At the time of his nomination, Paige was superintendent of schools for Houston, Texas. With his confirmation, he became the second black member of president Bush's cabinet, after Secretary of State Colin Powell. He was the first African American ever to be appointed Secretary of Education.

Paige was born on June 17, 1933, in Monticello, Mississippi. He was the first born of five children. His parents were both educators, and they pushed him to succeed at an early age. His mother was a librarian who worked in the then–segregated public schools in Mississippi, and his father was a school principal. Paige attended high school at the Lawrence County Training High School in the town of his birth, and then, helped by a sports scholarship, went on to earn a bachelor's degree at Mississippi's Jackson State University.

Paige excelled at Jackson State, making a lasting impression on his classmates. "It was an honor to outscore that joker on a test, and that didn't happen too often," Walter Reed, a fellow Jackson graduate, told Salatheia Bryant of the *Houston Chronicle.* "Everybody knew Rod was sitting at the top."

While at Jackson State, Paige brought in extra money by unloading milk trucks. He also ran on the track team and aspired to be an athletic coach. He succeeded in that goal, going on to become Jackson State's head football coach. At the same time, he studied for his master's degree at Indiana University. He earned his master's in 1964, and continued his education, earning a Ph.D. in physical education from the same university in 1969. His doctoral thesis was on football, specifically a study of offensive linemen's reaction times.

Paige's interest in coaching and football brought him to Houston, Texas, in 1971, where he took a job as head football coach at Texas Southern University. Paige served in this position for four years, turning down at least one offer to become a coach for the National Football League. He wanted to stay in academia.

Moving on from coaching, Paige accepted the job of Dean of the College of Education at Texas Southern University. He served in this post for ten years, establishing the Center for Excellence in Urban Education at the university. This research facility has as its focus the management of urban schools. Leaving coaching for academic administration proved to be the right decision for Paige; he took to the job well, and this interest naturally led to politics.

In 1989, Paige ran on the Republican ticket for a spot on the Board of Education of the Houston Independent School District. The Houston school district was then the largest school system in Texas, and it was the seventh–biggest in the country. Paige was elected, and he served on the school board until 1994.

As a school board member, Paige became known for facing difficult issues head on. Fellow board member Larry Marshall told Bryant of the *Houston Chronicle* that Paige didn't miss a beat when someone stood up in a meeting and asked Paige why he was a Republican. "He said," recalled Marshall, "'Because growing up in Mississippi, Democrats were lynching blacks.' It was such an inappropriate question, but it got such an appropriate answer."

While serving on the Houston school board, Paige was instrumental in the creation of a document called "A Declaration of Beliefs and Visions." This statement laid out a long–term plan for the school board, and it advocated a major overhaul of the way the Houston school system was run. Among the Declaration's recommendations was a call for decentralization of the school district, along with a demand for increased accountability at every level of the system, and a call for the development of a core curriculum to be taught at all the schools.

The Board appointed Paige to be Houston's superintendent of schools in 1994. This move angered many in the Hispanic community, who had the most students in the district, and who felt that Hispanic candidates had not been considered for the position. But Paige, as he has done throughout his career, managed to mollify his critics by working with them to address their concerns. By the end of Paige's tenure as superintendent, his opposition had all but evaporated. As Leonel Castillo, the educational liaison for Houston's mayor, put it to Claudia Kolker of the *Los Angeles Times,* "The way he reached out to the Latino community was with school construction and playing fields and numerous other programs."

Among Paige's achievements as superintendent was the creation of a program called Peer Examination, Evaluation, and Redesign (PEER). This program sought the recommendations of business and civic leaders in Houston for the improvement of Houston's schools. Paige sought to run the schools more like a business than a government institution, with administrators being held accountable for the performance of their students, and being required to adhere to strict quality control standards.

Also as superintendent, Paige sought to enforce a Texas state law that required students caught with weapons, or threatening violence, to be expelled from regular public schools and sent to a reform school. Following a model more commonly used in business, Paige also made continued employment of senior staff members contingent on performance, and he initiated incentive pay for teachers who demonstrated outstanding performance. Other steps he took included encouraging the retirement of, or the demotion of, numerous administrators. He hired private firms to handle garbage pickup, food preparation, and to run the school for violence–prone students. He also stopped promoting students who failed tests.

Paige's reform measures paid off; under his leadership, test scores in the predominantly black and Hispanic Houston school district steadily rose. By the time Paige left, it was one of the best school districts in the state, as measured by test schools. Test scores had risen 20 percent, and the dropout rate had been halved. School violence went down 20 percent under Paige. "Seventy–one percent of our students are classified as low income compared with 29 percent across the nation," he was quoted by *Texas Monthly*'s Brian D. Sweany as saying. "Yet our students are performing at the national average on test scores. That's phenomenal."

The school board expressed its approval of its superintendent by unanimously voting to raise his pay 26 percent, to $275,000 a year. This made him one of the best–paid superintendents in the country. It also meant that when he later became Secretary of Education, Paige had to take a reduction in salary; that post was to pay him only $157,000.

Much of Paige's success has been attributed to his ability to get along well with other decision makers, even with those who disagree with him. Texas state senator Rodney Ellis said of Paige on ABCNews. com, "His ability to inspire people and build a consensus comes from being an educator his whole life, an elected official, serving in a tough urban district and from having been a football coach. A lot of being a coach is the ability to get people to work as a team and go in one direction."

President Bush nominated Paige for the position of Secretary of Education at the close of 2000. Bush said at a press conference at the time, reported in *Jet*, "I looked for someone who is a reformer and someone who had a record of results, someone who understands that it is important for us to set the highest of high standards, and not accept ... any excuse for failure. I want an educator who had proven that urban schools can be excellent schools, and Rod Paige is the right person."

Paige and Bush have similar views on education, and when Bush was governor of Texas, he often held up Paige's work as a model that should be followed nationwide. Among the innovations Paige introduced to Texas that Bush would like to see extended to the nation was the introduction of annual standardized tests. Paige and Bush had been acquainted since the 1970s, and Paige helped with the campaign to elect Bush's father, George H.W. Bush, to the presidency.

Also in line with the younger President Bush's policies, Paige has been an advocate for using public tax money, in the form of vouchers, to help pay for parents to send their children to private schools. Paige, in initiating his Texas voucher program, said that he had no problem using public funds to finance private education, as long as the private schools thus supported had no religious ties. "We believe that public funds should go to students, not institutions, and there may be a time when vouchers will be part of the mix," Paige said in a column in *Education Week,* and quoted by Jacques Steinberg in the *New York Times* at the time of his nomination. Paige has also said that vouchers are a way to actually improve public schools—vouchers introduce healthy competition to the public schools and force them to do better. As he said in an interview with the *Detroit Free Press*, "My goal is to strengthen public schools. And you can't strengthen public schools by making them a monopoly and protecting them against the competition."

Paige is not without his detractors. At least one of these, Professor Linda McNeil of Rice University, believes that Houston's rise in test scores was the result of coaching students specifically for the tests, and, worse, pushing students who did not perform well out of the system. "I would certainly hope that Rod Paige does not push as a national agenda the policies which have proven so harmful to children here in Houston," she told Steinberg in the *New York Times.*

Accompanying Paige at his swearing–in ceremony in Washington in January of 2001, were his siblings, his son, his minister from Houston, and members of the Houston school board. Paige made a brief statement, in which he said, according to Patty Reinert of the *Houston Chronicle*, that he would work to bridge the "inexcusable achievement gap that exists among students attending public schools across this country—primarily among minority students and economically disadvantaged students."

Said Phyllis Hunter, the person Paige appointed to head the Houston school district reading program, of Paige to Mike Bowler of the *Baltimore Sun,* "You're going to see an educator on the Cabinet, really for the first time, and you're going to see heavy emphasis on reading. Educators will listen to Rod Paige, black educators especially, whereas they might not have listened to a former Republican governor."

The appointment of one of their own to the post of Education Secretary is an obvious source of pride to the residents of Monticello, Mississippi. As Paige's uncle, A.J. Bridges, put it to Bryant of the *Houston*

Chronicle, "Who would expect any black from Mississippi to become secretary of education? He's a very long way from Monticello. A very long way. If you ever lived in Mississippi, you'd know it was a long way. No doubt."

Sources

Periodicals

Baltimore Sun, January 7, 2001, p. 2B.
Houston Chronicle, January 20, 2001, p. A29; January 25, 2001, p. A3.
Jet, January 22, 2001, p. 8.
Los Angeles Times, December 30, 2000, p. A20.
New York Times, December 30, 2000, p. A10.
Texas Monthly, September 2000.

Online

"Houston's Top Scorer," ABCNews.com, http://abcnews.go.com/sections/politics/DailyNews/profile_paige.html (October 9, 2002).
"Rod Paige," NPR, http://www.npr.org/programs/npc/2001/010904.rpaige.html (October 9, 2002).
"Rod Paige, Q&A: Help All the Children Learn," *Detroit Free Press*, http://www.freep.com/voices/columnists/epaige30_20020830.htm (October 9, 2002).
"Rod Paige, U.S. Secretary of Education—Biography," U.S. Department of Education, http://www.ed.gov/offices/OPA/paigebio.html (October 9, 2002).

—Michael Belfiore

Samuel J. Palmisano

AP/Wide World Photos

President, Chief Executive Officer, and Chairman of IBM

Born c. 1952; married. *Education*—Attended John Hopkins University.

Addresses: *Office*—International Business Machines Corporation, New Orchard Rd., Armonk, NY 10504.

Career

Joined International Business Machines (IBM) Corporation as sales representative, 1973; named IBM senior managing director of operations, Japan; named president of IBM Integrated Systems Solutions Corp. (ISSC); named chief executive officer of ISSC; named senior vice president and group executive for IBM Personal Systems Group; named senior vice president and group executive for IBM Global Services, 1993; named senior vice president and group executive of IBM Enterprise Systems Group; named IBM president and chief operating officer; named IBM president and chief executive officer, 2002; named chairman of IBM, 2002.

Sidelights

Samuel J. Palmisano's nearly 30–year tenure at International Business Machines (IBM) Corporation culminated in his being named the company's chief executive officer (CEO) in 2002. His promotion was based upon his successes in previous positions at IBM, including senior vice president and group executive for IBM Global Services, where he oversaw a 30 percent rise in the business unit's revenues, which translated to a $32.2 billion increase. Palmisano replaced Louis V. Gerstner, Jr., who praised his successor in an IBM press release announcing Palmisano's promotion: "Over the last decade, Sam Palmisano has taken on a number of IBM's most significant challenges, from building the services business to transforming our server line. In each instance, Sam has done far more than manage operations effectively. He has made it both his personal mission and that of IBM to become the number–one competitor in each of these markets. Sam's unique mix of strategic vision, passion, and discipline, combined with his intimate understanding of IBM, make him the right person to become IBM's next CEO."

Palmisano is the son of an auto–repair shop owner from Baltimore, Maryland. He attended Calvert Hall College High School, a private Catholic boys school. While still in high school, he worked as a studio musician, earning up to $1,000 a week playing trumpet for such musical groups as the Temptations. An accomplished high school and college football player, he turned down an opportunity to try out for the Oakland Raiders. After graduating from John Hopkins University, Palmisano joined IBM in 1973 as a sales representative in the company's Baltimore offices. He moved from the sales organization to IBM Japan, followed by two tenures in the company's service organization, as well as heading up the company's personal computer and mainframe businesses. He also served as executive assistant to former CEO John Akers. He developed a reputation for implementing innovative ideas and challenging higher management. He reportedly harbors a deep hatred of corporate meetings and corporate red tape. Palmisano also managed to befriend the family of Presidents George H.W. and George W. Bush. Because Palmisano's in–laws vacationed for years near the Bushes in Kennebunkport, Maine, he became a frequent golf companion of the Bushes, and eventually purchased the senior Bush's Kennebunkport retreat.

Palmisano was instrumental in developing IBM's Integrated Systems Solutions Corp. (ISSC) Global Services into a major profit center for the company. An IBM business division that he was named to helm in 1993, Global Services was a consistent money loser until Palmisano instructed his management team to implement changes that would cause the division to first break even and eventually become a major source of corporate income. He challenged IBM's rigid corporate structure to make ISSC an independent company. *Fortune* writer Suzanne Koudsi reported, "To help drive sales, Palmisano gave stirring talks and was ready at a moment's notice to help seal a deal." Koudsi continued: "Palmisano instructed his lieutenants to turn the new unit around…. Gordon Myers, his right–hand man, dug into the project for a few months but reported back with bad news: There was no way it was going to happen. The group, which had lost tens of millions the year before, would break even. But make much more than that? Not likely." Palmisano, however, refused to accept Myers's forecast. According to Koudsi, he told Myers: "Gordon, we set an objective to be profitable this year, and you have to figure out how to get there. I'm not willing to accept that you can't." Myers beat the bushes for revenue streams and cost–cutting measures, and achieved profitability status by year's end. According to Koudsi: "It was classic Palmisano leadership: a mix of unflinching discipline and relentless optimism, bluntness with a smile. That combination of traits gained him loyal support from subordinates and helped him continue his corporate climb."

Not only did Palmisano envision ISSC as a profit center, he insisted on immediate profitability by refusing to sign any deals short of multi–million dollar contracts. This method eventually made ISSC the chief competitor of Electronic Data Systems, the former Ross Perot–owned company that also provided one–stop shopping for companies requiring both technology, customer support, and computer consulting. Palmisano's ability to produce results landed him a promotion to leadership of IBM's personal computer division. When his ISSC successor Dennie Welsh became seriously ill a few years later,

Palmisano was brought back to replace him. In 1999, he was promoted to senior vice president of IBM's server division. He changed the corporate culture to become more customer–focused and instituted streamlined manufacturing programs. He reduced the number of servers that IBM offered in order to minimize customer confusion, and oversaw the re-engineering of the company's Unix–servers. He then became president and, later, chief operating officer. Global Services eventually became the fastest-growing division of IBM, employing more individuals than any other IBM division. "He's a triple threat," consultant Sam Albert of Sam Albert Associates in Scarsdale, New York, told Koudis. "He's good for the customer, he's good for IBM, and he's good for the employees."

Palmisano was a leader in IBM's three–year project to develop and launch IBM's eServer product line. The eServer incorporated open standards and boasted mainframe–like reliability across all computer platforms. When he headed IBM's server and enterprise storage businesses, Palmisano was instrumental in IBM's initiative to adopt the open-source software Linux throughout IBM's server line. Eventually, all of IBM's hardware and software products supported Linux, a marked change from the variety of operating systems the company offered in the past. The effort began with a $1 billion investment by IBM in 2001, a move that prompted Palmisano to tell a LinuxWorld audience, as quoted at ZDNet News by Michael Kanellos, "We don't invest a billion dollars casually. Lou (Gerstner) and I don't write these checks without some scrutiny."

IBM, nicknamed Big Blue, officially began in 1911 as the Computing–Tabulating–Recording Company, an amalgamation of several companies that opened their doors in the 1880s. The company grew into one of the world's largest companies by developing computer mainframes, calculators, personal computers, networking, software, as well as several scientific breakthroughs. Four IBM research scientists have won Nobel prizes. The company also has become one of the corporate world's largest employers with more than 300,000 individuals on the payroll. By the 1990s, however, IBM was hemorrhaging money through lost market share in the lucrative personal computer market, as well as becoming a large, sprawling organization that seemingly had lost its focus. IBM reported losses in 1992 of $5 billion. Palmisano's predecessor, Gerstner, is credited with putting the company back on track. According to *ZDNet News*'s Kanellos, "[I]nstead of being a company that participates in nearly every market, IBM picks its battles."

As IBM chief executive officer, Gerstner has been credited with directing the company's focus on customer service and technology, an effort that increased the company's share price more than 800 percent and its market value by $180 billion. Gerstner also oversaw IBM as it gained market share in such products as computer servers, software, storage, and microelectronics. In addition, IBM received more United States patents than any other company for nine consecutive years under Gerstner's leadership. "I feel very fortunate to succeed Lou Gerstner as CEO," Palmisano said in an IBM press release. "Against all odds, he led IBM back from its darkest days. He transformed the company's culture and reignited growth. IBM's unflagging focus on both the customer and technology innovation is a direct result of Lou's leadership over the last nine years. He will leave a significant legacy." Among the changes instituted in IBM culture during Gerstner's tenure was a more down–to–earth approach. In the past, rumors abounded that IBM CEOs were treated like royalty, and that entire facilities would be repainted in anticipation of a CEO's visit. While continuing to compete in the hotly contested personal computer market of the 1990s, Gerstner also directed the efforts of IBM on computer consulting and services. The company also invested a tremendous effort toward research and development, eventually becoming a supplier of microchips, hard drives, and other technological advancements to such computer manufacturers as Apple Computer, Dell, and Compaq. By the end of 2001, IBM reported $88.4 billion in revenue and $7.7 billion in earnings, and earned a spot in the top ten of the *Fortune* 500.

Palmisano was named president of IBM in 2000, and its eighth CEO and successor to Gerstner on March 1, 2002. Palmisano's selection to succeed Gerstner was viewed by business analysts as a positive move due to Palmisano's more personable style and willingness to give interviews. "Palmisano ... is going to be in many ways the exact opposite [of Gerstner]," analyst Tom Bittman told *ZDNet News*'s Kanellos. "We see Palmisano being put much more in the limelight as a public personality for IBM. I think it's going to help IBM to be identified more with someone like Palmisano." Despite such apparent differences, *Fortune* journalist David Kirkpatrick also noted similarities: "Gerstner, 59, is gruff and often distant; Palmisao, 50, is personable—until crossed, when he lets you have it. But Palmisano was Gerstner's kind of guy even before Gerstner got to IBM. He thought nothing of flying off at a moment's notice to meet a customer halfway across the country. He held his reports to exacting financial targets. After a year of watching that kind of performance, Gerstner homed in on Palmisano, and the two would occasionally share cognac and cigars at the end of a long day." Kirkpatrick also recognized that "Palmisano may be the ultimate insider. He's had more diverse IBM experience than any CEO before him...." On October 29, 2002, Palmisano was named chairman of IBM, succeeding Gerstner who planned on retiring from the board at the end of 2002.

Predictions for Palmisano's success as IBM CEO vary. *Fortune*'s Kirkpatrick wrote, "Winning new sales, executing Gerstner's strategy, and developing modest new markets will be enough for Palmisano to succeed only if everything goes right. As we know from the past couple of years, things always go wrong in the technology business. To shield IBM from that kind of headache, Palmisano will have to deliver something big, something we can't yet envision. He can't be just a caretaker of Lou's legacy. He has to surprise us as much as Lou did." *Fortune*'s Koudsi offered her assessment, "No one is saying that IBM is in dire trouble. Palmisano is inheriting a company that, thanks largely to Global Services, is seemingly dominant. Yet outsiders are grumbling that while Palmisano is an admired leader, he hasn't proven to be a visionary, a trait he'll need to keep Global Services—and IBM—growing." Most business analysts acknowledge that Palmisano has a hard job ahead of him. IBM growth stalled during the last two years of Gerstner's tenure due to declining sales. In addition, IBM's personal computers continued to be priced higher than competitive models—factors that may force Palmisano to initiate layoffs or massive outsourcing. In addition, the company's cost of business has risen from 22.5 percent of revenues in 2000 to 23.9 percent in 2001, which may result in additional cost–cutting initiatives.

Sources

Periodicals

BusinessWeek, February 11, 2002, pp. 66–72.
Economist, February 2, 2002.
Fortune, August 13, 2001, p. 144; February 18, 2002, p. 60.
U.S. News & World Report, July 22, 2002, p. 33.

Online

"IBM names Palmisano as new CEO," *ZDNet News,* http://zdnet.com/2100–1104–825222.html, (September 28, 2002).
"IBM's Palmisano: Get into the grid," *CNet News.com,* http://www.news.com/2100–1001–841256.html (September 28, 2002).
"Samuel J. Palmisano Elected IBM CEO," IBM.com, http://www–916.ibm.com/press/prnews.nsf/jan/42CE5EC91D7983B985256B500058A102 (October 28, 2002).

—*Bruce Walker*

Suzan-Lori Parks

Playwright

Born in 1964, in Fort Knox, KY; daughter of Donald (a college professor) and Francis (a college administrator) Parks; married Paul Oscher (a blues musician), 2001. *Education:* Mount Holyoke College, B.A. (English and German), 1985.

Addresses: *Agent*—c/o Author Mail, Theatre Communications Group, 355 Lexington Ave., New York, NY 10017.

Career

Studied creative writing with author James Baldwin at Holyoke College, Massachusetts, 1985; produced plays include *Mutabilities in the Third Kingdom,* 1989; *The American Play,* 1994; *Venus,* 1996; *In the Blood,* 1999; and *Topdog/Underdog,* 2001. Parks has also written screenplays and teleplays, including the Spike Lee–directed film *Girl 6,* 1996, and a novel, *Getting My Mother's Body,* 2003.

Awards: Mary E. Woolley fellowship, 1989; Naomi Kitay fellowship, 1989; grant, Rockefeller Foundation, 1990; grant, New York Foundation for the Arts, 1990; OBIE Award, *Village Voice,* for *Imperceptible Mutabilities in the Third Kingdom,* 1990; National Endowment for the Arts Playwrighting Fellowship, 1990 and 1991; Whiting Foundation Writers Award, 1992; Ford Foundation, grant, 1995; Lila–Wallace Reader's Digest Award, 1995; CalArts/Alpert Award in Drama, 1996; OBIE Award, *Village Voice,* for *Venus,* 1996; PEN–Laura Pels Award for Excellence in Playwrighting, 2000; Guggenheim Fellowship, 2000; John T. and Catherine D. MacArthur Foundation Fellowship, 2001; John Gassner Playwright Award, 2002; Pulitzer Prize for drama, 2002.

Sidelights

Suzan–Lori Parks won the Pulitzer Prize for drama in 2002, becoming the first black female playwright to be awarded the prestigious prize. After winning the prize, she told Angeli R. Rasbury on the Women's eNews Web site, "As the first African–American woman to win the Pulitzer Prize [for theater], I have to say I wish I was the 101st."

Plays by Parks include *Imperceptible Mutabilities in the Third Kingdom* and *Topdog/Underdog.* The latter play opened at the Off–Broadway theater Joseph Papp Public Theater and later moved to a Broadway house. It was for this play that Parks won the Pulitzer. It is also the first play with more than one actor by a black woman to run on Broadway since *for colored girls who have considered suicide/when the rainbow is enuf* by Ntozake Shange opened in 1976.

Born in Fort Knox, Kentucky, Parks traveled a lot as a child; her father was a military officer and was stationed at different posts around the United States. She said of her childhood on the website of the publisher Bedford St. Martin's, "I've heard horrible stories about 12–step groups for army people. But I had a great childhood. My parents were really into experiencing the places we lived." She began writing at an early age, in the fourth grade writing a newspaper with her sister and brother called the *Daily Daily*, which they typed up in the attic of their house.

After living in a total of six states, Parks's family moved to Germany when Parks was in high school. She later described this as an important event in shaping her voice as a playwright. Since her parents enrolled her in the local German school system, rather than the school set up for the children of American military personnel, Parks had to learn German. This gave her a valuable perspective on her native language, English, that was to inform the dialogue she would later write for her plays.

Parks attended college at Mount Holyoke College in Massachusetts, where she majored in both English and German. There, while a sophomore, Parks took a creative writing class taught by one of the United States's most highly regarded African–American authors, James Baldwin. Baldwin, after hearing Parks read her work, encouraged her to pursue writing plays as a profession. It was the first time that anyone had suggested that to her, and it was a major turning point in Parks's life. As she later described the event to *People*, it was "like a kiss on the forehead to ward off all evil." She later told the *Christian Science Monitor*'s Iris Fanger, speaking of Baldwin, "He believed in me before I believed in me."

Parks wrote her first play before she left college. Called *The Sinner's Place*, it "was probably done in a basement room," Parks later told Rasbury of Women's eNews. Parks graduated from college in 1985 with Phi Beta Kappa and cum laude honors. She briefly moved to London, England, where she studied acting, and then relocated to the United States's theater capital, New York City. There, while working a day job as a legal assistant, she devoted most of her energies to writing plays.

The next work that Parks had produced was a play called *Betting on the Dust Commander*. Produced in 1987 in a Brooklyn bar, the show had no budget, and even required Parks herself to purchase chairs for the minimalist set. Her second produced play, called *Imperceptible Mutabilities in the Third Kingdom*, had a higher profile, and earned Parks recognition from the *New York Times* as the most promising playwright of the year. The play also earned Parks an OBIE award in 1990 for best Off–Broadway play. This play takes place in 1865 on the day that slaves in America were declared free, and it calls for black actors to perform the roles with their faces painted white.

In 1996, Parks again won an OBIE award, this time for her play *Venus*. *Venus* gives a fictional account of the true story of Saartji Baartman, a South African Khoi–San woman who was brought to Britain in 1810 and exhibited as a sideshow attraction as the "Venus Hottentot." *Venus* follows Baartman through her escape to Paris, France, where a doctor falls in love with her, and then makes plans to dissect her after her death. The play was produced at the New York Shakespeare Festival under the direction of Richard Foreman, one of New York's best–known avant–garde theater directors, and it was warmly received in the press.

Parks's work deals with, among other subjects, race relations in the United States, tapping historical figures and movements for added depth. Parks also considers the musicality of language, attempting to capture the English language as it is spoken on the street, giving it a stylistic spin to create a kind of spoken poetry.

She told Fanger in the *Christian Science Monitor*, "I've been writing plays for 20 years, and I've been experimental in lots of different ways. My plays aren't stylistically the same. Just being an African–American woman playwright on Broadway is experimental. As far as I know, there [are] four of us: Lorraine Hansberry, Ntozake Shange, Anna Deavere Smith, and now me." Speaking of her play *Topdog/Underdog*, she added, "It's also experimental as a woman to write a play that just involves two men and to write it so well that people think a man wrote it."

Speaking of her work in *American Theatre*, critic Shawn–Marie Garrett said "Parks has dramatized some of the most painful aspects of the black experience: Middle Passage, slavery, urban poverty, institutionalized discrimination, racist ethnographies. Yet even as her plays summon up the brutality of the past, they do so in a manner that is, paradoxically, both horrific and comic—irresistibly or disrespectfully so, depending on your point of view."

Although her work often addresses the strained relations between black and white Americans, Parks has said that that is not the primary focus of her work. Speaking on the subject, Parks told Rasbury on the Women's eNews Web site, "The real jungle is the jungle within, just empowering [our]selves. It's not just about racism in the world. It's not the only battle that African–American people have to fight." Once African–Americans realize this, said Parks, "then we can go out into the world and fight ... a better battle. But if we are just concentrating on what the white man is doing, that's pulling focus. We [have] got to focus on our own stuff in addition to him, but we really have to focus on our own stuff. That's the way to move forward most effectively."

Describing her writing process in an article she published in the journal *Theater*, Parks said, "I don't have readings of my plays before I have a good idea of what the play is. Sometimes artistic directors will plan a reading when they hear the writer has completed a first draft." She continued, "There are writers who enjoy thrashing out their plays in the workshop process. I do most of my writing at home, on my own. This has made me slightly unpopular on the workshop circuit."

In July of 2001, Parks married Paul Oscher, a blues musician. They had met in 1998, when they were introduced by a mutual friend. "It was love at first sight," Parks told *People*. Also in 2001, Parks won a MacArthur Foundation "genius grant" of $500,000. On winning the award, Parks told Mel Gussow of the *New York Times*, "It was a vote of confidence for what I've been doing. My husband, Paul, gets to call me Queen, Your Majesty, at least for a day. But I've got to get to work again." She said that she would use the grant to write more plays; the money would allow her to turn down more lucrative film and television work that nevertheless was less satisfying to her. She also said that she would work on a novel.

Parks opened her first Broadway play, *Topdog/Underdog*, on April 7, 2002. The play, which features two characters, brothers played by Jeffrey Wright, and rap star Mos Def, had finished a run the year before Off–Broadway, with Wright and Don Cheadle in the cast. The show opened to rave reviews in its Broadway production at the Ambassador Theatre. The *Christian Science Monitor*'s Iris Fanger called the play "a cross between a hip–hop riff and a Greek tragedy; as entertaining as the former and as gripping as the latter." Ben Brantley of the *New York Times* hailed it as a "dizzying spin" on the Cain and Abel story. In the play, said Brantley, "Brotherly love and hatred is translated into the terms of men who have known betrayal since their youth … and who will never be able entirely to trust anyone, including (and especially) each other."

Topdog/Underdog features two brothers named Lincoln and Booth. Lincoln is a former street scam artist who works in an arcade shooting booth dressed as Abraham Lincoln, allowing spectators to take turns shooting at him with cap pistols. His brother Booth makes his living as a shoplifter, and he ridi-

cules his brother's efforts to go straight, trying to entice him back to a life of petty crime. The play takes place in the run–down tenement they share, where their drinking and quarrelling leads to a violent end.

This play, Parks told Elizabeth Farnsworth on the PBS news program *NewsHour with Jim Lehrer*, was one of the easiest of her then–15 plays to date to write. "I've written plays that have taken six, seven, eight years, you know, eight, nine, ten, 12 drafts. And this one … took three days."

The day after the play opened on Broadway, Parks got word that she had won the Pulitzer Prize for drama. "I'm happy!" she told *Entertainment Weekly*'s Daniel Fierman and Gregory Kirschling soon afterward. "My head is going to swell so big I won't be able to get out of a cab! But can't let that happen. I gotta *write* tomorrow."

Parks told *People* that she gets the most satisfaction as a playwright from watching people attend her shows, especially people who normally don't spend a lot of time in the theater. Speaking of the Broadway production of *Topdog/Underdog*, she told *People*, "I love seeing the old hard–core theatergoers and the kids who have their baseball hats backward. We've got all kinds of people sitting there loving the play, and that's the most exciting thing."

Projects on Parks's desk following *Topdog/Underdog* included screenplays for a film production company founded by television talk show host Oprah Winfrey, a Disney musical based on the Harlem Globetrotters basketball team, and her debut novel, *Getting Mother's Body*. Asked to talk about her works in progress by the *Village Voice*'s James Hannaham, Parks responded, "I'm one of those writers who develops the piece long before developing the vocabulary with which to discuss it. My plays are much larger and more intelligent that I am. If I can reach out my hand like this, that's the limit of my physical grasp. The knowledge that is inside my plays can reach miles, hundreds of thousands of miles."

Selected writings

The Sinner's Place (play), c. 1985.
Betting on the Dust Commander (play), 1987.
Imperceptible Mutabilities in the Third Kingdom (play), Sun & Moon Press (Los Angeles), 1995.
The America Play: And Other Works, Theatre Communications Group (New York City), 1995.
Venus (play), Theatre Communications Group, 1997.

In the Blood (play), Dramatist's Play Service (New York City), 2000.

Red Letter Plays, Theatre Communications Group, 2000.

Topdog/Underdog (play), Theatre Communications Group, 2002.

Getting My Mother's Body (novel), Random House (New York City), 2003.

Sources

Periodicals

American Theatre, October 2000, p. 22.
Bomb, Spring 1994.
Christian Science Monitor, April 12, 2002.
Entertainment Weekly, April 19, 2002, p. 68.
New York Times, October 24, 2001, section A, p. 14; April 8, 2002.
People, June 3, 2002, pp. 143–44.
Theater, volume 29, issue 2, 1999, pp. 26–33.
Village Voice, November 3–9, 1999.

Online

"Historic Pulitzer Drama Victory," BBC.com, http://news.bbc.co.uk/1/hi/entertainment/arts/1918297.stm (October 9, 2002).

"Nominated Artists: Suzan–Lori Parks," Tony Awards, http://www.tonys.org/nominees/profiles/susanloriparks.html (October 9, 2002).

"Obies Search Results," VillageVoice.com, http://www.villagevoice.com/cgi–bin/obies/winner.cgi?selection=person&winner=Parks (October 9, 2002).

"Pulitzer Winner for Drama," Online NewsHour, http://www.pbs.org/newshour/conversation/jan–june02/parks_4–11.html (October 9, 2002).

"Pulitzer Winner Parks Talks About Being a First," Women's eNews, http://www.womensenews.org/article.cfm/dyn/aid/874 (October 9, 2002).

"Suzan–Lori Parks," Bedford St. Martin's, http://bedfordstmartins.com/litlinks/drama/parks.htm (October 9, 2002).

"Suzan–Lori Parks," *Contemporary Authors Online*, Gale Literature Resource Center 3.1 (October 10, 2002).

"Suzan–Lori Parks," MacArthur Foundation, http://www.macfound.org/programs/fel/2001fellows/parks.htm (October 9, 2002).

"Suzan–Lori Parks," Women of Color, Women of Words, http://www.scils.rutgers.edu/~cybers/parks2.html (October 9, 2002).

—*Michael Belfiore*

Amy Pascal

Mark Mainz/Getty Images

Movie studio executive

Born in 1958 in the United States; married to Bernard Weinraub (a writer for the *New York Times*); children: Anthony. *Education:* University of California–Los Angeles, B.A. (international relations/political science).

Addresses: *Office*—Columbia Pictures, 10202 Washington Blvd., Culver City, CA, 90232–3119, website: http://www.sonypictures.com.

Career

Assistant, Kestral production company; vice–president of production, 20th Century Fox, 1985–88; executive vice–president of production, Columbia Pictures, 1988–94; president of production, Turner Pictures Worldwide, 1994–96; studio president, Columbia Pictures, 1996–99; chairman, Columbia Pictures, 1999—; vice–chairman of Sony Pictures Entertainment, 2002—.

Awards: Showman of the Year, *Variety*, 2002; #26 of Most Powerful Women in Business, *Fortune*, 2002.

Sidelights

As chairman of Columbia Pictures and vice-chairman of Sony Pictures Entertainment, Amy Pascal has taken the once publicly ridiculed and failing film company and turned it into a success with such hits as *A League of Their Own*, *Charlie's Angels*, *Stuart Little*, and *Spiderman*. The box office receipts for Sony Pictures exceeded $1.25 billion in 2002, breaking every industry record and sealing Pascal's reputation in the film industry as a stellar businesswoman and groundbreaking leader.

Born in 1958, Amy Pascal grew up in Los Angeles, California. Although she told *Premiere*, "I knew I wanted to be in the movie business," Pascal majored in international relations/political science at the University of California–Los Angeles. She further told *Premiere* that she feared that her parents, a bookstore owner and economist, would disapprove and she would be "locked out of the house" if she pursued her dream of working in films.

After graduating, Pascal worked at Kestral, an independent production company run by producer Tony Garnett. Together they developed *Follow that Bird*, a film about the lovable character Big Bird from *Sesame Street*. In 1985, Pascal began working for 20th Century–Fox as vice–president of production where she helped developed the beloved John Cusack teen angst classic, *Say Anything*.

In 1988, Pascal jumped to Columbia Pictures and over the next six years moved up the ladder to executive vice president of production. At Columbia, Pascal earned praise for being an "incredibly creative and fierce champion of what she cares about," producer Lucy Fisher told *Daily Variety*. Successful films she championed included *Awakenings, Single White Female, Little Women,* and *A League of Their Own*. With such female–friendly audience films, Pascal soon earned the reputation for green–lighting, or supporting, chick flicks. However, she told *Variety*, "I'm so tired of that ... reputation. I mean, give me a break."

In 1994, Pascal switched studios again and became Turner Pictures Worldwide's president of production. For the next two years, she approved the production of both *Michael*, which helped John Travolta continue his career comeback, and *City of Angels*, which brought together two popular actors: Meg Ryan and Nicolas Cage.

In 1996, after Turner Pictures Worldwide merged with Warner Brothers, Pascal returned to Columbia Pictures as studio president. Over the next six years, Pascal and her boss, John Calley (Sony Pictures Entertainment president and chief executive officer), rebuilt Columbia Pictures. To do this, Pascal and Calley began "hitting moneymaking singles and doubles instead of swinging for the fences," noted *Entertainment Weekly*. This strategy, *Entertainment Weekly* further noted, "turned Columbia into one of Hollywood's smoothest–operating studios."

The keys to this successful strategy included choosing smaller–budgeted films, hiring little–known or about–to–become stars, spinning off TV shows, and sequels. "Well, it's an educated gamble," Pascal told *Entertainment Weekly*. "But sometimes you can think you know everything and be wrong." Some films Pascal was right about included the Adam Sandler comedy *Mr. Deeds*, the Drew Barrymore/Cameron Diaz/Lucy Liu action/comedy *Charlie's Angels*, and the high–flying special–effects action film *Spiderman*.

Pascal has also been wrong. Some of her clunkers included *8MM, Go,* and *All the Pretty Horses*. Yet, she has discovered that even though some films do not draw huge audiences, they are still worth making. "*8MM* was a really good script, Joel Schumacher is a great director ... and Nic Cage is a big–name star," she told *Entertainment Weekly*. Pascal also ignored critical reviews when she chose to green light the sequel to the not–so–kindly received *Godzilla*. "If a movie makes $400 million, you make

a sequel. It's that simple," she told *Entertainment Weekly*. This strategy worked with *Men in Black II*, which grossed $54 million over the July 4, 2002, holiday weekend. The huge success of movies such as *Spiderman, Men in Black II,* and *Panic Room* made 2002 a record–breaking year for Sony Pictures. Box office receipts totaling more than $1.25 billion broke the industry record for annual box office gross. *Spiderman* also broke an industry record, breaking the overall single–day record when it grossed $43.6 million in one day.

Her colleagues praise her down–to–earth demeanor, disarming friendliness, and hands–on work ethic. "First and foremost, she's not driven by overwhelming ego," says Howard Stringer, chairman–CEO of Sony Corp. of America, told *Variety*. "She's a team enthusiast. She likes bringing the best out of people. What I particularly like about her is that she's unthreatened by other people's ideas and suggestions." The magazine named Pascal its "Showman of the Year" in 2002.

In 2002, Pascal realized that the film industry has changed because more women have risen to the top of film studios. "The next sight that is left is ownership," she told *Daily Variety*. "There is no female Rupert Murdoch, no Ted Turner, no female power brokers on that level that control industries." She moved one step closer to this goal in late 2002, when she was named vice–chairman of Sony Pictures Entertainment, in addition to remaining chairman of Columbia Pictures. "I wake up every day," she commented to the *Los Angeles Times*, "even on the worst days, and I love this job."

Sources

Daily Variety, June 8, 2001.
Entertainment Weekly, June 18, 1999.
Hollywood Reporter, September 4, 2002.
Knight Ridder/Tribune News Service, October 28, 2002.
Los Angeles Times, October 27, 2000.
Premiere, May 1990.
PR Newswire, January 14, 2003.
Time, July 29, 2002.
USA Today, July 8, 2002.
Variety, December 20, 1999; August 19, 2002.

—Ann Schwalboski

Ann Patchett

Author

Born December 2, 1963, in Los Angeles, CA; daughter of Frank (a police captain) and Jeanne Ray (a nurse and author; maiden name, Wilkinson) Patchett; married and divorced. *Education:* Sarah Lawrence College, B.A., 1984; University of Iowa, M.F.A., 1987.

Addresses: *Agent*—Lisa Bankoff, International Creative Management, 40 West 57th St., New York, NY 10019. *Home*—Nashville, TN. *Website*—http://www. annpatchett.com.

Career

Began career in publishing as editorial assistant at Ecco Press, 1984; first short story published in the *Paris Review*, 1984; writer–in–residence, Allegheny College, Meadville, PA, 1989–90; visiting assistant professor, Murray State University, Murray, KY, 1992; debut novel, *The Patron Saint of Liars*, published by Houghton, 1992; Tennessee Williams fellow in Creative Writing, University of the South, Nashville, TN, 1997.

Awards: Award for Fiction, Trans–Atlantic Henfield Foundation, 1984; Editor's Choice Award for Fiction, *Iowa Journal of Literary Studies*, for "For Rita, Who Is Never Alice," 1986; Editor's Choice Award for Fiction, Columbia, for "The Magician's Assistant's Dream," 1987; residential fellow of Yaddo, 1989; Millay Colony for the Arts, 1989; James A. Michener/Copernicus Award, University of Iowa, for work on *Patron Saint of Liars*, 1989; residential fellow, Fine Arts Work Center, Provincetown,

RI, 1990–91; Janet Heidinger Kafka Prize for best work of fiction, for *Taft*, 1994; Tennessee Writers Award of the Year, Nashville Banner, for *The Magician's Assistant*, 1994; Guggenheim fellowship, for *The Magician's Assistant*, 1994; P.E.N./Faulkner Award, for *Bel Canto*, 2002; Orange Prize for Fiction, for *Bel Canto*, 2002.

Sidelights

American writer Ann Patchett won luminous praise for *Bel Canto*, her fourth novel. Within a year of its 2001 publication, *Bel Canto* had taken several prestigious honors, including the P.E.N./Faulkner Award and its $15,000 prize purse—the largest juried literary award in the United States—as well as the Orange Prize for Fiction in Britain. The story of a months–long hostage crisis in an unnamed South American country, Patchett's novel explores the complex connections between art, love, language, and the common bond that all humans, no matter their origins, ultimately share. "Patchett's psychological observations are usually intriguing and most often convincing," declared *Washington Post* writer Joseph McLellan in a review of one of her books. "Her style is fluent and highly readable."

Patchett was born in Los Angeles in 1963. Her parents divorced when she was six, which prompted her mother to relocate, with Patchett and her sister, to Nashville, Tennessee. The future writer was an admittedly poor student at the private Roman Catholic schools she attended, and recalled a two–year period in which she was forbidden to play outside at recess with her classmates because of a string of academic and disciplinary infractions. Patchett noted that her home life was part of the reason for her seeming indifference in the classroom. "We had peculiar circumstances," she said of her family in a *Publishers Weekly* interview with Elizabeth Bernstein. "She was a very loving mother, but we were scrambling; we had bigger things going on in our lives than whether or not I could read."

To compensate for her shortcomings in school, Patchett developed a penchant for storytelling, which impressed her teachers. By her teens, she was determined to become a poet, and was sending submissions to national magazines. She attended New York's Sarah Lawrence College, but midway through began to experience a case of writer's block; to remedy it, she enrolled in a fiction class taught by novelist Allan Gurganus (*Oldest Living Confederate Widow Tells All*), and began writing short stories. Not long after she graduated in 1984, the first story she had written was published in the prestigious *Paris Review.* "All Little Colored Children Should Learn to Play Harmonica," about a large African–American family in the 1940s, garnered Patchett a small measure of notice inside literary circles and went on to be included in several subsequent anthologies.

After a stint as an editorial assistant, Patchett enrolled in the graduate writing program at the University of Iowa, a noted professional training ground for upcoming writers. She finished her M.F.A. in 1987, but later said she learned little from her time at Iowa. Retreating to writers's colonies at Yaddo and Millay, she toyed with the idea of expanding the story of the Smileys, the family in her first short story, but was unable to develop a plot outline she liked. Married for a time, she taught at Allegheny College in Pennsylvania, but a sudden end to the union caused her to abandon the job and return to her mother's house in Nashville. She worked as a waitress at a T.G.I. Friday's restaurant, and wrote in her spare time.

Patchett eventually finished her first novel, 1992's *The Patron Saint of Liars,* which won an award even before it was published, the 1989 James A. Michener/Copernicus Award from the University of Iowa for a work in progress. This work is set in the 1960s and follows the story of Rose, a young married Californian who flees her marriage, though pregnant. She drives across the Plains and finds refuge at an abandoned hotel in Kentucky that has been refashioned by Roman Catholic nuns into a home for unwed mothers. Alice McDermott, writing in the *New York Times Book Review,* liked the way Patchett created a microcosm inside the "enchanted place" of that shelter. Patchett's "world of St. Elizabeth's, and of the novel itself … retains some sense of the miraculous, of a genuine, if unanticipated, power to heal," McDermott asserted.

Two years later Patchett's second novel, *Taft,* appeared in print. Its plot centers around a blues bar in Memphis on the city's famed Beale Street. The narrator is a 40ish bartender at Muddy's, John Nickel, whose girlfriend and young son have recently abandoned him. Once a blues drummer, Nickel is bereft, and when a teenage girl named Fay wanders into the bar one day, he befriends her and hires her. Nickel feels sorry for Fay and her brother, whose father has just died, and his sympathy causes Fay to develop a crush on him, despite the age difference and the still somewhat taboo nature of an interracial romance in the modern American South. Still, Fay and her brother—a drug abuser—help Nickel come to terms with the reasons his own son has left. Kathleen Hughes, reviewing *Taft* for in *Booklist,* called it a "compassionate and deeply moving" story that "deals swiftly and intelligently with the mystery of human behavior."

Patchett's own father had remained in California since his divorce and worked as a detective with the Los Angeles Police Department. Visiting him, Patchett attended a dinner show at a magic emporium, and was chosen from the audience to assist one of the performers. The experience gave her the idea for her third novel, *The Magician's Assistant,* and she won a Guggenheim Fellowship to complete it. The story follows several years in the life of Sabine, a beautiful and intelligent woman who confounded her family by eschewing architectural school in order to become a stage assistant to a gay magician named Parsifal, whom she eventually marries. Sabine's tale is told in flashback after Parsifal has died, and she becomes a caretaker to Phan, her late husband's lover, who is dying of AIDS. After Phan's death, she learns that Parsifal was not an orphan from an eccentric Eastern seaboard family, but rather the product of a rather prosaic Midwestern upbringing. She meets his mother and sisters when they come to Los Angeles to visit the grave, and she accepts an invitation to visit them during one Nebraska winter, during which she uncovers secrets about the husband who abandoned his identity. The deceptions of the magician were only a small part of Parsifal's persona, and Sabine reflects that the ultimate job of the assistant is "to misdirect the attention of the audience."

Published in 1997, *The Magician's Assistant* earned mostly positive reviews for Patchett, though *New York Times Book Review* writer Suzanne Berne felt that Sabine, as a character, remained "an enigma, a woman entranced by her own enchantment. Which explains why she never generates enough sympathy to make her predicament truly absorbing." Yet Berne also noted that the book was a "beguiling" novel, "and Patchett is an adroit, graceful writer who knows enough tricks to keep her story entertaining." Reviewing it for the *San Francisco Chronicle,* Alix Madrigal liked several things about the novel, including Patchett's "controlled, evocative prose" as well as "the uncanny way she makes the most surprising twists seem absolutely inevitable; not to mention the wisdom and tenderness with which she portrays the illusions that keep lovers and families together and those that rend them apart."

By then Patchett was working on conjuring the scenarios for her next novel, *Bel Canto.* As she once joked in a *New York Times Magazine* "Writers on Writing" article, "My life is a series of ranked priorities. At the top of the list is the thing I do not wish to do the very most, and beneath that is everything else." She explained further: "For a long time before I start to write a novel, anywhere from one year to two, I make it up.... The novel in my imagination travels with me like a small lavender moth making loopy circles around my head." The act of actually sitting down to write, however, was the difficult part, and she equated it to "grabbing my little friend (crushing its wings slightly in my thick hand), holding it down on a cork board and running it though with a pin."

In the case of her fourth book, *Bel Canto,* that process took four years. Published in 2001, it took several literary–world honors. The title means "beautiful singing" in Italian, and Patchett borrowed heavily from a real–life news event for its plot: in late 1996, members of a leftist guerrilla group in Peru stormed the Japanese Embassy in Lima, Peru's capital, and held several party–goers hostage for four months. Patchett's novel begins at a soiree held at the official home of the vice president of an unnamed South American country with a sizable elite minority of Japanese heritage, like Peru. A rebel group storms the party, hoping to capture the country's president—a man with a Japanese name, like Alberto Fujimori, president of Peru at the time of the real crisis—but Patchett's fictional President Masuda decides at the last minute to stay home in order to catch the latest episode of his favorite telenovela, or nighttime soap opera.

Bel Canto's party has been thrown to honor a visiting Japanese tycoon, Katsumi Hosokawa—the head of an electronics company—who travels with his skilled translator, Gen Watanabe. The government hopes to convince Hosokawa to build a factory in their country, and officials lure him by promising that the world–famous soprano, Roxane Coss, will deliver a private performance at the vice president's gala. Hosokawa is an ardent fan of hers, and attends only to be able to meet Coss in person. As the singer finishes her final aria, armed men emerge from heating and cooling vents and take everybody hostage. The rest of *Bel Canto* chronicles the relationships that develop between the polyglot of captives and the terrorists. Watanabe is pressed into constant service as a translator, and eventually finds his own voice as well. The vice president busies himself by playing host and spending more time in his unfamiliar home than he had ever before known; the hostage–takers, from a poor mountainous area, discover much about the modern world, and two emerge as chess and music prodigies. The opera singer and the electronics magnate, though they share no common language save for music, indeed fall in love through their passion for music.

Bel Canto prompted the occasional critical remark from a few reviewers, some of whom felt that its cast of characters were too archetypical and superlative. *Daily Telegraph* writer Helen Brown found that "the uptight chief executive, the compassionate diva, the rebel leader who wants only the best for his country, and the quiet translator are all disappointing, two–dimensional stereotypes. They are like opera characters who require soaring art, bel canto, to move their audience." James Polk, writing in the *New York Times Book Review,* saw the book and Patchett's achievement in a different light. "*Bel Canto* often shows Patchett doing what she does best—offering fine insights into the various ways in which human connections can be forged," Polk asserted, "whatever pressures the world may place upon them."

Bel Canto was a nominee for the National Book Critics Circle Award, and Patchett took the $15,000 P.E.N./Faulkner Award in 2001 for it. In Britain, her book beat out several top contenders for the Orange prize for fiction by women honoring "originality and creativity." American soprano Renee Fleming was interested into turning *Bel Canto* into a film project starring herself; Fleming's signature roles include Antonin Dvorák's opera *Rusalka,* which Coss is finishing just as the rebel group bursts into the room in the novel.

Patchett remains a resident of Nashville, and helped her mother, Jeanne Ray, find a publisher for her own first novel, *Julie and Romeo,* in 2000. In a piece she wrote about doing a book tour for the website

Bookreporter.com, she noted wryly that her mother's publisher decided to spend the marketing budget on well–placed ads, instead of sending her out on the road. She confessed that she herself "would rather not go on book tour[s].... There are some lovely moments of meeting people, but 98.9 percent of it takes place in an airport eating Cinnabuns."

Selected writings

The Patron Saint of Liars, Houghton (Boston, MA), 1992.
Taft, Houghton (Boston, MA), 1994.
The Magician's Assistant, Harcourt (New York, NY), 1997.
Bel Canto, HarperCollins (New York, NY), 2001.

Sources

Periodicals

Booklist, July 1994, p. 1923.
Bookseller, June 14, 2002, p. 6.
Daily News (Los Angeles, CA), July 29, 2001, p. L16.
Daily Telegraph (London, England), June 13, 2002.
Entertainment Weekly, July 31, 1992, p. 57; June 28, 2002, p. 96.
Independent (London, England), June 12, 2002, p. 7.
Independent Sunday (London, England), August 12, 2001, p. 16.
New Statesman, July 30, 2001, p. 43.
New York Times, August 26, 2002, p. E1.
New York Times Book Review, November 16, 1997, p. 17; June 10, 2001, p. 37.
Publishers Weekly, July 14, 1997, p. 62; July 18, 1994, p. 233; October 13, 1997, p. 52; April 16, 2001, p. 42.
San Francisco Chronicle, November 2, 1997, p. 12.
Seattle Post–Intelligencer, January 14, 2000, p. 19.
Washington Post, July 8, 2001, p. T6.
World Literature Today, Spring 2002, p. 152.

Online

"On the Road with Ann Patchett," Bookreporter. com, http://www.bookreporter.com/features/ road–patchett–1.asp (November 24, 2002).

—*Carol Brennan*

Danica Patrick

CART driver

Born March 25, 1982, in Roscoe, IL; daughter of T.J. (a mechanic) and Bev Patrick.

Addresses: *Office*—c/o Team Rahal, 4601 Lyman Dr., Hillard, OH 43026. *Website*—http://www.rahal.com.

Career

Began driving go–karts, 1992; switched to Formula Vauxhall and Formula Ford, 1998; signed with Team Rahal, 2002.

Awards: Winner, MRP Race Series in US820 Sportsman, 1993; breaks two track records in one day in Buchanan, MI, 1993; winner, national point championship in WKA Manufacturers Cup in the Yamaha Sportsman Class, 1994; winner, WKA Great Lakes Sprint Series in Yamaha Sportsman and US 820 Sportsman, 1994; winner, WKA Great Lakes Sprint Series in Yamaha Restricted Junior and US 820 Jr, 1995; winner, North American Championships in Yamaha Junior Division, 1995; winner of 39 of 49 feature races, including WKA Manufacturers Cup in Yamaha Jr. and Yamaha Restricted Jr. classes; WKA Grand National; WKA Great Lakes Sprint Series; WKA Midwest Sprint Series; and IKF Division 7 race, 1996; winner, WKA Grand National titles in the Yamaha Lite and HPV Lite classes, 1997; winner, WKA Summer National title in Yamaha Lite division, 1997; top woman finisher, England Formula Ford Festival, 2000.

Sidelights

Championship Auto Racing Team (CART) driver Danica Patrick inherited her love of machines and speed from her father, T.J., a mechanic; he and her mother, Bev, met at a snowmobile race. As a young girl, however, she didn't like getting dirty and having grease under her fingernails. This changed when Patrick was ten years old and her family went go–karting. On her first drive, her brakes failed, and she smashed head–on into a concrete wall. Patrick loved it, and couldn't wait to drive again.

In her first race, at the Sugar River Raceway in Wisconsin, the leaders lapped her after six turns around the track. However, that was the first of a 22–race series, and by the end of that season, she was second in points among 20 drivers and had set a new track record. By the time Patrick was 16, in 1998, she had already won three Grand National Karting championships. She had also won three national point championships and the 1995 North American championship in the Yamaha Junior Can class. She spent so much time at the track that she was kicked off her high school's cheerleading squad for missing too many practices.

In 1998, Patrick attended Track Speed School at Sebring International Speedway, one of three driving schools she attended in the two weeks before driving a sedan at an SCCA regional race at the Daytona International Speedway. The SCCA race, she told a reporter in the *Tampa Tribune,* was "the first step on the ladder in getting to Indy cars."

In that same year, Patrick left high school and moved to Milton Keyes, England, where she slept on a friend's couch at night and spent her days racing Formula Vauxhall. She then moved on to race Formula Ford. She was the first woman to place at the Formula Ford Festival at Brands Hatch, coming in second against drivers who later became Formula One testers. This was the highest finish for an American since 1978, and earned her a Formula 3 test with Carlin Motorsports in 2001.

By 2002, Patrick had attracted the attention of others in the racing field. She signed a contract to drive the BMW M3 in the American Le Mans series, but when BMW withdrew from the series, she was left without a driving slot.

Bobby Rahal, the 1986 Indianapolis 500 winner and owner of Team Rahal, told Ed Hinton in the Knight Ridder/Tribune News Service, "There is no question [that Patrick] can become the first woman to win the Indy 500." Famed racer and announcer Jackie Stewart had such faith in her ability that he supervised her racing in Europe, which Rahal told Hinton was "the most intense training ground there is in motor sports."

According to an article in WickedRacingNews.com, driver Ryan Hunter–Reay said, "I'm actually surprised she hasn't gotten a ride yet because she is the fastest girl out there and she's pretty marketable. I think it would be a good deal to get her out there to see what she can do." Similarly, Vickie O'Connor, president of the Toyota Atlantic Series, told WickedRacingNews.com, "Danica Patrick is the real thing.... With the right opportunities she'll be right at the top of her sport."

Patrick went to the 2002 Indianapolis 500 as a spectator, watching and learning from the other drivers. She told Doug Goodman of the *Rockford Register Star* that since she did not have the chance to race that year, "it's ... interesting and cool just to see it. I think it's nice to see a race before you do it."

In April of 2002, Patrick won the pro division in the Toyota Pro/Celebrity event at the Toyota Grand Prix of Long Beach, beating both Indianapolis 500 driver Sarah Fisher and four–time Trans–Am champion Tommy Kendall. In June of that year, Patrick signed a contract to drive for Rahal for the next two seasons, with the aim of eventually racing in the premier American open–wheel circuit, the CART FedEx Championship Series. She planned to drive in three races in the Barber Pro Dodge series, the entry–level CART series.

In 2003, Patrick was slated to race a full season with Team Rahal in the Toyota Atlantic Series, the final step before becoming a CART driver. She was the first woman since 1974 to drive in the Atlantic series. In a press release about her signing with Rahal, Patrick said, "There is no doubt that I can bring something different and something new to CART."

Historically, racing has been an almost completely male endeavor; female drivers are still a novelty in the sport. In 2000, for example, only two women raced in the Indianapolis 500, and they both crashed—into each other. Stereotypes of women as poor drivers, and the animosity of men who resented women entering the sport, made Patrick's rise through the ranks of racing more difficult than it was for her male counterparts.

Patrick said that being female in a traditionally male–dominated sport has been both a help and a hindrance to her career. "It gains attention very quickly," she told Goodman. "People notice you for being something different, and sponsors are looking for something different." However, Patrick added, "I'm under a magnifying glass—if I do well, it's great; if I do bad, I get bashed real bad. So everything I do gets magnified." She told a reporter for the *Seattle Post–Intelligencer,* "I'm there for a far deeper reason than just to go out there and stand pretty for pictures."

Sources

Periodicals

Knight Ridder/Tribune News Service, May 15, 2002, p. K0195.
Los Angeles Times, April 13, 2002, p. D11.
Plain Dealer (Cleveland, OH), July 13, 2002, p. D10.
Rockford Register Star, May 26, 2002, p. 1A, p. 1E.
Seattle Post–Intelligencer, June 20, 2002, p. C10.
Sports Illustrated, September 2, 2002, p. R14.
Tampa Tribune, April 11, 1998, p. 10.

Online

"Danica Patrick: Seeks Path To The Top In 2003," Team Argent Racing, http://www.amcwholesale. com/racing/personal.cfm (February 21, 2003).

"Danica Patrick," Team Argent Racing, http://www2.amcwholesale.com/racing/career.cfm (February 21, 2003).

"Danica Patrick," WickedRacingNews.com, http://www.wickedracingnews.com/danica_patrick_htm (February 25, 2003).

"Press Releases: Danica Patrick," Thunder Valley Racing, http://www.thundervalleyracing.com/press/releases/patrick/partrick02_1.htm (February 25, 2003).

—Kelly Winters

R. Donahue Peebles

Hotel and real estate developer

Born in 1960 in Washington, D.C.; married Katrina, 1991; children: R. Donahue III. *Education:* Attended Rutgers University, Newark, New Jersey.

Addresses: *Office*—Peebles Atlantic Development Corporation, 100 S.E. 2nd St., Ste. 4650, Miami, FL 33131–2113.

Career

Joined mother's real estate business in Washington, D.C., as an appraiser, early 1980s; opened his own real estate appraisal business, 1983; appointed to Washington's Board of Equalization and Review by Mayor Marion Barry, 1983; served as chairman of board, 1984–88; became involved in commercial real estate development, late 1980s; became interested in Miami area real estate market after vacation, mid–1990s; purchased hotel in South Beach, 1996; refurbished the property, which was reopened as Royal Palm Crowne Plaza Resort, the first African American–owned beachfront hotel in South Florida, 2002.

Sidelights

The leading African–American hotel developer in the United States, R. Donahue Peebles controls more than a million square feet of hotel and commercial property in Florida and Washington, D.C. The crown jewel of Peebles's properties, operated through a network of companies led by his Miami–based Peebles Atlantic Development Corporation (PADC), is the Royal Palm Crowne Plaza Resort in Miami Beach. Although the Royal Palm project was beset by costly delays and political wrangling, the resort stands as one of Peebles's proudest accomplishments. "This is a historic project on many levels," Peebles told Hospitality.net shortly after the resort's opening in May of 2002. "The opening of this hotel represents not only the completion of these magnificent buildings but also the fulfillment of a promise made to this community."

The Royal Palm project is more than just the largest African–American–owned and developed beachfront resort in America. The 1993 decision by Miami Beach's city fathers to allocate some of its oceanfront real estate, along with an investment of $10 million, to develop an African–American–owned hotel brought to an end a 30–month boycott of the city by black vacationers. Peebles helped to turn the dream into a reality. Perhaps the most telling indication that the rift between the resort city and African Americans had finally healed came with the decision of the National Association for the Advancement of Colored People (NAACP) to hold its 2003 annual convention in Miami Beach.

But for Peebles, the Royal Palm is just the beginning. Elsewhere in the Miami area, he is building a condominium tower and private villas at the Miami

Beach Bath Club, a private club that for most of its history excluded African Americans and other minorities from membership. In 1996 Peebles became the first African American to join the Bath Club and in 1998 he bought the club and announced his plan for the Bath Club Residences, scheduled to open in 2004. Ultimately, Peebles would like to see PADC, which he founded and serves as president and chief executive officer, develop a national hotel ownership company of 20 to 25 full–service hotels with 300 to 500 rooms each.

Peebles was born in the nation's capital in 1960. Although he lived briefly in Detroit, Michigan, most of his childhood was spent in Washington, D.C. At the age of 14 he enrolled in Capitol Page High School, located on the fourth floor of the Library of Congress. "I'd have school classes from six to ten–thirty in the morning and then work as a page until seven at night," Peebles told Wyatt Olson of *New Times Broward–Palm Beach*. His mother, Yvonne, operator of a small real estate business, fostered in Peebles an abiding appreciation for two things: real estate and the Democratic Party. Despite his interest in real estate, his original goal was a career in medicine. Inspired by an uncle who was a doctor, Peebles began taking classes at Rutgers University in Newark, New Jersey, with the intention of going on to medical school. However, after only a year at Rutgers, he dropped out and returned to Washington. He went to work as an appraiser in his mother's real estate office and in 1983 opened his own appraisal business.

Later in 1983 Peebles was appointed by D.C. Mayor Marion Barry to the city's powerful Board of Equalization and Review, a property assessment appeals board. A year later he was named chairman, a post in which he served until 1988, when he left the board to open up a tax assessment appeals business. Soon thereafter Peebles learned that the city was interested in leasing office space from a would–be developer in a blighted neighborhood of the nation's capital. "I thought, if Barry is going to lease from this developer, certainly he should lease from me," he told *New Times Broward–Palm Beach*. "After all, we're friends, and he's pro–minority business people." He moved quickly to seal a deal with the city, picking up the necessary land, and informing the mayor and the city commission that he was willing not only to build more office space but to lease it for less money. The project was finalized in 1989. Peebles's close ties with Barry, however, soured in September of 1995 when the mayor, under fire for a proposed $48 million plan to lease two office buildings from the developer, walked away from the deal.

Angry and frustrated, Peebles fled Washington, D.C., with his wife, Katrina, for a vacation in Miami Beach. While on vacation, he read an article in the local newspaper about a search by the City of Miami Beach for a black developer to refurbish the Royal Palm Hotel, an art deco hostelry of the 1930s that was long past its glory days. As an incentive, the city was offering to invest $10 million in the project. When Miami Beach invited proposals from prospective developers, Peebles submitted one. He quickly became a frontrunner but angered city fathers when he initiated negotiations to buy the adjacent Shorecrest Hotel, a property on which the city also had its eye. A selection committee appointed by the city commission picked another developer, but Peebles began lobbying the city commissioners who would have the ultimate say on who got the job. In June of 1996, Peebles was tapped by the city commission to develop the property.

More political wrangling and the consequent delays threw the Royal Palm project way behind schedule. It was not until mid–May 2002 that the hotel was finally opened. In the meantime Peebles moved his wife and son, R. Donahue III, from their home in suburban Washington to the Miami area. They first settled in a vacation house on Bay Harbor Islands, later moving to a waterfront home in Coconut Grove, before finally moving into a $2.2 million home in Coral Gables in 2000. Despite the time–consuming task of overseeing the delay–plagued Royal Palm project, Peebles moved ahead on other fronts, lining up projects in Washington, D.C.; New Orleans, Louisiana; San Francisco, California; and Fort Lauderdale, Florida. Some of these new deals were eventually abandoned because of political roadblocks, but Peebles was determined to keep his company on the move.

Peebles still has plenty to prove in his chosen field, but in an interview with Maria Mercedes of South Florida's *Entertainment News & Views*, he hinted that he may in time look to politics as a way to make a contribution. "At a certain point, I'll be looking to do something different. My motivation to be in business was never just driven by making a lot of money. I like to do projects that are challenging and exciting to me and that are going to make an impact socially, build a symbol. I like to consider that we have a company that's not building just buildings, but symbols of equal economic opportunity. I've mixed my business activity with politics. Who knows? Maybe I'll go into politics one day ... to add some diversity to the U.S. Senate or something like that."

Sources

Periodicals

Boston Globe, June 12, 2002.
Entertainment News & Views, February 15–22, 2002.

Forbes, April 15, 2002, pp. 235–38.
Lodging Hospitality,, August 1, 1998, p. 28.
Miami Herald, March 31, 2002.
Miami Times, June 25, 1998, p. 1A.
New Times Broward–Palm Beach, August 16, 2001.
New York Times, August 3, 2002.
South Florida Business Journal, May 2, 2002.

Online

"Nation's First African–American Developed and Majority–Owned Resort Hotel Open on Miami Beach," Hospitality Net, http://www.hospitalitynet.org/news/All_Latest_News/4011898.print (October 13, 2002).
"The School of Hospitality Management: Peebles Atlantic Development Corporation Visitor Industry Council Scholarship," Florida International University School of Hospitality Management, http://hospitality.fiu.edu/scholarships/scspeebles.html (October 13, 2002).

—Don Amerman

Michael J. Potter

President and Chief Executive Officer of Big Lots

Born c. 1960, in Oregon. *Education:* University of Oregon, B.S.; Capital University, M.B.A.

Addresses: *Office*—Big Lots, 300 Phillipi Rd., Columbus, OH, 43228–5311.

Career

Began retail career at Meier & Frank Department Stores, Portland, OR; worked at the May Department Store Co., Los Angeles, CA, and The Limited, Inc., Columbus, OH, until 1991; Consolidated Stores Corporation, Columbus, began as vice president and controller, 1991, became senior vice president and chief financial officer, 1994, executive vice president, 1998, president and chief executive officer, August 2000—.

Sidelights

In 2000, Michael J. Potter became one of the youngest chief executive officers (CEO) to head a Fortune 500 company when he rose to the top post at Big Lots, Inc., the Columbus, Ohio–based discount merchant. With more than 1,300 stores across 46 states, Big Lots is the largest closeout retailer in the United States. Potter is widely credited with revitalizing the company and returning it to its original focus—to provide consumers with steep discounts on name–brand merchandise discontinued or overstocked by more mainstream retailers. Big Lots also benefited from having no serious rival on the horizon, save for a few regional competitors.

"There is no one out there doing what we do on a national basis," the CEO told *Chain Store Age* writer Marianne Wilson. "Closeout retailing is still a new business segment to most of the population. It's ours to make."

A native of Oregon, Potter was born in the early 1960s and earned a degree in management and finance from the University of Oregon. He began his retail career at Meier & Frank Department Stores in Portland, before moving on to the May Department Store Company in Los Angeles, California. Tapped for an executive post at the hugely successful women's apparel retailer The Limited, Inc., in Columbus, Ohio, Potter relocated and returned to school to earn a master's degree in business administration from Capital University there. In 1991, he left The Limited for the Consolidated Stores Corporation in Columbus as a vice president and controller. Founded in 1967 by auto–parts manufacturer Sol Shenk, the company moved into the closeout–retailing sector in 1982 under the name Odd Lots (later called Big Lots). Eleven years later, it had more than 600 stores and was about to post its first billion–dollar year in sales. Buyers for its stores looked for and engineered deals to buy shipments of discontinued or overstocked merchandise from department stores and other mainstream retailers; the stores were bare–bones, no–frills operations, which helped keep costs down and profits high.

Consolidated Stores continued to add stores, but sales began to stagnate in the mid–1990s. Operating margins fell, and its stock, traded on the New York Stock Exchange, began performing poorly. By that point, Potter had risen to a senior vice presidency post and was serving as Consolidated's chief financial officer, and in 1998, he was made an executive vice president. He moved quickly to install a computerized inventory tracking system that year, which helped the chain focus on putting the right merchandise in its growing number of stores across the country; NASCAR merchandise, for example, was not the success in California that it proved with Big Lots shoppers in the Midwest, and East Coast shoppers preferred liquid laundry detergent over the powdered kind.

Potter faced more tremendous challenges in righting the company ship after some important deals soured: it bought a rival, MacFrugal's, for $1 billion in stock, which later proved an unwise buy, and then moved into Internet retailing by acquiring the inventory of Toy Liquidators and KB Toys in 1999; the Kbkids.com site proved a money–loser for Consolidated, and Potter okayed its sell–off, at a loss, when he became president and chief executive officer in August of 2000. At that point, Potter holed up with several key executives at a Columbus hotel for a marathon session to devise a turnaround strategy.

The first item was to re–brand all the stores (Big Lots, Odd Lots, Pic 'N Save, and MacFrugal's) with the Big Lots name, and then move on to making the stores cleaner, better lit, and more customer–friendly places to shop. Inventory problems had meant empty shelves at times in the past, and Potter was committed to ending that. "It takes years to get customers, but only minutes to lose them," he told *Forbes* writer Luisa Kroll. He also cut some advertising and moved the funds into focus–group research, and from that "came away with the conclusion that customers wanted more predictability and respectability in an inherently unpredictable and trashy business," Kroll remarked.

When he took over as CEO, Potter was one of the youngest executives to lead a Fortune 500 company. His leadership abilities were soon rewarded by increased figures: for 2000, Big Lots posted its first $3 billion–plus sales year, and numbers for 2001 climbed by more than six percent. He credited much of the turnaround on the new inventory tracking systems and market research. "We could never have done this before," he asserted in the *Forbes* interview. "It's bringing science to the unscientific. It's organized chaos." He hoped to increase sales even further with a savvy new national advertising campaign, and was committed to positioning Big Lots as a treasure trove for all shoppers of all income levels. Items such as Palm Pilots could be found in stores one week for just $70, or brand–name basketballs for $5, while heavily discounted consumer staples like diapers and batteries are kept on hand. Potter aimed at "expanding that next tier of customers that doesn't need to shop Big Lots but loves a bargain," Barbara Thau, a writer for *HFN: The Weekly Newspaper for the Home Furnishing Network*, quoted him as saying.

Since refocusing on its core discount business and moving out of cyber–retailing, Big Lots has actually benefited from some of the failures in the dotcom world; its buyers negotiated with furniture.com, for example, to take its unsold inventory. "There are a number of factors in the industry that are making our market strong," Potter said in an interview with *Point of Purchase* writers Lyndsey Erwin and Gareth Fenley. "One of them is the volatile shortened product life cycle that exists in the world today—products just don't last as long as they used to. New product introductions come at a rapid pace … and they're all trying to maximize their business with the large national retailers." Potter likes the freedom that running a closeout merchant, with its free–spirited marketing strategies, entails. "There aren't many rules and there isn't much bureaucracy here," he told *MMR* writer Scot Meyer.

Sources

Chain Store Age, October 2002.
Daily News Record, July 13, 1989, p. 10; May 12, 1994, p. 10.
Display & Design Ideas, June 2002, p. 40.
DSN Retailing Today, May 20, 2002, p. 60.
Forbes, May 27, 2002, p. 104.
HFN: The Weekly Newspaper for the Home Furnishing Network, June 24, 2002, p. 20.
MMR, March 19, 2001, p. 31; June 25, 2001, p. 137.
Point of Purchase, February 2002, p. 10.

—*Carol Brennan*

Paul Pressler

President and Chief Executive Officer of Gap, Inc.

Born c. 1956, in New York; married Mindy; children: Sean (son), Jordan (daughter). *Education:* State University of New York—Oneonta, B.A., 1978.

Addresses: *Office*—Gap, Inc., 2 Folsom St., San Francisco, CA 94105.

Career

Worked as an urban planner in New York City, late 1970s; joined Remco Toys and then Mego Toys; vice president, marketing and design, Kenner–Parker Toys, 1982–87; Walt Disney Company, Burbank, CA, senior vice president for product licensing, 1987–90, senior vice president for consumer products, 1990–92; Disney Store, Inc., Glendale, CA, executive vice president and general manager, 1992–94, president, July 1994–November 1994; president, Disneyland Parks and Hotels, Anaheim, CA, 1994–98; Walt Disney Parks and Resorts, Burbank, CA, president after 1998, made chair, 2000; Gap, Inc., San Francisco, CA, president and chief executive, September 2002, board member, October 2002.

Sidelights

Paul Pressler was the surprise choice in September of 2002 when San Francisco–based clothier Gap, Inc., announced that this Disney corporate veteran would become its next chief executive officer. Pressler's hire was seen as a bold move for the flagging retail giant, given the fact that he had no apparel–sector experience on his resume. Others

commended his talents as a strong, enigmatic leader and an ideal choice to revive the Gap brand. Pressler himself was enthusiastic. "At this stage in my career, it was an opportunity to lead what I also think is a fantastic brand," he told *Los Angeles Times* writers Abigail Goldman and Leslie Earnest. "They have 165,000 employees around the world. This is an opportunity that comes around once in a lifetime."

Born in the mid–1950s, Pressler grew up on Long Island and graduated from the State University of New York at Oneonta with a degree in economics in 1978. His first job was with New York City's urban planning department, but he soon moved over to the toy business. After two posts with smaller companies, he was hired as the vice president for marketing and design at Kenner–Parker Toys in 1982. He held the job for five years, and made a name for himself by guiding the company's "Care Bears" line into unprecedented success. The tie–ins to the popular dolls included a 1985 animated movie, for which Pressler served as an executive producer. In that capacity he came to the attention of Disney CEO Michael Eisner, who lured him over to the entertainment giant as a senior vice president for product licensing.

In 1990, Pressler was made Disney's senior vice president for all consumer products, and two years later was given one of the top spots within Disney's increasingly successful chain of retail stores. During his tenure the number of Disney stores more than doubled and enjoyed strong sales. Late in 1994 he was handed the proverbial keys to the Magic Kingdom as head of the company's flagship theme park, Disneyland, in Anaheim, California. He presided over a 1996 launch of Anaheim's $1.4–billion "California Adventure" theme park, the first new one to be built at the site in more than four decades. In 1998 he advanced to a job as president of Disney Theme Parks and Resorts, the company's $6 billion division that included some eleven Disney entertainment and adventure attractions around the world.

One of Pressler's most impressive achievements in his years at Disney—both with the retail stores and with the theme parks and resort division—was to position the Disney brand as one that lured a wide variety of age groups, from children to their grandparents. By most accounts he was a popular executive and leader at the company, publicly praised by Eisner and considered to be on the short list to one day replace Eisner at the helm. In 2001, former Disney executive Jeffrey Katzenberg described Pressler as "a general leading tens of thousands of troops," the film producer told *Los Angeles Times* writer Jerry Hirsch. "He instills loyalty and ambition. People want to deliver for him."

Such talents came to the attention of executive–search firms, and in the summer of 2002 Pressler was said to have turned down the top job at America Online, the world's largest Internet service provider. He then emerged as the top choice to run the Gap chain, the 33–year–old California retailer with a ubiquitous presence across urban and suburban America. The company had enjoyed terrific growth and prosperity throughout the 1990s, with more than 4,000 stores and retail square–footage that was in the billion–plus range; its empire included the Gap stores, Banana Republic, and the discount retailer Old Navy. But the company was faulted for expanding too quickly—perhaps cannibalizing its own sales in the process—and failing to keep customers coming in for affordable, trendy basic styles of jeans, t–shirts, and casual dress clothes. With the company's stock price in a free fall, a Gap press release in May of 2002 announced the retirement of longtime CEO Millard "Mickey" Drexler.

Pressler turned down one offer from the Gap board before accepting a second one on September 26, 2002. The company's stock took a brief upswing on Wall Street after the announcement, and *Money* writer Stephanie D. Smith observed that the choice of Pressler was not that unusual. "Gap's board of directors wanted a fundamentally different manager at the helm—a broad strategic thinker and market-

ing whiz rather than a fashion maven," Smith wrote. Pressler himself stressed that apparel–industry experience was not what the Gap seemed to need at the moment, telling *New York Times* journalist Sherri Day that he would not have much to do with the actual clothing lines. "I don't really see my job as the person picking the season's colors," he explained to Day. "I think we have fantastic merchants and talented people to do that."

Instead, Pressler saw his role as someone who could bring his brand–marketing expertise on board. "Needless to say, the opportunity to lead a company as prestigious as the Gap is very exciting and, in a lot of ways, I think it's analogous with Disney," he told *WWD*'s Evan Clark. "They're world–renowned brands; millions of people interact with the brands everyday." Pressler also announced that same day that he would immediately begin Gap's standard training program for all employees, which included 60 days of working in its stores. Within his first few months on the job, the company finally posted a profit after months of losses, and its share price rose nearly 50 percent. One of his fundamental decisions was to hire an advertising agency to conduct focus–group studies, so that a new campaign might target more specific demographic groups among Gap customers.

Around the Disney theme–park headquarters in Burbank back in the late 1990s, the genial, six–foot–two Pressler was known as "the Big Kahuna." His first–year salary at the Gap included a base of $1.5 million a year and an $885,000 bonus. He is married with two children.

Sources

Periodicals

Daily Variety, September 27, 2002, p. 1.
Los Angeles Times, July 18, 1996, p. 4; February 8, 2001, p. C1; September 27, 2002, p. C1.
Money, April 1, 2003, p. 61.
Newsweek, October 7, 2002, p. 48.
New York Times, September 27, 2002, p. C1.
WWD, September 27, 2002, p. 1; October 29, 2002, p. 2; December 31, 2002, p. 3.

Online

"The Challenge in Store for Gap," *BusinessWeek Online,* http://www.businessweek.com/bwdaily/dnflash/oct2002/nf2002109_2824.htm (October 9, 2002).
"Gap Starts Patching Its Holes," *BusinessWeek Online,* http://www.businessweek.com/bwdaily/dnflash/feb2003/nf20030224_7468_db014.htm (February 24, 2003).

—*Carol Brennan*

Philip Pullman

Author

Born Philip Nicholas Pullman, October 19, 1946, in Norwich, England; son of Alfred Outram (an airman) and Audrey (a homemaker; maiden name, Merrifield) Pullman; married Judith Speller (a therapist), August 15, 1970; children: James, Thomas. *Education*—Oxford University, B.A., 1968.

Addresses: *Agents*—Ellen Levine, 432 Park Ave. S., Ste. 1205, New York, NY 10016; A.P. Watt, 20 John St., London WC1N 2DR, England. *Home and Office*—24 Templar Rd., Oxford OX2 8LT, England. *Publisher*—Knopf, 299 Park Ave., 4th Fl., New York, NY 10171.

Career

Taught in a number of middle schools in and around Oxford, England, 1972–88; published his first adult novel, *Galatea*, 1978; joined faculty at Oxford University's Westminster College as a part–time lecturer, 1988; turned to children's fiction, publishing a number of novels and plays.

Awards: Lancashire County Libraries/National and Provincial Children's Book Award, for *The Ruby in the Smoke*, 1987; Best Books for Young Adults citation, School Library Journal, for *The Ruby in the Smoke*, 1987; Children's Book Award, International Reading Association, for *The Ruby in the Smoke*, 1988; Best Books for Young Adults citation, American Library Association (ALA), for *The Ruby in the Smoke*, 1988; Preis der Leseratten, ZDF Television (Germany), for *The Ruby in the Smoke*; Best Books for Young Adults citation, ALA, for *Shadow in the North*, 1988; Carnegie Medal, British Library Association, for *Northern Lights*, 1996; Publishing News British Children's Book of the Year Award, for *Northern Lights*, 1996; Children's Fiction Award, Guardian, for *Northern Lights*, 1996; Smarties Gold Award, Rowntree Mackintosh Co., for *The Firework Maker's Daughter*, 1996; Carnegie Medal short–list, British Library Association, for *Clockwork, or All Wound Up*, 1996; Smarties Silver Award, Rowntree Mackintosh Co., for *Clockwork, or All Wound Up*, 1997; British Book Award for best children's book, for *The Amber Spyglass*, 2000; May Hill Arbuthnot Honor Lecture Award, for "His Dark Materials" trilogy, 2001; Booker Prize long–list, for *The Amber Spyglass*, 2001; British Book Award for author of the year, for *The Amber Spyglass*, 2002; Whitbread Children's Award, for *The Amber Spyglass*, 2002; Whitbread Book of the Year Award, for *The Amber Spyglass*, 2002.

Sidelights

In a writing career spanning more than two decades, award–winning author Philip Pullman has written for a variety of audiences. Although he is perhaps best known for his books for children and young adults, Pullman also has written an adult novel and adapted several classic novels as plays. His most influential work thus far has been a fantasy trilogy entitled *His Dark Materials*. In an essay written for the teachers@random website, created and maintained by Random House, parent of Alfred A. Knopf, Pullman's American publisher, he took great care to describe himself as a "writer of stories." He explained, "I was sure that I was going to write stories myself when I grew up. It's important to put it like that: not 'I am a writer,' but rather

'I write stories.' If you put the emphasis on yourself rather than your work, you're in danger of thinking that you're the most important thing. But you're not. The story is what matters, and you're only the servant, and your job is to get it out on time and in good order." And lest there be any doubt about the importance Pullman attaches to stories, it's all spelled out quite clearly in his own words at Knopf's online profile of the author. "Stories are the most important thing in the world. Without stories, we wouldn't be human beings at all."

Although Pullman was born in Norwich, England, much of his early childhood was spent traveling the world because both his father and stepfather served in the Royal Air Force and were assigned to a series of international postings. While living briefly in Australia, Pullman discovered the joys of comics, reveling particularly in the exploits of Batman and Superman. When he was eleven, the family returned to Great Britain, settling in North Wales. It was an idyllic childhood, spent during a period when children were free to roam pretty much anywhere they chose. An early influence on Pullman was Enid Jones, his English teacher, to whom he still sends copies of all his newly published books. He studied English literature at Oxford University's Exeter College, earning his bachelor's degree in 1968. In the first four years after leaving Oxford, Pullman worked at a variety of odd jobs around England. During this period, he married therapist Judith Speller on August 15, 1970. The couple has two sons: James, a professional viola player, and Thomas, a university student.

In 1972, Pullman returned to the town of Oxford and took a position as a middle school teacher with the Oxfordshire Education Authority. In his spare time, he began to write. His first work to be published was an adult novel, *Galatea,* issued in 1978. Much of his subsequent work won its greatest popularity with children and young adults. Some of his early children's novels, including *The Ruby in the Smoke,* were based on plays that he'd written for his middle–school students. In an interview on the Random House website, the author was asked if he consciously targets any particular audience when he writes a book. "I don't know about this business of writing for this audience or that one.... If I think of my audience at all, I think of a group that includes adults, children, male, female, old, middle–aged, young, everyone who can read. If horses, dogs, cats, or pigeons could read, they'd be welcome to it as well. I don't want to shut anyone out."

While still teaching middle school, Pullman in 1985 published the first installment of his four–novel "Sally Lockhart" series of historical fiction, *The Ruby*

in the Smoke. Two years later, the second novel in the series, *The Shadow in the Plate* (published in the United States as *The Shadow in the North*) was published in England. After several years as a middle school teacher, Pullman in 1988 joined the faculty of Oxford's Westminster College as a part–time lecturer. He taught courses on the folk tale and Victorian novel and also a survey course that explored how words and pictures fit together. He continued to write extensively. While on the faculty at Westminster College, he completed the last two books in the "Sally Lockhart" series, *The Tiger in the Well,* published in 1990, and *The Tin Princess,* published in 1994. After finishing the "Sally Lockhart" series, Pullman began work on what was to become his most celebrated work, a trilogy collectively entitled "His Dark Materials."

An epic–scale fantasy, Pullman's "Dark Materials" trilogy borrows from Scandinavian mythology and Christian religious tradition to explore, in Pullman's words, the "temptation and the fall of humankind," as well as the complexities of good and evil and the possibility of parallel universes. The first book in the trilogy, *Northern Lights* (published as *The Golden Compass* in the United States), introduces the reader to a world similar to ours but different in some very important respects. Each human character in Pullman's fictional world has an animal alter ego that holds the person's soul. The author calls these alter egos "daemons." In the fictional worlds created by Pullman, daemons are the animal creatures that make human beings complete. The novel's central character, Lyra Belacqua, embarks on an epic quest from her childhood home in Oxford in search of several children who have been kidnapped for use in an Arctic research project. Lyra learns that the research facility is controlled by her mother, who wants to sever the link between human children and their daemons so that she can explore the power of "Dust," a mysterious invisible substance that surrounds all people after they reach puberty. In the end Lyra frees the captive children and continues her journey, now in search of her father, Lord Asriel, who has harnessed the power of Dust.

Asked in an interview on the Random House website how he came up with the idea of daemons, Pullman said: "When I first saw Lyra in my mind's eye, there was someone or something close by, which I realized was an important part of her. When I wrote the first four words of *Northern Lights,* 'Lyra and her daemon,' the relationship suddenly sprang into focus. One very important thing is that children's daemons can change shape, whereas they gradually lose the power to change during adolescence, and adults's daemons have one fixed animal shape which they keep for the rest of their lives. The daemon, and especially the way it grows and develops with its person, expresses a truth about human nature which it would have been hard to show so vividly otherwise."

Pullman followed the success of *Northern Lights* with *The Subtle Knife*, in which Lyra meets Will, a young boy in search of his long–lost father who disappeared shortly after Will's birth. Will, who is from our world, meets Lyra in a third universe known as Cittagazze, inhabited only by children because all adults have either been destroyed by soul–eating Specters or driven out. Will learns of the existence of a "subtle knife" capable of slicing through anything, including the walls of various universes. Together, Lyra and Will travel through all three universes—hers, his, and Cittagazze—in search of their fathers and the meaning of "Dust." At the conclusion of *The Subtle Knife*, Lyra discovers that her father, Lord Asriel, has himself been on a quest to overthrow the Church and make Lyra the new Eve in a newly created world.

In the final book of Pullman's "Dark Materials" trilogy—*The Amber Spyglass*—Lyra and Will escape from the clutches of Lyra's mother and embark on a search for Roger, a kitchen boy mistakenly betrayed by Lyra. In an effort to find Roger, the two scour the land of the dead for the kitchen boy's soul. At the end of this quest, they realize that war between the heavenly angels and rebel angels is imminent. With the overthrow of the old kingdom, Lyra and Will kiss to secure the fate of the new world that has replaced it. Writing in the *New Statesman*, critic Amanda Craig described *The Amber Spyglass* as "an intellectual challenge as to the essential nature of the human and the divine...."

Well received by both critics and the public, Pullman's "Dark Materials" trilogy helped to further secure the author's reputation as a writer for young people. Alfred A. Knopf, Pullman's publisher in the United States, likened the books in the trilogy to John Milton's classic *Paradise Lost*. Ironically, Milton's masterpiece is the source of the trilogy's title, which comes from a passage in Book II of *Paradise Lost*. And the story line of Pullman's trilogy bears a startling resemblance to the plot of Milton's work. Will and Lyra, Pullman's protagonists, seem to be the counterparts of Adam and Eve, while Lyra's parents collectively would appear to represent Satan.

In an interview after the publication of *The Subtle Knife*, Pullman denied that the trilogy was pure fantasy. To the contrary, he insisted, it represented stark realism. After the entire trilogy had been published, Pullman's characterization was revisited by Powells.com interviewer Dave Weich, who asked the author to elaborate on his reasoning. Pullman replied: "Well, when I made that comment I was trying to distinguish between these books and the kind of books most general readers think of as fantasy, the sub–Tolkien thing involving witches and elves and wizards and dwarves. Really, those authors are rewriting *The Lord of the Rings*. I'm trying to do something different: tell a story about what it means to grow up and become adult, the experience all of us have and all of us go through. I'm telling a story about a realistic subject, but I'm using the mechanism of fantasy. I think that's slightly unusual."

A lifelong lover of stories, Pullman wrote in his essay on the teachers@random website that he began telling stories as soon as he knew what stories were. "I was fascinated by them: that something could happen and be connected to another thing, and that someone could put the two things together and show how the first thing caused the second thing, which then caused a third thing. I loved it. I love it still."

Asked about his favorite author when he was a child, Pullman told teenreads.com writer Jennifer Abbots that he was very uncritical and liked almost every story he read. "I did really enjoy Conan Doyle's Sherlock Holmes stories in particular."

For a man who writes of multiple universes, Pullman hasn't strayed all that far from his roots. He and his wife, Jude, still live in Oxford, where Pullman tends to his writing chores in an outbuilding at the rear of his backyard garden. Pullman's writing studio boasts two comfortable chairs—one that he sits in while writing and another for using the computer. Other furnishings include a guitar, saxophone, a six–foot–long stuffed rat, several hundred books, and, of course, his computer.

Selected writings

Books

Galatea, Gollancz (London, England), 1978; Dutton (New York),1979.
Ancient Civilizations, Wheaton (Exeter, England), 1978.
Count Karlstein; or, The Ride of the Demon Huntsman, Chatto & Windus (London), 1982; Doubleday (London), 1991.

The Ruby in the Smoke, Oxford University Press (London), 1985; Knopf (New York), 1987.

How to Be Cool, Heinemann (London), 1987.

The Shadow in the Plate, Oxford University Press (London), 1987; published in the United States as *The Shadow in the North,* Knopf (New York), 1988.

Penny Dreadful, Corgi (London), 1989.

Spring–Heeled Jack, Doubleday (London), 1989; Knopf (New York), 1991.

The Tiger in the Well, Knopf (New York), 1990.

The Broken Bridge, Macmillan (London), 1990; Knopf (New York), 1992.

The White Mercedes, Macmillan (London), 1992; Knopf (New York), 1993.

Thunderbolt's Waxworks, Viking (London), 1994.

The Tin Princess, Knopf (New York), 1994.

The Gas–Fitter's Ball, Viking (London), 1995.

The Wonderful Story of Aladdin and the Enchanted Lamp, Scholastic (London), 1995.

Northern Lights, Scholastic (London), 1995; published in the United States as *The Golden Compass,* Knopf (New York), 1996.

Clockwork; or, All Wound Up, Doubleday (London), 1996; Arthur A. Levin (New York), 1998.

The Firework–Maker's Daughter, Corgi (London), 1996; Levine (New York), 1999.

The Subtle Knife, Scholastic (London), Knopf (New York), 1997.

The Amber Spyglass, Knopf (New York), 2000.

I Was a Rat, Knopf (New York), 2000.

His Dark Materials: The Trilogy, Ballantine (New York), 2001.

Puss in Boots: The Adventures of That Most Entertaining Feline, Knopf (New York), 2001.

Plays

The Three Musketeers (adapted from the novel by Alexandre Dumas), produced at Polka Children's Theatre, Wimbledon, England, 1985.

Frankenstein (adapted from the novel by Mary Shelley), Oxford University Press (London), 1990.

Sherlock Holmes and the Limehouse Horror, Nelson (Walton–on–Thames, England), 1993.

Puss in Boots, produced at Polka Children's Theatre, Wimbledon, England, 1997.

Sources

Periodicals

Entertainment Weekly, June 28–July 5, 2002, p. 97.

New Statesman, October 2000.

Online

Contemporary Authors Online, Gale, 2002.

"Philip Pullman: About the Author," Random House, http://www.randomhouse.com/features/Pullman/philippullman/index.html (November 27, 2002).

"Philip Pullman: Author Q & A," Random House, http://www.randomhouse.com/features/Pullman/philippullman/qanda.html (November 27, 2002).

"Philip Pullman: Author's Studio," Random House, http://www.randomhouse.com/features/Pullman/philippullman/studio.html (November 27, 2002).

"Philip Pullman: Bio," teenreads.com, http://www.teenreads.com/authors/au–pullman–philip.asp (November 27, 2002).

"Philip Pullman: Carnegie Medal Acceptance Speech," Random House, http://www.randomhouse.com/features/Pullman/philippullman/speech.html (November 27, 2002).

"Philip Pullman Reaches the Garden," Powells.com, http://www.powells.com/authors/pullman.html (November 27, 2002).

"Philip Pullman," teachers@random, http://www.randomhouse.com/teachers/rc/rc_ab_ppu.html (November 27, 2002).

"Philip Pullman, Writer of Stories," Mary Tise's School Library Media Resources, http://www.delanet.com/~ftise/pullman.html (November 27, 2002).

—Don Amerman

Marc Ravalomanana

President of Madagascar

Born c. 1950, in Madagascar. *Education:* Attended school in Sweden.

Addresses: *Office*—Embassy of the Republic of Madagascar, 2374 Massachusetts Ave. NW, Washington, D.C. 20008.

Career

Founded yogurt company in Antananarivo, Madagascar; acquired radio and television stations; elected mayor of Antananarivo, 1999; became president of Madagascar, 2002.

Sidelights

Marc Ravalomanana took office as president of Madagascar in mid–2002 after months of political turmoil in the Indian Ocean island nation. A self–made yogurt tycoon, Ravalomanana was hailed as harbinger of a new era for the impoverished country after decades of inefficient post–colonial rule. His ascension to the top office was a bitterly fought one that almost drew the country into civil war when longtime Malagasy leader Didier Ratsiraka refused to leave office. "This is not about good guys and bad guys, but about the awakening of this country to democracy," economist Pierre Rangera told *Guardian* writer James Astill about the election debacle. "After a popular revolution, you can never go back to dictatorship."

The son of a farmer, Ravalomanana was born around 1950 and grew up in Imerikasina, near the Malagasy capital of Antananarivo. Of Imerina heritage, a highlands people with Asian and African roots, Ravalomanana was educated in missionary schools and was determined to study abroad. He appealed to Denmark's ambassador to Madagascar to provide him with a financial stipend, and studied in Sweden. After returning to Madagascar, he founded a yogurt company and sold his wares around Antananarivo from the back of a bicycle. His Tiko brand was launched in earnest with a $1 million World Bank loan that helped him acquire a factory, and further support came from the Swedish packaging giant TetraPak. In time, Tiko grew into one of the island's most impressive economic successes.

The annual per capita income in Madagascar is about $260, making it one of the poorest countries in the world. Madagascar's 16 million citizens earn their living mainly as subsistence farmers, or as workers at foreign–owned textile plants. The island was a colonial possession of France until 1960, and independence only nominally improved its economic circumstances. A Francophile political establishment had held power for years, continuing with a Marxist–led military dictatorship led by Ratsiraka in 1975. A moribund economy and government corruption endured even after free–market reforms were established in 1987, but a growing pro–democracy movement brought free elections in 1993. Ratsiraka, however, remained in power almost unabated over the decade.

Meanwhile, Ravalomanana had become a media as well as food–business tycoon, acquiring some of the first non–government–run television and radio stations on the island. He decided to run for mayor of Antananarivo in 1999, and used his own personal wealth to finance a modern, professionally designed campaign centered on the slogan, "Tiako Iarivo," or "I love Antananarivo." He became one of the first Imerina ever to win significant political office in Madagascar, and quickly set about cleaning up the city. Municipal workers were given new uniforms and set about sweeping and washing the streets; houses were painted, new public latrines built, and lighting improved. Larger problems faced the rest of the island, however, with some villages without electricity and even inaccessible by roads. Interviewed by *San Francisco Chronicle* journalist Katya Robinson in 2000, Ravalomanana asserted that his success in Antananarivo could be amplified on a national level. "People are ready for big change," he said. "But the barrier is the old system, the old politics."

In 2001 Ravalomanana entered the upcoming presidential race. He faced Ratsiraka, but was able to impart his campaign messages on his Tiko product packaging, through his media outlets, and even with the help of his own helicopter, which he deployed on visits to rural areas. In these mountain areas, the candidate made history by delivering campaign speeches in his native Imerina tongue. In the December balloting, Ravalomanana took 80 percent of the urban vote, with rural tallies arriving more slowly. When the final results were announced in January, he had won 46 percent against Ratsiraka's 41 percent share of the votes. The lack of clear majority meant that a run–off election would be held, but Ravalomanana and his supporters claimed that the Ratsiraka side had committed election fraud. Demanding a recount, Ravalomanana was backed by citizens who began gathering daily outside of the Antananarivo government buildings. The country's top court reviewed the case, and ruled that the election had been conducted fairly. The protests grew larger in number, and Ravalomanana's supporters took over government buildings in early 2002. Ratsiraka fled to the countryside, asserted his was still the lawful government, and invited Antananarivo to secede. Meanwhile, Ravalomanana declared himself the winner, appointed a cabinet, and recalled parliament.

Antananarivo, a landlocked city, was put under martial law, and fuel supplies grew precariously meager in the weeks that followed. Negotiations between both sides took place in Senegal in April, which led to an agreement for a vote recount and a transitional Ravalomanana–Ratsiraka government, but the deal quickly fell apart after both sides accused each other of violating its terms. Madagascar's High Constitutional Court, with a new panel of judges, declared the December results legitimate, and this time Ratsiraka, bunkered down with his forces in Toamasina, the country's major port, challenged the ruling. Over the next month, Ravalomanana held out, and Ratsiraka retreated as the entire economy of the nation threatened to collapse.

Ravalomanana was inaugurated on May 6, 2002, and declared his intention to use his business expertise to right the Malagasy economy. "I am for wealth generation," he told Astill in the *Guardian* interview. "The development of a country is just like running a company." The stalemate with Ratsiraka continued, however, into the summer. Government troops advanced on the final pro–Ratsiraka stronghold of Toamasina, and the former president fled to the nearby Seychelles Islands in early July. Madagascar and Ravalomanana had won an important political coup when the United States formally recognized his government a few weeks before, with France following the lead, but a few days after Ratsiraka departed, the 53 delegates of a newly sat African Union rejected Madagascar, claiming that Ravalomanana had seized power unconstitutionally. Ravalomanana, who had been inaugurated as president in a football stadium before a crowd of 200,000, remained undaunted. "People want change," he told *Christian Science Monitor* writer Danna Harman. "In fact they want democracy—but they could not express it before. They did not know they had the power."

Sources

Periodicals

Christian Science Monitor, May 6, 2002.

Economist, December 22, 2001; March 9, 2002; April 13, 2002; June 1, 2002.

Financial Times, June 27, 2002, p. 7.

Guardian (London, England), May 10, 2002; May 12, 2002; July 6, 2002, p. 15.

Independent (London, England), February 28, 2002, p. 16; April 20, 2002, p. 15.

New York Times, April 13, 2002, p. A4; April 19, 2002, p. A12; May 6, 2002; May 7, 2002, p. A13; June 10, 2002; July 6, 2002, p. A6; July 10, 2002, p. A9.

Observer (London, England), May 12, 2002, p. 22.

San Francisco Chronicle, August 21, 2000, p. A8.

Online

"Profile: Marc Ravalomanana," BBC, http://news.bbc.co.uk/hi/english/world/africa/newsid_1866000/1866530.stm (May 19, 2002).

—*Carol Brennan*

Mike Rawlings

President and Chief Concept Officer of Pizza Hut

Born Michael Scott Rawlings, August 25, 1954, in Borger, TX; son of Eldon Rawlings; married Micki; children: Michelle, Gunnar. *Education:* Boston College, B.A. in philosophy and communication, 1976.

Addresses: *Office*—Pizza Hut, 14841 Dallas Parkway, Dallas, TX 75254.

Career

Joined the Dallas advertising firm of Tracy–Locke, 1979; rose through the corporate ranks to become chief executive, 1992; named president and chief concept officer of Pizza Hut, 1997.

Sidelights

As president and chief concept officer of Pizza Hut, Mike Rawlings oversees the largest chain of pizza restaurants in the United States. It is a job he enjoys as much as his painting and sculpture hobbies. "It's really the same thing at Pizza Hut," he told Steve Quinn in the *Dallas Morning News.* "How to take different elements and how to put it together in a fresh way."

Rawlings has revitalized Pizza Hut, a struggling brand when he took over, turning it into the most profitable of the three restaurants owned by its parent company, Tricon Global Restaurants. Under Rawlings, Pizza Hut has introduced some of the most popular products in its more–than–40–year history, boosted morale among its employees by offering bonuses and stock options, and even made history by launching the first corporate logo into space on the side of a Russian Proton rocket viewed on television by half a billion people around the world.

A high school football player, and a solid presence at 6–foot–3 inches and 250 pounds, Rawlings can appear imposing to his employees, but he is said to have a charisma that brings people together and makes them want to work hard from him. Pizza taste–tester Casey Haney described to the *Dallas Morning News*'s Quinn his first meeting with Rawlings: "He has this fill–the–room type presence. Right away, he was the center of attention, yet he wanted to talk to us. He made us feel like our time was valuable to him. He wanted to learn from us. He was a listener, kind of a facilitator, too." As Rawlings told Quinn, "Leadership is an honor; it's a gift."

Rawlings grew up in the upstate New York town of Liverpool. His grandparents were ministers at the Church of Nazarene, and he continues to be influenced by his religious background into adulthood, as he regularly attends services at the First Presbyterian Church in Dallas, Texas.

Also a leader in high school, Rawlings was president of his student council at Liverpool High in 1971. He excelled in athletics in high school, playing in three different sports, and helped his school football team win a league championship. Although he identified himself more with the jocks of his school than with the hippies who were challenging authority in institutions across the country, he sided with protestors at his school who wanted a designated smoking area. "I'm a very mainstream person in many ways," Rawlings explained to Quinn, "yet I love to be with people who have different points of view. It enriches me. You can be a hippie and an athlete and still be fighting for the same things."

Early jobs for Rawlings included that of garbage collector in his hometown, and valet car parker. After college, Rawlings went on to Boston College, earning a double bachelor's degree in philosophy and communication. He graduated in 1976, and moved to Dallas, Texas, the same year. Rawlings began his professional life in advertising, joining the Dallas advertising agency Tracy–Locke (which has since become DDB Needham Dallas) as a junior staffer in 1979. In his 18 years with the company, he steadily climbed the corporate ladder, rising to executive vice president/group account director, then general manager, then president, and finally becoming the company's chief executive in 1992.

Friend and colleague Tom Kerol told Quinn that Rawlings worked hard for his successes. "No one handed him anything," Kerol said. But the same year Rawlings became chief of Tracy–Locke, tragedy struck. His brother Mark, only 35 years old, suffered a fatal heart attack and died before Rawlings could see him one last time. "I still miss him," Rawlings told Quinn. His brother's death "matured" him, and taught him that "you'd better understand the different elements of life, how to get the most out of them and how to balance those things."

During his term at the advertising company, Rawlings worked on accounts for PepsiCo brands, the former parent company of Pizza Hut, and so became knowledgeable about Pizza Hut's business. Also during his tenure as an advertising executive, he helped to increase his company's revenues six fold, making his the biggest advertising company in the southern United States. Rawlings left the advertising agency in 1996. The following year he was hired by the chief of Tricon Global Restaurants, the company that by this time owned Pizza Hut, to helm the pizza chain. Tricon Global Restaurants had just spun off from PepsiCo, and consisted of former PepsiCo holdings KFC and Taco Bell in addition to Pizza Hut. As chief executive of Pizza Hut, Rawlings would also serve as the chain's chief concept officer, responsible for the brand's marketing and development. Rawlings described his reaction to the job offer to Cheryl Hall in the *Dallas Morning News:* "Here's a chance at the leadership brand, feeding people the food America loves better than anything else. I go, 'Wow! That's a pretty cool job.'"

At the time Rawlings took over Pizza Hut, the company was stumbling. Profits were down, and other pizza chains such as Papa John's, Little Caesars, and Domino's were eroding Pizza Hut's leadership position in the field. "The company needed some serious mojo," Rawlings told the *Dallas Morning News*'s Hall. "There were very talented people here and great brand equity. But it needed an internal belief in itself, direction and spirit." So Rawlings's first task at his new job was to pump $1 billion into a revitalization campaign to wake up the "sleepy" Pizza Hut brand, as he phrased it to Quinn. He also took pains to learn the pizza business at its most basic level, putting in time at one of the restaurants to learn how to make pizza dough himself. He was put to the test immediately when a rush order came through for 15 pizzas for a child's birthday party.

A major goal of the campaign was to get the Pizza Hut brand to appeal to a younger market by revamping its image. Some steps Rawlings took in this direction included adding more exciting offerings to the company's menu, adding employee incentives, redesigning restaurants and the corporate logo, shedding unprofitable restaurants, and selling hundreds of others to franchises.

Before Rawlings took over, turnover among Pizza Hut restaurant managers hovered around 30 percent each year. After Rawlings introduced a plan rewarding managers with $20,000 in stock options after four years of employment, turnover dropped to half its previous levels. Rawlings also took pains to formally recognize high–performing managers. One way he did this was to reward outstanding managers with bonuses and big yellow hats shaped like wedges of cheese. "It's a stupid piece of foam," Pizza Head human resources head Joe Bosch told Hall, "but you see these hard–core, 20–year veterans get tears in their eyes when they get one. It's a powerful thing." Manager Harold Edwards—a Big Cheese Award winner—agreed, telling Hall, "It shows that top management cares."

Product innovations introduced by Pizza Hut under Rawlings included the Big New Yorker, which proved to be one of the most successful new releases in the chain's existence. In large part because of the Big New Yorker, same–store sales increased 12 percent in a single year. Other new products produced under Rawlings included Insider Pizza, Twisted Crust and the P'Zone pizza. By all accounts, the innovations Rawlings introduced at the company were very successful, as Rawlings summed up for Hall: "People go, 'OK, this stuff works,'" he said. "We can have a fun culture, put money back into the pizza, and celebrate value."

In 1998, Pizza Hut sued rival pizza chain Papa John's, in a lawsuit arguing that Papa John's falsely represented itself as selling the best pizza. Rawlings saw this suit as essential to preserving the integrity of the Pizza Hut brand. As he told the Fox News Network, "I've got to make sure that this brand stays whole and as strong as it can be.... If we sit idly by, I'm sorry to say ... people will start to believe the gross mischaracterizations they've been making about our product." Rawlings saw the suit as an opportunity educate his customers about the merits of his product. He told Fox News Network, "Our pan pizza is made fresh every day in the store. We've got dough makers. We've got ... rollers. Their dough is made off–site in a factory.... They implied that their sauce is fresh and it's not."

Pizza Hut won its suit in 2000 when a federal district court judge ruled in its favor, forbidding Papa John's from claiming it made better pizza than Pizza Hut. Rawlings told *Business Wire*, "This is a landmark victory for consumers as much as it is for Pizza Hut. The Court ruled that truth in advertising outweighs hype and deceit, and it told Papa John's they no longer can deceive consumers as they've been doing in the past."

As part of the revitalization campaign, Pizza Hut made history in outer space; in 2000, it became the first company to officially commercialize space. In July of that year, a Russian Space Agency Proton rocket bearing Pizza Hut's revamped logo lifted off from Kazakhstan carrying a major component of the International Space Station.

With a reported cost of more than $1 million, the placement of the Pizza Hut logo represented a unique advertising opportunity for Pizza Hut. It was also a relative bargain, putting the Pizza Hut logo in front of an estimated 500 million television viewers around the world for about half the price

of an ad placed on television during the American Super Bowl. "We decided," Rawlings told the Associated Press, "that if we were going to launch this logo, to really launch it and find a big way to do it."

Pizza Hut's space campaign went even further in May of 2001, with the delivery of a specially made Pizza Hut pizza to the International Space Station. Vacuum–packed, the pizza took almost a year to develop, since a regular Pizza Hut pizza is not able to withstand the rigors of space travel.

The next step at Pizza Hut, as Rawlings envisions it, is no less than to challenge the dominance of fast food giants McDonald's and Burger King. "Pizza is the most important food in America today," Rawlings told the *Dallas Morning News*. "It's the number–one food for bringing families together at home." Getting Americans to eat more pizza than burgers, said Rawlings, is simply a matter of making it more available, for example at drive–in restaurants. "At our 3 'n' 1 store on Forest at Central," Rawlings told Hall, "we're selling Personal Pans by the carload at the drive–through window. That's our next venue."

In addition to his duties as chief of Pizza Hut, Rawlings considers it important to contribute time and money to civic projects in Dallas. He headed a task force appointed by the Dallas city government to improve programs for young people who needed social services, and he led Pizza Hut in a drive to contribute $250,000 to the Dallas Center for the Performing Arts Foundation.

Sources

Periodicals

Associated Press, September 30, 1999.
Business Wire, August 13, 2002.
Dallas Morning News, September 2, 1999; April 14, 2002.
Nation's Restaurant News, June 23, 1997, p. 5.
PR Newswire, July 12, 2000.

Online

"Pearson and Novak Name Senior Leadership Team for New Restaurant Company," PepsiCo, http://www.pepsico.com/press/19970610.shtml (August 13, 2002).

"Pizza Hut Celebrates Successful Delivery to Space," Space.com, http://www.space.com/news/spacestation/space_pizza_010522.html (August 14, 2002).

"Space Advertising Faces Hurdles in Russia," Space.com, http://www.space.com/businesstechnology/business/space_advertising_000612.html (August 14, 2002).

Transcripts

Cavuto Business Report (Fox News Network), transcript #081305cb.140, August 13, 1998.

CNBC/Dow Jones Business Video, transcript #071200cb.y50, July 12, 2000.

—*Michael Belfiore*

Judith Regan

Book publisher

Born Judith W. Regan in 1953, in Fitchburg, MA; daughter of Leo (a teacher) and Rita (a teacher) Regan; married Robert Kleinschmidt (a financial planner), 1987 (divorced, 2001); children: Patrick (with David Buckley, a psychologist), Lara (with Kleinschmidt). *Education:* Vassar College, B.A., 1975.

Addresses: *Office*—HarperCollins Publishers, 10 East 53rd St., New York, NY 10022.

Career

Reporter, *National Enquirer*, 1978–81; editor, *Woman's World* and *Real Life*; producer, *Entertainment Tonight* and *Geraldo*; editor, Simon & Schuster, 1988–94; president and senior editor, ReganBooks, 1994—; president, Regan Company; host of *Judith Regan Tonight*, Fox News, 1996—.

Sidelights

Judith Regan may not be a household name, but she knows how to capitalize on the popularity of her authors. Since her entrance into publishing, Regan has been responsible for some of the best-selling books on record. Her authors include right–wing commentator Rush Limbaugh, radio shock jock Howard Stern, and television personality Kathie Lee Gifford. She has earned a reputation as a hardball player in the world of publishing as well as in her personal life. She talks tough, plays rough, and seems to win most of the time.

Born in 1953, in Fitchburg, Massachusetts, she is the middle child of Leo and Rita Regan. Until she was ten years old, Regan lived with her family on her Sicilian grandparents's farm in Fitchburg. Afterward they moved to Bay Shore, New York. Her parents were both schoolteachers who valued education and achievement and instilled those ideals in their children. Regan credits her mother with her own will to succeed.

Regan earned a scholarship to attend Vassar College in Poughkeepsie, New York. During that time she indulged her wide–ranging interests and talents. She studied voice and spent a year in Boston studying art at the Museum School. After graduation she moved to New York City and continued to study voice with a teacher from Juilliard. While she found studying voice satisfying, she also needed to earn money. She described her frustration to Rebecca Mead of *New York*, "I was under so much stress to earn a living…. It was a horrible thing. You need to have a trust fund."

She worked odd jobs in several different cities, but then got a job as a reporter for the *National Enquirer*. She was responsible for the celebrity biography beat as well as writing the more common sensationalistic stories of the *Enquirer*. From writing for the *National Enquirer*, Regan went on to editing the magazines *Woman's World* and *Real Life*. She also spent a few years producing shows for *Entertainment Tonight* and *Geraldo*.

In 1987, she approached Simon & Schuster with ideas for some books that she'd like to write. Instead of signing her to write books, Simon & Schuster hired her as a consultant to bring in celebrity biographies. The next year Regan was promoted to full editor. It was during her tenure at Simon & Schuster that Regan established herself as a successful publisher. In one year, seven of her books hit the *New York Times* bestseller list. Those titles included Rush Limbaugh's *The Way Things Ought To Be*, Howard Stern's *Private Parts*, and a book featuring the MTV cartoon characters Beavis and Butthead called *This Sucks, Change It*.

In 1994, Rupert Murdoch offered Regan a position with his media company, News Corporation. He helped her set up her own company, Regan Company, so she could expand into movie and television development. He also gave her an imprint at HarperCollins, ReganBooks. In 1996, her television show *Judith Regan Tonight* began airing on Murdoch's Fox News channel. Her broad interest in all aspects of media is what originally sparked Murdoch's interest in her. Regan thinks that she and News Corporation are a good match. She explained in an interview with the MJM Entertainment Group, "It's a perfect environment for me because if you're very self starting, as I am, and you're very entrepreneurial, as I am, it's the kind of company that nurtures that, welcomes that, and embraces that."

Between 2000 and 2002, ReganBooks put 18 books on the *New York Times* best–seller list. It's a record that is hard to match anywhere else in the publishing business. Within the sphere of publishing though, Regan has fielded a lot of criticism for the types of books she publishes. She was the first publisher to release books focusing on the September 11, 2002, terrorist attacks on the United States. She has also courted World Wrestling Entertainment to publish biographies of its most popular stars. She explained her rationale to Mead, "I don't have to judge, because I am in the business of making money. All I want to do is publish books that make money. That is all I want to do. I want to be a successful businesswoman."

Regan's personal life has been subject to much critical viewing as well. She has been arrested more than once for scuffles with the New York police. Her grudges and her court battles are often fodder for gossip columns. She explained to Elizabeth Gleick of *People*, "I hold a grudge forever. I believe an eye for an eye…. No, I believe in two eyes for an eye."

The *New York Daily News* once named her the most annoying woman in New York. Regan blames this on sexist attitudes. She believes businessmen are allowed to be more aggressive. She explained to

Mead, "They are glorified, they are sanctified, they are deified. But if I, as a female, am aggressive about going after projects, about playing commander of those projects, I become a target." In order to address this issue, she is working on a book called *The Art of War for Women*, based on the classic Chinese text *The Art of War* by Sun Tzu.

In the 1970s, Regan and the American Civil Liberties Union (ACLU) took the state of Utah to court over their use of strip searches in the case of even minor offenses. Regan was stopped for improperly making a left turn. She was then arrested and strip–searched. Her case with the ACLU was successful.

Not so successful was her divorce from city financial planner Robert Kleinschmidt. The two married in 1987, had a daughter in 1991, then filed for divorce in 1992. Regan and Kleinschmidt fought for custody of their daughter for three years. Regan was finally awarded custody in 1995. It was another six years before the divorce was finalized. As a result of the extended court battle Regan brought charges against her lawyer for negligence.

Despite her hectic working schedule and tumultuous private life, Regan has visions of a calmer future. She described them in an interview with MJM Entertainment, "At some point when I make enough money, I'd like to become more philanthropic, get involved a little in politics, and change my life a little bit. And I'd like to spend more time with my children and have a happier and more wholesome family life. And perhaps have a loving relationship with a man."

Sources

Periodicals

Esquire, May 1996, p. 52.
Forbes, April 15, 2002, p. 118.
New York, October 25, 1993, p. 60.
People, February 14, 1994, p. 72.
U.S. News and World Report, December 25, 1995–January 1, 1996.

Online

"Interview with Judith Regan," MJM Entertainment Group, http://www.mjmgroup.com/Transcripts/Judith_Regan.htm (August 28, 2002).

—*Eve M. B. Hermann*

John C. Reilly

AP/Wide World Photos

Actor

Born John Christopher Reilly, May 24, 1965, in Chicago, IL; married Alison Dickey (a film producer); children: two sons. *Education:* DePaul University's Goodman School of Drama, B.F.A., 1987.

Addresses: *Agent*—United Talent Agency, 9560 Wilshire Blvd., Ste. 500, Beverly Hills, CA 90212–2427.

Career

Actor in films, including: *Casualties of War,* 1989; *We're No Angels,* 1989; *Days of Thunder,* 1990; *State of Grace,* 1990; *Shadows and Fog,* 1992; *Out on a Limb,* 1992; *Hoffa,* 1992; *What's Eating Gilbert Grape?* 1993; *The River Wild,* 1994; *Dolores Claiborne,* 1995; *Georgia,* 1995; *Hard Eight* (aka *Sydney*), 1997; *Boys,* 1996; *Boogie Nights,* 1997; *Chicago Cab,* 1998; *Nightwatch,* 1998; *Flagpole Special,* 1998; *The Thin Red Line,* 1998; *Never Been Kissed,* 1999; *For Love of the Game,* 1999; *Magnolia,* 1999; *The Perfect Storm,* 2000; *The Anniversary Party,* 2001; *Frank's Book,* 2001; *The Good Girl,* 2002; *Gangs of New York,* 2002; *Chicago,* 2002; *The Hours,* 2002; *Anger Management,* 2003. Television appearances include: *Martial Law* (series), 1998; *The Settlement* (movie), 1999. Stage appearances include: *The Grapes of Wrath,* Chicago, IL, 1988; *A Streetcar Named Desire,* Chicago, IL, 1997; *Exit the King,* Hollywood, CA, 1999; *True West,* New York, NY, 2000; *Marty,* Boston, MA, 2002.

Sidelights

One of the most popular character actors of the early 21st century, John C. Reilly has accomplished what no other film actor had done before. In 2002, Reilly appeared in three of the five films nominated for the Academy Awards Best Picture Award—*Chicago, Gangs of New York,* and *The Hours.* Although Thomas Mitchell in 1939 also had billing in three movies up for the Best Picture Award, that was done in an era when 10 films were nominated for the award. To make 2002 even sweeter for Reilly, his portrayal of the hapless Amos Hart in *Chicago* won for him an Oscar nomination as Best Supporting Actor. As convincing as a crooked, beat–hardened cop in *Gangs of New York* as he is as a cuckolded husband in *Chicago,* Reilly revels in his ability to be all things to all people on the big screen. Of his chameleon–like qualities, the actor told film director Paul Thomas Anderson in *Movieline,* "I think I'm appreciated by people who watch movies to the degree that they don't know who I am from movie to movie. That's actually a compliment. Some people think I'm stupid for this, but I try to think in long–term goals, to do work that I can be proud of in ten, 20 years, not just disposable crap that made everyone chuckle in the moment."

Interviewed by Bob Edwards for National Public Radio, Reilly credited his work in musicals as a child with helping to shape him as an actor. "Actually, where I learned to become an actor was through musicals, and that's all that I did from the age of about eight to about 17. Another really gratifying part of doing *Chicago* was that it felt like a return to my childhood in some way...." Asked by Edwards if any conclusion could be drawn from his portrayal of an unhappy husband in three of his 2002 films (*Chicago, The Good Girl,* and *The Hours*), Reilly replied, "I'm happy to say that life does not reflect art in this way for me. I've been happily married for about eleven years now, and people ask me, 'Why do you think people see you as this hapless, cuckolded husband?' or whatever. I don't really put a lot of thought into why people want me for what they want me for. I'm just happy to be able to play characters that are in conflict, that have some big issues to deal with, because, you know, happy couples are a great thing in life, but they're not always the most interesting things to watch in a story."

Born on May 24, 1965, in Chicago, Illinois, Reilly is the fifth of six children born to Irish Catholic parents; he grew up in the Windy City's Marquette Park neighborhood. His father, the owner of a Chicago–area linen supply company, loved to fish and took his children on numerous fishing trips to the Great Lakes and Florida. Reilly was bitten by the acting bug at the age of eight, when he accompanied a boyhood friend to a free acting class at a local park. From that point on, he was hooked, trying out for roles in musicals with the local community theater and taking part in whatever productions were staged at his school.

After graduating from high school, Reilly enrolled in DePaul University's Goodman School of Drama, from which he received his bachelor of fine arts degree in 1987. Fresh out of college, he joined Chicago's Organic Theater, with which group he made his professional acting debut in the fall of 1987. Not long thereafter he joined Chicago's prestigious Steppenwolf Theatre and in 1988 played Noah Joad in that company's production of *The Grapes of Wrath.* When the Steppenwolf production moved to New York, Reilly made his debut on Broadway.

Anxious to make the transition from stage to screen, Reilly sent a videotape of some of his stage work to film producer Brian De Palma. Not much later, De Palma, looking for actors to cast in his 1989 production of *Casualties of War,* selected Reilly to play the pivotal role of Hatcher in the Vietnam War drama. He followed up on his film debut with small roles

in that same year's *We're No Angels* and Woody Allen's 1992 film, *Shadows and Fog.* He began to win greater attention as an actor after taking somewhat meatier roles in 1990's *Days of Thunder* and *State of Grace* and 1993's *What's Eating Gilbert Grape?.* In *Days of Thunder,* Reilly played alongside Tom Cruise and Robert Duvall. Of that experience, he told Anderson at *Movieline,* "I love Tom and think he's a great actor, but at the time it was all about working with Robert Duvall. That movie was a bizarre experience. I was coming off serious movies, and suddenly there's Don Simpson and Jerry Bruckheimer in their heyday like Sodom and Gomorrah. It was a fall from grace for me as a young man to see the decadence that is movies and Hollywood at its most extreme—$100,000 parties and recruiting girls off the beach to come be extras. It was nuts."

In the early 1990s, Reilly married Alison Dickey, whom he'd met through actor Sean Penn. Although Dickey was working as an assistant to Penn in the area of project development when she and Reilly first met, she later became an independent film producer. The couple has two sons and lives in Los Angeles, California.

In 1997 Reilly graduated from the ranks of character actors to leading man, when he was selected to star opposite Gwyneth Paltrow in *Hard Eight.* The film also marked the beginning of an extremely fruitful collaboration with director Paul Thomas Anderson, who made his feature–length directorial debut with that movie. Sadly, although Reilly received wide critical praise for his work in the film, *Hard Eight* failed to excite much interest at the box office and was seen by relatively few moviegoers. Extremely impressed by Reilly's work, Anderson next cast the actor in 1997's *Boogie Nights* as a dimwitted porn actor who dreams of becoming a magician/songwriter. Anderson's second feature film was a big box office hit, winning for Reilly some long–overdue recognition.

Reilly, who has worked in three (*Hard Eight, Boogie Nights,* and *Magnolia*) of Anderson's four feature films, is as impressed with the director as Anderson is with him. As he told Nicole McEwan of *Ritz Filmbill,* "Paul finds things out about you. All the while you're hanging out, he's very casually mining your psyche for material. It's become a bit of a joke in our crowd; you know, be careful what you say or it'll wind up in the movie. Whatever you do, don't tell that embarrassing childhood story about how you wet your pants at the mall."

The recognition Reilly received for his work in *Boogie Nights* helped win to him meatier roles in a number of films released in the late 1990s. These included director Terrence Malick's *The Thin Red Line, Nightwatch, For Love of the Game, Never Been Kissed,* and *Magnolia.* For *Magnolia,* in which he played a lonely police officer involved with an emotionally unstable, crack–addicted woman, Reilly was re-united with director Anderson. In an interview with Liz Braun of the *Toronto Sun,* Reilly told how he had lobbied the director for a role in which he would end up with a romantic interest. "I said, 'Don't you know what a romantic I am? I'm always cast as these heavies or these semi–retarded child men. Can't you give me something I can relate to, like falling in love with a girl?' And he wrote in that emotional element."

Next up for Reilly was a supporting role in *The Perfect Storm,* the film adaptation of Sebastian Junger's 1997 best–seller about a crew of commercial fisher-men who in 1991 were caught in the vortex of three colliding storms in the Atlantic Ocean. Asked by Elizabeth A. Kennedy of the Associated Press if he felt any added responsibility because he was por-traying a true story, Reilly replied: "Oh, absolutely, it felt more serious than your typical job. One of the things that got us through how difficult the shoot-ing actually was was that we are telling a real story. This is real human drama; we're not creating some amusement park ride for the summer. Even though the movie is really exciting to watch, it's got a real pathos behind it."

In 2002 Reilly found himself thrust into the spot-light as never before. His work in four films released in 2002 was lavishly praised by most movie critics, and all four motion pictures performed reasonably well at the box office. Of his four 2002 films, three were among the five movies nominated for the 2002 Best Picture Oscar. Reilly himself was nominated as Best Supporting Actor for his role in *Chicago.* His portrayal of Amos Hart, the cuckolded husband of murdered chorus girl Roxie Hart in the film, which won Best Picture honors, gave Reilly an opportu-nity to get back to his roots in musical comedy. Ironically, the actor won his first Oscar nomination playing a character who—like Reilly—manages to go through life largely unnoticed. In *Chicago,* Reilly's character plaintively sings: "Cellophane, Mister Cellophane/Shudda been my name … /'Cause you can look right through me/Walk right by me/And never know I'm there."

Although that degree of transparency may have troubled Reilly's character, Amos Hart, it suits the actor just fine. As he told Steve Daly of *Entertain-ment Weekly,* "I treasure my anonymity. The more known I become as a name, the less I kinda like it. I like to have interactions with people. If everything is 'Hey, you're that guy,' that's the same interaction over and over again."

In the wake of Reilly's blockbuster year in 2002, the actor was interviewed by Alec Cawthorne for BBC.com. Cawthorne asked how he felt about being a character actor and whether he would like to trade those kinds of roles for life as a leading man. Reilly replied, "I'm friends of guys like Brad Pitt and George Clooney, and they'll come up to me quite often and say they want the parts I play because I get the interesting stuff. Yeah, but they get the girl! Let's switch for a day and see if they still want my parts. When people say I'm a character actor, that's a real honor. On bad days, I think that's just a limi-tation—that they're trying to keep me in my place and tell me I can't play larger roles. Most of the time I just think that 'character actor' means a good actor—someone who is not playing themselves for a living."

Sources

Books

Contemporary Theatre, Film, and Television, volume 32, Gale Group, 2000.

Periodicals

AP Online, June 28, 2000.
Entertainment Weekly, November 15, 2002, p. 76; Feb-ruary 21, 2003, p. 46.
Los Angeles, February 2003, p. 19.
Movieline, December/January 2000.
Ritz Filmbill, February 2000.
Tampa Tribune, January 3, 2003, p. 40.
Toronto Sun, January 11, 2000, p. 28.

Online

"Biography for John C. Reilly," Internet Movie Da-tabase, http://us.imdb.com/Bio?Reilly,%20John%20C (March 31, 2003).
"Films—Interviews: John C. Reilly," BBC.com, http://www.bbc.co.uk/films/2003/01/06/john_c_reilly_chicago_interview.shtml (March 31, 2003).
"John C. Reilly," Hollywood.com, http://www.hollywood.com/celebs/bio/celeb/1677828 (March 30, 2003).
"John C. Reilly," Internet Movie Database, http://us.imdb.com/Name?Reilly,+John+C. (March 31, 2003).
"John C. Reilly," Yahoo! Movies, http://movies.yahoo.com/shop?d=hc&id=1800019213&cf=biog&intl=us (March 30, 2003).

Transcripts

Morning Edition, National Public Radio, March 19, 2003.

—*Don Amerman*

John Ritter

Actor

Born Jonathan Southworth Ritter, September 17, 1948, in Burbank, CA; son of Tex (an actor and musician) and Dorothy Fay (an actress and musician) Ritter; married Nancy Morgan (an actress), October, 1977 (separated, 1993; divorced 1996); married Amy Yasbeck (an actress), September 18, 1999; children Jason, Carly, Tyler (first marriage), Stella (second marriage). *Education:* University of Southern California, B.F.A. (theater arts), 1971; Harvey Lembeck Comedy Workshop.

Addresses: *Office*—ABC, Inc. 500 S. Buena Vista St., Burbank, CA 91521–4551.

Career

Actor in films, including: *The Barefoot Executive,* 1971; *Scandalous John,* 1971; *The Other,* 1972; *The Stone Killer,* 1973; *Nickelodeon,* 1976; *Breakfast in Bed,* 1978; *Americathon,* 1978; *Hero at Large,* 1980; *Wholly Moses!,* 1980; *They All Laughed,* 1981; *Real Men,* 1987; *Skin Deep,* 1989; *Problem Child,* 1990; *Problem Child 2,* 1991; *Noises Off,* 1992; *Stay Tuned,* 1992; *Danielle Steele's Heartbeat,* 1993; *North,* 1994; *The Colony,* 1995; *Sling Blade,* 1996; *Mercenary,* 1997; *Nowhere,* 1997; *A Gun, A Car, A Blonde,* 1997; *Hacks,* 1997; *The Truth About Lying,* 1998; *Montana,* 1998; *Bride of Chucky,* 1998; *I Woke Up Early the Day I Died,* 1998; *Shadow of Doubt,* 1998; *Lost in the Pershing Point Hotel,* 2000; *Terror Tract,* 2000; *Panic,* 2000; *Tadpole,* 2002; *Man of the Year,* 2002; *Eli,* 2003; *Bad Santa,* 2003.

Television appearances include: *Dan August,* 1970; *Hawaii Five-O,* 1971, 1977; *Evil Roy Slade* (movie), 1971; *The Waltons,* 1972–80; *Medical Center,* 1973;

M*A*S*H, 1973; *Kojak,* 1974; *The Bob Newhart Show,* 1974; *Owen Marshall: Counselor at Law,* 1974; *The Night that Panicked America* (movie), 1975; *Phyllis,* 1975; *The Streets of San Francisco,* 1975; *Movin' On,* 1975; *Rhoda,* 1975–76; *Mannix,* 1975; *Petrocelli,* 1975; *Barnaby Jones,* 1975; *Mary Tyler Moore,* 1975; *The Rookies,* 1975; *Starsky and Hutch,* 1976; *Three's Company,* 1977–84; *The Love Boat,* 1977; *Leave Yesterday Behind* (movie), 1978; *Ringo* (movie), 1978; *The Ropers,* 1979; *The Associates,* 1980; *Omnibus,* 1980; *The Comeback Kid,* 1980; *Pray TV,* 1982; *In Love with an Older Woman,* 1982; *Sunset Limousine* (movie), 1983; *Love Thy Neighbor* (movie), 1984; *Pryor's Place,* 1984; *Three's A Crowd* (aka *Three's Company Too*), 1984; *Letting Go* (movie), 1985; *Life with Lucy,* 1986; *Unnatural Causes* (movie), 1986; *A Smoky Mountain Christmas* (movie), 1986; *The Flight of Dragons* (voice), 1986; *The Last Fling* (movie), 1986; *Hooperman,* 1987–89; *Tricks of the Trade* (movie), 1988; *My Brother's Wife* (movie), 1989; *The Dreamer of Oz: The L. Frank Baum Story* (movie), 1990; *It,* 1990; *Help Save Planet Earth: Easy Ways to Make a Difference* (documentary), 1990; *The Cosby Show,* 1991; *Anything But Love,* 1991; *The Summer My Father Grew Up* (movie), 1991; *Heartbeat* (movie), 1992; *Fish Police* (voice), 1992; *Hearts Afire,* 1992–95; *The Real Story of O Christmas Tree* (voice), 1992; *Prison for Children* (movie), 1993; *The Only Way Out* (movie), 1993; *The Larry Sanders Show,* 1993–94; *Dave's World,* 1994–95; *Gramps* (movie), 1995; *The*

Colony (movie), 1995; *NewsRadio*, 1995; *Wings*, 1996; *Unforgivable* (movie), 1996; *For Hope* (movie; uncredited), 1996; *Touched by an Angel*, 1996, 1999; *Over the Top*, 1997; *King of the Hill* (voice), 1997; *Mercenary* (movie), 1997; *A Child's Wish* (movie), 1997; *Dead Man's Gun* (movie), 1997; *Loss of Faith* (movie), 1997; *Buffy the Vampire Slayer*, 1997; *Ally McBeal*, 1998; *Dead Husbands* (movie), 1998; *Chance of a Lifetime* (movie), 1998; *It Came from the Sky* (movie), 1999; *Veronica's Closet*, 1999; *Holy Joe* (movie), 1999; *Lethal Vows* (movie), 1999; *Chicago Hope*, 2000; *Batman Beyond* (voice), 2000; *Family Law*, 2000; *Felicity*, 2000–02; *Clifford the Big Red Dog* (voice), 2000–01; *Tucker*, 2001; *The Ellen Show*, 2002; *Law & Order: Special Victims Unit*, 2002; *Scrubs*, 2002; *Breaking News*, 2002; *8 Simple Rules for Dating My Teenage Daughter*, 2002—.

Executive producer, including: *Anything But Love* (tv series), 1989; *Have Faith* (tv series), 1989; *Man of the Year*, 2002. Stage appearances include: *The Dinner Party*, Broadway, New York, NY, 2000; *J For J*, Los Angeles, CA, 2002.

Awards: Golden Globe Award for best actor in a series, Hollywood Foreign Press Association, for *Three's Company*, 1983; Emmy Award for outstanding actor in a comedy series, Academy of Television Arts and Sciences, for *Three's Company*, 1984; Emmy Award for outstanding host (with brother, Tom), for *Superfest: A Celebration of Ability*, 1986; Theatre World Award, for *The Dinner Party*, 2001.

Sidelights

Considered by many to be one of the most successful comic actors on television, John Ritter first captured the hearts of TV viewers in a big way as Jack Tripper on *Three's Company*, which ran from 1977 to 1984. But he also proved himself as a serious actor in the years following *Three's Company*. He continued working steadily after that show ended its run, next picking up the role of an indecisive cop on *Hooperman*, followed by the role of a legislative assistant in the political comedy *Hearts Afire*, which left the air in 1995. He also found time to appear in numerous movies, including *Sling Blade, Panic*, and *Tadpole*, and theater roles, including *The Dinner Party*, in which he appeared on Broadway with fellow 1970s TV star Henry Winkler.

Ritter was born in Burbank, California. His father was Tex Ritter, a well–known country musician from Texas. Tex won an Oscar for his rendition of "Do Not Foresake Me, Oh My Darlin'" in the 1952 western *High Noon*. Ritter's mother, Dorothy Fay, was also an actress and musician, initially from Arizona. Ritter's parents moved to Los Angeles, California, before Ritter was born in order to pursue their careers in entertainment. Ritter and his older brother, Tom (now an attorney), spent much of their childhood on the road with their parents as they traveled to gigs around the country. Although Ritter attended Hollywood High School, he grew up not around movie stars, but country–western musicians. In spite of this strong musical influence while growing up, Ritter has said that he inherited none of his parents' musical abilities.

Although his roles following *Three's Company* did not have the prominence of that hit show, Ritter remained busy into the 1990s and 2000 with guest spots on shows such as *Felicity, Scrubs, Ally McBeal*, and *Buffy the Vampire Slayer*. He also became the voice of *Clifford the Big Red Dog*, an educational cartoon series airing on PBS. His work on the dramedy *Ally McBeal* earned him an Emmy nomination.

In September of 2002, Ritter appeared in his first regular television series in seven years, *8 Simple Rules for Dating My Teenage Daughter*. The show features Ritter as the ham–handed father of three teenagers who think he is about as uncool as you can get. This was his first weekly series since *Hearts Afire* had ended its run in 1995.

Initially reluctant to sign on to the show because, as he put it to Michael A. Lipton and Todd Gold in *People*, "I didn't want to be [another] beleaguered dad [griping] to his children," Ritter warmed to the role after he was convinced by a friend to read the entire first script. One scene in the script in particular changed his mind about the show. This was a scene in which his character is asked by his younger daughter whether he thinks she is pretty. After he says "yes," they share a tender moment before she dismisses his opinion as irrelevant because he is too old. As Ritter explained to Lipton and Gold in *People*, "That's how life really is with kids." In other words, the show had the depth he felt was lacking in other shows. Interwoven with the comedy (always the main focus) in each episode is something more. Something, as Ritter put it to Judith S. Gillies in the *Washington Post*, "that you don't usually see."

In this respect, *8 Simple Rules* was a refreshing change from *Three's Company*, which sought only to make its audience laugh, not to be thought provoking. At one point while working on *Three's Company*, Ritter asked the writers, who had previously worked on *All in the Family* (a sitcom with more substance), if they could add a little depth to this show as well. Their response, according to Ritter, speaking to David Kronke in the *Houston Chronicle,* was, "This is just a soufflé. We did all the message stuff, and now we're doing farce."

Ritter also welcomed the chance to return to performing in sitcoms that *8 Simple Rules* presented. Although he had enjoyed his recent film roles and TV guest spots, nothing for him matched the enjoyment of working week after week with the same cast, developing and performing new scripts based on the same characters and situations. With *8 Simples Rules,* he was back in his element.

The show stars Ritter and fellow TV celebrity Katey Sagal (who made her mark in the TV series *Married ... with Children*); the two actors had previously worked together on the film *Chance of a Lifetime* in 1998. The new show hit the airwaves on the ABC network in a Tuesday–night time slot. Running in half–hour episodes, the sitcom features the two actors as the parents of three children, including two girls and a boy. The show was inspired by the book of the same name by W. Bruce Cameron. Much of the sitcom's humor comes as Ritter, an over–protective father, struggles to come to terms with his daughters' raging hormones.

The show, which is shot in front of a live audience, features Ritter as Paul Hennessy, a sports writer who has spent the last few years on the road for his job. He now finds himself staying at home more to pick up the slack from his wife, played by Sagal, who has started a new job as a nurse. Ritter's character finds that while he gets along well with his son, he has fallen out of touch with his teenage daughters; he expects them to still behave like the small children he last knew well. Instead, he has to contend with boyfriends and other teenage issues.

Initially, making people laugh didn't come easy to Ritter. In fact, his first career choice was politics, not performing. After suffering a head injury in an auto accident when he was 15, Ritter was forced to stay at home studying while his friends went out to parties. This serious, bookish teenager was elected president of his high school class, and, soon afterward, president of the entire student body. He enjoyed politics, even on this small level, and it was as a result of these experiences that he seriously considered politics as a career.

After graduating from high school, Ritter went on to the University of Southern California (USC) in Los Angeles, where he initially majored in psychology, with a minor in architecture, with dreams of becoming a senator. However, this ambition died with the assassinations of John F. Kennedy, Robert F. Kennedy, and Martin Luther King, Jr. When these leaders were killed, Ritter became disillusioned with a political system that allowed these crimes to happen, and he turned to acting, something he had always had fun doing, but which he had not taken seriously as a career choice. In 1968, Ritter began to study acting with teacher Nina Foch. Soon afterward, he switched his major at USC to acting.

Ritter graduated from college in 1971 with a theater degree, and he continued his studies with famed acting teacher Stella Adler at the Harvey Lembeck Comedy Workshop. His father died in 1974, three years after Ritter graduated from college.

Ritter landed his first film role right out of college, in 1971. This was a part in the film *The Barefoot Executive.* From there he moved on to more small film roles and guest spots on various television shows, including *The Waltons* and *The Mary Tyler Moore Show.* These roles led to his being cast in *Three's Company,* in which he played the male roommate of two single women, and his career was assured. First aired in 1977, *Three's Company* soon became the most–watched show on television, turning Ritter and his costars into celebrities.

The humor in *Three's Company* revolved around Ritter's character pretending to be gay so that his landlord will allow him to live with two beautiful, young, single women. Wild misunderstandings often resulted, forcing Ritter and his costars to extricate themselves from unfortunate situations. On the show, Ritter became known for his razor–sharp comic timing and his aptitude for physical comedy. His performances on *Three's Company* earned him an Emmy in 1984.

Having appeared in TV movies during the run of *Three's Company,* Ritter continued this work after *Three's Company* ended its run. Also following his work on the show, he appeared in numerous film roles, including *Real Men* in 1987, *Skin Deep* in 1989, and *Problem Child* in 1990, followed by a *Problem Child* sequel the following year. It was while working on *Problem Child* that Ritter met his future second wife, Amy Yasbeck.

In the 1990s, Ritter turned his attention more toward drama in his film work. Notable roles during this time included a gay storeowner in *Sling Blade* in 1996, and a psychiatrist who has a hit man for a patient in *Panic* in 2000. His TV appearances in the

1990s included guest spots on *Ally McBeal* and *Felicity*, in which he played an alcoholic father. On March 12, 2003, Ritter hosted the *TV Land Awards: A Celebration of Classic TV.*

In addition to his film and TV roles, Ritter became active in efforts to raise money for the treatment of cerebral palsy; his brother, Tom, is afflicted with the disease, and together they have hosted numerous telethons for United Cerebral Palsy. The pair won a shared Emmy in 1986 for their hosting of *Superfest: A Celebration of Ability.*

With his role as an over–protective father on *8 Simple Rules,* Ritter comes full circle from his role as dating machine Jack Tripper on *Three's Company.* "It's pretty funny," he told the *Washington Post's* Gillies. "Jack Tripper didn't think about the fact that these are somebody's daughters." The new show debuted on September 17, 2002, the day Ritter turned 54. By this time, he had appeared in more than two dozen made–for TV movies and 30 theatrical releases, in addition to his work on prime time television series.

Ritter brings first–hand experience to his new role. Now the father of teenagers himself, he has had his share of hair–raising experiences with boyfriends of his daughter, Carly, in college at Vassar at the time of *8 Simple Rules's* debut. He related one story to reporters in which one of Carly's boyfriends remarked, on meeting Ritter for the first time, that he planned on taking a break from school to, as quoted by Suzanne C. Ryan in the *Boston Globe,* "live a summer of debauchery." Although the boyfriend was not serious, Ritter was not amused, and he told the young man in no uncertain terms that this kind of joking was not appreciated.

Ritter has three children by his first wife, and a daughter with his second wife, actress Amy Yasbeck. One of Ritter's children by his first wife, Jason, is an actor in his own right, appearing in *Swimfan,* among other films. Although he enjoys his celebrity status, and especially his work as an actor, Ritter likens his time in the spotlight to spending time in the sun. As he told Gillies in the *Washington Post,* "It feels warm and you get a nice tan—but if you're out there too long, it can kill you."

Ritter told Luane Lee in the *Ottawa Citizen* that one of the principles by which he lives is life is "not to wait around to get people to love you but to really, truly spend your day doing acts of love and kindness...."

Sources

Periodicals

Boston Globe, September 16, 2002, p. B7.
Houston Chronicle, March 11, 2003, p. 8.
InStyle, March 2003, pp. 438–45.
Ottawa Citizen, August 23, 2002, p. E2.
People, December 16, 2002, pp. 127–31.
Seattle Times, July 29, 2002, p. E2.
Washington Post, December 1, 2002, p. Y7.

Online

"John Ritter," All Movie Guide, http://www.allmovie.com/cg/avg.dll?p=avg&sql=B60400~C (April 11, 2003).
"John Ritter," Internet Movie Database, http://www.imdb.com/Name?Ritter,+John (April 11, 2003).
"The Facts: John Ritter," E! Online, http://www.eonline.com/Facts/People/Bio/0,128,13317,00.html (April 11, 2003).

—Michael Belfiore

Doris Roberts

Actress

Born Doris May Roberts, November 4, 1930, in St. Louis, MO; daughter of Larry and Ann (Meltzer) Roberts; married Michael E. Cannata, June 21, 1950 (divorced, 1962); married William Goyen, November 10, 1963 (died, August, 1983); children: Michael R. (first marriage). *Education:* Attended New York University, 1950–51; attended Playhouse School of the Theater, 1953; attended Lee Strasberg Actors' Studio, New York, NY, 1956.

Addresses: Agency of the Performing Arts, 9200 Sunset Blvd., Los Angeles, CA 00069.

Career

Actress on stage, including: professional stage debut in Ann Arbor, MI, 1953; performed in summer stock, Chatham, MA, 1955; *The Time of Your Life* (Broadway debut), City Center, New York City, 1955; *The Desk Set,* Broadhurst Theatre, New York City, 1955; *The Death of Bessie Smith,* York Playhouse, New York City, 1961; *The American Dream,* York Playhouse, 1961; *Color of Darkness,* Writers Stage Theatre, New York City, 1963; *Cracks,* Writers Stage Theatre, 1963; *Marathon '33,* American National Theatre and Academy (ANTA) Theatre, New York City, 1963; understudy for Madame Girard and Eloisa, *Malcolm,* Shubert Theatre, New York City, 1966; *The Office,* Henry Miller's Theatre, New York City, 1966; *The Natural Look,* Longacre Theatre, New York City, 1967; *Last of the Red Hot Lovers,* Eugene O'Neill Theatre, New York City, 1969; *The American Dream,* Cherry Lane Theatre, New York City, 1971; *Felix,* Actors Studio, New York City, 1972; *The Opening,* summer tour, 1972; *The Secret Affairs of Mildred Wild,* Ambassador Theatre, New York City, 1972; *Bad Habits,* Astor Place Theatre, New York City, 1974; *Bad Habits,* Booth Theatre, New York City, 1974; *Ladies at the Alamo,* Actors Studio, 1975; *Mornings at Seven,* tour, 1976; *Cheaters,* Biltmore Theatre, New York City, 1978; *It's Only a Play,* Center Theatre Group, James A. Doolittle Theatre, Los Angeles, 1991–92.

Film appearances include: *Something Wild,* 1961; *Dear Heart* (uncredited), 1964; *Barefoot in the Park* (uncredited), 1968; *No Way to Treat a Lady,* 1968; *A Lovely Way to Die* (also known as *A Lovely Way to Go*), 1968; *The Honeymoon Killers* (also known as *The Lonely Hearts Killers*), 1970; *Such Good Friends,* 1971; *Little Murders,* 1971; *A New Leaf,* 1971; *The Heartbreak Kid,* 1972; *The Taking of Pelham 1–2–3,* 1974; *Hester Street,* 1975; *Blood Bath,* 1976; *Rabbit Test,* 1978; *Once in Paris,* 1978; *The Rose,* 1979; *Good Luck Miss Wykoff* (also known as *Secret Yearnings, The Shaming,* and *The Sin*), 1979; *Number One with a Bullet,* 1986; *National Lampoon's Christmas Vacation* (also known as *Christmas Vacation*), 1989; *Simple Justice,* 1989; *Honeymoon Academy* (also known as *For Better or for Worse*), 1990; *Used People,* 1992; *The Night We Never Met,* 1993; *The Grass Harp,* 1995; *My Giant,* 1998; *The Secret of NIMH 2: Timmy to the Rescue* (voice), 1998; *A Fish in the Bathtub,* 1999; *Full Circle,* 2001; *All Over the Guy,* 2001; *Dickie Roberts: Former Child Star,* 2003.

Television appearances include: *The Trouble with People* (special), NBC, 1972; *Bell, Book, and Candle* (special), 1976; *The Oath: Thirty–Three Hours in the Life of God* (special), 1976; *Mary Hartman, Mary Hartman*, 1977; *The Storyteller* (movie), NBC, 1977; *It Happened One Christmas* (movie), ABC, 1977; *Ruby and Oswald* (also known as *Four Days in Dallas*) (movie), CBS, 1978; *Angie*, ABC, 1979–80; *Jennifer: A Woman's Story* (movie), NBC, 1979; *Diary of Anne Frank* (movie), NBC, 1980; *In Trouble*, ABC, 1981; *Maggie*, ABC, 1981–82; *Love in the Present Tense* (movie), 1982; *Another Woman's Child* (movie), CBS, 1983; *Remington Steele*, NBC, 1983–87; *Me and Mrs. C.*, NBC, 1984; *A Letter to Three Wives* (movie), NBC, 1985; *California Girls* (movie), ABC, 1985; *Ordinary Heroes* (movie), ABC, 1986; *Alvin Goes Back to School* (special), 1986; *If It's Tuesday It Still Must Be Belgium* (movie), NBC, 1987; *The Fig Tree* (movie), 1987; *The Gregory Harrison Show*, CBS, 1989; *A Mom for Christmas* (movie), NBC, 1990; *The Ladies on Sweet Street*, ABC, 1990; *Blind Faith* (also known as *The Toms River Case*) (miniseries), NBC, 1990; *The Sunset Gang* (movie), 1991; *The Boys*, CBS, 1993; *The John Larroquette Show*, NBC, 1993; *A Time to Heal* (also known as *Jenny's Story* and *Out of the Darkness*) (movie), NBC, 1994; *Everybody Loves Raymond*, CBS, 1996—; *A Thousand Men and a Baby* (movie), 1997; *One True Love* (movie), 2000; *Sons of Mistletoe* (movie), 2001; *Turning Homeward* (movie), 2003.

Television guest appearances include: *Studio One*, CBS, 1952; *Naked City*, ABC, 1962; *The Defenders*, CBS, 1962–63; *Ben Casey*, ABC, 1963; *The Mary Tyler Moore Show*, CBS, 1975; *Joe and Sons*, CBS, 1975; *Medical Center*, CBS, 1975; *Baretta*, ABC, 1975; *All in the Family*, CBS, 1976; *Viva Valdez*, ABC, 1976; *The Streets of San Francisco*, ABC, 1976; *Rhoda*, CBS, 1976; *Family*, ABC, 1976; *Alice*, CBS, 1976, 1981; *Barney Miller*, ABC, 1977–80; *Blansky's Beauties*, ABC, 1977; *Soap*, ABC, 1978; *Fantasy Island*, ABC, 1979, 1981; *The Mary Tyler Moore Comedy Hour*, CBS, 1979; *The Love Boat*, ABC, 1980, 1983–84; *St. Elsewhere*, NBC, 1982; *Cagney and Lacey*, CBS, 1983, 1988; *The New Odd Couple*, ABC, 1983; *Faerie Tale Theatre*, Showtime, 1985; *Mr. Belvedere*, ABC, 1986; *You Are the Jury*, NBC, 1987; *WonderWorks*, PBS, 1987; *Perfect Strangers*, ABC, 1989; *Murder, She Wrote*, CBS, 1990, 1994; *Dream On*, HBO, 1990, 1993; *American Playhouse*, PBS, 1991; *Empty Nest*, 1991; *Step by Step*, 1994; *Walker, Texas Ranger*, CBS, 1994; *Burke's Law*, CBS, 1995; *The King of Queens*, CBS, 1999; *Touched by an Angel*, 2002; *Lizzie McGuire*, 2003.

Awards: Outer Critics Circle Award for best actress for *Bad Habits*, 1974; Emmy Award for best supporting actress in a drama series, Academy of Television Arts and Sciences, for *St. Elsewhere*, 1983; American Comedy Award for funniest female performer in a TV series, for *Everybody Loves Raymond*, 1999; Emmy Award for best supporting actress in a comedy series, Academy of Television Arts and Sciences, for *Everybody Loves Raymond*, 2001; TV Guide Comedy Award for supporting actress of the year in a comedy series, for *Everybody Loves Raymond*, 2001; Viewers for Quality TV Award for best supporting actress in a quality comedy, for *Everybody Loves Raymond*, 2001; Viewers for Quality TV Award for best supporting actress in a quality comedy, for *Everybody Loves Raymond*, 2002; Emmy Award for best supporting actress in a comedy series, Academy of Television Arts and Sciences, for *Everybody Loves Raymond*, 2002.

Sidelights

Adding to an already impressive list of stage and screen credits, Doris Roberts has become the queen of television sitcom comedy in the early 21st century. She is best known for her portrayal of a pushy, meddling mother on the hit television show *Everybody Loves Raymond* starring Ray Romano. Marie, as played by Roberts, has been described by reviewers in various ways but all of them agree that she is both funny and annoying. When asked if she resembles her television character in real life, Roberts replied to interviewer Jamie McKenna in an article for Gurney's Inn, Long Island, New York, "I hope to God for my children's sake I'm not. My character [Marie] could be a harridan; you could absolutely hate her and want to turn the knob. I walk a fine line, but I do it with love."

Roberts was born to Larry and Ann Roberts in St. Louis, Missouri, in 1930. She spoke with pride of her Russian–Jewish background to McKenna, noting that in films immigrants are often depicted as comic relief. "I wanted to be proud of my heritage. These people came over to a foreign country with nothing in their pockets and just the clothes on their backs," she told the *Independent*, as quoted by McKenna. "I love what they accomplished—adapting to an American culture, mastering a new language, working hard, and overcoming extreme difficulties. That's something to be proud of." Before she was of school age, she moved to New York City, and Roberts grew up in both the Bronx and Manhattan. By the time she was in first grade, she had written a play, and she wrote her first song at the age of seven. After graduating from high school, Roberts briefly attended New York University from 1950 to 1951. That led to the neighborhood Playhouse School of the Theater in New York City in 1953. By that time, she had met and married Michael E. Cannata. Their son, Michael R., has been her manager since the 1970s and is the father of her three grandchildren: Kelsey, Andy, and Devon. After her divorce from Cannata, Roberts married novelist William Goyen, who died in 1983. Roberts now makes her home in Los Angeles, California, but enjoys visiting her family back east, especially at the Long Island shore. She has spent many summers at the Hamptons and finds the atmosphere remarkably peaceful.

Although Roberts is now known for television work, she is a veteran of Broadway and Hollywood. Her break in the theatre came in 1955 when she appeared on Broadway in *The Time of Your Life*. Later that year she appeared in William Marchant's hit comedy *Desk Set*, about an efficiency expert and a research specialist. In 1961, she appeared in *The Death of Bessie Smith*, about the tragic death of the well-known singer. Other Broadways credits include *Marathon '33*, *Last of the Red Hot Lovers*, *The Secret Affairs of Mildred Wild*, and *Cheaters*. In addition, she won the Outer Critics Circle Award for her portrayal of Dolly Scupp in Terrence McNally's *Bad Habits*.

Roberts's film credits are many. They include 1968's *No Way to Treat a Lady*, a hit blend of romantic comedy and murder; 1970's *The Honeymoon Killers*, based on the Lonely Hearts Killers in which she played the roommate of the nurse-turned murderer; Alan Arkin's *Little Murders* in 1971 in which she played Elliott Gould's mother; 1979's *The Rose*, 1992's *Used People*; and 1995's *The Grass Harp*, based on Truman Capote's boyhood in the South. Her favorite film role was in 1975's *Hester Street*, a simple story about a young Jewish immigrant who joins her husband in New York City at the turn of the twentieth century.

During her Hollywood career, Roberts has earned the title of character actress, which she wears with pride. As she told Gloria Hillard of CNN.com, "The most important thing that I can say about myself is that I have the same passion for my work now as I did when I was 18 years old. It has never left me. If it ever leaves me, I'll quit."

Roberts has a long list of television film credits as well. Although she had many guest appearances on such shows as *Ben Casey* and *All in the Family*, she really began to make an impression on TV audiences in the 1970s. She appeared in TV movies such as *The Diary of Anne Frank*, *Ruby and Oswald*, *A Time to Heal*, and *1,000 Men and a Baby*. She received an Emmy for her guest appearance on *St. Elsewhere* as well as an Emmy nomination for her work in *Remington Steele*, which she joined in 1983. Her role on

Everybody Loves Raymond has won her much acclaim and many awards, including the 2001 and 2002 Emmys for Best Supporting Actress in a Comedy Series. The show has also won her two Viewers for Quality TV Awards for Best Supporting Actress in a Quality Comedy. The sitcom revolves around Raymond, an amiable sportswriter who copes with family situations that include his often-jealous brother and his meddling parents, played by Roberts and Peter Boyle, who happen to live across the street. They routinely drop by without an invitation and offer constant unasked-for advice. Raymond endures most of it with good nature.

When asked if she has any advice for up-and-coming actors, the veteran Roberts told McKenna that acting is hard work that takes passion and persistence in addition to talent. It's important to know whether you really want to act or merely want to be a celebrity, she explained. "You have to really study and be willing to accept rejection often," Roberts told McKenna. In May of 2003, St. Martin's Press published Roberts's book, *Are You Hungry, Dear? Life, Laughs, and Lasagna*. According to a *Booklist* review on Amazon.com, the memoir weaves together recipes from Roberts's own kitchen with anecdotes from her life in show business. Roberts also takes a passionate interest in other aspects of society. She attended a Senate hearing on the subject of ageism because she feels that the United States is the only country in the world that does not honor its elders. As a working, vital woman in her seventies, Roberts feels she has a lot to share and contribute.

Since her television work on *Everybody Loves Raymond*, Roberts has earned another title, according to Hillard at CNN.com: Everybody's Mother. She claims it is the best role she's ever had and it came at a perfect time for her. As she told Hillard, "I'm feeling good in my own skin. It takes too many years to get there. You should have that when you are a young person.... That I got it all is remarkable and wonderful. So it's a good life."

Selected writings

Are You Hungry, Dear? Life, Laughs, and Lasagna, St. Martin's Press, 2003.

Sources

Books

Who's Who in the Theatre, 17th edition, Gale Research, 1981.

Online

"*Are You Hungry, Dear? Life, Laughs, and Lasagna*," Amazon.com, http://www.amazon.com/exec/obidos/ASIN/0312312261/qid=1057686257/sr=2-1/ref=sr_2_1/104-6153531-6540754 (July 8, 2003).

"Doris Roberts," CBS.com, http://www.cbs.com/primetime/everybody_loves_raymond/bio_droberts.shtml (April 22, 2003).

"Doris Roberts: 'Everybody's mother,'" CNN.com, http://www-cgi.cnn.com/2000/showbiz/TV/09/08/emmy.doris.roberts/ (April 21, 2003).

"Doris Roberts," Internet Movie Database, http://us.imdb.com/Name?Roberts,+Doris (June 18, 2003).

"Doris Roberts," WVAH TV, http://www.wvah.com/programs/raymond/dorisroberts (April 21, 2003).

"It Seems Everybody Loves Doris Roberts," Gurney's Inn, http://www.gurneys-inn.com/Press/DorisRoberts.htm (April 20, 2003).

—*Rose Blue and Corinne J. Naden*

David Rockwell

Architect

Born David Katzenberg in 1956, in Chicago, IL; son of Maury Katzenberg and Joanne Rockwell, stepson of John Rockwell. *Education:* Syracuse University, B.S.; attended Architectural Association, London, England.

Addresses: *Office*—Rockwell Architecture, Planning and Design, P.G., 5 Union Square West, New York, NY 10003.

Career

Assistant to Broadway theater lighting designer, 1980s; founded architectural firm with partner Jay Haverson, 1984; bought Haverson out to form the Rockwell Group; designed his first full commission, Sushi Zen restaurant in New York City; designed 60 Planet Hollywood restaurants throughout the United States; designed Nobu sushi restaurant, New York City, 1994; designed Grand Central Terminal lower concourse, 1999; designed Mohegan Sun Casino; designed arena for Cirque du Soleil circus company; designed sets for Broadway musicals *The Rocky Horror Show* and *Hairspray,* 2002.

Sidelights

Known for his theatrical treatments of restaurants, hotels, casinos, stadiums, and other heavily trafficked areas, David Rockwell has been called an "entertainment architect," meaning, in the words of Belinda Luscombe, writing in *Time,* that he takes "the notion of entertainment to new places." In fact, some have stated that Rockwell cre-

ated the genre—a statement that Rockwell himself has denied, telling Ellen Lampert–Greaux in *Entertainment Design,* "I think entertainment architecture was invented back before the Roman Coliseum...." He said of his design firm, the Rockwell Group, "I don't think we invented anything; maybe we popularized something." If there is any single way in which Rockwell prefers his work to be regarded, it is that it is inventive. Not content to bring the tried–and–true architectural values to his creations, he wants his buildings to evoke an emotional response in the people who visit them, even a sense of play.

Rockwell was born in 1956, and spent the first four years of his life in Chicago, Illinois. His father, Maury Katzenberg, was killed in a plane crash when Rockwell was two years old. His mother, Joanne, subsequently married a businessman named John Rockwell, and the family relocated to New Jersey. Rockwell spent much of his childhood in Deal, New Jersey, a small town on the coast, where he and his four older brothers participated in local community theater productions.

Theater seemed to be in the blood of the Rockwell family—Rockwell's mother had started her professional life as a tap dancer who toured with the famous comedy team of Abbott and Costello, and when Rockwell was a boy, worked as a choreographer. She often directed the shows in which the Rockwell brothers appeared.

When Rockwell was ten years old, his stepfather abruptly retired from his job, packed up the family and headed south, to Guadalajara, Mexico. The transition from the subdued Jersey shore to the bright, vibrant colors of Guadalajara was to have an enormous influence on Rockwell's later work as an architect. His designs often feature abrupt transitions from a mundane, street–level reality, to a wild and vibrant interior.

Tragedy struck the Rockwell family yet again when Rockwell was 15 years old and his mother died. It seemed to the young Rockwell that the only constant in his life was change—big change—and this outlook was later to color everything he did, right down to a work style that obsessed over the fine details of his designs. As he told *Fast Company*'s Bill Breen, "You learn that the big things are uncontrollable. So you end up obsessing over all the little things."

It was while living in Mexico that Rockwell decided that he wanted to become an architect. As he told Lampert–Greaux in *Entertainment Design*, "I loved the marketplaces and started to think about public space–making. It seemed like a great way to combine my love of spaces and the theater…." After graduating from high school in Guadalajara at the age of 18, Rockwell moved to New York State to attend Syracuse University, where he studied architecture. He came to the school with no background in design. This became apparent immediately to Rockwell's professors when one of them asked Rockwell and his classmates to draw something from nature. Rockwell went outside, thought about the assignment, and came back with a drawing of his sandals. He realized he had badly misinterpreted the assignment when another student produced a drawing of the entire school campus. This episode gave Rockwell serious doubts about his decision to become an architect. But his professor prevailed upon him to stay in the program, telling him that his lack of prior design background could actually be an asset, since he had fewer bad habits to overcome than did the other, more experienced students.

Gradually, Rockwell found his own voice as a designer at the school. A breakthrough came when, asked to design a townhouse for a class assignment, Rockwell not only produced the drawings and model of the house called for in the assignment, but

a written narrative about the house, as well as biographies of the people who lived there. It was the first time that Rockwell had married the design of a structure with the story behind it, along with a strong focus on the people who would use it. This approach was to become a hallmark of Rockwell's work throughout his career.

After graduating from Syracuse, Rockwell moved on to the Architectural Association in London, England, to further his studies. Returning to the United States, he worked briefly as an assistant to a Broadway theater lighting designer before devoting himself fulltime to architecture. He quickly found that his interest in theater and his love of architecture were quite compatible, and lighting become an integral part of most of his designs. For instance, one of his more recent projects called for paper–thin sheets of wood glued to glass to be lit from behind. He later repeated the technique with thin slices of onyx, also lit from behind, to create a miniature mountain of glowing onyx for the Mohegan Sun Casino.

Rockwell first became an independent architect in 1984, when he formed a design firm with partner Jay Haverson. Rockwell later bought Haverson's half of the business to form the Rockwell Group. The firm grew to include nearly 100 designers, writers, lighting experts, modelers, and other creative professionals, all working to bring the grand visions of the company's founder to life.

Rockwell's first commissioned design as an independent architect was for a restaurant in New York called Sushi Zen. The centerpiece of the design was a silk mural covering an entire wall, backlit by neon to make it glow. The restaurant owners balked at the expense of the neon, and so Rockwell paid the $5,000 expense out of his own pocket. The result was a critically acclaimed design that, more than any other single project, was responsible for launching Rockwell's career.

Rockwell's designs have frequently been compared to stage sets, sometimes derisively. He does not deny the charge; as he told *Time*'s Luscombe, "Theater is an interesting laboratory for what we're doing as architects." In particular, Rockwell is intrigued by the notion of impermanence, and he seeks to evoke in his work the same sense of fleeting beauty intrinsic in a stage set that appears and then disappears during the course of a play or musical.

Many large commissions followed for Rockwell's firm, including designs for 60 Planet Hollywood restaurants around the United States, which put

Rockwell into a place of prominence on the national design scene. Another important project for which Rockwell has been nationally recognized is his re-design of New York City's famous Grand Central Terminal. After the terminal had fallen in a state of disrepair, the City of New York launched an extensive remodeling effort that sought to recapture the grand spirit in which the terminal was originally conceived. Rockwell was selected to remodel the terminal's lower concourse. Reopened in 1999, the lower concourse features a food court and a seating area for passengers waiting for trains.

Other notable Rockwell projects include the Kodak Theater, at which the Academy Awards were to be presented starting in 2002, and the viewing platforms at the site of the former World Trade Center in New York. Rockwell's designs have found their way back into the theater as well; he designed a building for the famed circus troupe Cirque du Soleil, designed sets for the Broadway musical *The Rocky Horror Show*, and, in 2002, he designed sets for the Broadway musical *Hairspray*.

Although lacking the financial backing of big, corporate projects, Rockwell's stage sets allow him to bring together his love of the theater and his design work as no other project can, and so he applies himself to these efforts with the same vigor he applies to any of his more permanent edifices. For his work on *Hairspray*, for instance, Rockwell designed no fewer than 18 sets, each as thoroughly researched and planned as any building project. As with all of his other projects, Rockwell started with research. In this case, the research involved studying the John Waters film on which the *Hairspray* musical was based.

To recreate the vivid realism of the film, Rockwell had a team of artists paint the Baltimore brown-stones that formed the basis of the sets in photo-realistic style. Then, to capture the wacky, off–kilter vision Waters created for his film, Rockwell had the sets constructed so that they leaned at crazy angles. All of which, Rockwell told Breen in *Fast Company*, was to "get the audience to buy in emotionally to this teenage girl's view of the world, which is very optimistic."

Rockwell has made it clear that one of the prime considerations his firm applies to accepting design projects is that at least one person on his senior staff feel a strong personal connection to it. In fact, he has said that his company turns down almost as much work as it accepts. In particular, Rockwell only accepts work from clients who have a clear vi-

sion for their project, a vision that Rockwell can use as a jumping–off point for his own inspiration. This also helps Rockwell to avoid "falling into the trap of repeating myself," as he told Clare Dowdy in *Design Week*.

Undoubtedly one of Rockwell's most inspired creations is the Mohegan Sun Casino in Uncasville, Connecticut. Extensive research into the history of the Mohegan tribe of Native Americans who own the casino resulted in a design based on the four seasons. Rockwell divided the casino's 600,000 square feet into four sections, each imbued with the aspects of one of the seasons. The seasons were then connected thematically by a "life trail." Dominating the space is a mountain of translucent onyx glowing with an inner light representing the Wombi Rock in Connecticut where the tribe originally made its home. Suspended from the ceiling of the casino are 30 million crystal beads. As with the set of *Hairspray*, Rockwell's intent with the Mohegan Sun design is to tell a story with space, and give the design a sense of drama, an "underlying intelligence," as *Fast Company*'s Breen described it.

For inspiration, Rockwell searches for the "secret narrative," as he told Breen, behind the spaces for which he designs. For the Japanese restaurant Nobu, for instance, his design was inspired by Japanese Kabuki theater. "You can't just look for interesting design devices," he told Breen. "You have to discover the heart and soul of a project. Only then will you have a fighting chance of bringing the space to life." Rockwell refuses to be quoted on where exactly his next flights of fancy will take him, saying only that he will continue to pursue projects which will allow him to try new approaches and to learn new techniques for creating drama with space.

Sources

Periodicals

Design Week, February 12, 1999, pp. 18–21.
Entertainment Design, November 1999.
Esquire, March 2002.
Fast Company, November 22, p. 77.
New York Times, December 18, 1994, p. 4; February 19, 1998, p. F1.
Time, September 16, 2002, pp. 64–67.

Online

"Rockwell Group: Who's Who: David Rockwell, President," Rockwell Group, http://www. rockwellgroup.com/printer.php3?page=aboutus/ whoswho.html&article=0 (March 2, 2003).

—*Michael Belfiore*

Bill Roedy

Tony Barson/WireImage.com

President of MTV Networks International

Born c. 1949, in Boston, MA; married; children: three. *Education:* Graduated from West Point Military Academy and Harvard Business School. *Military service:* U.S. Army, c. 1967–74.

Addresses: *Office*—MTV Networks, 1515 Broadway, New York, NY 10036. *Website*—http://www.mtv.com.

Career

Worked for HBO cable network; various positions including president, MTV Networks International, 1988—.

Sidelights

MTV, the music television network, is available to more than 375 million households—approximately one billion people—worldwide. In fact, 80 percent of the network's viewers live outside the United States. Bill Roedy, president of MTV Networks International, has almost single–handedly put it there. Roedy also is in charge of the 75–odd other channels worldwide, including VH1 and Nickelodeon operations. Global reach translates into enormous revenues for MTV's parent company, Viacom, but for Roedy it also means a unique corner on MTV's youthful viewers. Roedy, an AIDS activist who has been tireless in promoting AIDS education and fund–raising, has encouraged programming on the network that addresses AIDS, drugs, and racism targeted toward teens. *Business Week* counts Roedy as one of MTV's secrets of world domination, next to its profitable 10–34 year old demographic, the universal reach of the television medium, and the music itself.

Roedy was born in Boston, Massachusetts, but was raised in Miami, Florida. He graduated from North Miami Senior High in 1963 and then graduated from West Point Military Academy as a lieutenant. His father was a career military man, and Roedy himself was a decorated airborne ranger in Vietnam in the 1970s. After serving seven years in the Army, Roedy decided "It wasn't really for me," he said in an interview at Miami.com. "I always had a love for TV and music. I used to know the *TV Guide* by memory." Roedy got a job at HBO after earning his MBA from Harvard. "The pressure of dealing with friend or foe in Vietnam is much more than in any other business," he said in an interview with the British magazine *Campaign*. "Put that with Harvard Business School, which to me was a piece of cake. It gives you a sense of perspective."

When Roedy moved over to MTV in 1988, he helped launch the network's first overseas venture, MTV Europe. MTV Latin America followed in 1993, and the network began to capitalize on local talent, rather than just serving as an exporter of American music. Roedy has brought MTV into homes around the world virtually in person. He has met personally with such heads of state as former Israeli Prime Minister Shimon Peres, Singapore's founder Lee Kuan Yew, and Chinese leader Jiang Zemin. When Roedy met with Fidel Castro, the Cuban leader acknowledged his efforts in the campaign against AIDS and pondered the idea that Cuban kids could learn English from MTV. "We've had very little resistance once we explain that we're not in the business of exporting American culture," Roedy told *BusinessWeek*. Roedy has spent most of his adult life abroad, and has called London, England, home since the late 1980s. Even his family is international: He has dual U.S./British citizenship, his wife is Austrian/German, and their three children all have dual citizenship as well.

Roedy sends MTV producers out onto the streets of different countries to discover what is hot locally. Lena Katina and Julia Volkova were just two ordinary Russian teenagers until MTV made them one of Russia's hottest music groups: t.A.T.u. A little more than a year after the duo's first single appeared on MTV, they were courting major American record labels. Colombian rock singer Shakira went global with MTV's help—she has earned one Grammy award, two Latin Grammys, and has sold more than two million copies of her album, earning platinum status for sales. Pakistani pop singer Adnan Sami has crossed over into hostile territory on MTV—he became the most popular singer in India, a known enemy to Pakistan, after appearing on MTV India. Taiwanese pop star Jolin Tsai enjoyed the same kind of border–crossing exposure in mainland China thanks to the network. India and China are enormous markets that are hot on Roedy's list to infiltrate. "Music is an irrevocable step towards democracy," Roedy told Miami.com. "Music helps us forget conflict. It can be a vehicle that helps bring people together."

MTV's tailor–made formula results in a string of very different MTV franchises. Different videos, different programming, different on–air personalities (called VJs), and different languages produce different "attitude" and "tone," Roedy told Miami.com. "MTV Italy is very stylish. Brazil is very sexy." An animated VJ hosts MTV Japan, while MTV India plays mostly the popular Bollywood Hindi film videos, which would likely never make onto heavy rotation on American MTV. In 2001, when MTV was targeted in a *USA Today* editorial as a "vehicle of American imperialism," Roedy responded by de-fending the network, noting its celebration of "the vibrant diversity of culture globally," according to *Variety*.

As he watched friends succumb to AIDS, Roedy gradually became active in the campaign against the disease. He donates MTV's AIDS shows to any broadcaster who will air it. As a result, critical AIDS regions like South Africa and China receive AIDS–awareness programming. As chairman of the Global Business Council on HIV and AIDS (GBC), Roedy called major corporations to the mat, challenging them to step up and take action against the global AIDS crisis. "This disease is the defining humanitarian crisis of our times, and yet the corporate response to date has been inadequate given the scale of the epidemic," he is quoted as saying online at Worldbank.org. "The business community has a key role to play in the fight against HIV and AIDS…. I will do all I can to engage the private sector in this fight and scale up the global response to this pandemic—we have no choice but to get involved." While profit is the Viacom conglomerate's bottom line, Roedy has a wider view. "I always say to people, 'Money is important, it's very important, but it's not all about money,'" Roedy said on Miami.com. "How will we be judged in the future by our children and our children's children? Businesses are not doing enough. It's not an option; it's a responsibility."

Sources

Periodicals

BusinessWeek, February 18, 2001, p. 81.
Campaign (United Kingdom), August 8, 1997, p. 13.
Variety, August 13, 2001, p. 7.

Online

"MTV's other real world," Miami.com, http://www.miami.com/mld/miamiherald/entertainment/columnists/evelyn_mcdonnell/3586609.htm (October 30, 2002).
"New chair of Global Business Council on HIV and AIDS challenges companies to confront pandemic," World Band Group homepage, http://wbln0018.worldbank.org/news/pressrelease.nsf/673fa6c5a2d50a67852565e200692a79/98726fb0b6cd413d852569190063bdb9?OpenDocument (October 30, 2002).

—*Brenna Sanchez*

Al Roker

Weather forecaster and reporter

Jim Spellman/WireImage.com

Born Albert Lincoln Roker, August 20, 1954, New York, NY; son of Albert Lincoln (a bus driver and labor relations negotiator) and Isabel (a nurse) Roker; married Alice Bell, December 22, 1984 (divorced); married Deborah Roberts (a news correspondent), September 15, 1995; children: Courtney (from first marriage), Leila Ruth, Nicholas Albert. *Education:* State University of New York at Oswego, B.A., 1976.

Addresses: *Home*—315 E. 68th St. 14E, New York, NY 10021. *Office*—NBC-TV, 30 Rockefeller Plaza, New York, NY 10112.

Career

Weekday weathercaster, WTVH, Syracuse, NY, 1974–76; evening weathercaster, WTTG, Washington, D.C., 1976–78; WKYC, weekday weathercaster, Cleveland, OH, 1978–83; weekend weathercaster, WNBC, New York, NY, 1983–84; weekday weathercaster 1984–96; part–time weathercaster/ feature reporter, *Today*, NBC, 1987–96; host, *Al Roker*, CNBC, 1994–96; host, *Savage Skies*, PBS, 1995; host, *Remember This?*, MSNBC, 1996–97; president, Al Roker Productions, Inc, and RokerWare, Inc., 1996—; weathercaster/feature reporter, *Today*, NBC, 1996— ; host, *Going Places*, PBS, 1997; executive producer and host, *Al Roker's Championship Barbecue*, Food Network, 1999; executive producer and host, *Al Roker's Bahamas Reunion, Al Roker's Dining on the Strip, Al Roker's Midwest Fest*, Food Network, 2000; executive producer and host, *Al Roker's Around the World in New York City, Al Roker's Tailgating Party, Al Roker's New England Thanksgiving*, Food Network,

2001; executive producer and host, *Al Roker's Big Bad Book of Barbecue Show*, Food Network, 2002. Author of books, including: *Don't Make Me Stop This Car!*, 2000; *Al Roker's Big Bad Book of Barbecue*, 2002.

Member: American Federation of Television and Radio Artists, 1976—; Screen Actors Guild, 1996— ; American Meteorological Society Member, 1978—; AMS Seal of Approval, 1980; honorary chair, New York Race For the Cure/Three Miles of Men, 1997—; honorary celebrity committee, Guiding Eyes for the Blind, 1998; honorary chair, Greenwich House, 1998–99.

Awards: Emmy Award for best host, National Academy of Television Arts and Sciences, Cleveland chapter, 1981; Emmy Award for best on–air talent, National Academy of Television Arts and Sciences, New York chapter, 1984; best weatherman, *New York* magazine, 1985; Emmy Award for best on–air host, National Academy of Television Arts and Sciences, New York chapter, 1989; best weatherman, *New York* magazine, 1993; Distinguished Leadership Award, Fairfield University Alumni Association, 1994; Daytime Emmy Award for outstanding special class program, National Academy of Television Arts and Sciences, 1997; Distinguished Alumnus Award, State University of New York at Oswego, 1997; Emmy

Award for outstanding community service, National Academy of Television Arts and Sciences, 1997; America's Favorite Weather Reporter, National Science Foundation, 1998; Honorary Doctor of Humane Letters, State University of New York at Oswego, 1998; Daytime Emmy Award for outstanding special class program, National Academy of Television Arts and Sciences, 1998; Daytime Emmy Award for outstanding special class program, National Academy of Television Arts and Sciences, 1999; Pinnacle of Achievement Award, Salvation Army of Greater New York, 1999; Daytime Emmy Award for outstanding special class program, National Academy of Television Arts and Sciences, 2000.

Sidelights

Well-known and loved across the United States for his jovial antics and personable way, Al Roker has expanded his range beyond that of the loveable weatherman of NBC's morning news show *Today*. Besides weathercasting, Roker has hosted numerous television series, specials, and game shows, and has appeared in various sitcoms, usually playing himself. He is an author, a television producer, and the president of two companies. Roker has won seven Emmy awards. His 80 percent accuracy rate in weather forecasting earned him the American Meteorological Society's Seal of Approval in 1980. He is a man constantly on the go, whether producing specials for the Food Network, updating his personal website, or donating his time and energy to myriad charitable causes.

Born Albert Lincoln Roker on August 20, 1954, in New York City, Roker is the oldest of six children. His father, also named Albert Lincoln, was a bus driver who eventually became a labor relations negotiator for the New York City Transit Authority. Roker's mother, Isabel, worked as a nurse. Roker was raised in the Queens section of Brooklyn and credits his father with his drive to work hard.

Roker's blue-collar background made it impossible for him to attend a more prestigious university, so he ended up at State University of New York at Oswego. At the time he was interested in animation and cartooning and studied graphic communications. To fulfill the school's course requirements he took a meteorology class. It was in that class that Roker discovered an interest in science and a talent for meteorology. When Roker was a sophomore in college he started working part-time as the weekend weather forecaster for WTVH–TV in Syracuse. By the time he graduated in 1976, he had been promoted to the weekday weathercaster position.

After graduating from college, Roker landed a weathercasting job at WTTG–TV in Washington, D.C. While working there he met and came to admire Willard Scott, who took the time to mentor the rookie weathercaster, advising him to just be himself. From D.C., Roker moved on to a position in Cleveland, Ohio, working for WKYC–TV. In 1983, after five years in Cleveland, Roker was offered a position with New York's WNBC–TV as the weekend weather anchor. It didn't take long for him to prove himself and he was promoted to weekday weather forecaster in 1984. Three years later Roker began hosting the weather and also doing some reporting for the weekend edition of NBC's *Today* show, filling in for his former mentor Willard Scott. In 1996, when Scott announced his retirement Roker agreed to become the new weathercaster for the daily morning edition of the *Today* show. He continued working as the weather anchor for WNBC as well until 2000.

Roker is not one to sit on his laurels. Despite his premier position as weathercaster and reporter for *Today*, Roker saw opportunities to advance his career in a number of different directions. He hosts yearly events such as Macy's Thanksgiving Day Parade, the Tournament of Roses Parade, and NBC's Christmas at Rockefeller Center. For two years he was the host of his own show, *Al Roker*, on CNBC. He hosted the short-lived game show *Remember This?* for MSNBC. For PBS, he has hosted two acclaimed shows, *Savage Skies* and *Going Places*.

In 1996, Roker founded two companies. Al Roker Productions, Inc., was formed to develop and produce projects for television and video. Through his production company, Roker has produced close to a dozen shows, including nine specials for the Food Network. The other company he founded was RokerWare, which sells a variety of items designed by Roker including baseball caps, umbrellas, coffee mugs, and a line of baby clothes called WeatherBabies.

Roker has also made the *New York Times* bestseller list twice. In 2000, he gathered his knowledge of children and collected anecdotes for a book on parenting called *Don't Make Me Stop This Car!*. In 2002, Roker capitalized on the popularity of his Food Network series of specials and published a cookbook, *Al Roker's Big Bad Book of Barbecue*. Starting in 2001, Roker became a regular contributor to *Parents* magazine, addressing readers's questions about relationships and marriage.

Relationships and marriage are very important to Roker. He met his current wife, ABC news correspondent Deborah Roberts, in 1990. They were friends for years until Roker started taking the initiative to let her know he cared. In 1992, he watched her apartment while she was on special assignment. Seeing that her refrigerator was almost bare, he filled it with food and left flowers with a note for her return. Roberts took notice and they began dating. Roker proposed to her at the edge of the Grand Canyon, jokingly suggesting later that if she had said no, he would have jumped. The two married in New York on September 16, 1995. Together they have two children: Leila Ruth was born November 17, 1998, and Nicholas Albert was born July 18, 2002. Roker also has a daughter, Courtney, from his first marriage. He keeps his fans and other interested readers up to date on his relationships with his wife, kids, and other people through a journal he publishes online at http://www.roker.com.

Roker is also a tireless supporter of charities. He has been active in such organizations as the Children's Defense Fund, Fresh Air Fund, Read Across America, and numerous others. He is on the board of directors for the Family AIDS Network and is the honorary chair for both the Susan G. Komen Breast Cancer Foundation Race for the Cure/ Three Miles of Men and Greenwich House. The Salvation Army of Greater New York honored him in 1999 with the Pinnacle of Achievement Award, recognizing his outstanding philanthropic and humanitarian efforts. Roker has reached a level of celebrity that many might envy. There is a wax sculpture of him at the Las Vegas Madame Tussaud's Wax Museum. His easily recognized face led to his image being used in the 1997 movie *Men In Black*, where he was included with a lineup of other celebrities who are supposedly aliens posing as humans. Despite his success as a writer, producer, and designer, he told Marc Berman of *Daily Variety*, "No matter what I do in the future ... it won't, it can't, top my experience on the *Today* show."

After a lifetime of failed diets and obesity-related health problems, Roker underwent gastric bypass surgery in March of 2002. In eight months, he lost a third of his body weight. The surgery reduced his stomach from the size of a deflated football to an egg. Roker's surgeon, Dr. Marina Kurian, also bypassed a part of his small intestine, which ensured his body would absorb fewer calories and nutrients from food, which further reduced Roker's weight. As a result, Roker now takes an assortment of vitamin and mineral supplements daily. Plus, he began a regular workout regiman and a strictly portion-controlled diet, which Kurian said was important because over time, the stomach pouch would get bigger.

Sources

Periodicals

Daily Variety, January 14, 2002, p. B6.
Entertainment Weekly, January 31, 1997, p. 43.
People, October 5, 1995, p. 72; August 4, 1997, p. 124; April 12, 1999, p. 85. November 11, 2002, pp. 104-10.
PR Newswire, December 1, 1999.

Online

Al Roker.com, http://www.roker.com/ (September 6, 2002).

—*Eve M. B. Hermann*

Lea Salonga

Jim Spellman/WireImage.com

Singer and actress

Born February, 1971, in Manila, Philippines; daughter of Feliciano (an engineer and shipping company owner) and Ligaya (a homemaker) Salonga. *Education:* Attended Ateneo de Manila University, 1988.

Addresses: *Record company*—BMG/RCA Records, 1540 Broadway, Times Square, New York, NY 10036.

Career

Started acting in Manila theater productions, age eight; recorded first album, age ten; starred in own television show, *Love, Lea,* age 12; played Kim in *Miss Saigon,* London, England, 1990; played Kim in *Miss Saigon* on Broadway, New York, NY, 1991; played Eponine in *Les Miserables* on Broadway, 1992; performed singing voice of Jasmine in animated film *Aladdin,* 1992; played Eliza Doolittle in *My Fair Lady,* Manila, Philippines, 1993; appeared in *Into the Woods,* Singapore, 1994; starred in television movie *Redwood Curtain,* 1995; appeared in Broadway revival of *Grease* and Filipino film *I Wish It Happens Again;* performed singing voice of title character in animated film *Mulan,* 1998; reappeared in *Miss Saigon* on Broadway, 1999; starred in *They're Playing Our Song,* Singapore, 1999; released double album *Live, Vol. 1* and *Live, Vol. 2,* 2000; appeared in *They're Playing Our Song,* Manila, 2000; starred in *Flower Drum Song,* Los Angeles, CA, 2001; starred in *Flower Drum Song* on Broadway, 2002.

Awards: Lawrence Olivier Award for best actress in a musical, for *Miss Saigon,* 1990; Presidential Merit Medal, presented by Philippine President Corazon Aquino, 1990; Drama Desk Award for best actress in a musical, for *Miss Saigon,* 1991; Antoinette Perry (Tony) Award for best actress in a musical, League of American Theaters and Producers and the American Theatre Wing, for *Miss Saigon,* 1991; Drama Desk Award for best actress in a musical, for *Miss Saigon,* 1991; New York critics's Outer Circle Award for best actress in a musical, for *Miss Saigon,* 1991; Theatre World Award for best actress in a musical, for *Miss Saigon,* 1991.

Sidelights

The Philippine–born singer and actress Lea Salonga is best known for originating the role of Kim in the 1990 London stage hit *Miss Saigon.* Renowned for her enchanting voice, Salonga went on to bewitch Broadway audiences with the same show, earning every major New York drama award, including an Antoinette Perry (Tony) Award for Best Actress in 1991. She went on to perform the singing voices in two animated Disney films, *Aladdin* and *Mulan.*

Considered a national treasure in her native Philippines, Salonga was a child star in Manila, where she performed in theater and on television and released several successful albums. While Salonga has continued to sing and act on Broadway and internationally, she remains virtually synonymous with *Miss Saigon*, the long–running hit that launched her career.

Born in February of 1971, Salonga was a child of privilege who grew up in the suburbs of Manila. Her father, Feliciano, an engineer, served as a merchant marine officer before owning a successful shipping company. Her homemaker mother, Ligaya ("Joy" in English)—who later became Salonga's personal manager—was assisted by a maid and a driver. Salonga grew up with her younger brother and an adopted younger sister.

Young Salonga always knew she could sing; at age three she would sing along to television shows. When one of her cousins joined a theater group, Salonga grew interested in performing. The cousin helped eight–year–old Salonga land an audition for *The King and I*, in which she won her first part, as one of the children at court. "I didn't want to come down from the stage," she told Rita Zekas of the *Toronto Star*. The next year, she landed her first lead role, in a Manila production of *Annie*. When the young actress memorized the show's entire script, the director dubbed her "the stage computer." An accomplished student, Salonga followed a busy schedule of school, homework, and nighttime rehearsals. "There were always other kids to play with backstage," she told Hannah Pandian of Singapore's *Straits Times*.

At age ten Salonga recorded the first of several hit albums in the Philippines. "It was called *Small Voice* because I was so young, but in reality I could sing pretty big and loud," she told Eirik Knutzen of the *Toronto Star*. A child star, she appeared in such Manila stage productions as *Cat on a Hot Tin Roof* and *Fiddler on the Roof*. By age 12 she had her first national television show, *Love, Lea*. Her younger brother, Gerald, costarred in this musical variety show.

While she loved performing, young Salonga—once dubbed the Shirley Temple of the Philippines—felt that singing and acting would not provide enough income in the long run. She initially set her sights on a career in medicine, and even went so far as to finish one year of pre–med coursework at Ateneo de Manila University. But the London stage had other plans for her.

At age 17 Salonga auditioned for the lead in the London musical *Miss Saigon*, competing in a nine–month worldwide search that involved some 1,200 candidates. In this blockbuster show, an updated re–imagining of the Puccini opera *Madama Butterfly*, she won the role of Kim, an orphaned Vietnamese girl who must resort to prostitution in order to survive. The show opened in September 1989 to rave reviews, catapulting Salonga to stage fame. London reviewers hailed the 19–year–old actress as "a talent of shattering emotional depths" and "a remarkable find," according to Linda Joffee of the *Christian Science Monitor*.

Miss Saigon marked Salonga's first time performing outside of her native Philippines. Facing her first standing ovation in a theater of 2,500 spectators, she was stunned. "My jaw dropped," she told Joffee of the *Christian Science Monitor.* "I couldn't move. I didn't think I would have that kind of effect." The teenager also had to adjust to aspects of the performing life that conflicted with her conservative upbringing. Acting in love scenes and wearing call girls's clothes were challenges to Salonga, who was raised a Roman Catholic. Yet Salonga's father encouraged her; Salonga recounted to Pandian in the *Straits Times* that her father said, "They won't remember you for your skimpy clothes, they'll remember you for killing yourself onstage." And remember her they did. In 1990 Salonga won Britain's prestigious Lawrence Olivier Award for Best Actress in a Musical. As Salonga recalled years later to CNN.com, "Everything that came after [*Miss Saigon*] came as a result of that."

Soon plans were under way to bring *Miss Saigon* to New York City's Broadway. Salonga then found herself in the midst of a casting dispute between the American union Actors Equity and the show's British producer, Cameron Mackintosh. Actors Equity wanted to replace Salonga with an Asian–American actress, while Mackintosh lobbied on Salonga's behalf. Ultimately, Mackintosh brought the case to an arbitrator, who ruled in his favor. Salonga went to New York along with her British costar, Jonathan Pryce.

Opening on Broadway in April of 1991, *Miss Saigon* was a critical success, with both Salonga and Pryce winning Drama Desk and Tony awards. The show impressed audiences with its flashy special effects—including a scene in which a helicopter lands onstage. Soon *Miss Saigon* became a favorite of tourists. Its $100 ticket price set new records on Broadway. Salonga stayed with the show until March of 1992. Although she played Kim on Broadway for less than a year, Salonga had achieved international fame in the role. She would go on to cultivate a busy and versatile career as a singer and actress. But her name would always be synonymous with Miss Saigon and the title role that she had originated.

After she left the show, Salonga received several offers for film roles, but she demurred, claiming to Zekas of the *Toronto Star,* "I'm more of a singer than an actress." Salonga's recordings included a *King and I* soundtrack; she signed a contract with Atlantic Records in the early 1990s. After a brief rest from the stage, Salonga appeared in the 1992 Broadway production of *Les Miserables.* She played the part of Eponine, the French character who falls in love and dies unrequited. "It's a role I love," Salonga told Zekas of the *Toronto Star.* "It breaks down a few walls for Asian actors. Only Caucasians have been asked to do this role before now."

Also in 1992 Salonga performed the singing voice of Jasmine, the heroine of Disney's animated movie *Aladdin.* Her song "A Whole New World," from the *Aladdin* soundtrack, won an Oscar for Best Song in 1993. At the Academy Awards ceremony, she appeared live to sing the tune.

Other projects for Salonga included a return to Manila to play the female lead, Eliza Doolittle, in a 1993 Repertory Philippines production of *My Fair Lady.* When the Malaysian prime minister, Datuk Seri Dr. Mahathir Mohamad, wished to see her sold-out performance during a visit to Manila, the theater's managers constructed a makeshift "throne" for him.

The following year Salonga appeared in a Singapore production of Stephen Sondheim's Broadway hit musical *Into the Woods.* The play interwove such fairy tales as "Cinderella," "Jack and the Beanstalk," and "Little Red Riding Hood." Salonga played the part of a mischievous witch. During rehearsals, she flew back to the United States, where she had been granted residency, to sing for U.S. President Bill Clinton at a Democratic National Committee celebration.

Known for her wholesome character, Salonga lived with her mother in a Manhattan apartment well into her 20s. The deeply religious actress attended mass every Sunday and disliked going out. Always chaperoned on dates, Salonga preferred to invite men to a meal home-cooked by her mother.

Salonga appeared in 1995's *Redwood Curtain,* a television adaptation of Langford Wilson's Pulitzer Prize-winning play about an adopted Asian-American woman looking for her roots in the redwood forests of California. Playing the lead character, Geri Riordan, Salonga costarred with John Lithgow, who played Geri's adoptive father, Laird Riordan.

Other mid–1990s projects for Salonga included a few months in the Broadway revival of *Grease,* as well as the motion picture *I Wish It Happens Again.* The latter—a Filipino production and a Tagalog-language film—was shot in a mountain resort about six hours from Manila. Speaking Tagalog proved challenging for Salonga, for whom English was a first language. "I spoke [English] at home and in school," she told Knutzen of the *Toronto Star.* "My parents come from provinces separated by an ocean and could only communicate in English; I wasn't exposed to Tagalog until high school and college."

In 1998 Salonga performed the singing voice of the title character in Disney's animated film *Mulan.* Admired by critics, *Mulan* is the story of a young Chinese woman who disguises herself as soldier fighting to save her country. "I liked the story because it is about an Asian girl who became a hero—not a guy, a girl," Salonga told Helmi Yusof of the *Straits Times.* "It's very empowering for a lot of Asian girls to see that."

In spring of the following year, Salonga returned to the role of Kim in Broadway's *Miss Saigon.* "I'm not a kid anymore; I'm a woman," the 27-year-old actress told Valerie Gladstone of the *Plain Dealer.* "I no longer act the part of Kim. I live it." By fall, however, Salonga was off to new projects, including the star role in the Singapore Repertory Theatre (SRT)'s *They're Playing Our Song.* In this reprise of the 1977 Broadway musical by Neil Simon, she played Sonia, a New York lyricist. Salonga told the press that she enjoyed working with SRT because the company gave her the opportunity to play roles usually reserved for Caucasian performers.

Salonga would also appear in a Manila production of *They're Playing Our Song* in 2000. Just prior to her return to Philippine theater, she released a double album, *Live, Vol. 1* and *Live, Vol. 2.* The recording included songs ranging from show tunes (including "Tomorrow" from *Annie*) to pop hits (such as Cyndi Lauper's "True Colors"). To kick off the album, she performed in a solo concert in Manila, collaborating with her brother, Gerard, who served as the concert's music director.

In 2001 Salonga starred in the Los Angeles debut of *Flower Drum Song,* a remake of the 1958 Rodgers and Hammerstein musical. Once considered offensive to Asian Americans, the plot and dialogue of *Flower Drum Song* were completely overhauled by writer David Henry Hwang. Salonga played Mei-Li, a young Chinese immigrant who comes into her own in 1950s San Francisco. The show featured a pan–Asian cast—a fact that particularly delighted Salonga. "[Salonga] has one of the most engaging voices of musical comedy," the show's producer Benjamin Mordecai told CNN.com. "When you hear that voice you are just totally lost in it." Yet the star's mellifluous voice could not save the musical, which opened on Broadway to unfavorable reviews in the autumn of 2002 and closed in March of 2003. Leaving New York's Virginia Theater, *Flower Drum Song* would begin a national tour in autumn of 2003. The same year, Salonga announced that she was engaged to her Japanese–Chinese–American boyfriend, Robert Chien.

Meanwhile, she continues to adhere to a busy schedule of acting and singing commitments. Salonga remains a star in her native Philippines, but only true Broadway buffs recognize her face in the United States and beyond. Many will always associate her name with 1991's stage hit *Miss Saigon*. "I feel flattered by [the association]," Salonga told Karen D'Souza of the Montreal *Gazette*. "There are so many actors out there wishing they could become associated with a part like that, something they will be identified with forever. Like Carol Channing and Dolly. I'm lucky I got to experience that at such a young age."

Selected discography

(Contributor) *Aladdin* (soundtrack), Disney, 1992.

(Contributor) *The King and I* (soundtrack), Polygram, 1992.

Lea Salonga, Atlantic, 1993.

(Contributor) *Miss Saigon [London Cast Highlights]*, Geffen, 1993.

In Love, BMG, 1998.

By Heart, Mister C, 1999.

Live, Vol. 1 and *Live, Vol. 2*, BMG, 2000.

The Broadway Concert, BMG, 2002.

Sources

Periodicals

BusinessWorld (Philippines), June 9, 2000.
Christian Science Monitor, April 16, 1990, p. 13.
Daily News (New York), February 25, 2003, p. 42.
Gazette (Montreal, Canada), October 14, 2001, p. A11.
New York Times, April 28, 2000, p. E3.
Plain Dealer, March 21, 1999, p. 5I.
Straits Times (Singapore), January 12, 1994, p. 9; March 12, 1994, p. 1; October 1, 1999, p. 3.
Times (London, England), October 1, 1989; June 4, 1991.
Toronto Star, January 2, 1991, p. B8; May 31, 1991, p. D8; May 10, 1992, p. C1; April 23, 1995, p. C11.

Online

"Anonymous Salonga Sings Loud And Clear," CNN.com, http://www.cnn.com/2002/SHOW BIZ/Music/10/19/wkd.lea.salonga.ap/index. html (October 22, 2002).

"Lea Salonga," *All Music Guide*, http://www. allmusic.com (March 2, 2003).

—Wendy Kagan

Anita Shreve

Author

Born c. 1946, in Dedham, MA; married to John Osborn (an insurance agent); children: five. *Education:* Graduated from Tufts University.

Addresses: *Agent*—Virginia Barber, 101 Fifth Ave., New York, NY 10003. *Home*—Western Massachusetts.

Career

Worked as a high school teacher; served as a deputy editor for *Viva* magazine, Kenya, for three years in the 1970s; short stories she wrote early in her career include "Silence at Smuttynose," later the basis for her 1997 novel, *The Weight of Water,* and "Past the Island, Drifting" appeared in the *Ball State Forum,* 1975; freelance writer after 1986 and contributor to *Seventeen, Newsweek, Us* and the *New York Times Magazine;* first books were child–care tomes co–authored with Dr. Lawrence Balter; first novel, *Eden Close,* published by Harcourt, 1989; several of her subsequent books have been made into television and feature films. Has also taught writing at Amherst College, Amherst, MA.

Awards: O. Henry Prize for short fiction, for "Past the Island, Drifting," 1976; New England Book Award for Fiction, New England Booksellers' Association, for *The Weight of Water,* 1998.

Sidelights

Anita Shreve's popular fiction gained her a tremendous following in the 1990s. Shreve's heroines are strong, intelligent women searching for an-swers about the world and their place in it, especially in regard to love and family—a universal theme that seems to have struck a chord with readers. Shreve was a journalist and author of nonfiction books for several years before garnering critical attention and frequent appearances on the *New York Times* bestseller lists with novels like 1995's *Resistance.* When asked in an interview with *Writer's* Robert Allen Papinchak about the themes of love, passion, and betrayal in her work, Shreve admitted they intrigued her on several levels. "I don't examine this too closely, for fear of defusing the very thing that makes me want to write," she reflected. "I can tell you, however, that the arena of love is a wonderful place in which to place characters. It's something extraordinary that happens to ordinary people. It's often, as well, a terrific testing ground for moral character."

Shreve is a native of Dedham, Massachusetts, and grew up in the 1950s. She was an avid reader as a child, and was particularly drawn to the novels of L. Frank Baum, whose fantasy fiction inspired the classic 1939 film *The Wizard of Oz.* As a teen, she found herself drawn to the insightful, heroine–driven works of early twentieth century writer Edith Wharton. She studied English at Tufts University outside of Boston, and once took a writing course there taught by the poet Maxine Kumin. Penning her first short stories in the 1970s, Shreve found success when "Past the Island, Drifting," appeared in the *Ball State Forum* and won her an O. Henry Prize for short fiction in 1976.

Shreve lived in Nairobi, Kenya, for a three–year period in the 1970s. There she helped a friend who published a magazine called *Viva,* and met her husband–to–be. Returning to the United States, Shreve married, began a family, and enjoyed an increasingly successful freelance career. She wrote for *Newsweek, Seventeen,* and the *New York Times,* and her first few books were child–care tomes co-authored with Dr. Lawrence Balter in the mid–1980s. Some of Shreve's articles for the *New York Times Magazine* attracted favorable notice and led to her first nonfiction book as a solo author, *Remaking Motherhood: How Working Mothers Are Shaping Our Children's Future,* published by Viking in 1987. Interviews she conducted for her next work, 1989's *Women Together, Women Alone: The Legacy of the Consciousness–Raising Movement* led, indirectly, to a desire to explore some of these themes in a fictional setting. As she explained in a *Publishers Weekly* interview with Christina Frank, "I always had this fantasy that one of these days I would go back to writing fiction," Shreve said. "Fiction is my first love. I said to myself, 'You're either going to do it now, or it's not going to happen.'"

Shreve's first novel, *Eden Close,* appeared close on the heels of *Women Together, Women Alone* in 1989. Its story centers around Andrew and Eden, friends since their childhood in rural upstate New York. They almost become romantically involved as teens, but Eden's life changes abruptly one day when a home intruder sexually assaults her, kills her father, and leaves her blind from a shotgun blast. Andrew returns to her life several years later and tries to help Eden regain some ballast in her tragic life. Violence against women and its repercussions also served as a theme in Shreve's next work, *Strange Fits of Passion.* In this 1991 novel, Shreve weaves her fictional tale of a domestic–abuse survivor, Mary Amesbury, around a series of purported transcripts. Mary, formerly Maureen, fled an abusive life after killing her husband, and provides an account of her life to a reporter named Helen Scofield. Settling with her child under a new identity in a town on the coast of Maine, Mary's new life is destroyed when her whereabouts are betrayed by a jealous neighbor, and Scofield's account proves a self–serving, not entirely accurate one. *Publishers Weekly* contributor Sybil Steinberg liked the way Shreve's "elegiac, portentous prose provides effective pacing," and termed it "insightful and moving."

As for her own career as a journalist, Shreve found working in fiction more gratifying personally. "Quite simply, I have never felt as authentic as a journalist as I have as a novelist," she declared to Frank in *Publishers Weekly.* "Ironically, although a novel is fiction, it is easier, I believe, to tell the truth through fiction than through journalism." She wrote another novel for Harcourt, her longtime publisher, but after *Where or When* appeared in 1993 the house decided to cut back on its fiction list. A Boston publisher, Little, Brown, was interested in Shreve's work and offered her a new contract.

The first title from Shreve to appear under the Little, Brown logo was *Resistance,* published in 1995. The story is set during World War II and centers around Belgian housewife Claire Daussois, who is also a secret member of the underground resistance movement attempting to undermine the German Nazi occupying regime. When an American pilot, Ted Brice, is shot down near her farm, Claire hides the pilot in her attic and nurses him back to health; the two fall in love, but then her husband Henri is betrayed to the Nazis. "With deceptive simplicity and superb control, Shreve evokes the impersonal horrors of wartime and its heartbreaking personal tragedies," remarked a *Publishers Weekly* contributor.

Shreve's next novel, *The Weight of Water,* also won positive critical accolades. In it, photojournalist Jean Janes heads to a New England island called Smuttynose where a horrific double murder took place in 1873. On the boat trip are Jean's husband, Thomas—a renowned poet—their five–year–old daughter, and Jean's brother–in–law, Rich, and his girlfriend, Adaline. There is trouble brewing in Jean's marriage, and tensions on the trip are exacerbated by the flirtations between Thomas and Adaline. Yet Shreve also tells a parallel story about the two Norwegian immigrant sisters and the events leading up to the murder. Jean finds evidence in a local museum hinting that the wrong person may have been convicted, but her intuition cannot rescue the inevitable tragedy brewing in her own life. "Shreve has written the most moving book of her career so far," noted *San Francisco Chronicle* critic Rebecca Radner. "She makes us see how, acted on by tumultuous feelings, we may choose to pretend we are not accountable; yet even when wronged by others, we must reach for the uncompromising awareness that alone can save us."

Disaster also strikes in the first pages of *The Pilot's Wife,* Shreve's 1998 novel. A passenger jet explodes off the coast of Ireland, killing all aboard, and Kathryn Lyons is horrified to learn that her husband, its pilot, may have taken the plane down himself in an act of suicide. She soon learns that Jack harbored many secrets from her, including a mistress overseas. Kathryn has a difficult time facing the answers that her sleuthing has uncovered. Here, noted *Booklist* reviewer Joanne Wilkinson, Shreve "[weaves] a compelling plot through which she explores deeper issues, such as intimacy and grief." The book's theme of calculated deception struck such a chord that some months after it was published, television personality Oprah Winfrey called Shreve to tell her she had selected it for her popular "Oprah's Book Club" monthly feature—which would bring an appearance on *The Oprah Winfrey Show* for Shreve and concurrent jump in sales for her latest title. Winfrey told the author on the phone, according to *Record* writer Jane Gordon, "You are not going to believe how many women call in who this has happened to." When Shreve appeared to discuss her book, she was joined by five women who had experienced a shock about their husbands that was similar to the one in the book. The author admitted that such dual–life tales seemed to resonate with other readers as a universal theme as well. "How do you ever know you really know a person?" Shreve mused in an interview with Linda Du-Val for the Colorado Springs *Gazette*. "You can't, really. All you can know is what the other person lets you know."

The Pilot's Wife sold more than two million copies in paperback, and was made into a CBS movie that aired in 2002. Shreve's previous work, *The Weight of Water*, was also made into a telefilm that starred Catherine McCormack, Sean Penn, and Elizabeth Hurley, while *Resistance* was slated to become a feature film starring Bill Paxton and Julia Ormond. Shreve's next book, *Fortune's Rocks*, took place exactly 101 years before its 2000 publication. Its plot is a coming–of–age tale for one Olympia Biddeford, a 15–year–old girl from a wealthy Boston family. At her family's summer home on the coast of New Hampshire, she meets and unexpectedly falls in love with a physician friend of her father's. The ensuing affair scandalizes the town and results in pregnancy; she is forced to give the child up for adoption as well as her plans to attend Wellesley College because of the transgression. Later, Olympia attempts to win custody of her son. "The rigid decorum of the era is conveyed with the clarity of Edith Wharton," noted a *Publishers Weekly* critique, "and reflected in ... the moral code that regarded unwed mothers as despicable outcasts denied even the most minimal consolations of the social contract." A contributor to the *Seattle Post–Intelligencer* also gave it a terrific review, asserting that "there's pleasure in the conventional power of *Fortune's Rocks*. At its best—in the trial scenes, in the moral dilemma posed by the trial's conflict and in Olympia's stalwart character—it evokes those elemental emotions that are reborn in every new reader and that remain like bedrock in the most sophisticated of readers. Some stories never grow tiresome, and in *Fortune's Rocks*, Shreve has captured one of them and kept it alive and pacing in its cage."

Shreve revisited the story of the Janes family in her 2001 novel, *The Last Time They Met*. It centers on the now–widowed poet, Thomas, and an unrequited love from his teenage years. Some of it Shreve based on her time in Africa, during a section where Thomas and Linda meet again in their mid–twenties. Her next novel, *Sea Glass*, appeared the following year to, once again, an enthusiastic critical reception. The story begins with newlyweds Sexton and Honora Beecher, who buy a derelict house on the New Hampshire coast in the late 1920s. Sexton loses his job as a typewriter salesperson after the great Wall Street crash of 1929, and is forced to take a brutal job in a nearby textile mill. The couple become involved in a nascent unionizing movement at the mill, which turns ugly—but Honora is also dismayed to learn that her husband is not the honest man she thought she married. A *Publishers Weekly* critic termed this "one of Shreve's best," declaring that the author "is skilled at interpolating historical background, and her descriptions of the different social strata ... enhance a touching story about loyalty and betrayal, responsibility and dishonor."

Three of Shreve's novels—*The Pilot's Wife, Fortune's Rocks*, and *Sea Glass*—have been inspired by a house in Maine she finds particularly intriguing. A photograph of it hangs above her writing desk at her own home in western Massachusetts. It is, as readers of her work will know, an elaborate white clapboard dwelling with a mansard roof. "It had a real serenity," she told *New York Times* writer Roland Merullo. "At first, all I wanted to do was live there. Then, at a party, I overheard a snippet of conversation about an airline crash, and I began to imagine the pilot's wife. And there was this one split second in time when that idea came together with the house." It was a sentiment that she echoed in the interview with *Writer*'s Papinchak. "Stories unfold in houses," Shreve mused. "A house with any kind of age has dozens of stories to tell.... Sometimes, when I'm sitting by the hearth in the kitchen, I think about the people who have gone before me—the baby who was born in the room adjacent to the kitchen, the woman who cried at the inattentions of her husband in the upstairs bedroom, the girl who died of diphtheria croup in what is now my son's room. The house is full of stories."

Shreve's tenth novel, *All He Ever Wanted*, was published in 2003. Another work of historical fiction, this portrait of a Victorian–era American marriage is told in flashback: onetime professor of literature Nicholas Van Tassel is writing his memoirs aboard a train in 1933. He recalls the day he first met his wife, as he fled a hotel restaurant fire in the small New Hampshire college town where he lived and taught. Etna Bliss is a governess possessing hints of a more exciting past, and Van Tassel quickly becomes enamored of her. She marries him after warning him it will be a loveless match, but jealousy drives her husband to a desperate and treacherous act. "Shreve, with her renowned inventiveness, plays with time, moving the story now forward and now back, using this transference as an instrument of suspense," noted William Dieter in a review for the *Rocky Mountain News*.

Selected writings

(With Lawrence Balter) *Dr. Balter's Child Sense: Understanding and Handling the Common Problems of Infancy and Early Childhood*, Simon & Schuster (New York City), 1985.

(With Balter) *Dr. Balter's Baby Sense*, Poseidon Press (New York, NY), 1985.

(With Patricia Lone) *Working Woman: A Guide to Fitness and Health*, Mosby (St. Louis, MO), 1986.

Remaking Motherhood: How Working Mothers Are Shaping Our Children's Future, Viking (New York, NY), 1987.

(With Balter) *Who's in Control? Dr. Balter's Guide to Discipline without Combat*, Poseidon Press, 1988.

Women Together, Women Alone: The Legacy of the Consciousness–Raising Movement, Viking, 1989.

Eden Close, Harcourt (New York, NY), 1989.

Strange Fits of Passion, Harcourt, 1991.

Where or When, Harcourt, 1993.

Resistance, Little, Brown (Boston, MA), 1995.

The Weight of Water, Little, Brown, 1997.

The Pilot's Wife, Little, Brown, 1998.

Fortune's Rocks, Little, Brown, 2000.

The Last Time They Met, Little, Brown, 2001.

Sea Glass, Little, Brown, 2002.

All He Ever Wanted, Little, Brown, 2003.

Sources

Periodicals

Antioch Review, Spring 1998, p. 243.
Atlantic Monthly, April 2001, p. 105.
Booklist, January 1, 1997, p. 822; May 1, 1998, p. 1504.
Denver Post, April 8, 2001, p. G5.
Gazette (Colorado Springs, CO), February 6, 2000.
Library Journal, March 15, 2003, p. 117.
Los Angeles Times, April 14, 2002, p. TV3.
Milwaukee Journal Sentinel, April 1, 2001, p. 6.
New York Times, April 25, 2002, p. F1; November 1, 2002, p. E14.
Publishers Weekly, January 25, 1991, p. 47; April 12, 1991, p. 40; March 22, 1993, p. 68; March 6, 1995, p. 57; March 16, 1998, p. 52; September 13, 1999, p. 14; October 4, 1999, p. 61; December 6, 1999, p. 24; January 3, 2000, p. 40; March 19, 2001, p. 74; February 11, 2002, p. 160; April 22, 2002, p. 26; March 17, 2003, p. 50.
Psychology Today, October 1987, p. 69.
Record (Hackensack, NJ), March 30, 2000.
Rocky Mountain News, April 12, 2002, p. 29D; April 4, 2003, p. 25D.
San Francisco Chronicle, January 19, 1997, p. 5; May 3, 1998, p. 8.
Seattle Post–Intelligencer, January 21, 2000, p. 17.
Seattle Times, January 2, 2000, p. M12.
Writer, November 2001, p. 26.

Online

Contemporary Authors Online, Gale, 2002.

—Carol Brennan

M. Night Shyamalan

Filmmaker

Born Manoj Nelliyattu Shyamalan, August 6, 1970, in Pondicherry, India; son of Nelliate C. (a cardiologist) and Jayalakshmi (an obstetrician) Shyamalan; married Bhavna (a child psychologist), 1993; children: two. *Education:* New York University, B.F.A. in filmmaking, 1992.

Addresses: *Production company*—Blinding Edge Pictures, 100 Four Falls Corporate Center, Ste. 102, Conshohocken, PA 19428.

Career

Released first feature film that he wrote and directed, *Praying With Anger*, 1992; made first screenplay sale to a major movie studio, *Labor of Love*, 1994; released second feature as director and writer, *Wide Awake*, 1996; released *The Sixth Sense* as writer and director, 1999; screenwriter for *Stuart Little*, 1999; released *Unbreakable* as writer and director, 2000; released *Signs* as writer and director, 2002.

Awards: Distinguished Alumni Award, Episcopal Academy, 2001; Governor's Award for the Arts, State of Pennsylvania, 2002; Kodak Award, ShowEast Convention, 2002.

Sidelights

A Hollywood auteur who directs as well as writes major motion pictures, M. Night Shyamalan released one of the top–grossing films of all time, *The Sixth Sense*, in 1999. The film starred Bruce Willis and Haley Joel Osment as a child psychologist and a boy, respectively, coming to grips with death. The film combined strong writing and solid directing with outstanding performances to create one of that year's top–grossing films, second only to *Star Wars: The Phantom Menace*. *The Sixth Sense*, directed by Shyamalan when he was 28 years old, grossed more than $700 million, and it was nominated for six Academy awards, including best director, best screenplay, and best picture.

M. Night Shyamalan (pronounced SHAW–ma–lawn) was born in India to two doctors, mother Jayalakshmi Shyamalan, an obstetrician, and father Nelliate C. Shyamalan, a cardiologist. Then living in the Philadelphia, Pennsylvania, area in the United States, Shymalan's parents were visiting family in India when their son was born.

Shymalan grew up in the wealthy Penn Valley area of Philadelphia, and attended a private Catholic school, Episcopal Academy—not because his parents were Catholics, but because they valued the discipline such an education would give their son. He discovered a passion for filmmaking at the age of eight, when he was given a Super–8 movie camera. From then on he was hooked, making movies whenever he got the chance. He made a total of 45 amateur movies before becoming a professional filmmaker.

After graduating from high school, Shymalan attended New York University's Tisch School of the Arts, where he enrolled in the undergraduate film program. He had also been admitted to medical school, and his parents had hoped that he would follow in their footsteps and choose to become a doctor. As Shymalan said in the *Sydney Morning Herald,* "They weren't too happy that I wanted to go into movies although I think they saw it coming because I had been dabbling in film–making.... There was a certain icy silence when I chose film school in New York."

It was at New York University (NYU) that Shymalan came up with the easily–pronounced middle name, Night. "It's an American Indian name," he told Daryn Kagan on the Cable News Network show *CNN Live Today.* "At the time, I was studying American Indian culture, and I feel very close to that culture, the spirituality of it, the nature, the gentleness and the simpleness of it. And so that name I read, and I just thought, wow, I really connect to that, and now, as an adult, I feel like, gosh, it ... was meant to be, I think." It was also at NYU that Shymalan met his future wife, classmate Bhavna, now a child psychologist.

The first film Shymalan wrote and directed coming out of film school was *Praying with Anger,* a partly autobiographical piece that dealt with his return as an adult to the country of his birth. He raised the money to complete the project himself. Not only did he write, direct, and produce the feature, but he starred in it as well. It was shot in India, which allowed him to cut costs. Next, Shymalan wrote and sold a screenplay called *Labor of Love* to a major Hollywood studio. The film, about a man who sets out to show how much he loved his recently deceased wife by walking across the United States, was never produced.

Shymalan's next project was to write and direct *Wide Awake,* which was released in 1998 to a lukewarm public reception; the film was one of the smallest–grossing films of the year. It featured a boy in fifth grade who is prompted to wonder about the existence of God after his grandfather dies. Shymalan was more than vindicated, though, by the release of *The Sixth Sense* in 1999. The film was enormously popular, with a twist ending that prompted audiences to view it more than once to try to pick up clues they might have missed in the first viewing. The year 1999 also saw the release of a feature Shymalan had written, a screen adaptation of the children's book *Stuart Little* by E. B. White. This film also opened to critical and box office success.

The year following the release of *The Sixth Sense,* Shyamalan followed up his new–found success with another supernatural thriller, *Unbreakable,* which he also wrote and directed. This film also starred Willis, this time as a troubled husband and father with a powerful secret he has managed to keep even from himself, repressing memories of surviving a potentially deadly automobile crash as a young man. His ability to survive any physical calamity becomes impossible to ignore, however, when he survives a train wreck unscathed.

Inspired by comic book superheroes, the film establishes Willis as a force for good opposed only by a supervillain. "Comic books are modern–day mythology," Shymalan told the *Daily News of Los Angeles*'s Bob Strauss, "one of the many ways that people across time and [in] different countries have told stories. In Japan, in India, everywhere, comic books are still alive and well, and it was an interesting, untapped area of culture that hadn't really been delved into in a serious way. And I like taking things that are unbelievable and try to make you believe in them by the end of the two hours."

In order to achieve this believability, Shymalan took the unusual step of shooting the film in sequence, so that the actors and the crew could follow the story as it unfolded, just the way the audience would. Normally a film is shot out of sequence, with the order of the shooting dictated by the location of each scene—scenes that take place in one location are shot all at once. "It was quite a feat," Shymalan told Strauss, but, "I needed to keep a nice, clean line for Bruce [Willis] to follow in the arc of a belief."

So impressed were the stars of *Unbreakable,* Bruce Willis and Samuel L. Jackson, with Shymalan's last film, *The Sixth Sense,* that they agreed to act in *Unbreakable* even before they read the script. "I would like to do all my films with Night," Willis told Strauss. "Unfortunately, he needs to take a little time off in between." Jackson agreed with Willis, telling Strauss, "I read a lot of things that people tell me they've written for me that I wish they hadn't. But this [film] was a total compliment of who I am and what I try to do as an actor." In keeping with Shyamalan's increasing pull in Hollywood, *Unbreakable* earned the filmmaker $5–10 million (sources differ on the exact amount). In addition to writing and directing the film, he also acted as producer.

Following *Unbreakable,* Shyamalan released *Signs,* a UFO thriller staring Mel Gibson as a former priest who lost his faith with the death of his wife. Staying at a farmhouse with his brother, Gibson's character's life undergoes a transformation when the signs of extraterrestrial visitation of the film's title begin to appear in the form of large circles flattened in the family's corn fields. The film made Shyamalan the top–earning screenwriter in Hollywood when Disney paid him $5 million for the script. He earned a total of $10 million for writing and directing it.

Said Gibson of the film in the *Sydney Morning Herald,* "Films do three things if they're really great. They entertain, they educate, and they take you to a higher plane of existence or a spirituality, reaching outside your own realm. I think Night has pulled off the hat–trick with this one." Gibson said of Shyamalan's scriptwriting abilities in general in the *Press Trust of India,* "Night is uncompromising in the way he tells a story. He doesn't spoon–feed, and he doesn't pander to anyone."

Shymalan told Daryn Kagan on the Cable News Network's *CNN Live Today* program that the idea for the movie came out of a file he keeps of weird and unexplained phenomena around the world. The crop circle phenomenon also fit nicely with a theme he had been thinking about when brainstorming for a subject for a new movie. He told Kagan, "I always wanted to make a movie about ... a place that's been kind of marked by something, and we have to figure out what the meaning is...."

Shyamalan's film work bears his distinct style. Among his cinematic trademarks, he makes use of reflections in glass and other surfaces to frame his characters in various shots. He also frequently appears in small roles in his films, just like one of his filmmaking heroes, Alfred Hitchcock, who often appeared as an extra in his films. When asked by the *Houston Chronicle*'s Louis B. Parks whether he consciously emulated Hitchcock in this, Shymalan replied, "Oh no, no, no. It's more an attempt to just enjoy all the facets of filmmaking. I don't think I can be the best director I can unless I'm fully aware of how vulnerable and insecure it is to be an actor, and the personal choices you have to make, and how much you can risk out there, and how much you trust the director to say, 'I'm not going to make you look like a fool....' Basically," he added, "[acting] scares me to death, and I try to do anything that scares me to death."

Common themes in Shymalan's films include, in addition to the supernatural and unexplained, the point of view of children. As he told Parks, "I just always think of stories with little kids at the center, because that time in my life was a big time. It represents a kind of innocence and belief and faith. These movies are all about learning to believe in something." Family ties also feature prominently in Shymalan's work.

Of his writing in general, he told Parks, "I essentially just write about my life, and my feelings about things and 'what if,' you know, 'I got distant in my relationship with my wife?' Or 'what if I wasn't a good parent or didn't give enough time to my family?'" Shymalan also enjoys writing twist endings. "Not twists like plot movement," he told Robert Wilonsky of the *Riverfront Times,* "which is all there; it's all part of the storytelling already. I am talking about fundamental twists at the end. That's something I enjoy...." Most of all, as he told Strauss in the *Daily News of Los Angeles,* "I really enjoy it. That's what I would do for fun; it's a good thing to do that for a living."

Shyamalan makes his home in Wayne, Pennsylvania, a wealthy suburb of Philadelphia. "I have a very, very regular life," he told Parks in the *Houston Chronicle.* "I take out the garbage and fight with the dog next door so he doesn't eat the garbage."

Sources

Periodicals

Daily News of Los Angeles, L.A. Life section, November 19, 2000.
Houston Chronicle, November 19, 2000, p. 8.
New Straits Times, January 23, 2001, p. 7.
Newsweek, August 5, 2002, p. 48.
Press Trust of India, Nationwide International News section, August 1, 2002.
Riverfront Times, Columns section, December 13, 2000.
Sydney Morning Herald, August 9, 2002, p. 4.

Online

"Biography for M. Night Shyamalan," Internet Movie Database, http://us.imdb.com/Bio?Shyamalan,+M.+Night (November 11, 2002).

Transcripts

CNN Live Today, Cable News Network, #080909CN. V75, August 9, 2002.

—*Michael Belfiore*

Luiz Inácio Lula da Silva

AP/Wide World Photos

President of Brazil

Born October 27, 1945, in Garanhuns, Pernambuco, Brazil; son of Aristides Inácio da Silva (a farmer) and Eurídice Ferreira de Mello; married Marisa Letícia, 1974; children: five.

Addresses: *Ambassador's office*—3006 Massachusetts Ave., NW, Washington, D.C. 20008–3634. *E–mail*— webmaster@brasilemb.org. *Website*—www. brasilemb.org.

Career

Began as labor leader, 1969; elected to head of Partido dos Trabalhadores party, 1980; ran for president as head of Partido dos Trabalhadores party, 1989; ran for president as head of Partido dos Trabalhadores party, 1994; ran for president as head of Partido dos Trabalhadores party, 1998; elected president of Brazil, 2002—.

Member: Partido dos Trabalhadores party.

Sidelights

Luiz Inácio Lula da Silva, popularly known as 'Lula,' won the Brazilian presidency in October of 2002 by a landslide. An astounding 61 percent of the popular vote went to him. After three previous attempts at the office, he beat his opponent José Serra by 22.5 percentage points. Silva is the first leftist president to reach the office in Brazil's history but he faces an uphill battle to get the country's finances in order.

Silva was born in northern Brazil to an impoverished family in a poor community. One of eight children, his father was a farm worker—a common but difficult job—outside the cities of Brazil. Far from being a loving parent, he sent his children to work instead of school and, by some accounts, beat them regularly. At seven years old, Silva and his siblings traveled with their mother to São Paulo to live with the father, his mistress, and their family. The trip was difficult with all the family packed into the back of a pickup truck for 13 long days. The event would later become a legend of the adult Silva's political career.

Today, Brazil is the world's fourth largest democracy and the ninth biggest economy. But its history in the 20th century was filled with oppression and unfulfilled promise. After World War II, Brazilians felt that they had all the resources for a prosperous life: raw materials, an educated population, a large middle class. But due to crippling debt and a bad economy the promise never blossomed. In 1964, Brazilian president Joao Goulart was in trouble. Calls for radical changes were being made across the nation due to Brazil's miserable financial state. In an attempt to placate the International Monetary Fund, Goulart ordered the redistribution of privately owned land and the nationalization of private oil refineries. This only made people angrier. On April

1, 1964, the military removed Goulart and installed its own government, which would rule for more than 20 years.

It was under this regime that Silva had to make a life. Once his family arrived in São Paulo they settled into a single room at the back of a bar. He was, once again, forced to go to work instead of school. But this time around the boy had a few more options to choose from. Silva started as a shoe–shine boy, but ended up at Columbia Warehouse where he was registered as a worker for the first time. He would later transfer to Marte Screw Factory where his skilled metallurgical work allowed him to enroll in a technical school called SENAI. He studied for three years to become a mechanic, and for all intents and purposes could have led a quiet and comfortable life.

But Silva was convinced by his brother, José Ferreira da Silva, to join the union, which was a risky proposition in a military state. Many union leaders were killed or simply disappeared, which made Silva apprehensive, but he agreed to join up to satisfy his brother. He certainly didn't plan on rising in the ranks, but when his brother was imprisoned on charges that he was a communist subversive, things became personal. Silva claims that his brother's arrest helped him lose his own fear of being arrested. Emboldened by his brother's plight he began his own campaign to strengthen labor's political clout. He rapidly rose through the ranks and ended up heading the São Paulo car mechanics union. He found a natural talent for communicating the grievances of his fellow workers. But perhaps most importantly, his activities sparked a curiosity in him that would take him around the world in an impressive, educational journey. He traveled throughout Brazil, talking and listening to the working class in every state. When possible, he would try to get time with local leaders to get a feel for how his union could have an impact on the local political scene. His journeys eventually took him around the world, where he spoke to the press, took classes, and honed his debating and speaking skills in an effort to focus his message of fair pay and equal rights.

However, Brazil was still a dictatorship and it would not change easily. In 1978 Silva orchestrated a remarkable strike that was successful in raising the wages of workers around the country. He was making his name as a figure to watch in both labor and in national politics. Emboldened by their success, Silva and his fellow leaders ratcheted up the demands. Before Silva was arrested in 1980, three million workers around the country were striking.

However, the same year he was imprisoned the country's politicians opened a door for Silva to walk through. "Abertura" was a progressive policy of controlled political freedom that allowed for new political parties to enter the system. Brazil was suffering one of the most horrific economic downslides witnessed in the 20th century, with inflation reaching highs of 2,000 percent per year in the 1980s. By most measurements, the richest ten percent of the population controlled 50 percent of the national wealth, while the bottom 50 percent had only ten percent. The military rule decided it was time to open access to the political process, just a little, if they were to keep the country under control and avoid a revolution. Silva, sensing that this could be the end of the dictatorship, seized the chance to use the new "controlled openness" to start a political party.

The result of his union's efforts was Partido dos Trabalhadores (PT), a left–wing party designed to help the average Brazilian worker. With a deep knowledge of socialism, its history and its mistakes, Silva and his partners crafted a system where a majority of the influence came from the collective voice of the junior members. This went a long way toward avoiding the corruption that so many labor leaders had become infamous for in Brazil. Susan A. Berfield of *World Policy Journal* reported Silva as summing up his intentions with "[I want to create] a society with just income distribution, where the participation of the people is the fairest and most egalitarian as possible, where manual labor is valued, where basic needs of housing and schooling are rights, not privileges." Silva was elected the first president of the party, marking his official entrance into the world of national politics. By 1982 his party had almost 400,000 members. Silva ran for his first government post as governor of the State of São Paulo. Though he lost the election, his party managed to install eight federal congressmen, 12 state congressmen, and 78 council members.

As the 1980s wore on, the military rule was slowly giving way to democracy. With a new party to develop a platform around, Silva decided to go for the ultimate prize: the presidency. In 1989, Brazil held its first elections in more than 29 years. Silva ran on the liberal ticket and lost in an early round. He tried to run again in 1994, and again failed—though he did do better than his previous outing. In the meantime he continued to build a name for himself in Brazil and was gaining popularity with fellow politicians and, more importantly, the public. He became the point man on everything having to do with labor. His articulate style and humble beginnings were beginning to capture the imagination of Brazil's populace. Again, in 1998 he ran for the presidency. Hopes were high within his party this time since Silva had begun to moderate his politics and more centrist figures were beginning to see him as an ally they could work with. Unfortunately, with his extreme–left background he could not win in a country that many believed was far too conservative to consider him seriously. His education as a child ended when he was in grade school—another blow against him which his political enemies had no problem exploiting. He lost the election to Fernando Henrique Cardoso.

But something was different in the presidential race of 2002. The sitting president was popular since he had helped to control inflation and get the economic house back in order but his choice of a candidate to follow him was weak. Silva had reached the age of 56 and he was clearly a wiser and more determined candidate than he had ever been before. His outreaches to more moderate political figures, even some right–leaning figures, infuriated his liberal followers. But his crafty maneuvers only helped him in the eyes of the average Brazilian citizen. His efforts to appeal to the center of the political spectrum were starting to pay off. All through the 2002 election Silva held a substantial lead in the popularity polls. His choice of running mate was a popular centrist in Brazil and his image was cleaned up with nice suits and ties. Silva had gone mainstream and Brazil was ready to give him a shot at the country's problems. The rest of the world watched in fascination as a left–wing radical was elected to the presidency of Brazil, a first for the country.

Silva was inaugurated into office on January 1, 2003. His speech was articulate and detailed in what he wanted to do with his mandate. According to the *Economist*, he vowed to overcome Brazil's history of "inequality and social exclusion" to the delight of the crowd of 30,000. But that's when the hard work began. Now that he was in the international eye he came under fire not only from conservatives in his own country but from right–wing politicians around the world. According to Kenneth Maxwell in the *New York Review of Books*, Henry Hyde, chairman of the U.S. House of Representatives International Relations Committee wrote to President George W. Bush after Silva's electoral victory, "[Silva] is a pro–Castro radical who for electoral purposes had posed as a moderate." He went on to point out that Brazil could end up being part of an "axis of evil in the Americas." Silva is accustomed to these kinds of accusations. "When I started in the labor movement, the communists used to say I was a CIA agent. The right wing used to say I was a communist. I never was a communist and I never was a CIA agent," he told Lally Weymouth of *Newsweek*. "I was just a Brazilian who had the trust of my fellow workers, whom I represented in the metal workers' union."

Since occupying the office Silva has had to face the stinging reality of a country that is still deep in debt. But he promises to make do with the burden he has been given and hopes to get through his term without borrowing money anymore. Many believe his performance could determine the fate of democracy in the region. It will be a tough ride for the president but he insists he is ready.

Sources

Periodicals

Economist, Oct. 31, 2002, p. 57.
Newsweek, November 11, 2002, p. 38.
New York Review of Books, December 5, 2002.
World Policy Journal, Spring 1994, pp. 69–75.

Online

"Brazil inaugurates first leftist president," CNN.com, http://www.cnn.com/2003/WORLD/americas/01/01/brazil.inauguration.ap/index.html (March 27, 2003).

—*Ben Zackheim*

Russell and Kimora Lee Simmons

Jim Spellman/WireImage.com

Hip-hop mogul and fashion designer

Born Russell Simmons, c. 1957, in Queens, NY; son of Daniel (a college professor) and Evelyn (a recreation director) Simmons. *Education:* Attended City College, New York, NY. Born Kimora Lee, c. 1975, in St. Louis, MO; daughter of Joanne Kyoko Syng (a district manager for the Social Security Administration); married in 1998; children: Ming (daughter), Aoki Lee (daughter).

Addresses: *Office*—Phat Fashions LLC, 530 7th Ave., 14th Fl., New York, NY 10018. *Website*—www.phatfarm.com.

Career

Simmons heard first rap musician, 1977; started Rush Artist Management, representing Kurtis Blow, Grandmaster Flash, and other rap artists, late 1970s; co-founded music label Def Jam Recordings, 1984; produced film *Krush Groove,* 1985; founded Rush Communications, 1990; produced HBO show *Def Comedy Jam,* 1991; launched clothing company, Phat Farm, 1992. Lee attended a modeling workshop, age eleven; started modeling in Paris, age 13; chosen by designer Karl Lagerfeld to become face for Chanel, age 14. Simmons and Lee met, 1992; Simmons launched *One World* magazine, 1994; Lee launched women's fashion line, Baby Phat, 1999; Simmons published autobiography, *Life and Def,* 2001; Simmons produced HBO show *Russell Simmons Presents Def Poetry,* 2002.

Awards: Black Enterprise Company of the Year (awarded to Rush Communications), 2002.

Sidelights

The hip–hop entrepreneur Russell Simmons and his runway–model wife Kimora Lee Simmons made their fashion–world debut in the 1990s, when he launched Phat Farm, a men's clothing line, and she debuted Baby Phat, its female–oriented counterpart. While Simmons and Lee infuse their fashions with urban motifs, the couple's success has often been attributed to their ability to market their products across racial lines, bridging hip–hop and mainstream cultures.

Yet beyond Phat Fashions—the umbrella group for both the men's and women's clothing lines—Simmons and Lee run a range of other businesses, comprising something of an urban–culture enterprise. Simmons got his start in the music business as a representative for rap stars including LL Cool J, the Beastie Boys, Public Enemy, and Run–DMC—featuring his brother, Joseph (aka Run), as the group's lead rapper. With his knack for capitalizing on the hip–hop trend, he established the music label Def Jam Recordings, and then branched out into film and television via his Def Pictures production company. With Phat Farm, he made a foray into fashion in 1992, the year he met Lee. The pair—

known as much for their flashy, high–society lif-estyle as for their business successes—went on to build Simmons's empire, and to take no small share of the nearly $5 billion hip–hop industry.

Born and raised in Queens, New York, Russell Simmons was the second of three sons of Daniel, a college professor, and Evelyn, a recreation director for the New York City Parks Department. Growing up in the Hollis section of Queens, a working–class neighborhood, Simmons and his brothers became involved in an underground community of drug hangouts and street gangs. By age 13, Simmons—nicknamed Rush by his friends—was already dealing drugs; his brother Danny was an early heroin addict. The boys found themselves mixed up in a violent world, and when Simmons was 16, he was arrested for shooting a thug who had robbed him. Barely escaping a jail sentence, he was put on probation.

Looking to clean up his act, Simmons enrolled at Manhattan's City College in 1975. Not knowing what he wanted to do for a career, Simmons studied sociology and considered becoming a professor like his father. Yet a breakthrough came for him in the late 1970s, when he discovered a new passion: a little–known style of music called rap. "The first time I heard a rapper was in 1977," Simmons told Vanessa Grigoriadis of New York. "It was Kurtis Blow at the Charles Gallery on 125th Street [in Manhattan]. That changed my life."

Dropping out of school, Simmons started representing Blow and other rap artists, including Grandmaster Flash. "He was my promoter, and even when he was selling records from the trunk of his car, I knew he would do something," Grandmaster Flash told Associated Press writer Paul Shepard. Seeing the potential for rap to become a hot new style of music, Simmons rented dance halls, befriended party promoters, and began booking shows for his artists. Soon he was also representing his younger brother, lead–rapper Joey, whom he billed as "Run" in the now–famous rap group Run–DMC. Simmons dubbed his new business Rush Artist Management, as a nod to his childhood nickname.

"If there's anything I've done for urban culture, it was to expand on its base," Simmons told Grigoriadis of New York. For Simmons, that meant exposing rap and hip–hop music to a broader audience, and breaking any barriers of race. "I was making records that were based in urban culture and had been influenced more often than not by African Americans, but I never believed that their audience had to be black," he told Grigoriadis.

In 1984 Simmons teamed with producer Rick Rubin to found the music label Def Jam Recordings, which helped launch the hip–hop movement and expanded into a multimillion–dollar business. A year later Def Jam released its first album, LL Cool J's I Need a Beat. The label grew to include such names as Jay–Z and Foxy Brown, and Simmons came to be known as the Godfather of Hip–Hop. With his keen business acumen and entrepreneurial skills, Simmons helped steer the company to success, and became a millionaire in his twenties. His ability to recognize the potential of the hip–hop trend, and to translate it into a mainstream, commercial market, proved golden.

Soon the rap impresario branched out into film and television. In 1985 he produced a popular movie about Def Jam's beginnings, Krush Groove, with cameos by Run–DMC, the Fat Boys, Sheila E., and the Beastie Boys. His HBO show Def Comedy Jam, debuting in 1991, also became a hit. Just as he used his record label to discover new music talent, Simmons used his comedy show to launch a host of young new comedians, including Martin Lawrence and Chris Tucker. Simmons joined his multiple entrepreneurial ventures under one corporate umbrella, Rush Communications, in 1990.

Simmons's entrance to fashion came in 1992, when he created the hip–hop–inspired Phat Farm label. "Russell got into fashion because of his interest in models," Danny Simmons told Galina Espinoza of People. In November of that year, during New York City's Fashion Week, he met 17–year–old model Kimora Lee. He was twice her age, but Simmons courted her, sending the model a massive bouquet of flowers the next day.

Hailing from St. Louis, Missouri, Lee had inherited her beauty from a Japanese–American mother, Joanne Kyoko Syng, and an African–American father. Her parents never married, and Syng, a district manager for the Social Security Administration, raised the child on her own. By age ten, Lee, at 5' 8", towered over her classmates, who teased her. She would stop growing only when she reached a statuesque six–plus feet.

It was Syng's idea to enroll her shy eleven–year–old daughter in a modeling workshop, where Lee might gain confidence, which she did. Within two years she was modeling on the Paris runways, and at age 14 she was chosen by designer Karl Lagerfield to become the new face for Chanel. "Everything people thought was weird about me before was now good," Lee told Espinoza of People.

Simmons and Lee married on the Caribbean island of St. Bart's in 1998, amending their wedding vows to say they would stay together "for richer, for richer." The guest list included billionaires, princes, and celebrities from the entertainment, music, and fashion worlds.

To the media, the fashionable couple seems to epitomize the attraction of opposites: while Simmons holds to a vegan diet and practices yoga and meditation, Lee loves meat and dislikes exercise. Yet Lee and Simmons make their differences work to their advantage. "We're very competitive," Lee told Espinoza of *People*. "It makes us try harder."

Simmons launched Phat Farm in 1992; it started out as a mid–priced men's sportswear line that married a preppy, upscale look with a trendy hip–hop style. Top–selling products included baggy argyle sweaters and shiny–denim jeans. The label's appeal to celebrities—including rap star Eminem and basketball player Kobe Bryant—added to its allure on the mass market. Phat Farm later branched out to include fragrances—launching the men's cologne, Premium, in 2001—and footwear.

In 1999 the Simmonses launched Baby Phat, their new line of women's fashions, featuring Asian–inspired designs by Lee. The affordable offerings included sexy, streetwise separates like hip–hugger shorts ($24) and stretchy tube tops ($36). Like Phat Farm, Baby Phat became a favorite with celebrities, including singers Alicia Keys and Pink. Macy's, Bloomingdales, and other large, nationwide department stores carried the line, along with 3,000 clothing boutiques. By 2002, two Baby Phat stores had opened in New York City and Montreal. By May of that year, the line had grown to include lingerie, jewelry, and cosmetics. "[Baby Phat is] a lifestyle brand," Lee told Farrah Weinstein of the *New York Post*. "I want to offer everything that a woman needs to complete her life."

Lee gave birth to the couple's first child, a daughter named Ming, in 2000. While Lee balanced motherhood with her duties at Baby Phat, where she was president and creative director, she was anything but a typical working mother. "I have so much help," she told Farrah Weinstein of the *New York Post*. "There's 10 people around me at all times. It takes about 20 minutes [for me to get ready to go out]." Asked by Weinstein what she wears on a night on the town, Lee, then pregnant with her second child, replied, "I will always be in my stilettos and diamonds." At their 50,000–square–foot home in Saddle River, New Jersey, the Simmonses employed a butler, a live–in maid, and a full–time chef, among other helpers.

In 2001 Simmons published his autobiography, *Life and Def*, which chronicled his rise from a drug–dealing youth to an entrepreneur and philanthropist. In the book he cites his love for yoga as a key to his deepening spirituality. "The first 40 years of my life were about consumption," he told Isaac Guzman of the New York *Daily News*. "Now I still try to get [stuff] all day, but I don't care if I get it or not."

Simmons's company, Rush Communications, continued to diversify. In 1994 the company had delved into print media, launching the magazine *One World*, which aimed to blend urban and white mainstream culture. Later Simmons branched out into advertising and marketing with the launch of dRush LLC. Formed in a partnership with New York agency Deutsch Advertising, dRush brought a streetwise, hip–hop sensibility to the advertising campaigns of clients like Miller beer, HBO, and Courvoisier cognac.

Meanwhile, Simmons has kept up with film and television projects. He co–produced 1996's *The Nutty Professor*, starring Eddie Murphy. And in 2002 his production company created *Russell Simmons Presents Def Poetry*, an HBO program celebrating poetry slams—a trendy literary incarnation of hip–hop culture. Other ventures under the Rush Communications umbrella included a management/promotion company, Rush Street Team, and a company Web site, 360HipHop.com, which merged with BET.com in 2001. The following year, Simmons announced his co–founding of UniRush, a financial services firm, created as a partnership with the Cincinnati–based Unifund. Its first product would be a card, similar to a debit card, designed for use by individuals unable to open bank accounts.

As Russell and Kimora Lee Simmons's business ventures have multiplied, so have their philanthropic efforts. In 2001, Rush Philanthropic Arts Foundation put $300,000 into a program that exposed disadvantaged youths to the arts.

Lee and Simmons welcomed the birth of their second daughter, Aoki Lee, in August of 2002. They are busy parenting their successful companies as well. All along, perhaps the couple's biggest asset has been their ability to market products to a multi–ethnic, mainstream population, and to defy any racial barriers that stood in their way. "Black culture or urban culture is for all people who buy into it and not just for black people," Simmons told Grigoriadis of *New York* magazine. "Whether it's film or TV or records or advertising or clothing, I don't accept the box that [people] put me in."

Sources

Periodicals

Associated Press, July 20, 2002.

Black Enterprise, June 2002, p. 149.

Daily News (New York), December 23, 2001, p. 16.

New York, April 6, 1998.

New York Post, May 12, 2002, p. 48.

People, July 1, 2002, pp. 97–98.

St. Louis Post–Dispatch, November 30, 2001, p. D4.

Sunday Times (London, England), March 31, 2002.

Times Picayune (New Orleans, Louisiana), October 15, 2000, p. 1.

Transcripts

Business Center, CNBC, June 21, 2002.

—*Wendy Kagan*

Zadie Smith

Author

Born Sadie Smith, October 27, 1975, in Willesden, England. *Education:* Cambridge University, B.A., 1998; graduate study, Radcliffe Institute for Advanced Study at Harvard University, 2002.

Addresses: *Office*—c/o Author Mail, Random House, 299 Park Ave., New York, NY 10171–0002.

Career

Published first novel, *White Teeth,* 2000; published *The Autograph Man,* 2002; fellow at Radcliffe Institute for Advanced Study, 2002–03.

Awards: British Book Awards, Newcomer of the Year, for *White Teeth,* 2000; Frankfurt eBooks Award, Best Fiction Work, 2000; *Guardian* First Book Award, for *White Teeth,* 2000; James Tait Black Memorial Prize, 2000; Commonwealth Writers' First Book Award, 2000; Whitbread Book of the Year Award, for *White Teeth,* 2000; Whitbread First Novel Award, for *White Teeth,* 2000; Betty Trask Award, Debut Novel, Author Under Age 35, 2001; named one of the Granta Best of Young British Novelists, 2003; Wingate Prize, *Jewish Quarterly,* for *The Autograph Man,* 2003.

Sidelights

Throughout literary history, young writers have attracted widespread attention. In 2000, one such young writer with her debut novel, *White Teeth,* captured not only readers' fascinations but also critical acclaim. The author is Zadie Smith, a young woman who, according to Jeff Giles in *Newsweek,* is considered both by the media and readers as "drop–dead cool."

Smith was born on October 27, 1975, in England. Raised by a British father and Jamaican mother, Smith and her two younger brothers grew up in west London. As a young girl, Smith changed her name from "Sadie" to "Zadie," as the *Guardian* noted, "because it seemed right, exotic, different," and dreamed of becoming a dancer. However, she gave up that dream after discovering that Fred Astaire–Ginger Rogers dance movies were no longer being produced. In her early teen years, her parents divorced. To cope, Smith began writing. By the time she entered her teens, Smith had composed many short stories and poems. "I was not pretty at all," she told *Black Issues Book Review.* "That meant I had a great deal of time to do other things [because pretty girls spend all their time] being a pretty woman."

After surviving high school, where she was a bit of a trouble–maker, Smith entered Cambridge University. "I wanted to be an academic," she told the *Guardian,* "and all the writers I loved went there." While studying English literature, Smith wrote "The Newspaper Man," a short story which was published in *May Anthologies,* a collection of works by Cambridge University students. Harper-Collins, a renowned publishing house, saw the story, and contacted Smith. To protect her interests, a friend recommended that Smith not sign a contract with the publishers, but find a literary agent. To attract an agent's attention, she wrote an 80-page sample chapter—it worked. She was signed to the Andrew Wylie literary agency, a company that also represented author Salman Rushdie, whose first book, *Satanic Verses,* garnered him not only positive reviews, but also a death threat from the Shah of Iran. Smith did not attract such deadly attention, but she did catch the eye of Penguin Books, who offered her a two-book contract for almost $400,000.

In 1999, *White Teeth* burst into England's bookstores with a bang. The story, which time-traveled through 100 years and told the life stories of two men—Archie Jones, a middle-aged white man, and Samad Iqbal, a Muslim—and their families, challenged readers to "contemplate whether our choices determine our future or whether fate leads us to inevitable destiny," according to the *Library Journal.* Although popular with readers, *White Teeth* received a fair amount of both positive and negative reviews. *Black Issues Book Review* remarked that Smith's characters were "written with a multilateral depth." However, the *Wall Street Journal* noted that the characters were more "well-intentioned puppets rather than real people." Yet, most critics agreed that the book offered an amazing look into two divergent cultures. But Smith told the *New York Times Book Review* that the book presented "a utopian view," not a realist view, of "what it [race relations] might be, and what it should be and maybe what it will be." The television rights to *White Teeth* were sold to the British Broadcast Corporation and it was adapted into a four-part television miniseries which aired in the United Kingdom in 2002.

With *White Teeth*'s success, Smith became an overnight celebrity. Endless press tours and interviews turned her into a "professional hustler. It's not exactly what I wanted to do but it's OK, because people need to read the book," Smith commented in the *Boston Globe.* She was also expected to become a spokesperson for black writers. However, Smith dismisses this role because, as stated in the *San Francisco Chronicle,* "she considers herself, first and foremost, an artist, a novelist, and not a 'spokesman'." Smith is also her own harshest critic. She has written a scathing review of *White Teeth* herself and considers the book a pretentious, self-assigned writing exercise to prove to herself she could write. She succeeded beyond her expectations, however, as she commented in the *New York Times*

Book Review, "I have great ambitions of writing a very great book. I just don't think this [*White Teeth*] is it."

The public's obsessive interest in celebrities is one of the subjects in Smith's second novel, *The Autograph Man.* Alex-Li Tandem, half-Jewish and half-Chinese, is a dealer in the autographs of famous people. He is on a quest to find the autograph of his favorite screen star, Kitty Alexander, but she is retired now, reclusive, and was always reluctant to give out autographs. Once a week, Alex writes a letter to Kitty's fan club, hoping she will someday respond to his pleas. As time goes by without a response, Alex's obsession leads him to increasingly erratic behavior, including the sorting out of all behavior by whether it is "Jewish" or "Goyish." Among the novel's other characters are Alex's girlfriend, Esther, his two closest childhood friends—now a rabbi and an insurance salesman—and Adam, a black friend who combines Jewish mysticism with marijuana. "Smith's lively, descriptive prose drives a comic plot of labyrinthine complexity," wrote Shannon Olson in the *Minneapolis Star-Tribune.* A *Kirkus* reviewer found the novel to be "an uneasy mix of [the film] *Sunset Boulevard,* J. P. Donleavy's *The Ginger Man,* and James McCourt's fey romantic comedies about dementedly self-absorbed beautiful people." But Brad Hooper in *Booklist* concluded that Smith's second novel is "as bracingly intelligent and humorous as her first."

In *The Autograph Man* Smith paints a portrait of a society in which racial, religious, and ethnic distinctions are confused. "Smith likes to trample over the usual delimiters of identity," Laura Miller wrote in *Salon.com,* "on her way to portraying a new kind of mongrel world citizen: little bit of this, little bit of that." A critic for *Publishers Weekly* noted: "Smith paints portraits of a very multicultural Judaism: Adam, for instance, is a black Jew, while Alex is a disbelieving Chinese one." Daniel Zalewski in the *New York Times Book Review,* explained, "His unusual ethnicity aside, Alex is a safe choice for a character. He is the prevailing stereotype of his generation, the pop-culture-addled trivialist." Don McLeese in *Book* pointed out that "Alex is Smith's English Everyman, his ethnicity more matter-of-fact than life-defining." Sean Rocha of *Library Journal* concluded that "the novel's real pleasure lies in the masterfully crafted characters and the small insights that capture something so true of the world that they make the reader sit up in startled recognition." *Book*'s McLeese summed up: "Smith remains a virtuosic master of voices, a stylist who can be both playful and profound." In 2003, the novel won the *Jewish Quarterly* Wingate literary prize, which is Britain's leading award for fiction with a Jewish theme.

Following publication of *The Autograph Man,* Smith took a break from novel writing and accepted a prestigious fellowship for graduate study at Radcliffe Institute for Advanced Study at Harvard University in Boston, Massachusetts. While at Radcliffe, she planned to work on *The Morality of the Novel,* a "book of essays considering a selection of twentieth–century writers through the glass of moral philosophy," as described on the Radcliffe Institute website, as well as begin work on her third novel. Smith has great ambitions and even greater talent—she told *Newsweek,* "I'm enormously ambitious about being a part of English writing. But I don't feel as though I've written a book that has even a long shot of doing that."

Selected writings

White Teeth: A Novel, Random House (New York, NY), 2000.
The Autograph Man, Random House (New York, NY), 2002.

Sources

Books

Authors and Artists for Young Adults, volume 50, Gale Group, 2003.

Periodicals

Black Issues Book Review, September 2000.
Book, November–December 2002, p. 78; May–June 2003, p. 11.
Booklist, October 1, 2002, p. 276.
Boston Globe, June 13, 2000.
Chicago Sun–Times, June 7, 2000.
Entertainment Weekly, October 11, 2002, pp. 46–48.
Europe Intelligence Wire, October 7, 2002.
Guardian, December 11, 2000; September 16, 2002.
Kirkus Reviews, September 1, 2002, p. 1261.
Library Journal, April 1, 2000, p. 132; October 15, 2002, p. 95.
Minneapolis Star–Tribune, October 13, 2002.
Newsweek, May 1, 2000.
New York Times Book Review, April 30, 2000, pp. 7–8; October 6, 2002, p. 13.
Publishers Weekly, September 30, 2002, p. 47.
San Francisco Chronicle, June 13, 2000.
Time, September 30, 2002, p. 92.
Wall Street Journal, April 28, 2000.

Online

Salon.com, http://www.salon.com/ (May 27, 2003).
"Zadie Smith," Literature Awards, http://www.literature–awards.com/authors/zadie_smith.htm (April 17, 2003).
"Zadie Smith," Radcliffe Institute, http://www.radcliffe.edu/fellowships/current/2003/smith.html (May 27, 2003).
"Zadie Smith wins Jewish fiction prize," *Independent,* http://enjoyment.independent.co.uk/books/news/story.jsp?story=395388 (June 30, 2003).

—Ann Schwalboski

Aaron Sorkin

Television and film writer and producer

Born June 9, 1961; married to Julia Bingham (an attorney); children: Roxy. *Education:* Earned theater degree from Syracuse University.

Addresses: *Home*—Studio City, CA. *Office*—c/o *The West Wing,* John Wells's Productions, Warner Bros. Television, 4000 Warner Blvd., Building 133, Rm. 204, Burbank, CA 91522.

Career

Actor in New York City in mid–1980s; author of the play *Removing All Doubt;* author and actor of the one–act play *Hidden in This Picture,* 1988; authored the play *A Few Good Men,* which made its Broadway debut in 1989, toured several American cities beginning in 1992, and was made into a film by Columbia in 1992 based on Sorkin's screenplay; author of screenplay for *The American President,* 1995; credited with story idea for *Malice,* 1993; uncredited screenplay co–author for *The Rock,* 1996, and *Excess Baggage,* 1997; uncredited screenplay co–author, with David Marconi, of *Enemy of the State,* 1998. Has made on–screen cameo appearances in *A Few Good Men,* 1992, and *The American President,* 1995. Co–creator and executive producer, *Sports Night,* ABC, 1998–2000, and creator and executive producer, *The West Wing,* NBC, 1999-2003.

Awards: Humanitas Prize (with Matt Tarses, David Walpert, and Bill Wrubel) in the 30 Minute Category, Human Family Educational and Cultural Institute, for *Sports Night,* 1999; *TV Guide* Award for "the best show you're not watching," for *Sports Night,* 2000;

Golden Satellite Award for best television drama series, International Press Academy, for *The West Wing,* 2000; Nova Award, most promising producer in television, and Nova Award in Television, for *Sports Night* and *The West Wing,* 2000; Humanitas Prize (with Lawrence O'Donnell and Paul Redford) in the 60 Minute Category, Human Family Educational and Cultural Institute, for episodes of *The West Wing,* 2000; Humanitas Prize (with Lawrence O'Donnell and Paul Redford) in the 60 Minute Category, Human Family Educational and Cultural Institute, for episodes of *The West Wing,* 2002; Emmy Award for outstanding drama series, Academy of Television Arts and Sciences, for *The West Wing,* 2000; Emmy Award for outstanding drama series, Academy of Television Arts and Sciences, for *The West Wing,* 2001; Emmy Award for outstanding drama series, Academy of Television Arts and Sciences, for *The West Wing,* 2002.

Sidelights

Critics hail Aaron Sorkin's Emmy–winning series *The West Wing* as one of the finest hours on network television each week. Sorkin serves as head writer and executive producer for the hour–long NBC drama, which stars Martin Sheen as a fictional American president and depicts the behind–the–

scenes strife among White House staffers, and bipartisan deal–making, that is largely absent from standard media coverage of American politics. Sorkin's *West Wing* enjoys a cult following of viewers who gather weekly, an unusually high demographic of upper–income viewers, and a reputation for being the most–watched show in America's capital behind closed doors. "In America, we don't have shadow cabinets or governments–in–waiting," a writer for the *New Yorker* asserted. "What we have instead is *The West Wing*, NBC's drama about a White House staff that, compared with the Bush White House, has bigger offices, better haircuts, more Democrats, and many, many more people eager to filibuster about policy as they walk down the hall looking for coffee. As the show's creator and writer, Aaron Sorkin is essentially the country's loyal opposition." Sorkin, intensely involved in writing the show's scripts until the eleventh hour, has earned a reputation for consistently crafting superb dialogue for his flawed–yet–likable characters.

Sorkin was born in 1961 and grew up in Scarsdale, an affluent suburb of New York City. A drama major at Syracuse University, Sorkin moved to the city with the goal of becoming a stage actor. He performed in children's theater but eventually turned to writing for the stage himself. *Removing All Doubt* was his first play, and his second, *Hidden in This Picture,* earned solid reviews during its 1988 run. The idea for his next work was inspired by his sister, a Navy officer and judge. Deborah Sorkin had been sent to the U.S. Marine base at Guantanamo Bay, Cuba, to arbitrate a case involving some Marines accused of the murder of one of their own. Sorkin, intrigued by the tale, wrote a play based on it, *A Few Good Men.* After it debuted on Broadway in 1989, the drama attracted Hollywood interest, and Sorkin was offered a deal to write the screenplay.

The 1992 film version of *A Few Good Men* was directed by Rob Reiner and starred Tom Cruise, Demi Moore, and Jack Nicholson. The story remained: the base death was ostensibly an informal disciplinary action gone awry; Cruise played the lawyer defending the accused, Moore's character suspects a cover–up and turns her sights on the base commander, played by Nicholson. *Time* critic Richard Schickel found the plot "a little too neat structurally, its moral and human issues a little too clear–cut.... But Sorkin's dialogue is spit–shined, and the energy and conviction with which it is staged and played is more than a compensation; it's transformative. And hugely entertaining."

Sorkin earned an Academy Award nomination for best screenplay that year, an impressive achievement for a first–timer, and Reiner signed him to write another movie. *The American President,* released in 1995, starred Michael Douglas as fictional commander–in–chief Andrew Shepherd. When the widower president falls in love with a lobbyist played by Annette Bening, the romance triggers political troubles. *Entertainment Weekly* critic Owen Gleiberman called the film "pleasing fluff. The image of a chief executive as moonstruck single guy taps something buoyant and touching in our collective democratic imagination." Reviewing it for the *New Republic*, Stanley Kauffmann commented on Sorkin's playwriting background and rather speedy defection to Hollywood—a trend among writers and "part of the reason that Broadway is lacking in plays," Kauffmann noted, and concluded that in this particular case "Broadway has, apparently, lost another competent artisan."

Sorkin's script for *The American President,* which took him two years to write, was so enormous in its first draft that he delivered its 385 pages to Reiner in a shopping bag. Sorkin admitted to a substance abuse problem during the time he spent writing it at the Four Seasons Hotel. "I was the kind of addict who was functional—I was actually writing good material," he later told *Los Angeles Times* journalist Patrick Goldstein. "But I didn't see people or talk to people. I'd fax my pages over to Rob at 7 a.m. and after we'd talked about it, I'd close the curtains and start writing again." A stint at the Hazelden Institute in Minnesota helped Sorkin kick a cocaine habit, and also led to his marriage to entertainment attorney Julia Bingham, who worked for Reiner and helped arrange the Hazelden stay. They married and their daughter, Roxy, was born in late 2000.

Sorkin's first television series was a short–lived ABC sitcom called *Sports Night,* which debuted in 1998. Its premise was a behind–the–scenes look at the cast and crew of a fictional sports–highlights show, and starred Felicity Huffman as the high–strung producer romantically involved with her show's anchor, played by Peter Krause. The show earned enthusiastic critical accolades, but struggled in the ratings; ABC pulled the plug on it in early 2000. It gave Sorkin the freedom, however, to concentrate on his second television series, which was based on leftover material from *The American President. The West Wing* made its NBC debut in the fall of 1999 and was immediately hailed as one of the freshest, most tightly written new television dramas in recent memory. For his part, Sorkin was thankful to have been relieved of his *Sports Night* duties, after having managed to write, for one entire season, scripts for two weekly shows almost single–handedly. He told the *Houston Chronicle* that he was admittedly overworked, but it was more of a loyalty issue involving two different casts and crew. "[I]t was constantly feeling like I was cheating on my girlfriend," Sorkin told the paper. "It was like I had a secret family elsewhere." He also told the *Chronicle* that he saw his wife so rarely that Bingham "sends me a postcard from time to time, letting me know where I live," he joked. "Apparently we're redoing the kitchen and I'm going to like it a lot."

The West Wing garnered positive responses from both media critics and viewers for its depiction of the off–limits–to–the–public section of the White House that houses executive–branch staffers. Many liked the choice of veteran actor and renowned liberal activist Sheen to play President Josiah Bartlet, a centrist Democrat whom some pundits described as an idealized version of Bill Clinton. Sheen's character was immensely appealing, wrote *Entertainment Weekly* critic Ken Tucker, partly because the actor possessed "the right gruff–voiced intelligence and twinkly–eyed playfulness to pull off what is clearly Sorkin's goal: a combination of JFK and Teddy Roosevelt—an aging glamour–puss and Rough Rider, fair and tough."

The first season of *The West Wing* lured a steady number of loyal viewers, some 13 million each week, who tuned in to watch Sorkin's scripted Oval Office intrigue among Bartlet's staffers. Other cast members included Rob Lowe, in a barely disguised revision of Clinton's former policy advisor and deputy communications director George Stephanopoulos, and Allison Janney as press secretary C.J. Cregg. The show tackled topical subjects culled from the contemporary American political landscape, including racial tensions and inflammatory radio talk–show hosts, and Sheen's Bartlet regularly trumped his ideological foes with common sense, executive protocol, or strategic out–maneuvering; when these failed, he deployed a defense of American constitutional rights.

Sorkin's *West Wing* reportedly enjoyed a large fan base among Beltway insiders, and the cast even visited the Clinton White House in early 2000, meeting the President and taking a tour of the real West Wing. During the 2000 presidential campaign season, "Bartlet for President" bumper stickers began appearing in southern California, and when the Democratic National Convention was held in Los Angeles in August of 2000, *The West Wing* hosted a party on the show's set for some key party leaders. Sorkin, backed by a generous NBC budget, even lured actual political consultants to its writing staff, including former Clinton press secretary Dee Dee Myers.

The West Wing—and what was quickly perceived as its liberal slant—attracted the ire of conservative pundits. *The Weekly Standard* mocked it as the "Left Wing" on its cover, and Sorkin did admit to harboring a bias. In an interview with *Daily Variety*'s Josef Adalian, he recalled volunteering for Democratic White House hopeful George McGovern in 1972 as a middle–schooler. He held a McGovern sign aloft when the vehicle carrying incumbent Republican presidential candidate Richard Nixon drove past, and a woman approached him, took the sign, and stomped on it. "The only political agenda we have on *The West Wing* is the slim possibility that woman might be alive," Sorkin joked, "and I'm driving her out of her mind." Elsewhere, he defended the show and charges that it puts forth an anti–conservative, anti–Republican agenda. "Here's a show with no gratuitous violence, no gratuitous sex, that celebrates our institutions, is a valentine to public service, and has featured a character, the president of the United States, kneeling in the Oval Office and praying," Sorkin pointed out in the *Houston Chronicle* interview. He asserted that it was merely critics from the more conservative side of the ideological spectrum who condemned *The West Wing* because of "characters who disagree with them politically. And if that is to be the criterion for what is acceptable for what is up for discussion in this country, you have to get new writers."

In April of 2001, after finishing a second *West Wing* season, Sorkin was arrested for drug possession at the Burbank Airport before boarding a flight to Las Vegas. After he was released on bail, Sorkin appeared in court that summer and pled guilty to a misdemeanor and two felony charges for possession of marijuana, cocaine, and hallucinogenic mushrooms. He entered a diversion program for first–time criminal drug offenders which involved outpatient counseling and regular drug testing. Later that year he won his second Emmy Award for the show in the outstanding drama series category, and critics continued to pay homage to it as more than just 22 hours of scripted television each season. "The West Wing sets out, week after week," declared *Atlantic Monthly* writer Chris Lehmann, "to restore public faith in the institutions of our government, to shore up the bulwarks of American patriotism, and to supply a vision of executive liberalism—at once principled and pragmatic; mandating both estimable political vision and serious personal sacrifice; plying an understanding of the nation's common good that is heroically heedless of focus groups, opposition research, small–bore compromise, and re–election prospects—that exists nowhere else in our recent history."

In early 2002, Sorkin stepped out from behind the cover of his show to voice criticism of an NBC special, *The Bush White House: Inside the Real West Wing,* that was scheduled as a lead–in to his show. Sorkin, interviewed by the *New Yorker,* disparaged what he felt was a post–September 11 fawning over Republican President George W. Bush and his administration. "The media is waving pom–poms, and the entire country is being polite," Sorkin asserted.

The West Wing won its third Emmy later in 2002, and Sorkin enjoyed a lucrative deal with the network that would keep the show on the air at least until 2004. He admitted that being the chief writer for one show was still exhausting, but as he told Adalian in *Daily Variety,* the alternative was unappealing. "Not writing *The West Wing* is worse than writing *The West Wing,*" he reflected. It was a sentiment he also touched upon in the interview with Goldstein in the *Los Angeles Times*: when he and Bingham were dating, he took her to see *The American President.* "I thought, this is the ball game," he recalled. "If she likes the movie—meaning my writing—I'm all right. But if she doesn't, it's all over. Maybe that's why I spend so much time by myself writing. I've always felt that what I have that's most accessible or attractive comes out through my work. I just see myself as a guy who's better on paper than in real life."

According to CNN.com, on May 1, 2003, Sorkin unexpectedly announced that he was leaving *The West Wing* after the season finale. Thomas Schlamme, the director and co-executive producer, also left. Sorkin gave no reason for the departure, but the Associated Press said there were reports of tension between him and Warner Bros. (which produces the show) over budgets and production delays. In a joint statement issued with Schlamme, Sorkin said he plans to pursue other film, television, and theater projects.

Sources

Books

Contemporary Theatre, Film and Television, Volume 29, Gale, 2000.

Periodicals

American Enterprise, September 2001, p. 13.
Atlantic Monthly, March 2001, p. 93.
Daily Variety, August 30, 2002, p. 28.
Entertainment Weekly, December 18, 1992, p. 40; November 17, 1995, p. 56; October 22, 1999, p. 67; February 25, 2000, p. 32; May 4, 2001, p. 26.
Houston Chronicle, October 3, 1999, p. 8; July 23, 2000, p. 11.
Los Angeles Times, October 10, 1999, p. 2; November 21, 2001, p. F1.
New Republic, December 18, 1995, p. 28.
Newsweek, May 17, 1996, p. 68; October 11, 1999, p. 80.
New Yorker, March 4, 2002, p. 30.
New York Times, September 23, 2002, p. E1; October 21, 2002, p. C1.
Progressive, May 2000, p. 39.
Time, December 14, 1992, p. 70; November 20, 1995, p. 117.
U.S. News & World Report, October 7, 2002, p. 56.
Washington Post, April 17, 2002, p. C7.

Online

"*West Wing* creator leaving show," CNN.com, http://www.cnn.com/2003/SHOWBIZ/TV/05/01/west.wing.sorkin/index.html (May 2, 2003).

—*Carol Brennan*

Sissy Spacek

Actress

Born Mary Elizabeth Spacek, December 25, 1949, in Quitman, TX; daughter of Edwin (a state agricultural agent) and Virginia Spacek; married Jack Fisk (an art director for films), 1974; children: Schuyler (daughter), Madison (daughter). *Education:* Studied at the Lee Strasberg Theatrical Institute, New York, NY.

Addresses: *Agent*—Creative Artists Agency, 9830 Wilshire Blvd., Beverly Hills, CA 90212. *Home*—Virginia.

Career

Actress in films, including: *Trash*, 1970; *Prime Cut*, 1972; *Ginger in the Morning*, 1973; *Badlands*, 1973; *Carrie*, 1976; *Three Women*, 1977; *Welcome to L.A.*, 1977; *Coal Miner's Daughter*, 1980; *Heart Beat*, 1980; *Raggedy Man*, 1981; *Missing*, 1982; *The Man with Two Brains*, 1983; *The River*, 1984; *Marie*, 1985; *'night, Mother*, 1986; *Crimes of the Heart*, 1986; *Violets Are Blue*, 1986; *The Long Walk Home*, 1990; *JFK*, 1991; *Hard Promises*, 1992; *Trading Mom*, 1994; *The Grass Harp*, 1995; *Affliction*, 1997; *Blast From The Past*, 1999; *The Straight Story*, 1999; *In the Bedroom*, 2001. Television movie appearances include: *The Girls of Huntingdon House*, 1973; *The Migrants*, 1974; *Katherine*, 1975; *A Private Matter*, HBO, 1992; *A Place for Annie*, 1994; *The Good Old Boys*, 1995; *If These Walls Could Talk*, HBO, 1996. Television series appearances include: *The Waltons*. Performed in New York City as a folk–rock singer, late 1960s.

Awards: Best actress, National Society of Film Critics, for *Carrie*, 1976; best supporting actress, New York Film Critics Circle, for *Three Women*, 1977; best

actress, National Board of Review, for *Coal Miner's Daughter*, 1980; best actress, New York Film Critics Circle, for *Coal Miner's Daughter*, 1980; best actress, Los Angeles Film Critics Association, for *Coal Miner's Daughter*, 1980; best actress, National Society of Film Critics, for *Coal Miner's Daughter*, 1980; Academy Award for best actress, Academy of Motion Picture Arts and Sciences, for *Coal Miner's Daughter*, 1980; album of the year, Country Music Association, for *Coal Miner's Daughter*, 1980; Golden Globe Award for best actress in a motion picture (musical or comedy), Hollywood Foreign Press Association, for *Coal Miner's Daughter*, 1980; best actress, New York Film Critics Circle, for *Crimes of the Heart*, 1986; Golden Globe Award for best actress in a film (musical or comedy), Hollywood Foreign Press Association, for *Crimes of the Heart*, 1986; Golden Globe Award for best actress in a film, Hollywood Foreign Press Association, for *In the Bedroom*, 2001.

Sidelights

Veteran actress Sissy Spacek possesses a face that is often described as timeless. With her cascading strawberry–blond hair and waif–like physique, the Texas native appears to have aged little since she appeared opposite a young Martin Sheen in the classic 1973 crime–spree tale, *Badlands.* Spacek is also indelibly associated with her title role in *Carrie,* the 1976 thriller that launched the careers of writer Stephen King and actors John Travolta and Amy Irving. For it she earned her first Oscar nomination, and her sixth came more than a quarter–century later for *In the Bedroom,* an acclaimed independent film that emerged as a surprising box–office hit in early 2002. Only once has Spacek been awarded the Academy Award, however—for the 1980 Loretta Lynn biopic *Coal Miner's Daughter. Daily Telegraph* journalist Tim Robey granted that while such awards "don't matter much in the grand scheme of things," Spacek's moving portrayal of *In the Bedroom*'s griefstricken mother was indeed an Oscar–worthy one. "[I]t's the kind of performance—wrenchingly vulnerable and human, and almost unbearably sad—that has you caring intensely for it to get proper recognition," Robey continued.

Spacek hails from Quitman, a town in eastern Texas, where she was born on Christmas Day of 1949. Her tag–along, tomboyish ways prompted her two older brothers to bestow the "Sissy" nickname on her at an early age. As a teen, Spacek dreamed of moving to New York City to become a folk singer. In 1967, when she was a senior in high school, her 18–year–old brother Robbie was diagnosed with leukemia; in the hospital, she confessed her ambition, and he encouraged her to act on it. Her parents believed she was destined for the University of Texas at Austin, but after her brother died, they bravely approved of her move and supported her financially.

Spacek was fortunate to have a cousin in show business, actor Rip Torn, who was living in New York City at the time. A well–established television and film actor by then, Torn was married to actress Geraldine Page, and Spacek lived with them when she first arrived. Page was in a Broadway play at the time, and Spacek often went with her to work, partly because "I'd never been to a theater in my life," she told *Entertainment Weekly*'s Steve Daly. "I watched every show and played pinochle with the crew members underneath the stage." Spacek eventually signed a record deal to cut a novelty track, "John, You've Gone Too Far This Time," in 1968. The song was in reference to Beatle John Lennon, who had recently appeared nude on the cover of his *Two Virgins* album with Yoko Ono, and Spacek recorded it under the name Rainbo. When the single was quickly forgotten, she decided to explore other career options and enrolled in acting classes.

Spacek was drawn into Andy Warhol's "Factory" scene, the art/film studio–party pad of the era. She appeared in *Trash,* a 1970 cult classic directed by Warhol cohort Paul Morrissey, a role which entailed standing at a bar for nine hours next to transvestite Holly Woodlawn. She moved on to more mainstream jobs with *Prime Cut,* a 1972 thriller about a white slavery ring, and the title role in *Ginger in the Morning.* She was also cast as the girlfriend of John–Boy Walton in the popular television series *The Waltons* for two episodes. Her break came when Texas native Terrence Malick cast her as Holly in *Badlands,* a bleak romance that paired her with Sheen. When Holly's overprotective father forbids Kit, Sheen's rogue character, to see her, Kit murders him and the pair take to the road across some of the American West's most wind–swept scenery. The film was memorable for Spacek's voice–over narration in her Texas–twanged monotone.

Badlands, which wrapped by the end of 1972, also proved fortuitous in another way for Spacek: she met her future husband, Malick's art director Jack Fisk, on the set. The two were married in 1974, a year after *Badlands* finally arrived in theaters. It was a fortuitous moment for her career to launch. As Daly explained in *Entertainment Weekly,* Spacek "got in the door just as anti–glamorous faces were beginning to rule the business. Her luminous, slightly spooky features were an ideal canvas for a new crop of maverick filmmakers," and Daly listed Malick and Brian De Palma among them. Fisk had been hired by DePalma to art–direct his next film, a supernatural shocker called *Carrie.* The 1976 work was based on the first novel by horror writer Stephen King about a repressed and taunted high–schooler with telekinetic powers who wreaks havoc at her prom. Spacek was offered an audition one day when she came with Fisk to the set, but felt DePalma then tried to discourage her from the final tryout. On that occasion, Spacek decided to wear an odd sailor suit her mother had once sewed for her and greased her hair with Vaseline. She won the part, and *Carrie* became the surprise hit of the year and launched her career in earnest. In the film, when a boy riding a bike yells "Creepy Carrie!" at her, Spacek is wearing the sailor suit.

Carrie earned Spacek her first Academy Award nomination for Best Actress, and a smart deal that she signed with its producers netted her a small fortune: if the film did not do well, her take would have been miniscule; in the event that it did well in theaters, her earnings rose correspondingly. *Carrie,* made for just $2 million, grossed $34 million and soon Spacek and Fisk had acquired a thoroughbred horse farm in Virginia. Spacek could now afford to be choosy about her future roles as well: she worked with auteur–type writer–directors Alan Rudolph and Robert Altman on their respective 1977 releases, *Welcome to L.A.* and *Three Women.*

Spacek's next major part was also a star–making turn: she was cast in the biopic of country singer Loretta Lynn, *Coal Miner's Daughter*. Spacek was determined to sing Lynn's songs herself, without lip–synching to recorded versions, but director Michael Apted was uneasy; furthermore, Universal Pictures hoped to release a greatest–hits record by Lynn as a tie–in to the film. Spacek went to Nashville to work with Lynn, and convinced Apted finally by a telephone call in which she pretended to be Lynn. *Coal Miner's Daughter* won rave reviews, as did Spacek's performance, and for it she earned an Oscar.

During the next decade Spacek and Fisk began a family, and she took fewer roles. She appeared in the Costa–Gavras film *Missing* in 1982, based on a true story about an American who had vanished in a troubled South American country a decade earlier. She earned her third Academy Award nomination for it, and a fourth in 1984 for *The River*, a picturesque romance about a couple struggling to save their Tennessee farm; Mel Gibson played her husband. She also appeared in two movies based on acclaimed Broadway plays, *'night, Mother* and *Crimes of the Heart*, in 1986.

After a four–year hiatus, Spacek returned to the screen in 1990 with *The Long Walk Home*, a drama set during the Montgomery, Alabama, bus boycott in the 1950s. Her next role came as the wife of New Orleans district attorney Jim Garrison in the 1991 Oliver Stone film *JFK*. Still focused on raising her daughters Schuyler and Madison, Spacek kept work commitments to a minimum during much of the 1990s. She did the HBO projects *A Private Matter* and *If These Walls Could Talk*, both of which dealt with women's reproductive rights, and appeared in the comedy *Trading Mom* in 1994. She took a tougher role with *Affliction* in 1997, a Paul Schrader–directed story of murder in a small New Hampshire town in which she was cast as the paramour of lead Nick Nolte. Spacek was sanguine about her self–imposed hiatus. "I wasn't finding the roles, for whatever reason, that were really exciting to me," she told Robey in the *Daily Telegraph*. "But it worked out just perfectly, because I had my children, and I was so wonderfully involved in that that I had a hard time even reading scripts."

In 1999, Spacek appeared in the David Lynch film *A Straight Story*. The drama was based on the true story of two septuagenarian brothers, Alvin and Lyle Straight, who had not spoken in years. When Alvin learned his brother was terminally ill, he rode a tractor from Iowa to Wisconsin to see him. Spacek's husband had known Lynch since their teens, and Spacek and her husband were even thanked in the credits for Lynch's first film, 1977's cult–favorite *Eraserhead*, for providing money when production funds ran low. Spacek was also happy to help out a Virginia neighbor, Hugh Wilson, in his 1999 film *Blast from the Past*. She and Christopher Walken portrayed a pair of overly protective parents who have raised their son in an underground bomb shelter.

Spacek's most talked–about performance in years came with a small independent film, *In the Bedroom*, by first–time director Todd Field. Set in Maine, the screenplay was based on a short story by Andre Dubus and detailed the marital breakdown of a complacent, seemingly happy middle–class couple after their son is slain. Spacek was cast as Ruth Fowler, a high school choir teacher. British actor Tom Wilkinson played her husband, the small town's local doctor, and Nick Stahl their promising college–graduate son. Stahl's Frank returns home for the summer before entering architecture school, works on a lobster boat, and becomes involved with a "townie," a working–class New Englander named Natalie, played by Marisa Tomei. Natalie is separated from her husband and has two children, and Ruth does not hide her disdain for Natalie, nor her distaste for the overall situation. "This woman is not terribly likable," wrote *Los Angeles Times* journalist John Clark about Spacek's Ruth, whose vanity plate on her car reads "ART GAL." Clark called her "controlling, unforgiving, and wound very tight."

The film takes a shocking turn when Natalie's husband kills Frank in a jealous rage. The Fowlers's cozy world is shattered, with Ruth "holding in an ocean of rage," noted Rand Richards Cooper in a *Commonweal* review. Cooper called "Spacek's haggard face as she sits chain–smoking and staring blankly at late–night TV … a harrowing study in anguish." Husband and wife alternate between muteness and blame until another shocking episode. "*In the Bedroom* does what good art does with awful predicaments: You feel the dread of knowing not only that this could be you, but that it would be," asserted Cooper. Other reviews were similarly effusive. *Newsweek*'s film critic David Ansen noted that while much of the cast delivers solid performances, "it's the fierce honesty of Spacek and the stunned, haunted vulnerability of Wilkinson that provide the movie's soul. Fearlessly, they lead us inside the dark recesses of a marriage, where grief, love, and violence commingle in ways we might not care to acknowledge."

Spacek received her sixth Academy Award nomination in the Best Actress category for *In the Bedroom*— and her first since *Crimes of the Heart* in 1987—but lost to Halle Berry for *Monster's Ball*. She still lives with Fisk on her Virginia farm, and their college–age daughter, Schuyler, is now acting in films as well. In the *Daily Telegraph* interview with Robey, Spacek was realistic about the vagaries of a career in show business. After 30–odd years as an American actress, Spacek pointed out that she knew that one could not always be at the top of the Hollywood A–list. "You want to pick roles for all of the right reasons, and if you do pick roles to stay king of the mountain," she told Robey, "then you're getting yourself into serious trouble, and you're picking things out of fear as opposed to taking risks."

Sources

Books

International Dictionary of Films and Filmmakers, Volume 3: Actors and Actresses, St. James Press, 1996.

Periodicals

Commonweal, January 11, 2002, p. 19.
Daily Telegraph (London, England), March 11, 2002, p. 22.
Daily Variety, January 14, 2002, p. A16.
Entertainment Weekly, May 22, 1992, p. 82; June 19, 1992, p. 56; April 29, 1994, p. 60; May 27, 1994, p. 98; October 11, 1996, p. 77; November 16, 2001, p. 62; November 30, 2001, p. 60.
Los Angeles Times, November 20, 2001, p. F1.
Maclean's, February 8, 1999, p. 71.
Nation, January 20, 1992, p. 62.
New Republic, October 13, 1986, p. 26; February 2, 1987, p. 26.
Newsweek, January 11, 1999, p. 65; December 3, 2001, p. 72.
New York Times, April 20, 1980, p. D18; February 1, 2002, p. E1.
People, October 3, 1983, p. 92; September 15, 1986, p. 22; February 8, 1999, p. 10; March 1, 1999, p. 31; March 4, 2002, p. 111.
Time, October 7, 1985, p. 66; December 22, 1986, p. 70; December 17, 1990, p. 92.

Online

"Sissy Spacek," E! Online, http://www.eonline.com/Facts/People/Bio/0,128,14762.00.html (October 3, 2002).

—*Carol Brennan*

Kate Spade

Accessories designer

Born Katherine Noel Brosnahan in 1962, in Kansas City, MO; daughter of a construction company owner and a housewife; married Andy Spade (her business partner), 1994. *Education:* Arizona State University, B.A., 1985.

Addresses: *Email*—info@katespade.com. *Office*—48 W. 25th St., New York, NY 10010. *Website*—http://www.katespade.com.

Career

Assistant, *Mademoiselle* magazine, New York City, 1985; rose to senior fashion editor/accessories; quit *Mademoiselle* to found Kate Spade company with then–boyfriend Andy Spade, 1993; opened first shop, in New York City's SoHo neighborhood, 1996; opened several stores throughout the United States, late 1990s; sold 56 percent of her company to Neiman Marcus, 1999; launched Jack Spade, a men's accessories line, 1999; launched Kate Spade Home, a home furnishings line, 2002.

Awards: Perry Ellis Award for New Fashion Talent, Council of Fashion Designers of America (CFDA), 1996; Accessory Designer of the Year, CFDA, 1998.

Sidelights

Handbag designer Kate Spade started her own company with her then–boyfriend Andy Spade in 1993, and within three years her sleek, boxy, affordable totes had become favored accessories among stylish urban women. Fashion magazines featured handbags sporting the Kate Spade label, which began to appear in upscale department stores like Saks Fifth Avenue, Neiman Marcus, Bloomingdale's, and Bergdorf Goodman. Between 1996 and 1998, Spade opened freestanding stores in New York, Los Angeles, and Japan, and in 1999 Neiman Marcus bought 56 percent of her company for $33.6 million.

Spade's business grew to include not only handbags—retailing from about $100 to $500—but also sunglasses, shoes, luggage, paper products, leather goods, and increasingly, clothing. In 2001 her company announced that it would launch Kate Spade Home, a line of home furnishings. By 2002 the Kate Spade brand had grown into a $70 million business.

Born into a large Irish Catholic family in Kansas City, Missouri, Katherine Noel Brosnahan did not seem destined for a life in fashion. "When I was a kid, I didn't even know Chanel," she told Suzanne C. Ryan in the *Boston Globe*. "I would have called it Channel."

Spade attended Arizona State University, majoring in journalism and taking a part–time job at a department store in Phoenix. It was here that she met fellow University student Andy Spade (brother of comedian David Spade), who would become her boyfriend, business partner, and ultimately her husband.

Just after her graduation in 1985, Spade toured Europe, returning to the United States with only $2 in her pocket. Staying at a friend's apartment in New York City, she signed up with a temp agency to make some quick cash. Fortuitously, the agency placed her in the fashion department at *Mademoiselle* magazine, where she worked as an assistant, running errands, brewing coffee, and steaming clothes for the busy office. Spade remained at *Mademoiselle* for eight years, rising to Senior Fashion Editor/Accessories in her final year.

Meanwhile her boyfriend moved to New York City, and the couple saved money by sharing a tiny studio apartment. While Andy took a job as a copywriter at an advertising firm, Spade hatched a plan to leave the magazine and launch a small company of her own. "It was less about wanting to be a designer and more wanting to start a business," she told Bart Boehlert of *Urban Desires*. "I thought, 'What do I like?' I liked accessories and, specifically, I loved handbags." Also game to start a business, Andy became his girlfriend's partner, lending not only capital to the business but also his last name.

Spade quit her job in 1993, asking the magazine if they would take her back if her venture failed—just in case. Then she set up shop in her apartment, making handbag designs with paper cutouts and Scotch tape to adjust the proportions—and cashing in her $6,000 401(k) account to cover fabrics and expenses. When she was ready, she took her designs—six prototypes—to a manufacturer in the East New York section of Brooklyn, and the first Kate Spade bags made their debut. They were simple, sleek, utilitarian totes put together with colorful fabrics of satin-finish nylon or plush suede. "I wanted a functional bag that was sophisticated and had some style," she explained to Elizabeth Bumiller in the *New York Times*.

Soon Spade had enough handbags to fill a display booth at a 1993 accessories show at Manhattan's Javits Center. At the show, her bags caught the eye of a seller from Barneys, a New York department store. The seller bought a few bags, and the young designer's career was off to a strong start.

Yet Spade needed something to make her simple handbags seem a little more unique. The night before her second accessories show, she impulsively ripped her small logo tags out of the bags's interiors and sewed them on to their exteriors instead. Staying up all night, she completed her plan, altering every bag to fit the new look. The result was an eye–catching little accent that promoted her name brand.

By late 1993 Spade and her partner/boyfriend hired a third person, Pamela Bell Simotas, to help find materials and produce the handbags. In 1994 Elyce Arons, an old college friend of Spade, joined the team to lead its sales and public relations efforts. In these early days, before the company began to make a profit, the couple often drew money out of their personal checking accounts to pay their employees and to buy fabrics. Their apartment filled up with handbags during the shipping season. "We left a little trail to get to the bathroom," Spade told the *New York Times*'s Bumiller.

Spade and Andy married in 1994, and she officially took on the name she had sewn onto her handbags, which were enjoying increasing popularity. Soon both Barneys and Bergdorf Goodman were carrying Spade's totes, and fashion magazines started featuring her new accessories look. "Their response gave us the encouragement, told us we were on the right track," Andy told Jackie White in the *Buffalo News*.

Soon the fashion world was not just encouraging Spade but celebrating her. She received the Council of Fashion Designers of America's prestigious Perry Ellis Award for New Fashion Talent in 1996. The same year, the first Kate Spade boutique opened, in Manhattan's tony SoHo neighborhood. Andy quit his advertising–firm day job, joining his wife in the business on a full–time basis.

Spade—whose looks have been compared to the legendary film beauty Audrey Hepburn—has posed with her handbags in advertising spreads, and has become something of fashion icon. In 1999 she and her husband launched Jack Spade, a line of men's accessories, and in 2002 they debuted Kate Spade Home, her home furnishings line. In each of these new ventures, Spade has remained true to a personal style that prizes simplicity and timelessness. "Our point has always been to have a simple and clean approach while adding an element of interest or surprise," she told Leslie Newby in *Business and Industry*.

"I like things to endure because that's the way I shop," Spade explained to Bernadette Morra in the *Toronto Star*. "If I buy a cashmere sweater I want it to be something I wear for a long time. That's how I feel about this company. I want it to be like a fashion version of L.L. Bean, never in or out."

Sources

Periodicals

Boston Globe, July 14, 1999, p. F1.
Buffalo News, December 28, 1997, p. 2E.
Business and Industry, November 5, 2001, p. 4.
Denver Post, January 24, 2002, p. F1.
InStyle, August 2002, p. 272.
Newsday, January 18, 1996, p. B15.
New York Times, March 12, 1999, p. B2.
Toronto Star, April 24, 1997, p. C4.

Online

"Kate Spade and Her Hip Handbags," *Urban Desires,* http://desires.com/2.1/Style/Spade/Docs/spade1.html (August 12, 2002).
Kate Spade Official Web Site, http://www.katespade.com (August 19, 2002).
"Style in Spades," *New York* Magazine Online, http://www.newyorkmetro.com/nymetro/urban/home/design/features/4793 (August 12, 2002).

—Wendy Kagan

Elizabeth Spelke

Scientist

Born May 28, 1949, in New York, NY; children: Bridget, Joe. *Education:* Radcliffe College, bachelor's degree, 1971; Cornell University, master's degree, 1977; Cornell University, Ph.D.

Addresses: *Office*—Department of Psychology, Harvard University, William James Hall, 33 Kirkland St., Cambridge, MA 02138.

Career

Scientist, with a focus on developmental psychology; demonstrated that human infants associate sounds with the objects that produce them; professor of psychology at the University of Pennsylvania; professor at Cornell University; professor, Massachusetts Institute of Technology, 1996–2001; professor, Harvard, 2001—; named one of America's Best scientists by *Time,* 2001.

Sidelights

A developmental psychologist, Elizabeth Spelke was named one of America's best scientists by *Time* in 2001. Among her achievements is the demonstration that human infants are more capable mentally than had been previously thought.

Before Spelke published her research, scientists thought that babies younger than two years old perceive the world as a confusion of color, light, and sound with little coherence, and are unaware of the existence of objects unless they can see them. Not until they were older, the thinking went, did babies connect the images and other impressions that made up their world with actual people, places, and objects. Spelke changed this thinking by showing that babies were able to develop a coherent picture of the world around them by the time they are only a few months old.

She described her work to William Cromie in the *Harvard University Gazette* like this: "I'm trying to find out what infants are aware of and how they think about the world around them. Answers to such questions should help us understand the origins of human knowledge."

The daughter of a writer/filmmaker, Spelke spent much of her childhood abroad, traveling around the world with her father as he completed various projects. She grew to love travel, and still does so at every opportunity.

Spelke went to college at Radcliffe College at Harvard University in 1967. There, a course in developmental psychology taught by Jerry Kagan introduced her to the subject that was to become her lifelong calling. Spelke graduated from Radcliffe in 1971. In 1973, Spelke went on to graduate school at Cornell University, where she remained until 1977. It was in graduate school that Spelke made her first breakthrough in the field of infant cognition when she helped to demonstrate that infants were able to associate sounds with the objects that produced them. Spelke completed a Ph.D. at Cornell, and continued her research at the University of Pennsylvania as a professor of psychology. After nine years at the University of Pennsylvania, Spelke returned to Cornell, this time as a member of the faculty.

In 1996, Spelke took a professorship at the Massachusetts Institute of Technology's (MIT) Department of Brain and Cognitive Sciences. After five years at MIT, Spelke returned to Harvard in 2001. "I was not unhappy at MIT," she explained to Cromie in the *Harvard Gazette,* "but was pulled [to Harvard] by the opportunity to work directly with people I have known and admired for many years."

Spelke has two children of her own, and they, like Spelke herself as a child, have spent a great deal of time abroad as they travel with Spelke on various research projects. In fact, the family has spend so much time in France, that the children, Bridget and Joe, who were 16 and 13 respectively by 2001, have become fluent in French. Balancing her research with her teaching and her own childrearing duties, Spelke at times has felt that she has not been able to devote enough time to each activity. As she told Steven Pinker in *Time,* "There were times I felt I was cheating my science, my students, and my children. Sometimes there aren't enough hours in the day."

One difficulty facing scientists studying human development has been the challenge posed by subjects who are unable to communicate with researchers about their perceptions. This has required Spelke to find new ways to study infants. An approach Spelke uses to solve this problem is to pay close attention to where babies focus their attention during experiments. For instance, one experiment involves showing babies objects falling or rolling until the babies grow bored and look away. Next, Spelke shows the babies the same objects behaving in physically impossible ways—passing through solid objects, disappearing and reappearing, etc. These illusions illicit renewed interest from the babies; they stare more intently, as if they are trying to understand how these impossible events could happen. The same objects behaving normally, even if they fall or roll in different ways, elicit no special interest.

Spelke concludes from these and other experiments that babies are born with an innate set of assumptions about the way objects in the world ought to behave. Certain ideas about space, time, causation, and numbers, Spelke concludes, are inborn rather than learned. For instance, babies know without having to be taught that objects cannot pass through other solid objects, and that objects continue to exist even when we are not looking at them.

Spelke and her colleagues have also demonstrated that babies possess basic counting skills. In one experiment, a ball was shown to infants and then hidden in a box. A second ball was added to the box, and when the infants were asked to pull the ball out of the box, they reached inside the box twice, clearly expecting to find no more or less than two balls in the box. These experiments, Spelke told Cromie, "support the conclusion that babies add one and one to form a representation of two objects."

Further, Spelke and her associates showed that babies can distinguish between two sets of large numbers of objects; for instance, between a group of eight dots and a group of 16 dots. In experiments, the positioning of the dots was varied, showing that the infants really were recognizing the numbers of dots, not just patterns in the dots.

Spelke and her colleagues have also found that infants count the same way that monkeys, rats, and even pigeons do; they can perceive gross differences between groups of numbers, but cannot count them with precision. For example, babies, monkeys, rats, and pigeons can all tell the difference between one and two and between eight and 16, but not between 16 and 18. The more advanced counting ability that is unique to humans comes only with the development of language at about the age of three.

Spelke confirmed her conclusion that higher counting ability is directly related to language ability by studying brain activity in adult humans as they worked with numbers. "These results," Spelke told Cromie, "form part of converging evidence that two different systems are involved in representing numbers. The two systems come together when we learn verbal counting, which then allows us to represent numbers more precisely."

Spelke believes it important to combine insights from other fields of study with her own research. She has continued her education in philosophy, linguistics, computer science, anthropology, and neuroscience as she conducts her own research. "I believe," she told Cromie, "that important insights will emerge from looking at what each of these disciplines can contribute to our understanding of human nature."

Spelke has extended her research efforts to include studies of other creatures unable to communicate verbally, including monkeys. When asked for childrearing advice, Spelke tells parents to relax and enjoy their infants without pushing them to learn; their children's brains will develop just fine on their own.

Sources

Periodicals

Time, August 20, 2001, p. 24.

Online

"Numbers in Mind," *Science News Online,* http://www.sciencenews.org/20020622/bob9ref.asp (August 5, 2002).

"Toddling Toward the Birth of Knowledge," *Harvard University Gazette,* http:www.news.harvard.edu/gazette/2001/11.29/03–spelke.html (August 5, 2002).

—Michael Belfiore

Tony Stewart

AP/Wide World Photos

Professional race car driver

Born May 20, 1971, in Rushville, IN; son of Nelson and Pam Stewart.

Addresses: *Office*—c/o Joe Gibbs Racings, 13415 Reese Blvd. W., Huntersville, NC 28078–7933.

Career

Began racing career on the go–kart circuit at the age of eight; by the age of 18 had won every karting championship available and graduated from karts to bigger, faster cars—the midgets, sprints, and modifieds; began competing on the Indy Racing League (IRL) circuit, winning Rookie of the Year honors his first year, 1996; won IRL series championship, 1997; joined NASCAR's AAA Grand National Division circuit, 1998; began racing on NASCAR's Winston Cup circuit, winning Rookie of the Year honors and winning three races, 1999; won Winston Cup Series championship, 2002.

Sidelights

One of the fastest rising stars on the NASCAR racing circuit, Tony Stewart took only four years on the circuit to win its most coveted prize—the Winston Cup Series championship—in 2002. From the start, however, it was clear that Stewart was a comer. In his 1999 debut season on the Winston Cup circuit, he won three races and finished among the top five no less than 12 times. In addition to collecting more than $3 million in prize money his debut year, Stewart earned NASCAR's Rookie of the Year award. Driving the number 20

Home Depot Pontiac for Joe Gibbs Racing, Stewart finished the 1999 racing season fourth in Winston Cup championship points, the best finish by a rookie in more than three decades.

Most racing analysts seemed to agree that the sky is the limit for Stewart if he can only successfully vanquish his biggest enemy—Tony Stewart. The driver's hair–trigger temper has already cost him dearly. When he won the Winston Cup Series championship in 2002, he did so while still on NASCAR probation for shoving a photographer. Stewart's performance off the track has attracted almost as much attention as his brilliance behind the wheel. His costly confrontation with freelance photographer Gary Mook came in August of 2002 and cost Stewart $60,000 in fines—$10,000 from NASCAR and $50,000 from Home Depot, his sponsor. Both NASCAR and Home Depot also put Stewart on probation. Only a month later, a fan accused Stewart of pushing her after the Sharpie 500 race at Bristol, Tennessee/Virginia. That allegation was eventually determined to be unfounded. On the final weekend of the 2002 Winston Cup season at the Homestead–Miami Speedway, Stewart on November 17 again clashed with a photographer. Getty Images photographer Rusty Jarrett accused Stewart of deliberately running into him in the garage after the final practice for the race. Shortly after the incident

NASCAR summoned both parties to peace talks, during which Stewart apologized to Jarrett, closing the matter. However, NASCAR spokesman Jim Hunter did tell the *Atlanta Journal and Constitution,* "Tony could use a little work with his media relations."

Stewart was born on May 20, 1971, in Columbus, Indiana, just an hour south of the Indianapolis Motor Speedway, the Mecca of auto racing. The son of Nelson and Pam Stewart, he seemed destined almost from birth to become a race car driver. His father put him behind the wheel of a go–kart when he was only seven and before long Stewart hit the local karting circuit, his father serving as both kart owner and crew chief. In 1980, when he was only eight, the young karter won his first championship—winning a four–cycle, rookie junior class race on the speedway at the Columbus fairgrounds. Of the role his father played in shaping his winning ways, Stewart told FOX Sports: "He never let me settle for second. He didn't like it when we ran second, and he knew that I didn't like it when we ran second. If he saw that I wasn't giving 100 percent, then he was on me pretty hard about it. He pushed me to be better."

Stewart followed up his 1980 championship karting run at Columbus with two national championships—the 1983 International Karting Federation Grand National championship and the 1987 World Karting Association national championship. Having accomplished just about all that he could in the world of karting, Stewart in 1989 began to make the transition from go–karts to the faster open–wheel machines, including midgets, sprints, and modifieds. During the 1989 and 1990 seasons, he raced three–quarter midgets before joining the ranks of the United States Auto Club (USAC) in 1991, winning Rookie of the Year honors during his debut season. Three years later, in 1994, Stewart snared his first USAC championship in the National Midget category, winning five times in 22 starts. The following year, he made USAC history when he won the Triple Crown by grabbing the Skoal National Midget, True Value Silver Crown, and Loctite Sprint Car titles all in the same year. Only one other driver in USAC history has managed to win all three titles in a career, much less a single year.

On the strength of his singular success on the USAC circuit, Stewart in 1996 joined the fledgling Indy Racing League (IRL). His prowess as a driver earned him Rookie of the Year awards in 1996 and the IRL series championship in 1997. Stewart's winning ways with USAC and IRL brought him to the attention of Joe Gibbs Racing, which signed him to a contract in 1998. During his first season with the Gibbs team, which includes former Winston Cup champ Bobby Labonte, Stewart drove in a total of 22 NASCAR Busch Series, Grand National Division races to help prepare him for the more rugged schedule of the Winston Cup series. In 1999, Stewart moved into the majors, joining the Winston Cup circuit, which includes a total of more than 35 races each year.

Stewart's debut on the Winston Cup circuit in 1999 was impressive from the very start. At the Daytona 500, his first–ever Winston Cup race, he qualified for the outside front row and ended the race in 28th position. Even more impressive was his performance at Rockingham, North Carolina, where he finished 12th. In back–to–back races at the Tran-South Financial 400 in Darlington, South Carolina, and the Primestar 500 in Texas, Stewart finished in sixth place. By the end of the 1999 Winston Cup series, Stewart had collected more than $3 million in prize monies, winning three races and finishing among the top five 12 times. His brilliant debut earned for Stewart NASCAR Rookie of the Year honors. In total points for the 1999 Winston Cup series, Stewart finished in fourth place, the best showing by a rookie in more than three decades.

As if to prove that his performance in 1999 was more than beginner's luck, Stewart came back strong in 2000, finishing sixth in overall Winston Cup series points on the strength of six wins and 12 finishes among the top five. For his efforts, Stewart collected more than $3.6 million in winnings for 2000. Bobby Labonte, Stewart's teammate on Joe Gibbs Racing, took the Winston Cup championship for 2000. In 2001, his third season on the Winston Cup circuit, Stewart proved even more brilliant on the racetrack. He won three races, finished in the top five 15 times, and in the top 10 a total of 22 times. He earned more than $4.9 million in 2001 and, most importantly, he finished in second place in terms of overall Winston Cup series points.

While tearing up speedways around the country, Stewart also began to develop a reputation among the media as NASCAR's "bad boy." Never one for small talk, Stewart tended to be abrupt in his responses to reporters' inquiries, and before long many of them were dismissing him as sarcastic and condescending. For his part, Stewart admitted frankly that he was tired of having microphones and tape recorders shoved under his nose every time he went to the bathroom. Things came to a head in July of 2001. Stewart, upset with a ruling by NASCAR officials that he considered unfair, batted a tape recorder out of the hands of a reporter who approached him for comment. Stewart then kicked the recorder under a nearby truck. NASCAR took a dim view of Stewart's antics, fining him $10,000 for the incident and putting him on probation for the remainder of the season.

The crowning glory of Stewart's racing career to date came in 2002. Although it was a winning year for the driver overall, it did not get off to the most auspicious start. In the first of his 36 races in the 2002 Winston Cup series, Stewart finished 43rd after he was slowed down by engine trouble. He bounced back three weeks later to win the MBNA American 500 at Atlanta. For the season as a whole, he won three Winston Cup races and finished in the top five a total of 15 times. However, Stewart continued to be dogged by his strained relationship with the media. At Indy in August 2002 came Stewart's fateful confrontation with Mook, an incident that cost him $60,000 in fines and put him on probation with both NASCAR and Home Depot, his sponsor. Stewart managed to perform impressively on the speedway, despite the difficulties he was experiencing away from the track. His 2002 wins on the Winston Cup circuit included not only Atlanta but the Pontiac Excitement 400 at Richmond, Virginia, and the Sirius Satellite Radio run at Watkins Glen, New York.

Until late in the 2002 season, Stewart was trailing four other drivers in points. He vaulted into the ranks of the leaders in October when he placed second in the EA Sports 500 at Talladega, Alabama. The following weekend at Charlotte, North Carolina, he placed third in the UAW–GM Quality 500. He also made a strong showing at the NAPA 500 in Atlanta, in which he finished fourth. Although he performed fairly unimpressively in his last race of the season—the Homestead 400 at Homestead, Florida—he nevertheless managed to compile more points for the season than any other driver on the Winston Cup circuit, cinching the championship for Stewart.

Stewart's winnings for 2002 totaled a very impressive $9.2 million. But, more importantly, he accumulated a total of 4,797 Winston Cup points to win the 2002 championship, the proudest accomplishment of his career thus far. As he told FOX Sports after cinching the Winston Cup championship, "If I had to retype my resume tomorrow, I'd put the Winston Cup championship at No. 1. All of the championships I've been a part of were hard to acquire. None of them were easy. They had their unique set of circumstances, obstacles, and challenges to overcome. But my heart tells me that this championship—the Winston Cup championship—is my greatest accomplishment in racing."

Stewart's emergence as king of the hill in NASCAR racing in 2002 brought the driver a number of unaccustomed honors—including an audience with President George W. Bush and an opportunity to ring the opening bell on the New York Stock Exchange. By all accounts, the latter was the more impressive of the two events for Stewart. As reported by Martin Fennelly in the *Tampa Tribune,* Stewart told reporters: "Wall Street was cool. I got to ring a really obnoxiously loud bell for 30 seconds and nobody could hear anything."

In the first 17 races of the 2003 Winston Cup series, Stewart performed relatively well, finishing among the top five in five races (taking first place at the Pocono 500 on June 8) and in the top ten eight times. Whether he will manage to win the Winston Cup championship again in 2003 will depend, according to many observers, on his ability to harness his sometimes–explosive temper. Although Stewart has demonstrated clearly that he has no difficulty in maneuvering his way around a NASCAR speedway in winning time, he continues to have difficulty dealing with his growing fame. Fellow Hoosier and champion race car driver Jeff Gordon told Fennelly of the *Tampa Tribune,* "When you're successful, there are a lot of things that go with it. You can either go with it or butt heads. Sometimes, Tony still butts some heads."

Away from the racetrack, Stewart, who is single, lives in Davidson, North Carolina. He also owns his boyhood home in Columbus, Indiana. His sister, Natalie, helps run the Tony Stewart Fan Club.

Sources

Books

Complete Marquis Who's Who, Marquis Who's Who, 2003.

Periodicals

Atlanta Journal and Constitution, November 17, 2002, p. E3.
Sports Illustrated, October 21, 2002, p. 58; December 1, 2002, p. 18.
Sports Illustrated for Kids, February 2003, p. 48.
Tampa Tribune, February 13, 2003, p. 1.

Online

"1999 Statistics," Joe Gibbs Racing, http://www. joegibbsracing.com/tony_stewart/wc_20_stats99. php (March 29, 2003).

"2002 Statistics," Joe Gibbs Racing, http://www.joegibbsracing.com/tony_stewart/wc_20_stats02.php (March 29, 2003).

"Career Statistics," Joe Gibbs Racing, http://www.joegibbsracing.com/tony_stewart/wc_20_career.php (March 29, 2003).

"Tony Stewart Bio," FOX Sports.com, http://foxsports.lycos.com/content/view?contentId=310494 (March 28, 2003).

"Tony Stewart: Driver Profile," NASCAR.com, http://www.nascar.com/drivers/dps/tstewart00/wc/bio.html (March 28, 2003).

—Don Amerman

R. L. Stine

Reproduced by permission of R. L. Stine

Children's book author

Born Robert Lawrence Stine, October 8, 1943, in Columbus, OH; son of Lewis (a shipping manager) and Anne (Feinstein) Stine; married Jane Waldhorn (an owner/managing director of Parachute Press), June 22, 1969; children: Matthew Daniel. *Education:* Ohio State University, B.A., 1965; graduate study at New York University, 1966–67.

Addresses: *Office*—Parachute Press, 156 Fifth Ave., New York, NY 10010. *Websites*—http://www.scholastic.com/goosebumps/, http://www.thenightmareroom.com/.

Career

Social studies teacher at junior high schools in Columbus, OH, 1967–68; associate editor, *Junior Scholastic* magazine, New York City, 1968–71; editor, *Search* magazine, New York City, 1972–75; editor, *Bananas* magazine, New York City, 1975–84; published first children's humor book, *How to Be Funny*, 1978; freelance writer, 1982—; editor, *Maniac* magazine, New York City, 1984–85; published first scary novel for young audience, *Blind Date*, 1986; launched Fear Street series of novels with *The New Girl*, 1989; launched Goosebumps series with *Welcome to Dead House*, 1992; launched Nightmare Room series with *Liar, Liar*, 2000; head writer for Eureeka's Castle, Nickelodeon cable network; has also written a number of books targeted at older readers, including his autobiography, *It Came from Ohio: My Life as a Writer.*

Awards: American Library Association Children's Choice Award for several novels.

Sidelights

One of the most successful children's book authors of all time, R. L. Stine is also one of the most prolific. Best known for his wildly popular Fear Street, Goosebumps, and Nightmare Room series of novels, he churns out an average of two books every month, for an annual total of about 24 new novels. In 2000 Stine was recognized by the record–keeping folks at Guinness as the author of the world's top–selling children's series—namely Goosebumps. However, despite all these superlatives, he remains little known outside his target audience of young readers, who can't seem to get enough of the scary thrills supplied in abundance by Stine's creepy novels.

Stine admits to enjoying a good scare when he was a boy, a sensation he has happily shared with millions of young people since the mid–1980s, when he turned out *Blind Date*, the first of his trademark horror tales for teens and pre–teens. As he wrote on the Scholastic Books's website: "When I write, I try to think back to what I was afraid of or what was scary to me, and try to put those feelings into books." As inspiration, Stine has decorated his writing studio with a hanging skeleton and a tribal mask. The author prides himself on supplying younger readers with a safe—yet unforgettable—thrill. Asked by Tracy Rodrigues of the *Time* for Kids website what it took to scare kids or get under their skin, Stine replied: "Not much, because I think kids enjoy safe scares, like reading about a monster but knowing the book won't go too far or be too disgusting. So, at the same time they know they're safe, just reading in their room, and that there will always be a happy ending."

Stine was born on October 8, 1943, in Columbus, Ohio. The son of Lewis, a shipping manager, and Anne Stine, he began writing when he was only nine years old. As a child, he was inspired by some of the gruesome tales he found in comic books such as *Tales from the Crypt* and *The Vault of Horror*. He read the comic books as he waited for his turn in the chair at the neighborhood barber shop. "I used to get a haircut every Saturday so I would never miss any of the comic books," Stine told *Time* for Kids. "I had practically no hair when I was a kid!"

Not surprisingly, Stine's favorite holiday as a child was Halloween. In an article written for the Scholastic Kids Fun Online website, Stine recalled: "I always wanted to be something really scary. A ghost. A mummy. A—duck? One year, my mother bought me a duck suit. Other kids thought it was pretty funny, but I didn't think it was funny at all. When I wrote *The Haunted Mask* for Goosebumps, I remembered the duck costume and how embarrassing it was. So I gave Carly Beth, the girl in the book, a duck costume, too."

Although he was fascinated by tales of mystery and horror, some of Stine's earliest writings were in the humorous vein, an interest he continued to pursue during his years at Ohio State University, where he served for three years as editor of the campus humor magazine. After earning his bachelor's degree at Ohio State in 1965, Stine taught social studies for a year at a junior high school in Columbus. He then headed for New York City in the hopes of landing a writing job. For the next couple of years he worked for a variety of New York–based magazines. He eventually landed a job at Scholastic Books in 1968, working first as an assistant editor on *Junior Scholastic* magazine. In June of 1969, Stine married Jane Waldhorn, a fellow employee at Scholastic who several years later founded Parachute Press with Joan Waricha. The couple has a son, Matthew Daniel. In 1972 Stine was named editor of Scholastic's *Search* magazine, on which he worked until 1975 when he created *Bananas*, a humor magazine for pre–teens and teens. Stine also served as editor of *Bananas* un-

til 1984. That same year, Scholastic launched another Stine creation, *Maniac* magazine, which he edited for the first year of its existence.

The seeds for Stine's career as an author of children's books were sown in the late 1970s when he was approached by Ellen Rudin, an editor at Dutton. Rudin, impressed with Stine's work on *Bananas*, suggested that he give some thought to writing a humorous book for younger readers. Writing under the name Jovial Bob Stine, he turned out *How to Be Funny: An Extremely Silly Guidebook*, published by Dutton in 1978. This was followed by a number of humor books for kids published in the late 1970s and early 1980s.

Stine's childhood fascination with horror and mystery came in handy in the early 1980s when he began writing "Twistaplot" books for Scholastic and books with similar themes for Avon and Ballantine. Some of the latter were published under the pseudonyms of Eric Affabee and Zachary Blue. Somewhat ironically, the biggest impetus for his horror writing career came in the mid–1980s when he was laid off by Scholastic, which was experiencing financial problems. Stine suddenly found himself with plenty of time on his hands, time he devoted to writing more books. Acting on a suggestion from Jean Feiwel, the editorial director of Scholastic Books, that he try his hand at a horror novel, Stine turned out *Blind Date*, the tale of a teenage boy with a memory lapse and the mysterious girl who wants to date him. Like many of his novels, *Blind Date* had a title—suggested by Feiwel—long before it had a plot. Stine often starts his projects with nothing more than a title. In those cases, he tries to decide what scary possibilities the title suggests, giving rise to the outlines of a plot. Once his ideas have crystallized, he actually begins the writing process.

Stine followed *Blind Date* with a few other hit books, including 1987's *Twisted* and 1989's *The Baby–Sitter*. At the suggestion of his wife, he began trying to come up with ideas for a series of books that she might be able to sell through Parachute Press. Thus was the Fear Street series born. *The New Girl*, the first book in the series, was released in 1989. The connecting thread for most of the 100 titles in the series is the fact that most main characters live on Fear Street, which according to the cover copy on early titles in the series is a place "where your worst nightmares live." All characters in the Fear Street series of novels attend Shadyside High. With millions of copies in print, Stine's Fear Street series has been wildly popular. Almost all the novels in the series are stronger on plot than characterization and move at a hair–raising pace. Young fans of the series are particularly captivated by the author's trademark cliffhangers, with which almost all chapters end. Villains in the series range from supernatural forces to mere mortals with murderous tendencies.

Although young readers everywhere seemed to embrace Stine's novels with enthusiasm, many literary critics were decidedly less impressed with their formulaic nature. In a *Publishers Weekly* review of *Twisted*, the reviewer observed: "For shock value, this book adds up to a lot of cheap tricks." Caroline S. McKinney, reviewing *The Second Evil* in the pages of *Voice of Youth Advocates*, wrote that "these formula stories are very predictable and require very little thought on the part of the reader." Not all reviewers were so unkind. In a review of *The Sleepwalker* for *School Library Journal*, Alice Cronin declared that "Stine writes a good story. Teens will love the action." Even more positive was reviewer Sylvia C. Mitchell's assessment of *Silent Night* in *Voice of Youth Advocates* in which she observed that "if all series books were this good, I'd begin to drop my … prejudices against them."

The Fear Street series was so successful was that Stine in the early 1990s decided to launch yet another series, this one targeted at "tweens"—eight to 12 year olds. Encouraged by Waricha, his wife's partner in Parachute Press, Stine came up with the idea of the Goosebumps series, with stories a little less chilling than those he'd crafted for teens in the Fear Street series. The first book in the Goosebumps series—*Welcome to Dead House*—was published by Scholastic in 1992 and became an instant hit. Priced at only $3.99 a copy, the Goosebumps novels flew off the shelves, snatched up by pre–teens who could afford to buy the books out of their allowances. The success of the Goosebumps franchise—selling one to two million copies monthly—bowled over the publishing industry. Even more impressive was the ability of the Goosebumps stories to lure pre–teen boys into reading.

The unprecedented success of the Goosebumps series vaulted Stine into the public eye. Soon books in the series had become bestsellers in the United Kingdom, France, Germany, Italy, Spain, and Australia, and the series was translated into 16 languages in 31 countries. For three years running, Stine was named the best–selling author in the United States by *USA Today*. In the mid–1990s Fox launched a Goosebumps series on its Children's TV Network. Of his series's transformation to the small screen, Stine said, as quoted on the Real Answers website, "Goosebumps on TV is even scarier [than] books because it has real kids and real monsters."

Writing on Scholastic's Kids Fun Online website about how he got some of the ideas for his stories, Stine recalled: "The idea for the Goosebumps book *Stay Out of the Basement* all started with a crazy picture that flashed into my mind. I imagined a father taking off his baseball cap. Leaves were growing on his head instead of hair. How did the leaves get there? Who is the father? Is he turning into a plant? Is he *already* a plant?"

Whether it was attributable to the emergence of the Harry Potter phenomenon or simply changing tastes, Goosebumps books experienced a sharp drop in sales in the late 1990s. Scholastic Books, which marketed the series, reported that the Goosebumps series, which accounted for about 15 percent of revenues in 1996, had skidded to only 4 percent by 1999. As a consequence, Scholastic's stock took a beating, and the publisher's once–happy relationship with Stine and Parachute Press turned sour. Although the parties continued to work together, Scholastic filed a suit charging that Parachute had breached its contract and demanded back more than $10 million.

Looking to reinvigorate lagging sales, Stine in the late 1990s teamed up with HarperCollins to launch still another series he called the Nightmare Room. The first book in the series, *Liar, Liar*, was published in 2000. Nightmare Room differed from Stine's earlier series in that it combined each book with an online experience, marking the first time a children's author had created an interactive site as an online companion to his printed products. The Nightmare Room Web site can be found at http://www.thenightmareroom.com.

Of his latest series and its difference from Goosebumps, which proved a big seller with young readers, Stine told *Time*: "I always describe Goosebumps as a roller–coaster ride, all the twists and turns and crazy things jumping out at you. I see The Nightmare Room more like a fun house. You step inside this place, and everything seems normal at first. And then you look and you see, ah, the floor is tilted. And then it looks like the walls are closing in on you.... You're not in your old reality."

For wannabe writers, Stine offered this advice at the Scholastic Kids Fun Online website: "If you want to be a writer, don't worry so much about writing. Read as much as you can. Read as many different writers as you can. Soak up the styles. You can learn all kinds of ways to say things." Some of Stine's favorites as a boy were Norse legends, Greek myths, baseball stories, and almost anything by Edgar Allan Poe. The author and wife share their home on Manhattan's West Side with their dog, Nadine.

Selected writings

Young adult novels

Blind Date, Scholastic (New York, NY), 1986.

Twisted, Scholastic (New York, NY), 1987.

Broken Date ("Crosswinds" Series), Simon & Schuster (New York, NY), 1988.

The Baby–Sitter, Scholastic (New York, NY), 1989.

Phone Calls, Archway (New York, NY), 1990.

How I Broke up with Ernie, Archway (New York, NY), 1990.

Curtains, Archway (New York, NY), 1990.

The Boyfriend, Scholastic (New York, NY), 1990.

Beach Party, Scholastic (New York, NY), 1990.

Snowman, Scholastic (New York, NY), 1991.

The Girlfriend, Scholastic (New York, NY), 1991.

Baby–Sitter II, Scholastic (New York, NY), 1991.

Beach House, Scholastic (New York, NY), 1992.

Hit and Run, Scholastic (New York, NY), 1992.

Hitchhiker, Scholastic (New York, NY), 1993.

Baby–sitter III, Scholastic (New York, NY), 1993.

The Dead Girl Friend, Scholastic (New York, NY), 1993.

Halloween Night, Scholastic (New York, NY), 1993.

Call Waiting, Scholastic (New York, NY), 1994.

Halloween Night 2, Scholastic (New York, NY), 1994.

"Fear Street" series

The New Girl, Archway (New York, NY), 1989.

The Surprise Party, Archway (New York, NY), 1990.

The Stepsister, Archway (New York, NY), 1990.

Missing, Archway (New York, NY), 1990.

Halloween Party, Archway (New York, NY), 1990.

The Wrong Number, Archway (New York, NY), 1990.

The Sleepwalker, Archway (New York, NY), 1991.

Ski Weekend, Archway (New York, NY), 1991.

Silent Night, Archway (New York, NY), 1991.

The Secret Bedroom, Archway (New York, NY), 1991.

The Overnight, Archway (New York, NY), 1991.

Lights Out, Archway (New York, NY), 1991.

Haunted, Archway (New York, NY), 1991.

The Fire Game, Archway (New York, NY), 1991.

The Knife, Archway (New York, NY), 1992.

Prom Queen, Archway (New York, NY), 1992.

First Date, Archway (New York, NY), 1992.

The Best Friend, Archway (New York, NY), 1992.

Sunburn, Archway (New York, NY), 1993.

The Cheater, Archway (New York, NY), 1993.

The New Boy, Archway (New York, NY), 1994.

Bad Dreams, Archway (New York, NY), 1994.

The Dare, Archway (New York, NY), 1994.

Double Date, Archway (New York, NY), 1994.

The First Horror, Archway (New York, NY), 1994.

The Mind Reader, Archway (New York, NY), 1994.

One Evil Summer, Archway (New York, NY), 1994.

The Second Horror, Archway (New York, NY), 1994.

The Third Horror, Archway (New York, NY), 1994.

The Thrill Club, Archway (New York, NY), 1994.

College Weekend, Archway (New York, NY), 1995.

Final Grade, Archway (New York, NY), 1995.

The Stepsister 2, Archway (New York, NY), 1995.

Switched, Archway (New York, NY), 1995.

Truth or Dare, Archway (New York, NY), 1995.

Wrong Number 2, Archway (New York, NY), 1995.

What Holly Heard, Pocket Books (New York, NY), 1996.

The Face, Pocket Books (New York, NY), 1996.

Secret Admirer, Pocket Books (New York, NY), 1996.

The Perfect Date, Pocket Books (New York, NY), 1996.

The Boy Next Door, Simon & Schuster (New York, NY), 1996.

Night Games, Pocket Books (New York, NY), 1996.

Runaway, Archway (New York, NY), 1997.

Killer's Kiss, Archway (New York, NY), 1997.

All–Night Party, Archway (New York, NY), 1997.

The Rich Girl, Archway (New York, NY), 1997.

Cat, Archway (New York, NY), 1997.

Fear Hall: The Beginning, Archway (New York, NY), 1997.

Fear Hall: The Conclusion, Archway (New York, NY), 1997.

"Fear Street Super Chiller" series

Party Summer, Archway (New York, NY), 1991.

Goodnight Kiss, Archway (New York, NY), 1992.

Silent Night, Archway (New York, NY), 1992.

Broken Hearts, Archway (New York, NY), 1993.

Silent Night II, Archway (New York, NY), 1993.

The Dead Lifeguard, Archway (New York, NY), 1994.

Bad Moonlight, Archway (New York, NY), 1995.

Dead End, Archway (New York, NY), 1995.

High Tide, Archway (New York, NY), 1997.

"Fear Street Cheerleaders" series

The First Evil, Archway (New York, NY), 1992.

The Second Evil, Archway (New York, NY), 1992.

The Third Evil, Archway (New York, NY), 1992.

The New Evil, Archway (New York, NY), 1994.

"Fear Street Saga" series

The Betrayal, Archway (New York, NY), 1993.
The Secret, Archway (New York, NY), 1993.
The Burning, Archway (New York, NY), 1993.
A New Fear, Pocket Books (New York, NY), 1996.
House of Whispers, Simon & Schuster (New York, NY), 1996.
The Hidden Evil, Archway (New York, NY), 1997.
Daughters of Silence, Archway (New York, NY), 1997.
Children of Fear, Archway (New York, NY), 1997.

"Ghosts of Fear Street" series

Nightmare in 3–D, Pocket Books (New York, NY), 1996.
Stay Away from the Treehouse, Pocket Books (New York, NY), 1996.
Eye of the Fortuneteller, Pocket Books (New York, NY), 1996.
Fright Knight, Pocket Books (New York, NY), 1996.
Revenge of the Shadow People, Pocket Books (New York, NY), 1996.
The Bugman Lives, Pocket Books (New York, NY), 1996.
The Boy Who Ate Fear Street, Pocket Books (New York, NY), 1996.
Night of the Werecat, Pocket Books (New York, NY), 1996.
Body Switchers from Outer Space, Pocket Books (New York, NY), 1996.
Fright Christmas, Pocket Books (New York, NY), 1996.
Don't Ever Get Sick at Granny's, Pocket Books (New York, NY), 1997.

"Goosebumps" series

Welcome to Dead House, Scholastic (New York, NY), 1992.
Stay out of the Basement, Scholastic (New York, NY), 1992.
Monster Blood, Scholastic (New York, NY), 1992.
Say Cheese and Die, Scholastic (New York, NY), 1992.
The Curse of the Mummy's Tomb, Scholastic (New York, NY), 1993.
Let's Get Invisible, Scholastic (New York, NY), 1993.
Night of the Living Dummy, Scholastic (New York, NY), 1993.
The Girl Who Cried Monster, Scholastic (New York, NY), 1993.
Welcome to Camp Nightmare, Scholastic (New York, NY), 1993.
The Ghost Next Door, Scholastic (New York, NY), 1993.
The Haunted Mask, Scholastic (New York, NY), 1993.

Be Careful What You Wish For, Scholastic (New York, NY), 1993.
Piano Lessons Can Be Murder, Scholastic (New York, NY), 1993.
The Werewolf of Fever Swamp, Scholastic (New York, NY), 1993.
You Can't Scare Me, Scholastic (New York, NY), 1993.
One Day at Horrorland, Scholastic (New York, NY), 1994.
Why I'm Afraid of Bees, Scholastic (New York, NY), 1994.
Monster Blood 2, Scholastic (New York, NY), 1994.
Deep Trouble, Scholastic (New York, NY), 1994.
The Scarecrow Walks at Midnight, Scholastic (New York, NY), 1994.
Go Eat Worms!, Scholastic (New York, NY), 1994.
Ghost Beach, Scholastic (New York, NY), 1994.
Return of the Mummy, Scholastic (New York, NY), 1994.
Phantom of the Auditorium, Scholastic (New York, NY), 1994.
Attack of the Mutant, Scholastic (New York, NY), 1994.
My Hairiest Adventure, Scholastic (New York, NY), 1994.
A Night in Terror Tower, Scholastic (New York, NY), 1995.
The Cuckoo Clock of Doom, Scholastic (New York, NY), 1995.
Monster Blood 3, Scholastic (New York, NY), 1995.
It Came from beneath the Sink, Scholastic (New York, NY), 1995.
The Night of the Living Dummy 2, Scholastic (New York, NY), 1995.
The Barking Ghost, Scholastic (New York, NY), 1995.
The Horror at Camp Jellyjam, Scholastic (New York, NY), 1995.
Revenge of the Lawn Gnomes, Scholastic (New York, NY), 1995.
A Shocker on Shock Street, Scholastic (New York, NY), 1995.
The Haunted Mask 2, Scholastic (New York, NY), 1995.
The Headless Ghost, Scholastic (New York, NY), 1995.
The Abominable Snowman of Pasadena, Scholastic (New York, NY), 1995.
How I Got My Shrunken Head, Scholastic (New York, NY), 1996.
Night of the Living Dummy 3, Scholastic (New York, NY), 1996.
Bad Hare Day, Scholastic (New York, NY), 1996.
Egg Monsters from Mars, Scholastic (New York, NY), 1996.
The Beast from the East, Scholastic (New York, NY), 1996.
Say Cheese and Die—Again!, Scholastic (New York, NY), 1996.
Ghost Camp, Scholastic (New York, NY), 1996.

How to Kill a Monster, Scholastic (New York, NY), 1996.

Legend of the Lost Legend, Scholastic (New York, NY), 1996.

Attack of the Jack-o'-Lanterns, Scholastic (New York, NY), 1996.

Vampire Breath, Scholastic (New York, NY), 1996.

Calling All Creeps!, Scholastic (New York, NY), 1996.

Beware the Snowman, Scholastic (New York, NY), 1997.

How I Learned to Fly, Scholastic (New York, NY), 1997.

Chicken, Chicken, Scholastic (New York, NY), 1997.

Don't Go to Sleep!, Scholastic (New York, NY), 1997.

The Blob That Ate Everyone, Scholastic (New York, NY), 1997.

The Curse of Camp Cold Lake, Scholastic (New York, NY), 1997.

My Best Friend Is Invisible, Scholastic (New York, NY), 1997.

Deep Trouble II, Scholastic (New York, NY), 1997.

The Haunted School, Scholastic (New York, NY), 1997.

Werewolf Skin, Scholastic (New York, NY), 1997.

I Live in Your Basement!, Scholastic (New York, NY), 1997.

Monster Blood IV, Scholastic (New York, NY), 1997.

Also author of "Goosebumps Presents" books based on the television series, including *The Girl Who Cried Monster*, 1996, and *Welcome to Camp Nightmare*, 1996.

"Give Yourself Goosebumps" series

Escape from the Carnival of Horrors, Scholastic (New York, NY), 1995.

Tick Tock, You're Dead, Scholastic (New York, NY), 1995.

Trapped in Bat Wing Hall, Scholastic (New York, NY), 1995.

The Deadly Experiments of Dr. Eeek, Scholastic (New York, NY), 1996.

Night in Werewolf Woods, Scholastic (New York, NY), 1996.

Beware of the Purple Peanut Butter, Scholastic (New York, NY), 1996.

Under the Magician's Spell, Scholastic (New York, NY), 1996.

The Curse of the Creeping Coffin, Scholastic (New York, NY), 1996.

The Knight in Screaming Armor, Scholastic (New York, NY), 1996.

Diary of a Mad Mummy, Scholastic (New York, NY), 1996.

Deep in the Jungle of Doom, Scholastic (New York, NY), 1996.

Welcome to the Wicked Wax Museum, Scholastic (New York, NY), 1996.

Scream of the Evil Genie, Scholastic (New York, NY), 1997.

The Creepy Creations of Professor Shock, Scholastic (New York, NY), 1997.

Please Don't Feed the Vampire, Scholastic (New York, NY), 1997.

Secret Agent Grandma, Scholastic (New York, NY), 1997.

The Little Comic Shop of Horrors, Scholastic (New York, NY), 1997.

Attack of the Beastly Babysitter, Scholastic (New York, NY), 1997.

Escape from Camp Run for Your Life, Scholastic (New York, NY), 1997.

Toy Terror: Batteries Included, Scholastic (New York, NY), 1997.

The Twisted Tale of Tiki Island, Scholastic (New York, NY), 1997.

Return to the Carnival of Horrors, Scholastic (New York, NY), 1998.

Zapped in Space, Scholastic (New York, NY), 1998.

Lost In Stinkeye Swamp, Scholastic (New York, NY), 1998.

Shop Till You Drop ... Dead, Scholastic (New York, NY), 1998.

Alone in Snakebite Canyon, Scholastic (New York, NY), 1998.

Checkout Time at the Dead-End Hotel, Scholastic (New York, NY), 1998.

Night of a Thousand Claws, Scholastic (New York, NY), 1998.

You're Plant Food!, Scholastic (New York, NY), 1998.

Werewolf of Twisted Tree Lodge, Scholastic (New York, NY), 1998.

It's Only a Nightmare!, Scholastic (New York, NY), 1998.

It Came from the Internet, Scholastic (New York, NY), 1999.

Elevator to Nowhere, Scholastic (New York, NY), 1999.

Hocus-Pocus Horror, Scholastic (New York, NY), 1999.

Ship of Ghouls, Scholastic (New York, NY), 1999.

Escape from Horror House, Scholastic (New York, NY), 1999.

Into the Twister of Terror, Scholastic (New York, NY), 1999.

Scary Birthday to You!, Scholastic (New York, NY), 1999.

Zombie School, Scholastic (New York, NY), 1999.

Danger Time, Scholastic (New York, NY), 2000.

All-Day Nightmare, Scholastic (New York, NY), 2000.

"Give Yourself Goosebumps Special Edition" series

Into the Jaws of Doom, Scholastic (New York, NY), 1998.

Return to Terror Tower, Scholastic (New York, NY), 1998.

Trapped in the Circus of Fear, Scholastic (New York, NY), 1998.

One Night in Payne House, Scholastic (New York, NY), 1998.

The Curse of the Cave Creatures, Scholastic (New York, NY), 1999.

Revenge of the Body Squeezers, Scholastic (New York, NY), 1999.

Trick or … Trapped, Scholastic (New York, NY), 1999.

Weekend at Poison Lake, Scholastic (New York, NY), 1999.

"Goosebumps 2000" series

Cry of the Cat, Scholastic (New York, NY), 1998.

Bride of the Living Dummy, Scholastic (New York, NY), 1998.

Creature Teacher, Scholastic (New York, NY), 1998.

Invasion of the Body Squeezers Part 1, Scholastic (New York, NY), 1998.

Invasion of the Body Squeezers Part 2, Scholastic (New York, NY), 1998.

I Am Your Evil Twin, Scholastic (New York, NY), 1998.

Revenge R Us, Scholastic (New York, NY), 1998.

Fright Camp, Scholastic (New York, NY), 1998.

Are You Terrified Yet?, Scholastic (New York, NY), 1998.

Headless Halloween, Scholastic (New York, NY), 1999.

Attack of the Graveyard Ghouls, Scholastic (New York, NY), 1999.

Brain Juice, Scholastic (New York, NY), 1999.

Return to Horrorland, Scholastic (New York, NY), 1999.

Jekyll and Heidi, Scholastic (New York, NY), 1999.

Scream School, Scholastic (New York, NY), 1999.

The Mummy Walks, Scholastic (New York, NY), 1999.

The Werewolf in the Living Room, Scholastic (New York, NY), 1999.

Horrors of the Black Ring, Scholastic (New York, NY), 1999.

Return to Ghost Camp, Scholastic (New York, NY), 1999.

Be Afraid—Be Very Afraid!, Scholastic (New York, NY), 1999.

The Haunted Car!, Scholastic (New York, NY), 1999.

Full Moon Fever, Scholastic (New York, NY), 1999.

Slappy's Nightmare, Scholastic (New York, NY), 1999.

Earth Geeks Must Go!, Scholastic (New York, NY), 1999.

Ghost in the Mirror, Scholastic (New York, NY), 2000.

Also author of *Tales to Give You Goosebumps*, and *More Tales to Give You Goosebumps*.

"Nightmare Room" series

Liar, Liar, HarperCollins (New York, NY), 2000.

Don't Forget Me!, Avon (New York, NY), 2000.

Dear Diary, I'm Dead, HarperCollins (New York, NY), 2000.

Shadow Girl, Avon (New York, NY), 2001.

The Howler, Avon (New York, NY), 2001.

Camp Nowhere, HarperCollins (New York, NY), 2001.

They Call Me Creature, HarperCollins (New York, NY), 2001.

"Space Cadets" series

Jerks–in–Training, Scholastic (New York, NY), 1991.

Losers in Space, Scholastic (New York, NY), 1991.

Bozos on Patrol, Scholastic (New York, NY), 1992.

Juvenile

The Time Raider, illustrations by David Febland, Scholastic (New York, NY), 1982.

The Golden Sword of Dragonwalk, illustrations by David Febland, Scholastic (New York, NY), 1983.

Horrors of the Haunted Museum, Scholastic (New York, NY), 1984.

Instant Millionaire, illustrations by Jowill Woodman, Scholastic (New York, NY), 1984.

Through the Forest of Twisted Dreams, Avon (New York, NY), 1984.

The Badlands of Hark, illustrations by Bob Roper, Scholastic (New York, NY), 1985.

The Invaders of Hark, Scholastic (New York, NY), 1985.

Demons of the Deep, illustrations by Fred Carrillo, Golden Books (New York, NY), 1985.

Challenge of the Wolf Knight ("Wizards, Warriors, and You" Series), Avon (New York, NY), 1985.

James Bond in Win, Place, or Die, Ballantine (New York, NY), 1985.

Conquest of the Time Master, Avon (New York, NY), 1985.

Cavern of the Phantoms, Avon (New York, NY), 1986.

Mystery of the Imposter, Avon (New York, NY), 1986.

Golden Girl and the Vanishing Unicorn ("Golden Girl" series), Ballantine (New York, NY), 1986.

The Beast, Minstrel (New York, NY), 1994.

I Saw You That Night!, Scholastic (New York, NY), 1994.

The Beast 2, Minstrel (New York, NY), 1995.

When Good Ghouls Go Bad, Avon (New York, NY), 2001.

"Indiana Jones" series

Indiana Jones and the Curse of Horror Island, Ballantine (New York, NY), 1984.

Indiana Jones and the Giants of the Silver Tower, Ballantine (New York, NY), 1984.

Indiana Jones and the Cult of the Mummy's Crypt, Ballantine (New York, NY), 1985.

Indiana Jones and the Ape Slaves of Howling Island, Ballantine (New York, NY), 1987.

"G.I. Joe" series

Operation: Deadly Decoy, Ballantine (New York, NY), 1986.

Operation: Mindbender, Ballantine (New York, NY), 1986.

Serpentor and the Mummy Warrior, 1987.

Jungle Raid, Ballantine (New York, NY), 1988.

Siege of Serpentor, Ballantine (New York, NY), 1988.

Under name Jovial Bob Stine

The Absurdly Silly Encyclopedia and Flyswatter, illustrations by Bob Taylor, Scholastic (New York, NY), 1978.

How to Be Funny: An Extremely Silly Guidebook, illustrations by Carol Nicklaus, Dutton (New York, NY), 1978.

The Complete Book of Nerds, illustrations by Sam Viviano, Scholastic (New York, NY), 1979.

The Dynamite Do–It–Yourself Pen Pal Kit, illustrations by Jared Lee, Scholastic (New York, NY), 1980.

Dynamite's Funny Book of the Sad Facts of Life, illustrations by Jared Lee, Scholastic (New York, NY), 1980.

Going Out! Going Steady! Going Bananas!, photographs by Dan Nelken, Scholastic (New York, NY), 1980.

The Pig's Book of World Records, illustrations by Peter Lippman, Random House (New York, NY), 1980.

(With Jane Stine) *The Sick of Being Sick Book,* edited by Ann Durrell, illustrations by Carol Nicklaus, Dutton (New York, NY), 1980.

Bananas Looks at TV, Scholastic (New York, NY), 1981.

The Beast Handbook, illustrations by Bob Taylor, Scholastic (New York, NY), 1981.

(With Jane Stine) *The Cool Kids' Guide to Summer Camp,* illustrations by Jerry Zimmerman, Scholastic (New York, NY), 1981.

Gnasty Gnomes, illustrations by Peter Lippman, Random House (New York, NY), 1981.

Under the name Eric Affabee

Attack on the King, Avon (New York, NY), 1986.

G.I. Joe and the Everglades Swamp Terror, Ballantine (New York, NY), 1986.

Under the name Zachary Blue

The Jet Fighter Trap, Scholastic (New York, NY), 1987.

The Petrova Twist, Scholastic (New York, NY), 1987.

Other writings

Don't Stand in the Soup, illustrations by Carol Nicklaus, Bantam (New York, NY), 1982.

(With Jane Stine) *Bored with Being Bored!: How to Beat the Boredom Blahs,* illustrations by Jerry Zimmerman, Four Winds (New York, NY), 1982.

Blips!: The First Book of Video Game Funnies, illustrations by Bryan Hendrix, Scholastic (New York, NY), 1983.

(With Jane Stine) *Everything You Need to Survive: Brothers and Sisters,* illustrated by Sal Murdocca, Random House (New York, NY), 1983.

(With Jane Stine) *Everything You Need to Survive: First Dates,* illustrated by Sal Murdocca, Random House (New York, NY), 1983.

(With Jane Stine) *Everything You Need to Survive: Homework,* illustrated by Sal Murdocca, Random House (New York, NY), 1983.

(With Jane Stine) *Everything You Need to Survive: Money Problems,* illustrated by Sal Murdocca, Random House (New York, NY), 1983.

Jovial Bob's Computer Joke Book, Scholastic (New York, NY), 1985

Miami Mice, illustrations by Eric Gurney, Scholastic (New York, NY), 1986.

One Hundred and One Silly Monster Jokes, Scholastic (New York, NY), 1986.

The Doggone Dog Joke Book, Parachute Press, 1986.

Pork & Beans: Play Date, illustrations by José Aruego and Ariane Dewey, Scholastic (New York, NY), 1989.

Ghostbusters II Storybook, Scholastic (New York, NY), 1989.

One Hundred and One Vacation Jokes, illustrated by Rick Majica, Scholastic (New York, NY), 1990.

The Amazing Adventures of Me, Myself and I, Bantam (New York, NY), 1991.

Superstitious (adult horror), Warner Books (New York, NY), 1995.

It Came from Ohio: My Life as a Writer, (autobiography), Scholastic (New York, NY), 1997.

Nightmare Hour (short stories), HarperCollins (New York, NY), 1999.

The Haunting Hour (short stories), HarperCollins (New York, NY), 2001.

Beware! R. L. Stine Picks His Favorite Scary Stories, HarperCollins (New York, NY), 2002.

Also author of several "Twistaplot" books for Scholastic and "You Choose the Storyline" books for Ballantine and Avon.

Media adaptations

The Goosebumps series was produced by Scholastic Inc. as a live–action television series for the Fox Television Network beginning in 1995; *When Good Ghouls Go Bad* was adapted for video by Fox, 2001; The Nightmare Room series was adapted for a television show by Kids WB (Warner Brothers) network, 2001.

Sources

Books

Contemporary Popular Writers, St. James Press, 1997.

St. James Guide to Horror, Ghost & Gothic Writers, St. James Press, 1998.

St. James Guide to Young Adult Writers, second edition, St. James Press, 1999.

Periodicals

Publishers Weekly, July 10, 1987, p. 87.

School Library Journal, September 1990, p. 70.

Time, August 28, 2000.

U.S. News & World Report, October 23, 1995, p. 95.

Voice of Youth Advocates, April 1992, pp. 36–37; February 1993, p. 360.

Your Company, May 1, 1999, p. 68.

Online

"Author: R. L. Stine," KidsReads,com, http://www.kidsreads.com/authors/au–stine–rl.asp (August 19, 2002).

Contemporary Authors Online, Gale Group, 2002.

"Goosebumps," Real Answers with Steve Russo, http://www.24sevenvideos.com/gb.html (August 19, 2002).

"R. L. Stine, Author," *Time* for Kids, http://www.timeforkids.com/TFK/explore/story/0,6079,176635,00.html (August 17, 2002).

"Where Do You Get Your Ideas?" Scholastic Kids Fun Online, http://www.scholastic.com/goosebumps/books/stine/ideas.htm (August 17, 2002).

Transcripts

All Things Considered, National Public Radio, October 26, 1999.

—Don Amerman

Fritz Strobl

Downhill skier

Born August 24, 1972, in Steinfeld, Austria; married Bettina; children: two sons.

Addresses: *Office*—c/o Austrian Ski Federation (Österreichischer Skiverband), Olympiastrasse 10, A–6010 Innsbruck, Austria.

Career

Began skiing competitively in the late 1980s, while still a teenager; won berths on Austria's national downhill ski team through the late 1990s and into the new millennium; has won multiple

AP/Wide World Photos

World Cup downhill and Super–G events, as well as downhill gold medal at 2002 Winter Olympics in Salt Lake City. Serves as a policeman.

Sidelights

Although his skiing career spans three decades, Fritz Strobl's gold medal–winning downhill run at the 2002 Winter Olympics surprised just about everybody, except perhaps Strobl himself. The heavy favorite to win downhill gold at Salt Lake City was Strobl's teammate and countryman Stephan Eberharter, who had to settle for bronze at the Olympics. After all, Eberharter had finished first in the 2001–02 World Cup downhill competition (Strobl finished fifth) and, with countryman Hermann Maier sidelined by injuries from a motorcycle accident, was considered Austria's strongest downhill contender by far. Perhaps sensing that the near future held big things for him, Strobl only a month before his win at Salt Lake City had told reporters, according to *Sports Illustrated,* "Races aren't won by reputation. They are won by the fastest racer."

Strobl had managed to work his way up in World Cup standings dramatically during the decade preceding the 2002 Winter Olympics, climbing from a 116th–place finish in the 1993–94 competition to fifth place in 2001–02. In the five years of World Cup competition immediately preceding the Salt Lake City games, Strobl finished 27th in 1997–98; 14th in 1998–99; seventh in 1999–2000; 13th in 2000–01; and fifth in 2001–02. By contrast, Eberharter never finished below sixth place during the same period.

Strobl was born in Steinfeld, Austria, on August 24, 1972. He grew up in the mountains of Austria's alpine region and learned how to ski while still quite young. By the mid–1980s he was skiing competitively. It was not until the early 1990s, however, that he managed to win a berth on the Austrian national ski team and began racing on the World Cup circuit. In 1991, at the age of 19, Strobl made his World Cup debut at a downhill race in nearby Garmisch–Partenkirchen, Germany. Later that season, he tore ligaments in his left knee at a Nor–Am series event. By the latter half of the decade Strobl's performance had improved dramatically, and he began to make a creditable showing in competition. Although he had finished in 116th place in the World Cup standings for 1993–94, three years later, in 1996–97, he had climbed in the standings to a 12th–place finish. In a 1997 downhill race at Sestriere, Strobl finished fourth.

In the early 1990s, Strobl was plagued by injury, but he continued to race on both the World Cup and Europa Cup circuits. Although he did well in Europa Cup competition, he seemed to falter in World Cup events. In 1995, he told his coaches that he wanted to race exclusively in Europa Cup events. It proved to be a wise choice. In 1996 Strobl won the Europa Cup Super G title, guaranteeing him an automatic start position in World Cup Super G events the following year.

The next big challenge for Strobl was winning Austria's final spot in the Olympic men's downhill for the 1998 Winter Games in Nagano, Japan. Considered a long–shot, he astounded even himself with a super–fast training run at Hakuba, Japan, in early February of 1998. He raced down the 2.1–mile course in one minute, 52.26 seconds, three–quarters of a second faster than his nearest competitors. Strobl's sizzling run won for him the final berth on Austria's downhill team for Nagano, beating out some of his country's finest skiers, including not only Eberharter but Werner Franz, Hans Knaus, and Josef Strobl (no relation). Strobl's teammates for Nagano included Hermann Maier, Andreas Schifferer, and Hannes Trinkl. Maier, widely touted as "The Herminator," went on to win Olympic gold in the giant slalom and Super G events but is perhaps best remembered for his spectacular, airborne crash in the downhill. For his part, Strobl finished eleventh in the downhill event, in which Jean–Luc Cretier of France took gold.

In the run–up to the 2002 Winter Games in Salt Lake City, Strobl had compiled a total of seven wins in World Cup competition by the end of 2001. Six of those wins had come in downhill competition. Strobl won at Kitzbuehl, Vail, and Val d'Isere in 1997; Kitzbuehl in 2000; and Bormio and Garmisch–Partenkirchen in 2001. The seventh World Cup win had come in the super–giant slalom at St. Anton in 2000.

One of the most challenging courses for Strobl has been Kitzbuehl in his native Austria. On his first downhill at Kitzbuehl as a 19–year–old rookie, he crashed. Each year Kitzbuehl hosts two World Cup downhill races—one of them a traditional one–run event and the other a two–run sprint. Entered in the traditional downhill race, Strobl won World Cup races on what many consider the world's most feared course in both 1997 and 2000. In his first victory at Kitzbuehl, he set a new world record for the course: one minute and 51.58 seconds.

To grab the gold at Salt Lake City, Strobl knew that he would have to take some risks. His teammate, Stephan Eberharter, the odds–on favorite to take gold in the downhill, started ninth in a field of 55 racers, turning in a very impressive time of one minute and 39.41 seconds, putting him in first place at that point in the competition. Strobl was the next racer out of the gate, and he bested Eberharter's time by nearly half a second. As it turned out, it was the best time of the race, winning for Strobl the Olympic gold he'd sought for so long.

Looking back on the race he'd just run, Strobl told Scott Willoughby of MountainZone.com, "Basically, the downhill run is always technically difficult. I don't feel as if I skied aggressively at all. As a matter of fact, I skied with a lot of feeling. If you want to win, you have to risk something, and I did risk something today, and I got lucky, too."

Away from the ski slopes, Strobl works as a policeman in Austria, a job that exposes him to virtually all aspects of real life. The challenges of police work, he told SnowTime.com, are "good for the brain." He lives with his wife, Bettina, and their two young sons. Despite his win at Salt Lake City, Strobl says that privacy is not a problem. As he told SnowTime, "I have no bodyguards; I'm not Schwarzenegger or Herminator!"

Sources

Periodicals

Associated Press, February 7, 1998.
Boston Herald, February 11, 2002.
London Free Press, February 11, 2002, p. C3.
Reuters, December 12, 2001.
Rocky Mountain News, February 11, 2002.
Sports Illustrated, February 18, 2002, p. 46.
USA Today, February 11, 2002, p. 3D.

Online

"Fritz's Flash Down the Mountain Earns Him Gold," *SMH.com.au*, http://old.smh.com.au/news/0202/12/sport/sport2.html (February 24, 2003).

"Fritz Strobl (AUT)," *Alpine Ski World Database*, http://www.ski–db.com/db/profiles/strfr.asp (February 24, 2003).

"Fritz Strobl (AUT)," *SnowTime.com*, http://www.snowtime.com/AlpineSki/AlpineSki_ATHLETS.asp?page=1&id_player=107 (February 23, 2003).

"Fritz Strobl Did It," *SkiWorldCup.org*, http://www.skiworldcup.org/load/reports/SaltLake2002/03_2.html (February 24, 2003).

"Fritz Strobl Takes Risks for the Win," *Mountain Zone.com*, http://www.mountainzone.com/olympics/2002/html/ski_m_dh.html (February 23, 2003).

—Don Amerman

Kenzo Takada

Fashion designer

Born February 28, 1938 (some sources say February 27, 1939), in Himeiji City, Hyogo Prefecture, Japan; son of a tea–house manager. *Education:* Attended Kobe Gaibo University; earned degree from Bunka Fashion College (Bunkafukuso Gakuin), 1960.

Addresses: *Home*—Paris, France. *Office*—c/o Kenzo, 3 Place des Victoires, 75002 Paris, France.

Career

Designer for Sanai department store; pattern designer, *Soen* magazine, Tokyo, 1960–64; freelance fashion designer, Paris, after 1965; opened "Jungle Jap" boutique, Paris, 1970; Rue Cherche Midi Boutique opened, 1972; Kenzo–Paris boutique opened, New York, 1983; created menswear line, 1983; boutiques opened in Paris, Aix–en–Provence, Bordeaux, Lille, Lyon, Saint–Tropez, Copenhagen, London, Milan, and Tokyo, 1984–85; produced sportswear for American women's retailer The Limited, Inc. under "Album by Kenzo" label, after 1984; menswear and womenswear lines, Kenzo Jeans, and junior line launched, 1986; boutiques opened in Rome and New York City, 1987; fragrance and children's lines launched, both 1987; launched Kenzo City, a women's line, 1988; boutiques opened in Brussels, 1989, and Stockholm, 1990; bath products line, Le Bain, launched 1990; boutiques opened in Hong Kong, 1990, Bangkok, 1991, and Singapore, 1991; Kenzo Maison line launched, 1992; Bambou line launched, 1994; formally retired as designer for House of Kenzo, 1999; Yume lifestyle line launched, 2002. Has also designed costumes for the opera.

Awards: *Soen* Prize, 1960; Fashion Editors Club of Japan Prize, 1972; Bath Museum of Costume Dress of the Year Award, 1976, 1977; Chevalier de l'Ordre des Arts et des Lettres, 1984.

Sidelights

Kenzo Takada was the first Japanese émigré to establish himself in Paris's rarified world of designer fashion. This innovative creator of clothing for both sexes, who uses just "Kenzo" as his professional name, quickly acquired a cult following among the young jet–set of the 1970s for his vibrantly patterned and unusually cut women's fashions. His empire expanded over the next decade to include a men's line and an array of luxury items. After announcing his retirement as chief designer for the House of Kenzo in 1999, the exuberant trendsetter returned three years later with a new lifestyle line called Yume. "Fashion is like eating," Kenzo told *Newsweek* writer Steve Saler rather presciently in 1972. "You shouldn't stick with the same menu—it's monotonous. You need changes in your dress and your food to have changes in your spirit."

Kenzo was born in Japan in the late 1930s and grew up in the city of Himeiji. One of seven children, he liked to frequent the teahouse and hotel his parents ran, and developed an early interest in fabrics and design from contact with the kimono–fabric merchants who were its steady customers. As a child, he also liked to dress his sister's dolls, and copied designs of dresses from women's magazines. His sister entered fashion college, but at the time male students were not admitted to such institutions in Japan. After spending one term at Kobe Gaibo University studying English literature, Kenzo learned that Tokyo's prestigious Bunka Fashion College was prepared to enroll its first male students. He moved to the city and worked for a house painter in exchange for room, board, and a small salary to pay for the night–school courses in design he needed to qualify for entrance; his parents were staunchly opposed to his career plan. But at Bunka he proved to be a talented student and won the *Soen* prize, named after a fashion magazine and patternmaker, when he graduated in 1960.

For the next few years, Kenzo worked as a pattern designer for *Soen* and for a department store called Sanai, then decided to move to the center of the fashion world, Paris, France, though he did not yet speak French. He sailed to Marseilles and arrived in Paris in January of 1965. After taking quarters in the Montmartre section of the city, he established contacts and found work as a freelance designer for Louis Féraud and the magazines *Elle* and *Jardin des Modes*. At the time, he recalls being stunned by the conservative nature of fashion in Paris at the time. "Everything was in Shetland, with navy, British school–uniform–style coats, lots of kilts, Chanel and Hermes–style bags, pearls and Italian shoes," he told *Financial Times* journalist Jackie Wullschlager.

Kenzo also sold some of his designs to the venerable Paris department store Printemps, and took formal couture courses. In his spare time, he frequented the Paris flea markets, and a contact he made there led to an opportunity to open his own retail space and studio. He created his first collection of womenswear sewn from some Japanese fabrics he had picked up at Marche Saint Pierre flea market, and showed them in April of 1970. On the following day, he opened the doors of the cheekily named "Jungle Jap" store in the Galerie Vivienne, a nineteenth–century arcade near the Paris Opera.

During his first few years in business, Kenzo struggled to stay afloat financially; once, he was forced to borrow money from friends back in Japan to buy fabric to meet production costs. He then gambled at the casino in Deauville, a posh French resort, and won a sum large enough to repay his creditors. A steadier source of income came in the form of a French backer, Gilles Raysse, whose American wife, Carole, became one of Kenzo's first

models. His designs caught on with young, fashion–minded French women in the early 1970s, and *Elle* became an early champion of his work. The shirts, skirts, dresses, and trousers in his early collections usually took their inspiration from the vibrant street–youth culture of the era, and he also drew upon exotic locales from around the world. Native American, Russian, and Arabic elements found their way into his designs, which were characterized solely by their eclecticism and gleeful inconsistency from season to season. Rather than creating one single "Kenzo" signature look, the designer garnered a loyal following by constantly re–inventing his style, taking inspiration from his travels.

Often, several items were deployed to make up one Kenzo runway outfit, and the live models often acted out theme–driven scenarios, which made his semi–annual showings much–anticipated spectacles during the fall and spring ready–to–wear fashion weeks in Paris. He staged one in an actual circus tent; another devolved into a mob scene that took a detachment of Paris police to settle. His line was among the most successful and innovative in the ready–to–wear market during the 1970s. "Many fashion authorities credit Kenzo with starting such recent trends as kimono sleeves, the layered look, folklore fashion, winter cotton, the explosion of bright colors, vests, baggy pants, and workers's clothes," noted Hebe Dorsey in a 1976 *New York Times Magazine* profile. The article also credited a recent trend in Chinese–style tunics with a stopover the designer made in Hong Kong, where he bought a book on children in Communist–era China.

By 1979, the House of Kenzo was thriving, and posted $3.8 million in sales. The following decade would bring the expansion of the designer's visionary style into an array of other ventures. He was one of the first designers of women's clothing to launch a menswear line, in 1983, and his success was inspiring a slightly younger generation of Japanese designers to relocate to Paris. Soon, collections from Yohji Yamamoto, Issey Miyake, and other avant–garde Asians were being featured in the pages of French and American editions of *Vogue*. Kenzo, meanwhile, continued to forge his own path. Critiquing his spring 1983 collection, *New York Times* writer Bernardine Morris noted that it featured "vivid stripes and flower combinations in bulky clothes worn with turbans that were inspired by Afghanistan, according to the best guess. What he did was revive the ethnic element in fashion, one of the themes that has been neglected in recent seasons, and he did it with considerable charm." The designer himself admitted his look was a difficult one to define. "I'm much more for a woman who knows her style," he told *New York Times Magazine* writer

June Weir. "I don't try to design for everyone. I just do what I like; but it's important for me to see that many people can wear it."

His menswear was thriving as well. *Daily News Record* writers Richard Buckley and Melissa Drier reviewed a 1984 runway performance and asserted that "[b]y the end of the show, Kenzo had gone from tailored to the Tyrol, by way of the wild west and India—and somehow it all managed to work together." The designer was also credited with popularizing the flat shoe for women in the 1980s. "I am aware that high heels lend a better line of leg and that clingy dresses are sexy," he told Wullschlager in the *Financial Times*, "but they are not my style. Certainly eroticism exists in Japan, but it is different from sex appeal in the west. I prefer subtlety to overt sensuality and, to me, sexy fashion is always calculated."

Still, Kenzo's designs had failed to make a serious impact on the fashion–conscious American woman; in the early 1980s, sales in the United States remained moribund. To boost his North American presence, in 1984 the designer and his Paris–based company entered into a licensing agreement with The Limited, Inc., an apparel chain based in Ohio. Already known for its swift cornering of the mass–market women's retail industry, The Limited was hoping to offer its more forward–minded customers a line that bridged the realms of designer and mall fashion. The clothing was sold under the "Album by Kenzo" label and proved an instant hit. Yet the venture caused one upscale retailer to drop Kenzo's pricier designer line, and the Kenzo–Limited partnership eventually dissolved.

Kenzo's financial situation changed in 1985 when Jungle Jap S.A., the holding company for the House of Kenzo, was partially acquired by a French firm for $4.2 million. His attempts to conquer the North American market continued to prove unrewarding; in 1989, his New York City store at 70th and Madison avenues was shuttered. Sales remained strong in France and Japan, however, and in 1993 the company was acquired once more, this time by luxury–good giant Louis Vuitton Moet Hennessy (LVMH). The deal allowed Kenzo to launch a new bridge line, called Kenzo Studio, and expand his international licenses, which by then included a rather successful fragrance line. In the fall of 1995, a new Kenzo store opened on Madison Avenue to sell his still–avant garde wares. When asked about the seemingly paradoxical conundrum his strategy appeared to be—a Japanese designer working in Paris but creating for American women—Kenzo responded with characteristic confidence. "French

women, Japanese women, American women all dress pretty much in the same manner," the designer told *WWD* writer Janet Ozzard. "[In New York] one proposes a whole outfit, while a French woman might pick and choose and mix things more. Americans have an outfit for work and a different outfit for after work. But perhaps when [Americans] get more confident, they will change."

By 1997 the Kenzo empire was again thriving, with 100 stores in 20 countries. He retained creative control from his office at the company's Place des Victoires headquarters in Paris, and continued to earn accolades in the fashion press. Two years later, he surprised many when he announced his retirement as chief designer of the men's and women's ready–to–wear lines. To present his final collection, he hosted a lavish party in Paris attended by more than 3,000. Guests included designers Yamamoto, Sonia Rykiel, Donna Karan, Azzedine Alaïa, and Thierry Mugler, among others, and a small commemorative book of accolades was published in conjunction with his farewell that featured testimonials from Yves Saint Laurent, Karl Lagerfeld, Christian Lacroix, and Miyake, among others. Alaïa told *WWD* that it was "thanks to Kenzo that I started in fashion. He came at a time of enormous change, and he was at the beginning of ready–to–wear as we know it." At the runway show's finale, Kenzo appeared sitting atop a giant balloon in the shape of a globe, which then floated delightfully up to the ceiling. At the all–night party that followed, he rode a live elephant in between mingling with well–wishers. The designer admitted that his retirement might have been a bit premature and admitted that he had taken up painting. "I don't think I'll ever stop working. I will always have the need to create," he told *Daily News Record* reporter Nelson Mui. "I'm 60 now, and I want to be do a lot of things while I still can."

Design responsibility for the Kenzo women's line was assumed by his second–in–command, Gilles Rosier, while Roy Krejberg became chief designer for the men's label. Kenzo's retirement allowed him to spend even more time away from his Bastille-neighborhood Paris home, roaming the world on his travels, but in 2002 he announced his return to the world of design with a new line financed by LVMH. Called Yume, which translates as "dream" in Japanese, the new venture was launched as a "lifestyle" line featuring ready–to–wear, home linens, and accessories. The move copied those of fashion designers such as Calvin Klein, who had ventured into home products with great success. Kenzo noted that times had changed greatly since his start in Paris in the late 1960s. "When I began, I think it was easier, because there were fewer designers," he told Mui in the *Daily News Record.* "And everybody wanted fashion. Now, there are too many designers—the new ones do shows, but the business doesn't always follow. Young designers today want so much to be creative that they forget about the business side."

Sources

Books

Contemporary Designers, third edition, St. James Press, 1997.

Contemporary Fashion, St. James Press, 1995.

Periodicals

Daily News Record, February 3, 1984, p. 2; October 23, 1987, p. 6; November 29, 1999, p. 6.

Financial Times, May 24, 1997, p. 9.

Newsweek, May 1, 1972, p. 58.

New York Times, April 4, 1976; April 7, 1981, p. B6; October 22, 1982, p. B8.

New York Times Magazine, November 14, 1976; August 14, 1983, p. 34.

Times (London, England), October 3, 1998, p. 88.

WWD, October 20, 1983, p. 15; January 16, 1984, p. 2; July 13, 1984, p. 1; June 25, 1985, p. 3; January 19, 1987, p. 15; February 23, 1995, p. 12; September 18, 1995, p. 36; February 19, 1999, p. 7; October 11, 1999, p. 13; January 30, 2002, p. 13; May 13, 2002, p. 5.

—*Carol Brennan*

Lonnie Thompson

Glaciologist

Born July 1, 1948, in Huntington, WV; married to Ellen Mosley (a scientist). *Education:* Earned undergraduate geology degree from Marshall University; received graduate degree from Ohio State University.

Addresses: *Office*—Byrd Polar Research Center, Ohio State University, 1090 Carmack Rd., Columbus, OH 43210.

Career

Glaciologist. Affiliated with Ohio State University, Columbus, 1971—; distinguished professor of geological sciences and a team member of the Byrd Polar Research Center.

Awards: Common Wealth Award for Science and Invention (with wife Ellen Mosely–Thompson), PNC Financial Services Group, 2002; Dr. A. H. Heineken Prize for Environmental Sciences, Royal Netherlands Academy of Arts and Sciences, 2003.

Sidelights

Ohio State University glaciologist Lonnie Thompson has devoted his career to studying the planet's mountain ice caps. Thompson concentrates his research on the deep, millennia–old layers of snow and ice that sit atop some of the world's highest peaks in tropical climes, from Tanzania to the Peruvian Andes. His three–decade–old effort has yielded startling results about the effects of global warming on the world's ecosystem.

Thompson was born in Huntington, West Virginia, in 1948, and grew up on a small family farm in Gassaway. Both of his parents had left school after the eighth grade, and Thompson's father worked as an electrician. Still, the family struggled, and he became the first in his family to earn a college degree when he graduated from Marshall University with a degree in geology. Planning on entering the field of coal–mining research, he enrolled at the graduate school at Ohio State University in 1971. There, he signed on to a research project that the school's Institute of Polar Studies was conducting on an ice–core sample brought back from the Arctic regions. By carefully examining and testing various layers of this specimen from Greenland, Thompson discovered evidence in it of nuclear tests conducted by Soviet Union in early 1960s; delving further, he found sulfur from a 1815 volcanic eruption in Indonesia. Thompson was still in graduate school when he wrote his first paper and presented his findings, and recalled that just before he was about to present it at a conference, a senior colleague inquired about it. As Thompson told *Earth* magazine's John Fleischman, "He told me, 'If you get up there tomorrow and tell them that you can date ice cores with dust, that's the end of your career.'"

Thompson's paper was surprisingly well received, and it served to launch his career in ice research. After earning his graduate degree, he remained on at Ohio State, and decided to concentrate on ice samples taken from the more tropical regions of the planet, which bucked prevailing scientist wisdom of the era. Fellow glaciologists at the time were concentrating on studying ice from the polar regions, but Thompson was convinced that ice from high altitudes elsewhere might yield interesting scientific data as well. He was convinced that ages–old ice from tropical altitudes nearer the equator may have been much colder during the last Ice Age—some 20,000 years ago—than originally believed. He made his first venture into the Andes in 1973. As *Time*'s J. Madeleine Nash explained, "Thompson has helped overturn the long–standing belief that the planet's so–called Torrid Zone is merely a passive responder to swings of climate, as opposed to an active participant."

In the late 1970s, Thompson devised a way to bring solar drilling equipment to the Andes and other physically forbidding peaks. He used teams of pack mules and human porters, and initially had difficulties obtaining funding for such costs. In 1983, he led a team of researchers to the Quelccaya ice cap in Peru. Four years later, he ventured into China's Qingha–Tibetan Plateau, and the ice he found there was dated at an age of 40,000 years, making it the oldest ever recovered outside of the polar regions. Back in China in 1990, he sampled ice from the Guliya cap in the Kunlun Mountains, and found ice that was 100,000 years old. After another trip to Peru in 1993, Thompson's team successfully returned its first samples back to the labs at Ohio State to conduct further research there in more–controlled scientific conditions.

Thompson looks for markings on the ice's surface, which tell of changes in temperature and rainfall amounts over the decades. Traces of pollen show the type of plant life that flourished in the area at certain times. He was disturbed to find increasing evidence of global warming, shown by holes that signify water rivulets—a clear sign of melting ice inside. As Thompson explained in an article that appeared in *American Scientist*, he termed such tropical ice caps "the most sensitive spots on Earth.... These glaciers are very much like the canaries once used in coal mines," he continued. "They're an indicator of massive changes taking place and a response to the changes in climate in the tropics."

In 2001, Thompson caused a stir when he presented the findings of his team at the annual gathering of the American Association for the Advancement of Science. The data showed that more than a third of the ice atop Mount Kilimanjaro, the highest peak in Africa, had melted in the last 20 years alone. Thompson theorized that since Kilimanjaro's ice had

first been delineated by scientists in 1912, nearly 80 percent of it had disappeared. He warned that the same had taken place on Quelccaya in the Andes, displaying data that showed nearly a fifth of it had disappeared into a newly created lake since 1983 that was expanding annually. "At this rate, all of the ice will be gone between the years 2010 and 2020," a journalist for London's *Independent* newspaper, Steve Connor, quoted him as saying

Ignoring evidence of global warming portends disaster for the planet, Thompson asserts. Global warming describes the rise in the temperature of the earth's lower atmosphere as a result of human activity, and scientists already knew that so–called greenhouse gasses has been warming the planet in recent decades. As Thompson witnessed firsthand on his expeditions, local economies on these mountains were some of the first to feel the economic impact of global warming trends, but the larger implications could portend ecological disaster for the planet. "What we're doing is cashing in on a bank account that was built over thousands of years but isn't being replenished," Connor quoted him as saying in the *Independent*. "Once it's gone, it will be difficult to reform."

Thompson conducts much of his research with his wife, fellow glaciologist Ellen Mosley–Thompson. He has said that his hardscrabble West Virginia childhood helped him prepare for the rigors of his job, which often involves spending weeks at dizzying heights where altitude sickness is common, combined with bitter cold and meager meal rations. He has been recognized with several honors for his work, including being named one of *Time*'s top scientists in the United States. His accompanying profile, written by Nash, noted that he is well known "not only as a first–rate scientist but as a world–class adventurer—iron–willed, intrepid, and innovative."

Sources

American Scientist, July–August 2002, p. 389.
Business First–Columbus, August 24, 2001, p. A3.
Earth, October 1997, p. 38.
Independent (London, England), February 20, 2001, p. 8.
Time, August 20, 2001, p. 42.

—*Carol Brennan*

Amy Trask

Chief Executive Officer of the Oakland Raiders football team

Courtesy of Oakland Raiders

Born in 1961 in Los Angeles, CA; daughter of Marvin (an aerospace engineer) and Sel (an elementary education instructor); married Rob Trask (a real estate investor and developer), December, 1985. *Education:* University of California, Davis, 1978–80; University of California, Berkeley, bachelor's degree (political science), 1982; University of Southern California, law degree, 1985.

Addresses: *Office*—Oakland Raiders, 1220 Harbor Bay Pkwy., Alameda, CA 94502.

Career

Worked as intern in legal department of Los Angeles Raiders, 1983; joined Barger & Wolen, 1985; joined Raiders as attorney, 1987; named chief executive officer of the Raiders, 1997.

Sidelights

The first and thus far the only female chief executive in the National Football League (NFL), Amy Trask has been the right–hand woman of Oakland Raiders owner Al Davis since 1997. She's also the leading candidate to succeed Davis as the person responsible for day–to–day operations of the team if, as has been widely rumored, Davis steps down any time soon. Trask stands only five feet, three inches tall and tips the scale at just over 100 pounds, but she's proven time and time again she's as tough as any of her male counterparts in the NFL. Although she's rarely spotted without her trade-

mark strands of pearls, Trask can get down and dirty with the best of them when the need arises. As Davis told Alex Tresniowski and Vicki Sheff–Cahan of *People*, she's faced "some tough situations. The men tested her. They tried to intimidate her. They felt she didn't know enough about the game to speak about it."

Trask came to football as a dedicated fan of the game and an almost fanatical follower of the Raiders. It all began in the early 1980s when she was working toward her bachelor's degree in political science at the University of California in Berkeley. As she told Kathryn Schloessman of the Los Angeles Sports & Entertainment Commission, "I became a football fan, and more specifically a Raiders fan, while I was in college and went to a few games. The match–ups, the strategy, the intellectual and physical parts of the game—all aspects were completely fascinating to me." In her present position with the Raiders, Trask is responsible for the team's business operations. She also represents Davis at NFL owners' meetings. She freely admits that the club's ultimate goal—not surprisingly—is to win Super Bowls, a target the Raiders fell short of in Super Bowl XXXVII where they were defeated by the Tampa Bay Buccaneers, 48–21. Although the team has won no Super Bowls during Trask's tenure as CEO, the Raiders has three NFL championships to its credit with victories at Super Bowls XI (1977), XV (1981), and XVIII (1984).

Trask was born in Los Angeles in 1961 and raised in the sprawling city's exclusive Brentwood neighborhood. The youngest child of Marv (an aerospace engineer) and Sel (an elementary education instructor at UCLA), she was diagnosed with "behavioral problems" in grade and middle school, according to Tresniowski and Sheff–Cahan of *People*. To channel her overabundant energy into more constructive outlets, her parents steered her into horse jumping, a sport at which she excelled and in which she competed until a few years ago. By the time she got into Palisades High School, Trask's behavioral problems, real or imagined, had largely disappeared, and she became a model student.

After graduating from Palisades High in 1978, Trask enrolled at the University of California, Davis. Two years later she switched to the University of California, Berkeley, where she studied political science. It was during her years in Berkeley that she became hooked on football and the Raiders. She attended the team's home games in nearby Oakland and closely followed the Raiders' fortunes when they played away from home. Shortly after she received her bachelor's degree from Berkeley in 1982, Trask headed south to Los Angeles to study law at the University of Southern California (USC). Fortuitously, that same year the Raiders moved from their longtime home in Oakland to new digs in Los Angeles. The year after she began her law studies at USC, Trask worked briefly as an intern in the legal department of the Raiders.

While studying law at USC, Amy met and became romantically involved with fellow law student Rob Trask. Another classmate, Jerome Stanley, a close friend of both Amy and Rob, recalled that she was "the ultimate guy chick—a warm, bubbly, friendly woman you could go to the game with." But not even love could keep Amy from her fanatical following of the Raiders. On the day the couple was to be married in December of 1985, the bride–to–be asked that the start of the ceremony be delayed until the conclusion of a close game between the Raiders and the Denver Broncos. For his part, Rob claims that he had no objections to the brief delay. "Hey," he told Michael Silver of *Sports Illustrated*, "the guys and I were watching the finish in my room, too."

Shortly after she earned her law degree from USC in 1985, Trask took a job with the Los Angeles law firm of Barger & Wolen. Two years later she was approached by Raiders legal counsel Jeff Birren with an offer to join the team's legal department. Trask quickly impressed the team's owner with her firm resolve and total dedication to winning every case in which she became involved. Within a few years, Davis was sending her to NFL meetings as his representative. At almost all such meetings, particularly in the early years, Trask was the only woman present. But she didn't let that isolation intimidate her in any way. At an NFL meeting in 1997, Trask stood up to make a comment, only to be told by NFL Commissioner Paul Tagliabue, "The subject is closed." Trask refused to be silenced. She told Tresniowski and Sheff–Cahan of *People*, "And I said, 'Well, no, it's not. I have something to say.' We went back and forth, and finally he said, 'Okay, but be quick.'" It came as little surprise to anyone in the room that Trask took her time in making her point.

As a child growing up in Brentwood, Trask had dreamed of dozens of possible careers. "I was one of those young girls who wanted to be absolutely everything at different times," she told Nancy Laroche of the Women's Sports Foundation. "I can remember wanting to be an astronaut, an inventor, a scientist, veterinarian, a member of a symphony orchestra.... I grew up in an atmosphere where as children we were encouraged to dream. My parents told me I could be anything I wanted to be." How then did she turn a degree in political science into a career in football? "I've always been interested in learning for the sake of learning.... I took a lot of other courses in a lot of other disciplines. I took no courses on football. My interest in football and my passion for the game really developed when I was at Berkeley, but it was unrelated to the courses I was taking."

The role model who's had perhaps the greatest influence on Trask's life and career is Rosa Parks, who triggered the Montgomery, Alabama, bus boycott, one of the seminal events of the modern–day civil rights struggle. Trask told Ron Leuty of the *San Francisco Business Times*, "[Rosa Parks is] one of the greatest heroes of modern times. The strength and courage, the tenacity she had to say, 'I'm tired, and I'm not going to the back of the bus.' That is magnificent. What a strong and powerful and determined woman—and I don't think any of us can imagine just how daunting that was. She stood up against society."

Impressed with Trask's tenacity and business savvy, Davis in 1997 named his protégé chief executive of the Raiders, making her the first woman in NFL history to hold such a position. Although he's clearly one of the most–disliked men in the NFL, Davis has established a sterling record in the area of diversity. In 1989, he became the first modern–day NFL owner to hire an African–American coach when he brought in Art Shell. Davis also was among the first to give the head coach's job to a Hispanic person (Tom Flores in 1979). He's also given high–ranking executive positions to women in the franchise's legal affairs and business affairs departments.

Much of the criticism of Trask has centered on the extraordinarily close relationship between Davis and his CEO. As one former NFL executive told *Sports Illustrated,* "You just don't know where she stops and Al begins. My impression of her is that her veins run ice–cold water." Even former class-mate Stanley, now a sports agent, acknowledged that Trask has changed considerably in her years with the Raiders. He told Silver in *Sports Illustrated,* "She's not mean to me, but I know a lot of people in league circles who think she's heavy–handed. It's like she's been Raider–ized, turned into a Raider assassin."

Trask answers her critics by firmly insisting that she's far from being a yes–woman and in fact has been engaged in numerous contentious stand–offs with her boss. But she has no problem with being called "tough," which she sees as a compliment. "I can be very, very tough," she told Silver in *Sports Illustrated,* "and what's wrong with being tough? If 'tough' were used to describe a man in my position, I don't think it would be perceived as a negative."

For Trask, no two days on the job are ever the same. Her principal areas of responsibility cover such mat-ters as player contracts, chartering planes, stadium maintenance, financial oversight and analysis, inter-action with local officials and media representatives, and team logistics. However, the unifying theme in the front office of the Raiders is the overriding pas-sion of all the team's executives for football, the Raiders, and winning. Although Trask has no re-sponsibility for the actual management of the team, she becomes involved as much as is appropriate, she told Deborah Prussel, who interviewed her for IMDiversity.com. "On all other matters, I offer my opinions when asked, and even when I'm not asked."

Trask's legal training has come in handy from the very beginning of her years with the Raiders. When she first joined the team's legal department, she was assigned to handle the lawsuits arising from the Raiders' proposed move from the Los Angeles Coliseum to suburban Irwindale. More recently, she's had to oversee the continuing litigation be-

tween her team and the NFL. The Raiders filed a $1.2 billion suit against the NFL, charging the league had conspired to sabotage the team's plans to build a new stadium in suburban Los Angeles. In that le-gal filing, the Raiders also claimed that it still owned the NFL rights to the Los Angeles market. In a 9–3 vote in 2001, a Los Angeles Superior Court jury re-jected the Raiders' claims. However, in September of 2002, a Superior Court judge overturned the jury's decision and ordered a new trial. "We believe this is the right decision, a just decision," Trask told the Associated Press. "The NFL celebrated too soon."

As part of her job, Trask spearheads many of the Raiders' philanthropic initiatives, including those directed at young people. Programs sponsored by the Raiders include "Let Us Play" for elementary and junior high school girls, the Special Olympics, and a Responsible Fatherhood program with an ad-vertising campaign that features team players and carries the caption, "I may be tough on the field, but I'm not too tough to tickle." The team also worked recently with local police on a program to swap tickets to Raiders games for guns. More than 330 guns were turned in.

Both on and off the job, Trask is preoccupied with football. "We talk sports all the time," her husband, a real estate investor and developer, told Tresnio-wski and Sheff–Cahan of *People.* He also reported that he gives his wife "a very large berth" after Raiders losses and makes no plans for autumn Sundays. "If our wedding anniversary falls on a game day, we go to the game," his wife confirmed. "We have plenty of tender moments in the off–season." The couple lives in a two–story, four-bedroom hillside home in Oakland.

Sources

Periodicals

AP Worldstream, September 24, 2002.
People, December 9, 2002, p. 169.
San Francisco Business Times, December 18, 2000.
Sports Illustrated, October 14, 2002, p. 52.

Online

"Amy Trask: On the Gridiron," Women's Sports Foundation, http://www.womenssports foundation.org/cgi–bin/iowa/athletes/heroes/article.html?record=98 (February 23, 2003).

"Commitment to Equality," NFL.com, http://ww2.nfl.com/nflforher/001002trask.html (February 23, 2003).

"On the Job: Amy Trask," Los Angeles Sports & Entertainment Commission, http://www.lasec.net/whatsnew.htm (February 23, 2003).

"She's Chief Executive, Baby," RaiderDrive.com, http://www.raiderdrive.com/amy_trask.htm (February 23, 2003).

"She's Chief Executive of What?," IMDiversity.com, http://www.imdiversity.com/Article_Detail.asp?Article_ID=18 (February 23, 2003).

—Don Amerman

Stanley Tucci

Actor, director, and screenwriter

Born November 11, 1960, in Peekskill, NY; son of Stanley (a teacher) and Joan (Tropiano) Tucci; married Kate (a nursery–school teacher), April, 1995; children: two stepchildren, twins Nicolo Robert and Isabel Concetta. *Education:* Attended State University of New York at Purchase.

Addresses: *Agent*—Frank Trattaroli, William Morris Agency, 1325 Avenue of the Americas, New York, NY 10019. *Office*—First Cold Press Productions, c/o Rysher Entertainment, 885 Second Ave., 30th Fl., New York, NY 10017.

Career

Actor, director, and screenwriter. Began career on the stage and appeared in the Broadway productions *The Iceman Cometh; Brighton Beach Memoirs; The Misanthrope; The Queen of the Rebels; Frankie and Johnny in the Clair de Lune,* 2002. Actor on television, including: *Miami Vice, The Equalizer, Wiseguy, Thirtysomething, Crime Story, Equal Justice, Murder One, Winchell* (TV movie), HBO, 1998. Actor in films, including: *Prizzi's Honor,* 1985; *Who's That Girl,* 1987; *Slaves of New York,* 1989; *Quick Change,* 1990; *Billy Bathgate,* 1991; *Beethoven,* 1992; *Prelude to a Kiss,* 1992; *The Pelican Brief,* 1993; *Somebody to Love,* 1994; *It Could Happen to You,* 1994; *Mrs. Parker and the Vicious Circle,* 1994; *Jury Duty,* 1995; *Kiss of Death,* 1995; *Big Night,* 1996; *The Day Trippers,* 1996; *Life During Wartime,* 1997; *Deconstructing Harry,* 1997; *A Life Less Ordinary,* 1997; *The Imposters,* 1998; *A Midsummer Night's Dream,* 1999; *Joe Gould's Secret,* 2000; *America's Sweethearts,* 2001; *The Road to Perdition,* 2002. Co-writer and co–director of *Big Night,* 1996; director, producer, and screenwriter of *The Imposters,* 1998; director of *Joe Gould's Secret,* 2000.

Awards: Best First Film award, New York Film Critics Circle (with Joseph Tropiano), for *Big Night,* 1996; Waldo Salt Screenwriting Award, Sundance Film Festival (with Tropiano), for *Big Night,* 1996.

Sidelights

Until 1996 and the surprise success of his hit indie film *Big Night,* Stanley Tucci had spent years portraying criminal–underworld thugs in film and on television. Determined to show another side of Italian–American culture, he co–wrote a heartwarming script about two struggling restaurateurs in 1950s–era New Jersey, obtained a production deal, and then co–starred in and co–directed 1996's *Big Night.* The film's strong critical accolades and box–office receipts boosted Tucci's profile immensely in the entertainment industry, and he went on to helm the lens of two other features. After a hiatus of several years, the actor returned to Broadway in 2002 with his role in *Frankie and Johnny in the Clair de Lune,* a revival of Terrence McNally's two–person drama that also starred *Sopranos* actress Edie Falco.

Tucci was born in 1960 and grew up in Katonah, New York, the eldest of three siblings in an Italian–American family. A fan of the Marx Brothers comedies from the 1930s, the young Tucci was a born entertainer from an early age. "I always thought Stanley was an actor savant," his drama teacher from Katonah's John Jay High School, Gilbert Freeman, told *People* writer Toby Kahn. "He couldn't do anything else. He had to act." Tucci's father was an art teacher, and his mother a dedicated gourmand who concocted increasingly elaborate meals for family get–togethers. "In my house, food was the way to show love," Tucci recalled in an interview with Martha Frankel for *Cosmopolitan*. "Everything centered around the table.... Every memory I have is colored by what we ate, how it smelled, how it looked, how it tasted."

Tucci's high–school friend Campbell Scott, star of the 2002 comedy *Rodger Dodger,* was the son of actress Colleen Dewhurst, and Tucci received his first show–business break when he and Scott appeared as extras in a Broadway production that starred Dewhurst. After earning a theater degree from the acclaimed drama school at the State University of New York in Purchase, Tucci headed to New York City and worked in a restaurant, Alfredo's the Original of Rome, while taking parts in off–Broadway and Broadway productions. A second break came in 1985 when he was cast in a small part in director John Huston's crime farce, *Prizzi's Honor.* He went on to appear in episodes of *Miami Vice* and enjoyed some success as a mobster in the CBS drama *Wiseguy* during its 1988–89 season.

Tucci seemed a victim of typecasting, repeatedly winning roles that called for him to play criminal–world heavies or other sinister figures over the next few years. He was a dogcatcher in 1992's *Beethoven,* a Middle Eastern assassin in the film adaptation of John Grisham's *The Pelican Brief,* and the roundly disliked Richard Cross on TV's *Murder One* during its 1995–96 season. Tucci even earned an Emmy nomination for his portrayal of Cross, a scheming seducer and business tycoon. He had a small breakthrough role in the 1995 remake of the noir crime film *Kiss of Death,* opposite David Caruso and Nicholas Cage. Cast as a prosecutor hoping to nail a mob ring, Tucci won good reviews for his supporting role, but the film bombed at the box office. "What's most effective," opined *Time*'s Richard Schickel, "is Tucci's marvelously slimy prosecutor. This character was once a symbol of society's rectitude. Now he's as hard and amoral as the gangsters, someone we snicker at knowingly."

But Tucci, at 35, was dismayed at the direction his career had taken. He had appeared in two dozen or so films, but the work was never steady. "I would work, then nobody would hire me," he recalled in an interview with *Washington Post* writer Sharon Waxman. "I'd go through seven months where I couldn't get work. And it was always the same kind of stuff—gangsters, mafiosi, sometimes juicy, sometimes stock characters." His Italian heritage seemed to pigeonhole into playing a certain type, but Tucci believed that audiences were being hoodwinked into stereotypes about his ancestry. As the actor told Waxman, "the frustrating thing for me was I felt it was an insult to a wonderful culture, a wonderful tradition—and a personal insult too, the idea of this dumb, working–class people on the edge of illegal activity. Food and the Mafia, that's all Hollywood sees as Italian."

In the early 1990s, Tucci began writing his own project with his cousin Joseph Tropiano. After finishing the script about two Italian immigrant brothers and their failing restaurant, Tucci shopped the *Big Night* project around to production companies and won a deal to make it—though on a tightly restricted budget and shooting schedule. He cast himself as one of the brothers, and planned to direct as well—but nervous about the dual jobs, he asked his high–school friend Scott to help out behind the camera. Tony Shalhoub played Primo Pilaggi, a talented chef and co–owner of Paradise, a struggling New Jersey restaurant in the 1950s. Tucci, as Secundo—their first names are takeoffs on the Italian terms for the first and second dinner courses—portrayed the pragmatic frontman of the house, who harbors no delusions about the type of food his suburban patrons want—spaghetti and meatballs. Primo balks, and spends hours concocting elaborate, but ultimately money–losing fare for the restaurant. When the bank threatens to foreclose on the property, the brothers accept an ostensibly gracious offer of assistance from Pascal (Ian Holm), their across–the–street competitor, who tells them that he will ask famed Italian–American singer Louis Prima to stop by Paradise for dinner. The Pilaggis know that the resulting publicity will save their eatery, and sink all their energies—and remaining funds—into the "big night." The brothers's travails involving three female co–stars—Isabella Rossellini, Minnie Driver and Allison Janney—add a bit of romance to the cuisine–focused story.

Big Night won rave reviews at its Sundance Film Festival premiere, and Tucci and Tropiano even took home a festival award for screenwriting. One major Hollywood studio expressed interested in picking up *Big Night* for distribution, but asked that some elements in the beginning be changed, and the ending revised. Like the fictional Primo, Tucci and Tropiano balked on principle, and *Big Night* was released by the Samuel Goldwyn Company as originally filmed. Just a month after its release the movie broke even at the box office, and went on to pull in $12 million, boosted by good word-of-mouth and the rave reviews of critics. *Entertainment Weekly*'s Lisa Schwarzbaum called it a film that "sings with the kind of lyricism that fills the air when you're eating a great meal: All involved know they're in on something wonderful, and feel blessed to be sharing the table." Writing in *Time*, Schickel singled out *Big Night*'s moving, nearly wordless denouement in which Secundo makes Primo an omelet, terming it "spectacularly confident filmmaking, honoring our ability to draw our own conclusions about what we've seen and the medium's rarely employed ability to convey major emotions through minimal means." David Ansen, film critic for *Newsweek*, asserted that "Tucci's funny and delicious movie is about the clash of art and commerce, Old World and New, but no plot description can convey the delicate tone, the exquisite timing or the precision of the cast … that makes this small film so special."

For his next project, Tucci teamed with another longtime friend, actor Oliver Platt, and several other industry pals to revive the 1930s-era genre of the farce with *The Imposters*, a film that he also wrote and directed. *The Impostors* is set in a Depression-era New York City and stars Tucci and Platt as a pair of perpetually unemployed actors who hustle for food and spare change by delivering witty bouts of improvisational street theater. When they inadvertently insult a famed Shakespearean actor, they must flee the city and stow away aboard an ocean liner, but find their foe is also aboard. Rossellini, Lili Taylor, Aidan Quinn, Steve Buscemi, and even Woody Allen were also recruited for comedic roles in the film. Critics seemed less impressed after the compelling *Big Night*. Reviewing it for *Newsweek*, Jeff Giles declared that *The Impostors* "begins wonderfully but drifts farther and farther out to sea." Giles termed it "overly familiar and distressingly flat," but conceded that "Tucci and Platt are hugely gifted actors."

Giles's remark was a sentiment bolstered by Tucci's casting in several other big-budget projects, including the title role in the 1998 HBO film *Winchell* and *A Midsummer Night's Dream* in 1999. Still determined to make films on his own, the actor devoted time to his next project, *Joe Gould's Secret*, and directed it from a script originally penned by Howard Rodman. Tucci starred as *New Yorker* writer Joseph Mitchell, whose two pieces for the magazine about a Harvard-educated street poet won him acclaim; he cast Holm as Joe Gould, the eccentric author of a spurious "Oral History of Our Time." Mitchell's first 1942 *New Yorker* article helped make Gould a Greenwich Village celebrity, but he drank away the

contributions he panhandled for his "Joe Gould Fund" and died in 1957. Seven years later, Mitchell wrote another piece, "Joe Gould's Secret," revealing what the manuscript actually was, but Mitchell never wrote another article, though he remained on staff at the esteemed weekly until his death in 1996.

Joe Gould's Secret failed to replicate the box-office success of *Big Night*, but Tucci did win critical praise for his work both behind and before the camera. The scenes of the genteel but lonely Mitchell haunting the dive bars of New York seeking out Gould impressed *Nation* reviewer Stuart Klawans. "Sleek and long-faced, Tucci carries himself down to all these places with a slightly stiff modesty and emerges with equal decorum," Klawans declared. *Los Angeles Times* film critic Kenneth Turan called the film "a marvel of subtlety and restraint set in a carefully re-created 1940s and '50s Manhattan."

Tucci went on to appear in *Sidewalks of New York*, Edward Burns's 2001 comedy, and in *America's Sweethearts*, a Julia Roberts romantic comedy. He reprised his gangster role as real-life mobster Frank Nitti in 2002's *The Road to Perdition*, and later that year earned a torrent of publicity for his Broadway return in *Frankie and Johnny in the Clair de Lune* opposite HBO's fictional Carmela Soprano, Edie Falco. The tightly written drama opens with a first-time romantic encounter between Tucci's Johnny, a short-order cook, and the waitress Frankie, and Tucci's character then emerges naked from the bed. Absent from the stage since 1994, Tucci was pleased to co-star with Falco, another SUNY-Purchase theater grad, and *New York Times* writer John Leland asserted that both actors "bring a more earthy, New York agita to the roles" in McNally's acclaimed play.

Tucci took the nude scenes on stage in stride. He told the *New York Times*'s Leland that though the role instilled a certain anxiety in him, "I want it to be uncomfortable," Tucci told Leland. "You learn something when you go onstage that you don't in movies or television. It is your craft, but it is yourself as well. Those are your emotions up there. If you're naked, you're naked." The same paper's theater critic, Ben Brantley, gave it a mixed review, granting that the sex and nudity in the play did start the play off on an overly personal note, "but that doesn't begin to account for the enchanted spell of intimacy in which Mr. McNally's tale of two co-workers, a waitress and a cook in a greasy spoon, proceeds to enwrap its audience."

Tucci, married since 1995 to a former social worker turned nursery-school teacher, lives not far from where he grew up in Westchester County, New

York, with his two stepchildren and twin son and daughter (who were born in 2000), and is co–owner of a nearby restaurant called the Finch Tavern. "It's more like the way I grew up," he reflected in an interview with *San Francisco Chronicle* writer Ruthe Stein. "My dad was an art teacher and my mom worked in an office. My wife likes movies, but you know she can take them or leave them. We're not talking about the business all the time. Well, we are, because I talk about it all the time. But it's good to have a different perspective."

Selected writings

Screenplays

(With Joseph Tropiano) *Big Night*, Samuel Goldwyn, 1996.

The Imposters (also known as *Ship of Fools*), Twentieth Century–Fox/Fox Searchlight, 1998.

Books

(With Joan Tucci, Gianni Scappin, and Mimi Shanley Taft) *Cucina & Famiglia: Two Italian Families Share Their Stories, Recipes and Traditions*, William Morrow & Company (New York, NY), 1999.

Sources

Boston Herald, April 16, 2000, p. 62.

Cosmopolitan, October 1996, p. 120.

Crain's New York Business, September 22, 1997, p. 1.

Daily Variety, August 9, 2002, p. 2.

Entertainment Weekly, September 20, 1996, p. 20, p. 49; July 27, 2001, p. 43.

Esquire, December 1998, p. 44.

Guardian (London, England), October 25, 1996, p. 11.

Independent (London, England), May 29, 1997, p. 4.

Los Angeles Magazine, April 2000, p. 42.

Los Angeles Times, January 21, 2000, p. F1.

Nation, March 31, 1997, p. 35; October 26, 1998, p. 34; April 24, 2000, p. 42.

New Republic, May 31, 1999, p. 32.

Newsweek, February 12, 1996, p. 81; October 12, 1998, p. 88.

New York Times, August 4, 2002, p. 1; August 9, 2002; September 15, 2002, p. 13.

People, January 22, 1996, p. 57.

San Francisco Chronicle, September 27, 1998, p. 55; November 21, 2001, p. D5.

Time, May 1, 1995, p. 84; September 23, 1996, p. 72.

Washington Post, October 1, 1998, p. B1.

—*Carol Brennan*

Alvaro Uribe

President of Colombia

Born Alvaro Uribe Vélez, July 4, 1952, in Medellín, Colombia; son of a horse breeder and rancher; married Lina Moreno; children: Tomas, Jerónimo. *Education:* Received law degree from the Universidad de Antioquia; graduate work, Saint Anthony's College, Oxford University; graduate work, Harvard University, 1993.

Addresses: *Office*—Office of the President, Casa de Narino, Carrera 8a. 7–26, Santa Fe de Bogotá, Colombia.

Career

Began political–service career with the Empresas Públicas de Medellín (Medellín Public Works), Medellín, Colombia, as an assets manager, 1976; general secretary of the Ministerio de Trabajo (Labor Secretary) until 1980; director of national civil aeronautics for Colombia, 1980–82; elected mayor of Medellín, 1984; elected to national senate from Antioquia, 1986, 1990; elected governor of Antioquia, 1995; founded the Colombia First party, 2001; elected president of Colombia, 2002.

Sidelights

In a country rocked by years of violence, Álvaro Uribe Vélez managed to survive attempts on his life during his successful campaign to become the next president of Colombia. A law–and–order politician who promised Colombians an end to the 40–year–old internal war with leftist guerrillas that kills or maims thousands of civilians each year, Uribe

won a resounding victory in May of 2002. He again eluded well–placed bombs when he was sworn in three months later, and not long afterward took decisive action by declaring a national state of emergency. Uribe was described by *Newsweek International* writer Joseph Contreras as "slight and bespectacled," a figure who "looks more like a high–school math teacher than a hard–charging ideologue. But there's nothing wimpy about his message."

Uribe was born in 1952 in Colombia's Antioquia province, where his family owned estates and bred horses for several generations before him. He studied law and political science at Antioquia University in Medellín, the country's second largest city, and took his first job as a bureaucrat in 1976 as an assets manager in Antioquia's public–works department. After a stint in the department of labor, Uribe was appointed director of civil aeronautics for the entire country in 1980. He served two years in the post.

In 1983, Uribe's father was slain on the family ranch by rebels belonging to the Revolutionary Armed Forces of Colombia (FARC), one of the Marxist rebel groups that emerged in the 1960s. Winning converts among the rural peasantry and indigenous people of Colombia, such rebel groups had grown in number, but were either forced to make peace with the government or had faded away. FARC was the last remnant of this movement, and it grew increasingly powerful in the 1980s. FARC promised a more equitable distribution of Colombia's resources, a message that resonated with a populace in which 64 percent live at or below the poverty level. Yet FARC's tactics grew increasingly harsh in reaction to government attempts to annihilate its support, and it mounted a campaign of terror across the Colombian countryside that involved kidnappings for ransom and hijacking the country's coca crops in order to finance its political goals. Murders of journalists, trade–union activists, members of the clergy, human–rights workers, and landowners like Uribe's father also became common.

Uribe was elected Medellín mayor in 1984, and served a two–year term. In 1986, he stood for election as a senator on the Liberal Party ticket, and won the first of two four–year terms as a representative of Antioquia. Voters there elected him governor in 1995, and by then Uribe had forged "a reputation for fiscal skill and honesty—but also for having a prickly authoritarian streak," noted two South American correspondents for *Time*, Tim Padgett and Ruth Morris. As Antioquia's governor, Uribe dealt swiftly and harshly with the FARC menace in the state. He established rural security cooperatives called Convivirs, or community vigilance associations. These were citizen patrols that gathered information about FARC operatives in neighborhoods and other threats to national security and delivered the information to the police and army; the program was so successful that it was adopted by other provinces, but abuses followed, and much of the Convivirs' strength was truncated by the Colombian courts in 1997.

In 1998, a new president, Andrés Pastrana Arango, took office after promising to negotiate a cease–fire with FARC. To establish a neutral territory, he granted the group a wide swath of land in the jungle, but FARC quickly secured the area and used it as a base to launch a new offensive. Colombians were outraged, and Pastrana was vilified. Around this time, Uribe was studying social policy and education at St. Anthony's College of Oxford University in Britain. When he returned home to Colombia, Uribe moved onto the national political stage in 1999 by forming his breakaway political party, Colombia First. Its slogan—"strong hand, big heart"—summed up Uribe's strategy to deal with the FARC war: if elected, he promised to double the number of Colombian Army combat troops and members of the National Police in order to force the rebel group into submission.

Declaring his candidacy in the 2002 presidential elections, Uribe languished as a contender for much of 2001. Early the next year, however, FARC intensified its attacks, setting off a bomb in a Bogotá restaurant, attempting to blow up the city's main water reservoir, and hijacking a plane; in February of 2002 they kidnapped a senator, social activist, and presidential candidate, Ingrid Betancourt. Colombians swiftly rallied to Uribe's Colombia First party, and he began to gain steady point increases in the polls. He chose a journalist, Francisco Santos, as his running mate. The government–led peace talks with FARC finally collapsed, and the Pastrana regime was excoriated for, in the end, worsening the situation. Uribe stressed that his plan was the only rational one. "If we want a nation without guerrillas, without paramilitaries, we all have to get on the side of the armed forces," he was quoted as saying by *Financial Times* reporter Ruth Morris. Yet some observers still deemed an Uribe victory unlikely, as Contreras explained in *Newsweek International*—Colombia, the journalist noted, is "a country where ultraconservative politicians have seldom occupied the presidential palace."

Not surprisingly, there was said to be contract on Uribe's head as well. He survived a car–bombing in April that left three dead. Meanwhile, more moderate factions in the country voiced worries about the candidate's links to a right–wing paramilitary group, Autodefensas Unidas de Colombia (Colombian Self–Defense Units, or AUC), which publicly endorsed his candidacy. The AUC was an outgrowth of the Convivirs, and was said to have conducted a harsh campaign in Antioquia during the time there when Uribe governed the province. While calling for increased United States aid to fight Colombia's illegal drug traffickers, Uribe was also forced to answer to charges that his own connections linked him to the trade: in 1997 U.S. Drug Enforcement Administration (DEA) agents seized large amounts of a chemical commonly used for manufacturing cocaine; the man, a Medellín businessman, was a relative of Uribe's wife, but he was never indicted by the United States or Colombian governments. Uribe was also challenged in the press for his ties to top military brass. Contreras said that Uribe's presidential campaign was launched "at a 1999 gala dinner honoring two former Army generals cashiered by Pastrana for having collaborated with vigilante groups and right–wing paramilitary units charged with committing massacres and other atrocities in 1996 and 1997."

In an interview with *Newsweek International*'s Contreras as the election campaign entered its final weeks, Uribe laid out his strategy for dealing with FARC, which still called for doubling the ranks of the army and national police. "I don't rule out negotiations," he told the magazine. "But the guerrillas will have to accept a ceasefire and make a commitment to refrain from terrorist activity as preconditions." More temperate observers warned that Uribe's law–and–order promises could, if implemented, restrict human rights for all citizens in the bid to stamp out FARC. A political scientist at one of Bogotá's universities, Elizabeth Ungar, told the *Financial Times* that Uribe "presents a discourse about authority, but for many of us, it's a discourse of authoritarianism," she said in an interview with Morris of *Financial Times*. An *Economist* report defended the candidate, however. "[C]ontrary to some claims, he is no fascist," the magazine declared of Uribe, and dismissed rumors of possible ties to right–wing paramilitary groups or drug cartels. Uribe's "faults," the *Economist* stated, "are of a lesser order: he has some dubious friends, he is thin–skinned, he lacks a strong governmental team, and a few of his ideas are half–baked. Against this are useful qualities, including political skills and administrative experience."

In the elections held on May 26, 2002, Uribe bested former Liberal Party colleague Horacio Serpa to take the lead. After the ballots had been tallied, Uribe had taken 53 percent of the vote, which meant that a run–off election was not necessary; it was the first time in the history of Colombia's presidential elections that a candidate had won such a resounding majority. In his victory speech, Uribe declared that "the international community should know Colombia has expressed its desire to recover civility, to recover order," *New York Times* correspondent Juan Forero quoted him as saying. "That Colombia does not want the world to just know the bad news about the violence, but that the world be notified of our determination to defeat violence."

Uribe was inaugurated in Bogotá in August within a tightly controlled security parameter. Even commercial airline traffic was banned from the skies, but several bombs exploded on the ground that day that left 14 dead and 40 wounded. Not long after taking office, Uribe declared a state of emergency, which resulted in increased powers for government security forces. They were now allowed to search homes and offices of those with suspected links to FARC, for example, without the presence of an associate of the attorney–general's office. Some restrictions were lifted on the government's ability to use phone taps as well. Uribe claimed that such harsh measures were necessary to stop the violence. "If you read them carefully," a *New York Times* report quoted him as saying about his new acts, "you will see that they entirely respect human rights. I welcome the controversy. The measures aren't meant to silence controversy, but to face up to terrorism."

Uribe's hard–line tactics won support from the United States. President George W. Bush asked for and won from Congress an increase in aid to help the country's "Plan Colombia," a strategy that first went into operation in 2000 with a massive infusion of dollars to curb Colombia's illicit cocaine–trafficking business. The country is thought to produce about 80 percent of the cocaine consumed illegally in the United States, and both FARC and right–wing paramilitary groups have been linked to the drug trade in Colombia. Uribe stressed the need to cut off the source of funding for FARC arms and hideouts. "No country can ignore the kind of terrorist attacks against a democratic society that are taking place in Colombia," *Newsweek International*'s Contreras quoted Uribe as saying. "The state cannot allow [armed] groups to kill citizens or take part in drug trafficking, and that's why I'm asking for more international help, beginning with the United States." In 2003, American military operatives began training Colombian army troops in securing a crucial oil pipeline that is a favorite bombing target of FARC. Yet one Latin American political analyst warned that Uribe was unlikely to accept many strings attached to the American aid. "If anyone in the U.S. thinks they can impose their agenda through Uribe they are going to be mistaken," Michael Shifter told the *Financial Times*'s James Wilson. "He is not going to be an instrument of U.S. policy—he has very clear ideas, which may or may not coincide with those of Washington policymakers."

Uribe also began to work on implementing other campaign promises as well. He hoped to reduce the number of members of Congress, and vowed to root out the corruption endemic in Colombia politics. In his spare time, Uribe practices yoga. He is the father of two sons.

Sources

Christian Science Monitor, May 28, 2002, p. 1.
Economist, May 25, 2002; August 3, 2002; November 9, 2002.
European Report, December 11, 2002, p. 506.
Financial Times, February 20, 2002, p. 11; May 25, 2002, p. 7.
Global Agenda, August 8, 2002.
New Internationalist, November 2002, p. 8.
Newsweek International, March 25, 2002, p. 48, p. 50; June 24, 2002, p. 35.
New York Times, May 27, 2002, p. A1; August 8, 2002, p. A1; September 12, 2002, p. A7; December 12, 2002, p. A22;
NotiSur—South American Political and Economic Affairs, May 31, 2002.
Time, June 10, 2002, p. 35.

—Carol Brennan

Carmen Marc Valvo

Fashion designer

Born in 1954. *Education:* Manhattanville College, Purchase, NY, degree in fine arts; studied fashion at Parsons School of Design, New York, NY.

Addresses: *Office*—530 7th Ave., 23rd Floor, New York, NY 10018.

Career

Worked for Bill Atkinson, House of Ricci, Christian Dior, and other designers; designer of his own line, 1989—.

Awards: Best evening wear, Dallas Fashion Awards, 1996; Marymount College Designer of the Year Award, 2001; honoree at a gala hosted by the Fashion Group International, titled "Night of Stars: A Salute to American Icons," 2002; Neiman–Marcus $1 million dress award, 2002.

Sidelights

Carmen Marc Valvo grew up in a Spanish/Italian family in Greenwich, Connecticut, one of six children; his mother was a nurse. His father, an anesthesiologist, encouraged Valvo to become a plastic surgeon, and even took Valvo to witness an abdominal surgery at the age of nine. Valvo told Becky Homan in the *St. Louis Post–Dispatch*, "It was bloody, and I remember passing out on the [operating room] floor. I realized this was not going to happen for me." Far more interesting to Valvo was helping his sister with a school project, designing

medieval costumes for her Barbie dolls. He may have inherited his talent for clothing design from his grandmother, who was a skilled seamstress.

Throughout his childhood, Valvo had enjoyed sketching, painting, and doing art projects, and he eventually enrolled in a fine arts program at Manhattanville College in Purchase, New York. He then moved to Europe for three years, studying art in Vienna, and traveling to other countries to experience their culture. When he returned to the United States, he suffered severe whiplash as a result of an automobile accident. For the next nine months, he was immobilized, and he spent the time thinking about his future. He decided to go into fashion, and when he recovered, enrolled at the Parsons School of Design in New York City.

The registrar at the school tried to convince Valvo to enter fine arts, not fashion, but Valvo insisted on fashion. He had the talent for it, and knew it. "You can teach someone to draw or sketch," he told Linda Gillan Griffin in the *Houston Chronicle*, "but you can't teach style. Style is something unique. You either have it or you don't."

Valvo had it. After graduating from Parsons, he worked for sportswear designer Bill Atkinson. Atkinson had a lasting influence on Valvo, who would later design evening wear with a sportswear flair, such as beaded bustiers over skirts or pants, and stoles and opera coats sold separately.

Valvo worked for the House of Ricci in Paris for two years, designing Ricci's premier United States collection, but eventually moved on. He told Barbara de Witt in the *San Francisco Chronicle,* "The most valuable thing I learned from working there was not to be a prima donna because it's counterproductive, but I also learned to drape live models instead of fabric mannequins to get the best fit." After working for Ricci, he moved to Christian Dior, also in Paris, and then returned to the United States to study beading and handwork for a company that was contracting a great deal of such work from India.

In 1989, this company promised to give Valvo his own division, but the deal never materialized. "It was a promise made in bad faith," he told the *St. Louis Post–Dispatch*'s Homan. He moved on, and decided to take the plunge and start his own label. With the help of two friends who invested $5,000 each, and with the aid of his Asian contacts, he put together a line of clothing in nine days. By 1995, singer/actress Vanessa Williams had agreed to promote Valvo's glamorous gowns, and the promotion made his line take off.

By 1996, Valvo was producing six collections a year for upscale department stores, and also designed for couture clients. When he took time off, it was short—four days at the most. He told de Witt that because he owned his own company and was responsible for its success or failure, he did not have the luxury of taking time off, "unlike some designers who have financial backers."

Some of Valvo's best–known creations are his strapless evening gowns, which make use of a unique construction method: instead of using wires or bones to help them stay up, Valvo relies on heavy interfacing. He told the *San Francisco Chronicle*'s de Witt that he does not use bones "because they [are] uncomfortable and don't look natural." In designing his gowns, Valvo uses four models with different figure types, instead of relying on only one model. This allows him to create the perfect fit for a wide range of women. Before he approves a dress, it must fit all four of the models in the hips, waist, and bust; he also adds a generous allowance for alterations. When he designs a more difficult bias–cut gown, he uses eight different models.

Valvo specializes in evening wear because, he told Staci Sturrock in the *Palm Beach Post,* "We don't get dressed up enough." he added, "It's like a celebration of life." He also commented to Sturrock that he could make more money designing jeans, but preferred not to. "Evening wear designers are a very unusual breed because they do it for the love." Valvo's gowns are favorites among movie stars and other celebrities, who often wear them to awards ceremonies and gala banquets. However, Valvo told the *San Francisco Chronicle*'s de Witt that there is no guarantee that any star will like his designs, and he often does not know that a customer is going to keep a dress she has tried on until he sees her wearing it on television. De Witt noted, "Valvo knows when the star really likes the dress because she'll send a check back instead of the dress."

In 2001, Valvo won the Marymount College Designer of the year Award. In November of 2002, he was honored at a gala hosted by the Fashion Group International, titled "Night of Stars: A Salute to American Icons." In addition, Neiman Marcus department store presented him with a $1 million dress award for one of his signature dresses. Of the award ceremony in Dallas, Texas, Valvo said, "It was magical," according to Barbara Nachman in the *Journal News.*

Valvo told Homan that one of his strengths as a designer is his deep knowledge of how clothing is made, as well as other aspects of the fashion business. "My experience gave me the couture background," he told the *St. Louis Post–Dispatch*'s Homan. "And because of that, I don't have to answer to a board of directors. My collection can be purer. It is what I want it to be."

Sources

Periodicals

Honolulu Advertiser, March 6, 2001, p. C1.
Houston Chronicle, April 29, 2001, p. 6.
Journal News (Westchester, NY), April 1, 2001, p. 1E; September 17, 2002, p. 1E.
Palm Beach Post, January 17, 2003, p. 6D.
San Francisco Chronicle, November 7, 1996, p, E7.
St. Louis Post–Dispatch, October 15, 1998, p. 1.
WWD, September 25, 1996, p. 34.

Online

Carmen Marc Valvo, http://www.carmenmarc valvo.com/ (May 15, 2003).

—Kelly Winters

Nia Vardalos

Actress, playwright, and screenwriter

Born Antonia Eugenia Vardalos, September 24, 1962, in Winnipeg, Manitoba, Canada; daughter of Constantine (a businessperson) and Doreen Vardalos; married Ian Gomez (an actor), 1993. *Education:* Studied acting at Ryerson University, Toronto, Canada.

Addresses: *Agent*—Brillstein Grey Management, 9150 Wilshire Blvd., Ste. 350, Beverly Hills, CA 90212.

Career

Worked with Second City comedy team, 1988–94. Performer of one–woman show in Los Angeles, 1997–98. Film appearances include: *No Experience Necessary,* 1996; *Men Seeking Women,* 1997; *Short Cinema,* 1998; *Meet Prince Charming,* 1999; *My Big Fat Greek Wedding,* 2002. Television appearances include: *High Incident,* 1996; *Common Law,* 1996; *The Drew Carey Show,* 1997; *Team Knight Rider* (voice), 1997; *Boy Meets World,* 1998; *It's Like, You Know...,* 1999; *Two Guys, a Girl, and a Pizza Place,* 1999; *Curb Your Enthusiasm,* 2000; *Saturday Night Live,* 2002; *My Big Fat Greek Life,* 2003.

Awards: People's Choice Award for Favorite Motion Picture Comedy, for *My Big Fat Greek Wedding,* 2003.

Sidelights

Nia Vardalos is the writer and star of the 2002 hit film *My Big Fat Greek Wedding,* which tells the story of a Greek woman whose large, boisterous family is thrown into disarray when she decides to marry a non–Greek man. The film was based on a stage play written by Vardalos, and its success led to a television series, *My Big Fat Greek Life,* which also starred Vardalos.

Vardalos grew up in Winnipeg, Canada, the daughter of Constantine, a Greek immigrant and businessperson, and Doreen, a Canadian–born woman of Greek heritage. During her childhood and youth, Vardalos felt different from her peers because of her heritage and the emphasis her family placed on it. According to Les Spindle in *Back Stage West,* her father often said, "There are two kinds of people in the world: Greeks, and everybody else who wishes they were Greek."

When she was 20 years old, Vardalos moved to Toronto in order to study acting at Ryerson University, but the program there emphasized classical theater, which bored her. She left, and in 1988 found work with the Toronto branch of the Second City comedy troupe—but it was not acting work. She auditioned for the troupe three times, failing each time, and finally accepted a job in the box office. When one of the performers became sick three weeks later, she got her big break: she knew the whole show by heart, so she was asked to step in. The next day, she was hired as a permanent member of the London, Ontario troupe. She spent two years with the London company, and then performed for four years with Second City in Chicago, Illinois.

While in Chicago, Vardalos met Ian Gomez, another member of the troupe, and they fell in love. This initially caused some consternation in Vardalos's family, since Gomez was not Greek—he was of Puerto Rican and Jewish heritage. He agreed to convert to the Greek Orthodox Church, and the two married with her family's blessing in 1993.

In 1996 the couple moved to Los Angeles, California, to look for acting work, but it was difficult to find. Vardalos did commercial voiceovers and worked in a flower shop. During this time, Vardalos tried to find an agent who could get her work. However, her appearance and Greek ethnicity seemed to be working against her. According to Patricia Hluchy in *Maclean's*, her agent finally wrote her off, telling her, "You're not pretty enough to be a leading lady, you're not fat enough to be a character actor—you're Greek and there's nothing I can do for you."

Vardalos decided that since her heritage was such an issue, she would emphasize it even more. Her friends had always encouraged her to use her wealth of funny stories about her family in a performance, and now she did. She performed on her own, getting up on stage and telling stories about her large and eccentric Greek family, and eventually worked the stories into a 90–minute performance. She took this one–woman show, titled *My Big Fat Greek Wedding*, to three Los Angeles venues in 1997 and 1998. In the meantime, she spoke to producers about developing the show into a film, but those who were interested wanted to change it into a story about a large Italian or Hispanic family, which they considered more marketable. Vardalos adamantly refused, wanting to stay true to her own material. She quickly wrote and copyrighted a screenplay based on her act because she did not want anyone to steal her idea.

In 1999, actors Tom Hanks and Rita Wilson saw the show, and loved it. Wilson, who is half–Greek, told Vardalos that the show would make a great movie. Wilson agreed that Vardalos should play the lead in the film, and Wilson and Hanks helped Vardalos make the dream a reality. Wilson told *Back Stage West*'s Spindle, "For me, it was very important that, as a woman and an actress, she get to play the role that she created." Vardalos added, "I'm so grateful to Rita for her determination to make the film, and

that I was going to play the lead. Otherwise I wouldn't be sitting here right now. I call her my fairy godsister."

The film was produced by Hanks's Playtone Pictures and released in 2002. Vardalos was allowed to cast many roles in the film, and many members of her family appeared in it. It was an unexpected hit, making $350 million in eleven months.

Hluchy described the movie in *Maclean's* as "a charming, often hilarious tale about a large, larger–than–life Greek clan joined by marriage to a mute, tiny, haute WASP family." Vardalos drew on her real–life relatives for inspiration, creating a composite character based on the personalities of all her aunts, and inserting the names of all of her 27 first cousins into the script. Despite its ethnic focus, the film appealed to a wide audience. Vardalos told Hluchy, "Everyone relates to this story. I loved it when a Chinese woman came up to me and said, 'This is just like my family.'" In *Back Stage West*, Spindle wrote that the film was "buoyed by earthy, full–bodied characterizations, fine production values, and Vardalos's passion for the material," as well as "vibrant performances."

Early in 2003, Vardalos was woken up at 5:30 in the morning by a phone call. Although she initially feared someone in her family had died, she was pleasantly surprised to find she had been nominated for an Oscar. Her script for *My Big Fat Greek Wedding* was nominated for Best Screenplay Written Directly for the Screen. While she did not win an Oscar, Vardalos did receive a People's Choice Award for Favorite Motion Picture Comedy on January 12, 2003.

In 2003, CBS ordered seven episodes of a sitcom based on the film. Called *My Big Fat Greek Life*, it also starred Vardalos. Joel Stein wrote in *Time* that for the series, "The family will be a little less cartoonish, not as weapons–grade Greek as it was in the film." He quoted Vardalos, who said, "They will be a little hipper, a little less Old World. The risk is, we won't capture the feeling the movie had. It's a big risk." The show premiered in February of 2003 and won CBS one of its highest series–debut ratings in recent years.

Despite the show's auspicious beginning, its ratings dropped 54 percent after its debut, and Vardalos eventually decided that she did not want to continue doing it. After the season finale of the show was filmed in March of 2003, Vardalos asked CBS to cancel it. Vardalos's spokeswoman, Christina Papadopoulos, told *Entertainment Weekly* reporter Lynette Rice, "So many people had so many different visions. They were not able to have a unified direction." Vardalos's costar, Louis Mandylor, told Rice, "It wasn't easy. [Vardalos] had to act, produce, and do publicity."

In the meantime, Vardalos dealt with other troubles when she faced a lawsuit from Rick Siegel, her former manager. According to E! Online, Vardalos's former management company, Marathon Entertainment, filed a complaint on January 10, 2003, alleging that she reneged on a verbal deal to share 15 percent of her proceeds from *My Big Fat Greek Wedding*. Marathon also claimed that Siegel gave up a producing credit on the film in exchange for unconditional payment for his services. Vardalos's representatives claimed the suit was without merit and that Siegel had already been paid commission. In response to the lawsuit, Vardalos's attorney claimed Siegel unlawfully acted as an unlicensed talent agent and filed a complaint against the manager with the California Labor Commissioner. If it were proven that Siegel got Vardalos the movie gig he would have to forfeit his commission.

Vardalos's troubles continued when she—along with Playtone Productions, HBO, and Gold Circle Films—was named in a breach-of-contract lawsuit on July 1, 2003. "The suit, filed by ... Jim Milio, Melissa Jo Peltier, and Mark Hufnail, the three principals of MPH Entertainment, accuses the film's producers of using questionable accounting and seeks $20 million in compensatory damages," wrote Josh Grossberg at E! Online. According to the suit, MPH purchased Vardalos's script with the understanding that Milio would helm the film, then turned around and sold the rights to Playtone, HBO, and Gold Circle in return for a three percent share of the profits. MPH claimed they had received no money and had received a financial statement that the film had a net loss of $20 million and the company was owed nothing. Vardalos's attorney said she had nothing to do with the distribution of profits and should not have been named a party in the lawsuit. Playtone made a similar statement, saying the company was merely a profit participant and had no control of the money. Gold Circle Films issued a statement stating that the charge was exaggerated, as quoted by Grossberg: "We haven't seen the complaint, but we stand by the integrity of our accounting. It's ludicrous to suggest that this film will not be profitable. MPH Entertainment will see their appropriate participation in due course."

Vardalos moved on to a new project, a Universal film titled *Connie and Carla,* for which she wrote the screenplay. Scheduled for release in 2004, the film stars Vardalos and Toni Collette, who play two Chicago dinner theater performers who witness a Mafia killing and who then have to run for their lives. They decide that the Mafia thugs will not think of looking for them in Los Angeles, so they head there and assume new identities—as drag queens. Surprisingly, their ruse goes undetected, and they soon become celebrities, risking discovery. When Vardalos's character, Connie, meets a man she's interested in, she realizes she will have to choose between her false identity as a man, or revealing her true past.

Vardalos is still amazed at the success she has had. She told *Time*'s Stein, "I'm living an actor's dream. My mom says, 'You're working too hard.' I say, 'Coal mining is hard.' I'm a geek with a cool job."

Sources

Periodicals

Back Stage West, April 11, 2002, p. 13.
Daily Variety, January 8, 2003, p. 40.
Entertainment Weekly, July 26, 2002, p. 19; May 30, 2003, pp. 9–10.
Maclean's, August 5, 2002, p. 42.
People, December 30, 2002, p. 72; March 31, 2003, p. 57.
Time, March 3, 2003, p. 62.

Online

"Big Fat Greek Spat," E! Online, http://www.eonline.com/News/Items/0,1,12093,00.html (July 7, 2003).
Biography Resource Center Online, Gale Group, 2002.
"Nia's Big Fat Greek Lawsuit," E! Online, http://www.eonline.com/News/Items/0,1,11107,00.html (July 7, 2003).
"Principal Photography Begins On *Connie and Carla,*" CNNMoney, http://money.cnn.com/services/tickerheadlines/prn/laf054.P1.06132003180325.21527.htm (June 30, 2003).

—Kelly Winters

Peter Vitousek

Ecologist

Born Peter M. Vitousek, January 24, 1949, in Honolulu, HI; son of Roy and Betty Vitousek; married; children: two. *Education:* Amherst College, Massachusetts, B.A. in political science, 1971; Dartmouth College, New Hampshire, Ph.D. in biological sciences, 1975.

Addresses: *Office*—Stanford University, Department of Biology, Stanford, CA 94305.

Career

Ecologist; taught and conducted research at Indiana University and at the University of North Carolina; became professor at Stanford University, 1984; named one of America's best scientists by *Time* magazine, 2001.

Awards: Fellowship, Pew Fellows Program in Conservation and the Environment, 1990.

Sidelights

Peter Vitousek is an ecologist conducting most of his research in Hawaii. Based at Stanford University, he tries to understand how forests interact with the atmosphere and how the activities of people affect the delicate balance of nitrogen, oxygen, carbon dioxide, and other gases in the world's ecosystems.

A particular area of focus for Vitousek is the role that nitrogen plays in the earth's ecosystems. Nitrogen, which makes up almost 80 percent of the earth's atmosphere, is released by the burning of fossil fuels and the fertilization of cultivated land. Too much of it in the ecosystem causes explosive growth in some plant species, and causes others to suffocate. Human beings, Vitousek told the *Baltimore Sun,* "have altered nitrogen more than any other element." In fact, the amount of nitrogen in the biosphere has increased by a factor of two in the decades following World War II. "That's a huge alteration in how the world works," Vitousek told Jeffrey Kluger of *Time.*

Excess nitrogen introduced into the world's ecosystems has caused vast "dead–zones" in the world's oceans by stimulating the growth of algae that rob the water of oxygen, and has been blamed for health problems in humans ranging from cancer and brain damage to skin rashes. At the same time, because nitrogen is so useful as a fertilizer, Virtousek told the *Baltimore Sun,* it "is why around two billion of the six billion people on Earth are alive now." As Vitousek told *Time*'s Kluger, "Our capacity to change the earth means we must manage this."

Much of Vitousek's focus has been to demonstrate how organisms and the nutrients that sustain them can interact with each other thousands of miles apart. For instance, some plants in the Hawaiian islands survive on minerals blown to them on sea spray, and in the form of dust from Central Asia. "No ecosystem is entirely isolated," Virtousek told Kluger.

A colleague of Vitousek's, Oregon State University's Jane Lubchenco, told Kluger, "Peter is a real visionary. It's unusual to have someone who is simultaneously interested in the big picture and in taking a very detailed look at the processes themselves."

Vitousek was born on the Hawaiian island of Oahu. He developed an interest in the natural world early. As he told *Environment Hawaii*, "I ... spent a lot of time hiking in the Ko'olau as a kid, not knowing what I was looking at very much, but liking being outside a lot." Vitousek began his studies at Amherst College as a political science major, but he found his true calling when, in an English literature class, he read a book about the effect of invasive plants and animals on native ecosystems. "A lot of things came together for me then," he later told *Environment Hawaii*. "I had that experience, seeing it and then reading about it and realizing that it fit somewhere in the context of conservation and biology...."

The topic was especially relevant to Vitousek's home state, Hawaii, because plants and animals brought in by people have caused the extinction of many of that state's native species. "I decided I wanted to be an ecologist," he said later to Kluger, "so I jumped into science classes to catch up." It also helped that this career move would later allow him to work in Hawaii, something that was important to him.

Vitousek went to graduate school at Dartmouth College in New Hampshire, where he earned a Ph.D. in biological sciences in 1975. He accepted teaching posts at Indiana University and at the University of North Carolina, and continued his research. "I worked mostly on the mainland," he told *Environment Hawaii*. "Toward the end of that time, I started working in continental tropics in Costa Rica and Brazil a fair amount...." Finally, in 1984, Vitousek got his chance to conduct most of his research in Hawaii. This was when he became a professor at Stanford University.

In 1990, Vitousek was awarded a Pew Fellowship to study the effects on the local ecology of the introduction of non–native grasses to Hawaii. Also as part of his fellowship, he helped to educate the public about environmental changes taking place around the world. By 2001, Vitousek held an endowed chair at Stanford as Morrison Professor of Population and Resources.

Vitousek's base of operations in Hawaii is Hawaii Volcanoes National Park. "The park," he told *Environment Hawaii*, "has been really supportive of having a place where researchers from universities can come and set up and carry out work." A large part of Vitousek's work is geared toward aiding the conservation of native habitats—areas that still retain large numbers of native species and that are relatively untouched by invasive plants and animals. "I'd say the highest priority," he told *Environment Hawaii*, "has to be to take the areas that are in good shape, dominated by native communities and reasonably well protected, and take good care of them.... It's a lot cheaper and likely to be a lot more successful to keep them that way than it is to restore something that's gone down a path.... Those places ... are like no other places on earth. They are unique. They express Hawaii in a way that changed systems can't express Hawaii."

A recent project of Vitousek's included the study of sphagnum moss to determine its natural range in the Hawaiian islands, and whether its recent increase in range is due to the influence of people or of natural forces. Other goals of Virtousek's include spreading the word about Hawaii as a eco–tourist destination. "Galapagos is nothing compared to Hawaii," he told *Environment Hawaii*. "Nothing at all. And in terms of appreciating how the world works, evolutionarily, ecologically, culturally—there's nothing like Hawaii. And people who come here should see more of that, appreciate more of that, enjoy it more. Sure, the beaches and palm trees are great and drinks with umbrellas are fine, but beaches with palm trees and drinks with umbrellas are cheaper in Mexico."

At the same time, tourism has its price; the more people who visit Hawaii, the more pressure will be felt by its natural environment. The challenge, says Vitousek, is to draw tourists, and the corresponding attention tourists bring to ecological conservation, while at the same time protecting the environment from those tourists.

Sources

Periodicals

Baltimore Sun, September 24, 2000, p. 1A.
Time, August 20, 2001, pp. 44–45.

Online

"An Interview with Peter Vitousek," *Environment Hawaii*, http://www.environment–hawaii.org/701an.htm (August 5, 2002).
"Peter M. Vitousek, Ph.D.," Pew Fellows Program in Marine Conservation, http://www.pewmarine.org/PewFellows/pf_VitousekPeter_cv.html (August 26, 2002).

—*Michael Belfiore*

Sherron Watkins

Vice President for Corporate Development at Enron

Bill Pugliano/Getty Images

Born August 28, 1959; daughter of Dan C. Smith III (an attorney) and Shirley Klein Harrington (a business teacher); married Richard Watkins, 1997; children: Marion. *Education:* Received undergraduate degree from the University of Texas at Austin, 1981, and master's degree, 1982.

Addresses: *Home*—Houston, TX. *Office*—Enron Corp., 1400 Smith St., Houston, TX 77002.

Career

Certified public accountant; began as auditor at Arthur Andersen, Inc., Houston, TX, 1983; worked in New York City as auditor and accountant; began at Enron Corp., Houston, TX, 1993; rose to the post of vice president for corporate development, Enron Corp.

Sidelights

A formerly anonymous corporate executive became famous overnight in early 2002 when government investigators revealed that Sherron Watkins, Enron's vice president for corporate development, had sent Enron chair Kenneth L. Lay a memo months before warning about the potential fallout from the company's questionable accounting practices. Her memo proved that Lay and other Enron executives had indeed known about the falsely inflated numbers that caused hundreds of employees to lose their jobs and pension plans when the company declared bankruptcy in late 2001. "In the

sad tale of Enron's collapse," wrote *Time* journalist Michael Duffy, "Watkins is the closest thing to a hero in sight."

Watkins was born in 1959 and grew up in Tomball, Texas. Her maternal ancestors, originally from Germany, had settled the area in the nineteenth century. As a teen, she worked in the town supermarket, which her uncle owned, and displayed a talent for numbers early on. Her mother, a business teacher, counseled her to choose accounting as a profession, for she believed there were fewer hindrances to a woman's rise in it than in other fields. Watkins took that advice, graduating with a degree from the University of Texas at Austin in 1981, and a master's degree a year later. She went to work for Arthur Andersen, one of the largest corporate accounting firms in the United States, at its Houston office as an auditor.

Eager to leave Texas as a young woman, Watkins found similar work in New York City and lived there for several years. When she returned to Texas in the early 1990s, she began working at one of the most promising companies in Houston, the Enron Corporation. It was just eight years old when she joined in 1993, and had achieved a legendary reputation as a visionary leader in the realm of global energy resources and deals. She rose quickly through its ranks and, after her 1997 marriage, lived in a half–million–dollar house in a posh neighborhood near Rice University. She had a daughter in 1999 and drove a Lexus SUV. According to *Washington Post* journalist Jennifer Frey, "Watkins was just one of the legions of high–powered executive moms."

Transferred to the global finance unit run by Enron chief financial officer Andrew Fastow in July of 2001, Watkins went about her new duties, which involved finding assets for Enron to sell if it ran into financial trouble in its bid to become a full–fledged energy–trading company. Instead she kept discovering "off–the–books" partnerships and transactions in which Enron divisions loaned funds and stock shares to one another to camouflage losses. If the price of Enron stock rose, the strategy worked, but when the opposite happened, the financial quagmire grew exponentially. Of the two unorthodox partnerships named Condor and Raptor, one owed Enron more than $700 million. "Enron had booked huge profits from these entities while its stock price soared in 2000, despite the fact that neither Condor nor Raptor had any hard assets," journalist Duffy explained in *Time.* "But now that Enron's price was dropping, the company had to note these devaluations or pour more money into the companies when cash was short."

Others at Enron had noticed the practice—and realized that it made Enron stock worth far less than its actual trading price on Wall Street. A friend of Watkins's at the company had even questioned chief executive officer Jeffrey Skilling about it, and was promptly transferred out of his division. When Skilling resigned abruptly on August 14, 2001, rumors swirled that the company was in financial trouble. Lay, hoping to reassure employees and stockholders, invited employees to submit any worries or questions they might have to his mailbox. Watkins wrote an anonymous memo the next day, and a week later she confessed to writing it and handed Lay a far more detailed letter. "Has Enron become a risky place to work?," she asked in it, according to the *Washington Post.* "For those of us who didn't get rich over the last few years, can we afford to stay?" Watkins also declared herself "incredibly nervous that we will implode in a wave of accounting scandals."

On October 16 of that year, Enron announced a $618 million third–quarter loss. Investors panicked, Fastow was fired, and on the last day of the month the Securities and Exchange Commission began a formal inquiry. Both Skilling and Lay had sold large shares of their Enron stock in the past nine months, but regular Enron employees had been prevented from doing so during this crucial time; they were told that the company had recently switched its 401(k) plan administrator, and transfers of any 401(k) assets of Enron stock could not be made for the time being. As a result, hundreds of employees lost their retirement assets, and then their jobs, when 4,000 were let go in December.

Watkins's memo was included in the government–subpoenaed documents in one of 40 boxes of files handed over to investigators in mid–January, and she was heralded in the next day's newspapers. "Suddenly, she was the tough–talking Texas woman who had stood up to all the good old boys in the corporate hierarchy, the men who had been making millions while their employees and shareholders watched some, or all, of their life savings evaporate," noted the *Washington Post*'s Frey. Despite the news crews outside her house, Watkins went to work that day anyway. She testified a few weeks later before a House Energy and Commerce Committee subcommittee on oversight and investigations, and told Congress that Skilling and Fastow were the real culprits. She ventured that Lay had not properly understood the gravity of the accounting shell game. "I think Mr. Skilling and Mr. Fastow are highly intimidating, very smart individuals, and I think they intimidated a number of people into accepting some structures that were not truly acceptable," *Washington Post* journalist Susan Schmidt quoted her as telling the Congressional panel.

Skilling denied Watkins's charges, as did the Arthur Andersen executives implicated for condoning the very practices that corporate auditing firms are required by law to monitor when a company's stock is publicly traded. Watkins attained folk–hero status, and people began stopping her on the street around Houston to thank her. Still working at Enron in May of 2002, Watkins was writing a book, titled *Power Failure,* and there were plans for a Hollywood biopic of her story.

Selected writings

(With Mimi Swartz) *Power Failure,* Doubleday (New York City), 2003.

Sources

Periodicals

Daily Variety, March 27, 2002, p. 1.
Global Agenda, January 11, 2002.
Los Angeles Business Journal, January 21, 2002, p. 58.

New York Times, May 10, 2002, p. A1; June 6, 2002, p. A31.

Oil Daily, February 15, 2002.

People, February 4, 2002, p. 63.

Time, January 28, 2002, p. 16; February 4, 2002, p. 20.

Washington Post, January 25, 2002, p. C1; February 14, 2002, p. A2; February 15, 2002, p. A1.

Online

"The Right Way to Blow the Whistle," *BusinessWeek* Online, http://www.businessweek.com/bwdaily/dnflash/jan2002/nf20020130_7564.htm (January 30, 2002).

—*Carol Brennan*

Suzy Whaley

Professional golfer

Born November 10, 1966, in Syracuse, NY; daughter of Mick and Mary Ann McGuire; married Bill Whaley; children: Jennifer, Kelly. *Education:* University of North Carolina–Chapel Hill, 1989.

Addresses: *Office*—Blue Fox Run Country Club, 65 Nod Rd., Avon, CT 06001.

Career

LPGA Tour member, 1990, 1993; part–time golf teacher, Ibis Golf and Country Club, 1992–1996; head pro, Blue Fox Run Country Club, 1996—.

Awards: LPGA teaching and coaching division national title, 2002.

Sidelights

Suzy Whaley is one of the first women to play in an official Professional Golf Association (PGA) tournament since Babe Didrikson Zaharias played in a PGA tournament in 1938 and 1945. In May of 2003, Swedish golfer Annika Sorenstam played in a PGA tournament at the Bank of America Colonial in Fort Worth, Texas, but she was allowed in on a sponsor exemption. Whaley, on the other hand, earned the right to play in a PGA tournament when she won the Connecticut PGA sectional championship in September of 2002. Because Whaley earned this honor instead of being given it on a sponsor exemption, she is now considered a pioneer of women's golf.

Whaley grew up playing golf. Her mother, Mary Ann McGuire, was an avid golfer and often took Whaley with her to the course. As a teenager, Whaley worked summers at the Penn Oaks Country Club in West Chester, Pennsylvania, and eventually attended the University of North Carolina–Chapel Hill on a golf scholarship. She planned to go to law school after graduating in 1989, but instead received an offer from two business executives who said they were willing to sponsor her if she went professional. She accepted their offer, and in 1990 and 1993, she played on the Ladies' Professional Golf Association (LPGA) Tour. According to Joe Logan in the *Philadelphia Enquirer*, "She was young, lonely, miserable, and not good enough."

From 1992 to 1996, Whaley was a part–time teacher at Ibis Golf and Country Club. She left the LPGA Tour when she and her husband, Bill, who was also a golf pro, decided to start a family. They eventually had two daughters, Jennifer and Kelly.

In 2002, Whaley won the LPGA teaching and coaching division national title. In that same year, Whaley became the first woman since 1945 to qualify to play in a PGA tournament. That tournament was the Greater Hartford Open, scheduled to be held in July of 2003. Whaley qualified to play in it by winning the Connecticut PGA sectional championship in September of 2002. The PGA had only recently begun allowing women to play in chapter and section qualifying tournaments for the Club Professional Championship, opening the field to them in 1998.

Whaley's win, and her chance to play at the Hartford Open, set off a fiery controversy in the golf world. She told the *Philadelphia Enquirer*'s Logan that she had received a great deal of mail about the issue. Supporters told her she should play in the Hartford Open in order to serve as a role model for women and girls in golf. Other writers warned that women did not belong in a PGA tournament, and complained that she had won the sectional championship only because she was playing by different rules than those the male players had to follow. Under the rules, she did have an advantage over her male competitors in the sectional tournament. In that tournament, as a woman, Whaley played from tees that were only 90 percent as long as the tees that the men played from. In the Hartford Open, she would have to play the course the same way the men played it, from full–length tees.

After Whaley qualified by shooting on the shorter tees, the PGA, perhaps responding to the conservative contingent of golfer who believed that women didn't belong in PGA events, decided to change the rules that gave women players an advantage. In the *St. Petersburg Times*, Scott Purks noted that the new "Suzy Whaley Rule" stipulated that women must now play from the same tees as men in order to qualify for PGA Tour events.

Deciding whether or not to play in the Hartford Open was difficult for Whaley, who worried that if she did not play well there, her performance would reflect poorly on women's golf in general. In the end, however, she decided to play, and told Ron Sirak in *Golf World* that her decision was based on the fact that she could make a statement for female golfers, and also inspire younger players: "One of the biggest reasons is for my daughters, to show them that you do not have to be the best, but you can try." She also told Logan, "[M]y main goal—besides having a little fun—is to inspire young women to play anywhere they want to, to try out for the team they want to be on, whether it's a boys' or girls' team."

Whaley told Purks in the *St. Petersburg Times* that she knew she was an unlikely player to have achieved what she did. "It's been crazy," she said.

"You have to remember that I'm a 36–year–old club pro. I make tee times and sell golf gloves and balls. I'm not the best player in the world. Not by a long shot."

Lori VanSickle, director of golf at DuPont Country Club in Wilmington, Delaware, told the *Philadelphia Enquirer*'s Logan, "I like her decision and I like the reasons for her decision." On the fact that Whaley had no real chance of winning the Open, Van Sickle commented that this did not matter. "She is not going to be defined by what she shoots. She has already defined herself as a class act."

In the University of North Carolina at Chapel Hill's website, Whaley told an interviewer that in order to prepare for the Greater Hartford Open, she was "on an extremely heavy physical routine. I want to be in the best physical shape possible so I can remain emotionally strong when I am tired and so I can compete on the longer course."

In December of 2002, Whaley signed with Peter Jacobsen Productions, a publicity agency that would represent her in all her golf–related contracts, and which would also negotiate sponsor endorsements. In a press release, Ed Ellis, president of the agency, wrote, "We're delighted to work with Suzy. She's bright, articulate and, obviously, a very good athlete who is destined to impact golf history."

Whaley planned to play in six LPGA events in 2003, and hoped to play as many of these as possible before July so she could tune up her game for the PGA tournament.

After making the decision to play in the Greater Hartford Open, Whaley decided that she would use her position to make some points on behalf of women in golf. In the *Palm Beach Post*, Whaley referred to another boiling controversy in golf, over whether women should be allowed to play at the strictly men–only Augusta Country Club. She told the *Palm Beach Post*'s Craig Dolch, "If I can get people to talk about something other than Augusta, that would be terrific. Let's talk about why there's such a purse discrepancy between the LPGA and PGA Tour. One of the big reasons I'm doing this is to bring more attention to the LPGA."

In May of 2003, public attention shifted from Whaley to Sorenstam, who was allowed to play in a PGA tournament at the Bank of America Colonial in Fort Worth, Texas, thus becoming the first woman to do so since Babe Didrikson Zaharias played in 1945. Sorenstam was allowed in on a sponsor exemption, but she was widely regarded as "the best female golfer on the planet," according to *People*. Sorenstam's place in the tournament roster further fanned the flames of the controversy over whether women should be allowed to compete with men in golf. When asked about Sorenstam's foray into the PGA, Whaley told Purks in the *St. Petersburg Times*, "My hope is that people won't judge her on four days of golf, no matter what the result is. Bottom line is that she's a great player."

Whaley teed off at the Greater Hartford Open on July 24, 2003. She told Joel Schuchman at PGA.com that although she was nervous at first, she quickly settled down and played well, with a score of 75. She commented, "It was the most unbelievable moment walking up on that tee and having that many people cheering for me and supporting me and so many young kids out there yelling my name, and wishing me well. It was just an incredible, incredible moment."

Although Whaley scored 78 on the second day's play for a total score of 153, it was not good enough for her to make the final cut in the event. She told a *Hartford Courant* reporter that in the future, she would like to broaden her golf career, saying that she hoped to "do some golf commentating for a television network."

Whaley is the head pro at Blue Fox Run, a public golf course in Avon, Connecticut; her husband, Bill, is director of golf at River Highlands in Cromwell, Connecticut.

Sources

Periodicals

Austin American–Statesman, May 19, 2003, p. A1.
Golf World, September 27, 2002, p. 4; June 28, 2002, p. 6; December 13, 2002, p. 8.
Knight Ridder/Tribune News Service, January 17, 2003, p. K3187.
New York Times Upfront, February 7, 2003, p. 7.
Palm Beach Post, January 21, 2003, p. 1C.
People, May 26, 2003, p. 134.
Philadelphia Enquirer, January 14, 2003.
St. Petersburg Times (St. Petersburg, FL), April 4, 2003, p. 6C.

Online

"After Storm Over Annika, It's Smooth Sailing For Suzy," *Hartford Courant*, http://www.ctnow.com/sports/hc–media0725.artjul25,0,7191627.story?coll=hc–he adlines–sports (July 24, 2003).
"Interview with Suzy Whaley," PGA.com, http://www.pga.com/news/tours/pga–tour/whaleytranscript072403.cfm (July 24, 2003).
University of North Carolina at Chapel Hill, http://www.unc.edu/bw/feb_03/shorts.html (May 15, 2003).
"Why I'm Playing," CNNSI.com, http://www.sportsillustrated.cnn.com/golfonline/whaley/jan03 (December 3, 2002).
Peter Jacobsen Productions, http://www.pjp.com/pr.12.09.02.html (May 15, 2003).

—Kelly Winters

Peggy Whitson

AP/Wide World Photos

Astronaut

Born February 9, 1960, in Mount Ayr, IA; daughter of Keith (a farmer) and Beth (a farmer) Whitson; married Clarence F. Sams. *Education:* Iowa Wesleyan College, B.S., 1981; Rice University, Ph.D., 1985.

Addresses: *Office*—Lyndon B. Johnson Space Center, Houston, TX 77058.

Career

Postdoctoral fellow at Rice University, 1985–86; National Research Council Resident Research Associate, NASA Johnson Space Center, 1986–88; supervisor for Biochemical Research Group at KRUG International, a NASA medical sciences contractor, 1988–89; admitted into the NASA astronaut corps, 1996; flew to the International Space Station (ISS) aboard space shuttle *Endeavour* for a six–month stay, 2002; became the first astronaut designated science officer of the ISS, 2002.

Awards: Graduated Summa Cum Laude from Iowa Wesleyan College, 1981; NASA Sustained Superior Performance Award, 1990; NASA Certificate of Commendation 1994; NASA Exceptional Service Medal, 1995; NASA Silver Snoopy Award, 1995; NASA Space Act Board Award, 1995; NASA Tech Brief Award 1995; American Astronautical Society Randolph Lovelace II Award, 1995; Group Achievement Award for Shuttle–Mir Program, 1996; NASA Space Act Board Award, 1998.

Sidelights

In 2002, Peggy Whitson became the first astronaut to be named science officer of the International Space Station (ISS). She lived aboard the station for six months, for a total of 184 days and 22 hours in space, setting a record for the longest stay in space by any American astronaut who hadn't been in space before. A biochemist by training, Whitson's duties as science officer aboard the ISS included conducting experiments in physics, medicine, and biology. She also participated in the ongoing construction of the space station, installing structural components using the station's remote manipulator system, which she operated from the inside of the station. She also conducted a four–and–a–half hour spacewalk to install micrometeoroid shielding on the space station's exterior.

Whitson was born in 1960 in Mount Ayr, Iowa. She grew up on a pig farm near the town of Beaconsfield. Her parents, Keith and Beth Whitson, remained farmers throughout Whitson's training as a scientist and astronaut and after her return home from the ISS. Whitson was nine years old in the summer of 1969 when humans first set foot on the moon. Watching the event on television, she decided then and there that she wanted to be an astronaut. At the time, it was impossible for a woman to become an American astronaut—only men were admitted into the astronaut corps. But that changed in 1978, when the National Aeronautics and Space Administration (NASA) made its first selection of female astronauts. Whitson was then a senior in high school, and she knew that her dream could become a reality.

Realizing also that an advanced degree in science was one ticket into the astronaut corps, Whitson went on to Iowa Wesleyan College to study biology and chemistry. After graduating from Wesleyan, she attended Rice University to work toward a Ph.D. in biochemistry. Rice, from Whitson's point of view, was ideally located—in Houston, Texas, home of NASA's Johnson Space Center and Mission Control.

After earning her Ph.D. in biochemistry in 1985, Whitson spent ten years as a NASA scientist on the ground, helping to train NASA and Russian astronauts both in the United States and in Russia. Each year from 1986 (the year that the space shuttle *Challenger* exploded on launch, killing all seven astronauts on board) onward, Whitson applied to the astronaut corps.

Finally, in May of 1996, her persistence paid off when she was selected for the astronaut corps—one of an elite group of just 119 astronauts. And, six years later, on June 5, 2002, Whitson rocketed into space for the first time aboard the space shuttle *Endeavour* along with Russian cosmonauts Valeri Korzun, a veteran of previous missions to the Russian space station Mir, and Sergei Treschev, who, like Whitson, was a rookie. Together they would take over operation of the ISS from the three astronauts already there, staying for a total of six months in space.

With Whitson and her Russian crewmates on the shuttle were three American astronauts and one French astronaut who would help them make the transition to the ISS. Since this was Whitson's first time in space, it was unusual that she was asked to stay so long at the ISS; most rookie astronauts cut their teeth on shorter shuttle missions. But Whitson's 10-year association with NASA before becoming an astronaut allowed her to skip right past that usual requirement.

After a two-day journey, the space shuttle arrived at the 240-mile-high orbiting space station, and exchanged crewmembers with the ISS. Whitson be-

came the first American on the station with a Ph.D., the first without a military background, and only the second woman to become a resident of the station.

In one of her letters home, Whitson described her first view of the Earth from space, shortly after *Endeavour*'s launch. "To say that my first sight of the Earth from orbit was breathtaking or magnificent still seems such a paltry way to describe what I saw and felt.... The colors were so vibrant that they seemed to have a previously unseen texture. I would liken the feeling to having someone turn on the lights after having lived in semi-darkness for years. I had never really seen anything quite so clearly or with so much color!"

A high point of Whitson's stay aboard the ISS came on August 16, 2002, when she climbed into a Russian spacesuit and accompanied crewmate Korzun on a spacewalk outside the station. Her job on the spacewalk was to help Korzun install micrometeroid shields on the outside of the station, but her assigned tasks were momentarily forgotten when she floated out of the airlock and beheld the awe-inspiring beauty of a sunrise as the station sped around the curve of the Earth. As she said in one of her letters home, "I previously compared the view of being in space to having lived in semidarkness for several years and having someone turn on the lights. Well, the view from my helmet, continuing the same analogy, would be like going outside on a sunny, clear day after having lived in semidarkness for years!" Whitson and Korzun experienced three sunrises during their spacewalk as the ISS orbited the Earth three times in four hours, traveling at a speed of 17,500 miles per hour.

In September of 2002, Whitson was officially named the station's first science officer. From then on, said Sean O'Keefe, chief administrator of NASA, each succeeding space station crew would have one designated science officer. O'Keefe said that making science a priority on the orbiting outpost would allow NASA to "utilize it better," according to CNN. com.

The comparison of Whitson to the fictional character Spock, the science officer aboard the starship *Enterprise* on the *Star Trek* television series, was inevitable, and Whitson began to receive "an incredible amount of Star Trek/Mr. Spock–related e-mail" aboard the station, as she said in one of her letters home, published on the NASA website and in the *Houston Chronicle*. The association did not bother her though; she even signed the letter "Live long and prosper," a salutation used by Mr. Spock in the series.

Whitson was 42 years old at the time of her promotion to science officer. Her title merely put into name what was already fact—she was the first research scientist to live aboard the station. At the time of her appointment to science officer, she had been on the station for four months, and had two more months to go in her stay there. While the total length of her stay in space did not set a NASA record, it was the longest that a rookie astronaut had spent in space. She followed in the footsteps of Shannon Lucid, another American biochemist, who had spent six months on the Russian Mir space station in 1996, and who now serves as NASA chief scientist.

The ISS, still under construction at the time of Whitson's stay, could hold only three long–term residents, sharply limiting the time that could be spent purely on science—the crew's main duties were to keep the station and its myriad of systems running smoothly. The initial design for the station had called for a crew of six to seven astronauts, but budget cuts at both NASA and its Russian counterpart, which was an equal partner with NASA in the venture, forced the indefinite postponement of the planned expansion. Even so, the station, in its configuration at the time of Whitson's stay, had about as much living space as a three–bedroom house.

Since inhabitants of the space station are weightless, it is very important that they exercise regularly so that they do not lose bone mass and their ability to readapt to Earth's gravity when they return. Whitson's daily exercise regimen included a one–to–two–hour workout on the station's stationary bicycle and other equipment that could provide a workout in zero gravity.

Life in orbit required other adjustments as well. Since there are no laundry facilities on the ISS, the inhabitants must wear their clothing until they are too dirty to do so comfortably. They then pack them into an empty supply capsule attached to the station, along with all of their other garbage, and simply jettison it all, to burn up in Earth's atmosphere upon reentry.

After a record (for a rookie American astronaut) six–month stay in space, it was time for Whitson and her two crewmates to return home. On December 2, 2002, Whitson, Korzun, and Treschev floated aboard *Endeavour*, which had returned to retrieve them, for the return to Earth. Whitson, although craving fresh greens and a steak after six months of eating bagged and dehydrated food, found that her experience in space was every bit as exciting as she had imagined it would be.

As Whitson said in one of her letters home, published on the NASA website, "As my time aboard the station nears conclusion, I have lots of mixed feelings about leaving. While I, of course, want to see all of my family and friends, it is hard to let go of the idea of living here…. Being here, living here, is something that I will probably spend the rest of my life striving to find just the right words to try and encompass and convey just a fraction of what makes our endeavors in space so special and essential."

During her final days in space, Whitson was also struck by the power of the international cooperation that had made the space station possible. No less than 16 nations had contributed to the construction of the station, and Whitson saw that spirit of cooperation as one of the most important aspects of living and working on the station. "There is no way that I can imagine," she said, "especially after seeing our planet from this vantage point, that bringing our cultures closer together and proliferating understanding in our differences as well as our similarities, can be a bad endeavor." Whitson and her crewmates were replaced aboard the ISS by American astronauts Ken Bowersox and Don Petit and Russian cosmonaut Nikolai Budarin. Bowersox took over Whitson's role as science officer aboard the station.

On February 1, 2003, two months after Whitson left the ISS, the space shuttle *Columbia* broke up in the upper atmosphere as it returned from a mission in space. All seven astronauts aboard were killed. Following the disaster, NASA grounded its fleet of remaining shuttles indefinitely. It also canceled all public appearances by astronauts, including Whitman's scheduled visits to classrooms in her home state of Iowa.

The residents of the ISS at the time of the *Columbia* disaster were the same astronauts who had replaced Whitson and her Russian crewmates two months previously. Originally scheduled to return home aboard a NASA space shuttle, the ISS crew would be forced to return via the three–person Russian Soyuz lifeboat attached to the station. Future ISS residents would be brought to the station and returned via other Soyuz spacecraft. However, the limitations of the Soyuz meant that only two inhabitants could occupy the station at any given time— the bare minimum required to maintain the station's systems, leaving little or no time for science aboard the station. It seemed, at least until the space shuttles were ready to fly again, that no further science officers would inhabit the ISS.

Sources

Periodicals

Houston Chronicle, May 30, 2002, p. A4; November 10, 2002, p. A1; November 30, 2002, p. A27; December 3, 2002, p. A3.

Los Angeles Times, December 4, 2002, p. A36.

Omaha World–Herald, March 26, 1999, p. 15; February 2, 2003, p. 4A.

Ventura County Star, May 30, 2002, p. A8.

Online

"Astronaut Bio: Peggy Whitson," NASA, http://www.jsc.nasa.gov/Bios/htmlbios/whitson.html (February 24, 2003).

"Expedition Five Letters Home #8," NASA, http://spaceflight.nasa.gov/station/crew/exp5/lettershome8.html (February 24, 2003).

"Expedition Five Letters Home #9," NASA, http://spaceflight.nasa.gov/station/crew/exp5/lettershome9.html (February 24, 2003).

"Expedition Five Letters Home #13," NASA, http://spaceflight.nasa.gov/station/crew/exp5/lettershome.html (February 24, 2003).

"Russia to Taxi Space Station Crews," CNN.com, http://www.cnn.com/2003/TECH/space/02/27/sprj.colu.station.soyuz/index.html (March 1, 2003).

"Station Astronaut Named First Science Officer," CNN.com, http://www.cnn.com/2002/TECH/space/09/17/station.science.ap/index.html (September 17, 2002).

"STS–111 Satus Report #01 Wednesday, June 5, 2002 5 p.m. CDT," SpaceRef.com, http://www.spaceref.com/news/viewsr.html?pid=5666 (April 7, 2003).

—Michael Belfiore

Ranil Wickramasinghe

Prime minister of Sri Lanka

Born March 24, 1949, in Colombo, Sri Lanka; son of Esmond (a newspaper publisher) and Nalini (Wijewardene) Wickramasinghe; married to Maithree (a senior lecturer in English at the University of Kelaniya). *Education:* Royal College of Colombo; law degree, University of Colombo.

Addresses: *Office*—Office of the Prime Minister, No. 58, Sri Ernest de Silva Mawatha, Colombo 07, Sri Lanka. *Website*—http://www.priu.gov.lk/PrimeMinister/Indexpm.html.

Career

Briefly practiced law before entering politics; elected to the Parliament of Sri Lanka and appointed deputy minister of foreign affairs, 1977; elevated to cabinet status when appointed the country's first minister of youth affairs and employment by President J.R. Jayawardene, 1978; given additional portfolio of minister of education, 1980; appointed leader of the House in Parliament and appointed minister of industries, 1989; given additional portfolio of science and technology, 1990; named the cabinet's chief media spokesman, 1991; became prime minister after the death of President Premadasa, 1993; stepped down after general elections, 1994; became leader of United National Party and leader of the opposition in Parliament, 1994; sworn in as prime minister, 2001.

Sidelights

Ranil Wickramasinghe, a member of one of Sri Lanka's most distinguished families and a lawyer by profession, was swept into office as prime minister largely on the strength of his pledge to bring ethnic peace to his troubled island homeland. Officially sworn into office in early December of 2001, Wickramasinghe has worked tirelessly to fulfill that promise. Less than three months after taking office, Wickramasinghe's government, with the help of the Norwegian government, succeeded in reaching a permanent cease–fire agreement with the rebel Liberation Tigers of Tamil Eelam (LTTE). The cease–fire agreement was quickly followed up in 2002 by three rounds of peace talks between the government and the rebels, who have been fighting for an independent Tamil homeland since 1983. Wickramasinghe's quest for peace has not been without its detractors, mostly from the opposition party, who claim that Wickramasinghe has given away too much, too quickly to the rebels.

Two decades of ethnic conflict have deeply scarred Wickramasinghe's homeland, a densely populated island of about 25,350 square miles that is home to three main ethnic groups—Sinhalese, Tamils, and Muslims. The Sinhalese account for nearly 75 percent of the island's population. At the root of the current ethnic unrest in Sri Lanka is an insurgency mounted by the minority Tamils in support of their demand for an independent homeland. Sri Lanka's population of roughly 20 million has suffered the loss of about 65,000 citizens in the ethnic fighting, and more than 1.5 million Sri Lankans have been displaced or driven from the island altogether. Damage to the country's infrastructure has been considerable, and the landscape is littered with burnt–out buildings.

Born in the Sri Lankan capital of Colombo on March 24, 1949, Wickramasinghe is the son of Esmond and Nalini Wickramasinghe. His father served as managing director of the Associated Newspapers of Ceylon Ltd. from 1950 until 1968 and also chaired the International Press Institute. Esmond Wickramasinghe was also active in Sri Lanka's United National Party (UNP), serving on its working committee from 1973 to 1985. Wickramasinghe's mother is the daughter of Sri Lankan freedom fighter D.R. Wijewardene and best known for her support of the arts on the island. The prime minister's paternal grandfather, C.L. Wickramasinghe, was a leading government official during the country's colonial period.

Wickramasinghe first studied at Colombo's Royal College, graduating in 1969, after which he pursued a law degree at the University of Colombo. During his three years in law school, he was active in student politics, serving as president of the Law Students's Union and vice president of the University Students's Council. After earning his law degree in 1972, Wickramasinge enrolled as an advocate of the Supreme Court of Sri Lanka. Following in his father's footsteps, he also became active in the affairs of the UNP. His first serious foray into island politics came in 1977 when, at the age of 28, he was elected to Parliament and appointed deputy minister of foreign affairs by President Jayawardene. The following year Wickramasinghe became the youngest cabinet member in Sri Lanka when he was named by Jayawardene to be the country's first minister of youth affairs and employment. In 1980 he was given the additional portfolio of minister of education.

In his position as minister of youth affairs and employment, Wickramasinghe launched the country's first all–island Youth Development Program, which was established to promote youth clubs throughout Sri Lanka. He also established the National Youth Center and reorganized the country's industrial apprentice training schemes, significantly expanding the number of trainees. Even more far–reaching were Wickramasinghe's accomplishments as minister of education. Most importantly, he launched educational reforms designed to improve the quality of island education with a particular emphasis on the teaching of science and English. To encourage sports, Wickramasinghe introduced a school sports division. He also helped to bring the latest technology into Sri Lankan classrooms, initiating programs encouraging the use of computers and educational television. To improve the quality of teaching in Sri Lankan schools, Wickramasinghe oversaw the establishment of a National Institute of Education and Colleges of Education. To help attract better teachers, salaries of educators were significantly upgraded under Wickramasinghe's watch.

After the inauguration of President Ranasinghe Premadasa in 1989, Wickramasinghe was appointed leader of the House in Parliament and named minister of industries. He was given the additional portfolio of science and technology in March of 1990. Only a year later he was named the cabinet's chief media spokesman. As minister of industries, Wickramasinghe in 1989 launched the country's second round of economic liberalization. His Strategy for Industrialization eased regulation of the financial sector, deregulated other sectors, and privatized a number of state–owned enterprises. To help develop Sri Lanka's industrial infrastructure, Wickramasinghe set up a number of industrial estates and investment promotion zones. He also designed incentives to increase the presence of the information technology (IT) industry on the island.

In May of 1993, President Premadasa was assassinated by suspected Tamil Tiger guerillas. After his untimely death, Wickramasinghe became prime minister. While in office, he strengthened Sri Lanka's bilateral and multilateral ties with other countries in the region and throughout the Commonwealth. After 16 months in the post, he was forced to step down when the People's Alliance coalition, headed by Chandrika Kumaratunga, won parliamentary elections in the fall of 1994. During Wickramasinghe's relatively brief tenure as prime minister, Sri Lanka enjoyed its most vigorous economic growth of the decade. Shortly after stepping down as prime minister, the assassination of UNP leader Gamini Dissanayake by suspected LTTE rebels thrust Wickramasinghe into the leadership of his party and leader of the opposition in Parliament.

What followed was a period of change for both the UNP and Wickramasinghe himself. To improve his party's image and broaden its appeal, the new UNP leader spearheaded a campaign to rid the party of corruption and to open the party's membership to a more representative mix of ethnicity, gender, and youth. As to his personal image, Wickramasinghe experimented with a variety of hair styles in an effort to find one that was more appealing to the public. Like fellow party members Premadasa and Dissanayake, the UNP leader was a high–profile assassination target for the country's Tamil rebels. Wickramasinghe narrowly escaped death when a bomb exploded at a meeting he was addressing in the town of Eppawala. Also a target of the rebels was Kumaratunga, who was injured in an assassination attempt that was to prove critical in the next face–off between the ruling coalition and UNP.

Wickramasinghe ran for president in December of 1999 but lost in what many observers believe was a sympathy vote for Kumaratunga, who had been injured in a bomb explosion not long before. Although he failed in his bid to unseat the People's Alliance coalition from power, Wickramasinghe continued to pound away at the ruling coalition, criticizing its handling of the Tamil insurgency and citing its apparent inability to stabilize the economy. In the run–up to the general elections of 2001, Wickramasinghe pledged to bring a lasting peace to Sri Lanka and double the economic growth rate if his party was voted into office. He also promised to curtail presidential powers.

Wickramasinghe's promises apparently resonated with Sri Lanka's voters, for they voted the UNP into power in parliamentary elections in December of 2001. Although it was a humiliating loss for Kumaratunga, it did not spell an end to her presidency, which is scheduled to continue until 2005. However, the UNP victory made her a lame duck president. Wickramasinghe, sworn in as prime minister on December 9, 2001, moved quickly to consolidate power and make good on his campaign promises. Clearly, the most pressing issue on his agenda was finding a way to bring an end to years of ethnic conflict. In late February, Wickramasinghe's government and LTTE negotiators hammered out a permanent cease–fire agreement. Brokered by Norway, where talks between the two parties were held, the agreement halts hostilities and lays the groundwork for continuing peace talks to end the separatist war.

Citing objections to certain clauses in the agreement, Kumaratunga threatened to cancel the accord. "I can stop Ranil Wickramasinghe's agreement with one letter to the army commander," Kumaratunga told London's *Daily Mirror,* as quoted in AP Worldstream. She was also reportedly upset by Wickramasinghe's failure to keep her updated on the progress of the government's talks with the rebels. In the end, Kumaratunga never made good on her threat to scrap the agreement. In April of 2002, after Tamil Tiger leaders publicly rejected suicide bomb attacks, Wickramasinghe spoke optimistically of the prospects for peace. In return, the Tamil rebels demanded that the government lift its ban on the LTTE before planned peace talks could proceed. During the period from March through May, the decommissioning of rebel weapons got underway, under the terms of the February cease–fire agreement.

In early September of 2002, Wickramasinghe's government finally lifted its ban on the Tamil Tigers of the LTTE, clearing the way for the first round of peace talks since the cease–fire accord was struck earlier in the year. In two days of talks at Sattahip Naval Base, east of Bangkok, Thailand, in mid–September, government and rebel negotiators made substantial progress, reaching agreements in several areas, particularly in the realm of economic issues. Even more significantly, the rebels dropped their demand for a separate state and signaled their willingness to accept autonomy within Sri Lanka.

Speaking before the Investment Forum in New York City on September 19, 2002, Wickramasinghe urged investors to demonstrate their support of the peace process by investing in Sri Lanka. "Your endorsement of the peace process helps to give it credibility and momentum. Human rights activists are courageous pioneers. But when conservative, often apolitical, corporate leaders also stand up to be counted, then society takes notice and the peace train picks up speed," he said, as quoted on the High Commission of the Democratic Socialist Republic of Sri Lanka website.

A second round of peace talks got underway in Thailand at the end of October of 2002. During the course of those talks, the government and rebels agreed on a joint commission to develop areas of the country ravaged by the conflict. On November 25, 2002, Wickramasinghe and LTTE leader Anton Balasingham, in the highest–level meeting yet between the parties, jointly appealed for both economic and political help in ending Sri Lanka's two decades of ethnic strife. "Our success here will consolidate the peace process and propel it forward," Wickramasinghe told the Associated Press. Although Sri Lanka seems closer than ever to putting an end to the ethnic conflict that has shattered the country for nearly two decades, it remains uncertain whether Wickramasinghe's ambitious peace initiatives will ultimately accomplish that end. One ominous sign came in late November of 2002 when Tamil rebel leader Vellupillai Prabhakaran said he will push for secession and an independent state if the Tamil minority is not granted self–rule.

Wickramasinghe lives in Colombo with his wife, Maithree, a senior lecturer in English at the University of Kelaniya. In addition to her teaching duties, Maithree Wickramasinghe conducts research in the fields of gender and women's studies.

Sources

Periodicals

AP Online, November 24, 2002.
AP Worldstream, February 26, 2002; November 25, 2002, November 27, 2002.

Online

"Bio Data," Sri Lanka Department of Information, http://www.news.lk/bio_data.htm (November 27, 2002).

"Colombo Strives for United Front," Asia Times Online, http://atimes.com/atimes/South_Asia/DJ29Df04.html (November 28, 2002).

"Prime Minister Ranil Wickremesinghe: A Social Democrat with a Vision and a Mission," *Daily News,* http://origin.dailynews.lk/2002/01/03/fea04.html (November 28, 2002).

"Profile: Ranil Wickramasinghe," BBC News, http://news.bbc.co.uk/1/hi/world/south_asia/570222.stm (November 28, 2002).

"Progress at Sri Lanka Peace Talks," CNN.com, http://www.cnn.com/2002/WORLD/asiapcf/south/09/17/slanka.talks/index.html (November 28, 2002).

"Sri Lanka Prepared to Lift Tiger Ban," BBC News, http://news.bbc.co.uk/1/hi/world/south_asia/1922823.stm (November 28, 2002).

"Sri Lanka's Potential Political Stand–Off," BBC News, http://news.bbc.co.uk/1/hi/world/south_asia/1695593.stm (November 28, 2002).

"Sri Lanka Timeline," World News Map, http://www.mapreport.com/countries/sri_lanka.html (November 28, 2002).

"Statement by Honourable Ranil Wickramasinghe, Prime Minister of Sri Lanka, at the 'Investment Forum' in New York on 19th September 2002," High Commission of the Democratic Socialist Republic of Sri Lanka," http://www.srilankahcottawa.org/pressrelease/pr_investmentforuminnewyourk.htm (November 28, 2002).

—Don Amerman

Tom Wilkinson

Actor

Born Thomas Wilkinson, December 12, 1948, in Leeds, Yorkshire, England; married Diana Hardcastle (an actress); children: Alice, Molly. *Education:* University of Kent, B.A., 1970; attended Royal Academy of Dramatic Art (RADA), London.

Addresses: *Agency*—Lou Coulson Agency, 37 Berwick St., London W1V 3RF, England.

Career

Actor on stage, film, and television. Stage appearances include: student plays at the University of Kent, late 1960s; plays in Nottingham, Birmingham, Oxford, and London's National Theater, late 1970s; acted with London's Royal Shakespeare Company, early 1980s; *Hamlet,* 1981; *Tom and Viv,* 1983; *Ghosts,* c. 1985; *My Zinc Bed,* 2000. Television appearances include: *First Among Equals* (miniseries), BBC, 1986; *The Woman He Loved* (movie), 1988; *The Attic: The Hiding of Anne Frank* (movie), 1988; *Prime Suspect,* BBC, 1990; *Resnick: Lonely Hearts* (movie), BBC, 1991; *Resnick: Rough Treatment* (movie), 1991; *Charles Dickens's Martin Chuzzlewit* (movie), 1994. Film appearances include: *Weatherby,* 1985; *In The Name of the Father,* 1993; *Priest,* 1994; *Sense and Sensibility,* 1995; *The Ghost and the Darkness,* 1996; *The Full Monty,* 1997; *Wilde,* 1997; *Rush Hour,* 1998; *The Governess,* 1998; *Shakespeare in Love,* 1998; *Ride with the Devil,* 1999; *The Patriot,* 2000; *Black Night,* 2001; *In the Bedroom,* 2001; *The Importance of Being Earnest,* 2002.

Awards: British Academy of Film and Television Award for best supporting actor, for *The Full Monty,*

1998; New York Critics Film Circle Award for best actor, for *In the Bedroom,* 2001; Special Jury Prize, Sundance Film Festival, for *In the Bedroom,* 2001.

Sidelights

The British actor Tom Wilkinson was relatively unknown by American audiences when he appeared in 2001's acclaimed film *In the Bedroom,* for which he earned an Academy Award nomination for best actor. Yet Wilkinson had enjoyed a quiet fame—and had earned the ardent respect of his peers—for nearly two decades prior to playing opposite Sissy Spacek as a quiet Maine doctor facing the death of his only son. Critics praised the British thespian for his restrained yet powerful acting and for his pitch–perfect New England accent—and the New York Critics Film Circle honored Wilkinson with its best actor award.

Born in Yorkshire, England, in 1948, Wilkinson is the son of a Leeds farmer. When he was a toddler, his family left behind their financial hardships in England and emigrated to northern Canada. There Wilkinson's father found work as an aluminum smelter, and after six years, decided to return to England. "I was [in North America] between ages 5 and 11, which was just enough time for me to fall in love with [American] pop culture of the 1950s," Wilkinson told Gene Seymour of the *Los Angeles Times*. "Though I didn't see a television properly until I was 12 and we were back in England, I read Dell comics, listened to baseball and [would] go out every Saturday to the movies."

Back in England, the family settled in Cornwall, where Wilkinson's parents ran a pub. Upon the death of Wilkinson's father, his mother returned to Yorkshire, where her teenage son attended King James's Grammar School in Knaresborough. Here Wilkinson, age 16, met Headmistress Molly Sawdon, who took a particular interest in the lad. "[Sawdon] simply decided she would make something of me," Wilkinson told Alan Riding of the *New York Times*, "which meant being invited round to her house, being taught how to eat, which knives and forks to reach for first. We would go to the theater together. Having wandered aimlessly through school, suddenly someone took an interest in me."

It was at King James's that Wilkinson developed his passion for the theater, directing his first play, Ionesco's *Bald Soprano*. "After the first rehearsals, I decided this is what I want to do with my life," he told the *Los Angeles Times*'s Seymour. Although he went on to study English and American Literature at the University of Kent, entering the school in 1967, Wilkinson continued to cultivate his love for the theater. As a college student, he frequently acted in or directed student plays and revues. In 1970 he was accepted at the Royal Academy of Dramatic Art (RADA), London's foremost drama school.

At RADA, Wilkinson met other students from working–class families in the provinces, and discovered that opportunities now existed for young people like him to pursue artistic careers. "All the things that weren't cool became cool," he told the *New York Times*'s Riding. "I saw the young, provincial bohemian and thought, that role can be mine. I'll be in the arts."

Upon graduating from RADA, Wilkinson hit a lucky streak, catching the eye of British director Richard Eyre, who was then running the Nottingham Playhouse. He landed his first professional acting job there, performing in a range of plays that ran the gamut from Shakespeare to the contemporary British playwright David Hare. With this wide-ranging experience under his belt, Wilkinson acted in plays in London's National Theater, as well as in Birmingham, Oxford, and Edinburgh, Scotland.

By the early 1980s Wilkinson had landed a two–year contract with the prestigious Royal Shakespeare Company, where he earned distinction for his supporting role in a 1981 production of *Hamlet*. Yet his stint with the company left Wilkinson largely disillusioned. The actor did not get the roles that he felt he deserved, which left him feeling under-appreciated and frustrated. "It almost finished me off as an actor," he told the *New York Times*'s Riding. "I hated the sort of snobby atmosphere."

Other work for Wilkinson in the early to mid–1980s included a lead role as the poet T. S. Eliot, opposite Julie Covington, in 1983's *Tom and Viv*, a biographical drama at the Royal Court Theatre. Wilkinson played opposite acclaimed actress Vanessa Redgrave in 1985's David Hare feature film *Weatherby*, and teamed with Redgrave again in the stage version of Henrik Ibsen's *Ghosts*, at the Young Vic theatre. In the latter production, Wilkinson had his first chance to see his name in lights on a marquee in London's West End district. And in a high point of his early career, he starred in 1986's BBC television miniseries *First Among Equals*, an adaptation of a politically themed novel by Jeffrey Archer. The miniseries role garnered widespread exposure for Wilkinson, and earned him a kind of cult following. Next came a turn with American television, on CBS, where he appeared as Ernest Simpson in 1988's *The Woman He Loved*, which told the story of a love affair that deposed a king. The same year he appeared in the CBS movie *The Attic: The Hiding of Anne Frank*, which starred Mary Steenburgen and Paul Scofield.

Yet after a ten–year stretch of nonstop work and increasingly bigger stage, television, and film roles, Wilkinson suddenly found that the phone had stopped ringing. He had entered a dry spell, which lasted 18 months. Looking back at this low point, he told the *Los Angeles Times*'s Seymour that he stopped taking things for granted. "For a very long time early in my career, I tended to drift from job to job. I didn't have great financial ambitions. I always thought, if you've got enough money for a pack of cigarettes and an Italian meal, what else do you need?"

The dry spell ended, and Wilkinson was working again, picking up roles on television and in movies. These included a guest–star role as Peter Rawlins on 1990's popular BBC detective series *Prime Suspect* (shown on PBS two years later). The following year Wilkinson took the title role in two BBC adaptations of John Harvey detective novels: *Resnick: Lonely Hearts* and *Resnick: Rough Treatment*. Among his early–1990s film credits was a small role in 1993's drama by Jim Sheridan, *In the Name of the Father*, starring Daniel Day–Lewis and Emma Thompson. He returned to television for a memorable performance in 1994's *Charles Dickens' Martin*

Chuzzlewit (shown on PBS the following year). In a starring film role the same year, Wilkinson played a clergyman involved in a love affair with his house-keeper in Antonia Bird's controversial drama *Priest*. After *Priest* came a series of big–screen roles for Wilkinson, including a turn as Mr. Dashwood in 1995's Jane Austen adaptation *Sense and Sensibility*, and as a dastardly character in 1996's *The Ghost and the Darkness*.

In 1997 Wilkinson appeared in the hit comedy film *The Full Monty*, playing the proud, reluctant Gerald—one of six laid–off workers who turn to strip-tease dancing to support themselves. The film—an Academy Award nominee for best picture, screen-play, and director and winner for best original mu-sic score—brought Wilkinson an international audi-ence, and its popularity inspired the actor. "*The Full Monty* was a catalyst for me," he told Clodagh Hart-ley of the *Los Angeles Times*. "I decided at that point that I wanted to make films to the exclusion of tele-vision or theatre."

A slew of subsequent roles followed for Wilkinson, who appeared in such films as 1997's *Wilde*, 1998's period drama *The Governess*, and the same year's *Rush Hour* and *Shakespeare in Love*. In the latter he played Hugh Fennyman, a moneylender who be-comes a theater director, lending the film a comic role. Thought the part was relatively small, it earned him much praise.

Other film roles included 1999's *Ride with the Devil*, directed by Ang Lee of *Sense and Sensibility*, and 2000's *The Patriot*, in which Wilkinson played the reserved General Cornwallis. The same year, he re-turned to the London stage after an absence of more than a decade, co–starring with Julia Ormond in David Hare's *My Zinc Bed*.

Although the veteran film actor was highly re-spected by his industry peers, Wilkinson had not achieved mainstream fame until his starring role in 2001's *In the Bedroom*. Confident that Wilkinson had what it took for the part, first–time director Todd Field offered him the lead role over the telephone. Field had been seeking an actor unfamiliar to American audiences, and Wilkinson had been rec-ommended to him by filmmaker Stanley Kubrick's assistant. The British actor did not even meet the rest of the cast until he arrived for rehearsals in Maine. Playing opposite Sissy Spacek as Matt, a Maine doctor grieving for his murdered son, Wilkin-son seamlessly took on a native New England ac-cent, as well as the gestures and mannerisms that made the role so convincing.

When *In the Bedroom* screened at the Sundance Film Festival in January of 2001, the film stole the limelight. The festival's jurors heaped praise on Wilkinson and Spacek, who both took Special Jury Prizes for their acting. Critics lauded the British actor's complex performance, citing his quiet power and his deft handling of raw emotions. But when critics expressed surprise at his flawless American accent, he demurred. "I was brought up in Canada," he reminded CBSNews.com, "so when I first learned to speak, I talked like you guys with a little Cana-dian thing." Talking to Steven Rosen of the *Denver Post*, Wilkinson gave more credit to his acting train-ing than to his background: "I'm an actor; I'm meant to play anybody. The accent is the superficial bit—the 'inside' is what you need to know.... I got every-thing from the script, which was a particularly well–written one." Wilkinson also cited his Shakespearean training as an important touchstone for his work in the tragically charged film.

In the Bedroom landed Wilkinson a best actor award from the prestigious New York Film Critics Circle, as well as his first Oscar nomination from the Acad-emy of Motion Picture Arts and Sciences. The hype surrounding the Academy Awards surprised the British actor, who was invited to scores of inter-views with American journalists and reporters. In her interviews, Spacek praised her co–star for his inventive and "present" acting. On his part, Wilkin-son told the media that he did not expect to beat ac-tors Russell Crowe, running for his role in *A Beauti-ful Mind*; Sean Penn, for *I Am Sam*; Will Smith, for *Ali*; and Denzel Washington, for *Training Day*. (Ultimately, Crowe took the award.)

Also in 2001, Wilkinson co–starred in the less–popular Martin Lawrence comedy *Black Night*, por-traying a drunken, luckless knight. His next role, a small part in 2002's Oscar Wilde adaptation *The Im-portance of Being Earnest*, placed him aptly amid an all–star cast. He played Dr. Chausible in the late–nineteenth–century period comedy, which drew praise from critics. Yet, after the success of *Bedroom*, fans can expect to see Wilkinson in fewer bit roles, and in plenty of leading film roles in the future.

Sources

Periodicals

Denver Post, December 23, 2001, p. F1.
Guardian (London), November 9, 2001, p. 12.
Los Angeles Times, November 26., 2001, part 6, p. 10.
New York Times, March 10, 2002, sec. 2A, p. 9.
Sun, February 13, 2002, p. B1.

Online

"The Patriot Cast: Tom Wilkinson," The Patriot Resource, http://www.patriotresource.com/cast/tom.html (November 1, 2002).

"Tom Wilkinson," Hollywood.com, http://www.hollywood.com/celebs/bio/celeb/1677495; http://www.hollywood.com/celebs/detail/celeb/198204 (November 1, 2002).

"Tom Wilkinson's American Part," CBSNews.com, http://www.cbsnews.com/stories/2002/01/08/entertainment/main323564.shtml (November 1, 2002).

—Wendy Kagan

Will Wright

Game developer

Born in 1960, in Atlanta, GA; married; children: Cassidy (daughter).

Addresses: *Publisher*—Electronic Arts, 209 Redwood Shores Pkwy., Redwood City, CA 94065.

Career

Designer of games, including: *Raid on Bungeling Bay*, 1982; *SimCity*, 1989; *SimEarth: The Living Planet*, 1990; *SimAnt: The Electronic Ant Colony*, 1991; *SimCity 2000*, 1993; *SimCity Multimedia CD Version*, 1993; *SimCity 2000 Urban Renewal Kit*, 1994; *SimCity Classic*, 1994; *SimCopter*, 1998; *The Sims*, 2000; *The Sims: Unleashed*, 2002.

Awards: The TIME Digital 50, 1999; Invisionary Award, 2000; GDC Game of the Year Award for *The Sims*, 2001; Lifetime Achievement Award by the International Game Developers Association, 2001; Academy of Interactive Arts and Sciences Hall of Fame, 2002.

Sidelights

Computer games like *Doom* and *Quake* get a lot of press because of their controversial violent content. Consequently, many believe violent videogames are prevalent on the personal computer. But, in fact, the best–selling PC games of all time are an urban planner's dream come true. Will Wright's *Sim* series started with the game *SimCity*, an exploration of community micromanagement. In the mid–1980s Wright, the series creator, came up with the idea for a game where the player builds a city from scratch. Sewage design, community centers, and balancing the education budget would be the player's focus, a far cry from the interstellar gun fighting that dominated the industry at the time. But he had an even more revolutionary idea that would scare off more than a few game executives: the game would have no end. You could continue to play for as long as *SimCity* held your interest. Almost 15 years after its release the series still fascinates the public with 25 variations of the theme, including sequels and expansion packs (which add extra features to the games). Overall, 18 million copies of the *Sim* series have been sold worldwide.

As a boy, Wright was more interested in robots and board games than videogames. The son of a chemical engineer and a theater actress, Wright was a heavy reader and had a rich imagination. That imagination was probably a place of some comfort when his father, the owner of Wrights Plastic Company in Atlanta, died. Wright was only nine years old at the time. His mother eventually decided to move to Louisiana, the state she grew up in, to find the support she needed to raise two kids on her own. So, within a year he and his sister had lost their father and moved away from their friends.

While Wright attended high school, he began to show a talent for analyzing human behavior. He loved to build robots from found parts and Radio Shack kits. He tried to go the college route, studying architecture and mechanical engineering, but never found himself comfortable with the academic life. After five years of hopping from school to school he decided to move on with his life. He never graduated from college.

Wright spent every spare minute he had on building and analyzing a robot he called Mr. Rogers, a three-wheeled contraption that was able to map out the room it was in and send the coordinates to Wright's Apple II computer. He enjoyed seeing people's reactions to Mr. Rogers when he took him out on the town. He always tested how far he could stretch the humanization that people gave his robot. The way people decide to relate to technology is the foundation that he has built his career on. However, the technology of robotics did not allow for him to gather data or test his theories to the extent to which he would have liked.

Then, when he was 20, Wright played his first computer game and it changed his life. It was a flight simulator and it captivated the young man, more for its ability to create an entire world on the screen in front of him than for its impressive game play. He found himself just flying around, admiring the landscape on the monitor and imagining the little communities that slipped by below him. Later in his career he told Daniel Sieberg of Salon.com about how even a simple shape on the screen can excite the player if the world it is in feels real. "What inspires me is how much people were able to read into that little rectangle [in the old days of video gaming]. You only have to give people the briefest, most tentative scaffolding to hang something on and they'll build an elaborate narrative and fill in the gaps with their imagination. We humans are so good at that…. We can do a lot of really cool stuff with graphics and sound, but that's not where the magic happens."

He had enjoyed the flight simulator so much that he decided to design one of his own. Though he loved robotics, he yearned to reach a wider audience and videogames were part of the mainstream. Wright's first finished product was a helicopter action game called *Raid on Bungeling Bay,* for the Commodore 64. Once again, Wright had more fun flying around than he did playing the actual game. If his imagination could picture a whole world below him, then why not make a game that would take advantage of that? He saw an opportunity to create a game where people would feel comfortable ex-ploring their decision-making thought processes and sensibilities in a "real-world" setting. He knew that it was easy to appeal to our sense of violence, but how simple would it be to build a game that utilized our organizational skills or our instincts in an emergency situation? From this curiosity Wright developed the idea for *SimCity,* a real-time strategy game that would pit the player against real-life problems. Instead of gun-toting baddies the game would throw low SAT scores at the local high school or drop a tornado in the shopping district. In his imagination *SimCity* would challenge our sense of how we handle problems. In hindsight the idea still seems revolutionary. But Wright could barely sell the game to anyone outside of his immediate circle of friends, all of whom shared his enthusiasm for revealing our behavioral patterns.

After a lot of rejections, Wright realized he would have to be creative if he wanted to make his game. If the establishment would not support *SimCity* then he would have to find a way to do it himself. So Wright teamed up with his friend Jeff Braun and started Maxis, a game development company, which exists to this day. Wright and his small team, all friends, had to make the rules of the world we live in and then build an interface that would let the player have a good time following or breaking those rules. It was a huge task. But Wright tried to keep the premise as simple as possible, hoping that the final result would actually be fun to play. As *SimCity* got closer to completion, the game was hitting its stride and gluing game testers to their seats. Wright watched on as the testers micromanaged their cities and marveled at the barriers that the design team placed in their way. The potential publisher of *SimCity,* Broderbund, worried that the game was not really a game. But after adding some more natural disasters to the mix, Wright secured a distribution deal.

After *SimCity*'s release in 1989, the executives were happy with their decision to be careful with the game. It was not selling. Though it had captured the imagination of a niche market, it was not showing the kind of numbers that would designate a good seller. Then, *Time* magazine published an article on the odd little game. The idea, apparently, was being marketed incorrectly, because once the mainstream audience got word of *SimCity* it took off. Within months, hundreds of thousands of people were building and managing their own cities, glued to the screen for "just five more minutes." When teachers heard about *SimCity* they saw an opportunity to interest their students in subjects that would otherwise be difficult to explain. Schools around the country, to this day, use the game to teach students the intricacies and dynamics of cause and effect. Even the military took notice and got into the act. It has been funding the development of software similar to *SimCity* that could guess the behavior of an enemy before a war even begins. "Something about our culture has really disconnected the idea of play from what it should be, which is education," Wright told Nick Wadhams of the Associated Press for the *Chicago Tribune*. "We see play as kind of this disposable act that just adolescents are engaged in." Wright tapped into the way we think and feel and, as a result, *SimCity* has sold more than one million copies and continues to be a solid seller almost 15 years after its release.

With every success you can expect a sequel and *SimCity* has had its share. *SimCity* alone has spawned three sequels and the series has given gamers a number of variations on the *Sim* theme, including *SimEarth: The Living Planet, SimAnt: The Electronic Ant Colony*, and even *SimCopter* (since helicopters are one of Wright's obsessions). But it was the game that followed all of these which would define Wright's career as one of the most impressive in the history of the gaming industry: *The Sims*.

Released in 2000, *The Sims* started as a "dollhouse" game. The gamer would be given a plot of land and they would build a new life. The idea came from Wright's experience with the 1991 Oakland, California, fires. Wright's house burned down and he had to rebuild his family's life from scratch. Even in the face of personal disaster he found himself analyzing how he and his wife went about buying a new household. It might not have been very fun but it was fascinating to Wright.

If he could make a fun game where the player controlled a town, he wanted to take the next step and create a game that would make controlling a household just as entertaining. Once again, Wright found himself struggling against people, even peers, who could not see his vision. With years of respect in the budding game industry and millions of copies of his products sold, people still doubted the idea. After all, it is one thing to have thousands of options while minding a town but how fun could it be for a player to manage meals, throw parties and get a good night's sleep? "Internally, *The Sims* was a huge struggle getting it released, much more than *SimCity*," Wright told David Becker of CNET News.com. "We had an official product–selection committee, and I gave my spiel to the committee, and they actually rejected it; they thought we could not do it. At which point I kind of took the whole thing underground. It became my black box project."

When Electronic Arts, the largest game publisher in North America, bought Maxis in 1997 they saw that Wright was committed to the idea of *The Sims* and gave him a team with which to work. The heads of Electronic Arts thought if the man who designed *SimCity* believed he could make this new concept work, then he should be given the chance. It might have been the best decision the company ever made. When *The Sims* was released in 2000 it was an immediate and huge hit. People were enthralled by building a life from scratch. A massive community of players was given tools to build their own "skins" which lets their characters look like anyone they want. The skins and other items are traded online by the millions. Even Wright was blown away by the success of the game; he told a fan during an online CNN chat in 2000, "It's gotten to the point now where I surf the fan sites everyday and download cool things the fans have created, which is really ironic in a way! Because now it's the fans out there that are entertaining us, the developers, with their creations! This is something I never would have foreseen five years ago." *The Sims*, or one of its many expansion packs, has consistently sold in the top ten for three years and, to date, has sold more than eight million copies, making it the best–selling computer game of all time.

Wright still spends his spare time building robots and has appeared with his daughter on Comedy Central's *Battlebots*, a show where robots fight each other into submission. The machine they used for the show was the Chiabot, which hides its weapons in the shrubbery perched on top of its head.

Hollywood has also beaten on Wright's door. In 2003, he signed a first–look development deal with Fox Broadcasting for a new television series. Though *The Sims* is an obvious project for him to develop, Wright has not always done the obvious thing. In fact, his taste in telling a linear story has skewed toward the more "experimental," exemplified in a test show he made called *M.Y. Robot*, a mixture of animation and puppetry set in feudal Japan. In May of 2003, Wright's game *The Sims* was named one of the 100 greatest videogames of all time by *Entertainment Weekly*.

But as Wright's career options expand he seems to have a handle on the simplicity of his game designs and summed it up for John McLean–Foreman at Gamasutra.com: "One of the biggest things that I wanted to show was how ... the real resource everybody has in life is time. You can convert time to a lot of other things—you can convert it into money, objects, and friends—but how you choose to spend your time is how you're playing the game of life. That's the one thing that you don't get more of, really. So, time management was a big thing I wanted to at least make people more aware of. It's not so much preaching, 'Here's how you should spend your time.' It's just interesting when you sit back and think about how you choose to spend every minute of your day."

Sources

Periodicals

Chicago Tribune, November 21, 2002.
Entertainment Weekly, May 9, 2003, pp. 38–40.

Online

"A Chat with Will Wright," GIGnews.com, http://www.gignews.com/goddess_wright.htm (April 10, 2003)

"An Interview with Will Wright," Gamasutra.com, http://www.gamasutra.com/features/20010501/wright_01.htm (April 11, 2003).

"Digital 50," *Time,* http://www.time.com/time/digital/digital50/47.html (April 8, 2003).

"Military strategists could learn a thing or two from *The Sims*," Yahoo! News, http://story.news.yahoo.com/news?tmpl=story&u=/usatoday/20030402/tc_usatoday/5023808 (April 8, 2003).

"*Sims* Creator Inks TV Deal with Fox," Reuters, http://www.reuters.com/newsArticle.jhtml?type=topNews&storyID=2866628 (June 17, 2003).

"The secret behind *The Sims*," CNET News.com, http://news.com.com/2008–1082–254218.html (April 7, 2003).

"The World According to Will," Salon.com, http://www.salon.com/tech/feature/2000/02/17/Wright/index.html (April 11, 2003).

"Will Wright gets Invisionary Award," *Computer Games,* http://www.cdmag.com/articles/029/182/sims.html (April 7, 2003).

"Will Wright Interview," IGN.com, http://pc.ign.com/articles/095/095879p1.html (April 8, 2003).

"Will Wright," Moby Games, http://www.mobygames.com/developer/sheet/view/developerId=4217 (April 7, 2003).

"Will Wright on creating *The Sims* and *SimCity*," CNN.com, http://www.cnn.com/COMMUNITY/transcripts/2000/12/1/wright.chat (April 10, 2003).

"Will Wright's *Sims*: Unpredictably Perfect," TechTV, http://www.techtv.com/news/culture/story/0,24195,3411469,00.html (April 7, 2003).

—Ben Zackheim

Michelle Yeoh

Tony Barson/WireImage.com

Actress

Born Yeoh Chu–Kheng, August 6, 1962, in Ipoh, Perak, Malaysia; married Dickson Poon, 1988 (divorced, 1991). *Education:* Royal Academy of Dance, London, B.A.

Addresses: *Office*—c/o Han Entertainment Ltd., Room 2901–2903, 148 Electric Rd., North Point, Hong Kong.

Career

Won Miss Malaysia beauty pageant, and then starred in a commercial with Hong Kong action movie star Jackie Chan, 1983; tapped by film production company D&B films to act in small parts. Actress in films, including: *Yes, Madam,* 1985; *Royal Warriors,* 1986; *Easy Money,* 1987; *Magnificent Warriors,* 1987; *Police Story 3: Super Cop,* 1992; *Heroic Trio,* 1992; *Tai Chi Master,* 1993; *Wing Chun,* 1994; *Ah Kam,* 1995; *Tomorrow Never Dies,* 1997; *Crouching Tiger, Hidden Dragon,* 2000; *The Touch,* 2002. Founded Mythical Films, 2000. Producer of films, including: *The Touch,* 2002.

Awards: Award of Excellence in Acting for outstanding performance as an actor, Cineasia, 1999; International Star of the Year, ShoWest, 2001.

Sidelights

One of the biggest female film stars in Asia, Michelle Yeoh has been called the female Jackie Chan (an accolade she rejects) because, like Chan, she got her start in Hong Kong action films, she performs her own stunts, and has become an international superstar. She broke through to Western audiences when she costarred with Pierce Brosnan in the 1997 James Bond film *Tomorrow Never Dies,* and she won further acclaim in the West as costar of the Academy Award–winning Chinese–language film *Crouching Tiger, Hidden Dragon,* which was released in the United States in 2000.

Although she is famous in part for performing her own stunts, Yeoh nevertheless insisted in an interview with Lionel Seah of the *Straits Times,* "I've never done action for action's sake. What is action without dramatic development? Roger Spottiswoode, producer for *Tomorrow Never Dies,* once told me he could have a stand–in for me for the stunts. But he could never send in someone for me to do the drama. It's an added skill. In any case, I like to do my own stunts because I don't like other people to have the fun."

Michelle Yeoh was born Yeoh Chu–Kheng in 1962 in Ipoh, in western Malaysia. Her parents are both of Chinese heritage, and her father is a politician and lawyer. Yeoh learned Malay and English as her first languages, and she learned the Cantonese she would later speak in Hong Kong action films as her third language. When she was just four years old, Yeoh began taking ballet lessons. She knew that show business was her calling by the time she was 16 years old, and she then moved to London, England, to study at the Royal Academy of Dance. However, her dancing career ended almost as soon as it began when, after graduating from school, she suffered a back injury.

At the urging of her mother, Yeoh reluctantly entered the Miss Malaysia beauty pageant in 1983. She won the event, which directly led to a role in a commercial with Hong Kong movie star Jackie Chan. Yeoh's work in the commercial with Chan attracted the attention of executives at a small film production company, D&B Films. The company then hired Yeoh for a series of small parts in films without wide distribution, in which she acted under the name of Michelle Khan.

In 1985, Yeoh landed a role that was to set the tone for her later career. This was a part in D&B Film's *Yes, Madam,* an action–comedy in which Yeoh appeared with Cynthia Rothrock, a well–known martial arts action film star. The film called for Yeoh to defend herself in the opening scene with dazzling martial arts moves, first against a flasher, and then a band of robbers.

Without any previous martial arts experience, Yeoh had to hit the gym for nine hours a day to get up to speed for the film. Her hard work paid off; audiences loved her performance in *Yes, Madam,* and she quickly became one of the biggest female stars in Hong Kong action films. Films followed in rapid succession, including *Royal Warriors,* released in 1986, again featuring Yeoh with Rothrock, *Easy Money,* released in 1987, and *Magnificent Warriors,* also released in 1987. In this last film, she followed in Chan's footsteps by performing all of her own stunts. Also in 1987, Yeoh became engaged to one of the principals of D&B films, Dickson Poon. After marrying Poon, Yeoh dropped out of filmmaking to become a homemaker. The marriage failed, however, and the couple were divorced in 1991.

Fortunately for Yeoh's legions of fans in Asia, and for her future fans in the West, Yeoh returned to action films in a big way with her role in *Police Story 3: Super Cop,* released in 1992. In this film, she starred alongside Chan, matching his amazing stunts. Chan, said to be initially skeptical of a woman's ability to perform the same kind of death–defying stunts that had made him famous, was con-

cerned by the end of the shooting of the film that he might be upstaged by Yeoh. One of the most nerve–wracking stunts Yeoh performed in this picture was a motorcycle jump onto a moving train. She had learned to ride a motorcycle only the day before the shooting of that scene.

Now firmly established as a major star, Yeoh became the highest–paid female actor in Asia. Working under the name Michelle Yeoh, she went on to star in numerous action films, including *Heroic Trio,* released in 1992, *Tai Chi Master,* in 1993, along with fellow kung fu star Jet Li, and *Wing Chun,* released in 1994.

Performing her own stunts was not without its hazards. While she considered the shoulder dislocation and the occasional cracked rib she had already suffered while making films to be a normal part of her job, she was given a serious scare during the making of *Ah Kam* in 1995, when she mistimed a jump from an 18–foot wall. The star landed on her head and cracked a vertebra. Initially put in traction, and afraid that she might never walk again, Yeoh nevertheless made a spectacular recovery, and returned to the set of the film in full fighting form before a month had passed.

Yeoh has strenuously resisted the obvious comparisons many have made between her and Chan. "I'm not the female Jackie Chan," she told Cindy Pearlman of the *Chicago Sun–Times,* "and that's what I've heard. I'm not quite as foolish as Jackie." When asked how many broken bones her career has resulted in, she responded. "I have no broken bones. I have dislocated my shoulder. I've cracked my share of ribs. I've ruptured an artery. But I have never broken a bone."

After *Supercop* was released in the United States, American producers tapped Yeoh for the James Bond film *Tomorrow Never Dies,* released in 1997. In this film she starred opposite the charismatic Pierce Brosnan, who played James Bond, and very nearly stole the movie from him. "He's wonderful," Yeoh said of Brosnan to Pearlman in the *Chicago Sun–Times.* "He's handsome. Best of all, he's not intimidated by strong women in real life." Yeoh chose this role not only because it was a tremendous opportunity to reach new audiences, but also because, as she told Pearlman, "I love to see an Asian woman portrayed as something other than that demure, frightened, frail thing." Also, she told Pearlman, "This is the first really strong woman in a Bond movie who is not a villain. I've proven you don't have to be a b**** if you're a strong woman." As a result of her heightened profile in the United States, Yeoh was named one of *People*'s sexiest 50 people in 1997.

Working on a Hollywood film held unusual challenges for Yeoh. American insurance companies insisted that she not perform all of her own stunts, as she was accustomed to doing. Much to Yeoh's amusement and eventual frustration, the studio had difficulty finding stunt doubles who more or less matched Yeoh's diminutive frame, and who could perform the stunts as well as she could. "I knew I could do some of those stunts as well or better as most of the stunt people," she told Pearlman. "I like that they do have a difficult time finding a stunt double for me. I'm always sitting on the sidelines saying, 'I could do it.'"

Yeoh proved her versatility as a serious actress, as well as an action star, to Western audiences when she costarred in the Academy Award–winning *Crouching Tiger, Hidden Dragon,* released in the United States in 2000. As Jonathan Crow put it on the All Movie Guide website, with this film, "Yeoh cemented her status as an incredibly graceful fighter with the unusual ability to display a remarkable dramatic range as well." As in her previous films, Yeoh performed her own stunts in this film, sustaining a knee injury that required surgery.

Crouching Tiger, Hidden Dragon won the Academy Award for best foreign film of 2000, as well as three other Academy Awards. The film also shattered United States records for top–grossing Asian film and top grossing foreign–language film of all time. Affirming her commitment to remain based in Asia, Yeoh started her own Hong Kong film production company in 2000, called Mythical Films. "Why do I have the need to be a producer?" she asked Zainal Alam Kadiar of Malaysia's *New Straits Times.* "Well, it's a very personal decision, having a great passion for the industry.... It's more like a natural progression to what I have been doing. It is important to me to have a level of control, and ensure that I have enough creative input in my work." And she added, "Perhaps the decision to produce is also a selfish one.... So I can act my role according to how I want it. You see, as an actress, most of the time when I get a certain script, I always find myself wanting to do the male roles. I find them more challenging and demanding and it is in my nature to push myself."

Mythical Films immediately went into production on a romantic action film, with Shanghai, Xian, and the Himalayas as its principal locations. Called *The Touch,* the film features Yeoh as both producer and star of the film, and it was directed by Peter Pau, who won an Academy Award for best cinematography for *Crouching Tiger, Hidden Dragon.* Named one of the ten most anticipated films of 2002 at the 2001 Cannes Film Festival, the film features Yeoh as an acrobat charged with retrieving a sacred relic said to contain the spirit of a Buddhist holy man—a task impossible for an ordinary person to complete.

Speaking of the film to Chee–may Chow of Australia's *Newcastle Herald,* Yeoh said, "I believe there are so many tales to be told from our side, around our region, up in China and locations that we know better and stories that we can tell better." She continued, "I would not think that I would pack up my bags and go over there," she said of Hollywood. Especially when Hollywood comes to her; Miramax bought the right to distribute the film in the United States before it was even completed.

Mythical Films had four more films slated for eventual production at the time of the opening of *The Touch* in Asia, including the company's second production, *Hua Mulan,* in which Yeoh plays a woman who dresses as a man to go to war to help her ill father. In spite of heading her own production company, Yeoh told Mathew Scott of the *South China Morning Post* that she had no intention of becoming a director. "It's not something I've ever had any interest in doing. I think I'm very honest with myself; I know what I like to do and what I don't want to do."

Yeoh divides her time between Malaysia, where she helps to care for her elderly parents, and the United States. "I have the best of both worlds," she told Pearlman in the *Chicago Sun–Times.* "I'm a superstar in Asia. I'm in demand in Hollywood."

Sources

Periodicals

Chicago Sun–Times, December 14, 1997, p. 3.
Newcastle Herald, March 26, 2001, p. 48.
New Straits Times, July 9, 2002, p. 1.
South China Morning Post, August 1, 2002, p. 1.
Straits Times (Singapore), Life! section, August 2, 2002.

Online

"Crouching Tiger, Hidden Dragon," Yahoo! Movies, http://movies.yahoo.com/shop?d=hv&id=1800424121&cf=awards (October 14, 2002).

"Michelle Yeoh," All Movie Guide, http:www.
allmovie.com/cg/avg.dll?p=avg&sql=
B223709~C (October 9, 2002).

"People Profiles: Michelle Yeoh," People.com,
http://people.aol.com/people/profiles/basic
facts/0,9855,128037,00.html (October 9, 2002).

The Touch, http://www.thetouchmovie.com
(October 15, 2002).

—Michael Belfiore

Anthony Zinni

Diplomat

Born September 17, 1943, in Conshohocken, PA; son of Antonio (a chauffeur) and Lilla (a homemaker and seamstress) Zinni; married Deborah Bathke, 1966; children: Lisa, Maria, Anthony. *Education:* Villanova University, B.S. in economics, 1965; M.S. in international relations, M.S. in management and supervision.

Addresses: *Office*—Center for Strategic and International Studies, 1800 K St., NW, Washington, D.C.

Career

Enrolled in the United States Marine Corps, 1961; commissioned as an infantry second lieutenant, 1965; served two tours of duty in Vietnam, 1966–70; rose through the military ranks to become a four-star general; served as commander of the United States Central Command, 1997–2000; named U.S. special envoy to the Middle East, 2001.

Awards: Combat Action Ribbon; Bronze Star with Combat "V" and gold star; Defense Distinguished Service Medal with oak leaf cluster; Defense Superior Service Medal with two oak leaf clusters; Distinguished Sea Service Award, Naval Order of the United States, 2001.

Sidelights

As United States special envoy to the Middle East, Anthony Zinni was sent to Israel in 2001 to try to mediate peace between Israel and the na-

scent Palestinian state. A retired four-star U.S. Marine Corps general, Zinni was welcomed by officials on both sides of the conflict as a sign that the administration of U.S. President George W. Bush had gotten serious about helping to end the decades-old conflict.

Appointed to the envoy post in November of 2001, Zinni was 58 years old, and had retired from active military service the year before. He insisted that he receive no salary for his new duties, telling *People,* "I didn't want anyone to think that I'm in this for anything other than just a resolution of the conflict."

Zinni grew up in the industrial town of Conshohocken, Pennsylvania, near Philadelphia. He was his parents's youngest child. His father was a veteran of World War I, and his grandfather was a soldier in the Italian army. Even at an early age, Zinni knew he wanted to serve in his country's armed forces. "I would hear all these stories," he told *People.* "They fed my imagination."

Instead of getting a job at a local mill as many of his peers did, Zinni enrolled at Villanova University in 1961 and at the same time became a reservist in the U.S. Marine Corps. He graduated from college in 1965 with a commission as a second lieutenant, the first in his family to attend college. Intending to serve only three years in the military when he joined, he instead became a career Marine. "Once I got into the Marine Corps," he explained in *People,* "I got caught up in the whole ethos."

Zinni met his future wife, Debbie Bathke, while stationed at Quantico, Virginia. The two were married in 1966, just three months before Zinni was sent to the conflict brewing in Vietnam as an advisor to Vietnamese Marines. There he lived with Vietnamese soldiers and studied their language and culture. The process of learning all he could about the culture in which he was stationed would come to define all of his future deployments.

Toward the end of this first tour of duty, Zinni contracted malaria, hepatitis, and mononucleosis, and had to be brought home. After his recovery, he returned for a second tour of duty in Vietnam. He remained there until 1970, when, as a company commander, he was seriously wounded in battle. This time he left Vietnam for good.

Back home in the United States, Zinni again made a full recovery, and he continued his military career, adding the role of mediator to his duties in the 1990s. His assignments included helping ease tensions between Indian and Pakistani leaders, helping Kurdish refugees in Turkey and Iraq, and negotiating the release of an American prisoner of war held by Somali warlord General Aidid after the 1993 Black Hawk Down incident.

In 1997, Zinni, now a four-star general, was made commander of all U.S. forces deployed in the territory extending from East Africa through the Middle East to Central Asia. As head of Central Command, as this position was known, Zinni was stationed in Tampa, Florida. Now with two masters degrees, Zinni was known as a scholar as much as a soldier, and he applied his intellect to the task of command, each evening poring over newspapers from each of the 25 countries where his troops were stationed, seeking to remain as informed as he could about the politics of each country. He also did his best to take into account the cultural and political contexts in which his forces operated. As he told the *Villanovan,* a newspaper produced by his alma mater, and quoted in the *Washington Post,* "We learned the hard way the importance of appreciating the culture [and of] having a deeper understanding of the nature of the conflict."

It was in this post that Zinni developed the relationships that would serve him in his role as negotiator in some of the world's most troubled regions,

including Iraq, where Zinni supervised the daily combat air patrols the United States used to enforce no-fly zones. He also oversaw United States air strikes against Iraq in December of 1998.

Also during this period, Zinni developed a set of guidelines for United States forces engaged in the kinds of peacekeeping operations that have characterized that country's military involvement around the world since the end of the Cold War. Called "Twenty Lessons," and quoted in the *Washington Post,* these guidelines instruct U.S. commanders to "coordinate everything with everybody" and "don't make enemies [but] if you do, don't treat them gently." As retired Colonel Fred Peck, a colleague of Zinni's, put it in the *Washington Post,* "His attitude is, you try to make diplomacy work, but when it comes time for action, you're as swift and violent as you can be."

Zinni's standing in the military establishment was summed up in the *Washington Post* by one of his superiors, Lieutenant General James Jones, as: "He's very widely known in the Marine Corps as probably being the most operationally competent general officer that we have, meaning that he has done a little bit of everything, from war-fighting to humanitarian operations to peacekeeping to peace enforcement."

Zinni retired from military service in June of 2000, but he did not plan to retire from an active life. "I'm not ready to sit back and fish and watch the days go by," he told the *Atlanta Journal and Constitution.* "I will be up to something constructive."

That "something" turned out to be the job of President Bush's special envoy to the Middle East. It was an area Bush had tried to stay out of, trying to avoid the entanglements of his predecessors. The conflict between the Palestinians and the Israelis, in particular, was an area of which he wanted to steer clear. But increasing violence between the two sides in the conflict, as well as the September 11, 2001, terrorist attacks against the United States, required that the U.S. government take a more active role in the region. So, in November of 2001, Zinni was appointed special envoy to the Middle East.

The choice of Zinni as envoy was met with enthusiasm by the Palestinian government. "We have very much welcomed his presence," said Ghaleb Darabya, a Palestinian official based in Washington, D.C., speaking in the *Atlanta Journal and Constitution.* Darabya described Zinni as "fair and tough," and said "[t]hat's certainly what the Palestinians have wanted for a long time, which is to see a serious American involvement as a mediator in the Middle East peace process."

The Israeli government also welcomed Zinni, though there was said to be some trepidation about the close relationships Zinni had developed with Arab leaders during his time as head of Central Command. Determined to succeed in helping to negotiate peace between the Israelis and Palestinians where others have failed, Zinni counted among his assets the ability to question his superiors. As he told *People*, "Those of us who lived through Vietnam resented the fact that senior leaders knew something was wrong and didn't say anything at the time." He also saw his position as a soldier as a valuable asset. "If you look at history," he told *People*, "soldiers make the best peacemakers. In my mind it's because they've seen the worst of it. They're more understanding and more willing to find a way to make peace."

Sources

Periodicals

Atlanta Journal and Constitution, December 23, 2001, p. 2B.
Daily Telegraph, February 18, 1998, p. 35.
People, April 15, 2002, pp. 77–78.
Washington Post, March 6, 1998, p. A33.

Online

"Conversation with General Anthony Zinni," International Studies, UC Berkeley, http:// globetrotter.berkeley.edu/conversations/Zinni/ zinni–con0.html (August 20, 2002).
"Distinguished Sea Service Award 2001 Honoree— General Anthony C. Zinni, USMC (Ret.)," Naval Order of the United States, http://www. navalorder.org/dssa.html (August 19, 2002).

—Michael Belfiore

Barry Zito

Professional baseball player

Born Barry William Zito, May 13, 1978, in Las Vegas, NV; son of Joe (a composer) and Roberta (Singer) Zito. *Education:* Attended University of California, Santa Barbara, 1996; attended Pierce Junior College, Woodland Hills, CA, 1997; attended University of Southern California, 1998.

Addresses: *Agency*—Arn Tellem, Clear Channel Entertainment, 220 W. 42nd St., New York, NY 10036. *Office*—Oakland Athletics, Network Associates Coliseum, 7000 Coliseum Way, Oakland, CA 94621.

Career

Began pitching competitively in high school; drafted in first round to Minors team Sacramento Rivercats in 1999, drafted to Majors team Oakland Athletics, 2000; represented the A.L. in All–Star Game, 2002.

Awards: Freshman All–America honors, Collegiate Baseball, 1997; All–America selection, *USAToday Baseball Weekly,* 1998; named Pac–10 Pitcher of the Year, 1998; *The Sporting News* A.L. Pitcher of the Year, 2002; Players Choice Award for A.L. Pitching, 2002; A.L. Cy Young Award, 2002..

Sidelights

In the 2002 Major League Baseball season, Barry Zito led the American League (A.L.) in victories, ranked third in Earned Run Average (ERA), and tied Mike Mussina of the New York Yankees for third in strikeouts (182). Zito's opponents at the plate had a .185 average with runners in scoring position, the lowest in the A.L. Zito is known primarily for his fastball, changeup, and dangerous curveball, which many believe to be one of the best ever from an overhand pitcher. He was chosen to represent the A.L. in the 2002 All–Star game. His performance also netted him the coveted Cy Young Award, an honor given to the top pitchers in both the American and National Leagues. But 2002 was also a disappointing year for Zito because his team, the Oakland Athletics, were eliminated from the post–season in a first–round defeat by the Minnesota Twins. "It [the Cy Young Award] makes me less bummed out about what happened in the playoffs," he told CNNSI.com. "It hurt to see us not there. We thought this was the year, we thought this was the team. We almost knew it was."

Zito was born in Las Vegas, Nevada, but his family soon moved to the San Diego, California, area. From the time he was a toddler, Zito loved to throw things, as many children do. But what made him different was that he could throw things exactly where he wanted. His father, Joe, a former composer for Nat King Cole, built a pitching mound in the backyard of their home. Joe saw his son's talent and he was willing to spend the time needed to cultivate it. Every weekend they practiced for two hours, and Joe went as far as videotaping his son so they could go over his form in detail.

When Zito was old enough to get formal training, his father hired Randy Jones, a pitcher who won the Cy Young award in 1976 with the San Diego Padres. Jones had taken out a classified ad in a San Diego paper charging $50 per hour to train kids. Jones knew when he saw Zito throw that the boy had talent, but he also knew the youngster lacked discipline. "I remember vividly the four, five years we spent in the backyard with Randy," Zito told CNNSI.com. "When I did something incorrectly, he'd spit tobacco juice on my shoes, Nike high–tops we could barely afford." But Jones gave him a hard time for a reason. "I had to get his attention, and that worked with Barry," he told CNNSI.com. "He didn't focus really well when we first started." However, Jones saw a substantial talent and opened his house to Zito, a privilege only given to the best of his students. "I would use that as inspiration for the ones that showed a burning desire," he told CNNSI.com. The living room was filled with mementos from Jones's career, including the Cy Young award, and it left a deep impression on Zito. "It was sitting there in his living room every day," Zito told Chuck Johnson of USAToday. "I would marvel at it. I didn't know so much at the age of 12 or 13 what a Cy Young was. I just knew it was a great honor."

Zito developed into an independent teen who did not fit the stereotype of a jock. He wore his hair long and defied his peers's tastes in fashion. This strong sense of himself would later help him make some very difficult career decisions. His high school baseball record at University High, a private school in San Diego, was exceptional—especially his senior outing. His record of 8–4, 2.92 ERA and 105 strikeouts in 85 innings should have been enough to get the scouts to pay attention, but he lacked form and didn't display the strength they were looking for. His fastballs clocked at 85 mph, but 90 was the magic number. Craig Weissmann, a former Seattle Mariners scout, took on Zito for six weeks to work on the mechanics of his throws. Weissmann told Jeff Pearlman of Sports Illustrated, "He threw way too far across his body, and that killed his velocity. But there was something special about the kid." Over the next few weeks, Zito and Weissmann honed his technique until his fastballs clocked in at almost 90 mph, attracting interest from the scouts. The Seattle Mariners drafted him, at the age of 18, in the 59th round of the 1996 free agent draft. In addition to being drafted, he was offered a very unusual signing bonus for low–round picks of $90,000. But 59th was not to Zito's liking. His father recalled a moment during negotiations to Pearlman: "At one

point Craig turned to Barry and said, 'The offer is very good. What's the problem?' And my son said … 'I think I should be a first–rounder.'" Instead of getting his foot in the door, Zito decided to go to college.

In 1997, he continued to show his incredible talent as a college freshman at University of California, Santa Barbara, where he made Collegiate Baseball's All–America team with 123 strikeouts in 85 1/3 innings. Believing his chances of getting recruited to the Majors would be more likely at another school, he transferred to Pierce, a junior college in Woodland Hills, California. Indeed, in 1998, he was chosen by the Texas Rangers in the third round of the draft. However, Zito was not satisfied with the outcome; the signing offer of almost $300,000 was below what he thought he was worth. So, once again, he went back to school. This time he hung his hat at the University of Southern California. While there he racked up an even more impressive run, improving every game and pitching with a poise that got the Major League's attention. When he went 12–3 with an ERA of 3.28 and 154 strikeouts in 112 2/3 innings, the Oakland A's noticed. In 1999, they picked him in the first round, ninth overall, and offered a hefty $1.59 million signing bonus. This time, Zito signed. Both his talent and his instincts had served him well.

As with all new recruits, Zito went to the Minors first. In the 31 Minor League starts with the Sacramento River Cats he showed off his amazing curveball time and again. Soon enough, it caught the eye of upper management who wanted to see how well Zito could do under pressure. The lefty from California had not even spent a year with Sacramento when he was called up to the Major Leagues to start against the Anaheim Angels in July of 2000. His moment to shine came when the bases were loaded and he was up against the top of the Anaheim lineup: sluggers Mo Vaughn, Tim Salmon, and Garret Anderson. He struck them all out and served up his first win.

In 2000, Zito went on to start in 14 more games and exited his rookie season with an impressive 7–4 record and a 2.72 ERA—the lowest among Major League rookies with 30 or more innings pitched and the best in Oakland history by a rookie with 75 or more innings pitched. However, Zito was shaky in the first half of the 2001 season, with a 6–7 record and a 5.01 ERA in 22 starts. Then, on August 20, he started a nine–game winning streak with a four–hit shutout in a 9–0 win over the Cleveland Indians. He went 11–1 in his final 13 starts with 1.32 ERA, leaving his opponents with an embarrassing .174 batting average, after 200 strikeouts. The year 2001 was a complete success.

Zito's off–the–field behavior began to distract people from his athletic performance. He became known for doing bizarre things that consistently got the attention of the sports media. A favorite clubhouse tale is the time he introduced a reporter to his toy collection. According to Pearlman in *Sports Illustrated*, Zito told a reporter that he had a collection of toy animals, all of whom had Spanish names. He proceeded to list all of them on camera. Oakland A's outfielder Matt Stairs heard about this and bought a huge teddy bear named Mr. Jangles. Zito, being a rookie that year, had to carry the three–foot–tall stuffed animal around on all the road trips. In another account by Pearlman, Zito told a reporter that he would have no problem dressing like a girl. Whether he knew what the consequences of this statement were or not, he was soon walking around a hotel room in a wedding gown, with Mr. Jangles in tow.

Zito made 2002 a year where his talents made the news. He renegotiated his contract for a total of $9.3 million and proceeded to deliver a season that displayed the breadth of his talent. Zito cemented a reputation for a diverse arsenal that included a fastball, changeup, and stunning curveball that stymied his opponents. He did not hesitate to throw a risky pitch, no matter what the count. According to stats collected by the Sacramento River Cats's website, 2002 was a record breaking season. Zito became the A's third 20–game winner in the last three seasons as he won an A.L.–leading 23 games. He only lost five games and set an Oakland record with a .821 winning percentage. The win total was the fourth best single season in Oakland history and was the most by an Athletic since Bob Welch won 27 in 1990. Zito's 23 wins were also the most by an A.L. left–hander since Frank Viola won 24 for Minnesota in 1988. One of two A's All–Stars, Zito also had career highs in innings (229.1) and tied his career best in games started (35). He led the A.L. in games started (35), was second in winning percentage (.821), third in ERA (2.75), tied for third in strikeouts (182), fourth in opponent's batting average (.218), and fifth in innings pitched. Zito went 13–1 with a 3.01 ERA in his 17 starting assignments. He was 22–3 with a 2.39 ERA and .210 opponent's batting average over his final 29 starts beginning on May 5, including 12–2 with a 1.92 ERA and .203 opponent's batting average in 16 starts after the All–Star Break. Zito put together a career high tying nine–game winning streak from May 5 to June 22 and finished the regular season with an eight–game winning streak.

However, 2002 was also the year where his weaknesses were under scrutiny. Most believed he would rather pitch in low pressure situations than in a pinch, but few questioned that he would get more comfortable with do–or–die situations as his talents matured. Though the Oakland A's got into the post–season they were quickly eliminated by Minnesota in the first round. The loss surprised baseball fans since the A's pitching depth was exceptional. Soon after their defeat Zito was awarded the Cy Young Award and given a $100,000 bonus. According to *USAToday* statistics, Zito received 17 first place votes, nine second place votes and two third place votes and was named on all 28 ballots. The 24–year–old left–hander totaled 114 points to beat out Pedro Martinez of Boston. Zito won the award after just two and a half seasons in the majors. He was the youngest Cy Young Award winner since Roger Clemens of the Yankees in 1986. Zito was 23–5 in 2002, with 182 strikeouts and a 2.75 ERA. His 47–17 career record with a 3.04 ERA in 84 career starts and his .734 career winning percentage is the best in Major League history since 1900 among pitchers with 50 or more decisions.

Sources

Periodicals

Sports Illustrated, January 15, 2001, p. 44.

Online

"Barry Zito," Oakland Athletics Team Online, http://oakland.athletics.mlb.com/NASApp/mlb/oak/team/oak_player_bio.jsp?club_context=oak&playerid=21709 (December 12, 2002).

"Former River Cat Barry Zito Wins A.L. Cy Young Award," Sacramento River Cats Online, http://www.rivercats.com/doc.asp?ID=1565 (December 12, 2002).

"Zito edges Pedro to win A.L. Cy Young Award", CNNSI.com, http://sportsillustrated.cnn.com/baseball/news/2002/11/07/alcy_ap/ (November 2, 2002).

"Zito named A.L. Cy Young winner," *USAToday*, http://www.usatoday.com/sports/baseball/al/2002–11–07–zito–cy–young_x.htm (December 19, 2002).

—*Ben Zackheim*

Obituaries

Joaquin Balaguer

Born Joaquin Balaguer y Ricardo, September 1, 1907, in Navarette, Dominican Republic; died of heart failure, July 14, 2002, in Santo Domingo, Dominican Republic. Politician. As president of the Dominican Republic for 22 years, Joaquin Balaguer ruled the Caribbean nation with an iron fist at times, and almost always with the foreign–aid largesse that came from cordial relations with a succession of White House administrations. "Balaguer was one of Latin America's last great *caudillos,*" noted *Los Angeles Times* writer Mark Fineman, "the strongmen rulers who blended paternal beneficence with an authoritarian omnipresence to build a rock–solid power base, largely with the poor."

Balaguer was born in 1907 in Navarette, a town in the northern part of the Dominican Republic, which shares its land mass with Haiti. The island was named "Hispaniola" when Christopher Columbus landed there in 1492, and is adjacent to Puerto Rico, from where Balaguer's father had emigrated. His mother was a Dominican with Spanish blood, and he grew up in a household that included six sisters. Of a literary mind at an early age, he wrote his first book of poetry at the age of 14, *Pagan Psalms.* He studied philosophy and then went on to earn a law degree from the University of Santo Domingo, in the Dominican Republic's capital city, in 1929.

After leaving school, Balaguer accepted a government job offer to serve as a state attorney, and from there moved into the Dominican Republic's foreign service with diplomatic postings in Madrid and Paris. While stationed in the latter city, he earned a doctorate in law and political science from the University of the Sorbonne in 1934. He returned to Santo Domingo and entered the government of newly installed Rafael Leonides Trujillo, a general who had led an army coup in 1930 and installed a

ruthlessly efficient dictatorship. Balaguer held various cabinet positions in the Trujillo administration, including secretary for education and culture, and also taught at the University of Santo Domingo. In 1957, Trujillo made him vice president and then president as the regime began to topple. His long-time ties to the General would haunt the rest of his political career, providing much fodder for his political opponents. Balaguer himself was not unaffected, however: in his 1988 autobiography, he claimed that the waning years of the Trujillo era had been "the saddest and most humiliating" period of his career, according to *Washington Post* writer Richard Pearson.

When Trujillo was assassinated in 1961, Balaguer took over and quickly launched a liberalization plan, but he had a tenuous hold on power and was forced to flee the country when a leftist leader, Juan Bosch, took over. Balaguer lived in New York City for a time, where he planned a new Dominican political group, the right–wing Reformist Party. Meanwhile, the situation back in Santo Domingo was deteriorating, and U.S. State Department observers warned President Lyndon B. Johnson that it could become Latin America's second Communist country, after Cuba. Johnson sent 20,000 Marines to quell the situation, and in American–controlled elections the following year Balaguer bested Bosch with a 57 percent majority.

The Dominican Republic was a poor country of eight million people, a large majority of them illiterate, when Balaguer was sworn in for the second of what would be six presidential terms. Unemployment was at 60 percent, and the country was physically wrecked from four years of strife. Balaguer quickly launched public–works projects that restored streets and buildings, and enacted agricultural reforms as well. He enjoyed the support of the country's Roman Catholic hierarchy, and for years made weekly walking tours of villages, where he met with citizens and passed out toys and bicycles to children.

During the first decade of Balaguer's rule, the army and police carried out a decisive campaign to destroy the leftist political opposition. Human–rights agencies believed that as many as 1,000 citizens died at the hands of right–wing death squads between 1966 and 1971, and critics of Balaguer claimed he did little to stop these abuses of power. The president remained a staunch ally of the United States in Latin American politics, and in return received large amounts of United States aid. Bosch and other opposition groups boycotted the 1970 and 1974 elections, claiming that the process invited vote fraud. Balaguer lost his 1978 re–election bid, but within a few years had merged his group with the Revolutionary Social Christian Party to become the Social Christian Reform Party. The new slate won in 1986 and Balaguer was returned to the presidency.

By this time he was nearly 80 and blind, and critics claimed he was not up to the job. His retort to them, according to Pearson in the *Washington Post*, was succinct: "I will not be asked to thread needles when in office." His politics and ability to tolerate dissent were said to have mellowed over the years, but the paternalistic style remained, and Balaguer was said to know the country's bank balance every night before he left the office. He still wrote poetry and showed a keen interest in arcane literary debates.

When Balaguer was elected again in 1994, in what some viewed as suspect balloting, he agreed to serve only two years. Against Balaguer's 22–year–record, only Cuba's Fidel Castro had served longer in office in this part of the world. He still remained active behind the scenes, however, with an important party vote, and his successor, Hipolito Mejia, often visited the modest Balaguer home for counsel. Hospitalized with a bleeding ulcer in early July of 2002, he died of heart failure on July 14, 2002; he was 95. Balaguer is survived by a sister. Thousands turned out in Santo Domingo—many of them from the poorest parts of the country—to gather in mourning outside his house. **Sources:** *Chicago Tribune*, July 15, 2002, section 2, p. 6; *Los Angeles Times*, July 15, 2002, p. B9; *New York Times*, July 15, 2002, p. A19; *Times* (London), http://www.timesonline.co.uk (July 15, 2002); *Washington Post*, July 15, 2002, p. B4.

—*Carol Brennan*

Gilbert Bécaud

Born François Gilbert Silly, October 24, 1927, in Toulon, France; died of lung cancer, December 18, 2001, in Paris, France. Singer and songwriter. The French crooner Gilbert Bécaud wrote and performed some 400 songs and rose to fame during the 1950s with his dramatic and romantic compositions. Among his string of hit songs was "Et Maintenant," which became a worldwide favorite in English when American singer Frank Sinatra recorded it as "What Now, My Love." Although the Sinatra version was perhaps the most famous, some 150 more renditions of the song were recorded by a range of artists, including Shirley Bassey, Sarah Vaughan, Judy Garland, Elvis Presley, and Barbra Streisand.

A beloved composer among contemporary singers—including Sammy Davis Jr., Liza Minnelli, and Neil Diamond—Bécaud was also a memorable performer in his own right. In 1954, after an energetic performance at the Olympia Theater in Paris, fans dubbed him "Mr. 100,000 Volts." His other nicknames included "Monsieur Dynamite" and "The Atomic Mushroom." Although he toured internationally, Bécaud found his most loyal audiences in his native France.

Born in the French Mediterranean city of Toulon, Bécaud took an early interest in music, beginning his studies in the piano at a conservatory in Nice at age nine. Toward the end of World War II, Bécaud joined the French Resistance. He settled in Paris after the war, playing the piano in bars and nightclubs, and often accompanying the singer Jacques Pills. At this time he also began to write his own compositions.

When Pills married the famed French singer Edith Piaf in the early 1950s, Bécaud benefitted from the connection, which gave his career a boost. Piaf, along with French crooner Charles Aznavour, helped launch Bécaud's prolific songwriting career. It was Piaf who sang one of his first successes, 1950's "Je t'ai Dans la Peau," which Bécaud co–wrote with Pierre Delanoe.

Bécaud made his own very successful recording debut in 1953. The following year, he performed at the opening of the celebrated Olympia Theater in Paris, where—legend has it—his fans became so excited they tore up the theater's seats. Bécaud came back for more than 40 appearances at the Olympia. One of his last, in 1997, came on the heels of an extensive renovation for the theater. Throughout his career, he was known for his kinetic, physical style of performing, and for his signature onstage outfit: a navy blue suit, white shirt, and polka–dot tie (of which he owned more than 200).

Although Bécaud took part in a golden age of music in France—during a movement known as "la chanson française" (French song)—he never enjoyed the level of fame achieved by Piaf, Yves Montand, Charles Trenet, and some other contemporaries. However, his peers, who particularly appreciated his songwriting skills, tremendously respected him. Upon Bécaud's death, Aznavour told the *New York Times*, "He was a great composer of melodies. Nowadays, when all melodies sound alike, if you look at Gilbert's songs, you'll see that every melody is different."

Jane Morgan recorded his "Le Jour où la Pluie Viendra" ("The Day the Rains Came"), and Vicki Carr made a hit of his "Seul sur Son Etoile" ("It Must Be Him"). His composition "Je T'appartiens" ("Let It Be Me") spawned a range of recordings from such artists as the Everly Brothers, Bob Dylan, Roberta Flack, Nina Simone, James Brown, and Sonny and Cher. Other Bécaud hits include "Nathalie," "L'Important C'Est la Rose" ("What's Important Is the Rose"), and "Quand Il Est Mort le Poète" ("When the Poet Dies").

In 1966 Bécaud performed a one–man show on Broadway for a three–week run. He came back to the United States in the 1980s with the musical *Roza*, based on a Romain Gary novel about a former prostitute who raises a young Arab boy in Paris. The production, which was developed in Baltimore and Los Angeles, received mixed reviews, although critics generally praised Bécaud's music.

Bécaud announced his retirement from touring in 1991, ending a hectic schedule of up to 249 concerts worldwide each year. He continued to write music, however, and released his final album, *Faut Faire Avec* (Have to Make Do) in 1999. A more serious tone characterized this last album, which was recorded during the singer's battle with cancer. Although he prevailed over cancer of the jaw, the singer was later diagnosed with lung cancer, to which he eventually succumbed.

At age 74, Bécaud died on December 18, 2001, on his houseboat on the Seine River in Paris, surrounded by family and friends. He is survived by his second wife, Kitty St.–John; their two children, Jennifer and Emily; and three children from his first marriage, Gaya, Philippe, and Anne. **Sources:** *Chicago Times*, December 19, 2001, section 2, p. 12; CNN.com, http://www.cnn.com/2001/SHOWBIZ/Music/12/18/death.Becaud/index.html (December 18, 2001); *Los Angeles Times*, December 19, 2001, p. B11; *New York Times*, December 19, 2001, p. C19; *Washington Post*, December 22, 2001, p. B4.

—*Wendy Kagan*

Milton Berle

Born Milton Berlinger, July 12, 1908, in New York, NY; died of colon cancer, March 27, 2002, in Beverly Hills, CA. Comedian, actor, and songwriter. Known variously as "Mr. Television," "Uncle Miltie," and the "Thief of Bad Gags" (the last name bestowed on him by columnist Walter Winchell), Milton Berle was TV's first star. His *Texaco Star Theater* was perhaps vaudeville's last gasp—a mixture of comedy sketches and other variety entertainment—that endeared Berle to millions of Americans and won him an Emmy.

Berle, who was born in New York City's Harlem neighborhood, was pushed by his mother, Sarah, into entering a number of amateur contests. At the age of 5 he got his first real taste of show business when he won a Charlie Chaplin impersonation contest in Mount Vernon, New York; he later appeared in the Chaplin film, *Tillie's Punctured Romance*. Berle was also a child model for Buster Brown Shoes. Berle's other silent film appearances included 1914's *The Perils of Pauline*, starring Pearl White, and 1920's *The Mark of Zorro*, featuring Douglas Fairbanks, Sr. It was in 1920, while teamed with Elizabeth Kennedy, that the already–savvy Berle shortened his name from Berlinger so that it would be spelled in larger letters on theater marquees. In 1921 Kennedy and Berle played the Palace Theater in New York, the mecca of vaudeville.

Berle soon outgrew the act—literally, since it was based on two child performers. In the early 1920s he began to hone his craft as a solo performer: learning how to tell jokes and performing card tricks among other things. During these years he first dressed in women's clothes as part of his act, supposedly getting the idea from the annual drag balls at the Rockland Palace on 155th Street in New York. Berle's formal education was scant—he briefly attended the Performing Children's School in New

York City—but by 1924, at age 16, he was performing at Times Square's Loews State Theater at a salary of $600 a week, which more or less ended his schooling. Throughout the 1920s Berle's star continued to rise on the vaudeville circuit.

In the 1930s Berle appeared in the Broadway revues *The Ziegfield Follies* and *Earl Carroll Vanities*. Vaudeville began to wane with the popularity of talking pictures in the early 1930s and Berle attempted the transition to radio and Hollywood, first appearing on Rudy Vallee's national radio show and then in the 1934 Warner Brothers Vitaphone film, *Gags to Riches*. Berle's other films during this period were 1937's *New Faces of 1937*, 1938's *Radio City Revels*, 1941's *Tall, Dark and Handsome, Sun Valley Serenade*, and *Rise and Shine*, 1942's *Whispering Ghosts* and *Over My Dead Body*, and 1943's *Margin for Error*. Although he appeared in movies almost to the end of his life Berle's film career never really did take off. In 1939 he was the star of the radio series *Stop Me If You've Heard This*, but the show soon failed. During the next ten years Berle made the rounds of the nightclub circuit. By 1939 he was commanding $6,000 per week at the International Casino on Broadway. After World War Two he was earning as much as $10,000 per week. In 1941 he married dancer Joyce Matthews. They were divorced in 1947, remarried in 1949 (whereupon Berle joked, "She reminded me of my first wife," according to *People*), and divorced a second time later that year.

As successful a club comic as he was, it was television that catapulted Berle to superstardom. Likewise, Berle's show changed the popular entertainment habits of America. When the variety radio show *Texaco Star Theater* debuted in June of 1948, Berle signed on as one of four rotating hosts that included Henny Youngman, Morey Amsterdam, and Jack Carter. Berle's outrageous physical humor, unsuited for radio and even the big screen, was perfect for television, and his popularity was such that in September of 1948 he was named as the show's permanent host when it moved to the fledgling medium. Propelled by Berle's anything–for–a–laugh ethos, *Texaco Star Theater* commanded the television airwaves on Tuesday nights, and Berle became one of America's most famous entertainers, considered television's first superstar. His program helped cement the medium in American culture and was one of the main reasons for the increase in television sales in the early 1950s. Many other comedians soon followed him to the promised land of television, in-

cluding Jack Benny, Bob Hope, Red Skelton, George Burns and Gracie Allen, Phil Silvers, Jackie Gleason, and Lucille Ball.

Berle won an Emmy Award in 1950 and on May 3, 1951, he signed an unprecedented "lifetime" deal with NBC that paid him $200,000 per year. The deal actually lasted for 30 years and was altered in the 1960s. The show, though, began to take its toll on Berle. By the fall of 1951 he was taking off every fourth week to recharge his batteries. By his own account, according to the *New York Times*, that decision "was a big mistake" as his ratings fell.

In 1953, Berle married movie–industry publicist Ruth Cosgrove. They remained married until her death in 1989. The year 1953 also marked the end of Texaco's sponsorship of Berle's show; Berle continued with sponsorship by Buick, though the name of the show was changed to the *Buick–Berle Show*. Buick sponsorship lasted one season, and in 1954 the show became simply *The Milton Berle Show*. It was cancelled in 1955.

Berle hosted the *Kraft Music Hall* during the 1958–59 television season, but by 1960 his career was at its nadir. He was reduced to hosting a show called *Jackpot Bowling Starring Milton Berle*. In 1966 he attempted a comeback with another show titled *The Milton Berle Show*, but the times had changed and it too failed. From then on Berle made numerous guest star appearances on television shows such as *Batman, F Troop*, and *Amazing Stories*, and also in dramatic programs. Among his later films were 1960's *Let's Make Love*, 1963's *It's a Mad Mad Mad Mad World*, 1966's *The Oscar*, 1984's *Broadway Danny Rose*, in which he played himself; and 1990's *Driving Me Crazy*. Berle also composed and wrote the lyrics to hundreds of songs.

The National Academy of Television Arts and Sciences named Berle Man of the Year in 1959 and in 1979 awarded him a special Emmy. In 1984 he was the first inductee into the Television Hall of Fame, and in 1992 he was the first inductee into the Comedy Hall of Fame. The New York Chapter of the Academy of Television Arts and Sciences gave him a lifetime achievement award in 1996.

Along with numerous joke books (one of Berle's running routines was that he stole jokes from everyone), Berle published *Milton Berle: An Autobiography* in 1974. It was cowritten with Haskel Frankel. In 1985 Berle underwent quadruple bypass surgery. In 1991 he married fashion designer Lorna Adams.

Berle died in his sleep on March 27, 2002, in Beverly Hills, California; he was 93. He is survived by Adams; an adopted daughter, Victoria; an adopted son, William Berle; and two stepdaughters, Susan and Leslie. **Sources:** CNN.com, http://www.cnn.com/2002/SHOWBIZ/News/03/27/milton.berle.obit/index.html (March 28, 2002); *People*, April 15, 2002, pp. 144–48; *New York Times*, March 28, 2002, p. A1; *Washington Post*, March 28, 2002, p. A1, p. A10.

—*Frank Caso*

Bill Blass

Born William Ralph Bass, June 22, 1922, in Fort Wayne, IN; died of throat cancer, June 12, 2002, in New Preston, CT. Fashion designer. In a career that spanned six decades, Bill Blass created innovative, understated fashions for many of America's best–known women, as well as ready–to–wear clothing for both men and women. One of the first American designers to win acclaim on the international fashion scene, Blass more than any other figure helped to create the phenomenon of the celebrity designer.

A consummate businessman as well as a designer, Blass personally appeared at stores and gala events all over the United States to promote his designs, which grew to encompass not only clothing but fragrances, linens, and even chocolates and automobile interiors. He later attributed much of his success to these frequent road trips, which allowed him to interact directly with the women who wore his designs, and to learn firsthand what they wanted to wear.

Blass was the only child of Ralph Aldrich Bass, who owned a hardware store, and Ethyl Keyser Blass, a dressmaker. His father committed suicide when Blass was five years old. As a child, Blass idolized female screen stars like Marlene Dietrich and Carole Lombard. "Those women inspired me," he was later quoted by Enid Nemy in the *New York Times*, "and I had to get out [of Indiana]."

Soon after Blass graduated from high school, in 1939, he won second place in a design contest run by the *Chicago Tribune*. This gave him the confidence to travel to New York and try to make a career for himself in fashion. He arrived in New York in 1940, enrolling in classes at the McDowell School of Fashion. Also at this time, he took a job as a sketch artist for a clothing manufacturer.

With the onset of World War II, Blass joined the Army, where he was posted to the 603 Camouflage Battalion. He saw action in a total of 21 engagements in Europe, including the Battle of the Bulge and the crossing of the Rhine that led to Germany's defeat. After the war, Blass returned to New York, where he joined the staff of fashion designer Anne Klein. This job did not last long, however; he was fired by the designer, who felt that although he was well–mannered, he lacked talent. Blass's next job was with a clothing manufacturer named Anna Miller. After Miller's retirement in 1959, her company combined with that of her brother, the well–respected designer Maurice Rentner. Blass moved up through the company ranks, and gradually his designs found acceptance with the label. Rentner died in 1960, and after that, Blass was able to add his name to the label. Blass's takeover of the company was complete by 1970, when he changed its name to Bill Blass Ltd.

In 1967, Blass became the first American designer of women's clothing to successfully incorporate men's fashions into his lines. After an initial rocky start, during which he tried to introduce Scottish kilts to American men, his plaid suits became popular. In 1968, he became the first person to receive the Coty American Fashion Critics Award for menswear— this on top of the two Coty Awards he had already received for his womenswear. He was to win a total of seven Coty Awards (the Academy Awards of fashion) by the end of his career.

Blass's work was instrumental to the acceptance of American designers on the international fashion scene. Significantly, he was invited in 1973 to participate in a Palace of Versailles fashion show in France. This major fashion event was one of the first in which an American designer was presented on an equal basis with major European designers. Blass remained successful throughout the 1970s and 1980s, and in 1987 he was awarded a Lifetime Achievement Award by the Council of Fashion Designers of America.

By the 1990s, Blass had built a fashion empire that included 97 separate licensing arrangements grossing more than $700 million around the world, with his initial ready–to–wear styles constituting only a little more than one percent of his total sales. During this time he became known for his philanthropy; in 1994, for instance, he donated $10 million to the New York Public Library. Other charities Blass contributed significantly to included AIDS research efforts and organizations caring for AIDS patients. The Council of Fashion Designers of America honored Blass for his charitable contributions with its first–ever Humanitarian Leadership Award in 1996.

Bass retired from the fashion business in 1999, selling his company for $50 million. Shortly thereafter, he was diagnosed with throat cancer. In his final years Blass wrote an autobiography titled *Bare Blass* and completed a catalog for a retrospective of his fashions presented at Indiana University in Bloomington.

Never married, Blass lived his last years on a 22–acre estate in New Preston, Connecticut, accompanied by his Labrador retriever, Barnaby. He died on June 12, 2002, at his home, just ten days short of his 80th birthday. **Sources:** *Los Angeles Times,* June 13, 2002, p. 13; *New York Times,* June 13, 2002, p. A1; *People,* July 1, 2002, p. 106; *Washington Post,* June 14, 2002, p. B7.

—*Michael Belfiore*

J. Carter Brown

Born October 8, 1934, in Providence, RI; died of pulmonary failure, June 17, 2002, in Boston, MA. Museum director. J. Carter Brown spent nearly a quarter–century as head of the National Gallery of Art in Washington, D.C., one of the world's leading repositories of fine art. Patrician by birth but possessed of a keen sense for what drew museum visitors from all walks of life, Brown was said to have created the "blockbuster" show back in the 1970s. "He transformed the museum world from an ivory tower into an immensely popular place," his successor, Earl A. Powell III, told *New York Times* writer Michael Kimmelman. "He was a great aristocrat, but a real populist."

Brown hailed from Rhode Island, where his family roots stretched back to Roger Williams, founder of a community there in 1635 that later became one of the 13 colonies. Others in the family owned some of the first textile factories in New England in the 1790s, and their largesse later established the Ivy League university in Providence that bears the family name. Brown's father inherited a $10–million fortune when still a child, and became a renowned art collector. His mother, Anne Kinsolving, had been the music critic of the *Baltimore News* as well as an orchestra violinist. After attending a boarding school in Arizona, Brown was first in his graduating class at the elite Groton School in 1951, and when he entered Harvard College a year later, he brought with him a Henri Matisse drawing and a watercolor by Paul Cézanne to hang in his dorm room. He earned an M.B.A. from the school following his undergraduate degree, and spent time in Tuscany under the tutelage of art critic and historian Bernard Berenson. Back in the United States in 1961, Brown was studying at New York University for a master's degree in fine arts when he was offered a job at Washington's National Gallery as assistant to its director. Three years later he became assistant director, and in 1967 he was put in charge of planning a new East Building for the museum. When the I.M. Pei–designed wing opened in 1978, it set a new benchmark for modern American museum design as an innovative, light–filled architectural space on par with the treasures it was created to house.

Brown was named director of the National Gallery in 1969, and the exemplary record of his 23 years at the helm could be measured in figures: he began with a budget of $3.2 million in federal monies, plus a $34 million endowment; in 1992, when he retired, government arts dollars earmarked for the museum were $52.3 million annually, and it had an endowment of $186 million. In his time, more some 20,000 works were added to its collections, including "The Artist's Father" by Cézanne, Picasso's "Nude Woman," and the Jackson Pollock painting "Lavender Mist." Thanks to Brown's skill in courting important donors, the Gallery received important works from the John Hay Whitney collection and Old Master drawings from industrialist Armand Hammer's famed hoard. Visitors to the museum on the National Mall, just slightly more than a million when Brown came on board in the late 1960s, numbered as high as seven million some years. Those attendance figures were often the result of the large–scale shows organized around attention–grabbing themes that Brown dreamed up: "Treasure of Tutankhamun" in 1976, "The Splendor of Dresden: Five Centuries of Art Collecting" in 1978, 1985's "Treasure Houses of Britain," and the controversial "Helga" paintings from Andrew Wyeth two years later. During his 23–year tenure, noted Kimmelman in the *New York Times,* Brown "made what had been a fairly sleepy, albeit grand gallery of old master paintings where few exhibitions happened into a legitimate rival of the much bigger, older Met as the nation's premier art attraction."

The final "blockbuster"—as these highly publicized shows came to be called—under Brown's watch was "Circa 1492: Art in the Age of Exploration" in 1991. As museum director, he spared no expense on mounting these exhibits, and his voice was a familiar one to visitors who strolled through them with the gallery-guide cassette tapes. He formally retired in 1992, but continued to be active in the arts. For many years he sat on the Commission of Fine Arts for the District of Columbia, which oversaw the monuments in the nation's capital; in that realm he had been an ardent supporter of the Vietnam Veterans Memorial and the winning, but initially controversial design from Maya Lin. He served as jury chair for the Pritzker Prize in architecture, and was one of the co-founders of Ovation, a cable arts network. Brown was committed to the ideal that art should enrich the lives of all, not just those who would afford access to it. "I come from a great line of preachers," Kimmelman quoted him as saying in a *New York Times* obituary. "I believe in the arts and I have a sort of messianic zeal about broadening their audience."

Brown died on June 17, 2002, of pulmonary failure, at the age of 67. He had previously undergone treatment for multiple myeloma. He was twice married and divorced, first to Constance Mellon, and then to Pamela Braga Drexel. Brown is survived by his fiancée, Anne Hawley, the director of Boston's Isabella Stewart Gardner Museum; his son, Jay; and his daughter, Elissa. **Sources:** *Los Angeles Times,* June 19, 2002; *New York Times,* June 19, 2002; *Times* (London), June 20, 2002; *Washington Post,* June 19, 2002.

—*Carol Brennan*

Camilo Jose Cela

Born May 11, 1916, in Iria Flavia, Spain; died of heart disease, January 17, 2001, in Madrid, Spain. Author. The Spanish author Camilo Jose Cela, winner of the 1989 Nobel Prize in Literature, penned 12 novels and 60 other books of stories, poetry, and nonfiction. Perhaps the most-lauded Spanish writer of the second half of the twentieth century, Cela garnered praise for the 1942 publication of his novel *La Familia de Pascual Duarte* (The Family of Pascual Duarte)—his first and, according to some critics, his best work. Known for the dark nature of his subject matter and the original style of his fiction, Cela grew more experimental with every work, writing stories without punctuation or plot development, or with multiple unreliable narrators.

After he won the Nobel Prize, Cela, who had been relatively unknown outside the Spanish-speaking world, enjoyed international celebrity. Throughout Spain, he was known as much for his writing as for his brash personality and sarcastic humor. Cela took delight in challenging conventions and in shocking his readership, as he did with 1968's *Secret Dictionary,* a compilation of coarse and irreverent Spanish slang. Contributing to his controversial reputation in Spain was his former sympathy for General Francisco Franco's military dictatorship, which ruled from the late 1930s to the mid-1970s. Yet despite this, Cela was a celebrated writer in his native country, which awarded him its highest literary honor, the Cervantes Prize, in 1995.

The oldest of nine children, Cela (pronounced SAY-lah) was the son of a Spanish father, a civil servant and part-time writer, and a British mother. His upper-middle-class family moved often, according to his father's work assignments, taking residence in the Galicia region and in other parts of Spain, and eventually settling in Madrid. Although he was known to remark about his happy childhood, Cela fought tuberculosis as a teenager, and spent a year in a sanatorium. He would later chronicle this experience in his second novel, 1944's *Pabellon de Reposo* (Convalescence Wing).

Cela studied law, medicine, and philosophy at Madrid University, and published a volume of Surrealist poetry in 1936, when he was barely 20 years old. Yet his studies were interrupted that year with the outbreak of the Spanish Civil War. Siding with the right-wing rebel forces led by Franco, Cela was recruited as a private. After sustaining wounds in battle, he was released from the army and became a censor. Upon the war's end, Cela resumed his studies but did not complete his degrees.

Only 26 when he published *La Familia de Pascual Duarte,* Cela rose to national literary fame. This astonishingly realistic novel told the story of an illiterate murderer awaiting his execution. Replete with violent details and grotesque characters, the novel offended church and government officials and was banned in its second edition. The book remained an illicit favorite, however, and was made into a film in 1976. It is second only to Miguel de Cervantes's *Don Quixote* as the most widely translated Spanish literary work.

An extremely prolific author, Cela delved into travel writing with 1948's *The Voyage to the Alcarria,* which chronicled his journey on foot through a remote, poverty-stricken region of the Guadalajara province.

He went on to write many travel books alongside his fiction and other works. One of his most famous early novels, 1951's *La Colmena* (The Hive), portrayed 1943 Madrid in a series of short scenes featuring more than 200 characters. "*La Colmena* is just a slice of life," Cela once wrote (quoted in the *Guardian*), "a pale reflection of daily, bitter, loveable, painful reality." Banned in Spain, the book found its first publisher in Buenos Aires, Argentina.

It was *La Colmena* that led to Cela's exile to the island of Mallorca, where he moved from Madrid in 1954. Here he founded *Papeles de Son Armadans*, a literary magazine with a political edge, featuring exiled writers. In the 1960s he owned the Alfaguara publishing house, which printed scholarly books as well as works by new novelists. After the death of Franco in 1975, Cela emerged from exile and went on to serve as a senator.

Cela was married twice, first to Rosario Conde in 1944. In the late 1980s he made headlines in Spain when he left his wife of 44 years to live with Marina Castano, a radio journalist who was less than half his age; the pair married in 1991. In the midst of this scandal, it was announced that the author had won the Nobel Prize, awarded to Cela for what the Swedish Academy called his "rich and inventive prose, which with restrained compassion forms a challenging vision of man's vulnerability," as quoted in the *New York Times*.

After winning the Nobel, Cela relished his international celebrity, touring Spain in his Rolls Royce and dining with his young wife in fashionable restaurants. He continued to write, publishing 1992's *Mazurka for Two Dead Men* to warm reviews.

In a Madrid hospital on January 17, 2002, Cela died of heart disease at the age of 85. He is survived by his second wife and a son, Camilo Jose, from his first marriage. **Sources:** *Guardian* (London), January 18, 2002, p. 20; *Independent* (London), January 18, 2002, p. 6; *Los Angeles Times*, January 18, 2002, p. B15; *New York Times*, January 18, 2002, p. C15; *Times* (London), January 18, 2002, p. 23; *Washington Post*, January 19, 2002, p. B7.

—*Wendy Kagan*

Eduardo Chillida

Born January 10, 1924, in San Sebastian, Spain; died August 19, 2002, in San Sebastian, Spain. Sculptor.

Considered one of the premiere sculptors of the 20th century, Eduardo Chillida created monolithic abstract works primarily in steel and iron. His works are renowned throughout the world and can be found in Paris, France, Dallas, Texas, and Frankfurt, Germany, as well as his native San Sebastian, Spain. A prolific artist, Chillida worked steadily for more than 30 years and opened in more than 100 one-man exhibitions.

Chillida (pronounced Chee–YEE–dah) was athletic in his youth and played goalkeeper for his town's soccer team. To keep him out of harm's way during the Spanish civil war, Chillida's parents sent him to live in France during part of the 1930s. After finishing his studies at a classical high school, he attended the University of Madrid where he majored in architecture.

In 1947, he left the University of Madrid and began studying art, focusing on sculpture and painting. The following year he moved to Paris and set up his first studio where he worked in plaster and clay. In Paris his work was exhibited in several group exhibitions, including two shows at the Salon Mai. His sculptures for the Salon Mai impressed the curators of the Maeght Gallery in Paris who asked him to submit pieces for another exhibition. Chillida worked closely with the Maeght Gallery for years afterward.

Before moving to Paris, Chillida married Pilar Belzunce, also a native of San Sebastian. In 1951, Chillida and Belzunce returned to northern Spain for the birth of their first child. Around that time he became interested in working in iron and created his first work in the medium, *Ilarik*, with the help of a blacksmith. Inspired, he set up his own forge. In 1952, Chillida destroyed all of his previous work and redirected his efforts toward forging pieces in iron.

In 1954, the Clan Gallery in Madrid hosted Chillida's first one-man show. In the succeeding years his reputation grew. He received commissions from Franciscan monks as well as the San Sebastian city council. His works were featured in the Milan, Italy, Triennales as well as at the Galerie Denise Rene in Paris. He expanded his work to include stone carvings.

In 1957, Chillida was recognized by the Graham Foundation of Chicago, an organization that focuses on architecture and art as it relates to built environments. The next year he exhibited for the first time at the Venice Biennale and won the Grand International Prize for sculpture. That same year he exhibited works at the Guggenheim Museum in New York and in the Pittsburgh International at the Carnegie Institute.

In 1960, Chillida was awarded the Kandinsky Prize, an award created to recognize promising young abstract artists. During the following decade, Chillida's work would become more mature, distinguishing itself from the works of other well–known abstract sculptors like Alexander Calder. His style became blocky and condensed while remaining open to the environment that surrounded it. He had abandoned the more linear aspects of his previous works.

Throughout the 1960s, the Maeght Gallery launched several major exhibitions of Chillida's work. In 1961, his one–man show included 23 of his sculptures. In 1964, the gallery hosted another one–man show entitled *La Poésie de l'espace chez Eduardo Chillida*. In the late 1960s, Chillida traveled throughout Greece and Tuscany. He began carving in alabaster, inspired by the sights he saw in these areas. He also set up a studio in Pietrasanta, Italy, a city renowned for its history in sculpture. In 1964, he won the Carnegie Prize for sculpture at the Pittsburgh International.

As the '60s came to an end, Chillida earned more commissions. He created a monumental granite carving for the Houston Museum of Fine Arts called *Abesti Gogora V*. For the UNESCO building in Paris, France, he forged a steel sculpture called *Comb of the Wind IV*. Two other steel sculptures were installed, one in Washington, D.C., and the other in Dusseldorf, Germany.

Chillida was not only recognized for his sculptures, he also received major awards for his artist's books. The books were created using a form of abstract collage that he had invented. In 1974, he won the Diano Marina Prize for illustrations he had made using wood engravings. The illustrations were for the poem, "Mas alla," by Spanish poet Jorge Guillen, whom he had met while a visiting professor at Harvard.

In 1977, Chillida installed his most well–known work. *Comb of the Wind XV*, a large iron sculpture that juts out from the rocks along the coastline of the Bay of San Sebastian, is a monument held in high regard in Spain. It is even featured on some Spanish coins. The work, situated in the politically tumultuous Basque region of Spain, is considered a symbol of the ongoing conflict and a call for peace.

Throughout the '80s and into the '90s, Chillida continued to accumulate awards and recognition. He gained honorary memberships in the Royal Academy in London, the American Academy of Arts and Letters, and the Real Academia de Bellas Artes de San Fernando in Spain. The French Ministry of Culture awarded him the Grand Prix des Arts et des Lettres.

Chillida died on August 19, 2002, following a long illness; he was 78. He is survived by his wife, eight children, and 26 grandchildren. Chillida's monumental sculptures will remain as a testament to his honored place in the world of abstract art. **Sources:** *Chicago Tribune*, August 20, 2002, section 2, p. 9; Eduardo Chillida website, http://www.eduardo-chillida.com/en_biografia.htm (May 12, 2003); *Los Angeles Times*, August 23, 2002, p. B12; *New York Times*, August 22, 2002, p. A19; *Smithsonian*, July 2000, pp. 56-63; *Times* (London), http://www.timesonline.co.uk (August 21, 2002).

—*Eve M. B. Hermann*

Rosemary Clooney

Born May 23, 1928, in Maysville, KY; died of lung cancer, June 29, 2002, in Beverly Hills, CA. Singer. Rosemary Clooney hit the charts in 1951 with the tune "Come On–a My House," a quirky song penned by William Saroyan and Ross Bagdasarian. Her career took many turns in the following decades, ending with a major comeback in the 1990s that solidified her status as one of America's finest classic pop singers. Richard Severo of the *New York Times* wrote, "[S]he sang with so much assuredness, simplicity, and honesty that these elements became her trademark and endeared her to audiences and critics alike."

Clooney's family life was unstable and she and her siblings were shuffled around to various relatives' houses. She and her sisters ended up living in Cincinnati, Ohio, with her maternal grandparents. As a toddler she sang around the house, eventually performing at her grandfather's political rallies in the small Kentucky town of Maysville where she was born. In 1945, she and her younger sister, Betty, won a contest sponsored by Cincinnati radio station WLW and began singing nightly on one of the station's shows.

The radio job led to gigs with local bands. In 1946, Tony Pastor hired the sisters to sing for his traveling big band. The two, still in their teens, traveled around the country chaperoned by their uncle. By 1947, *Downbeat* magazine was comparing Clooney's voice to that of noted singer Ella Fitzgerald. Her first solo recording was the song "I'm Sorry I Didn't Say I Was Sorry When I Made You Cry Last Night."

In 1949, Betty retired from singing and went home to Cincinnati. Clooney had her sights set on a solo career and left Pastor's band to head to New York. The following year she signed a contract with Columbia Records. She had a minor hit with her recording of "Beautiful Brown Eyes" in 1951. That same year she hit Number One with the novelty song based on an Armenian folk tune, "Come On–a My House."

She continued with a string of hits that included "Tenderly" and "Botch–a–me" as well as duets like "Too Old to Cut The Mustard" with actress Marlene Dietrich and "The Night Before Christmas Song" with Gene Autry. In 1953, she made the cover of *Time* magazine and debuted in her first film, a musical called *The Stars Are Singing*. Her film career was short and mostly unremarkable. Her most notable role was in the classic Bing Crosby film *White Christmas*.

During the late '50s, Clooney worked primarily in television hosting her own show, *The Rosemary Clooney Show,* and appearing on other variety programs. She was also busy giving birth to her five children during that time. She was pregnant from 1955 to 1960 with children from her marriage to actor Jose Ferrer. In 1961, the two divorced, only to remarry that same year. They divorced for good in 1967.

By 1968, relationship troubles, including a failed affair with a younger man, drove Clooney to abuse sleeping pills and tranquilizers. In attendance at the Ambassador Hotel when Robert Kennedy was assassinated, she was devastated by his death. Not long afterward, Clooney experienced a complete mental breakdown that required her to stay in a psychiatric ward for a period of time.

After her recovery, Clooney started over at the bottom. She could only find gigs in hotel lounges but throughout the '70s she continued to perform and slowly rebuilt her career. For a time she appeared in commercials for paper towels. Her big break came in 1976 when Crosby asked her to join him on the tour celebrating his 50th anniversary in show business. The next year she signed a contract with Concord Jazz, a small jazz label, and began recording tribute albums to classic pop writers like Cole Porter and Duke Ellington.

The 1990s saw the culmination of Clooney's career. In 1991, she debuted at Carnegie Hall and returned for another performance two years later. In 1994, she had a recurring role on the television show *ER* in which her nephew George Clooney starred. For her performance she earned an Emmy nomination. In 1996, she had her first number–one album, *Rosemary Clooney's White Christmas*. That same year she married Dante DiPaolo, whom she had first met in the 1950s.

A longtime smoker, Clooney was diagnosed with lung cancer in January of 2002 during a routine physical. The next day she underwent surgery at the Mayo Clinic in Rochester, Minnesota, to remove the upper lobe of her left lung. Although doctors expected a quick recovery, complications led to an extended stay, and she was not released from the hospital until May. Her recovery in the hospital kept her from attending the Grammy ceremonies where she was awarded a lifetime achievement award.

Clooney died on June 29, 2002, from complications as a result of lung cancer; she was 74. Clooney is survived by her second husband, Dante DiPaolo; sons Miguel, Gabriel, and Rafael (with Ferrer); daughters Maria and Monsita (with Ferrer); and ten grandchildren. Even during her lowest moments she remained dedicated to her art and persevered to make a lasting impression in music. **Sources:** *BBC News,* http://news.bbc.co.uk/hi/english/entertainment/showbiz/newsid_2075000/2075534.stm (July 1, 2002); *Cincinnati Enquirer,* http://www.enquirer.com/editions/2002/01/15/tem_clooney_has.html (May 8, 2002); *Entertainment Weekly,* July 12, 2002, p. 26; *E! Online,* http://www.eonline.com/News/Items/0,1,10179,00.html?tnews (July 1, 2002); *Kentucky Post,* http://www.kypost.com/2002/jan/15/cancer011502.html (May 8, 2002); *Los Angeles Times,* June 30, 2002, p. B14; *New York Times,* July 1, 2002, p. A14; *People,* July 15, 2002, p. 70; *Times* (London), http://www.timesonline.co.uk (July 1, 2002); *Washington Post,* July 1, 2002, p. B4.

—Eve M. B. Hermann

John Entwistle

Born John Alec Entwistle, October 4, 1944, in Chiswick, England; died of a heart attack, June 27, 2002, in Las Vegas, NV. Rock musician. A founding member of the influential rock group the Who, John Entwistle played bass for the band and also wrote many of its songs, played trumpet, and sang backing vocals. Nicknamed "Ox" and "Thunderfingers," he played a powerful, understated counterpoint to band mates Roger Daltrey (vocals), Pete Townsend (guitar), and Keith Moon (drums), whose wild stage personae included smashing their instruments on stage.

Entwistle grew up London's working class Shepard's Bush neighborhood. His parents were Herbert, a trumpet player, and Maude Entwistle, a piano player. Entwistle's parents broke up when Entwistle was a boy, and he moved in with his grandparents. While still a boy, he began singing in clubhouses in his neighborhood, and took up several instruments, including the French horn, which he later played on a number of Who songs. Other instruments he learned to play included the trumpet and the piano, as well as the bass.

Entwistle met fellow future Who band member Pete Townshend in high school, and in 1959 they played in a Dixieland band together, with Entwistle on trumpet and Townsend on banjo. In 1962, Entwistle joined Roger Daltrey in a rock band called the Detours. Entwistle recruited Townshend for the band, and with the addition of Keith Moon, the band's lineup was complete. During this time, Entwistle supported himself by working as a clerk at Britain's tax-collection agency. After making several recordings as the High Numbers, the group changed its name to the Who.

The Who played local clubs and eventually landed on the British charts with their first hit, "I Can't Explain." Several British and United States hits followed, including "My Generation," which featured Entwistle's solo bass work. After the Who played in the United States at the Monterey Pop Festival in 1967, at Woodstock in 1969, and released their hit rock opera *Tommy,* the band was firmly established as one of the top rock groups in the world, alongside the Rolling Stones and the Beatles. Entwistle married his first wife, Alison Wise, in 1967, and they had a son named Christopher.

Within a year of the release of *Tommy,* Entwistle released the first of what was to be a total of four solo albums in a four-year period. This first solo effort was titled *Smash Your Head Against the Wall.* Entwistle also formed his own band, called the John Entwistle Band, which went on tour. An anthology of Entwistle's music called *Thunderfingers* was released in 1996, and the John Entwistle Band put out an album called *Music from Van–Pires* in 1997.

The Who played off and on together through the 1980s, engaging in various so-called farewell and reunion tours. Their last studio recording was released in 1982, and the latest reunion tour, in 2002, was planned as the first step on a road that would lead them back to the studio for the first time in 20 years. But the tour was halted even as it began by Entwistle's death.

Entwistle had checked into the Hard Rock Hotel and Casino in Las Vegas (where the Who was to open their United States tour) a day before his band mates, so that he could attend an exhibition of his drawings at the Aladdin Hotel and Casino. Drawing had long been a passion for Entwistle, and one of his drawings had been used for a Who album cover (*The Who by Numbers).* He died of a heart attack in his room, and his body was found by his road assistant. He had been on medication for a heart condition. The Clark County, Nevada, coroner said that Entwistle died when a "significant amount of cocaine" brought on a heart attack. The death was ruled accidental, not an overdose. A British pathologist later confirmed that Entwistle did indeed die from a deadly mix of cocaine and a pre-existing heart condition.

With Entwistle's death, only half of the Who's original members remained—Moon had died of a drug overdose in 1978. The initial tour dates were cancelled, but the band vowed to go ahead with the rest of the tour, dedicating it to Entwistle's memory.

Entwistle was the most understated of his band mates; while Daltrey, Townshend, and Moon all delighted in onstage theatrics, even occasionally destroying their instruments at the end of a show, Entwistle was content merely to play his bass, in the words of Geoff Boucher of the *Los Angeles Times,* "like a ramrod-straight commuter awaiting a morning train." Nevertheless, Entwistle quietly established himself as one of the greatest bass players in rock, admired by fans and fellow musicians alike.

Entwistle had married and divorced twice. He died at the age of 57 on June 27, 2002, in Las Vegas, Nevada. Entwistle is survived by his girlfriend, Lisa Pritchard-Johnson; and his son, Christopher.

Sources: *Chicago Tribune,* June 28, 2002, p. 11; CNN. com, http://www.cnn.com/2002/SHOWBIZ/ News/06/28/entwistle.lead/index.html (July 1, 2002); E! Online, http://www.eonline.com/News/ Items/0,1,10169,00.html (July 1, 2002), http://www. eonline.com/News/Items/0,1,10175,00.html (July 1, 2002); *Los Angeles Times,* June 28, 2002, p. B12; *New York Times,* June 27, 2002, p. C15; *Times* (London), June 29, 2002, p. 40.

—*Michael Belfiore*

Maria Felix

Born Maria de los Ángeles Felix Guereña, May 4, 1914, in Alamos, Sonora, Mexico; died of congestive heart failure, April 8, 2002, in Mexico City, Mexico. Actress. Maria Felix was the goddess of Mexico's golden age of cinema during the 1930s–50s. She conquered the screen with her beauty and a strength that had not been seen in any earlier female stars. She spent three decades making films worldwide, including Mexico, Spain, Italy, France, and Argentina. Despite her iconic status in Mexico, she never made a film in Hollywood. She refused to learn English and also refused to be denigrated by the stereotypical roles that were available.

Felix was one of 16 children, 12 of whom survived. Her father was a civil servant who ruled over his family in typical machismo fashion. Sam Dillon of the *New York Times* wrote that Felix described her father as a "classic macho who hid his emotions, beat his sons, and ignored his daughters." The family lived in Sonora until Felix was 10 and then moved to Guadalajara. Perhaps it was her fiery nature, which would later dominate her public persona, that caused Felix to be expelled from several schools. Despite her problems, she ended up attending university.

While attending university, Felix was elected Queen of the Carnival, in recognition of her beauty. Her first husband, Enrique Álvarez, proposed to her after demonstrating on her the cosmetics that he sold. She agreed and was married before the age of 20. In 1934, she gave birth to their son, Enrique Álvarez Felix. The two divorced not long afterward and Felix moved to Mexico City to get away from her ex-husband.

Felix took a job as a secretary to support herself in Mexico City. One day as she walked down the street she was spotted by a director. He convinced her that with her beauty she should try to be an actress. He helped her get her first role in the film *The Rock of Spirits.* Although the film did not fare well with the critics, Felix was launched into stardom.

Her beauty, combined with a forceful personality, helped distinguish her from other contemporary Mexican actresses. While women's characters had been traditionally submissive, Felix stood out as a dominating and controlling force on and off the screen. At the height of her career, she gained a level of control over the production of her film that is usually only accorded to producers and directors. She had a say in everything from lighting and camera angles to scenarios and wardrobe.

In 1946 Felix made her first film with director Emilio Fernandez and cinematographer Gabriel Figueroa. The romantic comedy *Enamorada* would become known as one of her best works. The film was one of many that Felix made with Fernandez and Figueroa.

With Felix's rise to stardom came increasing popularity. She was admired throughout the Spanish–speaking world, and was the object of adoration. Many men were said to have fallen in love with her. The preeminent Mexican muralist Diego Rivera became so enamored of her that he painted an entire series of portraits. Her second husband, Agustín Lara, Mexico's greatest songwriter, wrote a popular song about her called "Maria Bonita" (Pretty Maria).

Her popularity also had its critics. Mexican writer Carlos Fuentes based a character in his novel *Zona Sagrada* upon Felix. Portrayed as an egomaniac in the book, Felix reacted strongly to the criticism. Undaunted, Fuentes wrote a play 15 years later, *Orchids in the Moonlight,* that held her and her cinematic rival Dolores del Rio in a negative light. Upon her death, despite having been critical of her, Fuentes said of Felix to the *New York Times's* Dillon, "She was a magnificent character, and ... the greatest beauty of the golden age of the Mexican cinema."

In the 1950s, Felix made films with two of Europe's most prominent filmmakers. She starred in *French Cancan* directed by noted French director Jean Renoir. She also starred in Spanish director Luis Buñuel's *La Fièvre Monte à El Pao.* In 1958, she and del Rio delighted fans by starring together in the film *La Cucaracha.*

Felix stopped making films in 1970. Her last films were *La Constitucion* and *La Generala*. One of the reasons she may have stopped making films was her self–consciousness about aging. When she was 66, a fan told her she should make more films because she was still beautiful. The *Times* wrote that Felix's response was an indignant, "What do you mean *still*?"

Even after she no longer made films, Felix remained a fixture in Mexican cinema's constellation of stars. With 47 films to her credit, Felix was awarded the Los Angeles Latino International Film Festival's lifetime achievement award in 2000. She maintained three homes, one in Paris and two others in Cuernavaca and Mexico City, Mexico. Her extravagance was notorious. She once arrived in London with 40 trunks of clothing. Asked why she had so many outfits, she explained that her fans expected it of her.

Felix divorced her first husband, Enrique Álvarez, sometime after 1934. She married musician and poet Agustín Lara in 1943, and divorced him in 1947. In 1952 she married Mexican film star Jorge Negrete, but he died in 1953. In 1956, she married French millionaire Alex Berger who died in 1974. Felix's son, Enrique Álvarez Felix, died of a heart attack in 1996. Felix was strong, opinionated, and beautiful. Her presence during the height of Mexican cinema left a legacy of strong female characters that influences the modern world cinema. American actor Edward James Olmos explained to Chris Kraul of the *Los Angeles Times*, "She was a true giant of Mexico's golden age, and she helped make world cinema." Felix died on April 8, 2002, at her home in Mexico City, Mexico, of congestive heart failure; she was 87. **Sources:** *Los Angeles Times*, April 9, 2002, p. B10; *New York Times*, April 9, 2002, p. A29; *Times* (London), http://www.thetimes.co.uk (April 13, 2002); *Washington Post*, April 10, 2002, p. B6.

—*Eve M. B. Hermann*

John Frankenheimer

Born February 19, 1930, in New York, NY; died of a stroke, July 6, 2002, in Los Angeles, CA. Director. John Frankenheimer directed one of the most critically acclaimed political thrillers of the 1960s, *The Manchurian Candidate*. Throughout the '60s he continued to make films that were visually challenging and socially relevant. His work in live television established his prowess as a director, having learned to work fast and hard with few rehearsals. His career took a hit in the '70s and '80s as he faced personal problems. Before his death he had reestablished himself in television, winning four Emmys for his dramatic television movies.

Frankenheimer grew up in a religiously mixed household. His father was Jewish and made a living as a stockbroker. His mother was Irish American and raised Frankenheimer as a Catholic. He attended La Salle Military Academy, a private military high school in Oakdale, New York. Frankenheimer studied acting at Williams College, graduating in 1951. He gave up acting when he realized that he was too self–concious to be successful.

After college, Frankenheimer served in the Air Force. Stationed in Burbank, California, he learned to make documentaries as part of the film squadron. In 1953, he moved to New York and became an assistant director at CBS. He worked primarily on news and weather shows. He was quickly promoted to directing more prestigious shows like Edward R. Murrow's celebrity talk show *Person to Person*, and *You Are There*, which re–enacted historical events as if they were contemporary.

Frankenheimer made his biggest impact on television in the late '50s and early '60s as director of more than 100 live television plays. His work on anthology series like *Playhouse 90* established him as an up–and–coming director. He directed some of the most critically acclaimed plays for live television, including *Turn of the Screw* starring Ingrid Bergman, *Days of Wine and Roses*, and *The Young Stranger*, which he later turned into a film.

Frankenheimer did not enjoy the experience he had making his first film, *The Young Stranger*, in 1957. He had decided he didn't want to make films, but live television was no longer an option once technology advanced to allow pre–recorded shows. CNN.com quoted Frankenheimer, who said, "I became kind of like the village blacksmith after the invention of the automobile.... There just was nowhere to go. Obviously, the next thing for me was directing movies."

With nowhere else to turn, Frankenheimer unleashed his directorial talents in a flurry of his finest films from 1961 to 1964. He directed six films during those years. In 1962, he released three films, two of which have become classics of American cinema. *Birdman of Alcatraz* stars Burt Lancaster as Robert Stroud, a convicted murderer who becomes an expert on birds while serving out his life sentence. The film was a critical success and Lancaster went on to star in several other Frankenheimer films.

One of the other films released that year, *The Manchurian Candidate,* is listed as one of the 100 best American films by the American Film Institute. It stars Frank Sinatra, Angela Lansbury, and Laurence Harvey. An adaptation of a novel by Richard Condon, *The Manchurian Candidate* weaves political and social commentary into a story about a Korean War veteran brainwashed by communists to assassinate a politician. The film has been recognized for its superior juxtaposition of the thriller genre with satire. Angela Lansbury was nominated for an Oscar for her role in the film. Other exceptional films that Frankenheimer directed from that time period include *Seven Days in May* and *The Train,* both starring Lancaster.

By the end of the '60s, Frankenheimer's films were becoming less well–received. In 1968, he suffered a major personal setback. A close friend of presidential candidate Robert Kennedy, Frankenheimer was overcome by depression and disillusion when Kennedy was assassinated. Frankenheimer withdrew from filmmaking and moved to France for five years. He studied cooking at the Cordon Bleu chef's school and made a few films. He also became seriously addicted to alcohol.

Frankenheimer's filmmaking career suffered during the following decade and into the '80s. It wasn't until the 1990s that his career began to rebound. Coming full circle, Frankenheimer found his niche again in directing dramas for television. Based on true events, *Against the Wall, The Burning Season, Andersonville,* and *George Wallace* each earned Emmy awards for best director. His final television film, *Path to War,* about the United States' involvement in Vietnam was aired after his death in 2002.

Frankenheimer died on July 6, 2002, after he suffered a stroke caused by complications from spinal surgery; he was 72. He is survived by his wife, Evans, who he married in 1964; and daughters Elise and Kristi from his first marriage to Carolyn Miller (they divorced in 1961). "John revolutionized everybody's way of looking at films. He had such a highly charged visual style.... Movies began to look different after John came along," said longtime friend and president of the Academy of Motion Picture Arts and Sciences Frank Pierson to the *New York Times.* **Sources:** CNN.com, http://www.cnn. com/2002/SHOWBIZ/Movies/07/06/

frankenheimer.obit/index.html (July 8, 2002); *Entertainment Weekly,* July 19, 2002, p. 19; *Los Angeles Times,* July 7, 2002, p. B16; *New York Times,* July 8, 2002, p. A17; *Times* (London), http://www. timesonline.co.uk (July 8, 2002); *Washington Post,* July 7, 2002, p. C8.

—*Eve M. B. Hermann*

Stephen Jay Gould

Born September 10, 1941, in Queens, NY; died of lung cancer, May 20, 2002, in New York, NY. Paleontologist and evolutionary theorist. As controversial as he was popular, Stephen Jay Gould was perhaps the most well–known evolutionary biologist since Charles Darwin. He published more than 20 books that effectively translated the theories and science of evolutionary biology into works that a layperson could understand. Titles like *Bully for Brontosaurus, Hen's Teeth and Horses Toes,* and *The Panda's Thumb* were required introductory reading for biology students as well as hits on bestseller lists. As fellow Harvard professor Andrew Knoll noted to CNN.com, "[He] was able to reach an audience that most of us would never reach and not nearly so effectively. He really was paleontology's public intellectual."

Gould made an impact on public debate with his outspoken opposition to creationism. He fueled debate within academia as well with his theory of punctuated equilibrium. His work is credited with inspiring new fields of study including evolution and development as well as macroevolution. He was also a dedicated fan of the New York Yankees and member of the Cecilia Society where he sang in the choir for years.

Gould's father, a court stenographer, took him to the American Museum of Natural History when he was five years old. Gould's experience at the museum would set the course for the rest of his life. The *New York Times* reported that Gould once wrote, "I dreamed of becoming a scientist, in general, and a paleontologist, in particular, ever since the Tyrannosaurus skeleton awed and scared me." He graduated from Antioch College in Yellow Springs, Ohio, in 1963, with a degree in geology. From there he went on to earn his doctorate in paleontology from Columbia University in 1967.

As a graduate student, Gould focused on a tropical land snail known as the Cerion. His work took him to Central America where he searched for the small snails while avoiding drug smugglers and gunfire. Studies of the fossil records led him and a fellow student, Niles Eldredge, to develop their theory of punctuated equilibrium. Because of gaps in the fossil record, Gould and Eldridge came to the conclusion that evolution, rather than changing slowly over time, had periods of stasis followed by rapid periods of change. Their theory challenged the deeply held belief of gradual evolution.

He also inspired controversy with his theory that not all adaptations have a purpose. This theory put forth the idea that structural requirements created some adaptations as accidental byproducts—much as the decorated spandrels (mosaic–filled spaces) in ancient cathedrals were the byproduct of building arches. The other idea was that some adaptations were really "exaptations" (a word Gould coined), which are features that get used for something other than that for which they were originally intended.

Gould introduced these theories early in his career as a Harvard professor, having joined the faculty as an assistant professor in 1967. He was promoted quickly in the following years and by 1973 he was professor of geology and curator of invertebrate paleontology at the Museum of Comparative Zoology. Beginning in 1974, Gould wrote a column called "This View of Life" for every issue of *Natural History* until 2001. The essays numbered close to 300 and were the basis for many of his books.

In 1981, he was named scientist of the year by *Discover* magazine. He also won the National Book Award for *The Panda's Thumb*. The next year he won the National Book Critics Award for *The Mismeasure of Man*, which challenged the basis for intelligence testing as inherently biased. He was also named Alexander Agassiz Professor of Zoology at Harvard.

In 1982, Gould battled a rare form of cancer called abdominal mesothelioma. A champion of statistics, he used it to explain biological events like extinction as well as trends in baseball. This time he used it to bolster his hope of fighting his cancer. His hope was to prove that the median survival time of eight months that he had been told he had was not the mean; he succeeded.

Gould had other interests outside of paleontology. He was devoted to the New York Yankees even though he spent his entire academic career in the home territory of the Boston Red Sox. In 1999, he wrote a tribute to famous Yankees player Joe DiMaggio, which was published by the Associated Press. He was also a commentator in the PBS documentary about baseball that was directed by Ken Burns. Other topics he could write about with knowledge included art, architecture, music, and history.

His best–selling books and outspoken opinions also garnered him an unprecedented popularity with the general public. He portrayed himself in an episode of the television cartoon *The Simpsons*. Treating him much like a celebrity, *Architectural Digest* did a story of the renovations Gould made on his Manhattan apartment. As Carol Kaesuk Yoon of the *New York Times* wrote, "Outside academia, Dr. Gould was almost universally adored by those familiar with his work."

Gould had a profound impact on the natural sciences. David Jablonski told the *Chicago Tribune*, "It's hard to think of another scientist who was as visible, articulate, or skilled at helping the public see the world view of an evolutionist." Shortly before his death, Gould finally published his magnum opus, *The Structure of Evolutionary Theory*, which synthesized his ideas with those of Darwin. Twenty years after overcoming the odds to beat one form of cancer, Gould died of lung cancer at age 60 on May 20, 2002. He is survived by his wife, Rhonda Roland Shearer, a sculptor; his two sons from his previous marriage to Deborah Lee: Jesse and Ethan; his stepson, Jade; and stepdaughter, London. **Sources:** *Chicago Tribune*, May 21, 2002, section 2, p. 9; CNN. com, http://www.cnn.com/2002/TECH/science/ 05/20/obit.gould.ap/index.html (May 23, 2002); *Guardian* (London), May 22, 2002, p. 20; *New York Times*, May 21, 2002, p. A1, p. A24; *Washington Post*, May 21, 2002, p. B6.

—*Eve M. B. Hermann*

Charles Guggenheim

Born Charles Eli Guggenheim, March 31, 1924, in Cincinnati, OH; died of pancreatic cancer, October 9, 2002, in Washington, D.C. Filmmaker. Director and producer Charles Guggenheim earned four Academy Awards for his documentary films over the course of an esteemed five–decade career. He was also the creator of the first political campaign commercials for television during the early days of the medium in the mid–1950s, but later gave up the highly lucrative work, remarking, "If you play a piano in a house of ill repute, it doesn't make a difference how well you play the piano," *Washington Post* writer Bart Barnes quoted him as saying.

Of German–Jewish extraction, Guggenheim was born in 1924 in Cincinnati, Ohio, where his father and grandfather ran a furniture business. As a boy, he suffered from dyslexia, but the learning disability went unrecognized at the time, and he was simply thought to be slow learner. Teased by his classmates, he did not learn to read until he was nine years old, and satisfied his curiosity about the world by looking at photographs in *Life* magazine. Guggenheim later said that had he not endured such rough experiences in his early life and learned to compensate, he likely would have joined the family business.

Guggenheim spent time at the Colorado State College of Agriculture and Mechanic Arts before enlisting in the U.S. Army during World War II. He was hospitalized with a foot infection, however, just before his division was posted overseas, and was forced to remain stateside. His division went on to suffer heavy casualties during the Battle of the Bulge, and thousands became prisoners–of–war of Nazi Germany. After the war, Guggenheim finished his education at the University of Iowa in 1948, and worked in New York City for a time at CBS Radio. Recognizing the importance of the new medium of television, he moved to Chicago, Illinois—at the time, broadcasting's epicenter—and worked behind the scenes on children's shows for CBS. From there he went to St. Louis, Missouri, where he worked in public television for a time before founding his documentary–filmmaking company in 1954.

Guggenheim Productions produced the first political ad that ever aired on television, for the 1956 Democratic presidential candidate, Adlai E. Stevenson. In time, the company moved to Washington, D.C., to be nearer the political nexus, and went on the produce campaign spots for several Democratic frontrunners, among them the three Kennedy brothers. "We were winning races no one thought we could," the *Washington Post*'s Barnes quoted him as saying about these early days of media campaigning. Guggenheim's longtime friend and tennis partner Jack Valenti, president of the Motion Picture Association of America, told the *Los Angeles Times*'s Dennis McLellan that as an advertising whiz, Guggenheim "recognized early on, before almost any political filmmakers, that people vote viscerally, not intellectually. So he tried to appeal to the emotions—the heart rather than the head. And that's what made his campaign stuff not only unique but powerful."

Healthy and fit, Guggenheim often rode his bike the three miles from home to office in the Georgetown section of Washington for many years. When not making political ads, he concentrated on documentary films, his first passion. His work won four Academy Awards, and he was nominated in his category 12 times, meeting an Oscar–history record held only by animator Walt Disney. Among his most powerful works were the 1964 film *Nine from Little Rock,* about the school–desegregation battle in Arkansas in 1957, and *RFK Remembered*, shown at the Democratic National Convention in late August of 1968 just weeks after the Senator and brother of a slain president was assassinated himself. While anti–war protesters clashed with Chicago police outside, convention delegates marched through the venue singing "The Battle Hymn of the Republic" as Guggenheim's film played. Similar works that served as documentaries of three Democratic presidential administrations—those of Harry S Truman, John F. Kennedy, and Lyndon B. Johnson—later became part of the presidential libraries of each man.

In the mid–1980s, having grown disillusioned with contemporary American political campaigning, Guggenheim decided to quit making the candidate ads. "These 30–second and 60–second inquisitions are becoming more and more a part of the electoral process," *New York Times* writer Wolfgang Saxon quoted him as saying. "It doesn't take much ability or judgment or ethical restraint to use the 30–second spots to slander someone, to make an inference, to hit, to run, to oversimplify." He continued to make acclaimed documentary films, often shown on the Public Broadcasting Service (PBS) network. These included 1986's *The Making of Liberty* for the centenary of the Statue of Liberty's arrival in New York, and *The Johnstown Flood,* which won him another Oscar. Tales of ordinary heroics, such as the ones he uncovered in chronicling the deadly Johnstown disaster in 1889, fascinated Guggenheim. "There are great stories in what is very common," Barnes quoted him as saying in the *Washington Post* obituary.

Guggenheim's final work was one that had a deeply personal significance: among the American and Allied forces who were captured at Battle of the Bulge, the ones who had Jewish–sounding surnames were sent by the Nazis to a slave labor camp, Berga, in eastern Germany, where many perished from exhaustion, starvation, and beatings. "Guggenheim was long haunted by the fact he had been spared while his comrades faced death or imprisonment," noted his *Times* of London obituary. His final work, *Berga: Soldiers of Another War,* was a homage to his fellow soldiers, though he was already ill from pancreatic cancer and struggled to complete it. Guggenheim died on October 9, 2002, in Washington, D.C.; he was 78. He is survived by his wife, Marion Streett Guggenheim; his sons, Davis and Jonathan; his daughter, Grace; and four grandchildren. **Sources:** *Chicago Tribune*, October 11, 2002, section 2, p. 10; *Los Angeles Times*, October 11, 2002, p. B14; *New York Times*, October 11, 2002, p. C11; *Times* (London), http://www.timesonline.co.uk (October 12, 2002); *Washington Post*, October 10, 2002, p. B6.

—*Carol Brennan*

Lionel Hampton

Born April 20, 1908, in Louisville, KY; died of a heart attack, August 31, 2002, in New York, NY. Musician. The leading vibraphone player in the United States, Lionel Hampton's career lasted decades and encompassed musical styles from jazz and bebop to big band and rhythm and blues. Claudia Levy wrote in the *Washington Post*, "[He] played the vibes with lightning swiftness and harmonic and melodic simplicity." His style set the standard for future vibraphonists.

Hampton was a contemporary of such musical stars as Louis Armstrong and Benny Goodman. His association with Goodman's orchestra made a social as well as musical impact: it was the first time blacks and whites performed on the same stage. When he struck out on his own, Hampton continued to make contributions to music that impacted jazz as well as rock and roll.

Hampton's musical education began early in his life. For part of his childhood, he was raised in Birmingham, Alabama, by his grandmother. Church services that they attended there introduced him to the bass drum. Peter Watrous of the *New York Times* quoted Hampton, who said, "They'd have a whole band in the church ... and they'd be rocking.... I'd be sitting by the sister who was playing the big brass drum and when she'd get happy and start dancing ... I'd grab that bass drum and start in on that beat. After that, I always had that beat in me."

Later Hampton was sent to Kenosha, Wisconsin, where he attended Holy Rosary Academy, a Catholic school for black and Native American children. He learned to play drums from the nuns at the school and was a member of the fife and drum band. His family relocated to Chicago while he was still in school and he grew up surrounded by some the era's best musicians while continuing to learn new instruments.

In school and as part of a band of newsboys sponsored by the *Chicago Defender*, a black newspaper in Chicago, Hampton played the timpani, xylophone, orchestra bells, and the snare drum. His uncle was a well–known bootlegger in Chicago who often held parties at his home that included guests like blues and jazz pioneers Alberta Hunter, Jelly Roll Morton, and Bessie Smith. By the time he was in high school, Hampton had his own drum set and was playing professionally.

In 1926, Hampton moved to Los Angeles, California, to play with Les Hite's orchestra. Eventually, they became the house band for the Cotton Club in Culver City, California. As the house band they played backup for Armstrong when he performed at the club. At a recording session with Armstrong, Hampton played the vibraphones for the first time. The instrument was sitting in a corner and Armstrong asked if anyone could play it. Hampton saw that it was laid out similarly to a piano and xylophone and said he could. The first recorded jazz vibraphone was played by Hampton on Armstrong's recording of "Memories of You."

In 1936, big band leader Benny Goodman caught Hampton's performance at the Paradise Club in Los Angeles. Goodman invited Hampton to record with him and then offered him a job in his orchestra. Hampton debuted with Goodman's quartet at the Madhattan Room in the Pennsylvania Hotel in New York City that year. For the next four years, Hampton was an integral part of Goodman's orchestra as well as his quartet, quintet, and sextet.

As part of Goodman's big band, Hampton contributed to some of the era's most popular music. In addition, his presence on the stage with a mostly white band helped integration gain a foothold. Because of the segregation that was prevalent throughout the United States at that time, Goodman always made sure that Hampton traveled with him, ensuring that Hampton had a place to stay. The *Times* related this Hampton quote, "As far as I'm concerned, what he [Goodman] did in those days ... made it possible for [blacks] to have their chance in baseball and other fields."

In those early years, the RCA Victor recording company gave Hampton recording time in their studios. With that opportunity, Hampton recorded with small ensembles throughout the late '30s, recordings that have become some of the most highly acclaimed of their kind. By 1940, Hampton was ready to step out on his own and formed his own big band. For the next 25 years, Hampton's orchestra entertained enthusiastic crowds around the world.

By the time he dissolved the group, they had been credited in some circles with setting the tone for rock and roll performances to come. His concerts would elicit hand clapping from audiences as Hampton bounced from drums to piano to vibraphones. Often he would march out into the aisles with his brass section. Sometimes criticized for his over–the–top antics, Hampton always felt he was there to entertain first.

Hampton wrote some of the swing eras most popular tunes, including "Flying Home," which he claimed to have played more than 300 times over 50 years. With more than 200 pieces of music to his credit, Hampton made a lasting contribution to the genre. Throughout his career he was voted the best vibes player in the business.

Due to his wife Gladys's exceptional fiscal management (she was his manager), Hampton was one of the wealthiest musicians in the business. He used his wealth to fund scholarships, festivals, and even a low–income housing development in Harlem, New York. Hampton's generosity was returned in kind. He received dozens of honorary doctorates, has a street in Berlin, Germany, named after him, and is the namesake for the University of Idaho School of Music.

Hampton was married for 35 years to Gladys Neal, who died in 1971. They had no children and Hampton has no survivors; he never remarried. He continued to perform into his old age at music festivals and other venues around the world. He died on August 31, 2002, from complications resulting from a heart attack at the age of 94. Music critic Nat Hentoff told the *Los Angeles Times*, "He was the definition of swinging. The core of jazz flowed out of him, just as it did out of Armstrong." **Sources:** *Los Angeles Times*, September 1, 2002, p. A1, p. A28; *New York Times*, September 1, 2002, p. A1, p. A23; *Times (London)*, http://www.timesonline.co.uk (September 2, 2002); *Washington Post*, September 1, 2002, p. A1, p. A10.

—Eve M. B. Hermann

Ruth Handler

Born November 4, 1916, in Denver, CO; died of complications following colon surgery, April 27, 2002, in Los Angeles, CA. Toy company executive. Mattel co–founder Ruth Handler was the woman behind the Barbie doll, one of the most potent pop–culture icons of twentieth–century America. Handler created what became the world's best–selling toy in 1959 after realizing that young girls preferred to play with dolls that had interesting outfits and accessories, rather than play–act a maternal role with a faux infant. "Every little girl needed a doll through which to project herself into her dream of her future," Handler told the *New York Times* in a 1977 interview quoted in her obituary notice.

The child of Polish immigrants, Handler was born Ruth Mosko in 1916 in Denver, Colorado, the youngest of ten children. At the age of 19, she moved to Los Angeles, California, and found work as a secretary at Paramount Studios. In 1938, she married her boyfriend from high school, Elliot Handler, who had followed her to California and then studied at what became the Art Center College of Design in Pasadena. During the early 1940s, her husband began making small items for their home out of a revolutionary new material, plastic, and she encouraged him to make enough for her to sell at local stores; after some success in this, they founded the Mattel Company in 1945 with a third partner. Within a few years the company had racked up impressive sales with toy guns and musical instruments, and Mattel became the first company ever to advertise its wares on American television year–round.

The idea for "Barbie" came to Handler after watching her young daughter, Barbara, play with paper dolls, which had different outfits. Barbara seemed uninterested in baby dolls—Handler had disdained them as well as a child—and the mother/marketing whiz thought that a teenage–type doll might fill a niche in the toy market. "When she took the idea to Mattel's executives, who were men, they sneered that no mother would buy her daughter a grown–up doll with a bosom," explained *Los Angeles Times* journalist Elaine Woo. The idea was shelved until Handler made a trip to Germany in 1956 and brought back a voluptuous little doll named Lilli, which was modeled after an adult–oriented cartoon character. Based on the Lilli figure, the first Barbie went on display—wearing a bathing suit, high heels, and perky ponytail—at the 1959 American Toy Fair in New York. Mattel's "Barbie Teen–Age Fashion Model" had sales of 350,000 the first year, and the company began adding new outfits and accessories that filled out the fictional glamour girl's fabulous life as demand skyrocketed. Barbie took ski vacations, drove a convertible, and lived in a posh townhouse. Her "career" wardrobe evolved over the years as well, from a ballerina or flight attendant to astronaut and surgeon. In the end, Handler's creation proved a phenomenal success, and made Mattel a powerhouse in the toy industry.

Handler's Barbie doll was derided in the more feminist–conscious 1970s as a poor role model. "Critics said the doll gave girls misguided goals, whether for their careers or for their own physical development," explained *New York Times* writer Sarah Kershaw, but Handler defended her creation in her 1994 autobiography, *Dream Doll: The Ruth Handler Story*. "My whole philosophy of Barbie was that through the doll the little girl could be anything she wanted to be," she wrote. "Barbie always represented the fact that a woman has choices." Handler embodied that take–charge spirit herself: in 1970, she was diagnosed with breast cancer and underwent a mastectomy. Unhappy with the post–surgery alternatives offered, she founded her own prosthesis company, the Ruthton Corporation, and began making artificial breasts from a foam and silicon blend marketed under the name Nearly Me. At the time, there was little public awareness or discussion of the disease, and Handler emerged as one of the first courageous spokespersons for early–detection measures. Ruthton was later sold to Kimberly–Clark, but Handler had not earned any great fortune from it. "It sure rebuilt my self–esteem," the *Los Angeles Times* obituary by Woo quoted her as saying, "and I think I rebuilt the self–esteem of others."

In the mid–1970s, Handler and her husband were ousted from the company they had founded after a scandal over Mattel's financial records erupted. They pleaded guilty to fraud and false reporting to the Securities and Exchange Commission, and paid a hefty fine. Handler later said that the bout with cancer had distracted her from her duties, especially when she returned to the office. "I had been running a company making hundreds of millions of dollars a year," Woo quoted her as saying. "I had a big job. But suddenly I was supposed to whisper about what I'd been through."

A longtime Los Angeles resident, Handler underwent surgery on her colon in early 2002, but suffered from post–operative complications. She died on April 27, 2002; she was 85. Handler is survived by her husband, daughter, five grandchildren, and one great–granddaughter. A son, Ken, whose name inspired Barbie's male counterpart, died in 1994. **Sources:** *Los Angeles Times*, April 28, 2002, p. A1, p. A32; *New York Times*, April 29, 2002, p. A1, p. A23; *People*, May 13, 2002, pp. 66-67; *Times* (London), http://www.thetimes.co.uk (April 29, 2002); *Washington Post*, April 29, 2002, p. B4.

—*Carol Brennan*

George Harrison

Born George Harold Harrison, February 25, 1943, in Liverpool, England; died of cancer, November 29, 2001, in Los Angeles, CA. Musician. As the youngest member of the Beatles, one of the most influential bands in rock history, George Harrison rose to worldwide fame while in his early twenties. Harrison was the most introspective of the quartet, and was dubbed the "Quiet Beatle" by journalists. However those who knew him well attested to a raucous sense of humor that belied his public image.

Harrison came from a working–class background in Liverpool. His father, Harold, was a bus driver and his mother, Louise, was a housewife. He was two years behind John Lennon (whom he did not know at the time) at Dovedale Primary School and a year behind Paul McCartney at Liverpool Institute. Harrison and McCartney met while on the school bus and discovered they shared common interests in guitars and guitarists—by then Harrison had formed a skiffle band with his brother Peter. Skiffle was a musical style with a high–energy, folk–based sound. At the time McCartney was in a band called the Quarrymen, and he introduced to Harrison to his bandmates, including Lennon. Harrison joined the group in 1958, and in 1960 they changed their name to the Beatles, though it wasn't until drummer Ringo Starr joined that the quartet's final configuration was set.

After performing in Hamburg, Germany, the Beatles returned to Liverpool where they met Brian Epstein, a local record store owner who became their manager. The songwriting team of Lennon and McCartney went on to write most, but not all, of the band's 27 number–one hit songs in the United States and Great Britain. Harrison, who at times felt creatively stifled by his more extroverted colleagues, wrote such hits as "Taxman," Something" (which singer/actor Frank Sinatra called the greatest love song of all time), "Here Comes the Sun" and "While My Guitar Gently Weeps."

During the filming of the first Beatles film, *A Hard Day's Night*, Harrison met model Patti Boyd, who appeared briefly in the film. They were married in January of 1966. It was Boyd who introduced the receptive Harrison to the Maharishi Mahesh Yogi. Harrison, in turn, influenced the other Beatles's decisions to embrace transcendental meditation (TM) and the Maharishi Mahesh Yogi as their guru. While the others's interest in Eastern spirituality eventually waned, Harrison's gathered strength. He was associated with the International Society for Krishna Consciousness, and was one of its biggest financial benefactors. Harrison's interest in Indian culture naturally extended to music; he introduced the sitar to Western pop music on the Beatles's song "Norwegian Wood."

Following the Beatles's breakup in 1970 Harrison struck out on a solo career. In fact the breakup has been partly attributed to his desire to record more of his songs. He once remarked, as quoted at CNN.com by Graham Jones, "The biggest break in my career was getting into the Beatles. The second biggest break was getting out of them." Harrison was the first of the four Beatles to record a solo album. Actually he had recorded a soundtrack, *Wonderwall Music,* in 1968 and *Electronic Sound* in 1969, but his breakout album was the triple–record set *All Things Must Pass,* released in 1970. It was indicative of both Harrison's spirituality and his pent–up creative urges. Critics praised the album and one of the songs, "My Sweet Lord," swept the charts. Later the song and Harrison were engulfed in a copyright controversy when Harrison was sued because of the song's similarity to the 1962 Chiffons hit "He's So Fine." Allan Kozinn of the *New York Times* reported that Harrison was found guilty of "unconscious plagiarism."

In 1971 Harrison staged two benefit concerts at New York's Madison Square Garden with an all–star lineup that featured Bob Dylan and Eric Clapton. The concert's proceeds were earmarked for the people of Bangladesh. The three–record set that resulted from the shows won a Grammy, and Harrison was at the height of his solo career. Approximately $10 million was raised for Bangladesh, but the money was held up for 10 years due to tax inquiries.

Harrison's next two efforts, 1973's *Living in the Material World* and 1974's *Dark Horse,* continued in the same spiritual vein, but by the time the latter album came out Harrison discovered that the critics and a good deal of his fans had drifted away from Eastern spirituality. Harrison would seldom reach his earlier heights of success. He also went through personal hard times when his marriage to Boyd ended in 1974. Though she began living with Harrison's best friend, Clapton, his friendship with both remained strong. In 1978 Harrison married Olivia Arias soon after the birth of their son, Dhani. Harrison's other 1970s albums were 1975's *Extra Texture,* 1976's *The Best of George Harrison* and *33 1/3,* and 1979's *George Harrison.* The latter two were on his own label, Dark Horse.

During the 1980s, in addition to his own recordings, Harrison served as a record and film producer. He was the financial backer for Monty Python's *Life of Brian,* and afterward started a production company, Handmade Films. Among the 27 films the company produced were *The Long Good Friday, Mona Lisa, Time Bandits,* the cult favorite *Withnail and I,* and *Shanghai Surprise.* Harrison sold his interest in Handmade Films in 1994.

Harrison released *Somewhere in England* in 1981 and *Gone Troppo* in 1982, but it wasn't until 1987 that Harrison returned to the top of the music charts with the single, "Got My Mind Set On You" from the album *Cloud Nine.* The song was number two on the British charts and reached number one in the United States. Also in the late 1980s Harrison became a member of the supergroup the Traveling Wilburys, whose members included Bob Dylan, Roy Orbison, Tom Petty, and Jeff Lynne. "Wilbury" was the term Harrison and Lynne used for studio gremlins. Harrison won a second Grammy Award for their 1988 album. In 1989 he released *Best of Dark Horse 1976–1989.* And in 1990 another Wilburys album came out. Harrison released his final album, *George Harrison Live in Japan,* in 1992.

That same year the normally reclusive Harrison ventured into politics when he publicly supported the Natural Law Party in Britain. The Party, which has since gone defunct in the United Kingdom, had a political philosophy based on TM and bipartisanship. In 1996 Harrison was the plaintiff in a lawsuit against a former financial advisor whom he accused of mishandling funds. Harrison was awarded £6 million. In 1998 Harrison was diagnosed with throat cancer, which went into remission following radiation treatment. The following year Harrison was stabbed by an intruder in his Oxfordshire mansion. The stabbing punctured one of his lungs.

By June of 2001 the world discovered that Harrison was being treated for lung cancer and a brain tumor at a Swiss clinic. Harrison denied reports that death was imminent, and in October was back in the studio where he recorded "Horse to the Water," with Jools Holland. Harrison cowrote the song with his son, Dhani. The song was released in November of 2001 on Holland's CD, *Small World Big Band.*

Weeks before his death Harrison underwent treatment at the Staten Island University Hospital in New York City and the UCLA Medical Center. He died of cancer on November 29, 2001, at the age of 58. He is survived by his wife, Olivia, and son, Dhani. **Sources:** CNN.com, http://www.cnn.com/2001/SHOWBIZ/music/11/30/harrison.londonobit/index.html (November 30, 2001); CNN.com, http://www.cnn.com/2001/SHOWBIZ/music/11/

30/harrison.obit/ (November 30, 2001); Disco graphynet.com, http://www.discographynet.com/ harrison/harrison.html (August 20, 2002); *New York Times*, December 1, 2001, p. A1.

—*Frank Caso*

Alfred Heineken

Born Alfred Henry Heineken, November 4, 1923, in Amsterdam, Netherlands; died of pneumonia, January 3, 2002, in Noordwijk, Netherlands. Head of Heineken brewery. Alfred Heineken is credited with transforming his family's brewery from a relatively small company into an international giant, second only to the American Anheuser Busch and the Belgian Interbrew companies in worldwide beer sales.

Heineken started in his family's beer company when he was 18 years old, in 1942. The company had been started in 1864 when Heineken's grandfather, Gerard Adriaan Heineken, bought a small brewery in Amsterdam called The Haystack when he was 22 years old. The brewery began operating under the Heineken name in 1873. At the time, the company was just one of hundreds of small breweries operating in Holland.

In 1946, Heineken moved to the United States to become his company's sales manager at its distributor in that country. Much of his job consisted of pounding the pavement in New York City trying to convince bartenders to carry his company's beer. It was in the United States that he met and married an American woman named Lucille Cummins, the daughter of a bourbon maker in Kentucky.

Influenced by American marketing and advertising practices, Heineken returned to his native Holland after two years in the United States, determined to boost his company's sales around the world. One of his first moves in that direction was to reintroduce the company's distinctive green bottle and red–star–and–black–banner logo, which had been discontinued. He said, according to the *Times* of London, "The stomach is very conservative."

The green bottles cost more to produce than the bottles the company had been using, but they did boost sales, and they helped to establish his company as a brand that symbolized more than just beer. As the *Washington Post* reported, his motto was: "I don't sell beer, I sell warmth." Heineken also established the company's advertising department at its headquarters in Amsterdam. As he was quoted as saying in the *New York Times*, "Had I not been a beer brewer I would have become an advertising man." In 1964, Heineken was made a member of the company's management board. In 1971 he became the company's chief executive officer (CEO).

Heineken was the victim of kidnappers in 1983. As he was leaving his office and heading to his car, he was captured by three gunmen. His chauffeur tried to intervene, but he too was captured, and they were both hustled into a waiting getaway van. The kidnappers held Heineken and his chauffeur for three weeks in an abandoned factory outside of Amsterdam, demanding $14 million in ransom money. They were held in primitive conditions, chained to a wall, and given only one meal a day, and a bucket of water so that they could wash themselves. Heineken tried to keep his hair combed with a plastic fork, and he did his best to keep his sense of humor, "although," as he told the *Times* of London, "there wasn't much chance to exercise it."

Police finally rescued Heineken and his driver after receiving an anonymous tip pinpointing their location. Heineken's family had handed over the ransom money only two days before, having disregarded Heineken's insistence that, in the event of his kidnapping, ransom not be paid. However, the police were able arrest two dozen conspirators involved in the kidnapping. Nevertheless, Heineken became a recluse after this experience, venturing into the public eye only when absolutely necessary, and closely guarding his privacy.

Heineken remained CEO of his company until 1989, at which time he became head of the company's supervisory board. He served in this position until 1995. Heineken was also management board chairman of Heineken Holdings NV, the company that controlled the brewery. He assumed this post in 1979. Even though in later years he no longer was responsible for the day–to–day operations of the brewery, he retained ultimate control through Heineken Holdings. He announced his retirement from that post in November of 2001, less than two months before his death. His daughter, Charlene, was set to assume the family's controlling interest in Heineken Holdings.

At the time of his death, Heineken was the wealthiest man in Holland, with more than $3.6 billion to his name. The product that he helped become a household name around the world was sold in 170 countries, and made by 110 breweries in 50 countries. His company was the third largest brewery in the world at the time of his death. His family retained a controlling stake in the company, which was smaller only than Anheuser Busch of the United States and Interbrew of Belgium.

"It is not all that dreadful to die," the *Washington Post* reported Heineken as saying in a rare interview, "because it was not all that bad before you were born." Heineken died on January 3, 2002, at his home in the Dutch seaside resort town of Noordwijk. The cause of death was pneumonia, though he had been ailing since suffering a mild stroke the year before. He was 78 years old. He is survived by his wife, Lucille; their daughter, Charlene; and five grandchildren. **Sources:** *Chicago Tribune,* January 5, 2002, p. 17; *Los Angeles Times,* January 5, 2002, p. B13; *New York Times,* August 22, 2001, p. C15; *Times* (London), http://www.thetimes.co.uk (January 5, 2002); *Washington Post,* January 5, 2002, p. B6.

—*Michael Belfiore*

Waylon Jennings

Born Waylon Arnold Jennings, June 15, 1937, in Littlefield, TX; died from complications related to diabetes, February 13, 2002, in Chandler, AZ. Country musician and songwriter. One of the original "outlaws" of country music, Waylon Jennings recorded more than 60 albums and had 53 Top 10 country music hits, of which 16 went to Number One. Jennings was the winner of two Grammy Awards, and four Country Music Association Awards; he was inducted into the Country Music Hall of Fame in 2001.

Jennings's father was a truck driver by profession and also a guitar player. The younger Jennings began to play guitar at an early age and entered talent shows. While still in his early teens Jennings formed his first band, the Texas Longhorns. Music so consumed his young life that he dropped out of high school and began working as a disc jockey. In the early years he was interested in rock 'n' roll. While working as a disk jockey in Lubbock, Texas, Jennings met Buddy Holly, at that time another aspiring musician like himself. Jennings became the bassist in Holly's band, the Crickets, and with Holly's assistance made his own recordings in 1958: "Jolé Blon" and "When Sin Stops." Holly was the producer and guitarist on those songs; King Curtis

played saxophone. "Mainly what I learned from Buddy was an attitude," Jennings said years later, according to CNN.com. "He loved music, and he taught me that it shouldn't have any barriers to it."

Jennings was not on Holly's ill-fated flight, which crashed on February 3, 1959, killing Holly and fellow rock 'n' roll stars Richie Valens and J.P. "The Big Bopper" Richardson. At the last moment Jennings gave up his seat on the plane to Richardson. With the dissolution of the Crickets, Jennings's music began to take a different turn.

While Jennings undeniably moved toward country music (county and western as it was known at the time), and eventually became one of its major influences, he himself was influenced by sources outside the genre. These included trumpeter Herb Alpert, Bob Dylan, the Beatles, and the Rolling Stones. Alpert signed Jennings to a contract on his A&M label in 1963. But Jennings was veering away from pop and soon went to Nashville, Tennessee, where guitar legend Chet Atkins signed him to a contract with RCA in 1965. During his early days in Nashville, Jennings became a friend and roommate of another legend–in–the–making, Johnny Cash. Jennings made numerous appearances on the *Grand Ole Opry,* and by the mid–1960s he was recording his first hits. These included "Stop the World (and Let Me Off)," "Walk On Out of My Mind," "I Got You," "Only Daddy That'll Walk the Line," "I'm a Ramblin' Man," "Luckenbach, Texas," "I've Always Been Crazy," "Amanda," and "Rose in Paradise." In 1966 Jennings appeared in the film, *Nashville Rebel,* which also starred Loretta Lynn and Tex Ritter. He won his first Grammy Award in 1969 for "MacArthur Park," on which he collaborated with the Kimberlys. Also in 1969 Jennings married singer Jessi Colter, his fourth wife. Jennings and Coulter recorded the albums *Suspicious Minds* in 1970 and *Under Your Spell Again* in 1971.

As the years passed Jennings grew increasingly dissatisfied with the overproduced Nashville sound. His biggest impact on country music came in 1976 when he, Colter, Willie Nelson, and Tompall Glaser recorded the album *Wanted: The Outlaws*. It was the first country album to reach the one million sales mark, thus certifying it as a platinum record. *Wanted: The Outlaws* was not only a crossover success, attracting thousands of new fans, it solidified Jennings's and Nelson's images as outlaw musicians who bucked the Nashville system. Nashville, however, was more than willing to accommodate two of its biggest stars, which led the iconoclastic Jennings to later claim that the outlaw image was merely a convenient marketing tool. Jennings and Nelson also had a hit with their duet, "Mammas Don't Let Your Babies Grow Up to Be Cowboys."

In 1979 Jennings made the leap to television as the narrator of the series *The Dukes of Hazzard.* His recording of the show's theme song reached Number One on the Country charts and was also a pop hit. That same year Jenning's *Greatest Hits* album sold four million copies.

Jennings's personal life, aside from three failed marriages, was plagued by poor health and drug addiction. By his own account, Jennings's cocaine habit reached $1,500 per day. In 1977 he was arrested at a Nashville recording studio and charged with conspiracy and possession of cocaine with intent to distribute; the charges were later dropped. In 1984 Jennings, an estimated $2.5 million in debt, decided being on drugs 21 years was enough. He leased a house in Arizona where he kicked his cocaine habit by going cold turkey. Though he successfully ended his addiction, his health problems began to mount during this time. In the mid–1980s he underwent heart surgery (coincidentally, Cash was his roommate in the hospital); Jennings also suffered from diabetes.

In 1985 Jennings, Nelson, Cash, and Kris Kristofferson formed the Highwaymen. Their first album, *The Highwaymen,* reached Number One. The group recorded two more albums during the next ten years, *Highwaymen 2* in 1990 and *The Road Goes On Forever* in 1995.

Both Jennings's health and his popularity with the new generation of country music fans declined in the 1990s though he still recorded critically acclaimed CDs. His final album, *Never Say Die,* was released in 2000. In October of 2001 Jennings was inducted into the Country Music Hall of Fame, though he did not attend the ceremony. In December of 2001 his left foot was amputated due to complications from diabetes.

Jennings died in his sleep at his home in Chandler, Arizona, on February 13, 2002; he was 64. He is survived by Colter; their son, Shooter; a daughter, Tammy Lynn; a step–daughter, Jennifer; and four children from previous marriages: sons Terry and Buddy; and daughters Julie and Deanna. **Sources:** CNN.com, http://www.cnn.com/2002/SHOWBIZ/Music/02/13/jennings.obit.ap/index.html (February 14, 2002); E! Online, http://www.eonline.com/News/Items/0,1,9523,00.html (February 14,

2002); *Los Angeles Times,* February 14, 2002, p. B14; *New York Times,* February 14, 2002, p. C21; *Times* (London), February 15, 2002; *Washington Post,* February 14, 2002, p. B6.

—*Frank Caso*

Yousuf Karsh

Born December 23, 1908, in Mardin, Turkey; died July 13, 2002, in Boston, MA. Photographer. Famous for his portraits of famous and powerful people, including British Prime Minister Winston Churchill, author Ernest Hemingway, and many others, Karsh was known professionally as Karsh of Ottawa. Reproduced in countless books, magazines, and newspapers around the world, his portraits have become among the best known of many of his subjects.

Karsh was born in Turkey to Armenian parents in 1908. When he was five years old, to escape Turkish persecution he immigrated to Sherbrooke, Montreal, in Canada, where his uncle worked as a studio photographer. It was from his uncle that Karsh learned the rudiments of photography. His uncle, recognizing his nephew's talent, sent him to Boston, Massachusetts, as a young man to become an apprentice to well–known portrait photographer John H. Garo.

After working for three years with Garo, who was also an Armenian, Karsh returned to Canada, where he opened a portrait studio of his own in Ottawa in 1932. The decision to relocate to Ottawa was a strategic one; he felt that it would give him the best chance to met world leaders as they traveled between London and Washington.

The dramatic lighting style that Karsh adopted for his work came from his study of artificial lighting techniques used at the Little Theater in Ottawa, for which he photographed theatrical productions. Garo had always worked with natural light, but Karsh discovered that artificial lighting was best suited for the heroic portraits that were to become his trademark.

Karsh's association with the Little Theater proved advantageous in other ways: it was there that he met the son of Lord Bessborough, governor general of Canada. The son persuaded his father to be photographed by Karsh. Lord Bessborough was delighted with the result, and thus was born a long association between Karsh and Canadian political leaders. This association led to Karsh's introduction to Britain's Prime Minister Winston Churchill when Churchill visited Canada in 1941.

Churchill gave Karsh only two minutes to take his portrait, but in that short time, Karsh captured the English leader in a pose that was to become world famous. The portrait, with Churchill glowering at the camera with an expression of defiance, seemed to symbolize Britain's resolve to defend itself against conquest by German leader Adolf Hitler. One story has it that Karsh snapped the picture immediately after snatching away Churchill's cigar, thus capturing the leader in a moment of anger. The picture quickly landed on the cover of *Life* magazine and in newspapers around the world. It has since been called by *Lens Magazine* "the most reproduced photograph in the history of photography," according to Richard Pearson of the *Washington Post*.

The portrait of Churchill catapulted Karsh to international success as a portrait photographer. Afterward, the Canadian magazine *Saturday Night* (some sources say the Canadian government) paid his way to London, England, so that he could photograph other British wartime leaders. Next he picked up an assignment from *Life* magazine to photograph American political leaders in Washington. In 1946, Karsh published many of the resulting photographs in his first book, *Faces of Destiny*.

Other books Karsh published during his career include *Portraits of Greatness*, which saw print in 1959, *Faces of Our Time*, published in 1971, and 1976's *Karsh Portraits*. His photographs have also been added to the permanent collections of some of the great museums of the world, including the National Portrait Gallery of London, the Museums of Modern Art in New York and Tokyo, and the Metropolitan Museum of Art in New York. In addition, several countries have based postage stamps on his portraits of political leaders, including those of Canadian Prime Minister William Lyon Mackenzie King, Queen Elizabeth of Britain, and Konrad Adenauer of Germany.

Other famous portraits by Karsh include renowned playwright George Bernard Shaw, Supreme Commander of the Allied Expeditionary Force, General Dwight D. Eisenhower; author Ernest Hemingway, and painter Georgia O'Keeffe. He also photographed U. S. Presidents Harry S. Truman and John F. Kennedy, Russian leader Nikita Khrushchev, Cu-

ban leader Fidel Castro, writers Robert Frost, John Updike, and Norman Mailer, and artists Pablo Picasso and Andy Warhol.

Karsh preferred to photograph his subjects in formal studio settings, with careful attention paid to lighting. His techniques resulted in powerful, almost statuesque portraits in which the faces of his subjects emerged from dark backgrounds looking thoughtful and serious. Photographing his subjects was only the final stage of a process that began long before he met his subjects. Before his subjects entered his studio, Karsh studied them thoroughly, reading biographies, newspaper articles, and interviews. If possible, he tried to get to know people who knew his subjects so that he could more easily engage them in conversation.

In the last decade of his life, Karsh moved back to Boston, where he lived until his death. He retired in the early 1990s, and President Clinton was the subject of his final portrait. Karsh died on July 13, 2002, at the age of 93 after surgery for undisclosed reasons in Boston. His first wife, Solange Gauthier, died in 1961. He is survived by his second wife, Estrellita Maria Nachbar, and his brother, Salim Karsh. **Sources:** *Independent* (London), July 15, 2002, p. 14; *Los Angeles Times*, July 14, 2002, p. B16; *New York Times*, July 15, 2002, p. B7; *Washington Post*, July 14, 2002, p. C6.

—*Michael Belfiore*

Ken Kesey

Born Ken Elton Kesey, September 17, 1935, in La Junta, CO; died November 10, 2001, in Eugene, OR. Author and 1960s counter–culture figure. Best known as the author of the novel *One Flew Over the Cuckoo's Nest*, Kesey's life, like his best fiction, epitomized anti–authoritarianism.

Kesey was born in La Junta, Colorado, to Fred and Geneva Smith Kesey, both dairy farmers. In 1943, the family moved to Springfield, Oregon, a suburb of Eugene. Fred Kesey later founded the Eugene Farmers Cooperative. Growing up in a prosperous suburban setting, Kesey thrived in outdoor activities such as hunting and fishing, swimming and river rafting. He also boxed and wrestled. He was a star high school football player and wrestler and voted "most likely to succeed" by his graduating class of 1953. Kesey went on to attend the University of Oregon. In 1956, he married his high school sweetheart, Norma Faye Haxby, and graduated from college a year later.

After graduating, Kesey spent a brief time in Hollywood where he managed to gain bit parts in a few films, but he soon moved north to Palo Alto to attend Stanford University's graduate writing program. Kesey's instructors in the program were Wallace Stegner and Malcolm Cowley; his classmates included Larry McMurtry, Wendell Berry, Robert Stone, Ernest Gaines, and Ken Babbs.

In 1959 Kesey volunteered as a guinea pig for government-sponsored LSD experiments at the Menlo Park Veterans Administration Hospital. The experience forever changed his perception of society and his place in it. He later became a night attendant in the hospital's mental ward. The job gave him access to the hallucinogen and allowed him to finish a manuscript, titled "Zoo," about beatniks in San Francisco's North Beach neighborhood. "Zoo," as well as an earlier novel, "End of Autumn," went unpublished, but the job and the drug experience provided the impetus for his best-known work: *One Flew Over the Cuckoo's Nest*. The book, published in 1962, is a story about a con man who fakes mental illness to avoid prison and instead winds up fighting a losing battle against a tyrannical nurse. The story is narrated by a schizophrenic patient, Chief Bromden.

One Flew Over the Cuckoo's Nest enjoyed an incarnation as a Broadway play starring Kirk Douglas, and was made into one of the most successful films in Hollywood history in 1975. However, Kesey earned relatively little from these latter endeavors. He was excluded from any creative role in the film by director Milos Forman, and thereafter vowed never to see the film. He even criticized the choice of Jack Nicholson as the lead.

Kesey's next novel, *Sometimes a Great Notion*, was published in 1964. It tells the story of the Stamper family, who are loggers and individualists. This, too, was made into a film, titled *Never Give An Inch*, starring Paul Newman and Henry Fonda. Though it is overshadowed in popular culture by *Cuckoo's Nest*, *Sometimes a Great Notion* is considered by most critics to be Kesey's best novel.

The year 1964 was also when Kesey began organizing the acid tests in San Francisco, public parties in rented halls that featured music by the Grateful Dead, then known as the Warlocks, and punch laced with LSD, which at that time was not illegal. Later that year Kesey and his friends, known as the Merry Pranksters, set out on a cross-country trip in a 1939 school bus painted in the swirling, colorful, psychedelic style of the era. The destination sign on the front of the bus read "Furthur," which became the name for the bus. On the back another sign read "Weird Load." The Pranksters's ostensible destination was the New York World's Fair, but the trip was really about spreading anarchic fun across the United States. To drive the bus, Kesey had enlisted the legendary Neal Cassady, prototype for the character of Dean Moriarty in Jack Kerouac's novel, *On the Road*. The cross-country trip, the acid tests, and Kesey's subsequent legal problems were chronicled by Tom Wolfe in *The Electric Kool-Aid Acid Test*.

In New York City, Kesey met with Kerouac and poet Allen Ginsburg. The pranksters then headed upstate to meet with Timothy Leary, a former Harvard professor and another well-known advocate for LSD. When they arrived, Leary was involved in a three-day meditation and their meeting was brief.

Back in San Francisco Kesey took up where he had left off, and the acid tests became bigger events than before. They gained such notoriety—LSD itself had become popular—that the drug was made illegal. Kesey himself ran into trouble with the law when he was arrested for possession of marijuana. To avoid prison Kesey faked his suicide in January of 1966 and traveled to Mexico with some of the Pranksters. He was rearrested in 1968 when he returned to the United States and served five months in the San Mateo county jail.

In 1973 Kesey published *Kesey's Garage Sale*, a collection of letters and nonfiction pieces. In 1974 he and Babbs cofounded a magazine, *Spit in the Ocean*. *Demon Box*, another nonfiction collection, came out in 1986. In 1990 he published *The Furthur Inquiry*, a chronicle of the Prankster bus trip, and the children's tale, *Little Tricker the Squirrel Meets Big Double Bear*. Another children's book followed in 1991, *The Sea Lion: A Story of the Cliff People*. He published his third novel, *Sailor Song*, in 1992. Over the years critics had contended that Kesey's extensive drug use was responsible for his limited fiction output. Kesey acknowledged that drugs may have slowed down his output, but he thought his fame was more responsible. "Famous isn't good for a writer," he said in a 1990 Associated Press interview, as reported at CNN.com. "You don't observe well when you're being observed." Many felt his son Jed's 1984 death in a van crash also slowed his writing. In 1994 Kesey co–wrote *Last Round Up,* a book about Oregon rodeo riders, with Babbs.

Toward the end of his life, Kesey had been ill with diabetes and cancer of the liver. Two weeks before his death at the age of 66 he underwent surgery to remove 40 percent of his liver. He is survived by his wife; son, Zane; daughters Shannon and Sunshine; his mother, brother, and three grandchildren. **Sources:** CNN.com, http://www.cnn.com/2001/US/11/10/ken.kesey.obit.ap/index.html (November 12, 2001); *Los Angeles Times,* November 11, 2001, p. A1; *New York Times,* November 11, 2001, p. 47; *Times* (London), November 12, 2001, p. 19.

—Frank Caso

John Knowles

Born September 16, 1926, in Fairmont, WV; died November 29, 2001, in Ft. Lauderdale, FL. Author. As the author of the best–selling novel *A Separate Peace* in 1959, John Knowles won the William Faulker Foundation Award as well as the Rosenthal Award presented by the National Institute of Arts and Letters, and the book was made into a movie by Paramount Pictures in 1972. The novel was the first that Knowles wrote, and although he later wrote eight others, along with several nonfiction pieces and a collection of short stories, his later work never matched the popularity of his initial effort.

A Separate Peace concerns boys coming of age in a boarding school in World War II New England, and has found enduring resonance in young people throughout the world for decades. In fact, it was named one of the best English–language works of literature of all time in a poll at Radcliffe College conducted in 1989. The book has also been required reading for millions of junior high and high school students. *Washington Post* critic Paul Piazza wrote of the novel in 1981 that it "movingly chronicled the struggle between two adolescents who, too young to enlist, discover the enemy not in Europe or the Pacific, but in themselves."

A pivotal moment in the book comes when a character named Phineas falls out of a tree and breaks his leg. Readers of the book have argued for decades about whether another character, Forrester, deliberately caused Phineas to fall. Knowles refused to respond to the question and took the answer to his grave.

Knowles was born in West Virginia in 1926. His father was a vice president at the Consolidated Coal Company, and he sent Knowles to a boarding school in New Hampshire when he was 15 years old. This school, Phillips Exeter Academy, was to form the basis for the fictional boarding school, Devon, detailed in *A Separate Peace.*

Knowles summed up his experience at Phillips Exeter Academy in the school's magazine years later, and was quoted by CNN.com. The school, said Knowles, "picked me up out of the hills of West Virginia, forced me to learn to study, tossed me into Yale, and inspired me to write a book, my novel *A Separate Peace,* which, eschewing false modesty, made me quite famous and financially secure." Knowles graduated from Exeter in 1945, and immediately enlisted in the United States Army Air Corps's Aviation Cadet Program. He was discharged eight months later, after qualifying as a pilot. He went on to Yale University, from which he graduated in 1949.

In 1950, Knowles landed a job as a reporter and drama critic for the *Hartford Courant.* He stayed at this position until 1952. Afterward, he traveled around Europe, where he met author and playwright Thornton Wilder. Wilder became a mentor to Knowles, suggesting that he base his first novel on his strongest memories.

Knowles returned to the United States in 1955, and the following year, took a job as associate editor at the New York–based magazine *Holiday* while working on the book that was to become *A Separate Peace.* He also helped to pay the bills during this time by working as a freelance writer. He remained at *Holiday* until 1959, when *A Separate Peace* was published in England. The novel was rejected by every major publisher in the United States before Knowles sold it to a London publisher, Secker and Warburg. Rave reviews finally convinced Macmillan to publish the book in the United States in 1960, and it eventually sold more than eight million copies.

The 1960s found Knowles at the University of North Carolina and at Princeton University as a writer–in–residence. He continued to write and publish books, including several novels. In the 1980s, Knowles moved to Fort Lauderdale. There he took a position as a creative writing teacher at Florida Atlantic University in Boca Raton.

Knowles returned to the setting of his first book in the 1981 novel *Peace Breaks Out.* He published his last novel, called *The Private Life of Axie Reed,* in

1986. His last published book was *Backcasts: Memories and Recollections of Seventy Years as a Sportsman*, published in 1993.

Although none of his subsequent books matched the popularity or critical acclaim of his first, Knowles told an interviewer that he didn't mind. He said of *A Separate Peace*, quoted in the *New York Times*, "It's paid the bills for 30 years. It has made my career possible. Unlike most writers, I don't have to do anything else to make a living."

Knowles died on November 29, 2001, at the age of 75 in Fort Lauderdale, Florida, after a short illness. He is survived by his sisters, Dorothy Maxwell and Marjorie Johnson; and his brother, James. **Sources:** CNN.com, http://www.cnn.com/2001/SHOWBIZ/books/11/29/obit.knowles.ap/index.html (November 30, 2001); *Los Angeles Times*, December 1, 2001, p. B20; *New York Times*, December 1, 2001, p. A25; *Times* (London), December 21, 2001, p. 19; *Washington Post*, December 1, 2001, p. B7.

—*Michael Belfiore*

Spyros Kyprianou

Born October 28, 1932, in Limassol, Cyprus; died of pelvic cancer, March 12, 2002, in Nicosia, Cyprus. Politician. Spyros Kyprianou, Cyprus's former president, was a leading political figure on the Mediterranean island nation for a number of years. Of Greek Cypriot heritage, he opposed concessions to Cyprus's Turkish minority after militant Turk Cypriots created a separate republic on the island in 1974. The situation remained unresolved at the time of Kyprianou's passing.

Born in 1932 in Limassol, one of Cyprus's chief ports, Kyprianou traveled to Britain as a young man to study economics at the City of London College and later became a lawyer. The charismatic leader of the Orthodox Church of Cyprus, Archbishop Makarios, made Kyprianou, at age of just 20, his secretary in London. At the time, the isle was a British possession, but moving toward independence. Makarios hoped for "enosis," or union with mainland Greece, and Kyprianou's duty was to shore up British support toward this goal. In the late 1950s, he traveled extensively on behalf of Cypriot politics, meeting with Greek allies in Athens and with United Nations delegates in New York City. In 1960,

Cyprus attained its independence, and Makarios became its first elected president. Just 28 years old at the time, Kyprianou was named the country's minister of justice by his mentor. He then served as Cyprus's foreign minister until 1972, when his opposition to interference from Athens brought pressure on Makarios, who asked him to resign.

Meanwhile, the Mediterranean island was becoming a battleground between Greek and Turkish nationalist sentiments. Turk Cypriots remained dissatisfied with the political concessions granted to them in the constitution, and when a Greek–led coup ousted Makarios in the summer of 1974 and established a pro–enosis government, Turkey sent a military force to the island which seized its northern third. The Greek coup failed, but the Turkish action held. Makarios was restored to power and Kyprianou again served as his advisor; he also served on Cyprus's delegation to the United Nations. There, Kyprianou urged the General Assembly to condemn the partition of the island.

In 1976, Kyprianou founded Cyprus's Democratic Party, which won a majority of political offices in elections later that year. Kyprianou, as party chief, became president of the House of Representatives. When Makarios died in August of 1977, Kyprianou—under the terms of the constitution—was appointed to serve the remainder of Makarios's presidency. The political problems continued, however, and an extremist group kidnapped Kyprianou's 21–year–old son in December of 1977. His release, they asserted, would be linked to the release of Turkish political prisoners on Cyprus. Kyprianou rejected this term, and "won great popularity by refusing to negotiate," according to *New York Times* writer Paul Lewis, "saying he was ready to sacrifice his son but 'never my country.'" His son survived the kidnapping.

In the 1978 elections on Cyprus, Kyprianou ran unopposed for the presidency, and the following year agreed to meet with Turk Cypriot leader Rauf Denktash. A peace settlement was reached, with the island divided into a two–zone federal state, but subsequent talks faltered. By 1981 Kyprianou's Democratic Party was losing mainstream support, and problems with mainland Greece continued, especially when Kyprianou struck a political deal with a Communist group on Cyprus. After his 1983 re-election, however, Kyprianou moved toward reconciliation with Athens. He remained adamant about the Turk Cypriot claims. "Kyprianou resisted a new initiative by the U.N. Secretary–General, which laid down guidelines for a Cyprus settlement," the *Times* noted about this era. "His attitude prompted the resignation of his Foreign Minister and strong reactions from other political parties."

Kyprianou and his hard–line stance prompted Denktash to proclaim Turkish Republic of Northern Cyprus (TRNC) in November of 1983. Self–governing, it is recognized as legitimate only by mainland Turkey. Over the next few years, Kyprianou occasionally met with Denktash, but continued to reject United Nations peace proposals, a stance that eroded his political support at home. In 1987 Kyprianou suffered a heart attack and went to London for treatment. He lost his re–election bid for the presidency the next year.

Despite the setbacks, Kyprianou's eleven–year tenure as president of Cyprus was one that brought prosperity to the island and closer ties to Europe as well. In his post–presidential years, Kyprianou continued to argue against granting concessions to the TRNC, and even criticized his successor for what he viewed as far too conciliatory gestures. His name was ventured as a possible candidate for the presidency again in 1993, but he declined the offer to run. Ongoing talks at the time of his death in March of 2002 seemed more promising of a peaceful resolution of Cyprus's civil strife, for the island nation was compelled to resolve the problem before it could be admitted into the European Union. Kyprianou died on March 12, 2002, of pelvic cancer; he was 69. He is survived by his wife, Mimi Pagathrokliton, whom he wed in 1956, and two sons. **Sources:** *Chicago Tribune*, March 13, 2002, section 2, p. 9; *Los Angeles Times*, March 13, 2002, p. B10; *New York Times*, March 14, 2002, p. C13; *Times* (London), March 13, 2002, p. 32; *Washington Post*, March 13, 2002, p. B6.

—*Carol Brennan*

Ann Landers

Born Esther Pauline Friedman, July 4, 1918, in Sioux City, IA; died of cancer, June 22, 2002, in Chicago, IL. Advice columnist. Under the pen name "Ann Landers," Esther Lederer was the most read and beloved advice columnist in the world for 47 years. She broke the stereotype of the staid and moralizing advice columnist to dispense common–sense and sometimes controversial counsel to the confused masses in a down–to–earth manner. By the time she died, more than 90 million readers turned

to her column in 1,200 papers. John W. Madigan, chief executive officer and chairman of the *Chicago Tribune*, told CNN.com, "She helped people with her advice and made important contributions to society through the causes she supported."

Lederer was one of four daughters born to Abraham and Rebecca Friedman, Russian immigrants who eventually ended up owning a string of movie theaters. Lederer's closest companion while growing up was her twin sister Pauline Esther, born 17 minutes after Lederer. The twins were inseparable—dressing alike and sharing a bed. Once out of high school they both attended Morningside College in Sioux City where they co–wrote a gossip column called "The Campus Rats."

In 1939, the sisters dropped out of college and were married in a double ceremony. Esther married Jules William Lederer, the founder of Budget Rent–a–Car, and Pauline married prominent businessman Morton Phillips. Lederer spent the next 16 years raising their daughter, Margo, and working as a volunteer for various organizations. She was an active member of the Democratic Party, serving for a time as the county party chairman in Eau Claire, Wisconsin. She also volunteered for the Red Cross.

In 1955, the Lederers relocated to Chicago. Looking for something to put her energy into, Lederer felt she could be of help to the advice columnist of the *Chicago Sun–Times* and offered her assistance. When she contacted the newspaper she found out that the original columnist had recently died and that a contest was being held to find a replacement.

Lederer entered the competition and set herself to the task of answering a small batch of letters. Her first questions ranged from the legal to the religious, and Lederer called upon several resources at her disposal to help sort them out. Her resources included Justice William O. Douglas of the Supreme Court and Rev. Theodore M. Hesburgh, the president of Notre Dame. When she returned the letters with the accompanying answers, the editors thought she had fabricated her sources. She assured them that they were valid and a few days later she was offered the job as columnist for "Ask Ann Landers." She wrote for the *Sun–Times* until 1987 when she moved her column to the competing *Chicago Tribune*.

In the beginning, the letters that Lederer received reflected the more conservative times. She often answered questions about dating, hygiene, or simple legal matters. But she didn't back away from the hard questions. One letter she received during the

'50s dealt with the issue of homosexuality. Her column published the letter and her answer, but not without a little controversy. A newspaper in St. Joseph, Michigan, refused to publish the column. Not one to be silenced, Lederer explained to the paper that they would lose readership when people flocked to buy the competing paper that was publishing this particular article. As she explained in a quote in the *New York Times*, "From then on, boy, that St. Joe paper printed every damn word I wrote."

Lederer often used her column to support causes in which she believed. She opposed the actions in Vietnam, and supported abortion rights and gun control. As a result of her column, President Nixon signed a bill that created the National Cancer Act, allocating $100 million to cancer research. Her readers had responded by the hundreds of thousands to her plea to cut out the column discussing this issue and send it to the White House.

Lederer faced some of her own controversies during her tenure as the world's advice columnist. Not long after Lederer began her column, her sister, Pauline, took up writing one of her own under the pen name Abigail Van Buren. As the creator of Dear Abby, Pauline competed for the same market as her sister. Pauline's actions caused a rift between the sisters that was not healed until many years later.

Other moments of embarrassment for Lederer included having to admit that she recycled old letters for newer columns and adding her own remarks to a letter from a reader regarding fraudulent charities. She also had to publicly apologize for calling Pope John Paul II a "polack" in a *New Yorker* interview, according to the *New York Times*.

Perhaps the hardest issue Lederer ever had to broach was the disintegration of her marriage of more than 30 years to Jules Lederer. She had dedicated herself so fully to her husband that she had the lining of her coats stitched with the phrase "Jules's Wife." In 1975, Jules left her for another woman. In response, Lederer removed the lining from her coats and wrote the most personal column of her career. The response from her readership was an astounding 35,000 letters of support, all of which she kept.

While Lederer changed her attitudes regarding marriage and sexuality as society changed, she still stuck by a few old standards. Up until she died, she composed her columns on an old typewriter. Often she would soak in the bath in her Lake Shore Drive apartment for hours, tapping out replies. She read all the letters she answered, sifting through hundreds that had been pre–selected from the thousands she received daily.

Lederer was diagnosed with multiple myeloma, a form of bone marrow cancer, in early 2002 and refused treatment. She died on June 22, 2002, at age 83 taking the name Ann Landers—to which she owned all the rights—with her. Divorced from Jules Lederer in 1975, she never remarried. She is survived by her sister, Pauline; her daughter, Margo Howard, who writes as Dear Prudence for the online publication *Slate;* three grandchildren, and four great–grandchildren. **Sources:** CNN.com, http://www.cnn.com/2002/US/06/23/ann.landers.obit/index.html (June 24, 2002); *Los Angeles Times,* June 23, 2002, p. A1; *New York Times,* June 24, 2002, p. B7; *People,* July 8, 2002, pp. 67-68; *Times* (London), June 24, 2002, p. 36.

— *Eve M. B. Hermann*

Peggy Lee

Born Norma Deloris Egstrom, May 27, 1920, in Jamestown, ND; died of a heart attack, January 23, 2002, in Los Angeles, CA. Singer, songwriter, arranger, and actress. Sultry, cool and sexy, at the height of her popularity in the 1950s and 1960s Peggy Lee presented an image of the modern torch singer: somewhat heartbroken, yet iconoclastic and unbowed. Though her career waned after 1970 her output, nevertheless, was stupendous; she made more than 700 recordings and recorded more than 60 albums.

Lee was born in Jamestown, North Dakota. Her mother, Selma, died when she was four years old, and Lee was physically abused by her stepmother, while her alcoholic father, Marvin, did little to intervene. Music provided an escape for the young girl. She sang in her church choir and her school glee club. By age 14 she was singing professionally at a local radio station. From there she moved on to station WDAY in Fargo, North Dakota; it was the Fargo station manager who changed her name to Peggy Lee.

After graduating from high school, Lee bought a train ticket to Hollywood, arriving with $18. She secured a few brief nightclub engagements, but ended up working as a waitress and a carnival spieler. It was at this time that Lee developed her trademark soft, sultry sound, lowering her voice instead of raising it to be heard above the din of the nightclub audiences. Little work left her no choice and Lee returned to WDAY. From there she struck out to a less ambitious locale: she moved to Minneapolis where she caught on with Will Osborne's band.

Lee's big break came in 1941 when Benny Goodman heard her performing in the Ambassador West Hotel in Chicago. He signed her to replace Helen Forrest as the vocalist in his band. Despite a rocky beginning with the Goodman band, stardom came to Lee in 1942 with her first hit, "Why Don't You Do Right?" It was one of the United States's best-selling records that year. She also had recorded "Blues in the Night" and "The Way You Look Tonight" with Goodman. Lee left the Goodman band in 1943 and married Dave Barbour, the band's guitarist. Their daughter, Nikki, was born in 1944.

Striking off on their own, Lee and Barbour collaborated on a number of songs and performed and recorded together. Her hits in her post–Goodman period included "Golden Earrings" and "Mañana." Although Lee and Barbour were divorced in 1951—their split-up was caused by his alcoholism—they continued to be friends. Married four times, it was Barbour whom Lee described as the love of her life. In fact, discussing her first marriage in a 1984 *People* interview she said, "I finally understood what Sophie Tucker used to say: You have to have your heart broken at least once to sing a love song." They continued to write songs together after the divorce, and even planned to reconcile after Lee's fourth marriage ended. The reconciliation was never to be: Barbour died prematurely in 1965. Lee was also married to actor Brad Dexter in 1955, actor Dewey Martin from 1956–59, and percussionist Jack Del Rio from 1964–65.

Lee had a brief film career. She made a number of cameo appearances beginning with *Stagedoor Canteen* in 1943. She also filmed a number of musical shorts with Barbour. She had a minor role in the 1950 Bing Crosby film, *Mr. Music,* in which Lee and Crosby sang a duet. In 1953 she had a featured role in the remake of *The Jazz Singer* that starred Danny Thomas. Ironically, the height of her acting career was also her last movie. Lee was nominated for an Academy Award for best supporting actress for her performance as an alcoholic blues singer in the 1955 film *Pete Kelly's Blues.* Years later she admitted, as quoted in the *Los Angeles Times,* "I loved acting, but my agents never brought me another script. I was

worth a lot more to them on the road." Perhaps the film she is most closely associated with is the 1952 animated Disney feature *Lady and the Tramp.* Lee supplied the voices for several of the characters, co–wrote one of the songs, and sang three songs for the film. One of the characters was even named for her. Years later, when Disney reissued the film on videocassette, Lee sued for royalties and was awarded $2.3 million in 1992.

Lee was nominated for 12 Grammy Awards, garnering her first two nominations in 1958 for "Fever," perhaps the song that best epitomizes the sultry Lee style. Other nominations included 1959's "Alright, Okay, You Win." In 1960 Lee garnered three nominations for her performances of the songs "I'm Gonna Go Fishin'" and "Heart" and the album *Latin a la Lee.* She won her first Grammy in 1969 with the Lieber–Stoller song "Is That All There Is?" Her second Grammy came in 1995 when she was given a Lifetime Achievement award. She had already received the Pied Piper Award in 1990, the lifetime achievement award of the American Society of Composers, Authors and Publishers (ASCAP).

Early in her career Lee performed on the radio, and from 1946 until the 1990s she made numerous television appearances, including her own specials. One of her few professional setbacks came in 1983 when *Peg,* her musical autobiography, flopped on Broadway after just 13 previews and five performances. Undaunted, in 1989 she published her autobiography, *Miss Peggy Lee.*

Among the people with whom she collaborated as a songwriter were Duke Ellington, Cy Coleman, and Quincy Jones. On her recordings she collaborated with George Shearing, Benny Carter, and Frank Sinatra. Sinatra even conducted the Nelson Riddle orchestra for her 1957 album, *The Man I Love.*

Beginning with double pneumonia in 1961, Lee was troubled by many ailments. These included diabetes and glandular problems that brought on heart trouble. In 1985 she underwent double–bypass heart surgery. In 1987 she fractured her pelvis in a fall. Yet she managed to recover and go back on the road to perform. If need be, she took an oxygen tent and a wheelchair with her. Her career ended in 1998 after she suffered a stroke that impaired her speech.

Lee died on January 21, 2002, of a heart attack; she was 81. She is survived by her daughter, three grandchildren, and three great–grandchildren.

Sources: *Los Angeles Times,* January 23, 2002, p. A1, p. A8; *New York Times,* January 23, 2002, p. A21; *People,* February 4, 2002, p. 77; *Times* (London), http://www.thetimes.co.uk (January 23, 2002); *Washington Post,* January 23, 2002, p. B6.

—*Frank Caso*

Astrid Lindgren

Born Astrid Anna Emilia Ericsson, November 14, 1907, in Vimmerby, Sweden; died of a viral infection, January 28, 2002, in Stockholm, Sweden. Children's book author. As a writer, Astrid Lindgren rose to prominence as the creator of Pippi Longstocking, the adventurous heroine in a series of children's books. The inaugural installment, *Pippi Longstocking,* which was first published in 1945, was immediately embraced by Swedish children but derided by adults because of the character's anti–authoritarian approach to life. Left to raise herself, nine–year–old Pippi appealed to younger audiences because, as the first book begins, according to the *New York Times,* "there was no one to tell her to go to bed when she was having the most fun, and no one who could make her take cod liver oil when she much preferred caramel candy." Lindgren's books were translated into more than 75 languages and sold in the millions.

Lindgren was the second of four children born to Samuel August and Hanna Jonsson Ericsson. The couple were tenant farmers at Nas, a 500–year–old farm in southern Sweden. Lindgren grew up in a red house that was built in the middle of apple orchards. "Rocks and trees were as close to us as living beings, and nature protected and nurtured our playing and our dreaming," she wrote in her 1973 memoir, as quoted in the *New York Times.* "Whatever our imagination could call forth was enacted in the land around us—all fairy tales, all adventures we invented or read about or heard about, all of it happened there, and only there. Even our songs and prayers had their places in surrounding nature."

Lindgren remained at Nas until 1926, when she became pregnant. Unmarried, she moved to Copenhagen, and gave birth to her son, Lars. She later moved to Stockholm, where she accepted a secretarial job at the Royal Automobile Club. In 1931, she married Sture Lindgren, a man with whom she worked. While publishing stories for the magazine *Countryside Christmas* throughout the 1930s, as well as a book, *Twenty–Five Automobile Tours in Sweden,* in 1939, Lindgren didn't actually embark upon a career as an author of children's books until 1941. Her second child, daughter Karin, was bedridden with pneumonia and implored her mother to tell her stories. When Lindgren asked Karin what story she should tell, the daughter spontaneously replied, "Tell about Pippi Langstrump (Longstocking)," according to a *New Yorker* anecdote recounted in the *New York Times.* "I didn't ask her who Pippi Longstocking was. I just began the story, and since it was a strange name it turned out to be a strange girl as well."

Pippi—whose full name is Pippilotta Delicatessa Windowshade Mackrelmint Efraim's daughter Longstocking—wears unmatched socks, oversized shoes, and sports trademark pigtails that stick out from both sides of her head. Her mother is dead and her father is a sailor lost at sea, although Pippi is convinced he is stranded on a South Sea island, where he is king of all the cannibals. Her father had left her a trunk of gold pieces with which she provides for her needs in the comically decrepit Villa Villekulla. She also has a horse and monkey. She boasts coarse manners and superhuman strength with which she both amazes and exasperates her more "normal" friends, Tommy and Annika. Published in 1945, *Pippi Longstocking* was followed by the sequels *Pippi Goes on Board* in 1946, *Pippi in the South Seas* in 1948, *Pippi on the Run* in 1971, as well as several other adventures featuring such characters as Karlsson–on–the–Roof, Master Detective Bill Bergson, Emil, Mio, Mischievous Meg, Ronja Rovardotter, and the Children of Troublemaker Street, most of which were never translated into English.

From 1946 to 1970, Lindgren worked as editor–in–chief at the publishing house Raben and Sjorgen. In the 1970s, Lindgren became an outspoken advocate of tax reform in Sweden. While she had been a member of the Social Democrat Party, she protested that she and other Swedish artists were being taxed unfairly. Prior to the 1976 election, she published a satirical editorial in which she wrote that the combination of local and national taxes equaled more than 102 percent of her income. The article was credited for helping to end more than 40 years of Social Democrat rule in Sweden. The subsequent ruling party rolled back taxes. In addition to tax reform, Lindgren concerned herself with children's rights and the humane treatment of farm animals. Her work on behalf of the latter resulted in her receiving the Albert Schweitzer award from the Animal Welfare Institute.

Lindgren's died on January 28, 2002, in Stockholm, Sweden, at the age of 94 of a viral infection. Sture Lindgren died in 1952, and her son, Lars, died in 1986. Lindgren is survived by her sister, Stina Hergin; daughter, Karin; seven grandchildren, and eleven great–grandchildren. She is immortalized by a statue in Stockholm's Tenerlunden park. **Sources:** *Guardian* (London, England), January 29, 2002, p. 18; *Independent* (London, England), January 29, 2002, p. 6; *New York Times*, January 29, 2002, p. B9; *Washington Post*, January 29, 2002, p. C1.

—*Bruce Walker*

Lisa Lopes

Born May 27, 1971, in Philadelphia, PA; died in a car accident, April 26, 2002, in La Ceiba, Honduras. R&B singer and rapper. Lisa "Left Eye" Lopes made her name as a musician and performer with the hit trio TLC, but where she got her nickname was something of a puzzle. According to one source, the moniker came from a boyfriend who noticed that Lopes's left eye was slightly larger than the right. In other accounts, the flamboyant performer came to be known as "Left Eye" when she replaced the left lens of a pair of spectacles with a condom to promote safe sex. In any case, Lopes was a much–loved figure in modern music, dominating the hip–hop and R&B charts for a decade as part of the group TLC. Her untimely death at age 30 in a car accident drew headlines worldwide.

Born into a close–knit family, Lopes came by her musical leanings early in life. Her father, who died when Lopes was 17, was an authoritarian figure who also encouraged young Lisa to sing; the girl's mother, Wanda, lived close by her daughter even after TLC shot to fame. After the family moved to Atlanta, Georgia, the teenage Lopes was already working for an rhythm–and–blues group when she was approached by Ian Burke, a talent scout, to audition for a new group, one described by a *New York Times* article as "streetwise, approachable girls." Lopes fit that description perfectly, and TLC was born. Lopes, the "L" of the title, joined Tionne "T–Boz" Watkins and Rozonda "Chilli" Jones; the trio's 1992 debut album produced three Top 10 singles: "What About Your Friends," "Ain't 2 Proud 2 Beg," and "Baby–Baby–Baby."

Audiences quickly took to TLC's high–energy style, lively choreography, and arresting costumes; at the same time, the group endeavored to educate their young fans with lyrics that encouraged self–reliance and made reference to such issues as crime and AIDS. With the success of TLC's two subsequent albums, *CrazySexyCool* and *Fanmail*, the trio surpassed the Supremes as the best–selling female group in terms of album sales. (Diana Ross and company still reigned supreme in terms of number–one hits.)

Even with TLC's success, there was some discord in the group. Some of it was instigated by the outspoken Lopes, known as the "crazy" member of the company. In one incident, the trio separated in 2000 after Lopes challenged her bandmates to produce solo works to see who was the best performer. (Lopes's own contribution, *Supernova*, was not kindly received by critics.) Other conflicts came from monetary matters; in 1995, with the group still in top form, TLC filed for Chapter 7 bankruptcy protection and endured battles over royalties with their record company and management.

Perhaps Lopes's most dramatic non–musical encounter came in 1994 when she was convicted of first–degree arson after the mansion she shared with her ex–boyfriend, Atlanta Falcons player Andre Rison, burned to the ground. An avowed alcoholic, Lopes admitted to setting the flame that destroyed the million–dollar estate; she was sentenced to five years of probation and ordered into an alcohol treatment program. Lopes and Rison reconciled and split numerous times during their tempestuous relationship.

But there was another side to the "crazy" Lopes. She worked tirelessly for children's causes, one of which had brought the singer to Honduras in 2002. In that nation—where Lopes owned a condominium that provided frequent respite—she set up a literacy program and a child–development center. Likewise, she joined forces with an organization that provided services to youths in impoverished Sudan. On a more personal note, Lopes took under her wing (and later adopted) an eight–year–old girl named Snow, who was the daughter of a friend going through difficult times. A musical mentor, Lopes was guiding the way of a new group, Egypt, some of whose members were with the singer during her fateful car ride.

According to reports, Lopes was at the wheel of a rented Mitsubishi Montero that day. The car, built to carry seven, held ten passengers. After passing a truck on a two–lane highway, the Montero careened off the road and flipped several times before coming to rest upside down. Lopes, who was thrown from the vehicle, suffered fatal injuries to her head and chest. She died at the age of 30. The other nine passengers survived, though some were treated for injuries.

Hip–hop fans met the news with dismay, particularly in the wake of the plane–crash death of another young R&B talent, Aaliyah, the previous August. A funeral procession in Lithonia, Georgia, turned into a mob scene when thousands of fans flocked to surround the hearse. The singer's white casket was engraved with lyrics she performed as part of TLC: "Dreams are hopeless aspirations, in hopes of coming true/Believe in yourself, the rest is up to me and you."

Among those in attendance at her funeral and memorial service were her TLC bandmates, Rison, and several notables from the music industry. Antonio Reid, president of TLC's label Arista Records, acknowledged that the petite performer enjoyed a larger–than–life reputation. "She was difficult for the right reasons," he was quoted in a CNN.com report. "Her creativity never stopped. Lisa, your exuberance will be missed, your passion will be missed." Watkins and Thomas told CNN.com, "We have truly lost our sister. She did so much for us," Egypt singer Sophia Gibson told a *People* reporter, "She was like an angel." Lopes is survived by her mother, brother, sister, and adopted daughter. **Sources:** CNN.com, http://www.cnn.com/2002/SHOWBIZ/Music/05/02/lopes.funeral.ap/index.html (May 2, 2002); *Los Angeles Times*, April 27, 2002, p. B20; *New York Times*, April 27, 2002, p. A10; *People*, May 13, 2002, pp. 69-71; *Times* (London), April 27, 2002; *Washington Post*, April 27, 2002, p. B7.

—Susan Salter

Stanley Marcus

Born April 20, 1905, in Dallas, TX; died January 22, 2002, in Dallas, TX. Retailer. Stanley Marcus elevated the American retail experience to a stratosphere of luxury unparalleled in its era. For decades Marcus ran "The Store," as he deemed his family's Neiman Marcus company, and single–handedly made the Texas retailer an unlikely paragon of taste and style. His influence continued long after his official retirement in 1975, as Neiman Marcus continued to set a standard pursued by its competitors well into the next century.

Marcus was a colorful character and known as a consummate salesperson. Nicknamed "Mr. Stanley," he was one of Dallas, Texas's pre–eminent citizens

and a champion of the arts. He was born in 1905, the eldest of four boys in a Jewish family of retailers. Two years later, his father founded Neiman Marcus with an aunt and uncle in Dallas, and the store thrived.

Sent East for his education, Marcus failed the Harvard College entrance exam and was forced to enroll at Amherst College for a year. There, a fraternity revoked its pledge offer when they learned he was Jewish; irate over the incident, Marcus told his parents that he wanted to come home and enter the University of Texas, but they refused. He transferred to Harvard the next year, finishing in 1925 and earning a graduate business degree a year later.

As a young man, Marcus dreamed of a literary career in New York publishing, but his parents were once more adamant, and he returned to Dallas to enter the family business. He began at Neiman Marcus as a stock boy, but quickly advanced to the posts of secretary, treasurer, and director. Marcus proved an enthusiastic, creative salesperson and even keener marketing genius. He launched a series of weekly fashion shows, said to be the first ever in an American department store, and Neiman Marcus was also the first of its kind to carry designer apparel, which had customarily been available only in a few select boutiques or through designer showrooms.

When Marcus started his career, Dallas was awash in money from newly minted Texas cattle and oil barons, and as he rose through the executive ranks his push to make Neiman Marcus the premier luxury–goods emporium dovetailed perfectly with the times. The store's "emphasis on quality, luxury, and rarity appealed to newly rich customers who were uncertain in matters of taste," explained *New York Times* writer Eric Pace. "It suggested that they could buy quantities of costly Neiman Marcus goods with the comforting certainty that everything was truly first class."

Marcus advanced to the duties of president and chief executive officer in 1950. The Neiman Marcus empire expanded quickly, and became the first retailer outside of the New York area to advertise in national magazines such as *Vogue*. Realizing that celebrity tie–ins served as priceless advertising, Marcus offered to provide the inaugural gowns for First Ladies Mamie Eisenhower and Lady Bird Johnson. Neiman Marcus also supplied the bridesmaids's dresses for Grace Kelly's 1956 wedding to Prince Rainier of Monaco. Again, Marcus's talent for marketing helped make Neiman Marcus a pioneer in its field: in 1957 the store launched its "Fortnights," in which a different country or culture was showcased for two weeks with relevant merchandise and cultural events around Dallas. Over the next decade, more Texas stores were added, and profits soared: sales were $20 million in 1950 when Marcus took over, and had more than tripled by 1969 to $62 million.

In 1969, the Marcus family sold the company to a larger retailing conglomerate, but Marcus and his relatives retained a controlling amount of stock. By the 1980s, Neiman Marcus had become famous for its annual Christmas catalog, another example of "Mr. Stanley's" talent for promotion: it offered items of unrestrained extravagance, such as his and her airplanes, helicopters, submarines—the undersea vessels sold for $20 million—live camels, and black Angus steer.

Marcus authored two autobiographies that detailed his business sense and became must-reads for those in the retail industry: *Minding the Store,* published in 1974, and *Quest for the Best,* which appeared five years later. He formally retired in 1975, but began his own consulting business with a marketing focus soon afterward. A patron of the arts in Dallas, Marcus was also slightly infamous for his rather liberal views in a politically conservative city. When he publicly supported the 1960 presidential campaign of Democrat John F. Kennedy, the company received scores of irate letters from Neiman Marcus customers demanding that their charge accounts be closed in protest; Marcus answered each letter personally. In 1966, three teenage boys were expelled from a Dallas public high school because they had long hair and the court case made national headlines; Marcus supported them on constitutional grounds. Leon Harris, one of Marcus's competitors in the Texas retail scene, once said that Marcus "stood politically for what he thought was right when a lot of people didn't," the *Dallas Morning News* quoted him as saying. "He has been courageous in political matters in a city of gutless wonders."

In his later years, Marcus wrote a weekly opinion piece for that same newspaper, and not long before his death accompanied one of his college-age granddaughters on a shopping jaunt around New York City. He had remarried in the late 1970s, after the 1978 death of his wife Mary Cantrell, a sportswear buyer for Neiman's before their 1932 union. Marcus died on January 22, 2002, at the age of 96. He is survived by his second wife, Linda Cumber Robinson; his children from his first marriage: daughters Jerrie and Wendy and a son, Richard; and 10 grandchildren and 12 great-grandchildren.

Sources: *Dallas Morning News,* January 23, 2002, p. 1A; *New York Times,* January 23, 2002, p. A16; *Times* (London), January 24, 2002, p. 21; *Washington Post,* January 24, 2002, p. C1.

—Carol Brennan

Spike Milligan

Born Terence Alan Milligan, April 16, 1918, in Ahmednagar, India; died February 27, 2002, in Rye, East Sussex, England. Comedy writer, performer, author, and poet. Spike Milligan was one of the great innovators of post–World War II British comedy whose influence and partnerships extended from Peter Sellers to the Monty Python troupe.

Milligan's father was a sergeant–major in the Royal Artillery and Milligan received his early education in India. Milligan first took to the stage as a six–year–old clown in a school performance in Poona. When the entire family returned to England in 1933, following his father's retirement from the army, the 15–year–old Milligan left school for a succession of menial jobs to help make ends meet. He never gave up hope of becoming an entertainer, though his interests in those days were musical. Milligan sang, played trumpet, and eventually had his own jazz band.

He saw military action during World War II in North Africa and Italy. During the Italian campaign in 1943, Milligan suffered shrapnel wounds in the leg and, most probably, a nervous breakdown—the first of ten. While recovering in Naples, Milligan began playing jazz guitar in the Bill Hall Trio, entertaining the troops. He also toured with the Ann Lenor Trio. Milligan eventually was given a medical discharge from the army.

Back in the United Kingdom he was first encouraged to write comedy by Jimmy Grafton, a scriptwriter for Derek Roy on a BBC radio show titled *Variety Bandbox.* The turning point in Milligan's career came when Grafton introduced him to Harry Secombe. Secombe then introduced Milligan to Sellers and Michael Bentine, and this quartet eventually came to be known as the Goons. They took their name from characters in the *Popeye* comic.

Soon the foursome managed to convince BBC radio producers of the value of their anarchic comedy. Their BBC radio show, *Those Crazy People,* made its debut in August of 1951 as a bimonthly program. A year later it was retitled *The Goon Show*. The now-weekly program literally turned British comedy on its head, lasting until January of 1960 for a total of 243 programs. However an attempt to transfer the program to television in 1960 failed. A final performance of *The Goon Show* was given in 1972 as part of the 50th anniversary of the BBC. The show catapulted its stars, especially Sellers, to fame, but it took its toll on Milligan. The strain of comedy writing and performing on a weekly basis for half the year was too much for him and led to another nervous breakdown, in which he tried to kill Sellers (though they remained friends thereafter) and led to the end of his marriage to June Marlowe in 1961, whom he had married in 1952. Yet Milligan, once he recovered from both traumas, never slowed down. Simultaneous with *The Goon Show*, Milligan worked on the television program, *A Show Called Fred*, for which he won the TV Writer of the Year Award in 1956. Milligan also created *The Idiot Weekly, Son of Fred*, and *Q5*.

In 1961 Milligan played Ben Gunn in a stage version of *Treasure Island*. The following year Milligan cowrote, with John Antrobus, *The Bedsitting Room*—a play about England after a nuclear war—in which he starred. In 1964 Milligan performed in an adaptation of Ivan Goncharov's nineteenth-century novel, *Oblomov*. The play evolved into a sendup and became a hit comedy under the title *Son of Oblomov*. In 1962 Milligan married Patricia Ridgeway; she died of cancer in 1978.

Milligan's influence was particularly seen in the British comedy show *Monty Python's Flying Circus*. Interviewed in a 1996 documentary, John Cleese, one of the Python troupe, admitted were it not for the groundbreaking work of *The Goon Show* there "would have been no Python," reported the *New York Times*. Milligan became a writer for *Monty Python's Flying Circus* and occasionally appeared in skits. He also appeared in two Python films: 1979's *The Life of Brian* and 1980's *Monty Python and the Holy Grail*. Milligan's other films were 1960's *The Running, Jumping and Standing Still Film*, 1969's *The Bedsitting Room*, 1973's *Adolf Hitler: My Part in His Downfall*, 1974's *The Three Musketeers*, 1977's *The Last Remake of Beau Geste*, and 1981's *History of the World, Part One*.

Milligan was a prolific writer. In addition to his numerous television, theater, and film scripts, he published 60 books, which included six volumes of war memoirs, two volumes of letters, poetry, novels, and the children's books *Milliganimals* (1968),

Milligan's Ark (1971), *Badjelly the Witch* (1973), and *Condensed Animals* (1991). His first book was the comic novel, *Puckoon,* about the partitioning of Ireland.

A 1956 British immigration law temporarily deprived the India-born Milligan of citizenship pending certification and in anger he applied for and received Irish citizenship. Despite that he was named honorary commander of the British Empire (CBE) in 1992 and made an honorary knight in 2000. Milligan was given a Lifetime Achievement Award for comedy in 1994.

In later years Milligan was equally known for the causes he supported, which included Greenpeace, Friends of the Earth, and the World Wildlife Fund. Milligan died on February 27, 2002, in his home in Rye, Sussex, England; he was 83. He is survived by his third wife Shelagh Sinclair, whom he married in 1983; a son, Sean, and two daughters, Sile and Laura (with Marlowe); a daughter, Jane (with Ridgeway); and two children with other women. **Sources:** *Independent* (London), February 28, 2002, p. 6; *New York Times,* February 28, 2002, p. A25; *Times* (London), February 28, 2002, p. 39.

—*Frank Caso*

Dudley Moore

Born Dudley Stuart John Moore, April 19, 1935, in Dagenham, Essex, England; died of pneumonia, March 27, 2002, in Plainfield, NJ. Comedian, actor, musician, and composer. Dudley Moore first gained fame in a groundbreaking comedy revue and afterward when teamed with Peter Cook, but his comedic talent was fully recognized in a number of films directed by Blake Edwards.

The son of working-class parents, Moore was born with a clubfoot and a deformed leg. Numerous childhood operations corrected both deformities, but Moore spent a good deal of his childhood recovering from the surgeries. Psychologically, he was affected by schoolyard taunts and his own mother's coldness. He later claimed that that was why he turned to comedy. As a child he proved a virtuoso musician whose accomplishments on the piano and organ won him a scholarship to a private music high school. From there he went on to attend Magdalen College at Oxford University in 1954, also on a music scholarship. Besides the classical music he studied at Oxford, Moore ventured into jazz, playing in clubs; cabaret, where he composed songs for student revues; and pop music. After he graduated from Oxford in 1958, Moore was offered the position as organist at King's College. He turned it down, however, to become a jazz pianist. His first single was a jazz number titled "Strictly for the Birds." It was produced by George Martin, who went on to produce the Beatles.

Moore's career turned toward comedy in 1960 when he joined with Alan Bennett, Jonathan Miller, and Peter Cook to create *Beyond the Fringe,* their wildly successful satiric revue, which premiered at the 1960 Edinburgh festival. *Beyond the Fringe* was a hit in 1961 in London's West End; it played on Broadway in New York City in 1962. After the quartet broke up in 1964 Moore and Cook formed a comedy team that lasted for nearly 12 years, but ended acrimoniously.

Cook and Moore transferred their comedy success to BBC television with the 1965 series *Not Only ... But Also,* which featured the unforgettable "Pete and Dud dialogues" in which the pair came on as Cockney versions of themselves. They also acted in films. These included cameo roles in 1966's *The Wrong Box,* which starred Peter Sellers, Ralph Richardson, and Michael Caine; and 1967's *Bedazzled,* their first starring vehicle. The Cook–Moore team broke up for a time but reteamed for the successful revue, *Beyond the Fringe* in the early 1970s. After success in Australia and London the revue played on Broadway with a new title—*Good Evening.* Moore and Cook won Tony Awards for the show.

During the late 1960s Moore publicly admitted he suffered from depression, but throughout his years with Cook, whom the diminutive Moore often deferred to, he had continued playing jazz piano and composing. Moore had even composed the film scores to, among others, *Bedazzled* and 1968's *Thirty Is a Dangerous Age, Cynthia,* in which he also acted. He had another West End success in *Play It Again, Sam* (in the role made famous by Woody Allen). In 1968 Moore married actress Suzy Kendall; they divorced in 1972. Moore married actress Tuesday Weld in 1975 and they had a son, Patrick. At this time Moore was a tax exile living in Hollywood, but he returned to Great Britain in 1976. He and Cook released a series of recordings, *Derek and Clive,* hoping to cash in on the earlier success of the Pete and Dud dialogues. But these latter dialogues reflected the loss of innocence which their partnership had endured. Moore especially was no longer willing to put up with the alcoholic and abusive

Cook; the team broke up for good in 1977. A year later Moore was lured back to Hollywood to appear in the film *Foul Play,* which starred Chevy Chase and Goldie Hawn.

In 1979, thanks to director Blake Edwards, Moore became, for a time, one of Hollywood biggest stars. Edwards chose Moore for the part of the man undergoing a midlife crisis in the popular film *10.* The film costarred Julie Andrews and Bo Derek. Moore followed this up with a bust—the biblical comedy *Wholly Moses!* It was his performance in his next film, *Arthur,* that cemented Moore's star reputation. The film about a lonely, alcoholic millionaire costarred Liza Minnelli and John Gielgud. Moore infused the role of the millionaire with a pathos that earned him a Golden Globe award. Unfortunately, this was the pinnacle of his career.

In his next film, *Six Weeks,* Moore played against type as a politician involved with the mother of a dying girl. This and most of Moore's subsequent films were either critical or box office flops—often both. The one exception to this was 1984's *Micki and Maude,* another comedy directed by Edwards. Moore won a second Golden Globe award for his role of a television newsman who juggles a wife and mistress, both of whom are pregnant. Moore's other films of this period include 1983's *Lovesick,* and 1984's *Unfaithfully Yours* and *Best Defense.* Just prior to his Hollywood breakthrough, in 1979, Moore divorced Weld. In 1988 he married model Brogan Lane, but their marriage lasted only 16 months. Moore's fourth marriage was to Nicole Rothschild in 1994. They had a son, Nicholas, in 1995, but their marriage ended bitterly in 1999.

In the early 1990s Moore tried his hand at television again—1993's *Dudley* and 1994's *Daddy's Girls*—but neither series took off. Comedy aside, classical and jazz music remained his twin passions. He performed with jazz singer Cleo Laine and in such venues as New York City's Metropolitan Museum of Art, Carnegie Hall, and the Hollywood Bowl.

In 1997 Moore was diagnosed with progressive supranuclear palsy (PSP), a degenerative disease similar to Parkinson's. The disease gradually eroded his memory and sapped his physical ability, but during its early stages Hollywood gossip attributed Moore's memory loss to drug and alcohol abuse. In November of 2001 Moore was made a commander of the British Empire (CBE) by Prince Charles. It was Moore's final public appearance.

Moore died on March 27, 2002, of pneumonia as a complication of PSP at his home in Plainfield, New Jersey; he was 66. He is survived by his sons, Patrick and Nicholas, and a sister, Barbara Stevens. **Sources:** *Independent* (London), March 29, 2002, p. 6; *Los Angeles Times*, March 28, 2002, p. B14; March 31, 2002, p. A2; *New York Times*, March 28, 2002, p. A28; *People*, April 15, 2002, pp. 92-98; *Times* (London), March 28, 2002, p. 43; *Washington Post*, March 27, 2002, p. B6.

—*Frank Caso*

Max Perutz

Born Max Ferdinand Perutz, May 19, 1914, in Vienna, Austria; died of cancer, February 6, 2002, in Cambridge, England. Scientist. Max Perutz discovered and mapped the structure of the protein hemoglobin, thus establishing the foundation for molecular biology. He worked constantly until his death, intrigued by molecules of protein, their function, and their role in disease. His creativity and energy aided him in establishing one of the most prestigious and successful research laboratories in Britain, the Medical Research Council Laboratory for Molecular Biology. He spent every day in the lab, excluding Christmas, and was able to communicate as easily with elementary students as he was with the world's top scientists. Erica Goode wrote in the *New York Times* that Perutz's discovery "opened a window on proteins ... and provided a cornerstone for many fundamental advances in molecular medicine and genetics over the last three decades."

Perutz's parents had become wealthy in the textile industry, and had wanted him to study law at college. Unfortunately for their hopes of him joining the family business, Perutz became fascinated with chemistry. In 1932, he enrolled at Vienna University, studying mineral chemistry and glaciology. He wanted to continue his studies but found Vienna's adherence to 19th century models for science unsuitable. He was intrigued by the work of Sir Frederick Gowland Hopkins, who was a professor at Cambrige University in England. With the full financial support of his family, Perutz chose to earn his doctorate at Cambridge.

In 1936, Perutz began his studies at Cambridge's Cavendish Laboratory. By the following year he had figured out how to view the structure of hemoglobin crystals using x–ray crystallography, which was invented in 1912. It is a method where a crystalized substance is rotated in a beam of x–rays. The resulting photos are mathematically interpreted, reconstructing the location and position of linked atoms in the crystal.

In 1939, Perutz suffered a major setback when his parents's business was seized by Nazis. His family had been Jewish, but had converted to Catholicism. His parents were left penniless and at Perutz's urging, moved to England to be with him. Sir Lawrence Bragg, unwilling to see a gifted and promising student forced out of school, managed to secure a position for Perutz as his research assistant. This allowed Perutz to continue his studies and earn his doctorate.

In 1940, the same year he earned his doctorate, Perutz and his father, along with many other foreign residents, were arrested by the British government due to fears of their being Nazi sympathizers. They were held at several internment camps, eventually ending up at a camp in Canada. Perutz was unstoppable in his intellectual seeking and while interned, formed a haphazard university within the camp made up himself and other scientists, including theoretical physicist Karl Fuchs and cosmologist Thomas Gold.

After a year of internment, Perutz was allowed to return to Cambridge. The British government set him up to work on a secret project called Project Habbakuk hoping to use his knowledge of glaciology. Perutz was assigned the task of discovering a way to make ice stronger and less brittle. The hope was to build giant landing strips made of ice in the middle of the North Atlantic to make air shipments between North America and England less dangerous. Although he did succeed in helping to create a strong and bullet–proof form of ice, the project was deemed impractical and shelved.

After the war ended, Perutz was able to return to his studies of hemoglobin. Even though he had made a major discovery, there was still more work ahead figuring out the entire structure of hemoglobin. In 1953, he was able to interpret more of the structure by comparing ordinary hemoglobin crystals with ones that had mercury atoms added to them. By 1959, he had worked out the complete structure of the molecule, although he continued to add to the details of it for years afterward. The *Daily Telegraph* related Perutz's decription of the discovery, "It was an overwhelming experience to see a vital part of ourselves that is a thousand times smaller than anything visible under a light microscope revealed in detail for the first time."

In 1962, Perutz won the Nobel Prize in Chemistry along with his colleague, Sir John Kendrow, who had detailed the structure of a similar but smaller molecule. That same year the Medical Research Council founded the Laboratory for Molecular Biology (LMB). Headed by Perutz, the LMB would produce in the following years ten Nobel prize winners, including James Watson and Francis Crick, the discoverers of DNA. The *Times* quoted Perutz's theory on how to create an atmosphere that fosters scientific discovery, "Well–run laboratories can foster [creativity in science], but hierarchical organization, inflexible, bureaucratic rules, and mountains of futile paperwork can kill it. Discoveries cannot be planned; they pop up, like Puck, in unexpected corners."

Perutz's endless curiosity and love of science helped advance science in many areas. In particular, his research helped pave the way for identifying the cause of diseases like sickle cell anemia, and established important links between proteins and Alzheimer's and Huntington's. He earned many awards throughout his career and in 1988 was given the highest civil honor accorded in England, the Order of Merit. Perutz died of cancer on February 6, 2002; he was 87. He is survived by his wife, Gisela Peiser, whom he married in 1942; a son, Robin; a daughter, Vivien; and two grandchildren. **Sources:** *Daily Telegraph* (London), February 7, 2002, p. 1; *Guardian* (London), February 7, 2002, p. 24; *Independent* (London), February 7, 2002, p. 6; *Los Angeles Times,* February 9, 2002, p. B18; *New York Times,* February 8, 2002, p. A21; *Times* (London), February 7, 2002, p. 21.

—*Eve M. B. Hermann*

George Porter

Born December 6, 1920, in Stainforth, Yorkshire, England; died August 31, 2002, in Canterbury, England. Scientist. George Porter, more formally known as Lord Porter of Luddenham, was a co–recipient of the 1967 Nobel Prize in chemistry for his work in light–driven chemical reactions. The longtime professor of physical chemistry was also one of British science's best–known propagandists for the field, hectoring politicians for funding and appearing frequently as the host of popular television programs that explained esoteric concepts in lay terms. "[N]o heavyweight scientist in the last 40 years has done more to promote the public understanding of science than he," declared Ronald Mason in a tribute to Porter for London's *Independent* newspaper.

Porter was born in Stainforth, a city in South Yorkshire, in 1920. An early interest in chemistry was encouraged by his father, and the youngster even had his own laboratory—but it was a mobile one, separate from the family home. Recalling his youth, Porter admitted to being "very fond of explosions," according to *Washington Post* writer Martin Weil. He studied at Leeds University, and served in the Royal Naval Volunteer Reserve as a radar operator during World War II. Intrigued by this relatively new field, Porter brought what he knew about radar science to Cambridge University after the war. There he worked with a mentor, Dr. Ronald G. W. Norrish, to solve one of the most pressing dilemmas in physical chemistry at the time: scientists were determined to learn what happens when molecules divide and reassemble, but the process was so quick that it was undetectable to the human eye.

Together, Porter and Norrish developed what became known as called flash photolysis. Norrish was already working on the idea of using light flashes to view the reactions, but these proved too short to provide measurement; it was Porter's idea to use the same pulses of energy that radar technology deployed. As *New York Times* writer Kenneth Chang explained, the pair "started chemical reactions in a gas with a bright flash of light that shattered chemical bonds. The molecular fragments, known as free radicals, are highly reactive and quickly recombine into new molecules." Another flash then "identified the free radicals; the colors of light they absorbed acted as identifying fingerprints." At the time, these flashes of light were just a thousandths of a second, but within a decade advances in science had reduced that time to a millionth of a second.

Porter would not be formally recognized by the Nobel Prize committee for some years, however. He remained at Cambridge until 1954, did a brief stint in the private sector as an assistant director of research for the British Rayon Research Association, and in 1955 was made a professor at Sheffield University. Named its Firth Professor of Chemistry in 1963 and serving as head of the department for the next three years, he helped make Sheffield one of the top schools in the field of chemistry. He shared the 1967 Nobel Prize with Norrish and Manfred Eigen of the Max Planck Institute for Physical Chemistry in Germany.

Porter also conducted research quite early in his career that bore fruit much later. While at Cambridge, he conducted experiments involving chlorine dioxide. "I had to confess that I could not see any possible use of my work," Weil's *Washington Post* obituary quoted him as saying, but some three decades later it was learned that a byproduct of his process, chlorine monoxide, was tied to the destruction of the Earth's ozone layer. Porter's subsequent research continued apace with developments in the scientific world; he believed that photosynthesis—the process by which green plants convert sunlight to energy—was the key to cleaner energy sources for the planet, but remained stymied by finding a way to replicate the process in the lab. A colleague, Dr. David Phillips, told the *New York Times*'s Chang that Porter was fond of saying, "Nature is miserably inefficient in converting light into usable energy; surely with modern science, we can do better than that." Phillips told the newspaper that years later, Porter would reflect, "Nature is miserably inefficient at converting light into usable energy, but it would be presumptuous of mere mortals to beat nature."

Porter was a media–savvy scientist. He hosted several British television series, from the *Laws of Disorder* in the mid–1960s to *Natural History of a Sunbeam* a decade later. In the late 1960s he began a long tenure as professor and director of the Royal Institution of Great Britain, whose mission is to make science and its discoveries known to and understood by the public. He was also a co–founder of the Committee on the Public Understanding of Science. For his achievements he was created Baron Porter of Luddenham in 1990. In his first speech before the House of Lords, Porter spoke about the need for increased government funding for scientific research.

Later in his career, Porter was a member of the faculty of Imperial College in London, where he established its Centre for Photomolecular Sciences. He also served as president of Britain's Royal Society after 1985, an august body founded in 1640 and one of whose past presidents had been Sir Isaac Newton. Porter died on August 31, 2002, in Canterbury, England; he was 81. He is survived by his wife, Stella Brooke Porter; and two sons, John and Andrew. **Sources:** *Independent* (London, England), September 4, 2002, p. 16; *Los Angeles Times*, September 4, 2002, p. B11; *New York Times*, September 4, 2002, p. B8; *Washington Post*, September 5, 2002, p. B6.

—*Carol Brennan*

Chaim Potok

Born Herman Harold Potok, February 17, 1929, in Bronx, NY; died of cancer, July 23, 2002, in Merion, PA. Author. Chaim Potok chronicled the world of Hasidic Judaism from a unique vantage point: like many of his protagonists, Potok had struggled with

a decision to leave its insular world behind as he became an adult. In his case, he turned to a less conservative sect of Judaism, and was ordained a rabbi in it; he was also a philosophy professor before he became a best–selling author. Daniel Walden, writing in London's *Independent* newspaper, called him "the first American Jewish novelist who opened up the field from the inside."

Born in 1929, Potok was the son of two Polish immigrants to New York City who brought with them their Hasidic faith. This strain of Judaism dates back to Eastern Europe in the 1700s, and despite a diaspora its members still maintain a rigorous observance to dress, religious worship, and community standards. Throughout his life, Potok was called by his Hebrew name, Chaim—meaning "life" or "alive"—which he also used professionally. Potok recalled growing up in a strict household, and though he showed an aptitude for art at an early age, his parents discouraged this as frivolous. He was schooled at a local yeshiva, but read forbidden secular books on the sly at the public library. While commuting from his home to Manhattan's Yeshiva University daily, he dissected works from Ernest Hemingway and others with the skills he had already learned studying the Talmud. He was especially drawn to two important novels by Roman Catholic writers, *Brideshead Revisited* by Evelyn Waugh and James Joyce's *Portrait of the Artist as a Young Man,* saying later that they guided him toward a career in letters.

First, however, Potok became a rabbi. After graduating from Yeshiva University in 1950, he chose to begin rabbinical studies at the Jewish Theological Seminary in New York. This was not a Hasidic institution, but rather one that adhered to the less stringent Conservative Jewish sect. His decision stunned his family and neighbors, and Potok noted years later there were some from his youth who refused to speak to him even decades later. With a master's degree in Hebrew literature, he was ordained a rabbi in 1954. He served in the United States Army as a chaplain in the mid–1950s, posted in South Korea, and then moved to Los Angeles, California, to take a teaching post at the University of Judaism.

Potok went on to earn a doctorate in philosophy from the University of Pennsylvania in 1965. Two years later, his first novel, *The Chosen,* appeared, and it was the first–ever literary work with a Hasidic Jewish community as its setting. The story takes place during the late 1940s inside Brooklyn's Williamsburg neighborhood—long the epicenter of Hasidic life in North America—and centers on two teenagers. Danny Saunders is the son of a tzaddik (spiritual leader) in the community, and he is expected to follow suit. His best friend is Reuven Malter, who is from a more progressive Jewish household. Danny struggles with his decision to leave the Hasidic community behind. "In almost painterly detail," noted *New York Times* writer Margalit Fox, "Potok conjured up a universe of men in dark caftans and fur–trimmed hats; Sabbath dinners awash in candlelight; the sounds of Yiddish in the streets and Hebrew in the synagogues...."

The Chosen spent six months on the *New York Times* best–seller list, and was a National Book Award finalist. Potok followed it with a sequel, *The Promise,* in 1969, but for a number of years afterward still kept his job as editor–in–chief of the Jewish Publication Society. He wrote another well–received work, 1972's *My Name Is Asher Lev,* about a young artist who outrages his conservative Jewish family in Crown Heights when he begins painting crucifixion scenes. Critics were not entirely in agreement about Potok's style in these and later works, which included *In the Beginning,* published in 1975, *The Book of Lights*—the tale of an army chaplain—and *Davita's Harp,* both from 1985. As the *New York Times*'s Fox noted, he "wrote in a straightforward prose that some critics found unpolished and others likened to that of an urban Hemingway."

The appeal and significance of Potok's fiction was easier to assess, however. Writing in the *Los Angeles Times,* Reed Johnson asserted that his body of work "bore a profoundly humanist stamp," adding, "although that secular quality upset some Jewish readers and scandalized some members of the Jewish press, many other readers and critics applauded Potok's fearlessness and skill in exploring the internal fissures in modern Jewish life and belief." In 1981, a Hollywood adaptation of *The Chosen,* with Rod Steiger, Maximilian Schell, and Robby Benson, was released; it also enjoyed a run as a Broadway musical during the 1988 season. Potok was also the author of a 1978 history of the Jews, and wrote children's books as well. Under contract with Alfred A. Knopf in New York for his entire career, his final book was the novel *Old Men at Midnight,* published in 2001, not long after he was diagnosed with cancer.

Potok died on July 23, 2002, in his home in Merion, Pennsylvania, of brain cancer; he was 73. He is survived by his wife, Adena Sarah Mosevitzky, to whom he had been married since 1958; his daughters, Rena and Naama; his son, Akiva; and two grandchildren. Walden, assessing Potok's career for the *Independent,* termed him "a world–class writer

and scholar. Though critics often underrated him, it is my judgement that in the long run he will emerge as one of the major American Jewish writers of the 20th century." **Sources:** *Chicago Tribune,* July 24, 2002, section 2, p. 8; *Independent* (London), August 7, 2002, p. 14; *Los Angeles Times,* July 24, 2002, p. B11; *New York Times,* July 24, 2002, p. A17; *Washington Post,* July 24, 2002, p. B5.

—*Carol Brennan*

Princess Margaret, Countess of Snowdon

Born August 21, 1930, at Glamis Castle, Angus, Scotland; died after a stroke, February 9, 2002, in London, England. Princess of Great Britain and Northern Ireland. Margaret Rose Windsor, known throughout the English–speaking world simply as Princess Margaret, was the younger sister of Queen Elizabeth II. A stunning beauty in her younger days and a known bon vivant, Margaret's well–publicized romantic travails gave the British public a foretaste of the scandals that later beset the royal family in the 1980s when three of the Queen's four children divorced.

Margaret was born in 1930 at Glamis Castle in Scotland, the second daughter of the Duke and Duchess of York. Her life changed irrevocably in 1936 when her father's older brother, King Edward VIII, abdicated the throne in order to marry an American woman, Wallis Simpson. Margaret's father, next in line to the throne, became king. Upon learning that her sister would someday become Queen of England, Margaret reportedly said, "Poor you," according to a *Los Angeles Times* obituary.

The two royal sisters were educated at home, and their every move was chronicled by the press. After World War II and its hardships they emerged as hard–working ambassadors for England, both at home and abroad. A famously beautiful debutante in her day, the younger princess led what the newspapers dubbed the "Margaret Set" of fashionable, well–heeled nightclubbers in heady postwar London. She was slim, with porcelain skin and blue eyes, and had several prominent suitors, but was unfortunate enough to fall in love with her father's equerry, a World War II hero named Peter Townsend. The Royal Air Force captain was divorced, however, and when rumors of the romance emerged—after a clearly smitten Margaret was photographed flicking a piece of lint from Townsend's uniform on her sister's 1953 Coronation Day—several prominent leaders of the Anglican Church argued that a union between a member of the royal family and a divorced commoner was unthinkable. There was some public support for her plight, but Margaret would have been forced to give up her royal title, succession rights, and generous allowance in the event that she and Townsend decided to wed. On October 31, 1955, the Princess issued a statement that she would not marry Townsend, declaring herself "conscious of my duty to the Commonwealth," according to a *New York Times* obituary.

Five years later Margaret wed Antony Armstrong–Jones, a photographer, in a spectacular wedding at Westminster Abbey. Their son, David, was born in 1961, followed by daughter Sarah in 1964. The discord between the Princess and her husband, now Lord Snowdon, became apparent even in public over the years, and there were accusations of infidelity on both sides. In the early 1970s, Margaret became linked to Roddy Llewellyn, described in the *New York Times* by Joseph R. Gregory as "an upper-class drifter 17 years her junior whose main accomplishment appeared to be a talent for gardening." The pair vacationed on the Caribbean island of Mustique, where Margaret maintained a villa, and the media attention eventually caused the Snowdons to divorce in 1978. She was the first member of Britain's royal family to do so in the modern era.

At times, Margaret endured criticism for scheduling a limited number of royal duties in correlation to her generous allowance—$100,000 at the time of her divorce—and for living lavishly. She was known to travel by helicopter, sometimes appeared to sulk during her public engagements, and stood firmly on royal protocol: even in private, all were required to address her as "Ma'am," but her friends were said to be allowed to call her "Ma'am darling." Those who knew her countered that Margaret was a loyal and vivacious companion, a talented mimic, and a lover of music. She remained on friendly terms with Townsend, Llewellyn, and even her ex-husband.

Margaret's excesses of the previous era seemed tame compared to the scandals surrounding the dissolution of the marriages of two of her nephews, Charles, the Prince of Wales, from the former Lady Diana Spencer, and Prince Andrew and Sarah, Duchess of York. The thwarted romance between Margaret and Townsend was said to have been the harbinger of doom for the Windsor house, according to *New York Times*, "the turning point to disaster for the royal family," quipped Harold Brooks–Baker, the publishing director of *Burke's Peerage*, a British society register, in 1995 after Group Captain

Townsend's death. "After Princess Margaret was denied marriage, it backfired and more or less ruined Margaret's life. The queen decided that from then on, anyone someone in her family wanted to marry would be more or less acceptable. The royal family and the public now feel that they've gone too far in the other direction."

A heavy smoker for much of her life and said to possess a fondness for Famous Grouse whiskey, Margaret was plagued by ill health in her later years. In 1998, she suffered a stroke, burned her feet in the bathtub the next year, and was felled by another stroke in March of 2001. She made only a few public appearances the remainder of the year. Margaret died on February 9, 2002, at the age of 71. She is survived by her son, daughter, and three grandchildren. **Sources:** *Chicago Tribune*, February 10, 2002, section 1, p. 6; *Independent* (London), February 11, 2002, p. 6; *Los Angeles Times*, February 10, 2002, p. B16; *New York Times*, February 10, 2002, p. A30; *Times* (London), http://www.thetimes.co.uk (February 9, 2002); *Washington Post*, February 10, 2002, p. C8.

—Carol Brennan

Queen Elizabeth the Queen Mother

Born Elizabeth Angela Marguerite Bowes–Lyon, August 4, 1900, in London, England; died in her sleep, March 30, 2002, in Windsor Castle, Berkshire, England. Royal consort. Queen Elizabeth the Queen Mother, the formal title of the woman born Elizabeth Angela Marguerite Bowes–Lyons but known around the world as the "Queen Mum," was Britain's most beloved royal figure. In a life that spanned the twentieth century and a few years beyond, the mother of Queen Elizabeth II lived a remarkably scandal–free life, and she was known for her graciousness and charm, both publicly and in private. "With her death," noted *Independent* writer Hugo Vickers, " it is no cliché to say that an era of British life comes to a close."

The Queen Mother was born in 1900, the ninth of ten children in the well–connected Bowes–Lyon family of Scotland. She grew up on a large country estate in Hertfordshire as well as at the family's ancestral castle, Glamis. As a young debutante in London, she was ardently courted by the second in line to the English throne, Prince Albert. A frail, shy man with a temper and prone to stammer, he seemed an unlikely spouse for the vivacious, good–

natured Elizabeth, but she acquiesced, and their 1923 union made her the first commoner to marry so near the throne since the 1600s.

The Duke and Duchess of York, as they were known, had two daughters in quick succession, Elizabeth and Margaret, but when Prince Albert's brother, King Edward VIII, fell in love with Wallis Simpson, an American divorcée, Edward abdicated the throne in order to marry her. Albert, next in the line of succession, took the name King George VI, but the scandal surrounding his ascendancy made it "an intolerable honor," the new Queen Consort was said to have remarked at the time, according to *People*. Privately, she worked tirelessly to support her husband and help him meet the challenges of his new job. She urged him to visit a speech therapist, and it was said that her strength helped both the king and the nation endure the tragedies and terror of World War II. Bombs fell in the forecourt of the royal home, Buckingham Palace, when the couple and their daughters were inside, but she and her husband refused to send the daughters to Canada for safety. Instead she toured the British countryside, visiting service personnel and bombed cities, and promoted war rationing efforts and other domestic measures. She proved so popular a figure during the war years that German chancellor Adolf Hitler famously declared her "the most dangerous woman in Europe," according to the *Independent*.

When George VI died in 1952, the Queen Consort officially became the "Queen Mother" after her eldest daughter advanced to the throne. She was a young widow, too energetic to retire as her predecessors had done, and so instead undertook a heavy schedule of public engagements on behalf of the Crown. She served as patron or president of 312 organizations, regiments, and charities, and enjoyed spending time at the Windsors's country estate at Sandringham (Windsor is the surname of the British royal family). In her private life, she was a keen fan of thoroughbred horseracing and kept a stable of her own winners.

Though Britain's royal family endured a number of scandals in the 1970s and '80s, the Queen Mother remained a hugely popular public figure. Her broad smile, quick wit, and pastel suits topped by her signature plumed hats helped give her a reputation as England's unofficial national grandmother. Though she once called Simpson "the woman who killed my husband," according to the *New York Times*, the Queen Mother graciously followed her sister–in–law's coffin during the Duchess of Windsor's funeral procession in 1986.

Though she suffered declining health in her later years, the Queen Mother remained an indefatigable figure, still dancing at parties until well into her 90s. At the age of 97, she walked the entire length of Westminster Abbey during the funeral of Prince Charles's former wife, Diana, Princess of Wales. "Her presence was the more poignant when it is recalled she had attended the funeral of another Princess of Wales, Queen Alexandra, some 72 years before, and that that princess had married into the Royal Family in 1863," noted Vickers in his chronicle of the Queen Mother's remarkably long life. The nation celebrated her 100th birthday in August of 2000, and she gave up her royal duties only later the following year. One of her last appearances was at another funeral, this one for her younger daughter, Princess Margaret, in February of 2002. The Queen Mother died in her sleep on March 30, 2002, at the age of 101. "She was, quite simply, the most magical grandmother you could possibly have," *People* quoted Prince Charles as saying in a television tribute to her a few weeks after her death. **Sources:** *Independent* (London), April 1, 2002, p. 4; *Los Angeles Times*, March 31, 2002, p. A1, p. A6; *New York Times*, April 1, 2002, p. A20; *People*, April 15, 2002, pp. 50-55; *Time*, April 8, 2002, p. 51; *Times* (London), http://www.thetimes.co.uk (April 4, 2002); *Washington Post*, March 31, 2002, p. A1, p. A10.

—*Carol Brennan*

Dick Schaap

Born September 27, 1934, in Brooklyn, NY; died from acute respiratory distress following hip surgery, December 21, 2001, in New York, NY. Journalist. Dick Schaap is thought to be the first print journalist to segue into a career in television sports broadcasting. A veteran New York City newspaper editor and columnist, Schaap began chronicling the increasingly celebrity–oriented world of professional sports in the early 1970s. He was a regular on both ESPN, the cable sports channel, and ABC News programs like *20/20*. Schaap also authored more than 30 books, many of them "as told to" biographies of sports figures. *Guardian* writer Michael Carlson called him "one of America's great sportswriters, although most of his best work was done outside daily papers, and much of it transcended sport."

Schaap grew up in Long Island, New York. His journalism career began at the age of 15 when he began filing stories for the sports section of the *Nassau*

Daily Review–Star, a job that introduced him to another cub reporter, Jimmy Breslin, who would go on to an equally stellar career in journalism. Schaap played lacrosse at Cornell University, and later entered Columbia University's School of Journalism to earn his graduate degree. After a stint with the *Long Island Press,* he joined the staff of *Newsweek* in 1959, covering sports for the weekly magazine. In 1964, Schaap reunited with Breslin when he took a job at the *New York Herald Tribune* as city editor. He progressed to writing a column for the paper with a focus on New York City matters and national politics.

Schaap was a colorful figure with the gift of gab and ability to turn a flip, memorable phrase. At the *Herald Tribune,* he capitalized on a remark made by new Mayor John V. Lindsay on his first day in office, which coincided with a paralyzing transit strike. Lindsay had responded, when asked by reporters if he was still happy to be the mayor on such a challenging day, "I still think it's a fun city." Schaap turned phrase into sarcastic dig, and the "Fun City" jibe became a standard for pundit writers and newspaper headlines for years.

Schaap's prominent job and exuberant personality introduced him to many well–known figures. *New York Times* writer Richard Sandomir characterized the journalist as "a gleeful, unrepentant name–dropper, playing on his talent for usually being in the right, or fortuitous, place most of the time." Yet Schaap also collected friends from all walks of life. "My favourite sport is people," the *Guardian*'s Carlson quoted him as saying. In some cases he knew celebrities long before they achieved prominence: while at *Newsweek,* he brought a young prizefighter named Cassius Clay to Harlem, where they witnessed an African American man delivering a politically charged speech. The Kentucky native was stunned to hear such polemic, but within a few years had become a Black Muslim and changed his name to Muhammad Ali. In the early 1970s, Schaap hired an up–and–coming comedian named Billy Crystal to perform at a roast in Ali's honor, which launched the actor's career.

Schaap ventured into sports biographies when he co–authored a 1968 bestseller, *Instant Replay,* with Green Bay Packer football player Jerry Kramer. He went on to write three others with Kramer and continued the "as told to Dick Schaap" credit with a host of other sports personalities, including Hank Aaron, Joe Montana, Tom Seaver, Joe Namath, and Bo Jackson. During this period, Schaap made a move into television journalism, working first with the local NBC affiliate in New York City and then becoming a regular correspondent for *NBC News.*

In the early 1980s, Schaap jumped ship to the ABC news organization, where he appeared on the weekly newsmagazine *20/20* and the weekday evening broadcast, *World News Tonight.* "Schaap was widely respected by colleagues and interview subjects as a journalist with an even hand," noted *Los Angeles Times* journalist Mike Penner, "unafraid to ask a tough question but unwilling to embarrass his subject." He earned three Emmy awards for his profiles, which included one of comedian Sid Caesar admitting his substance abuse and recovery efforts, and a story on Olympic decathlete Tom Waddell, who was battling AIDS.

An avid theater–goer, Schaap also delivered reviews of Broadway shows for ABC News programs. He was thought to be the sole American eligible to cast annual votes for both the Heisman Trophy, bestowed on the best college football player, and the Antoinette Perry (Tony) Awards for outstanding Broadway theater productions. Schaap also hosted a boisterous weekly panel show for ESPN, *The Sports Reporters,* for many years before his death. His son, Jeremy, also became a sports broadcaster. In 2001, Schaap's own autobiography finally appeared, *Flashing Before My Eyes,* which the *Washington Post* reported contained 531 instances of name–dropping. ESPN aired a two–hour profile on Schaap's life and career based on the book.

On December 21, 2001, Schaap underwent hip replacement surgery and died at the age of 67 from post–operative complications. He is survived by his third wife, Trish; son, Jeremy; and five other children. **Sources:** *Capital Times* (Madison, WI), December 22, 2001, p. 1C; *Guardian* (London, England), January 10, 2002, p. 22; Knight-Ridder/Tribune News Service, February 23, 2001; *Los Angeles Times,* December 22, 2001, p. B14; *New York Times,* December 22, 2001, p. C15; December 31, 2001, p. A2; *Washington Post,* December 22, 2001, p. B5.

—*Carol Brennan*

Leopold Senghor

Born Leopold Sedar Senghor, October 9, 1906, in Joal, Senegal; died December 20, 2001, in Normandy, France. Poet and politician. By turns a poet, a professor, a philosopher, and a politician, Senghor was the first president of post–colonial Senegal, Africa. He saw his country through its transformation from a French colony to a fully independent nation, and was elected to the presidency four times, serving a total of 21 years in that capacity. In 1981, he became the first African leader to voluntarily step down from office.

The product of equal parts African and European cultures, Senghor was the son of a Senegalese peanut farmer and merchant. He was a schoolteacher in French schools and fought as a soldier in the second World War in the French army. He also helped to found a cultural movement he and his peers called "negritude," a celebration of African heritage and its resonances in cultures around the world. "I wear European clothing, and the Americans dance to jazz which derives from our African rhythms," Senghor was quoted by Albin Krebs of the *New York Times* as saying. "Civilization in the 20th century is universal."

Although Senghor wanted political freedom for his nation, he also felt that France should remain involved in the political affairs of Senegal. For him, the end of colonialism meant, as he said in the *Independent* of London, "the abolition of all prejudice, of all superiority complex in the mind of the colonizer and the abolition of all inferiority complex in the mind of the colonized."

Senghor was born in the fishing village of Joal on the coast of Senegal in 1906. He grew up in Djilor, a town inland of the coast about 20 kilometers. As he later wrote, as quoted in the *Washington Post,* "I grew up in the heartland of Africa, at the crossroads/ Of castes and races and roads." His father was a successful merchant and peanut farmer, and a member of the Serer ethnic group. His mother was a Roman Catholic and belonged to the Fulani ethnic group. A convert to Christianity, Senghor's father nevertheless had more than one wife, and some said that as a result, Senghor had perhaps two dozen siblings.

Senghor's mother sent him to a missionary school, but he also learned traditional Fulani folklore and traditions from his uncle on his mother's side. It was his mother, Senghor said years later, and quoted by the *New York Times*'s Krebs, who instilled in him a desire to become "a teaching priest to work toward the intellectual emancipation of my race." He decided not to go become a priest, however, and when he turned 20, he attended, instead of a seminary, a secular school in Dakar, Senegal. Then, in 1928, he won a scholarship to the Lycee Louis–le–Grand at the Sorbonne in Paris. While at the Sorbonne, Senghor met and befriended Georges Pompidou, who went on to become president of France. The two remained friends throughout their lives.

His time in France taught Senghor that Africa's contribution to world civilization was considerable, apparent in art forms ranging from music to painting to literature. It was also in France that Senghor helped to develop the concept of "negritude," a philosophy that black civilization had its own values, achievements, and aspirations. The philosophy retained a respect for European and Western art and political thought, but Senghor pled with his fellow Africans to "assimilate, not be assimilated," according to the *New York Times*'s Krebs. An accomplished poet, Senghor denounced in his poetry what he called the "soullessness" of European civilization, and celebrated what he felt was African civilization's close ties to the natural world.

Senghor graduated from the Sorbonne in 1935, and was the first of African heritage to be named agrege, the highest level of French school teacher. After graduation, he worked as a schoolteacher in Tours, France. When he first stepped into a classroom at Tours, he was reported by the *Independent* as having said, "I am black. Let's spend the next few minutes in silence so that you can look at me and see how black I am. Then we can get on with our work."

Senghor was still teaching in 1939, this time in a school near Paris, when he was drafted into the French Army. In 1940, he was captured by German soldiers and spent two years as a German prisoner. In captivity, he worked to help fellow prisoners escape. He also wrote poetry, which was later published in a book called *Chantes d'Ombre.* At the end of the war, in 1945, Senghor began his political career, serving as deputy for Senegal to the French Constituent Assembly. The following year, he was elected to serve as one of two deputies from Senegal in the French National Assembly, where he served until 1958. Senghor also published his first book of poems in 1945. Called *Songs of the Shadow,* it was well received, as were the other volumes of poetry he published over the next 20 years.

In 1946, Senghor married his first wife, a Guyanese woman named Ginette Eboue. They eventually divorced after nine years of marriage. Senghor married again, this time to a French woman named Colette Hubert.

Senegal was granted independence from France in 1960, and Senghor was elected the newly formed country's first president. Only two years into his first term as president, a former friend of Senghor's, Prime Minister Mamadou, attempted a coup. The take–over attempt was unsuccessful, and Senghor had Mamadou put in prison for the rest of his life. Elections in 1963, 1968, and 1973 kept Senghor in the president's office until he voluntarily stepped down in 1980, handing the reins of power to a hand–picked successor. He was the first African president to leave office voluntarily. He retired with his wife to the French village of Verson, and there concentrated on poetry and academic pursuits. Senghor became the first African member of the Academie Francaise in 1984.

Senghor died on December 20, 2001, in his home in Normandy, France, at the age of 95. As reported by the *New York Times*'s Krebs, French president Jacques Chirac said on hearing of Senghor's death, "Poetry has lost one of its masters, Senegal a statesman, Africa a visionary, and France a friend." Senghor is survived by his wife, Colette; and a son. **Sources:** *Independent*, December 21, 2001, p. 6; *Los Angeles Times*, December 21, 2002, p. B12; *New York Times*, December 21, 2001, p. C15; *Times* (London), December 21, 2001, p. 19; *Washington Post*, December 21, 2001, p. B6.

—*Michael Belfiore*

Howard K. Smith

Born Howard Kingsbury Smith, Jr., May 12, 1914, in Ferriday, LA; died of pneumonia aggravated by congestive heart failure, February 15, 2002, in Bethesda, MD. Journalist. Howard K. Smith delivered eyewitness accounts of some of the most dramatic events of the twentieth century, and his "daring, analytical reporting from the front lines of World War II helped launch a golden age in broadcast journalism," noted *Los Angeles Times* writer Elaine Woo. A native of Louisiana, Smith was the son of a railroad conductor and attended Tulane University in New Orleans on a scholarship. Traveling to Germany in 1936 for graduate study, Smith then spent a year at Oxford University in 1937 as a Rhodes Scholar, becoming the first American to serve as president of Oxford's Labor Club and leading demonstrations against the rising tide of fascism in Europe. In 1939, his fluency in German helped him land a job with United Press. He reported from Berlin, home to one of those fascist governments, and quickly moved over to the CBS radio network as a correspondent. Smith's reports on the increasingly aggressive policies of the Nazi German government attracted the interest of rigorous Nazi censors, and in late 1941 he was forced to flee the country just a day before the United States entered World War II.

Smith wrote a book about his adventure, *Last Train from Berlin*, that was published in 1942, the same year he wed Danish journalist Benedicte Traberg.

For CBS he spent the next three years following troops as one of several highly regarded young American journalists posted to Europe during the war. Known as the "Murrow Boys" in honor of their doyen, Edward R. Murrow, the group also included William L. Shirer and Eric Sevareid. Smith and his colleagues made broadcast history with their stirring battlefield reports; he was present when the remnants of the German Army made their historic surrender in Berlin to Russian forces in May of 1945. In the postwar era, Smith reported from London, succeeding Murrow as CBS's chief European correspondent. He returned to the United States in 1957 to become a commentator on CBS's nightly newscast. Three years later he moderated the first televised presidential debate between candidates Richard M. Nixon and John F. Kennedy.

In 1961 Smith advanced to the post of chief correspondent and general manager of CBS's Washington bureau. Filming with a crew in Birmingham, Alabama, in 1961, Smith was the only national reporter on the scene when white supremacists attacked a group of civil–rights workers while the police steered clear of the melee; at the end of his television special, Smith warned that should the United States not take stronger measures to prevent such atrocities, the country could become "a racial dictatorship, like Nazi Germany," Smith said, according to the *New York Times*. He concluded his report with a quote from Edmund Burke, an eighteenth–century British politician: "The only thing necessary for the triumph of evil is for good men to do nothing." Network executives ordered the line edited out, which angered Smith. He met with the president of CBS News, Richard Salant, who reportedly told him, "We won't allow you to adopt causes," the *New York Times* report stated. Firm in his belief that it was indeed the responsibility of journalism to take sides, Smith argued his cause personally with CBS chair William S. Paley, but Paley remained adamant and Smith resigned in anger. Within a few years other CBS correspondents had used the Burke line on the air. "I remembered the old adage that it is smart to be right, but it is stupid to be right at the wrong time," Smith reflected, according to a *Los Angeles Times* obituary.

Smith was hired by ABC News and given his own weekly program for a time. In 1969 he became co–anchor of network's *Evening News* with Frank Reynolds. Somewhat to the surprise of those accustomed to his unabashedly liberal views, Smith argued for escalation of the war in Vietnam in order to end the conflict swiftly. His son, Jack, was serving in the Seventh U.S. Cavalry, and when he was wounded Smith journeyed there himself to conduct an unprecedented interview. The footage aired on

Smith's 1966 ABC News special, *A Father, a Son and War*. Over the years, Smith was considered so emblematic of the archetypical silver–haired, resonant–voiced newscaster that he was invited to appear in feature and television films as one; his credits include Robert Altman's *Nashville* in 1975 and the 1977 blockbuster *Close Encounters of the Third Kind*. He retired from ABC in 1979. An autobiography, *Events Leading Up To My Death: The Life of a Twentieth–Century Reporter,* was published in 1996. Smith died on February 15, 2002, at his home in Ferriday, Louisiana; he was 87. He is survived by his wife, Bennie; a daughter, and his son, who also became an ABC News correspondent. **Sources:** *Chicago Tribune,* February 19, 2002, section 2, p. 8; *Los Angeles Times,* February 19, 2002, p. A1; *New York Times,* February 19, 2002, p. C9; *Times* (London), February 21, 2002, p. 37; *Washington Post,* February 19, 2002, p. B6.

—Carol Brennan

Sam Snead

Born May 27, 1912, in Hot Springs, VA; died May 23, 2002, in Hot Springs, VA. Professional golf player and author. Sam Snead was called "Slammin' Sam," and for good reason. Snead's effortless–looking golf swing endeared the veteran player to generations of fans and competitors alike. For more than four decades, Snead was a fixture on the professional golf circuit, winning the Masters tournament three times, the Professional Golf Association (PGA) Championship three times, and the British Open once.

As a child growing up in Virginia, Snead used sticks for golf clubs and acorns for balls. The family lived a backwoods life, with Snead saying "we never wore shoes until it snowed." Early on, he developed a light hand on the club, comparing his grip to that of holding a bird. Snead also had the advantage of being double–jointed, which facilitated his wide driving arc. In his 1946 book *How to Play Golf*—one of at least 13 books he published on the subject—Snead used his characteristic folksy humor to drive home that point that a swing should be approached "easily and lazily, because the golf ball isn't going to run away from you while you're swinging." At the same time, Snead helped disprove an old golf assumption that long hitters weren't good players; he was said to be an ideal "long putter."

A teenage caddy, Snead turned professional in 1933, beginning as the house pro at the Greenbrier resort in White Sulpher Springs, West Virginia. The next year, at age 24, Snead shot 61 in that state's professional championship, foretelling his future of PGA success. Soon Snead was hitting the road in search of new golf challenges. In those post–Depression days, the young player was given to displays of thrift, driving a used car and watching for $1.50–per–night motels. In 1946 Snead "chafed," as a *New York Times* article put it, when his expenses for competing in and traveling to the British Open exceeded his winnings. It would be another two decades before Snead returned to that tournament.

But Snead showed little resistance to dominating United States contests. By 1938 he had set a record for PGA winnings. However, one prize did elude "Slammin' Sam"—the U.S. Open, whose tournaments he played from 1937 to 1977, finishing second four times. His loss in 1939—when, on the last hole, holding a one–stroke lead, Snead's putting proved disastrous—is considered one of the great heartbreaks of the golfer's career.

The caliber of Snead's opponents no doubt helped his game. The golfer regularly played against such names as Ben Hogan, Byron Nelson, and Arnold Palmer. Snead accumulated numerous honors, including the Vardon Trophy for the lowest stroke average, which he won four times. He played in the Ryder Cup eight times. In 1949 Snead was the winner of the Masters Tournament, the first man to wear the coveted green jacket of the Augusta National Golf Club; he won again in 1952 and 1954, the latter time beating Hogan by one stroke in an 18–hole playoff.

Though Snead's expertise was rarely in question, time eventually caught up with the star. In the 1960s he developed what golfers call the "yips," which, according to Bart Barnes's *Washington Post* article, "is common to golfers of middle age and beyond. For reasons said to be partly physical and partly psychological, golfers suffering from the yips find short putts extremely difficult." Snead coped by developing what Barnes called "a 'sidesaddle' style of putting in which he faced the hole, feet together, holding the top of the putter with his left hand clenched into a fist, his right hand positioned well down the shaft."

Seemingly unstoppable, Snead continued professional play into his late sixties. In 1979, he was the youngest pro to shoot his age, 67. As late as 2002, in the face of failing health, Snead drove the ceremonial first ball at the Masters. But a series of strokes felled the great champion. He died on May 23, 2002, at the age of 89. Snead is survived by his two sons; his wife, Audrey, died in 1990.

The occasion of Snead's passing brought remembrances from his peers. Jack Nicklaus told *GolfOnline* that Snead "brought so much to the game with his great swing and the most fluid motion ever to grace a golf course." He was "probably the greatest athlete that golf has ever had," declared Gary Player to the *Los Angeles Times*. "Maybe in time, Tiger [Woods] will prove to be the athlete of this century in golf, but in the last, Sam Snead was the best athlete." The same article quoted a 1995 remark by the paper's late columnist Jim Murray, who said of Snead: "He was as loose–jointed as an ocelot, as uninhibited as a cub bear. The golf club was a wand. Watching Snead play golf was like watching [Gene] Kelly dance, [Babe] Ruth bat, [Spencer] Tracy act, [Sandy] Koufax pitch, or [Jack] Dempsey punch. A work of art." **Sources:** *GolfOnline*, http://sportsillustrated.cnn.com/golfonline/news/2002/05/23/snead_obit_ap/ (May 23, 2002); *Guardian* (London), May 25, 2002, p. 22; *Los Angeles Times*, May 24, 2002, p. A1; *New York Times*, May 24, 2002, p. C11; *Washington Post*, May 24, 2002, p. D1, p. D4.

—*Susan Salter*

Rod Steiger

Born Rodney Stephen Steiger, April 14, 1925, in Westhampton, NY; died of pneumonia and kidney failure, July 9, 2002, in Los Angeles, CA. Actor. A Method actor known for his ability to transform himself completely for his roles in television, stage, and film, Rod Steiger performed alongside another Method actor of his generation, Marlon Brando, in *On the Waterfront,* and a won an Oscar in 1967 for his role as a bigoted sheriff in the film *In the Heat of the Night.*

Steiger was born in 1925 in the Long Island, New York, town of Westhampton. He came from a family of performers; both of his parents made their living on stage. Steiger's parents, Lorraine and Frederick Steiger, split up when Steiger was one year old. He was an only child, and spent his childhood with his mother, who suffered from alcoholism after Steiger's father left her.

After the divorce, Steiger and his mother moved to New Jersey, where he had his first acting experiences while still in elementary school. He later re-

called searching for his mother in local saloons to make her come home. His mother's difficulties, he later said, gave him the intense focus on the craft of acting for which he was to become famous; embarrassed by his mother's behavior, he determined to bring respectability to the name of Steiger.

Steiger put his acting aspirations on hold, however, when the United States entered World War II in 1942. Then only 16 years old, and with only a year of high school under his belt, he lied about his age and joined the Navy. There he served in the South Pacific as a torpedoman on the destroyer *Taussig,* seeing combat on such famous battlefields as Iwo Jima and Okinawa.

Home from the war in 1945, Steiger returned to the New York area, settling in Newark, New Jersey. Supporting himself as a clerk for the Veterans Administration, he began to study acting at the New School for Social Research in New York. In 1946 and 1947, Steiger continued his studies with famed acting teacher Lee Strasberg at New York's Actors Studio. It was under Strasberg that Steiger became a proponent of the Method, which has an actor drawing on memories of personal experiences to fuel raw, intensely personal performances. Steiger began his acting career in earnest in 1948, appearing in more than 250 television shows between then and 1953.

He made his Broadway theater and film debuts in 1951. His first Broadway role was in the drama by Clifford Odets, *Night Music.* He first appeared in film in a small role in *Teresa.* Another notable performance at this time was his portrayal of Marlon Brando's brother in *On the Waterfront.* The performance won Steiger his first Oscar nomination. The film itself won no less than seven Oscars, including one for Best Picture.

The success of *On the Waterfront* brought Steiger to a new level in his acting career. Film roles followed at a rapid pace, including that of Judd in the 1955 film version of the musical *Oklahoma!* Steiger's career continued to do well in the 1960s, and it was then that he turned in what many considered his best performance: his portrayal of a Holocaust survivor operating a pawnshop in Harlem in *The Pawnbroker,* directed by Sidney Lumet. But although Steiger was certain he would win an Oscar for that role, the Best Actor award went to Lee Marvin that year, for his performance in *Cat Ballou.* Steiger would have to wait two more years to earn an Oscar; in 1967, he won an Oscar for his performance as the bigoted Sheriff Gillespie in *In the Heat of the Night*. Also in the 1960s, Steiger appeared in the epic film *Doctor Zhivago*.

One of Steiger's few regrets in life was turning down the role of World War II General George S. Patton in the film of the same name, which was shot soon after Steiger's Oscar win. The role instead went to George C. Scott, who won an Oscar for his performance. Steiger's star began to fade. While his performances remained strong, he performed in mostly supporting roles, leaving the spotlight to other actors. One notable exception was his portrayal of the title characters in the 1969 film *The Illustrated Man*, which was based on a collection of short stories by science fiction author Ray Bradbury.

Steiger struggled with personal problems through the 1970s and 1980s, battling depression and alcoholism. He made two suicide attempts during this time—once by taking pills, another by trying to drown himself in the ocean near his Malibu, California, home. The actor made no secret about his difficulties, and in the 1990s, he testified before Congress about the illness of depression. This testimony was instrumental in the passage of a bill releasing almost $24 million in funds for the study of mental health issues. Steiger also became the public face of a decade–long public awareness campaign about depression. Through a combination of therapy and medication, Steiger got himself back together, and he continued to act through the 1990s, appearing in such films as *The Hurricane, Mars Attacks!*, and *Crazy in Alabama*. His last film appearance was as a grandfather searching for his son in the 2001 film *A Month of Sundays*.

Steiger died on July 9, 2002, of pneumonia and kidney failure at a hospital in Los Angeles; he was 77. His marriages to Sally Gracie, Claire Bloom, Sherry Nelson, and Paula Ellis ended in divorce. He is survived by his fifth wife, Joan Benedict; his daughter, Anna, by his second wife; and his son, Michael, by his fourth wife. **Sources:** *Los Angeles Times*, July 10, 2002, p. A1, p. A14; *New York Times*, July 10 2002, p. A23; *Washington Post*, July 10, 2002, p. B6.

—*Michael Belfiore*

Dave Thomas

Born Rex David Thomas, July 2, 1932, in Atlantic City, NJ; died of liver cancer, January 8, 2002, in Ft. Lauderdale, FL. Founder of Wendy's International.

Thomas helped to attract customers to his restaurants by starring in his own commercials as a down–home, grandfatherly figure. He made more than 800 commercials, earning recognition in the Guinness Book of World Records as having starred in more advertisements than any other company founder. According to a survey conducted by Wendy's, fully 90 percent of Americans recognized Thomas as the founder of Wendy's. "Dave was our patriarch, a great, big, lovable man," Wendy's International CEO Jack Schuessler told Ameet Sachdev of the *Chicago Tribune* after Thomas's death. "He was the heart and soul of our company."

Adopted when he was a baby, Thomas lost his adoptive mother to rheumatic fever when he was still a young boy. His adoptive father, Rex, moved around a lot, and married three more times, causing Thomas to lose two stepmothers by the time he was ten years old. Of his remaining relatives, Thomas was closest to his adoptive maternal grandmother, Millie Sinclair, whose insistence on doing a job right was to become a life–long motto for Thomas. "Don't cut corners," his grandmother told him, according to Douglas Martin of the *New York Times*. And so he didn't, later creating distinctive, square–shaped hamburgers for his restaurants.

Thomas and his grandmother spent a lot of time eating in lunch counters, an activity he loved so much, that by the time he was eight years old, he determined that he would one day run his own restaurant. "Popeye wasn't my hero," he later said, according to the *New York Times*'s Martin. "Wimpy was, because he loved hamburgers." When Thomas was 15 years old, he landed a restaurant job with a boss who was to become a role–model for him. Still wearing a three–piece suit, Thomas's boss would help to clean his restaurant, scrubbing floors, and wiping counters. Thomas thought to himself, according to Martin, "If my boss can do everything, I can, too."

Thomas's adoptive father moved again when Thomas was in the tenth grade, and Thomas made the decision not to go with him, dropping out of high school to support himself with full–time work. He later joined the U.S. Army, serving as an enlisted-men's club manager in West Germany. Out of the Army, Thomas went back to work for his old restaurant boss. The boss acquired four down–on–their luck Kentucky Fried Chicken restaurants in Columbus, Ohio, and he gave Thomas an ownership stake in exchange for making them profitable. Thomas succeeded, and he sold his stake in 1968 for more than $1 million. Thomas opened the first Wendy's in downtown Columbus, Ohio, in November of

1969. The restaurant's name was the nickname of one of his daughters, Melinda Lou, a freckle–faced redhead who later graced the restaurant chain's logo, and she came to the opening to help greet customers. Thomas's stated goal for the restaurant at the time was simply to be able to provide employment for each of his five children. But less than ten years later, Thomas found himself at the helm of a 1,000–restaurant chain. By 2002, that number had grown to 6,000 restaurants. In 1995, Wendy's International bought a Canadian chain called Tim Hortons, and so ran an additional 2,000 stores.

Said National Restaurant Association president Steven C. Anderson in the *New York Times*, of Thomas, "he achieved an unprecedented level of success in a highly competitive segment of the restaurant business." Thomas relinquished control of day–to–day management of his company in 1982, but the chain began to falter in his absence, so he took a more active role again in the late 1980s, including starring in the company's commercials.

Because he was an orphan himself, Thomas devoted much of his free time to the cause of helping foster children find adoptive homes. U.S. President George H.W. Bush appointed him a national spokesperson on the issue, and President Bill Clinton, too, recognized Thomas as an influential leader in this area.

Because of his own less–than–ideal upbringing, Thomas, by his own admission, was not a perfect father. And, as his son Ken told *People* in 1993, and reported by Martin in the *New York Times*, "He doesn't seem to know how to be with us. For him, home is a nice place to visit, but he doesn't want to live there." Thomas said of his own father in his 1991 book *Dave's Way*, and quoted in the *Washington Post*, "I never remember him hugging me or showing any affection." Thomas called dropping out of high school a life–long regret, and in 1993, he earned his General Equivalency Diploma (G.E.D.).

Thomas died of liver cancer on January 8, 2002, at the age of 69, in his home in Ft. Lauderdale, Florida. He is survived by his wife, Lorraine; their son, Ken; daughters Melinda Lou ("Wendy"), Pam, Molly, and Lori; and 16 grandchildren. **Sources:** *Chicago Tribune*, January 9, 2002, section 3, p. 1, p. 3; *Los Angeles Times*, January 9, 2002, p. B10; *New York Times*, January 9, 2002, p. A23; *Washington Post*, January 9, 2002, p. B5.

—*Michael Belfiore*

Johnny Unitas

Born John Constantine Unitas, May 7, 1933, in Pittsburgh, PA; died September 11, 2002, in Timonium, MD. Professional football player. A quarterback for most of his career for the Baltimore Colts, Johnny Unitas broke almost every National Football League (NFL) passing record. He is credited with helping to bring the game of football into the modern era, and has twice been voted the greatest quarterback in the history of the game. He was inducted into the Football Hall of Fame in 1979.

Unitas was born in 1933 in Pittsburgh, Pennsylvania. When he was four years old (some sources say five), he lost his father, who owned a coal delivery business, to pneumonia. Left with four children, Unitas's mother went to night school to learn how to be a bookkeeper so that she could support her family.

Turned down for college at Notre Dame, Unitas went to the University of Louisville, where on his first day on the football field, the head coach mistook him for the water boy because of his small stature. By the time he was a sophomore, however, there was no doubt that he was a force to be reckoned with on the field. That year, 1952, he attracted the attention of pro football recruiters when he completed 17 out of a total of 22 passes to lead his team to victory against Florida State.

Graduating from college in 1955, Unitas was signed by the Pittsburgh Steelers, but, astonishingly, was cut from the team in training camp. To add insult to injury, Unitas was handed $10 and told to buy himself a bus ticket home. He decided instead to keep the money and hitchhike back to Pittsburgh.

Unitas found a job as a construction worker, and managed to continue playing football, with the Bloomfield Rams, a team of the Greater Pittsburgh League. It was a fan who convinced recruiters at the Baltimore Colts to give Unitas another shot at playing pro football. After Colts coach Weeb Eubank saw Unitas in action, he signed him to the team in 1956.

In 1958, Unitas played in the game that has since come to be called the greatest game ever played. The game featured the Colts against the Giants. With only 90 seconds remaining on the clock, Unitas completed four passes that moved the Colts forward a crucial 85 yards and set the team up for a field goal that tied the game. Unitas was instrumental in gaining the Colts the tie–breaking, game-winning point. The game, nationally televised, made football fans out of millions of Americans, and is credited with helping to make the game of American football a national obsession.

Unitas played for a total of 18 years for the Colts, winning three championships for the team. He was three times (some sources say twice) voted the NFL's most valuable player (MVP). For 47 games in a row, from 1956 to 1960, Unitas threw at least one touchdown pass. This is a record that remains undefeated.

In 1969, Unitas was named by the NFL 50th Anniversary Committee the greatest quarterback of all time. The following year he was named player of the decade by the Associated Press. He was also named to the All–Pro team a total of five times. In 2000, Unitas was again voted the best quarterback in the history of the game, this time by the 36–member panel responsible for electing players to the Football Hall of Fame.

Unitas played for the Colts for all but the last five games of his pro football career. In 1973, he was sold to the San Diego Chargers for $150,000. The Chargers doubled the $125,000 salary he had been paid by the Colts. It was with the Chargers that Unitas became the first quarterback to top a career total of 40,000 yards passed. Unitas retired from the game in 1974 with one year remaining on his contract.

Unitas retired with a career total of 5,186 passes, 2,830 of which were completed. His total yardage on passes was 40,239. He led the Colts to two consecutive NFL Championships, in 1958 and 1959. In 1970 he led his team to victory in the Super Bowl. At the time of his retirement he held no less than 22 NFL records, including those for most passes attempted, most passes completed, most yards gained passing, and most seasons as the top touchdown passer in the NFL.

After retiring from playing football, Unitas went to work as a football commentator for CBS. This career choice turned out to be less than ideal for Unitas, who at times found himself tongue–tied on the air. Classes to improve his diction failed to appease his superiors at CBS, and the network let him go after five years. According to Sam Farmer in the *Los Angeles Times*, Unitas said, "I was expected to be glib, funny, insightful and speak perfectly. But I wasn't prepared." In his later years, Unitas pursued several business interests, including a Baltimore–area

restaurant called the Golden Arm. For a few years, he broadcast a radio show from the restaurant. He also became a frequent public speaker.

Unitas suffered a heart attack while exercising at a Timonium, Maryland, physical therapy center. After he collapsed, medical personnel at the therapy center tried to revive him, but without success. He was taken to the nearby St. Joseph Medical Center, where he was pronounced dead. The heart attack was the second for Unitas. His first had been in 1993, after which he had undergone emergency triple–bypass surgery.

Unitas died on September 11, 2002, at the age of 69. He is survived by his second wife, Sandra; daughters Janice and Paige; and sons Kenneth, Robert, Chris, John Jr., Joe, and Chad. **Sources:** *Chicago Tribune*, September 12, 2002, p. 4/1, p. 4/10; *Los Angeles Times*, September 12, 2002, p. D1, p. D11; *New York Times*, September 12, 2002, p. C11; *Times* (London), September 13, 2002, p. 40; *Washington Post*, September 12 2002, p. D1, p. D5.

—*Michael Belfiore*

Robert Urich

Born December 19, 1946, in Toronto, OH; died April 16, 2002, in Thousand Oaks, CA. Actor. The archetypical made–for–TV heartthrob, Robert Urich held the record for the most starring roles—15—in television series both dramatic and comedic. "He was just one of the sweetest men I've ever met," producer Aaron Spelling told the *Los Angeles Times*. "No matter what you put him in, the audience loved him."

Urich was a product of blue–collar Toronto, Ohio, just west of Pittsburgh, Pennsylvania. He grew to a ruggedly handsome six–foot–two, distinguishing himself as a hometown football star who went on to study at Florida State University on an athletic scholarship. As a student Urich began working in front of the camera, hosting his own local series. He earned his bachelor's degree in radio and television communications in 1968, and added a master's degree in 1971 from Michigan State University. On–camera and behind–the–scenes work at a Chicago news station followed, but Urich found his true calling when he agreed to portray a soldier for a Jewish United Bond appeal. Hooked on acting, the young man made his way to the Chicago stage. After playing Burt Reynolds's younger brother in a 1972 production of *The Rainmaker,* Urich heeded his co-star's advice to move to Hollywood.

It didn't take long for television to discover Urich. His first series, the 1973 sitcom *Bob & Carol & Ted & Alice,* was based on the risqué 1969 film about marital infidelity. As the "swinging" Bob, Urich played a character who urged his neighbors to join in the free-love culture. The series was cancelled in one season, but by then the actor was a recognizable face. That exposure led to Urich's next series, the controversial police drama *S.W.A.T.* He played Officer Jim Street, part of a police battalion whose violent ways led some viewers to mount a protest. *S.W. A.T* lasted 34 episodes.

By 1977 Urich was again trying his hand at comedy, playing playboy tennis pro Peter Campbell on the critically acclaimed soap opera spoof *Soap.* His character was murdered in the first season, but the "who killed Peter" subplot helped usher in an era of television season-ending "cliffhangers." Leaving *Soap* opened Urich to his first starring role in a show lasting more than one year. *Vega$,* which aired 1978–81, revolved around private eye Dan Tanna, a man who, the actor once noted, "wears wool jackets and a leather vest in 115-degree heat and drives his car into his living room." As the suave detective, Urich made *Vega$* a popular, if not a critical, success.

Perhaps Urich's most fleshed-out television role came in 1985, when he starred in *Spenser: For Hire,* a series based on Robert B. Parker's popular detective novels. Urich's Spenser (no first name) was a Boston-based private eye whose tough exterior masked a sense of morality and a love for the more refined pleasures of life, including gourmet cooking. The show lasted three seasons. The character was so popular that Urich starred in four feature-length Spencer made-for-television films.

While television was his forte, Urich also appeared on the big screen. He made his movie debut in 1973's *Magnum Force,* a sequel to *Dirty Harry.* In classic struggling-actor fashion, Urich told producers he was skilled at riding a motorcycle. The truth came out when in his big scene Urich—playing a vigilante biker—slid off a ramp and crashed into the other actors' bikes. Later, Urich was featured in such movies as *Ice Pirates, Turk 182!,* and *Cloverbend.* In 1999 he returned to the stage as conniving lawyer Billy Flynn in the Broadway revival of the musical *Chicago.*

Urich was starring in *The Lazarus Man* in 1996 when he made public his diagnosis of synovial cell sarcoma, a rare cancer that attacks the body's joints. Though he told producers he would be able to work, the show was cancelled; Urich subsequently sued for breach of contract. The news of Urich's illness made headlines, and the actor began a second career as a health advocate, establishing the Heather and Robert Urich Fund for Sarcoma Research. He made television appearances during his chemotherapy, not afraid to be seen bald or bloated.

His optimism made Urich a popular public speaker and fund-raiser. He received his star on the Hollywood Walk of Fame in 1995; other honors included the Gilda Radner Courage Award from the Roswell Park Cancer Institute. In 1998 Urich was named national spokesman for the American Cancer Society.

For a while, it seemed Urich was beating the disease. He continued acting on television, starring as the ship's captain in *Love Boat: The Next Wave* in 1998. As late as 2001 the actor was still well enough to take a supporting role in the short-lived sitcom *Emeril.* In early 2002 he played on a celebrity edition of *Who Wants to Be A Millionaire,* donating his winnings to cancer research. Urich died April 16, 2002, at the age of 55; he is survived by his wife, Heather Menzies; and three children. **Sources:** E! Online, http://www.eonline.com/News/Items/0,1,9812,00.html (April 16, 2002); *Independent* (London), April 17, 2002, p. 18; *Los Angeles Times,* April 17, 2002, p. B10; *New York Times,* April 17, 2002, p. A21; *Times* (London), April 19, 2002, p. 37; *Washington Post,* April 17, 2002, p. B5.

—*Susan Salter*

Lew Wasserman

Born Lewis Robert Wasserman, March 15 (some sources say March 22), 1913, in Cleveland, OH; died June 3, 2002, in Beverly Hills, CA. Chairman and Chief Executive of Music Corporation of America. Called "the last of the legendary movie moguls" by Jonathan Kandell in the *New York Times,* Lew Wasserman was one of the most powerful figures in Hollywood following World War II. During his company's early years as a talent agency, Music Corporation of America (MCA) had under contract such stars as Bette Davis, Jimmy Stewart, Judy Garland, Henry Fonda, Fred Astaire, Ginger Rogers, Gregory Peck, Billy Wilder, Alfred Hitchcock, and many others. Later, as a production company, MCA produced such blockbusters as *Airport, Jaws, Star Wars, E.T., Jurassic Park,* and *Back to the Future.* His company also produced numerous hit television series, including *Alfred Hitchcock Presents, Magnum P.I.,* and *Miami Vice,* and its music division put out albums by top recording artists such as Nirvana, Reba McEntire, and Elton John.

Wasserman was born and raised in Cleveland, Ohio, the son of Russian immigrants. It was the dream of Wasserman's parents, Isaac and Minnie, to run a successful restaurant in Cleveland, but the business never got off the ground. Wasserman started his career in entertainment as an usher in a movie and vaudeville theater while still in high school, and there met some of the best performers of the time, including Edgar Bergen and the comedy team of Burns and Allen.

After graduating from high school in 1930, Wasserman landed a job as a public relations specialist for a nightclub in Cleveland, and there worked mostly with clients of the MCA talent agency. Executives at MCA were impressed by Wasserman's deft handling of their clients, and they hired him away from the nightclub to work directly for them. In 1938, Wasserman and his wife, Edie, moved with MCA to California, where the company hoped to move from representing vaudeville acts to movie stars. The Wasserman's only child, Lynne Kay, was born in 1940.

Moving up the corporate ranks, Wasserman became president of MCA in 1946. Soon, his client list included most of Hollywood's top stars, whom he attracted by securing unprecedented freedoms for them. Wasserman's biggest achievement during this time was to do away with the seven–year studio contracts that actors were normally expected to sign, thus freeing his clients to sign on to individual projects with any studio they chose. With Wasserman's help, his clients's power grew to allow them to approve directors for their films, make script changes, and even earn percentages of box office revenues.

Early in the 1950s, Wasserman decided to turn his company into not only a talent agency, but a movie production house as well. Throughout the 1950s, MCA acquired assets from other production companies, including old films from Paramount Pictures, which he licensed for television broadcast, and Universal's back lot. MCA gradually acquired the rest of Universal's assets, turning the back lot into not only MCA's production facilities, but its corporate headquarters and the site of the Universal Studios amusement park as well.

In the early 1960s, MCA faced pressure from the United States government to sell off its talent agency, citing conflicts of interest with its movie studio. Wasserman initially fought this action, but finally acquiesced, thereafter vowing to use his vast influence to turn governmental politics in his favor. During the 1960s, Wasserman set a precedent for Hollywood political activism by organizing big fund–raisers for political campaigns, mostly for the Democratic Party.

The 1970s saw Wasserman at the vanguard of a new movie genre—the summer blockbuster. This phenomenon started with Wasserman's inspired marketing of director Steven Spielberg's first big hit, *Jaws,* in 1975, and he continued the successful formula with *Star Wars* in 1977, as well as other MCA blockbusters in the 1980s.

Wasserman's influence finally began to decline with the advent of big media conglomerates like Time Warner and the News Corporation. He sold MCA in 1990 to the Matsushita Electric Industrial Company of Japan. Although he retained managing control, he was at odds with his new bosses almost immediately; his power was effectively curtailed. In perhaps the biggest indication of the split between Wasserman and his parent company, Matsushita Electric sold MCA in 1995 to the Seagram company without telling Wasserman. Renamed Universal Studios by Seagram's parent company, Wasserman's old company kept him on as a consultant, but his days as a Hollywood mogul were over.

Along with his contribution to the film and television industry, Wasserman was known for supporting civil rights causes, and for donating large amounts of money to Jewish organizations and Catholic charities. In 1973, he received the Jean Hersholt Humanitarian Award from the Academy of Motion Picture Arts and Sciences, and in 1995, he was awarded the Presidential Medal of Freedom—the United States government's highest civilian honor—by President Clinton in a ceremony at the White House.

Wasserman died at the age of 89 in his home in Beverly Hills, California, after an extended illness following a stroke. He is survived by his wife, daughter, a grandson, Casey; and a granddaughter,

Carol. **Sources:** *Los Angeles Times*, June 4, 2002, p. A1; *New York Times*, June 4, 2002, p. A1; *Times* (London), June 5, 2002.

—*Michael Belfiore*

Byron White

Born June 8, 1917, in Fort Collins, CO; died of complications from pneumonia, April 15, 2002, in Denver, CO. Supreme Court justice. The conservative "odd man out" in the liberal Supreme Court of the John F. Kennedy administration, Justice Byron White dissented several notable rulings of the 1960s but always stood by his principles of accountability and responsibility.

White's appointment to the highest court in the United States capped a distinguished life that saw the Colorado native excelling in both sports and law. Born in Fort Collins, White was the son of parents who never completed high school; even still, his lumberman father served as the Republican mayor of Wellington, Colorado. As a youth White was as committed to his studies as he was to football, graduating with a straight–A average. "Byron was so smart," his classmate Ella Mae Doyle recalled in a *Denver Post* article, "that the teacher had to mark a few wrong answers on his tests, just to let him know he wasn't perfect."

A gifted running back, White entered the University of Colorado on a scholarship. In 1937 the 20–year–old was a star athlete, named All–American in football and leading Colorado's basketball team to the championships a year later. It was during his college years that the future judge obtained his life-long—and despised—nickname of "Whizzer." The valedictorian of his college class, White went on to win on a Rhodes scholarship to Oxford University. He deferred his trip to England, however, for another big chance—to play professional football for the Pittsburgh Pirates (later called the Pittsburgh Steelers). At that time, his starting salary, $15,800, was a record for a rookie.

Still the scholar–athlete, White, who led the professional league in rushing, attended Yale Law School when not playing ball for Pittsburgh and, later, the Detroit Lions. Eventually White made it to England, where he met the young John F. Kennedy. The two peers (born just ten days apart) became fast friends.

The advent of World War II interrupted White's dual careers; a Navy intelligence officer, he crossed paths with Kennedy again when White was assigned to write the official report on the sinking of the future president's PT–109 ship.

The postwar years found White finishing his legal studies and clerking for Supreme Court Chief Justice Fred Vinson. An attorney specializing in bankruptcy and tax issues, the low–key White shunned the political spotlight. It was Kennedy who brought White into the public eye, beginning in 1960 when the Massachusetts senator tapped White to head his presidential campaign in Colorado. With Kennedy's election came the offer for White to serve as deputy attorney general at the Justice Department under J.F.K.'s brother, Robert. Both Kennedy brothers, in fact, "admired White as a model for the new administration," according to a *Los Angeles Times* article by David Savage. "He was smart and tough, a skeptic but one who was committed to public service." In 1961 White was put to a difficult test when he accompanied 600 National Guardsmen to Alabama with a mission to protect the civil–rights "Freedom Riders" from opposition violence. "As a leader, White was calm, organized and definitely in charge," noted Savage.

In March of 1962, Supreme Court Justice Charles Whittaker retired, and John and Robert Kennedy nominated White to fill the open seat. It was a controversial move, said Savage: "They passed over a long list of Harvard academics and other distinguished lawyers in favor of a rookie Justice Department official with no judicial experience." The Senate confirmed the nomination and Justice Byron White was sworn in on April 1, 1962. At age 44 White was the youngest man to date to be named to the Supreme Court. He served 31 years and at the time of his death was the only living former Supreme Court judge.

White's years on the top bench were marked by dissenting opinion. He argued against the landmark *Roe v. Wade* abortion–rights decision, for example, stating that "the court apparently values the convenience of the pregnant mother more than the continued existence and development of the life or potential life that she carries," as quoted in the *Denver Post*. The *Miranda v. Arizona* ruling, which gives accused criminals "the right to remain silent," prompted another dissent: "I see nothing wrong or immoral, and certainly nothing unconstitutional in the police's asking a suspect whether or not he killed his wife," he wrote, as quoted at CNN.com.

Over the decades the Supreme Court shifted in tenor from the liberal days of Chief Justice Earl Warren to the more conservative environment of Chief Justice William Rehnquist. White stayed true to his beliefs; in 1991, for example, he dissented with an Indiana law that banned nude dancing, arguing that such a ban violated the right to free expression. Nude dancing "may not be high art, to say the least," he wrote, but "that should not be the determining factor in deciding this case." Such an opinion, in the words of *Independent* reporter Rupert Cornwell, "illustrated the unshakable conservatism of White's jurisprudence, and his belief that the court should confine itself to a narrow legal function."

White announced his retirement in March of 1993. Characteristically, he shied away from a press conference; instead, he sent a letter of thanks to his judicial colleagues. White lived to see a federal building in Washington, D.C., named in his honor; he spent the last year of his life in his home state of Colorado. White died of complications from pneumonia on April 15, 2002; he was 84. On the occasion of White's death, his peers recalled him as a man of substance. "Anyone who ever met Byron White will recall his painfully firm handshake," Justice Antonin Scalia was quoted in the *Los Angeles Times*. "I always thought that was an apt symbol for his role on this court.... If there is one adjective that never could, never would, be applied to Byron White, it is wishy–washy." White is survived by his wife, Marion; a son, Charles; a daughter, Nancy; and six grandchildren. **Sources:** CNN.com, http://www.cnn.com/2002/LAW/04/15/white.obit/index.html (April 15, 2002); *Denver Post*, April 16, 2002, p. A01; *Independent* (London), April 17, 2002, p. 18; *Los Angeles Times*, April 16, 2002, p. B10; *New York Times*, April 15, 2002, p. A1, p. A28; *Washington Post*, April 16, 2002, p. A1, p. A11.

—Susan Salter

Robert Whitehead

Born March 3, 1916, in Montréal, Quebec, Canada; died of cancer, June 15, 2002, in Pound Ridge, NY. Broadway producer. Robert Whitehead's more than 60 years in theater made him one of the most renowned producers of artful yet commercially successful Broadway plays. He collaborated with some of the 20th century's best actors, playwrights, producers, and directors. The *New York Times* described him as "a class act, the opposite of razzle–dazzle."

Whitehead was the son of William Thomas Whitehead, owner of textile mills throughout Canada, and Lena Mary Labatt Whitehead, an opera singer and member of the family that owned Labatt's brewery. He grew up in Montréal, often spending summers playing with his cousin, Hume Cronyn, who went on to a successful career in theater and film. He attended college at Trinity College School in Port Hope, Ontario. After graduation he worked as a commercial photographer. His stint with photography was short lived and soon he ventured to New York City with the vague idea of working in the theater.

In New York he studied acting at the New York School of Theatre. In 1936, he had his New York debut in the play *Night Must Fall*. Later he joined the Barter Theater in Abingdon, Virginia, where he took on several roles including acting, stage managing, and building scenery.

As World War II began to loom larger in the American consciousness, Whitehead had doubts about his desire to work in theater. The *New York Times* quoted him in his indecisiveness, "I was haunted by the question of whether I had any talent for any aspect of the theater—or was this a vagabond escape from responsible activities?" An essay by noted director and critic Harold Clurman changed Whitehead's mind and inspired him to achieve success within the world of theater. But first Whitehead enlisted in the American Field Service. From 1942 to 1945, Whitehead served as an ambulance driver in North Africa, Italy, and India.

Upon his return from the war, Whitehead abandoned acting for producing. The first play he produced was *Medea* as interpreted by Robinson Jeffers. Whitehead filled the lead roles with famed Australian actress Judith Anderson and noted Shakespearean actor John Gielgud. *Medea* and Whitehead's second production (also starring Gielgud), *Crime and Punishment*, were commercially successful. These successes earned Whitehead a reputation as someone who could produce financially lucrative works that were also considered art.

He continued his successful streak with an award–winning production of Carson McCuller's *Member of the Wedding* in 1950. Known as a quiet man, Whitehead was also capable of taking extraordinary chances. For *Member of the Wedding* he cast the relatively unknown actress Julie Harris, who was 24 at the time, to play the lead role of a 12–year–old child. He also sought out Ethel Waters, a popular singer and revue performer from the 1920s through the

1940s, to play the role of the cook. His choices were perfect, and the play was later made into a movie starring the same actors who had been in the play.

In 1956, his first play—*Bus Stop*—was nominated for a Tony Award. In 1957, Whitehead had five plays on Broadway: *Separate Tables, Orpheus Descending, The Waltz of the Toreadors, A Hole in the Head,* and *Major Barbara.* In 1962, his production of *A Man for All Seasons* won Tony Awards for best dramatic production and best play.

In 1960, Whitehead and Elia Kazan were asked to head the first Lincoln Center theater company. By 1964 the Lincoln Center Repertory Theater was established and opened for its first season. Their first production was *After the Fall,* written by Arthur Miller and starring Jason Robards. Unfortunately, *After the Fall* and the other plays that opened that first season were not well received. Kazan and Whitehead left the company that year amid controversies involving conflicts with the board of directors.

Whitehead continued to produce and sometimes direct plays. He had a longstanding relationship with Arthur Miller, producing many of Miller's later plays. He earned a Tony Award in 1984 for his highly successful restaging of *Death of a Salesman* starring Dustin Hoffman. Other outstanding playwrights that he worked with included Tennessee Williams, Carson McCullers, Eugene O'Neill, Thornton Wilder, Friedrich Dürrenmatt, Jean Anouilh, and Robert Bolt.

Not everything that Whitehead attempted was a success. His ability with drama did not appear to include musicals. His productions of musicals were well–publicized flops including 1958's *Goldilocks,* 1961's *The Conquering Hero,* and 1976's *1600 Pennsylvania Avenue,* which closed after playing for only one week.

In total, Whitehead won six Tony Awards. In 1996, his production of the play *Master Class* starring his wife, Australian actress Zoe Caldwell, earned a Tony for best play. In 2002, only a few weeks before his death, Whitehead was presented with a Special Lifetime Achievement Tony Award for his more than 60 years of work in theater.

Whitehead's first wife, Virginia, died in 1965; he married Caldwell in 1968. He died on June 15, 2002, at his home in Pound Ridge, New York, of cancer; he was 86. Whitehead is survived by his wife and their two sons, Sam and Charlie. As a man whose name often guaranteed the quality of play, Whitehead will be remembered, as this quote from the *New York Times* described, as "a quiet, assertive force, often a mediator and a man with impeccable taste." **Sources:** *Los Angeles Times,* June 18, 2002, p. B10; *New York Times,* June 17, 2002, p. A18; *Times* (London), July 4, 2002; *Washington Post,* June 18, 2002, p. B6.

—*Eve M. B. Hermann*

Billy Wilder

Born Samuel Wilder, June 22, 1906, in Sucha, in the Austro–Hungarian Empire; died of pneumonia, March 27, 2002, in Beverly Hills, CA. Screenwriter, director, and producer. The son of middle–European Jewish parents, Billy Wilder worked in the German and French film industries before emigrating to Hollywood in 1934. Collaborating with native English-speaking writers, Wilder was a sought–after screenwriter in the 1930s. After a successful directorial debut in 1942, he became a major figure, co–writing and directing such films as *Sunset Boulevard, Some Like It Hot,* and *The Apartment.* Besides receiving 21 Academy Award nominations (winning six times), he was the recipient of numerous life achievement honors, which he jokingly referred to as "Quick, before they croak" awards, according to a *New York Times* obituary.

As a writer–director, Wilder was known for his caustic wit and sometimes criticized for his hard–nosed cynicism, personified by decidedly unsympathetic heroes, such as Fred MacMurray's murderous insurance agent in 1944's *Double Indemnity,* Kirk Douglas's exploitative reporter in 1951's *Ace in the Hole,* and William Holden's mercenary screenwriter who narrates 1950's *Sunset Boulevard* from the pool of a Beverly Hills mansion, where he floats dead.

The younger of two brothers born in the town of Sucha (now in Poland), in the Austro–Hungarian Empire, Samuel "Billie" Wilder was born to an entrepreneurial father, Max Wilder, and the former Eugenie Baldinger, who was so taken by American culture she nicknamed her son after Buffalo Bill Cody, the touring showman. Wilder's father died while he was still a child. His brother emigrated to the United States around 1922. His mother, grandmother, and stepfather all died in the Auschwitz concentration camp during the Holocaust.

After attending the rough equivalent of high school in Vienna, Wilder enrolled in the University of Vienna to please his family who expected him to study law. He dropped out after only three months, taking a job as a copy boy for the Viennese daily *Die Stunde.* Initially he reported on sports and culture, but soon was entrusted with interviews. In one infamous effort, he tried to interview Sigmund Freud by posing as a patient, only to be thrown out.

Another legendary encounter allegedly got him into the motion picture business. Wilder had moved to Berlin, where he was working as a freelance journalist. One day, in his apartment, he was confronted by a man escaping discovery by a jealous boyfriend next door who came home unexpectedly. In the lover's hasty flight, he had left his clothes behind. Wilder instantly recognized him as Galitzenstein, a famous movie producer, and offered his help on one condition: that Galitzenstein read a screenplay Wilder had written. "I'll buy it," responded the producer, script in hand. "It feels like a good story," he said, according to a *Los Angeles Times* obituary. The encounter in any of its several reported versions bears a dubious likeness to the kind of oddball situations Wilder devised for his films.

When Adolf Hitler came to power in 1933, Wilder, who had by then established himself as a screenwriter in Berlin, did not wait to pack his bags for France. During a 10–month stay in Paris he wrote and co–directed the film *Bad Seed.* Then came an invitation to Hollywood from a film producer, Joe May, whom Wilder had known in Germany. Accepting a one–way ticket, Wilder started as a writer at Columbia pictures at $150 a week. Learning English by listening to baseball games on the radio and acquiring 20 new words a day, Wilder contributed to a number of films during his early years in Hollywood, scoring huge successes with 1938's *Bluebird's Eighth Wife* and 1939's *Ninotchka,* both directed by fellow émigré and idol Ernst Lubitsch. During Wilder's long retirement, visitors to his office in Beverly Hills noticed a large plaque that read, "How would Lubitsch do it?"

From his directorial debut with 1942's *The Major and the Minor,* starring Ginger Rogers, Wilder always worked as both writer and director, sometimes producing his films as well. Although he thoroughly mastered the English language, throughout his Hollywood career he never wrote a script without the assistance of a native English–speaking collaborator. Two partnerships stand out. From 1936 to 1950 he worked with Charles Brackett, a Harvard–educated New York State senator's son. Together they penned the two Lubitsch comedies, winning an Oscar nomination for *Ninotchka,* and later the classics *The Lost Weekend* (1945), starring

Ray Milland as a struggling alcoholic, and 1950's masterpiece *Sunset Boulevard,* a gritty drama featuring Gloria Swanson as a forgotten silent movie queen. An exception during this period was the 1944 "film noir" *Double Indemnity,* co–written by Raymond Chandler, author of the Philip Marlowe detective novels. Starting with 1957's *Love in the Afternoon,* a romance which paired Gary Cooper with Audrey Hepburn, Wilder collaborated with I.A.L. "Izzy" Diamond. This monumental partnership lasted through Wilder's last film, the Jack Lemmon and Walter Matthau reunion *Buddy Buddy,* in 1981. Among the Wilder–Diamond triumphs are 1959's *Some Like It Hot,* 1960's *The Apartment,* and 1966's *The Fortune Cookie.* All three films starred Jack Lemmon, Wilder's "everyman," with whom he collaborated seven times. Wilder directed Lemmon three times opposite his frequent co–star Matthau, and twice directed Marilyn Monroe (in 1955's *The Seven Year Itch* and in *Some Like It Hot*). Monroe required up to 59 takes to get her lines right. Asked if he would ever work with her again, he said, "In the United States, I'd hate it. In Paris, it might not be so bad. While we were waiting, we could all take painting lessons," he said, according to the *Independent.*

Other hits included 1953's *Stalag 17,* starring Holden; 1954's *Sabrina,* with Holden, Hepburn, and Humphrey Bogart; 1957's *The Spirit of St. Louis,* starring James Stewart as Charles Lindbergh; 1958's *Witness for the Prosecution,* with Marlene Dietrich, Charles Laughton, and Tyrone Power; 1961's *One, Two, Three,* starring James Cagney; and his highest grossing film, 1963's *Irma la Douce,* with Lemmon and Shirley MacLaine. Wilder's string of critical and box–office successes, beginning in the 1940s, is unparalleled in cinema history.

In addition to his 21 Academy Award nominations, leading to six wins in the directing, writing and producing categories—for *The Lost Weekend* and *The Apartment*—Wilder was honored by the Cannes International Film Festival in 1979, the Screen Writers Guild in 1980, the Film Society of Lincoln Center in 1982, the American Film Institute in 1986, and the Academy of Motion Picture Arts and Sciences in 1987.

As a film student, this writer used to visit Wilder at his Beverly Hills office when the long–retired director was in his eighties. On one occasion, Wilder remarked, "Any critic who likes your picture is a good critic," adding that he preferred those from the *New York Times,* "because even when they don't like your picture they still call you *mister.*"

Wilder's first marriage was to Judith Coppicus Iribe, in 1936 (they divorced in 1947), with whom he had one daughter, Victoria. In 1949, he married actress Audrey Young. He died in his sleep of pneumonia on March 27, 2002, in Beverly Hills, at the age of 95. He is survived by his wife, daughter, and a granddaughter. **Sources:** "Billy Wilder," pamphlet, University of Southern California Filmic Writing Program, produced for its Wilder film retrospective, 1991; *Independent* (London), March 30, 2002, p. 6; *Los Angeles Times*, March 29, 2002, p. A1; *New York Times*, March 29, 2002, p. A1; personal interview with Billy Wilder, c. 1990s.

—*D. László Conhaim*

Ted Williams

Born Teddy Samuel Williams, August 30, 1918, in San Diego, CA; died July 5, 2002, in Inverness, FL. Professional baseball player. Hailed as perhaps the greatest hitter in the history of baseball, Ted Williams played 19 seasons with the Boston Red Sox from 1939 to 1960. In 1941 he became the last pro league player to hit an average of .400 in a single season. Interrupted from playing baseball a total of five seasons during his prime playing years while he flew fighter planes in World War II and the Korean War, Williams nevertheless retired with one of the best records in the history of baseball.

Williams's stated goal was to become the greatest baseball hitter in the world. By most accounts, he succeeded; although Babe Ruth hit more home runs, and Ty Cobb had a better lifetime average, no other player matched Williams for his combination of power and average. He co–authored a book with John Underwood in 1970 called *The Science of Hitting*, which is today considered the most important book on batting. Williams attributed his phenomenal success as a hitter to an unswerving dedication to the study of batting, and to his superb eyesight, at one time measured as 20/10.

Williams was born in San Diego, California, in 1918, and he grew up in the San Diego neighborhood of North Park. His parents were Sam and May Williams. Williams was the oldest of two boys born to the couple, and he was named Teddy (Williams preferred Theodore) in honor of President Teddy Roosevelt, with whom Sam Williams claimed to ridden while they both served in the United States Calvary. Williams's mother worked in the Salvation Army, helping the homeless of Tijuana, Mexico, just across the border from San Diego.

Williams later said in his autobiography, *My Turn at Bat*, published in 1969, that he was ashamed of his home life growing up, because he never had nice clothes to wear and his mother spent more time among homeless people than with her own family. He also said that his relationship with his father was equally distant.

First playing baseball in high school, Williams went within two years of graduating to playing first for his local Pacific Coast League, and then joining the Boston Red Sox in April of 1939. Williams hit .327 in his rookie season with the Red Sox, quickly earning the nickname the Splendid Splinter because he was tall and thin and had a graceful swing. In his second season, he did even better, batting .344. In 1941, Williams hit .356, and had 137 runs batted in (RBI), including 36 home runs. These accomplishments earned him the Triple Crown, a title that honors a player who leads the league in home runs, batting average, and RBI. Williams also won a Triple Crown in 1947.

In 1942, the United States entered World War II, and Williams, then at the top of his game at the age of 24, joined the United States Navy. He entered the Navy as an aviation cadet, and eventually earned his wings as an officer in the Marines. Slated to see action in the South Pacific, Williams was called home when the war ended in 1945, before he could be sent to the front. He rejoined the Red Sox in time for the 1946 season.

In his first season back with the Red Sox, Williams batted .342, hit 38 home runs, and had 123 RBI. He led the Red Sox to the pennant that year, earning himself American League most valuable player (MVP) honors. Although he brought his team to the World Series, the Red Sox did not win. It was Williams's only World Series. Also in 1946, Williams hit the longest home run in the history of Boston's Fenway Park. His hit landed in the 33rd row of seats, a distance of more than 500 feet from home plate. The seat where the ball landed was later painted red to contrast with the surrounding green seats to mark the spot.

The United States entered the Korean War in the 1950s, and this time Williams saw combat. Leaving the Red Sox to fly fighter planes, he fought in 39 missions. On two separate occasions, his plane was hit by antiaircraft fire, forcing him to land—fortunately not in enemy territory.

Williams retired from playing baseball in 1960, after hitting a slump in the 1959 season, in which he slipped to a .254 batting average. Williams was disappointed in this performance, and for his final season, he insisted on a 30% pay cut, receiving $90,000 instead of his previous pay of $125,000. Williams went out with a bang, however, at his last at–bat, hitting a home run off pitcher Jack Fisher of the Baltimore Orioles. His hitting record for the 19 seasons he played between 1939 and 1960 stood at .344. He was inducted into the Baseball Hall of Fame in 1966.

At the end of the 1960s, Williams became manager of the Washington Senators. He held this position until 1972, the year the team moved to Texas and became the Texas Rangers. In addition to his activities as a pro ball player, Williams donated time and money to charities aiding children with cancer. His favorite leisure pursuits during retirement were fishing and playing golf and tennis. In 1982 Williams wrote another book with Underwood titled *Fishing the Big Three*, which focused on tarpon, bonefish, and Atlantic salmon. He also made regular appearances at Red Sox spring training to coach young hitters in the art in which he was the master. He engaged in these activities for more than 30 years, until he suffered a stroke in 1991. In 1999, the *Boston Globe* named Williams the New England sports figure of the 20th century. The city of Boston also named its $2.3 billion harbor tunnel after Williams.

Williams was married and divorced three times. His first marriage was to Doris Soule, whom he married in 1944; they divorced in 1955. He married Lee Howard in 1961. This marriage lasted until 1966, and the following year, he married Dolores Wettach, whom he divorced in 1972. His companion after this was Louise Kaufman, whom he did not marry, and who died in 1993. Williams died of cardiac arrest in a hospital in Inverness, Florida, on July 5, 2002 at the age of 83. He is survived by his daughter, Bobbie Jo, by his first wife; and a son and a daughter, John Henry and Claudia, by his third wife. **Sources:** *Los Angeles Times*, July 6, 2002, p. A1, p. A14; *New York Times*, July 6, 2002, p. A1, p. B18; *Times* (London), July 8, 2002, p. 33; *Washington Post*, July 6, 2002, p. A1, p. A8.

—*Michael Belfiore*

Irene Worth

Born Harriet Abrams, June 23, 1916, in Fairbury, NE; died of a stroke, March 10, 2002, in New York, NY. Actress. Considered one of the greatest stage actresses of her time, Irene Worth epitomized the classical actor. During her long career she won three

Tony awards, a British Film Academy Award, and received an honorable Commander of the British Empire (CBE).

Worth was the daughter of Nebraska schoolteachers, both of whom were Mennonites. In 1920 the family relocated to California, settling first in a Mennonite community in Reedley, then (in 1928) in San Luis Obispo, and later in Saticoy, near Ventura, in 1930. The latter moves marked the family's break with the Mennonite life. Harriet attended high school in San Luis Obispo, Ventura, and Costa Mesa. Her first stage role came in high school when she appeared in *The Mikado*. After graduation she enrolled in Santa Ana Junior College (now Santa Ana College), then transferred to the University of California–Los Angeles (UCLA) after two years. While at UCLA she appeared in a number of student productions including, *A Bill of Divorcement*, *The Children's Hour*, and *Ethan Frome*. She also had a bit role in a Hollywood film. She graduated in 1937 with a degree in education and began teaching kindergarten, but in 1942 she struck out for New York and a career in the theater. In New York she took the name Irene (pronounced I–ree–nee) Worth. Her first post–college acting job was with a touring company of *Escape Me Never* in 1942. She scored her first Broadway role in 1943 in *The Two Mrs. Carrolls*. Elizabeth Bergner, the star of *The Two Mrs. Carrolls*, persuaded Worth to move to London, England, where she studied drama with Elsie Fogarty, aspiring to be a classical actress. Worth performed in various plays throughout the 1940s in the lesser theaters, prior to taking on the role of Celia in T. S. Eliot's *The Cocktail Party*. She originated the role at the Edinburgh festival and also played it in London and on Broadway. According to the *New York Times*, renowned critic Brooks Atkinson—in his review of her Broadway performance—wrote that Worth gave "a remarkably skillful, passionate and perceptive performance." From then on the indefatigable Worth alternated between New York and London with occasional stops in Canada.

Worth joined the Old Vic company in 1951 and appeared in *A Midsummer Night's Dream* in the role of Helena, directed by Tyrone Guthrie. She also gave her first performance as Lady Macbeth at the Old Vic, and appeared in *The Other Heart*, about poet François Villon. She later toured South Africa with the company.

In 1953 Worth became a founding member of the Shakespeare festival in Stratford, Ontario; she was the principal leading lady opposite Alec Guinness. The two appeared together in *All's Well That Ends Well*. In his review of the play Atkinson captured

Worth's talent in a sentence, calling her performance "superb" and one that "overflows with loveliness, devotion, ceremony and modest guile." Worth also appeared in *Richard III* that season. She was soon back on the London stage in *A Day by the Sea*, which costarred John Gielgud and Ralph Richardson. Worth proved her versatility in the late 1950s when she costarred with Guinness in the farce, *Hotel Paradiso*, had the title role in Schiller's *Mary Stuart* (Eva Le Gallienne played Queen Elizabeth), and played Rosalind in *As You Like It*. She also performed on radio and television, usually reprising her theater roles. Although she made very few films she nevertheless won a British Film Academy Award for her performance in Anthony Asquith's 1958 thriller, *Orders to Kill*.

In 1962 Worth joined the Royal Shakespeare Company where, directed by Peter Brook, she played Goneril opposite Paul Scofield's Lear. Worth later reprised her role for a film version of *King Lear*. She also reprised her Lady Macbeth, and appeared in *The Physicists* by Friedrich Dürrenmat, the latter play also directed by Brook. In 1964 she appeared on Broadway in Edward Albee's *Tiny Alice* and won her first Tony award; her costar was Gielgud. In 1968 Worth was reunited with director Brook and Gielgud when she played Jocasta in *Oedipus* at the Old Vic.

The 1960s was a busy decade for Worth. In addition to plays she began doing dramatic readings, often with Gielgud. Their collaboration in this regard encompassed work by Eliot, Edith Sitwell, and Shakespeare. Worth continued to do dramatic reading throughout her career and later expanded her repertoire to include Virginia Woolf, Ivan Turgenev, and Noel Coward.

In 1975 she was awarded an honorable CBE (Commander of the British Empire). Her second Tony, in 1976, came for her performance in the revival of Tennessee Williams's *Sweet Bird of Youth*. Among her other notable performances during that decade were Madame Ranevskaya in Anton Chekhov's *The Cherry Orchard* (1977) and Winnie in Samuel Beckett's *Happy Days* (1979). In the mid–1980s Worth played Volumnia in *Coriolanus* both in London and New York.

Worth won her third Tony award in 1991 for her portrayal of Grandma Kurnitz in *Lost in Yonkers*, the Pulitzer Prize–winning play by Neil Simon. This role, too, she reprised for the film version. In 1999 Worth suffered a stroke prior to the preview performances of Jean Anouilh's *Ring Around the Moon* and had to retire from the play. However she made a recovery and eventually went back to work. In 2001 she appeared opposite Scofield in *I Take Your Hand in Mine*, a play based on the love letters of Chekhov and Olga Knipper.

Worth suffered another stroke at a Manhattan post office and died in Roosevelt Hospital in New York City on March 10, 2002, at the age of 85. She is survived by a sister, Carol Johnson, and a brother, Luke Evans. **Sources:** *Chicago Tribune*, March 12, 2002, section 2, p. 9; *Los Angeles Times*, March 12, 2002, p. B11; *New York Times*, March 12, 2002, p. A27; *Times* (London), http://www.thetimes.co.uk (March 12, 2002).

—*Frank Caso*

Cumulative Nationality Index

This index lists all newsmakers alphabetically under their respective nationalities. Indexes in softbound issues allow access to the current year's entries; indexes in annual hardbound volumes are cumulative, covering the entire *Newsmakers* series.

Listee names are followed by a year and issue number; thus **1996**:3 indicates that an entry on that individual appears in both 1996, Issue 3, and the 1996 cumulation. For access to newsmakers appearing earlier than the current softbound issue, see the previous year's cumulation.

AFGHAN
Karzai, Hamid **2002**:3

ALGERIAN
Zeroual, Liamine **1996**:2

AMERICAN
Aaliyah **2001**:3
Abbey, Edward
Obituary **1989**:3
Abbott, George
Obituary **1995**:3
Abbott, Jim **1988**:3
Abdul, Paula **1990**:3
Abercrombie, Josephine **1987**:2
Abernathy, Ralph
Obituary **1990**:3
Abraham, S. Daniel **2003**:3
Abraham, Spencer **1991**:4
Abrams, Elliott **1987**:1
Abramson, Lyn **1986**:3
Abzug, Bella **1998**:2
Achtenberg, Roberta **1993**:4
Ackerman, Will **1987**:4
Acuff, Roy
Obituary **1993**:2
Adair, Red **1987**:3
Adams, Patch **1999**:2
Adams, Scott **1996**:4
Addams, Charles
Obituary **1989**:1
Affleck, Ben **1999**:1
Agassi, Andre **1990**:2
Agee, Tommie
Obituary **2001**:4
Agnew, Spiro Theodore
Obituary **1997**:1
Aguilera, Christina **2000**:4
Aiello, Danny **1990**:4
Aikman, Troy **1994**:2
Ailes, Roger **1989**:3
Ailey, Alvin **1989**:2
Obituary **1990**:2
Ainge, Danny **1987**:1
Akers, John F. **1988**:3
Akers, Michelle **1996**:1

Akin, Phil
Brief Entry **1987**:3
Alba, Jessica **2001**:2
Albee, Edward **1997**:1
Albert, Marv **1994**:3
Albert, Stephen **1986**:1
Albom, Mitch **1999**:3
Albright, Madeleine **1994**:3
Alda, Robert
Obituary **1986**:3
Alexander, Jane **1994**:2
Alexander, Jason **1993**:3
Alexander, Lamar **1991**:2
Alexie, Sherman **1998**:4
Ali, Laila **2001**:2
Ali, Muhammad **1997**:2
Alioto, Joseph L.
Obituary **1998**:3
Allaire, Paul **1995**:1
Allard, Linda **2003**:2
Allen, Bob **1992**:4
Allen, Debbie **1998**:2
Allen, Joan **1998**:1
Allen, John **1992**:1
Allen, Mel
Obituary **1996**:4
Allen, Ray **2002**:1
Allen, Steve
Obituary **2001**:2
Allen, Tim **1993**:1
Allen, Woody **1994**:1
Alley, Kirstie **1990**:3
Allred, Gloria **1985**:2
Alter, Hobie
Brief Entry **1985**:1
Altman, Robert **1993**:2
Altman, Sidney **1997**:2
Alvarez, Aida **1999**:2
Ambrose, Stephen **2002**:3
Ameche, Don
Obituary **1994**:2
Amory, Cleveland
Obituary **1999**:2
Amos, Tori **1995**:1
Amos, Wally **2000**:1
Amsterdam, Morey
Obituary **1997**:1

Anastas, Robert
Brief Entry **1985**:2
Ancier, Garth **1989**:1
Anderson, Gillian **1997**:1
Anderson, Harry **1988**:2
Anderson, Laurie **2000**:2
Anderson, Marion
Obituary **1993**:4
Anderson, Poul
Obituary **2002**:3
Andreessen, Marc **1996**:2
Andrews, Maxene
Obituary **1996**:2
Angelos, Peter **1995**:4
Angelou, Maya **1993**:4
Angier, Natalie **2000**:3
Aniston, Jennifer **2000**:3
Annenberg, Walter **1992**:3
Anthony, Earl
Obituary **2002**:3
Anthony, Marc **2000**:3
Antonini, Joseph **1991**:2
Applegate, Christina **2000**:4
Applewhite, Marshall Herff
Obituary **1997**:3
Arad, Avi **2003**:2
Archer, Dennis **1994**:4
Arden, Eve
Obituary **1991**:2
Aretsky, Ken **1988**:1
Arison, Ted **1990**:3
Arkoff, Samuel Z.
Obituary **2002**:4
Arledge, Roone **1992**:2
Arlen, Harold
Obituary **1986**:3
Arman **1993**:1
Armstrong, C. Michael **2002**:1
Armstrong, Henry
Obituary **1989**:1
Armstrong, Lance **2000**:1
Arnaz, Desi
Obituary **1987**:1
Arnold, Tom **1993**:2
Arquette, Patricia **2001**:3
Arquette, Rosanna **1985**:2

Castillo, Ana **2000**:4
Catlett, Elizabeth **1999**:3
Cattrall, Kim **2003**:3
Caulfield, Joan
  Obituary **1992**:1
Cavazos, Lauro F. **1989**:2
Cerf, Vinton G. **1999**:2
Chabon, Michael **2002**:1
Chamberlain, Wilt
  Obituary **2000**:2
Chamberlin, Wendy **2002**:4
Chancellor, John
  Obituary **1997**:1
Chaney, John **1989**:1
Channing, Stockard **1991**:3
Chapman, Tracy **1989**:2
Chappell, Tom **2002**:3
Chase, Chevy **1990**:1
Chast, Roz **1992**:4
Chastain, Brandi **2001**:3
Chatham, Russell **1990**:1
Chaudhari, Praveen **1989**:4
Chavez, Cesar
  Obituary **1993**:4
Chavez, Linda **1999**:3
Chavez-Thompson, Linda **1999**:1
Chavis, Benjamin **1993**:4
Cheadle, Don **2002**:1
Cheatham, Adolphus Doc
  Obituary **1997**:4
Cheek, James Edward
  Brief Entry **1987**:1
Chenault, Kenneth I. **1999**:3
Cheney, Dick **1991**:3
Cheney, Lynne V. **1990**:4
Cher **1993**:1
Chia, Sandro **1987**:2
Chihuly, Dale **1995**:2
Chiklis, Michael **2003**:3
Child, Julia **1999**:4
Chittister, Joan D. **2002**:2
Cho, Margaret **1995**:2
Chouinard, Yvon **2002**:2
Christopher, Warren **1996**:3
Chu, Paul C.W. **1988**:2
Chung, Connie **1988**:4
Chyna **2001**:4
Cisneros, Henry **1987**:2
Claiborne, Liz **1986**:3
Clancy, Tom **1998**:4
Clark, J. E.
  Brief Entry **1986**:1
Clark, Jim **1997**:1
Clark, Marcia **1995**:1
Clark, Mary Higgins **2000**:4
Clarke, Richard A. **2002**:2
Clarke, Stanley **1985**:4
Clarkson, Kelly **2003**:3
Clavell, James
  Obituary **1995**:1
Clay, Andrew Dice **1991**:1
Cleaver, Eldridge
  Obituary **1998**:4
Clemens, Roger **1991**:4
Clements, George **1985**:1
Cleveland, James
  Obituary **1991**:3
Cliburn, Van **1995**:1
Clinton, Bill **1992**:1
Clinton, Hillary Rodham **1993**:2
Clooney, George **1996**:4

Clooney, Rosemary
  Obituary **2003**:4
Close, Glenn **1988**:3
Clyburn, James **1999**:4
Cobain, Kurt
  Obituary **1994**:3
Coca, Imogene
  Obituary **2002**:2
Cochran, Johnnie **1996**:1
Coco, James
  Obituary **1987**:2
Codrescu, Andre **1997**:3
Coen, Joel and Ethan **1992**:1
Coffin, William Sloane, Jr. **1990**:3
Cohen, William S. **1998**:1
Colasanto, Nicholas
  Obituary **1985**:2
Colby, William E.
  Obituary **1996**:4
Cole, Johnnetta B. **1994**:3
Cole, Kenneth **2003**:1
Cole, Natalie **1992**:4
Coleman, Dabney **1988**:3
Coleman, Sheldon, Jr. **1990**:2
Coles, Robert **1995**:1
Collier, Sophia **2001**:2
Collins, Albert
  Obituary **1994**:2
Collins, Billy **2002**:2
Collins, Cardiss **1995**:3
Collins, Eileen **1995**:3
Collins, Kerry **2002**:3
Colwell, Rita Rossi **1999**:3
Combs, Sean Puffy **1998**:4
Commager, Henry Steele
  Obituary **1998**:3
Como, Perry
  Obituary **2002**:2
Condit, Phil **2001**:3
Condon, Richard
  Obituary **1996**:4
Conigliaro, Tony
  Obituary **1990**:3
Connally, John
  Obituary **1994**:1
Connelly, Jennifer **2002**:4
Conner, Dennis **1987**:2
Connerly, Ward **2000**:2
Connick, Harry, Jr. **1991**:1
Conrad, Pete
  Obituary **2000**:1
Convy, Bert
  Obituary **1992**:1
Conyers, John, Jr. **1999**:1
Cook, Robin **1996**:3
Coolio **1996**:4
Cooper, Alexander **1988**:4
Cooper, Cynthia **1999**:1
Coors, William K.
  Brief Entry **1985**:1
Copeland, Al **1988**:3
Copland, Aaron
  Obituary **1991**:2
Copperfield, David **1986**:3
Coppola, Carmine
  Obituary **1991**:4
Coppola, Francis Ford **1989**:4
Corea, Chick **1986**:3
Cornwell, Patricia **2003**:1
Cosby, Bill **1999**:2
Cosell, Howard
  Obituary **1995**:4

Costas, Bob **1986**:4
Costner, Kevin **1989**:4
Couples, Fred **1994**:4
Couric, Katherine **1991**:4
Courier, Jim **1993**:2
Cousteau, Jean-Michel **1988**:2
Covey, Stephen R. **1994**:4
Cowley, Malcolm
  Obituary **1989**:3
Cox, Courteney **1996**:2
Cox, Richard Joseph
  Brief Entry **1985**:1
Cozza, Stephen **2001**:1
Craig, James **2001**:1
Cram, Donald J.
  Obituary **2002**:2
Crandall, Robert L. **1992**:1
Craven, Wes **1997**:3
Crawford, Broderick
  Obituary **1986**:3
Crawford, Cheryl
  Obituary **1987**:1
Crawford, Cindy **1993**:3
Cray, Robert **1988**:2
Cray, Seymour R.
  Brief Entry **1986**:3
  Obituary **1997**:2
Crichton, Michael **1995**:3
Cronkite, Walter Leland **1997**:3
Crosby, David **2000**:4
Crothers, Scatman
  Obituary **1987**:1
Crow, Sheryl **1995**:2
Crowe, Cameron **2001**:2
Cruise, Tom **1985**:4
Crumb, R. **1995**:4
Cruzan, Nancy
  Obituary **1991**:3
Crystal, Billy **1985**:3
Cugat, Xavier
  Obituary **1991**:2
Culkin, Macaulay **1991**:3
Cunningham, Merce **1998**:1
Cunningham, Michael **2003**:4
Cunningham, Randall **1990**:1
Cunningham, Reverend William
  Obituary **1997**:4
Cuomo, Mario **1992**:2
Curran, Charles E. **1989**:2
Curren, Tommy
  Brief Entry **1987**:4
Curry, Ann **2001**:1
Curtis, Jamie Lee **1995**:1
Cusack, John **1999**:3
Cyrus, Billy Ray **1993**:1
Dafoe, Willem **1988**:1
Dahmer, Jeffrey
  Obituary **1995**:2
Daily, Bishop Thomas V. **1990**:4
D'Alessio, Kitty
  Brief Entry **1987**:3
Daly, Carson **2002**:4
D'Amato, Al **1996**:1
Damon, Matt **1999**:1
Danes, Claire **1999**:4
Daniels, Faith **1993**:3
Daniels, Jeff **1989**:4
Danza, Tony **1989**:1
D'Arby, Terence Trent **1988**:4
Darden, Christopher **1996**:4
Daschle, Tom **2002**:3
Davenport, Lindsay **1999**:2

David, Larry **2003**:4
Davis, Angela **1998**:3
Davis, Bette
  Obituary **1990**:1
Davis, Eric **1987**:4
Davis, Geena **1992**:1
Davis, Miles
  Obituary **1992**:2
Davis, Noel **1990**:3
Davis, Patti **1995**:1
Davis, Sammy, Jr.
  Obituary **1990**:4
Davis, Terrell **1998**:2
Day, Dennis
  Obituary **1988**:4
Day, Pat **1995**:2
Dean, Laura **1989**:4
Dearden, John Cardinal
  Obituary **1988**:4
DeBartolo, Edward J., Jr. **1989**:3
DeCarava, Roy **1996**:3
De Cordova, Frederick **1985**:2
Dees, Morris **1992**:1
DeGeneres, Ellen **1995**:3
de Kooning, Willem **1994**:4
  Obituary **1997**:3
De La Hoya, Oscar **1998**:2
Delany, Sarah
  Obituary **1999**:3
DeLay, Tom **2000**:1
Dell, Michael **1996**:2
DeLuca, Fred **2003**:3
de Mille, Agnes
  Obituary **1994**:2
Deming, W. Edwards **1992**:2
  Obituary **1994**:2
Demme, Jonathan **1992**:4
De Niro, Robert **1999**:1
Dennehy, Brian **2002**:1
Dennis, Sandy
  Obituary **1992**:4
Denver, John
  Obituary **1998**:1
de Passe, Suzanne **1990**:4
Depp, Johnny **1991**:3
Dern, Laura **1992**:3
Dershowitz, Alan **1992**:1
Desormeaux, Kent **1990**:2
Destiny's Child **2001**:3
Deutch, John **1996**:4
Devine, John M. **2003**:2
DeVita, Vincent T., Jr. **1987**:3
De Vito, Danny **1987**:1
Diamond, I.A.L.
  Obituary **1988**:3
Diamond, Selma
  Obituary **1985**:2
Diaz, Cameron **1999**:1
DiBello, Paul
  Brief Entry **1986**:4
DiCaprio, Leonardo Wilhelm **1997**:2
Dickerson, Nancy H.
  Obituary **1998**:2
Dickey, James
  Obituary **1998**:2
Dickinson, Brian **1998**:2
Diebenkorn, Richard
  Obituary **1993**:4
Diemer, Walter E.
  Obituary **1998**:2
DiFranco, Ani **1997**:1
Diggs, Taye **2000**:1

Diller, Barry **1991**:1
Dillon, Matt **1992**:2
DiMaggio, Joe
  Obituary **1999**:3
Di Meola, Al **1986**:4
Dinkins, David N. **1990**:2
Disney, Lillian
  Obituary **1998**:3
Disney, Roy E. **1986**:3
Divine
  Obituary **1988**:3
Dixie Chicks **2001**:2
Dr. Demento **1986**:1
Dr. Dre **1994**:3
Doherty, Shannen **1994**:2
Dolan, Terry **1985**:2
Dolan, Tom **2001**:2
Dolby, Ray Milton
  Brief Entry **1986**:1
Dole, Bob **1994**:2
Dole, Elizabeth Hanford **1990**:1
Dolenz, Micky **1986**:4
Donahue, Troy
  Obituary **2002**:4
Donghia, Angelo R.
  Obituary **1985**:2
Donnellan, Nanci **1995**:2
Dorati, Antal
  Obituary **1989**:2
Dorris, Michael
  Obituary **1997**:3
Dorsey, Thomas A.
  Obituary **1993**:3
Doubleday, Nelson, Jr. **1987**:1
Douglas, Buster **1990**:4
Douglas, Marjory Stoneman **1993**:1
  Obituary **1998**:4
Douglas, Michael **1986**:2
Dove, Rita **1994**:3
Dowd, Maureen Brigid **1997**:1
Downey, Bruce **2003**:1
Downey, Morton, Jr. **1988**:4
Dravecky, Dave **1992**:1
Drescher, Fran **1995**:3
Drexler, Clyde **1992**:4
Drexler, Millard S. **1990**:3
Dreyfuss, Richard **1996**:3
Drysdale, Don
  Obituary **1994**:1
Duarte, Henry **2003**:3
Dubrof, Jessica
  Obituary **1996**:4
Duchovny, David **1998**:3
Dudley, Jane
  Obituary **2002**:4
Duffy, Karen **1998**:1
Dukakis, Michael **1988**:3
Dukakis, Olympia **1996**:4
Duke, David **1990**:2
Duke, Doris
  Obituary **1994**:2
Duke, Red
  Brief Entry **1987**:1
Duncan, Tim **2000**:1
Duncan, Todd
  Obituary **1998**:3
Dunham, Carroll **2003**:4
Dunlap, Albert J. **1997**:2
Dunne, Dominick **1997**:1
Dunst, Kirsten **2001**:4
Dupri, Jermaine **1999**:1

Durocher, Leo
  Obituary **1992**:2
Durrell, Gerald
  Obituary **1995**:3
Duval, David **2000**:3
Duvall, Camille
  Brief Entry **1988**:1
Duvall, Robert **1999**:3
Dykstra, Lenny **1993**:4
Dylan, Bob **1998**:1
Earle, Sylvia **2001**:1
Earnhardt, Dale
  Obituary **2001**:4
Eastwood, Clint **1993**:3
Eaton, Robert J. **1994**:2
Eazy-E
  Obituary **1995**:3
Ebert, Roger **1998**:3
Eckert, Robert A. **2002**:3
Eckstine, Billy
  Obituary **1993**:4
Edelman, Marian Wright **1990**:4
Edmonds, Kenneth Babyface **1995**:3
Edwards, Bob **1993**:2
Edwards, Harry **1989**:4
Eggers, Dave **2001**:3
Ehrlichman, John
  Obituary **1999**:3
Eilberg, Amy
  Brief Entry **1985**:3
Eisenman, Peter **1992**:4
Eisenstaedt, Alfred
  Obituary **1996**:1
Eisner, Michael **1989**:2
Elders, Joycelyn **1994**:1
Eldridge, Roy
  Obituary **1989**:3
Elfman, Jenna **1999**:4
Ellerbee, Linda **1993**:3
Elliott, Missy **2003**:4
Ellis, Perry
  Obituary **1986**:3
Ellison, Ralph
  Obituary **1994**:4
Ellroy, James **2003**:4
Elway, John **1990**:3
Eminem **2001**:2
Engelbreit, Mary **1994**:3
Engibous, Thomas J. **2003**:3
Engler, John **1996**:3
Englund, Richard
  Obituary **1991**:3
Engstrom, Elmer W.
  Obituary **1985**:2
Ensler, Eve **2002**:4
Ephron, Henry
  Obituary **1993**:2
Ephron, Nora **1992**:3
Epps, Omar **2000**:4
Epstein, Jason **1991**:1
Epstein, Theo **2003**:4
Erin Brockovich-Ellis **2003**:3
Ertegun, Ahmet **1986**:3
Ervin, Sam
  Obituary **1985**:2
Esiason, Boomer **1991**:1
Estefan, Gloria **1991**:4
Estes, Pete
  Obituary **1988**:3
Estevez, Emilio **1985**:4
Estrich, Susan **1989**:1
Etheridge, Melissa **1995**:4

Evans, Dale
  Obituary **2001**:3
Evans, Janet **1989**:1
Evans, Joni **1991**:4
Evans, Nancy **2000**:4
Evers-Williams, Myrlie **1995**:4
Ewing, Patrick **1985**:3
Eyler, John. H., Jr. **2001**:3
Factor, Max
  Obituary **1996**:4
Fagan, Garth **2000**:1
Fairbanks, Douglas, Jr.
  Obituary **2000**:4
Fairstein, Linda **1991**:1
Falconer, Ian **2003**:1
Falkenberg, Nanette **1985**:2
Fallon, Jimmy **2003**:1
Faludi, Susan **1992**:4
Fanning, Shawn **2001**:1
Farley, Chris
  Obituary **1998**:2
Farmer, James
  Obituary **2000**:1
Farrakhan, Louis **1990**:4
Farrell, Perry **1992**:2
Farrell, Suzanne **1996**:3
Farrow, Mia **1998**:3
Faubus, Orval
  Obituary **1995**:2
Faulkner, Shannon **1994**:4
Favre, Brett Lorenzo **1997**:2
Favreau, Jon **2002**:3
Fawcett, Farrah **1998**:4
Fehr, Donald **1987**:2
Feinstein, Dianne **1993**:3
Feld, Eliot **1996**:1
Feld, Kenneth **1988**:2
Feldman, Sandra **1987**:3
Fell, Norman
  Obituary **1999**:2
Fender, Leo
  Obituary **1992**:1
Fenley, Molissa **1988**:3
Fenwick, Millicent H.
  Obituary **1993**:2
Fernandez, Joseph **1991**:3
Ferraro, Geraldine **1998**:3
Ferrell, Trevor
  Brief Entry **1985**:2
Fertel, Ruth **2000**:2
Fetchit, Stepin
  Obituary **1986**:1
Fieger, Geoffrey **2001**:3
Field, Patricia **2002**:2
Field, Sally **1995**:3
Fielder, Cecil **1993**:2
Fields, Debbi **1987**:3
Fields, Evelyn J. **2001**:3
Filo, David and Jerry Yang **1998**:3
Finley, Karen **1992**:4
Fiorina, Carleton S. **2000**:1
Fireman, Paul
  Brief Entry **1987**:2
Firestone, Roy **1988**:2
Fish, Hamilton
  Obituary **1991**:3
Fishburne, Laurence **1995**:3
Fisher, Carrie **1991**:1
Fisher, Mary **1994**:3
Fisher, Mel **1985**:4
Fitzgerald, A. Ernest **1986**:2

Fitzgerald, Ella
  Obituary **1996**:4
Flanders, Ed
  Obituary **1995**:3
Flatley, Michael **1997**:3
Fleischer, Ari **2003**:1
Fleiss, Mike **2003**:4
Fleming, Art
  Obituary **1995**:4
Fleming, Renee **2001**:4
Flockhart, Calista **1998**:4
Flood, Curt
  Obituary **1997**:2
Florio, James J. **1991**:2
Flutie, Doug **1999**:2
Flynn, Ray **1989**:1
Flynt, Larry **1997**:3
Foley, Thomas S. **1990**:1
Folkman, Judah **1999**:1
Fomon, Robert M. **1985**:3
Fonda, Bridget **1995**:1
Foote, Shelby **1991**:2
Forbes, Malcolm S.
  Obituary **1990**:3
Forbes, Steve **1996**:2
Ford, Harrison **1990**:2
Ford, Henry II
  Obituary **1988**:1
Ford, Tennessee Ernie
  Obituary **1992**:2
Ford, Tom **1999**:3
Ford, William Clay, Jr. **1999**:1
Foreman, Dave **1990**:3
Forsythe, William **1993**:2
Foss, Joe **1990**:3
Fosse, Bob
  Obituary **1988**:1
Fossey, Dian
  Obituary **1986**:1
Foster, David **1988**:2
Foster, Jodie **1989**:2
Foster, Phil
  Obituary **1985**:3
Foster, Sutton **2003**:2
Foster, Tabatha
  Obituary **1988**:3
Foster, Vincent
  Obituary **1994**:1
Fox, Matthew **1992**:2
Fox, Vivica **1999**:1
Foxworthy, Jeff **1996**:1
Foxx, Jamie **2001**:1
Foxx, Redd
  Obituary **1992**:2
France, Johnny
  Brief Entry **1987**:1
Franciscus, James
  Obituary **1992**:1
Frank, Barney **1989**:2
Frank, Robert **1995**:2
Franken, Al **1996**:3
Frankenheimer, John
  Obituary **2003**:4
Frankenthaler, Helen **1990**:1
Franklin, Aretha **1998**:3
Franklin, Melvin
  Obituary **1995**:3
Franz, Dennis **1995**:2
Franzen, Jonathan **2002**:3
Fraser, Brendan **2000**:1
Frazier, Charles **2003**:2
Freeh, Louis J. **1994**:2

Freeman, Cliff **1996**:1
Freeman, Morgan **1990**:4
Freleng, Friz
  Obituary **1995**:4
Friedan, Betty **1994**:2
Friend, Patricia A. **2003**:3
Frist, Bill **2003**:4
Fudge, Ann **2000**:3
Fulbright, J. William
  Obituary **1995**:3
Fulghum, Robert **1996**:1
Funt, Allen
  Obituary **2000**:1
Furman, Rosemary
  Brief Entry **1986**:4
Futrell, Mary Hatwood **1986**:1
Futter, Ellen V. **1995**:1
Gabor, Eva
  Obituary **1996**:1
Gacy, John Wayne
  Obituary **1994**:4
Gaines, William M.
  Obituary **1993**:1
Gale, Robert Peter **1986**:4
Galindo, Rudy **2001**:2
Gallo, Robert **1991**:1
Galvin, John R. **1990**:1
Galvin, Martin
  Brief Entry **1985**:3
Gandolfini, James **2001**:3
Gandy, Kim **2002**:2
Ganzi, Victor **2003**:3
Garbo, Greta
  Obituary **1990**:3
Garcia, Andy **1999**:3
Garcia, Cristina **1997**:4
Garcia, Jerry **1988**:3
  Obituary **1996**:1
Garcia, Joe
  Brief Entry **1986**:4
Gardner, Ava Lavinia
  Obituary **1990**:2
Gardner, David and Tom **2001**:4
Gardner, Randy **1997**:2
Garner, Jennifer **2003**:1
Garnett, Kevin **2000**:3
Garofalo, Janeane **1996**:4
Garr, Teri **1988**:4
Garrison, Jim
  Obituary **1993**:2
Garson, Greer
  Obituary **1996**:4
Garzarelli, Elaine M. **1992**:3
Gates, Bill **1993**:3 **1987**:4
Gates, Robert M. **1992**:2
Gathers, Hank
  Obituary **1990**:3
Gault, Willie **1991**:2
Gebbie, Kristine **1994**:2
Geffen, David **1985**:3 **1997**:3
Gehry, Frank O. **1987**:1
Geisel, Theodor
  Obituary **1992**:2
Gellar, Sarah Michelle **1999**:3
Geller, Margaret Joan **1998**:2
George, Elizabeth **2003**:3
Gephardt, Richard **1987**:3
Gerba, Charles **1999**:4
Gere, Richard **1994**:3
Gergen, David **1994**:1
Gerstner, Lou **1993**:4

Harris, Thomas **2001**:1
Harry, Deborah **1990**:1
Hart, Mary
  Brief Entry **1988**:1
Hart, Melissa Joan **2002**:1
Hart, Mickey **1991**:2
Hartman, Phil **1996**:2
  Obituary **1998**:4
Harvard, Beverly **1995**:2
Harvey, Paul **1995**:3
Harwell, Ernie **1997**:3
Haseltine, William A. **1999**:2
Hassenfeld, Stephen **1987**:4
Hastert, Dennis **1999**:3
Hatch, Orin G. **2000**:2
Hatch, Richard **2001**:1
Hatem, George
  Obituary **1989**:1
Hawk, Tony **2001**:4
Hawke, Ethan **1995**:4
Hawkins, Jeff and
  Donna Dubinsky **2000**:2
Hawkins, Screamin' Jay
  Obituary **2000**:3
Hawn, Goldie Jeanne **1997**:2
Hayes, Helen
  Obituary **1993**:4
Hayes, Isaac **1998**:4
Hayes, Robert M. **1986**:3
Hayes, Woody
  Obituary **1987**:2
Hayworth, Rita
  Obituary **1987**:3
Headroom, Max **1986**:4
Healey, Jack **1990**:1
Healy, Bernadine **1993**:1
Healy, Timothy S. **1990**:2
Heard, J.C.
  Obituary **1989**:1
Hearst, Randolph A.
  Obituary **2001**:3
Heat-Moon, William Least **2000**:2
Heche, Anne **1999**:1
Heckerling, Amy **1987**:2
Heckert, Richard E.
  Brief Entry **1987**:3
Hefner, Christie **1985**:1
Heid, Bill
  Brief Entry **1987**:2
Heifetz, Jascha
  Obituary **1988**:2
Heinz, H.J.
  Obituary **1987**:2
Heinz, John
  Obituary **1991**:4
Helgenberger, Marg **2002**:2
Heller, Joseph
  Obituary **2000**:2
Heller, Walter
  Obituary **1987**:4
Helms, Bobby
  Obituary **1997**:4
Helms, Jesse **1998**:1
Helmsley, Leona **1988**:1
Heloise **2001**:4
Helton, Todd **2001**:1
Hemingway, Margaux
  Obituary **1997**:1
Henderson, Rickey **2002**:3
Hennessy, John L. **2002**:2
Henning, Doug
  Obituary **2000**:3

Hensel Twins **1996**:4
Henson, Brian **1992**:1
Henson, Jim **1989**:1
  Obituary **1990**:4
Hepburn, Katharine **1991**:2
Hernandez, Willie **1985**:1
Hero, Peter **2001**:2
Hershey, Barbara **1989**:1
Hershiser, Orel **1989**:2
Herzog, Doug **2002**:4
Heston, Charlton **1999**:4
Hewitt, Jennifer Love **1999**:2
Hewlett, William
  Obituary **2001**:4
Highsmith, Patricia
  Obituary **1995**:3
Hilbert, Stephen C. **1997**:4
Hilfiger, Tommy **1993**:3
Hill, Anita **1994**:1
Hill, Faith **2000**:1
Hill, Grant **1995**:3
Hill, Lauryn **1999**:3
Hill, Lynn **1991**:2
Hillegass, Clifton Keith **1989**:4
Hills, Carla **1990**:3
Hines, Gregory **1992**:4
Hinton, Milt
  Obituary **2001**:3
Hirschhorn, Joel
  Brief Entry **1986**:1
Hirt, Al
  Obituary **1999**:4
Hiss, Alger
  Obituary **1997**:2
Hoffa, Jim, Jr. **1999**:2
Hoffman, Abbie
  Obituary **1989**:3
Hoffs, Susanna **1988**:2
Hogan, Ben
  Obituary **1997**:4
Hogan, Hulk **1987**:3
Holbrooke, Richard **1996**:2
Holden, Betsy **2003**:2
Holl, Steven **2003**:1
Holmes, John C.
  Obituary **1988**:3
Holtz, Lou **1986**:4
Holyfield, Evander **1991**:3
Hooker, John Lee **1998**:1
  Obituary **2002**:3
hooks, bell **2000**:2
Hootie and the Blowfish **1995**:4
Horne, Lena **1998**:4
Horner, Jack **1985**:2
Hornsby, Bruce **1989**:3
Horovitz, Adam **1988**:3
Horowitz, Paul **1988**:2
Horowitz, Vladimir
  Obituary **1990**:1
Horrigan, Edward, Jr. **1989**:1
Horwich, Frances
  Obituary **2002**:3
Houseman, John
  Obituary **1989**:1
Houston, Cissy **1999**:3
Houston, Whitney **1986**:3
Howard, Desmond Kevin **1997**:2
Howard, Ron **1997**:2
Howser, Dick
  Obituary **1987**:4
Hubbard, Freddie **1988**:4
Hudson, Kate **2001**:2

Hudson, Rock
  Obituary **1985**:4
Huerta, Dolores **1998**:1
Hughes, Cathy **1999**:1
Hughes, Karen **2001**:2
Hughes, Mark **1985**:3
Hughes, Sarah **2002**:4
Hughley, D.L. **2001**:1
Huizenga, Wayne **1992**:1
Hull, Jane Dee **1999**:2
Hullinger, Charlotte
  Brief Entry **1985**:1
Hundt, Reed Eric **1997**:2
Hunt, Helen **1994**:4
Hunter, Catfish
  Obituary **2000**:1
Hunter, Holly **1989**:4
Hunter, Howard **1994**:4
Hunter, Madeline **1991**:2
Hurt, William **1986**:1
Huston, Anjelica **1989**:3
Huston, John
  Obituary **1988**:1
Hutton, Timothy **1986**:3
Hwang, David Henry **1999**:1
Hyatt, Joel **1985**:3
Hyde, Henry **1999**:1
Hynde, Chrissie **1991**:1
Iacocca, Lee **1993**:1
Ice Cube **1999**:2
Ice-T **1992**:3
Ifill, Gwen **2002**:4
Iglesias, Enrique **2000**:1
Ilitch, Mike **1993**:4
Immelt, Jeffrey R. **2001**:2
Imus, Don **1997**:1
Inatome, Rick **1985**:4
Indigo Girls **1994**:4
Ingersoll, Ralph II **1988**:2
Inkster, Juli **2000**:2
Inman, Bobby Ray **1985**:1
Ireland, Patricia **1992**:2
Irvin, Michael **1996**:3
Irwin, Bill **1988**:3
Irwin, James
  Obituary **1992**:1
Isaacson, Portia
  Brief Entry **1986**:1
Isaacson, Walter **2003**:2
Ito, Lance **1995**:3
Iverson, Allen **2001**:4
Ives, Burl
  Obituary **1995**:4
Ivins, Molly **1993**:4
Jackson, Alan **2003**:1
Jackson, Bo **1986**:3
Jackson, Cordell **1992**:4
Jackson, Janet **1990**:4
Jackson, Jesse **1996**:1
Jackson, Jesse, Jr. **1998**:3
Jackson, Michael **1996**:2
Jackson, Phil **1996**:3
Jackson, Samuel L. **1995**:4
Jackson, Thomas Penfield **2000**:2
Jacobs, Joe **1994**:1
Jacobs, Marc **2002**:3
Jacuzzi, Candido
  Obituary **1987**:1
Jahn, Helmut **1987**:3
James, Etta **1995**:2
Jamison, Judith **1990**:3
Janklow, Morton **1989**:3

Janney, Allison **2003**:3
Janzen, Daniel H. **1988**:4
Jarmusch, Jim **1998**:3
Jarrett, Keith **1992**:4
Jarvik, Robert K. **1985**:1
Jay, Ricky **1995**:1
Jeffords, James **2002**:2
Jemison, Mae C. **1993**:1
Jen, Gish **2000**:1
Jenkins, Sally **1997**:2
Jennings, Waylon
   Obituary **2003**:2
Jeter, Derek **1999**:4
Jewel **1999**:2
Jillian, Ann **1986**:4
Jobs, Steve **2000**:1
Joel, Billy **1994**:3
Joffrey, Robert
   Obituary **1988**:3
John, Daymond **2000**:1
Johnson, Betsey **1996**:2
Johnson, Don **1986**:1
Johnson, Earvin Magic **1988**:4
Johnson, Jimmy **1993**:3
Johnson, Kevin **1991**:1
Johnson, Keyshawn **2000**:4
Johnson, Larry **1993**:3
Johnson, Michael **2000**:1
Johnson, Philip **1989**:2
Johnson, Randy **1996**:2
Johnson, Robert L. **2000**:4
Jolie, Angelina **2000**:2
Jones, Arthur A. **1985**:3
Jones, Bill T. **1991**:4
Jones, Cherry **1999**:3
Jones, Chuck **2001**:2
Jones, Etta
   Obituary **2002**:4
Jones, Gayl **1999**:4
Jones, Jerry **1994**:4
Jones, Marion **1998**:4
Jones, Quincy **1990**:4
Jones, Tommy Lee **1994**:2
Jong, Erica **1998**:3
Jonze, Spike **2000**:3
Jordan, Barbara
   Obituary **1996**:3
Jordan, Charles M. **1989**:4
Jordan, James
   Obituary **1994**:1
Jordan, King **1990**:1
Jordan, Michael **1987**:2
Jordan, Vernon, Jr. **2002**:3
Jorgensen, Christine
   Obituary **1989**:4
Jovovich, Milla **2002**:1
Joyner, Florence Griffith **1989**:2
   Obituary **1999**:1
Joyner-Kersee, Jackie **1993**:1
Judd, Ashley **1998**:1
Judge, Mike **1994**:2
Judkins, Reba
   Brief Entry **1987**:3
Junck, Mary E. **2003**:4
Justin, John Jr. **1992**:2
Justiz, Manuel J. **1986**:4
Kael, Pauline **2000**:4
   Obituary **2002**:4
Kahane, Meir
   Obituary **1991**:2
Kahn, Madeline
   Obituary **2000**:2

Kallen, Jackie **1994**:1
Kamali, Norma **1989**:1
Kamen, Dean **2003**:1
Kanokogi, Rusty
   Brief Entry **1987**:1
Kapor, Mitch **1990**:3
Karan, Donna **1988**:1
Kasem, Casey **1987**:1
Kashuk, Sonia **2002**:4
Kaskey, Ray
   Brief Entry **1987**:2
Kassebaum, Nancy **1991**:1
Katz, Alex **1990**:3
Katz, Lillian **1987**:4
Katzenberg, Jeffrey **1995**:3
Kaufman, Elaine **1989**:4
Kavner, Julie **1992**:3
Kaye, Danny
   Obituary **1987**:2
Kaye, Nora
   Obituary **1987**:4
Kaye, Sammy
   Obituary **1987**:4
Keating, Charles H., Jr. **1990**:4
Keaton, Diane **1997**:1
Keaton, Michael **1989**:4
Keitel, Harvey **1994**:3
Keith, Brian
   Obituary **1997**:4
Keith, Louis **1988**:2
Kelleher, Herb **1995**:1
Kelley, DeForest
   Obituary **2000**:1
Kelley, Virginia
   Obituary **1994**:3
Kelly, Ellsworth **1992**:1
Kelly, Gene
   Obituary **1996**:3
Kelly, Jim **1991**:4
Kelly, Patrick
   Obituary **1990**:2
Kelly, R. **1997**:3
Kelly, William R.
   Obituary **1998**:2
Kemp, Jack **1990**:4
Kemp, Jan **1987**:2
Kemp, Shawn **1995**:1
Kendricks, Eddie
   Obituary **1993**:2
Kennedy, John F., Jr. **1990**:1
   Obituary **1999**:4
Kennedy, Rose
   Obituary **1995**:3
Kennedy, Weldon **1997**:3
Kenny G **1994**:4
Keno, Leigh and Leslie **2001**:2
Kent, Corita
   Obituary **1987**:1
Keough, Donald Raymond **1986**:1
Keplinger, Dan **2001**:1
Kerkorian, Kirk **1996**:2
Kerr, Walter
   Obituary **1997**:1
Kerrey, Bob **1986**:1 **1991**:3
Kerrigan, Nancy **1994**:3
Kesey, Ken
   Obituary **2003**:1
Kessler, David **1992**:1
Ketcham, Hank
   Obituary **2002**:2
Kevorkian, Jack **1991**:3
Keyes, Alan **1996**:2

Kidd, Jason **2003**:2
Kid Rock **2001**:1
Kilborn, Craig **2003**:2
Kilby, Jack **2002**:2
Kilmer, Val **1991**:4
Kilts, James M. **2001**:3
Kimsey, James V. **2001**:1
King, Bernice **2000**:2
King, Coretta Scott **1999**:3
King, Don **1989**:1
King, Larry **1993**:1
King, Mary-Claire **1998**:3
King, Stephen **1998**:1
Kingsborough, Donald
   Brief Entry **1986**:2
Kingsley, Patricia **1990**:2
Kinison, Sam
   Obituary **1993**:1
Kiraly, Karch
   Brief Entry **1987**:1
Kissinger, Henry **1999**:4
Kissling, Frances **1989**:2
Kistler, Darci **1993**:1
Kite, Tom **1990**:3
Klass, Perri **1993**:2
Klein, Calvin **1996**:2
Kline, Kevin **2000**:1
Kloss, Henry E.
   Brief Entry **1985**:2
Kluge, John **1991**:1
Knievel, Robbie **1990**:1
Knight, Bobby **1985**:3
Knight, Philip H. **1994**:1
Knight, Ted
   Obituary **1986**:4
Knight, Wayne **1997**:1
Knowles, John
   Obituary **2003**:1
Koch, Bill **1992**:3
Kohnstamm, Abby **2001**:1
Koogle, Tim **2000**:4
Koons, Jeff **1991**:4
Koontz, Dean **1999**:3
Koop, C. Everett **1989**:3
Kopits, Steven E.
   Brief Entry **1987**:1
Koplovitz, Kay **1986**:3
Kopp, Wendy **1993**:3
Koppel, Ted **1989**:1
Kordich, Jay **1993**:2
Koresh, David
   Obituary **1993**:4
Kornberg, Arthur **1992**:1
Kors, Michael **2000**:4
Kostabi, Mark **1989**:4
Kozinski, Alex **2002**:2
Kozol, Jonathan **1992**:1
Kramer, Larry **1991**:2
Kramer, Stanley
   Obituary **2002**:1
Krantz, Judith **2003**:1
Kravitz, Lenny **1991**:1
Krim, Mathilde **1989**:2
Kroc, Ray
   Obituary **1985**:1
Krol, John
   Obituary **1996**:3
Kroll, Alexander S. **1989**:3
Krone, Julie **1989**:2
Kruk, John **1994**:4
Krzyzewski, Mike **1993**:2

Zappa, Frank
  Obituary **1994**:2
Zech, Lando W.
  Brief Entry **1987**:4
Zellweger, Renee **2001**:1
Zemeckis, Robert **2002**:1
Zetcher, Arnold B. **2002**:1
Ziff, William B., Jr. **1986**:4
Zigler, Edward **1994**:1
Zinnemann, Fred
  Obituary **1997**:3
Zinni, Anthony **2003**:1
Zito, Barry **2003**:3
Zucker, Jeff **1993**:3
Zucker, Jerry **2002**:2
Zuckerman, Mortimer **1986**:3
Zwilich, Ellen **1990**:1

ANGOLAN
  Savimbi, Jonas **1986**:2 **1994**:2

ARGENTINIAN
  Barenboim, Daniel **2001**:1
  Bocca, Julio **1995**:3
  Duhalde, Eduardo **2003**:3
  Herrera, Paloma **1996**:2
  Maradona, Diego **1991**:3
  Pelli, Cesar **1991**:4
  Sabatini, Gabriela
    Brief Entry **1985**:4
  Timmerman, Jacobo
    Obituary **2000**:3

AUSTRALIAN
  Allen, Peter
    Obituary **1993**:1
  Anderson, Judith
    Obituary **1992**:3
  Bee Gees, The **1997**:4
  Blanchett, Cate **1999**:3
  Bond, Alan **1989**:2
  Bradman, Sir Donald
    Obituary **2002**:1
  Clavell, James
    Obituary **1995**:1
  Freeman, Cathy **2001**:3
  Gibb, Andy
    Obituary **1988**:3
  Gibson, Mel **1990**:1
  Helfgott, David **1997**:2
  Hewitt, Lleyton **2002**:2
  Hughes, Robert **1996**:4
  Humphries, Barry **1993**:1
  Hutchence, Michael
    Obituary **1998**:1
  Irwin, Steve **2001**:2
  Kidman, Nicole **1992**:4
  Klensch, Elsa **2001**:4
  Luhrmann, Baz **2002**:3
  Minogue, Kylie **2003**:4
  Murdoch, Rupert **1988**:4
  Norman, Greg **1988**:3
  Powter, Susan **1994**:3
  Rafter, Patrick **2001**:1
  Rush, Geoffrey **2002**:1
  Summers, Anne **1990**:2
  Travers, P.L.
    Obituary **1996**:4
  Tyler, Richard **1995**:3
  Webb, Karrie **2000**:4

AUSTRIAN
  Brabeck-Letmathe, Peter **2001**:4
  Brandauer, Klaus Maria **1987**:3
  Djerassi, Carl **2000**:4
  Drucker, Peter F. **1992**:3
  Falco
    Brief Entry **1987**:2
  Frankl, Viktor E.
    Obituary **1998**:1
  Hrabal, Bohumil
    Obituary **1997**:3
  Lamarr, Hedy
    Obituary **2000**:3
  Lang, Helmut **1999**:2
  Lorenz, Konrad
    Obituary **1989**:3
  Perutz, Max
    Obituary **2003**:2
  Porsche, Ferdinand
    Obituary **1998**:4
  Puck, Wolfgang **1990**:1
  Strobl, Fritz **2003**:3
  von Karajan, Herbert
    Obituary **1989**:4
  von Trapp, Maria
    Obituary **1987**:3

BANGLADESHI
  Nasrin, Taslima **1995**:1

BELGIAN
  Hepburn, Audrey
    Obituary **1993**:2
  von Furstenberg, Diane **1994**:2

BOSNIAN
  Izetbegovic, Alija **1996**:4

BRAZILIAN
  Cardoso, Fernando Henrique **1996**:4
  Castaneda, Carlos
    Obituary **1998**:4
  Collor de Mello, Fernando **1992**:4
  Fittipaldi, Emerson **1994**:2
  Ronaldo **1999**:2
  Salgado, Sebastiao **1994**:2
  Senna, Ayrton **1991**:4
    Obituary **1994**:4
  Silva, Luiz Inacio Lula da **2003**:4
  Xuxa **1994**:2

BRITISH
  Adamson, George
    Obituary **1990**:2
  Baddeley, Hermione
    Obituary **1986**:4
  Beckett, Wendy (Sister) **1998**:3
  Branson, Richard **1987**:1
  Chatwin, Bruce
    Obituary **1989**:2
  Cleese, John **1989**:2
  Cummings, Sam **1986**:3
  Dalton, Timothy **1988**:4
  Davison, Ian Hay **1986**:1
  Day-Lewis, Daniel **1989**:4 **1994**:4
  Dench, Judi **1999**:4
  Egan, John **1987**:2
  Eno, Brian **1986**:2
  Ferguson, Sarah **1990**:3
  Fiennes, Ranulph **1990**:3
  Foster, Norman **1999**:4

Gift, Roland **1990**:2
Goodall, Jane **1991**:1
Hamilton, Hamish
  Obituary **1988**:4
Harrison, Rex
  Obituary **1990**:4
Hawking, Stephen W. **1990**:1
Hockney, David **1988**:3
Hounsfield, Godfrey **1989**:2
Howard, Trevor
  Obituary **1988**:2
Ireland, Jill
  Obituary **1990**:4
Knopfler, Mark **1986**:2
Laing, R.D.
  Obituary **1990**:1
Lawrence, Ruth
  Brief Entry **1986**:3
Leach, Robin
  Brief Entry **1985**:4
Lennox, Annie **1985**:4 **1996**:4
Livingstone, Ken **1988**:3
Lloyd Webber, Andrew **1989**:1
Macmillan, Harold
  Obituary **1987**:2
MacMillan, Kenneth
  Obituary **1993**:2
Maxwell, Robert **1990**:1
Michael, George **1989**:2
Milne, Christopher Robin
  Obituary **1996**:4
Moore, Henry
  Obituary **1986**:4
Murdoch, Iris
  Obituary **1999**:4
Norrington, Roger **1989**:4
Oldman, Gary **1998**:1
Olivier, Laurence
  Obituary **1989**:4
Philby, Kim
  Obituary **1988**:3
Rattle, Simon **1989**:4
Redgrave, Vanessa **1989**:2
Rhodes, Zandra **1986**:2
Roddick, Anita **1989**:4
Runcie, Robert **1989**:4
  Obituary **2001**:1
Saatchi, Charles **1987**:3
Steptoe, Patrick
  Obituary **1988**:3
Stevens, James
  Brief Entry **1988**:1
Thatcher, Margaret **1989**:2
Tudor, Antony
  Obituary **1987**:4
Ullman, Tracey **1988**:3
Wilson, Peter C.
  Obituary **1985**:2
Wintour, Anna **1990**:4

BRUNEI
  Bolkiah, Sultan Muda
    Hassanal **1985**:4

BULGARIAN
  Christo **1992**:3
  Dimitrova, Ghena **1987**:1

BURMESE
  Suu Kyi, Aung San **1996**:2

Durrell, Gerald
  Obituary **1995**:3
Gandhi, Indira
  Obituary **1985**:1
Gandhi, Rajiv
  Obituary **1991**:4
Gandhi, Sonia **2000**:2
Gowda, H. D. Deve **1997**:1
Mahesh Yogi, Maharishi **1991**:3
Mehta, Zubin **1994**:3
Mother Teresa **1993**:1
  Obituary **1998**:1
Musharraf, Pervez **2000**:2
Narayan, R.K.
  Obituary **2002**:2
Prowse, Juliet
  Obituary **1997**:1
Rajneesh, Bhagwan Shree
  Obituary **1990**:2
Ram, Jagjivan
  Obituary **1986**:4
Rao, P. V. Narasimha **1993**:2
Rushdie, Salman **1994**:1
Vajpayee, Atal Behari **1998**:4
Wahid, Abdurrahman **2000**:3

INDONESIAN
Habibie, Bacharuddin Jusuf **1999**:3
Megawati Sukarnoputri **2002**:2
Megawati Sukarnoputri **2000**:1

IRANIAN
Khatami, Mohammed **1997**:4
Khomeini, Ayatollah Ruhollah
  Obituary **1989**:4
McCourt, Frank **1997**:4
Rafsanjani, Ali Akbar
  Hashemi **1987**:3
Schroeder, Barbet **1996**:1

IRAQI
Hussein, Saddam **1991**:1
Kamel, Hussein **1996**:1
Saatchi, Maurice **1995**:4

IRISH
Adams, Gerald **1994**:1
Ahern, Bertie **1999**:3
Beckett, Samuel Barclay
  Obituary **1990**:2
Bono **1988**:4
Branagh, Kenneth **1992**:2
Brosnan, Pierce **2000**:3
Byrne, Gabriel **1997**:4
de Valois, Dame Ninette
  Obituary **2002**:1
Enya **1992**:3
Geldof, Bob **1985**:3
Heaney, Seamus **1996**:2
Herzog, Chaim
  Obituary **1997**:3
Hume, John **1987**:1
Huston, John
  Obituary **1988**:1
Jordan, Neil **1993**:3
McGuinness, Martin **1985**:4
Neeson, Liam **1993**:4
O'Connor, Sinead **1990**:4

O'Sullivan, Maureen
  Obituary **1998**:4
Robinson, Mary **1993**:1
Trimble, David **1999**:1
U **2002**:4

ISRAELI
Arens, Moshe **1985**:1
Arison, Ted **1990**:3
Barak, Ehud **1999**:4
Begin, Menachem
  Obituary **1992**:3
Herzog, Chaim
  Obituary **1997**:3
Levinger, Moshe **1992**:1
Levy, David **1987**:2
Mintz, Shlomo **1986**:2
Netanyahu, Benjamin **1996**:4
Peres, Shimon **1996**:3
Rabin, Leah
  Obituary **2001**:2
Rabin, Yitzhak **1993**:1
  Obituary **1996**:2
Shcharansky, Anatoly **1986**:2

ITALIAN
Agnelli, Giovanni **1989**:4
Armani, Giorgio **1991**:2
Bartoli, Cecilia **1994**:1
Benetton, Luciano **1988**:1
Benigni, Roberto **1999**:2
Berlusconi, Silvio **1994**:4
Capra, Frank
  Obituary **1992**:2
Clemente, Francesco **1992**:2
Coppola, Carmine
  Obituary **1991**:4
Fabio **1993**:4
Fano, Ugo
  Obituary **2001**:4
Fellini, Federico
  Obituary **1994**:2
Ferrari, Enzo **1988**:4
Ferri, Alessandra **1987**:2
Fo, Dario **1998**:1
Gardenia, Vincent
  Obituary **1993**:2
Gassman, Vittorio
  Obituary **2001**:1
Gucci, Maurizio
  Brief Entry **1985**:4
Lamborghini, Ferrucio
  Obituary **1993**:3
Leone, Sergio
  Obituary **1989**:4
Masina, Giulietta
  Obituary **1994**:3
Mastroianni, Marcello
  Obituary **1997**:2
Michelangeli, Arturo
  Benedetti **1988**:2
Montand, Yves
  Obituary **1992**:2
Pavarotti, Luciano **1997**:4
Pozzi, Lucio **1990**:2
Prada, Miuccia **1996**:1
Sinopoli, Giuseppe **1988**:1
Staller, Ilona **1988**:3
Tomba, Alberto **1992**:3
Versace, Donatella **1999**:1

Versace, Gianni
  Brief Entry **1988**:1
  Obituary **1998**:2
Zanardi, Alex **1998**:2
Zeffirelli, Franco **1991**:3

JAMAICAN
Marley, Ziggy **1990**:4
Tosh, Peter
  Obituary **1988**:2

JAPANESE
Akihito, Emperor of Japan **1990**:1
Aoki, Rocky **1990**:2
Doi, Takako
  Brief Entry **1987**:4
Hirohito, Emperor of Japan
  Obituary **1989**:2
Honda, Soichiro
  Obituary **1986**:1
Hosokawa, Morihiro **1994**:1
Isozaki, Arata **1990**:2
Itami, Juzo
  Obituary **1998**:2
Katayama, Yutaka **1987**:1
Koizumi, Junichiro **2002**:1
Kurosawa, Akira **1991**:1
  Obituary **1999**:1
Masako, Crown Princess **1993**:4
Matsuhisa, Nobuyuki **2002**:3
Mitarai, Fujio **2002**:4
Miyake, Issey **1985**:2
Miyazawa, Kiichi **1992**:2
Mori, Yoshiro **2000**:4
Morita, Akio
  Obituary **2000**:2
Morita, Akio **1989**:4
Nagako, Empress Dowager
  Obituary **2001**:1
Nomo, Hideo **1996**:2
Obuchi, Keizo
  Obituary **2000**:4
Obuchi, Keizo **1999**:2
Oe, Kenzaburo **1997**:1
Sasakawa, Ryoichi
  Brief Entry **1988**:1
Shimomura, Tsutomu **1996**:1
Suzuki, Ichiro **2002**:2
Suzuki, Sin'ichi
  Obituary **1998**:3
Takada, Kenzo **2003**:2
Takei, Kei **1990**:2
Takeshita, Noboru
  Obituary **2001**:1
Tanaka, Tomoyuki
  Obituary **1997**:3
Toyoda, Eiji **1985**:2
Uchida, Mitsuko **1989**:3
Yamamoto, Kenichi **1989**:1

JORDANIAN
Abdullah II, King **2002**:4
al-Abdullah, Rania **2001**:1
Hussein I, King **1997**:3
  Obituary **1999**:3

KENYAN
Kibaki, Mwai **2003**:4
Moi, Daniel arap **1993**:2

SOMALIAN
Iman **2001**:3

SOUTH AFRICAN
Barnard, Christiaan
Obituary **2002**:4
Blackburn, Molly
Obituary **1985**:4
Buthelezi, Mangosuthu
Gatsha **1989**:3
de Klerk, F.W. **1990**:1
Duncan, Sheena
Brief Entry **1987**:1
Fugard, Athol **1992**:3
Hani, Chris
Obituary **1993**:4
Makeba, Miriam **1989**:2
Mandela, Nelson **1990**:3
Mandela, Winnie **1989**:3
Matthews, Dave **1999**:3
Mbeki, Thabo **1999**:4
Oppenheimer, Harry
Obituary **2001**:3
Paton, Alan
Obituary **1988**:3
Ramaphosa, Cyril **1988**:2
Slovo, Joe **1989**:2
Suzman, Helen **1989**:3
Tambo, Oliver **1991**:3
Theron, Charlize **2001**:4
Treurnicht, Andries **1992**:2
Woods, Donald
Obituary **2002**:3

SOVIET
Asimov, Isaac
Obituary **1992**:3
Chernenko, Konstantin
Obituary **1985**:1
Dalai Lama **1989**:1
Dubinin, Yuri **1987**:4
Dzhanibekov, Vladimir **1988**:1
Erte
Obituary **1990**:4
Federov, Sergei **1995**:1
Godunov, Alexander
Obituary **1995**:4
Gorbachev, Mikhail **1985**:2
Grebenshikov, Boris **1990**:1
Gromyko, Andrei
Obituary **1990**:2
Karadzic, Radovan **1995**:3
Milosevic, Slobodan **1993**:2
Molotov, Vyacheslav Mikhailovich
Obituary **1987**:1
Nureyev, Rudolf
Obituary **1993**:2
Sakharov, Andrei Dmitrievich
Obituary **1990**:2
Smirnoff, Yakov **1987**:2
Vidov, Oleg **1987**:4
Yeltsin, Boris **1991**:1
Zhirinovsky, Vladimir **1994**:2

SPANISH
Almodovar, Pedro **2000**:3
Banderas, Antonio **1996**:2
Blahnik, Manolo **2000**:2

Carreras, Jose **1995**:2
Cela, Camilo Jose
Obituary **2003**:1
Chillida, Eduardo
Obituary **2003**:4
Cruz, Penelope **2001**:4
Dali, Salvador
Obituary **1989**:2
de Pinies, Jamie
Brief Entry **1986**:3
Domingo, Placido **1993**:2
Juan Carlos I **1993**:1
Lopez de Arriortua, Jose Ignacio
1993:4
Miro, Joan
Obituary **1985**:1
Moneo, Jose Rafael **1996**:4
Montoya, Carlos
Obituary **1993**:4
Samaranch, Juan Antonio **1986**:2
Segovia, Andres
Obituary **1987**:3
Wences, Senor
Obituary **1999**:4

SRI LANKAN
Bandaranaike, Sirimavo
Obituary **2001**:2
Ondaatje, Philip Michael **1997**:3
Wickramasinghe, Ranil **2003**:2

SUDANESE
Turabi, Hassan **1995**:4

SWEDISH
Bergman, Ingmar **1999**:4
Cardigans, The **1997**:4
Carlsson, Arvid **2001**:2
Garbo, Greta
Obituary **1990**:3
Hallstrom, Lasse **2002**:3
Lindbergh, Pelle
Obituary **1985**:4
Lindgren, Astrid
Obituary **2003**:1
Olin, Lena **1991**:2
Palme, Olof
Obituary **1986**:2
Renvall, Johan
Brief Entry **1987**:4
Sorenstam, Annika **2001**:1

SWISS
del Ponte, Carla **2001**:1
Frank, Robert **1995**:2
Vollenweider, Andreas **1985**:2

SYRIAN
Assad, Hafez
Obituary **2000**:4
Assad, Hafez al- **1992**:1
Assad, Rifaat **1986**:3

TAHITIAN
Brando, Cheyenne
Obituary **1995**:4

TAIWANESE
Chen Shui-bian **2001**:2
Ho, David **1997**:2
Lee Teng-hui **2000**:1

TANZANIAN
Nyerere, Julius
Obituary **2000**:2

TRINIDADIAN
Ture, Kwame
Obituary **1999**:2

TUNISIAN
Azria, Max **2001**:4

TURKISH
Ocalan, Abdullah **1999**:4

UGANDAN
Museveni, Yoweri **2002**:1

UKRAINIAN
Baiul, Oksana **1995**:3

VENEZUELAN
Herrera, Carolina **1997**:1
Perez, Carlos Andre **1990**:2

VIETNAMESE
Dong, Pham Van
Obituary **2000**:4
Le Duan
Obituary **1986**:4
Le Duc Tho
Obituary **1991**:1

WELSH
Bale, Christian **2001**:3
Dahl, Roald
Obituary **1991**:2
Hopkins, Anthony **1992**:4
Jones, Tom **1993**:4
William, Prince of Wales **2001**:3
Zeta-Jones, Catherine **1999**:4

YEMENI
Saleh, Ali Abdullah **2001**:3

YUGOSLAVIAN
Filipovic, Zlata **1994**:4
Kostunica, Vojislav **2001**:1
Pogorelich, Ivo **1986**:4
Seles, Monica **1991**:3

ZAIRAN
Mobutu Sese Seko **1993**:4
Obituary **1998**:1

ZAMBIAN
Chiluba, Frederick **1992**:3

ZIMBABWEAN
Mugabe, Robert **1988**:4

Cumulative Occupation Index

This index lists all newsmakers alphabetically by their occupations or fields of primary activity. Indexes in softbound issues allow access to the current year's entries; indexes in annual hardbound volumes are cumulative, covering the entire *Newsmakers* series.

Listee names are followed by a year and issue number; thus **1996**:3 indicates that an entry on that individual appears in both 1996, Issue 3, and the 1996 cumulation. For access to newsmakers appearing earlier than the current softbound issue, see the previous year's cumulation.

ART AND DESIGN

Adams, Scott **1996**:4
Addams, Charles
  Obituary **1989**:1
Agnes B **2002**:3
Allard, Linda **2003**:2
Anderson, Laurie **2000**:2
Arman **1993**:1
Armani, Giorgio **1991**:2
Aucoin, Kevyn **2001**:3
Avedon, Richard **1993**:4
Azria, Max **2001**:4
Baldessari, John **1991**:4
Banks, Jeffrey **1998**:2
Barbera, Joseph **1988**:2
Barks, Carl
  Obituary **2001**:2
Barnes, Ernie **1997**:4
Barry, Lynda **1992**:1
Bean, Alan L. **1986**:2
Beuys, Joseph
  Obituary **1986**:3
Blahnik, Manolo **2000**:2
Blass, Bill
  Obituary **2003**:3
Boone, Mary **1985**:1
Botero, Fernando **1994**:3
Bourgeois, Louise **1994**:1
Bowie, David **1998**:2
Brown, Bobbi **2001**:4
Brown, J. Carter
  Obituary **2003**:3
Bunshaft, Gordon **1989**:3
  Obituary **1991**:1
Cameron, David
  Brief Entry **1988**:1
Campbell, Ben Nighthorse **1998**:1
Campbell, Naomi **2000**:2
Cardin, Pierre **2003**:3
Castelli, Leo
  Obituary **2000**:1
Catlett, Elizabeth **1999**:3
Chagall, Marc
  Obituary **1985**:2
Chalayan, Hussein **2003**:2
Chast, Roz **1992**:4
Chatham, Russell **1990**:1

Chia, Sandro **1987**:2
Chihuly, Dale **1995**:2
Chillida, Eduardo
  Obituary **2003**:4
Christo **1992**:3
Claiborne, Liz **1986**:3
Clemente, Francesco **1992**:2
Cole, Kenneth **2003**:1
Cooper, Alexander **1988**:4
Crumb, R. **1995**:4
Dali, Salvador
  Obituary **1989**:2
DeCarava, Roy **1996**:3
de Kooning, Willem **1994**:4
  Obituary **1997**:3
Diebenkorn, Richard
  Obituary **1993**:4
Donghia, Angelo R.
  Obituary **1985**:2
Duarte, Henry **2003**:3
Dubuffet, Jean
  Obituary **1985**:4
Dunham, Carroll **2003**:4
Eisenman, Peter **1992**:4
Eisenstaedt, Alfred
  Obituary **1996**:1
Ellis, Perry
  Obituary **1986**:3
Engelbreit, Mary **1994**:3
Erickson, Arthur **1989**:3
Erte
  Obituary **1990**:4
Fekkai, Frederic **2003**:2
Field, Patricia **2002**:2
Finley, Karen **1992**:4
Fisher, Mary **1994**:3
Ford, Tom **1999**:3
Foster, Norman **1999**:4
Frank, Robert **1995**:2
Frankenthaler, Helen **1990**:1
Freud, Lucian **2000**:4
Gaines, William M.
  Obituary **1993**:1
Gaultier, Jean-Paul **1998**:1
Gehry, Frank O. **1987**:1
Giannulli, Mossimo **2002**:3
Gober, Robert **1996**:3

Golden, Thelma **2003**:3
Goody, Joan **1990**:2
Gould, Chester
  Obituary **1985**:2
Graham, Nicholas **1991**:4
Graham, Robert **1993**:4
Graves, Michael **2000**:1
Graves, Nancy **1989**:3
Greenberg, Robert **2003**:2
Groening, Matt **1990**:4
Guccione, Bob **1986**:1
Gund, Agnes **1993**:2
Gursky, Andreas **2002**:2
Halston
  Obituary **1990**:3
Handford, Martin **1991**:3
Haring, Keith
  Obituary **1990**:3
Hilfiger, Tommy **1993**:3
Hockney, David **1988**:3
Holl, Steven **2003**:1
Hughes, Robert **1996**:4
Isozaki, Arata **1990**:2
Jacobs, Marc **2002**:3
Jahn, Helmut **1987**:3
Johnson, Betsey **1996**:2
Johnson, Philip **1989**:2
Jordan, Charles M. **1989**:4
Judge, Mike **1994**:2
Kahlo, Frida **1991**:3
Kamali, Norma **1989**:1
Karan, Donna **1988**:1
Karsh, Yousuf
  Obituary **2003**:4
Kashuk, Sonia **2002**:4
Kaskey, Ray
  Brief Entry **1987**:2
Katz, Alex **1990**:3
Kelly, Ellsworth **1992**:1
Kelly, Patrick
  Obituary **1990**:2
Kent, Corita
  Obituary **1987**:1
Keplinger, Dan **2001**:1
Ketcham, Hank
  Obituary **2002**:2
Kiefer, Anselm **1990**:2

Boyer, Herbert Wayne **1985**:1
Boyle, Gertrude **1995**:3
Brabeck-Letmathe, Peter **2001**:4
Bradley, Todd **2003**:3
Branson, Richard **1987**:1
Bravo, Ellen **1998**:2
Breitschwerdt, Werner **1988**:4
Brennan, Edward A. **1989**:1
Brennan, Robert E. **1988**:1
Bronfman, Edgar, Jr. **1994**:4
Brooks, Diana D. **1990**:1
Brown, Tina **1992**:1
Buffett, Jimmy **1999**:3
Buffett, Warren **1995**:2
Burnison, Chantal Simone **1988**:3
Burns, Robin **1991**:2
Burr, Donald Calvin **1985**:3
Busch, August A. III **1988**:2
Busch, August Anheuser, Jr.
    Obituary **1990**:2
Bushnell, Nolan **1985**:1
Buss, Jerry **1989**:3
Cain, Herman **1998**:3
Callaway, Ely
    Obituary **2002**:3
Calloway, D. Wayne **1987**:3
Campeau, Robert **1990**:1
Canfield, Alan B.
    Brief Entry **1986**:3
Carter, Billy
    Obituary **1989**:1
Case, Steve **1995**:4 **1996**:4
Chalayan, Hussein **2003**:2
Chappell, Tom **2002**:3
Chenault, Kenneth I. **1999**:3
Chouinard, Yvon **2002**:2
Chung Ju Yung
    Obituary **2002**:1
Claiborne, Liz **1986**:3
Clark, Jim **1997**:1
Cole, Kenneth **2003**:1
Coleman, Sheldon, Jr. **1990**:2
Collier, Sophia **2001**:2
Combs, Sean Puffy **1998**:4
Condit, Phil **2001**:3
Cooper, Alexander **1988**:4
Coors, William K.
    Brief Entry **1985**:1
Copeland, Al **1988**:3
Covey, Stephen R. **1994**:4
Cox, Richard Joseph
    Brief Entry **1985**:1
Craig, James **2001**:1
Craig, Sid and Jenny **1993**:4
Crandall, Robert L. **1992**:1
Crawford, Cheryl
    Obituary **1987**:1
Cray, Seymour R.
    Brief Entry **1986**:3
    Obituary **1997**:2
Cummings, Sam **1986**:3
D'Alessio, Kitty
    Brief Entry **1987**:3
Davison, Ian Hay **1986**:1
DeBartolo, Edward J., Jr. **1989**:3
Dell, Michael **1996**:2
DeLuca, Fred **2003**:3
Deming, W. Edwards **1992**:2
    Obituary **1994**:2
de Passe, Suzanne **1990**:4
Devine, John M. **2003**:2

Diemer, Walter E.
    Obituary **1998**:2
DiFranco, Ani **1997**:1
Diller, Barry **1991**:1
Disney, Lillian
    Obituary **1998**:3
Disney, Roy E. **1986**:3
Dolby, Ray Milton
    Brief Entry **1986**:1
Doubleday, Nelson, Jr. **1987**:1
Downey, Bruce **2003**:1
Drexler, Millard S. **1990**:3
Drucker, Peter F. **1992**:3
Dunlap, Albert J. **1997**:2
Dupri, Jermaine **1999**:1
Eagleson, Alan **1987**:4
Eaton, Robert J. **1994**:2
Ebbers, Bernie **1998**:1
Eckert, Robert A. **2002**:3
Egan, John **1987**:2
Eisner, Michael **1989**:2
Ellis, Perry
    Obituary **1986**:3
Engibous, Thomas J. **2003**:3
Engstrom, Elmer W.
    Obituary **1985**:2
Epstein, Jason **1991**:1
Ertegun, Ahmet **1986**:3
Estes, Pete
    Obituary **1988**:3
Evans, Nancy **2000**:4
Eyler, John. H., Jr. **2001**:3
Factor, Max
    Obituary **1996**:4
Fekkai, Frederic **2003**:2
Feld, Kenneth **1988**:2
Fender, Leo
    Obituary **1992**:1
Ferrari, Enzo **1988**:4
Fertel, Ruth **2000**:2
Fields, Debbi **1987**:3
Fiorina, Carleton S. **2000**:1
Fireman, Paul
    Brief Entry **1987**:2
Fisher, Mel **1985**:4
Flynt, Larry **1997**:3
Fodor, Eugene
    Obituary **1991**:3
Fomon, Robert M. **1985**:3
Forbes, Malcolm S.
    Obituary **1990**:3
Ford, Henry II
    Obituary **1988**:1
Ford, William Clay, Jr. **1999**:1
Frank, Anthony M. **1992**:1
Freeman, Cliff **1996**:1
Fudge, Ann **2000**:3
Ganzi, Victor **2003**:3
Garcia, Joe
    Brief Entry **1986**:4
Garzarelli, Elaine M. **1992**:3
Gates, Bill **1993**:3 **1987**:4
Gatien, Peter
    Brief Entry **1986**:1
Gaultier, Jean-Paul **1998**:1
Gerstner, Lou **1993**:4
Gilbert, Walter **1988**:3
Gillett, George **1988**:1
Glass, David **1996**:1
Goizueta, Roberto **1996**:1
    Obituary **1998**:1
Goldberg, Leonard **1988**:4

Goody, Sam
    Obituary **1992**:1
Gorman, Leon
    Brief Entry **1987**:1
Grace, J. Peter **1990**:2
Graham, Bill **1986**:4
    Obituary **1992**:2
Graham, Donald **1985**:4
Graham, Katharine Meyer **1997**:3
    Obituary **2002**:3
Graham, Nicholas **1991**:4
Greenberg, Robert **2003**:2
Gregory, Dick **1990**:3
Grove, Andrew S. **1995**:3
Grucci, Felix **1987**:1
Gucci, Maurizio
    Brief Entry **1985**:4
Guccione, Bob **1986**:1
Gund, Agnes **1993**:2
Gutierrez, Carlos M. **2001**:4
Haas, Robert D. **1986**:4
Hahn, Carl H. **1986**:4
Hakuta, Ken
    Brief Entry **1986**:1
Hamilton, Hamish
    Obituary **1988**:4
Hammer, Armand
    Obituary **1991**:3
Handler, Ruth
    Obituary **2003**:3
Haney, Chris
    Brief Entry **1985**:1
Haseltine, William A. **1999**:2
Hassenfeld, Stephen **1987**:4
Hawkins, Jeff and
    Donna Dubinsky **2000**:2
Hearst, Randolph A.
    Obituary **2001**:3
Heckert, Richard E.
    Brief Entry **1987**:3
Hefner, Christie **1985**:1
Heineken, Alfred
    Obituary **2003**:1
Heinz, H.J.
    Obituary **1987**:2
Helmsley, Leona **1988**:1
Herrera, Carolina **1997**:1
Herzog, Doug **2002**:4
Hilbert, Stephen C. **1997**:4
Hilfiger, Tommy **1993**:3
Hillegass, Clifton Keith **1989**:4
Holbrooke, Richard **1996**:2
Holden, Betsy **2003**:2
Honda, Soichiro
    Obituary **1986**:1
Horrigan, Edward, Jr. **1989**:1
Hughes, Cathy **1999**:1
Hughes, Mark **1985**:3
Huizenga, Wayne **1992**:1
Hyatt, Joel **1985**:3
Iacocca, Lee **1993**:1
Ilitch, Mike **1993**:4
Iman **2001**:3
Immelt, Jeffrey R. **2001**:2
Inatome, Rick **1985**:4
Ingersoll, Ralph II **1988**:2
Isaacson, Portia
    Brief Entry **1986**:1
Jacuzzi, Candido
    Obituary **1987**:1
Janklow, Morton **1989**:3
Jobs, Steve **2000**:1

Tharp, Twyla **1992**:4
Tudor, Antony
  Obituary **1987**:4
Tune, Tommy **1994**:2
Varone, Doug **2001**:2
Verdi-Fletcher, Mary **1998**:2
Verdon, Gwen
  Obituary **2001**:2
Whelan, Wendy **1999**:3

EDUCATION

Abramson, Lyn **1986**:3
Alexander, Lamar **1991**:2
Bakker, Robert T. **1991**:3
Bayley, Corrine
  Brief Entry **1986**:4
Billington, James **1990**:3
Bollinger, Lee C. **2003**:2
Botstein, Leon **1985**:3
Bush, Millie **1992**:1
Campbell, Bebe Moore **1996**:2
Casper, Gerhard **1993**:1
Cavazos, Lauro F. **1989**:2
Cheek, James Edward
  Brief Entry **1987**:1
Cheney, Lynne V. **1990**:4
Clements, George **1985**:1
Cole, Johnetta B. **1994**:3
Coles, Robert **1995**:1
Commager, Henry Steele
  Obituary **1998**:3
Curran, Charles E. **1989**:2
Davis, Angela **1998**:3
Delany, Sarah
  Obituary **1999**:3
Deming, W. Edwards **1992**:2
  Obituary **1994**:2
Dershowitz, Alan **1992**:1
Dove, Rita **1994**:3
Drucker, Peter F. **1992**:3
Edelman, Marian Wright **1990**:4
Edwards, Harry **1989**:4
Etzioni, Amitai **1994**:3
Feldman, Sandra **1987**:3
Fernandez, Joseph **1991**:3
Folkman, Judah **1999**:1
Fox, Matthew **1992**:2
Fulbright, J. William
  Obituary **1995**:3
Futter, Ellen V. **1995**:1
Ghali, Boutros Boutros **1992**:3
Giamatti, A. Bartlett **1988**:4
  Obituary **1990**:1
Goldhaber, Fred
  Brief Entry **1986**:3
Gray, Hanna **1992**:4
Green, Richard R. **1988**:3
Gregorian, Vartan **1990**:3
Gund, Agnes **1993**:2
Hackney, Sheldon **1995**:1
Hair, Jay D. **1994**:3
Harker, Patrick T. **2001**:2
Hayakawa, Samuel Ichiye
  Obituary **1992**:3
Healy, Bernadine **1993**:1
Healy, Timothy S. **1990**:2
Heaney, Seamus **1996**:2
Heller, Walter
  Obituary **1987**:4
Hennessy, John L. **2002**:2
Hill, Anita **1994**:1

Hillegass, Clifton Keith **1989**:4
Horwich, Frances
  Obituary **2002**:3
Hunter, Madeline **1991**:2
Janzen, Daniel H. **1988**:4
Jordan, King **1990**:1
Justiz, Manuel J. **1986**:4
Kemp, Jan **1987**:2
King, Mary-Claire **1998**:3
Kopp, Wendy **1993**:3
Kozol, Jonathan **1992**:1
Lagasse, Emeril **1998**:3
Lamb, Wally **1999**:1
Lang, Eugene M. **1990**:3
Langston, J. William
  Brief Entry **1986**:2
Lawrence, Ruth
  Brief Entry **1986**:3
Laybourne, Geraldine **1997**:1
Leach, Penelope **1992**:4
Lerner, Michael **1994**:2
Levine, Arnold **2002**:3
MacKinnon, Catharine **1993**:2
Malloy, Edward Monk **1989**:4
Marier, Rebecca **1995**:4
McAuliffe, Christa
  Obituary **1985**:4
McMillan, Terry **1993**:2
Morrison, Toni **1998**:1
Mumford, Lewis
  Obituary **1990**:2
Nemerov, Howard
  Obituary **1992**:1
Nye, Bill **1997**:2
Owens, Delia and Mark **1993**:3
Pagels, Elaine **1997**:1
Paglia, Camille **1992**:3
Paige, Rod **2003**:2
Parizeau, Jacques **1995**:1
Peter, Valentine J. **1988**:2
Riley, Richard W. **1996**:3
Rodin, Judith **1994**:4
Rosendahl, Bruce R.
  Brief Entry **1986**:4
Rowland, Pleasant **1992**:3
Scheck, Barry **2000**:4
Schuman, Patricia Glass **1993**:2
Shalala, Donna **1992**:3
Sherman, Russell **1987**:4
Silber, John **1990**:1
Simmons, Adele Smith **1988**:4
Simmons, Ruth **1995**:2
Smoot, George F. **1993**:3
Sowell, Thomas **1998**:3
Spock, Benjamin **1995**:2
  Obituary **1998**:3
Steele, Shelby **1991**:2
Swanson, Mary Catherine **2002**:2
Tannen, Deborah **1995**:1
Thiebaud, Wayne **1991**:1
Thomas, Michel **1987**:4
Tilghman, Shirley M. **2002**:1
Tribe, Laurence H. **1988**:1
Tyson, Laura D'Andrea **1994**:1
Unz, Ron **1999**:1
Van Duyn, Mona **1993**:2
Vickrey, William S.
  Obituary **1997**:2
Warren, Robert Penn
  Obituary **1990**:1
West, Cornel **1994**:2
Wexler, Nancy S. **1992**:3

Wiesel, Elie **1998**:1
Wigand, Jeffrey **2000**:4
Wiles, Andrew **1994**:1
Wilson, Edward O. **1994**:4
Wilson, William Julius **1997**:1
Wu, Harry **1996**:1
Zanker, Bill
  Brief Entry **1987**:3
Zigler, Edward **1994**:1

FILM

Abbott, George
  Obituary **1995**:3
Adjani, Isabelle **1991**:1
Affleck, Ben **1999**:1
Aiello, Danny **1990**:4
Alda, Robert
  Obituary **1986**:3
Alexander, Jane **1994**:2
Alexander, Jason **1993**:3
Allen, Debbie **1998**:2
Allen, Joan **1998**:1
Allen, Woody **1994**:1
Alley, Kirstie **1990**:3
Almodovar, Pedro **2000**:3
Altman, Robert **1993**:2
Ameche, Don
  Obituary **1994**:2
Anderson, Judith
  Obituary **1992**:3
Andrews, Julie **1996**:1
Aniston, Jennifer **2000**:3
Applegate, Christina **2000**:4
Arad, Avi **2003**:2
Arden, Eve
  Obituary **1991**:2
Arkoff, Samuel Z.
  Obituary **2002**:4
Arlen, Harold
  Obituary **1986**:3
Arnaz, Desi
  Obituary **1987**:1
Arnold, Tom **1993**:2
Arquette, Patricia **2001**:3
Arquette, Rosanna **1985**:2
Arthur, Jean
  Obituary **1992**:1
Ashcroft, Peggy
  Obituary **1992**:1
Astaire, Fred
  Obituary **1987**:4
Astor, Mary
  Obituary **1988**:1
Autry, Gene
  Obituary **1999**:1
Aykroyd, Dan **1989**:3 **1997**:3
Bacall, Lauren **1997**:3
Backus, Jim
  Obituary **1990**:1
Bacon, Kevin **1995**:3
Baddeley, Hermione
  Obituary **1986**:4
Bailey, Pearl
  Obituary **1991**:1
Bakula, Scott **2003**:1
Baldwin, Alec **2002**:2
Bale, Christian **2001**:3
Ball, Lucille
  Obituary **1989**:3
Banderas, Antonio **1996**:2
Banks, Tyra **1996**:3
Barker, Clive **2003**:3

Vidov, Oleg **1987**:4
Villechaize, Herve
  Obituary **1994**:1
Vincent, Fay **1990**:2
Voight, Jon **2002**:3
Walker, Nancy
  Obituary **1992**:3
Wallis, Hal
  Obituary **1987**:1
Warhol, Andy
  Obituary **1987**:2
Washington, Denzel **1993**:2
Wasserman, Lew
  Obituary **2003**:3
Waters, John **1988**:3
Watson, Emily **2001**:1
Wayans, Damon **1998**:4
Wayans, Keenen Ivory **1991**:1
Wayne, David
  Obituary **1995**:3
Weaver, Sigourney **1988**:3
Wegman, William **1991**:1
Weinstein, Bob and Harvey **2000**:4
Weintraub, Jerry **1986**:1
Whitaker, Forest **1996**:2
Wiest, Dianne **1995**:2
Wilder, Billy
  Obituary **2003**:2
Wilkinson, Tom **2003**:2
Williams, Robin **1988**:4
Williams, Vanessa L. **1999**:2
Willis, Bruce **1986**:4
Wilson, Owen **2002**:3
Winfrey, Oprah **1986**:4 **1997**:3
Winger, Debra **1994**:3
Winslet, Kate **2002**:4
Witherspoon, Reese **2002**:1
Wolfman Jack
  Obituary **1996**:1
Wong, B.D. **1998**:1
Woo, John **1994**:2
Wood, Elijah **2002**:4
Woods, James **1988**:3
Wyle, Noah **1997**:3
Wynn, Keenan
  Obituary **1987**:1
Yeoh, Michelle **2003**:2
Young, Loretta
  Obituary **2001**:1
Young, Robert
  Obituary **1999**:1
Zanuck, Lili Fini **1994**:2
Zeffirelli, Franco **1991**:3
Zellweger, Renee **2001**:1
Zemeckis, Robert **2002**:1
Zeta-Jones, Catherine **1999**:4
Zucker, Jerry **2002**:2

LAW
Abzug, Bella **1998**:2
Achtenberg, Roberta **1993**:4
Allred, Gloria **1985**:2
Angelos, Peter **1995**:4
Archer, Dennis **1994**:4
Astorga, Nora **1988**:2
Babbitt, Bruce **1994**:1
Bailey, F. Lee **1995**:4
Baker, James A. III **1991**:2
Bikoff, James L.
  Brief Entry **1986**:2
Blackmun, Harry A.
  Obituary **1999**:3

Boies, David **2002**:1
Bradley, Tom
  Obituary **1999**:1
Brennan, William
  Obituary **1997**:4
Breyer, Stephen Gerald
  1994:4 **1997**:2
Brown, Willie **1996**:4
Brown, Willie L. **1985**:2
Burger, Warren E.
  Obituary **1995**:4
Burnison, Chantal Simone **1988**:3
Campbell, Kim **1993**:4
Cantrell, Ed
  Brief Entry **1985**:3
Casey, William
  Obituary **1987**:3
Casper, Gerhard **1993**:1
Clark, Marcia **1995**:1
Clinton, Bill **1992**:1
Clinton, Hillary Rodham **1993**:2
Cochran, Johnnie **1996**:1
Colby, William E.
  Obituary **1996**:4
Cuomo, Mario **1992**:2
Darden, Christopher **1996**:4
Dees, Morris **1992**:1
del Ponte, Carla **2001**:1
Dershowitz, Alan **1992**:1
Deutch, John **1996**:4
Dole, Elizabeth Hanford **1990**:1
Dukakis, Michael **1988**:3
Eagleson, Alan **1987**:4
Ehrlichman, John
  Obituary **1999**:3
Ervin, Sam
  Obituary **1985**:2
Estrich, Susan **1989**:1
Fairstein, Linda **1991**:1
Fehr, Donald **1987**:2
Fieger, Geoffrey **2001**:3
Florio, James J. **1991**:2
Foster, Vincent
  Obituary **1994**:1
France, Johnny
  Brief Entry **1987**:1
Freeh, Louis J. **1994**:2
Fulbright, J. William
  Obituary **1995**:3
Furman, Rosemary
  Brief Entry **1986**:4
Garrison, Jim
  Obituary **1993**:2
Ginsburg, Ruth Bader **1993**:4
Giuliani, Rudolph **1994**:2
Glasser, Ira **1989**:1
Gore, Albert, Sr.
  Obituary **1999**:2
Grisham, John **1994**:4
Harvard, Beverly **1995**:2
Hayes, Robert M. **1986**:3
Hill, Anita **1994**:1
Hills, Carla **1990**:3
Hirschhorn, Joel
  Brief Entry **1986**:1
Hoffa, Jim, Jr. **1999**:2
Hyatt, Joel **1985**:3
Ireland, Patricia **1992**:2
Ito, Lance **1995**:3
Janklow, Morton **1989**:3
Kennedy, John F., Jr. **1990**:1
  Obituary **1999**:4

Kennedy, Weldon **1997**:3
Kunstler, William
  Obituary **1996**:1
Kunstler, William **1992**:3
Kurzban, Ira **1987**:2
Lee, Henry C. **1997**:1
Lee, Martin **1998**:2
Lewis, Loida Nicolas **1998**:3
Lewis, Reginald F. **1988**:4
  Obituary **1993**:3
Lightner, Candy **1985**:1
Liman, Arthur **1989**:4
Lipsig, Harry H. **1985**:1
Lipton, Martin **1987**:3
MacKinnon, Catharine **1993**:2
Marshall, Thurgood
  Obituary **1993**:3
McCloskey, James **1993**:1
Mitchell, George J. **1989**:3
Mitchell, John
  Obituary **1989**:2
Mitchelson, Marvin **1989**:2
Morrison, Trudi
  Brief Entry **1986**:2
Nader, Ralph **1989**:4
Napolitano, Janet **1997**:1
Neal, James Foster **1986**:2
O'Connor, Sandra Day **1991**:1
O'Leary, Hazel **1993**:4
O'Steen, Van
  Brief Entry **1986**:3
Panetta, Leon **1995**:1
Pirro, Jeanine **1998**:2
Powell, Lewis F.
  Obituary **1999**:1
Puccio, Thomas P. **1986**:4
Quayle, Dan **1989**:2
Raines, Franklin **1997**:4
Ramaphosa, Cyril **1988**:2
Ramo, Roberta Cooper **1996**:1
Rehnquist, William H. **2001**:2
Reno, Janet **1993**:3
Rothwax, Harold **1996**:3
Scalia, Antonin **1988**:2
Scheck, Barry **2000**:4
Schily, Otto
  Brief Entry **1987**:4
Sheehan, Daniel P. **1989**:1
Sheindlin, Judith **1999**:1
Sirica, John
  Obituary **1993**:2
Skinner, Sam **1992**:3
Slater, Rodney E. **1997**:4
Slotnick, Barry
  Brief Entry **1987**:4
Souter, David **1991**:3
Starr, Kenneth **1998**:3
Steinberg, Leigh **1987**:3
Stern, David **1991**:4
Stewart, Potter
  Obituary **1986**:1
Strauss, Robert **1991**:4
Tagliabue, Paul **1990**:2
Thomas, Clarence **1992**:2
Thompson, Fred **1998**:2
Tribe, Laurence H. **1988**:1
Vincent, Fay **1990**:2
Violet, Arlene **1985**:3
Wapner, Joseph A. **1987**:1
Watson, Elizabeth **1991**:2
White, Byron
  Obituary **2003**:3

Williams, Edward Bennett
Obituary **1988**:4
Williams, Willie L. **1993**:1
Wilson, Bertha
Brief Entry **1986**:1

MUSIC

Aaliyah **2001**:3
Abdul, Paula **1990**:3
Ackerman, Will **1987**:4
Acuff, Roy
Obituary **1993**:2
Aguilera, Christina **2000**:4
Albert, Stephen **1986**:1
Allen, Peter
Obituary **1993**:1
Amos, Tori **1995**:1
Anderson, Marion
Obituary **1993**:4
Andrews, Julie **1996**:1
Andrews, Maxene
Obituary **1996**:2
Anthony, Marc **2000**:3
Arlen, Harold
Obituary **1986**:3
Arnaz, Desi
Obituary **1987**:1
Arrau, Claudio
Obituary **1992**:1
Arrested Development **1994**:2
Astaire, Fred
Obituary **1987**:4
Autry, Gene
Obituary **1999**:1
Backstreet Boys **2001**:3
Badu, Erykah **2000**:4
Baez, Joan **1998**:3
Bailey, Pearl
Obituary **1991**:1
Baker, Anita **1987**:4
Barenboim, Daniel **2001**:1
Bartoli, Cecilia **1994**:1
Basie, Count
Obituary **1985**:1
Battle, Kathleen **1998**:1
Beastie Boys, The **1999**:1
Becaud, Gilbert
Obituary **2003**:1
Beck **2000**:2
Bee Gees, The **1997**:4
Benatar, Pat **1986**:1
Bennett, Tony **1994**:4
Berlin, Irving
Obituary **1990**:1
Bernhard, Sandra **1989**:4
Bernstein, Leonard
Obituary **1991**:1
Berry, Chuck **2001**:2
Bjork **1996**:1
Blades, Ruben **1998**:2
Blakey, Art
Obituary **1991**:1
Blige, Mary J. **1995**:3
Bolton, Michael **1993**:2
Bon Jovi, Jon **1987**:4
Bono **1988**:4
Bono, Sonny **1992**:2
Obituary **1998**:2
Borge, Victor
Obituary **2001**:3
Botstein, Leon **1985**:3
Bowie, David **1998**:2

Bowles, Paul
Obituary **2000**:3
Boxcar Willie
Obituary **1999**:4
Boyz II Men **1995**:1
Brandy **1996**:4
Branson, Richard **1987**:1
Braxton, Toni **1994**:3
Brooks, Garth **1992**:1
Brown, James **1991**:4
Brown, Les
Obituary **2001**:3
Buckley, Jeff
Obituary **1997**:4
Buffett, Jimmy **1999**:3
Bush, Kate **1994**:3
Butterfield, Paul
Obituary **1987**:3
Cage, John
Obituary **1993**:1
Calloway, Cab
Obituary **1995**:2
Cardigans, The **1997**:4
Carey, Mariah **1991**:3
Carlisle, Belinda **1989**:3
Carpenter, Mary-Chapin **1994**:1
Carreras, Jose **1995**:2
Carter, Ron **1987**:3
Cash, Johnny **1995**:3
Cerovsek, Corey
Brief Entry **1987**:4
Chapman, Tracy **1989**:2
Cheatham, Adolphus Doc
Obituary **1997**:4
Cher **1993**:1
Clapton, Eric **1993**:3
Clarke, Stanley **1985**:4
Clarkson, Kelly **2003**:3
Cleveland, James
Obituary **1991**:3
Cliburn, Van **1995**:1
Clooney, Rosemary
Obituary **2003**:4
Cobain, Kurt
Obituary **1994**:3
Cole, Natalie **1992**:4
Collins, Albert
Obituary **1994**:2
Combs, Sean Puffy **1998**:4
Como, Perry
Obituary **2002**:2
Connick, Harry, Jr. **1991**:1
Coolio **1996**:4
Copland, Aaron
Obituary **1991**:2
Coppola, Carmine
Obituary **1991**:4
Corea, Chick **1986**:3
Costello, Elvis **1994**:4
Cowell, Simon **2003**:4
Crawford, Michael **1994**:2
Cray, Robert **1988**:2
Crosby, David **2000**:4
Crothers, Scatman
Obituary **1987**:1
Crow, Sheryl **1995**:2
Crowe, Russell **2000**:4
Cugat, Xavier
Obituary **1991**:2
Cyrus, Billy Ray **1993**:1
D'Arby, Terence Trent **1988**:4

Davis, Miles
Obituary **1992**:2
Davis, Sammy, Jr.
Obituary **1990**:4
Day, Dennis
Obituary **1988**:4
Dean, Laura **1989**:4
Denver, John
Obituary **1998**:1
de Passe, Suzanne **1990**:4
Destiny's Child **2001**:3
DiFranco, Ani **1997**:1
Di Meola, Al **1986**:4
Dimitrova, Ghena **1987**:1
Dion, Celine **1995**:3
Dixie Chicks **2001**:2
Dr. Demento **1986**:1
Dr. Dre **1994**:3
Dolenz, Micky **1986**:4
Domingo, Placido **1993**:2
Dorati, Antal
Obituary **1989**:2
Dorsey, Thomas A.
Obituary **1993**:3
Duncan, Todd
Obituary **1998**:3
Dupri, Jermaine **1999**:1
Dylan, Bob **1998**:1
Eazy-E
Obituary **1995**:3
Eckstine, Billy
Obituary **1993**:4
Edmonds, Kenneth Babyface **1995**:3
Eldridge, Roy
Obituary **1989**:3
Elliott, Missy **2003**:4
Eminem **2001**:2
Eno, Brian **1986**:2
Entwistle, John
Obituary **2003**:3
En Vogue **1994**:1
Enya **1992**:3
Ertegun, Ahmet **1986**:3
Esquivel, Juan **1996**:2
Estefan, Gloria **1991**:4
Etheridge, Melissa **1995**:4
Everything But The Girl **1996**:4
Falco
Brief Entry **1987**:2
Farrell, Perry **1992**:2
Fender, Leo
Obituary **1992**:1
Fitzgerald, Ella
Obituary **1996**:4
Fleming, Renee **2001**:4
Ford, Tennessee Ernie
Obituary **1992**:2
Foster, David **1988**:2
Franklin, Aretha **1998**:3
Franklin, Melvin
Obituary **1995**:3
Garbage **2002**:3
Garcia, Jerry **1988**:3
Obituary **1996**:1
Geffen, David **1985**:3 **1997**:3
Geldof, Bob **1985**:3
Getz, Stan
Obituary **1991**:4
Gibb, Andy
Obituary **1988**:3
Gifford, Kathie Lee **1992**:2
Gift, Roland **1990**:2

POLITICS AND GOVERNMENT--FOREIGN

Obuchi, Keizo
  Obituary **2000**:4
Obuchi, Keizo **1999**:2
Ocalan, Abdullah **1999**:4
Olav, King of Norway
  Obituary **1991**:3
Palme, Olof
  Obituary **1986**:2
Papandreou, Andrea
  Obituary **1997**:1
Parizeau, Jacques **1995**:1
Pastrana, Andres **2002**:1
Paton, Alan
  Obituary **1988**:3
Patten, Christopher **1993**:3
Paz, Octavio **1991**:2
Peckford, Brian **1989**:1
Peres, Shimon **1996**:3
Perez, Carlos Andre **1990**:2
Perez de Cuellar, Javier **1991**:3
Peterson, David **1987**:1
Philby, Kim
  Obituary **1988**:3
Pinochet, Augusto **1999**:2
Pol Pot
  Obituary **1998**:4
Preval, Rene **1997**:2
Primakov, Yevgeny **1999**:3
Princess Margaret, Countess of
  Snowdon
  Obituary **2003**:2
Putin, Vladimir **2000**:3
Qaddhafi, Muammar **1998**:3
Queen Elizabeth the Queen Mother
  Obituary **2003**:2
Rabin, Leah
  Obituary **2001**:2
Rabin, Yitzhak **1993**:1
  Obituary **1996**:2
Rafsanjani, Ali Akbar
  Hashemi **1987**:3
Rahman, Sheik Omar
  Abdel- **1993**:3
Ram, Jagjivan
  Obituary **1986**:4
Ramos, Fidel **1995**:2
Rao, P. V. Narasimha **1993**:2
Ravalomanana, Marc **2003**:1
Reisman, Simon **1987**:4
Robelo, Alfonso **1988**:1
Robinson, Mary **1993**:1
Saleh, Ali Abdullah **2001**:3
Salinas, Carlos **1992**:1
Sarkis, Elias
  Obituary **1985**:3
Saro-Wiwa, Ken
  Obituary **1996**:2
Savimbi, Jonas **1986**:2 **1994**:2
Schily, Otto
  Brief Entry **1987**:4
Schroder, Gerhard **1999**:1
Sharon, Ariel **2001**:4
Shipley, Jenny **1998**:3
Silva, Luiz Inacio Lula da **2003**:4
Simpson, Wallis
  Obituary **1986**:3
Slovo, Joe **1989**:2
Staller, Ilona **1988**:3
Strauss, Robert **1991**:4
Suu Kyi, Aung San **1996**:2
Suzman, Helen **1989**:3

Takeshita, Noburu
  Obituary **2001**:1
Tambo, Oliver **1991**:3
Terzi, Zehdi Labib **1985**:3
Thatcher, Margaret **1989**:2
Treurnicht, Andries **1992**:2
Trimble, David **1999**:1
Trudeau, Pierre
  Obituary **2001**:1
Tudjman, Franjo **1996**:2
Tudjman, Franjo
  Obituary **2000**:2
Turabi, Hassan **1995**:4
Uribe, Alvaro **2003**:3
Vajpayee, Atal Behari **1998**:4
Vander Zalm, William **1987**:3
Wahid, Abdurrahman **2000**:3
Walesa, Lech **1991**:2
Wei Jingsheng **1998**:2
Werner, Ruth
  Obituary **2001**:1
Wickramasinghe, Ranil **2003**:2
William, Prince of Wales **2001**:3
Wilson, Bertha
  Brief Entry **1986**:1
Ye Jianying
  Obituary **1987**:1
Yeltsin, Boris **1991**:1
Zedillo, Ernesto **1995**:1
Zeroual, Liamine **1996**:2
Zhao Ziyang **1989**:1
Zhirinovsky, Vladimir **1994**:2
Zia ul-Haq, Mohammad
  Obituary **1988**:4
Chirac, Jacques **1995**:4

POLITICS AND GOVERNMENT--U.S.

Abraham, Spencer **1991**:4
Abrams, Elliott **1987**:1
Abzug, Bella **1998**:2
Achtenberg, Roberta **1993**:4
Agnew, Spiro Theodore
  Obituary **1997**:1
Ailes, Roger **1989**:3
Albright, Madeleine **1994**:3
Alexander, Lamar **1991**:2
Alioto, Joseph L.
  Obituary **1998**:3
Alvarez, Aida **1999**:2
Archer, Dennis **1994**:4
Ashcroft, John **2002**:4
Aspin, Les
  Obituary **1996**:1
Atwater, Lee **1989**:4
  Obituary **1991**:4
Babbitt, Bruce **1994**:1
Baker, James A. III **1991**:2
Baldrige, Malcolm
  Obituary **1988**:1
Banks, Dennis J. **1986**:4
Barry, Marion **1991**:1
Barshefsky, Charlene **2000**:4
Beame, Abraham
  Obituary **2001**:4
Begaye, Kelsey **1999**:3
Bennett, William **1990**:1
Benson, Ezra Taft
  Obituary **1994**:4
Bentsen, Lloyd **1993**:3
Berger, Sandy **2000**:1
Berle, Peter A.A.
  Brief Entry **1987**:3

Biden, Joe **1986**:3
Bonner, Robert **2003**:4
Bono, Sonny **1992**:2
  Obituary **1998**:2
Boxer, Barbara **1995**:1
Boyington, Gregory Pappy
  Obituary **1988**:2
Bradley, Bill **2000**:2
Bradley, Tom
  Obituary **1999**:1
Brady, Sarah and James S. **1991**:4
Braun, Carol Moseley **1993**:1
Brazile, Donna **2001**:1
Brennan, William
  Obituary **1997**:4
Brown, Edmund G., Sr.
  Obituary **1996**:3
Brown, Jerry **1992**:4
Brown, Ron
  Obituary **1996**:4
Brown, Ron **1990**:3
Brown, Willie **1996**:4
Brown, Willie L. **1985**:2
Browner, Carol M. **1994**:1
Buchanan, Pat **1996**:3
Bundy, McGeorge
  Obituary **1997**:1
Bundy, William P.
  Obituary **2001**:2
Bush, Barbara **1989**:3
Bush, George W., Jr. **1996**:4
Bush, Jeb **2003**:1
Caliguiri, Richard S.
  Obituary **1988**:3
Campbell, Ben Nighthorse **1998**:1
Campbell, Bill **1997**:1
Card, Andrew H., Jr. **2003**:2
Carey, Ron **1993**:3
Carmona, Richard **2003**:2
Carnahan, Jean **2001**:2
Carnahan, Mel
  Obituary **2001**:2
Carter, Billy
  Obituary **1989**:1
Carter, Jimmy **1995**:1
Casey, William
  Obituary **1987**:3
Cavazos, Lauro F. **1989**:2
Chamberlin, Wendy **2002**:4
Chavez, Linda **1999**:3
Chavez-Thompson, Linda **1999**:1
Cheney, Dick **1991**:3
Cheney, Lynne V. **1990**:4
Christopher, Warren **1996**:3
Cisneros, Henry **1987**:2
Clark, J. E.
  Brief Entry **1986**:1
Clinton, Bill **1992**:1
Clinton, Hillary Rodham **1993**:2
Clyburn, James **1999**:4
Cohen, William S. **1998**:1
Collins, Cardiss **1995**:3
Connally, John
  Obituary **1994**:1
Conyers, John, Jr. **1999**:1
Cuomo, Mario **1992**:2
D'Amato, Al **1996**:1
Daschle, Tom **2002**:3
DeLay, Tom **2000**:1
Dinkins, David N. **1990**:2
Dolan, Terry **1985**:2
Dole, Bob **1994**:2

SOCIAL ISSUES

SPORTS

Abbott, Jim **1988**:3
Abercrombie, Josephine **1987**:2
Agassi, Andre **1990**:2
Agee, Tommie
  Obituary **2001**:4
Aikman, Troy **1994**:2
Ainge, Danny **1987**:1
Akers, Michelle **1996**:1
Albert, Marv **1994**:3
Albom, Mitch **1999**:3
Ali, Laila **2001**:2
Ali, Muhammad **1997**:2
Allen, Mel
  Obituary **1996**:4
Allen, Ray **2002**:1
Alter, Hobie
  Brief Entry **1985**:1
Angelos, Peter **1995**:4
Anthony, Earl
  Obituary **2002**:3
Aoki, Rocky **1990**:2
Armstrong, Henry
  Obituary **1989**:1
Armstrong, Lance **2000**:1
Ashe, Arthur
  Obituary **1993**:3
Austin, Stone Cold Steve **2001**:3
Axthelm, Pete
  Obituary **1991**:3
Azinger, Paul **1995**:2
Babilonia, Tai **1997**:2
Baiul, Oksana **1995**:3
Baker, Kathy
  Brief Entry **1986**:1
Barkley, Charles **1988**:2
Barnes, Ernie **1997**:4
Baumgartner, Bruce
  Brief Entry **1987**:3
Becker, Boris
  Brief Entry **1985**:3
Beckham, David **2003**:1
Bell, Ricky
  Obituary **1985**:1
Belle, Albert **1996**:4
Benoit, Joan **1986**:3
Bias, Len
  Obituary **1986**:3
Bird, Larry **1990**:3
Blair, Bonnie **1992**:3
Bledsoe, Drew **1995**:1
Boggs, Wade **1989**:3
Boitano, Brian **1988**:3
Bonds, Barry **1993**:3
Bonilla, Bobby **1992**:2
Bosworth, Brian **1989**:1
Boudreau, Louis
  Obituary **2002**:3
Bourque, Raymond Jean **1997**:3
Bowe, Riddick **1993**:2
Bowman, Scotty **1998**:4
Bradman, Sir Donald
  Obituary **2002**:1
Brady, Tom **2002**:4
Bremen, Barry **1987**:3
Brown, Jim **1993**:2
Brown, Paul
  Obituary **1992**:1
Bryant, Kobe **1998**:3
Busch, August Anheuser, Jr.
  Obituary **1990**:2
Buss, Jerry **1989**:3

Butcher, Susan **1991**:1
Callaway, Ely
  Obituary **2002**:3
Campanella, Roy
  Obituary **1994**:1
Canseco, Jose **1990**:2
Capriati, Jennifer **1991**:1
Caray, Harry **1988**:3
  Obituary **1998**:3
Carter, Gary **1987**:1
Carter, Joe **1994**:2
Carter, Rubin **2000**:3
Carter, Vince **2001**:4
Chamberlain, Wilt
  Obituary **2000**:2
Chaney, John **1989**:1
Chastain, Brandi **2001**:3
Chen, T.C.
  Brief Entry **1987**:3
Cherry, Don **1993**:4
Chyna **2001**:4
Clemens, Roger **1991**:4
Coffey, Paul **1985**:4
Collins, Kerry **2002**:3
Conigliaro, Tony
  Obituary **1990**:3
Conner, Dennis **1987**:2
Cooper, Cynthia **1999**:1
Copeland, Al **1988**:3
Cosell, Howard
  Obituary **1995**:4
Costas, Bob **1986**:4
Couples, Fred **1994**:4
Courier, Jim **1993**:2
Cunningham, Randall **1990**:1
Curren, Tommy
  Brief Entry **1987**:4
Danza, Tony **1989**:1
Davenport, Lindsay **1999**:2
Davis, Eric **1987**:4
Davis, Terrell **1998**:2
Day, Pat **1995**:2
DeBartolo, Edward J., Jr. **1989**:3
De La Hoya, Oscar **1998**:2
Desormeaux, Kent **1990**:2
DiBello, Paul
  Brief Entry **1986**:4
DiMaggio, Joe
  Obituary **1999**:3
Dolan, Tom **2001**:2
Donnellan, Nanci **1995**:2
Doubleday, Nelson, Jr. **1987**:1
Douglas, Buster **1990**:4
Dravecky, Dave **1992**:1
Drexler, Clyde **1992**:4
Drysdale, Don
  Obituary **1994**:1
Duncan, Tim **2000**:1
Durocher, Leo
  Obituary **1992**:2
Duval, David **2000**:3
Duvall, Camille
  Brief Entry **1988**:1
Dykstra, Lenny **1993**:4
Eagleson, Alan **1987**:4
Earnhardt, Dale
  Obituary **2001**:4
Edwards, Harry **1989**:4
Elway, John **1990**:3
Epstein, Theo **2003**:4
Esiason, Boomer **1991**:1
Evans, Janet **1989**:1

Ewing, Patrick **1985**:3
Faldo, Nick **1993**:3
Favre, Brett Lorenzo **1997**:2
Federov, Sergei **1995**:1
Fehr, Donald **1987**:2
Ferrari, Enzo **1988**:4
Fielder, Cecil **1993**:2
Fiennes, Ranulph **1990**:3
Firestone, Roy **1988**:2
Fittipaldi, Emerson **1994**:2
Flood, Curt
  Obituary **1997**:2
Flutie, Doug **1999**:2
Foss, Joe **1990**:3
Freeman, Cathy **2001**:3
Fuhr, Grant **1997**:3
Galindo, Rudy **2001**:2
Garcia, Joe
  Brief Entry **1986**:4
Gardner, Randy **1997**:2
Garnett, Kevin **2000**:3
Gathers, Hank
  Obituary **1990**:3
Gault, Willie **1991**:2
Gerulaitis, Vitas
  Obituary **1995**:1
Giamatti, A. Bartlett **1988**:4
  Obituary **1990**:1
Gibson, Kirk **1985**:2
Gilmour, Doug **1994**:3
Glaus, Troy **2003**:3
Gomez, Lefty
  Obituary **1989**:3
Gooden, Dwight **1985**:2
Gordeeva, Ekaterina **1996**:4
Gordon, Jeff **1996**:1
Graf, Steffi **1987**:4
Granato, Cammi **1999**:3
Grange, Red
  Obituary **1991**:3
Graziano, Rocky
  Obituary **1990**:4
Greenberg, Hank
  Obituary **1986**:4
Gretzky, Wayne **1989**:2
Griffey, Ken Jr. **1994**:1
Grinkov, Sergei
  Obituary **1996**:2
Gruden, Jon **2003**:4
Gumbel, Greg **1996**:4
Gwynn, Tony **1995**:1
Hagler, Marvelous Marvin **1985**:2
Hamilton, Scott **1998**:2
Hamm, Mia **2000**:1
Hanauer, Chip **1986**:2
Hardaway, Anfernee **1996**:2
Harkes, John **1996**:4
Harmon, Tom
  Obituary **1990**:3
Harwell, Ernie **1997**:3
Hasek, Dominik **1998**:3
Hawk, Tony **2001**:4
Hayes, Woody
  Obituary **1987**:2
Helton, Todd **2001**:1
Henderson, Rickey **2002**:3
Hernandez, Willie **1985**:1
Hershiser, Orel **1989**:2
Hewitt, Lleyton **2002**:2
Hextall, Ron **1988**:2
Hill, Grant **1995**:3
Hill, Lynn **1991**:2

Smith, Emmitt **1994**:1
Smith, Jerry
  Obituary **1987**:1
Snead, Sam
  Obituary **2003**:3
Snyder, Jimmy
  Obituary **1996**:4
Sorenstam, Annika **2001**:1
Sosa, Sammy **1999**:1
Sprewell, Latrell **1999**:4
Stargell, Willie
  Obituary **2002**:1
Steger, Will **1990**:4
Steinberg, Leigh **1987**:3
Steinbrenner, George **1991**:1
Stern, David **1991**:4
Stewart, Dave **1991**:1
Stewart, Payne
  Obituary **2000**:2
Stewart, Tony **2003**:4
Stockton, John Houston **1997**:3
Stofflet, Ty
  Brief Entry **1987**:1
Strange, Curtis **1988**:4
Street, Picabo **1999**:3
Strobl, Fritz **2003**:3
Strug, Kerri **1997**:3
Suzuki, Ichiro **2002**:2
Swoopes, Sheryl **1998**:2
Tagliabue, Paul **1990**:2
Tarkenian, Jerry **1990**:4
Taylor, Lawrence **1987**:3
Testaverde, Vinny **1987**:2
Thomas, Debi **1987**:2
Thomas, Derrick
  Obituary **2000**:3
Thomas, Frank **1994**:3
Thomas, Isiah **1989**:2
Thomas, Thurman **1993**:1
Thompson, John **1988**:3
Tomba, Alberto **1992**:3
Torre, Joseph Paul **1997**:1
Trask, Amy **2003**:3
Trinidad, Felix **2000**:4
Turner, Ted **1989**:1
Tyson, Mike **1986**:4
Unitas, Johnny
  Obituary **2003**:4
Upshaw, Gene **1988**:1
Van Dyken, Amy **1997**:1
Van Slyke, Andy **1992**:4
Vaughn, Mo **1999**:2
Veeck, Bill
  Obituary **1986**:1
Ventura, Jesse **1999**:2
Villeneuve, Jacques **1997**:1
Vincent, Fay **1990**:2
Vitale, Dick **1988**:4 **1994**:4
Waddell, Thomas F.
  Obituary **1988**:2
Walsh, Bill **1987**:4
Warner, Kurt **2000**:3
Webb, Karrie **2000**:4
Webber, Chris **1994**:1
Weber, Pete **1986**:3
Welch, Bob **1991**:3
Wells, David **1999**:3
Whaley, Suzy **2003**:4
White, Bill **1989**:3
White, Byron
  Obituary **2003**:3
White, Reggie **1993**:4

Wilkens, Lenny **1995**:2
Williams, Doug **1988**:2
Williams, Edward Bennett
  Obituary **1988**:4
Williams, Ricky **2000**:2
Williams, Serena **1999**:4
Williams, Ted
  Obituary **2003**:4
Williams, Venus **1998**:2
Witt, Katarina **1991**:3
Woodard, Lynette **1986**:2
Woods, Tiger **1995**:4
Woodson, Ron **1996**:4
Worthy, James **1991**:2
Yamaguchi, Kristi **1992**:3
Young, Steve **1995**:2
Yzerman, Steve **1991**:2
Zamboni, Frank J.
  Brief Entry **1986**:4
Zanardi, Alex **1998**:2
Zatopek, Emil
  Obituary **2001**:3
Zito, Barry **2003**:3

TECHNOLOGY
Adair, Red **1987**:3
Allaire, Paul **1995**:1
Andreessen, Marc **1996**:2
Barksdale, James L. **1998**:2
Belluzzo, Rick **2001**:3
Berners-Lee, Tim **1997**:4
Bezos, Jeff **1998**:4
Bloch, Erich **1987**:4
Bose, Amar
  Brief Entry **1986**:4
Boyer, Herbert Wayne **1985**:1
Bradley, Todd **2003**:3
Burum, Stephen H.
  Brief Entry **1987**:2
Bushnell, Nolan **1985**:1
Case, Steve **1995**:4 **1996**:4
Cerf, Vinton G. **1999**:2
Chaudhari, Praveen **1989**:4
Clarke, Richard A. **2002**:2
Cray, Seymour R.
  Brief Entry **1986**:3
  Obituary **1997**:2
Davis, Noel **1990**:3
Dell, Michael **1996**:2
Dolby, Ray Milton
  Brief Entry **1986**:1
Dunlap, Albert J. **1997**:2
Dzhanibekov, Vladimir **1988**:1
Engibous, Thomas J. **2003**:3
Engstrom, Elmer W.
  Obituary **1985**:2
Evans, Nancy **2000**:4
Fanning, Shawn **2001**:1
Fender, Leo
  Obituary **1992**:1
Filo, David and Jerry Yang **1998**:3
Gardner, David and Tom **2001**:4
Garneau, Marc **1985**:1
Gates, Bill **1993**:3 **1987**:4
Gould, Gordon **1987**:1
Hagelstein, Peter
  Brief Entry **1986**:3
Hewlett, William
  Obituary **2001**:4
Hounsfield, Godfrey **1989**:2
Inman, Bobby Ray **1985**:1

Irwin, James
  Obituary **1992**:1
Jacuzzi, Candido
  Obituary **1987**:1
Jarvik, Robert K. **1985**:1
Jemison, Mae C. **1993**:1
Kamen, Dean **2003**:1
Kilby, Jack **2002**:2
Kimsey, James V. **2001**:1
Kloss, Henry E.
  Brief Entry **1985**:2
Koch, Bill **1992**:3
Kurzweil, Raymond **1986**:3
Kwoh, Yik San **1988**:2
Lamborghini, Ferrucio
  Obituary **1993**:3
Land, Edwin H.
  Obituary **1991**:3
Langer, Robert **2003**:4
Lanier, Jaron **1993**:4
MacCready, Paul **1986**:4
McGowan, William **1985**:2
McLaren, Norman
  Obituary **1987**:2
Minsky, Marvin **1994**:3
Moody, John **1985**:3
Morita, Akio
  Obituary **2000**:2
Morita, Akio **1989**:4
Newman, Joseph **1987**:1
Noyce, Robert N. **1985**:4
Ollila, Jorma **2003**:4
Pack, Ellen **2001**:2
Palmisano, Samuel J. **2003**:1
Parsons, Richard **2002**:4
Perlman, Steve **1998**:2
Perry, William **1994**:4
Pfeiffer, Eckhard **1998**:4
Ramsay, Mike **2002**:1
Raskin, Jef **1997**:4
Rifkin, Jeremy **1990**:3
Ritchie, Dennis and Kenneth
  Thompson **2000**:1
Roberts, Brian L. **2002**:4
Roberts, Steven K. **1992**:1
Rutan, Burt **1987**:2
Schank, Roger **1989**:2
Schmidt, Eric **2002**:4
Scholz, Tom **1987**:2
Schroeder, William J.
  Obituary **1986**:4
Sculley, John **1989**:4
Semel, Terry **2002**:2
Shirley, Donna **1999**:1
Sinclair, Mary **1985**:2
Taylor, Jeff **2001**:3
Tito, Dennis **2002**:1
Titov, Gherman
  Obituary **2001**:3
Tom and Ray Magliozzi **1991**:4
Toomer, Ron **1990**:1
Torvalds, Linus **1999**:3
Treybig, James G. **1988**:3
Wang, An **1986**:1
  Obituary **1990**:3
Wright, Will **2003**:4
Yamamoto, Kenichi **1989**:1

TELEVISION
Affleck, Ben **1999**:1
Alba, Jessica **2001**:2
Albert, Marv **1994**:3

Price, Vincent
  Obituary **1994**:2
Priestly, Jason **1993**:2
Prince, Faith **1993**:2
Prinze, Freddie, Jr. **1999**:3
Pryor, Richard **1999**:3
Quaid, Dennis **1989**:4
Queen Latifah **1992**:2
Quinn, Martha **1986**:4
Quivers, Robin **1995**:4
Radecki, Thomas
  Brief Entry **1986**:2
Radner, Gilda
  Obituary **1989**:4
Raimi, Sam **1999**:2
Randi, James **1990**:2
Raphael, Sally Jessy **1992**:4
Rashad, Phylicia **1987**:3
Raye, Martha
  Obituary **1995**:1
Reasoner, Harry
  Obituary **1992**:1
Redgrave, Lynn **1999**:3
Redgrave, Vanessa **1989**:2
Reed, Donna
  Obituary **1986**:1
Reed, Robert
  Obituary **1992**:4
Reese, Della **1999**:2
Reeve, Christopher **1997**:2
Reiner, Rob **1991**:2
Reiser, Paul **1995**:2
Remick, Lee
  Obituary **1992**:1
Reuben, Gloria **1999**:4
Reubens, Paul **1987**:2
Ricci, Christina **1999**:1
Richards, Michael **1993**:4
Riddle, Nelson
  Obituary **1985**:4
Ripa, Kelly **2002**:2
Ritter, John **2003**:4
Rivera, Geraldo **1989**:1
Robbins, Tim **1993**:1
Roberts, Cokie **1993**:4
Roberts, Doris **2003**:4
Roberts, Julia **1991**:3
Robertson, Pat **1988**:2
Robinson, Max
  Obituary **1989**:2
Rock, Chris **1998**:1
Rock, The **2001**:2
Roddenberry, Gene
  Obituary **1992**:2
Rogers, Fred **2000**:4
Rogers, Roy
  Obituary **1998**:4
Roker, Al **2003**:1
Roker, Roxie
  Obituary **1996**:2
Rolle, Esther
  Obituary **1999**:2
Rollins, Howard E., Jr. **1986**:1
Romano, Ray **2001**:4
Rose, Charlie **1994**:2
Rourke, Mickey **1988**:4
Rowan, Dan
  Obituary **1988**:1
Rudner, Rita **1993**:2
Russell, Keri **2000**:1
Ryan, Meg **1994**:1
Sagansky, Jeff **1993**:2

Sajak, Pat
  Brief Entry **1985**:4
Sandler, Adam **1999**:2
Saralegui, Cristina **1999**:2
Sarandon, Susan **1995**:3
Savage, Fred **1990**:1
Savalas, Telly
  Obituary **1994**:3
Sawyer, Diane **1994**:4
Schaap, Dick
  Obituary **2003**:1
Schneider, Rob **1997**:4
Schwimmer, David **1996**:2
Scott, Gene
  Brief Entry **1986**:1
Sedelmaier, Joe **1985**:3
Seinfeld, Jerry **1992**:4
Sevareid, Eric
  Obituary **1993**:1
Seymour, Jane **1994**:4
Shaffer, Paul **1987**:1
Shandling, Garry **1995**:1
Sharkey, Ray
  Obituary **1994**:1
Shawn, Dick
  Obituary **1987**:3
Sheedy, Ally **1989**:1
Sheen, Charlie **2001**:2
Sheindlin, Judith **1999**:1
Shepherd, Cybill **1996**:3
Shields, Brooke **1996**:3
Shore, Dinah
  Obituary **1994**:3
Short, Martin **1986**:1
Shriver, Maria
  Brief Entry **1986**:2
Shue, Andrew **1994**:4
Silverman, Jonathan **1997**:2
Silvers, Phil
  Obituary **1985**:4
Silverstone, Alicia **1997**:4
Sinise, Gary **1996**:1
Siskel, Gene
  Obituary **1999**:3
Skelton, Red
  Obituary **1998**:1
Slater, Christian **1994**:1
Smigel, Robert **2001**:3
Smirnoff, Yakov **1987**:2
Smith, Buffalo Bob
  Obituary **1999**:1
Smith, Howard K.
  Obituary **2003**:2
Smith, Jeff **1991**:4
Smith, Kate
  Obituary **1986**:3
Smits, Jimmy **1990**:1
Snipes, Wesley **1993**:1
Somers, Suzanne **2000**:1
Sondheim, Stephen **1994**:4
Sorkin, Aaron **2003**:2
Southern, Terry
  Obituary **1996**:2
Spade, David **1999**:2
Spheeris, Penelope **1989**:2
Spielberg, Steven **1993**:4 **1997**:4
Springer, Jerry **1998**:4
Stein, Ben **2001**:1
Stern, Howard **1988**:2 **1993**:3
Stevenson, McLean
  Obituary **1996**:3
Stewart, Jon **2001**:2

Stewart, Martha **1992**:1
Stewart, Patrick **1996**:1
Stiller, Ben **1999**:1
Stone, Sharon **1993**:4
Stoppard, Tom **1995**:4
Streisand, Barbra **1992**:2
Studi, Wes **1994**:3
Susskind, David
  Obituary **1987**:2
Sutherland, Kiefer **2002**:4
Swaggart, Jimmy **1987**:3
Swayze, John Cameron
  Obituary **1996**:1
Tandy, Jessica **1990**:4
  Obituary **1995**:1
Tartikoff, Brandon **1985**:2
  Obituary **1998**:1
Taylor, Elizabeth **1993**:3
Tesh, John **1996**:3
Thomas, Danny
  Obituary **1991**:3
Thompson, Emma **1993**:2
Thornton, Billy Bob **1997**:4
Tillstrom, Burr
  Obituary **1986**:1
Tilly, Jennifer **1997**:2
Tisch, Laurence A. **1988**:2
Tomei, Marisa **1995**:2
Totenberg, Nina **1992**:2
Travolta, John **1995**:2
Trotter, Charlie **2000**:4
Trudeau, Garry **1991**:2
Tucci, Stanley **2003**:2
Tucker, Chris **1999**:1
Tucker, Forrest
  Obituary **1987**:1
Turner, Janine **1993**:2
Turner, Lana
  Obituary **1996**:1
Turner, Ted **1989**:1
Ullman, Tracey **1988**:3
Urich, Robert **1988**:1
  Obituary **2003**:3
Vanilla Ice **1991**:3
Vardalos, Nia **2003**:4
Varney, Jim
  Brief Entry **1985**:4
  Obituary **2000**:3
Vaughn, Vince **1999**:2
Ventura, Jesse **1999**:2
Vidal, Gore **1996**:2
Vieira, Meredith **2001**:3
Villechaize, Herve
  Obituary **1994**:1
Vitale, Dick **1988**:4 **1994**:4
Walker, Nancy
  Obituary **1992**:3
Walters, Barbara **1998**:3
Wapner, Joseph A. **1987**:1
Ward, Sela **2001**:3
Washington, Denzel **1993**:2
Wasserman, Lew
  Obituary **2003**:3
Wayans, Damon **1998**:4
Wayans, Keenen Ivory **1991**:1
Wayne, David
  Obituary **1995**:3
Weitz, Bruce **1985**:4
Whitaker, Forest **1996**:2
White, Jaleel **1992**:3
Whittle, Christopher **1989**:3
Wilkinson, Tom **2003**:2

Weaver, Sigourney **1988**:3
Weitz, Bruce **1985**:4
Wences, Senor
  Obituary **1999**:4
Whitaker, Forest **1996**:2
Whitehead, Robert
  Obituary **2003**:3
Wiest, Dianne **1995**:2
Wilkinson, Tom **2003**:2
Willis, Bruce **1986**:4
Wong, B.D. **1998**:1
Woods, James **1988**:3
Worth, Irene
  Obituary **2003**:2
Wyle, Noah **1997**:3
Youngman, Henny
  Obituary **1998**:3
Zeffirelli, Franco **1991**:3

WRITING
Adams, Douglas
  Obituary **2002**:2
Adams, Scott **1996**:4
Albom, Mitch **1999**:3
Alexie, Sherman **1998**:4
Amanpour, Christiane **1997**:2
Ambler, Eric
  Obituary **1999**:2
Ambrose, Stephen **2002**:3
Amis, Kingsley
  Obituary **1996**:2
Amory, Cleveland
  Obituary **1999**:2
Anderson, Poul
  Obituary **2002**:3
Angelou, Maya **1993**:4
Angier, Natalie **2000**:3
Asimov, Isaac
  Obituary **1992**:3
Atwood, Margaret **2001**:2
Axthelm, Pete
  Obituary **1991**:3
Bacall, Lauren **1997**:3
Bakker, Robert T. **1991**:3
Baldwin, James
  Obituary **1988**:2
Ball, Edward **1999**:2
Baraka, Amiri **2000**:3
Barber, Red
  Obituary **1993**:2
Barker, Clive **2003**:3
Barry, Dave **1991**:2
Barry, Lynda **1992**:1
Beckett, Samuel Barclay
  Obituary **1990**:2
Bloodworth-Thomason,
  Linda **1994**:1
Blume, Judy **1998**:4
Bly, Robert **1992**:4
Blyth, Myrna **2002**:4
Bombeck, Erma
  Obituary **1996**:4
Bowles, Paul
  Obituary **2000**:3
Bradford, Barbara Taylor **2002**:4
Bradshaw, John **1992**:1
Branagh, Kenneth **1992**:2
Brodsky, Joseph
  Obituary **1996**:3
Brokaw, Tom **2000**:3
Brooks, Gwendolyn **1998**:1
  Obituary **2001**:2

Brown, Tina **1992**:1
Buffett, Jimmy **1999**:3
Burgess, Anthony
  Obituary **1994**:2
Burroughs, William S.
  Obituary **1997**:4
Burroughs, William S. **1994**:2
Buscaglia, Leo
  Obituary **1998**:4
Busch, Charles **1998**:3
Bush, Millie **1992**:1
Butler, Octavia E. **1999**:3
Byrne, Gabriel **1997**:4
Caen, Herb
  Obituary **1997**:4
Campbell, Bebe Moore **1996**:2
Caplan, Arthur L. **2000**:2
Carcaterra, Lorenzo **1996**:1
Carey, George **1992**:3
Carlson, Richard **2002**:1
Carver, Raymond
  Obituary **1989**:1
Castaneda, Carlos
  Obituary **1998**:4
Castillo, Ana **2000**:4
Cela, Camilo Jose
  Obituary **2003**:1
Chabon, Michael **2002**:1
Chatwin, Bruce
  Obituary **1989**:2
Chavez, Linda **1999**:3
Cheney, Lynne V. **1990**:4
Child, Julia **1999**:4
Chopra, Deepak **1996**:3
Clancy, Tom **1998**:4
Clark, Mary Higgins **2000**:4
Clavell, James
  Obituary **1995**:1
Cleaver, Eldridge
  Obituary **1998**:4
Codrescu, Andre **1997**:3
Cole, Johnetta B. **1994**:3
Coles, Robert **1995**:1
Collins, Billy **2002**:2
Comfort, Alex
  Obituary **2000**:4
Condon, Richard
  Obituary **1996**:4
Cook, Robin **1996**:3
Cornwell, Patricia **2003**:1
Cosby, Bill **1999**:2
Covey, Stephen R. **1994**:4
Cowley, Malcolm
  Obituary **1989**:3
Crichton, Michael **1995**:3
Cronenberg, David **1992**:3
Cunningham, Michael **2003**:4
Dahl, Roald
  Obituary **1991**:2
Darden, Christopher **1996**:4
David, Larry **2003**:4
Davis, Patti **1995**:1
Delany, Sarah
  Obituary **1999**:3
Dershowitz, Alan **1992**:1
Diamond, I.A.L.
  Obituary **1988**:3
Diamond, Selma
  Obituary **1985**:2
Dickey, James
  Obituary **1998**:2
Dickinson, Brian **1998**:2

Djerassi, Carl **2000**:4
Dorris, Michael
  Obituary **1997**:3
Douglas, Marjory Stoneman **1993**:1
  Obituary **1998**:4
Dove, Rita **1994**:3
Dowd, Maureen Brigid **1997**:1
Drucker, Peter F. **1992**:3
Dunne, Dominick **1997**:1
Duras, Marguerite
  Obituary **1996**:3
Durrell, Gerald
  Obituary **1995**:3
Ebert, Roger **1998**:3
Edwards, Bob **1993**:2
Eggers, Dave **2001**:3
Elliott, Missy **2003**:4
Ellison, Ralph
  Obituary **1994**:4
Ellroy, James **2003**:4
Ephron, Nora **1992**:3
Epstein, Jason **1991**:1
Etzioni, Amitai **1994**:3
Evans, Joni **1991**:4
Fabio **1993**:4
Falconer, Ian **2003**:1
Faludi, Susan **1992**:4
Fielding, Helen **2000**:4
Filipovic, Zlata **1994**:4
Fish, Hamilton
  Obituary **1991**:3
Fisher, Carrie **1991**:1
Flynt, Larry **1997**:3
Fo, Dario **1998**:1
Fodor, Eugene
  Obituary **1991**:3
Foote, Shelby **1991**:2
Forbes, Steve **1996**:2
Foxworthy, Jeff **1996**:1
Franken, Al **1996**:3
Frankl, Viktor E.
  Obituary **1998**:1
Franzen, Jonathan **2002**:3
Frazier, Charles **2003**:2
Friedan, Betty **1994**:2
Frye, Northrop
  Obituary **1991**:3
Fugard, Athol **1992**:3
Fulbright, J. William
  Obituary **1995**:3
Fulghum, Robert **1996**:1
Gaines, William M.
  Obituary **1993**:1
Gao Xingjian **2001**:2
Garcia, Cristina **1997**:4
Geisel, Theodor
  Obituary **1992**:2
George, Elizabeth **2003**:3
Gibson, William Ford, III **1997**:2
Gillespie, Marcia **1999**:4
Ginsberg, Allen
  Obituary **1997**:3
Goldman, William **2001**:1
Gore, Albert, Jr. **1993**:2
Goren, Charles H.
  Obituary **1991**:4
Grafton, Sue **2000**:2
Graham, Billy **1992**:1
Graham, Katharine Meyer **1997**:3
  Obituary **2002**:3
Grass, Gunter **2000**:2
Gray, John **1995**:3

Cumulative Subject Index

This index lists all newsmakers by subjects, company names, products, organizations, issues, awards, and professional specialties. Indexes in softbound issues allow access to the current year's entries; indexes in annual hardbound volumes are cumulative, covering the entire *Newsmakers* series.

Listee names are followed by a year and issue number; thus **1996**:3 indicates that an entry on that individual appears in both 1996, Issue 3, and the 1996 cumulation. For access to newsmakers appearing earlier than the current softbound issue, see the previous year's cumulation.

Kaye, Danny
  Obituary **1987**:2
Keaton, Diane **1997**:1
Kline, Kevin **2000**:1
Kubrick, Stanley
  Obituary **1999**:3
Kurosawa, Akira **1991**:1
  Obituary **1999**:1
Lange, Jessica **1995**:4
Lardner Jr., Ring
  Obituary **2001**:2
Lemmon, Jack **1998**:4
  Obituary **2002**:3
Levinson, Barry **1989**:3
Lithgow, John **1985**:2
Loy, Myrna
  Obituary **1994**:2
Lucas, George **1999**:4
Malle, Louis
  Obituary **1996**:2
Mancini, Henry
  Obituary **1994**:4
Marvin, Lee
  Obituary **1988**:1
Matlin, Marlee **1992**:2
Matthau, Walter **2000**:3
McCartney, Paul **2002**:4
McDormand, Frances **1997**:3
McDowall, Roddy
  Obituary **1999**:1
McLaren, Norman
  Obituary **1987**:2
Milland, Ray
  Obituary **1986**:2
Newman, Paul **1995**:3
Nichols, Mike **1994**:4
Nicholson, Jack **1989**:2
North, Alex **1986**:3
Pacino, Al **1993**:4
Page, Geraldine
  Obituary **1987**:4
Pakula, Alan
  Obituary **1999**:2
Park, Nick **1997**:3
Pesci, Joe **1992**:4
Phillips, Julia **1992**:1
Poitier, Sidney **1990**:3
Prince **1995**:3
Puzo, Mario
  Obituary **2000**:1
Quinn, Anthony
  Obituary **2002**:2
Redford, Robert **1993**:2
Redgrave, Vanessa **1989**:2
Reed, Donna
  Obituary **1986**:1
Riddle, Nelson
  Obituary **1985**:4
Robards, Jason
  Obituary **2001**:3
Robbins, Jerome
  Obituary **1999**:1
Rogers, Ginger
  Obituary **1995**:4
Rollins, Howard E., Jr. **1986**:1
Ruehl, Mercedes **1992**:4
Rush, Geoffrey **2002**:1
Sainte-Marie, Buffy **2000**:1
Scott, George C.
  Obituary **2000**:2
Sinatra, Frank
  Obituary **1998**:4

Soderbergh, Steven **2001**:4
Sorvino, Mira **1996**:3
Spacek, Sissy **2003**:1
Spacey, Kevin **1996**:4
Stallone, Sylvester **1994**:2
Steiger, Rod
  Obituary **2003**:4
Streep, Meryl **1990**:2
Streisand, Barbra **1992**:2
Styne, Jule
  Obituary **1995**:1
Swank, Hilary **2000**:3
Tan Dun **2002**:1
Tandy, Jessica **1990**:4
  Obituary **1995**:1
Taylor, Elizabeth **1993**:3
Thompson, Emma **1993**:2
Tomei, Marisa **1995**:2
Trudeau, Garry **1991**:2
Vinton, Will
  Brief Entry **1988**:1
Voight, Jon **2002**:3
Wallis, Hal
  Obituary **1987**:1
Washington, Denzel **1993**:2
Wiest, Dianne **1995**:2
Wilder, Billy
  Obituary **2003**:2
Zanuck, Lili Fini **1994**:2
Zemeckis, Robert **2002**:1

ACLU
  See: American Civil Liberties Union

Acoustics
  Kloss, Henry E.
    Brief Entry **1985**:2

Acquired Immune Deficiency Syndrome
  Ashe, Arthur
    Obituary **1993**:3
  Bennett, Michael
    Obituary **1988**:1
  Bergalis, Kimberly
    Obituary **1992**:3
  Berkley, Seth **2002**:3
  Dolan, Terry **1985**:2
  Eazy-E
    Obituary **1995**:3
  Fisher, Mary **1994**:3
  Gallo, Robert **1991**:1
  Gebbie, Kristine **1994**:2
  Gertz, Alison
    Obituary **1993**:2
  Glaser, Elizabeth
    Obituary **1995**:2
  Halston
    Obituary **1990**:3
  Haring, Keith
    Obituary **1990**:3
  Ho, David **1997**:2
  Holmes, John C.
    Obituary **1988**:3
  Hudson, Rock
    Obituary **1985**:4
  Kramer, Larry **1991**:2
  Krim, Mathilde **1989**:2
  Kushner, Tony **1995**:2
  Liberace
    Obituary **1987**:2
  Louganis, Greg **1995**:3

Mapplethorpe, Robert
  Obituary **1989**:3
Matlovich, Leonard P.
  Obituary **1988**:4
McKinney, Stewart B.
  Obituary **1987**:4
Mullis, Kary **1995**:3
Robinson, Max
  Obituary **1989**:2
Shilts, Randy **1993**:4
  Obituary **1994**:3
Smith, Jerry
  Obituary **1987**:1
Taylor, Elizabeth **1993**:3
Waddell, Thomas F.
  Obituary **1988**:2
White, Ryan
  Obituary **1990**:3
Zamora, Pedro
  Obituary **1995**:2

ACT-UP
  See: AIDS Coalition to Unleash
  Power

Adolph Coors Co.
  Coors, William K.
    Brief Entry **1985**:1

Adoption
  Clements, George **1985**:1

Advertising
  Ailes, Roger **1989**:3
  Beers, Charlotte **1999**:3
  Freeman, Cliff **1996**:1
  Kroll, Alexander S. **1989**:3
  Lazarus, Shelly **1998**:3
  McElligott, Thomas J. **1987**:4
  Ogilvy, David
    Obituary **2000**:1
  O'Steen, Van
    Brief Entry **1986**:3
  Peller, Clara
    Obituary **1988**:1
  Proctor, Barbara Gardner **1985**:3
  Riney, Hal **1989**:1
  Saatchi, Charles **1987**:3
  Saatchi, Maurice **1995**:4
  Sedelmaier, Joe **1985**:3
  Vinton, Will
    Brief Entry **1988**:1
  Whittle, Christopher **1989**:3

AFL-CIO
  See: American Federation of Labor
  and Congress of Industrial
  Organizations

African National Congress
  Buthelezi, Mangosuthu
    Gatsha **1989**:3
  Hani, Chris
    Obituary **1993**:4
  Mandela, Nelson **1990**:3
  Mbeki, Thabo **1999**:4
  Slovo, Joe **1989**:2
  Tambo, Oliver **1991**:3

Leakey, Richard **1994**:2
Montagu, Ashley
Obituary **2000**:2

AOL
See: America Online

Apartheid
Biehl, Amy
Obituary **1994**:1
Blackburn, Molly
Obituary **1985**:4
Buthelezi, Mangosuthu
Gatsha **1989**:3
Carter, Amy **1987**:4
de Klerk, F.W. **1990**:1
Duncan, Sheena
Brief Entry **1987**:1
Fugard, Athol **1992**:3
Hoffman, Abbie
Obituary **1989**:3
Makeba, Miriam **1989**:2
Mandela, Winnie **1989**:3
Paton, Alan
Obituary **1988**:3
Ramaphosa, Cyril **1988**:2
Suzman, Helen **1989**:3
Tambo, Oliver **1991**:3
Treurnicht, Andries **1992**:2
Woods, Donald
Obituary **2002**:3

APBA
See: American Power Boat
Association

Apple Computer, Inc.
Jobs, Steve **2000**:1
Perlman, Steve **1998**:2
Raskin, Jef **1997**:4
Sculley, John **1989**:4

Archaeology
Soren, David
Brief Entry **1986**:3

Architecture
Bunshaft, Gordon **1989**:3
Obituary **1991**:1
Cooper, Alexander **1988**:4
Eisenman, Peter **1992**:4
Erickson, Arthur **1989**:3
Foster, Norman **1999**:4
Gehry, Frank O. **1987**:1
Goody, Joan **1990**:2
Graves, Michael **2000**:1
Holl, Steven **2003**:1
Isozaki, Arata **1990**:2
Jahn, Helmut **1987**:3
Johnson, Philip **1989**:2
Kiefer, Anselm **1990**:2
Lapidus, Morris
Obituary **2001**:4
Lasdun, Denys
Obituary **2001**:4
Lin, Maya **1990**:3
McDonough, William **2003**:1
Meier, Richard **2001**:4

Moneo, Jose Rafael **1996**:4
Mumford, Lewis
Obituary **1990**:2
Pedersen, William **1989**:4
Pei, I.M. **1990**:4
Pelli, Cesar **1991**:4
Portman, John **1988**:2
Predock, Antoine **1993**:2
Roche, Kevin **1985**:1
Rockwell, David **2003**:3
Rouse, James
Obituary **1996**:4
Venturi, Robert **1994**:4
Yamasaki, Minoru
Obituary **1986**:2

Argus Corp. Ltd.
Black, Conrad **1986**:2

Arizona state government
Hull, Jane Dee **1999**:2

Arkansas state government
Clinton, Bill **1992**:1

Artificial heart
Jarvik, Robert K. **1985**:1
Schroeder, William J.
Obituary **1986**:4

Artificial intelligence
Minsky, Marvin **1994**:3

Association of Southeast Asian Nations
Bolkiah, Sultan Muda
Hassanal **1985**:4

Astronautics
Bean, Alan L. **1986**:2
Collins, Eileen **1995**:3
Conrad, Pete
Obituary **2000**:1
Dzhanibekov, Vladimir **1988**:1
Garneau, Marc **1985**:1
Glenn, John **1998**:3
Lucid, Shannon **1997**:1
McAuliffe, Christa
Obituary **1985**:4
Whitson, Peggy **2003**:3

Astronomy
Bopp, Thomas **1997**:3
Geller, Margaret Joan **1998**:2
Hale, Alan **1997**:3
Hawking, Stephen W. **1990**:1
Hoyle, Sir Fred
Obituary **2002**:4
Smoot, George F. **1993**:3

AT&T
Allen, Bob **1992**:4
Armstrong, C. Michael **2002**:1

Atari
Bushnell, Nolan **1985**:1
Kingsborough, Donald
Brief Entry **1986**:2
Perlman, Steve **1998**:2

Atlanta Braves baseball team
Lofton, Kenny **1998**:1
Maddux, Greg **1996**:2
Sanders, Deion **1992**:4
Turner, Ted **1989**:1

Atlanta Falcons football team
Sanders, Deion **1992**:4

Atlanta Hawks basketball team
Maravich, Pete
Obituary **1988**:2
McMillen, Tom **1988**:4
Turner, Ted **1989**:1
Wilkens, Lenny **1995**:2

Atlantic Records
Ertegun, Ahmet **1986**:3

Automobile racing
Ferrari, Enzo **1988**:4
Fittipaldi, Emerson **1994**:2
Gordon, Jeff **1996**:1
Muldowney, Shirley **1986**:1
Newman, Paul **1995**:3
Penske, Roger **1988**:3
Porsche, Ferdinand
Obituary **1998**:4
Prost, Alain **1988**:1
St. James, Lyn **1993**:2
Senna, Ayrton **1991**:4
Obituary **1994**:4
Villeneuve, Jacques **1997**:1
Zanardi, Alex **1998**:2

Aviation
Burr, Donald Calvin **1985**:3
Dubrof, Jessica
Obituary **1996**:4
Lindbergh, Anne Morrow
Obituary **2001**:4
MacCready, Paul **1986**:4
Martin, Dean Paul
Obituary **1987**:3
Moody, John **1985**:3
Rutan, Burt **1987**:2
Schiavo, Mary **1998**:2
Wolf, Stephen M. **1989**:3
Yeager, Chuck **1998**:1

Avis Rent A Car
Rand, A. Barry **2000**:3

Avon Products, Inc.
Jung, Andrea **2000**:2
Waldron, Hicks B. **1987**:3

Bad Boy Records
Combs, Sean Puffy **1998**:4

Ballet West
Lander, Toni
Obituary **1985**:4

Ballooning
Aoki, Rocky **1990**:2

Baltimore, Md., city government
Schaefer, William Donald **1988**:1

Biogen, Inc.
Gilbert, Walter **1988**:3

Biosphere 2
Allen, John **1992**:1

Biotechnology
Gilbert, Walter **1988**:3
Haseltine, William A. **1999**:2

Birds
Berle, Peter A.A.
Brief Entry **1987**:3
Pough, Richard Hooper **1989**:1
Redig, Patrick **1985**:3
Toone, Bill
Brief Entry **1987**:2

Birth control
Baird, Bill
Brief Entry **1987**:2
Baulieu, Etienne-Emile **1990**:1
Djerassi, Carl **2000**:4
Falkenberg, Nanette **1985**:2
Morgentaler, Henry **1986**:3
Rock, John
Obituary **1985**:1
Wattleton, Faye **1989**:1

Black Panther Party
Cleaver, Eldridge
Obituary **1998**:4
Newton, Huey
Obituary **1990**:1
Ture, Kwame
Obituary **1999**:2

Black Sash
Duncan, Sheena
Brief Entry **1987**:1

Blockbuster Video
Huizenga, Wayne **1992**:1

Bloomingdale's
Campeau, Robert **1990**:1
Traub, Marvin
Brief Entry **1987**:3

Boat racing
Aoki, Rocky **1990**:2
Conner, Dennis **1987**:2
Copeland, Al **1988**:3
Hanauer, Chip **1986**:2
Turner, Ted **1989**:1

Bodybuilding
Powter, Susan **1994**:3
Reeves, Steve
Obituary **2000**:4
Schwarzenegger, Arnold **1991**:1

Body Shops International
Roddick, Anita **1989**:4

Boston Bruins hockey team
Bourque, Raymond Jean **1997**:3

Bose Corp.
Bose, Amar
Brief Entry **1986**:4

Boston Celtics basketball team
Ainge, Danny **1987**:1
Bird, Larry **1990**:3
Lewis, Reggie
Obituary **1994**:1
Maravich, Pete
Obituary **1988**:2

Boston, Mass., city government
Flynn, Ray **1989**:1
Frank, Barney **1989**:2

Boston Properties Co.
Zuckerman, Mortimer **1986**:3

Boston Red Sox baseball team
Boggs, Wade **1989**:3
Clemens, Roger **1991**:4
Conigliaro, Tony
Obituary **1990**:3
Epstein, Theo **2003**:4
Henderson, Rickey **2002**:3
Vaughn, Mo **1999**:2
Williams, Ted
Obituary **2003**:4

Boston University
Silber, John **1990**:1

Bowling
Anthony, Earl
Obituary **2002**:3
Weber, Pete **1986**:3

Boxing
Abercrombie, Josephine **1987**:2
Ali, Laila **2001**:2
Armstrong, Henry
Obituary **1989**:1
Bowe, Riddick **1993**:2
Carter, Rubin **2000**:3
Danza, Tony **1989**:1
De La Hoya, Oscar **1998**:2
Douglas, Buster **1990**:4
Graziano, Rocky
Obituary **1990**:4
Hagler, Marvelous Marvin **1985**:2
Holyfield, Evander **1991**:3
Kallen, Jackie **1994**:1
King, Don **1989**:1
Leonard, Sugar Ray **1989**:4
Lewis, Lennox **2000**:2
Moore, Archie
Obituary **1999**:2
Robinson, Sugar Ray
Obituary **1989**:3
Trinidad, Felix **2000**:4
Tyson, Mike **1986**:4

Boys Town
Peter, Valentine J. **1988**:2

BrainReserve
Popcorn, Faith
Brief Entry **1988**:1

Branch Davidians religious sect
Koresh, David
Obituary **1993**:4

Brewing
Busch, August A. III **1988**:2
Coors, William K.
Brief Entry **1985**:1
Stroh, Peter W. **1985**:2

Bridge
Goren, Charles H.
Obituary **1991**:4

British Columbia provincial government
Vander Zalm, William **1987**:3

British royal family
Charles, Prince of Wales **1995**:3
Diana, Princess of Wales **1993**:1
Obituary **1997**:4
Ferguson, Sarah **1990**:3

Broadcasting
Albert, Marv **1994**:3
Allen, Mel
Obituary **1996**:4
Ancier, Garth **1989**:1
Barber, Red
Obituary **1993**:2
Bell, Art **2000**:1
Brown, James **1991**:4
Caray, Harry **1988**:3
Obituary **1998**:3
Cherry, Don **1993**:4
Chung, Connie **1988**:4
Cosell, Howard
Obituary **1995**:4
Costas, Bob **1986**:4
Couric, Katherine **1991**:4
Daniels, Faith **1993**:3
Dickerson, Nancy H.
Obituary **1998**:2
Diller, Barry **1991**:1
Dr. Demento **1986**:1
Donnellan, Nanci **1995**:2
Drysdale, Don
Obituary **1994**:1
Edwards, Bob **1993**:2
Ellerbee, Linda **1993**:3
Firestone, Roy **1988**:2
Gillett, George **1988**:1
Goldberg, Leonard **1988**:4
Grange, Red
Obituary **1991**:3
Gumbel, Bryant **1990**:2
Gunn, Hartford N., Jr.
Obituary **1986**:2
Harvey, Paul **1995**:3
Imus, Don **1997**:1
Jones, Jenny **1998**:2
Kasem, Casey **1987**:1
Kent, Arthur **1991**:4 **1997**:2
King, Larry **1993**:1
Kluge, John **1991**:1
Koppel, Ted **1989**:1
Kuralt, Charles
Obituary **1998**:3
Madden, John **1995**:1
Moyers, Bill **1991**:4
Murdoch, Rupert **1988**:4

CAT Scanner
Hounsfield, Godfrey **1989**:2

Cattle rustling
Cantrell, Ed
Brief Entry **1985**:3

Caviar
Petrossian, Christian
Brief Entry **1985**:3

CBC
See: Canadian Broadcasting Corp.

CBS, Inc.
Cox, Richard Joseph
Brief Entry **1985**:1
Cronkite, Walter Leland **1997**:3
Paley, William S.
Obituary **1991**:2
Reasoner, Harry
Obituary **1992**:1
Sagansky, Jeff **1993**:2
Tisch, Laurence A. **1988**:2
Yetnikoff, Walter **1988**:1

CDF
See: Children's Defense Fund

Center for Equal Opportunity
Chavez, Linda **1999**:3

Centers for Living
Williamson, Marianne **1991**:4

Central America
Astorga, Nora **1988**:2
Cruz, Arturo **1985**:1
Obando, Miguel **1986**:4
Robelo, Alfonso **1988**:1

Central Intelligence Agency
Carter, Amy **1987**:4
Casey, William
Obituary **1987**:3
Colby, William E.
Obituary **1996**:4
Deutch, John **1996**:4
Gates, Robert M. **1992**:2
Inman, Bobby Ray **1985**:1
Tenet, George **2000**:3

Centurion Ministries
McCloskey, James **1993**:1

Cesar Awards
Adjani, Isabelle **1991**:1
Deneuve, Catherine **2003**:2
Depardieu, Gerard **1991**:2

Chanel, Inc.
D'Alessio, Kitty
Brief Entry **1987**:3
Lagerfeld, Karl **1999**:4

Chantal Pharmacentical Corp.
Burnison, Chantal Simone **1988**:3

Charlotte Hornets basketball team
Bryant, Kobe **1998**:3
Johnson, Larry **1993**:3
Mourning, Alonzo **1994**:2

Chef Boy-ar-dee
Boiardi, Hector
Obituary **1985**:3

Chess
Kasparov, Garry **1997**:4
Polgar, Judit **1993**:3

Chicago Bears football team
McMahon, Jim **1985**:4
Payton, Walter
Obituary **2000**:2

Chicago Bulls basketball team
Jackson, Phil **1996**:3
Jordan, Michael **1987**:2
Kukoc, Toni **1995**:4
Pippen, Scottie **1992**:2

Chicago Blackhawks
Hasek, Dominik **1998**:3

Chicago Cubs baseball team
Caray, Harry **1988**:3
Obituary **1998**:3
Sosa, Sammy **1999**:1

Chicago, Ill., city government
Washington, Harold
Obituary **1988**:1

Chicago White Sox baseball team
Caray, Harry **1988**:3
Obituary **1998**:3
Leyland, Jim **1998**:2
Thomas, Frank **1994**:3
Veeck, Bill
Obituary **1986**:1

Child care
Hale, Clara
Obituary **1993**:3
Leach, Penelope **1992**:4
Spock, Benjamin **1995**:2
Obituary **1998**:3

Children's Defense Fund
Clinton, Hillary Rodham **1993**:2
Edelman, Marian Wright **1990**:4

Chimpanzees
Goodall, Jane **1991**:1

Choreography
Abdul, Paula **1990**:3
Ailey, Alvin **1989**:2
Obituary **1990**:2

Astaire, Fred
Obituary **1987**:4
Bennett, Michael
Obituary **1988**:1
Cunningham, Merce **1998**:1
Dean, Laura **1989**:4
de Mille, Agnes
Obituary **1994**:2
Feld, Eliot **1996**:1
Fenley, Molissa **1988**:3
Forsythe, William **1993**:2
Fosse, Bob
Obituary **1988**:1
Glover, Savion **1997**:1
Graham, Martha
Obituary **1991**:4
Jamison, Judith **1990**:3
Joffrey, Robert
Obituary **1988**:3
Jones, Bill T. **1991**:4
MacMillan, Kenneth
Obituary **1993**:2
Mitchell, Arthur **1995**:1
Morris, Mark **1991**:1
Nureyev, Rudolf
Obituary **1993**:2
Parsons, David **1993**:4
Ross, Herbert
Obituary **2002**:4
Takei, Kei **1990**:2
Taylor, Paul **1992**:3
Tharp, Twyla **1992**:4
Tudor, Antony
Obituary **1987**:4
Tune, Tommy **1994**:2
Varone, Doug **2001**:2

Christian Coalition
Reed, Ralph **1995**:1

Christic Institute
Sheehan, Daniel P. **1989**:1

Chrysler Motor Corp.
Eaton, Robert J. **1994**:2
Iacocca, Lee **1993**:1
Lutz, Robert A. **1990**:1

CHUCK
See: Committee to Halt Useless
College Killings

Church of England
Carey, George **1992**:3
Runcie, Robert **1989**:4
Obituary **2001**:1

Church of Jesus Christ of Latter-Day Saints
See: Mormon Church

CIA
See: Central Intelligence Agency

Cincinatti Bengals football team
Esiason, Boomer **1991**:1

Banks, Jeffrey **1998**:2
Benetton, Luciano **1988**:1
Blahnik, Manolo **2000**:2
Blass, Bill
  Obituary **2003**:3
Cameron, David
  Brief Entry **1988**:1
Cardin, Pierre **2003**:3
Chalayan, Hussein **2003**:2
Claiborne, Liz **1986**:3
Cole, Kenneth **2003**:1
Crawford, Cindy **1993**:3
D'Alessio, Kitty
  Brief Entry **1987**:3
Duarte, Henry **2003**:3
Ellis, Perry
  Obituary **1986**:3
Erte
  Obituary **1990**:4
Ford, Tom **1999**:3
Gaultier, Jean-Paul **1998**:1
Giannulli, Mossimo **2002**:3
Gucci, Maurizio
  Brief Entry **1985**:4
Haas, Robert D. **1986**:4
Halston
  Obituary **1990**:3
Herrera, Carolina **1997**:1
Hilfiger, Tommy **1993**:3
Jacobs, Marc **2002**:3
Johnson, Betsey **1996**:2
Kamali, Norma **1989**:1
Karan, Donna **1988**:1
Kelly, Patrick
  Obituary **1990**:2
Klein, Calvin **1996**:2
Klensch, Elsa **2001**:4
Kors, Michael **2000**:4
Lagerfeld, Karl **1999**:4
Lang, Helmut **1999**:2
Lange, Liz **2003**:4
Lauren, Ralph **1990**:1
Mellinger, Frederick
  Obituary **1990**:4
Mello, Dawn **1992**:2
Miller, Nicole **1995**:4
Mills, Malia **2003**:1
Miyake, Issey **1985**:2
Mizrahi, Isaac **1991**:1
Natori, Josie **1994**:3
Nipon, Albert
  Brief Entry **1986**:4
Oldham, Todd **1995**:4
Picasso, Paloma **1991**:1
Porizkova, Paulina
  Brief Entry **1986**:4
Potok, Anna Maximilian
  Brief Entry **1985**:2
Prada, Miuccia **1996**:1
Pressler, Paul **2003**:4
Rhodes, Zandra **1986**:2
Rykiel, Sonia **2000**:3
Sander, Jil **1995**:2
Smith, Paul **2002**:4
Smith, Willi
  Obituary **1987**:3
Spade, Kate **2003**:1
Sui, Anna **1995**:1
Takada, Kenzo **2003**:2
Tilberis, Elizabeth **1994**:3
Tompkins, Susie
  Brief Entry **1987**:2

Trump, Ivana **1995**:2
Tyler, Richard **1995**:3
Valvo, Carmen Marc **2003**:4
Versace, Donatella **1999**:1
Versace, Gianni
  Brief Entry **1988**:1
  Obituary **1998**:2
von Furstenberg, Diane **1994**:2
Wachner, Linda **1988**:3 **1997**:2
Westwood, Vivienne **1998**:3

FBI
  See: Federal Bureau of Investigation

FDA
  See: Food and Drug Administration

Federal Bureau of Investigation
  Freeh, Louis J. **1994**:2
  Kennedy, Weldon **1997**:3

Federal Communications Commission (FCC)
  Hundt, Reed Eric **1997**:2

Federal Express Corp.
  Smith, Frederick W. **1985**:4

Federal Reserve System
  Greenspan, Alan **1992**:2

Federal Trade Commission
  Oliver, Daniel **1988**:2

Feminism
  See: Women's issues

Fiat
  See: Fabbrica Italiana Automobili
    Torino SpA

Film Criticism
  Kael, Pauline **2000**:4
    Obituary **2002**:4

Fire fighting
  Adair, Red **1987**:3

Fireworks
  Grucci, Felix **1987**:1

First Jersey Securities
  Brennan, Robert E. **1988**:1

Florida Marlins baseball team
  Leyland, Jim **1998**:2
  Lowell, Mike **2003**:2
  Sheffield, Gary **1998**:1

Flying
  See: Aviation

FOE
  See: Friends of the Earth

Food and Drug Administration
  Kessler, David **1992**:1

Football
  Aikman, Troy **1994**:2
  Barnes, Ernie **1997**:4
  Bell, Ricky
    Obituary **1985**:1
  Bledsoe, Drew **1995**:1
  Bosworth, Brian **1989**:1
  Brown, Jim **1993**:2
  Brown, Paul
    Obituary **1992**:1
  Cunningham, Randall **1990**:1
  Davis, Terrell **1998**:2
  Elway, John **1990**:3
  Esiason, Boomer **1991**:1
  Flutie, Doug **1999**:2
  Gault, Willie **1991**:2
  Grange, Red
    Obituary **1991**:3
  Hayes, Woody
    Obituary **1987**:2
  Holtz, Lou **1986**:4
  Irvin, Michael **1996**:3
  Jackson, Bo **1986**:3
  Johnson, Jimmy **1993**:3
  Johnson, Keyshawn **2000**:4
  Jones, Jerry **1994**:4
  Kelly, Jim **1991**:4
  Kemp, Jack **1990**:4
  Landry, Tom
    Obituary **2000**:3
  Lewis, Ray **2001**:3
  Madden, John **1995**:1
  Matuszak, John
    Obituary **1989**:4
  McMahon, Jim **1985**:4
  Monk, Art **1993**:2
  Montana, Joe **1989**:2
  Moon, Warren **1991**:3
  Moss, Randy **1999**:3
  Okoye, Christian **1990**:2
  Payton, Walter
    Obituary **2000**:2
  Rice, Jerry **1990**:4
  Rypien, Mark **1992**:3
  Sanders, Barry **1992**:1
  Sanders, Deion **1992**:4
  Schembechler, Bo **1990**:3
  Sharpe, Sterling **1994**:3
  Shula, Don **1992**:2
  Smith, Emmitt **1994**:1
  Smith, Jerry
    Obituary **1987**:1
  Tagliabue, Paul **1990**:2
  Taylor, Lawrence **1987**:3
  Testaverde, Vinny **1987**:2
  Thomas, Derrick
    Obituary **2000**:3
  Thomas, Thurman **1993**:1
  Trask, Amy **2003**:3
  Unitas, Johnny
    Obituary **2003**:4
  Upshaw, Gene **1988**:1
  Walsh, Bill **1987**:4
  Warner, Kurt **2000**:3
  White, Reggie **1993**:4
  Williams, Doug **1988**:2
  Young, Steve **1995**:2

Forbes, Inc.
  Forbes, Steve **1996**:2

Ford Foundation
Berresford, Susan V. **1998**:4

Ford Motor Co.
Devine, John M. **2003**:2
Ford, Henry II
Obituary **1988**:1
Ford, William Clay, Jr. **1999**:1
Lutz, Robert A. **1990**:1
McNamara, Robert S. **1995**:4
Petersen, Donald Eugene **1985**:1
Trotman, Alex **1995**:4

Fox Broadcasting Co.
Ancier, Garth **1989**:1
Carter, Chris **2000**:1
Diller, Barry **1991**:1
Murdoch, Rupert **1988**:4
Wayans, Keenen Ivory **1991**:1

Frederick's of Hollywood
Mellinger, Frederick
Obituary **1990**:4

Freedom House
Lord, Bette Bao **1994**:1

FRELIMO
See: Mozambique Liberation Front

Friends of the Earth
Brower, David **1990**:4
Ngau, Harrison **1991**:3

Friends of the Everglades
Douglas, Marjory Stoneman **1993**:1
Obituary **1998**:4

FTC
See: Federal Trade Commission

Future Computing, Inc.
Isaacson, Portia
Brief Entry **1986**:1

Gallaudet University
Jordan, King **1990**:1

Gannett Co., Inc.
Neuharth, Allen H. **1986**:1

Gap Inc.
Drexler, Millard S. **1990**:3
Pressler, Paul **2003**:4

Garth Fagan Dance
Fagan, Garth **2000**:1

Gateway 2000
Waitt, Ted **1997**:4

Gay rights
Achtenberg, Roberta **1993**:4
Cammermeyer, Margarethe **1995**:2
Crisp, Quentin
Obituary **2000**:3
Frank, Barney **1989**:2
Goldhaber, Fred
Brief Entry **1986**:3

Matlovich, Leonard P.
Obituary **1988**:4
Tafel, Richard **2000**:4

Genentech, Inc.
Boyer, Herbert Wayne **1985**:1

General Electric Co.
Fudge, Ann **2000**:3
Immelt, Jeffrey R. **2001**:2
Welch, Jack **1993**:3

General Motors Corp.
Devine, John M. **2003**:2
Estes, Pete
Obituary **1988**:3
Jordan, Charles M. **1989**:4
Lutz, Robert A. **1990**:1
Moore, Michael **1990**:3
Smith, Jack **1994**:3
Smith, Roger **1990**:3
Stempel, Robert **1991**:3

Genetics
Boyer, Herbert Wayne **1985**:1
Gilbert, Walter **1988**:3
Haseltine, William A. **1999**:2
King, Mary-Claire **1998**:3
Kornberg, Arthur **1992**:1
Krim, Mathilde **1989**:2
Nuesslein-Volhard, Christiane **1998**:1
Rifkin, Jeremy **1990**:3
Rosenberg, Steven **1989**:1
Wigler, Michael
Brief Entry **1985**:1

Genome Corp.
Gilbert, Walter **1988**:3

Geology
Rosendahl, Bruce R.
Brief Entry **1986**:4

Georgetown University
Healy, Timothy S. **1990**:2

Georgetown University basketball team
Thompson, John **1988**:3

Gesundheit! Institute
Adams, Patch **1999**:2

Gianni Versace Group
Versace, Donatella **1999**:1
Versace, Gianni
Brief Entry **1988**:1
Obituary **1998**:2

Gillett Group
Gillett, George **1988**:1

GM
See: General Motors Corp.

Golden Globe Awards
Affleck, Ben **1999**:1
Bacall, Lauren **1997**:3
Bakula, Scott **2003**:1
Beatty, Warren **2000**:1

Blanchett, Cate **1999**:3
Burnett, Carol **2000**:3
Caine, Michael **2000**:4
Carter, Chris **2000**:1
Cattrall, Kim **2003**:3
Cheadle, Don **2002**:1
Cher **1993**:1
Chiklis, Michael **2003**:3
Connelly, Jennifer **2002**:4
Cosby, Bill **1999**:2
Curtis, Jamie Lee **1995**:1
Damon, Matt **1999**:1
Danes, Claire **1999**:4
Dench, Judi **1999**:4
De Niro, Robert **1999**:1
Dennehy, Brian **2002**:1
Depardieu, Gerard **1991**:2
Duvall, Robert **1999**:3
Elfman, Jenna **1999**:4
Farrow, Mia **1998**:3
Fell, Norman
Obituary **1999**:2
Fiennes, Ralph **1996**:2
Finney, Albert **2003**:3
Flockhart, Calista **1998**:4
Garner, Jennifer **2003**:1
Goldberg, Whoopi **1993**:3
Hallstrom, Lasse **2002**:3
Hanks, Tom **1989**:2 **2000**:2
Harris, Ed **2002**:2
Heston, Charlton **1999**:4
Irons, Jeremy **1991**:4
Johnson, Don **1986**:1
Jolie, Angelina **2000**:2
Keaton, Diane **1997**:1
Lansbury, Angela **1993**:1
Lemmon, Jack **1998**:4
Obituary **2002**:3
Lucas, George **1999**:4
Luhrmann, Baz **2002**:3
Matlin, Marlee **1992**:2
Matthau, Walter **2000**:3
Moore, Dudley
Obituary **2003**:2
Moore, Mary Tyler **1996**:2
Norton, Edward **2000**:2
Pakula, Alan
Obituary **1999**:2
Peters, Bernadette **2000**:1
Redgrave, Lynn **1999**:3
Ritter, John **2003**:4
Roberts, Julia **1991**:3
Russell, Keri **2000**:1
Sheen, Martin **2002**:1
Spacek, Sissy **2003**:1
Streisand, Barbra **1992**:2
Sutherland, Kiefer **2002**:4
Swank, Hilary **2000**:3
Taylor, Lili **2000**:2
Thompson, Emma **1993**:2
Ullman, Tracey **1988**:3
Washington, Denzel **1993**:2

Golden State Warriors basketball team
Sprewell, Latrell **1999**:4
Webber, Chris **1994**:1

Golf
Azinger, Paul **1995**:2
Baker, Kathy
Brief Entry **1986**:1
Callaway, Ely
Obituary **2002**:3

Green Bay Packers football team
Favre, Brett Lorenzo **1997**:2
Howard, Desmond Kevin **1997**:2
Sharpe, Sterling **1994**:3
White, Reggie **1993**:4

Greenpeace International
McTaggart, David **1989**:4

Greens party (West Germany)
Schily, Otto
Brief Entry **1987**:4

GRP Records, Inc.
Grusin, Dave
Brief Entry **1987**:2

Gucci
Ford, Tom **1999**:3

Gucci Shops, Inc.
Gucci, Maurizio
Brief Entry **1985**:4
Mello, Dawn **1992**:2

Gun control
Brady, Sarah and James S. **1991**:4

Gulf + Western
Diller, Barry **1991**:1

Gymnastics
Retton, Mary Lou **1985**:2
Strug, Kerri **1997**:3

Hampshire College
Simmons, Adele Smith **1988**:4

Handicap rights
Brady, Sarah and James S. **1991**:4
Dickinson, Brian **1998**:2

H & R Block, Inc.
Bloch, Henry **1988**:4

Hanna-Barbera Productions
Barbera, Joseph **1988**:2
Hanna, William
Obituary **2002**:1

Hard Candy
Mohajer, Dineh **1997**:3

Harlem Globetrotters basketball team
Woodard, Lynette **1986**:2

Harley-Davidson Motor Co., Inc.
Beals, Vaughn **1988**:2

Hartford, Conn., city government
Perry, Carrie Saxon **1989**:2

Hasbro, Inc.
Hassenfeld, Stephen **1987**:4

Hasidism
Schneerson, Menachem Mendel
1992:4
Obituary **1994**:4

Hasty Pudding Theatricals
Beatty, Warren **2000**:1
Burnett, Carol **2000**:3
Hanks, Tom **1989**:2 **2000**:2
Peters, Bernadette **2000**:1

Hearst Magazines
Black, Cathleen **1998**:4
Ganzi, Victor **2003**:3

Heisman Trophy
Flutie, Doug **1999**:2
Howard, Desmond Kevin **1997**:2
Jackson, Bo **1986**:3
Testaverde, Vinny **1987**:2
Williams, Ricky **2000**:2

Helmsley Hotels, Inc.
Helmsley, Leona **1988**:1

Hemlock Society
Humphry, Derek **1992**:2

Herbalife International
Hughes, Mark **1985**:3

Hereditary Disease Foundation
Wexler, Nancy S. **1992**:3

Herut Party (Israel)
Levy, David **1987**:2

HEW
See: Department of Health,
Education, and Welfare

Hewlett-Packard
Fiorina, Carleton S. **2000**:1
Hewlett, William
Obituary **2001**:4
Packard, David
Obituary **1996**:3

HGS
See: Human Genome Sciences, Inc.

HHR
See: Department of Health and
Human Services

High Flight Foundation
Irwin, James
Obituary **1992**:1

Hitchhiking
Heid, Bill
Brief Entry **1987**:2

Hobie Cat
Alter, Hobie
Brief Entry **1985**:1
Hasek, Dominik **1998**:3

Hockey
Bourque, Raymond Jean **1997**:3
Cherry, Don **1993**:4
Coffey, Paul **1985**:4
Eagleson, Alan **1987**:4
Federov, Sergei **1995**:1
Fuhr, Grant **1997**:3
Gilmour, Doug **1994**:3
Granato, Cammi **1999**:3
Gretzky, Wayne **1989**:2
Hextall, Ron **1988**:2
Hull, Brett **1991**:4
Jagr, Jaromir **1995**:4
Klima, Petr **1987**:1
Konstantinov, Vladimir **1997**:4
LaFontaine, Pat **1985**:1
Lemieux, Claude **1996**:1
Lemieux, Mario **1986**:4
Lindbergh, Pelle
Obituary **1985**:4
Lindros, Eric **1992**:1
Messier, Mark **1993**:1
Pocklington, Peter H. **1985**:2
Richard, Maurice
Obituary **2000**:4
Roy, Patrick **1994**:2
Sakic, Joe **2002**:1
Yzerman, Steve **1991**:2
Zamboni, Frank J.
Brief Entry **1986**:4

Honda Motor Co.
Honda, Soichiro
Obituary **1986**:1

Hong Kong government
Lee, Martin **1998**:2
Patten, Christopher **1993**:3

Horror fiction
Barker, Clive **2003**:3
Harris, Thomas **2001**:1
King, Stephen **1998**:1
Koontz, Dean **1999**:3
Stine, R. L. **2003**:1

Horse racing
Day, Pat **1995**:2
Desormeaux, Kent **1990**:2
Krone, Julie **1989**:2
Lukas, D. Wayne **1986**:2
McCarron, Chris **1995**:4
Mellon, Paul
Obituary **1999**:3
O'Donnell, Bill
Brief Entry **1987**:4
Pincay, Laffit, Jr. **1986**:3
Secretariat
Obituary **1990**:1

Houston Astros baseball team
Lofton, Kenny **1998**:1
Ryan, Nolan **1989**:4

Houston Oilers football team
Moon, Warren **1991**:3

Houston Rockets basketball team
Olajuwon, Akeem **1985**:1

Freij, Elias **1986**:4
Ghali, Boutros Boutros **1992**:3
Hussein, Saddam **1991**:1
Hussein I, King **1997**:3
 Obituary **1999**:3
Jumblatt, Walid **1987**:4
Khatami, Mohammed **1997**:4
Khomeini, Ayatollah Ruhollah
 Obituary **1989**:4
Levy, David **1987**:2
Nidal, Abu **1987**:1
Rafsanjani, Ali Akbar
 Hashemi **1987**:3
Redgrave, Vanessa **1989**:2
Sarkis, Elias
 Obituary **1985**:3
Schwarzkopf, Norman **1991**:3
Terzi, Zehdi Labib **1985**:3

Military
 Abacha, Sani **1996**:3
 Arens, Moshe **1985**:1
 Aspin, Les
 Obituary **1996**:1
 Babangida, Ibrahim
 Badamosi **1992**:4
 Boyington, Gregory Pappy
 Obituary **1988**:2
 Cammermeyer, Margarethe **1995**:2
 Cedras, Raoul **1994**:4
 Doe, Samuel
 Obituary **1991**:1
 Dzhanibekov, Vladimir **1988**:1
 Fitzgerald, A. Ernest **1986**:2
 Galvin, John R. **1990**:1
 Garneau, Marc **1985**:1
 Hess, Rudolph
 Obituary **1988**:1
 Hussein, Saddam **1991**:1
 Inman, Bobby Ray **1985**:1
 Jumblatt, Walid **1987**:4
 Lansdale, Edward G.
 Obituary **1987**:2
 Le Duan
 Obituary **1986**:4
 Le Duc Tho
 Obituary **1991**:1
 Marier, Rebecca **1995**:4
 McCain, John S. **1998**:4
 McSally, Martha **2002**:4
 North, Oliver **1987**:4
 Paige, Emmett, Jr.
 Brief Entry **1986**:4
 Pinochet, Augusto **1999**:2
 Powell, Colin **1990**:1
 Rickover, Hyman
 Obituary **1986**:4
 Schwarzkopf, Norman **1991**:3
 Shalikashvili, John **1994**:2
 Taylor, Maxwell
 Obituary **1987**:3
 Ventura, Jesse **1999**:2
 Willson, S. Brian **1989**:3
 Yeager, Chuck **1998**:1
 Ye Jianying
 Obituary **1987**:1
 Zech, Lando W.
 Brief Entry **1987**:4
 Zia ul-Haq, Mohammad
 Obituary **1988**:4

Milwaukee Brewers baseball team
 Sheffield, Gary **1998**:1
 Veeck, Bill
 Obituary **1986**:1

Minimalist art
 Richter, Gerhard **1997**:2

Minnesota state government
 Ventura, Jesse **1999**:2

Minnesota Timberwolves basketball team
 Garnett, Kevin **2000**:3
 Laettner, Christian **1993**:1

Minnesota Vikings football team
 Moss, Randy **1999**:3
 Payton, Walter
 Obituary **2000**:2

Miramax
 Weinstein, Bob and Harvey **2000**:4

Miss America Pageant
 Wells, Sharlene
 Brief Entry **1985**:1
 Williams, Vanessa L. **1999**:2

Miss Manners
 Martin, Judith **2000**:3

Mister Rogers
 Rogers, Fred **2000**:4

Modeling
 Brando, Cheyenne
 Obituary **1995**:4
 Campbell, Naomi **2000**:2
 Crawford, Cindy **1993**:3
 Diaz, Cameron **1999**:1
 Fabio **1993**:4
 Fawcett, Farrah **1998**:4
 Hurley, Elizabeth **1999**:2
 Leslie, Lisa **1997**:4
 MacDowell, Andie **1993**:4
 Marky Mark **1993**:3
 McCarthy, Jenny **1997**:4
 Moss, Kate **1995**:3

Molecular biology
 Gilbert, Walter **1988**:3
 Kornberg, Arthur **1992**:1
 Mullis, Kary **1995**:3
 Sidransky, David **2002**:4

Montreal Canadiens hockey team
 Lemieux, Claude **1996**:1
 Richard, Maurice
 Obituary **2000**:4
 Roy, Patrick **1994**:2

Monty Python
 Cleese, John **1989**:2
 Milligan, Spike
 Obituary **2003**:2

Mormon Church
 Benson, Ezra Taft
 Obituary **1994**:4
 Hunter, Howard **1994**:4

Mothers Against Drunk Driving
 Lightner, Candy **1985**:1
 Potts, Annie **1994**:1

Motivational speakers
 Brown, Les **1994**:3
 Peters, Tom **1998**:1

Motown Records
 de Passe, Suzanne **1990**:4
 Franklin, Melvin
 Obituary **1995**:3
 Kendricks, Eddie
 Obituary **1993**:2
 Payton, Lawrence
 Obituary **1997**:4
 Ruffin, David
 Obituary **1991**:4
 Wells, Mary
 Obituary **1993**:1

Motorcycles
 Beals, Vaughn **1988**:2
 Knievel, Robbie **1990**:1

Mountain climbing
 Wood, Sharon
 Brief Entry **1988**:1

Moving Earth (dance company)
 Takei, Kei **1990**:2

Mozambique Liberation Front
 Chissano, Joaquim **1987**:4
 Machel, Samora
 Obituary **1987**:1

Mrs. Fields Cookies, Inc.
 Fields, Debbi **1987**:3

Ms. magazine
 Gillespie, Marcia **1999**:4
 Morgan, Robin **1991**:1
 Steinem, Gloria **1996**:2
 Summers, Anne **1990**:2

MTV Networks, Inc.
 Daly, Carson **2002**:4
 Duffy, Karen **1998**:1
 Kutcher, Ashton **2003**:4
 Laybourne, Geraldine **1997**:1
 Osbournes, The **2003**:4
 Pittman, Robert W. **1985**:1
 Quinn, Martha **1986**:4
 Roedy, Bill **2003**:2

Multiple birth research
 Keith, Louis **1988**:2

Muppets
 Henson, Brian **1992**:1
 Henson, Jim **1989**:1
 Obituary **1990**:4

Museum of Modern Art (New York City)
Gund, Agnes **1993**:2

NAACP
See: National Association for the Advancement of Colored People
Chavis, Benjamin **1993**:4

NARAL
See: National Abortion Rights Action League

NASA
See: National Aeronautics and Space Administration

Nation of Islam
Cleaver, Eldridge
Obituary **1998**:4
Farrakhan, Louis **1990**:4
Shabazz, Betty
Obituary **1997**:4

National Abortion Rights Action League
Falkenberg, Nanette **1985**:2
Michelman, Kate **1998**:4

National Academy of Science
Djerassi, Carl **2000**:4

National Aeronautics and Space Administration
Bean, Alan L. **1986**:2
Collins, Eileen **1995**:3
Conrad, Pete
Obituary **2000**:1
Garneau, Marc **1985**:1
Glenn, John **1998**:3
Jemison, Mae C. **1993**:1
Lucid, Shannon **1997**:1
McAuliffe, Christa
Obituary **1985**:4
Shepard, Alan
Obituary **1999**:1

National Association for the Advancement of Colored People
Chavis, Benjamin **1993**:4
Evers-Williams, Myrlie **1995**:4
Johnson, Robert L. **2000**:4
LL Cool J **1998**:2
Mfume, Kweisi **1996**:3

National Audubon Society
Berle, Peter A.A.
Brief Entry **1987**:3

National Baptist Convention
Shaw, William **2000**:3

National Basketball Association
Bryant, Kobe **1998**:3
Duncan, Tim **2000**:1
Garnett, Kevin **2000**:3

Malone, Karl **1990**:1 **1997**:3
O'Malley, Susan **1995**:2
Stockton, John Houston **1997**:3

NBA
See: National Basketball Association

National Cancer Institute
DeVita, Vincent T., Jr. **1987**:3
King, Mary-Claire **1998**:3
Rosenberg, Steven **1989**:1

National Center for Atmospheric Research
Thompson, Starley
Brief Entry **1987**:3

National Coalition for the Homeless
Hayes, Robert M. **1986**:3

National Coalition on Television Violence
Radecki, Thomas
Brief Entry **1986**:2

National Commission on Excellence
Justiz, Manuel J. **1986**:4

National Conservative Political Action Committee
Dolan, Terry **1985**:2

National Education Association
Chavez, Linda **1999**:3
Futrell, Mary Hatwood **1986**:1

National Endowment for the Arts
Alexander, Jane **1994**:2
Alexie, Sherman **1998**:4
Anderson, Laurie **2000**:2
Bishop, Andre **2000**:1
Brooks, Gwendolyn **1998**:1
Obituary **2001**:2
Castillo, Ana **2000**:4
Fagan, Garth **2000**:1
Jones, Gayl **1999**:4
Marshall, Susan **2000**:4
Miller, Bebe **2000**:2
Oates, Joyce Carol **2000**:1
Parks, Suzan-Lori **2003**:2
Reeve, Christopher **1997**:2
Ringgold, Faith **2000**:3
Serrano, Andres **2000**:4
Wagner, Catherine F. **2002**:3

National Endowment for the Humanities
Cheney, Lynne V. **1990**:4
Hackney, Sheldon **1995**:1

National Federation for Decency
Wildmon, Donald **1988**:4

National Football League
Favre, Brett Lorenzo **1997**:2
Flutie, Doug **1999**:2

Howard, Desmond Kevin **1997**:2
Moss, Randy **1999**:3
Shula, Don **1992**:2
Tagliabue, Paul **1990**:2

National Football League Players Association
Upshaw, Gene **1988**:1

National Hockey League Players Association
Bourque, Raymond Jean **1997**:3
Eagleson, Alan **1987**:4
Fuhr, Grant **1997**:3

National Hot Rod Association
Muldowney, Shirley **1986**:1

National Institute of Education
Justiz, Manuel J. **1986**:4

National Institutes of Health
Healy, Bernadine **1993**:1
Jacobs, Joe **1994**:1

National Organization for Women
Abzug, Bella **1998**:2
Friedan, Betty **1994**:2
Gandy, Kim **2002**:2
Ireland, Patricia **1992**:2
Yard, Molly **1991**:4

National Park Service
Mott, William Penn, Jr. **1986**:1

National Public Radio
Codrescu, Andre **1997**:3
Edwards, Bob **1993**:2
Gross, Terry **1998**:3
Magliozzi, Tom and Ray **1991**:4
Maynard, Joyce **1999**:4
Roberts, Cokie **1993**:4
Tom and Ray Magliozzi **1991**:4
Totenberg, Nina **1992**:2

National Restaurant Association
Cain, Herman **1998**:3

National Rifle Association
Foss, Joe **1990**:3
Helms, Jesse **1998**:1
Heston, Charlton **1999**:4

National Science Foundation
Bloch, Erich **1987**:4
Colwell, Rita Rossi **1999**:3
Geller, Margaret Joan **1998**:2

National Security Agency
Inman, Bobby Ray **1985**:1

National Union for the Total Independence of Angola
Savimbi, Jonas **1986**:2 **1994**:2

National Union of Mineworkers
Ramaphosa, Cyril **1988**:2

National Wildlife Federation
Hair, Jay D. **1994**:3

Native American issues
Banks, Dennis J. **1986**:4
Begaye, Kelsey **1999**:3
Campbell, Ben Nighthorse **1998**:1
Castaneda, Carlos
Obituary **1998**:4
Grant, Rodney A. **1992**:1
Greene, Graham **1997**:2
LaDuke, Winona **1995**:2
Mankiller, Wilma P.
Brief Entry **1986**:2
Peltier, Leonard **1995**:1
Sidney, Ivan
Brief Entry **1987**:2
Studi, Wes **1994**:3

NATO
See: North Atlantic Treaty
Organization

Nautilus Sports/Medical Industries
Jones, Arthur A. **1985**:3

Navajo Nation
Begaye, Kelsey **1999**:3

Nazi Party
Hess, Rudolph
Obituary **1988**:1
Klarsfeld, Beate **1989**:1
Mengele, Josef
Obituary **1985**:2

NBC Television Network
Brokaw, Tom **2000**:3
Curry, Ann **2001**:1
Gumbel, Greg **1996**:4
Tartikoff, Brandon **1985**:2
Obituary **1998**:1

NCPAC
See: National Conservative Political
Action Committee

NCTV
See: National Coalition on
Television Violence

NDP
See: New Democratic Party
(Canada)

NEA
See: National Education Association

Nebraska state government
Kerrey, Bob **1986**:1 **1991**:3
Orr, Kay **1987**:4

Nebula Awards
Asimov, Isaac
Obituary **1992**:3
Brooks, Mel **2003**:1

Negro American League
Pride, Charley **1998**:1

NEH
See: National Endowment for the
Humanities

Netscape Communications Corp.
Andreessen, Marc **1996**:2
Barksdale, James L. **1998**:2
Clark, Jim **1997**:1

Neurobiology
Goldman-Rakic, Patricia **2002**:4
LeVay, Simon **1992**:2

New Democratic Party (Canada)
Lewis, Stephen **1987**:2
McLaughlin, Audrey **1990**:3

New England Patriots football team
Bledsoe, Drew **1995**:1
Brady, Tom **2002**:4

Newfoundland provincial government
Peckford, Brian **1989**:1

New Hampshire state government
Sununu, John **1989**:2

New Jersey Devils hockey team
Lemieux, Claude **1996**:1

New Orleans Saints football team
Williams, Ricky **2000**:2

New York City Ballet
Kistler, Darci **1993**:1
Whelan, Wendy **1999**:3

New York City Board of Education
Green, Richard R. **1988**:3

New York City government
Dinkins, David N. **1990**:2
Fairstein, Linda **1991**:1
Giuliani, Rudolph **1994**:2
Kennedy, John F., Jr. **1990**:1
Obituary **1999**:4

New Yorker magazine
Brown, Tina **1992**:1
Chast, Roz **1992**:4
Shawn, William
Obituary **1993**:3

New York Giants football team
Collins, Kerry **2002**:3
Taylor, Lawrence **1987**:3

New York Islanders hockey team
LaFontaine, Pat **1985**:1

New York Knicks basketball team
Bradley, Bill **2000**:2
Ewing, Patrick **1985**:3
McMillen, Tom **1988**:4
Riley, Pat **1994**:3
Sprewell, Latrell **1999**:4

New York Mets baseball team
Agee, Tommie
Obituary **2001**:4
Bonilla, Bobby **1992**:2
Carter, Gary **1987**:1
Doubleday, Nelson, Jr. **1987**:1
Gooden, Dwight **1985**:2
Piazza, Mike **1998**:4
Ryan, Nolan **1989**:4

New York Philharmonic Orchestra
Masur, Kurt **1993**:4

New York Public Library
Gregorian, Vartan **1990**:3
Healy, Timothy S. **1990**:2

New York Rangers hockey team
Messier, Mark **1993**:1

New York City public schools
Fernandez, Joseph **1991**:3

New York State Government
Cuomo, Mario **1992**:2
Florio, James J. **1991**:2
Pataki, George **1995**:2
Rothwax, Harold **1996**:3

New York Stock Exchange
Fomon, Robert M. **1985**:3
Phelan, John Joseph, Jr. **1985**:4
Siebert, Muriel **1987**:2

New York Times
Dowd, Maureen Brigid **1997**:1
Lelyveld, Joseph S. **1994**:4
Sulzberger, Arthur O., Jr. **1998**:3

New York Titans football team
Barnes, Ernie **1997**:4

New York Yankees baseball team
DiMaggio, Joe
Obituary **1999**:3
Gomez, Lefty
Obituary **1989**:3
Howser, Dick
Obituary **1987**:4
Jeter, Derek **1999**:4
Mantle, Mickey
Obituary **1996**:1
Maris, Roger
Obituary **1986**:1
Martin, Billy **1988**:4
Obituary **1990**:2

Mattingly, Don **1986**:2
Steinbrenner, George **1991**:1
Torre, Joseph Paul **1997**:1
Wells, David **1999**:3

NFL
See: National Football League

NHLPA
See: National Hockey League
Players Association

NHRA
See: National Hot Rod Association

NIH
See: National Institutes of Health

Nike, Inc.
Hamm, Mia **2000**:1
Knight, Philip H. **1994**:1 9 to 5
Bravo, Ellen **1998**:2
Nussbaum, Karen **1988**:3

Nissan Motor Co.
Katayama, Yutaka **1987**:1

No Limit (record label)
Master P **1999**:4

Nobel Prize
Altman, Sidney **1997**:2
Arias Sanchez, Oscar **1989**:3
Beckett, Samuel Barclay
Obituary **1990**:2
Begin, Menachem
Obituary **1992**:3
Blobel, Gunter **2000**:4
Carlsson, Arvid **2001**:2
Cela, Camilo Jose
Obituary **2003**:1
Cram, Donald J.
Obituary **2002**:2
Fo, Dario **1998**:1
Gao Xingjian **2001**:2
Grass, Gunter **2000**:2
Heaney, Seamus **1996**:2
Hounsfield, Godfrey **1989**:2
Kilby, Jack **2002**:2
Kissinger, Henry **1999**:4
Kornberg, Arthur **1992**:1
Lederman, Leon Max **1989**:4
Lorenz, Konrad
Obituary **1989**:3
Menchu, Rigoberta **1993**:2
Morrison, Toni **1998**:1
Mother Teresa **1993**:1
Obituary **1998**:1
Mullis, Kary **1995**:3
Nuesslein-Volhard, Christiane **1998**:1
Oe, Kenzaburo **1997**:1
Pauling, Linus
Obituary **1995**:1
Paz, Octavio **1991**:2

Perutz, Max
Obituary **2003**:2
Porter, George
Obituary **2003**:4
Prusiner, Stanley **1998**:2
Sakharov, Andrei Dmitrievich
Obituary **1990**:2
Saramago, Jose **1999**:1
Singer, Isaac Bashevis
Obituary **1992**:1
Suu Kyi, Aung San **1996**:2
Szent-Gyoergyi, Albert
Obituary **1987**:2
Trimble, David **1999**:1
Walesa, Lech **1991**:2
Wiesel, Elie **1998**:1

NORAID
See: Irish Northern Aid Committee

North Atlantic Treaty Organization
Galvin, John R. **1990**:1

NOW
See: National Organization for
Women

NRA
See: National Rifle Association

NRC
See: Nuclear Regulatory
Commission

NPR
See: National Public Radio
Tom and Ray Magliozzi **1991**:4

NSF
See: National Science Foundation

Nuclear energy
Gale, Robert Peter **1986**:4
Hagelstein, Peter
Brief Entry **1986**:3
Lederman, Leon Max **1989**:4
Maglich, Bogdan C. **1990**:1
Merritt, Justine
Brief Entry **1985**:3
Nader, Ralph **1989**:4
Palme, Olof
Obituary **1986**:2
Rickover, Hyman
Obituary **1986**:4
Sinclair, Mary **1985**:2
Smith, Samantha
Obituary **1985**:3
Zech, Lando W.
Brief Entry **1987**:4

Nuclear Regulatory Commission
Zech, Lando W.
Brief Entry **1987**:4

NUM
See: National Union of
Mineworkers

NWF
See: National Wildlife Federation

Oakland A's baseball team
Canseco, Jose **1990**:2
Caray, Harry **1988**:3
Obituary **1998**:3
Stewart, Dave **1991**:1
Welch, Bob **1991**:3
Zito, Barry **2003**:3

Oakland Raiders football team
Matuszak, John
Obituary **1989**:4
Trask, Amy **2003**:3
Upshaw, Gene **1988**:1

Obie Awards
Albee, Edward **1997**:1
Baldwin, Alec **2002**:2
Bergman, Ingmar **1999**:4
Close, Glenn **1988**:3
Coco, James
Obituary **1987**:2
Daniels, Jeff **1989**:4
Dewhurst, Colleen
Obituary **1992**:2
Dukakis, Olympia **1996**:4
Duvall, Robert **1999**:3
Ensler, Eve **2002**:4
Fo, Dario **1998**:1
Fugard, Athol **1992**:3
Hurt, William **1986**:1
Hwang, David Henry **1999**:1
Irwin, Bill **1988**:3
Kline, Kevin **2000**:1
Leguizamo, John **1999**:1
Miller, Arthur **1999**:4
Pacino, Al **1993**:4
Parks, Suzan-Lori **2003**:2
Shepard, Sam **1996**:4
Streep, Meryl **1990**:2
Tune, Tommy **1994**:2
Turturro, John **2002**:2
Vogel, Paula **1999**:2
Washington, Denzel **1993**:2
Woods, James **1988**:3

Occidental Petroleum Corp.
Hammer, Armand
Obituary **1991**:3

Oceanography
Cousteau, Jacques-Yves
Obituary **1998**:2
Cousteau, Jean-Michel **1988**:2
Fisher, Mel **1985**:4

Office of National Drug Control Policy
Bennett, William **1990**:1
Martinez, Bob **1992**:1

Cumulative Subject Index

Random House publishers
Evans, Joni **1991**:4

RCA Corp.
Engstrom, Elmer W.
Obituary **1985**:2

Real estate
Bloch, Ivan **1986**:3
Buss, Jerry **1989**:3
Campeau, Robert **1990**:1
Portman, John **1988**:2
Trump, Donald **1989**:2

Reebok U.S.A. Ltd., Inc.
Fireman, Paul
Brief Entry **1987**:2

Renaissance Motion Pictures
Raimi, Sam **1999**:2

RENAMO
Dhlakama, Afonso **1993**:3

Renault, Inc.
Besse, Georges
Obituary **1987**:1

Republican National Committee
Abraham, Spencer **1991**:4
Atwater, Lee **1989**:4
Obituary **1991**:4
Molinari, Susan **1996**:4

Resistancia Nacional Mocambican
See: RENAMO

Restaurants
Aoki, Rocky **1990**:2
Aretsky, Ken **1988**:1
Bushnell, Nolan **1985**:1
Copeland, Al **1988**:3
Fertel, Ruth **2000**:2
Kaufman, Elaine **1989**:4
Kerrey, Bob **1986**:1 **1991**:3
Kroc, Ray
Obituary **1985**:1
Lagasse, Emeril **1998**:3
Melman, Richard
Brief Entry **1986**:1
Petrossian, Christian
Brief Entry **1985**:3
Puck, Wolfgang **1990**:1
Thomas, Dave **1986**:2 **1993**:2
Obituary **2003**:1

Retailing
Drexler, Millard S. **1990**:3
Marcus, Stanley
Obituary **2003**:1

Reuben Awards
Gould, Chester
Obituary **1985**:2
Schulz, Charles
Obituary **2000**:3

Revlon, Inc.
Duffy, Karen **1998**:1
Perelman, Ronald **1989**:2

Rhode Island state government
Violet, Arlene **1985**:3

Richter Scale
Richter, Charles Francis
Obituary **1985**:4

Ringling Brothers and Barnum & Bailey Circus
Burck, Wade
Brief Entry **1986**:1
Feld, Kenneth **1988**:2

RJR Nabisco, Inc.
Horrigan, Edward, Jr. **1989**:1

Robotics
Kwoh, Yik San **1988**:2

Rock Climbing
Hill, Lynn **1991**:2

Rockman
Scholz, Tom **1987**:2

Roller Coasters
Toomer, Ron **1990**:1

Rolling Stone magazine
Wenner, Jann **1993**:1

Rotary engine
Yamamoto, Kenichi **1989**:1

Running
Benoit, Joan **1986**:3
Joyner, Florence Griffith **1989**:2
Obituary **1999**:1
Knight, Philip H. **1994**:1
Zatopek, Emil
Obituary **2001**:3

Russian Federation
Putin, Vladimir **2000**:3
Yeltsin, Boris **1991**:1

SADD
See: Students Against Drunken Driving

Sailing
Alter, Hobie
Brief Entry **1985**:1
Conner, Dennis **1987**:2
Koch, Bill **1992**:3
Morgan, Dodge **1987**:1
Turner, Ted **1989**:1

St. Louis Blues hockey team
Fuhr, Grant **1997**:3
Hull, Brett **1991**:4

St. Louis Browns baseball team
Veeck, Bill
Obituary **1986**:1

St. Louis Cardinals baseball team
Busch, August A. III **1988**:2
Busch, August Anheuser, Jr.
Obituary **1990**:2
Caray, Harry **1988**:3
Obituary **1998**:3
McGwire, Mark **1999**:1

St. Louis Rams football team
Warner, Kurt **2000**:3

San Antonio Spurs basketball team
Duncan, Tim **2000**:1
Robinson, David **1990**:4

San Antonio, Tex., city government
Cisneros, Henry **1987**:2

San Diego Chargers football team
Barnes, Ernie **1997**:4
Bell, Ricky
Obituary **1985**:1
Unitas, Johnny
Obituary **2003**:4

San Diego Padres baseball team
Dravecky, Dave **1992**:1
Gwynn, Tony **1995**:1
Kroc, Ray
Obituary **1985**:1
Sheffield, Gary **1998**:1

San Francisco city government
Alioto, Joseph L.
Obituary **1998**:3
Brown, Willie **1996**:4

San Francisco 49ers football team
DeBartolo, Edward J., Jr. **1989**:3
Montana, Joe **1989**:2
Rice, Jerry **1990**:4
Walsh, Bill **1987**:4
Young, Steve **1995**:2

San Francisco Giants baseball team
Bonds, Barry **1993**:3
Dravecky, Dave **1992**:1

SANE/FREEZE
Coffin, William Sloane, Jr. **1990**:3

Save the Children Federation
Guyer, David
Brief Entry **1988**:1

SBA
See: Small Business Administration

Schottco Corp.
Schott, Marge **1985**:4

Schwinn Bicycle Co.
Schwinn, Edward R., Jr.
Brief Entry **1985**:4

Sakharov, Andrei Dmitrievich
Obituary **1990**:2
Smith, Samantha
Obituary **1985**:3
Vidov, Oleg **1987**:4

Speed skating
Blair, Bonnie **1992**:3

Spin magazine
Guccione, Bob, Jr. **1991**:4

Spinal-cord injuries
Reeve, Christopher **1997**:2

Starbucks Coffee Co.
Schultz, Howard **1995**:3

Strategic Defense Initiative
Hagelstein, Peter
Brief Entry **1986**:3

Stroh Brewery Co.
Stroh, Peter W. **1985**:2

Students Against Drunken Driving
Anastas, Robert
Brief Entry **1985**:2
Lightner, Candy **1985**:1

Submarines
Rickover, Hyman
Obituary **1986**:4
Zech, Lando W.
Brief Entry **1987**:4

Sun Microsystems, Inc.
McNealy, Scott **1999**:4

Sunbeam Corp.
Dunlap, Albert J. **1997**:2

Suicide
Applewhite, Marshall Herff
Obituary **1997**:3
Dorris, Michael
Obituary **1997**:3
Hutchence, Michael
Obituary **1998**:1
Quill, Timothy E. **1997**:3

Sundance Institute
Redford, Robert **1993**:2

Sunshine Foundation
Sample, Bill
Brief Entry **1986**:2

Superconductors
Chaudhari, Praveen **1989**:4
Chu, Paul C.W. **1988**:2

Supreme Court of Canada
Wilson, Bertha
Brief Entry **1986**:1

Surfing
Curren, Tommy
Brief Entry **1987**:4

SWAPO
See: South West African People's
Organization

Swimming
Evans, Janet **1989**:1
Van Dyken, Amy **1997**:1

Tampa Bay Buccaneers football team
Bell, Ricky
Obituary **1985**:1
Gruden, Jon **2003**:4
Johnson, Keyshawn **2000**:4
Testaverde, Vinny **1987**:2
Williams, Doug **1988**:2
Young, Steve **1995**:2

Tandem Computers, Inc.
Treybig, James G. **1988**:3

Teach for America
Kopp, Wendy **1993**:3

Tectonics
Rosendahl, Bruce R.
Brief Entry **1986**:4

Teddy Ruxpin
Kingsborough, Donald
Brief Entry **1986**:2

Tele-Communications, Inc.
Malone, John C. **1988**:3 **1996**:3

Televangelism
Graham, Billy **1992**:1
Hahn, Jessica **1989**:4
Robertson, Pat **1988**:2
Rogers, Adrian **1987**:4
Swaggart, Jimmy **1987**:3

Temple University basketball team
Chaney, John **1989**:1

Tennis
Agassi, Andre **1990**:2
Ashe, Arthur
Obituary **1993**:3
Becker, Boris
Brief Entry **1985**:3
Capriati, Jennifer **1991**:1
Courier, Jim **1993**:2
Davenport, Lindsay **1999**:2
Gerulaitis, Vitas
Obituary **1995**:1
Graf, Steffi **1987**:4
Hewitt, Lleyton **2002**:2
Hingis, Martina **1999**:1
Ivanisevic, Goran **2002**:1
Kournikova, Anna **2000**:3
Navratilova, Martina **1989**:1
Pierce, Mary **1994**:4
Riggs, Bobby
Obituary **1996**:2

Sabatini, Gabriela
Brief Entry **1985**:4
Safin, Marat **2001**:3
Sampras, Pete **1994**:1
Seles, Monica **1991**:3
Williams, Serena **1999**:4
Williams, Venus **1998**:2

Test tube babies
Steptoe, Patrick
Obituary **1988**:3

Texas Rangers baseball team
Rodriguez, Alex **2001**:2
Ryan, Nolan **1989**:4

Texas State Government
Bush, George W., Jr. **1996**:4
Richards, Ann **1991**:2

Therapeutic Recreation Systems
Radocy, Robert
Brief Entry **1986**:3

Timberline Reclamations
McIntyre, Richard
Brief Entry **1986**:2

Time Warner Inc.
Ho, David **1997**:2
Levin, Gerald **1995**:2
Ross, Steven J.
Obituary **1993**:3

TLC Beatrice International
Lewis, Loida Nicolas **1998**:3

TLC Group L.P.
Lewis, Reginald F. **1988**:4
Obituary **1993**:3

Today Show
Couric, Katherine **1991**:4
Gumbel, Bryant **1990**:2
Norville, Deborah **1990**:3

Tony Awards
Abbott, George
Obituary **1995**:3
Alda, Robert
Obituary **1986**:3
Alexander, Jane **1994**:2
Alexander, Jason **1993**:3
Allen, Debbie **1998**:2
Allen, Joan **1998**:1
Bacall, Lauren **1997**:3
Bailey, Pearl
Obituary **1991**:1
Bennett, Michael
Obituary **1988**:1
Bloch, Ivan **1986**:3
Booth, Shirley
Obituary **1993**:2
Brooks, Mel **2003**:1
Brynner, Yul
Obituary **1985**:4
Buckley, Betty **1996**:2
Burnett, Carol **2000**:3
Channing, Stockard **1991**:3

Women's issues

Allred, Gloria **1985**:2
Baez, Joan **1998**:3
Boxer, Barbara **1995**:1
Braun, Carol Moseley **1993**:1
Butler, Brett **1995**:1
Cresson, Edith **1992**:1
Davis, Angela **1998**:3
Doi, Takako
    Brief Entry **1987**:4
Faludi, Susan **1992**:4
Faulkner, Shannon **1994**:4
Ferraro, Geraldine **1998**:3
Finley, Karen **1992**:4
Finnbogadottir, Vigdis
    Brief Entry **1986**:2
Flynt, Larry **1997**:3
Friedan, Betty **1994**:2
Furman, Rosemary
    Brief Entry **1986**:4
Grant, Charity
    Brief Entry **1985**:2
Harris, Barbara **1989**:3
Hill, Anita **1994**:1
Ireland, Jill
    Obituary **1990**:4
Jong, Erica **1998**:3
Kanokogi, Rusty
    Brief Entry **1987**:1
Love, Susan **1995**:2
MacKinnon, Catharine **1993**:2
Marier, Rebecca **1995**:4
Mikulski, Barbara **1992**:4
Monroe, Rose Will
    Obituary **1997**:4
Morgan, Robin **1991**:1
Nasrin, Taslima **1995**:1
Nussbaum, Karen **1988**:3

Paglia, Camille **1992**:3
Profet, Margie **1994**:4
Steinem, Gloria **1996**:2
Summers, Anne **1990**:2
Wattleton, Faye **1989**:1
Wolf, Naomi **1994**:3
Yard, Molly **1991**:4

Woods Hole Research Center
Woodwell, George S. **1987**:2

World Bank
McCloy, John J.
    Obituary **1989**:3
McNamara, Robert S. **1995**:4

World Cup
Hamm, Mia **2000**:1

World Health Organization
Brundtland, Gro Harlem **2000**:1

World of Wonder, Inc.
Kingsborough, Donald
    Brief Entry **1986**:2

World Wrestling Federation
Austin, Stone Cold Steve **2001**:3
Hogan, Hulk **1987**:3
McMahon, Vince, Jr. **1985**:4
Ventura, Jesse **1999**:2

Wrestling
Baumgartner, Bruce
    Brief Entry **1987**:3
Chyna **2001**:4

Hogan, Hulk **1987**:3
McMahon, Vince, Jr. **1985**:4
Rock, The **2001**:2
Ventura, Jesse **1999**:2

WWF
See: World Wrestling Federation

Xerox
Allaire, Paul **1995**:1
McColough, C. Peter **1990**:2
Mulcahy, Anne M. **2003**:2
Rand, A. Barry **2000**:3

Yahoo!
Filo, David and Jerry Yang **1998**:3
Koogle, Tim **2000**:4
Semel, Terry **2002**:2

Young & Rubicam, Inc.
Kroll, Alexander S. **1989**:3

Zamboni ice machine
Zamboni, Frank J.
    Brief Entry **1986**:4

ZANU
See: Zimbabwe African National
    Union

Ziff Corp
Ziff, William B., Jr. **1986**:4

Zimbabwe African National Union
Mugabe, Robert **1988**:4

Cumulative Newsmakers Index

This index lists all newsmakers included in the entire *Newsmakers* series.

Listee names are followed by a year and issue number; thus **1996**:3 indicates that an entry on that individual appears in both 1996, Issue 3, and the 1996 cumulation.

Gallagher, Noel 1967(?)-
See Oasis
Gallo, Robert 1937- **1991**:1
Galvin, John R. 1929- **1990**:1
Galvin, Martin
Brief Entry **1985**:3
Gandhi, Indira 1917-1984
Obituary **1985**:1
Gandhi, Rajiv 1944-1991
Obituary **1991**:4
Gandhi, Sonia 1947- **2000**:2
Gandolfini, James 1961- **2001**:3
Gandy, Kim 1954(?)- **2002**:2
Ganzi, Victor 1947- **2003**:3
Gao Xingjian 1940- **2001**:2
Garbage **2002**:3
Garbo, Greta 1905-1990
Obituary **1990**:3
Garcia, Andy 1956- **1999**:3
Garcia, Cristina 1958- **1997**:4
Garcia, Jerome John
See Garcia, Jerry
Garcia, Jerry 1942-1995 .... **1988**:3
Obituary **1996**:1
Garcia, Joe
Brief Entry **1986**:4
Gardenia, Vincent 1922-1992
Obituary **1993**:2
Gardner, Ava Lavinia 1922-1990
Obituary **1990**:2
Gardner, David and Tom **2001**:4
Gardner, Randy 1957- **1997**:2
Garneau, Marc 1949- **1985**:1
Garner, Jennifer 1972- **2003**:1
Garnett, Kevin 1976- **2000**:3
Garofalo, Janeane 1964- **1996**:4
Garr, Teri 1949- **1988**:4
Garrison, Earling Carothers
See Garrison, Jim
Garrison, Jim 1922-1992
Obituary **1993**:2
Garson, Greer 1903-1996
Obituary **1996**:4
Garzarelli, Elaine M. 1951- **1992**:3
Gassman, Vittorio 1922-2000
Obituary **2001**:1
Gates, Bill 1955- **1993**:3 **1987**:4
Gates, Robert M. 1943- **1992**:2
Gates, William H. III
See Gates, Bill
Gather, Temelea (Montsho Eshe)
See Arrested Development
Gathers, Hank 1967(?)-1990
Obituary **1990**:3
Gatien, Peter
Brief Entry **1986**:1
Gault, Willie 1960- **1991**:2
Gaultier, Jean-Paul 1952- **1998**:1
Gbagbo, Laurent 1945- **2003**:2
Gebbie, Kristine 1944(?)- **1994**:2
Geffen, David 1943- **1985**:3 **1997**:3
Gehry, Frank O. 1929- **1987**:1
Geisel, Theodor 1904-1991
Obituary **1992**:2
Geldof, Bob 1954(?)- **1985**:3
Gellar, Sarah Michelle 1977- **1999**:3
Geller, Margaret Joan 1947- **1998**:2
George, Elizabeth 1949- **2003**:3
Gephardt, Richard 1941- **1987**:3
Gerba, Charles 1945- **1999**:4
Gere, Richard 1949- **1994**:3
Gergen, David 1942- **1994**:1

Gerstner, Lou 1942- **1993**:4
Gerstner, Louis Vincent, Jr.
See Gerstner, Lou
Gertz, Alison 1966(?)-1992
Obituary **1993**:2
Gerulaitis, Vitas 1954-1994
Obituary **1995**:1
Getz, Stan 1927-1991
Obituary **1991**:4
Ghali, Boutros Boutros 1922- **1992**:3
Giamatti, A. Bartlett 1938-1989 ..... **1988**:4
Obituary **1990**:1
Giamatti, Angelo Bartlett
See Giamatti, A. Bartlett
Giannulli, Mossimo 1963- **2002**:3
Gibb, Andy 1958-1988
Obituary **1988**:3
Gibb, Barry
See Bee Gees, The
Gibb, Maurice
See Bee Gees, The
Gibb, Robin
See Bee Gees, The
Gibson, Kirk 1957- **1985**:2
Gibson, Mel 1956- **1990**:1
Gibson, William Ford, III 1948- **1997**:2
Gielgud, John 1904-2000
Obituary **2000**:4
Gifford, Kathie Lee 1953- **1992**:2
Gift, Roland 1960(?)- **1990**:2
Gilbert, Walter 1932- **1988**:3
Gilford, Jack 1907-1990
Obituary **1990**:4
Gill, Vince 1957- **1995**:2
Gillespie, Dizzy 1917-1993
Obituary **1993**:2
Gillespie, John Birks
See Gillespie, Dizzy
Gillespie, Marcia 1944- **1999**:4
Gillett, George 1938- **1988**:1
Gilmour, Doug 1963- **1994**:3
Gilruth, Robert 1913-2000
Obituary **2001**:1
Gingrich, Newt 1943- **1991**:1 **1997**:3
Ginsberg, Allen 1926-1997
Obituary **1997**:3
Ginsburg, Ruth Bader 1933- **1993**:4
Gish, Lillian 1893-1993
Obituary **1993**:4
Giuliani, Rudolph 1944- **1994**:2
Glaser, Elizabeth 1947-1994
Obituary **1995**:2
Glass, David 1935- **1996**:1
Glass, Philip 1937- **1991**:4
Glasser, Ira 1938- **1989**:1
Glaus, Troy 1976- **2003**:3
Gleason, Herbert John
See Gleason, Jackie
Gleason, Jackie 1916-1987
Obituary **1987**:4
Glenn, John 1921- **1998**:3
Gless, Sharon 1944- **1989**:3
Glover, Corey
See Living Colour
Glover, Danny 1947- **1998**:4
Glover, Savion 1973- **1997**:1
Gobel, George 1920(?)-1991
Obituary **1991**:4
Gober, Robert 1954- **1996**:3
Godard, Jean-Luc 1930- **1998**:1
Godunov, Alexander 1949-1995
Obituary **1995**:4

Goetz, Bernhard Hugo 1947(?)- **1985**:3
Goff, Helen Lyndon
See Travers, P.L.
Goizueta, Roberto 1931-1997 .... **1996**:1
Obituary **1998**:1
Goldberg, Gary David 1944- **1989**:4
Goldberg, Leonard 1934- **1988**:4
Goldberg, Whoopi 1955- **1993**:3
Goldblum, Jeff 1952- **1988**:1 **1997**:3
Golden, Thelma 1965- **2003**:3
Goldhaber, Fred
Brief Entry **1986**:3
Goldman, William 1931- **2001**:1
Goldman-Rakic, Patricia 1937- **2002**:4
Goldwater, Barry 1909-1998
Obituary **1998**:4
Gomez, "Lefty" 1909-1989
Obituary **1989**:3
Gong Li 1965- **1998**:4
Goodall, Jane 1934- **1991**:1
Gooden, Dwight 1964- **1985**:2
Gooding, Cuba, Jr. 1968- **1997**:3
Goodman, Benjamin David
See Goodman, Benny
Goodman, Benny 1909-1986
Obituary **1986**:3
Goodman, John 1952- **1990**:3
Goody, Joan 1935- **1990**:2
Goody, Sam 1904-1991
Obituary **1992**:1
Gorbachev, Mikhail 1931- **1985**:2
Gorbachev, Raisa 1932-1999
Obituary **2000**:2
Gordeeva, Ekaterina 1972- **1996**:4
Gordon, Dexter 1923-1990 . **1987**:1 **1990**:4
Gordon, Gale 1906-1995
Obituary **1996**:1
Gordon, Jeff 1971- **1996**:1
Gore, Albert, Jr. 1948(?)- **1993**:2
Gore, Albert, Sr. 1907-1998
Obituary **1999**:2
Gore, Mary Elizabeth
See Gore, Tipper
Gore, Tipper 1948- **1985**:4
Gorelick, Kenny
See Kenny G
Goren, Charles H. 1901-1991
Obituary **1991**:4
Gorman, Leon
Brief Entry **1987**:1
Gossard, Stone
See Pearl Jam
Gossett, Louis, Jr. 1936- **1989**:3
Gould, Chester 1900-1985
Obituary **1985**:2
Gould, Gordon 1920- **1987**:1
Gould, Stephen Jay 1941-2002
Obituary **2003**:3
Gowda, H. D. Deve 1933- **1997**:1
Grace, J. Peter 1913- **1990**:2
Graf, Steffi 1969- **1987**:4
Grafton, Sue 1940- **2000**:2
Graham, Bill 1931-1991 .... **1986**:4
Obituary **1992**:2
Graham, Billy 1918- **1992**:1
Graham, Donald 1945- **1985**:4
Graham, Heather 1970- **2000**:1
Graham, Katharine Meyer 1917- .. **1997**:3
Obituary **2002**:3
Graham, Lauren 1967- **2003**:4
Graham, Martha 1894-1991
Obituary **1991**:4